LONGMAN STUDY EDITION

American and Texas Government

POLICY AND POLITICS

Tenth Edition

D0124441

NEAL TANNAHILL
Houston Community College

Longman

Boston   Columbus   Indianapolis   New York   San Francisco   Upper Saddle River
Amsterdam   Cape Town   Dubai   London   Madrid   Milan   Munich   Paris   Montreal   Toronto
Delhi   Mexico City   São Paulo   Sydney   Hong Kong   Seoul   Singapore   Taipei   Tokyo

Editor-in-Chief: Eric Stano
Supplements Editor: Corey Kahn
Senior Media Editor: Regina Vertiz
Marketing Manager: Lindsey Prudhomme
Production Manager: Bob Ginsberg
Project Coordination, Text Design, and Electronic Page Makeup: S4Carlisle Publishing Services
Cover Design Manager: John Callahan
Cover Designer: Kay Petronio
Cover Illustration/Photo: iStockphoto, Photographer: Soubrette
Pearson Image Resource Center/Photo Researcher: Jody Potter
Image Permission Coordinator: Frances Toepfer
Senior Manufacturing Buyer: Alfred C. Dorsey
Printer and Binder: RR Donnelley & Sons Company/Crawfordsville
Cover Printer: RR Donnelley & Sons Company/Crawfordsville

For permission to use copyrighted material, grateful acknowledgment is made to the copyright holders
on p. 925, which is hereby made part of this copyright page.

Library of Congress Cataloging-in-Publication Data
Tannahill, Neal, date.
    American government : policy and politics / Neal Tannahill. — 10th ed., Longman study ed.
      p. cm.
    Includes bibliographical references and index.
    ISBN-13: 978-0-205-74672-9
    ISBN-10: 0-205-74672-1
    1. United States—Politics and government —Textbooks. I. Title.
JK276.T35 2009
320.473—dc22 2009015545

1 2 3 4 5 6 7 8 9 10—DOC—12 11 10 09

Longman
is an imprint of

www.pearsonhighered.com

ISBN-13: 978-0-205-74672-9
ISBN-10:   0-205-74672-1

Contents

CHAPTER 19 • The Texas Constitution   513

CHAPTER 20 • The Federal Context of Texas Policymaking   537

CHAPTER 27 • The Judicial Branch in Texas   727

CHAPTER 28 • City Government in Texas   755

To the Instructor

New to This Edition

This edition of *American and Texas Government* includes a number of changes designed to reflect recent political developments, including the 2008 election and the early months of the Obama administration. The edition takes account of the latest in scholarly research and responds to requests from faculty using the textbook. I have also deleted the chapter on regulatory policymaking from the American Government section and added a chapter on criminal justice in Texas. The most important revisions in each chapter are the following:

Introduction   The Americans with Disabilities Act (ADA) remains as the unifying example, but I retired Casey Martin and used the controversy over global warming to illustrate some of the details of agenda setting.

Chapter 1   The aging of the population opens the chapter. I added a section based on an essay by Professor Robert H. Frank on the "winner-take-all economy" and included a new Global Perspective on immigration policy and politics in France.

Chapter 2   The failed effort of the newly elected Democratic Congress in 2007 to force President Bush to begin the withdrawal of U.S. combat forces from Iraq introduces the chapter.

Chapter 3   I have rewritten the description of No Child Left Behind (NCLB) to ensure that students understand that schools must assess student progress not just as a whole but also by subgroups based on race/ethnicity, income level, English proficiency, and special education status. I revised the Global Perspective on federalism in Germany to focus on education policy. I illustrate the concept that states are laboratories of democracy by discussing healthcare reform in Massachusetts.

Chapter 4   The chapter includes a new Global Perspective on civil unions in Denmark.

Chapter 5   The chapter discusses turnout in the 2008 presidential election, focusing on younger adults in particular. I have replaced the concept of voting age population (VAP) with voting eligible population (VEP).

Chapter 6   The introduction discusses the political impact of new communications media such as YouTube, blogs, and the Internet by focusing on the effect of the macaca incident on George Allen's 2006 senatorial campaign. I have added a discussion of the communication operation of the G. W. Bush administration.

Chapter 7   The chapter introduction focuses on the NRA as one of the most powerful interest groups in American politics, noting that a relatively small group of people who are well organized and highly motivated can have more political influence than a large group that is disorganized and disinterested. The chapter has a new Global Perspective on church and state in Mexico.

Chapter 8   The chapter begins with a summary of the results of the 2008 election and its impact on the nature of party competition. I reorganized the section on party identification to focus more on the different types of independents. The Democratic Party has gained an advantage since 2004 because fewer people now identify with the Republican Party, and independents are more likely to vote Democratic than Republican. The section on party history has been deleted.

Chapter 9   The chapter begins with a discussion of the Obama–Clinton Democratic presidential nomination contest. I infuse discussion of the 2008 primary and general election campaigns throughout the chapter, dropping most of the old references to the 2004 campaign. I discuss base voters and swing voters, examining their impact on election outcomes. I discuss the underlying factors affecting the outcome of a presidential election, noting that campaigns have an impact but that underlying factors are more important. I revised the section on issues to reflect current research, which has identified issues as almost as important as party ID in determining voter choice.

Chapter 10   I eliminated the section on the factors affecting the legislative process and moved its elements to other parts of this and other chapters. I deleted the discussion of pork barrel spending from this chapter because it is also discussed in the chapter on economic policymaking.

Chapter 11   The introduction focuses on the challenge facing President Obama in reforming America's healthcare system. The section on presidential powers has been updated to include inherent powers. It also shifts focus somewhat to note that the Constitution provides an outline of presidential powers, which has gained definition and expanded through the give-and-take of the political process.

Chapter 12   I have eliminated Chapter 15 on regulatory policymaking and folded some of that material into this chapter. I added a paragraph discussing recess appointments.

Chapter 13   The chapter introduction discusses the likelihood that President Obama will have the opportunity to change the philosophical balance on a closely divided Supreme Court. The chapter has a new Global Perspective on Islamic law in Nigeria.

Chapter 14   The chapter begins with a discussion of the economic crisis facing the nation in late 2008 and 2009 and the efforts of the Bush and Obama administrations to address that crisis. The Global Perspective examines healthcare in Canada.

Chapter 15   I updated the controversy over civil liberties and the war on terror to include both the latest Supreme Court decisions and the executive orders issued by President Obama concerning the use of torture and the closing of the detention center at Guantanamo Bay.

Chapter 16   The section on school desegregation includes a discussion of *Parents Involved in Community Schools v. Seattle School District No. 1,* which holds that the Supreme Court will apply strict scrutiny to any school assignment decision that considers race, even decisions taken with the goal of enhancing racial integration. The chapter has a new Global Perspective on women's rights in Saudi Arabia.

Chapter 17   I included a section on the Bush administration's focus on expanding democracy abroad and introduced the concept of a democratic peace. I revised the definition of two key terms: "rogue states" and "military preemption."

Chapter 18   I expanded the discussion of illegal immigration and its impact on Texas government and the economy.

Chapter 19   I updated the feature on gay marriage in Massachusetts and included coverage of the 2007 constitutional amendment election.

Chapter 20   The controversy surrounding the Real ID Act is the new chapter opener.

Chapter 21   I added a discussion of the contentious struggle in the legislature between Republicans and Democrats over requiring prospective voters to present a picture ID in order to cast ballots. The chapter also evaluates turnout in the 2006 election.

Chapter 22   The chapter opener focuses on the lobbying fight between liquor wholesalers and package stores that developed in the 2007 legislative session. The chapter examines the legislative agenda of the religious right in the Texas legislature.

Chapter 23   The chapter discusses the gains made by the Democratic Party in the 2006 election and considers whether the Democrats are making a comeback sufficient to restore them to power in the foreseeable future.

Chapter 24   The chapter opener focuses on the battle in the 2006 Republican primary between candidates supported by James Leininger and candidates backed by the Texas Parent PAC.

Chapter 25   The chapter opener focuses on the battle over Tom Craddick and the office of speaker in the Texas legislature.

Chapter 26   The chapter opener focuses on an executive order issued by Governor Rick Perry to require schoolgirls to be vaccinated for human papilloma virus (HPV). The chapter discusses both the merits of the order and the legal/constitutional authority of the governor to act.

Chapter 27   The chapter opener examines the role of the courts in deciding whether the Texas Constitution requires the state to cover abortion in its Medicaid program.

Chapter 28   The chapter opener examines the effort by the city of Farmers Branch to adopt a set of ordinances designed to address the issue of illegal immigration.

Chapter 29   The chapter discusses legislation passed in 2007 that will eventually replace the TAKS graduation test with end-of-course exams. I have added a section on merit pay and included a feature on school choice in Cleveland, Ohio.

Chapter 30   I have added a feature on universal healthcare in Massachusetts.

Chapter 31   This chapter on criminal justice is new for this edition.

APPROACH AND FEATURES OF THIS BOOK

My experience as a classroom teacher has taught me that a textbook needs to work well for both students and faculty. Students prefer a text that is interesting, easy to read, and designed for effective study. Faculty members want a textbook with solid scholarship, thorough coverage of the subject, and features that support effective teaching. I have written *American and Texas Government* to address all of these goals.

The underlying premise of my writing is that many students are unfamiliar with American culture and unaware of the basic principles of American national, state, and local government and politics. I teach at a large urban community college with a diverse student population that includes many international students and students who are first-generation Americans. I recognize that these students have not had the decades of immersion in American culture that I have had. References that may be obvious to me, such as calling Texas the Lone Star State or the use of a football analogy, may flummox them. I also write with the knowledge that many students, even some native-born Americans, do not know the basics of American government. When I first began teaching, I assumed that students already knew how bills become law, how the governor is chosen, how the courts operate, and so forth, but I soon learned that I was mistaken.

I believe that a government textbook should address the major policy controversies of the day in order to be interesting and relevant to students and instructors as well. How better to introduce the foreign and defense policy issues facing the United States than with a discussion of American policy toward Iran and North Korea, the two remaining charter members of the axis of evil? My goal is for students to understand course materials by relating them to the major events and critical policy issues of the day.

A good textbook should show students how to become participants in their own government. The quality of American democracy depends on citizen participation. I am proud to say that two current members of the Texas legislature are former students of mine; one a Democrat and the other a Republican. I am especially gratified that one of the legislators credits my class with stimulating his interest in government and politics. The 2008 presidential election produced a revival of political interest in young people in Texas and across the nation, giving faculty an opening in the classroom to help students develop real understanding of the democratic process. My goal is for this textbook to be an ally in that endeavor.

A good textbook should introduce students to the discipline of political science. Although I do not expect many of my students to major in political science, I believe that all students should recognize and appreciate the difference between scholarship and advocacy. I expose students to as much political science research as possible and expect them to be able to relate political science concepts to current political developments and controversies.

A good textbook should stress skills. Introductory government classes should be about more than just description. I want students to be able to use the Internet, read graphs and charts, identify points of view, and apply scholarly concepts to contemporary events. In my class, students gain experience reading, writing, speaking, researching, and thinking critically. Those are skills that assist students throughout their academic and professional careers.

Finally, a good textbook should be a learning guide for students and a teaching resource for instructors. This textbook includes a number of features that will benefit both students and faculty:

- **Learning Outcomes** Each chapter begins with a list of learning outcomes that assist students in organizing their study by helping them identify the most important points in the chapter.

- **Key Terms** Words and phrases that have a specific meaning in the context of the subject matter appear in bold type, followed by a clear, straightforward definition. Each key term with its definition is also highlighted in the margin of the text.

- **Getting Involved** In the American Government chapters, this feature is a set of student projects that are designed to enable students to learn by doing, such as visiting a political party headquarters, recording a weekly journal on the impact of government on their lives, or registering to vote. The activity for Chapter 2 is a service-learning project. Instructors may want to work with local governments and nonprofit organizations to identify possible placement opportunities for students. Many colleges have service-learning offices that can provide support for instructors and students. Furthermore, several activities, such as asking students to complete the paperwork to apply for financial aid or attending a meeting of a student organization, are designed to foster student retention in college.

  In the Texas Government section, the Getting Involved feature tells students how they can get involved in their communities, the college, and their government by doing volunteer work, joining an interest group, or becoming a court appointed special advocate.

- **Glossary** The glossary in the back of the textbook enables students to quickly review the definitions of key terms used in the text.

- **Let's Debate** The Let's Debate feature, in the Texas Government section only, is designed to promote classroom discussion and serves as a starting point for term papers by examining various sides of a contemporary political issue. Topics include the implementation of the recommendations of the 9/11 Commission, the use of polling by the media, congressional war powers, and the selection of judges in Texas.

- **What Is Your Opinion?** Each chapter includes a number of highlighted focus questions that ask students their opinions on some of the political controversies discussed in the text. The questions are designed to hold student interest as they read; some questions may also serve as the starting point for an interesting class discussion.

- **Global Perspectives/National Perspectives** Each chapter in the American Government section includes a short essay on the government and politics of another nation. The Texas Government chapters include an essay on policy and policymaking in another American state. The comparative approach gives students added insight into how government works.

- **Practice Test Questions** I have written a set of multiple-choice questions for each chapter that is designed to allow students to assess their understanding of chapter content. I wrote the questions myself to ensure that they focus on the meat of the subject and that they challenge students to think critically about course topics. Although some questions are fairly straightforward, a good many of them require students to apply concepts to real-world situations. Instructors should encourage students to use the questions as a study guide. They should also anticipate that students will be asking them to explain some of the answers to them.

ACKNOWLEDGMENTS

Many persons contributed to the writing and production of this book. Eric Stano, Donna Garnier, and Bob Ginsberg at Pearson gave me sympathetic and professional help from the beginning of work on the edition to its completion. Frank Ubhaus, Valdosta State University; Omar Purdue, Maranatha Baptist College; Michael Brittingham, Louisville University; Gary Brown, Montgomery College; Jasmine Farrier, Louisville University; and Joanna Sabo, Monroe Community College; Amanda Bigelow, Illinois Valley Community College read the previous edition of this book and offered guidance for its revision.

I am grateful to my friends and colleagues among the Government faculty at Houston Community College for their friendship and support. I have learned most of what I know about teaching from them. Thank you Ghassan Abdallah, Cecile (Cammy) Shay, Evelyn Ballard, Harold "Hal" Comello, Dale Foster, Larry Gonzalez, Mark Hartray, Edmund "Butch" Herod, Brenda Jones, Aaron Knight, Heidi Lange, Gary LeBlanc, Raymond Lew, Joe C. Martin, Vinette Meikle Harris, David Ngene, Carlos Pierott, Donna Rhea, John Speer, Jaye Sutter, John Ben Sutter, Mark Tiller, Linda Webb, and Celia Wintz. I am also grateful for the hard work and dedication of my support staff at Houston Community College, especially Susan Howard, Rose Andrus, Charles Cook, Sue Cox, and Mary David.

Finally, I wish to dedicate this book to my friends: Anup Bodhe, Anderson Brandao, Jason Orr, Luis Arturo Nava, Ron Rueckert, Kim Galle, and Hal Stockbridge.

NEAL TANNAHILL
HOUSTON COMMUNITY COLLEGE
neal.tannahill@hccs.edu
ntannahill@aol.com

To the Student

I designed this textbook with students in mind. I have been a member of the political science faculty at Houston Community College for more than 30 years, teaching hundreds of introductory American government classes, probably much like the one you are taking now. Some of my students have been older adults, returning to school after years in the workplace or at home raising a family, whereas other students have been recent high school graduates. I have worked with international students, full-time students, part-time students, working students, and students with disabilities. I have taught dual-credit classes in high schools and distance education courses online.

I have learned from experience that students want a textbook that is easily read. Consequently, my primary goal as a textbook author is to write clearly. Because I know that not every student is already familiar with American government, I have taken care to define terms and explain the importance of historical events that are mentioned in the text. I want students to be able to understand every sentence, every paragraph, and every chapter without having to read them over and over again.

I also know that students want a textbook that is interesting. To catch and hold the interest of students, I have organized the textbook around the major policy controversies of today. Student readers will learn about American government and politics in the context of the debate over immigration reform, capital punishment in Texas, abortion rights, gay marriage, school finance reform, and other issues.

Students want a textbook that will guide their study. The text includes a number of features designed to help students understand course materials and prepare for tests.

- **Learning Outcomes** Each chapter begins with a set of learning outcomes, which are designed to help students organize their study by identifying the most important concepts in each chapter.
- **Key Terms** Words and phrases that have a specific meaning in the context of the subject matter appear in bold type, followed by a clear, straightforward definition. Students should avoid memorizing the definitions of each term. Instead, they should learn what the terms mean in the context of each chapter and be able to define and explain them in their own words. The list of these key terms at the end of each chapter can also help students focus their study.
- **Glossary** The textbook contains a glossary that includes the definitions of the key terms listed in the text. Students who forget what a term means can look it up quickly in the glossary.

- **Global Perspectives/National Perspectives** Each chapter includes a short essay on the politics and government of another country (in the American Government section) or another state (in the Texas Government section).
- **Let's Debate** Each chapter, in the Texas Government Section only, contains a feature focusing on a major policy controversy, such as the debate over gay marriage. The give-and-take of the debate exchange will help students understand the issue and form their own opinions.
- **Getting Involved** The American Government chapters include a set of projects that are designed to enable students to learn by doing, such as visiting a political party headquarters, volunteering at a local government office or nonprofit agency, interviewing a police officer about implementing the *Miranda* warning, or registering to vote.

  Each chapter in the Texas section includes a feature telling students how they can get involved in their communities, the college, and their government by doing volunteer work, joining an interest group, or becoming a court appointed special advocate.
- **Practice Test Questions** A set of multiple-choice questions for each chapter is provided at the end of the text that enables students to test their knowledge.

I am proud to have the opportunity to be part of your education. If you have questions about the textbook or American government, you can write to me at neal.tannahill@hccs.edu or ntannahill@aol.com. I hope to hear from you!

NEAL TANNAHILL

Introduction

Government, Politics, and the Policymaking Process

CHAPTER OUTLINE

The Importance of Government

Government and Politics

The Public Policy Approach
    The Policymaking Environment
    Agenda Building

Policy Formulation
Policy Adoption
Policy Implementation
Policy Evaluation

LEARNING OUTCOMES

After studying the Introduction, students should be able to do the following:

▸ Assess the impact of government on the lives of individuals as well as society as a whole. (pp. 2–4)

▸ Describe the policymaking environment, especially the environment for the adoption of the Americans with Disabilities Act (ADA). (pp. 5–6)

▸ Identify the five stages of the public policy approach. (pp. 6–10)

▸ Describe the process whereby disability rights became part of the policy agenda. (pp. 6–7)

▸ Analyze the formulation, adoption, and implementation of the ADA. (pp. 7–8)

▸ Identify the criteria that could be used for evaluating the ADA. (pp. 8–9)

▸ Define the key terms listed on page 10 and explain their significance.

Americans with Disabilities Act (ADA) A federal law designed to end discrimination against persons with disabilities and eliminate barriers to their full participation in American society.

The **Americans with Disabilities Act (ADA)** of 1991 is a federal law designed to end discrimination against persons with disabilities and eliminate barriers to their full participation in American society. The ADA protects people with disabilities from discrimination in all employment practices, including hiring, firing, promotions, and compensation. The ADA does not force employers to hire unqualified individuals who happen to be disabled, but it does require companies to make "reasonable accommodation" for otherwise qualified job applicants or current employees who happen to be disabled unless the business can show that the accommodation would put an "undue hardship" on its operation. The ADA also requires that private businesses that are open to the public—such as restaurants, hotels, theaters, retail stores, funeral homes, healthcare offices, pharmacies, private schools, and day care centers—be accessible to persons with disabilities. Business owners may have to modify their premises or change their way of doing business so long as the necessary modifications or accommodations do not unduly burden the business or force business owners fundamentally to alter the nature of the goods or services they provide.[1]

THE IMPORTANCE OF GOVERNMENT

The ADA illustrates the importance of government. For millions of Americans with disabilities, the act offers the promise of opportunity to compete in the workplace without discrimination, and it guarantees access to restaurants, hotels, shops, and clinics. The ADA forces employers to review their employment practices to ensure compliance with the law and to take reasonable steps to accommodate the needs of workers and customers with disabilities. For society as a whole, the ADA gives millions of people with disabilities the opportunity to become full participants in the nation's economy, both as workers and consumers.

Government affects individual Americans through regulations, taxes, and services. Government regulates many aspects of daily life, either directly or indirectly. Government sets speed limits and other driving regulations, establishes a minimum age to purchase and consume alcoholic beverages, and determines the educational and technical qualifications required for practicing many occupations and professions. Government regulations affect the quality of air and water, gasoline mileage performance of automobiles, and working conditions in factories. In addition, regulation attempts to protect consumers from unsafe products, untested drugs, misleading package labels, and deceptive advertising.

Government services provide benefits to all Americans. Public hospitals, schools, and transportation networks serve millions of people. Many college students receive financial aid and attend institutions that benefit from public funding. Government welfare programs assist millions of low-income families. Elderly people and many individuals with disabilities receive Social Security and Medicare benefits.

Gross Domestic Product (GDP) The total value of goods and services produced by a nation's economy in a year, excluding transactions with foreign countries.

Government regulations and services cost money. Federal, state, and local taxes combined represent 29 percent of the nation's **Gross Domestic Product (GDP)**, which is the total value of goods and services produced by a nation's economy in a year, excluding transactions with foreign countries.[2] Workers pay income and payroll taxes on the wages they earn. Consumers pay sales taxes on retail purchases and excise taxes on tobacco, alcohol, tires, gasoline, and other products. Homeowners and business owners pay property taxes on their homes and businesses.

Government not only touches the lives of individual Americans, but it also affects the nation's quality of life. Most people would not want to live, work, or run a business in a country without a fully functioning government. Government regulations and services help ensure safe neighborhoods, a healthy environment, an efficient transportation system, and an educated workforce. The tax system provides a mechanism for government to spread the cost of its operation to a broad range of individuals and groups in society. In times of emergency, such as a terrorist attack or a natural disaster, people turn to government to respond to the crisis, assist the victims, and rebuild damaged communities.

Studying American government is important because of its great impact on individuals and society. People who understand how government works will be better equipped to take advantage of the benefits and services government provides and more able to prepare themselves to live effectively under government regulation and taxation. Studying American government helps citizens understand how they can influence government policies through voting, participating in political organizations, and contacting public officials.

The study of American government raises important philosophical questions about the role of government. What services should government provide? What limits should be placed on government activity? Is it preferable to have an active government that attempts to solve societal problems, such as the lack of access of people with disabilities to employment opportunities and public accommodations, or a relatively passive government that performs a limited set of functions?

 WHAT IS YOUR OPINION?

Do you favor a small government that provides relatively modest services but holds down taxes or an active government that provides more services but costs more?

GOVERNMENT AND POLITICS

Government The institution with authority to set policy for society.

Government and *politics* are distinct but closely related terms. **Government** is the institution with authority to set policy for society. Congress, the president, courts, and government agencies, such as the Social Security Administration (SSA) and the Food and Drug Administration (FDA), are all structures of American national government. Each state has a governor, legislature, court system, and administrative departments in addition to a series of local governments, such as municipalities, townships, counties, and school districts.

Politics The process that determines who shall occupy the roles of leadership in government and how the power of government shall be exercised.

Whereas government is an *institution*, politics is a *process*. One political scientist says that **politics** is the way in which decisions for a society are made and considered binding most of the time by most of the people.[3] Another scholar declares that the study of politics is "the attempt to explain the various ways in which power is exercised in the everyday world and how that power is used to allocate resources and benefits to some people and groups, and costs and burdens to other people and groups."[4] We could add a third definition: Politics is the process that determines who shall occupy the roles of leadership in government and how the power of government shall be exercised.

Each of these definitions of politics emphasizes different aspects of the concept. Taken together, they enable us to identify certain key elements of politics as well as the relationship between politics and government:

- Government and politics are entwined. The selection of government personnel and the adoption of government policies are political. The enactment of the ADA, for example, took place through the political process.
- Politics is broader than government. In addition to the institutions of government and government officials, politics also involves individuals, groups, and organizations that are not officially part of the government, such as voters, the media, interest groups, political parties, individual political activists, and policy experts.
- Politics involves making decisions about the distribution of government benefits and the allocation of their costs.
- Politics is competitive. In American politics, individuals and groups compete with one another over the selection of the persons who will occupy government office and over the policies government will enact and enforce.

Politics is the process that determines who shall occupy the roles of leadership in government and how the power of government shall be exercised.

THE PUBLIC POLICY APPROACH

Public policy The response, or lack of response, of government decision-makers to an issue.

Public policy approach A comprehensive method for studying the process through which issues come to the attention of government decision-makers and through which policies are formulated, adopted, implemented, and evaluated.

Policymaking environment The complex of factors outside of government that has an impact, either directly or indirectly, on the policymaking process.

The public policy approach is one of the models that political scientists use for studying government and politics. **Public policy** is the response, or lack of response, of government decision-makers to an issue. Government policies can take the form of laws, executive orders, regulations, court decisions, or, in some cases, no action at all. The decision by government decision-makers *not* to act is just as much a policy decision as the choice to take a particular action.

The **public policy approach** is a comprehensive method for studying the process through which issues come to the attention of government decision-makers and through which policies are formulated, adopted, implemented, and evaluated. The public policy approach goes beyond an examination of the content of laws and regulations to consider the broader scope of policymaking. A study of government policy toward persons with disabilities would begin by examining the legal, cultural, socioeconomic, and political factors shaping the environment for the policy. It would consider how the rights of people with disabilities became an issue of public concern, and it would examine the process through which the government formulated and adopted the ADA. The study would also consider the policy's implementation and evaluation.[5]

The public policy approach is a particularly useful basis for organizing an introductory textbook. The public policy approach focuses attention on what government actually *does* rather than just its structures and organization. It also provides students with a mechanism for organizing political information and concepts. Finally, the public policy approach is broad enough to allow discussion of a wide range of scholarly studies.

The Policymaking Environment

The **policymaking environment** is the complex of factors outside of government that has an impact, either directly or indirectly, on the policymaking process. The types of issues that the government addresses, the set of policy alternatives that government decision-makers are willing to consider, and the resources available to the government depend on the international, cultural, demographic, economic, constitutional, and political environments.

- The international environment affects American economic, military, diplomatic, and defense policy. The terrorist attacks of September 11, 2001, focused the nation's attention on the danger of international terrorism, leading to heightened security at airports and other public places, as well as increased defense expenditures.
- The nation's cultural values, customs, and beliefs affect policymaking. The increased visibility of people with disabilities in American society, including actor Christopher Reeve and former presidential candidate Bob Dole, helped create a positive environment for the adoption of the ADA.
- The size, distribution, and composition of the nation's population constitute the demographic environment. The proportion of the population with disabilities

or who have friends or family members with disabilities influences the policy process because it determines the number of people who must be accommodated, as well as the potential strength of forces advocating disability rights.

- The size, growth rate, and structure of the economy influence the policy process. Business executives are more willing to provide access to people with disabilities when the economy is robust than when the economy is stagnant.
- The U.S. Constitution constitutes an important part of the policymaking environment by setting the legal ground rules for policy adoption and implementation.
- The political environment for policymaking includes political parties, interest groups, the media, public opinion, and the participation of individual citizens. The emergence of organized groups advocating disability rights was a key factor in the passage of the ADA.

Agenda Building

Agenda building The process through which problems become matters of public concern and government action.

Agenda building is the process through which problems become matters of public concern and government action. The politics of agenda building involves government officials and groups outside of the government competing to determine which problems government will address. Whereas some interests want to promote the consideration of certain issues, other forces that oppose change work to block discussion by denying that a problem exists or by arguing that the government either cannot or should not address it.[6] Consider the controversy surrounding **global warming,** which is the gradual warming of the Earth's atmosphere reportedly caused by the burning of fossil fuels and industrial pollutants. Many scientists believe that global warming is a threat to the planet which, if left unchecked, will lead to serious consequences for life in the United States and around the world. Environmentalists want the government to take action to reduce the greenhouse gas emissions that cause global warming. In contrast, people who oppose government efforts to address global warming are skeptical that it exists, doubt that it is caused by human action, and/or question the effectiveness of government actions to address the problem. They want government to take no action or to take minimal action.

Global warming The gradual warming of the Earth's atmosphere reportedly caused by the burning of fossil fuels and industrial pollutants.

Agenda building not only identifies problems for government attention but also defines the nature of those problems, and therefore the eventual thrust of a policy solution.[7] Consider the issue of disability rights. During the debate in Congress on the ADA, spokespersons for advocacy groups for the disabled, such as the Disability Rights Education and Defense Fund (DREDF) and the Americans Disabled for Attendant Programs Today (ADAPT), noted that the employment rate for persons with severe disabilities was only 23 percent compared with an employment rate for adults without disabilities of nearly 80 percent.[8] The supporters of disability rights argued that discrimination or a lack of access to public facilities prevented many persons with disabilities from working. They proposed passage of federal legislation prohibiting discrimination against people with disabilities and ensuring access to business facilities as a solution to the problem. In contrast, business groups opposed government regulation. They denied that employment discrimination against people with disabilities was a major problem, suggesting instead that the employment rate for people with disabilities was low because many people with disabilities either cannot work or do not want to work. Furthermore, they said, individuals with disabilities who have few skills can make more money from government disability payments than they can earn in low-wage jobs.

Policy Formulation

Policy formulation The development of strategies for dealing with the problems on the official policy agenda.

Policy formulation is the development of strategies for dealing with the problems on the official policy agenda. Government officials as well as individuals and organizations outside of government—such as interest groups, political parties, policy experts, and the media—participate in policy formulation. The formulation of ADA legislation, for example, involved negotiations among members of Congress, executive branch officials, business interests, and advocacy groups for people with disabilities. Although most business groups supported the goals of the ADA, they were concerned that the law would require businesses to hire unqualified applicants or make extensive (and expensive) physical modifications in their facilities. Business owners also worried that the new law would subject them to lawsuits and the possibility of expensive jury settlements.

The wording of the ADA reflects a compromise between the supporters of people with disabilities and business interests. The advocacy groups succeeded in writing a broad definition of disability into the law. The ADA declares that an individual with a disability is "a person who has a physical or mental impairment that substantially limits one or more major life activities, a record of such an impairment, or is regarded as having such an impairment."[9] Major life activities include the ability of individuals to care for themselves, perform manual tasks, walk, see, hear, speak, breathe, learn, work, sit, stand, lift, and reach. Under the law, persons with learning disabilities, epilepsy, mental illness, muscular dystrophy, HIV infection, cancer, diabetes, mental retardation, alcoholism, and cosmetic disfigurement are all considered disabled.

Business groups succeeded in limiting the scope of the law. Although the ADA prohibits discrimination, it does not establish a quota system for hiring people with disabilities. It requires only that employers hire and promote qualified candidates without regard to disability. Furthermore, the ADA declares that a business need only make "reasonable accommodation" for employees and customers with disabilities that does not place an "undue hardship" on its operations.

Issue network A group of political actors that is actively involved with policymaking in a particular issue area.

Political scientists use the term **issue network** to describe a group of political actors that is actively involved with policymaking in a particular issue area. Issue networks vary from issue to issue. The issue network for disability rights includes advocacy groups for people with disabilities, business organizations, individual spokespersons for disability rights, journalists who focus on disability issues, members of Congress and the executive branch who are involved with the issue, and the courts. Although not all participants in an issue network are equally influential, no one individual or group is usually able to dominate policymaking on the issue. Instead, policy reflects the result of conflict and occasionally compromise among the participants.

Policy Adoption

Policy adoption is the official decision of a government body to accept a particular policy and put it into effect. The ADA, for example, was enacted through the legislative process. Congress passed the measure and the president signed it into law.

Not all policies are drafted into formal legislation and adopted through the legislative process. Courts adopt policies when they decide cases. Government agencies, such as the Environmental Protection Agency (EPA), adopt policies by issuing regulations. The president can adopt policy by issuing executive orders. Government officials also make policy when they decide either to take no action or continue policies already in place.

Policy Implementation

Policy implementation is the stage of the policy process in which policies are carried out. Implementation involves not just government officials but also individuals and groups outside of the government. Private businesses, individuals with disabilities, the Equal Employment Opportunity Commission (EEOC), and the courts all participate in the implementation of the ADA. The law requires private businesses to take reasonable steps to accommodate employees and customers with disabilities. If individuals with disabilities believe they have suffered discrimination, the law allows them to file a lawsuit against the offending business and/or file a complaint with the EEOC. Penalties for violators can be as high as $110,000 for repeat offenders.[10] During 2006, the EEOC, which also hears charges of racial, ethnic, gender, and age discrimination, handled 15,575 complaints based on the ADA, more than a fifth of the total complaints filed with the agency.[11]

The implementation process often involves supplying details and interpretations of policy that are omitted, either intentionally or unintentionally, during policy formulation. The ADA, as noted, requires businesses to make "reasonable accommodations" for employees and customers with disabilities that do not place an "undue hardship" on their operations. How these terms apply to hundreds of specific circumstances depends on their interpretation by the EEOC and the courts. The EEOC, for example, has ruled that employers may not refuse to hire people with disabilities because of concerns about their impact on health insurance costs.[12] More often than not, the courts have sided with employers, narrowing the scope of the ADA and making it difficult for individuals to prevail in disability discrimination lawsuits filed against businesses. Employers win more than 90 percent of the workplace discrimination cases filed under the ADA.[13]

Policy Evaluation

Policy evaluation is the assessment of policy. It involves questions of equity, efficiency, effectiveness, and political feasibility. *Equity* is the concept that similarly situated people should be treated equally. *Efficiency* is a comparison of a policy's costs with the benefits it provides. *Effectiveness* is the extent to which a policy achieves its goals. *Political feasibility* refers to the ability of a policy to obtain and hold public support. Equitable policies are not always efficient. Similarly, some policies that are effective are not politically feasible, and vice versa.[14]

Normative analysis A method of study that is based on certain values.

Evaluation can be either normative or empirical. A **normative analysis** is a method of study that is based on certain values. A normative evaluation of the ADA, for example, might consider the merits of the goals of the law or the wisdom of trying to achieve those goals through government regulation. In contrast, an **empirical analysis** is a method of study that relies on experience and scientific observation. An empirical evaluation might focus on changes in the employment rate for people with disabilities, the number of lawsuits filed under the law, or the average cost of compliance to employers and business owners.

Empirical analysis A method of study that relies on experience and scientific observation.

Evaluation studies show that the ADA has had a mixed impact:

- A survey of corporate executives found that the median cost of making the workplace more accessible was only $223 per individual with disabilities. Two-thirds of the executives surveyed reported that the ADA had not spawned an increase in lawsuits.[15]

- A majority of ADA complaints filed with the EEOC have involved issues that members of Congress did not discuss in drafting the law, such as back problems and psychological stress. Only 10 percent of the complaints have come from people with spinal cord injuries or other neurological problems—the conditions most frequently mentioned when the ADA was written.[16]

GETTING INVOLVED   Government and You

Government policies affect each of us every day in ways that are obvious and in ways that may not always be readily apparent. If a police officer stops you for speeding on your way to class, the government has touched you in a fashion that is direct and clear. In contrast, when you pick up a relative at the airport for a holiday visit, it may not occur to you that tax dollars paid to build the airport.

An important goal of this course is for students to recognize the relevance of government to their own lives and to the life of their community. To help achieve that goal, your assignment is to keep a journal documenting the impact of government on your life throughout the semester. You can write in longhand in a notebook or create your journal entries in a computer file to be submitted at the end of the term. Each entry will identify and discuss a daily event in your life that involved your interaction with government, either directly or indirectly.

Your instructor will grade your journal on the following criteria:

- **Number and frequency of entries.** Your journal must include at least four dated entries for each week of the course.

- **Evidence of growth in your understanding of American government.** As the course progresses, your journal entries should reveal a higher level of sophistication than entries made in the first few weeks of the term.

- **Quality of journal entries.** Some of your entries should identify a connection to course materials, citing concepts discussed in your textbook or in the classroom. At least one entry a week should include a personal evaluation of the role of government. You will not be graded on your point of view, but you should display evidence that you have thought critically about the role of government in your life and in society as a whole.

- Despite the ADA, the employment rate for people with disabilities actually declined between 1992 and 2000.[17]

Feedback The impact of the results of policy evaluation on the policy process.

The impact of the results of policy evaluation on the policy process is known as **feedback.** If a policy is judged successful and the problem solved, officials may terminate the policy. Should the problem persist, the policy process may begin anew as groups and individuals once again push the issue to the forefront of the policy agenda. Evaluation studies frequently result in initiatives to modify policies or improve their implementation. In 1999, for example, Congress passed, and President Bill Clinton signed, legislation making it easier for people with disabilities to keep their government-funded healthcare coverage after taking a job. The supporters of the act hoped that it would enable thousands of people with disabilities who had previously been kept out of the job market, despite the ADA, because of fear of losing their health coverage, to take jobs.

 WHAT IS YOUR OPINION?

Has the ADA been a success or failure? What is the basis for your answer?

KEY TERMS

agenda building

Americans with Disabilities Act (ADA)

empirical analysis

feedback

global warming

government

Gross Domestic Product (GDP)

issue network

normative analysis

policy adoption

policy evaluation

policy formulation

policy implementation

policymaking environment

politics

public policy

public policy approach

NOTES

1. Civil Rights Division, U.S. Department of Justice, "A Guide to Disability Rights Laws," September 2005, available at www.usdoj.gov.
2. Office of Management and Budget, "Total Government Receipts in Absolute Amounts and as a Percentage of GDP: 1948–2006," *The Budget for Fiscal Year 2008, Historical Tables*, available at www.omb.gov.
3. David Easton, "Political Science in the United States," in David Easton, John G. Gunnell, and Luigi Graziano, eds., *The Development of Political Science* (London: Routledge, 1991), p. 275.
4. Thomas A. Birkland, *An Introduction to the Policy Process: Theories, Concepts, and Models of Public Policy Making* (Armonk, NY: M.E. Sharpe, 2001), pp. 4–5.
5. Thomas A. Birkland, *An Introduction to the Policy Process: Theories, Concepts, and Models of Public Policy Making*, 2nd ed. (Armonk, NY: M. E. Sharpe, 2005), p. 6.
6. Roger W. Cobb and Marc Howard Ross, "Agenda Setting and the Denial of Agenda Access: Key Concepts," in Roger W. Cobb and Marc Howard Ross, eds., *Cultural Strategies of Agenda Denial: Avoidance, Attack, and Redefinition* (Lawrence, KS: University of Kansas Press, 1997), pp. 19–20.
7. David A. Rochefort and Roger W. Cobb, "Problem Definition: An Emerging Perspective," in David A. Rochefort and Roger W. Cobb, eds., *The Politics of Problem Definition: Shaping the Policy Agenda* (Lawrence, KS: University of Kansas Press, 1994), pp. 1–31.

8. Jack M. McNeil, *Employment, Earnings, and Disability*, U.S. Bureau of the Census, 2000, available at www.census.gov.

9. Civil Rights Division, "A Guide to Disability Rights Laws."

10. U.S. Equal Employment Opportunity Commission, Department of Justice, Civil Rights Division, *The Americans with Disabilities Act: Questions and Answers,* available at www.usdoj.gov.

11. U.S. Equal Employment Opportunity Commission, "Charge Statistics FY 1997 through FY 2006," available at www.eeoc.gov.

12. U.S. Equal Employment Opportunity Commission, "Selected Enforcement Guidelines and Other Policy Documents on the ADA," available at www.eeoc.gov.

13. National Resource Center on AD/HD, "Workplace and Higher Education Issues," available at www.help4adhd.org.

14. Christine H. Rossell, "Using Multiple Criteria to Evaluate Public Policies: The Case of School Desegregation," *American Politics Quarterly* 21 (April 1993), p. 162.

15. Jill Smolowe, "Noble Aims, Mixed Results," *Time*, July 31, 1995, p. 55.

16. U.S. Equal Employment Opportunity Commission, "ADA Charge Data by Impairments/Bases—Merit Factor Resolutions, 1997–2007," available at www.eeoc.gov.

17. David C. Stapleton and Richard Burkhauser, eds., *Decline in Employment of People with Disabilities: A Policy Puzzle* (Kalamazoo, MI: W. E. Upjohn Institute, 2003).

Chapter 1

A Changing America in a Changing World

CHAPTER OUTLINE

LEARNING OUTCOMES

After studying Chapter 1, students should be able to do the following:

- Assess the impact of demographic change on the policymaking environment, especially the aging of the population and the retirement of the baby-boom generation. (p. 14)

- Describe America's political culture, focusing in particular on the key elements of democracy and capitalism. (pp. 15–17)

- Assess the impact of the international environment on the nation's policymaking process. (p. 17)

- Assess the impact of immigration, both legal and illegal, on the policymaking process. (pp. 18–20)

- Describe the population of the United States in terms of size, growth rate, race and ethnicity, and geographic distribution. (pp. 20–21)

- Assess the size and strength of the economy of the United States relative to the economies of other countries. (p. 23)

- Evaluate the impact of the global economy on policymaking in the United States. (pp. 23–25)

- Describe patterns of wealth and poverty in America, comparing the economic status of families and individuals based on race, ethnicity, gender, residence, region, and family composition. (pp. 25–27)

- Describe the relationship between the cultural, international, demographic, and economic environments and the policymaking process. (pp. 27–29)

- Define the key terms listed on page 30 and explain their significance.

The population of the United States is aging. In 2007, 37.9 million Americans were age 65 and older. The U.S. Census Bureau estimates that the number of older Americans will increase steadily for at least the next two decades. The number of people at least 65 years old will be 40.2 million in 2010, 46.8 million in 2015, 54.6 million in 2020, and 63.5 million in 2025. As a percentage of the total population, the group of people 65 years and above will steadily increase from 12.6 percent in 2007 to 18.1 percent in 2025. While the older population is increasing rapidly, the number of people between 16 and 64 years of age, the prime working years, is growing slowly and actually falling as a percentage of the total population. According to the U.S. Census Bureau, the population age 16 to 64 will fall from 65.6 percent of the total population in 2010 to only 60.6 percent in 2025.[1]

The aging of the population threatens the financial solvency of the government's major healthcare and pension programs—Medicare, Medicaid, and Social Security. Medicare and Medicaid are healthcare programs. **Medicare** is a federally funded health insurance program for the elderly. As the population ages, the number of people eligible for Medicare will climb and the cost of the program will grow. **Medicaid** is a federal program designed to provide health insurance coverage to low-income persons, people with disabilities, and elderly people who are impoverished. Although older people are a minority of Medicaid recipients, the cost of their healthcare is greater than it is for other groups of beneficiaries. **Social Security** is a federal pension and disability insurance program funded through a payroll tax on workers and their employers. Its costs will rise as more and more people reach retirement age and begin collecting benefits. Because the traditional working age population is growing slowly, payroll tax revenues will be unable to keep up with program expenditures, forcing the government to cut benefits or find other revenue sources to fund the program.

The slow growth of the population of traditional working age threatens the economy as well as the ability of the government to raise sufficient revenue to cover the costs of Medicare, Medicaid, Social Security, and other government programs. Who will fill the jobs currently held by older Americans as they reach retirement age? Will many people age 65 and above decide to remain in the workforce beyond the traditional retirement age of 65? Will their places be taken by new waves of immigrants and their children?

Demographic change, such as the aging of the population, is an important element of the **policymaking environment,** which is the complex of factors outside of government that has an impact, either directly or indirectly, on the policymaking process. The policymaking environment influences the types of issues that appear on the policy agenda, the policy options government decision makers consider during policy formulation, the policy alternatives selected during policy adoption, the resources available for policy implementation, and the values that influence policy evaluation. Chapter 1 is the first of a series of chapters that deal with the environment for policymaking. The chapter examines some of the more important aspects of the cultural, international, and socioeconomic environments for policymaking in America. Subsequent chapters address the legal/constitutional environment and the political environment.

Medicare A federally funded health insurance program for the elderly.

Medicaid A federal program designed to provide health insurance coverage to low-income persons, people with disabilities, and elderly people who are impoverished.

Social Security A federal pension and disability insurance program funded through a payroll tax on workers and their employers.

Policymaking environment The complex of factors outside of government that has an impact, either directly or indirectly, on the policymaking process.

POLITICAL CULTURE

Political culture
The widely held, deeply rooted political values of a society.

Political culture refers to the widely held, deeply rooted political values of a society. These values are important for the policymaking process because they define the terms of political debate and establish the range of acceptable policy options available to policymakers.

Democracy and Capitalism

Democracy A system of government in which ultimate political authority is vested in the people.

Attitudes toward democracy and capitalism constitute the core of America's political culture. A **democracy** is a system of government in which ultimate political authority is vested in the people. Political scientist Robert A. Dahl identifies eight criteria of democracy:

1. **The Right to Vote**   All or nearly all citizens enjoy the right to vote and have their votes counted equally. In the United States, every adult citizen has the right to vote except people who have lost their voting rights because they have been convicted of a serious crime. Significant restrictions on the right to vote are undemocratic. For example, Saudi Arabia held elections for the first time in 2006 to select members of municipal councils but only allowed men to cast ballots. Although holding an election is a step toward democracy, excluding women is undemocratic.

2. **The Right to Be Elected**   Citizens have the right to compete for elective office, including people who oppose the policies of the current government. In 2002, Vietnam held elections for the National Assembly with 759 candidates competing for 498 positions. The election fell short of democracy, however, because the only candidates who were allowed to compete were either members of the Communist Party or had been approved by the party organization.[2]

3. **The Right of Political Leaders to Compete for Support and Votes**   Candidates have an opportunity to conduct campaigns in order to win support. If candidates cannot campaign, voters are unable to make informed choices.

4. **Free and Fair Elections**   All candidates compete under the same set of rules, without legal advantage or disadvantage. Democratic governments respect the outcomes of elections, peacefully stepping down from office and allowing opposition political parties and leaders to take power.

5. **Freedom of Association**   Citizens have the right to form political parties and organize groups. They can attend meetings, participate in political rallies, and take part in peaceful demonstrations.

6. **Freedom of Expression**   People living in a democracy have the right to express their political views without censorship or fear of government retaliation. Governments that jail their critics are not democracies. For example, an Egyptian court sentenced an opposition political leader to five years in prison at hard labor for allegedly forging the signatures on the petition he used to create his own political party, including those of his wife and father.[3]

7. **Alternative Sources of Information**   The citizens in a democracy have access to information sources that are not controlled by the government. Elections cannot be free and fair if the only information voters have about government policies and candidates is information supplied and controlled by the government. In Russia, for example, the government has shut down or taken over all private television networks with a national reach. Journalists who dare to report information that contradicts the official government line face the danger of lawsuits, imprisonment, and even death.[4]

8. **Institutions for Making Public Policies Depend on Votes and Other Expressions of Citizen Preference**   In a democracy, citizens elect policymakers. Free and fair elections are meaningless if military leaders or religious figures that do not answer to the voters are the real policymakers.[5] Saudi Arabia, despite its recent elections for municipal councils, is an **absolute monarchy,** which is a country ruled by one person, usually a king or queen. King Abdullah rules Saudi Arabia. In contrast, Great Britain is both a democracy and a constitutional monarchy. A **constitutional monarchy** is a country in which the powers of the ruler are limited to those granted under the constitution and the laws of the nation. The British monarch, Queen Elizabeth, is a tourist attraction rather than an actual ruler.

Absolute monarchy A country ruled by one person, usually a king or queen.

Constitutional monarchy A country in which the powers of the ruler are limited to those granted under the constitution and the laws of the nation.

Capitalism An economic system characterized by individual and corporate ownership of the means of production, and a market economy based on the supply and demand of goods and services.

Capitalism is the other principal element of America's political culture. It is an economic system characterized by individual and corporate ownership of the means of production, and a market economy based on the supply and demand of goods and services. Under capitalism, the marketplace, in which buyers and sellers freely exchange goods and services, determines what goods and services are produced, how they are produced, and for whom they are produced. The proponents of capitalism argue that it is good for consumers because businesses compete to provide quality goods and services at prices that consumers are willing to pay. They believe that capitalism promotes economic growth because only the most efficient business enterprises survive the competition of the marketplace.

Political Culture and Policymaking

Political culture is an important part of the policymaking environment because it helps determine which problems make the policy agenda and sets the boundaries of permissible solutions available to policymakers for dealing with those problems. When a number of coal miners were killed in a series of coal mining accidents in West Virginia in early 2006, union leaders and government officials demanded tougher safety standards for mines, better equipment for miners, and closer inspections by government agencies. No one, not even the most radical union leaders, demanded that the government take over the coal mining industry. Public (i.e., government) ownership of coalmines or major industries in general is not a policy option within the permissible limits of America's political culture because it contradicts the basic principles of capitalism. Similarly, most Americans responded to the terrorist attacks of September 11, 2001, by demanding tighter airport security, better law enforcement, and a military response abroad. Few people called for the government to halt immigration or imprison individuals who have criticized American foreign policy. In fact, President George W. Bush and other national leaders were quick to warn against targeting Muslims or Arab Americans for retaliation.

THE INTERNATIONAL ENVIRONMENT

The United States is the preeminent nation in the world, militarily, economically, and culturally. Since the collapse of the Soviet Union in 1991, the United States has become the world's only military superpower. The United States spends more money on its military than the next 14 countries combined.[6] The United States is also the foremost economic power with the world's largest and most productive economy. Furthermore, American culture permeates the world. American fashion, music, and entertainment are pervasive.

Nonetheless, the events of September 11, 2001, demonstrated that the United States is vulnerable to attack despite the strength of its armed forces. American military might proved to be no deterrent to terrorists willing to give their own lives in order to inflict casualties on the United States. The challenge American armed forces faced after September 11 was to respond effectively to international terrorism with armed forces developed with the goal of fighting a conventional war against other nations rather than against terrorists who are not directly associated with another government.

The terrorist attacks of September 11, 2001, changed the international environment for policymaking in the United States.

The American economy is more closely tied to the global economy than ever before. Russia, Eastern Europe, the new nations that were once part of the Soviet Union, and China now participate in the world economy, buying and selling goods and services internationally. The opportunities for American companies to sell goods and services abroad are greater, but competition has increased as well. As a result, trade issues enjoy a more prominent place on the nation's policy agenda. The global economy also means that economic disruptions in one nation affect other countries as well. The financial crisis that engulfed the U.S. economy in 2008 soon produced a worldwide **recession,** which is an economic slowdown characterized by declining economic output and rising unemployment.

Recession An economic slowdown characterized by declining economic output and rising unemployment.

THE DEMOGRAPHIC ENVIRONMENT

The United States has more than 300 million people. Figure 1.1 traces the population growth rate of the United States during the twentieth century. The nation's population increased rapidly in the early decades of the century before the Depression years of the 1930s, when the growth rate fell sharply. The population growth rate accelerated in the late 1940s and 1950s with the birth of the **baby-boom generation,** which is the exceptionally large number of Americans born during the late 1940s, 1950s, and early 1960s. Many American families delayed having children during the Great Depression of the 1930s and during World War II in the early 1940s.

Baby-boom generation The exceptionally large number of Americans born during the late 1940s, 1950s, and early 1960s.

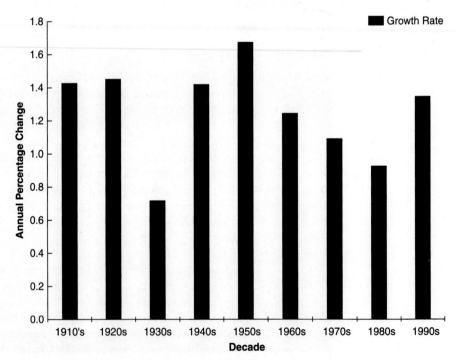

FIGURE 1.1   Average Annual Population Growth.
Source: U.S. Census Bureau.

After the war, the birthrate soared because families reunited and people grew optimistic about the future. With the end of the baby boom, the rate of population growth slowed in each subsequent decade until the 1990s, when the nation's population increased more rapidly than it had in any decade since the 1950s. Even though birthrates fell during the 1990s, the population growth rate climbed because of increased immigration.

Immigration

Immigrants constitute an eighth of the nation's population.[7] Whereas earlier waves of immigration to the United States were primarily from Europe, most recent immigrants come from Latin America or Asia. The primary countries of origin for recent legal immigrants to the United States are, in order of importance, Mexico, India, Philippines, and China. The states in which immigrants most frequently settle are California, New York, Texas, Florida, New Jersey, and Illinois.[8]

Professor Dowell Myers believes that the United States should welcome immigration to balance an otherwise top-heavy age structure in the population. The retirement of the baby-boom generation will leave a void in the workforce too large for the smaller generations that followed the baby-boomers to occupy. Millions of jobs may go unfilled and payroll tax collections may be inadequate to cover healthcare and pension benefits for retirees unless the nation adopts a liberal immigration policy to allow skilled and unskilled workers into the country to fill the employment gap.[9]

Illegal Immigration

More than 11 million people live in the United States illegally—and the number is growing.[10] The undocumented population is evenly divided between people who entered the country legally on temporary visas, such as student visas and tourist visas, and people who crossed the border illegally. More than half of the unauthorized immigrants are from Mexico. One of every nine Mexicans now lives in the United States. A quarter of illegal immigrants are from other Latin American countries, particularly Honduras, El Salvador, Guatemala, Nicaragua, and Brazil. The rest comes from Canada, Europe, Asia, and Africa. Although the population of undocumented immigrants is growing in every region of the country, a majority of illegal immigrants live in the states of California, Texas, Florida, New York, Arizona, Illinois, and New Jersey.

People migrate to the United States primarily for economic reasons. Unauthorized workers account for 5 percent of the civilian workforce. They are concentrated in low-wage occupations such as farming, cleaning, construction, and food preparation. Although unauthorized workers in the United States earn only about half as much per person as do American citizens and permanent residents, they make substantially more money than they earned in their home countries.

Most undocumented immigrants live in families rather than alone as single adults. The ratio of men to women is 56 percent to 44 percent. Undocumented families include more than three million children who are U.S. citizens because they were born in the United States. Most unauthorized families live at or near the poverty level and lack health insurance.[11]

Illegal immigration is controversial. Critics charge that undocumented workers drive down wage rates for American citizens while overcrowding schools and hospital emergency rooms. They argue that unauthorized immigrants undermine the nation's cultural integrity because they create cultural enclaves that resemble their home countries instead of learning English and adopting the customs of the United States. The opponents of illegal immigration favor tighter border controls, strict enforcement of immigration laws, and punishment for American citizens who provide unauthorized immigrants with jobs, housing, healthcare, and other services.

 WHAT IS YOUR OPINION?

Should U.S. immigration policies favor people from countries that speak English?

In contrast, immigration advocates contend that the United States benefits from immigration, even illegal immigration. They argue that undocumented workers take jobs that citizens do not want and that they pay more in taxes than they receive in government services. An influx of hard-working, well-motivated manual workers enhances the competitiveness of American industry and provides additional jobs for citizens as managers. The defenders of immigration believe that today's immigrants enrich the nation's culture just as did earlier waves of immigrants from Great Britain, Germany, Ireland, Italy, and Poland. Furthermore, the proponents of immigration contend that most recent immigrants are quick to learn English and eager to become citizens so they can participate in the nation's political life. Immigration advocates believe that the United States should grant legal status to undocumented workers who have helped build the nation's economy, while enacting a realistic immigration system to enable foreign workers to enter the country legally to find jobs.

Population Diversity

The United States is a multiracial/multiethnic society. The 2000 U.S. Census found that the nation's population was 75 percent white, 12 percent African American, 4 percent Asian American, 1 percent Native American, and 6 percent another race. More than 7 million people, 2.5 percent of the total population, classified themselves as biracial or multiracial.[12] Nearly 13 percent of the nation's population identified as Latino (who may be any race). Latinos were the fastest growing American ethnic group during the 1990s, increasing by more than 50 percent.[13] Because of continued immigration and relatively high birthrates for Latino women, demographers expect that the Latino population will continue to grow rapidly, increasing from 12.6 percent of the population in 2000 to 24.4 percent in 2050.[14]

The United States has the largest economy in the world.

Sunbelt The Southern and Western regions of the United States.

Frostbelt The Northeastern and Midwestern regions of the United States.

The population of the United States has been shifting to the South and the West, the region known as the **Sunbelt,** and away from the Northeast and Midwest, the **Frostbelt.** In 1970, a majority of the nation's population, 52 percent, lived in the Frostbelt. The population has subsequently shifted steadily to the South and West. In 2000, 58 percent of Americans lived in the Sunbelt.[15] The Sunbelt population is growing because of relatively higher birthrates in the region, immigration from abroad, and intrastate migration from the Frostbelt.

Population changes have affected the political balance in the U.S. House of Representatives. Because the Northeast and Midwest have lost population, they have lost seats in the House. After the 2000 U.S. Census, New York and Pennsylvania each lost two House seats, whereas eight other states lost one seat each. In contrast, the South and West gained seats. Arizona, Texas, Florida, and Georgia each gained two seats in the House. Four other states added one seat apiece. Sunbelt politicians have also dominated the race for the White House. Barack Obama of Illinois was the first successful presidential candidate from a Frostbelt state since 1960 when John Kennedy of Massachusetts won the White House.

The United States is an urban country. According to the 2000 U.S. Census, 80 percent of the nation's people reside in metropolitan areas, with a majority of Americans living in urban centers of more than a million residents. Furthermore, metropolitan areas are growing more rapidly than non-metropolitan areas. During the 1990s, the population of metropolitan areas increased by 13.9 percent compared to a 10.2 percent growth rate in nonmetropolitan areas.[16]

GLOBAL PERSPECTIVE   Immigration Policy and Politics in France

The government of France encouraged immigration after World War II to provide labor for postwar reconstruction. France experienced a postwar labor shortage because it suffered 600,000 casualties during the war. It also had the lowest birthrate in Europe between World War I and World War II. The steel, mining, and electric power industries in particular needed foreign workers to meet the postwar demand. Many foreign workers took jobs in service industries as well. Over the next 30 years, millions of foreign workers migrated to France. Sometimes they were joined by their families. Immigrants came to France from Southern Europe, especially Italy and Portugal, and from North Africa. Algeria, which had been a French colony prior to its independence in 1962, was the most important North African nation of origin.*

The presence in France of a large number of North African immigrants has been controversial. Some French see North Africans as a threat to social cohesion and even national security. North Africans, most of whom are Arab Muslims, are ethnically and culturally different from the French European majority, most of which is nonobservant Catholic. Some French also consider North Africans a threat to national security because of the association of some European Islamic immigrants with 9/11 and other terrorist acts. Nonetheless, many European French reject anti-immigrant appeals because they believe that anti-immigrant sentiments contradict the fundamental principles of French democracy, which are *Liberté, Égalité, Fraternité* (liberty, equality, and brotherhood). They believe that France should embrace the cultural diversity of immigrant populations rather than forcing their assimilation.[†]

France has adopted a series of laws and regulations aimed at addressing the issue of non-European immigration. France has halted the immigration of non-European workers but continues to allow family reunification, which has increased the number of North Africans living in France. To reduce the size of the immigrant population, France has offered financial incentives to immigrants to return home, but the program has had little success. It has threatened to fine employers who use illegal workers. France has also attempted to pressure North African immigrants to assimilate into French culture. A 2004 law, for example, bans headscarves from public schools, preventing Muslim girls from covering their heads.[‡]

QUESTIONS TO CONSIDER

1. How important is it for immigrants to adopt the culture of the majority of people in their new country?
2. Are Mexican immigrants in the United States as culturally different as North African immigrants in France?
3. Is opposition to non-European immigration in France (and the United States) racist?

*Chistopher Rudolph, *National Security and Immigration: Policy Develops in the United States and Western Europe Since 1945* (Stanford, CA: Stanford University Press, 2006), pp. 126–142.

†Mari-Claude Blanc-Chaléard. "Old and New Migrants in France: Italians and Algerians," in Leo Lucassen, David Feldman, and Jochen Oltmer, eds., *Paths of Integration: Migrants in Western Europe (1880–2004)* (Amsterdam: Amsterdam University Press, 2006), p. 54.

‡Alec G. Hargreaves, *Multi-Ethnic France: Immigration, Politics, Culture, and Society* (NY: Routledge, 2007), p. 201.

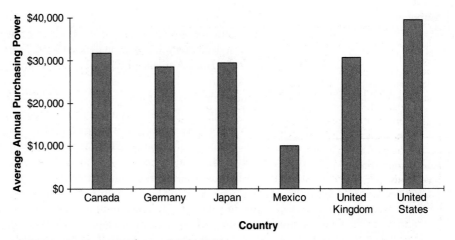

FIGURE 1.2   Per Capita Purchasing Power, 2004.
Source: U.S. Census Bureau, "Gross Domestic Product (GDP) by Country: 1990-2004," *2008 Statistical Abstract,* available at www.census.gov.

THE ECONOMIC ENVIRONMENT

Gross Domestic Product (GDP) The total value of goods and services produced by a nation's economy in a year, excluding transactions with foreign countries.

Per capita Per person.

Standard of living A term that refers to the goods and services affordable by and available to the residents of a nation.

Developing countries Nations with relatively low levels of per capita income.

The United States has the largest economy in the world. The **Gross Domestic Product (GDP)** is the total value of goods and services produced by a nation's economy in a year, excluding transactions with foreign countries. The U.S. GDP stood at $13.8 trillion at the end of 2007. No other country's economy is nearly as large. Even though the United States contains only 4.6 percent of the world's population, it generates 21.1 percent of world economic output.[17]

Figure 1.2 shows GDP **per capita** (per person) adjusted for purchasing power differences for Canada, Germany, Japan, Mexico, the United Kingdom, and the United States. Because the cost of goods and services varies from country to country, the same amount of money does not purchase the same quantity of goods and services from one nation to another. Adjusting GDP per capita to reflect differences in purchasing power is a good measure of a nation's **standard of living,** which is a term that refers to the goods and services affordable by and available to the residents of a nation. As the figure indicates, the average American enjoys greater purchasing power than people living in the other countries listed. Americans are somewhat better off than people living in other industrialized countries, such as Canada, Germany, Japan, and the United Kingdom. Meanwhile, the standard of living in the United States is substantially higher than it is in Mexico and other **developing countries,** which are nations with relatively low levels of per capita income.

Global Economy

The United States emerged from World War II as the world's foremost economic power. With European and Asian competitors devastated by war, American companies dominated the domestic market and shipped manufactured goods around the globe. Millions of Americans with only a high school education found good-paying jobs working in steel plants or on automobile assembly lines.

Global economy
The integration of national economies into a world economic system in which companies compete worldwide for suppliers and markets.

North American Free Trade Agreement (NAFTA) An international accord among the United States, Mexico, and Canada to lower trade barriers among the three nations.

Today, the United States is part of a **global economy,** which is the integration of national economies into a world economic system in which companies compete worldwide for suppliers and markets. International treaties and agreements, such as the **North American Free Trade Agreement (NAFTA),** have reduced the barriers to trade among the world's countries. NAFTA is an international accord among the United States, Mexico, and Canada to lower trade barriers among the three nations. The move toward free trade has allowed American companies to compete for business abroad, but it has forced them to compete at home as well against overseas competitors.

Some American companies and workers have prospered in the global economy. American agriculture and major retailers such as Wal-Mart have benefited from international trade because their markets (and profits) have grown.[18] Companies that have lowered their cost of doing business through outsourcing or the use of modern technology have also done well. Their investors have profited from higher stock prices, and their managers and executives have reaped the reward in higher salaries and bonuses. Skilled workers who understand and can operate the latest technology in their fields are in high demand, especially workers who have the ability to adapt quickly as technology changes.

In contrast, international trade has been a disaster for workers in fields that have been unable to compete against low-wage competition from abroad. Less expensive transportation and communication systems make it possible to produce goods in areas of the world where production costs are low and then transport those goods to markets worldwide. How can an American manufacturer afford to pay $15 an hour to low-skill assembly workers in the United States if low-skill workers in Indonesia, China, or the Caribbean will do the same work for less than $2 an hour? The American firm must either move its production process to a country with lower wage costs or lose market share because it cannot compete. Since 1995, textile employment in the United States has fallen from 850,000 jobs to 200,000 as companies either go out of business or move their operations overseas where wage rates are lower.[19] American companies have also begun to cut costs by outsourcing information technology work and some business process functions to India, China, and Russia—countries that have a large number of college-educated workers who will work for much lower wages than their counterparts in the United States. Computer programming jobs that pay $60,000 to $80,000 a year in the United States can be performed for as little as $9,000 a year in China, $6,000 in India, and $5,000 in Russia.[20]

Low-skill, poorly educated American workers have also been damaged by technological change. Modern technology has enabled companies to replace low-skill workers with machines, generating the same output or more with fewer workers. Between 1979 and 2000, U.S. factory output nearly doubled even though the number of manufacturing jobs fell by more than two million. A quarter century ago, General Motors (GM) employed 454,000 workers to manufacture five million vehicles. In 2004, GM produced the same number of cars and trucks, but its payroll had shrunk to 118,000 employees.[21] Even though the American workers who lose their jobs because of international trade and technological change usually find new positions, their new jobs typically pay $2 or more an hour less than their old jobs and often come without benefits.[22] In 1979, General Motors, Ford, and General Electric were the nation's largest employers, whereas today the companies employing the most workers are Wal-Mart, Mc-Donald's, and UPS.[23]

Wal-Mart is the largest private employer in the United States.

TABLE 1.1   Share of National Income Received by Each Fifth of Families: 1980–2007

Year	Poorest 5th	Second 5th	Third 5th	Fourth 5th	Wealthiest 5th
1980	5.3%	11.6%	17.6%	24.4%	41.4%
1985	4.8	11.0	16.9	24.3	43.1
1990	4.6	10.8	16.6	23.8	44.3
1995	4.4	10.1	15.6	23.2	46.5
2000	4.3	9.8	15.5	22.8	47.4
2007	3.7	9.6	15.3	22.9	48.5

Sources: U.S. Census Bureau, *2008 Statistical Abstract,* available at www.census.gov;
U.S. Census Bureau, "Income and Earnings Summary Measures by Selected Characteristics:
2006 and 2007," *Income, Poverty, and Health Insurance Coverage in the United States: 2007,*
available at www.census.gov.

Income Distribution

As the economy has changed, the gap between the rich and other income groups has widened. Table 1.1 shows the share of national income earned by each of five income groups, from the poorest fifth of American families through the wealthiest fifth. Over a 27-year period from 1980 through 2007, the proportion of national income received by the wealthiest fifth of the population increased from 41.4 percent to 48.5 percent. The rich got richer. In the meantime, the share of national income earned by the four other groups of families declined. In particular, the share of income earned by the poorest families fell by more than 30 percent, from 5.3 percent of the total in 1980 to 3.7 percent in 2007. The poor got poorer.

Another way to explain the concept of income distribution is to compare the earnings of people at the top of the income ladder with those of ordinary wage earners.

In 1992, the 400 individuals and families with the highest incomes in the country received, on average, $12.9 million in wages and salaries. That figure represented the combined salaries of 287,400 retail clerks. In 2000, the average income for the top 400 had more than doubled to $29 million, an amount equal to the total earnings of 504,600 retail clerks.[24] In short, the wealthiest 400 Americans earned more money in 2000 than more than half a million retail clerks earned combined.

Economist Robert H. Frank attributes the growth of income inequality to changes in the economy and in tax policy. Professor Frank says that the United States has a winner-take-all economy in which small differences in performance often translate into huge differences in economic reward. Corporate executives, sports stars, and well-known entertainers earn huge paychecks, many times greater than the earnings of ordinary workers, average athletes, and entertainers without the star power. In the meantime, income tax reductions adopted during the Ronald Reagan and George W. Bush administrations significantly reduced income tax rates for upper-income earners, effectively shifting wealth toward the top of the income ladder.[25]

Household income in the United States varies, depending on race, ethnicity, residence, region, and gender. Whites and Asian Americans/Pacific Islanders are better off than Latinos and African Americans. In 2007, the median household income in the United States was $50,233. Asian American/Pacific Islander households had the highest average income—$66,103. The average income for white households was $54,920. In contrast, the average household income for African Americans and Latino households was significantly lower—$33,916 and $38,679, respectively. Incomes vary depending on whether families live in metropolitan or nonmetropolitan areas. In 2007, the average household income for families living in metropolitan areas was higher than it was for families located outside big cities. Suburban households had higher incomes than families living in the inner city. Family incomes differ based on region. In 2007, household income was lower in the South than it was in any other region of the country. Household income was highest in the Northeast. Income also varies by gender. In 2007, the average income of male full-time, year-round workers was $45,113 compared with $35,102 for women.[26]

Income differences among racial and ethnic groups, and between men and women, reflect disparities in education and training, social factors, and discrimination. As a group, Asian Americans and whites are better educated than African Americans and Latinos. Women often fall behind their male counterparts on the career ladder because many women leave the workforce for years to raise children. Jobs that are traditionally held by women, such as nursing and education, typically pay less than jobs that are traditionally male. Finally, many observers believe that the incomes of women and minorities lag behind those of white males because of employment discrimination.

Poverty threshold
The amount of money an individual or family needs to purchase basic necessities, such as food, clothing, health care, shelter, and transportation.

Poverty

The government measures poverty on a subsistence basis. The **poverty threshold** is the amount of money an individual or family needs to purchase basic necessities, such as food, clothing, healthcare, shelter, and transportation. The actual dollar amount varies with family size and rises with inflation. In 2008, the official government poverty threshold was $21,200 for a family of four.[27] More than 37 million Americans lived in poverty in 2007, 12.5 percent of the population.[28]

Although the poverty rate for racial and ethnic minority groups and for families headed by women has declined over the past 50 years, it is still higher than it is for other groups. In 2007, the poverty rate for Latinos, African Americans, and Asian Americans stood at 21.5 percent, 24.5 percent, and 10.2 percent, respectively, compared with 8.2 percent for whites. Poverty also affects children and families headed by women in disproportionate numbers. Eighteen percent of the nation's children under 18 lived in families that were poor in 2007. The poverty rate for families headed by women was 28.3 percent.[29]

 WHAT IS YOUR OPINION?

Should the government do more to reduce poverty?

Nearly 46 million Americans, 15.3 percent of the population, lack health insurance coverage. Almost 60 percent of the population enjoys health insurance through their employers, although that figure has been falling because some companies have dropped coverage for existing employees or have chosen not to offer coverage to new employees.[30] Government-funded health insurance programs—Medicare, Medicaid, and military healthcare—cover about a fourth of the population. Most of the people who lack health insurance work in jobs that do not provide coverage. They have too much income to be eligible for Medicaid and are too young to qualify for Medicare. Without health insurance, they and their families must do without healthcare, pay for health services out of pocket, or go to hospital emergency rooms.

CONCLUSION: THE CULTURAL, INTERNATIONAL, AND SOCIOECONOMIC CONTEXT FOR POLICYMAKING

The cultural, international, demographic, and economic environments affect every stage of the policymaking process.

Agenda Building

The policymaking environment creates the context in which individuals and groups raise issues to the policy agenda. Dramatic events can have an immediate impact on the policy agenda. For example, the terrorist attacks of September 11, 2001, were startling events that focused the nation's attention on the issues of national defense and homeland security. Other developments, such as the aging of the nation's population, are less dramatic but nonetheless important. As the baby-boom generation reaches retirement, the policy agenda will increasingly reflect the interests and demands of older adults. Healthcare and retirement income security will claim a higher place on the policy agenda. Patterns of income distribution affect attitudes about government programs. African Americans and Latinos are more likely to favor government healthcare and income security programs than are whites and Asian Americans because they are more in need of government assistance. The recession of 2008-2009 focused attention on the economy.

GETTING INVOLVED

A Changing Nation, Changing Communities

Data from the 2000 U.S. Census show that the United States is changing. The population is both aging and growing more diverse. Whereas the huge baby-boom generation is aging, immigration, especially from Latin America and Asia, is transforming the face of America. The economy is changing as well. "Smokestack industries," such as automobile manufacturing and steel production, are in decline; high-tech industries, such as biotechnology and robotics, are expanding.

Is your local community changing as well? Your assignment is to research the ways in which your community has changed by interviewing one or more people who are longtime residents. The individuals you interview should be persons who have lived in the community for at least 15 or 20 years. They can be relatives, friends, coworkers, or classmates. Your questions should cover the following topics:

- **Population change.** Has the population of the area grown? Have people immigrated to the community from other states or other nations? How has the racial/ethnic makeup of the population changed? Has the population as a whole grown younger or older?
- **Economic change.** Has the mix of businesses and industries changed? Have any major

employers gone out of business? Are there new industries?

- **Cultural change.** Does the community have places of worship for religious faiths that are new to the area? Are there new types of restaurants? Do grocery stores carry different varieties of produce to match the tastes of new residents? Does the community celebrate different or additional holidays and festivals?

Take careful notes on what you are told because your instructor plans to organize a class discussion around the research that you and other students have completed. The instructor will ask students to relate the information they learned from their interviews and then analyze the impact of socioeconomic change on the policymaking process. Prepare for the discussion by considering the following questions: Would you expect different issues to appear on the policy agenda today as compared with 20 years ago based on the changes that have taken place in your community? Do you think the capacity of government to respond to policy demands has changed? Would you expect that the community's standard for evaluating government performance has changed?

Policy Formulation and Adoption

The environment affects policy formulation. Political culture limits the range of acceptable policy alternatives available to policymakers. Policy solutions that are widely perceived as undemocratic or contrary to the nation's capitalist traditions are not politically feasible. The nation's economy affects policy formulation as well. A healthy economy generates tax revenues that can be used to tackle policy problems, whereas a stagnant economy reduces the options of policymakers. Defense spending reflects the perceived level of threat to American interests in the international environment.

Policy adoption is affected by environmental factors. Consider the impact of population aging on the budget process. The aging of the population is draining the budget of resources that could be used to support new government programs. When the baby-boom generation retires, the cost of programs targeting the elderly will consume so much of the budget that they will crowd out most other spending.

Major agriculture producers say that they need immigrant labor to take positions that American citizens are unwilling to fill.

Policy Implementation and Evaluation

Cultural, international, demographic, and economic factors affect policy implementation. The ability of the government to implement expensive policies successfully may depend on long-term economic growth sufficient to generate revenue. Illegal immigration from Mexico may slow in the next few years because the Mexican economy is growing, whereas the size of the Mexican population is increasing more slowly than it was before.[31]

Environmental factors also influence policy evaluation. Americans evaluate policies from the perspectives of the broad political culture—capitalism and democracy. Groups of Americans that are numerous and groups that are economically advantaged are better positioned to make their voices heard in evaluating policies than smaller groups with relatively fewer resources.

Studying America's political culture, international environment, demographic environment, and economic environment is important for students of American government because these factors provide the context for policymaking. They determine the types of political issues that make the official policy agenda, establish the boundaries of acceptable policy options available to public officials during the policy formulation and adoption stages, set the ground rules for policy implementation, and establish standards for evaluating policies. Furthermore, changes in the nation's political culture, population, and economy, as well as changes in the international environment, will lead to changes in public policies.

KEY TERMS

absolute monarchy	global economy	policymaking environment
baby-boom generation	Gross Domestic Product (GDP)	political culture
capitalism	Medicaid	poverty threshold
constitutional monarchy	Medicare	recession
democracy	North American Free Trade	Social Security
developing countries	Agreement (NAFTA)	standard of living
Frostbelt	per capita	Sunbelt

NOTES

1. U.S. Census Bureau, "Resident Population Projection by Sex and Age: 2010–2050," 2008 *Statistical Abstract*, available at www.census.gov.
2. "Vietnam Gears Up for Single-Party Election," May 18, 2002, available at cnn.com.
3. Michael Slackman, "Testing Egypt, Mubarak Rival Is Sent to Jail," *New York Times*, December 25, 2005, available at www.nytimes.com.
4. M. Steven Fish, *Democracy Derailed in Russia: The Failure of Open Politics* (New York: Cambridge University Press, 2005), p. 71.
5. Robert A. Dahl, *Polyarchy: Participation and Opposition* (New Haven, CT: Yale University Press, 1971), p. 3.
6. Stockholm International Peace Research Institute, "Fifteen Major Spenders in 2006," available at www.sipri.org.
7. U.S. Census Bureau, "Census Bureau Data Show Key Population Changes Across Nation," available at www.census.gov.
8. U.S. Citizenship and Immigration Services (USCIS), *Fiscal Year 2004 Yearbook of Immigration Statistics*, available at http://uscis.gov/graphics/.
9. Dowell Myers, *Immigrants and Boomers: Forging a New Social Contract for the Future of America* (New York: Russell Sage Foundation, 2007), pp. 4–43.
10. Jeffrey S. Passel, "Size and Characteristics of the Unauthorized Migrant Population in the U.S.," available at http://pewhispanic.org.
11. Jeffrey S. Passel, "Unauthorized Migrants: Numbers and Characteristics," Pew Hispanic Center Report, June 2005, available at http://pewhispanic.org.
12. U.S. Census Bureau, "Population by Race, Including All Specific Combinations of Two Races, for the United States, 2000," available at www.census.gov.
13. U.S. Census Bureau, *The Population Profile of the United States: 2000*, available at www.census.gov.
14. U.S. Census Bureau, "Projected Population of the United States, by Race and Hispanic Origin: 2000 to 2050," available at www.census.gov.
15. U.S. Census Bureau, "Resident Population by Region, Race, and Hispanic Origin: 2000," 2001 *Statistical Abstract of the United States*, available at www.census.gov.
16. U.S. Census Bureau, "Metropolitan and Non-Metropolitan Population by State: 1980–2000," 2001 *Statistical Abstract of the United States*, available at www.census.gov.
17. Bureau of Economic Analysis, "Current Dollar and 'Real' Gross Domestic Product," available at www.bea.gov/.
18. Tim Weiner, "Free Trade Accord at 10: Growing Pains Are Clear," *New York Times*, December 27, 2003, available at www.nytimes.com.
19. John M. Berry, "Doing More with Fewer Workers," *Washington Post National Weekly Edition*, December 8–14, 2003, p. 19; Department of Labor, Bureau of Labor Statistics, "Textile Mills Employment: March 2006," available at www.bls.gov.
20. Gary Schneider, "Another Kind of Homeland Security," *Washington Post National Weekly Edition*, February 9–15, 2004, p. 16.
21. Ibid.
22. David Finkel, "The American Dream, Revisited," *Washington Post National Weekly Edition*, December 22, 2003–January 4, 2004, p. 19.
23. Scott Burns, "Jobs and Benefits Are a la Carte Now," *Dallas Morning News*, May 18, 2004, available at www.dallasnews.com.
24. Donald L. Barlett and James B. Steele, "Has Your Life Become a Game of Chance?" *Time*, February 2, 2004, p. 42.
25. Robert H. Frank, "Income Inequality and the Protestant Ethic," in Victor Nee and Richard Swedberg, eds., *Capitalism* (Stanford, CA: Stanford University Press, 2007), pp. 73–79.

26. U.S. Census Bureau, *Income, Poverty, and Health Insurance Coverage in the United States: 2007*, available at www.census.gov.

27. U.S. Department of Health and Human Services, "2008 Annual Update of the HHS Poverty Guidelines," available at www.hhs.gov.

28. U.S. Census Bureau, *Income, Poverty, and Health Insurance Coverage in the United States: 2007*.

29. Ibid.

30. Ibid.

31. Passel, "Unauthorized Migrants: Numbers and Characteristics."

Chapter 2

The American Constitution

CHAPTER OUTLINE

The Background of the Constitution
   Historical Setting
   American Political Thought

Constitutional Principles
   Representative Democracy
   Rule of Law
   Limited Government
   Separation of Powers with Checks and Balances
   Federalism
   Bicameralism

The Living Constitution
   Constitutional Change Through Practice and Experience
   Constitutional Change Through Amendment
   Constitutional Change Through Judicial Interpretation

The Constitution, Politics, and Public Policy

Conclusion: The Constitutional Environment for Policymaking
   Agenda Building
   Policy Formulation and Adoption
   Policy Implementation and Evaluation

LEARNING OUTCOMES

After studying Chapter 2, students should be able to do the following:

- Describe the role that the U.S. Constitution plays in structuring policymaking, focusing on the effort of the newly elected Democratic majorities in the U.S. House and Senate to change American policy in Iraq. (pp. 34–35)

- Trace the historical background of the Constitution, identifying the events that influenced the development of the Constitution of 1787. (pp. 35–37)

- Identify the elements of American political thought that had a significant impact on the development of American government, describing their influence on the Constitution. (pp. 37–39)

- Evaluate the significance for contemporary policymaking of the following constitutional principles: representative democracy, rule of law, limited government, separation of powers with checks and balances, federalism, and bicameralism. (pp. 40–46)

- Identify the ways in which the Constitution changes, including the amending process, change through practice and experience, and change through judicial interpretation. (pp. 47–52)

- Evaluate the arguments for and against the American constitutional system. (pp. 52–54)

- Assess the impact of the Constitution on each stage of the policymaking process. (pp. 54–56)

- Define the key terms listed on page 56 and explain their significance.

The Democratic Party won the 2006 congressional election, capturing narrow majorities in both the U.S. House and Senate. When the 110th session of Congress convened in January 2007, Democrats outnumbered Republicans in the House, 233–202. The margin in the Senate was 51–49, counting two independents as Democrats because they voted with the Democrats to organize the chamber.

The foremost goal for the new Democratic majority in Congress was ending the war in Iraq. Public opinion polls registered strong opposition to the war, especially among Democratic voters, and most Democratic members of Congress had campaigned on the issue. In May 2007, Congress passed a funding bill for the wars in Iraq and Afghanistan that included a provision requiring the president to begin withdrawing troops in October with the goal of getting all U.S. combat forces out of Iraq by the end of March 2008. The measure failed to become law, however, because President George W. Bush vetoed it and Congress was unable to override the veto. Congress eventually passed, and the president signed, a war-funding bill that did not include a withdrawal provision.

The failure of the newly elected Democratic congressional majority to force an end to the war in Iraq illustrates the role of the U.S. Constitution in the policymaking process. The Constitution specifies that legislation cannot pass Congress unless both the House and Senate approve identical measures. Furthermore, legislation cannot become law without presidential support or acquiescence, unless both houses of Congress are able to override a presidential veto by a two-thirds vote of each chamber. Even though the two houses of Congress passed a provision to require a troop withdrawal from Iraq, President Bush did not agree and vetoed the measure. Congress was unable to override the veto.

The framers of the U.S. Constitution designed a system of government in which change usually happens slowly rather than quickly and tends to reflect compromise among contending interests. The Democrats won control of Congress in 2006 by opposing the war in Iraq, but their margin of control was narrow, especially in the Senate. When President Bush vetoed the measure that contained the troop withdrawal provision, anti-war Democrats in Congress fell well short of the two-thirds margin needed to override the veto.

The Constitution erects a buffer between short-term public opinion and public policy, especially if opinion is closely divided on an issue. Consider the relationship between public opinion on the war in Iraq and the country's war policy. President Bush ordered American forces to overthrow the government of Saddam Hussein in 2003 and won reelection the following year against Democrat John Kerry, an opponent of the war. The Republican Party gained seats in Congress as well. The voters supported the war by reelecting the president and keeping his party in control of Congress. By 2006, the war had grown unpopular, and the Democratic Party used the issue to help win majorities in the House and Senate. The election indicated that the public had turned against the war. Nonetheless, the margins in both chambers were narrow and Bush continued in office as president. Democratic opponents of the war in Congress lacked the strength to overturn the Bush veto and force the president to begin withdrawing troops. In the long run, the voters would decide the issue in the 2008 presidential election, which pitted candidates with opposite views on the war. Senator John McCain, the Republican nominee, supported the war effort and promised to keep American forces in Iraq until "the job was done." In contrast, Senator Barack Obama, his Democratic opponent, promised to bring the troops home.

This is the first of two chapters that explore the legal/constitutional environment for policymaking. The chapter examines the U.S. Constitution. The next chapter focuses on the federal system.

THE BACKGROUND OF THE CONSTITUTION

Constitution The fundamental law by which a state or nation is organized and governed, and to which ordinary legislation must conform.

A **constitution** is the fundamental law by which a state or nation is organized and governed, and to which ordinary legislation must conform. It establishes the framework of government, assigns the powers and duties of government bodies, and defines the relationship between the people and their government. The U.S. Constitution, which is more than 220 years of age, is the oldest written national Constitution still in effect in the world today.

Historical Setting

The Americans who wrote the Constitution of 1787 had lived through two difficult periods: the late colonial period under British rule and the period under the government created by the Articles of Confederation. To a considerable degree, the Constitution was a reaction to these two experiences.

The Colonial Period   The American colonists were initially satisfied with the political relationship with Great Britain. Preoccupied with matters at home, the British authorities allowed the Americans a substantial measure of self-government. Each colony had a governor, appointed by the king, and a legislative assembly whose members were locally elected. The colonial assemblies could levy taxes, appropriate money, approve or reject the governor's appointments, and pass laws for their colony. Although the governor had the power to veto legislation, the assemblies exercised considerable leverage over the governor by virtue of their control of the budget. This **power of the purse,** which is the authority to raise and spend money, made the locally elected legislative assemblies the dominant bodies of colonial government.

Power of the purse The authority to raise and spend money.

After 1763, the British chose to reorganize their colonial system. The French and Indian War (1756–1763), in which the British and the Americans fought against the French and their Indian allies for control of North America, left the British with a sizable war debt. The British also faced the problem of governing Canada and enforcing treaties with the Indians, which limited westward expansion by the colonists.

British officials decided that the American colonists should pay part of the cost of defending and administering the empire in North America. The British imposed new taxes, such as the Stamp Act of 1765, and attempted to crack down on smuggling to prevent colonists from avoiding customs taxes. To enforce their policies, the British increased the number of officials in North America and permanently stationed troops in the colonies.

To the surprise of the British, the Americans were outraged. Over the years, the colonists had grown accustomed to self-government and they were unwilling to surrender the privilege. They regarded the new policies as a violation of local traditions and an abridgment of their rights as British citizens. Before 1763, the only taxes the Americans paid to London were duties on trade, and the colonists interpreted the duties as measures to regulate commerce rather than taxes. Now, however, London attempted to impose levies that were clearly taxes. The Americans argued that as English citizens they could be taxed only by their own elected representatives and not by the British Parliament. No taxation without representation, they declared. This argument made no sense to the British. In their view, every Member of Parliament represented every British citizen; it was irrelevant that no Americans sat in Parliament. The dispute over taxation and other issues worsened, leading eventually to revolution and American independence.

During the Revolutionary War, the American colonies became the United States, loosely allied under the leadership of the Continental Congress, which was a **unicameral** (one-house) **legislature** in which each state had a single vote. Although the Continental Congress had no official governing authority, it declared America's independence, raised an army, appointed George Washington commander-in-chief, coined money, and negotiated with foreign nations. The Continental Congress also drafted a plan for national union. This plan, known as the Articles of Confederation, went into effect in 1781, upon approval by the 13 states.

Unicameral legislature A one-house legislature.

Ending the war in Iraq was the foremost goal of Democratic congressional leaders after their party won control of Congress in the 2006 election.

The Articles of Confederation   The Articles of Confederation created a league of friendship, a "perpetual union" of states, with a unicameral congress. Although state legislatures could send as many as seven delegates to the Confederation Congress, each state possessed a single vote, and nine states (of 13) had to approve decisions. Amending the Articles required unanimous approval of the states. The Articles provided for no independent national executive or national judiciary.

The states were the primary units of government in the new nation rather than the Confederation government. Each of the 13 states had its own state constitution that established a framework for state government. These state constitutions typically provided for a **bicameral** (two-house) **legislature,** a governor, and a court system. Because Americans feared executive power as a source of tyranny, they adopted state constitutions that limited the powers of state governors, making legislatures the dominant branch of state government.[1]

Bicameral legislature A two-house legislature.

The Americans who wrote the Articles of Confederation were determined to create a government whose powers would be strictly limited. Having just freed themselves from British rule, they did not want to create a strong national government that might become as oppressive as the British colonial government. The Americans who wrote the Articles apparently went too far, however, because the Confederation proved too weak to deal effectively with the new nation's problems. It lacked the power to collect taxes from individuals, having to rely instead on contributions from the states. When state governments failed to pay—as many did—the confederation government was left without financial support. The Confederation also lacked authority to regulate commerce, prohibit states from printing worthless currency, enforce the provisions of the peace treaty with Great Britain, or even defend itself against rebellion. When small farmers in western Massachusetts engaged in an armed uprising against the government over debt and taxes in 1786–1787, the Confederation government failed to respond. After a private army finally crushed the insurrection, which was known as Shays' Rebellion after its leader, Daniel Shays, public opinion began to coalesce in favor of a stronger national government than the one provided by the Articles of Confederation. Attempts to amend the Articles to correct deficiencies failed because Rhode Island refused to agree and the amendment process required the unanimous consent of the states.

American Political Thought

The Americans who wrote the Constitution were educated people who studied the important political writings of their day. The work of Englishman John Locke (1632–1704) was particularly influential. In his *Second Treatise on Government* (1689), Locke declared that people in their natural state were born free and equal, and possessed certain natural rights, which were life, liberty, and property. Unfortunately, Locke said, evil people disrupt the good life of the state of nature by conspiring to deprive others of their life, liberty, or property. To protect their rights, people voluntarily join together to form governments. The power of government, then, stems from the consent of the governed, who entrust the government with responsibility for protecting their lives, liberty, and possessions. Should government fail in this task, Locke declared, the people have the right to revolt and institute a new government.

Americans drew three important principles from Locke's thought. First, Locke's theory of revolution offered the perfect theoretical rationale for the American Revolution. In the Declaration of Independence, which is reprinted in the Appendix of this text, the founders used Locke's theory to justify independence from Great Britain. The Americans were justified in revolting against the King, the founders declared, because the King deprived them of their rights to "Life, Liberty, and the pursuit of Happiness." Thomas Jefferson, the principal author of the Declaration, substituted the phrase *pursuit of Happiness* for the word *property* in order to give the document a more idealistic tone. Second, Locke provided a theoretical basis for the creation of a national government that could be a positive force in society instead of just a necessary evil. According to Locke, the people create government in order to accomplish certain goals, that is, to protect life, liberty, and property from the dangers inherent in a state of nature. In theory, then, government can play an active, positive role in society. Third, Locke's concept of natural rights offered a theoretical foundation for limiting government authority over the individual. The **doctrine of natural rights** is the belief that individual rights transcend the power of government. People create government to protect their rights, not to abridge them. Locke's theory of natural rights provided a basis for a **bill of rights,** which is a constitutional document guaranteeing individual rights and liberties.

Doctrine of natural rights The belief that individual rights transcend the power of government.

Bill of rights A constitutional document guaranteeing individual rights and liberties.

Although the nation's founders frequently cited the writings of European philosophers such as Locke, they did more than just apply the theories developed in Europe to the United States. They created a nation and wrote a Constitution based on American events, experiences, and ideas, citing European writings selectively to reinforce what they already believed. Furthermore, the Americans were not afraid to disregard the advice of the political theorists when it did not fit their image of American political reality.[2]

The most important element of American political thought was the changing conception of the nature of politics and government. At the time of the Revolution, American political theorists believed that politics was a never-ending struggle between the people and the government. In their view, the people were virtuous and united in support of the public good. In contrast, the government, personified by the king, was corrupt and oppressive. After declaring their independence, the Americans knew that they needed a national government, but they did not want a strong one. The government established by the Articles of Confederation fit the bill nicely.

After a few years of independence, many Americans recognized that they were wrong about the nature of the people and the role of government. Instead of society being united behind a common perception of the public good, they saw that it was composed of a variety of interests or factions, which opposed one another on a number of policy issues. Furthermore, practical political experience in the states demonstrated that the people were not so virtuous after all. When one faction gained control of the government of a particular state or locality, it would often use its power to enforce its will over opposing interests.

By 1787, many Americans had decided that a strong national government could play a positive role in society. First, the national government could reconcile the divergent concerns of various groups in society to produce policies

In May 2007, Congress passed a funding bill for the wars in Iraq and Afghanistan that included a provision requiring the president to begin withdrawing troops in October with the goal of getting all U.S. combat forces out of Iraq by the end of March 2008.

designed to achieve the public good. A large nation, such as the United States, includes a wide range of interests competing for power. Although a particular group or faction might be strong enough to control the government in one state or a local area, no single group would be able to dominate nationwide. A strong national government would provide a forum in which groups would be able to reconcile their differences. The result would be policies that would be acceptable to a broad range of interests.

Second, a strong national government could protect individual liberty and property from the power of oppressive majorities. At the state or local level, a dominant faction could adopt policies designed to advance its own religious or economic interests at the expense of the minority. At the national level, however, no one group or faction would be powerful enough to enforce its will on the entire nation. Because every group held minority status in one state or another, it would be in each group's interest to protect minorities against the power of oppressive local majorities.[3] For example, the framers of the Constitution included a provision prohibiting a state-supported church because of the multiplicity of religious sects in America. Although many of the early American religious groups would have liked nothing better than to establish their faith as the official state religion, they lacked the power to achieve that goal. Consequently, they preferred an official government policy of religious freedom to risking the possibility that another religious group would gain official recognition.[4]

CONSTITUTIONAL PRINCIPLES

To understand the American Constitution, we must study the principles behind it. Let's look in detail at some of the Constitution's most important themes.

Representative Democracy

Democracy A system of government in which ultimate political authority is vested in the people.

A **democracy** is a system of government in which the people hold ultimate political power. Although the framers of the Constitution favored a government that would answer to the people, they did not want to give too much power to majority opinion. The framers were particularly wary of **direct democracy,** which is a political system in which the citizens vote directly on matters of public concern. The framers of the Constitution worried that ordinary citizens lacked the information to make intelligent policy decisions. They feared that direct democracy would produce policies reflecting hasty, emotional decisions rather than well-considered judgments.

Direct democracy A political system in which the citizens vote directly on matters of public concern.

The framers also worried that direct democracy would enable a majority of the people to enact policies that would silence, disadvantage, or harm the minority point of view, thus producing a **tyranny of the majority,** which is the abuse of the minority by the majority. The danger of majority rule is that the majority may vote to adopt policies that unfairly disadvantage the minority. The challenge for the framers of the Constitution was to create a form of government that would provide for majority rule while protecting the rights and liberties of minorities.

Tyranny of the majority The abuse of the minority by the majority.

Instead of a direct democracy, the framers created a **representative democracy** or a **republic,** which is a political system in which citizens elect representatives to make policy decisions on their behalf. The framers believed that elected representatives would act as a buffer between the people and government policies. Representatives would be more knowledgeable than ordinary citizens would be about policy issues. They would also be more likely than the general public to recognize the legitimate interests of different groups in society and seek policy compromises designed to accommodate those interests.

Representative democracy or **republic** A political system in which citizens elect representatives to make policy decisions on their behalf.

? WHAT IS YOUR OPINION?

Assuming that modern technology would overcome any logistical problems, do you think the United States would be better off today with a direct democracy rather than a republic? Why or why not?

Competition is the essence of democracy.[5] Candidates compete by offering the programs and policies designed to appeal to the voters. In 2008, for example, McCain and Obama offered contrasting positions on healthcare, taxes, and the war in Iraq. Once in office, elected officials do their best to please the public because they want to win reelection.

Supermajority A voting margin which is greater than a simple majority.

To further guard against the tyranny of the majority, the framers provided that some policy actions could be taken only with the consent of a **supermajority,** that is, a voting margin that is greater than a simple majority. Constitutional amendments

Rule of law The constitutional principle that holds that the discretion of public officials in dealing with individuals is limited by the law.

Writ of *habeas corpus* A court order requiring government authorities either to release a person held in custody or demonstrate that the person is detained in accordance with law.

Bill of attainder A law declaring a person or a group of persons guilty of a crime and providing for punishment without benefit of a judicial proceeding.

***ex post facto* law** A retroactive criminal statute that operates to the disadvantage of accused persons.

Due process of law The constitutional principle holding that government must follow fair and regular procedures in actions that could lead to an individual's suffering loss of life, liberty, or property.

must be proposed by two-thirds of the members of both the House and the Senate and ratified by three-fourths of the states. Treaties must be approved by two-thirds of the Senate. Presidential vetoes can only be overridden by a two-thirds' vote of each chamber of Congress. Executive and judicial officials can be removed from office only by a two-thirds' vote of the Senate. In each of these cases, a simple majority of 50 percent plus one does not prevail. Instead, policy actions require the support or at least acceptance of a supermajority of two-thirds or more.

Rule of Law

The **rule of law** is the constitutional principle that holds that the discretion of public officials in dealing with individuals is limited by the law. The very existence of a written Constitution implies the rule of law, but certain constitutional provisions deserve special notice. In Article I, Section 9, the Constitution guarantees the privilege of the writ of *habeas corpus* except in cases of invasion, rebellion, or threat to public safety. A **writ of *habeas corpus*** is a court order requiring that government authorities either release a person held in custody or demonstrate that the person is detained in accordance with law. *Habeas corpus* is designed to prevent arbitrary arrest and imprisonment. The Constitution protects Americans from being held in custody by the government unless they are charged and convicted in accordance with the law.

? WHAT IS YOUR OPINION?

Should the government be allowed to arrest American citizens and hold them without charges and without trial if it believes that they are involved in planning terrorist attacks against the United States?

The Constitution prohibits the passage of bills of attainder and *ex post facto* laws. A **bill of attainder** is a law declaring a person or a group of persons guilty of a crime and providing for punishment without benefit of a judicial proceeding. An ***ex post facto* law** is a retroactive criminal statute that operates to the disadvantage of accused persons. It makes a crime out of an act that was not illegal when it was committed.

Due process of law is the constitutional principle holding that government must follow fair and regular procedures in actions that could lead to an individual's suffering loss of life, liberty, or property. In both the Fifth and Fourteenth Amendments, the Constitution provides that neither Congress (the Fifth Amendment) nor the states (the Fourteenth Amendment) may deprive any person of "life, liberty, or property, without due process of law." Due process of law generally protects individuals from the arbitrary actions of public officials. Before individuals may be imprisoned, fined, or executed, they must be given their day in court in accordance with law. Among other rights, the Constitution guarantees accused persons the right to a speedy, public trial by an impartial jury, the right to confront witnesses, and the right to legal counsel.

Limited Government

Limited government The constitutional principle that government does not have unrestricted authority over individuals.

Limited government is the constitutional principle that government does not have unrestricted authority over individuals. The government of the United States is not a dictatorship with absolute authority; its power is limited. Perhaps the most important constitutional restriction on the authority of government is the **Bill of Rights,** the first ten amendments to the Constitution.

Bill of Rights The U.S. Bill of Rights is the first ten amendments to the U.S. Constitution.

The Bill of Rights was not part of the original Constitution because a majority of the framers of the Constitution believed that such a provision was unnecessary, redundant, useless, and possibly even dangerous. The framers thought that a bill of rights would be unnecessary because each state constitution had a bill of rights and the national government lacked sufficient power to threaten individual liberty. They considered a bill of rights redundant because the Constitution already contained a number of provisions designed to protect individual liberty, such as the prohibition against *ex post facto* laws and bills of attainder, and the guarantee of due process of law. They thought that a bill of rights would be useless because they believed that a paper guarantee of individual liberty would mean little in the face of public pressure. Finally, the framers resisted the inclusion of a bill of rights in the Constitution because they worried that some rights might be inadvertently left out and that any right omitted from the document would be lost.[6]

The failure of the proposed Constitution to include a bill of rights became a political issue during the debate over ratification. After the Constitution was written in 1787, it still had to be approved (or ratified) by 9 of the 13 states. The **Antifederalists** were Americans opposed to the ratification of the new Constitution because they thought it gave too much power to the national government. They raised the issue of a bill of rights in hopes of defeating the Constitution and forcing the convening of a new constitutional convention. The **Federalists** were Americans who supported the ratification of the Constitution. Although most Federalists initially opposed inclusion of a bill of rights in the constitution, they switched sides on the issue in order to secure ratification and prevent a new convention. They promised to add a bill of rights once the Constitution was ratified and the new government took office.[7]

Antifederalists Americans opposed to the ratification of the new Constitution because they thought it gave too much power to the national government.

Federalists Americans who supported the ratification of the Constitution.

The Federalists kept their promise. In 1789, the First Congress of the United States proposed 12 amendments, 10 of which were ratified by a sufficient number of states to become part of the Constitution by 1791. One of the rejected amendments, a provision requiring that a congressional pay raise could not go into effect before an intervening election take place, was finally ratified in 1992 to become the Twenty-seventh Amendment.

The authors of the Bill of Rights intended that it would apply only to the national government and not the states because the states already had bills of rights. The U.S. Constitution and the national Bill of Rights would protect individual rights against abuse by the national government. State constitutions and state bills of rights would secure individual rights from infringement by state governments.

The Fourteenth Amendment, which was added to the Constitution immediately after the Civil War, provided the constitutional basis for applying the national Bill of Rights to the states. Congress proposed the Fourteenth Amendment in 1866

Selective incorporation of the Bill of Rights against the states The process through which the U.S. Supreme Court interpreted the Due Process Clause of the Fourteenth Amendment of the U.S. Constitution to apply most of the provisions of the national Bill of Rights to the states.

Legislative power The power to make laws.

Executive power The power to enforce laws.

Judicial power The power to interpret laws.

Separation of powers The division of political power among executive, legislative, and judicial branches of government.

Checks and balances The overlapping of the powers of the branches of government designed to ensure that public officials limit the authority of one another.

to protect the rights of the former slaves from infringement by state governments. The amendment defined U.S. citizenship, making it clear that all Americans are citizens of both the United States and the state in which they live. The amendment declared that state governments could not take life, liberty, or property without "due process of law," or deny to any person within their jurisdiction "equal protection of the laws." The Fourteenth Amendment also prohibited states from making laws abridging the "privileges or immunities" of citizens.

The Fourteenth Amendment did not play a major role in the protection of individual rights until the twentieth century. Initially, the Fourteenth Amendment had little impact on individual rights because the Supreme Court of the United States refused to interpret its provisions to protect individual rights. Not until the twentieth century did the Court begin the process known as the **selective incorporation of the Bill of Rights against the states.** This is the process through which the U.S. Supreme Court interpreted the Due Process Clause of the Fourteenth Amendment of the U.S. Constitution to apply most of the provisions of the national Bill of Rights to the states. Although the Supreme Court has never ruled that the Bill of Rights as a whole applies to the states, it has selectively held that virtually all of its key provisions apply against the states through the Due Process Clause of the Fourteenth Amendment. As a result, the national Bill of Rights now protects individual rights against infringement by both the national government and the state governments as well.

Separation of Powers with Checks and Balances

The framers of the U.S. Constitution adopted separation of powers with checks and balances as a means for controlling the power of government. Although the roots of these concepts went back a century, their modern development was the work of Baron de Montesquieu, an eighteenth-century French political philosopher. Montesquieu identified three kinds of political power: the power to make laws (**legislative power**), enforce laws (**executive power**), and interpret laws (**judicial power**). Montesquieu warned against allowing one person or a single group of people from exercising all three powers because that person or group would become so powerful as to pose a threat to individual liberty. To protect freedom, Montesquieu advocated **separation of powers,** that is, the division of political power among executive, legislative, and judicial branches of government. He called for a system of checks and balances to prevent any one of the three branches from becoming too strong. **Checks and balances** refer to the overlapping of the powers of the branches of government designed to ensure that public officials limit the authority of one another.

James Madison was the principal architect of America's system of separation of powers with checks and balances. In fact, scholars sometimes refer to the nation's constitutional apparatus as the Madisonian system. Madison and two other proponents of the new constitution, Alexander Hamilton and John Jay, wrote a series of essays known as the *Federalist Papers* to advocate the ratification of the new Constitution. In *The Federalist* No. 51, Madison identified two threats to liberty: (1) **factions,** which are special interests who seek their own good at the expense of the common good, and (2) the excessive concentration of political power in the

Federalist Papers
A series of essays written by James Madison, Alexander Hamilton, and John Jay advocating the ratification of the Constitution.

Factions Special interests who seek their own good at the expense of the common good.

hands of government officials. Madison's remedy for these dangers was the creation of a strong national government with separation of powers and checks and balances.

Madison believed that the nation needed a strong national government to control the power of factions. In this regard, Madison noted the advantage of a large nation with many diverse interests. At the local or state level, he said, a single faction might be powerful enough to dominate. It could unfairly force its will on the minority, creating a tyranny of the majority. Over the breadth of the entire nation, however, the narrow perspectives of that faction would be checked by the interests of other factions entrenched in other areas. A strong national government would provide an arena in which factions would counterbalance one another. National policies, therefore, would reflect compromise among a range of interests.

Madison also favored separation of powers with checks and balances as a means to control the power of government officials. Madison said that the goal of the system was "to divide and arrange the several offices [of government] in such a manner as that each may be a check on the other."[8] In this fashion, the selfish, private interests of officeholders would counterbalance each other to the public good. "Ambition," Madison wrote, "must be made to counteract ambition."[9]

The Constitution contains an elaborate network of checks and balances. The executive branch, for example, checks the judicial branch through the power of the president to appoint members of the Supreme Court and other federal courts. Congress, in turn, checks the president and the courts in that the Senate must confirm judicial appointments. Similarly, the Constitution declares that Congress has the authority to declare war, but it names the president commander-in-chief of the armed forces. The president negotiates treaties, but the Senate must ratify them.

Separation of powers with checks and balances creates tension among the branches of government because the framers of the Constitution refused to draw clear lines of demarcation among Congress, the president, and the judiciary. In fact, the phrase *separation of powers* is misleading. What really exists is a system in which separate institutions *share* power.[10] Friction is inevitable.

The 2008 presidential election gave voters the opportunity to break the constitutional deadlock over the course of the war in Iraq.

Federalism

The Americans who gathered in Philadelphia in 1787 for the constitutional convention had lived under both a unitary system and a confederation. The British North American colonies were part of a **unitary government,** which is a governmental system in which political authority is concentrated in a single national government. The local colonial governments could constitutionally exercise only those powers specifically granted to them by the British parliament. The defenders of unitary government argue that it provides for consistent policy administration throughout a country and allows for efficient handling of nationwide problems. In contrast, the critics of unitary government say that it fails to permit sufficient local variation to accommodate differing local circumstances. American dissatisfaction with the policies of Britain's centralized administration led to the Revolution.

The Articles of Confederation established a **confederation,** which is a league of nearly independent states, similar to the United Nations today. Under the confederation government, individual Americans were citizens of their respective states but not the national government. As a result, the government under the Articles lacked the authority to deal directly with individuals (e.g., to tax them); it could deal only with the governments of the 13 states. The advantage of a confederation is that it allows states to cooperate without surrendering any of their basic powers. The disadvantage is that it provides for a weak central government, which proved the undoing of the confederation.

The framers of the Constitution set out to establish a government that would be capable of effective administration but would not undermine the American tradition of local control. Their solution was to create a federation. A **federation** or **federal system** is a political system that divides power between a central government, with authority over the whole nation, and a series of state governments.

A federation is a compromise between unitary government and a confederation. In a unitary system, the national government is sovereign. **Sovereignty** is the authority of a state to exercise its legitimate powers within its boundaries, free from external interference. The powers of state and local governments (if they exist) are granted to them by the national government. In a confederation, the states are sovereign. The national government's authority flows from the states. In a federal system, the national (or federal) government and the state governments are both sovereign. They derive their authority not from one another but from the Constitution. Both levels of government act directly on the people through their officials and laws, both are supreme within their proper sphere of authority, and both must consent to constitutional change.

A federation offers Americans several advantages. A federal system provides a means of political representation that can accommodate the diversity of American society. Individual Americans are citizens of their states and the nation as well and participate in the selection of representatives to both levels of government. In a federal system, local interests shape local policy. The national government, meanwhile, is an arena in which local interests from different regions can check and balance one another, permitting the national interest to prevail.

Federalism can help protect against the tyranny of the majority. The federal system creates a series of overlapping state and district election systems that select both

---

Unitary government A governmental system in which political authority is concentrated in a single national government.

Confederation A league of nearly independent states, similar to the United Nations today.

Federation or **federal system** A political system that divides power between a central government, with authority over the whole nation, and a series of state governments.

Sovereignty The authority of a state to exercise its legitimate powers within its boundaries, free from external interference.

members of Congress and the president. The federal election system gives minorities of all kinds—racial, ethnic, religious, regional, local, occupational, social, and sexual—the opportunity to be part of a majority because they may comprise the swing vote in a closely divided state or district. Consequently, they must be consulted; their interests must be considered.[11]

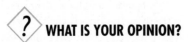

? WHAT IS YOUR OPINION?

Which is the best form of government—a unitary government, a confederation, or a federal government?

Nonetheless, a federal system imposes certain disadvantages. Local variations confuse citizens and hinder business. Traveling Americans face different traffic laws in each state. People who move from one state to another must adapt to different laws regarding such matters as marriage, divorce, wills, and occupational licensing. A couple approved as foster parents in one state may have to go through the approval process again if they move to another state. Businesses must adjust to variations in tax laws and regulations. California, for example, imposes tougher automobile emissions standards than the national government or most other states, forcing manufacturers to specially equip cars to be sold in that state. Federalism also sets the stage for conflict. American history is filled with examples of disputes between states and the national government; the Civil War was the most serious. Issues such as the 55 mile-per-hour speed limit requirement and the 21-year-old minimum legal drinking age are contemporary examples of conflicts between states and the national government.

Bicameralism

The framers of the Constitution expected the legislative branch to be the dominant institution of American national government because it was the dominant branch of state governments. To prevent the national legislature from becoming too powerful, the framers divided Congress into two houses with different sizes, terms of office, responsibilities, and constituencies. The precise organization of America's bicameral Congress was the product of an agreement between large-state and small-state forces known as the Connecticut Compromise. Members of the House of Representatives would be chosen by direct popular election to serve two-year terms with the number of representatives from each state based on population. Each state would have two senators chosen by their state legislatures to serve six-year terms. The adoption of the Seventeenth Amendment in 1913 provided for direct popular election of senators.

The framers expected that the popularly elected house would be constrained by a more conservative senate. With a two-year term, members of the house would be closer to the people and more likely to act hastily in accordance with short-term popular sentiment. In contrast, senators, chosen by state legislatures and serving longer terms, would be insulated from popular pressures, thus enabling them to act more cautiously and put the national interest ahead of short-term political gain.[12]

Senator John McCain, the Republican candidate for president, promised to keep American forces in Iraq until "the job was done."

THE LIVING CONSTITUTION

The Constitution has not just survived for more than 220 years, but it has grown and matured with the nation, serving still as the fundamental framework for policymaking. When the original document was written in 1787, the United States was a nation of only about four million people, most of whom lived on farms and in small towns. Many Americans—slaves, women, and individuals without property—were denied full rights of participation in the policymaking process. Today, the country is dramatically changed, but the Constitution, with only 27 official amendments, endures as the centerpiece of policymaking.

The genius of the Constitution lies in its ability to adapt to changing times while maintaining adherence to basic principles. The Constitution is a brief, general document that is full of phrases that lack clear definition. The Eighth Amendment, for example, prohibits "cruel and unusual punishments." Article I, Section 8 gives Congress the power to regulate "commerce." Article II, Section 4 declares that the president may be impeached and removed from office for "treason, bribery, or other high crimes and misdemeanors." The Fourth Amendment prohibits "unreasonable searches and seizures." What do these terms mean? What punishments are "cruel and unusual?" What is "commerce?" What are "high crimes and misdemeanors"? Which searches and seizures are "reasonable" and which are "unreasonable"?

The Constitution is often vague, and so the framers intended. They set down certain basic, fundamental principles, but omitted details in order to allow succeeding generations to supply specifics in light of their own experiences. The basic idea behind the concept of "cruel and unusual punishments," for example, is that government must not go too far in punishing criminals. The prohibition against "unreasonable searches and seizures" places limits on the police. Had the framers of the Constitution decided to spell out everything in detail, they would have produced a document far longer and less satisfactory than the one we have. Eventually, the nation would have outgrown it and either cast it aside or been forced to amend it repeatedly.

 WHAT IS YOUR OPINION?

Is the Constitution too general? Would the nation be better served had the framers created a more specific document?

Constitutional Change Through Practice and Experience

The Constitution has adapted to changing times through practice and experience. Consider the role of the presidency. The historical development of the office has given definition to the powers of the presidency beyond the scope of the office that was foreseen by the framers. Other elements of American government have developed despite slight mention in the Constitution. Even though the federal bureaucracy is barely discussed in the Constitution, its importance in American government has grown to the point that some observers refer to it as the fourth branch of government. Furthermore, some important contemporary features of American government are not mentioned at all in the Constitution, including the committee system in Congress, the executive cabinet, and the political party system. To an important extent, the meaning of the Constitution is found in its historical development over time as succeeding generations of Americans have addressed policy issues within its framework.

Constitutional Change Through Amendment

Constitutional amendment A formal, written change or addition to the nation's governing document.

A **constitutional amendment** is a formal, written change or addition to the nation's governing document. A major flaw of the Articles of Confederation was that the articles could be amended only by unanimous vote. In practice, correcting weaknesses in the document proved impossible because of the obstinacy of only one or a few states. In 1787, then, the Constitution's framers were careful to include a reasonable method of amendment that was difficult enough to preclude hasty, ill-conceived changes, but not impossible.

The Constitution provides two methods for proposing amendments and two methods for their ratification. An amendment can be proposed by either a two-thirds' vote of each house of Congress or by a constitutional convention called by Congress upon petition by two-thirds of the states. The former method of proposal has been used many times: Congress proposed all 27 amendments that have been added to the Constitution. The convention procedure has never been used, and no one knows for sure just how the process would work. Must state petitions be written

The British Parliamentary System

Most of the world's democracies are patterned after the British parliamentary system rather than the checks and balances system of the United States. A **parliamentary system** is a system of government in which political power is concentrated in a legislative body and a cabinet headed by a prime minister. The British legislature, which is called the **Parliament,** has two chambers, a House of Commons and a House of Lords. Real power is in the hands of the House of Commons, which is composed of 660 members elected from districts. The House of Lords, which includes the bishops of the Church of England and other members appointed for life by the king or queen, is now little more than a debating society with the power only to delay legislation, not defeat it.

British voters understand that when they vote for Parliament that they are also choosing a government. At election time, each British political party presents the voters with a detailed set of policy proposals that it promises to implement if given the opportunity. Voters know that a vote for a particular parliamentary candidate is a vote for the policies offered by that candidate's political party. It is also a vote for the election of that party's leader as prime minister.

In the 1997 national election, the Labour Party won a majority of seats in Commons, ending 18 years of rule by the Conservative Party. The new Parliament proceeded to elect Tony Blair, the Labour Party leader, as prime minister, to replace John Major, the Conservative prime minister. With a majority in Parliament, the Labour government was able to enact its program without worrying about constitutional checks and balances.

The primary check on the government in Great Britain is the electorate. The government must hold a new parliamentary election within five years, giving voters the opportunity to keep the current government in power or turn the government over to the opposition. Labour has continued in office because it has been able to maintain its parliamentary majority, winning elections in both 2001 and 2005. When Blair resigned as prime minister in 2007, the Labour members of Parliament chose Gordon Brown as their new leader, and he consequently became prime minister.

QUESTIONS TO CONSIDER

1. Which political system is more responsive to citizen demands—the American or the British system?
2. Which political system is more likely to produce dramatic policy change?
3. Which political system is better equipped to protect the rights of minorities?

Parliamentary system A system of government in which political power is concentrated in a legislative body and a cabinet headed by a prime minister.

Parliament The British legislature.

in identical form? Could a state withdraw a petition after submitting it? Would Congress *have* to call a convention if the required number of states submitted petitions? Would the convention be limited to the subject identified in the petitions, or could the convention rewrite the entire document? Because of these unanswered questions, many constitutional scholars are apprehensive about the possibility of a new constitutional convention.

After an amendment is proposed, either by Congress or convention, three-fourths of the states must ratify it. Ratification can be accomplished either by vote of the state legislatures or by specially called state conventions. The former method has been used successfully 26 times, the latter only once, to ratify the Twenty-first Amendment repealing Prohibition.

The road to constitutional amendment may be difficult, but a number of groups believe their cause is worth the effort. In the 1970s and early 1980s, the **Equal Rights Amendment (ERA),** which was a proposed amendment guaranteeing equality before the law, regardless of sex, passed Congress but fell three states short of ratification. In recent years, Congress has considered but failed to pass other proposed

Equal Rights Amendment (ERA) A proposed amendment guaranteeing equality before the law, regardless of sex.

amendments dealing with such issues as prayer in schools, flag burning, term limitation, abortion, electoral college reform, a balanced budget, and gay marriage.

 WHAT IS YOUR OPINION?

Is amending the Constitution too difficult, too easy, or just right?

Constitutional Change Through Judicial Interpretation

A final means of constitutional change is judicial interpretation. In fact, it may be no exaggeration to say that what counts most in constitutional law is the interpretation of the Constitution by the courts, particularly the U.S. Supreme Court, rather than the words of the document itself. Many phrases important to constitutional law are not even in the Constitution, including "war power," "clear and present danger," "separation of church and state," "right of privacy," "separate but equal," and "police power." These famous words appear not in the Constitution but in judicial opinions.

Judicial interpretation of the Constitution is ineviatable because of the document's general nature. Many of the phrases of the Constitution are purposely ambiguous, requiring continuous reinterpretation and adaptation. Indeed, one constitutional scholar says that we have an unwritten constitution, whose history is the history of judicial interpretation.[13]

Judicial review The power of courts to declare unconstitutional the actions of the other branches and units of government.

The power of courts to declare unconstitutional the actions of the other branches and units of government is known as **judicial review.** Although the Constitution is silent about the power of judicial review, many historians believe that the founders expected the courts to exercise the authority. Ironically, the Supreme Court assumed the power of judicial review through constitutional interpretation, first holding an act of Congress unconstitutional in 1803 in the case of *Marbury v. Madison*.[14]

The case had its roots in the election of 1800 when President John Adams was defeated and his political party, the Federalist Party, lost its majority in Congress. In the period between the election and the inauguration of the new president, Adams proceeded to nominate, and the Senate to confirm, the appointments of a number of loyal Federalists to serve in the judicial branch of government.

One of these judicial appointments went to William Marbury, who was named justice of the peace for the District of Columbia. President Adams signed and sealed Marbury's official commission on the day before he left office, but the secretary of state neglected to deliver the commission. When Thomas Jefferson, the newly elected president, took office, he ordered his secretary of state, James Madison, not to deliver the commission. Marbury subsequently sued, asking the Supreme Court to issue a writ of *mandamus* to order Madison to deliver the commission. A **writ of mandamus** is a court order directing a public official to perform a specific act or duty.

Writ of mandamus A court order directing a public official to perform a specific act or duty.

The case presented the Supreme Court with a dilemma. Chief Justice John Marshall and the other members of the Court were Federalists who would have liked nothing better than to blast the Jefferson administration and order Madison to deliver the commission. Had the Court done so, however, Jefferson would probably have defied the order. Marshall knew that defiance by the president would destroy the Court's prestige, but he also wanted to avoid ruling for the administration.

Judicial review provided Marshall and the Court a way out of their dilemma. Marshall used the Court's opinion to scold Jefferson and Madison for refusing to deliver the commission. Marbury was entitled to his commission, said Marshall, and a writ of *mandamus* was in order. Marshall ruled, however, that the Supreme Court lacked authority to issue the writ. Marshall pointed out that the Constitution lists the types of cases that may be tried before the Supreme Court in Article III, Section 2 and that the list does not include the power to issue writs of *mandamus* to federal officials. Congress had given the Court the authority to issue the writ legislatively in the Judiciary Act of 1789. Marshall held that Congress had no constitutional authority to expand the Court's **jurisdiction,** which is the authority of a court to hear a case. Therefore, the section of the Judiciary Act that gave the Court the power to issue writs of *mandamus* was unconstitutional. By this means, Marshall was able to attack Jefferson without giving the president the opportunity to defy the Court's authority.

Jurisdiction The authority of a court to hear a case.

The long-term significance of *Marbury v. Madison* is that it is the first case in which the Supreme Court exercised the power to hold acts of Congress unconstitutional. In his ruling, Marshall stated that the Constitution is the "fundamental and paramount law of the nation" and that it is the duty of the courts to interpret the law. "Thus," Marshall continued, "the particular phraseology of the Constitution of the United States confirms and strengthens the principle . . . that a law repugnant to the Constitution is void." Marshall concluded that in conflicts between the Constitution and acts of Congress, it was the Court's duty to enforce the Constitution by refusing to uphold the law.

Judicial review is an instrument of constitutional change because the process involves constitutional interpretation. Professor Richard H. Fallon, Jr., says that today's justices interpret the Constitution in light of history, precedent (i.e., earlier interpretations), and considerations of moral desirability and practical workability.[15] Consider the history of judicial interpretation of the **Equal Protection Clause,** which is the provision found in the Fourteenth Amendment of the U.S. Constitution that declares that "No State shall . . . deny to any person within its jurisdiction the equal protection of the laws." Historians believe that Congress proposed this phrase to safeguard the civil rights of former slaves and their offspring by requiring states to treat all of their residents equally under state law, regardless of race.

Equal Protection Clause A provision of the Fourteenth Amendment of the U.S. Constitution that declares that "No State shall . . . deny to any person within its jurisdiction the equal protection of the laws."

The U.S. Supreme Court's initial interpretation of the Equal Protection Clause came in 1896 in *Plessy v. Ferguson.* The case centered on the constitutionality of a Louisiana law that required racial segregation (separation) in passenger railcars. Could a state government prohibit African American travelers from sharing a railcar with white passengers without violating the Equal Protection Clause? The Supreme Court answered that it could as long as the accommodations were equal. "Separate but equal" facilities, said the Court, were sufficient to satisfy the requirements of the Fourteenth Amendment.[16] Almost 60 years later, the Supreme Court addressed a similar issue in the case of *Brown v. Board of Education of Topeka* (1954). The *Brown* case involved a constitutional challenge to a Kansas law requiring racial segregation in public schools. Could a state government prohibit African American youngsters from sharing a school with white children without violating the Equal Protection Clause? In this case, the Supreme Court overruled *Plessy,* holding that the Equal Protection Clause of the Fourteenth Amendment prohibits state

Barack Obama, the Democratic candidate for president in 2008, promised to withdraw combat forces from Iraq.

laws requiring racial segregation in public schools. The Court declared that "separate but equal" was a contradiction because the legal requirement of separation placed the stamp of inferiority on the black race.[17] And so the Constitution was changed, not through the adoption of a constitutional amendment (the wording of the Equal Protection Clause remained the same), but because of changing judicial interpretation.

THE CONSTITUTION, POLITICS, AND PUBLIC POLICY

The U.S. Constitution affects the policymaking process by fragmenting political power. Separation of powers divides power at the national level among legislative, executive, and judicial branches. Bicameralism splits the legislative branch in two, dividing power between the House and Senate. Federalism distributes power between the national government and the states.

The fragmentation of political power in the United States produces slow, incremental change. Presidents need the cooperation of Congress to have their programs enacted. In turn, Congress has difficulty acting without presidential initiative or at least acquiescence. Both the president and Congress need the support of the bureaucracy if their policies are to be faithfully executed. Frequently, they require the cooperation of state and local officials as well. The courts, meanwhile, can reverse or delay policies adopted at other levels or by other branches of government. With so many steps and so many power centers involved in the policy process, change is usually slow in coming if it comes at all. When policy changes occur, they are generally incremental and gradual, reflecting compromise among the various political actors involved in the process.

The framers of the U.S. Constitution favored a system that would ensure deliberation and delay rather than precipitous action. They were cautious people, wary of rapid change and none too confident about the judgment of popular majorities. Consequently, they created a constitutional apparatus that would work slowly and be unlikely to produce dramatic upheavals in public policy. The founders feared that rapid, major change would too often produce more harm than good. Consider the controversy over American policy in Iraq. After the 2006 election, a majority of the members of the U.S. House and Senate favored withdrawing American combat forces from Iraq, but the proponents of withdrawal lacked sufficient numbers to override a presidential veto. Any change in American policy had to await the 2008 election of a new president and a new Congress.

The Constitution promotes policy stability.[18] The election of new president or a change in control of Congress is unlikely to produce dramatic policy change because the Constitution works against dramatic change. A new president with bold new ideas must convince both Congress and the federal courts that the policy ideas are not only wise but also constitutional.

The framers of the Constitution wanted to ensure that the diversity of political interests in American society would be represented in the policy process. During the debates at the constitutional convention of 1787, one of the major issues was how best to protect the small states from large-state domination. In response to the controversy, the authors of the Constitution established a system that would provide opportunity for the varied groups and interests of American society to participate in policymaking. Today, many Americans still see this as a virtue.

Nonetheless, America's constitutional arrangements have their critics. The oldest complaint, first voiced by the Antifederalists, is that the Constitution favored the rich and wellborn over the interests of the common people. In the early twentieth century, historian Charles Beard echoed the position of the Antifederalists by arguing that the framers of the Constitution had been members of a small group of wealthy Americans who set out to preserve and enhance the economic and political opportunities of their class.[19] Although modern historians have refuted most of Beard's research, a number of contemporary observers nonetheless believe that the Constitution benefits special interests. The constitutional fragmentation of power that presents a range of forums in which different groups may be heard also provides a series of power centers that interest groups can control. Because of the complexity of the constitutional process, entrenched groups can frequently muster the influence to halt policy changes they consider unfavorable, sometimes overriding the wishes of a majority in Congress and the nation. The supermajority provisions in the Constitution allow a determined minority to block the will of the majority.

The most basic criticism of the Constitution is that it is a blueprint for political deadlock among the branches and units of government. By dividing government against itself, the founders ensured that all proposals for policy change must pass through a maze of power centers. The complexity of the arrangement not only slows the policymaking process but also gives most of the trump cards to the forces opposing whatever measure is under consideration. It is easier to defeat policy proposals than to pass them.

Professor James Sundquist believes that American history is filled with the failures of the system to respond effectively to policy crises. Consider the dilemma of the Vietnam War. Congress and the president were unable to agree either to withdraw American forces or do what was necessary to win the war. As a result, the nation was condemned to a half-in, half-out compromise policy that satisfied no one and, in the long run, proved disastrous. Sundquist says the same constitutional paralysis hindered the nation's ability to deal with secession in the 1860s, the Great Depression in the 1930s, and federal budget deficits of the 1980s.[20]

Nonetheless, constitutional stalemate is not inevitable. Sundquist's list tells only half the story. The nation did eventually rise to the challenge of secession and preserved the Union. The constitutional deadlock over the Great Depression ended. The budget deficit of the 1980s was finally eliminated. Furthermore, we can point to national crises such as World War II and the Cuban Missile Crisis that American government was able to address in a forthright, spirited manner, without constitutional gridlock.

Policy deadlocks are as much political as they are constitutional. The Constitution structures the policy process by setting the ground rules for policymaking. It does not dictate the outcome of the policy process. The failure of American government to resolve the Vietnam War reflected a lack of political consensus on a proper course of action rather than a constitutional breakdown.[21] We could say the same about the failure of Congress to dictate the withdrawal of American combat forces from Iraq. Whereas public opinion polls showed that a clear majority of Americans believed that the war in Iraq was a mistake, they found the public conflicted on the best course of action to end American involvement.[22]

 WHAT IS YOUR OPINION?

Does the Constitution need to be rewritten for the twenty-first century? If so, how?

CONCLUSION: THE CONSTITUTIONAL ENVIRONMENT FOR POLICYMAKING

The U.S. Constitution affects every stage of the policymaking process.

Agenda Building

Constitutional principles often define issues during the agenda setting stage of the policymaking process. Because of the Constitution, Americans debate the role of religion in public life from the perspectives of the First Amendment, considering both the constitutional guarantee of free exercise of religion and the prohibition against an establishment of religion. Discussions of the wisdom of state-sponsored prayers in public-school classrooms inevitably revolve around issues of constitutionality.

GETTING INVOLVED

Service Learning

Service learning is based on the concept that students can learn more about a subject through participation and experience combined with traditional coursework than they can through classroom instruction alone. Students benefit from service learning because they have an opportunity to participate in the implementation of government policies in their communities. As a result, they can relate course concepts to the real world and have the satisfaction that their volunteer work will benefit others. Students will also gain valuable knowledge and skills from the experience beyond those normally acquired in a classroom.

Use the following checklist to guide you through your service-learning project:

- Identify a government office or agency that welcomes student volunteers. The government pages of the telephone book list local government offices. You may wish to begin with the mayor's office, a county commissioner or county supervisor, school district, hospital district, or state legislator. Ask for suggestions and a referral. You may wish to seek a placement in an agency that deals with issues related to your career goals. If you plan to pursue a degree in the health field, for example, you may want to volunteer at a hospital. Prospective teachers may wish to complete their service-learning project at a school.
- Call the agency or department that interests you, and ask to speak to the volunteer coordinator. Explain that you are completing a service-learning project for your college and want to know about volunteer opportunities. You will want to arrange a placement that matches your interests and the needs of the agency.

- Your instructor will set the number of hours you should volunteer over the course of the term. Normally, students should expect to work from 20 to 40 hours over a long semester to receive full benefit from the activity.
- As you complete your assignment at the agency, ask the volunteer coordinator to provide you with documentation of the hours of your work to present to your instructor.

You will be required to keep a reflective journal documenting your service. Journal entries should discuss your work in the project and your reaction to the experience. Your journal should cover the following topics:

- What you did for the organization.
- What you thought of the clients served by the organization.
- What you thought of the other people working for the organization.
- What you thought of the work done by the organization.
- How your experience relates to course materials.
- How your experience relates to topics in the news.

Write at least one journal entry for every two hours you spend at your placement. Each journal entry should be at least four sentences long. You will be evaluated on the amount of time you spent at your placement, the number and length of your journal entries, and the quality of your entries. In particular, at least some of your entries should draw a connection between your volunteer experience and course concepts.

Constitutional considerations frame the abortion controversy as well, with a constitutional "right to life" counterbalanced against a "right to choose."

Policy Formulation and Adoption

The Constitution limits the policy options available to policymakers during the policy formulation stage to those policy approaches that are consistent with the Constitution. A policy aimed at shielding children from offensive materials on the Internet must be formulated with the Constitution in mind because it will likely face legal challenge from critics who believe that it violates the free speech provision of the First Amendment. Similarly, policies designed to control illegal immigration must be formulated to pass constitutional scrutiny because the Constitution protects all *persons* in the United States, not just citizens.

The Constitution sets the ground rules for policy adoption. Legislative policies require passage by both houses of Congress and the signature of the president. If the president vetoes a measure, the Constitution provides that it dies unless the House and Senate pass it again by a two-thirds' margin. Not all policies are adopted through the legislative process. The Constitution also establishes procedures, either explicitly or implicitly, for the adoption of policies through treaties, constitutional amendments, executive orders, judicial decisions, and rulemaking by government agencies.

Policy Implementation and Evaluation

The Constitution influences the implementation of policy. At the national level of government, policy implementation is primarily the responsibility of the executive branch. State and local governments also participate in policy implementation because of the federal system.

Finally, the Constitution affects policy evaluation. The separation of powers system with checks and balances ensures that each branch of government can evaluate policies adopted by the other branches. Congress oversees policy implementation by the executive branch. The judicial branch evaluates policies adopted by the other branches by interpreting laws and reviewing the constitutionality of executive and legislative policies.

KEY TERMS

Antifederalists
bicameral legislature
bill of attainder
Bill of Rights
bill of rights
checks and balances
confederation
constitution
constitutional amendment
democracy
direct democracy
doctrine of natural rights
due process of law
Equal Protection Clause
Equal Rights Amendment (ERA)

executive power
ex post facto law
factions
Federalist Papers
Federalists
federation *or* federal system
judicial power
judicial review
jurisdiction
legislative power
limited government
Parliament
parliamentary system
power of the purse

representative democracy *or* republic
rule of law
selective incorporation of the Bill of Rights against the states
separation of powers
sovereignty
supermajority
tyranny of the majority
unicameral legislature
unitary government
writ of *habeas corpus*
writ of *mandamus*

NOTES

1. Gordon S. Wood, *The Creation of the American Republic 1776–1787* (Chapel Hill: University of North Carolina Press, 1969), pp. 131–148.

2. Donald S. Lutz, "The Changing View of the Founding and a New Perspective on American Political Theory," *Social Science Quarterly* 68 (December 1987): 669–686.

3. Wood, pp. 601–614.

4. Lutz, p. 677.

5. Michael P. M. McDonald and John Samples, *The Marketplace of Democracy: Electoral Competition and American Politics* (Washington, DC: Cato Institute, 2006), p. 1.

6. Paul Finkelman, "James Madison and the Bill of Rights: A Reluctant Paternity," in Gerhard Casper, Dennis J. Hutchison, and David Strauss, eds., *The Supreme Court Review* (Chicago: University of Chicago Press, 1990), pp. 309–311.

7. Richard Labunski, *James Madison and the Struggle for the Bill of Rights* (New York: Oxford University Press, 2006), pp. 96–255.

8. *The Federalist*, No. 51.

9. Ibid.

10. Richard Neustadt, *Presidential Power*, rev. ed. (New York: Wiley, 1976), p. 33.

11. Robert A. Dahl, *A Preface to Democratic Theory*, expanded edition (Chicago: University of Chicago Press, 2006), p. 137.

12. Edward C. Carmines and Lawrence C. Dodd, "Bicameralism in Congress: The Changing Partnership," in Lawrence C. Dodd and Bruce I. Oppenheimer, eds., *Congress Reconsidered*, 3rd ed. (Washington, DC: Congressional Quarterly Press, 1985), pp. 414–436.

13. Leonard Levy, *Judgments: Essays on American Constitutional History* (Chicago: Quadrangle Books, 1972), p. 17.

14. *Marbury v. Madison*, 1 Cranch 137 (1803).

15. Richard H. Fallon, Jr., *The Dynamic Constitution: An Introduction to American Constitutional Law* (New York: Cambridge University Press, 2004), p. 193.

16. *Plessy v. Ferguson*, 163 U.S. 537 (1896).

17. *Brown v. Board of Education of Topeka*, 347 U.S. 483 (1954).

18. Thomas A. Birkland, *An Introduction to the Policy Process: Theories, Concepts, and Models of Public Policy Making* (Armonk, NY: M. E. Sharpe, 2001), p. 39.

19. Charles A. Beard, *An Economic Interpretation of the Constitution of the United States* (New York: Macmillan, 1913).

20. James L. Sundquist, *Constitutional Reform and Effective Government*, rev. ed. (Washington, DC: Brookings Institution, 1986), pp. 5–6.

21. Peter F. Nardulli, "The Constitution and American Politics: A Developmental Perspective," in Peter F. Nardulli, ed., *The Constitution and American Political Development* (Chicago: University of Chicago Press, 1992), p. 12.

22. Jeffrey M. Jones, "Majority Continues to Consider Iraq War a Mistake," February 6, 2008, available at www.gallup.com.

Chapter 3

The Federal System

CHAPTER OUTLINE

LEARNING OUTCOMES

After studying Chapter 3, students should be able to do the following:

▸ Summarize the arguments for and against federal government involvement in education policy, focusing in particular on No Child Left Behind (NCLB). (pp. 60–61)

▸ Distinguish between the delegated powers and the implied powers. (pp. 61–63)

▸ Describe the powers of the national government, identifying at least one specific power granted by the Constitution to each of the three branches of the federal government. (p. 63)

▸ Identify the provisions in the Constitution that address the relationship of states to one another and to the national government. (pp. 63–65)

▸ Compare and contrast the arguments presented by the proponents of states' rights with those offered by the advocates of national government supremacy. (pp. 65–66)

▸ Describe the significance of *McCulloch v. Maryland*. (pp. 66–68)

▸ Evaluate the current status of the federal system in light of recent Supreme Court rulings. (pp. 68–69)

▸ Describe the process through which federal programs are adopted. (pp. 70–71)

▸ Distinguish between categorical grants and block grants and between project grants and formula grants. (pp. 72–73)

▸ Identify and discuss the various types of restrictions Congress places on the receipt of federal money, including matching funds requirements and federal mandates. (pp. 73–75)

▸ Discuss the impact of the federal system on each stage of the policymaking process. (pp. 75–78)

▸ Define the key terms listed on page 79 and explain their significance.

No Child Left Behind (NCLB) A federal law that requires state governments and local school districts to institute basic skills testing in reading and mathematics for students in grades three through eight, and use the results to assess school performance.

No Child Left Behind (NCLB) is a federal law that requires state governments and local school districts to institute basic skills testing in reading and mathematics for students in grades three through eight and to use the results to assess school performance. Schools must assess student progress not just for the entire school but also by subgroups based on race/ethnicity, income level, English proficiency, and special education status. NCLB requires schools to report student progress separately for students in a subgroup, forcing them to be accountable for the progress of all of their students. Even if a school's overall performance is good, it will receive a failing grade under the law if, for example, the performance of Latino or special education students lags.[1] The goal of NCLB is that schools regularly improve their performance so that all students will be proficient in reading and math by 2014, including low-income students, minority students, students with disabilities, and students with limited English proficiency. Schools that fail to show adequate yearly progress face an escalating series of sanctions, ultimately including the replacement of faculty and staff or having the state or a private company take over school management.

NCLB, which was named for a slogan used by the George W. Bush presidential campaign, substantially increases the role of the federal government in public education.[2] Historically, state and local governments have been primarily responsible for making education policy. They operate the nation's public education system and provide more than 90 percent of the money.[3] The role of the federal government has been limited to funding certain targeted activities. In exchange for the money, state and local governments have had to comply with some federal requirements. NCLB goes well beyond earlier federal education initiatives.

The proponents of federal involvement in public education believe that federal resources can ensure access to a quality education for all the nation's children. Some states and school districts are too poor or perhaps unwilling to spend enough money to provide a quality education for all children, especially youngsters with special needs that are expensive to address. Federal money supports the education of children with disabilities and students with limited English proficiency. Federal dollars provide computers for schools in low-income areas and training for teachers. The **School Lunch Program** is a federal program that provides free or reduced-cost lunches to children from poor families.

School Lunch Program A federal program that provides free or reduced-cost lunches to children from poor families.

The supporters of federal education policy argue that federal regulations improve the quality of education nationwide by setting standards for fairness and performance. Federal laws and regulations prohibit discrimination on account of race and ethnicity and require school districts to educate all children, even students with severe learning disabilities. The federal government has compelled school districts to adopt policies designed to ensure safe and drug-free schools. Congress and the president have also begun to set national goals for school performance. In addition to annual testing for all students, NCLB requires states to administer a standardized basic skills test to a sample of students every other year in order to compare student performance across states.[4]

The critics of federal involvement in public education question the wisdom of setting education policy in Washington, DC. Who is better positioned to understand the problems of local schools, they ask, federal bureaucrats or officials at the state and local level? Federal education programs may not address the needs of local school districts in the ways that local educators think are most effective. NCLB forces states to neglect their own education reform plans to concentrate instead on creating an intricate system of high-stakes, basic skills testing. With administrative careers, teacher assignments, and student promotions all depending on test results, principals and teachers have a strong incentive to drop everything else and concentrate on the test. Instead of learning to read, write, and do math, students will learn how to take multiple-choice exams to pass a particular test. The school may even pressure weak students to drop out of school before the test is administered in order to inflate school test scores.[5]

The controversy over the federal role in public education demonstrates the relevance of the federal system to the policymaking process. The United States does not have just one set of policymaking institutions but, literally, thousands. In addition to the national government, 50 states and more than 80,000 local governments formulate, adopt, implement, and evaluate policies. Many public policies reflect the interplay among the levels of government. Education policy, for example, reflects decisions made at the national, state, and local levels.

This is the second of two chapters focusing on the legal/constitutional environment for policymaking. Chapter 2 examined the U.S. Constitution, including a brief introduction to the concept of federalism. This chapter develops the material presented in Chapter 2 by exploring federalism in more depth.

 WHAT IS YOUR OPINION?

If you were a member of Congress, would you have voted for the No Child Left Behind Act?

Federal system or **federation** A political system that divides power between a central government, with authority over the whole nation, and a series of state governments.

Delegated or **enumerated powers** The powers explicitly granted to the national government by the Constitution.

Legislative power The power to make laws.

THE CONSTITUTIONAL BASIS OF FEDERALISM

Power of the purse The authority to raise and spend money.

Tariffs Taxes on imported goods.

Excise taxes Taxes levied on the manufacture, transportation, sale, or consumption of a particular item or set of related items.

The United States has a federal system of government. A **federal system** or **federation** is a political system that divides power between a central government with authority over the whole nation and a series of state governments. The Constitution delegates certain powers to the national government while leaving other powers to the states.

The Powers of the National Government

The powers explicitly granted to the national government by the Constitution are known as the **delegated** or **enumerated powers.** The Constitution grants each branch of the national government certain powers. It gives the legislative branch the most extensive list of powers and the judicial branch, the least extensive.

The Powers of the Legislative Branch   The Constitution vests the **legislative power,** the power to make laws, in Congress. In Article I, Section 8, the Constitution gives Congress broad legislative authority. Congress has the **power of the purse,** which is authority to raise and spend money. Congress can levy taxes, including **tariffs,** which are taxes on imported goods, and **excise taxes,** which are levies assessed on the manufacture, transportation, sale, or consumption of a particular item or set of related

No Child Left Behind (NCLB) is a federal law that requires state governments and local school districts to institute basic skills testing in reading and mathematics for students in grades three through eight and to use the results to assess school performance and track the progress of individual students.

Necessary and Proper Clause or **Elastic Clause** The Constitutional provision found in Article I, section 8 that declares that "[Congress shall have the power] to make all laws which shall be necessary and proper for carrying into execution the foregoing powers, and all other powers vested by this Constitution in the government of the United States, or in any department or office thereof." It is the basis for much of the legislation passed by Congress because it gives Congress the means to exercise its delegated authority.

Implied powers Those powers of Congress not explicitly mentioned in the Constitution, but derived by implication from the delegated powers.

items. The Constitution charges Congress with providing for the "common defense and general welfare." It authorizes Congress to borrow money and repay the nation's debt.

The Constitution grants Congress the power to promote economic development. Congress can regulate commerce among the states and trade with other nations. It can coin money, enact laws governing bankruptcy, set standards for weights and measures, provide for the punishment of counterfeiters, create post offices and post roads, and establish rules for copyright and patent protection.

The Constitution also gives Congress an important role in foreign affairs and the nation's defense. Congress can suppress insurrection and repel invasion. It can declare war, raise and support armies, and maintain a navy.

Article I, Section 8 concludes with the **Necessary and Proper Clause** or **Elastic Clause.** "[Congress shall have the power] to make all laws which shall be necessary and proper for carrying into execution the foregoing powers, and all other powers vested by this Constitution in the government of the United States, or in any department or office thereof." The Necessary and Proper Clause is the basis for much of the legislation passed by Congress because it gives Congress the means to exercise its delegated authority.

The Necessary and Proper Clause is the constitutional basis for the doctrine of implied powers. **Implied powers** are those powers of Congress not explicitly mentioned in the Constitution but derived by implication from the delegated powers. Because the Constitution explicitly grants Congress the authority to raise armies, the power to draft men and women into the armed forces would be an example of an implied power. The authority to draft is not explicitly granted as a delegated power, but it can

Due Process Clause The constitutional provision that declares that no state shall "deprive any person of life, liberty, or property, without due process of law."

Equal Protection Clause A provision of the Fourteenth Amendment of the U.S. Constitution that declares that "No State shall . . . deny to any person within its jurisdiction the equal protection of the laws."

Executive power The power to enforce laws.

Judicial power The power to interpret laws.

National Supremacy Clause The constitutional provision that declares that the Constitution and laws of the United States take precedence over the constitutions and laws of the states.

be inferred as an action "necessary and proper" for carrying out one of the delegated powers—raising armies.

Several constitutional amendments expand the authority of Congress beyond those powers listed in Article I. The Fourteenth Amendment includes the Due Process and the Equal Protection Clauses. The **Due Process Clause** is the constitutional provision that declares that no state shall "deprive any person of life, liberty, or property, without due process of law." The **Equal Protection Clause** declares that "No State shall . . . deny to any person within its jurisdiction the equal protection of the laws." The amendment gives Congress the power to enforce both provisions through "appropriate legislation." Congress also has the power to enforce the Fifteenth Amendment, which declares that the rights of citizens to vote shall not be abridged on account of race, color, or previous condition of servitude. The Sixteenth Amendment grants Congress the authority to levy an income tax.

The Powers of the Executive Branch   The Constitution grants **executive power,** the power to enforce laws, to the president, declaring that the president should "take Care that Laws be faithfully executed." In Article II, the Constitution says that the president shall be commander-in-chief of the nation's armed forces. It states that the president may require reports from the heads of the executive departments, grant pardons and reprieves, make treaties with "the Advice and Consent" of the Senate, and appoint ambassadors, judges, and other officials. The president may make policy recommendations to Congress, receive ambassadors, and convene special sessions of Congress.

The Powers of the Judicial Branch   The Constitution vests **judicial power,** the power to interpret laws, in a Supreme Court and whatever other federal courts Congress sees fit to create. In Article III, the Constitution declares that the judicial power extends to all cases arising under the Constitution, federal law, and treaties. The Constitution gives the Supreme Court of the United States the authority to try a limited range of cases, such as cases affecting ambassadors and cases in which a state is a party. The Constitution empowers Congress to determine the types of cases on which the Court may hear appeals.

National Supremacy   The Constitution addresses the question of the relative power of the national and state governments in Article VI in a passage known as the **National Supremacy Clause.** This is the constitutional provision that declares that the Constitution and laws of the United States take precedence over the constitutions and laws of the states. In short, the National Supremacy Clause declares that the constitutional exercise of national power supersedes state action. The U.S. Constitution is superior to national law, state constitutions, and state laws. National law is superior to state constitutions and state laws.

The Constitutional Status of the States

The Constitution discusses the relationship of states with one another and with the national government. Article IV contains the **Full Faith and Credit Clause,** which is the constitutional provision requiring that states recognize the official acts of other

The School Lunch Program is a federal program that provides free or reduced-cost lunches to children from poor families.

Full Faith and Credit Clause The constitutional provision requiring that states recognize the official acts of other states, such as marriages, divorces, adoptions, court orders, and other legal decisions.

Defense of Marriage Act The federal law stipulating that each state may choose either to recognize or not recognize same-sex marriages performed in other states.

Civil union A legal partnership between two men or two women that gives the couple all the benefits, protections, and responsibilities under law as are granted to spouses in a traditional marriage.

Privileges and Immunities Clause The constitutional provision prohibiting state governments from discriminating against the citizens of other states.

states, such as marriages, divorces, adoptions, court orders, and other legal decisions. The constitutional meaning of the Full Faith and Credit Clause may soon be tested by the controversy over gay marriage. In 2004, the Massachusetts Supreme Court interpreted the state constitution of Massachusetts to hold that the state could not legally restrict the right of marriage to heterosexual couples. Same-sex couples who marry in Massachusetts may move to other states and then ask their new home states to recognize their marriage under the Full Faith and Credit Clause. Consequently, the U.S. Supreme Court may eventually be asked to rule on the meaning of the Full Faith and Credit Clause and the constitutionality of the **Defense of Marriage Act,** which is a federal law stipulating that each state may choose either to recognize or not recognize same-sex marriages performed in other states. Although many states have adopted measures to prevent the spread of gay marriage, other states have begun to recognize same-sex unions performed in Canada, Massachusetts, and other areas where they are legal. New Jersey treats gay marriages as equivalent to civil unions, which are legal in New Jersey. (A **civil union** is a legal partnership between two men or two women that gives the couple all the benefits, protections, and responsibilities under law as are granted to spouses in a traditional marriage.) In New York, meanwhile, some state courts and government agencies have recognized gay marriages as legal even though the state has neither gay marriage nor civil unions.[6]

Article IV also addresses the concepts of privileges and immunities, and extradition. The **Privileges and Immunities Clause** is a constitutional provision prohibiting state governments from discriminating against the citizens of other states. This provision ensures that visitors to a state are accorded the same legal protection, travel rights, and property rights as a state's own citizens. The courts

Extradition The return from one state to another of a person accused of a crime.

have held, however, that states may deny out-of-state residents certain privileges such as voting and paying lower tuition at state colleges and universities. **Extradition** is the return from one state to another of a person accused of a crime. A person charged with a crime in California who flees to Nevada, for example, could be extradited back to California.

The Constitution prohibits states from taking certain actions. States may not negotiate international treaties, form alliances with foreign countries, or engage in war unless they are invaded. States may not create their own currency or levy taxes on commerce with other states or foreign nations.

The Constitution includes a number of guarantees to the states. In Article IV, the Constitution declares that states may not be divided or consolidated without their permission. The Constitution also promises states defense against invasion, protection from domestic violence when requested, equal representation in the U.S. Senate, and a republican form of government. A **republic** is a representative democracy in which citizens elect representatives to make policy decisions on their behalf. The Eleventh Amendment prohibits foreign residents or the citizens of other states from suing a state in federal court.

Republic A representative democracy in which citizens elect representatives to make policy decisions on their behalf.

The best-known constitutional guarantee given the states is the Tenth Amendment: "The powers not delegated to the United States by the Constitution, nor prohibited by it to the states, are reserved to the states respectively, or to the people." This provision forms the basis for the doctrine of reserved or residual powers. The powers of the national government are enumerated in the Constitution—the delegated powers. According to the Tenth Amendment, the powers not delegated to the national government are reserved to the states or to the people. **Reserved** or **residual powers,** then, are the powers of government left to the states. In other words, the national government may exercise only those powers granted to it by the Constitution, whereas state governments possess all the powers not given to the national government, except those that are prohibited to the states by the Constitution.

Reserved or **residual powers** The powers of government left to the states.

This description of the federal system implies that the division of powers between the national government and the states resembles a layer cake, with each level of government exercising authority in its own sphere without overlap. In practice, however, the authority of the national government and the powers of the states overlap considerably. For example, both the states and the national government participate in education policymaking. Those powers of government that are jointly exercised by the national government and state governments are known as **concurrent powers.** Both levels of government have authority to tax, spend, and regulate. Instead of a layer cake, the federal system today more closely resembles a marble cake with its overlapping textures.

Concurrent powers Those powers of government that are jointly exercised by the national government and state governments.

The States' Rights/National Government Supremacy Controversy

States' rights An interpretation of the Constitution that favors limiting the authority of the federal government while expanding the powers of the states.

The supporters of states' rights and the proponents of national government supremacy have long debated the role of the states and the national government in the federal system. The doctrine of **states' rights** is an interpretation of the Constitution that favors limiting the authority of the federal government while expanding the powers of the states. The advocates of states' rights believe that the Constitution is a compact among the states that restricts the national government to those powers explicitly granted to it by the Constitution, that is, to the delegated powers. They would question, for example, whether the federal government should be involved in public education at all. The advocates of states' rights argue that the scope of the implied powers should be strictly limited. In contrast, the supporters of national government supremacy contend that the Constitution is a compact among the people rather than the states. They note that the document begins with the following phrase: "We the people . . ." The supporters of a strong national government believe that the implied powers should be construed broadly in order to further the interests of the people. The federal government has a role to play in public education, they say, because it has a duty to "promote the general Welfare."

The controversy over the respective roles of the national government and the states has also been argued on the basis of practical politics. States' rights advocates believe that local control makes for more efficient government because it permits a closer match between the services government provides and the policy preferences of constituents. Who should know better what public policies citizens favor—national officials or local officeholders? Furthermore, the supporters of states' rights believe that local control of public policy enhances the opportunity for citizen participation. State and local governments are closer to the people. If citizens disapprove of policy decisions, they can work to affect state policies and policymakers more effectively than they can influence policies and officeholders at the national level.

The supporters of a strong national government believe that national control makes for better public policy. A strong national government can set policy standards for the entire country in such areas as poverty relief, racial integration, and environmental protection. In contrast, state governments may lack both the resources and the will to assist the poor. State and local officials may choose to discriminate against racial minorities or be indifferent to environmental hazards. Only the federal government can supply the resources and the political will to achieve national goals.

 WHAT IS YOUR OPINION?

Which side more closely reflects your point of view: the supporters of a strong national government or the advocates of states' rights?

The Federal System and the Supreme Court

Constitutional controversies about the relative powers of the states and the national government are a recurrent theme of American history. On several occasions, the Supreme Court of the United States has addressed federalism issues. The Court first dealt with the controversy over the relationship between the states and the national government in the famous case of *McCulloch v. Maryland* (1819).

In 1791, Congress chartered a national bank, the First Bank of the United States, amid great controversy. Thomas Jefferson, who was then secretary of state, opposed the bank because the authority to create it was not among the powers

Although many states have adopted measures to prevent the spread of gay marriage, other states have begun to recognize same-sex unions performed in Canada, Massachusetts, and other areas where they are legal.

specifically enumerated by the Constitution. In contrast, Alexander Hamilton, who was secretary of the treasury, supported the bank and the power of Congress to establish it. He believed that the action of Congress was justified as an exercise of authority reasonably *implied* by the delegated powers. Despite the controversy, no legal challenge to the bank arose, and it operated until its charter expired in 1811.

Congress chartered the Second Bank of the United States in 1816, and it, too, became the object of controversy, particularly in the West and South. Critics accused the bank of corruption and inefficiency. The most serious charge was that the bank was responsible for an economic downturn that ruined thousands of investors. Several states responded to the public outcry against the bank by adopting restrictions on it or levying heavy taxes against it. Maryland, for example, required payment of an annual tax of $15,000 on the bank's Baltimore branch, which, in those days, was a sum large enough to drive the bank out of business in the state. Of course, that was just what the Maryland legislature wanted. When James W. McCulloch, the bank's cashier, refused to pay the tax, Maryland sued. The case presented two important constitutional issues: (1) Does the national government have authority to charter a bank? And (2) Does a state have the power to tax an arm of the national government?

Chief Justice John Marshall wrote the unanimous opinion of the U.S. Supreme Court, answering both questions. First, the Court upheld the authority of Congress to charter a bank on the basis of the doctrine of implied powers. Marshall noted that although the Constitution does not specifically grant Congress the power to incorporate a bank, the Constitution does say that Congress may lay and collect taxes, borrow money, and raise and support armies. What if, Marshall asked, tax money collected in the North is needed in the South to support an army? The creation of a national bank to transport that money would be a "necessary and proper" step to that end. The power to charter the bank, Marshall held, was implied by the Necessary and Proper Clause.[7]

Second, the Court ruled that Maryland's tax was unconstitutional. The power to tax, said Marshall, is the power to destroy because a high tax can drive the object of the taxation out of existence. If Maryland or any state has the authority to tax an arm of the national government, it could effectively shut it down and that would be contrary to the nature of the federal union as stated in the National Supremacy Clause.

In sum, the Supreme Court's decision in *McCulloch v. Maryland* supported the position of those who favored national government supremacy. By giving broad scope to the doctrine of implied powers, the Court provided the national government with a vast source of power. By stressing the importance of the National Supremacy Clause, the Court denied states the right to interfere in the constitutional operations of the national government.

The Supreme Court has not always been as receptive to the exercise of federal power as it was in *McCulloch v. Maryland*. In 1857, a few years before the outbreak of the Civil War, the Court held that the national government lacked authority to regulate slavery in the territories in the infamous *Dred Scott* decision.[8] Similarly, in the early 1930s, the Supreme Court limited the power of the national government to respond to the Great Depression by striking down much of the New Deal as unconstitutional. The **New Deal** was a legislative package of reform measures proposed by President Franklin Roosevelt for dealing with the Great Depression. It involved the federal government more deeply in the nation's economy than ever before.

Both the Supreme Court's decision in *Dred Scott* and its anti–New Deal rulings were eventually reversed. Congress and the states overturned the *Dred Scott* decision by proposing and ratifying the Thirteenth, Fourteenth, and Fifteenth Amendments to the Constitution. The Supreme Court reversed itself in the late 1930s, eventually holding New Deal legislation constitutional. For half a century thereafter, the Supreme Court found few constitutional limitations on the exercise of federal power. If Congress could present a plausible constitutional basis for an action, the Court would uphold it as constitutional.

Congress took advantage of the Supreme Court's broad interpretation of the doctrine of implied powers to exercise authority in a wide range of policy areas. In particular, Congress made frequent use of the Commerce Clause to justify legislation. The **Commerce Clause** is the constitutional provision giving Congress authority to "regulate commerce . . . among the several states." Congress used the Commerce Clause as a basis for legislation dealing with such diverse subjects as child labor, agricultural price supports, and racial discrimination in public places. In each instance, Congress argued that the particular activity it sought to regulate was part of interstate commerce, which Congress is empowered to regulate, and in each instance, the Supreme Court eventually accepted the argument.

In recent years, however, the Supreme Court has issued a series of states' rights rulings. In 1995, the Supreme Court ruled that Congress had overstepped its authority when it enacted the Gun-Free School Zones Act of 1990, a federal law banning firearms within 1,000 feet of a school. The Court found the act unconstitutional, ruling that Congress can only regulate economic activity that "substantially affects"

New Deal A legislative package of reform measures proposed by President Franklin Roosevelt for dealing with the Great Depression.

Commerce Clause The constitutional provision giving Congress authority to "regulate commerce . . . among the several states."

interstate commerce and that the possession of a firearm in the vicinity of a school does not meet that criterion.[9] In 1997, the Supreme Court overturned a provision in the **Brady Act,** which is a federal gun control law that requires a background check on an unlicensed purchaser of a firearm in order to determine whether the individual can legally own a weapon. The Court ruled unconstitutional a provision in the bill that required local law enforcement agencies to conduct background checks on potential gun purchasers. The Court said that the national government did not have the authority to force state governments to carry out its regulatory policies.[10] In 2000, the Supreme Court threw out a provision in the federal Violence Against Women Act that gave the victims of sexual assault the right to sue their attackers for damages. Congress based the measure on its constitutional power to regulate interstate commerce, but the Court ruled that violent crime is insufficiently connected to interstate commerce to justify Congress taking action.[11]

What is the constitutional relationship between the federal government and the states? Twenty years ago, the answer was that the national government was clearly the dominant partner in the federal system. Although the authority of the federal government was limited to the delegated powers, the Supreme Court's interpretation of the implied powers was broad enough to enable the federal government to justify almost any action. Today, however, the pendulum has begun to swing back toward the states' rights position. In several recent cases, the Supreme Court has made it clear that it will not uphold the constitutionality of federal actions unless they are closely tied to one of the delegated powers. This is an area of constitutional law that is evolving.

Brady Act A federal gun control law that requires a background check on an unlicensed purchaser of a firearm in order to determine whether the individual can legally own a weapon.

Millions of Americans benefit from the Food Stamp Program.

FEDERAL GRANT PROGRAMS

Federal grant program A program through which the national government gives money to state and local governments to spend in accordance with set standards and conditions.

A **federal grant program** is a program through which the national government gives money to state and local governments to spend in accordance with set standards and conditions. NCLB is an example of a federal program that deals with public education. Other federal programs address such policy areas as transportation, childhood nutrition, healthcare, public housing, vocational education, airport construction, hazardous waste disposal, job training, law enforcement, scientific research, neighborhood preservation, mental health, and substance abuse prevention and treatment. In 2007, the federal government gave $444 billion in grants to state and local governments, 16 percent of federal outlays.[12]

Program Adoption

Congress and the president adopt federal programs through the legislative process. Both houses of Congress must agree to establish a program and the president must either sign the legislation or allow it to become law without signature. If the president vetoes the measure, it can only become law if Congress votes to override the veto by a two-thirds' margin in each house. Congress passed the No Child Left Behind Act in late 2001, and President Bush signed it into law in early 2002.

Authorization process The procedure through which Congress legislatively establishes a program, defines its general purpose, devises procedures for its operation, specifies an agency to implement the program, and indicates an approximate level of funding for the program but does not actually provide money.

Federal programs must be authorized and funds appropriated for their operation. The **authorization process** is the procedure through which Congress legislatively establishes a program, defines its general purpose, devises procedures for its operation, specifies an agency to implement the program, and indicates an approximate level of funding for the program but does not actually provide money. Although Congress authorizes some federal programs on a permanent basis, it stipulates that other programs must be reauthorized periodically. NCLB is the reauthorizing legislation for the Elementary and Secondary Education Act (ESEA) of 1965, which was the authorization legislation for most federal education programs. Over the years, Congress and the president have added new education programs or revised old ones by adopting amendments to ESEA. NCLB is a significant revision of the original measure. It faced reauthorization in 2007, but Congress failed to act. Instead, Congress extended the reauthorization deadline until 2009 when a new president would have input in the process.

Appropriations process The procedure through which Congress legislatively allocates money for a particular purpose.

The **appropriations process** is the procedure through which Congress legislatively allocates money for a particular purpose. The appropriations process takes place annually. Federal programs do not function unless Congress authorizes them *and* appropriates money for their operation. Without money, programs go out of business or, if they are new programs, never begin functioning. Even if the opponents of a federal program cannot prevent its authorization, they can accomplish their goal by cutting or eliminating the program's funding.

President Bush's support for NCLB was out of character for most Republican politicians. In general, Republicans believe that public education should be the responsibility of state and local governments and they want to minimize federal education funding. Republican President Ronald Reagan even asked Congress to eliminate the federal Department of Education. In contrast, most Democrats want the federal government to play an active role in the nation's education system to ensure equitable access for all youngsters and to provide financial resources to the nation's schools.

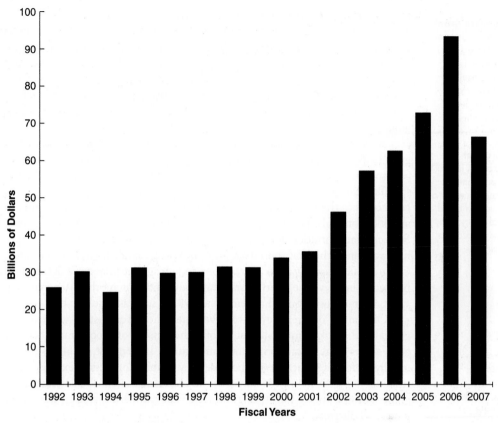

FIGURE 3.1   Department of Education Budget.
Source: Office of Management and Budget.

Figure 3.1 graphs the annual appropriation for the U.S. Department of Education from 1992 through 2007. During most of the 1990s, Republicans in Congress and President Bill Clinton battled over education funding. The Republicans wanted to reduce federal involvement in public education, whereas President Clinton favored increasing education spending. As the figure indicates, neither side achieved its goal. Education spending increased in 1993 after Clinton won the White House and the Democratic Party enjoyed a majority in both the House and the Senate, but fell in 1994 when the Republican Party won control of Congress. Education spending remained fairly flat for the rest of the decade. Ironically, federal education funding rose dramatically after the election of Republican President Bush. Democrats, who held a Senate majority in 2001, refused to support NCLB unless the president also agreed to a substantial increase in federal funding for education.[13] Funding growth continued even after the GOP won a Senate majority in the 2002 election. Education spending peaked in 2006 before falling back in 2007.

Types of Federal Programs

Federal programs come in a variety of forms.

Categorical grant program A federal grant program that provides funds to state and local governments for a narrowly defined purpose.

Block grant program A federal grant program that provides money for a program in a broad, general policy area, such as childcare or job training.

Categorical and Block Grants A **categorical grant program** is a federal grant program that provides funds to state and local governments for a narrowly defined purpose, such as removing asbestos from school buildings or acquiring land for outdoor recreation. In this type of program, Congress allows state and local officials little discretion as to how the money is spent. Categorical grants comprise more than 90 percent of all federal grants and provide nearly 90 percent of federal grant money to state and local governments.[14] Most federal education programs are categorical grant programs.

A **block grant program** is a federal grant program that provides money for a program in a broad, general policy area, such as childcare or job training. State and local governments have more discretion in spending block grant funds than they have in spending categorical grant money. Nonetheless, Congress tends over time to attach conditions to the receipt of block grant money, thus reducing the flexibility of state and local officials. For example, Congress and the president originally created the Surface Transportation Program to give states a lump sum of money to spend on highways and other transportation projects in accordance with statewide objectives. Congress subsequently added restrictions, requiring that 10 percent of the funds must be used to improve the safety of state highways and that another 10 percent must be spent on transportation enhancement activities, such as hike and bike trails.[15]

Officials at different levels of government hold contrasting views about categorical and block grants. Most state officeholders favor block grants because they allow states more discretion in implementation. In contrast, members of Congress usually prefer categorical grants because they enable Congress to exercise more control over implementation. Members of the U.S. House, in particular, like categorical grants because they entail special projects that can be targeted to individual congressional districts.[16]

 WHAT IS YOUR OPINION?

If you were a member of Congress, would you prefer block grants or categorical grants?

Project grant program A grant program that requires state and local governments to compete for available federal money.

Formula grant program A grant program that awards funding on the basis of a formula established by Congress.

Project and Formula Grants Federal grants differ in the criteria by which funding is awarded. A **project grant program** is a grant program that requires state and local governments to compete for available federal money. State and local governments make detailed grant applications that federal agencies evaluate in order to make funding decisions. The Department of Education, for example, administers project grants dealing with a range of educational initiatives, such as teacher training, math and science education, bilingual education, and preparing students for the demands of today's workforce. Public schools, colleges, and universities make application to the agency, which then decides which grant proposals merit funding.

A **formula grant program** is a grant program that awards funding on the basis of a formula established by Congress. In contrast to project grants, formula grants provide money for every state and/or locality that qualifies under the formula. The Community Development Program, for example, is a federal grant program that awards annual grants to metropolitan cities and urban counties to implement a wide

GLOBAL PERSPECTIVE

Education Policy and Federalism in Germany

Germany created a federal system after World War II at the encouragement of the allied powers. Having fought two world wars against Germany, the allies wanted the Germans to create a political system that would disperse power among the national government and a series of states, rather than concentrate it in a central government. The German federal system divides power between a national government and 16 states called länder.*

Although the German Constitution grants the länder exclusive jurisdiction over education policy, the German public supports a uniform national approach to education. Unlike the American states, the länder are more accurately described as administrative units rather than historically or culturally distinct regions. Public opinion favors centralized education policy-making with a uniform national policy because German society is culturally homogeneous and the public wants the schools to promote national unity. The German public also believes that a consistent national educational policy promotes academic excellence, whereas educational diversity produces mediocrity.

The länder use the Standing Conference of Ministers of Culture (KMK) as a mechanism to circumvent the constitutionally required decentralization of educational policy. The KMK has negotiated an agreement to standardize the curriculum, establish uniform educational assessment criteria, and coordinate the timing and duration of the school year among the länder. Consequently, Germany has a uniform national education policy despite the constitutional requirement of decentralization.†

QUESTIONS TO CONSIDER

1. Would the German public favor or oppose an educational initiative such as No Child Left Behind? Why or why not?
2. Why do Americans, unlike the Germans, resist a national set of educational policies?
3. Do you believe states should be able to set their own education policies or should education policy be determined at the national level?

*Karen Adelberger, "Federalism and Its Discontents: Fiscal and Legislative Power-Sharing in Germany, 1948–1999," *Regional and Federal Studies* 11 (Summer 2000): 43–68.
†Jan Erk, *Explaining Federalism: State, Society and Congruence in Austria, Belgium, Canada, Germany, and Switzerland* (New York: Routledge, 2008), pp. 58–70.

Matching funds requirement The legislative provision that the national government will provide grant money for a particular activity only on condition that the state or local government involved supplies a certain percentage of the total money required for the project or program.

variety of community and economic development activities directed toward neighborhood revitalization, economic development, and the provision of improved community facilities and services. The program awards funds based on a formula that includes population, poverty, and overcrowded housing. Most formulas are based on state population, with modifications designed to focus on areas of greater need and to ensure that every state receive at least a minimal amount of money.[17] Formula grants outnumber project grants by a four-to-one ratio. Most federal money is awarded through formula grants as well.[18]

Grant Conditions

Federal grants usually come with conditions. A **matching funds requirement** is the legislative provision that the national government will provide grant money for a particular activity only on condition that the state or local government involved supplies a certain percentage of the total money required for the project or program. For example, the federal government covers only 75 percent of the cost of highway

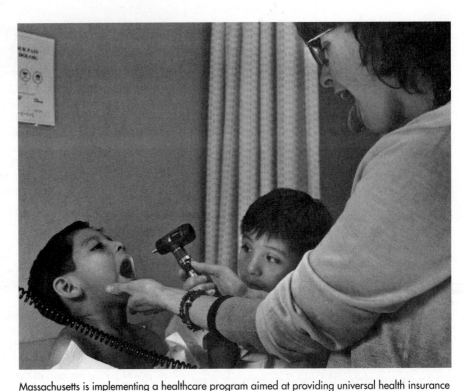

Massachusetts is implementing a healthcare program aimed at providing universal health insurance coverage, which, if it proves successful, could serve as a model for a national healthcare program.

Food Stamp Program A federal program that provides vouchers to low-income families and individuals that can be used to purchase food from grocery stores.

Medicaid A federal program designed to provide health insurance coverage to low-income persons, people with disabilities, and elderly people who are impoverished.

Federal mandate A legal requirement placed on a state or local government by the national government requiring certain policy actions.

construction projects, requiring states to provide a 25 percent match. About half of all federal grant programs require funding participation by the recipient.[19] Even federal programs that do not mandate financial participation by state and local governments usually require contributions in-kind. The **Food Stamp Program** is a federal program that provides vouchers to low-income families and individuals that can be used to purchase food from grocery stores. Even though the national government covers the cost of food stamps, it requires that states administer the program.

Matching funds requirements sometimes force states and localities to devote ever-growing sums of money to particular programs. Consider the impact on state budgets of **Medicaid,** which is a federal program designed to provide health insurance coverage to low-income persons, people with disabilities, and elderly people who are impoverished. The federal government and the states split the cost of Medicaid, with the federal government picking up 50 to 80 percent of the cost, depending on a state's wealth. Because healthcare costs are rapidly rising, especially the cost of prescription drugs, Medicaid is the fastest growing item in most state budgets, accounting for 13 percent of state general fund expenditures.[20]

Congress also imposes mandates on recipients of federal funds. A **federal mandate** is a legal requirement placed on a state or local government by the national government requiring certain policy actions. Some mandates apply to grants recipients in general. These include provisions in the area of equal rights, equal access for the disabled, environmental protection, historic preservation, and union wage rates for contractors' personnel. Individual programs often have particular strings attached as well. To receive federal law enforcement grants, for example, states must collect data on sex offenders, include DNA samples, and prepare a statewide sex offender registry database.[21] Each of these requirements is an example of an **unfunded mandate,** which is a requirement imposed by Congress on state or local governments without providing federal funding to cover its cost. In 1995, Congress passed and the president signed the Unfunded Mandates Reform Act to curb the growth in unfunded mandates, but it has been ineffective.

Unfunded mandate A requirement imposed by Congress on state or local governments without providing federal funding to cover its cost.

Grant conditions and federal mandates impose substantial costs on state and local governments. The National Conference of State Legislatures estimates the annual cost of federal mandates to states at $30 billion.[22] The most expensive federal programs for states and localities are federally mandated special education programs, NCLB, and prescription drug costs for people eligible for both Medicare and Medicaid.[23]

 WHAT IS YOUR OPINION?

Do you think state officials should turn down federal money in order to avoid federal mandates?

CONCLUSION: FEDERALISM AND PUBLIC POLICY

The federal system is a fundamental part of the legal/constitutional environment for policymaking, affecting every stage of the policy process.

Agenda Building

The United States does not have a single government but rather thousands of interconnected governments. Each level of government has its own policy agenda and procedures for policy adoption. Individuals and groups seeking to influence the official policy agenda may lobby Congress or an executive agency at the national level, a state legislature, or a unit of local government. Groups who fail to have their issues addressed at one level of government may find redress at another.

The levels of government influence the policy agendas of each other. The actions of state and local governments sometimes affect the policy agenda of the national government. For example, Congress passed legislation designed to shield gun manufacturers from lawsuits after more than 20 cities and counties filed suit against the gun industry seeking to recover damages caused by the illegal use of firearms.[24]

The actions of the national government frequently influence the policy agendas of state and local governments. The federal government has passed on much of the cost of homeland security to state and local governments, forcing local officials to make budget cuts or find additional sources of revenue. Whenever the Secretary of Homeland Security raises the threat advisory from yellow (elevated risk of terror attack) to orange (high risk of terror attack), state and local governments have to respond by increasing security at airports, power plants, public buildings, sports

Frustrated by a lack of action from the federal government, a number of states have adopted measures designed to address the issue of illegal immigration.

facilities, and other potential terror targets. Although the federal government has provided states with some money to fund homeland security activities, the amount has not been sufficient to cover the cost.

State and local governments have adopted legislation to address some policy issues because the federal government has failed to act. Frustrated with a lack of federal action on illegal immigration, many states have adopted measures designed to address the issue. In Arizona, for example, employers who knowingly hire an illegal immigrant face suspension and eventual loss of their business license. Several states have passed legislation to prevent illegal immigrants from obtaining driver's licenses.[25]

Policy Formulation and Adoption

The federal system affects policy formulation. To a degree, each state is a policy laboratory. Both the federal government and other states draw from the experiences of particular states in formulating their own policies. For example, policymakers across the nation are closely watching the implementation of a healthcare program in

GETTING INVOLVED

Federal Programs and You

Federal grants and loans are important for students and the institutions they attend. Many students depend on federal financial aid to complete their degrees. Furthermore, federal grant and loan programs effectively subsidize higher education by making it possible for students to go to college. Institutions that lose their accreditation must often close their doors because they forfeit their ability to award federal financial aid to their students.

Federal financial assistance to students comes in the form of grants and loans. Students need not repay grant money, but loans must be repaid. Pell Grants provide federal financial assistance to students based on their financial need. The amount of money that students can receive depends on the cost of their education and their available financial resources. Federal Family Education Loans (FFEL) and the Stafford Loan Program enable students to borrow money to attend college. Depending on their financial need, students may be eligible for subsidized federal loans, which do not begin assessing interest until recipients begin repayment.

Your assignment is to complete the paperwork to apply for federal financial aid. Visit your college's financial aid office, or go to its website to obtain the appropriate documents. You may wish to attend a financial aid seminar to learn what aid is available and whether you are eligible. Complete the paperwork, and submit the original or a copy to your instructor to document that you have completed the assignment.

The purpose of this assignment is both to give you insight into the relationship between federal programs and your college and to encourage you to apply for financial aid if you qualify and do not currently receive assistance. If you already have financial aid or you do not qualify for assistance, you will at least learn how the process works so that you can advise other students or prospective students about the resource. If you discover that you do qualify for a grant or a loan, this may be your opportunity to get the assistance you need to complete your degree.

Massachusetts aimed at providing universal health insurance coverage. The plan uses a series of penalties and incentives to close the insurance gap. People who can afford health insurance are required to purchase it much the way drivers in most states are required to have automobile liability insurance. Individuals who fail to get health insurance initially lose their personal exemption on the state income tax, which was worth $219 in 2007. In subsequent years, they face a penalty up to half the cost of a monthly insurance premium for each month they remained uninsured. Businesses with at least ten employees are required to provide them with health insurance coverage or face a fine as well. The government subsidizes the cost of health insurance for lower income people based on a sliding scale.[26] If the Massachusetts plan proves successful, it could be the basis of a national program.

Units of government and public officials at one level of government lobby other units and levels of government to influence the formulation of policies that may affect them. States and localities often retain professional lobbyists to represent their interests in Washington, DC. State and local governments also lobby through national associations, including the National League of Cities, U.S. Congress of Mayors, National Governors Association, and National Conference of State Legislatures.

The federal system influences policy adoption. With the exception of foreign and defense policy issues, which are the exclusive domain of the federal government, most policy issues in the United States are addressed by policies adopted by more than one unit and level of government. The national government, state governments, and local governments all adopt policies concerning issues such as education, healthcare, the environment, resource development, and law enforcement.

The national government affects state and local policy adoption through mandates and preemption. Federal mandates require states and localities to take certain actions. The Clean Air Act requires state and local governments to adopt regulations designed to decrease air pollution. The National Voter Registration Act (also known as the Motor Voter Act) forces state governments to make it easier for people to register to vote. The Asbestos Hazard Emergency Response Act requires state and local governments to remove asbestos from all public buildings.

The federal government prevents state and local governments from making policy in some policy areas. An act of Congress adopting regulatory policies that overrule state policies in a particular regulatory area is known as **federal preemption of state authority.** Since 1965, Congress and the president have adopted more than 350 laws preempting state regulation, including preemptions of state policies dealing with cellular phone rates, nuclear power safety, nutrition labeling, and private pension plans.[27] States may not regulate airlines, bus and trucking companies, mutual funds, or the telecommunications industry. For example, federal law prevents cities and other units of local government from banning the construction of cell towers, even though many local residents would like to keep the towers out of their neighborhoods because they are unsightly and negatively affect property values.[28]

Federal preemption of state authority An act of Congress adopting regulatory policies that overrule state policies in a particular regulatory area.

Policy Implementation and Evaluation

Federalism affects policy implementation. Many of the policies adopted by the national government require implementation by state and local officials, including federal policies dealing with welfare, transportation, environmental protection, and healthcare. NCLB is a federal education program that must be implemented by state and local governments. Federal regulations also affect the implementation of public policies adopted at the state level. The **Americans with Disabilities Act (ADA),** which is a federal law intended to end discrimination against individuals with disabilities and eliminate barriers preventing their full participation in American society, requires that new buses purchased by mass transit systems must have wheelchair lifts.[29]

Americans with Disabilities Act (ADA) A federal law designed to end discrimination against persons with disabilities and eliminate barriers to their full participation in American society.

Finally, the federal system influences policy evaluation. Public officials at all levels of government evaluate policy and give feedback. State and local officials frequently communicate their evaluations of federal programs to members of Congress and senators from their state. Federal officials often evaluate the effectiveness of federal programs by assessing their implementation at the state and local level. Congress uses feedback from evaluation reports to redesign federal programs. Evaluation studies on the impact of NCLB show that it has failed to make significant progress toward closing the achievement gap between white students and minority students, especially African Americans and Latinos. When Congress considered reauthorization legislation for the program in 2007, it debated how the law could be changed to help states improve minority student test scores.[30] Critics also warn that the NCLB requirement that all students be proficient in reading and math by 2014 is unrealistic. In some states, most schools, even schools that have achieved great progress, will be branded chronic failures and face restructuring.[31]

KEY TERMS

Americans with Disabilities Act (ADA)

appropriations process

authorization process

block grant program

Brady Act

categorical grant program

civil union

Commerce Clause

concurrent powers

Defense of Marriage Act

delegated or enumerated powers

Due Process Clause

Equal Protection Clause

excise taxes

executive power

extradition

federal grant program

federal mandate

federal preemption of state authority

federal system or federation

Food Stamp Program

formula grant program

Full Faith and Credit Clause

implied powers

judicial power

legislative power

matching funds requirement

Medicaid

National Supremacy Clause

Necessary and Proper Clause or Elastic Clause

New Deal

No Child Left Behind (NCLB)

power of the purse

Privileges and Immunities Clause

project grant program

republic

reserved or residual powers

School Lunch Program

states' rights

tariffs

unfunded mandate

NOTES

1. Kenneth Wong and Gail Sunderman, "Education Accountability as a Presidential Priority: No Child Left Behind and the Bush Presidency," *Publius: The Journal of Federalism* 37 (Summer 2007): 333–350.
2. Public Law 107-110.
3. Claudia Wallis and Sonja Steptoe, "How to Fix No Child Left Behind," *Time*, June 4, 2007, p. 36.
4. Paul E. Peterson and Martin R. West, eds., *No Child Left Behind? The Politics and Practice of School Accountability* (Washington, DC: Brookings Institution Press, 2003), pp. 1–9.
5. Diana Jean Schemo, "Failing Schools Strain to Meet U.S. Standard," *New York Times*, October 16, 2007, available at www.nytimes.com.
6. Anemona Hartocollis, "Gay Marriage Gains Notice in State Court," *New York Times*, March 6, 2008, available at www.nytimes.com.
7. *McCulloch v. Maryland*, 4 Wheaton 316 (1819).
8. *Dred Scott v. Sandford*, 19 Howard 393 (1857).
9. *United States v. Lopez*, 514 U.S. 549 (1995).
10. *Printz v. United States*, 521 U.S. 98 (1997).
11. *United States v. Morrison*, 529 U.S. 598 (2000).
12. Office of Management and Budget, "Summary Comparison of Total Outlays for Grants to State and Local Governments, 1940 to 2013," *The Budget for Fiscal Year 2009, Historical Tables*, available at www.whitehouse.gov/omb/budget.
13. David S. Broder, "How the Education Bill Was Born," *Washington Post National Weekly Edition*, December 24, 2001–January 6, 2002, pp. 14–15.
14. Larry N. Gerston, *American Federalism: A Concise Introduction* (Armonk, NY: M. E. Sharpe, 2007), p. 69.
15. Texas Comptroller of Public Accounts, "Theory of Devolution," *Fiscal Notes*, July 1996, p. 4.
16. Frances E. Lee, "Bicameralism and Geographic Politics: Allocating Funds in the House and Senate," *Legislative Studies Quarterly* 29 (May 2004): 185–214.
17. Frances E. Lee and Bruce I. Oppenheimer, *Sizing Up the Senate: The Unequal Consequences of Equal Representation* (Chicago: University of Chicago Press, 1999), pp. 203–220.
18. *Characteristics of Federal Grant Programs to State and Local Governments: Grants Funded 1995* (Washington, DC: Advisory Commission on Intergovernmental Relations, 1995).
19. David B. Walker, *The Rebirth of Federalism* (Chatham, NJ: Chatham House, 1995), p. 242.
20. Trinity D. Tomsic, "Managing Medicaid in Tough Times," *State Legislatures*, June 2002, pp. 13–17.
21. Paul Posner, "The Politics of Coercive Federalism in the Bush Era," *Publius: The Journal of Federalism* 37 (Summer 2007), p. 399.
22. Gerston, *American Federalism: A Concise Introduction*, p. 20.
23. Molly Stauffer and Carl Tubbesing, "The Mandate Monster," *State Legislatures*, May 2004, pp. 22–23.
24. Posner, "The Politics of Coercive Federalism in the Bush Era," p. 399.
25. Julia Preston, "Surge in Immigration Laws Around U.S.," *New York Times*, August 6, 2007, available at www.nytimes. com.

26. Pam Belluck, "Massachusetts Sets Health Plan for Nearly All," *New York Times*, April 5, 2006, available at www.nytimes.com.

27. Joseph F. Zimmerman, "The Nature and Political Significance of Preemption," *PS: Political Science & Politics*, July 2005, p. 361.

28. Jonathan Walters, "'Save Us from the States!'" *Governing*, June 2001, p. 20.

29. John M. Goshko, "The Big-Ticket Costs of the Disabilities Act," *Washington Post National Weekly Edition*, March 20–26, 1995, p. 31.

30. Sam Dillon, "Schools Slow in Closing Gaps Between Races," *New York Times*, November 20, 2006, available at www.nytimes.com.

31. Schemo, "Failing Schools Strain to Meet U.S. Standard."

Chapter 4

Public Opinion

CHAPTER OUTLINE

Political Socialization
   Process of Socialization
   Agents of Socialization
   Are Political Attitudes Genetically
   Transmitted?

Measuring Public Opinion
   Sampling
   Question Wording
   Question Sequencing
   Attitudes, Nonattitudes, and Phantom
   Opinions
   Interviewer–Respondent Interaction
   Timing

Political Knowledge

Support for Democratic Principles

Political Trust and Political Legitimacy

Political Efficacy

Political Philosophy
   Are Americans Liberal or Conservative?
   Opinion Differences Among Groups

Conclusion: Public Opinion and Public Policy
   Agenda Building
   Policy Formulation and Adoption
   Policy Implementation and Evaluation

LEARNING OUTCOMES

After studying Chapter 4, students should be able
to do the following:

▶ Describe the process of political socialization from
early childhood throughout the lifecycle.
(pp. 83–84)

▶ Discuss the role played by each of the following
agents of socialization: family, school, peer groups,
religious institutions, and the media. (pp. 84–88)

▶ Evaluate research assessing the genetic basis for
political attitudes and beliefs. (p. 88)

▶ Explain the theory and practice of survey
research, focusing on sampling, question wording,
sequencing, phantom opinions, interviewer–
respondent interaction, and timing. (pp. 89–94)

▶ Assess the level of political knowledge in the
United States, and discuss the impact of that
level on the policymaking process. (pp. 94–95)

▶ Evaluate the level of support Americans express
for the principles of majority rule and minority
rights. (pp. 95–98)

▶ Assess the significance of research on political
trust. (p. 99)

▶ Evaluate the level of political efficacy in the
United States. (pp. 99–100)

▶ Compare and contrast liberalism and
conservatism. (pp. 100–102)

▶ Evaluate whether Americans are liberal or
conservative. (pp. 102–103)

▶ Compare and contrast the political views of various subgroups of Americans based on social class, race and ethnicity, religion, generation, region, and gender. (pp. 103–106)

▶ Describe the roll of public opinion in the policymaking process. (pp. 106–108)

▶ Define the key terms listed on page 109 and explain their significance.

Gay and lesbian rights are among the most controversial and emotional subjects in American politics. The supporters of gay and lesbian rights define the issue in terms of civil rights and human dignity. They believe that gay men and lesbians should be afforded the same rights and privileges under the law as all other Americans. Gay rights advocates sometimes accuse their opponents of intolerance and bigotry. In contrast, the opponents of gay and lesbian rights regard the issue as a matter of traditional family values and social permissiveness. Many critics of the gay and lesbian rights movement believe that homosexuality is an immoral, deviant lifestyle at odds with nature and God's laws. They are against the government granting civil rights protections to gay men and lesbians and oppose any legal recognition of homosexual relationships.

Public opinion toward gay rights is complex and varies depending on the particular issue. Almost all Americans (89 percent) believe that gay men and lesbians "should . . . have equal rights in terms of job opportunities," but the nation is divided on other gay and lesbians rights issues. Although a majority of Americans (57 percent) believe that homosexuality should be considered an acceptable alternative lifestyle, the country is almost evenly divided on whether homosexuality is morally acceptable or morally wrong. Furthermore, a majority of Americans (53 percent) tell researchers that same-sex unions should not be recognized as valid.[1]

The topic of gay and lesbian rights provides a good introduction to the study of public opinion by raising a number of questions:

- How do scholars measure public opinion on issues such as gay and lesbian rights? Are opinion surveys accurate, especially on controversial or complex subjects?

- Why do different groups of Americans hold different views on such topics as the issue of gay and lesbian rights? What factors account for the development of individual attitudes and beliefs?

- What is the nature of public opinion in America? What is the relationship between attitudes on gay and lesbian rights and the democratic principles of majority rule and minority rights? Does public opinion on issues such as gay and lesbian rights vary among different groups of Americans? Do people vary in the intensity with which they hold an opinion on a subject?

- Finally, to what extent does public opinion influence public policy?

This chapter continues the examination of the environment for policymaking. Chapter 1 considered the cultural, international, and socioeconomic environments for policymaking. Chapters 2 and 3 focused on the constitutional/legal environment, with Chapter 2 examining the U.S. Constitution and Chapter 3 addressing the federal system. Chapters 4 through 9 will explore various aspects of the political environment. This chapter deals with public opinion; Chapter 5 considers political participation; Chapter 6 addresses the media; Chapter 7 examines interest groups; Chapter 8 focuses on political parties; Chapter 9 looks at elections.

 WHAT IS YOUR OPINION?

Should gay men and lesbians enjoy civil rights protection similar to other minority groups?

POLITICAL SOCIALIZATION

Political socialization The process whereby individuals acquire political knowledge, attitudes, and beliefs.

Individual attitudes about gay and lesbian rights and all other political issues are shaped through **political socialization,** which is the process whereby individuals acquire political knowledge, attitudes, and beliefs. Although socialization is a learning process, much of what individuals know and believe about politics and government does not come from formal classroom teaching but rather through informal learning that takes place throughout a lifetime. Filling out an income tax return, applying for a student loan, listening to a newscast on the radio, serving on a jury, helping a relative apply for permanent residency, and standing for the playing of the National Anthem at a sporting event are all opportunities for political socialization.

Process of Socialization

Children recognize political figures and symbols before they understand political processes. When asked about government, youngsters mention the president, police officers, and firefighters. Although grade school students recognize political terms such as *Congress, political party,* and *democracy,* they do not understand their meaning. Most children think of Congress as a group of men and women who help the president. Many youngsters can name the political party their family supports, but they are unable to distinguish between the two major parties on issues. Even though most children declare democracy to be the best form of government, few understand the term's meaning.

Young children have a positive attitude toward the government and its symbols. They see police officers as friends and helpers and tell researchers that the president is someone who is smarter and more honest than other people are. Most youngsters can also distinguish the American flag from the flags of other nations and say that it is their favorite.[2]

In adolescence, young people begin to resemble adults politically. They are able to separate individual roles from institutional roles, recognizing that it is possible to criticize the president, for example, while still supporting the office of the presidency. Procedures and processes such as voting and lawmaking are more visible and important to adolescents than they are for young children, and their general knowledge of the political process is more sophisticated.

The attitudes of different groups toward the political system begin to diverge during the adolescent years. During adolescence, many African American children grow less trustful of authority figures, especially police officers. In contrast, young people from middle-class white families remain positive.[3] Disillusionment with authority figures diminishes as young adults enter the workforce.[4]

Political events drive socialization during adolescence. For example, young people gain knowledge and develop political party attachments during a presidential election campaign. The more intense a particular political event is for an individual adolescent, the more enduring the political views. Major events such as the Civil War and the Great Depression had a lifelong impact on generations of Americans.[5]

Political socialization continues into adulthood although at a slower pace than during childhood or adolescence. Both attitudes and basic knowledge levels about politics and government crystallize during early adulthood and tend to persist with comparatively little change in later years of life.[6] Nonetheless, as young adults enter the workforce, purchase homes, start families, change careers, and eventually retire, they may change their views on specific political issues.

Agents of Socialization

Agents of socialization Those factors that contribute to political socialization by shaping formal and informal learning.

Those factors that contribute to political socialization by shaping formal and informal learning are known as **agents of socialization.** These factors affect the level, intensity, and direction of thoughts and actions about politics. In American society, the agents of socialization include the family, school, peer groups, religious institutions, and the media.

Family   Children acquire certain attitudes and orientations toward politics from their families. Adults whose parents were politically active are more likely to be involved in politics themselves as compared with their peers whose parents were uninvolved in the political process. Voters are usually the children of voters.[7] Young people whose parents are politically knowledgeable are more likely to be well informed about government and politics than are children with uninformed parents.[8] Young people who discuss politics and current events with their parents are more knowledgeable about government and politics and more committed to future voting than are other youth.[9]

Families influence at least the initial development of political party affiliation. As parents talk with one another and with their children, they are unconsciously constructing a "family identity" that can include a party identification.[10] A study of fourth graders found that 60 percent of the youngsters identified with a party even though they had virtually no knowledge of party history, issues, or candidates. The children merely adopted the party of their parents in much the way that they accepted their parents' religious preference. Declaring "We're Democrats" was as natural for the children as it was for them to say "We're Catholics."[11] Political independence (the absence of party identification) is passed along from parents to children as well.[12]

The political similarities between parents and their offspring diminish over time. Young adults frequently change their political views and party affiliation in response to new socializing experiences. By the age of 25, young adults often adjust their political party identification to place it in line with the party they prefer on the issues about which they care.[13]

School   The school is an important agent of political socialization. Civics classes enhance student knowledge of American government and politics, especially if the classes include discussions of current events. Coursework may lead students to watch news programs or read about current events online. Students taking civics classes may ask their parents more questions about political affairs than students not enrolled.[14] Furthermore, young people who volunteer to work in community organizations, perhaps as part of a high school course requirement, often develop a lifetime habit of civic engagement that includes participation in community organizations and voting.[15]

Schools teach patriotism. Historically, the public schools have trained the children of immigrants to be patriotic Americans, and schools continue to play that role today. In the classroom, students pledge allegiance to the flag, sing patriotic songs, commemorate national holidays, and study the lives of national heroes, such as George Washington, Abraham Lincoln, and Martin Luther King, Jr. Schools provide students with opportunities to participate in extracurricular activities, including political clubs and student government organizations. Young people who learn participatory skills in school typically become participatory adults.[16]

 WHAT IS YOUR OPINION?

Should schools teach youngsters to be patriotic Americans?

Schools also give young people firsthand experience working within a power structure. A school is a self-contained political system, with peers, authorities, rules, rewards, and punishments. Youngsters inevitably develop attitudes about authority and their roles as participants in the system. Schools are not democracies, of course; principals and teachers are often more interested in discipline than participation. Some scholars believe that the primary focus of schools on compliance with rules hinders the development of political participation skills. This phenomenon is particularly true of schools in low-income areas.[17]

The effects of college on political socialization are difficult to measure. Students who attend college differ politically from young people who do not continue their education beyond high school, but college-bound youngsters tend to vary from their peers even before they enter college. High-school graduates who go to college are more knowledgeable and interested in politics and feel more capable of influencing the policy process than do young people who are not college-bound.[18] Nevertheless, college life does appear to loosen family ties as far as political attitudes are concerned. College can be a broadening experience because students are exposed to a greater variety of ideas and people than they were in high school. As a result, collegians are less likely to share their family's political views than are people who do not attend college.

Religious Institutions   Churches, synagogues, mosques, and other religious institutions are important agents of political socialization for many Americans. Sixty percent of Americans tell survey researchers that religion is very important in their lives. Nearly two-thirds belong to a church, synagogue, or another religious body.

Schools teach patriotism by engaging students in the rituals of American democracy, such as the pledge of allegiance.

Although the proportion of Americans who declare that they are religious has decreased since the 1950s, Americans are more religious than are the people in most other industrialized nations. According to the Gallup Poll, 41 percent of Americans report that they attend religious services once a week compared with 26 percent of Canadians and 17 percent of people living in the United Kingdom.[19]

Personal involvement in religious organizations is associated with political participation. People who attend worship services, especially people who are active in churches and other religious bodies, are more likely to be politically engaged than are people who are uninvolved in a religious institution.[20] The association between religious activism and political activism is particularly important for African Americans.[21] Historically, the black church has been an important training ground for political leadership. Dr. Martin Luther King, Jr., the Reverend Jessie Jackson, and many other African American civil rights leaders learned skills in church that served them well in the political arena.

Religious institutions may also foster the development of particular political attitudes. Even though people tend to join religious organizations that promote political beliefs that are similar to their own, churches, temples, and other religious bodies have an independent effect on political views.[22] This is particularly true for religious organizations that feature an intense commitment of faith and a belief in religion as a source of truth and community. Members of churches or other religious bodies who are accustomed to accepting the religious organization as the authoritative interpreter of the word of God often respect the political pronouncements of religious leaders as well.[23]

 ### ? WHAT IS YOUR OPINION?

Should churches and other religious institutions take positions on political issues and candidates?

Peer Groups   Personal communications among friends and coworkers help shape political attitudes and beliefs. Individuals who personally know someone who is gay or lesbian are more supportive of gay rights than are other people.[24] Interpersonal discussions are more important than the media in influencing voter decisions.[25] When adults change peer groups because of a new job or a move to a different city, their political views may change as well.[26]

The impact of a peer group on an individual's political views depends on the significance of the group to the individual. People are more likely to share the values of a group that is important to them than they are those of a group that is less significant. Nonetheless, not all members of a group think alike. Many persons remain in a group even though they disagree with its values because they overlook the conflict. A study of conservative Christian churches found that nearly 40 percent of women members held feminist views that were contrary to the values of their church. The feminist women remained in the church despite the conflict because they perceived little or no connection between their religious beliefs and their political views.[27]

Media   Mass media outlets are important agents of socialization. Political participation is closely associated with media usage, especially newspaper and newsmagazine readership. Nearly everyone who votes reads a newspaper and about half of regular voters read newsmagazines as well.

The most important media sources for political information in order of usage are local television news, newspapers, radio, evening network news, online news, Fox News, CNN, and the morning network shows.[28] Young people who are frequent media users are more informed about politics and government than are young people who are less frequent users. They understand American government more clearly than less frequent media users, and they are more supportive of American values, such as free speech.[29]

Political scientists believe that the media, especially television, determine the relative importance Americans attach to various national problems. In other words, the media help set the policy agenda. Television news stories influence the priorities Americans assign to various national problems.[30] Media reports also help define the criteria by which the public evaluates a president's performance. The more attention the media pay to a particular policy issue, the more the public incorporates what they know about that issue into their overall judgment of the president.[31]

Are Political Attitudes Genetically Transmitted?

Political scientists have begun to explore whether differences in political attitudes and beliefs have a genetic basis. Researchers comparing the political attitudes and ideologies of monozygotic (identical) and dizygotic (nonidentical) twins in the United States and Australia have found a genetic basis for the way individuals respond to environmental conditions. Political similarities between parents and children may have as much or more to do with genetics than socialization. The scholars who conducted the research even suggest that the ideological division in American politics may have a genetic basis, and they identify two distinct ideological orientations that reflect the interaction of genes and the environment. People with an "absolutist" orientation are suspicious of immigrants, yearn for strong leadership and national unity, and seek an unbending moral code. They favor swift and sure punishment for those who violate society's moral code, tolerate economic inequality, and hold a pessimistic view of human nature. In contrast, people with a "contextualist" orientation are tolerant of immigrants and seek a context-dependent rather than rule-dependent approach to proper social behavior. They dislike predetermined punishments for those who violate moral codes, distrust strong leaders, disapprove of economic inequality, and hold an optimistic view of human nature.[32]

Religious organizations are important agents of socialization for many Americans.

MEASURING PUBLIC OPINION

Survey research
The measurement of public opinion.

Survey research, the measurement of public opinion, is a familiar part of the American scene. Businesses use market surveys to assess public tastes for their products and services. Political campaigns employ polls to plan strategy. Public officials use surveys to assess public understanding of problems and issues.[33] The media use opinion surveys to gauge public reaction to political events and assess the popularity of officeholders and candidates. Scholars rely on survey research as a tool for studying public opinion and political behavior.

Sampling

Universe The population survey researchers wish to study.

Sample A subset of a universe.

Margin of error (or sample error) A statistical term that refers to the accuracy of a survey.

Survey research enables scholars to examine the characteristics of a large group, the universe, by studying a subset of that group, a sample. In survey research, a **universe** is the population researchers wish to study. It may consist of all adult Americans, likely voters, Californians, or people who attend religious services regularly. A **sample** is a subset or part of a universe.

A properly chosen sample will reflect the universe within a given **margin of error (or sample error),** which is a statistical term that refers to the accuracy of a survey. The margin of error for a sample of 1,065 persons out of a universe of 500,000 or more is ± 3 percentage points, 95 percent of the time. Suppose that we know for a fact that 10 percent of all adults are left-handed. Sampling theory dictates that 95 percent of the time, a randomly selected sample of 1,065 people will include 7, 8, 9, 10, 11, 12, or 13 percent left-handers, that is, ± 3 percentage points from the true proportion of left-handed people in the universe. Five percent of the randomly selected samples of 1,065 persons will produce an error that is greater than 3 percentage points. In other words, 5 samples out of 100 will contain a proportion of left-handed people less than 7 percent or more than 13 percent.

The size of the margin of error depends on the sample size. Table 4.1 lists the margin of error for various sample sizes for a large universe. The margin of error decreases as the sample size increases and vice versa. The margin of error for samples of 100 or fewer is so large as to make the survey meaningless. Researchers can reduce the margin of error by increasing the sample size but cannot eliminate it unless, of course, they survey every member of the universe. In practice, most professional survey research firms aim for a margin of error of ± 3 to 4 percentage points.

Survey research is not exact. Because of the margin of error, a survey more closely resembles a shotgun than a rifle. Suppose a survey shows that Candidate X is

TABLE 4.1   Margins of Error for a Universe Greater Than 500,000

Margin of Error	Sample Size
±4%	600
±3%	1,065
±2%	2,390
±1%	9,425

leading Candidate Y by a 48 percent to 46 percent margin, while another survey indicates that Candidate Y is leading by 49 percent to 45 percent. The margin of error in each survey is ± 4 percentage points. Statistically, the surveys show the same result—support for the two candidates is within the margin of error. Neither candidate leads the other.

Statistical chance dictates that 5 percent of the samples taken will produce results that miss the true value by a margin greater than the margin of error. For example, even if two candidates are actually tied in voter support, an occasional sample will show one or the other with a lead greater than the margin of error. Over the course of an election campaign, surveys may show a good deal of relatively small voter movement between candidates with an occasional major shift in public support even if no actual change in voter support for the two candidates takes place.

To be an accurate reflection of a universe, a sample must be representative of the universe. If researchers are interested in the views of all Americans, a sample of a thousand people from Atlanta, a thousand women, or a thousand callers to a radio talk show would not likely be representative. An unrepresentative sample is a **biased sample,** that is, a sample that tends to produce results that do not reflect the true characteristics of the universe because it is unrepresentative of the universe. For example, radio talk programs present a distorted picture of public opinion because callers and listeners are disproportionately conservative Republican men with strong opinions on political issues.[34]

Biased sample A sample that tends to produce results that do not reflect the true characteristics of the universe because it is unrepresentative of the universe.

Internet polls are notoriously (and sometimes hilariously) unreliable because the sample consists of people who choose to participate, sometimes more than once. For example, *People* magazine once conducted an online poll to select the Most Beautiful Person of the Year. The editors at *People* expected that the winner would be a glamorous celebrity. When Howard Stern, a nationally syndicated radio talk show host, heard about the poll, he encouraged his listeners to vote for Hank, the Angry, Drunken Dwarf. Wrestling fans got into the act as well, flooding the *People* website with votes for Ric "Nature Boy" Flair, a professional wrestler. Hank, the Angry, Drunken Dwarf won the vote as *People*'s Most Beautiful Person and Flair finished second.[35]

A biased sample led to one of the most famous polling mistakes in history. During the 1920s and 1930s, a magazine called *Literary Digest* conducted presidential polls every four years. In 1936, the magazine mailed ten million ballots to individuals whose names and addresses were taken from telephone directories and automobile registration lists across the country. About two million people responded. On that basis, *Literary Digest* predicted that Alf Landon, the Republican challenger, would defeat incumbent Democratic President Franklin Roosevelt by a resounding 57 percent to 43 percent margin. In fact, Roosevelt was reelected by the largest landslide in American history!

What went wrong? *Literary Digest*'s sample was unrepresentative of the universe of likely voters. In the midst of the Great Depression, most of the people who owned telephones and automobiles were middle- and upper-income folks, who tended to vote Republican. In contrast, many poor and working-class people could not afford cars and telephones and were not sampled by the poll. Most of them voted for Roosevelt.

Random sample
A sample in which each member of a universe has an equal likelihood of being included.

Although nothing can guarantee a representative sample 100 percent of the time, the ideal approach is to employ a random sample. A **random sample** is a sample in which each member of a universe has an equal likelihood of being included; it is unbiased. If the universe were composed of the students at a particular college, researchers could select a random sample by picking every 10th or 20th student from a master list. In contrast, taking a random sample of Roman Catholics or people who will vote in the next election is difficult because no master list exists. Identifying samples of likely voters is especially challenging for pollsters because people tend to overestimate the probability that they will cast a ballot. Surveys conducted before relatively low turnout elections are frequently inaccurate because pollsters are often unable to separate voters from nonvoters.

National survey research firms generate samples using computerized systems to select a random set of telephone numbers. The researchers start with a list of all telephone exchanges in the United States along with an estimate of the number of households served by each exchange. A computer uses that information to create a master list of telephone numbers and then selects a random sample from the list. Because the computer is working from a list of possible numbers rather than actual telephone listings, people who have unlisted telephone numbers will be as likely to be included in the sample as will people with listed numbers. Survey researchers then use the list of numbers to conduct telephone interviews. To correct for the possible bias of including only those people in the survey who are usually home and answer their telephones, professional polling firms call back repeatedly at different times over several days. Once someone answers the telephone, the researchers do not necessarily interview the person who answered the phone. Instead, they ask for a list of all the adults in the household and then randomly select someone to interview, even if they have to call back at another time to find that person at home.

Many people refuse to participate in opinion polls. The response rate for major national surveys conducted over several days with callbacks to people who do not answer their phones initially is less than 30 to 40 percent. It is much less for snapshot polls taken overnight. Cell phones are another problem for survey researchers. Because wireless carriers charge users by the minute, cell phone users are less likely to agree to participate than are people using landlines.[36] Scholars are particularly concerned that low response rates may make surveys inaccurate because the people who respond to surveys differ demographically from the people who refuse to participate. Researchers attempt to compensate for differential response rates by weighting their samples to add men, young adults, and other people whose demographic groups would otherwise be underrepresented in the sample.[37]

Measuring public opinion about controversial issues is especially difficult. Respondents may not honestly answer questions concerning attitudes about race, for example, because they do not want to appear prejudiced. Researchers have found that public opinion polls attempting to measure voter preferences in election contests between African American and white candidates typically overestimate the vote for African American candidates because some white voters apparently misreport their candidate preferences.[38]

Question Wording

The best sample is worthless if survey questions are invalid. Questions that are confusing, oversimplified, or biased are unlikely to produce valid results. Consider the following survey questions:

1. If you are now covered by Medicare, or if you soon will be, would you be willing to pay higher premiums, deductibles, or income tax surcharges for: (a) Catastrophic hospital coverage, (b) Catastrophic nursing home coverage, (c) Both, (d) Neither?

2. Do you believe abortion should be legal: (a) Yes, (b) No, (c) No Opinion?

3. Should scientists and doctors be allowed to pursue stem cell research for the treatment of Alzheimer's, Parkinson's, diabetes, spinal cord injuries, and other tragic conditions: (a) Yes, (b) No, (c) Not sure?

Question 1 is confusing. It also forces respondents to choose among an unrealistically limited set of options. Some people might be willing to pay higher premiums and deductibles but not income tax surcharges or vice versa. How would they respond to the question?

Question 2 is oversimplified. Many people believe that abortion should be legal under certain circumstances but illegal under others. The question, with its oversimplified answer alternatives, would force these people to misstate their views.

Biased question A survey question that produces results tilted to one side or another.

Question 3 is a **biased question,** which is a survey question that produces results tilted to one side or another. The question is biased because it misstates the issue. The policy debate over stem cell research is not over whether scientists should be allowed to conduct research but whether federal funds should support it. Furthermore, the question is biased because it ignores the concerns of stem cell research opponents while calling attention to the "tragic conditions" that stem cell research might be able to help.

Question wording can affect survey responses because it provides a frame of reference to a question.[39] Consider the issue of granting legal status to same-sex couples. Although a majority of Americans say that they oppose gay marriage, the nation is evenly divided on whether homosexual couples should be allowed "to legally form civil unions, giving them some of the legal rights of married couples." If the wording is changed slightly to mention "healthcare benefits and Social Security survivor benefits," then the level of approval rises to more than 60 percent.[40] Many Americans react negatively to gay marriage apparently because the word *marriage* provides a religious frame of reference and they are reluctant to sanction homosexuality in that context. In contrast, questions that mention healthcare and Social Security benefits elicit a more positive response because those words frame the issue in a legal context rather than a religious one.

? WHAT IS YOUR OPINION?

Should public officials use opinion surveys to determine what policies are most popular and then adopt those policies?

Question Sequencing

The order in which questions are asked can affect a survey's results because question sequence can determine the context within which respondents consider a question. For example, asking about presidential job performance after questions about a particular government policy affect the president's popularity depending on whether the policy is perceived as successful or unsuccessful. Professional researchers attempt to control for the impact of question sequencing by rotating the order in which question are asked among survey respondents.[41]

Attitudes, Nonattitudes, and Phantom Opinions

A survey sponsored by the *Washington Post* asked a national sample of Americans the following question: "Some people say the 1975 Public Affairs Act should be repealed. Do you agree or disagree that it should be repealed?" The survey found that 24 percent of the sample agreed that the act should be repealed, while 19 percent said that it should not be repealed. The other 57 percent had no opinion. Ironically, the people with no opinion were the best informed because the Public Affairs Act was a totally fictitious law. The survey researchers made it up in order to test how many respondents would express an opinion on an issue about which they obviously had no knowledge.[42]

Phantom opinions invalidate the results of survey research. Survey respondents make up responses to questions about which they have little or no information because they do not want to appear uninformed.[43] Professional pollsters guard against distorting their poll results with uncommitted opinions by offering respondents a relatively painless opportunity to confess that they have not heard of an issue or do not have an opinion. Some survey researchers also ask respondents to indicate the intensity with which they hold their views and then take that intensity into account in interpreting the results of a survey.

Interviewer–Respondent Interaction

The race or gender of an interviewer can affect survey results when sensitive issues are involved because respondents sometimes attempt to say the "right thing" based on the race or gender of the interviewer.[44] For example, a survey measuring racial attitudes found black respondents were considerably more likely to say that white people could be trusted when the interviewer was white than when an African American interviewer asked the same questions.[45] Similarly, women are much more likely to give pro-choice responses to questions about abortion to female interviewers than they are to male interviewers.[46]

Timing

Even the most carefully conducted survey is only a snapshot of public opinion on the day of the poll because public opinion can change. In March 1991, for example, immediately after the American victory in the First Gulf War, the Gallup Poll showed that the approval rating of the first President Bush was 89 percent. Many political

Harry Truman gets the last laugh. (Photo Courtesy: Corbis/Bettmann)

observers predicted that the president would win reelection easily. By August 1992, however, Bush's popularity rating had fallen below 35 percent. Three months later, he was defeated for reelection.[47]

Using poll results to predict the future can be risky: ask Thomas E. Dewey. In 1948, Democratic President Harry Truman was running for election against Dewey, the Republican Party nominee. Throughout the summer and early fall, the polls showed Dewey well ahead, and it was generally assumed that Dewey would win handily. Because the major polling firms stopped surveying voters more than a week before the election, they missed a late voter shift in favor of President Truman. Consequently, Truman's election victory was a surprise to many people, including the editors of the *Chicago Tribune*, who rushed to press on election night with the famous headline: "Dewey Defeats Truman."

POLITICAL KNOWLEDGE

Many Americans are poorly informed about politics and government. Although some Americans are quite knowledgeable about public affairs, a majority of the nation's adults cannot accurately name their own representative in Congress or even one of the U.S. senators from their state. Most Americans are unable to identify the Bill of Rights. Less than a fifth can name the current chief justice of the United States.[48]

Political scientist W. Russell Neuman divides the public into three groups based on their knowledge about and interest in government and politics. At one end of the spectrum, we find a large group of people, about a fifth of the population, who are indifferent to politics; they have no opinions. At the other end are political junkies, a small group, probably less than 5 percent of the population, who are interested in politics and are well informed. The great majority of Americans fit in the middle category. Most of the time, they follow political developments halfheartedly. Although they have carefully developed opinions on some issues, their views on most issues are vague and incomplete.[49]

Some groups of Americans are more knowledgeable than are others. As a group, men know more about politics than do women. Whites are better informed than are African Americans. Wealthy people are more knowledgeable than are poor persons. Republicans know more than do Democrats. Well-educated people are better informed than are people with less formal schooling.[50]

Political information affects political behavior and beliefs. Knowledgeable Americans are more likely to vote and more likely to cast an informed ballot than are the uninformed. In 1994, 70 percent of survey respondents who were well informed about politics and government reported voting in that year's congressional elections compared with only 25 percent of less knowledgeable respondents. Furthermore, knowledgeable respondents typically voted for candidates whose views on issues of importance to them coincided with their own. In contrast, there was almost no relationship between the political issues that low-knowledge voters said mattered most to them and the issue positions of the candidates for whom they voted.[51]

Some observers believe that the political ignorance of many Americans has led to a dumbing down of political campaigns and contributes to the onslaught of negative campaign advertising. Political scientist Samuel Popkin says that candidates now conduct two campaigns. Candidates direct one campaign at informed voters, stressing issues and policy positions. They conduct a second campaign directed at less well-informed voters, attacking the character of their opponents.[52]

 WHAT IS YOUR OPINION?

Are people who neglect to keep up with the news unpatriotic?

SUPPORT FOR DEMOCRATIC PRINCIPLES

Survey data on gay and lesbian rights raise questions about support among the American public for basic democratic principles of majority rule and minority rights. Americans believe that "homosexuals should . . . have equal rights in terms of job opportunities" by a substantial 87 percent to 11 percent margin, with the other 3 percent expressing no opinion. When asked about specific professions, however, support for equal employment opportunities for gay men and lesbians falls. The survey found that 43 percent opposed hiring gays and lesbians as elementary school teachers, and 47 percent opposed homosexuals in the clergy.[53]

Do Americans support the democratic principles of majority rule and minority rights? Political scientists have studied this question for decades. During the 1950s, Professor Samuel Stouffer conducted a major study to evaluate public opinion toward civil liberties and found a high level of intolerance toward persons with unpopular views. For example, only 27 percent of the persons interviewed in his sample would permit "an admitted communist" to make a speech.[54]

In 1960, political scientists James W. Prothro and C. W. Grigg published what has become a classic study on the subject of political tolerance. They conducted a survey in which respondents overwhelmingly endorsed the sentiment that public officials should be chosen by majority vote and that people whose opinions were in the minority should have the right to convince others of their views. When Prothro and Grigg asked about specific, concrete situations, however, they found dramatically less support for the practice of majority rule and minority rights. Many respondents said that a communist should not be allowed to take office, even if legally elected. Many persons also stated that atheists should not be allowed to speak publicly against religion.[55] In the years since the Prothro and Grigg study first appeared, other research has confirmed that Americans are more likely to endorse democratic principles in the abstract than in specific application. One study even found that a majority of Americans opposed many of the specific guarantees of individual rights found in the Bill of Rights.[56]

A number of studies conducted in the 1970s concluded that Americans were growing more tolerant of political diversity. Using questions almost identical to those asked by Stouffer two decades earlier, political scientists found significantly larger percentages of Americans willing to tolerate atheists, socialists, and communists. Some scholars concluded that the trend toward greater tolerance reflected the views of a younger, more urban, and better-educated population.[57]

Recent research contradicts the conclusion that Americans have grown more accepting of political diversity. Although attitudes toward socialists, communists, and atheists have generally become more tolerant, many Americans express intolerant attitudes towards racists and persons advocating military rule in the United States. Americans are apparently no more tolerant of persons with unpopular views today than they were in the 1950s. The difference is that the targets of intolerance have changed and the number of unpopular groups is less than it was 50 years ago.[58] Furthermore, some Americans do not feel free. More than half of fundamentalist Christians and abortion rights opponents tell researchers that they believe that they cannot exercise full political freedom.[59]

Civil liberties The protection of the individual from the unrestricted power of government.

A number of political scientists believe that the general public has little understanding or concern for **civil liberties,** which is the protection of the individual from the unrestricted power of government. "[T]he only time many people consider . . . [civil liberties]," one scholar says, "is when they are being queried about it in public opinion surveys."[60] Consequently, people respond to questions about civil liberties based on their perception of a particular group's threat to society. In the 1950s, many Americans favored limiting free speech for communists because they feared communism. Americans today feel less threatened by communists than by racist groups such as the Ku Klux Klan. When answering survey questions, then, they express more tolerance for communists than for members of the Klan.[61] In sum, Americans favor civil liberties for groups they like; they oppose civil liberties for groups they dislike.

Americans favor civil liberties for groups they like; they oppose civil liberties for groups they dislike.

 WHAT IS YOUR OPINION?

Should the Ku Klux Klan be allowed to hold political rallies to spread its political philosophy of racial intolerance?

The apparent indifference of most Americans to civil liberties, at least as they apply to controversial groups, disturbs a number of observers. Tolerance for people of other races, ethnicities, religions, and political beliefs is an important underpinning for democracy.[62] Many political theorists believe that the maintenance of a free society requires a high degree of popular support for civil liberties. How, then, can we explain the stability of democracy in the United States in the face of research that has often found a lack of support for the fundamental principles of democracy?

Political scientists identify three factors accounting for the preservation of political freedom in the United States, despite the ambivalence and occasional hostility of many Americans to civil liberties. First, the Constitution protects individual rights. Although paper guarantees of individual freedom are not sufficient to ensure civil liberties, they provide an important legal foundation for individual rights.[63] Second, Americans do not agree on the target groups to be suppressed. Some people believe that communists should be kept from expressing their views or holding public office, whereas others favor silencing members of the Klan or people who oppose abortion rights. Because Americans do not agree on which groups should be suppressed, they are unable to unite behind undemocratic public policies. Finally, a number of political scientists believe that the attitudes of the general public about civil liberties issues are not nearly as important as the views of **political elites,** who are persons

Political elites
Persons that exercise a major influence on the policymaking process.

GLOBAL PERSPECTIVE

Civil Unions in Denmark

In 1989, Denmark became the first country in the world to grant legal recognition to same-sex relationships. The Danish arrangement, which is a form of civil union, is known as registered partnership. (A **civil union** is a legal partnership between two men or two women that gives the couple all the benefits, protections, and responsibilities under law as are granted to spouses in a traditional marriage.) Since Denmark adopted registered partnerships, five nations (Belgium, Spain, Canada, South Africa, and The Netherlands) have approved same-sex marriage. More than a dozen other countries allow civil unions or registered partnerships, including France, Germany, and the United Kingdom.

The debate over the Danish Registered Partnership Act resembled the current debate over gay marriage in the United States. The proponents of the legislation spoke of the importance of the nation treating all couples equally under the law. They argued that legal recognition of gay unions would promote the development of stable relationships. By discouraging sexual promiscuity, registered partnership would reduce the spread of AIDS and other sexually transmitted diseases. In contrast, opponents of the measure warned that government recognition of same-sex partnerships would weaken support for traditional marriage. The government should protect traditional marriage, they said, by reserving it for traditional couples.

The Danish Registered Partnership Act passed the Danish parliament by a vote of 71 to 47. "Two people of the same sex may have their partnership registered," the law declared. Whenever the word "marriage" or the word "spouse" appears in Danish law, it is construed to include registered partners. For all intents and purposes, then, registered partners are married in the eyes of Danish law.*

Nearly 6,000 Danes were classified as registered partners in 2005 compared with more than 2 million married people. Although the number of registered partners has been rising, most gay men and lesbians are not involved in partnerships. About a sixth of same-sex couples are raising children.†

Registered partnerships have apparently had no appreciable effect on the marriage rate in Denmark. The long-term trend in countries throughout the region, a trend that predates registered partnerships and same-sex marriage, has been toward lower marriage rates, higher divorce rates, and higher birthrates outside of marriage. In Denmark, the marriage rate was higher in 2000 than it was in 1989 when the Registered Partnership Act was adopted. The divorce rate was roughly the same.‡

QUESTIONS TO CONSIDER

1. Are registered partnerships (or civil unions) second-class marriages, or are they an acceptable compromise between the proponents and opponents of same-sex marriage?
2. Would you expect the adoption of same-sex marriage throughout the United States to have an impact on traditional marriage rates? Why or why not?
3. Why do you think most gay men and lesbians in Denmark are not involved in registered partnerships?

*William N. Eskridge, Jr. and Darren R. Spedale, *Gay Marriage: For Better or Worse?* (New York: Oxford University Press, 2006), pp. 50–54.
†Ibid., p. 94.
‡Ibid., pp. 173–174.

that exercise a major influence on the policymaking process. Support for democratic principles in specific situations, not just in the abstract, is stronger among people who are politically active and well informed than it is among individuals who are politically uninvolved. Democracy endures because those who are most directly involved in policymaking—political elites—understand and support the principles of majority rule and minority rights.[64]

POLITICAL TRUST AND POLITICAL LEGITIMACY

Civil union A legal partnership between two men or two women that gives the couple all the benefits, protections, and responsibilities under law as are granted to spouses in a traditional marriage.

Political legitimacy The popular acceptance of a government and its officials as rightful authorities in the exercise of power.

Many scholars believe that political trust is essential to political legitimacy in a democracy. **Political legitimacy** is the popular acceptance of a government and its officials as rightful authorities in the exercise of power. For the most part, democracy depends on the voluntary cooperation of its citizens rather than coercion. People pay taxes and obey laws because they accept the authority of the government. They seek political change through the electoral process and peacefully accept the outcomes of election contests because they recognize the decisions of the electoral process as binding. If a significant proportion of the population loses trust in the political system, the quality of democracy declines. Tax evasion and disrespect for the rule of law increase. The potential for a revolutionary change in the political order may develop. Political battles may be fought with bullets, not ballots.

Political scientists attempt to measure the level of political trust in society through a set of questions developed by the Center for Political Studies (CPS), which is a social science research unit housed at the University of Michigan. The questions probe the degree to which citizens believe that government leaders are honest (or crooked) and competent (or incompetent). One question asks, "How much of the time do you think you can trust the government in Washington to do what is right—just about always, most of the time, or only some of the time?" Another question reads, "Do you think that quite a few of the people running the government are a little crooked, not very many are, or do you think hardly any of them are crooked at all?"[65]

Political scientists average the answers to the questions to create a Trust Index. The index fell during the 1960s and 1970s, rose in the 1980s, fell again in the 1990s, increased dramatically after the terrorist attacks on September 11, 2001, and then dropped yet again.[66] Political scientists disagree as to how to interpret these data. Some scholars believe that the figures show that many Americans have lost confidence in their government. In contrast, other political scientists argue that public support for democracy in the United States remains solid. They believe that the questions that the CPS uses to measure trust in government are poorly worded and that they actually measure public approval (or disapproval) of current government officials rather than support for the political system.[67]

POLITICAL EFFICACY

Political efficacy The extent to which individuals believe they can influence the policymaking process.

Political efficacy is the extent to which individuals believe they can influence the policymaking process. Political efficacy is related to participation. People who believe that they can affect government policies would logically be more inclined to participate politically than people who have no confidence in their ability to influence what government does.

Political scientists identify two components of this concept. **Internal political efficacy** is the assessment by an individual of his or her personal ability to influence the policymaking process. The concept addresses a person's self-assessment of his or her knowledge of the political system and ability to communicate with political

Internal political efficacy The assessment by an individual of his or her personal ability to influence the policymaking process.

decision-makers. Scholars measure internal political efficacy by asking the following agree/disagree question: "Sometimes politics and government seem so complicated that a person like me can't really understand what's going on." Agreement with the statement indicates a low level of internal political efficacy and vice versa. In 2000, 60 percent agreed with the statement compared with 32 percent who disagreed.[68] Because internal political efficacy rose during the 1980s and 1990s, when voting turnout was in decline, most political scientists do not believe that the concept is related to voter participation. Low levels of internal political efficacy may explain why many Americans do not participate politically in other ways, but they apparently do not account for changes in voter participation rates.

External political efficacy The assessment of an individual of the responsiveness of government to his or her concerns.

External political efficacy refers to the assessment of an individual of the responsiveness of government to his or her concerns. This concept deals with an individual's evaluation of the willingness of government officials to respond to the views of ordinary citizens. Political scientists have created a Government Responsiveness Index based on responses to questions such as the following: "Over the years, how much attention do you feel the government pays to what the people think when it decides what to do?" The index generally declined from the mid-1960s through the early 1980s, but it has subsequently increased.[69] Scholars believe that external political efficacy is associated with voter participation.[70]

POLITICAL PHILOSOPHY

Liberalism The political philosophy that favors the use of government power to foster the development of the individual and promote the welfare of society.

In American politics, the terms *liberalism* and *conservatism* are often used to describe political philosophy. **Liberalism** is the political philosophy that favors the use of government power to foster the development of the individual and promote the welfare of society. Liberals believe that the government can (and should) advance social progress by promoting political equality, social justice, and economic prosperity. Liberals usually favor government regulation and high levels of government spending for social programs. Liberals value social and cultural diversity and defend the right of individual adult choice on issues such as access to abortion. In contrast, **conservatism** is the political philosophy that government power undermines the development of the individual and diminishes society as a whole. Conservatives argue that government regulations and social programs generally do harm rather than good. Charities, private businesses, and individuals can solve societal problems if the government will just leave them alone. Conservatives also believe that the government should defend the traditional values of society.

Conservatism The political philosophy that government power undermines the development of the individual and diminishes society as a whole.

The terms *right* and *left* are also used to describe political ideology. In American politics, the **political right** refers to conservatism, the **political left** to liberalism. Similarly, **right wing** means conservative; **left wing** means liberal. The use of these terms comes from the traditional practice in European legislatures of seating members of liberal parties on the left side of the meeting hall, whereas members of conservative parties sit on the right side.

Political right Conservatism.

Liberals and conservatives disagree about the capacity of government to solve problems. Although liberals and conservatives both acknowledge that the nation faces certain social problems, they disagree as to whether those problems

Political left
Liberalism.

Right wing
Conservatism.

Left wing
Liberal.

can be best addressed by the government or private initiative. Liberals advocate government action to assist disadvantaged groups in society, such as the elderly, poor, minorities, and people with disabilities. They generally support such programs as Social Security, Medicare, welfare assistance for the poor, national health insurance, federal aid for education, and affirmative action programs for women and minorities. In contrast, conservatives argue that government, especially the national government, is too inefficient to solve the nation's social problems. They believe that government should reduce spending on social programs and cut taxes in order to promote economic growth, which, the conservatives argue, benefits everyone. As President Ronald Reagan once put it, "The best anti-poverty program is a job."

Liberals and conservatives disagree about the efficacy of government regulation. Liberals believe in the use of government power to regulate business in the public interest. They support environmental-protection laws to safeguard air and water quality, consumer-protection regulations to protect the buying public, occupational safety and health standards to ensure safe working conditions, and strict regulation of utilities to guarantee efficiency. Liberals are more likely than conservatives are to endorse trade restrictions to protect American companies and workers from foreign competition. In contrast, conservatives warn that government regulations usually involve undue interference with the market economy. They believe that government regulations drive up the cost of doing business, increasing prices for consumers and lowering wage rates for workers. In this policy area, at least, conservatives agree with the motto: "The government that governs least governs best."

Consider the issue of the environment. Liberals value a clean environment even if it means sacrificing some economic growth. They advocate government regulation to ensure clean air and water. They favor government actions designed to respond to the threat of **global warming,** which is the gradual warming of the Earth's atmosphere reportedly caused by the burning of fossil fuels and industrial pollutants. In contrast, conservatives want to proceed slowly in addressing environmental issues such as global warming so as not to negatively impact economic growth. They prefer market-oriented solutions to the pollution problem rather than government mandates.

Global warming
The gradual warming of the Earth's atmosphere reportedly caused by the burning of fossil fuels and industrial pollutants.

 WHAT IS YOUR OPINION?

Do you consider yourself a liberal, conservative, or moderate?

Conservatives and liberals trade positions on the role of government when it comes to social issues, such as pornography, gay and lesbian rights, abortion, school prayer, and women's rights. On these issues, conservatives favor a more active government, whereas liberals prefer less government involvement. Conservatives define social issues in terms of traditional family values. They regard pornography, gay and lesbian rights, abortion, assisted suicide, stem cell research, and the Supreme Court's refusal to allow government-mandated spoken prayer in public schoolrooms as direct assaults on God, family, and country. Conservatives generally support the rigorous enforcement of pornography laws, the adoption of a constitutional amendment against abortion, and the enactment of an amendment permitting school prayer. Conservatives oppose assisted suicide, most stem cell research, and laws protecting gay men and lesbians from discrimination. They also reject efforts to legalize same-sex marriage.

In contrast, liberals believe that adults should be free to decide for themselves what books to read or films to watch. They hold that women should be allowed to pursue the career goals of their choice and should be treated equally with men under the law. Liberals believe that women should not be forced to bear unwanted children; gay men and lesbians should not suffer discrimination; and the government should not dictate prayers for children to recite in the public schools. They favor government support for stem cell research aimed at finding cures for disease.

Ironically, both liberals and conservatives criticize government. Liberals believe that government should act more aggressively to promote the democratic value of equality by helping disadvantaged individuals and groups gain economic and political power. Furthermore, when government does act, liberals say that it often favors the interests of the rich and powerful. In contrast, conservatives criticize government for undercutting capitalism by interfering with the efficient working of the free enterprise system, thus lowering economic productivity. Conservatives believe that government economic intervention hurts everyone, including the poor.

Although the terms *liberalism* and *conservatism* help define the contours of the policy debate in America, their usefulness is limited. The real-life differences between liberals and conservatives are often matters of degree and emphasis rather than dramatic contrast. Also, a number of policy issues, including many foreign policy issues, cannot easily be defined along liberal/conservative lines. Finally, few Americans are consistently liberal or conservative, with most people holding conservative views on some issues, liberal opinions on others.

Are Americans Liberal or Conservative?

Public opinion surveys typically find more self-identified conservatives than liberals. According to the American National Election Studies (ANES), 23 percent of Americans described themselves as slightly liberal, liberal, or extremely liberal in 2004 compared with 32 percent who said they were slightly conservative, conservative, or extremely conservative. Meanwhile, 26 percent described themselves as moderate or middle of the road.[71] Nonetheless, political scientists warn against putting too much stock in self-appraisals of political philosophy. Studies have found that many Americans cannot accurately define *liberalism* and *conservatism*. Furthermore, research shows that relatively few people structure their thinking along liberal/conservative lines.[72]

Another approach to assessing political philosophy is to inquire about the role of government. When asked to choose between "more government services and more spending" or "fewer services to reduce spending," survey respondents favored the former 43 percent to 20 percent, with the rest either in the middle or declaring they don't know.[73] Furthermore, when asked about specific government activities, most Americans want government involved in a wide range of policy areas. Surveys show that few Americans favor decreasing or ending federal government involvement in consumer protection, medical research, financing college education, or job training for low-income people.[74]

Survey researchers Albert H. and Susan Davis Cantril have developed an index to classify Americans as to their attitudes about the role of government, including responses to both general and specific questions. The Cantril index shows that although many Americans have mixed feelings about the role of government in society, more people support an active government than oppose it. The Cantrils classify 39 percent of adult Americans as steady supporters of government compared with only 10 percent who are steady critics of government. They classify 12 percent of their sample as ambivalent supporters of government and 20 percent as ambivalent critics. Eleven percent of the sample could not be classified.[75]

 WHAT IS YOUR OPINION?

Do you consider yourself liberal, conservative, or middle of the road? Why?

Opinion Differences Among Groups

Surveys show that political attitudes vary among individuals according to such factors as social class, race, and gender. For example, support for gay and lesbian rights is strongest among women, younger adults, people who live on the East or West Coast, college graduates, higher-income groups, people who live in urban and suburban areas, Democrats and independents, self-identified liberals, and Catholics. In contrast, opposition to gay and lesbian rights is greatest among men, older adults, Southerners, people with relatively little formal education, lower-income groups, self-identified conservatives, Republicans, and Protestants.[76]

Social Class   Lower-income persons are more liberal than middle- and upper-income people on some issues but more conservative on others. On social welfare issues, lower-income people tend to be more liberal than middle- and upper-income Americans apparently because they see themselves as beneficiaries of social welfare programs. In contrast, lower-income individuals are often more conservative than other income groups on such noneconomic issues as women's rights and the rights of persons accused of crimes. Furthermore, lower-income whites are less supportive of civil rights for African Americans than are middle-income whites.

In foreign policy matters, lower-income individuals are more isolationist than middle-income people, but also more supportive of the use of military force in dealing with other nations. **Isolationism** is the view that the United States should stay out of the affairs of other nations. Working-class people often oppose free trade, fearing the loss of jobs to international competition. In contrast, middle- and upper-income people have a more internationalist perspective; they tend to favor free trade, foreign aid, and negotiated settlements of disputes.[77]

Race and Ethnicity   African Americans and Latinos are more liberal than whites on economic issues, favoring activist government with strong job training and welfare programs. Members of both minority groups typically support **affirmative action,** which is a program designed to ensure equal opportunities in employment and college admissions for racial minorities and women. African Americans in particular

Isolationism The view that the United States should stay out of the affairs of other nations.

Affirmative action A program designed to ensure equal opportunities in employment and college admissions for racial minorities and women.

perceive widespread racial discrimination in society and believe that it is the major reason many African Americans have trouble finding good jobs and adequate housing. They want government to play an active role in the quest for racial equality. In contrast, many whites think racism is a thing of the past.[78] They believe that African Americans have already achieved equality with whites. (In fact, African Americans continue to lag behind whites in employment, income, education, and access to healthcare.) Whites who believe that African Americans are as well off or better off than white Americans are opposed to affirmative action and government programs designed to assist blacks to improve their status.[79]

African Americans and Latinos are more conservative than whites on some social issues. Although African Americans and Latinos are less likely to support the death penalty than whites, they are more likely to hold conservative views than the general population on the issues of abortion and gay marriage. African American and Latino conservatism on these issues reflects relatively high rates of church attendance for both minority groups.[80]

Religious left
Individuals who hold liberal views because of their religious beliefs.

Religious right
Individuals who hold conservative views because of their religious beliefs.

Religion   Religious beliefs motivate many Americans to participate in politics. The **religious left** refers to individuals who hold liberal views because of their religious beliefs, whereas the phrase **religious right** refers to individuals who hold conservative views because of their religious beliefs. During the 1960s and early 1970s, many people supported civil rights for African Americans or opposed the Vietnam War because of religious principles. Today, poverty, peace, immigration, and the environment are important issues for religious liberals. Most members of the religious left are associated with mainline Protestant Christian churches, such as the Presbyterians, Episcopalians, and Church of Christ (Disciples), or with the Jewish faith. It also includes Buddhists and many people who declare that they are "spiritual" but not associated with organized religion.[81] The most important political issues for the religious right are opposition to abortion, pornography, and gay and lesbian rights. Christian conservatives support prayer in school and the right of parents to educate their children as they see fit. Christian conservatives tend to be associated with white evangelical Protestant churches, such as Assemblies of God and the Southern Baptist Convention.[82] Not all religious groups are in the camp of the left or right. Roman Catholics, for example, oppose abortion and gay marriage, positions associated with the religious right, but also oppose the death penalty, support civil rights and immigrant rights, and favor government efforts to end poverty. The latter positions are typically associated with the religious left. Furthermore, some conservative Christian groups have begun broadening their focus to include global warming, AIDS, and other traditionally liberal concerns.

In contemporary American politics, the religious right is more influential than the religious left. This development reflects the relative strength of the religious organizations associated with each cause. Whereas most mainline Protestant churches have been losing members for years, conservative evangelical churches have been growing. In the 1960s, twice as many white adults claimed membership in mainline Protestant denominations than were members of evangelical Protestant churches. Today, conservative evangelical Protestants outnumber members of mainline denominations. Furthermore, church attendance is higher among conservative evangelicals.[83]

African Americans are relatively conservative on the issues of abortion and gay and lesbian rights, reflecting their high rates of church attendance.

Because of the growth of conservative Christian churches, active church participation is now associated with political conservatism. At least among whites, the more actively involved people are with religious organizations, the more likely they are to hold conservative political views, and vice versa. For African Americans, the church is a basis for liberal activism on economic issues. Nonetheless, African Americans who are active church members hold more conservative views on social issues, such as abortion and gay and lesbian rights, than do African Americans who do not participate actively in a church.[84]

Generation   Younger Americans are more tolerant of ethnic, racial, and social diversity than older adults. People below the age of 30 are more sympathetic with affirmative action programs that aid minorities than are older people and are more likely to favor gay and lesbian rights.[85] Despite conventional wisdom, studies find no evidence that people grow more conservative with age. Instead, age-related differences in political views reflect the impact of socializing events common to a generation.[86] Younger Americans today, for example, came of age after the appearance of individual rights movements for African Americans, women, and homosexuals. In contrast, older people grew up at a time when African Americans were segregated, most women worked at home, and gay men and lesbians were in the closet. Differences in political views between generations may also represent different levels of education. Younger Americans may be more tolerant because they are better educated than previous generations.[87]

Region   Differences in political views among people from different geographical regions are fewer now than they once were, but they still exist. In general, people from the East and West coasts are more liberal than are people from the South, Midwest, or Rocky Mountain region. Although most regional differences can be explained by other factors such as class, race, and religion, some genuine regional variations based on unique cultural and historical factors may play a role in the political fabric of the nation. The South's lingering identification with the Old Confederacy is perhaps the most notable example of how history can affect the political thinking of a region.

Gender gap
Differences in party identification and political attitudes between men and women.

Gender   Men and women are different politically. The phrase **gender gap** refers to differences in party identification and political attitudes between men and women. Women are more likely than men to vote for Democratic candidates. They are also more likely than men to favor government programs to provide healthcare and education and to protect the environment. Women are less likely than men to favor increased defense spending and to believe that the wars in Afghanistan and Iraq are worth it.[88] Women and men hold similar views on the issues of abortion rights, women's equality, and gay marriage.[89] Although women and men vote in similar proportions, men are more knowledgeable about and more interested in politics. They are also more likely to feel politically efficacious.[90]

CONCLUSION: PUBLIC OPINION AND PUBLIC POLICY

Public opinion affects every stage of the policymaking process.

Agenda Building

Candidates and officeholders usually talk about the issues that interest voters. If polls show that voters are concerned about healthcare, then candidates and officials discuss healthcare. If polls indicate that immigration is a major concern, they talk about immigration. To be sure, not every issue on the policy agenda is an issue that is a high priority for a substantial proportion of the general public. Some issues become part of the policy agenda because of the actions of interest groups or public officials. Nonetheless, government officials are unlikely to ignore an issue that is important to a large part of the general public.

Latent opinion
What public opinion would be at election time if a political opponent made a public official's position on the issue the target of a campaign attack.

Policy Formulation and Adoption

Years ago, political scientist V. O. Key, Jr., introduced the concept of latent opinion to explain the relationship between public opinion and policy formulation and adoption. **Latent opinion** is not what voters think about an issue today, but what

GETTING INVOLVED

Family Politics

Political scientists believe that families play an important role in the socialization process. Politically active families typically raise children who become politically active adults. Families also pass along their party identification to their offspring, at least initially. Young adults may eventually change their party allegiance to join the party that more closely matches their adult policy preferences.

How did your family affect your political socialization, particularly your level of political involvement and your party identification? Your instructor is going to conduct a class discussion on this topic during an upcoming class session. Prepare to join in the discussion by taking the following steps:

1. Jot down some information about your own level of political involvement and party affiliation. Are you registered to vote? Are you a regular voter? Have you ever joined a political group or participated in a political campaign? How closely do you follow current events? Do you consider yourself a Republican, Democrat, an independent, or a supporter of another political party? Have you always had the same party affiliation?

2. Record your recollections of your family's political involvement and party loyalties. Were your parents or the adults who raised you politically active? What was their political party allegiance?

3. Speak with your parents or other members of your family to verify the accuracy of your recollections. Do their memories match your recollections?

4. Finally, consider the role your family played in your personal political socialization, and be prepared to discuss the topic in class.

---

public opinion would be at election time if a political opponent made a public official's position on the issue the target of a campaign attack.[91] Elected officials make thousands of policy decisions. Except for a relatively few high profile actions, such as President Bush ordering the American armed forces to attack Iraq, most of these decisions are invisible to the overwhelming majority of Americans. Nonetheless, public officials consider public opinion during policy formulation and adoption because they recognize that a future political opponent could raise the issue during an election campaign.

Contemporary political scientist James A. Stimson discusses the impact of public opinion on the decision-making calculus of public officials by introducing the concept of a **zone of acquiescence,** which is the range of policy options acceptable to the public on a particular issue. Stimson says that some policy options are too liberal to be acceptable to a majority of the public, whereas other options are too conservative. The zone of acquiescence encompasses those policy options that lie between the two extremes. The size of the zone varies from issue to issue and may change if public opinion grows more conservative or more liberal. Rational policymakers choose policy options within the zone of acquiescence; otherwise, they risk electoral defeat.[92]

The concept of a zone of acquiescence draws attention to a number of important points about the relationship between public opinion and public policy. First, public opinion affects policy formulation and adoption not by dictating policy but by

Zone of acquiescence The range of policy options acceptable to the public on a particular issue.

limiting options. On most issues, the zone of acquiescence is broad enough to include a number of policy options from which public officials may choose. Public opinion sets the range of acceptable alternatives, but it does not determine which options policymakers select. Other factors, including the influence of interest groups and political parties, come into play.

Second, the concept of a zone of acquiescence does not imply that policies are not controversial. The zone of acquiescence is based on majority preferences. Although abortion is legal in the United States, it remains controversial, and many Americans find it totally unacceptable.

Third, the zone of acquiescence affects elected officials differently because they are chosen from different constituencies. A **constituency** is the district from which an officeholder is elected. **Constituents** are the people an officeholder represents. A member of Congress elected from a district where a majority of constituents are African American, for example, faces a more liberal zone of acquiescence on economic issues than does a representative whose constituents are mostly upper-income whites. The president, meanwhile, must deal with a nationwide constituency.

Fourth, the zone of acquiescence for a particular issue changes as public opinion changes. During the 1980s, public opinion grew more conservative on law and order issues such as the death penalty. Consequently, the range of acceptable policy options available to officials grew more conservative as well. States adopted laws giving harsher sentences to violent criminals, and more states began implementing the death penalty. On other issues, such as gay and lesbian rights, public policy became more liberal as public opinion grew more liberal, especially in large urban areas whose residents are more likely to hold liberal views on the issue than people living in small towns and rural areas.[93] Policy positions that were not acceptable in the 1950s have now become acceptable.

Constituency The district from which an officeholder is elected.

Constituents The people an officeholder represents.

Policy Implementation and Evaluation

Policymakers consider public opinion, at least indirectly, during policy implementation. Officials enforce policies that enjoy broad public support more aggressively than policies that are controversial. As public sentiment against drunk driving has grown, officials have responded not just by adopting tougher DWI laws, but also by enforcing laws more aggressively. In contrast, the Supreme Court's decision against state-sponsored prayer in schools enjoys relatively little public support. Many school officials ignore violations unless parents complain.

Finally, public opinion influences evaluation. Public officials are more likely to scrutinize policies that have proved unpopular as compared with policies that enjoy strong public support. Congress and the press are more likely to investigate a program that is perceived as ineffective or that is unpopular with the public than they are to scrutinize a program that is widely regarded as successful.

KEY TERMS

affirmative action

agents of socialization

biased question

biased sample

civil liberties

civil union

conservatism

constituency

constituents

external political efficacy

gender gap

global warming

internal political efficacy

isolationism

latent opinion

left wing

liberalism

margin of error (*or* sample error)

political efficacy

political elites

political left

political legitimacy

political right

political socialization

random sample

religious left

religious right

right wing

sample

survey research

universe

zone of acquiescence

NOTES

1. Lydia Saad, "Tolerance for Gay Rights at High-Water Mark," May 29, 2007, available at www.gallup.com.

2. Fred I. Greenstein, *Children and Politics* (New Haven, CT: Yale University Press, 1956).

3. Edward Greenberg, "Orientations of Black and White Children to Political Activity," *Social Science Quarterly* 5 (December 1970): 561–571.

4. Doris A. Graber, *Mass Media and American Politics*, 7th ed. (Washington, DC: CQ Press, 2006), p. 116.

5. David O. Sears and Nicholas A. Valentino, "Politics Matters: Political Events as Catalysts for Pre-adult Socialization," *American Political Science Review* 91 (March 1997): 45–65.

6. M. Kent Jennings, "Political Knowledge Over Time and Across Generations," *Public Opinion Quarterly* 60 (Summer 1996): 228–252.

7. Eric Plutzer, "Becoming a Habitual Voter: Inertia, Resources, and Growth in Young Adulthood," *American Political Science Review* 96 (March 2002): 54.

8. Richard G. Niemi and Jane Junn, *Civic Education: What Makes Students Learn* (New Haven, CT: Yale University Press, 1998), p. 148.

9. Hugh McIntosh, Daniel Hart, and James Youniss, "The Influence of Family Political Discussion on Youth Civic Development: Which Parent Qualities Matter?" *PS: Political Science & Politics*, July 2007, pp. 495–499.

10. Cyntria Gordon, "Al Gore's Our Guy: Linguistically Constructing a Family Political Identity," *Discourse and Society* 15 (2004): 607–631.

11. Greenstein, *Children and Politics*, pp. 71–75.

12. Franco Mattei and Richard G. Niemi, "Unrealized Partisans, Realized Independents, and the Intergenerational Transmission of Partisan Identification," *Journal of Politics* 53 (February 1991): 161–174.

13. Paul Allen Beck and M. Kent Jennings, "Family Traditions, Political Periods, and the Development of Partisan Orientations," *Journal of Politics* 53 (August 1991): 742–763.

14. Niemi and Junn, *Civic Education*, p. 148.

15. Edward Metz and James Youniss, "A Demonstration that School-Based Required Service Does Not Deter—But Heightens—Volunteerism," *PS: Political Science & Politics* (April 2003): 281–286.

16. Molly W. Andolina, Krista Jenkins, Cliff Zukin, and Scott Keeter, "Habits from Home, Lessons from School: Influences on Youth Civic Engagement," *PS: Political Science & Politics* (April 2003): 278–279.

17. Edgar Lott, "Civic Education, Community Norms, and Political Indoctrination," *American Sociological Review* 28 (February 1963): 69–75.

18. Kenneth P. Langton, *Political Socialization* (New York: Oxford University Press, 1969), p. 116.

19. Lydia Saad, "Religion Is Very Important to Majority of Americans," December 5, 2003, available at www.gallup.com.

20. Robert Wuthnow, "Mobilizing Civic Engagement: The Changing Impact of Religious Involvement," in Theda Skocpol and Morris P. Fiorina, eds., *Civic Engagement in American Democracy* (Washington, DC: Brookings Institution Press, 1999), p. 352.

21. Frederick C. Harris, "Something Within: Religion as a Mobilizer of African American-Political Activism," *Journal of Politics* 56 (February 1994): 42–68.

22. Kenneth D. Wald, Dennis E. Owen, and Samuel S. Hill, Jr., "Churches as Political Communities," *American Political Science Review* 82 (June 1988): 531–548.

23. Kenneth D. Wald, Dennis E. Owen, and Samuel S. Hill, Jr., "Political Cohesion in Churches," *Journal of Politics* 52 (February 1990): 197–215.

24. Katharine Q. Seelye and Janet Elder, "Strong Support Is Found for Ban on Gay Marriage," *New York Times,* December 21, 2003, available at www.nytimes.com.

25. Paul Allen Beck, Russell J. Dalton, Steven Greene, and Robert Huckfeldt, "The Social Calculus of Voting: Interpersonal, Media, and Organizational Influences on Presidential Choices," *American Political Science Review* 96 (March 2002): 57–73.

26. Herbert P. Hyman, *Political Socialization* (Glencoe, IL: Free Press, 1959), pp. 109–115.

27. Clyde Wilcox, "Feminism and Anti-Feminism Among Evangelical Women," *Western Political Quarterly* 42 (March 1989): 147–160.

28. Graber, *Mass Media and American Politics,* p. 4.

29. Ibid., p. 185.

30. Shanto Iyengar and Donald R. Kinder, *News That Matters: Television and American Opinion* (Chicago: University of Chicago Press, 1987), pp. 112–113.

31. Jon A. Krosnick and Donald R. Kinder, "Altering the Foundations of Support for the President Through Priming," *American Political Science Review* 84 (June 1990): 497–512.

32. John R. Alford, Carolyn L. Funk, and John R. Hibbing, "Are Political Orientations Genetically Transmitted?" *American Political Science Review* 99 (May 2005): 153–167.

33. Jeffrey M. Stonecash, *Political Polling: Strategic Information in Campaigns* (Lanham, MD: Rowman & Littlefield, 2003), pp. 141–143.

34. Richard Morin, "Look Who's Talking," *Washington Post National Weekly Edition,* July 19–25, 1993, p. 37.

35. Richard Morin, "The Jokers Stacking the Deck," *Washington Post National Weekly Edition,* August 17, 1998, p. 42.

36. Megan Thee, "Cellphones Challenge Poll Sampling," *New York Times,* December 7, 2007, available at www.nytimes.com.

37. Herbert Asher, *Polling and the Public: What Every Citizen Should Know,* 6th ed. (Washington, DC: CQ Press, 2004) pp. 82–86.

38. Adam J. Berinsky, "The Two Faces of Public Opinion," *American Journal of Political Science* 43 (October 1999): 1209–1230.

39. Larry M. Bartels, "Democracy with Attitudes," in Michael B. MacKuen and George Rabinowitz, eds., *Electoral Democracy* (Ann Arbor: University of Michigan Press, 2003), pp. 56–57.

40. Frank Newport, "Six Out of 10 Americans Say Homosexual Relations Should Be Recognized as Legal," May 15, 2003, available at www.gallup.com.

41. Asher, *Polling and the Public,* p. 61.

42. Richard Morin, "What Informed Public Opinion?" *Washington Post National Weekly Edition,* April 10–16, 1995, p. 36.

43. John Zaller and Stanley Feldman, "A Simple Theory of the Survey Response: Answering Questions versus Revealing Preferences," *American Journal of Political Science* 36 (August 1992): 579–616.

44. Robert M. Worcester and Kully Kaur-Ballagan, "Who's Asking?" *Public Perspective,* May/June 2002, pp. 42–43.

45. Howard Schuman and Jean Converse, "The Effects of Black and White Interviewers on Black Response in 1968," *Public Opinion Quarterly* 35 (Spring 1971): 44–68; and Shirley Hatchett and Howard Schuman, "White Respondents and Race of Interviewer Effects," *Public Opinion Quarterly* 39 (Winter 1975): 523–528.

46. Asher, *Polling and the Public,* p. 96.

47. *Gallup Poll Monthly,* July 1992, pp. 8–9.

48. George H. Gallup, Jr., "How Many Americans Know U.S. History? Part I," October 21, 2003, available at www.gallup.com.

49. W. Russell Neuman, *The Paradox of Mass Politics: Knowledge and Opinion in the American Electorate* (Cambridge, MA: Harvard University Press, 1986), ch. 1.

50. Richard Morin, "Tuned Out, Turned Off," *Washington Post National Weekly Edition,* February 5–11, 1996, p. 6.

51. Ibid.

52. Quoted Ibid., p. 8.

53. "Homosexual Relations," available at www.gallup.com.

54. Samuel A. Stouffer, *Communism, Conformity, and Civil Liberties: A Cross Section of the Nation Speaks Its Mind* (Garden City, NY: Doubleday, 1955), pp. 28–42.

55. James W. Prothro and C. W. Grigg, "Fundamental Principles of Democracy: Bases of Agreement and Disagreement," *Journal of Politics* 22 (Spring 1960): 276–294.

56. Robert Chandler, *Public Opinion: Changing Attitudes on Contemporary Social and Political Issues,* A CBS News Reference Book (New York: R. R. Bowker, 1972), pp. 6–13.

57. Clyde Z. Nunn, Harry J. Crockett, Jr., and J. Allen Williams, Jr., *Tolerance for Nonconformity: A National Survey of Americans' Changing Commitment to Civil Liberties* (San Francisco: Jossey-Bass, 1978); and James A. Davis, "Communism, Conformity, Cohorts, and Categories: American Tolerance in 1954 and 1972–73," *American Journal of Sociology* 81 (November 1975): 491–513.

58. Jeffrey J. Mondak and Mitchell S. Sanders, "Tolerance and Intolerance, 1976–1998," *American Journal of Political Science* 47 (July 2003): 492–502.

59. James L. Gibson, "Intolerance and Political Repression in the United States: A Half Century After McCarthyism," *American Journal of Political Science* 52 (January 2008), p. 105.

60. John Mueller, "Trends in Political Tolerance," *Public Opinion Quarterly* 52 (Spring 1988): 19.

61. Donald Philip Green and Lisa Michele Waxman, "Direct Threat and Political Tolerance," *Public Opinion Quarterly* 51 (Summer 1987): 149–165.

62. James L. Gibson, "Enigmas of Intolerance: Fifty Years after Stouffer's *Communism, Conformity, and Civil Liberties,*" *Perspectives on Politics* 4 (March 2006): 21–34.

63. David G. Barnum and John L. Sullivan, "The Elusive Foundations of Political Freedom in Britain and the United States," *Journal of Politics* 52 (August 1990): 719–739.

64. Dennis Chong, "How People Think, Reason, and Feel about Rights and Liberties," *American Journal of Political Science* 37 (August 1993): 867–899.

65. "The ANES Guide to Public Opinion and Electoral Behavior," available at www.electionstudies.org.

66. Robert S. Erikson and Kent L. Tedin, *American Public Opinion: Its Origins, Content, and Impact*, 7th ed. (New York: Pearson Longman, 2005), pp. 163–166.

67. Timothy E. Cook and Paul Gronke, "The Skeptical American: Revisiting the Meanings of Trust in Government and Confidence in Institutions," *Journal of Politics*, 67 (August 2005): 784–803.

68. "The ANES Guide to Public Opinion and Electoral Behavior," available at www.electionstudies.org.

69. Ibid.

70. Ruy A. Teixeira, *Why Americans Don't Vote: Turnout Decline in the United States 1960–1984* (New York: Greenwood Press, 1987), p. 78.

71. "The ANES Guide to Public Opinion and Electoral Behavior."

72. William G. Jacoby, "The Sources of Liberal-Conservative Thinking: Education and Conceptualization," *Political Behavior* 10 (Winter 1988): 316–332.

73. "The ANES Guide to Public Opinion and Electoral Behavior."

74. Albert H. Cantril and Susan Davis Cantril, *Reading Mixed Signals: Ambivalence in American Public Opinion About Government* (Washington, DC: Woodrow Wilson Center Press, 1999), pp. 10–14.

75. Ibid., p. 20.

76. The Gallup Poll, available at www.gallup.com.

77. Eugene R. Wittkopf and Michael R. Maggiotto, "Elites and Masses: A Comparative Analysis of Attitudes Toward America's World Role," *Journal of Politics* 45 (May 1983): 303–334.

78. Scott B. Blinder, "Dissonance Persists: Reproduction of Racial Attitudes Among Post-Civil Rights Cohorts of White Americans," *American Politics Research* 35 (May 2007): 299–335.

79. Richard Morin, "It's Not as It Seems," *Washington Post National Weekly Edition*, July 16–22, 2001, p. 34.

80. Barbara A. Bardes and Robert W. Oldendick, *Public Opinion: Measuring the American Mind*, 3rd ed. (Belmont, CA: Thomson Wadsworth), p. 96.

81. Caryle Murphy and Alan Cooperman, "Seeking to Reclaim the Moral High Ground," *Washington Post National Weekly Edition*, May 29–June 4, 2006, p. 12.

82. James L. Guth, John C. Green, Corwin E. Smith, and Margaret M. Poloma, "Pulpits and Politics: The Protestant Clergy in the 1988 Presidential Election," in James L. Guth and John C. Green, eds., *The Bible and the Ballot Box* (Boulder, CO: Westview Press, 1991), pp. 73–93.

83. Allen D. Hertzke and John David Rausch, Jr., "The Religious Vote in American Politics: Value Conflict, Continuity, and Change," in Craig, *Broken Contract?* p. 191, Stephen C. Craig, *Broken Contract: Changing Relationships Between Americans and their Government* (Boulder, CO: Westview Press, 1966).

84. Steven A. Peterson, "Church Participation and Political Participation: The Spillover Effect," *American Politics Quarterly* 20 (January 1992): 123–139.

85. Amy Goldstein and Richard Morin, "The Squeaky Wheel Gets the Grease," *Washington Post National Weekly Edition*, October 28–November 3, 2002, p. 34.

86. Nicholas L. Danigelis and Stephen J. Cutler, "Cohort Trends in Attitudes About Law and Order: Who's Leading the Conservative Wave?" *Public Opinion Quarterly* 55 (Spring 1991): 24–49.

87. Thomas C. Wilson, "Trends in Tolerance Toward Rightist and Leftist Groups, 1976–1988," *Public Opinion Quarterly* 58 (Winter 1994): 539–556.

88. Laurel Elder and Steven Greene, "The Myth of 'Security Moms' and 'Nascar Dads,' Parenthood, Political Stereotypes, and the 2004 Election," *Social Science Quarterly* 88 (March 2007): 11.

89. Karen M. Kaufmann, "The Gender Gap," *PS: Political Science & Politics* (July 2006): 447–453.

90. Sidney Verba, Nancy Burns, and Kay Lehman Schlozman, "Knowing and Caring about Politics: Gender and Political Engagement," *Journal of Politics* 59 (November 1997): 1051–1072.

91. V. O. Key, Jr., *Public Opinion and American Democracy* (New York: Alfred Knopf, 1961), p. 499.

92. James A. Stimson, *Public Opinion in America: Moods, Cycles, and Swings* (Boulder, CO: Westview Press, 1991), pp. 19–21.

93. Kenneth D. Wald, James W. Button, and Barbara A. Rienzo, "The Politics of Gay Rights in American Communities: Explaining Antidiscrimination Ordinances and Policies," *American Journal of Political Science* 40 (November 1996): 1152–1178.

Chapter 5

Political
Participation

CHAPTER OUTLINE

LEARNING OUTCOMES

After studying Chapter 5, students should be able to do the following:

- List the methods individuals use to participate in the policy process, explaining why some methods are used more frequently than others are used. (pp. 114–116)

- Identify and discuss the most important factors influencing individual participation in the policy process. (pp. 116–117)

- Describe the relationship between participation and the following factors: income, age, race/ethnicity, and gender. (pp. 117–120)

- Compare and contrast the five groups of nonvoters identified by Doppelt and Sheerer. (p. 120)

- Trace trends in voter turnout in presidential elections since the 1960s. (p. 121)

- Identify the reasons voter participation rates in the United States are lower than participation rates in most other democracies. (pp. 121–123)

- Identify potential reforms aimed at increasing voter turnout, and assess their likely effectiveness. (pp. 123–125)

- Compare and contrast the political and policy preferences of those people who participate with the preferences of adult Americans in general. (pp. 125–127)

- Describe the role of participation in the policymaking process. (pp. 127–129)

- Define the key terms listed on page 129 and explain their significance.

More people voted in 2008 than in any previous American presidential election. The political year began with a record turnout in the New Hampshire presidential primary in early January. As the election year progressed, one state after another set turnout records. Primary election participation increased by 47 percent in Missouri and 69 percent in New Jersey.[1]

The election year concluded in November when more than 131 million Americans cast ballots for president, the largest election turnout in American history in terms of the total vote. Participation increased on a percentage basis as well, with an estimated 61.6 percent of the voting eligible population turning out to vote, the largest turnout since 1968. After a period of declining voter turnout, 2008 marked the third consecutive presidential election in which voter participation increased.

Voter turnout in the 2008 presidential election introduces this chapter on political participation. The chapter discusses voting and other forms of political participation in the United States, considering participation rates and the impact of political participation on the policymaking process. The chapter is the second in a series of chapters dealing with the political environment for policymaking. Chapter 4, the previous chapter, examined public opinion. The next four chapters—6, 7, 8, and 9—focus on the media, interest groups, political parties, and elections, respectively.

FORMS OF PARTICIPATION

Political participation An activity that has the intent or effect of influencing government action.

Political participation is an activity that has the intent or effect of influencing government action. Voting is the most common form of political participation. Substantially more Americans tell survey researchers that they vote than claim to participate through any other type of political activity. More than three-fourths of the respondents to the American National Election Survey reported casting ballots for president in 2004. (*Reported* turnout typically exceeds *actual* turnout because people do not want to admit to an interviewer that they neglected to vote.) In contrast, 48 percent said that they tried to influence people how to vote, 21 percent indicated that wore political buttons or put bumper stickers on their cars, 13 percent contributed money to candidates or a party, 7 percent attended a political meeting, and 3 percent worked for a candidate or a party.[2]

Election turnout is closely related to the level of interest in a particular contest.[3] Presidential races typically attract more voters on a percentage basis than other types of elections because of their high-profile nature. In contrast, voter turnout for congressional elections held in nonpresidential (midterm) election years seldom exceeds 40–45 percent of the voting eligible population. The voter participation rate in the 2006 midterm election was 40 percent. Even though that was the highest midterm election turnout since 1970, the figure was substantially less than the turnout in the presidential election years of 2004 and 2008.[4]

People participate in election contests in ways other than voting. Individuals who want to do more for a candidate or political party than just casting a ballot take part in election campaigns. They contribute money, prepare campaign mailers, telephone potential voters, put up yard signs, and work the polls on Election Day. Not

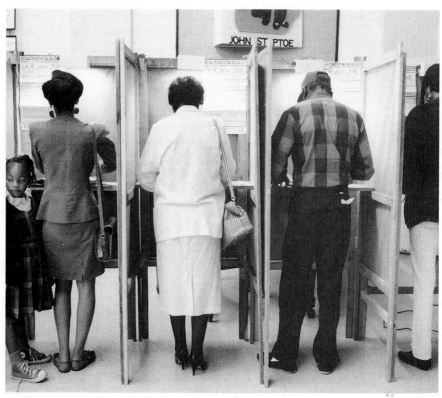

Voting is the most common form of political participation.

all forms of political participation are election centered. People attempt to influence the policy process by contacting public officials. Surveys show that about a third of Americans have contacted public officials, usually officials at the state or local level.[5] Many citizens write their representatives in Congress, telephone state legislators, or appear in person before the local city council or school board. Sometimes people concerned about a particular issue or policy gather signatures on a petition to present to government officials.

Americans also try to influence the policy process by joining or supporting interest groups. People interested in the reform of laws dealing with drunk driving join Mothers Against Drunk Driving (MADD) or Students Against Drunk Driving (SADD). Individuals concerned with animal rights contribute money to groups such as the American Society for the Prevention of Cruelty to Animals (ASPCA) or People for the Ethical Treatment of Animals (PETA). Opponents of gun control laws join the National Rifle Association (NRA).

Some Americans participate through unconventional political acts, such as protest demonstrations, sit-ins, or violence. During the 1960s, thousands of people took to the streets on behalf of the civil rights movement or in opposition to the war in Vietnam. Today, political activists engage in demonstrations in an effort to influence government policy on issues such as the war in Iraq and immigration. Some individuals and groups resort to violence to further their political cause, including bombing federal buildings and shooting physicians who perform abortions.

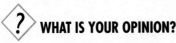 **WHAT IS YOUR OPINION?**

Is political violence ever justified?

EXPLAINING PARTICIPATION

The most important factors influencing individual participation are personal resources, psychological engagement, voter mobilization, and community involvement.[6]

Personal Resources

The personal resources most closely associated with political participation are time, money, and civic skills, such as communication skills and organizational ability. Each form of political activity requires a different configuration of resources. Some political activities take time; others require money; still others demand civic skills. People who want to contribute money to candidates and political parties must have financial resources. Individuals who work in campaigns or participate in political groups and activities must have both time and civic skills.[7] Participation rates are higher for activities that require relatively little time, few skills, and little or no expense. Voting is the most common form of political participation because it requires a relatively small amount of time and no expense. In contrast, relatively few people work in political campaigns or give money to candidates because those activities require significant amounts of time, civic skills, and money.

Psychological Engagement

People take part in the policymaking process when they are knowledgeable, interested, and have a strong sense of political efficacy. People participate in political campaigns for candidates and parties in whom they are interested, contact public officials over issues about which they are knowledgeable, and join political groups whose causes they support. Individuals who believe that a particular government policy affects their personal welfare are more likely to participate politically than would otherwise be expected. For example, lower-income Social Security recipients are more likely to participate on that issue than are upper-income recipients, probably because they are more dependent financially on their Social Security checks than are wealthier beneficiaries.[8] In contrast, people who are uninformed or disinterested in politics are usually uninvolved. Participation also depends on a sense of **political efficacy,** which is the extent to which individuals believe that they can influence the policymaking process. People are more likely to participate when they have confidence in their ability to affect the policy process and believe that policymakers are willing to accept their input.[9]

Political efficacy
The extent to which individuals believe they can influence the policymaking process.

Voter Mobilization

Political participation depends on **voter mobilization,** which is the process of motivating citizens to vote. Although some people are self-starters, the likelihood that individuals will vote, participate in an election campaign, join a political group, or engage in some other form of political participation increases if those individuals are asked to participate.[10] Political parties encourage people to vote and volunteer for campaigns. Interest groups, such as labor unions, the League of United Latin American Citizens (LULAC), and the AARP, educate citizens about political issues and urge their involvement in the policy process. Research shows that face-to-face contacts significantly increase the likelihood that individuals will go to the polls, especially if the contacts take place near Election Day.[11] In contrast, direct mail and telephone calls are less effective at increasing turnout.[12]

Community Involvement

Finally, people participate politically because of their involvement in the community. Individuals who have close community ties, such as home ownership and membership in community organizations, are more likely to participate than people without community ties. They regard voting and other forms of political participation as their civic duty because they can see the connection between participation and the quality of life in their community.[13]

PATTERNS OF PARTICIPATION

Participation rates vary among individuals based on such factors as income, age, race/ethnicity, and gender.

Income

Affluence and activity go together for every form of political participation. The higher the family income, the more likely a person will vote. According to the U.S. Census Bureau, the reported rate of voter turnout in 2004 for people in families earning more than $100,000 a year was 79 percent, compared with a turnout rate for people with family incomes less than $20,000 of 40 percent.[14] The participation gap between high- and low-income groups is less for voting than it is for other types of participation, especially giving money to candidates and parties. A majority of citizens with incomes of $75,000 or more report making campaign contributions, compared with only 6 percent of Americans with incomes under $15,000. Ninety-five percent of major donors earn more than $100,000 a year.[15] People who are well-off financially are also more likely than low-income people to join organizations, contact public officials, and engage in political protests.[16]

Participation rates and income are associated because resources and psychological attachment rise with income. Obviously, people in higher income groups have more money to contribute to political causes. Because income and education are closely related, more affluent citizens are better informed about government and politics than are less wealthy individuals. They have better communication and organizational skills. Wealthy citizens are also more likely to have a relatively high level of political efficacy than less affluent people.

Age

Figure 5.1 graphs reported voter participation rates by age group in the 2004 presidential election. As the figure indicates, voter turnout is lowest for the youngest group. Younger adults have fewer resources and are less interested in the policy process than older adults. As adults mature, their incomes increase and their skills develop. Older adults establish roots in their communities that increase their interest and awareness of the political process. Consequently, participation increases with each successive age group, with the peak voting years coming between 65 and 74 years of age. After age 75, voter participation begins to decline because illness and infirmity force the elderly to reduce their involvement in the policy process.

Race/Ethnicity

Participation varies among racial and ethnic groups. The voter turnout in 2004 was 66 percent for whites, 56 percent for African Americans, 30 percent for Asian Americans, and 28 percent for Latinos.[17] African Americans are more likely to engage in protests and participate in political campaigns than whites, but they are less likely to contribute campaign money than whites. Participation rates for Latinos are lower than they are for other groups across the full range of political activities. Compared with African Americans and whites, Latinos are underrepresented in every form of participation.[18]

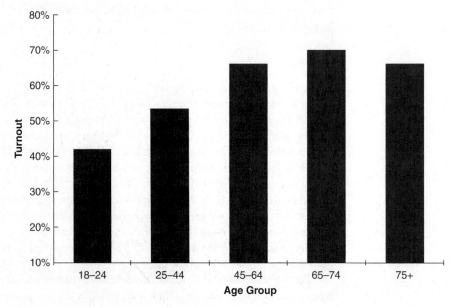

FIGURE 5.1 Voter Turnout by Age Group, 2004.
Source: U.S. Census Bureau.

Many members of racial/ethnic minority groups are ineligible to vote either because they are not citizens or are disqualified by criminal convictions. Only 2 percent of whites 18 years of age or older were unable to register and vote in 2004 because they were not citizens. The percentage of noncitizens among African Americans was 6 percent. It was 33 percent for Asian Americans and 41 percent for Latinos.[19] Meanwhile, 5.3 million Americans are disqualified from voting because they are incarcerated or have prior criminal convictions. Eleven states permanently disfranchise individuals convicted of serious crimes. The policy of denying voting rights to criminal offenders disproportionately affects minority Americans, particularly African American males, 14 percent of whom are disfranchised because of criminal convictions.[20]

Racial/ethnic patterns of participation also reflect the importance of recruitment to political participation. We would expect that participation rates for African American and Latino citizens would be lower than participation rates for whites because of income and age differences. As a group, minority citizens are less affluent and younger than whites. Nonetheless, participation rates for African Americans exceed expectations because of the effectiveness of organizations in the African American community, such as churches and political groups, at stimulating participation. Latino voter turnout, meanwhile, increases when Latino candidates are on the ballot.[21]

Gender

Women are more likely to vote than men, but men are more likely than women to engage in many other forms of participation. In 2004, 60 percent of women reported that they voted, compared with 56 percent for men.[22] Substantially more men than women

Participation rates for African Americans exceed expectations because of the effectiveness of organizations in the African American community, such as churches and political groups, of stimulating participation.

are disqualified from voting because of criminal convictions. Women are just as likely as men are to participate in election campaigns, but they are less likely to contribute money to political campaigns, contact public officials, and join political organizations.[23]

These data reflect differences in resources and psychological engagement between men and women. Women on average have lower average incomes than do men. Income is closely associated with participation, especially forms of participation other than voting. Furthermore, surveys indicate that men are more informed about and interested in politics and government than women are, even when they have the same level of education.[24]

NONVOTERS

People do not vote for a variety of reasons. After the 2004 presidential election, the U.S. Census Bureau surveyed nonvoters, asking them why they were ballot-box no-shows. About a fifth of nonvoters said they were too busy or had conflicting schedules. Another 15 percent of nonvoters suffered illness or disability; 9 percent were out of town on Election Day. Other people said that they did not vote because they were not interested (11 percent), disliked the candidates (10 percent), or did not care about the campaign issues (8 percent). Finally, 7 percent of nonvoters blamed registration problems for their failure to participate in the election.[25]

Political scientists Jack C. Doppelt and Ellen Sheerer identify five different groups of nonvoters.

1. **Doers (29 percent of nonvoters)**   The "Doers" are busy people, too busy to register and vote unless they are highly motivated to support (or oppose) a particular candidate. Except for their relative youth, the people in this category resemble voters. They are affluent, educated, active in community affairs, and follow the news.

2. **Unpluggeds (27 percent)**   The "Unpluggeds" do not believe that the policy process affects their lives. Compared with voters, they are relatively young, poorly educated, and uninformed about government and politics.

3. **Irritables (18 percent)**   The "Irritables" know what government is doing and do not like it. They are angry with public officials and the institutions of government, such as Congress and the presidency. As a group, they are relatively educated and affluent.

4. **Don't Knows (14 percent)**   Individuals in the "Don't Know" category are indifferent to government, focusing instead on their jobs and families. The people in this group are poorly educated and have low incomes.

5. **Alienateds (12 percent)**   The "Alienateds" are the most pessimistic nonvoters. They dislike candidates, political parties, and the institutions of government. They come from every demographic group.

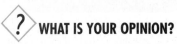 **WHAT IS YOUR OPINION?**

Does it really matter that Americans do not vote?

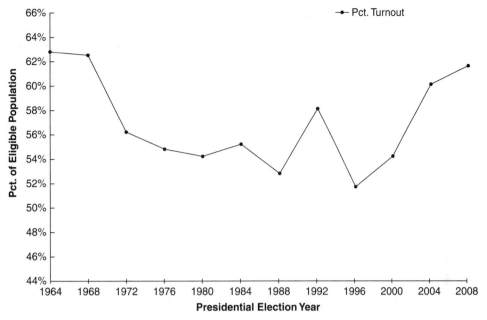

FIGURE 5.2   Voter Turnout 1964–2008.
Source: Vital Statistics in American Politics 2007–2008; Michael P. McDonald, U.S. Election Project.

TRENDS IN VOTER TURNOUT

Voting eligible population (VEP)
The number of U.S. residents who are eligible to vote.

Political scientists who study election participation measure voter turnout relative to the size of the **voting eligible population (VEP),** which is the number of U.S. residents who are legally qualified to vote. The VEP differs from the **voting age population (VAP),** which is the number of U.S. residents who are 18 years of age or older, because it excludes individuals who are ineligible to cast a ballot. In contrast to the VAP, the VEP does not include noncitizens, convicted criminals (depending on state law), and people who are mentally incapacitated.[26]

Voting age population (VAP)
The number of U.S. residents who are 18 years of age or older.

Figure 5.2 charts changes in presidential election turnout relative to the size of the VEP from 1964 through the 2008 election. More than 62 percent of the VEP cast ballots in the 1964 presidential election, capping a steady 36-year rise in voter turnout in the United States. For the next 30 years, voter participation rates generally fell, reaching a 70-year low in 1996 at 51.7 percent of the VEP. Election turnout subsequently rebounded, increasing to 54.2 percent in 2000, 60.1 percent in 2004, and 61.6 percent in 2008.

PARTICIPATION RATES IN COMPARATIVE PERSPECTIVE

Voting turnout in the United States is relatively low compared with other industrialized democracies. According to data collected by the International Institute for Democracy and Electoral Assistance, the United States lags behind most other countries in the world in electoral participation in national legislative elections. In 2006, for example, turnout in the Italian election surpassed 80 percent. Participation in Germany in 2005 was more than 75 percent. It was 65 percent in Canada.[27]

Political scientists identify three factors as primarily responsible for the United States having a relatively lower voter turnout rate than most other democracies. First, American election procedures are more cumbersome than they are in most other democracies. Before Americans can cast a ballot in most states, they must register to vote, usually no later than 30 days before an election. More than a fourth of the VAP in the United States is not registered to vote.[28] In most other democracies, the government takes the initiative to register eligible voters. American elections traditionally take place on Tuesday, whereas other countries declare a national holiday so citizens can vote without missing work. Compared with most other democracies, the United States holds frequent elections and elects large numbers of public officials. Many Americans stay home, confused by the length and complexity of the ballot.[29]

 WHAT IS YOUR OPINION?

Should the United States reform its voting procedures to make it easier and more convenient for citizens to cast their ballots?

Second, voter participation rates in the United States are relatively low because the nation's political parties are relatively weak. Strong political parties enhance voter turnout by educating citizens about candidates and issues, stimulating interest in election outcomes, and mobilizing citizens to go to the polls. They recruit voters. In the United States, citizen ties to political parties are relatively weak. Political scientist G. Bingham Powell, Jr., estimates that if American political parties were more centralized and had stronger ties to other social organizations, such as labor unions, religious bodies, and ethnic groups, then voter participation would rise by as much as 10 percent.[30] Labor unions in particular have an effect on voter turnout of low- and middle-income people.[31]

Finally, many citizens in the United States stay home from the polls because they do not perceive that elections have much impact on policy. The candidates who win elections may not be able to deliver on their promises because of **separation of powers,** which is the division of political authority among executive, legislative, and judicial branches of government. During the 2006 election campaign, Democratic congressional candidates called for the withdrawal of American combat forces from Iraq. Even though the Democratic Party captured majorities in both the House and Senate, it could not keep its promise, either because proposals to bring home the troops failed to pass both chambers of Congress or because President George W. Bush vetoed them.

Ironically, Americans are at least as active as are the citizens of other countries when it comes to forms of political activity other than voting. People in the United States are more likely to engage in campaign activity, contact public officials, attend political meetings, and participate in nonpolitical organizations than are people in other countries. Furthermore, the rate of participation in forms of political participation other than voting has been increasing since the 1960s.[32]

Separation of powers The division of political power among executive, legislative, and judicial branches of government.

Voter turnout surged in the 2004 and 2008 presidential elections.

Political scientists have done relatively little research on the question of why participation rates for forms of political participation other than voting are greater than they are in other countries. Perhaps the best explanation for the relatively high levels of nonvoting participation in the United States is that Americans have more resources—including time, money, and civic skills—than people in other countries. As a group, Americans are better educated, more affluent, and more experienced at working in nonpolitical groups such as clubs and religious institutions than the citizens of other democracies.[33]

INCREASING VOTER TURNOUT

Those observers who worry about low voter turnout favor the enactment of election-law reforms to enhance participation rates. The U.S. Government Accountability Office (GAO), an investigative arm of Congress, recommends the adoption of the following three election procedures: (1) registration deadlines that fall on or close to election day, (2) toll-free telephone numbers to allow voters to request absentee ballots, and (3) the increased use of mail balloting.[34] The state of Oregon has been using mail elections since the mid-1990s. Research indicates that mail elections have increased election participation by 10 percent.[35] Some states have also begun experimenting with Internet voting. Seven states allow same-day registration, which means that citizens can register to vote on Election Day.

In 1993, Congress passed and President Clinton signed the **National Voter Registration Act (NVRA),** which is also known as the Motor Voter Act. It is a federal law designed to make it easier for citizens to register to vote by requiring states to allow mail registration and provide an opportunity for people to register when applying for or renewing driver's licenses or when visiting federal, state, or local agencies, such as welfare offices. The law also prohibited states from removing names from the voter registration rolls merely for failure to vote.

Although the NVRA dramatically increased the number of people registered to vote, it did not increase voter turnout. The NVRA helped add 11.5 million people to the voter rolls between January 1995, when states were required to implement the law, and November 1996. Nonetheless, the voter turnout rate hit a 70-year low in 1996. "You may be able to spoon-feed someone and make it almost automatic to get them registered," said one election official, "but if it takes that much effort just to get

National Voter Registration Act (NVRA) A federal law designed to make it easier for citizens to register to vote by requiring states to allow mail registration and provide an opportunity for people to register when applying for or renewing driver's licenses or when visiting federal, state, or local agencies, such as welfare offices.

them registered, how do you expect them to take the initiative to actually come out and vote?"[36]

Political science research indicates that voting has two stages: registration and the actual vote itself. The NVRA failed to increase voter turnout in 1996 because it affected only the ease with which people can register. It did not make anyone more interested in politics or better informed about candidates and issues. The NRVA did not increase political efficacy or strengthen the efforts of political parties and groups to draw citizens to the polls. Voter registration reform alone is not sufficient to increase citizen participation in the electoral process.[37]

Research on nonvoters helps explain the failure of the NRVA. Consider the five categories of nonvoters identified by Doppelt and Sheerer: Doers, Unpluggeds, Irritables, Don't Knows, and Alienateds. Although changes in registration rules and other election procedures might increase turnout somewhat by making it easier for Doers to register, it seems unlikely that election-law reforms would have much impact on other groups of nonvoters. After all, election-law reforms will do nothing to make people better informed, less alienated, or more efficacious.

Compulsory voting The legal requirement that citizens participate in national elections.

GLOBAL PERSPECTIVE   Compulsory Voting in Australia

Compulsory voting, which is the legal requirement that citizens participate in national elections, is a low-cost, efficient remedy to the problem of low turnout. Voter participation rates are almost 20 percent higher in nations with compulsory voting than they are in other democracies.* Almost everyone votes in Australia, a nation that has had compulsory voting since 1924. For example, voter turnout was 94 percent in the 2004 national election.†

The Australian Election Commission (AEC) enforces the nation's compulsory voting law. The AEC sends a "please explain" letter to people who fail to vote in a particular election. Election no-shows can either pay a fine or offer an explanation. If the AEC decides that the explanation is valid, it can waive the fine. The courts settle disputes between the AEC and individual nonvoters over the validity of excuses. The proportion of Australians fined for failing to vote never exceeds 1 percent of the electorate.‡

Political scientists believe that compulsory voting strengthens political parties in general and working class parties in particular. Because parties do not have to devote their resources to turning out the vote, they can focus on persuasion and conversion. Compulsory voting builds party loyalty among citizens who must regularly choose among party candidates. Survey research in Australia finds that most Australian voters express firm and longstanding commitments to a party. Compulsory voting also benefits political parties representing the working class relative to parties that reflect the interests of middle- and upper-income voters because lower-income people are less likely to vote than middle-income citizens.

QUESTIONS TO CONSIDER

1. Is nonvoting such an important problem that it needs a legal remedy?
2. Do you think compulsory voting would work in the United States to increase turnout substantially?
3. Do you think that the United States will ever adopt compulsory voting? Why or why not?

---

*Mark N. Franklin, "Electoral Engineering and Cross-National Turnout Differences: What Role of Compulsory Voting?" *British Journal of Political Science* 29 (January 1999): 205.

†International Institute for Democracy and Electoral Assistance, "Voter Turnout," www.idea.int/vt/.

‡M. Mackerras and I. McAllister, "Compulsory Voting, Party Stability, and Electoral Advantage in Australia," *Electoral Studies,* 18 (June 1999): 217–233.

The 2004 and 2008 presidential elections suggest that the United States is experiencing a voting revival. After years of declining or flat electoral participation rates, voter turnout has surged to a level not seen in nearly 40 years. The increase reflected the result of massive voter mobilization efforts coupled with high public interest in the election. The two major political parties, supported by their interest group allies, organized sophisticated get-out-the-vote (GOTV) campaigns in 2004 and 2008, focusing on the **battleground states,** which are swing states in which the relative strength of the two major party presidential candidates is close enough so that either candidate could conceivably carry the state. Campaign volunteers and paid organizers telephoned, mailed, e-mailed, or visited millions of potential voters, encouraging them to go to the polls. Exposure to intense campaign activity increases political engagement, especially among low-income voters, a group with typically low voter turnout rates.[38] In the meantime, hot-button issues such as the war in Iraq, the War on Terror, gay marriage, healthcare reform, taxes, and the economy energized citizens to go to the polls. According to the NES, 40 percent of Americans said they were "very much interested" in the 2004 presidential campaign, the highest level of interest in the history of the poll and 14 percentage points higher than the level of interest expressed in 2000.[39] Interest in the 2008 election may have been even higher.

Battleground states Swing states in which the relative strength of the two major party presidential candidates is close enough so that either candidate could conceivably carry the state.

PARTICIPATION BIAS

Is participation biased in favor of some groups and against others? If everyone voted, would election outcomes change? Do those people who participate in campaigns, contact public officials, give money to candidates, and join political groups have issue preferences that are similar to all citizens? In short, does political participation bias public policy toward candidates and policy preferences that are not shared by Americans as a whole?

Conventional political wisdom holds that low election turnout helps the Republicans, whereas Democrats benefit from a large turnout. Studies indicate that young people, the unemployed, laborers, lower-income persons, individuals with relatively little formal education, people who are not married, Latinos, and people who seldom if ever attend religious services are disproportionately represented among nonvoters.[40] Because surveys show that these groups of people tend to vote for Democratic candidates more frequently than they support Republicans, Democrats in Congress and state legislatures often favor reforming registration laws and other voting procedures to enhance voter turnout. For the same reason, Republican officials generally oppose election law reform. Nonetheless, the 2004 election demonstrated that relative high voter turnout does not necessarily advantage the Democratic Party. Even though the Kerry campaign increased the Democratic vote by 16 percent over Al Gore's showing in 2000, it was not enough because the Republican presidential vote grew by 23 percent.[41] (Incidentally, research shows that bad weather helps the Republican Party because Democrats are significantly more likely to stay home if it rains or snows than are Republicans.[42])

Political scientists are skeptical that increased voter turnout would have much impact on the fortunes of either political party.[43] Many nonvoters are disinterested and uninformed. Although surveys show that nonvoters are somewhat more likely to support the Democrats as the party best able to solve their problems, two-thirds of

Voting is a two-step process: registration and the actual vote itself.

nonvoters (compared with half of voters) see no difference between parties and candidates on the issues.[44]

Furthermore, scholarly studies rarely uncover evidence that nonvoters would have chosen a different president from the person actually elected.[45] In fact, political scientists have found that nonvoters are often more supportive of the candidate who actually did win the presidency than are voters. In 1988, for example, George H. W. Bush led Michael Dukakis in the actual popular vote by 8 percentage points, whereas a

New York Times/CBS News poll of nonvoters showed Bush with a 16 percentage-point lead. Had everyone voted, Bush would have won by an even larger margin.[46] Increased voter turnout will change the outcome of an election only when the election is closely fought, the increased turnout is relatively large in comparison with the normal electorate, and most of the new voters support the same candidate or party.[47] These three conditions are seldom met in American presidential politics and only occasionally met at the state and local level.

Research does, however, show a bias in political attitudes. Political activists are more conservative than the population as a whole on economic issues. Compared with the general population, people who participate in the policy process are less likely to support government spending for public services, government help for minority groups, and programs to assist the poor. Individual campaign contributors tend to be more conservative and more Republican than the electorate as a whole.[48] Furthermore, African American and Latino activists are more conservative on economic issues than African Americans and Latinos as a group. In sum, political activity underrepresents those people who favor government programs for disadvantaged groups and overrepresents those who oppose them.[49] To the extent that elected officials respond to the demands of voters, public policies will be consistent with the interests of middle- and upper-income groups rather than the working class.

Interest group and political party activities contribute to the participation bias as well. In the nineteenth and early twentieth centuries, the nation's most important interest groups were large membership organizations that drew people from all strata of society, rich and poor alike. These groups advocated government policies that benefited people across class lines, such as Social Security, Medicare, public schools, and programs for war veterans. Since the middle of the twentieth century, large membership organizations, such as labor unions, have declined, whereas professionally managed advocacy groups composed mainly of middle- and upper-middle class professionals have proliferated. These groups push middle-class agendas.[50] Political parties contribute to the imbalance in participation rates as well by targeting their campaigns at people with voting histories. With rare exceptions, political campaigns focus on turning out their core supporters rather than trying to expand the electorate.[51]

Direct democracy
A political system in which the citizens vote directly on matters of public concern.

CONCLUSION: POLITICAL PARTICIPATION AND PUBLIC POLICY

Representative democracy A political system in which citizens elect representatives to make policy decisions on their behalf.

The nature of America's constitutional system of government makes it difficult to identify the connection between individual participation and public policy. In most cases, citizens do not make policy directly as they would in a **direct democracy;** instead, they elect representatives to make policy decisions on their behalf. The United States is a **representative democracy.** Furthermore, federalism, the bicameral Congress, and the separation of powers with checks and balances ensure that most public policies reflect the interaction of numerous public officials, both elected and appointed, at different levels and in different branches of government. Establishing a linkage between a particular policy and one person's vote, campaign contribution, letter to a representative, or protest would be difficult. Nonetheless, individual participation plays a role in the nation's policy process.

Agenda Building

Individuals can sometimes affect the national policy agenda. The modern campaign to ratify the Twenty-seventh Amendment to the U.S. Constitution was begun not by an organized group but by an individual. The amendment, which requires that a congressional pay raise not take effect until after the next election, was proposed in 1789 but not ratified by the requisite number of states. The amendment was presumed dead until 1982, when an aide to a state legislator in Texas read about the amendment and began a campaign for its ratification. Ten years later a sufficient number of states had ratified the amendment for it to become part of the Constitution.

In general, an individual is most effective at influencing the policy agenda at the local level. Although one person is unlikely to have a significant impact on the national policy agenda, an individual's participation can set the agenda for a local government, such as a city, county, or school district. City residents who are worried about rising crime in their neighborhood, for example, can often succeed in putting their issue on the agenda of their local city council.

Policy Formulation and Adoption

Most of the nation's elected officials are self-starters in the sense that they decide for themselves to seek office. Individual citizens who choose to run for office can often have a major effect on policy formulation and adoption. Carolyn McCarthy was a nurse living in Garden City, New York, when her husband was killed and her son seriously wounded in the "Long Island Railroad Massacre" when a gunman opened fire on rail passengers traveling between New York City and the Long Island suburbs. McCarthy, who initially knew little about politics, became a gun-control activist. When Dan Frisa, the congressman from her district, voted against gun-control legislation that she supported, McCarthy decided to run against him and she won.

GETTING INVOLVED   Registering to Vote

Voting is a two-step process: registration and the actual vote itself. Before Americans can vote, they must register. Registration involves citizens providing voter registration officials with their names and addresses, and establishing or at least asserting that they meet the legal requirements to vote. Registration is important because most people who register subsequently cast their ballots.

Your assignment is to learn how the voter registration process works in your state by completing the paperwork to register. You can obtain voter registration information from an office of county government, driver's license bureau, welfare office, and some public libraries. Complete the voter registration card for submission to your instructor to document that you have done the assignment. If you recognize that you are not eligible to vote, perhaps because you are not an American citizen, write the word VOID on the card. If you are already a registered voter or do not wish to register at this time, write DO NOT PROCESS on the card so that your instructor will not forward the document to the voter registration office. Otherwise, this is your opportunity to register to vote. You may even want to obtain extra voter registration cards to share with friends and family members.

Since 1997, Carolyn McCarthy has served in the U.S. House of Representatives, working in particular to formulate and pass gun-control legislation.

The chances for individuals to influence policy formulation and adoption are greater at the local level than at the state or national levels. Although relatively few individuals can win election or appointment to a major state or national office, thousands of people have the opportunity to serve in an elected office at the local level on school boards, city councils, or local utility boards. Furthermore, individual voices can be heard at the local level on issues of concern much more readily than on the national level.

Policy Implementation and Evaluation

Individuals can sometimes affect policy implementation. For example, the owners of Adarand Constructors, a Colorado construction company, decided to file suit against the federal Department of Transportation (DOT) over the procedures followed by the agency in the construction of federal highway projects. The lawsuit challenged the practice of the DOT to prefer contractors owned by individuals who are "black, Hispanic, Asian Pacific, Subcontinent Asian, and Native American." The U.S. Supreme Court eventually ruled against the DOT, declaring that the agency could grant a minority preference only in those circumstances when it could show a clear history of discrimination against minority contractors.[52] The DOT had to abandon its practice of granting preference to minority contractors.

Finally, individuals can participate in policy evaluation. Citizens can express their pleasure or displeasure with government policies by contacting their elected officials. Members of Congress or at least members of their staff read the mail. A clearly written, thoughtful letter or e-mail message can have an impact. Individuals can also participate informally in policy evaluation by writing letters to the editor of their local newspaper or calling a radio talk program.

KEY TERMS

battleground states

compulsory voting

direct democracy

National Voter Registration Act (NVRA)

political efficacy

political participation

representative democracy

separation of powers

voter mobilization

voting age population (VAP)

voting eligible population (VEP)

NOTES

1. David Mark, "2008 Could See Turnout Tsunami," March 24, 2008, available at www.politico.com.
2. "The ANES Guide to Public Opinion and Electoral Behavior," available at www.electionstudies.org.
3. John R. Petrocek and Daron Shaw, "Nonvoting in America: Attitudes in Context," in William Crotty, ed., *Political Participation and American Democracy* (New York: Greenwood Press, 1991), p. 83.
4. "National Voter Turnout in Federal Elections: 1960–2004," available at www.infoplease.com.
5. Sidney Verba, Kay Lehman Schlozman, and Henry E. Brady, *Voice and Equality: Civic Volunteerism in American Politics* (Cambridge, MA: Harvard University Press, 1995), p. 51.
6. André Blais, *To Vote or Not to Vote?* (Pittsburgh: University of Pittsburg Press, 2000), pp. 12–13.

7. Henry E. Brady, Sidney Verba, Kay Lehman Schlozman, "Beyond SES: A Resource Model of Political Participation," *American Political Science Review* 89 (June 1995): 3.

8. Andrea Louise Campbell, "Self-Interest, Social Security, and the Distinctive Participation Patterns of Senior Citizens," *American Political Science Review* 96 (September 2002): 565–574.

9. Verba, Schlozman, and Brady, *Voice and Equality: Civic Volunteerism in American Politics*, p. 354.

10. Thomas M. Holbrook and Scott D. McClurg, "The Mobilization of Core Supporters: Campaigns, Turnout, and Electoral Composition in the United States Presidential Elections," *American Journal of Political Science* 49 (October 2005): 689–703.

11. Donald P. Green, Alan S. Gerber, and David W. Nickerson, "Getting Out the Vote in Local Elections: Results from Six Door-to-Door Canvassing Experiments," *Journal of Politics* 65 (November 2003): 1083–1096.

12. Alan S. Gerber and Donald P. Green, "The Effects of Canvassing, Telephone Calls, and Direct Mail on Voter Turnout: A Field Experiment," *American Political Science Review* 94 (September 2000): 653–663.

13. Blais, *To Vote or Not to Vote?*, p. 13.

14. U.S. Census Bureau, "Voting and Registration in the Election of November 2004," available at www.census.gov.

15. Campaign Finance Institute Task Force on Presidential Nomination Financing, *Participation, Competition, and Engagement: How to Revive and Improve Public Funding for Presidential Nomination Politics* (Washington, DC: Campaign Finance Institute, 2003), quoted in APSA Task Force Report, "American Democracy in an Age of Rising Inequality," *Perspectives on Politics* 2 (December 2004), p. 656.

16. APSA Task Force Report, "American Democracy in an Age of Rising Inequality," p. 656.

17. U.S. Census Bureau, "Voting and Registration in the Election of November 2004."

18. Verba, Schlozman, and Brady, *Voice and Equality: Civic Volunteerism in American Politics*, pp. 332–338.

19. U.S. Census Bureau, "Voting and Registration in the Election of November 2004."

20. Jeff Manza and Christopher Uggen, *Locked Out: Felon Disenfranchisement and American Democracy* (New York: Oxford University Press, 2006), pp. 76–80.

21. Matt A. Barreto, "¡Sí Se Puede! Latino Candidates and the Mobilization of Latino Voters," *American Political Science Review* 101 (August 2007): 425–441.

22. U.S. Census Bureau, "Voting and Registration in the Election of November 2004."

23. Verba, Schlozman, and Brady, *Voice and Equality: Civic Volunteerism in American Politics*, p. 255.

24. Richard Morin, "Tuned Out, Turned Off," *Washington Post National Weekly Edition*, February 5–11, 1996, p. 6.

25. U.S. Census Bureau, "Voting and Registration in the Election of November 2004."

26. Michael P. McDonald, United States Election Project, available at http://elections.gmu.edu.

27. International Institute for Democracy and Electoral Assistance, available at www.idea.int.

28. U.S. Census Bureau, "Voting and Registration in the Election of November 2004."

29. Gary W. Cox, "Electoral Rules and the Calculus of Mobilization," *Legislative Studies Quarterly* 24 (August 1999): 387–419.

30. G. Bingham Powell, Jr., "American Voter Turnout in Comparative Perspective," *American Political Science Review* 80 (March 1986): 17–43.

31. Jan E. Leighley and Jonathan Nagler, "Unions, Voter Turnout, and Class Bias in the U.S. Electorate, 1964–2004," *Journal of Politics* 69 (May 2007): 430–441.

32. Verba, Schlozman, and Brady, *Voice and Equality: Civic Volunteerism in American Politics*, p. 72.

33. Ibid.

34. *Voting: Some Procedural Changes and Informational Activities Could Increase Turnout* (Washington, DC: General Accounting Office, 1990), p. 2.

35. Sean Richey, "Voting by Mail: Turnout and Institutional Reform in Oregon," *Social Sciences Quarterly* 89 (December 2008): 902–915.

36. Ronald D. Michaelson, Illinois State Board of Elections, quoted in Peter Baker, "An All-Time High for Ballot Box No-Shows," *Washington Post National Weekly Edition*, November 11–17, 1996, p. 11.

37. Michael D. Martinez and David Hill, "Did Motor Voter Work?" *American Politics Quarterly* 27 (July 1999): 296–315.

38. James G. Gimpel, Karen M. Kaufmann, and Shanna Pearson-Markowitz, "Battleground States Versus Blackout States: The Behavioral Implications of Modern Presidential Campaigns," *Journal of Politics* 69 (August 2007): 786–797.

39. U.S. Census Bureau, "Voting and Registration in the Election of November 2004."

40. Petrocek and Shaw, "Nonvoting in America: Attitudes in Context," pp. 71–72.

41. Gary C. Jacobson, *A Divider, Not a Uniter: George W. Bush and the American People* (New York: Pearson Longman, 2007), p. 186.

42. Brad T. Gomez, Thomas G. Hansford, and George A. Krause, "The Republicans Should Pray for Rain: Weather, Turnout, and Voting in U.S. Presidential Elections," *Journal of Politics* 69 (August 2007): 649–663.

43. Jack H. Nagel and John E. McNulty, "Partisan Effects of Voter Turnout in Presidential Elections," *American Politics Quarterly* 28 (July 2000): 408–429.

44. William Crotty, "Political Participation: Mapping the Terrain," in Crotty, ed., *Political Participation and American Democracy*, pp. 7–15.

45. Michael M. Gant and William Lyons, "Democratic Theory, Nonvoting, and Public Policy," *American Politics Quarterly* 21 (April 1993): 185–204.

46. E. J. Dionne, Jr., "If Nonvoters Had Voted: Same Winner, But Bigger," *New York Times*, November 21, 1988, p. 10.

47. Thomas E. Cavanagh, "When Turnout Matters: Mobilization and Conversion as Determinants of Election Outcomes," in Crotty, *Political Participation and American Democracy*, p. 106.

48. Peter L. Francia, Rachel E. Goldberg, John C. Green, Paul S. Herrnson, and Clyde Wilcox, "Individual Donors in the 1996 Federal Elections," in John C. Green, ed., *Financing the 1996 Election* (Armonk, NY: M. E. Sharpe, 1999), p. 128.

49. Verba, Schlozman, and Brady, *Voice and Equality: Civic Volunteerism in American Politics*, pp. 475–493.

50. Theda Skocpol, *Diminished Democracy: From Membership to Management in American Civic Life* (Norman: University of Oklahoma Press, 2003), pp. 6–13, 224–244.

51. APSA Task Force Report, "American Democracy in an Age of Rising Inequality," p. 657.

52. *Adarand Constructors v. Pena*, 515 U.S. 200 (1995).

Chapter 6

The Media

CHAPTER OUTLINE

The Media Landscape

Government Regulation of the News Media
   Obscenity and Defamation
   Prior Restraint and National Security
   The FCC and the Broadcast Media
   Reporters, Confidential Sources, and Criminal
   Prosecutions

Covering the News

Media Biases

Conclusion: The Media and Public Policy
   Agenda Building
   Policy Formulation and Adoption
   Policy Implementation and Evaluation

LEARNING OUTCOMES

After studying Chapter 6, students should be able
to do the following:

▸ Assess the impact of YouTube and other new
communication technologies on the
policymaking environment. (p. 134)

▸ Describe the media landscape in the United
States. (pp. 135–136)

▸ Describe government regulation of the media in
the United States. (pp. 137–141)

▸ Explain how media consolidation affects news
coverage. (p. 141)

▸ Describe how candidates and officeholders
attempt to manipulate news coverage.
(pp. 142–144)

▸ Evaluate whether the news media are biased.
(pp. 144–145)

▸ Describe the role of the media in the
policymaking process. (pp. 145–147)

▸ Define the key terms listed on page 147 and
explain their significance.

YouTube A video sharing Internet website where users can upload, view, and share video clips.

YouTube is a video-sharing Internet website where users can upload, view, and share video clips. Even though it has been online only since 2005, it has become a significant media outlet with the capacity to make or break a political campaign. Ask former Virginia Senator George Allen. In 2006, Allen was a heavy favorite to win reelection to the U.S. Senate and a potential frontrunner for the 2008 Republican presidential nomination until his campaign unraveled after an incident at a political rally in Southwest Virginia. S. R. Sidarth, a 20-year-old college student, was videotaping Allen's remarks on behalf of the campaign of James Webb, Allen's Democratic opponent. Taping an opponent's speeches is a standard campaign practice, and it was not the first time that Sidarth had recorded an Allen speech. This time, however, Allen chose to introduce Sidarth to the crowd. "Let's give a welcome to Macaca, here," said the senator. "Welcome to America and the real world of Virginia."[1] Sidarth, a native-born American citizen of Indian descent, was embarrassed and offended by the remark.

The Macaca incident became Allen's undoing. Sidarth, who was taping Allen's speech, had a video of Allen calling him out. The Webb campaign quickly posted the tape on YouTube[2] and leaked the story to the *Washington Post*, the largest newspaper in the area. The campaign e-mailed supporters with links to the video, and before long, cable television and other media outlets were covering the controversy. Although Allen tried to explain later that he called Sidarth Macaca in reference to his Mohawk-style haircut, bloggers pointed out that in some European cultures Macaca is considered a racial slur against African immigrants. Allen made other mistakes and Webb ran a strong campaign, but the extensive coverage of the Macaca incident was probably the single most important factor in Allen's defeat for reelection.[3]

YouTube and other new communication technologies have changed the political environment for candidates and officeholders. Before camcorders, YouTube, weblogs, and cable television, the Macaca incident might have gone unreported. At the most, it would have been a one-day newspaper story with little impact on the campaign. Camcorders enable campaign workers, reporters, and even ordinary citizens to tape candidate speeches, campaign rallies, government meetings, and other events that would have gone unrecorded in the past. Videotape is critical for coverage on cable news outlets. YouTube provides a means for spreading the videotape of the incident not just to media outlets but to anyone with a computer. Millions of people watched the video of Allen calling out the young college student and formed their own opinion about his behavior.

George Allen's Macaca episode and its YouTude airing introduce our discussion on the place of the media in the policymaking environment. The chapter describes the media landscape in the United States, discusses government regulation of the news media, examines the way the media cover the news, and explores the question of media bias. This chapter is the third in a series focusing on the political environment for the policymaking process. Chapter 4 dealt with public opinion; political participation was the subject of Chapter 5. The next three chapters—7, 8, and 9—will focus on interest groups, political parties, and elections, respectively.

THE MEDIA LANDSCAPE

Public Broadcasting Service (PBS) A nonprofit private corporation that is jointly owned by hundreds of member television stations throughout the United States.

National Public Radio (NPR) A nonprofit membership organization of radio stations.

Corporation for Public Broadcasting A government agency chartered and funded by the U.S. government with the goal of promoting public broadcasting.

Print media Newspapers and magazines.

Broadcast media Television, radio, and the Internet.

New media A term used to refer to alternative media sources, such as the Internet, cable television, and satellite radio.

In contrast to much of the world, direct government ownership of media outlets in the United States is relatively limited. The federal government operates the Armed Forces Radio and Television Service, which provides news and entertainment to members of the U.S. armed forces worldwide. Many local governments, including cities, schools, and colleges, operate cable television stations. City governments may use their cable television channel to air city council meetings and other public service programming. Universities and colleges sometimes operate radio stations.

The **Public Broadcasting Service (PBS)** and **National Public Radio (NPR)** are private nonprofit media services with public and private financial support. PBS is a nonprofit private corporation that is jointly owned by hundreds of member television stations throughout the United States; NPR is a nonprofit membership organization of radio stations. The **Corporation for Public Broadcasting** is a government agency chartered and funded by the U.S. government with the goal of promoting public broadcasting. It provides some funding for both PBS and NPR. Public radio and television stations also benefit from corporate donations and financial contributions from the general public. PBS and NPR regularly interrupt their programming to ask their viewers and listeners to pledge their financial support.

Private businesses, often large corporations, own and operate most media outlets in the United States. Most **print media** (newspapers and magazines) and **broadcast media** (television, radio, and the Internet) outlets are part of large chains. Consolidation is an important trend in media ownership. The ten largest newspaper groups control a majority of newspaper circulation in the nation. Most television stations belong to national networks, such as CBS, NBC, ABC, Fox, or CW. Clear Channel Communication and Cumulus Media own hundreds of radio stations, including many in the same city.[4] Cross-media ownership is common as well, in which one corporation owns several types of media. The Tribune Company, for example, owns the *Chicago Tribune* newspaper as well as several radio and television stations in the Chicago area and dozens of other newspapers, television stations, and radio stations around the country.[5]

The media landscape is changing. Many mainstream media outlets, especially newspapers, newsmagazines, and the network evening news, have been in decline for years, at least in terms of circulation and ratings. Newspaper circulation and advertising revenue is in decline. Some papers have filed for bankruptcy and others have cut back on home delivery. Circulation for the "big three" newsmagazines (*Time, Newsweek,* and *U.S. News & World Report*) is falling. Ratings for the network evening news and morning news shows are in a long decline as well. Over the past 25 years, the combined audience for the network evening news has fallen, on average, by a million viewers a year.[6]

While traditional media sources are losing readers, listeners, and watchers, the **new media,** which is a term used to refer to alternative media sources, such as the Internet, cable television, and satellite radio, are growing in importance. Young people in particular are turning away from traditional media sources in favor of the new media.[7] In 1992, newspapers and television network news were the most important

CBS Evening News hired celebrity journalist Katie Couric as news anchor in hopes of boosting ratings, but ratings continued to fall, faster than ever.

reported media sources for news about that year's presidential campaign. By 2004, however, the most important reported sources of information about the presidential contest were newspapers, cable television, network television, radio, and the Internet.[8] Fox News, CNN, and MSNBC offer news coverage around the clock. Radio talk shows offer news and opinion much of the day. In the meantime, anyone with a computer can create a website or write a **weblog** or **blog,** which is an online personal journal or newsletter that is regularly updated. Although online news sources vary considerably in quality and credibility, some of them have become important sources of information. The Matt Drudge website called the Drudge Report was the first media source to break the news about the relationship between White House intern Monica Lewinsky and President Bill Clinton. Blogs in particular are important opinion outlets. In fact, liberal bloggers have become such an important source of opinion leadership in the Democratic Party that presidential candidates have hired some of them to write blogs for their campaign websites.

Candidates and elected officials have adapted to the new media environment by using the Internet for communication and fundraising. Between 1996 and 2004, the percentage of major party candidates for Congress with campaign websites increased from 22 percent to 81 percent.[9] Although every major presidential candidate had an online presence in 2008, Barack Obama used the Internet more effectively than any of his opponents, raising millions of dollars and online.

Weblog or **blog**
An online personal journal or newsletter that is regularly updated.

GLOBAL PERSPECTIVE

Government Control of the Media in Cuba

The government tightly controls the media in Cuba. The government owns the electronic media and controls its content. Foreign news agencies that wish to cover news stories in Cuba are forced to hire local journalists through government offices. Independent journalists are subject to harassment, detention, and physical attacks. Journalists found guilty of publishing anti-government propaganda or insulting government officials can be sentenced to long prison terms. According to Reporters Without Borders, an international nonprofit organization that advocates for freedom of the press, two dozen journalists were held in Cuban prisons in poor conditions in 2008.[*]

The Cuban government attempts to control Internet access by banning private Internet connections. As a result, less than 2 percent of the Cuban population has Internet access. People who want to surf the Web or check their e-mail must go to Internet cafés, universities, or other public sites where their activities can be closely monitored. The computers in Internet cafés and hotels have software installed that alerts police whenever it spots "subversive" words. Cuban residents who write articles critical of the Cuban government for foreign websites are subject to 20-year prison terms.[†]

The U.S. government attempts to break the Cuban government's monopoly on information with Radio Martí, which broadcasts on shortwave and medium-wave transmitters from Miami, Florida. Miami's most popular Spanish-language AM radio station, which is powerful enough to be heard throughout Cuba, also carries an hour of news from Radio Martí each night at midnight. The Cuban government jams the shortwave and medium-wave Radio Martí broadcasts throughout the island and the AM radio station in Havana, so the program's effectiveness is questionable.

QUESTIONS TO CONSIDER

1. Can a country be a democracy without a free press? Why or why not?
2. Is it ever appropriate for a government to manage the news media?
3. Should the United States continue to fund Radio Martí?

*"Cuba—Annual Report 2007," available at www.rsf.org.
†Ibid.

GOVERNMENT REGULATION OF THE NEWS MEDIA

The U.S. Constitution guarantees freedom of the press. "Congress shall make no law," declares the First Amendment, "abridging the freedom of speech, or of the press." As a result, the news media enjoy broad freedom to report the news, even news that is critical of the government. The tradition of press freedom is so strong in the United States that even publicly funded media outlets are expected to operate without government interference. For example, Kenneth W. Tomlinson, the chair of the Corporation for Public Broadcasting, which provides some funding for PBS and NPR, was forced to resign over allegations that he was trying to influence the content of PBS programming.

Obscenity and Defamation

Freedom of the press is not absolute. The First Amendment does not protect media outlets from prosecution for violating obscenity laws or from being sued for defamation of character. The U.S. Supreme Court narrowly defines obscenity. In order for material to be legally obscene, it must meet all three elements of the following criteria:

1. It must depict or describe sexual conduct. Although depictions of graphic violence may offend many people, the legal definition of obscenity does not encompass violent images.
2. The material must be such that the "average person, applying contemporary . . . standards, would find that the work taken as a whole appeals to prurient interest."
3. The work taken as a whole must lack serious literary, artistic, political, or scientific value.[10]

The definition of obscenity is so narrowly drawn as to exclude most material that ordinary citizens consider pornographic. With the exception of cases involving child pornography, obscenity prosecutions are rare and have no direct impact on the news media.

Libel False written statements which lower a person's reputation or expose a person to hatred, contempt, or ridicule.

Defamation involves false written (**libel**) or spoken (**slander**) statements that lower a person's reputation or expose a person to hatred, contempt, or ridicule. Defamation lawsuits are fairly common and sometimes successful. In 2007, for example, the *National Enquirer* settled a defamation lawsuit filed by actress Cameron Diaz over an allegation that she had an affair with a married man.[11]

Slander False spoken statements which lower a person's reputation or expose a person to hatred, contempt, or ridicule.

The U.S. Supreme Court has long held that the First Amendment does not protect defamatory expression. In recent decades, however, the Court has adopted a relatively strict standard for the defamation of public figures, which the Court defines as individuals who thrust themselves to the forefront of a particular public controversy in order to influence the resolution of the issues involved. Ordinary citizens can win defamation suits merely by proving that a statement is false and that it lowers their reputation or exposes them to hatred, contempt, or ridicule. In contrast, public figures must also show that the statement was made with malice or reckless disregard for the truth. The justification for this approach is that public figures, in contrast to private individuals, have access to channels of effective communication to combat allegations about their conduct. Furthermore, public figures have voluntarily subjected themselves to public scrutiny.[12] Consequently, elected officials and high-profile government appointees seldom file defamation suits against the media and are almost never successful.

Prior Restraint and National Security

In early 1979, *Progressive* magazine announced plans to publish an article on how to build an H-bomb. The magazine's editors explained that their purpose in printing the article was to inform the public about nuclear weapons. Because the information in the article was gleaned from unclassified sources, the article would divulge no real secrets. Nonetheless, the federal government asked a judge to block publication of the article on national security grounds.

Prior restraint Government action to prevent the publication or broadcast of objectionable material.

This is an example of **prior restraint,** that is, government action to prevent the publication or broadcast of objectionable material. Expression involving defamation or obscenity can be held punishable *after* its utterance or publication. The issue of prior restraint considers whether government can block the expression of objectionable material *before* the fact. The Supreme Court has held that prior restraint is such an extreme limitation on freedom of the press that it can be used only in exceptional circumstances, such as time of war.[13]

The Supreme Court has had difficulty deciding prior restraint cases involving national security. In the *Pentagon Papers Case* (1971), the Court refused to block newspaper publication of government documents detailing the history of American involvement in Vietnam. Although the Nixon administration claimed the documents included military secrets, the newspaper charged that the government's only real concerns were political because no national security issues were at stake. The Court was deeply divided, however, and its opinion gave little guidance as to how similar disputes might be resolved in the future.[14] Nor did the *Progressive* controversy enable the Court to clarify the law in this area. After several newspapers published H-bomb articles, the government dropped its case against the magazine and the issue never reached the Supreme Court. The Court has yet to clarify the matter.

The FCC and the Broadcast Media

Congress created the Federal Communications Commission (FCC) in 1939 to regulate the broadcast media using the public airwaves, which include VHF and UHF television and AM/FM radio. The Supreme Court has allowed government regulation of these media, despite the First Amendment, because the public airwaves spectrum is limited.[15] FCC regulation of broadcast frequency and transmission power ensures that stations do not interfere with one another. The FCC has no authority to regulate cable TV, satellite radio, or the Internet.

Equal-time rule
An FCC regulation requiring broadcasters to provide an equivalent opportunity to opposing political candidates competing for the same office.

Some FCC regulations affect broadcast content. The **equal-time rule** is an FCC regulation requiring broadcasters to provide an equivalent opportunity to opposing political candidates competing for the same office. For example, if a television station gives Candidate A one minute of free airtime during prime time, then it must offer the equivalent opportunity to other candidates for the same office. The purpose of the equal-time rule is to prevent broadcasters from giving an unfair advantage to one candidate or a group of candidates. The rule does not apply to documentaries, interviews, newscasts, and news event coverage. The FCC exempts political debates from the rule as long as the media station itself is not hosting the debate. The equal-time rule also does not apply to paid campaign advertisements as long as the media outlet is willing to sell advertising time to all qualified candidates for an office.

Fairness Doctrine
An FCC regulation requiring broadcasters to present controversial issues of public importance and to present them in an honest, equal, and balanced manner.

Some media observers favor greater government regulation of the broadcast media. They want Congress or the FCC to reenact the **Fairness Doctrine,** which was an FCC regulation requiring broadcasters to present controversial issues of public importance and to present them in an honest, equal, and balanced manner. The FCC repealed the Fairness Doctrine in 1987, arguing that it inhibited rather than enhanced public debate and that it appeared to violate the First Amendment. Congress passed legislation to restore the Fairness Doctrine, but President Ronald Reagan vetoed the measure and Congress was unable to override the veto. The proponents of the Fairness Doctrine believe that it is needed to provide for the public discussion of controversial issues and to ensure that all voices are heard. In contrast, critics of

The FCC fined CBS for Janet Jackson's "wardrobe malfunction" during the 2004 Super Bowl halftime show.

the Fairness Doctrine argue that it inhibits free speech because broadcasters sometimes will not discuss controversial political issues because they want to avoid having to provide free airtime for opposing views. Furthermore, they say, the Fairness Doctrine is unnecessary because the proliferation of media outlets, including Internet websites and blogs, ensures broad exposure to all sorts of competing points of view.

While the FCC has been reducing regulation of political views, it has adopted a more aggressive approach to regulating indecency. For example, the FCC fined CBS for Janet Jackson's "wardrobe malfunction" during the 2004 Super Bowl halftime show. Congress subsequently passed legislation to allow the FCC to impose fines as high as $325,000 for each violation of its decency standard.[16] Howard Stern, a radio talk show host famous for off-color remarks and sexual humor, moved his syndicated broadcast radio show to Sirius Satellite Radio to escape FCC scrutiny.

Reporters, Confidential Sources, and Criminal Prosecutions

Journalists frequently base their stories on information received from confidential sources, typically government officials who request that their identities be kept secret. Reporters honor the request because they know that their information sources will dry up if they cannot maintain their anonymity. The issue of confidential sources becomes especially troublesome if the reporter has information that may be relevant in a criminal prosecution or may affect national security. Journalists believe that the

First Amendment shields reporters from being compelled to reveal their sources, but the courts have not agreed.[17] In 2005, for example, a federal judge ordered Judith Miller, a *New York Times* reporter, jailed for contempt of court for refusing to reveal her information source in the investigation of who illegally leaked the information that Valerie Plame was a covert Central Intelligence Agency (CIA) agent.

Shield law A statute that protects journalists from being forced to disclose confidential information in a legal proceeding.

A **shield law** is a statute that protects journalists from being forced to disclose confidential information in a legal proceeding. A majority of states have enacted shield laws, but not the federal government.[18] The proponents of shield laws believe that they protect the public's right to know. Without shield laws, confidential sources would hesitate to reveal government inefficiency and corruption to reporters for fear that they will lose their jobs when their identities are revealed. In contrast, the opponents of shield laws argue that journalists should not be above the law. They should be required to appear in court and present evidence just like other citizens.

⟨?⟩ WHAT IS YOUR OPINION?

Do you favor the adoption of shield laws?

COVERING THE NEWS

A major goal of news media outlets is to attract as large an audience as possible. Newspaper advertising rates depend on readership. Arbitron ratings of listeners determine advertising rates for ratio stations; Nielson ratings count television viewers. Online advertising rates depend on website traffic. Even nonprofit media outlets such as PBS and NPR want to attract a large audience to support their pledge drives.

Media outlets take different approaches to building an audience. Television networks, big city newspapers, and newsmagazines aim to attract as large an audience as possible. They cover mainstream news from a middle-of-the-road perspective with an eye to entertainment value by highlighting dramatic events and celebrities. Stories about Britney Spears get more coverage than do in-depth analyses of budget policy. Reports on crime, traffic accidents, and severe weather dominate local news to the near exclusion of serious coverage of local policy issues. In contrast, other media outlets try to build a niche audience by targeting audiences based on political philosophy, issue focus, or religious values. Political activists can find a set of websites, blogs, radio talk shows, magazines, and television shows that reinforce their point of view.

Media consolidation impacts news coverage. Because of chain ownership, newspaper stories written for the *New York Times* or *Washington Post* may appear in local newspapers around the nation in identical form. In any given week, all three major newsmagazines may feature the same cover story. Meanwhile, local radio and television stations rely on network news feeds for national news. As a result, news outlets around the country tend to focus on the same handful of national stories each day, often told from the same perspective and sometimes in the same words. Because of staff reductions, local media outlets focus on national election coverage rather than state and local contests.[19]

"If it bleeds, it leads." Reports on crime, traffic accidents, and severe weather dominate local news to the near exclusion of serious coverage of local policy issues.

Campaign organizations attempt to manage news coverage to present the candidates they favor in the most positive light. Indeed, the presidential campaigns of Reagan in 1980 and 1984 and George H. W. Bush in 1988 were the prototype of campaign control of news media coverage. The Reagan–Bush strategy, which most campaigns now attempt to copy, was based on several principles. First, campaign managers choose a single theme to emphasize each campaign day, such as crime, the environment, or defense. If the candidate and the members of the candidate's team address the same issue and only that issue, the news media will be more likely to focus on that issue in their daily campaign reports.

Second, the campaign selects an eye-catching visual backdrop for their candidate that reemphasizes the theme of the day, such as the Statue of Liberty, a retirement home, or a military base. In 1988, George H. W. Bush even staged a campaign event in a factory that made American flags. Campaign organizers try to ensure that everyone in the audience is friendly so that television images convey the impression of popular support. When President George W. Bush ran for reelection in 2004, he typically appeared at invitation-only rallies to ensure that news reports would be filled with pictures of smiling faces and cheering crowds.

Finally, campaign managers carefully brief the candidate to stick with the campaign script. Each speech includes one or two carefully worded phrases that can be used as sound bites on the evening news. A **sound bite** is a short phrase taken from a candidate's speech by the news media for use on newscasts. "Read my lips," said Bush in 1988, "no new taxes." Candidates who lack discipline or who are prone to gaffes distract from their own message.

Sound bite A short phrase taken from a candidate's speech by the news media for use on newscasts.

Once in office, elected officials establish sophisticated communications operations to manage the news. President George W. Bush's communications operation had 63 full-time employees organized among offices of communication, media affairs, speechwriting, global communications, press, and photography. Other communication employees worked in the offices of the vice president, first lady, and the National Security Council. Altogether, the Bush administration employed more than 300 people full-time to manage and support its communications operation.[20]

The Bush administration's communications strategy attempted to tie policy, politics, and communications together. Professor Bruce Miroff says that the Bush administration depicted the war in Iraq as if it were a professional wrestling match in which the audience (the American people) watches the good guy (President Bush) overpower the bad guy (Saddam Hussein). President Bush declared victory on May 1, 2003, after landing in a jet on the deck of the aircraft carrier *Abraham Lincoln*. Bush, dressed in a green flight suit, used the aircraft carrier as a stage to announce that combat operations in Iraq were over. A large banner over the president's head read "Mission Accomplished."[21]

Candidates and officeholders do not always succeed in managing the media. The proliferation of media outlets along with the emergence of new communications technologies such as YouTube and weblogging increases the likelihood that candidate bloopers will be caught on tape and broadcast widely. George Allen's Macaca remark dominated news about his campaign for months. His campaign's efforts at damage control proved ineffective because of new allegations reported online and in the broadcast media that he used racial slurs when he played college football and wore a Confederate flag lapel pin for his high school senior class photo.

Events sometimes overwhelm an officeholder's communications strategy. Hurricane Katrina, for example, was a communications catastrophe for George W. Bush's

President Bush used an aircraft carrier as a backdrop to declare victory in the War in Iraq.

administration. Rather than interrupt his vacation to address the crisis, President Bush left Secretary of Homeland Security Michael Chertoff in charge. While television viewers saw images of thousands of people stranded on roofs and huddled in the New Orleans Superdome, Chertoff declared his pleasure with the response of the federal government to the disaster. When President Bush finally arrived in the region, several days after the hurricane struck, his rhetoric seemed out of touch with the reality in New Orleans. "Brownie," he said to Federal Emergency Management Administration (FEMA) Director Michael Brown, "You're doing a heck of a job."[22]

MEDIA BIASES

Objective journalism A style of news reporting that focuses on facts rather than opinion, and presents all sides of controversial issues.

Objective journalism is a style of news reporting that focuses on facts rather than opinion and presents all sides of controversial issues. Major newspapers, broadcast television news, and the major cable news networks pride themselves on their commitment to objective journalism. The trademark slogan for Fox News is "fair and balanced." Even though newspapers endorse candidates on their editorial page, the ideal of objective journalism is that candidate endorsements have no impact on the content or tone of their news coverage.

Nonetheless, many political activists believe that the press is biased. Conservatives accuse the media of a liberal bias. For evidence, they cite a survey showing that 44 percent of news journalists identified with the Democratic Party compared with only 16 percent who said they were Republicans; another 34 percent were independent.[23] Conservatives believe that the media slant the news in favor of liberal policy perspectives while ignoring conservative points of view. In contrast, many liberals believe that the media have a conservative bias. Conservative commentators such as Rush Limbaugh dominate talk radio, and most newspaper editorial endorsements typically go to Republicans. The liberals dismiss talk of a Democratic bias among reporters because the newspapers, television networks, and newsmagazines for which journalists work are large corporations, owned and operated in most cases by conservative Republicans. Management sets editorial policy, they say, not reporters.

Research suggests that media sources may indeed play favorites. The network evening news treats Democratic candidates more favorably than it does Republicans. The Democratic candidate for president has enjoyed more favorable coverage on the network evening news than the Republican candidate in three of the last five presidential elections. Coverage was balanced in the other two elections. In 2004, for example, 57 percent of the network news reports on Democratic presidential candidate John Kerry were positive, compared with 37 percent of the news reports on President George W. Bush. Nonetheless, scholars have no evidence that news coverage affects election outcomes. Kerry lost the election, despite receiving more favorable network news coverage than Bush. Furthermore, citizens have more news sources available to them than the network news, including newspapers, radio, Internet websites, and cable television. Fox News coverage of the 2004 presidential election was decidedly Bush-friendly. Fifty-three percent of Fox News stories on the president were positive, compared with only 21 percent of the Kerry stories.[24] In practice, news consumers often choose media outlets that reflect their particular biases. The CNN and Fox cable news audiences perceive political reality differently. Conservative Republicans watch Fox, while liberal Democrats tune in to CNN.[25]

Political science research has also identified media biases that are not based on party affiliation or political ideology. Research on Senate races has found that newspapers tend to slant the information on their news pages to favor the candidate endorsed by the paper on its editorial page, regardless of that candidate's party affiliation.[26] Furthermore, studies show that the press is biased against presidential incumbents, without regard for party and ideology. An **incumbent** is a current officeholder. All recent presidents, Democrats and Republicans alike, received more negative press coverage than did their opponents when they ran for reelection.[27]

Incumbent Current officeholder.

The press has grown increasingly negative. Since the 1960s, bad news has increased by a factor of three and is now the dominant theme of news coverage of national politics. Thirty years ago, press coverage of public affairs emphasized the words of newsmakers and stressed the positive. The press grew more critical during the 1970s as journalists began to counter the statements of government officials rather than just report them. By the late 1970s, the focus of the Washington, DC, press corps was **attack journalism,** which is an approach to news reporting in which journalists take an adversarial attitude toward candidates and elected officials. Reporters decided to critically examine the actions of newsmakers, countering the statements of public officials with the responses of their critics and adversaries.[28] As a result, campaign coverage has grown negative. In 1960, 75 percent of press references to both major party presidential candidates (Richard Nixon and John Kennedy) were positive. In contrast, only 40 percent of references to the major party presidential candidates in 1992 (George H. W. Bush and Bill Clinton) were positive.[29]

Attack journalism An approach to news reporting in which journalists take an adversarial attitude toward candidates and elected officials.

 WHAT IS YOUR OPINION?

Are the media too negative about government and public officials?

CONCLUSION: THE MEDIA AND PUBLIC POLICY

The media play an important role in the policymaking process, especially during the agenda building and policy evaluation stages.

Agenda Building

Signaling role A term that refers to the accepted responsibility of the media to alert the public to important developments as they happen.

Political scientists say that the press plays a **signaling role,** which is a term that refers to the accepted responsibility of the media to alert the public to important developments as they happen. The media may be unable to tell people what to think, but they generally succeed in telling people what to think about. In early 2007, the *Washington Post* published a series of stories about the poor quality of care injured service personnel had been receiving from Walter Reed Army Medical Center in Washington, DC. Other media outlets quickly picked up on the coverage, and the issue of medical care for Iraq war veterans soon rose to the forefront of the policy agenda. Several congressional committees held hearings on the issue, the Bush

GETTING INVOLVED

Favorite News and Information Links

Do you have a favorite set of online sources of information and opinion? Your assignment is to create an annotated inventory of online sites. For each entry, indicate the name of the site, give its URL, describe it, and explain why you have selected it. Select at least one site in each of the following categories:

- National news source that emphasizes objective journalism.
- State and local news source that emphasizes objective journalism.

- Political commentary, combining news and opinion.
- Issue-oriented website that focuses on a particular issue, either objectively or subjectively.
- Educational or professional website that is related to your college major or career goals.
- Personal interest website that deals with a hobby, sports team, or entertainment source that you enjoy.

administration called for an investigation, and the Secretary of Defense removed the military commanders in charge of veterans' care at Walter Reed.

Policy Formulation and Adoption

Framing The process by which a communication source, such as a news organization, defines and constructs a political issue or public controversy.

The media play an indirect role in policy formulation and adoption. The media influence policy adoption through **framing,** which is the process by which a communication source, such as a news organization, defines and constructs a political issue or public controversy. The way the media present an issue helps define the approaches that policymakers will take to its resolution. The vivid images of flooded homes and people seeking shelter in the New Orleans Superdome along with accounts of bureaucratic bungling ensured that policymakers would regard Hurricane Katrina as not just a natural disaster but also the failure of the government to respond effectively to a crisis. The media do not adopt policies, but they do publicize policy adoption by reporting on acts of Congress, Supreme Court decisions, and presidential actions. The press also provides political leaders with a means to communicate with the public to explain government policies and ask for support.

Policy Implementation and Evaluation

Empirical analysis A method of study that relies on experience and scientific observation.

Normative analysis A method of study that is based on certain values.

The media have a larger role in policy evaluation than policy implementation. Other than carrying out FCC rules, the media do not implement public policies. They are, however, important participants in policy evaluation, offering both empirical and normative policy analyses. An **empirical analysis** is a method of study that relies on experience and scientific observation, whereas a **normative analysis** is a method of study that is based on certain values. The media are an important source of empirical policy evaluation. In recent years, media outlets have issued a broad range of empirical analyses of government programs and activities, including investigative reports on the conduct of the war in Iraq, the implementation of the Medicare prescription drug program, and the effectiveness of airport luggage screening. The media also publicize empirical reports completed by government agencies and independent groups. In addition to empirical evaluation of policy, the media offer a broad spectrum of normative policy evaluations, ranging from newspaper editorials to radio talk show commentaries and blog postings. Media policy evaluations often set the agenda for policy modifications and the adoption of new policies.

KEY TERMS

attack journalism

broadcast media

Corporation for Public Broadcasting

empirical analysis

equal-time rule

Fairness Doctrine

framing

incumbent

libel

National Public Radio (NPR)

new media

normative analysis

objective journalism

print media

prior restraint

Public Broadcasting Service (PBS)

shield law

signaling role

slander

sound bite

weblog *or* blog

YouTube

NOTES

1. Tim Craig and Michael D. Shear, "Allen Quip Provokes Outrage, Apology," *Washington Post*, August 15, 2006, p. A01.

2. www.youtube.com/watch?v=r90z0PMnKwI.

3. Claude R. Marx, "The Media and Campaign 2006," in Larry J. Sabato, ed., *The Sixth Year Itch: The Rise and Fall of the George W. Bush Presidency* (New York: Pearson, 2008), pp. 159–160.

4. Project for Excellence in Journalism, available at www.stateofthenewsmedia.org.

5. "2006 Annual Report," available at www.tribune.com.

6. "The State of the News Media 2009," available at www.stateofthenewsmedia.org.

7. Pew Center for the People and the Press, available at http://people-press.org.

8. Stephen J. Farnsworth and S. Robert Lichter, *The Nightly News Nightmare: Television's Coverage of U.S. Presidential Elections, 1988–2004*, 2nd ed. (Lanham, MD: Rowman & Littlefield, 2007), p. 25.

9. Philip N. Howard, *New Media Campaigns and the Managed Citizen* (New York: Cambridge University Press, 2006), p. 27.

10. *Miller v. California*, 413 U.S. 15 (1973).

11. Richard Johnson, "A Win for Diaz," *New York Post*, February 17, 2007, available at www.nypost.com.

12. *New York Times v. Sullivan*, 376 U.S. 254 (1964).

13. *Near v. Minnesota*, 283 U.S. 697 (1931).

14. *New York Times v. United States*, 403 U.S. 713 (1971).

15. *Red Lion Broadcasting v. FCC* (395 U.S. 367 (1969).

16. Broadcast Decency Enforcement Act of 2005, PL No. 109–235.

17. *Herbert v. Lando*, 441 U.S. 153 (1979).

18. Doris A. Graber, *Mass Media and American Politics*, 7th ed. (Washington, DC: CQ Press, 2006), p. 77.

19. Erika Franklin Fowler and Kenneth M. Goldstein, eds., "Free Media in Campaigns," in Stephen C. Craig, ed., *The Electoral Challenge: Theory Meets Practice* (Washington, DC: CQ Press, 2006), pp. 112–115.

20. Martha Joynt Kumar, "Managing the News: The Bush Communications Operation," in George C. Edwards III and Desmond. S. King, eds., *The Polarized Presidency of George W. Bush* (New York: Oxford University Press, 2007), pp. 353–354.

21. Bruce Miroff, "The Presidential Spectacle," in Michael Nelson, ed., *The Presidency and the Political System*, 8th ed. (Washington, DC: CQ Press, 2006), p. 277.

22. White House Press Release, "President Arrives in Alabama, Briefed on Hurricane Katrina," September 2, 2005, available at www.whitehouse.gov.

23. S. Robert Lichter, Linda S. Lichter, and Stanley Rothman, *The Media Elite: America's New Powerbrokers* (Bethesda, MD: Adler and Adler, 1986), pp. 54–71.

24. Farnsworth and Lichter, *The Nightly News Nightmare*, pp. 118–161.

25. Jonathan S. Morris, "Slanted Objectivity? Perceived Media Bias, Cable News Exposure, and Political Attitudes," *Social Science Quarterly* 88 (September 2007): 707–728.

26. Kim Fridkin Kahn and Patrick J. Kenney, "The Slant of the News: How Editorial Endorsements Influence Campaign Coverage and Citizens' Views of Candidates," *American Political Science Review* 96 (June 2002): 381–394.

27. Tim Groeling and Samuel Kernell, "Is Network News Coverage of the President Biased?" *Journal of Politics* 60 (November 1998): 1063–1087; Larry Sabato, "Is There an Anti-Republican, Anti-Conservative Media Tilt?" *Campaigns and Elections*, September 1993, p. 16.

28. Thomas E. Patterson, "Bad News, Period," *PS: Political Science and Politics*, March 1996, pp. 17–20.

29. Elizabeth A. Skewes, *Message Control: How News Is Made on the Presidential Campaign Trail* (Lanham, MD: Rowman & Littlefield, 2007), p. 13.

Chapter 7

Interest Groups

CHAPTER OUTLINE

Why People Join Groups

Types of Interest Groups
    Business Groups
    Labor Unions
    Professional Associations
    Agricultural Groups
    Racial and Ethnic Minority Rights Groups
    Religious Groups
    Citizen, Advocacy, and Cause Groups

Interest Group Tactics
    Electioneering
    Lobbying

Creating Public Pressure
Protest Demonstrations
Litigation
Political Violence

The Strength of Interest Groups

Conclusion: Interest Groups and Public Policy
    Agenda Building
    Policy Formulation and Adoption
    Policy Implementation and Evaluation

LEARNING OUTCOMES

After studying Chapter 7, students should be able to do the following:

- Explain why the NRA achieves most of its policy goals despite the ambivalence of public opinion toward its policy objectives. (pp. 150–151)

- Identify why people join interest groups in spite of the free-rider barrier to group membership. (pp. 151–152)

- Identify the various types of groups active in American politics, assess their strength, and discuss their goals. (pp. 152–160)

- Identify the various methods interest groups use to influence the outcomes of elections. (pp. 160–168)

- Compare and contrast the approaches taken by business-oriented PACs and labor PACs to contributing money to candidates for Congress. (p. 162)

- Compare and contrast the insider and outsider approaches to lobbying. (pp. 164–165)

- Identify the factors that affect the effectiveness of interest groups on the policy process. (pp. 168–170)

- Describe the role of interest groups in the policymaking process. (pp. 170–171)

- Define the key terms listed on page 172 and explain their significance.

National Rifle Association (NRA)
An interest group organized to defend the rights of gun owners and defeat efforts at gun control.

The **National Rifle Association (NRA)** is one of the most successful interest groups in American politics. The NRA, which is an interest group organized to defend the rights of gun owners and defeat efforts at gun control, has largely succeeded in defining the gun debate in terms of the right to own, sell, and carry a weapon, as opposed to limiting criminal access to firearms. As a result, Congress has not seriously considered passing gun-control legislation in more than a decade. Furthermore, in 2004, Congress failed to reauthorize the federal Assault Weapons Ban, which prohibited the sale of certain semi-automatic "assault weapons," including Uzis and AK-47s.

Gun control is no longer a significant part of the policy agenda because the Democratic Party has decided that the issue costs Democratic candidates more votes than it gains for them. Gun control was an issue in the 2000 and 2004 presidential elections. Democratic presidential candidates Al Gore (2000) and John Kerry (2004) both supported gun control, whereas George W. Bush, the Republican candidate each year, opposed gun control. The NRA endorsed Bush and helped turn out the vote to elect him president. Many Democratic strategists blamed Gore's loss in West Virginia and Tennessee in 2000 and Kerry's defeat in Ohio in 2004 on the gun issue. Had Gore won either state in 2000, he would have been elected president. Similarly, Ohio proved decisive to the outcome of the 2004 election. After 2004, the Democratic Party wanted no part of gun control. Most Democratic candidates avoided the issue in both 2006 and 2008. In fact, Barack Obama's 2008 campaign website omitted mention of gun control entirely, including instead a tribute to sportsmen who hunt and fish.

Ironically, the NRA is successful despite public opinion, which is divided on issues of gun control. Most Americans believe that the Second Amendment to the Constitution guarantees an individual right to own a gun. A Gallup poll taken in 2008 found that 73 percent of respondents believe that the Second Amendment grants individuals the right to own a firearm, compared with 20 percent who think that the Constitution only guarantees the right of militia members to be armed. Nonetheless, many Americans favor strict gun-control regulations. According to the 2008 survey, 49 percent of Americans believe that gun-control regulations should be made "more strict," compared with 11 percent who think they should be made "less strict." Another 38 percent of respondents favor keeping gun-control laws as they are.[1]

The success of the NRA illustrates an important point about interest group politics: A relatively small group of people who are well organized and highly motivated have more political influence than a large group that is disorganized and disinterested. Gun-rights enthusiasts as a group feel more strongly about the issue than do gun-control advocates. Because ordinary citizens who favor gun control are less likely to base their voting decisions on the issue alone than are ordinary citizens opposed to gun control, the gun-control side has less political power than gun-rights forces. Furthermore, the NRA is far better organized than opposing groups. The Brady Campaign to Prevent Gun Violence, which is the largest gun-control organization, is no match for the NRA in terms of money, membership, organization, and political influence.

The role of the NRA in American politics introduces this chapter on interest groups. The chapter begins by considering why people join groups. It then identifies the various types of interests groups in American politics, discusses their political goals, and assesses their relative strength. The chapter examines the tactics interest

Many members of the NRA believe passionately in a constitutional right to keep and bear arms.

groups employ to achieve their goals and discusses the factors that affect the relative strength of groups. Finally, the chapter examines the role of interest groups in the policymaking process.

Chapter 7 is the third in a series of chapters focusing on the political environment for policymaking. Chapter 4 dealt with public opinion, whereas political participation was the subject of Chapter 5. Chapter 6 examined the media. The next two chapters, Chapter 8 and Chapter 9, will focus on political parties and elections, respectively.

WHY PEOPLE JOIN GROUPS

AARP An interest group representing the concerns of older Americans (formerly known as the American Association of Retired Persons).

George and Inez Martinez are an older couple living in El Paso, Texas. They recently received a letter from the AARP inviting them to join that organization. The **AARP** is an interest group representing the concerns of older Americans (formerly known as the American Association of Retired Persons). Mr. and Mrs. Martinez have heard of the AARP and approve of its work on behalf of older people. Annual AARP dues are relatively low. Nonetheless, why should the Martinez's join? Surely, the few dollars the Martinez's contribute in dues will be too little to have any appreciable effect on the fortunes of the organization. Furthermore, as senior citizens, Mr. and Mrs. Martinez stand to benefit from whatever legislative gains the AARP achieves whether or not they join the organization.

The situation facing the Martinez's illustrates what Professor Mancur Olson calls the **free-rider barrier to group membership,** which is the concept that individuals will have little incentive to join a group and contribute resources to it if the

Free-rider barrier to group membership The concept that individuals will have little incentive to join a group and contribute resources to it if the group's benefits go to members and nonmembers alike.

group's benefits go to members and nonmembers alike. Olson says that groups attempt to compensate for the free-rider barrier by offering selective benefits that go only to group members. The AARP, for example, provides members with a number of selective benefits, including the opportunity to purchase discounted dental, health, and long-term care insurance.[2]

Political scientists identify three types of incentives individuals have for joining and participating in a group: material, solidary, and purposive incentives, which are sometimes also called expressive incentives. *Material incentives* to group membership are tangible benefits that can be measured monetarily. For example, the NRA offers its members firearms training classes; life insurance for the families of police officers killed in the line of duty; gun-loss insurance; and discounts on car rentals, hotel reservations, and airline tickets. *Solidary incentives* to group membership are social benefits arising from association with other group members. The NRA has more than 10,000 state associations and local clubs. Members participate in training programs, clinics, and shooting tournaments. *Purposive incentives* to group membership are the rewards individuals find in working for a cause in which they believe. Many members of the NRA believe passionately in a constitutional right to keep and bear arms.[3] Some groups offer members one type of incentive to join, whereas other groups offer two types or all three kinds of incentives.

TYPES OF INTEREST GROUPS

Interest group An organization of people who join together voluntarily on the basis of some shared interest for the purpose of influencing policy.

An **interest group** is an organization of people who join together voluntarily on the basis of some interest they share for the purpose of influencing policy. Sometimes the shared interest is economic. Dairy farmers, for example, work through the National Milk Producers Federation. Small business owners join the National Federation of Independent Business (NFIB). At other times, the interests that unite people involve morals, culture, and social values. Individuals concerned about safeguarding the environment may become involved in an environmental organization, such as the Sierra Club or Greenpeace. Gun enthusiasts may join the National Rifle Association (NRA).

Business Groups

Business groups are the most numerous and probably the most potent of America's interest groups. Although their voices are heard on virtually every major policy issue, business interests are especially concerned with tax laws, interest rates, environmental regulations, trade policy, labor laws, government contracts, and other matters that affect their costs, profits, and operations.

Business interests attempt to influence public policy both as individual firms and through a variety of front organizations. Northrup Grumman, ExxonMobil, Microsoft Corp., Verizon Communications, and other large firms are major players in national politics, aggressively promoting their particular interests with government officials. For example, ExxonMobil Corp. and other energy companies favor the relaxation of federal environmental standards to enhance energy production.

They support legislation designed to open the Alaska National Wildlife Refuge (ANWR) to oil and gas production. Wal-Mart, Target, and other retailers with credit card programs favored the recent adoption of bankruptcy reform legislation designed to make it more difficult for consumer debtors to go bankrupt.

Business interests join together across industry lines to promote pro-business public policies. The **Chamber of Commerce** is a business federation representing the interests of more than 3 million businesses of all sizes, sectors, and regions.[4] It has a national organization with headquarters in Washington, DC, state organizations in every state, and chapters in thousands of cities throughout the nation. The National Federation of Independent Business (NFIB) is a federation representing the interests of small and independent businesses. The Business Roundtable is an association of chief executive officers of major U.S. corporations.

Business groups work through **trade associations,** which are organizations representing the interests of firms and professionals in the same general field. Large financial institutions, such as Bank of America and JPMorgan Chase, belong to the American Bankers Association. Other trade associations include the National Association of Manufacturers (NAM), National Restaurant Association, and the National Association of Wholesale-Distributors.

Business groups also sometimes create front organizations to promote particular issue positions. Wal-Mart, Intel Corp., GlaxoSmithKline, and other firms fund an organization called the Class Action Fairness Coalition to support legislation designed to make it more difficult to file class action lawsuits. A **class action lawsuit** is a suit brought by one or more people on behalf of themselves and others who are similarly situated. For example, if a large number of people have allegedly been injured by a defective or hazardous product, such as a breast implant or tobacco, attorneys can file a class action suit on behalf of a small number of named individuals and a large number of other people who have also been affected.

Business groups are well positioned to influence policy. They are numerous, dispersed throughout the country, organized, and well funded. Small business owners and corporate executives are prominent figures in communities around the nation. They often know their member of Congress personally and understand how to articulate effectively their views to policymakers. Furthermore, business groups have funds to contribute to political causes. During the 2008 presidential election cycle, business interests gave $1.8 billion to political campaigns, substantially more than the $68 million contributed by organized labor.[5]

Labor Unions

Organized labor is an important political force in America, although it is not as powerful as it once was. More than a fourth of the civilian labor force belonged to a union in 1970, compared with only 12.1 percent in 2007.[6] The manufacturing industries in which unions have historically had their best organizing successes, such as automobile assembly and steel manufacturing, now employee significantly fewer workers than they did 40 years ago. More than 20 states have adopted **right-to-work laws,** which are statutes that prohibit union membership as a condition of employment.[7] Furthermore, many employers aggressively resist unionization. Wal-Mart,

Chamber of Commerce A business federation representing the interests of more than 3 million businesses of all sizes, sectors, and regions.

Trade associations Organizations representing the interests of firms and professionals in the same general field.

Class action lawsuits Lawsuits brought by one or more people on behalf of themselves and others who are similarly situated.

Right-to-work laws Statutes that prohibit union membership as a condition of employment.

Wal-Mart, the nation's biggest employer, has aggressively resisted efforts to unionize its workforce.

the nation's largest employer, has successfully fought off efforts to unionize its work-force. Not one of Wal-Mart's 3,500 American stores is unionized.[8] The unions that have had the most organizing success in recent years have been unions targeting public sector (government) employees and low-wage workers, such as janitors, agricultural workers, and people employed by nursing homes.

The largest union group in the nation is the **American Federation of Labor-Congress of Industrial Organizations (AFL-CIO).** It is composed of 56 separate unions with a combined membership of 10.5 million. Some of the better known unions affiliated with the AFL-CIO are the American Federation of Teachers, American Postal Workers Union, International Brotherhood of Teamsters, United Mine Workers of America, and the American Federation of State, County, and Municipal Employees (AFSCME).[9] The AFL-CIO recently suffered the defection of several large unions, including the Teamsters, Service Employees International Union (SEIU), and unions representing carpenters, bricklayers, and iron workers. Union leaders who left the AFL-CIO criticized the federation for failing to recruit union members aggressively.[10]

Organized labor is strongest in the **Frostbelt** (the Northeast and Midwest), weakest in the **Sunbelt** (the South and West). Unions are powerful in the large, industrialized states of the Northeast and Midwest. In Michigan, for example, the United Auto Workers (UAW) may be the state's single most potent political force. In these regions of the country, labor is well organized and skilled at flexing its political muscle. In contrast, labor is not as well organized or as politically influential in the Sunbelt, the nation's fastest growing area. In many Sunbelt states,

American Federation of Labor-Congress of Industrial Organizations (AFL-CIO) A labor union federation.

Frostbelt The Northeastern and Midwestern regions of the United States.

Sunbelt The Southern and Western regions of the United States.

organized labor is hurt by anti-union laws and by a diverse and divided workforce, many of whose members are hostile to organized labor. Unionization in the South and Southwest has taken hold in only a few places. As a result, labor's power in most of the Sunbelt is confined to certain localities. In fact, the general political climate in the region is often so anti-union that labor support for a candidate or a cause can be counterproductive.

Organized labor endorses public policies that promote workplace health and safety, supports efforts to build union membership, and favors attempts to improve the quality of life for working-class Americans. Unions believe that the federal government should aggressively enforce laws affecting workplace health and safety. They support government policies requiring the use of union labor and union wage scales on construction projects built with federal funds. They favor increasing the federal **minimum wage,** which is the lowest hourly wage that an employer can legally pay covered workers. Unions endorse efforts to strengthen the private pension system and Social Security.

Conventional wisdom holds that organized labor and big business counterbalance each other, invariably taking opposing views on public policy issues. At times, that is the case. Management and labor generally disagree on labor-relations laws, occupational safety and health regulations, and minimum wage laws. At other times, however, big business and big labor find themselves on the same side in policy disputes. Labor leaders and business executives both favor higher defense spending, for example, because it means more defense contracts and more jobs. The United Steelworkers and steel manufacturers join forces to push for import restrictions on foreign competition. Both business and labor oppose environmental regulations that could threaten the closing of offending plants and the loss of jobs.

Minimum wage
The lowest hourly wage that an employer can legally pay covered workers.

Professional Associations

Doctors, lawyers, realtors, and other professionals form associations to advance their interests. Professional associations are influential because of the relatively high socioeconomic status of their membership. Professionals have the resources to make their voices heard, and they enjoy an added advantage because many elected officials come from the ranks of the professions, especially the legal profession.

Professional associations are concerned with public policies that affect their members. The **American Medical Association (AMA),** an interest group representing the concerns of physicians, would like government to limit the amount of money judges and juries can award in medical malpractice lawsuits. The **American Bar Association (ABA),** a lawyers' group, opposes the AMA on the issue. Professional associations sometimes take stands on policy issues outside the immediate concerns of their membership, such as tax policy, defense spending, and women's rights.

American Medical Association (AMA) An interest group representing the concerns of physicians

American Bar Association (ABA) An interest group representing the concerns of lawyers.

Agricultural Groups

Agricultural groups are influential on farm issues at the national level and in state legislatures in farming states. Farmers are knowledgeable about issues that affect them. They are organized and enjoy a favorable public image. Furthermore, agricultural interests are also business interests because much of agriculture has

GLOBAL PERSPECTIVE

Church and State in Mexico

Mexico is an overwhelmingly Catholic country. In 2000, 85 percent of the population told surveyors that they were Roman Catholic, compared with 4 percent who claimed to be Protestant, 4 percent who identified with another religion, and 6 percent who declared that they had no religious affiliation. Furthermore, most Mexicans are practicing Catholics. More than 40 percent of Mexican Catholics attend church on a weekly basis; another 20 percent attend at least once a month.*

Nonetheless, Mexico has a strong history of **anticlericalism,** which is a movement that opposes the institutional power of religion and the involvement of the church in all aspects of public and political life. Even though individual citizens enjoyed the right to worship as they pleased, the government restricted the power of the Catholic Church for years. The Mexican Constitution of 1917 established state superiority over religion, limited the role of the church in education, and deprived clergy of the right to vote. Public education incorporated anti-church rhetoric in student lessons.[†]

The Mexican government suppressed the church in order to keep it from becoming a threat to state authority. Until recently, the Mexican government was semi-democratic at best. Although Mexico held regular elections, one political party, the Institutional Revolutionary Party (PRI), always won because it manipulated election laws and rigged the vote count to ensure the success of its candidates. Undemocratic governments attempt to restrict all sources of opposition. Government officials in Mexico regarded the Roman Catholic Church as a potential threat to their control because the overwhelming majority of Mexicans were practicing Catholics.

As Mexico has become more democratic, the government has eased restrictions on the church and its political involvement has grown. Clergy now enjoy the right to vote and speak out on political issues. As a result, the church has become an important interest group in Mexican politics.[‡] It has addressed a number of political issues including the distribution of wealth, illicit drugs, and democratization. In particular, the church has criticized the government for not doing more to help the poor.[§]

QUESTIONS TO CONSIDER

1. Should churches take positions on political issues?
2. Do religious organizations play the role of interest groups in American politics?
3. Are interest groups essential to democratic development?

*Roderi Ai Camp, *Politics in Mexico: The Democratic Consolidation* (New York: Oxford University Press, 2007), pp. 89.

[†]Ibid., pp. 144–145.

[‡]Daniel C. Levy and Kathleen Bruhn, *Mexico: The Struggle for Democratic Development*, 2nd ed. (Berkeley: University of California Press, 2006), pp. 123–124.

[§]Camp, *Politics in Mexico*, p. 146.

Anticlericalism A movement that opposes the institutional power of religion, and the involvement of the church in all aspects of public and political life.

become agribusiness with all the advantages that business interests enjoy. The most important farm groups include the American Farm Bureau and the National Farmers Union. Associations representing farm interests related to a particular crop or commodity, such as the National Milk Producers Federation, are important as well.

In general, agricultural groups want government loan guarantees, crop subsidies, and the promotion of farm exports. Of course, each farm group has its own particular cause. Tobacco growers are concerned that government efforts to limit smoking will reduce demand for their products. Western cattle interests want to ensure continued low-cost access to public lands to graze their herds. Fruit and vegetable growers favor immigration policies designed to ensure a steady supply of farm workers.

Racial and Ethnic Minority Rights Groups

African Americans, Latinos, Asian Americans, Native Americans, and other racial and ethnic minority groups have created interest groups to promote their political causes. The **National Association for the Advancement of Colored People (NAACP)** is an interest group organized to represent the concerns of African Americans. The **League of United Latin American Citizens (LULAC)** is a Latino interest group. The **American Indian Movement (AIM)** is a group representing the views of Native Americans.

Racial and ethnic minority groups share the goals of equality before the law, representation in elective and appointive office, freedom from discrimination, and economic advancement. Minority groups are interested in the enforcement of laws against discrimination; the election and appointment of minorities to federal, state, and local offices; and the extension of government programs geared toward fighting poverty. Racial and ethnic minority groups generally support the enforcement of the Voting Rights Act and the implementation of affirmative action programs. The **Voting Rights Act (VRA)** is a federal law designed to protect the voting rights of racial and ethnic minorities. **Affirmative action** is a program designed to ensure equal opportunities in employment and college admissions for racial minorities and women. LULAC and other Latino rights organizations favor the adoption of immigration reforms that would allow longstanding undocumented workers the opportunity to work in the United States legally and eventually become citizens.

Organizations that represent the interests of racial and ethnic minorities are an important political force in most big cities and in states where minority populations are large enough to translate into political power. In addition, minorities, especially African Americans and Latinos, play an important role in national politics. Nonetheless, minority citizens, particularly Latinos, are underrepresented at the ballot box because of low voter turnout. All minority citizens are underrepresented among people who contribute money to election campaigns.[11] Furthermore, the problems facing minority groups in America today—subtle discrimination, inadequate housing, substandard healthcare, malnutrition, poverty, and illiteracy—are particularly difficult to solve.

Religious Groups

Throughout American history, religious organizations have been actively involved in the policy process. Both the abolition (of slavery) and the prohibition (of alcoholic beverages) movements had strong religious overtones, as did the civil rights and anti–Vietnam War movements of the 1960s and early 1970s. State aid to parochial schools has long been a cause dear to many members of the Roman Catholic Church, and Catholic organizations have been heavily involved in the fight against abortion. Jewish groups have kept close watch over American policy toward Israel.

National Association for the Advancement of Colored People (NAACP) An interest group organized to represent the concerns of African Americans.

League of United Latin American Citizens (LULAC) A Latino interest group.

American Indian Movement (AIM) A group representing the views of Native Americans.

Voting Rights Act (VRA) A federal law designed to protect the voting rights of racial and ethnic minorities.

Affirmative action A program designed to ensure equal opportunities in employment and college admissions for racial minorities and women.

Religious right
Individuals who hold conservative views because of their religious beliefs.

Religious left
Individuals who hold liberal views because of their religious beliefs.

Citizen groups
Organizations created to support government policies that they believe will benefit the public at large.

Common Cause A group organized to work for campaign finance reform and other good-government causes.

Sierra Club An environmental organization.

American Civil Liberties Union (ACLU) A group organized to protect the rights of individuals as outlined in the U.S. Constitution.

Advocacy groups
Organizations created to seek benefits on behalf of groups of persons who are in some way incapacitated or otherwise unable to represent their own interests.

Organizations that represent the interests of racial and ethnic minorities are an important political force in most big cities and in states where minority populations are large enough to translate into political power.

Today, the most active religiously oriented political groups are associated with the **religious right,** which is a term that refers to individuals who hold conservative views because of their religious beliefs. Focus on the Family, Family Research Council, and other conservative religious organizations are concerned with such causes as abortion, same-sex marriage, and prayer in school. Since the 2004 presidential election, religious liberals have begun organizing to counter the influence of the religious right. The **religious left,** which is a term that refers to people who hold liberal views because of their religious beliefs, has established a number of organizations and created websites. Issues important to the religious left include opposition to the war in Iraq and the adoption of government programs to fight poverty and protect the environment.[12]

Conservative Christian organizations have been more successful at the ballot box than they have in building influence in Washington, DC, because many Christian conservatives are uncomfortable with the policy compromises necessary to move legislation through Congress to passage.[13] Conservative Christian groups benefit from a core of highly committed supporters who can be mobilized to go to the polls and contact members of Congress over issues that are important to them, such as abortion and gay marriage. In 2004, for example, Christian conservatives turned out in large numbers in states that held referenda on the issue of gay marriage.[14] Most Christian conservative voters also supported the reelection of President Bush. Nonetheless, many conservative Christian activists are frustrated with the inability of Congress and the president to outlaw abortion and prohibit gay marriage through constitutional amendment.

? WHAT IS YOUR OPINION?

Is it wrong for churches and other religious organizations to be involved politically?

Citizen, Advocacy, and Cause Groups

Citizen groups are organizations created to support government policies that they believe will benefit the public at large. For example, **Common Cause,** which calls itself "the citizen lobby," is a group organized to work for campaign finance reform and other good-government causes. Other citizen groups include the **Sierra Club,** an environmental organization, and the **American Civil Liberties Union (ACLU),** a group organized to protect the rights of individuals as outlined in the U.S. Constitution.

Advocacy groups are organizations created to seek benefits on behalf of groups of persons who are in some way incapacitated or otherwise unable to represent their own interests. The Children's Defense Fund, for example, promotes the welfare of children. The Coalition for the Homeless is an organization that works on behalf of homeless persons. Other examples of advocacy groups include the Alzheimer's Association and the American Cancer Society.

Cause groups are organizations whose members care intensely about a single issue or small group of related issues. The **National Right to Life Committee** is an organization opposed to abortion, whereas the **NARAL Pro-Choice America** favors abortion rights. The **Club for Growth** is a cause group that favors a low-tax and limited government agenda. Other cause groups include the NRA, AARP, **National Organization for Women (NOW),** a group organized to promote women's rights, and the **Human Rights Campaign (HRC),** an organization formed to promote the cause of gay and lesbian rights.

Citizen, advocacy, and cause groups have achieved some victories in American politics. Many of these groups are expert at attracting media attention to their issues by releasing research reports or conducting high-profile public demonstrations. Earth Day, for example, is an annual event designed to call attention to environmental concerns. The National Right to Life Committee holds a demonstration in Washington, DC, every year on the anniversary of *Roe v. Wade*, the Supreme Court decision that recognized that a woman's constitutional right to privacy includes the right to abortion during the first two trimesters of a pregnancy.

Many public policies reflect the policy values of citizen, advocacy, and cause groups. The Endangered Species Act, the Clean Air Act, and other pieces of environmental legislation are testimony to the effectiveness of the Sierra Club and other environmental organizations. **Mothers Against Drunk Driving (MADD),**

Cause groups
Organizations whose members care intensely about a single issue or small group of related issues.

National Right to Life Committee An organization opposed to abortion.

National Abortion Rights Action League (NARAL Pro-Choice America) An organization that favors abortion rights.

Club for Growth A cause group that favors a low-tax and limited government agenda.

National Organization for Women (NOW) A group organized to promote women's rights.

Human Rights Campaign (HRC) An organization formed to promote gay and lesbian rights.

Mother's Against Drunk Driving (MADD) An interest group that supports the reform of laws dealing with drunk driving.

Abortion opponents make their views known on the anniversary of the Supreme Court's decision in *Roe v. Wade.*

Social Security A federal pension and disability insurance program funded through a payroll tax on workers and their employers.

which is an interest group that supports the reform of laws dealing with drunk driving, is the motivating force behind a successful effort to stiffen the nation's DWI laws. The AARP is influential on policy issues affecting older Americans such as Social Security and Medicare. **Social Security** is a federal pension and disability insurance program funded through a payroll tax on workers and their employers. **Medicare** is a federally funded health insurance program for the elderly.

Medicare A federally funded health insurance program for the elderly.

Although the policy impact of citizen, advocacy, and cause groups has been significant, the policy influence of these groups seldom extends beyond the issues on which they specialize. The NRA is a powerful interest group, but its effectiveness is limited to gun issues. Environmental groups are not influential beyond environmental issues. Abortion groups only address abortion-related issues.

INTEREST GROUP TACTICS

Interest groups employ a variety of tactics in an effort to achieve their goals.

Electioneering

Many interest groups seek policy influence by participating in the electoral process. A number of groups try to affect election outcomes by targeting enemies and endorsing friends. Each congressional election year, Friends of the Earth, an environmental group, targets for defeat a "Dirty Dozen," 12 members of Congress who voted consistently against the group's position on environmental legislation. The group publicizes its list in hopes that environmentally conscious citizens will vote against the representatives on the list. Other groups endorse candidates friendly to their cause. During the 2008 presidential campaign, the AFL-CIO and NARAL Pro-Choice America endorsed Democrat Barack Obama, whereas the NRA and the National Right to Life Committee threw their support behind Republican John McCain.

Some interest groups focus on educating their members and supporters about the merits of candidates. The AFL-CIO uses newsletters, phone banks, and rallies to encourage union members to support endorsed candidates. Many interest groups keep scorecards, showing how members of Congress voted on issues important to the group and assigning scores to senators and representatives indicating whether they are friend or foe. Groups hope that people sympathetic to group goals will consult the scorecards before deciding how to vote and for whom to contribute campaign contributions.

Groups with financial resources participate in the electoral process financially. Group members with high incomes give money to candidates and parties individually. During the 2008 election cycle, lawyers contributed $232 million to political candidates, with 76 percent of the money going to Democrats. Most lawyers supported Democratic candidates because they opposed Republican efforts to enact lawsuit reforms, such as restrictions on class action lawsuits. In contrast, oil and gas executives gave $35 million in campaign contributions, with 77 percent going to Republicans.[15] Energy executives generally favored Republican candidates because they agreed with Republican efforts to expand energy exploration, including opening ANWR for drilling.

Federal law requires that interest groups that want to contribute money directly to candidates must make their contributions through a **political action committee (PAC),** which is an organization created to raise and distribute money in election campaigns. Although organized labor created the first PACs in the 1940s, the modern PAC era did not begin until the 1970s, when Congress passed the Federal Election Campaign Act to reform campaign finance. Since the 1970s, the number of PACs active in American politics at the national level of government has grown from fewer than a thousand to more than 4,600.[16] The biggest spenders among PACs during the 2008 election cycle were PACs associated with Service Employees International Union ($64 million), Act Blue ($53 million), Moveon.org ($36 million), and EMILY's List ($34 million).[17] **EMILY's List** is a PAC whose goal is the election of pro-choice Democratic women to office. (EMILY is the acronym for Early Money Is Like Yeast, rather than a woman's name.) **Moveon.org** is an advocacy group that raises money for Democratic candidates. Act Blue is a liberal advocacy group.

Political Action Committee (PAC) An organization created to raise and distribute money in election campaigns

EMILY's List A PAC whose goal is the election of pro-choice Democratic women to office.

Moveon.org An advocacy group that raises money for Democratic candidates.

Interest groups follow different campaign funding strategies. Labor unions work to increase the number of members of Congress sympathetic to their point of view, usually Democrats. In the 2007–2008 election period, PACs associated with organized labor made 92 percent of their contributions to Democratic candidates. Although most labor money goes to incumbent members of Congress, unions are willing to fund challengers and candidates for open seats who stand a reasonable chance of winning. About a third labor PAC donations goes to challengers and candidates for open seats.[18]

Many cause groups pursue strategies similar to that of organized labor in that they are primarily interested in increasing the number of elected officials who share their views. Although some cause groups work to elect friends and defeat enemies without regard for party affiliation, most groups are more closely associated with one party than the other. The bulk of NRA support goes to Republican Party candidates, for example, whereas most of the candidates backed by NOW are Democrats. Some cause groups aggressively fund challengers to incumbents who vote against their interests. Because groups such as the NRA and the National Right to Life Committee have narrow policy interests, they see little risk in working to defeat unfriendly incumbents.

Business groups are more pragmatic than either organized labor or most cause groups and advocacy groups because they have broad policy interests. Business interests recognize that a public official who opposes them today on one issue may support them tomorrow on another issue. Business PACs contribute money to candidates with the goal of obtaining **access,** which is the opportunity to communicate directly with legislators and other government officials in hopes of influencing the details of policy. Many business-oriented PACs follow the **Friendly Incumbent Rule,** which is a policy whereby an interest group will back any incumbent who is generally supportive of the group's policy preferences, without regard for the party or policy views of the challenger. Because business-oriented groups favor incumbents, they tend to divide their contributions between the two political parties, despite the traditional alliance between business interests and the Republican Party.

Interest groups in general, not just business-oriented groups, tend to support incumbents. Most interest groups would rather give to a strong candidate who is only somewhat supportive of their cause than throw their money away on an almost certain loser who is completely behind the group's goals. Because incumbents win more often than challengers, especially in races for the U.S. House, most interest-group money goes to them.

Some interest groups funnel money to candidates they support through **bundling,** which is a procedure in which an interest group gathers checks from individual supporters made out to the campaigns of targeted candidates. The group then passes those checks along to the candidates. EMILY's List bundles money to give to Democratic women candidates who support abortion rights. The advantage of bundling for an interest group is that it allows the group to route more money to a candidate than it could legally contribute under its own name because the group is simply acting as a clearinghouse for checks written by hundreds of individuals.

Access The opportunity to communicate directly with legislators and other government officials in hopes of influencing the details of policy.

Friendly Incumbent Rule A policy whereby an interest group will back any incumbent who is generally supportive of the group's policy preferences, without regard for the party or policy views of the challenger.

Bundling A procedure in which an interest group gathers checks from individual supporters made out to the campaigns of targeted candidates.

EMILY's List endorsed Hillary Clinton for president in 2008.

527 Committees
Organizations created by individuals and groups to influence the outcomes of elections by raising and spending money that candidates and political parties raise and spend legally.

Some interest groups participate in elections through **527 Committees,** which are organizations created by individuals and groups to influence the outcomes of elections by raising and spending money that candidates and political parties cannot raise and spend legally. Federal law limits the amount of money individuals and groups can legally give to candidates and parties, but it does not apply to 527 committees. Groups can contribute as much money as they like to a 527 committee, which can then use the money for voter mobilization and "issue advocacy." Although the law prevents 527 committees from running advertisements either for or against particular candidates, it allows issue advertisements that are typically designed to influence voter opinion on the candidates without explicitly telling people how to cast their vote. In 2004, America Coming Together, a 527 committee created by wealthy Democratic donors, spent $79 million in an effort to defeat President Bush for reelection. The largest contributors to America Coming Together included wealthy individuals, such as financier George Soros and businessman Peter Lewis, and interest groups, such as the Sierra Club and various labor unions.[19]

Lobbying

Lobbying The communication of information by a representative of an interest group to a government official for the purpose of influencing a policy decision.

Interest groups attempt to influence policymaking by **lobbying,** which is the communication of information by a representative of an interest group to a government official for the purpose of influencing a policy decision. Groups lobby both the legislative and executive branches of government, attempting to influence every stage of the policy process. The number of Washington, DC, lobbyists, including support staffs, is estimated at more than 250,000.[20] Some interest groups have full-time lobbyists on their professional staffs, whereas other groups hire Washington law firms or consulting agencies to lobby on their behalf. More than 150 former members of Congress are lobbyists.[21] Former senator and presidential candidate Bob Dole, for example, became a lobbyist with the firm of Alston & Bird after his unsuccessful run for the White House in 1996, earning far more money as a lobbyist than he would have made had he been elected president. Other lobbyists are former congressional staff members, former employees of the executive branch, and even relatives of current members of Congress.

Lobbying is expensive whether interest groups employ full-time lobbyists or contract with established Washington lobbyists. In 2008, interest groups reported spending more than $3.24 billion for lobbying expenses. The U.S. Chamber of Commerce, for example, spent $92 million on its lobby activities. ExxonMobil spent $29 million.[22]

Information is the key to lobbying. Successful lobbyists provide members of Congress with accurate facts and figures. Although lobbyists offer their own interpretation of data and voice arguments to support their group's particular policy preferences, they are honest because they know that their effectiveness depends on their credibility. In fact, lobbyists are an important information source for government officials.[23]

The most successful lobbying efforts of Congress are those that are supported by campaign contributions and buttressed by pressure from people living in a representative's district or a senator's home state.[24] Interest groups lay the groundwork for effective lobbying by giving money to political campaigns. Lobbyists sometimes serve as campaign treasurers for members seeking reelection. Major trade associations have purchased Capitol Hill townhouses for fundraisers so that members of Congress can quickly go back to the Capitol to cast votes and then return to the event.[25] Although campaign contributions do not necessarily buy votes, they do generally guarantee access to decision-makers by lobbyists. Once Congress is in session, well-organized groups attempt to support their lobbyists in Washington by encouraging group members in the home districts of key legislators to contact their representatives.

Interest groups use different approaches to influencing policy. Most labor unions and business groups employ what might be called an insider's approach to achieving influence. These groups have a long-range interest in several policy areas. They give PAC contributions to gain access to officeholders for lobbyists who then work to get to know the public officials on a personal basis. Whatever pressure these groups bring to bear on public officials is subtle and unspoken. They believe threats are counterproductive and harmful to the construction of a long-term relationship between the interest group and the officeholder. In fact, interest groups give highest priority to lobbying their allies on the committees that formulate legislation. Lobbyists give friendly legislators facts, figures, and talking points in order to counter arguments raised by legislative opponents.[26] Groups taking an insider's approach are usually able to take the outcome of elections in stride because they cultivate relationships with members of both political parties. After the 2006 election, which swept Republicans out and put Democrats in control of Congress, Steven C. Anderson, the president of the National Restaurant Association, a Republican-leaning group, summarized the impact of the election on his group as follows: "We lost many friends in this election, but that doesn't mean we can't make new friends, and that's what we'll do."[27]

Lobbyists using the insider approach do not expect to affect the way members of Congress vote on final passage of high-visibility legislation. Instead, their goal is to influence the details of legislation to include loopholes that benefit the interest group they represent. For example, a recent tax bill contained a provision limited to a single company, identified as a "corporation incorporated on June 13, 1917, which has its principal place of business in Bartlesville, Oklahoma." The only company fitting that description is Phillips Petroleum. Recent legislation increasing the minimum wage included a provision that "clarifies that foreign trade income of an FSC and export trade income of an ETC do not constitute passive income for purposes of the PFIC definition." That particular phrase was worth $22 million in tax savings for Hercules, Inc., a chemical manufacturer.[28]

In contrast, other groups, whose policy goals are more narrowly focused, follow an outsider's approach to influencing policy. The NRA, National Right to Life Committee, and some other cause groups focus on a relatively small set of high-profile issues. Members of Congress either support them on their pet issues or they are against them. Groups using an outsider's strategy are more heavy-handed in dealing with public officials than are interest groups with a broader range of policy concerns. Groups taking an outside approach are less willing to compromise on policy issues than are insider groups, and more likely to threaten (and attempt to carry out) political reprisals against officeholders who oppose them.

Protesters demonstrating against the war in Iraq.

Creating Public Pressure

Some interest groups attempt to achieve their goals by generating public support for their policy positions and focusing it on government officials. Groups launch public relations campaigns to convince the general public that their particular point of view embodies the public interest. The NRA, for example, purchased a series of magazine advertisements designed to improve the public image of the group. The advertisements featured hunters, police officers, and business people with the caption, "I am the NRA." Some tobacco companies have conducted high-profile media campaigns against underage smoking to counter criticism that tobacco advertisers have targeted youngsters.

The most sophisticated public relations campaigns are aimed at orchestrating citizen pressure on members of Congress and other public officials. The AFL-CIO ran radio and television advertisements in selected congressional districts attacking Republican members of the House for preventing legislation raising the minimum wage from coming to a vote. More than 20 Republican House members broke with the position of their party leadership by voting to increase the minimum wage and their votes proved the difference. The legislation passed the House and eventually became law.[29]

Some interest groups with large memberships have developed sophisticated procedures for mobilizing their members to pressure government officials. The NFIB, which has more than 600,000 members, divides its membership list into four categories:

- An "A" list of 400,000 members who have responded to at least one direct mail request that they contact their legislators in support of the group's policy preferences.
- An "AA" list of 200,000 members who have responded to more than one direct mail request.
- A "Guardian" list of 40,000 members who are the most active.
- A "Key Contact" list of 3,000 members who have personal relationships with public officials.

The NFIB uses its membership lists to influence the legislative process. NFIB lobbyists first identify which senators and representatives are the swing votes in Congress on issues important to the group. The professional staff of the NFIB then sends direct mail or e-mail messages to NFIB members who live in the states and districts of the targeted lawmakers, asking them to contact their senator or representative in support of the group's goals.[30]

Protest Demonstrations

Groups that cannot afford public relations experts and advertising costs pursue their goals by means of protest demonstrations. Civil rights organizations used this technique in the 1960s. Today, it is employed by groups pursuing a variety of goals, ranging from organizations opposing construction of a nuclear power plant

GETTING INVOLVED

Participating in a Student Group

Colleges and universities typically host a range of student clubs and organizations. Students may participate in such organizations as an international student association, Campus Crusade for Christ, the chess club, a Young Democrats/Young Republicans group, a gay/lesbian/bisexual students association, the black student union, the bridge club, a Muslim students association, the computer science club, a Jewish life organization, Latino students association, the karate club, a premedical society, the Catholic Student Union, the math club, or an Asian students association. The student life office at your college will have a list of student groups active on your campus.

Attend a meeting of the student club or organization of your choice, and identify the incentives the group provides its participants. Does the organization offer material, solidary, or purposive incentives? Keep in mind that some organizations offer more than one type of incentive. Some students may participate because of material incentives (such as a scholarship opportunity), whereas others may join a group because of solidary incentives (they just want to make friends).

Write a paragraph for submission to your instructor describing the organization you attended and discussing the incentives it offers to students. Clearly identify the type or types of incentives the group offers, giving specific examples from activities at the meetings or information provided in the group's literature or on its website.

The assignment does not require that you join a student group or continue attending meetings. Nonetheless, you should consider participation in at least one student organization. Student organizations enrich the educational experience for college students and increase the likelihood that students will successfully complete their education.

to anti-pornography crusaders picketing convenience stores that sell *Playboy* magazine. In general, protest demonstrations are a tactic used by groups unable to achieve their goals through other means. Sometimes the protest catches the attention of the general public, which brings pressure to bear on behalf of the protesting group. In most cases, though, protests have only a marginal impact on public policy.

Litigation

A number of interest groups specialize in the use of litigation (i.e., lawsuits) to achieve their goals. The ACLU provides legal assistance to individuals and groups involved in controversies involving individual rights and liberties, including disputes over freedom of religion, free speech, and the death penalty. The American Center for Law and Justice and the Liberty Counsel are organizations that litigate to support conservative Christian goals, such as opposition to abortion rights and gay marriage. Other interest groups use litigation as one of several approaches to achieving their policy goals. In 2008, the NRA won a major legal victory when the U.S. Supreme Court held for the first time that the Second Amendment protects an individual right to possess a firearm without being a member of a militia.[31]

Is animal research unethical?

Political Violence

Some groups employ unconventional methods to achieve their goals. The Animal Liberation Front, Stop Animal Exploitation Now, and some other animal rights groups take aggressive action to oppose animal research. Although most animal rights demonstrations are peaceful and legal, some opponents of animal research resort to violence. Protestors have broken into university laboratories, releasing lab animals and destroying property. Some researchers have been threatened with physical assault and death and had their homes vandalized.[32]

 WHAT IS YOUR OPINION?

If you were a scientist, would animal rights protestors prevent you from using animals in laboratory research?

THE STRENGTH OF INTEREST GROUPS

The policymaking influence of interest groups depends on several factors:

- **Alliances with political parties** In American politics, some interest groups have loose, informal alliances with political parties. Labor unions, African American rights groups, women's organizations, environmentalists, gun-control groups, abortion-rights organizations, and gay and lesbian rights groups are generally aligned with the Democratic Party. Business groups, the NRA, National Right to Life Committee, anti-tax organizations, and conservative Christian organizations are tied to the Republican Party. Interest groups have more policymaking influence when the party with which they are allied is successful than when it is out of office. After the Democrats took control of Congress in the 2006 election, labor unions, consumer groups, environmental organizations, minority rights groups, and other interest groups typically allied with the Democratic Party saw their influence rise, whereas business groups and trade associations lost influence.

- **Alliances with members of Congress and executive branch officials** The policymaking influence of interest groups depends on their ability to cultivate relationships with key officials in the legislative and executive branches of government, regardless of which party controls Congress or the White House. Business groups compensate for Democratic control of Congress by establishing ties with committee and subcommittee chairs through campaign contributions and effective lobbying. Frequently, business lobbyists succeeded in softening the impact of regulatory legislation on their particular industry.

- **Public opinion** Public opinion affects the ability of interest groups to achieve their policy goals. The chief goal for the president and most members of Congress is reelection. They are not going to support policy proposals that the public strongly opposes or adopt programs that they believe will prove unpopular, regardless of PAC contributions, lobbying, or other interest group activities. Groups are most successful when their policy goals enjoy strong public support.

- **Unity among groups representing the same cause** Interest groups have more influence when organizations representing the same or similar interests or points of view share goals and speak with one voice. For example, at least 11 major environmental organizations participate in national politics. Many more environmental groups operate at the state and local levels. Although environmental groups agree on the broadly defined goal of protecting the environment, they emphasize different aspects of the cause and disagree on tactics and strategy, sometimes quite vocally.[33] On those issues on which environmental groups agree, members of Congress already predisposed to be friendly to the environmental cause have clear direction for their efforts. When environmental groups disagree about policy, however, members of Congress who usually support their cause are less likely to proceed with enthusiasm. Furthermore, opponents of the environmentalist position will use the division among the environmental groups to undermine their initiative.

- **Opposition from other groups** The policy influence of groups depends on the extent of opposition from other groups. Interest groups are most successful on issues over which there is no conflict among groups.[34] Conflict among groups is least likely on specific provisions of detailed legislation, such as an amendment to the Tax Code to grant a narrow tax break to a particular industry. Conflict is most likely on major policy issues that are high profile. Doctors' groups and lawyers associations, for example, butt heads over the issue of medical malpractice insurance reform. Environmental and business groups often oppose one another on environmental issues. On many issues, public officials can choose which interests to court, playing one group off against another.

- **Resources** Finally, groups with resources, especially money, organization, and volunteers, are more influential than groups without resources. The most effective interest group tactics—electioneering, lobbying, and creating public pressure—all require financial resources. Groups with a substantial number of committed members can generate pressure on Congress on behalf of group goals. Well-organized groups can provide campaign assistance to favored candidates through communications to members and perhaps volunteer support.

CONCLUSION: INTEREST GROUPS AND PUBLIC POLICY

Interest groups are an important part of the policymaking process in a democracy. Interest groups moderate the interaction between ordinary citizens and government officials. They educate citizens about political issues, mobilize supporters to go to the polls, make policy demands on the government, and attempt to hold elected officials accountable for their actions. A healthy mix of interest groups is an essential component of a civic society critical to the success of democracy. Democracy is strongest in societies with large number of competing interest groups because they help prevent the concentration of power.[35]

Agenda Building

Interest groups are prominent participants in the process that determines the issues that are part of the nation's policy agenda. The National Right to Life Committee, for example, works to define abortion as a national problem that needs to be addressed by government policy. In contrast, NARAL tries to frame the issue in terms of a woman's right to choose. Much of American politics involves similar battles between groups on different sides of an issue trying to sell their perspective on the issue to the general public and government decision-makers. Whereas public health groups address the issue of government regulation of tobacco from a health perspective, tobacco companies attempt to frame the issue in terms of economics or government regulation. Tobacco interests partner with restaurant associations to oppose state and local efforts to prohibit smoking in restaurants and other public places, arguing that the restriction would hurt business. The added advantage of this strategy for the tobacco industry is that it allows a group with a more favorable public image than tobacco companies to take the public relations lead on the issue.

The relative strength of interest groups affects public policy. Consider the impact of declining labor union membership on social welfare policy. As labor union membership has fallen, public policy has become less aligned with the interests of the working class. The inflation-adjusted value of the minimum wage, unemployment benefits, Food Stamps, and other programs aimed at assisting low-income families, workers, and the unemployed have all declined.[36]

Interest groups contribute to the polarization of American politics because groups tend to represent issue extremes rather than more moderate policy options. Consider the issue of abortion. NARAL and the National Right to Life Committee push policy alternatives on either extreme of the issue. People who believe that abortion should but legal but greatly restricted have no group to speak for them even though they represent the majority.[37] Polls show that only a minority of Americans believe that abortion should be illegal in all circumstances (18 percent) or legal in all circumstances (26 percent).[38]

Policy Formulation and Adoption

Interest groups play a major role in policy formulation. Groups are seldom satisfied with putting their particular issue on the policy agenda. They also want government to address the issue from their perspective. The oil and gas industry favors energy policies that focus on expanding production, including the authorization of energy exploration in ANWR. In contrast, environmentalists push for an energy policy that emphasizes conservation and the development of alternative fuels. Sometimes government policies reflect the triumph of one set of interest groups over another. More frequently, public policies are the result of compromise among competing interests over the details of policy.

Interest groups do not adopt policies directly because adoption is the responsibility of members of Congress, the president, and other government officials. Nonetheless, interest groups try to affect policy adoption. By contributing money to candidates and making endorsements, groups attempt to influence the selection of officeholders. After the election is over, groups lobby for and against the adoption of particular policies. Americans for Tax Reform, a cause group that advocates tax reform, asks candidates and officeholders to sign a Taxpayer Protection Pledge, which is a written promise to oppose any and all efforts to increase taxes. The list of elected officials who have signed the pledge includes 193 members of the House, 41 senators, 8 governors, and more than 1,200 state legislators.[39]

Policy Implementation and Evaluation

Interest groups work to influence policy implementation. Groups that have been successful during the policy formulation and adoption stages try to ensure that the policies are implemented favorably, whereas groups who lost at earlier stages work to minimize the impact of a policy. The AARP and pharmaceutical companies are actively involved in the implementation of the prescription drug benefit that Congress and the president added to the Medicaid program in 2003. The AARP wants to ensure that older Americans receive maximum benefit from the program, whereas pharmaceuticals focus on reimbursement issues.

Finally, interest groups attempt to put their interpretation on a policy's evaluation in hopes that government officials will change it to reflect their perspective. Environmental organizations blame the nation's energy policy for global warming and rising gasoline prices, arguing that the nation needs to focus on conservation and the development of alternative fuels. In contrast, the oil and gas industry insists that the solution to high gasoline prices is more energy development, both in the ANWR and offshore.

KEY TERMS

527 Committees

AARP

access

advocacy groups

affirmative action

American Bar Association (ABA)

American Civil Liberties Union (ACLU)

American Federation of Labor-Congress of Industrial Organizations (AFL-CIO)

American Indian Movement (AIM)

American Medical Association (AMA)

anticlericalism

bundling

cause groups

Chamber of Commerce

citizen groups

class action lawsuits

Club for Growth

Common Cause

EMILY's List

free-rider barrier to group membership

Friendly Incumbent Rule

Frostbelt

Human Rights Campaign (HRC)

interest group

League of United Latin American Citizens (LULAC)

lobbying

Medicare

minimum wage

Mothers Against Drunk Driving (MADD)

Moveon.org

NARAL Pro-Choice America

National Association for the Advancement of Colored People (NAACP)

National Organization for Women (NOW)

National Rifle Association (NRA)

National Right to Life Committee

Political Action Committee (PAC)

religious left

religious right

right-to-work laws

Sierra Club

Social Security

Sunbelt

trade associations

Voting Rights Act (VRA)

NOTES

1. Jeffrey M. Jones, "Public Believes Americans Have Right to Own Guns," March 27, 2008, available at www.gallup.com.

2. Mancur Olson, *The Logic of Collective Action* (Cambridge, MA: Harvard University Press, 1971).

3. Kelly D. Patterson and Matthew M. Singer, "Targeting Success: The Enduring Power of the NRA," in Allan J. Ciglar and Burdett A. Loomis, eds., *Interest Group Politics* (Washington, DC: CQ Press, 2007), pp. 41–42.

4. Anthony J. Nownes, *Total Lobbying: What Lobbyists Want (And How They Try to Get It)* (New York: Cambridge University Pres, 2006), p. 13.

5. Center for Responsive Politics, available at www.opensecrets.org.

6. U.S. Census Bureau, "Labor Union Membership by Sector: 2006," 2009 *Statistical Abstract of the United States*, available at www.census.gov.

7. Peter L. Francia, "Protecting America's Workers in Hostile Territory: Unions and the Republican Congress," in Paul S. Herrnson, Ronald G. Shaiko, and Clyde Wilcox, eds., *The Interest Group Connection: Electioneering, Lobbying, and Policymaking in Washington*, 2nd ed. (Washington, DC: CQ Press, 2005), p. 214.

8. Amy Joyce, "Divided Unions," *Washington Post National Weekly Edition*, August 1–7, 2005, p. 20.

9. American Federation of Labor-Congress of Industrial Organizations, available at www.aflcio.org.

10. Steven Greenhouse, "Two Major Construction Unions Plan to Leave A.F.L.-C.I.O.," *New York Times*, February 15, 2006, available at www.nytimes.com.

11. Sidney Verba, Kay Lehman Schlozman, and Henry E. Brady, *Voice and Equality: Civic Volunteerism in American Politics* (Cambridge, MA: Harvard University Press, 1995), pp. 332–338.

12. Caryle Murphy and Alan Cooperman, "Seeking to Reclaim the Moral High Ground," *Washington Post National Weekly Edition*, May 29–June 4, 2006, p. 12.

13. John C. Green and Nathan S. Bigelow, "The Christian Right Goes to Washington: Social Movement Resources and the Legislative Process," in Herrnson, Shaiko, and Wilcox, eds., *The Interest Group Connection*, pp. 191–206.

14. John C. Green, Mark J. Rozell, and Clyde Wilcox, eds., *The Values Campaign? The Christian Right and the 2004 Election* (Washington, DC: Georgetown University Press, 2006), p. 4.

15. Center for Responsive Politics, available at www.opensecrets.org.

16. Federal Election Commission, "Summary of PAC Financial Activity," available at www.fec.gov.

17. Center for Responsive Politics, available at www.opensecrets.org.

18. Federal Election Commission, "PAC Financial Activity," available at www.fec.gov.

19. Center for Responsive Politics, available at www.opensecrets.org.

20. Professor James A. Thurber, quoted in Jeffrey H. Birnbaum, "Mickey Goes to Washington," *Washington Post National Weekly Edition*, February 25–March 2, 2008, p. 6.

21. Ronald G. Shaiko, "Making the Connection: Organized Interests, Political Representation, and the Changing Rules of the Game in Washington Politics," in Herrnson, Shaiko, and Wilcox, eds., *The Interest Group Connection*, p. 32.

22. Center for Responsive Politics, available at www.opensecrets.org.

23. Rogan Kersh, "The Well-Informed Lobbyist: Information and Interest Group Lobbying," in Ciglar and Loomis, ed., *Interest Group Politics*, pp. 390–406.

24. John R. Wright, "Contributions, Lobbying, and Committee Voting in the U.S. House of Representatives," *American Political Science Review* 84 (June 1990): 417–438.

25. Thomas B. Edsall, "A Chill but Not the Cold Shoulder," *Washington Post National Weekly Edition*, January 16–22, 2006, p. 15.

26. Marie Hojnacki and David C. Kimball, "Organized Interests and the Decision of Whom to Lobby in Congress," *American Political Science Review* 92 (December 1998): 775–790.

27. Quoted in Jeffrey H. Birnbaum, "A U-Turn on K Street," *Washington Post National Weekly Edition*, December 4–10, 2006, p. 13.

28. Dan Clawson, Alan Neustadtl, and Mark Weller, *Dollars and Votes: How Business Campaign Contributions Subvert Democracy* (Philadelphia: Temple University Press, 1998), pp. 67–69.

29. Ruth Markus and Charles R. Babcock, "Feeding the Election Machine," *Washington Post National Weekly Edition*, February 17, 1997, p. 7.

30. Steven E. Schier, *By Invitation Only: The Rise of Exclusive Politics in the United States* (Pittsburgh, PA: University of Pittsburgh Press, 2000), p. 179–181.

31. *District of Columbia v. Heller*, 07–290 (2008).

32. Richard Monastersky, "Protesters Fail to Slow Animal Research," *Chronicle of Higher Education*, April 18, 2008, pp. A1, A26–A28.

33. Tom Arrandale, "The Mid-Life Crisis of the Environmental Lobby," *Governing*, April 1992, pp. 32–36.

34. Diana Evans, "Before the Roll Call: Interest Group Lobbying and Public Policy Outcomes in House Committees," *Political Research Quarterly* 49 (June 1996): 287–304.

35. Marcella Ridlan Ray, *The Changing and Unchanging Face of U.S. Civil Society* (New Brunswick, NJ: Transaction Publishers, 2002), pp. 2–3.

36. Jacob S. Hacker, "Privatizing Risk without Privatizing the Welfare State: The Hidden Politics of Social Policy Retrenchment in the United States," *American Political Science Review* 98 (May 2004): pp. 251–256.

37. Richard M. Skinner, *More Than Money: Interest Group Action in Congressional Elections* (Lanham, MD: Rowman & Littlefield, 2007), pp. 165–167.

38. Lydia Saad, "Public Divided on 'Pro-Choice' versus 'Pro-Life' Abortion Labels," *Gallup News Service*, May 21 2007, available at www.gallup.com.

39. Americans for Tax Reform, available at www.atr.org.

Chapter 8

Political Parties

CHAPTER OUTLINE

The Party System

Party Organization

Political Cycles and Party Realignment

The Party Balance: Democrats, Republicans, and Independents

Voting Patterns
    Income
    Race and Ethnicity
    Education
    Gender
    Age

Family and Lifestyle Status
Region
Political Ideology
Religion
Place of Residence

Issue Orientation

Divided Government

Conclusion: Political Parties and Public Policy
    Agenda Building
    Policy Formulation and Adoption
    Policy Implementation and Evaluation

LEARNING OUTCOMES

After studying Chapter 8, students should be able to do the following:

▸ Assess the effect of the 2008 election on the party balance in American politics. (p. 176)

▸ Compare and contrast political parties and interest groups. (pp. 176–177)

▸ Identify the reasons given by political scientists to explain the two-party system in the United States. (pp. 177–179)

▸ Describe the structures of the Democratic and Republican Party organizations, and identify the tasks that the national party organizations perform for party candidates. (pp. 179–180)

▸ Assess the fundraising capacity of each of the two major political parties. (pp. 180–182)

▸ Discuss the factors underlying the alternation in power between political parties in the American political system. (p. 182)

▸ Assess the strength of the Democratic and Republican Parties today in terms of party identification. (p. 183)

▸ Describe the different groups of people who consider themselves as political independents. (pp. 183–184)

▸ Compare and contrast the Democratic and Republican Parties today in terms of group support among voters. (pp. 184–188)

▶ Compare and contrast the party platforms of the two parties. (pp. 189–192)

▶ Identify the reasons political scientists give to explain divided government. (pp. 192–195)

▶ Describe the role of political parties in the policymaking process. (pp. 195–197)

▶ Define the key terms listed on page 197 and explain their significance.

The Democratic Party won the 2008 election, capturing the presidency for the first time in three elections and strengthening its hold in Congress. In the race for the White House, Democratic presidential candidate Barack Obama defeated Republican John McCain. Obama carried 28 states and the District of Columbia with a total of 365 electoral votes, while McCain took 22 states with 172 electoral votes. Obama also claimed a majority of the popular vote—53 percent to 46 percent for his Republican opponent. Obama's share of the popular vote was the largest for any Democrat running for president since Lyndon Johnson in 1964.

Democrats did well in other races as well. While Obama was winning the White House, the Democratic Party expanded its majorities in Congress, picking up 8 seats in the Senate and 21 seats in the House. When the new Senate convened in 2009, it contained 59 Democrats and 41 Republicans. The new House included 257 Democrats and 178 Republicans. At the state level, Democrats held the governorships of 29 states, compared with 21 state governors who were Republican. In 27 states, Democrats held majorities in both legislative chambers, compared with 14 states in which the Republican Party enjoyed full control. The legislatures in eight states were split; the Nebraska legislature is nonpartisan, which means that candidates run for seats without party labels.

This chapter is the fifth in a series of six chapters dealing with the political background of policymaking in America. Chapters 4, 5, 6, and 7 address the topics of public opinion, political participation, the media, and interest groups, respectively. Chapter 9 considers elections. This chapter examines political parties in America and their role in the policymaking process. It considers the party system, party organization, and party strength. It compares the Democratic and Republican Parties in terms of their support groups and issue orientations. Finally, the chapter explores the role of political parties in the policymaking process.

THE PARTY SYSTEM

Political party A group of individuals who join together to seek government office in order to make public policy.

A **political party** is a group of individuals who join together to seek government office in order to make public policy. A party differs from an interest group in its effort to win control of the machinery of government. Both parties and interest groups participate in election campaigns, but only parties actually run candidates for office. Candidates for Congress run as Democrats or Republicans, not as representatives of labor unions or corporations.

The United States has a two-party system.

The major political parties in the United States also have a broader base of support than interest groups and take positions on a wider range of policy issues than do most interest groups. The United Auto Workers (UAW), for example, is a labor union representing automobile workers. Its political concerns are limited to matters relevant to auto workers and their families, such as tax policy, Social Security, Medicare, laws affecting the ability of unions to organize workers, and the enforcement of workplace safety regulations. The National Rifle Association (NRA), meanwhile, focuses narrowly on gun issues. In contrast to the UAW, NRA, and other interest groups, the Democratic and Republican Parties have broad bases of support and take positions on the full spectrum of political issues. In fact, political scientists sometimes use the terms *umbrella party* or *big tent* to refer to the two major political parties in the United States because each party encompasses a broad set of social, political, and economic interests.

The number of political parties varies from country to country. The United States has a **two-party system,** which is the division of voter loyalties between two major political parties, resulting in the near exclusion of minor parties from seriously competing for a share of political power. After the 2008 election, 98 of 100 U.S. senators were elected as either Democrats or Republicans. Bernie Sanders of Vermont and Joe Liebermann of Connecticut won election as independents but caucus with the Democrats and are counted as Democrats for purpose of committee assignments. Liebermann calls himself an "independent Democrat." The two major parties held all 435 seats in the U.S. House and all 50 offices of state governor.

A **third party** is a minor party in a two-party system. Third-party candidates and independents may compete for office in a two-party system, but usually with a notable

Two-party system The division of voter loyalties between two major political parties.

Third party A minor party in a two-party system.

GLOBAL PERSPECTIVE

The Israeli Party System

Israel has a **multiparty system,** which is the division of voter loyalties among three or more major political parties. The Knesset, the lower house of the Israeli national legislature, included 12 parties after the 2009 elections. Kadima, the largest party in the Knesset, held 28 of 120 seats. The LiKud Party was the second largest party in the Knesset with 27 seats. Yisrael Beiteinu had 12 seats. The Labor Party won 13 seats. No other party had more than five seats.* To achieve a majority in the Knesset, several parties had to form a coalition.

Israel has **proportional representation (PR),** which is an election system that awards legislative seats to each party approximately equal to its popular voting strength. As long as a party receives at least 2 percent of the total vote, the minimum threshold for gaining representation, the party wins seats in the Knesset in proportion to its share of the vote. In 2009, for example, Kadima won 23 percent of the seats in the Knesset based on 22 percent of the popular vote. Proportional representation is related to multiparty systems because voters know that their votes will count. Unless a party has almost no popular support, each vote it receives will enable it to increase its representation in the Knesset.

Voters in Israel cast their ballots for the party rather than individual candidates by choosing a letter symbol. Before the election, each party prepares a list of candidates for the Knesset and ranks them in order, placing party leaders at the top. If the party wins five seats, the first five candidates on the list become members of the Knesset. If it wins ten seats, the first ten candidates are elected. Candidates are chosen to represent their party in the Knesset rather than individual geographic districts as in the United States.[†]

Democracies with multiparty systems are countries with intense social and political divisions. People who disagree fundamentally about the nature of society and the role of government are less likely to form broad-based coalition parties such as those that exist in the United States. Instead, they create smaller, more narrowly based parties. Societies that are deeply divided are likely to have several political parties. The multiplicity of political parties in Israel reflects a nation deeply divided over the peace process, the creation of a Palestinian state, the economy, and the role of religion in society.

Many political scientists believe that electoral laws and a nation's social structure interact. Nations with deep social and political divisions create electoral systems based on proportional representation in order to allow the democratic expression of those divisions at the ballot box. In contrast, countries with fewer divisions establish election procedures that favor a two-party system.[‡]

QUESTIONS TO CONSIDER

1. If the United States were to adopt proportional representation, do you think that a multiparty system would soon develop? Why or why not?
2. If Israel were to adopt a plurality election system, do you think a two-party system would eventually emerge in that country? Why or why not?
3. What are the advantages and disadvantages of each type of party system?

*Knesset website, "Current Parliamentary Groups in the Knesset," available at www.knesset.gov.

[†]Asher Arian, *Politics in Israel: The Second Republic*, 2nd ed. (Washington, DC: CQ Press, 2005), p. 203.

[‡]Octavio Amorim Neto and Gary W. Cox, "Electoral Institutions, Cleavage Structures, and the Number of Parties," *American Journal of Political Science* 41 (January 1997): 149–174.

Multiparty system The division of voter loyalties among three or more major political parties.

lack of success. The roster of third parties in the United States includes Green, Reform, Libertarian, Natural Law, Official Constitution, Workers World, Socialist, and Socialist Equality Parties. The Green and the Libertarians are the most successful, winning a handful of local races in recent elections.

Proportional representation (PR) An election system that awards legislative seats to each party approximately equal to its popular voting strength.

Plurality election system A method for choosing public officials that awards office to the candidate with the most votes, favors a two-party system.

Electoral college The system established in the Constitution for indirect election of the president and vice president.

? WHAT IS YOUR OPINION?

Would you ever seriously consider voting for a third-party candidate for president? Why or why not?

Why does the United States have a two-party system as opposed to a system with three or more major political parties as in most other democracies? Political scientists offer two sets of explanations—the electoral system and the absence of deep-seated political divisions in American society. Maurice Duverger, a French political scientist, wrote in the 1950s that a **plurality election system,** which is a method for choosing public officials that awards office to the candidate with the most votes, favors a two-party system.[1] Candidates for executive and legislative office in the United States run from geographic areas and the candidate with the more votes wins the office. Candidates who finish second or third win nothing, no matter how close the race. The **electoral college,** which is the system established in the Constitution for indirect election of the president and vice president, is especially inhospitable to third-party candidates because it awards electoral votes, the only votes that really count, to candidates who win the most popular votes in a state. In 1992, for example, Reform Party candidate Ross Perot won no electoral votes, despite taking 19 percent of the popular vote, because he carried no states. The dilemma for minor parties in the United States is that if they do not quickly develop enough popular support to win elections, the voters will not take them seriously. If voters believe that a party and its candidates are unlikely to win, they often decide to choose between the major party candidates because they do not want to throw away their votes.[2]

Scholars also believe that a nation's party system reflects the fundamental social and political divisions of society. The more intense the divisions, the more likely the nation will have a multiparty system. The United States has a two-party system, they say, because Americans are relatively united. Americans may disagree about the role of government in society, but they generally share the basic values of capitalism and democracy. People with opposing views on some issues can unite under the same party banner because they agree on other issues.

PARTY ORGANIZATION

The organization of political parties in the United States reflects the federal system, with organizations at both the state and national levels of government. At the state level, the Democratic and Republican Party organizations are led by executive party committees, which are elected by party activists who participate in local party meetings, district conventions, and state party conventions. The executive committee usually elects the state party chair. In Texas, for example, the Texas Republican Executive Committee selects the chair of the Texas Republican Party, whereas the Democratic Executive Committee chooses the chair of the Texas Democratic Party.

A national committee and a national chair lead the national party organizations. The national committee consists of a committeeman and committeewoman

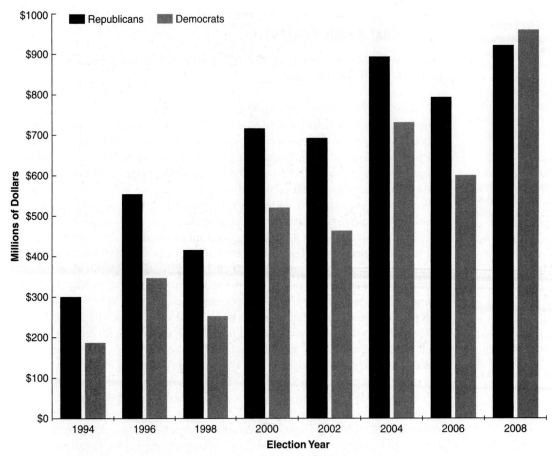

FIGURE 8.1   Party Fundraising, 1994–2008.
Source: Federal Election Commission.

chosen by the party organizations of each state and the District of Columbia. The national committee elects the national committee chair. When the party controls the White House, the president usually handpicks the national chairperson.

The Democratic National Committee (DNC) and Republican National Committee (RNC) work to increase the number of party officeholders. Each party tries to recruit a strong list of candidates for the next election. Although the national party organizations do not control nominations, they can encourage potential candidates to run. They also provide candidates with technical assistance and campaign advice. The DNC and RNC support their candidates with polling data, issue research, media assistance, and advice on campaign strategy. Both national parties offer campaign seminars, teaching inexperienced candidates how to do everything from raising money to dealing with the media. The most important service the national party organizations provide for their candidates is money.

Figure 8.1 tracks Democratic and Republican Party fundraising from 1994 through the 2008 election. The Republicans have historically enjoyed a significant

Republican Party losses in the 2006 and 2008 elections reflected the widespread unpopularity of President George W. Bush and his administration's policies.

fundraising advantage over the Democrats because of the socioeconomic status of their support base and because of their fundraising expertise. People who identify with the Republican Party have more money than do people who consider themselves Democrats. Moreover, the Republicans have also benefited from a more efficient fundraising operation, especially direct mail. As the figure shows, however, the Democrats have closed the fundraising gap, primarily because they have taken better advantage of the Internet than their Republican opponents. The Democratic Party and its candidates now raise substantially more money online than the Republican Party and its candidates.[3] In 2008, the Democratic and Republican national campaign organizations raised more than $900 million each to support their candidates with the Democratic Party enjoying a small fundraising advantage.

Access The
opportunity to
communicate directly
with legislators and
other government
officials in hopes of
influencing the details
of policy.

Political parties take a different approach to campaign finance than interest groups. Most interest groups contribute primarily to incumbent officeholders because they want to develop positive relationships with influential members of Congress. Their goal is **access,** which is the opportunity to communicate directly with legislators and other government officials in hopes of influencing the details of policy. In contrast, the goal of political parties is to control the government. Consequently, they contribute most of their money to candidates in competitive races, whether incumbents or challengers.[4]

POLITICAL CYCLES AND PARTY REALIGNMENT

Alternation in power among political parties is an inevitable and essential element of democracy. Over time, the political party in power loses popularity because it adopts policies that prove unpopular with a large segment of the population, mishandles a natural disaster, or is unlucky enough to be in charge during an economic downturn. Eventually, the party in power loses majority support and the opposition party takes power. The success of the Democratic Party in the 2006 and 2008 elections, for example, reflected popular displeasure with the performance of the Republican Congress (before the 2006 election) and the George W. Bush administration. In early 2008, less than one in three Americans approved of President Bush's performance as president, seriously damaging the prospects of Republican Party candidates in that year's election.[5] Alternation in power is a critical component of democracy because it is the mechanism for holding the government accountable to the voters. President Obama and the Democratic Congress have an incentive to do their best to provide an effective government because they know that they, too, will eventually be held accountable at the ballot box.

Political scientists Samuel Merrill III, Bernard Grofman, and Thomas L. Brunell offer a theory to explain partisan cycles in American politics. They note that the average American voter is moderate—less liberal on most policy issues than the Democratic Party and less conservative than the Republicans. When the Republicans are in power, the public mood grows more liberal because the Republicans adopt policies that are more conservative than the policy preferences of the average voter. Over a period of time, generally 12 to 15 years, the public grows dissatisfied and votes for change, putting a Democrat in the White House and electing a Democratic majority in Congress. The opposite happens when the Democrats are in power.[6]

Party era A period
of time characterized
by a degree of
uniformity in the
nature of political
party competition.

**Party
realignment**
A change in the
underlying party
loyalties of voters that
ends one party era
and begins another.

Other political sciences use the concepts of party era and political party realignment to explain changes in the party balance. A **party era** is a period of time characterized by a degree of uniformity in the nature of political party competition. A **party realignment** is a change in the underlying party loyalties of voters that ends one party era and begins another. The 1932 election in which Democrat Franklin Roosevelt swept into office in the midst of the Great Depression is the classic example of a realigning election. The voters blamed the Republican Party for the Depression and turned control of the government over to the Democrats who held onto their majority status for nearly 50 years.

THE PARTY BALANCE: DEMOCRATS, REPUBLICANS, AND INDEPENDENTS

Grand Old Party (GOP) Nickname of the Republican Party.

Political scientists measure party identification by asking survey respondents if they consider themselves Democrats, Republicans, or independents. In 2008, Democrats outnumbered Republicans by a 36 percent to 27 percent margin, with another 36 percent declaring that they were independents. The figures represented a slight gain in party ID for the Democratic Party since 2004 but a sizable decline for the **Grand Old Party (GOP),** which is a nickname for the Republican Party. In 2004, the two parties were on nearly equal footing among the electorate; 35 percent identified with the Democratic Party, compared with 33 percent for the Republicans. Between 2004 and 2008, the proportion of people identifying with the Democratic Party increased by 1 percentage point, whereas Republican Party identification fell by 6 percentage points. In the meantime, the proportion of people calling themselves independents rose by 3 percentage points, from 33 percent in 2004 to 36 percent in 2008.[7]

 WHAT IS YOUR OPINION?

Is it better to identify with a political party or to be an independent?

Independents are a diverse group. They mirror the population in terms of age, income, and education, but they are disproportionately male. A majority of Democrats are women; Republicans are divided evenly between men and women. Independents are less likely to be religious than are people who identify with either the Democratic Party or the GOP. In terms of political attitudes, researchers identify five categories of independents:

- **Deliberators** These are classic swing voters who could go with one party or the other. They are satisfied with the political system and have a positive image of both political parties.
- **Disillusioned** These are people who are alienated from the political system. They do not like either party and are open to voting for an independent candidate.
- **Dislocated** These people are liberal on social issues but conservative on economic issues. They prefer the Democratic Party on the former; the Republican Party on the latter.
- **Disguised** These are people who reject party labels, but typically vote for one party or the other. They are Democrats or Republicans in all respects but the party label.
- **Disengaged** These people have little or no interest in politics. They are the least likely to be registered to vote among all the groups of independents.[8]

The Democratic Party has made electoral gains since 2004 not just because the proportion of Republican Party identifies has declined, but also because independents are more likely to vote Democratic. In 2004, independents divided almost equally among independents who leaned Democratic, independents who leaned Republican, and true independents. The ratio of Democrats and Democratic-leaning independents to Republicans and Republican-leaning independents was close,

Both Senator John McCain and Senator Barack Obama conducted campaigns designed to appeal to independent voters.

47 percent to 44 percent. (The Republican Party won the 2004 election because Democratic turnout was less than Republican turnout.) In contrast, independents leaning Democratic outnumbered independents who leaned Republican by a three-to-two margin in 2008. The combination of Democrats and Democratic-leaning independents represented 51 percent of the electorate, compared with 37 percent Republican and Republican-leaning independents.[9]

VOTING PATTERNS

Voting patterns reflect differences in income, race and ethnicity, education, gender, age, family and lifestyle status, region, ideology, and religion.

Income

Exit polls Surveys based on random samples of voters leaving the polling place.

Economic status is one of the most enduring bases for voting divisions in America. Since the 1930s, Republican candidates have typically done better among upper-income voters, whereas Democrats have scored their highest vote percentages among lower-income groups. In 2008, **exit polls,** which are surveys based on random samples of voters leaving the polling place, found that Obama outpolled McCain among voters with family incomes less than $50,000 a year by 60 percent to 38 percent. The two candidates evenly split the votes of people in families with annual incomes greater than $50,000.[10]

Race and Ethnicity

Voting patterns reflect the nation's racial divisions. White voters lean Republican. In 2008, whites backed McCain 55 percent to 45 percent for Obama. In contrast, minority voters support the Democrats. In 2008, African Americans supported Obama over McCain by a lopsided 95 percent to 4 percent. Asian Americans gave Obama 61 percent of their votes compared with 35 percent who supported McCain. Democratic candidates also enjoy strong support from most Latinos. In 2008, Obama won the Latino vote 66 percent to 32 percent for McCain.[11] Latino voters were especially important for Obama because they apparently provided his margin of victory in Colorado, Florida, Nevada, and New Mexico, four hotly contested states that George W. Bush won in 2004.[12] Not all groups of Latinos share the same perspective on party affiliation. Whereas Mexican Americans and Puerto Ricans typically vote Democratic, most Cuban Americans support the GOP because of the Republican Party's strong anti-Castro position.[13]

Education

The Democratic Party is strongest with voters at either end of the education ladder. In 2008, Obama led McCain by 63 percent to 35 percent among voters who had not

White voters lean Republican; minority voters tend to support the Democrats.

graduated from high school. Obama won the votes of high school graduates as well by a more modest 52 percent to 46 percent for his Republican opponent. The two parties evenly split the votes of college graduates. Among voters with postgraduate degrees, however, Obama led his Republican opponents by 58 percent to 40 percent.[14] For the most part, the relationship between education and party support reflects differences in income. As people move up the education ladder, they also move up the income ladder. Individuals in higher income brackets are more likely to vote Republican than are lower income voters. The pattern holds through college but not into graduate and professional school. People who have postgraduate college degrees tend to vote Democratic because many of them hold liberal positions on social issues such as abortion rights, environmental protection, gay and lesbian rights, the war in Iraq, and affirmative action.

Gender

Gender gap
Differences in party identification and political attitudes between men and women.

For more than 40 years, American voters have divided along gender lines, producing a **gender gap,** the differences in party identification and political attitudes between men and women. The gender gap has emerged in American politics because men have moved away from the Democratic Party. In 1952, a majority of both men and women identified with the Democratic Party. Since then, the percentage of women identifying with the Democrats has risen while the proportion of men declaring themselves Democrats has declined. The gender gap was greatest in the 1996 presidential election at 14 percentage points. Since then, the gap has somewhat narrowed. In 2008, half of male voters supported Obama compared with 56 percent of women voters who backed the Democrat, a 6 percentage point gender gap.[15]

Age

Polling data reveal that younger voters have been moving toward the Democratic Party and away from the GOP. In fact, Obama won the presidency in 2008 because of his support from younger voters. He outpolled McCain among voters under the age of 30 by 66 percent to 32 percent. Obama won the 30–44 age bracket as well, but by a closer margin of 52 percent to 46 percent. The two candidates split the votes of people age 45 to 64. McCain won a majority of voters over the age of 65, 53 percent to 45 percent for Obama.[16]

Family and Lifestyle Status

People who are members of traditional families tend to vote Republican, whereas unmarried adults and people who are gay, lesbian, or bisexual generally back the Democrats. In 2008, married voters supported McCain by 51 percent to 47 percent for Obama. In contrast, Obama led his Republican opponent among single people by 65 percent to 33 percent. Voters who identified as gay, lesbian, or bisexual supported Obama by 70 percent to 27 percent for McCain.[17]

Region

Regional voting patterns have changed. The South was once the strongest region for the Democratic Party, whereas the Midwest was a stronghold for the GOP.

Today, Democrats run best in the Northeast and on the West Coast. The GOP is strongest in the South, the Great Plains, and the Rocky Mountain West. The Midwest has become a battleground region between the two parties. In 2008, Obama was strongest in the Northeast, winning 59 percent of the vote and carrying every state in the region. McCain ran best in the South, outpolling Obama 53 percent to 46 percent, and winning every southern state except Florida, North Carolina, and Virginia.[18]

Political Ideology

The Democratic and Republican Parties are ideologically polarized. Conservatives are aligned with the GOP; liberals vote Democratic. In 2008, liberals supported Obama over McCain by a substantial 88 percent to 10 percent. In contrast, conservatives backed McCain by an impressive 78 percent to 20 percent. Moderates tend to be swing voters. Obama won the White House because he captured the votes of moderates, 60 percent to 39 percent for McCain.[19]

The political parties were once more ideologically diverse than they are today. Many conservatives identified with the Democratic Party, especially in the South, whereas the Republican Party had a liberal wing based principally in the Northeast. Important legislation frequently passed Congress with the support of bipartisan coalitions. For example, the Civil Rights Act of 1964 passed Congress because moderate and liberal Republicans joined with liberal Democrats to overcome the intense opposition of conservative southern Democrats.

The political parties are more ideologically distinct today because their coalitions of supporters have changed. The move of southern white conservatives from the Democratic Party to the GOP has made the Democrats more liberal and the Republicans more conservative. The Democratic Party has adopted liberal positions on a range of social issues in order to appeal to middle-class voters concerned with abortion rights, the environment, and gay and lesbian rights. The Republican Party, meanwhile, has taken conservative positions on social issues to bolster its support among conservative Christians.[20]

Religion

Religion and party support are closely related. During the last party era, voting patterns reflected religious affiliation. Protestants generally supported the Republican Party, Catholics leaned to the Democratic Party, and Jews were strongly Democratic. Today, party divisions based on religion have grown more complex. Although most Jews still vote for Democrats, Catholics have become a swing group. Conservative white evangelical Protestants (including Southern Baptists, Pentacostals, and members of the Assemblies of God) are firmly Republican as are members of the Church of Jesus Christ of Latter-day Saints (the Mormons). Latinos as a whole typically support the Democrats, but the GOP is stronger among Latino evangelicals than among Latino Catholics, who remain firmly Democratic.[21] White members of mainline Protestant denominations (including Methodists, Episcopalians, and Presbyterians) lean Republican as well, but less so than do evangelicals. Most African Americans are Democrats, regardless of their religious preferences.[22] In 2008, Jews supported Obama over McCain by 78 percent to 21 percent. Catholics backed Obama as well, but the margin was more narrow, 54 percent to 45 percent. Protestants voted for McCain by 54 percent to 45 percent for Obama.[23]

In the current party system, voting patterns are also based on frequency of attendance at religious services. White Protestants and Catholics who attend worship services regularly are more likely to vote Republican than are people who attend services less frequently.[24] In 2008, McCain led among voters who said that they attended religious services more than once a week by 55 percent to 43 percent for Obama. In contrast, voters who declared that they seldom attended religious services voted for Obama by 59 percent to 40 percent. People who never attended services backed the Democrat by 67 percent to 30 percent.[25]

Place of Residence

Voting patterns reflect place of residence. Democrats win urban areas, Republicans carry rural areas, and the suburbs are a battleground between the two parties. In 2008, Obama outpolled McCain in large urban areas by 63 percent to 35 percent, whereas the Republican candidate won rural areas by 53 percent to 45 percent. The vote in the suburbs was 50 percent for Obama to 48 percent for the Republican.[26]

White Christians who attend church regularly are more likely to vote Republican than are people who attend services rarely or not at all.

ISSUE ORIENTATION

Liberalism The political philosophy that favors the use of government power to foster the development of the individual and promote the welfare of society.

Conservatism The political philosophy that government power undermines the development of the individual and diminishes society as a whole.

Party platform A statement of party principles and issue positions.

Since 1960, the parties have grown further apart philosophically, with the Democrats generally taking liberal positions and the Republicans expressing conservative views. **Liberalism** is the political philosophy that favors the use of government power to foster the development of the individual and promote the welfare of society. Democrats believe that a strong government is needed to provided essential services and remedy social inequalities. Democrats make an exception to their endorsement of a strong government when it comes to cultural issues, such as abortion and homosexuality. They believe that government should leave decisions on those sorts of issues to the individual. In contrast, the Republican Party embraces **conservatism,** which is the political philosophy that government power undermines the development of the individual and diminishes society as a whole. Republicans believe that a strong government interferes with business and threatens individual freedom. The exception to this approach for Republicans is that they believe that government should enforce traditional values on issues such as abortion and homosexuality.

A **party platform** is a statement of party principles and issue positions. The 2008 Democratic and Republican Party platforms, which are excerpted in Table 8.1, show clear philosophical differences between the parties on many issues. The parties disagreed on tax policy, labor laws, abortion, gay and lesbian rights, and affirmative action. By no means, however, do the parties take opposite sides on all issues. Some differences are nuanced. Consider gun control. Both parties endorse a right of gun ownership, but they disagree on the efficacy of gun regulation. The Democrats endorse "reasonable regulation," while the Republicans declare that gun control

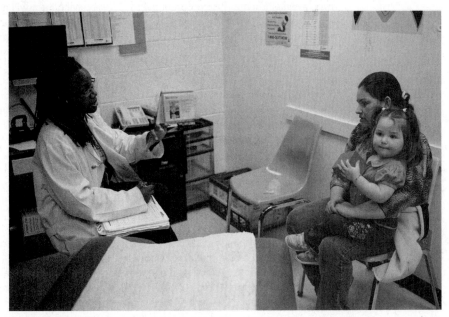

The Democratic and Republican Parties disagree about the best approach to healthcare reform.

TABLE 8.1   Selected 2008 Democratic and Republican Party Platform Positions

Issue	Democratic Position	Republican Position
Healthcare	Declares that every American should be guaranteed affordable, comprehensive healthcare and that healthcare should be a shared responsibility between employers, workers, insurers, providers and government. Endorses government support for embryonic stem cell research. Favors emphasis on wellness and preventative care.	Supports health savings accounts that provide tax breaks to individuals who save money to pay for their own health insurance coverage. Says that individually purchased health insurance and employer provided health insurance should be given the same tax status. Calls for expansion of research using adult stem cells but opposes embryonic stem cell research. Favors focus on wellness and preventative care.
Education	Supports innovative ways to increase teacher pay that are negotiated between schools and teachers rather than imposed on teachers. Endorses $4,000 higher education tax credit; in exchange, students will perform community service. Supports age-appropriate sex education.	Supports school choice programs with vouchers for private schools, including religious schools. Advocates merit pay for teachers. Endorses abstinence-only sex education.
Environmental policy	Endorses a cap-and-trade system to reduce carbon emissions that cause global warming.	Favors market-based solutions for decreasing emissions, reducing greenhouse gasses, and mitigating the impact of climate change.
Social Security	Opposes Social Security privatization and increasing the retirement age. Promises to raise revenue to support the program by applying the Social Security payroll tax on income over $250,000 a year.	Promises that anyone now receiving Social Security benefits or close to receiving them will not have their benefits cut or their taxes increased. Calls for partial privatization through the creation of personal investment accounts.
Iran	Declares that the United States and its allies should use diplomacy, sanctions, and incentives to ensure that Iran not be allowed to develop nuclear weapons; all options for dealing with Iran should be on the table.	Declares that the United States, in solidarity with the international community, should not allow Iran to develop nuclear weapons.
Iraq and Afghanistan	Promises to bring the War in Iraq to a responsible end. Declares that the War in Afghanistan and the fight against the Taliban should be the nation's top military priority.	Says that the waging of war—and the achieving of peace—should never be micromanaged in a party platform. Calls for increasing troop strength in Afghanistan
Israel	Declares that under all circumstances that the United States must ensure that Israel enjoys a qualitative edge for its national security and its right to self-defense.	Declares support for Israel and pledges that the United States will ensure that Israel enjoy a qualitative edge in defense technologies over any potential adversaries.

Issue	Democratic Position	Republican Position
Energy	Declares the United States must reduce oil consumption by 35 percent by 2030. Says that the government should provide incentives to increase domestic production of clean and renewable energy. Calls for more fuel efficient automobiles.	Calls for increasing energy development in the United States in an environmentally responsible way, including drilling in the Artic National Wildlife Refuge (ANWR), on federal lands in the western United States, and offshore. Supports the construction of new nuclear power plants as well as alternative sources of energy, such as wind, solar, and geothermal. Advocates the use of free market incentives to promote energy conservation.
Trade	Calls for the inclusion of international labor and environmental standards in trade agreements. Wants to amend the North American Free Trade Agreement (NAFTA).	Supports free trade and open markets because free trade means more American jobs, higher wages, and a better standard of living.
Tax policy	Promises to eliminate income taxes on retirees making less than $50,000 a year. Says that families earning more than $250,000 a year will have to give back some of the tax cuts granted them during the Bush administration. Promises to increase the Earned Income Tax Credit (EITC) with the goal of cutting the poverty rate in half in ten years. Calls for tax simplification.	Favors making the tax cuts enacted during the early years of the Bush administration permanent. Proposes a major reduction in the corporate income tax rate. Calls for giving tax-payers the option of filing under the current tax code or under a two-rate flat-tax alternative.
Budget policy	Supports a pay-as-you-go budget process in which Congress would have to balance any spending increases or tax reductions with equal spending reductions or tax increases.	Calls for the adoption of a Balanced Budget constitutional amendment. Says that additional spending should be offset by reductions in another program. Opposes **earmarks,** which are legislative provision which direct that funds be spent for particular purposes. Advocates a one-year freeze on all non-defense discretionary spending.
Immigration reform	Calls for securing the nation's borders. Promises to improve the legal immigration system. Endorses immigration reform that requires undocumented immigrants who are in good standing to pay a fine, pay taxes, learn English, and then have the opportunity to become citizens.	Declares that border security is essential to national security. Oppose amnesty. Supports English as the official language of the nation. Opposes drivers' licenses and in-state college tuition for illegal aliens.
Labor laws	Promises to raise the minimum wage and index it to the rate of inflation. Calls for expanding the Family and Medical Leave Act so workers can take care of an elderly parent or attend a PTA meeting. Says that workers should be able to earn at least seven paid sick leave days a year.	Supports the right of states to enact **right-to-work laws,** which are statutes that prohibit union membership as a condition of employment.

(Continued)

TABLE 8.1 *(Continued)*

Issue	Democratic Position	Republican Position
Gun control	Promises to preserve the right to own and use firearms, while recognizing the need for reasonable regulation.	Strongly supports the individual right to own and bear arms. Declares that gun control only penalizes law-abiding citizens and is ineffective at preventing crime.
Affirmative action	Supports affirmative action to redress discrimination and achieve diversity in federal contracting and higher education.	Opposes discrimination while rejecting all preferences, quotas, and set-asides based on skin color, ethnicity, or gender.
Abortion	"Strongly and unequivocally supports *Roe v. Wade* and a woman's right to choose a safe and legal abortion, regardless of ability to pay."	Favors a constitutional amendment to prohibit abortion.
Gay and lesbian rights	Endorses federal legislation to prohibit job discrimination based on sexual orientation. Supports "equal responsibility, benefits, and protections" for same-sex couples, but does not mention gay marriage. Declares that all men and women should be allowed to serve in the military without regard for sexual orientation.	Endorses a constitutional amendment to define marriage as between one man and one woman. Opposes legal recognition of same-sex relationships or granting benefits to same-sex couples.

Earmarks
Legislative provision that direct that funds be spent for particular purposes.

penalizes the law abiding without having an impact on crime. Finally, the two parties take similar positions on some issues. Both the Democratic and the Republican platforms declared support for Israel, even using the same phrase to pledge that the United States would ensure that Israel would always have better weapons ("a qualitative edge") than its adversaries.

DIVIDED GOVERNMENT

Divided government The phenomenon of one political party controlling the legislative branch of government while the other holds the executive branch.

Divided government refers to the phenomenon of one political party controlling the legislative branch of government while the other holds the executive branch. Consider the information contained in Table 8.2. During the 24-year period between 1969 and 1993, the Democratic Party controlled both the presidency and Congress for only six years. During the rest of the period, the Republican Party held the White House and the Democrats controlled at least one house of Congress. Political scientists explained divided government by declaring that the Republican Party enjoyed an advantage in presidential elections, whereas the Democrats had become the party of Congress, especially the House of Representatives. The 1992 and 1994 elections turned this explanation on its head when Democrat Bill Clinton broke the Republican lock on the White House (in 1992) and the GOP captured control of both houses of Congress (in 1994). Consequently, political scientists began to look for explanations of divided government in general.

TABLE 8.2   Party Control of Executive and Legislative Branches of American National Government Since 1969

Year	Divided or Unified Control	Party Controlling Executive and Legislative Branches
1969–1977 (eight years)	Divided	Republican president, Democratic Congress
1977–1981 (four years)	Unified	Democratic president, Democratic Congress
1981–1987 (six years)	Divided	Republican president, Democratic House, Republican Senate
1987–1993 (six years)	Divided	Republican president, Democratic Congress
1993–1995 (two years)	Unified	Democratic president, Democratic Congress
1995–2001 (six years)	Divided	Democratic president, Republican Congress
2001–2003 (two years)	Divided	Republican president, Republican House, Democratic Senate*
2003–2007	Unified	Republican president, Republican Congress
2007–2009	Divided	Republican president, Democratic Congress
Since 2009	Unified	Democratic president, Democratic Congress

*After the 2000 election, the Senate was evenly divided between the two parties, and the vote of Republican Vice President Richard Cheney enabled the GOP to claim majority status. In 2001, however, Republican Senator James Jeffords of Vermont switched his party allegiance from Republican to independent to allow the Democrats to claim the majority.

Right-to-work laws Statutes that prohibit union membership as a condition of employment.

 WHAT IS YOUR OPINION?

Do you prefer divided government, or would you rather have both the legislative and executive branches controlled by the same party?

Historical research shows that divided government is not unique to the late twentieth century, although it has become more frequent. The first instances of divided government occurred before the Civil War. In the nineteenth century, 16 of 50 elections produced divided government, with different parties controlling the White House and at least one chamber of Congress.[27] Between 1900 and 1952, 22 elections produced unified government; four resulted in divided government.

Divided government has now become commonplace. Between 1952 and 2008, 12 elections resulted in unified government, while 17 elections produced divided government.[28] Divided government is common at the state level as well.

The Constitution sets the stage for divided government. In a parliamentary system, the national legislature chooses the chief executive (often called a prime minister) by majority vote. Consequently, the party or coalition of parties that controls the legislature also controls the executive. In contrast, the United States has **separation of powers,** which is the division of political power among executive, legislative, and judicial branches of government. Members of Congress and the president are elected independently from one another. They have different constituencies, serve terms of different length, and stand for election at different times. In particular, midterm elections are more likely to produce divided government than presidential election years. With relatively few exceptions, the president's party loses seats in the House in a midterm election. On nine occasions since 1894, midterm elections have produced divided government or added a second chamber to opposition control.[29] In 2006, for example, the Democratic Party won control of Congress,

Separation of powers The division of political power among executive, legislative, and judicial branches of government.

Polling data show that younger voters have been moving toward the Democratic Party and away from the GOP.

producing divided government after a period of unified Republican control. The 2008 election ended divided government because Democrats won control of both the White House and Congress.

Elections for president, Congress, and the Senate usually feature different issues. Whereas candidates for president stress national issues involving foreign policy, defense, and the strength of the nation's economy, candidates for the House of Representatives focus on local issues, such as cleaning up an area waterway or the proposed closure of a regional military base. Local voters may choose the presidential candidate they believe will work the hardest to cut taxes while voting for the candidate for Congress who promises to support increased federal spending in the region.[30]

At any given time, Party A may have an advantage on national issues while Party B is perceived by voters as being stronger on local issues. During the 1980s, presidential elections focused on defense, tax rates, and cultural values—issues that favored the Republicans. In contrast, races for Congress focused on more specific policy concerns, such as protecting Social Security, helping farmers or unemployed workers, and promoting local economic development. These were issues that advantaged Democrats.[31] Divided government reflects the divided issue preferences of Americans. Voters want low inflation, a less obtrusive government, and low taxes—positions associated with the GOP. Voters also want the government to ensure a safe environment, promote education, and protect the integrity of the Social Security and Medicare programs—issues that favor the Democratic Party.[32]

Political scientists disagree as to whether divided government is the result of conscious voter choice. Some research indicates that even though the proportion of voters who split their ticket in order to balance the House with a president of the other party is small, the number is large enough to affect election outcomes.[33] Other research, however, finds that voters who split their tickets in hopes of producing divided control of government are more than offset by people who cast straight tickets in order to minimize gridlock. In other words, strategic voting makes divided government less common, not more common.[34]

CONCLUSION: POLITICAL PARTIES AND PUBLIC POLICY

Political parties are similar to interest groups in that they both connect individuals and groups to the government. The concept of democracy is that government policies reflect the policy preferences of citizens. In large, complex societies such as the United States, political parties are a means whereby individuals and groups can make their policy preferences known to government decision-makers and then hold those officials accountable for the adoption and successful implementation of those policy preferences.

Agenda Building

Political parties help set the policy agenda. Individuals and groups work through political parties to identify problems and raise issues for government action. In recent years, for example, religious conservatives have worked within the Republican Party to call attention to what they see as the moral decay of American society. The GOP has articulated their concerns in its party platform, and Republican candidates and elected officials have raised moral issues during election campaigns and while in office. Similarly, the Democratic Party has been a vehicle to advance the cause of groups and individuals concerned with safeguarding the environment, advancing the cause of minority rights, and protecting abortion rights.

Policy Formulation and Adoption

Political parties play an important role in policy formulation and adoption. Parties not only raise issues, but they develop policy solutions to address the problems they identify. For example, the 2000 Republican Party platform included an outline of a tax cut proposal that eventually became the Economic Growth and Tax Reconciliation Act, which became law in 2001 after Republicans captured the White House and won control of both houses of Congress. In Congress, Democrats and Republicans meet in separate groups to formulate policy proposals and plan strategy for their adoption. The passage of the Economic Growth and Tax Reconciliation Act in 2001 represented a victory for Republicans in Congress over the organized opposition of the congressional Democrats.

Although political parties do not directly adopt policies, they facilitate policy adoption by bridging the separation of powers between the legislative and executive branches. The president works with fellow party members in Congress to pass legislation they support or defeat legislation favored by the other party. President George W. Bush worked closely with Republican congressional leaders in Congress to pass his

GETTING INVOLVED

Party Politics at the Grassroots

Political parties are organized along the lines of the federal system, with national, state, and local structures. The latter are responsible for building grassroots support for candidates and getting out the vote on Election Day. Depending on the size of your community and the nature of party competition in your state, one or more political parties may be active in your area.

Your assignment is to learn about the organization and activities of a political party in your area by visiting its local office. Use the business pages of the telephone directory or an Internet search engine to locate the local offices of the Democratic, Republican, Libertarian, or Green Party in your area. After you identify a local party office, call to learn its location and hours of operation so you can visit. When you arrive at the office, chat with the office staff, ask questions, collect any literature that might be available, and observe the layout. Do

your best to learn the answers to the following research questions:

- What does the local party office do?
- Had you been a potential volunteer, ready to get involved in party activities, would the local party have been able to take advantage of your energy? Did you feel welcome?
- Was the office well supplied with literature and information about party officeholders, candidates, and issue positions?
- Would you describe the office as well organized or disorganized? Why?

Once you return from your visit, write a short essay describing your experience at the local party office. Discuss the answers to the questions. Conclude the essay with your personal evaluation of the activity. Be sure to use correct grammar.

tax cut proposal, making compromises when necessary to ensure majority support. In the end, the measure won unanimous Republican support and the votes of a few Democrats, mostly members of Congress from states and districts that voted for Bush in the 2000 presidential election.

Political parties play an especially important role in America's separation of powers system because they reduce the number of political actors necessary to achieve policy compromises. Without political parties, congressional leaders would have to negotiate with dozens, perhaps hundreds, of members of the House and Senate in order to build majority support for policy proposals. In practice, the party leadership in each chamber, along with the White House, negotiates policy compromises on the final version of major legislation.[35]

Policy Implementation and Evaluation

Political parties participate indirectly in policy implementation. Presidential appointees are responsible for administering the agencies and departments of the executive branch of government. Most of the men and women that presidents select as department heads and agency administrators are fellow party members. Appointed executive branch officials typically bring their partisan perspectives with them to the task of policy implementation. For example, Democratic presidents typically appoint administrators to head the Environmental Protection Agency (EPA) who have a background in environmental activism with the Sierra Club or other environmental organizations. They are committed to aggressively enforcing the nation's environmental laws. In contrast, EPA administrators appointed by Republican presidents usually come from an industry background. They approach enforcement from the perspective of working with business and industry to achieve voluntary compliance with the law whenever possible.

Governing party
The political party or party coalition holding the reins of government in a democracy.

Political parties play a key role in policy evaluation. Every democracy in the world has at least two political parties. The political party or party coalition holding the reins of government in a democracy is the **governing party.** It plays the most important role in policy adoption and implementation. The political party out of power in a democracy is the **opposition party.** The opposition party criticizes the policies of the governing party and offers alternatives. The opposition party ensures that citizens receive more information about government policies and programs than the official statements of government leaders. The opposition party has an incentive to highlight failures and seek out inefficiency and corruption. The opposition also presents alternative policies and offers its leaders to the voters at the next election. Opposition parties help make democracy work by providing information to citizens and offering voters alternative policies and alternative sets of leaders to those put forward by the governing party.

Opposition party
The political party out of power in a democracy.

KEY TERMS

access

conservatism

divided government

earmarks

electoral college

exit polls

gender gap

governing party

Grand Old Party (GOP)

liberalism

multiparty system

opposition party

party era

party platform

party realignment

plurality election system

political party

proportional representation (PR)

right-to-work laws

separation of powers

third party

two-party system

NOTES

1. Maurice Duverger, *Political Parties* (New York: Wiley, 1954), p. 217.
2. A. James Reichley, "The Future of the American Two-Party System at the Beginning of a New Century," in John C. Green and Rick Farmer, eds., *The State of the Parties: The Changing Role of Contemporary American Parties,* 4th ed. (Lanham, MD: Rowman & Littlefield, 2003), pp. 20–21.
3. Michael Toner, "The Impact of the New Campaign Finance Law on the 2004 Presidential Election," in Larry Sabato, ed., *Divided States of America: The Slash and Burn Politics of the 2004 Presidential Election* (New York: Pearson Longman, 2006), p. 197.
4. Timothy P. Nokken, "Ideological Congruence versus Electoral Success: Distribution of Party Organization Contributions in Senate Elections, 1990–2000," *American Politics Research* 31 (January 2003): 3–26.
5. "Bush Approval Static, Congress' Sinks Further," Gallup, March 14, 2008, available at www.gallup.com.
6. Samuel Merrill III, Bernard Grofman, and Thomas L. Brunell, "Cycles in American National Electoral Politics, 1854–2006: Statistical Evidence and an Explanatory Model," *American Political Science Review* 102 (February 2008): 1–17.
7. Pew Center for the People & the Press, "Fewer Voters Identify as Republicans," March 20, 2008, available at http://perresearch.org.

8. Dan Balz and Jon Cohen, "A Political Force with Many Philosophies," *Washington Post*, July 1, 2007, available at www.washingtonpost.com.

9. Pew Center for the People & the Press, "Fewer Voters Identify as Republicans."

10. Exit poll data, available at www.cnn.com.

11. Ibid.

12. Juan Castillo, "Latinos Deliver on Poetential, Turn Out Big for Obama," *Austin American-Statesman*, November 6, 2008, available at www.statesman.com.

13. David L. Leal, Stephan A. Nuño, Jongho Lee, and Rodolpho O. de la Garza, "Latinos, Immigration, and the 2006 Midterm Election," *PS: Political Science & Politics*, April 2008, p. 312.

14. Exit poll data.

15. Ibid.

16. Ibid.

17. Ibid.

18. Ibid.

19. Exit poll data.

20. Morris P. Fiorina, *Culture War? The Myth of a Polarized America*, 2nd ed. (New York, NY: Pearson Education, 2006), pp. 61–70.

21. Jongho Lee and Harry P. Pachon, "Leading the Way: An Analysis of the Effect of Religion on the Latino Vote," *American Politics Research* 35 (March 2007): 252–272.

22. John C. Green, Lyman A. Kellstedt, Corwin E. Smidt, and James L. Guth, "How the Faithful Voted: Religious Communities and the Presidential Vote," in David E. Campbell, ed., *A Matter of Faith: Religion in the 2004 Presidential Election* (Washington, DC: Brookings Institution Press, 2007), pp. 1–28.

23. Exit poll data.

24. Frank Newport, "Church Attendance and Party Identification," Gallup News Service, May 18, 2005, available at www.gallup.com.

25. Exit poll data.

26. Ibid.

27. Joel H. Silbey, "Divided Government in Historical Perspective, 1789–1996," in Peter F. Golderisi, ed., *Divided Government: Change, Uncertainty, and the Constitutional Order* (Lanham, MD: Rowman & Littlefield, 1996), pp. 9–34.

28. Morris Fiorina, *Divided Government*, 2nd ed. (Cambridge, MA: Harvard University Press, 1996), p. 7.

29. Andrew E. Busch, *Horses in Midstream: U.S. Midterm Elections and Their Consequences, 1894–1998* (Pittsburgh: University of Pittsburgh Press, 1999), pp. 15–22.

30. John R. Petrocik and Joseph Doherty, "The Road to Divided Government: Paved Without Intention," in Golderisi, ed., *Divided Government: Change, Uncertainty, and the Constitutional Order*, p. 105.

31. Gary C. Jacobson, "The Persistence of Democratic House Majorities," in Gary W. Cox and Samuel Kernell, eds., *The Politics of Divided Government* (Boulder, CO: Westview, 1991), pp. 57–84.

32. Gary C. Jacobson, "Divided Government and the 1994 Elections," in Golderisi, ed., *Divided Government: Change, Uncertainty, and the Constitutional Order*, p. 62.

33. Walter R. Mebane, Jr., "Combination, Moderation, and Institutional Balancing in American Presidential Elections," *American Political Science Review* 94 (March 2000): 37–57.

34. Michael Peress, "Strategic Voting in Multi-Office Elections," *Legislative Studies Quarterly* 33 (November 2008): 619–640.

35. Richard D. Forgette, *Congress, Parties, and Puzzles: Politics as a Team Sport* (New York: Peter Lang, 2004), p. 176.

Chapter 9

Elections

CHAPTER OUTLINE

LEARNING OUTCOMES

After studying Chapter 9, students should be able to do the following:

- Assess the historic significance of the 2008 Democratic presidential nomination race. (p. 200)
- Identify the various types of elections held in the United States. (pp. 200–201)
- Compare and contrast at-large and district election systems. (pp. 202–203)
- Describe the impact of one-person, one-vote on representation and policy. (pp. 203–204)
- Describe the impact of the Voting Rights Act (VRA) on the redistricting process and representation. (pp. 204–206)

- Describe and discuss the role of money in election campaigns, considering the cost of campaigns, how money is used in campaigns, the sources of money, and campaign finance regulations. (pp. 206–210)
- Identify the goals of an election campaign and the approaches candidates take to achieving those goals. (pp. 210–212)
- Compare and contrast elections for the U.S. House and U.S. Senate. (pp. 213–216)
- Describe the process through which delegates to the national party conventions are chosen and the changes that have taken place in that process since the early 1960s. (pp. 216–221)

▶ Identify and discuss the stages of the presidential nomination process, using Obama-Clinton as an example. (pp. 221–225)

▶ Evaluate the 2008 vice presidential selections, considering how closely each vice presidential choice fit the traditional criteria of ticket balancing. (pp. 225–226)

▶ Explain the electoral college system, and evaluate its role in presidential elections. (pp. 226–231)

▶ Compare and contrast the role of base voters and swing voters in an election. (pp. 231–235)

▶ Describe the effect of each of the following factors on voter choice: party identification, issues, personal qualities and image, campaigns, and retrospective and prospective voting. (pp. 236–237)

▶ Describe the role of elections in the policymaking process. (pp. 237–240)

▶ Define the key terms listed on page 240 and explain their significance.

The race for the 2008 Democratic presidential nomination was historic. Although several well-known party leaders launched presidential bids, the field soon narrowed to two contenders attempting to make history—Illinois Senator Barack Obama and New York Senator Hillary Clinton. The son of a white woman from Kansas and a black immigrant from Kenya, Obama hoped to become America's first African American president. Clinton, the wife of former President Bill Clinton, would be the nation's first woman president.

The contest between Obama and Clinton was notable for its duration and closeness. In 2000 and 2004, the Democratic Party had identified a nominee before the end of March. With the 2008 nomination schedule more frontloaded than ever before, most observers expected that one candidate would have the nomination wrapped up no later than the end of February. Nonetheless, neither Obama nor Clinton was able to pull away from the other until early June, when Obama finally captured enough delegates to claim the nomination. Furthermore, the margin of victory was quite narrow—fewer than 200 delegates separated the two candidates of more than 4,000 total delegates.

This chapter on elections is the last in a series of chapters addressing the political background of policymaking in America. Chapters 4, 5, 6, 7, and 8 dealt with public opinion, participation, the media, interest groups, and political parties, respectively. This chapter focuses on elections, considering types of elections, election districts and redistricting, political campaigns, congressional elections, presidential elections, the factors that influence voter choice, and the relationship between elections and public policy.

TYPES OF ELECTIONS

Americans have the opportunity to cast ballots in several types of elections. A **general election** is an election to fill state and national offices held in November of even-numbered years. Voters choose among Democratic and Republican candidates

General election
An election to fill state and national offices held in November of even-numbered years.

Split ticket ballot
Voters casting their ballots for the candidates of two or more political parties.

Straight ticket ballot Voters selecting the entire slate of candidates of one party only.

Runoff An election between the two candidates receiving the most votes when no candidate got a majority in an initial election.

Primary election An election held to determine a party's nominees for the general election ballot.

Closed primary An election system that limits primary election participation to registered party members.

Open primary An election system that allows voters to pick the party primary of their choice without regard to their party affiliation.

and sometimes third-party candidates and independent candidates not affiliated with any political party.

General election voters may cast a split ticket or a straight ticket ballot. A **split ticket ballot** involves voters casting their ballots for the candidates of two or more political parties. In contrast, a **straight ticket ballot** refers to voters selecting the entire slate of candidates of one party only. Ticket splitting was once more common than it is today. In 1972, 30 percent of voters chose presidential and congressional candidates from different political parties, whereas only 17 percent of voters split their tickets in 2004.[1] Political scientists believe that ticket splitting has diminished because the parties are more ideologically polarized than they were in the 1970s, especially in the South. Conservative white voters in the South once voted Republican for president while casting their ballots for conservative Democrats for Congress. Today, they vote Republican for both offices.[2]

Most general elections are plurality elections. In every state but Georgia, the candidate with the most votes wins the general election, regardless of whether the candidate has a majority of ballots cast. Georgia requires a **runoff,** which is an election between the two candidates receiving the most votes when no candidate won a majority in an initial election.

In most states, major parties choose their general election candidates in primary elections scheduled a month or more before the November general election. A **primary election** is an election held to determine a party's nominees for the general election ballot. Democrats compete against other Democrats; Republicans compete against Republicans. In a number of states, a candidate must achieve a certain threshold level of support at a state party convention in order to qualify for the primary ballot. The candidate with the most votes wins the primary election in most states, regardless of whether the candidate has a majority. Some states, including most southern states, require a runoff between the top two candidates if no one receives a majority in the first vote.

Some states conduct closed primaries, whereas other states hold open primaries. A **closed primary** is an election system that limits primary election participation to registered party members. Only registered Republicans can compete in the GOP primary; participants in the Democratic primary must be registered Democrats. In contrast, an **open primary** is an election system that allows voters to pick the party primary of their choice without regard to their party affiliation.

Louisiana selects state and local officials by means of a **blanket primary,** which is a primary election system that allows voters to select candidates without regard for party affiliation. If no candidate receives a majority in the primary, the two leading candidates face each other in the general election regardless of party affiliation. A few states use the blanket primary for local offices only and a number of states, including Washington and Oregon, are considering its adoption for all state elections.

Republican Bobby Jindal became governor of Louisiana in 2007, taking 54 percent of the blanket primary vote to win a four-way race without a runoff.

ELECTION DISTRICTS AND REDISTRICTING

Blanket primary
A primary election system that allows voters to select candidates without regard for party affiliation.

American voters select public officials in a combination of at-large and district elections. An **at-large election** is a method for choosing public officials in which the citizens of an entire political subdivision, such as a state, vote to select officeholders. U.S. senators, state governors, and other state executive branch officials are elected at-large in statewide elections. States that are so sparsely populated that they have only one representative in the U.S. House of Representatives (such as Alaska, Delaware, and Wyoming) choose their member of Congress in statewide at-large elections as well.

A **district election** is a method for choosing public officials that divides a political subdivision, such as a state, into geographic areas called districts and each district elects one official. States with more than one U.S. representative choose their members of Congress from districts. Michigan, for example, with 15 members in the U.S. House, has 15 U.S. congressional districts, each of which elects one representative. The members of state legislatures are also chosen in district elections.

Reapportionment

Legislative district boundaries must be redrawn every ten years after the national census is taken. Census data are used for apportioning the 435 seats of the U.S. House of Representatives among the states. **Apportionment** is the allocation of legislative seats among the states. States that have grown rapidly since the last census gain seats in the House, whereas slowly growing states lose representation. After the 2000 Census, nine states lost one or more seats in the House, whereas eight states gained one or more seats. New York, which lost two House seats, had to shuffle district boundaries to reduce the number of congressional districts in the state from 31 to 29. In contrast, Florida, which gained two seats, increased the number of its House districts from 23 to 25.

Legislative districts must also be redrawn because of population movement within a state. **Redistricting** is the process through which the boundaries of legislative districts are redrawn to reflect population movement. During the first half of the twentieth century, a number of states failed to redistrict despite dramatic population movement from rural to urban areas because rural state legislators did not want to relinquish control. As a result, the population size of some legislative districts varied dramatically. In Illinois, one U.S. congressional district in Chicago had a population of 914,053 by the early 1960s, whereas another district in rural southern Illinois contained only 112,116 people.[3]

The U.S. Supreme Court dealt with the issue of legislative reapportionment in a series of cases, the most important of which were *Baker v. Carr* (1962) and *Wesberry v. Sanders* (1964).[4] **Reapportionment** is the reallocation of legislative seats. In these and other cases, the Supreme Court established the doctrine of **one person, one vote,** which is the judicial ruling that the Equal Protection Clause of the Fourteenth Amendment to the U.S. Constitution requires that legislative districts be apportioned on the basis of population. The Supreme Court has also stipulated that legislative district boundaries be drawn to ensure nearly equal population size. Although the Court allows some leeway in state legislative and local district size, it requires that U.S. congressional districts contain almost exactly the same number of people. In 2002, for example, a federal court overturned Pennsylvania's redistricting plan because two U.S. House districts varied in size by 19 people—646,361 compared with 646,380.[5]

The Court's one-person, one-vote decisions have affected legislative representation and policy. When the rulings were first implemented in the 1960s, rural areas lost representation, whereas the nation's big cities gained seats. As a result, urban problems, such as housing, education, unemployment, transportation, and race relations took center stage on legislative agendas. Congress and many state legislatures became more liberal.[6] The distribution of public funds changed as well. Counties that were overrepresented before redistricting in the 1960s received relatively more government funds per person than they deserved on the basis of their population, whereas areas that were underrepresented received fewer government dollars per capita than their population size would dictate. After redistricting, the distribution of government funds changed to conform closely to relative population size. Nationwide, the effect of redistricting was to shift $7 billion of public funds annually from rural to urban areas.[7]

At-large election A method for choosing public officials in which the citizens of an entire political subdivision, such as a state, vote to select officeholders.

District election A method for choosing public officials that divides a political subdivision, such as a state, into geographic areas called districts and each district elects one official.

Apportionment The allocation of legislative seats among the states.

Redistricting The process through which the boundaries of legislative districts are redrawn to reflect population movement.

Reapportionment The reallocation of legislative seats.

One person, one vote The judicial ruling that the Equal Protection Clause of the Fourteenth Amendment to the U.S. Constitution requires that legislative districts be apportioned on the basis of population.

Recent census figures have shown that America's population has shifted away from generally liberal inner cities to more conservative suburbs and surrounding metropolitan areas. This time, redistricting changes have led to fewer representatives from constituencies demanding big government and more representatives from areas where people are wary of government. Congress and many state legislatures have grown more conservative.[8]

Voting Rights Act

Voting Rights Act (VRA) A federal law designed to protect the voting rights of racial and ethnic minorities.

Pre-clearance A requirement of the Voting Rights Act that state and local governments in areas with a history of voting discrimination must submit redistricting plans to the federal Department of Justice for approval *before* they can go into effect.

Majority-minority districts Legislative districts whose population was more than 50 percent African American and Latino.

The **Voting Rights Act (VRA)** is a federal law designed to protect the voting rights of racial and ethnic minorities. The VRA makes it illegal for state and local governments to enact and enforce election rules and procedures that diminish the voting power of racial, ethnic, and language minority groups. Furthermore, the VRA requires state and local governments in areas with a history of voting discrimination to submit redistricting plans to the U.S. Department of Justice for approval *before* they can go into effect. This procedure is known as **pre-clearance.** Congress and the president included the pre-clearance provision in the VRA in order to stay one step ahead of local officials who adopted new discriminatory electoral practice as soon as the federal courts threw out an old procedure. The pre-clearance provision of the VRA only applies to states and parts of states that have substantial racial and language minority populations with relatively low rates of voter participation, including all or part of Alaska, Alabama, Arizona, California, Florida, Georgia, Louisiana, Michigan, Mississippi, New Hampshire, New York, North Carolina, South Carolina, South Dakota, Texas, and Virginia.

In the late 1980s and early 1990s, the Department of Justice in the George H. W. Bush administration interpreted amendments to the VRA adopted in 1982 to require that state legislatures create legislative districts designed to maximize minority representation. In short, the Justice Department declared that if a district *could* be drawn that would likely elect an African American or Latino candidate then it *must* be drawn. State legislatures would have to create the maximum possible number of **majority-minority districts,** which are legislative districts with populations that are more than 50 percent minority.[9]

Why would a Republican administration choose to implement the VRA to increase African American and Latino representation in Congress and state legislatures? After all, most minority lawmakers are Democrats. The reason was simple: The policy also helped the Republican Party gain seats.[10] To construct majority African American and Latino districts, state legislatures redrew district lines to shift minority voters away from adjacent districts into new majority-minority districts. Because most African American and Latino voters are Democrats, the redistricting reduced Democratic voting strength in surrounding districts, threatening the political survival of some white Democratic members of Congress. The Georgia congressional delegation, for example, went from one African American Democrat, eight white Democrats, and one white Republican before redistricting in 1991 to three African American Democrats and eight white Republicans after the 1994 election. Nationwide, the creation of majority-minority districts after the 1990 Census helped white Republicans pick up about nine seats in Congress, defeating white Democrats who were stripped of some of their minority voter support.[11]

In the mid-1990s, the U.S. Supreme Court overruled the Justice Department's interpretation of the VRA. The Court responded to legal challenges filed against majority-minority districts created in Louisiana, Georgia, and other southern states by ruling that state governments cannot use race as the predominant, overriding factor in drawing district lines unless they have a compelling reason. The Court declared that the goal of maximizing the number of majority-minority districts is not a sufficient reason for race-based redistricting because Congress did not enact the VRA with the intent of forcing states to maximize the number of districts that would elect African American and Latino candidates. The purpose of the VRA was to prevent discrimination.[12] The Court has held that states are free to redistrict as long as the districts they draw do not diminish the political influence of minorities. The VRA does not require states to create additional majority-minority districts in order to increase minority representation.[13] Furthermore, the Court ruled in 2003 that states have the leeway to create "coalitional districts," in which minority voters do not form a numerical majority but are numerous enough so that black and white coalitional voting will give an African American candidate a realistic opportunity to be elected.[14]

In sum, the judicial climate for redistricting under the VRA has changed. After the 1990 Census, states acted under the assumption that they had to maximize the number of legislative districts that would elect African American and Latino candidates. State redistricting after the 2000 Census worked under the guidance of Supreme Court decisions interpreting the VRA to prohibit discrimination but not to require state legislatures to create majority-minority districts. In fact, the Supreme Court had held that a legislature could not consider race in creating districts unless it had a compelling reason. Finally, after the 2010 Census, states will have the freedom to create coalitional districts instead of majority-minority districts if they wish.[15]

 WHAT IS YOUR OPINION?

Are people who voted against (or for) Barack Obama because he is African American racist?

Gerrymandering

Redistricting can be used to advance the interests of a political party or a particular individual. In fact, the practice is so common that there is a word for it, **gerrymandering,** which is the drawing of legislative district lines for political advantage. The term dates from early-nineteenth-century Massachusetts when Governor Elbridge Gerry was behind the creation of a district that observers said resembled a salamander, hence the term Gerry-*mander*.

Political science research shows that gerrymandering can have an important but not overwhelming effect on election outcomes. A political party with complete control of the redistricting process can put itself in position to increase its representation in the U.S. House by about 6 percent. It can also protect between 17 and 25 percent of its incumbents from significant challenges from the other party.[16] After the 2000 redistricting, the number of congressional districts that were competitive between the two major political parties declined significantly.[17] Nonetheless, the impact of gerrymandering is short-lived, disappearing after two or three elections.[18]

The federal courts have been more tolerant of political gerrymandering than they have efforts to draw districts to increase minority representation in Congress. The U.S. Supreme Court has held that partisan gerrymandering is unconstitutional if it can be demonstrated that the "electoral system is arranged in such a manner that will consistently degrade a . . . group of voters' influence on the political process as a whole."[19] In practice, however, this standard is so high that it has never been satisfied. The U.S. Supreme Court has yet to find a political gerrymander unconstitutional.[20]

Mid-Cycle Redistricting

Mid-cycle redistricting The practice of redrawing legislative districts outside the regular redistricting cycle in order to gain political advantage.

The latest redistricting controversy involves **mid-cycle redistricting,** which is the practice of redrawing legislative districts outside the regular redistricting cycle in order to gain political advantage. In 2003, Colorado and Texas adopted new redistricting schemes to replace legal redistricting plans already in place that had been used in the previous year's election. In Colorado, the Republican-controlled legislature and the Republican governor changed the boundaries of the state's Seventh Congressional District in order to help GOP Congressman Bob Beauprez win reelection. In 2002, Beauprez defeated his Democratic opponent by fewer than 300 votes. Meanwhile in Texas, the Republican legislature and the Republican governor redistricted in hopes of changing the ratio of the Texas congressional delegation from a 17 to 15 Democratic advantage to a 22 to 10 Republican majority. Although the Colorado Supreme Court overturned the Colorado mid-cycle redistricting plan as a violation of the Colorado Constitution, the Texas plan survived, helping the Republicans pick up five congressional seats in the 2004 election.

ELECTION CAMPAIGNS

Election campaign An attempt to get information to voters that will persuade them to elect a candidate or not elect an opponent.

An **election campaign** is an attempt to get information to voters that will persuade them to elect a candidate or not elect an opponent. Although many local election contests are modest affairs, presidential campaigns, statewide races, local elections in big cities, and many elections for Congress and state legislatures feature professional campaign consultants, sophisticated organizations, and big money.

The Role of Money

Money is the most controversial feature of American electoral politics.

The Cost of Campaigns   Election campaigns cost money. In 2008, Barack Obama and John McCain raised and spent more than $1 billion in their race for the White House, with Obama raising almost twice as much as his Republican opponent. Races for Congress are expensive as well. In 2006, the average winning candidate for a seat in the U.S. House spent nearly $1.3 million. The cost of Senate races varied, depending on the size of the state. Running for office is far more expensive in a large urban state with multiple media markets than it is in a small rural state without a major media market. In 2006, major-party Senate candidates averaged $8 million in campaign spending.[21]

Money is a campaign necessity, but it does not guarantee success. In 2006, incumbent members of the House who won reelection outspent their opponent by an average $1.2 million to $300,000. Similarly, Senate incumbents who won reelection spent more than twice as much as their losing challengers, $9.3 million compared with $4.2 million. Nonetheless, money alone does not ensure victory. In 2006, the U.S. Senate candidates who raised and spent the most money were Democrat Hillary Clinton of New York ($41 million), Republican Rick Santorum of Pennsylvania ($28 million), Republican James Talent of Missouri ($24 million), and Democrat Ned Lamont of Connecticut ($21 million).[22] Clinton won her race, but the others lost.

Critics charge that campaigns are too expensive. Many potential candidates for office choose not to run because they do not think they can raise the necessary funds. Incumbents, meanwhile, must devote an inordinate amount of time to fundraising. The critics of the current campaign funding system worry that public officials will make policy decisions with an eye to pleasing contributors rather than serving the policy interests of ordinary constituents.

In contrast, some policymakers believe that election campaigns are not especially expensive, at least not compared with commercial advertising campaigns. Procter & Gamble, ExxonMobil, McDonalds, and other retail advertisers spend more money to promote their products than candidates spend informing voters. Citizens need more information to make intelligent choices at the ballot box, they say, not less. The problem with campaign spending is not the total amount of money spent but the disparity in resources among candidates. These policymakers favor reforming the campaign finance system to make it easier for candidates and parties to raise and spend money. Then, voters will have more information on which to base their choices. An analysis of the campaigns for the U.S. House suggests that campaign spending enhances the quality of democracy. The study finds that campaign spending increases voter knowledge, improves the ability of the public to accurately identify the issue positions of the candidates, and increases voter interest in the campaign.[23]

Many observers believe that the media and the general public exaggerate the importance of money in the policy process. Money alone does not determine election results nor does it dictate policy outcomes. Political parties, the media, experts, elected and appointed officials, public opinion, individual policy entrepreneurs, and interest groups (both well-funded and poorly funded) all play a role. To be sure, money matters, but it would be a mistake, they say, to believe that it dominates everything. Furthermore, the number of individuals and groups who contribute to campaigns is so large that the influence of individual contributors is diluted.

The Campaign Budget   The largest item in most campaign budgets is advertising, particularly television. The cost of advertising time varies greatly, depending on the market and the medium. Television, especially network television during primetime, is the most expensive. Cable television, radio, and newspapers are less costly. Advertising in larger markets, such as New York City or Los Angeles, is substantially more expensive than advertising in smaller markets, such as Baton Rouge, Louisiana, or Albuquerque, New Mexico. Running a serious political campaign in a populous state with several major media markets is many times more costly than running a campaign in a less populous state without a major media market.

Political campaigns have expenses other than advertising. Campaigns have offices with telephone banks, computers, fax machines, furniture, supplies, and utility costs. Campaigns hire consultants and employ professionals for fundraising, event coordination, media relations, Internet connection, and volunteer coordination. In 2000, the George W. Bush presidential campaign rented 34 offices and employed a full-time staff of 175.[24] Candidates for president or statewide office also spend a good deal of money for travel. Fundraising itself is a campaign expense. In 2004, the Bush campaign spent $50 million on fundraising, $1 for every $4.87 raised.[25]

Sources of Campaign Money   Wealthy individuals sometimes finance their own election campaigns. In 2008, Jared Polis ($6 million) of Colorado, Sandy Treadwell of New York ($6 million), and Doug Ose ($5 million) of California headed a list of 16 candidates for the U.S. House or Senate who invested at least $1 million of personal funds in an attempt to win elective office. Polis won, but the other two lost, as did all but 4 of the 16 big-spending candidates.[26] Self-financing is usually a sign of weakness because candidates with enough support to win office can raise money for their campaigns.

Candidates who are not wealthy enough to bankroll their own campaigns (or who choose to hold onto their money) must rely on others to finance their election efforts. Individual campaign contributors are the most important overall source of campaign cash, accounting for 54 percent of total receipts for U.S. House and Senate candidates and 75 percent of the money raised by the two major-party presidential candidates in 2008, not counting federal funds.[27] Candidates raise money from individuals through direct solicitations, usually on the telephone or at fundraising dinners or receptions; by means of direct mail; and over the Internet. Candidates spend hours on the phone calling wealthy supporters asking for the maximum contribution under federal law, which in 2008 was $2,300 per individual contributor.

George W. Bush developed a sophisticated system for raising money from individuals that netted millions of dollars for his two presidential campaigns. In 2000, more than 500 Bush supporters called Pioneers (mostly wealthy energy company officials, lobbyists, and corporate executives) raised $100,000 each in individual contributions up to $1,000, which was, at the time, the maximum amount an individual could give.[28] Each of the Pioneers tapped at least 100 people for contributions and earmarked their contribution checks with a special identification code in order to get credit. The Bush campaign rewarded Pioneers with special receptions and individual meetings with the candidate. Subsequently, President Bush appointed at least 19 of the Pioneers as ambassadors to other countries.[29] In 2004, with the contribution limit raised to $2,000 a person, the Bush campaign created a second category of fundraisers called Rangers, who agreed to raise at least $200,000 for the president's reelection.

Direct mail is another important fundraising tool. Typically, Candidate A sends a long, detailed letter to supporters warning of dire consequences if the other candidate wins the election. The only way to prevent the calamity and save the country, the letter declares, is to contribute money to Candidate A by writing a check today and inserting it in the return envelope included in the mailing. Direct mail is an expensive fundraising tool because it takes time and money to develop an address list of people who are likely to respond positively to appeals for campaign money. Mailing expenses are costly as well. Nonetheless, direct mail can be effective. For years, the

Political Action Committee (PAC) An organization created to raise and distribute money in election campaigns.

Bipartisan Campaign Reform Act (BCRA) A campaign finance reform law designed to limit the political influence of big money campaign contributors.

Soft money The name given to funds that are raised by political parties that are not subject to federal campaign finance regulations.

Hard money Funds that are raised subject to federal campaign contribution and expenditure limitations.

Independent expenditures Money spent in support of a candidate but not coordinated with the candidate's campaign.

527 Committees Organizations created by individuals and groups to influence the outcomes of elections by raising and spending money that candidates and political parties raise and spend legally.

Republican Party held a fundraising advantage over the Democrats because it had a more sophisticated direct mail operation.

The Internet is the latest innovation in campaign fundraising. Campaigns create a sharp-looking website designed to attach the attention of supporters who can donate online with a credit card and a few mouse clicks. The advantage of Internet fundraising is that it is relatively inexpensive, especially compared with direct mail. Campaigns can send e-mail again and again to supporters, giving them campaign updates and asking for funds at virtually no expense.[30] In 2008, the Obama campaign raised millions of dollars in online contributions, mostly from people giving relatively small amounts.

Interest groups give money directly to candidates through **political action committees (PACs),** which are organizations created to raise and distribute money in election campaigns. PACs are an important source of funds in races for the U.S. House, accounting for more than a third of the total money raised by House candidates. In contrast, PACs gave relatively little money directly to Senate or presidential candidates.[31] Federal law limits the amount of money a PAC can give a candidate for federal office to $5,000 for each election.

The role of political parties in campaign fundraising has changed because of the adoption of the **Bipartisan Campaign Reform Act (BCRA)** of 2002, which is a campaign finance reform law designed to limit the political influence of big money campaign contributors. The BCRA, which is also know as McCain-Feingold after its two Senate sponsors, Senator John McCain and Senator Russ Feingold, prohibited political parties from raising **soft money,** which is the name given to funds that are raised by political parties that are not subject to federal campaign finance regulations. Before the adoption of the BCRA, parties raised hundreds of millions of dollars in unregulated large contributions from individuals, corporations, and unions. The BCRA prohibited parties from raising soft money beginning with the 2004 election, forcing them to rely on **hard money,** which are funds that are raised subject to federal campaign contribution and expenditure limitations.[32]

Political parties support their candidates primarily with **independent expenditures,** which is money spent in support of a candidate but not coordinated with the candidate's campaign. Although parties can contribute a limited amount of money directly to candidates, they can make unlimited independent expenditures. Parties also back candidates by providing them with polling data and conducting get-out-the-vote efforts.

Much of the millions of dollars in soft money contributions that once went to political parties now goes to **527 committees,** which are organizations created by individuals and groups to influence the outcomes of elections by raising and spending money that candidates and political parties cannot legally raise. As long as 527 committees operate independently of political campaigns and stop short of explicitly calling for a candidate's election or defeat, they can raise and spend unlimited amounts of unregulated soft money. In the 2004 presidential campaign, 527 committees raised and spent millions of dollars to support one side or the other. MoveOn.org, America Coming Together, and the Media Fund were 527 committees that helped the Democrats by registering voters, organizing activists, and purchasing political advertisements designed to defeat Bush and elect Kerry. In the meantime, Progress for America Voter Fund and Swift Boat Veterans for Truth were 527 committees that worked to defeat Kerry and reelect the president. In particular, the Swift Boat Veterans for Truth undermined Kerry's status as a decorated war hero with advertisements attacking Kerry's service in Vietnam. Because the 527 committees did not explicitly coordinate their work with either political party or presidential campaign, they claimed that the BCRA did not apply to them.[33]

Federal funds are an important source of campaign money for candidates for president. Although some reformers favor government funding for congressional elections, money is currently available only for presidential races. We discuss presidential campaign funding in more detail later in the chapter.

Campaign Organization and Strategy

Big-time campaigns are long, drawn-out affairs. Challengers begin planning and organizing their campaigns years before the election. Incumbents, meanwhile, never really quit campaigning. Many observers believe that American politics now features constant election campaigns because newly elected officeholders start work on their reelection the day they take the oath of office.

Campaigns start early because much has to be done. Candidates spend the early months of the race raising money, building an organization, seeking group endorsements, and planning strategy. One of the first tasks of a campaign is to prepare the candidate. This often means outfitting the candidate with a new wardrobe, a new hairstyle, and a slimmer waistline. Some critics of George W. Bush believe that he purchased his ranch in Crawford, Texas, in 1999 because it would provide an attractive backdrop for television reports on the candidate during the 2000 presidential election campaign. It would also help him project an image as a regular guy rather than the privileged son of a famous family who graduated from Harvard and Yale. Candidates also memorize a basic speech and rehearse answers to questions reporters might ask.

Many factors shape the course of a campaign and influence strategy, including the type of office at stake, the nature of the constituency, the personalities and images of the candidates, the issues that concern the electorate, and whether one of the candidates is an incumbent seeking reelection. Incumbents generally use a different campaign strategy than do challengers seeking to unseat incumbents. Presidents running for reelection often employ a **rose garden strategy,** which is a campaign approach in which an incumbent president attempts to appear presidential rather than political. The president holds press conferences, meets foreign heads of state, makes "nonpolitical" trips to dedicate public works projects, and announces the awarding of federal grants for projects in closely fought cities and states.

Rose garden strategy A campaign approach in which an incumbent president attempts to appear presidential rather than political.

An important goal for many campaigns is to improve the candidate's name recognition, especially if the candidate is not an incumbent. Citizens generally will not vote for someone with whom they are unfamiliar. Races for less visible offices may never move beyond the name-recognition stage. It helps if voters are already familiar with the candidate. Tom Osborne easily won a seat in Congress from Nebraska after retiring from a long and successful career as the head football coach at the University of Nebraska.

Besides building name recognition, campaigns attempt to create a favorable image of the candidate. Candidates air campaign advertisements that stress their qualifications for the office and associate the candidate with popular themes and

Movie actor Arnold Schwarzenegger enjoyed near universal name recognition before he decided to run for governor of California.

images. In 2008, for example, Senator McCain used his personal history as a prisoner of war in Vietnam as evidence that he was strong enough to be an effective commander-in-chief. Obama's image as an energetic relatively young man helped reinforce his message of change and reform.

Campaigns try to create an unfavorable impression of the opponent. Negative campaigning is nothing new in American politics. Thomas Jefferson's enemies denounced him as the anti-Christ. Opponents accused President Grover Cleveland of beating his wife and fathering an illegitimate child. Critics attacked Theodore Roosevelt as a drunkard and a drug addict. In 1950, George Smathers defeated Senator Claude Pepper in Florida by calling Pepper "a shameless EXTROVERT" who has "a sister who was once a THESPIAN."[34] (If your dictionary is not handy, an *extrovert* is someone who is outgoing and a *thespian* is an actor or actress.)

Research is mixed on the effectiveness of negative campaigning. Sometimes it works, but sometimes it backfires. In general, negative campaigning is a more effective strategy for challengers than it is for incumbents, who are more successful with a positive campaign. Nonetheless, incumbents are often able to effectively counter a challenger's attacks. Political scientists find no evidence that personal attacks or attacks that distort the record are effective.[35] Political scientists also disagree as to whether negative campaign advertisements affect voter turnout. Some political scientists believe that negative campaign advertising diminishes the turnout of independents and people with weak ties to political parties. Negative advertisements make the public disenchanted with both candidates, they say, causing supporters of both sides to stay home.[36] In contrast, other scholars think that negative campaign accusations may actually engage voters in a campaign and increase turnout.[37] Some analysts even believe that negative campaigns are good for democracy because they inform the public about important issues and concerns.[38]

Early in a campaign, candidates work to build name identification and establish their credibility by producing a message that is primarily positive. As the election approaches, candidates who trail in the polls often decide that positive advertising alone will not close the gap with their opponents, so they go on the attack in hopes of undermining their opponent's support.[39] Incumbents sometimes launch attach ad campaigns against their challengers early in the election season in hopes of giving voters a negative image of the challenger before the challenger has a chance to establish a positive identification. Candidates who suffer attack are likely to respond in kind because they know that voters presume that an unanswered attack is true.[40]

Campaign advertising increases citizen knowledge of issues and candidates, affects voter evaluations of candidates, and increases a candidate's share of the vote.[41] Campaign advertising that is broadcast close to the election has a greater impact than advertising early in the contest. Research shows that advertising has its greatest influence on people who are moderately aware of the campaign. The least politically alert do not get the message, whereas the best informed citizens have already made up their minds.[42]

Most candidates do their best to meet as many voters as possible. They shake hands in front of factory gates, discuss issues at town hall meetings, and wade into the crowd at campaign rallies. Voters like and know more about candidates that they meet in person although people who seek out a particular candidate are disposed to like that candidate already. The effect of the meeting is primarily to reinforce an already established preference.[43]

Election campaigns for major offices are fought on the ground and in the air. Campaign professionals use the term **ground war** to refer to campaign activities featuring direct contact between campaign workers and citizens, such as door-to-door canvassing and personal telephone contacts. In 2008, the Obama and McCain campaigns deployed small armies of volunteers and paid campaign workers to register voters and get out the vote. The Democrats targeted inner-city minority residents, whereas the Republican campaign focused on increasing the turnout of conservative Christian voters. Both parties concentrated their efforts on the **battleground states,** which are swing states in which the relative strength of the two major party presidential candidates is close enough so that either candidate could conceivably carry the state. The **air war** refers to campaign activities that involve the media, including television, radio, and the Internet. In 2008, campaign professionals focused their television advertising on network shows and cable channels that data analyses showed were popular with people most likely to support the candidates of their party.

Ground war Campaign activities featuring direct contact between campaign workers and citizens, such as door-to-door canvassing and personal telephone contacts.

Battleground states Swing states in which the relative strength of the two major party presidential candidates is close enough so that either candidate could conceivably carry the state.

Air war Campaign activities that involve the media, including television, radio, and the Internet.

CONGRESSIONAL ELECTIONS

In America's representative democracy, citizens elect the Congress. Voters choose members of the House from districts to serve two-year terms, except in states that have only one representative, who runs statewide. Senators run statewide for six-year terms. Because Senate terms are staggered, voters elect one-third of the Senate every two years.

House Elections

The most striking feature of elections for the U.S. House of Representatives is that most incumbents are reelected. In 2006, only 25 incumbents were defeated for reelection, three in a primary election and 22 in the general election, for a success rate of 94 percent for those members seeking reelection.[44] Since 1986, more than 95 percent of incumbent representatives seeking reelection have won. Furthermore, many races are not close. In 2008, only 53 House races were decided by a margin of 10 percentage points or less.[45]

Incumbency affords sitting members of Congress a number of electoral advantages. Members of Congress enjoy the benefits of free postage (known as the **franking privilege**), money to staff one or more offices in the district, and an allowance to fund numerous trips home during congressional sessions. Incumbents can also generate free publicity by sending press releases to local media outlets and giving speeches in the district. Consequently, most incumbent House members are much better known than challengers.

Incumbents are almost always better funded than challengers. In 2008, the average House incumbent raised $1.4 million compared with $337,000 for the average challenger.[46] To become known, and hence competitive, challengers need to spend hundreds of thousands of dollars on their campaigns. Most serious candidates for Congress will not run unless they believe they have a realistic chance of winning—and that means raising more than $500,000.[47] Potential challengers who doubt they can raise enough money to be competitive usually decide to wait for another opportunity. Furthermore, incumbent members of Congress try to scare off challengers by raising as much money as they can as early as they can. Most serious challengers are reluctant to run against an incumbent who already has several hundred thousand dollars in the bank.

House incumbents benefit from the tendency of voters to regard House races as local contests. House members running for reelection stress personal qualities and the services they provide their districts. Even though polls show that a majority of Americans often disapprove of the job that Congress as a whole is doing, many incumbent members of Congress enjoy strong approval ratings in their districts.[48] Unless the incumbent is involved in a personal scandal or appears to lose touch with the district, challengers have few grounds on which to base a successful campaign.

Another reason for the high reelection rate for incumbents is that many congressional districts are safe for one party or the other. Most state officials who draw district lines are not interested in close elections; their primary concern is that their favored party and candidates win. A Democratic-controlled legislature, for example, tries to

Franking privilege Free postage provided members of Congress.

ensure the reelection of Democratic incumbents by concentrating Democratic voters in their districts. In the process, the legislature invariably draws a number of districts with heavy concentrations of GOP supporters. Legislators have no interest in creating districts that are evenly balanced along party lines. In 2002, the first election following the 2001 redistricting, only about 45 out of 435 U.S. Congressional districts were closely enough balanced between the two major parties to be legitimately competitive.[49] Incumbents in districts that are safe for their party may face serious challengers in the party primary, but they will probably not be unseated in a general election.

Historically, the political party holding the White House loses seats in the House of Representatives in midterm elections. Between 1920 and 1980, the president's party lost ground in the House in 15 out of 16 midterm elections, dropping an average of 35 seats. The phenomenon was so pronounced and appeared so regularly that political scientists developed theories to explain it. One set of theories focused on the withdrawal of coattails. The **coattail effect** is a political phenomenon in which a strong candidate for one office gives a boost to fellow party members on the same ballot seeking other offices. Coattails are particularly important in election contests in which voters have relatively little information about either candidate, such as open-seat races for the U.S. House. In presidential election years, some of the people who turn out to cast their ballots for a popular presidential candidate either vote a straight ticket or support candidates from the same party as their presidential choice, even though they have no real candidate preference. Two years later, without a presidential race on the ballot, many of the congressional candidates who benefited from the coattail effect lose without it. A second set of theories attempts to explain the tendency of the president's party to lose House seats in the midterm on the basis of ideological balancing. Moderate voters support the opposition party in order to restrain the president from pushing policies that they perceive to be ideologically extreme. Some voters may also use their vote at midterm to punish the president's party for poor performance, especially the performance of the economy.[50]

Today, the midterm election phenomenon of the president's party losing seats in the House is no longer so pronounced. Since 1980, the president's party has lost ground in the House in five of seven midterm elections with an average loss of 15 seats. The incumbent president's party actually gained seats in midterm elections in 1998 and 2002. Relatively few seats now change hands at midterm now because relatively few districts are competitive between the two parties and because incumbents enjoy such a substantial advantage that they are difficult to defeat under any circumstances.

Senate Elections

Senate races are more competitive than House elections. Incumbency is a factor in Senate contests, but it is not the overwhelming advantage that it is in House races. Furthermore, Senate races are typically closer than House contests, even when the incumbent wins. In 2008, 8 of 35 Senate races were decided by less than 10 percent of the vote.

Political scientists identify a number of differences between Senate and House races that account for the relatively greater vulnerability of Senate incumbents. First, Senate constituencies are more diverse than most House constituencies and hence

Coattail effect A political phenomenon in which a strong candidate for one office gives a boost to fellow party members on the same ballot seeking other offices.

GLOBAL PERSPECTIVE

Legislative Elections in Brazil

Brazil elects the members of its national legislature using a system in which each state is an at-large, multimember district. The size of a state's legislative delegation varies from 8 to 70 members, depending on its population. Political parties can nominate as many candidates as there are seats at stake, but only the names of the parties appear on the ballot. Voters can cast their ballots either for a party or for a particular candidate by writing in the candidate's name or number. The total number of votes a party receives is the sum of its party votes and the votes cast for its individual candidates.

The number of seats a party wins is based on **proportional representation (PR),** which is an election system that awards legislative seats to each party approximately equal to its popular voting strength. If the combined votes for a party and its candidates total 25 percent of the votes cast in the state, then the party wins 25 percent of the seats at stake. The candidates on the party slate with the most individual votes actually claim the seats. If a party has enough combined party and candidate votes to win five seats, for example, the five individual candidates on its party list who received the most votes are the individuals chosen to serve in the national legislature. *

The Brazilian electoral system provides for competition not just among political parties but also among candidates in the same party. In practice, legislative candidates focus on building their personal vote totals, often by campaigning in a geographical stronghold or targeting a particular group of voters, such as industrial workers, ethnic minorities, or members of Protestant Christian churches (who are a minority in Catholic Brazil). The electoral system affects policymaking because legislators worried about winning reelection focus their energy on **pork barrel spending,** which are expenditures to fund local projects that are not critically important from a national perspective. Political scientists also believe that the system increases the power of Brazil's president, who trades support on local projects for legislative votes on national issues.[†]

QUESTIONS TO CONSIDER

1. How does the Brazilian legislative electoral system differ from the American system?
2. Is the Brazilian system democratic? Why or why not?
3. Do you think Brazilian legislators focus more on pork barrel spending than do the members of the U.S. Congress? Why or why not?

---

*David J. Samuels, "Incentives to Cultivate a Party Vote in Candidate-Centric Electoral Systems: Evidence from Brazil," *Comparative Political Studies* 32 (June 1999): 487–518.

[†]Barry Ames, "Electoral Rules, Constituency Pressures, and Pork Barrel: Bases of Voting in the Brazilian Congress," *Journal of Politics* 57 (May 1995): 324–343.

Proportional representation (PR) An election system that awards legislative seats to each party approximately equal to its popular voting strength.

more competitive. U.S. House districts are often drawn to the clear electoral advantage of one party or the other. In contrast, senators must run at-large statewide, and both parties are capable of winning statewide races in any state.

Second, incumbent senators generally face stronger challengers than House incumbents. A seat in the Senate is an important enough prize to attract the candidacies of governors; big-city mayors; members of the House; and well-known figures such as astronauts, war heroes, sports stars, and show business celebrities. As a result, Senate challengers can usually attract enough media attention and raise sufficient money to run at least a minimal campaign.[51]

Finally, research has found that voters tend to perceive Senate races as national election contests. As a result, national issues often play a prominent role in Senate campaigns and national trends frequently affect Senate election outcomes. A study of the impact of presidential coattails on Senate contests found that a 10 percent gain in a party's presidential vote in a state adds about two percentage points to the vote of its Senate candidate.[52] Presidential popularity affects Senate races in off-year elections as well.[53]

PRESIDENTIAL ELECTIONS

Pork barrel spending
Expenditures to fund local projects that are not critically important from a national perspective.

The presidential election process consists of two distinct phases with different rules, requiring candidates to wage two separate campaigns. The first phase is the contest for the nomination. Candidates compete for their party's nomination, which is awarded at a national party convention by majority vote of the delegates in attendance. The second phase is the general election contest. The two major party candidates along with third-party candidates and independents compete to win an electoral college majority in the November general election.

The Presidential Nomination Phase

In the first phase of the presidential election process, candidates compete for their political party's nomination. In the summer of a presidential election year, the two major parties hold national conventions to which the party organizations in each state, the District of Columbia, and the various territories send delegates. The Democratic Party traditionally invites more delegates to its convention than does the GOP. In 2008, 4,049 delegates attended the Democratic National Convention in Denver, whereas 2,380 delegates attended the Republican National Convention in Minneapolis.

The size of each state's convention delegation varies, depending on a formula set by the party that includes both the state's population and the success of the party in the state. In 2008, for example, California, the nation's largest state, sent 363 delegates to the Democratic convention and 161 delegates to the Republican convention. Arkansas, a relatively small state, sent 35 delegates to the Democratic convention, 31 to the GOP meeting.

The convention selects the presidential and vice presidential nominees to run on the party's ticket in the November general election by majority vote of the convention delegates. Until the conventions have done their work, the real contest is not between Democrats and Republicans, but among Democrats for the Democratic presidential nomination and among Republicans for their party's nomination. Because the convention delegates make the actual selection, candidates focus on the delegate-selection process in each state, hoping to get their supporters selected as delegates to the national convention. In 2008, Clinton, Obama, and former North Carolina Senator John Edwards were the leading candidates for the Democratic nomination. McCain, former Massachusetts Governor Mitt Romney, former Arkansas Governor Mike Huckabee, and former New York City Mayor Rudy Giuliani contended for the GOP nomination.

Presidential preference primary An election in which party voters cast ballots for the presidential candidate they favor and in so doing help determine the number of national convention delegates that candidate will receive.

The Delegate-Selection Process   The process of selecting delegates to the national party conventions varies from state to state. Most delegates are chosen in presidential preference primaries. A **presidential preference primary** is an election in which

The 2008 Democratic National Convention was designed to present the nation with an image of a party united after a bruising nomination fight between Hillary Clinton and Barack Obama.

party voters cast ballots for the presidential candidate they favor and in so doing help determine the number of national convention delegates that candidate will receive. Democratic voters select among Democratic candidates; Republican voters choose among GOP presidential contenders.

Presidential primary election campaigns are similar to other election campaigns except that the candidates must appeal to a different voter pool. Primary elections typically attract fewer voters than the general election. In 2008, 530,000 voters participated in the New Hampshire presidential preference primary compared with 700,000 who turned out for the November general election in that state.[54] Primary election voters differ from general election voters in that most people who participate in primaries identify strongly with the party in whose primary they vote. In contrast, the electorate for the general election includes a larger proportion of independents and people who identify weakly with a party.

The nature of the primary electorate affects the approaches candidates must take to winning the nomination. People who identify strongly with the GOP are more conservative than voters as a group, whereas people who identify strongly with the Democratic Party are more liberal.[55] Consequently, Republican presidential contenders usually stress conservative themes during the nomination phase, whereas Democratic candidates emphasize liberal positions. Primary voters do not just consider policy preferences in choosing among candidates; they also evaluate each candidate's chances of winning the November general election.[56] The most liberal Democratic candidate and the most conservative Republican candidate may not win the nomination if large numbers of their party's primary voters believe they would not be strong candidates in the general election.

Caucus method of delegate selection
A procedure for choosing national party convention delegates that involves party voters participating in a series of precinct and district or county political meetings.

States that do not conduct presidential preference primaries use the caucus method to choose national convention delegates. The **caucus method of delegate selection** is a procedure for choosing national party convention delegates that involves party voters participating in a series of precinct and district or county political meetings. The process begins with party members attending local precinct meetings or caucuses that elect delegates to district or county meetings. The district/county meetings in turn select delegates for the state party convention. Finally, the state convention chooses national convention delegates.

Candidates who do well in presidential preference primaries and caucuses win delegates pledged to support their nomination at the national convention. The Democratic Party awards delegates in rough proportion to a candidate's level of support as long as the candidate surpasses a 15 percent threshold. Figures 9.1 and 9.2 compare the 2008 Democratic primary vote in California with the distribution of delegates. As Figure 9.1 shows, Clinton won the primary with 52 percent of the vote to Obama's 42 percent. Edwards and several other candidates split the remaining 6 percent of the ballots. Figure 9.2 graphs the distribution of delegates in California, with Clinton getting 55 percent of the 370 delegates at stake compared with 45 percent of the delegates going to Obama. The other candidates failed to earn delegates because none of them surpassed the minimum vote threshold.

Republican Party rules award delegates on a winner-take-all basis in most states. Figures 9.3 and 9.4 graph the 2008 Republican primary vote and delegate distribution in Florida. As Figure 9.3 indicates, McCain won the Florida primary with a little more than a third of the vote. Three other candidates—Romney, Giuliani, and Huckabee—each earned a significant number of votes. Nonetheless, as Figure 9.4 shows, McCain won all of Florida's 57 delegates because of the Republican Party's winner-take-all allocation of delegates.

Candidates use a different strategy for competing in caucus states than they employ in states with primary elections. Because caucus meetings require more time

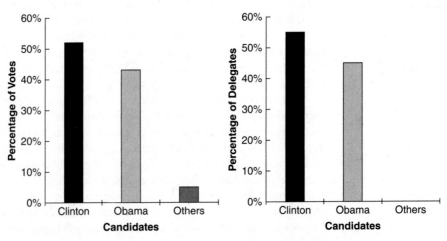

FIGURE 9.1 California Democratic Primary Vote, 2008.

FIGURE 9.2 California Democratic Convention Delegate Allocation, 2008.

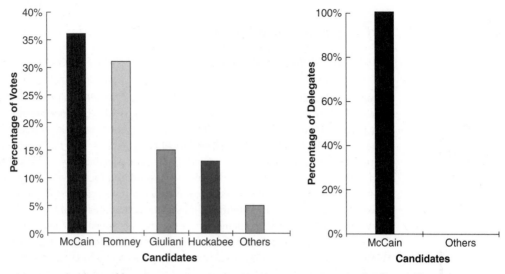

FIGURE 9.3   Florida Republican Primary Vote, 2008.

FIGURE 9.4   Florida Republican Convention Delegate Allocation, 2008.

and effort than simply voting in a primary, the number of people who participate in them is generally fewer than primary participants and far fewer than the number of people who turn out for general elections. In 2004, for example, 350,000 people took part in the Iowa caucus compared with 1.5 million who voted in the general election.[57]

Most caucus participants are party activists who tend to be more liberal (in the Democratic Party) or more conservative (in the Republican Party) than party voters or the electorate as a whole. Furthermore, a fairly high percentage of party activists who participate in caucuses are "true believers" who are more interested in imposing their policy preferences on the public agenda than electing their party's candidates to office.[58] Consequently, in each party, ideologically extreme candidates (i.e., strong conservatives in the GOP, strong liberals in the Democratic Party) do better in caucus states than primary states.[59]

In addition to delegates selected through presidential preference primaries and caucuses, the national Democratic Party convention includes several hundred Democratic officeholders and party officials who are called **superdelegates.** The 2008 Democratic National Convention included 796 superdelegates, 19 percent of the total. The superdelegates are chosen on the basis of the offices they hold rather than their support for a particular candidate. In contrast to delegates selected through presidential preference primary elections and caucuses, superdelegates are officially uncommitted, pledged to support no candidate. The superdelegate system ensures that Democratic officeholders and party leaders can attend the convention as delegates, regardless of their candidate preferences. The system also bolsters the position of insider candidates who enjoy the support of party leaders. In 2008, superdelegates found themselves in a position to name a presidential nominee because the closeness of the Obama–Clinton race prevented either candidate from winning a majority of pledged delegates. Most superdelegates chose to go with Obama because he was the candidate who won the most pledged delegates.

Superdelegates
Democratic Party officials and officeholders selected to attend the national party convention on the basis of the offices they hold.

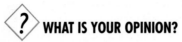

WHAT IS YOUR OPINION?

Should superdelegates play a role in choosing a party's presidential nominee?

Reforming the Delegate-Selection Process   The delegate-selection process has changed a great deal in recent years. For more than a century, the Democratic and Republican parties nominated their presidential candidates at national conventions that were dominated by elected officials and local party leaders. The main concern of the party leaders was the selection of a candidate whose popularity would boost the election chances of their party's candidates at the state and local level. They also hoped that their party's nominee would cooperate with state party leaders once elected. Fewer than 20 states held primaries, and serious candidates would focus on only one or two primaries in order to demonstrate their voter appeal to the party leadership. Critics of this system charged that it was undemocratic because it allowed for relatively little input from ordinary party members and voters. In 1952, for example, Senator Estes Kefauver of Tennessee won 12 of the 13 Democratic primaries he entered, but he did not get the nomination because party leaders did not like him.[60]

The 1968 Democratic National Convention was the catalyst for reforming the delegate-selection process. Although party leaders' control over the presidential selection process had already begun to slip because of the long-term decay of party organization in the United States, the process of change accelerated in 1968. Party reformers were outraged that Vice President Hubert Humphrey was able to win the Democratic presidential nomination without entering a single primary. The reformers charged that too much power was in the hands of party bosses such as Mayor Richard J. Daley of Chicago. Because Humphrey and the party leadership needed the support of the reformers to win the general election against Republican Richard Nixon (they lost anyway), they granted them a major concession: the formation of a reform commission chaired by Senator George McGovern of South Dakota.

The McGovern Commission revised the Democratic Party delegate-selection process in a fashion consistent with the goals of the reformers. First, the commission opened the process to greater participation for rank-and-file party members and activists, giving no special advantage to party insiders. Second, the commission mandated representation in the process by groups favored by the reformers—African Americans, women, and young people. Later, the party added Latinos, Native Americans, and gay men and lesbians to the list. Finally, the commission pushed for a system that would award convention delegates to candidates in rough proportion to their voting strength in a state rather than a winner-take-all system.

By the end of the 1970s, a number of Democrats thought that the reforms had gone too far. The attempt to reduce the power of party leaders had worked so well that many Democratic members of Congress and Democratic governors did not attend the 1972 and 1976 conventions. The power of the leaders over delegates had been largely lost to candidates and interest-group representatives. Furthermore, many Democrats feared that the new process produced weak nominees outside the mainstream of the party, such as McGovern in 1972 and Jimmy Carter in 1976. After Carter's defeat for reelection in 1980, Democratic Party regulars pushed through rules changes that would reserve delegate seats for party officials and elected officeholders—superdelegates. Nonetheless, few observers believed that party leaders had regained their lost power over presidential selection.

While the Democrats struggled over reforming delegate-selection procedures, the national Republican Party was content to leave most delegate-selection decisions to state parties, acting only to ensure more participation by poorly represented groups, especially women. Nonetheless, the Republican nomination process did not go unchanged. As political parties grew weaker, GOP leaders, similar to their Democratic counterparts, were hard pressed to maintain control over the presidential nomination process. Furthermore, many state legislatures responded to the Democratic Party reforms by changing delegate-selection procedures in their states.

The effect of the changes in the presidential nomination process in both parties has been to weaken the authority of party leaders in the presidential nomination process while increasing the power of party voters and activists. The nomination process has been opened to millions of ordinary Americans voting in primaries and participating in caucuses. In 2008, for example, 55 million people participated in the presidential nomination process.[61]

The Road to the Nomination   In 2008, the presidential nomination process had six stages:

1. **Pre-Primary Positioning Stage**   The men and women who want to be president begin the process of seeking their party's nomination more than a year before any votes are cast by assembling campaign teams, collecting endorsements, establishing campaign organizations in key primary and caucus states, building name recognition among party voters and activists, and raising money. Obama established himself as a serious contender for the Democratic nomination in 2007 by raising millions of dollars, mobilizing an army of dedicated volunteers, and creating organizations in early primary and caucus states. Although Obama trailed Clinton in the national polls at the end of 2007, he had raised nearly as much money as she and probably had the better organization in place.

   Raising money is particularly important for candidates during the pre-primary positioning stage. Because the nomination process is frontloaded, candidates need to have millions of dollars on hand in order to conduct campaigns in dozens of states in the space of just a couple of months. Furthermore, media attention mirrors fundraising success. Obama was able to compete against Clinton and eventually win the nomination because of his remarkable fundraising operation.

   Federal campaign finance laws allow for partial federal funding of presidential campaigns during the nomination stage. To qualify for federal matching funds, candidates must prove they are serious contenders by raising at least $5,000 in each of 20 states in individual contributions of $250 or less. Once a candidate qualifies for federal funding, the government will match individual contributions dollar for dollar up to $250. Candidates who accept the money must agree to an overall pre-convention spending ceiling and state-by-state limits that vary based on the population of a state.

Candidates who reject federal funding are free to raise and spend as much money as they can.

Most serious presidential candidates no longer participate in the federal funding system because they are unwilling to accept the spending and fundraising limits. In 2004, candidates who took federal matching funds were limited to $51 million during the nomination period, including federal funds. In contrast, Kerry and Bush, both of whom rejected federal financing, each raised and spent more than $200 million on their campaigns. In 2008, Obama and Clinton, both of whom rejected federal funds, collected well over $250 million in campaign contributions for the nomination fight.[62]

2. **Iowa and New Hampshire—Narrowing the Field** The first caucus (in Iowa) and the first primary (in New Hampshire) help define the candidate field by establishing some candidates as frontrunners and eliminating others as serious contenders. The Iowa Caucus and New Hampshire Primary receive enormous media attention because they are the first caucus and the first primary of the nomination process. Each of the two contests receives 10 to 20 percent of the total media coverage devoted to the nomination campaign, compared with no more than 2 percent that other states receive.[63] Consequently, candidates who do well in Iowa and New Hampshire gain name recognition and momentum that can be used to raise money and win votes in later contests, whereas candidates who do poorly are doomed to failure, with neither media attention nor an ability to raise campaign money. The eventual nominee almost always finishes in the top three in Iowa and the top two in New Hampshire.

Success or failure in Iowa and New Hampshire depends on media interpretation based on expectations. Candidates build momentum by exceeding expectations; they lose momentum by falling short of expectations. In 1972, for example, Senator Edmund Muskie, the early frontrunner for the Democratic nomination, was expected to do especially well in New Hampshire because he was from the neighboring state of Maine. Although Muskie won the New Hampshire primary, the media discounted his victory because his margin over runner-up George McGovern was less than anticipated. Muskie's campaign never recovered, and McGovern went on to win the nomination.

The strategy of the Obama campaign was to finish ahead of Clinton in Iowa. The Clinton campaign initially had misgivings about even competing in Iowa because Bill Clinton had not campaigned there when he won the nomination in 1992. (He conceded the caucus to Iowa Senator Tom Harkin, who was running for president as well.) When a memo surfaced suggesting that she skip Iowa, Senator Clinton declared that she was going all out to win the Iowa Caucus. That was a mistake. Obama outspent Clinton in Iowa, held more campaign events in the state, and had a better organization. Obama was a political phenomenon, attracting tens of thousands of people to his campaign events. At each speech or rally, his organizers gathered thousands of names, telephone numbers, and e-mail addresses, and then used the information to create a grassroots campaign organization and to raise money. Obama won the Iowa Caucus; Clinton finished third, just behind former senator and vice presidential candidate John Edwards.[64]

Obama hoped to become the clear frontrunner for the nomination by winning the New Hampshire primary, held in early January just a few days after the Iowa Caucus. Riding a wave of favorable publicity generated by his Iowa Caucus win, Obama moved up in the polls in New Hampshire and seemed poised to deliver another blow to the Clinton campaign.[65] Nonetheless, Clinton won a narrow victory in New Hampshire by capturing a large majority of white working-class women voters.

 WHAT IS YOUR OPINION?

Do Iowa and New Hampshire play too great a role in the presidential nomination process?

3. **Super Tuesday**   Over the years, state legislatures around the country have moved their nomination contests to early in the year in hopes that their states will have more influence in the nomination process. In 2008, 24 states scheduled primaries or caucuses on February 5, including the big states of California, New York, Illinois, and New Jersey. Candidates with money, organization, and name recognition benefit from the frontloaded nomination process because they have the resources to compete in dozens of states within a matter of a few days. Both Obama and Clinton were able to compete in 2008 because they had well-funded campaign organizations in place in all of the Super Tuesday states.

Super Tuesday often settles the nomination contest, at least for the Republicans. With so many delegates at stake, one candidate usually wins enough delegates to claim the nomination or at least build an insurmountable delegate lead. The GOP contest is likely to wrap up first because of the party's winner-take-all delegate rule. Senator McCain became the inevitable Republican nominee because he won the most votes and, consequently, all of the delegates at stake in California, New York, New Jersey, and Illinois. The other major contenders soon dropped out of the race.

The Democratic nomination may take longer to settle because the Democratic Party awards delegates on a proportional basis. In 2008, Clinton and Obama split the Super Tuesday contests. Even though Clinton won New York, California, and New Jersey, she earned only a few more delegates than her opponent in each state because the vote was relatively close and the party's proportional rule ensured a near equal division of delegates between the two candidates. The two candidates emerged from the Super Tuesday voting nearly even in delegates won.

Although Clinton and Obama each enjoyed broad-based support, the electorate divided by race, ethnicity, and gender. Obama carried several rural, overwhelmingly white states, including Iowa and Colorado, and a number of high-profile African American political leaders endorsed Clinton. Nonetheless, most African American voters supported Obama, whereas a majority of whites, Latinos, and women, especially older working-class white women, backed Clinton. In Pennsylvania, for example, Clinton outpolled Obama among white women by a 68 percent to 32 percent margin. In the meantime, 90 percent of African American voters in Pennsylvania supported Obama compared with 10 percent who voted for Clinton.[66]

4. **The Post–Super Tuesday Contests**   Obama emerged from Super Tuesday better positioned to win the nomination than Clinton. The Clinton campaign assumed that she would effectively capture the nomination on Super Tuesday, whereas the Obama organization prepared for the nomination fight to continue well beyond the Super Tuesday voting. The Obama campaign created an organization in each of the states holding caucuses and primaries in the days and weeks immediately following Super Tuesday, but Clinton did not. Obama also took the fundraising lead. At the end of April 2008, more than halfway through the nomination process, Obama had raised $272 million compared with Clinton's $222 million.[67] Between February 5 and March 5, Obama won 11 consecutive contests, building a delegate lead of more than 150. Clinton recovered to win primaries in Texas, Ohio, Pennsylvania, and other states, but Obama won contests as well and she failed to close the gap. When the last primaries were held in early June, Obama had a clear delegate lead and enough superdelegates announced their support to give him the nomination.

5. **The Transition**   The period from the end of the nomination contest until the national party conventions in mid-summer is a time of transition. Once the frontrunner has enough delegates to ensure nomination, party leaders begin urging the remaining candidates still in the race to drop out in the name of party unity. In the meantime, the campaign of the eventual nominee begins to change focus. The candidate's speeches start to emphasize themes geared toward general election voters rather than the hardcore party voters who participate in primaries and caucuses. Campaign spokespersons redirect their attacks from their nomination opponents to the candidate of the other party. In 2008, the transition began for McCain shortly after Super Tuesday, whereas Obama had to wait until early June to begin the transition phase.

6. **The National Party Conventions**   The national party conventions are the last step in the nomination process. The official role of a convention is to adopt a party platform and nominate a presidential and a vice presidential candidate. A **party platform** is a statement of party principles and issue positions. Traditional wisdom holds that platforms are meaningless documents, forgotten by Labor Day. To be sure, platforms often include general language because they represent compromise among different factions within the party. Nonetheless, research shows that administrations fulfill about 70 percent of their platform promises.[68]

Party platform A statement of party principles and issue positions.

The most important business of a convention is the official selection of the presidential nominee, ratifying the choice made during the primary season. Traditionally, the nomination takes place during primetime on the third evening of the convention. Festivities begin as speakers place the names of prospective nominees before the convention and their supporters respond with exuberant (and planned) demonstrations. Eventually, the time comes to call the roll of the states and the delegates vote. A majority of the delegates must agree on a nominee. At every convention for more than 60 years, the delegates have selected a winner on the first ballot. Unless the nomination process changes dramatically, that pattern is likely to continue.

The final official business of the convention is to pick a vice presidential candidate. Although the selection process is formally identical to the method for choosing a presidential nominee, the presidential candidate usually makes the choice weeks before the convention meets and the delegates ratify it. Above all else, presidential nominees look for running mates who will help them win in November. Historically, presidential candidates have tried to **balance the ticket,** which is an attempt to select a vice presidential candidate who will appeal to different groups of voters than the presidential nominee. Presidential candidates consider different types of balances in selecting a vice presidential running mate:

Balance the ticket An attempt to select a vice presidential candidate who will appeal to different groups of voters than the presidential nominee.

- Racial, ethnic, religious, and gender diversity.
- Regional balance.
- Ideological balance.
- Experience.
- Factional balance (in hopes of healing divisions produced by a bruising primary battle).
- Personal characteristics, such as age, style, and personal appeal.[69]

Also, it is helpful if the vice presidential candidate comes from a populous state, such as California, Texas, New York, or Florida. (Ironically, research finds that voter evaluations of vice presidential candidates have no impact on voter choice for president.[70])

Both Obama and McCain used their vice presidential selections to shore up perceived weaknesses by adding balance to their tickets. Obama chose Senator Joe Biden of Delaware, a 35-year veteran of the U.S. Senate and Chair of the Senate Foreign Relations Committee. Obama wanted Biden to balance his own relative lack of experience, especially in foreign and defense policymaking. Obama may have also hoped that Biden, a Roman Catholic who was born in Pennsylvania, would attract white working-class voters in the Midwest and Catholic voters nationwide. McCain, meanwhile, surprised almost everyone by choosing Alaska's 44-year-old governor, Sarah Palin, as his running mate. McCain hoped to energize the conservative base of his party by choosing Palin because she is an outspoken opponent of abortion and gay marriage. He may have also hoped to attract the support of some women who were disappointed that Hillary Clinton had not won the Democratic nomination.

Biden probably did more to help Obama than Palin did to assist McCain. Except for occasional verbal missteps, Biden avoided controversy while campaigning vigorously for the ticket. **Exit polls,** which are surveys based on random samples of voters leaving the polling place, found that two-thirds of the electorate believed that Biden would be qualified to be president should it become necessary. Palin excited the conservative base of the Republican Party, attracting large crowds at campaign

Exit polls Surveys based on random samples of voters leaving the polling place.

events and mobilizing volunteers to work for the ticket, but her lack of experience and shaky interview performances left many observers questioning her fitness for the job. According to the exit polls, 60 percent of the electorate said she was not qualified to be president should it become necessary.[71]

The national party conventions are political rituals. The presidential candidates, vice presidential choices, and platform positions are all known well in advance of the convention and approved without significant opposition. For roughly a week, each party presents itself and its candidates in the best possible light while trashing the opposition. Nonetheless, conventions are important to the election process because many citizens decide how to vote at the time of the conventions.[72] On average, the party convention is worth from 5 to 7 percentage points in the polls for the party's ticket.[73]

The General Election Phase

After the party conventions, the presidential election process enters its second and decisive phase. The field of presidential candidates has narrowed to one Democrat, one Republican, and several other candidates running on third-party tickets or as independents. The rules of the political game have changed as well as each campaign considers what it must do to win an electoral college majority.

The Electoral College   True or false: The candidate with the most votes is elected president. Answer: Not necessarily. Ask Al Gore. In 2000, Gore won 51 million votes nationwide compared with 50.5 million votes for George W. Bush, a difference of more than 500,000 votes. Nonetheless, Bush captured the White House because he won a majority of the votes in the electoral college, 271 for Bush to 267 for Gore.

Electoral college
The system established in the Constitution for indirect election of the president and vice president.

The **electoral college** is the system established in the Constitution for the indirect election of the president and vice president. The framers of the Constitution disagreed on a procedure for selecting a president. Some delegates at the Constitutional Convention of 1787 favored letting Congress choose the president, but a majority rejected the idea because they worried that congressional selection would make the chief executive subservient to Congress. Another group of delegates favored direct popular election, but they faced opposition as well. Delegates from less populous states were afraid that popular election would afford their states little influence. A number of delegates also believed that voters scattered across the nation would be unaware of the merits of all of the candidates for president. Citizens would vote for local favorites from their region of the country, perhaps overlooking better-qualified candidates from other states. The electoral college was a compromise between a system of congressional selection of the president and direct popular election.[74] The electoral college also reflected the **Federal system,** which is the division of power between a central government, with authority over the whole nation, and a series of state governments. By basing electoral votes in the states, the electoral college ensured that presidents would respond to the interests of the states.[75]

Federal system A political system that divides power between a central government, with authority over the whole nation, and a series of state governments.

Under the electoral college system, each state is entitled to as many electoral votes as the sum of its representatives in the U.S. House and Senate. Florida, for example, with 25 representatives and two senators, has 27 electoral votes; California, with 53 representatives and two senators, has 55. Altogether, the number of electoral votes is 538, based on 435 members of the House, 100 senators, and three electors for the District of Columbia. It takes a majority, 270 electoral votes, to elect a president.

Electors are individuals selected in each state officially to cast that state's electoral votes. Each state selects as many electors as it has electoral votes. The framers of the Constitution anticipated that the members of the electoral college would be experienced state leaders who would exercise good judgment in the selection of a president and vice president. In practice, however, the electors have been people chosen by party leaders to cast the state's electoral ballots for their party's nominees for president and vice president if their party's ticket carries the state. Electors are usually long-time party activists selected as a reward for their service to the party. (The U.S. Constitution prohibits members of Congress from serving as electors.) Instead of exercising their own judgment to choose candidates for president and vice president, electors almost always cast their votes for their party's candidates.

The Constitution empowers the states to determine the manner for selecting electors. Every state but Maine and Nebraska uses a winner-take-all election system. The entire slate of electors backing the presidential candidate winning the most popular votes in the state earns the right to serve as the official set of electors, regardless of the margin of victory or whether the candidate won a majority of the state's vote. Bush won the presidency in 2000 because he was finally declared the winner of Florida's electoral votes after weeks of recounts and lawsuits over recounts and allegations of election irregularities. Bush claimed all of Florida's electoral votes, even though his official margin of victory was less than 600 votes out of almost 6 million ballots cast and he won only 49 percent of the state's vote.

The states of Maine and Nebraska award electors based on the total statewide vote *and* the vote in each congressional district. In 2008, Obama and McCain split Nebraska's five electoral votes four to one. Obama earned one electoral vote because he had the most votes in the state's Second Congressional District. McCain took Nebraska's other four electoral votes by winning the First and Third Congressional Districts and having the most votes statewide.

When voters choose among candidates in November, they are literally casting their ballots for electors pledged to support particular presidential and vice presidential candidates. In 32 states, the names of the electors do not even appear on the ballot. A California voter casting a ballot for Obama in 2008 was really voting for a slate of 55 electors pledged to vote for the Obama–Biden ticket for president and vice president. A McCain voter in California cast a ballot for a different set of 55 electors, a slate pledged to back the McCain–Palin ticket.

The electoral college meets to vote for presidential candidates more than a month after the popular vote. In December, the electors selected on Election Day in November gather in their state's capital city to officially mark their ballots for president and vice president. The electors chosen by the voters of Georgia, for example, meet in Atlanta, the state's capital city. New York's electors gather in Albany, that state's capital. In January, Congress convenes in joint session (both chambers meeting together), opens the ballots, and announces the official outcome.

Electors Individuals selected in each state to officially cast that state's electoral votes.

If no candidate receives a majority of electoral votes, Congress picks the president and vice president. The Constitution states that the House chooses the president from among the three presidential candidates with the most electoral votes. Each state delegation has one vote, and a majority (26 states) is needed for election. In the meantime, the Senate names the vice president from the top two vice presidential candidates. Each senator has one vote and a majority is required for election.

The 2000 presidential election made the electoral college the center of controversy. Gore won the popular vote because he piled up huge margins of victory in California and New York, whereas Bush won other states by smaller margins. Gore carried California and New York, the two largest states he won, by a combined victory margin of 2.9 million votes. In contrast, Bush won Texas and Florida, the two states with the most electoral votes in his column, by a combined margin of only 1.4 million votes. Bush also benefited from the federalism bonus that awards every state three electoral votes (because of its two senators and one representative) regardless of size. Because Bush carried 11 of 18 smaller states, he won more electoral votes than he would have received on the basis of population alone.[76]

Bush is not the only person to be elected president despite losing the national popular vote. In 1876, Samuel Tilden lost to Rutherford B. Hayes even though he received more popular votes than did his opponent. Similarly, Grover Cleveland won the popular vote in 1888 but lost the electoral college—and the presidency—to Benjamin Harrison. The chances of a "wrong winner" electoral vote outcome are about one in three when the popular vote margin is 500,000 votes or fewer.[77] Nonetheless, election outcomes that close are rare. Only two presidential races in the twentieth century had popular vote margins of fewer than 500,000 votes—the Kennedy–Nixon election in 1960 and the Nixon–Humphrey contest in 1968.

The critics of the electoral college warn that the electors may vote for persons other than their party's presidential and vice presidential candidates. Fewer than half the states legally require the electors to cast their ballots for their party's nominees. In 2004, for example, one Democratic elector from Minnesota cast an official presidential ballot for vice presidential candidate John Edwards instead of John Kerry, apparently by accident because none of the state's ten electors owned up to the action. The 2000 election was so close that two Bush electors could have changed the outcome had they switched their votes from Bush to Gore. Nonetheless, academic observers downplay the seriousness of this problem because most electoral vote margins are large enough that dozens of electors would have to change their votes to affect an election's outcome. Also, electors rarely prove unfaithful. Since 1789, only 10 out of nearly 22,000 electors have voted "against instructions."[78] None affected the outcome of an election.

Another criticism of the electoral college is that Congress picks the president and vice president if no candidate receives a majority of the electoral vote. Although this procedure is part of the Constitution, many Americans would likely be disturbed by the prospect of a chief executive chosen through behind-the-scenes maneuvering. It might also weaken the office of the presidency by making the incumbent dependent on congressional selection.[79] In 1824, the last time Congress named the president (the selection of John Quincy Adams over Andrew Jackson) was marred by dark rumors of a backroom deal. In recent years, the closest the nation has come to seeing an election go to Congress was in 1968, when independent candidate George Wallace won 46 electoral votes. Despite winning 19 percent of the popular vote in 1992 and 8.5 percent in 1996, Ross Perot won no electoral votes because he failed to carry any states.

The strength of the electoral college is that it conveys political legitimacy to the winner in closely fought presidential elections. **Political legitimacy** is the popular acceptance of a government and its officials as rightful authorities in the exercise of power. If citizens and other public officials believe that a president lacks political legitimacy, the president will have difficulty exercising authority. The proponents of the electoral college argue that it enhances the legitimacy of the president by ensuring that even fairly close presidential elections produce a clear winner. Even though Bill Clinton took only 43 percent of the popular vote in 1992, he won 69 percent of the electoral vote. The electoral college turned a badly divided popular vote, split 43 percent for Clinton to 38 percent for Bush to 19 percent for Perot, into a one-sided electoral college victory. The morning after the election some newspapers even used the word *landslide* to describe Clinton's victory. Figure 9.5 compares the popular vote with the electoral vote percentage for the winning presidential candidate from 1940 through 2008. In every election, the winning candidate's electoral vote percentage was greater than the popular vote percentage, even in the 2000 election when the electoral college turned a popular vote loser into an electoral college winner. The defenders of the electoral college believe that it is beneficial because it gives the

Political legitimacy The popular acceptance of a government and its officials as rightful authorities in the exercise of power.

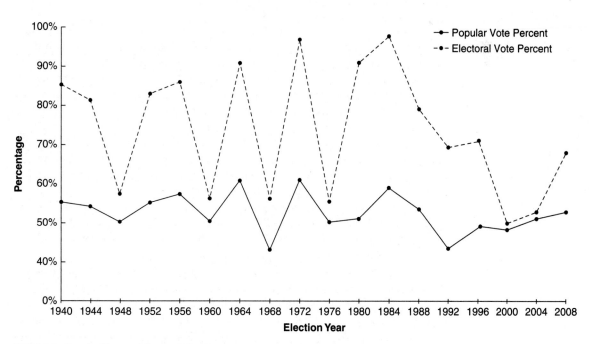

FIGURE 9.5   Popular Vote and Electoral Vote Percent.

winning presidential candidate the appearance of the majority support necessary to be an effective president.

Nonetheless, the 2000 election showed that the electoral college sometimes undermines the political legitimacy of a president. The outcome of the national electoral college vote depended on the result of the popular vote in Florida, which was too close to call. For more than a month, county canvassing boards, state officials, the Florida legislature, Florida judges, the Florida Supreme Court, and the U.S. Supreme Court struggled over ballot-counting issues. The outcome of the Florida vote ultimately hinged on the decision whether and how to count more than 40,000 ballots that voting machines had failed to count. Many observers believed that a hand count of 40,000 additional ballots would give the election to Gore because most of the ballots were from counties that voted heavily for the vice president. After a district court judge in Florida ruled against a hand count, the Florida Supreme Court, all of whose members were Democrats, voted four to three to order a hand count. Within less than a day, the U.S. Supreme Court voted five to four to halt the count. The five justices in the majority were all appointees of President Reagan or President George H. W. Bush, the father of the presidential candidate who benefited from the decision. Many observers believed that the involvement of the courts in the election outcome would undermine the legitimacy of the new president, regardless of the outcome of the dispute. Had Gore won because the Florida Supreme Court ordered a hand recount, Republicans would have charged that his victory was tainted by the intervention of a partisan court. As it were, many Democrats argued that Bush's election was illegitimate because of the intervention of a narrow partisan majority on the U.S. Supreme Court.

In the aftermath of the 2000 election, some members of Congress proposed constitutional amendments to abolish the electoral college and replace it with direct popular election. The advocates of direct election point out that their system is simpler than the electoral college and more democratic because it ensures that the candidate with the most votes nationwide wins. They also think direct election would increase turnout because every vote would count equally regardless of the state in which it was cast.[80]

Nonetheless, direct election of the president has its detractors. Some critics complain that candidates would make fewer public appearances, concentrating even more on television than they do now. Other opponents fear that a proliferation of independent and minor-party candidates would undermine the legitimacy of the eventual winner. Once again, consider the 1992 presidential election. Had Clinton won the presidency based on 43 percent of the popular vote instead of 69 percent of the electoral vote, would his administration have enjoyed the same level of political legitimacy as it did with his solid electoral college victory?

Most political scientists think that it is unlikely that Congress and the states will adopt a constitutional amendment to abolish the electoral college, despite the 2000 election. Constitutional amendments must be proposed by a two-thirds' vote of the House and Senate and then ratified by three-fourths of the states, margins not easily achieved. Will small states agree to an amendment that would reduce their influence in the presidential election process? Furthermore, interest groups that are disproportionately powerful in states with large numbers of electoral votes will oppose eliminating the electoral college because it would reduce their influence. African Americans, Latinos, Jews, gay men and lesbians, and organized labor all enjoy considerable influence in large states rich in electoral votes. No candidate who hopes to win in California, for example, can afford to ignore the interests of Latino voters. Similarly, Jewish voters are disproportionately important in the large states of New York and Florida. Cuban American voters enjoy considerable influence in American politics because of their concentration in Florida.

 WHAT IS YOUR OPINION?

Do you think the electoral college should be replaced with direct popular election of the president?

The Fall Campaign   The goal of the general election campaign is to win 270 electoral votes. Each campaign targets states based on their electoral votes and the perception of the closeness of the race in the state and allocates campaign resources accordingly.[81] Wyoming, Alaska, Montana, Delaware, and other states with few electoral votes receive little attention from the candidates, whereas California, Texas, New York, Florida, and other large states are preeminently important. If polls in a state show that one candidate leads the other by a substantial margin, then neither side is likely to devote many campaign resources to that state, focusing instead on places where the race is closer. In recent presidential elections, Texas, California, and New York have seen relatively little campaign activity because they have not been politically competitive. The Republicans have dominated presidential races in Texas, whereas the Democrats have had a lock on California and New York. In contrast, Florida, Ohio, Pennsylvania, and Michigan have been battleground states.

The campaign funding rules are different for the general election period than they are during the primary season. Once the major party nominees are chosen, they are eligible for complete funding for the general election campaign, $84.1 million in 2008. Candidates who accept the money may neither raise nor spend additional funds. In 2008, McCain accepted public financing, but Obama refused it because he thought he would be able to raise and spend more money than federal funding would have provided; he was right. Obama raised several hundred million dollars for the general election campaign, giving him a substantial financial advantage over McCain.

Third-party and independent candidates may also benefit from federal funding. Third-party and independent candidates receive federal money *if* they win 5 percent or more of the popular vote in November. The catch is that the amount of money they receive depends on the size of their vote, and they must wait until after the election to collect, at least in their initial year. If a third party does well enough to qualify for federal funds, it receives a proportional amount of money at the beginning of the next general election period. Third-party and independent candidates who

Although presidential debates are highly publicized affairs, they usually have little impact on the outcome of the election.

apply for federal funds must abide by contribution and spending limits, including the requirement that they spend no more than $50,000 of personal funds.

The presidential and vice presidential debates are often the most publicized events of the fall campaign. They are watched closely by the public and reported extensively by the media. Debates affect peoples' views of the candidates both because of the presentations made by the candidates themselves and because of media analyses.[82] Nonetheless, research shows that debates typically have little impact on election outcomes. The debate between John Kennedy and Richard Nixon is widely regarded as the turning point of the 1960 presidential race—but only because of the closeness of that contest. Most people who watched or heard the debate thought that the candidate they already favored had won. Most debates have little lasting effect on either voter preferences or knowledge about candidates and issues.[83]

Most campaign events, not just debates, have relatively little impact on the election outcomes because relatively few voters are open to persuasion. In 2008, 60 percent of the electorate decided how to vote before the national party conventions. Only 10 percent of the 2008 electorate made their voting choice within a week of election day.[84]

The electorate includes both base voters and swing voters. **Base voters** are rock-solid Republicans or hardcore Democrats, firmly committed to voting for their party's nominee. In contrast, **swing voters** are citizens who could vote for either the Democratic or the Republican nominee. Base voters typically outnumber swing voters by a large margin. In 2004, polling indicated that 42 percent of voters were the Democratic base; 45 percent were the Republican base. Only 13 percent could be classified as swing voters.[85]

Base voters Rock solid Republicans or hardcore Democrats, firmly committed to voting for their party's nominee.

Swing voters are citizens who could vote for either the Democratic or the Republican nominee.

The base vote decides most elections. Bush won the 2004 election because his party had the larger base that year and the Republicans did a better job than the Democrats at turning out their base. Swing voters make a difference only when the base vote for each party is nearly equal size and one candidate or the early attracts a substantial majority of the swing vote. Political scientist William G. Mayer calculates that the swing vote was critical to the outcome of the close elections of 1976, 1980, 1992, and 2000, but other recent elections were decided by the base.[86] In 2008, voters identifying with the Democratic Party outnumbered Republican Party identifiers 39 percent to 32 percent, giving Obama a distinct advantage. Obama also captured 52 percent of independents, which represented 29 percent of the electorate.[87]

In the last few days of the campaign, the candidates frantically crisscross the country, making as many appearances as possible in large states that are expected to be close. Research shows that candidate appearances increase turnout, especially late in the campaign season, but have relatively little impact on voter choice.[88] Consequently, the candidates focus on party strongholds. Republicans hold rallies in the suburbs; Democrats campaign in inner-city neighborhoods.

Blue States, Red States, and the 2008 Election   Some political observers believe that the United States is deeply and closely divided along regional lines into Republican **red states** and Democratic **blue states,** so named because of the colors used on the electoral college map to show states that went Republican (red) or Democratic (blue). In this view, red states are pro-gun, pro-life, anti-gay Christian conservative strongholds opposed to government regulation and high taxes, whereas blue states are secular liberal bastions that favor gun control, abortion rights, gay rights, and well-funded government programs aimed at alleviating societal problems.

The 2004 electoral college map, which is shown in Figure 9.6, graphically illustrates the blue state/red state divide. President Bush won reelection by carrying every state in the South, every state in the Great Plains, and every state in the Rocky Mountains. Kerry won the Northeast and every state on the West Coast except Alaska. The two candidates split the Midwest. The 2004 electoral vote division closely resembled the 2000 election. The only states that flipped from one party to the other were New Mexico and Iowa, which went for Gore in 2000 but Bush in 2004, and New Hampshire, which switched from Bush in 2000 to Kerry in 2004.

Political scientist Morris P. Fiorina believes that the red state–blue state division is overblown. He points out that most of the red states have major enclaves of blue voters and vice versa. Even though Texas is a red state on the electoral college map, many of its cities voted for Kerry as did the region along the border with Mexico. Meanwhile, a majority of the counties in California, a blue state, voted for Bush.[89]

In 2008, Obama broke out of the blue state–red state stalemate by winning a number of formerly red states. In addition to holding onto every state that Kerry took in 2004, Obama expanded his base in the Northeast by winning New Hampshire. He shored up his position in the Midwest, taking Ohio, Indiana, and Iowa. Obama made inroads in the South, the reddest region in the nation, winning Virginia, North Carolina, and Florida. Finally, he carved out a section of the Southwest, taking Colorado, New Mexico, and Nevada.

Red states States that voted for Republican George W. Bush for president in 2000 and 2004 symbolized by the color red on the Electoral College map.

Blue states States that voted for Democratic presidential candidates in 2000 and 2004 symbolized by the color blue on the Electoral College map.

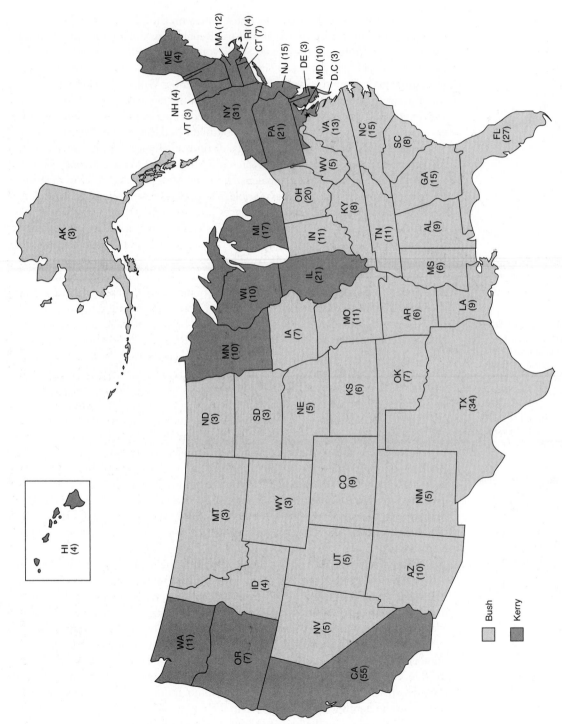

FIGURE 9.6 President Bush won reelection in 2004 by capturing 31 states with 286 electoral votes, sweeping the South, the Great Plains, and the Rocky Mountain States.

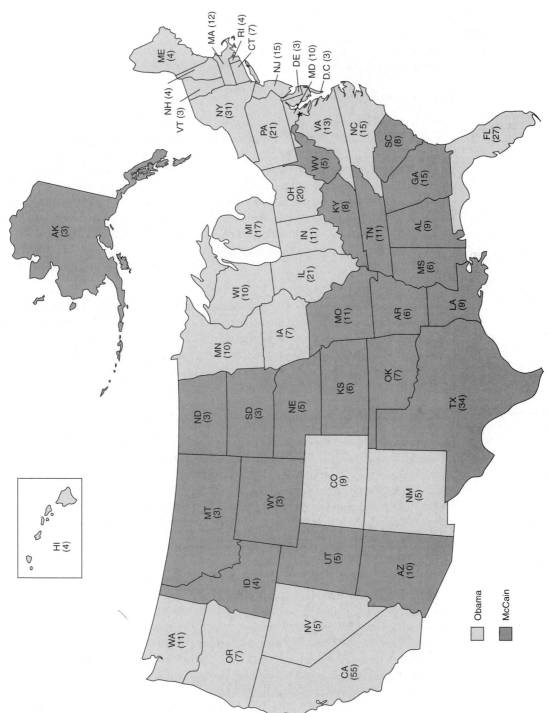

FIGURE 9.7 Barack Obama won the White House in 2008 by carrying 28 states and the District of Columbia for a total of 365 electoral votes. Obama won every state taken by Kerry and added several formerly red states, including the large states of Ohio, Florida, North Carolina, Virginia, and Indiana.

235

THE VOTERS DECIDE

Why do voters decide as they do? Political scientists identify a number of factors influencing voter choice.

Party Identification

Voter choice is closely related to political party identification.[90] Democrats vote for Democratic candidates; Republicans back Republicans. On average, 75 percent of voters cast their ballots for the candidate of the party with which they identify.[91] Keep in mind, however, that party identification is a complex phenomenon. People identify with one party or the other because they agree with its issue positions, have confidence in its leaders, or feel comfortable with groups associated with the party. When citizens decide to vote for Candidate A because Candidate A is a Democrat (or Republican), their choice is more than blind allegiance to a party label, it is also a response to the perceived issue positions and image of the party.

Issues

The role of issues varies. Informed voters select candidates based on ideology and the issue positions of the candidates. Intense campaigns make it easier for citizens to obtain information, increasing the level of issue voting. Less-well-informed voters fall back on party identification. Poorly informed voters and people who are ambivalent on parties and issues base their voting decisions on other factors, such as their judgment about the state of the economy.[92]

Personal Qualities and Image

Political science research shows that perceptions of a candidate's personal qualities influence voter choice. One study finds that voters evaluate presidential candidates on the basis on their mental image of what a president should be. According to the study, citizens want a president who is competent, honest, and reliable, and they pick the candidate they believe best matches those qualities.[93] Another study concludes that voters respond to candidates on the basis of their emotional evaluation of a candidate's moral leadership and competence.[94]

Campaigns

Campaigns educate voters about candidates and issues.[95] Candidates who choose not to conduct a campaign or who lack the necessary funding to get their message across almost never win. Challengers for congressional seats who have less than a quarter million dollars to spend have less than a 1 percent chance of winning.[96]

Research shows that campaign tactics vary in their effectiveness. Campaign advertising affects voters in concert with their party identification, making Democrats more likely to vote Democratic and Republicans more likely to support GOP candidates. The issues that work best for the Democrats are education, childcare, and healthcare. In contrast, Republicans benefit when they can shift the issue focus to taxes, morality, economic growth, and foreign policy.[97]

Political scientists believe that election campaigns affect election outcomes, but they are not as important as the state of the economy and the political context in which the race is run. The three most important underlying factors affecting the outcome of a presidential race are the following: (1) the incumbent president's approval rating in the months before the election, (2) the growth rate of the economy in the quarter prior to the election, and (3) the length of time the president's party has held the White House.[98] All three factors worked against McCain in the 2008 presidential campaign. He was a Republican trying to keep his party's hold on the White House for the third election in a row, despite incumbent President Bush's low approval rating and a serious economic downturn. In 2008, 71 percent of the voters told pollsters that they disapproved of the way Bush was handling his job, and two-thirds of them cast their ballots for Obama. Half the electorate described the economy as "poor" or "not so good"; 54 percent of them voted for Obama compared with 44 percent for McCain.[99]

Retrospective and Prospective Voting

Retrospective voting The concept that voters choose candidates based on their perception of an incumbent candidate's past performance in office or the performance of the incumbent party.

Citizens make voting decisions based on their evaluations of the past and expectations for the future. **Retrospective voting** is the concept that voters choose candidates based on their perception of an incumbent candidate's past performance in office or the performance of the incumbent party. If voters perceive that things are going well, incumbent officeholders and their party usually get the credit. They get the blame, though, if voters think the situation is poor. The economy is the most important factor affecting retrospective voter, but war and peace matter as well.[100] In 2008, 75 percent of the electorate told survey researches that the country was "seriously off on the wrong track"; 62 percent of them voted for Obama.[101]

Prospective voting The concept that voters evaluate the incumbent officeholder and the incumbent's party based on their expectations of future developments.

Voter evaluations of candidates have a prospective component as well. **Prospective voting** is the concept that voters evaluate the incumbent officeholder and the incumbent's party based on their expectations of future developments. One study finds that voter expectations of economic performance have a strong influence on voter choice.[102] Another study shows that voters reward or punish the president based on their view of the nation's economic prospects rather than the current standard of living.[103]

 WHAT IS YOUR OPINION?

What are the most important qualities a candidate for president should have in order to get your vote?

CONCLUSION: ELECTIONS AND PUBLIC POLICY

Elections play a significant role in the policymaking process.

Agenda Building

Election campaigns focus public attention on issues and shape the policy agenda. Challengers identify issues that incumbents have rejected in hopes of convincing voters to turn the incumbent officials out of office. When challengers are successful,

GETTING INVOLVED   In-Person Politics

Although this is the age of television campaigns and Internet websites, volunteers still have a place in election campaigns. They mail campaign literature to registered voters, telephone supporters to encourage them to vote, and drive citizens to the polls on Election Day. Whereas volunteers augment the work of campaign professionals in races for major office, they are often the backbone of campaigns for local office.

Your assignment is to research campaign activity by volunteering for the candidate of your choice. Contact the local political party organizations to identify local campaigns that are seeking volunteers. Your instructor may be able to assist you in making contact with a campaign as well. To verify your volunteer work, bring your instructor a signed note from the campaign office manager on letterhead stationery indicating the time you spent on the campaign. Also, prepare a written report discussing your volunteer work and your impressions of the campaign. Your report should cover the following points:

- Identify the candidate and the office the candidate seeks, noting whether the candidate is the incumbent.
- Identify the location and describe the physical layout of the campaign office.
- Describe the other people working in the campaign as to age, gender, race, and ethnicity.
- List the task(s) you completed for the campaign, explaining why you believe your work was important to the campaign.
- Assess whether the campaign office was well organized or disorganized.
- Describe your impression of the experience, discussing whether you had a good time and if you ever plan to volunteer to work for a campaign again.

they have an incentive to address the issues they raised in the campaign or risk being accused of failing to deliver in the next election. Even when incumbents win reelection, they are likely to respond to the most popular issues raised by their challengers in order to prevent them from being used against them in future contests.[104]

Policy Formulation and Adoption

Electoral mandate
The expression of popular support for a particular policy demonstrated through the electoral process.

Political commentators sometimes use the concept of electoral mandate to discuss the relationship between elections and public policy. An **electoral mandate** is the expression of popular support for a particular policy demonstrated through the electoral process. The concept of electoral mandate reflects the democratic ideal that elections enable citizens to shape the course of public policy by selecting candidates who endorse policies the voters favor. In theory, candidates and parties offer competing sets of policy proposals. The voters choose the set of policies they prefer and the newly elected officials then proceed to enact the set of policies on which they campaigned. In other words, they have a mandate to carry out their policy proposals.

In the United States, the relationship between elections and specific public policies is indirect at best. Election constituencies overlap. Whereas the president is chosen nationally through the electoral college, senators and governors are elected in statewide elections. Members of the U.S. House and state legislatures are chosen from districts. One group of voters, desiring one set of policy outcomes, selects the president while other groups of voters, preferring other policy outcomes, elect members of the Congress.

Elections are fought over many issues. The war in Iraq, the war on terror, health-care reform, taxes, global warming, gasoline prices, the federal budget deficit, and abortion all played a role in the 2008 presidential election contest between Obama and McCain. Races for Congress and the U.S. Senate featured those issues and others as well. Without a single dominant issue or a group of dominant issues, the election outcome cannot reflect clear policy preferences on the part of the elec-torate. Nonetheless, winning candidates often declare a mandate, claiming that their election signifies popular support of their policies. After President George W. Bush won reelection, he declared that his victory gave him the political capital he needed to push for Social Security reform.

The constitutional system tempers the short-term impact of electoral change. Because of separation of powers with checks and balances, and the federal system, no newly elected president can achieve dramatic change without the cooperation of other political actors. Bush was unable to achieve his goal of Social Security reform despite his claim of a mandate and his party's control of Congress. The measure proved so unpopular that it never came to a vote in Congress.

Political scientists identify three ways in which elections influence policy. First, elections change the composition of the government. Elections do not make policy, but they select the people who do. Democrats and Republicans differ about the role of government. Furthermore, contrary to popular belief, research shows that candi-dates keep their campaign promises most of the time.[105] Second, policymakers calcu-late the electoral implications of policy positions and act accordingly. Public officials, concerned about their reelection and the future electoral prospects of their party, take policy actions with an eye on the next election. In short, elections make policy re-sponsive to voters either through changing the occupants of government or by influ-encing officeholders to modify their policies to conform to the preferences of the electorate.[106] Finally, unexpected election results shock the political system, giving the impression of a mandate (whether voters intended one or not). The perception of a mandate is critical to overcoming the institutional barriers to policy change.[107]

Policy Implementation and Evaluation

Elections have an indirect influence on policy implementation. Public officials may interpret an election outcome as an indication that the voters want the government to implement a policy more or less aggressively. When the Republican Party lost seats in the House in the 1998 midterm election, many observers judged the outcome as an indication that the voters were unenthusiastic about the pending impeachment of President Clinton. Even though the House continued with the process and im-peached Clinton, the Senate refused to remove him from office.

Elections are a means for citizens to evaluate the policy performance of govern-ment officials. The concept of retrospective voting is that citizens base their election decisions on their evaluation of the performance of incumbent officials. Indeed, the history of elections in America is one of the voters tossing officials out of office when they believe that government policies have failed and reelecting incumbents when times are good. For example, an analysis of the 2006 midterm election suggests that the war in Iraq may have cost the Republican Party control of the U.S. Senate.

According to a study conducted by political scientist Jeffrey E. Cohen, each additional death per 100,000 residents in a state reduced the Republican vote total by 14 percentage points. The 2006 midterm Senate elections were effectively a referendum on the president's Iraq War policy.[108]

KEY TERMS

527 committees
air war
apportionment
at-large election
balance the ticket
base voters
battleground states
Bipartisan Campaign Reform Act (BCRA)
blanket primary
blue states
caucus method of delegate selection
closed primary
coattail effect
district election
election campaign
electoral college
electoral mandate

electors
exit polls
federal system
franking privilege
general election
gerrymandering
ground war
hard money
independent expenditures
majority-minority districts
mid-cycle redistricting
one person, one vote
open primary
party platform
political action committees (PACs)
political legitimacy
pork barrel spending
pre-clearance

presidential preference primary
primary election
proportional representation (PR)
prospective voting
reapportionment
red states
redistricting
retrospective voting
rose garden strategy
runoff
soft money
split ticket ballot
straight ticket ballot
superdelegates
swing voters
Voting Rights Act (VRA)

NOTES

1. "Split-Ticket Voting Presidential/Congressional 1952–2004," The ANES Guide to Public Opinion and Electoral Behavior, available at www.electionstudies.org.

2. David C. Kimball, "A Decline in Ticket Splitting and the Increasing Salience of Party Labels," in Herbert F. Weisberg and Clyde Wilcox, eds., *Models of Voting in Presidential Elections: The 2000 U.S. Election* (Stanford, CA: Stanford Law and Politics, 2004), pp. 161–176.

3. Robert E. Cushman and Robert F. Cushman, *Cases in Constitutional Law*, 3rd ed. (New York: Appleton-Century-Crofts, 1968), p. 42.

4. *Baker v. Carr*, 369 U.S. 186 (1962), and *Wesberry v. Sanders*, 376 U.S. 1 (1964).

5. *Vieth v. Commonwealth of Pennsylvania*, 195 F. Supp. 2d 672 (M.D. Pa. 2002).

6. Mathew D. McCubbins and Thomas Schwartz, "Congress, the Courts, and Public Policy: Consequences of the One Man, One Vote Rule," *American Journal of Political Science* 32 (May 1988): 388–415.

7. Stephen Ansolabehere, Alan Gerber, and James Snyder, "Equal Money: Court-Ordered Redistricting and Public Expenditures in the American States," *American Political Science Review* 96 (December 2002): 767–777.

8. Harold Wolman and Lisa Marckini, "The Effect of Place on Legislative Roll-Call Voting: The Case of Central-City Representatives in the U.S. House," *Political Science Quarterly* 81 (September 2000): 763–781.

9. Mark Monmonier, *Bushmanders and Bullwinkles: How Politicians Manipulate Electronic Maps and Census Data to Win Elections* (Chicago: University of Chicago Press, 2001), p. 62.

10. David Lublin and D. Stephen Voss, "Racial Redistricting and Realignment in Southern State Legislatures," *American Journal of Political Science* 44 (October 2000): 792–810.

11. David Lublin, "Race and Redistricting in the United States: An Overview," in Lisa Handley and Bernie Grofman, eds., *Redistricting in Comparative Perspective* (New York: Oxford University Press, 2008), p. 148.

12. *Shaw v. Reno*, 509 U.S. 630 (1993); and *Miller v. Johnson*, 515 U.S. 900 (1995).

13. *Reno v. Bossier Parish School Board*, 528 U.S. 320 (2000).

14. *Georgia v. Ashcroft*, 539 U.S. 461 (2003).

15. Richard H. Pildes, "Political Competition and the Modern VRA," in David L. Epstein, Richard H. Pildes, Rodolfo O. de la Garza, and Sharyn O'Halloran, eds., *The Future of the Voting Rights Act* (New York: Russell Sage Foundation, 2006), p. 7.

16. Thomas L. Wyrick, "Management of Political Influence: Gerrymandering in the 1980s," *American Politics Quarterly* 19 (October 1991): 396–416.

17. Michael P. McDonald, "Redistricting and Competitive Districts," in Michael P. McDonald and John Samples, eds., *The Marketplace of Democracy: Electoral Competition and American Politics* (Washington, DC: Cato Institute, 2006), p. 225.

18. Richard G. Niemi and Laura R. Winsky, "The Persistence of Partisan Redistricting Effects in Congressional Elections in the 1970s and 1980s," *Journal of Politics* 54 (May 1992): 565–572.

19. *Davis v. Bandemer*, 478 U.S. 109 (1986).

20. Richard L. Engstrom, "The Post-2000 Round of Redistricting: An Entangled Thicket within the Federal System," *Publius: The Journal of Federalism* 32 (Fall 2002): 60–64.

21. Center for Responsive Politics, available at www .opensecrets.org.

22. Ibid.

23. John J. Coleman and Paul F. Manna, "Congressional Campaign Spending and the Quality of Democracy," *Journal of Politics* 62 (August 2000): 757–789.

24. John Mintz and Ruth Marcus, "Bush's Bucks Have a High Burn Rate," *Washington Post National Weekly Edition*, March 6, 2000, p. 11.

25. Ken Herman, "Campaigns Spend Millions to Seek Yet More Millions," *Austin American-Statesman*, August 22, 2004, available at www.statesman.com.

26. Center for Responsive Politics.

27. Federal Election Commission, available at www.fec.gov.

28. Richard A. Oppel Jr., "Campaign Documents Show Depth of Bush Fund-Raising," *New York Times*, May 5, 2003, available at www.nytimes.com.

29. Wayne Slater, "Elite Donors Lifted Bush," *Dallas Morning News*, May 5, 2003, available at www.dallasnews.com.

30. Kirsten A. Foot and Steven M. Schneider, *Web Campaigning* (Cambridge, MA: MIT Press, 2006), pp. 197–198.

31. Center for Responsive Politics.

32. Michael J. Malbin, *The Election After Reform: Money, Politics, and the Bipartisan Campaign Reform Act* (Lanham, MD: Rowman & Littlefield, 2006), pp. 3–4.

33. Glen Justice and Jim Rutenberg, "Advocacy Groups Step Up Costly Battle of Political Ads," *New York Times*, September 25, 2004, available at www.nytimes.com.

34. Kerwin C. Swint, *Mudslingers: The Top 25 Negative Political Campaigns of All Time* (Westport, CT: Praeger, 2006), p. 47.

35. Richard R. Lau and Gerald M. Pomper, "Effectiveness of Negative Campaigning in U.S. Senate Elections," *American Journal of Political Science* 46 (January 2002): 47–66.

36. Stephen Ansolabehere and Shanto Iyengar, *Going Negative: How Attack Ads Shrink and Polarize the Electorate* (New York: Free Press, 1995), pp. 89–113.

37. Ken Goldstein and Paul Freedman, "Campaign Advertising and Voter Turnout: New Evidence for a Stimulation Effect," *Journal of Politics* 64 (August 2002): 721–740.

38. John G. Geer, *In Defense of Negativity: Attack Ads in Presidential Campaigns* (Chicago, IL: University of Chicago Press, 2006), pp. 153–164.

39. David E. Damore, "Candidate Strategy and the Decision to Go Negative," *Political Research Quarterly*, 55 (September 2002): 669–685.

40. Steven Ansolabehere and Shanto Iyengar, "Winning Through Advertising: It's All in the Context," in James A. Thurber and Candice J. Nelson, eds., *Campaigns and Elections American Style* (Boulder, CO: Westview, 1995), p. 109.

41. Lynda Lee Kaid, "Political Advertising," in Stephen C. Craig, ed., *The Electoral Challenge: Theory Meets Practice* (Washington, DC: CQ Press, 2006), p. 82.

42. Gregory A. Huber and Kevin Arceneaux, "Identifying the Persuasive Effects of Presidential Advertising," *American Journal of Political Science* 51 (October 2007): 957–977.

43. Lynn Vavreck, Constantine J. Spiliotes, and Linda L. Fowler, "The Effects of Retail Politics in the New Hampshire Primary," *American Journal of Political Science* 46 (July 2002): 595–610.

44. Paul R. Abramson, John H. Aldrich, and David Rohde, *Change and Continuity in the 2004 and 2006 Elections* (Washington, DC: CQ Press, 2007), pp. 265–266.

45. Center for Responsive Politics.

46. Ibid.

47. Michael E. Toner and Melissa L. Laurenza, "Emerging Campaign Finance Trends and Their Impact on the 2006 Midterm Election," in Larry J. Sabato, ed., *The Sixth Year Itch: The Rise and Fall of the George W. Bush Presidency* (New York: Pearson, 2008), p. 132.

48. Charles Franklin, "Congressional vs. Presidential Approval," May 15, 2007, available at www.pollster.com.

49. Jeffrey M. Stonecash, Mark D. Brewer, and Mack D. Marieni, *Diverging Parties: Social Change, Realignment, and Party Polarization* (Boulder, CO: Westview, 2003), p. 25.

50. Robert S. Erikson and Gerald C. Wright, "Voters, Candidates, and Issues in Congressional Elections," in Lawrence C. Dodd and Bruce I. Oppenheimer, eds., *Congress Reconsidered*, 7th ed. (Washington, DC: CQ Press, 2001), p. 72.

51. Jonathan S. Krasno, *Challengers, Competition, and Reelection: Comparing Senate and House Elections* (New Haven, CT: Yale University Press, 1994), p. 154.

52. James E. Campbell and Joe A. Sumners, "Presidential Coattails in Senate Elections," *American Political Science Review* 84 (June 1990): 513–524.

53. Stephen D. Shaffer and George A. Chressanthis, "Accountability and U.S. Senate Elections: A Multivariate Analysis," *Western Political Quarterly* 44 (September 1991): 632.

54. Secretary of State of New Hampshire, available at www.sos.nh.gov.

55. John S. Jackson, Nathan S. Bigelow, and John C. Green, "The State of Party Elites: National Convention Delegates, 1992–2000," in John C. Green and Rick Farmer, eds., *The State of the Parties: The Changing Role of Contemporary American Parties* (Lanham, MD: Rowman & Littlefield, 2003), pp. 54–78.

56. Paul R. Abramson, John H. Aldrich, Phil Paolino, and David W. Rohde, "'Sophisticated' Voting in the 1988 Presidential Primaries," *American Political Science Review* 86 (March 1992): 55–69.

57. "State-by-State Election Results," available at www.govote.com.

58. John M. Bruce, John A. Clark, and John H. Kessel, "Advocacy Politics in Presidential Politics," *American Political Science Review* 85 (December 1991): 1091–1105.

59. Barbara Norrander, "Nomination Choices: Caucus and Primary Outcomes, 1976–88," *American Journal of Political Science* 37 (May 1993): 343–364.

60. William G. Mayer, "Voting in Presidential Primaries: What Can We Learn from Three Decades of Exit Polling?" in William G. Mayer, ed., *The Making of the Presidential Candidates 2008* (Lanham, MD: Rowman & Littlefield, 2008), p. 169.

61. Available at www.realclearpolitics.com.

62. Federal Election Commission.

63. Paul-Henri Gurian and Audrey A. Haynes, "Presidential Nomination Campaigns: Toward 2004," *PS: Political Science & Politics* April 2003, p. 177.

64. Mark Z. Barabak, "How Obama Went from Underdog to Alpha," *Los Angeles Times*, June 4, 2008, available at www.latimes.com.

65. Jackie Calmes, "Clinton Braces for Second Loss; Union, Senators May Back Obama," *The Wall Street Journal*, January 8, 2008, available at www.wsj.com.

66. Exit polls, available at www.msnbc.com.

67. Federal Election Commission.

68. Gerald M. Pomper, "Parliamentary Government in the United States: A New Regime for a New Century?" in Green and Farmer, eds., *The State of the Parties*, p. 273.

69. Jody C. Baumgartner, *The American Vice Presidency Reconsidered* (Westport, CT: Praeger, 2006), p. 78.

70. David W. Romero, "Requiem for a Lightweight: Vice Presidential Candidate Evaluation and the Presidential Vote," *Presidential Studies Quarterly* 31 (September 2001): 454–463.

71. Exit polls, available at www.cnn.com.

72. Gerald M. Pomper, "The New Role of the Conventions as Political Rituals," in Costas Panagopoulos, ed., *Rewiring Politics: Presidential Nominating Conventions in the Media Age* (Baton Rouge, LA: LSU Press, 2007), pp. 189–197.

73. James E. Campbell, Lynn L. Cherry, and Kenneth A. Wink, "The Convention Bump," *American Politics Quarterly* 20 (July 1992): 287–307.

74. Lawrence D. Longley and Neal R. Peirce, *The Electoral College Primer* (New Haven, CT: Yale University Press, 1996), pp. 17–19.

75. Randall E. Adkins and Kent A. Kirwan, "What Role Does the 'Federalism Bonus' Play in Presidential Selection?" *Publius: The Journal of Federalism* 32 (Fall 2002): 71–90.

76. Ibid.

77. David W. Abbott and James P. Levine, *Wrong Winner: The Coming Debacle in the Electoral College* (New York, NY: Praeger, 1991), p. 32.

78. Lawrence D. Longley and Neal R. Peirce, *The Electoral College Primer 2000* (New Haven, CT: Yale University Press, 1999), p. 24.

79. George C. Edwards III, *Why the Electoral College Is Bad for America* (New Haven, CT: Yale University Press, 2004), p. 150.

80. Ann N. Crigler, Marion R. Just, and Edward J. McCaffery, *Rethinking the Vote: The Politics and Prospects of American Electoral Reform* (New York: Oxford University Press, 2004).

81. Daron R. Shaw, *The Race to 270: The Electoral College and the Campaign Strategies of 2000 and 2004* (Chicago: University of Chicago Press, 2006), p. 143.

82. Kim J. Fridkin, Patrick J. Kenney, Sarah Allen Gershon, Karen Shafer, and Gina Serignese Woodall, "Capturing the Power of a Campaign Event: The 2004 Presidential Debate in Tempe," *Journal of Politics* 69 (August 2007): 770–785.

83. David J. Lanoue, "The 'Turning Point': Viewers' Reactions to the Second 1988 Presidential Debate," *American Politics Quarterly* 19 (January 1991): 80–95.

84. Exit Poll, available at www.cnn.com

85. Mayer, ed., *The Swing Voter in American Politics*, p. 19.

86. Ibid.

87. Exit poll.

88. Jeffrey M. Jones, "Does Bringing Out the Candidate Bring Out the Vote?" *American Politics Quarterly* 26 (October 1998): 395–419.

89. Morris P. Fiorina, *Culture War? The Myth of a Polarized America*, 2nd ed. (New York: NY: Pearson Education, 2006), pp. 57–60.

90. Warren E. Miller, "Party Identification, Realignment, and Party Voting: Back to the Basics," *American Political Science Review* 85 (June 1991): 557–568.

91. John R. Petrocik, "Reporting Campaigns: Reforming the Press," in Thurber and Nelson, eds., *Campaigns and Elections American Style*, p. 128.

92. Scott J. Basinger and Howard Lavine, "Ambivalence, Information, and Electoral Choice," *American Political Science Review* 99 (May 2005): 169–184.

93. Arthur H. Miller, Martin P. Wattenberg, and Oksana Malachuk, "Schematic Assessments of Presidential Candidates," *American Political Science Review* 80 (June 1986): 521–540.

94. George E. Marcus, "The Structure of Emotional Response: 1984 Presidential Candidates," *American Political Science Review* 82 (September 1988): 737–761.

95. Thomas M. Holbrook, "Do Campaigns Matter?" in Craig, ed., *The Electoral Challenge: Theory Meets Practice*, pp. 12–13.

96. Edward Roeder, "Not Only Does Money Talk, It Often Calls the Winners," *Washington Post National Weekly Edition*, September 26–October 2, 1994, p. 23.

97. Brian F. Schaffner, "Priming Gender: Campaigning on Women's Issues in U.S. Senate Elections," *American Journal of Political Science* 49 (October 2005): 803–817.

98. Alan I. Abramowitz, "Can McCain Overcome the Triple Whammy?" May 29, 2008, Larry J. Sabato's Crystal Ball 2008, available at www.centerforpolitics.org.

99. Exit polls.

100. David Karol and Edward Miguel, "The Electoral Cost of War: Iraq Casualties and the 2004 U.S. Presidential Election," *Journal of Politics* 69 (August 2007): 633–648.

101. Exit polls.

102. Brad Lockerbie, "Prospective Voting in Presidential Elections, 1956–1988," *American Politics Quarterly* 20 (July 1992): 308–325.

103. Michael B. MacKuen, Robert S. Erikson, and James A. Stimson, "Peasants or Bankers? The American Electorate and the U.S. Economy," *American Political Science Review* 86 (September 1992): 597–611.

104. Tracy Sulkin, *Issue Politics in Congress* (New York: Cambridge University Press, 2005), pp. 168–175.

105. Evan J. Ringquist and Carl Dasse, "Lies, Damned Lies, and Campaign Promises? Environmental Legislation in the 105th Congress," *Social Science Quarterly* 85 (June 2004): 400–419.

106. James A. Stimson, Michael B. McKuen, and Robert S. Erikson, "Dynamic Representation," *American Political Science Review* 89 (September 1995): 543–565.

107. Lawrence J. Grossback, David A. M. Peterson, and James A. Stimson, *Mandate Politics* (New York: Cambridge University Press, 2007), pp. 179–192.

108. Jeffrey E. Cohen, "The Polls: Presidential Referendum Effects in the 2006 Midterm Elections," *Presidential Studies Quarterly* 37 (September 2007): 545–557.

Chapter 10

Congress

CHAPTER OUTLINE

LEARNING OUTCOMES

After studying Chapter 10, students should be able to do the following:

- Compare and contrast the structures, responsibilities, and characteristics of the two houses of Congress. (pp. 247–248)

- Profile the membership of Congress, considering qualifications, personal backgrounds, and compensation. (pp. 248–250)

- Compare and contrast the different personal styles of members of Congress. (pp. 250–251)

- Describe the relationship members of Congress have with their constituents, focusing on the different constituencies identified by Fenno and on constituency service. (pp. 251–252)

- Evaluate the arguments for and against term limits. (pp. 252–253)

- Describe the organization of Congress on the floor of the House and Senate, focusing on the role of the party leadership in each chamber. (pp. 254–258)

- Describe how the role of the party leadership in Congress changes depending on the political party affiliation of the president. (p. 258)

- Outline the organization of congressional committees and subcommittees. (pp. 258–261)

- Compare and contrast the modern legislative process with the traditional "bill-becomes-a-law" model of the legislative process. (pp. 261–262)

- Trace the steps in the legislative process, including origin and introduction, committee and subcommittee action, floor action, conference committee action, and presidential action. (pp. 262–272)

▶ Chart the progress of immigration reform legislation through Congress, and explain how it illustrates the legislative process. (pp. 262–272)

▶ Compare and contrast procedures in the House and Senate for bringing legislation to the floor after it has cleared committee. (pp. 267–269)

▶ Describe the role of the filibuster in the lawmaking process. (pp. 269–271)

▶ Describe the role of Congress in the policymaking process. (pp. 273–274)

▶ Define the key terms listed on page 274 and explain their significance.

The issue of illegal immigration divides Congress and the nation. In late 2005, the U.S. House of Representatives passed legislation aimed at enforcing the nation's immigration laws. The bill called for improved border security, including the construction of a 700-mile fence to partially seal the 2,000-mile Mexican border. The legislation would make it a crime to be in the country illegally and would provide criminal penalties for people who helped illegal immigrants enter or stay in the United States. Finally, employers would be required to use an electronic verification system to ensure their workers were in the country legally.

A few months later, the U.S. Senate passed its own version of immigration reform. The Senate bill, similar to its House counterpart, provided for tougher border security (albeit with a shorter, 300-mile fence). The Senate bill also resembled the House measure in requiring stricter employer verification of worker eligibility. In other respects, however, the Senate bill differed dramatically from the House version. The Senate measure included a pathway to permanent legal status for most of the 11 million people in the United States illegally. It also created a new temporary worker program. Finally, although the Senate bill penalized smugglers, it exempted from criminal penalties people who provide humanitarian assistance to immigrants.

Immigration reform proved too hot for Congress to handle. Legislation cannot pass Congress unless both houses approve identical measures. When the House and Senate pass different bills addressing the same issue, congressional leaders often appoint a **conference committee,** which is a special congressional committee created to negotiate differences on similar pieces of legislation passed by the House and Senate. Although the Senate was ready to begin the conference committee process on immigration reform, the House leadership chose instead to hold a series of hearings around the country designed to stress border security and attack the Senate bill. The Senate responded with hearings of its own, which emphasized the merits of the Senate approach to the issue. A few weeks before adjourning to campaign for the November 2006 election, Republican leaders in the House and Senate brought to a vote a bill to construct a 700-mile fence along the Mexican border, and it passed easily. Congress failed to address other aspects of the issue.

The 2006 election failed to break the congressional deadlock over immigration reform. The Democratic Party won a majority of seats in both houses of Congress in the 2006 election, at least in part because of the failure of the Republicans to deal with illegal immigration. Nonetheless, the new Democratic Congress was no more willing or able to pass immigration reform legislation than the Republican Congress that preceded it. Perhaps President Barack Obama and the Congress elected in 2008 will act on the issue.

Conference committee A special congressional committee created to negotiate differences on similar pieces of legislation passed by the House and Senate.

The debate over immigration reform provides a backdrop for studying the U.S. Congress. It highlights the differences in the two chambers of Congress, illustrates the steps of the lawmaking process work, and demonstrates the role of politics in the legislative process. This chapter examines the structure, membership, organization, and processes of the U.S. Congress. It explores the policymaking role of Congress using the struggle to pass immigration reform legislation to illustrate the dynamics of the process.

Chapter 10 is the first of a series of four chapters examining the policymaking institutions of American national government. The next chapter, Chapter 11, focuses on the presidency, and Chapter 12 considers the federal bureaucracy. Chapter 13, the last chapter in the series, looks at the federal court system. Each chapter describes the structures of government, outlines their constitutional responsibilities, and examines their role in the policymaking process.

BICAMERALISM

Bicameralism The division of the legislative branch of government into two chambers.

Bicameral legislature A two-house legislature.

The debate over immigration reform illustrates **bicameralism,** which is the division of the legislative branch of government into two chambers. Article I of the Constitution declares that the legislative power of the United States is vested in a **bicameral** (two-house) **legislature,** consisting of a Senate and a House of Representatives. Legislation does not pass Congress unless it passes both the House and the Senate in identical form. The debate over immigration reform required policy agreement between the House and Senate, two distinctly different legislative bodies.

States enjoy equal representation in the U.S. Senate. The Constitution originally stipulated that each state be represented by two senators chosen by its state legislature. The Seventeenth Amendment, ratified in 1913, provided for the direct popular election of senators. Today, the 50 states elect 100 senators, running statewide to serve six-year staggered terms, with one-third of the Senate standing for reelection each election year. Because senators run for election statewide, they have more diverse constituencies than members of the House, most of which run from relatively small districts. The size of a state's delegation in the U.S. House depends on the state's population with the requirement that each state, no matter how small, must have at least one representative. In 1911, Congress capped the size of the House at 435 representatives. Today, the House membership also includes nonvoting delegates from the District of Columbia, American Samoa, the Virgin Islands, and Guam, as well as a resident commissioner from Puerto Rico. Representatives run for election from districts to serve two-year terms, with the entire House standing for reelection every other year. The Constitution assigns certain responsibilities exclusively to the Senate. The Senate ratifies treaties by a two-thirds' vote. It confirms presidential appointments of federal judges, ambassadors, and executive branch officials, all by majority vote. The only major appointment also requiring House approval is for the office of vice president. The Twenty-fifth Amendment provides that both the House and Senate confirm the president's nomination for vice president if the office becomes vacant.

The Senate and House share other duties. Both chambers must vote by a two-thirds' margin to propose constitutional amendments, and both houses must agree by majority vote to declare war. The government can neither raise nor spend money

Impeach The act of formally accusing an official of the executive or judicial branches of an impeachable offense.

Supermajority A voting margin which is greater than a simple majority.

without majority approval of both chambers. The Constitution specifies that the House of Representatives can **impeach** (formally accuse) an executive or judicial branch officeholder by majority vote. The accused official can be removed from office by a two-thirds' vote of the Senate.

Because of their different constitutional structures and responsibilities, the House and Senate have developed into distinct legislative bodies. The Senate is often likened to a great debating society, where senators discuss the grand design of national policy. It is individualistic and dependent on informally devised decision-making practices. Many of the decisions made in the Senate require the approval of a **supermajority,** which is a voting majority that is greater than a simple majority. Because the Senate conducts much of its business under agreements requiring the unanimous consent of its members, individual senators enjoy considerable power over the legislative process.[1] Furthermore, the rules of debate in the Senate allow a minority of 41 senators to extend debate endlessly, preventing a measure from ever coming to a vote.

The House of Representatives is a less prestigious body than the Senate, whose Members of the House have a reputation for devotion to technical expertise, personalized constituency service, and responsiveness to local political interests. Because of its size, the House is a relatively impersonal institution that depends on formal rules to structure the decision-making process. In contrast to the Senate, the House makes decisions by majority vote. As long as a measure enjoys the support of a bare majority of the members of the House, its opponents are powerless to stop it.

The contrasting approaches taken to immigration reform by the House and Senate reflect the differences in the two legislative bodies. The Senate agreed on a balanced immigration reform plan because senators represent constituents holding a range of views. Most states include immigrant families concerned about the status of their relatives, business interests wanting to ensure an adequate supply of workers, low-skilled American workers worried about competition from illegal immigrants, and political activists on both sides of the issue. The Senate bill was able to attract enough votes to pass the Senate because it included something for everyone—tough border security, a pathway to legalization, employer verification of worker status, and a guest worker program. In contrast, the House passed a tough border security bill because most Republicans in the House were under heavy constituent pressure from conservative activists angry over illegal immigration. The Republican leadership in the House did not need to propose a balanced immigration reform bill or accept compromise because the chamber operates on a strict majority basis and the leadership had enough votes to pass its bill. The House Republican leadership eventually decided that passing a bill to authorize construction of a fence along the border was preferable to passing a comprehensive immigration reform bill that would anger the party's core supporters.

MEMBERSHIP

The U.S. Constitution requires that members of the House be no less than 25 years of age, American citizens for at least seven years, and residents of the state in which their district is located. Senators must be at least 30 years old, citizens for nine years, and residents of the state they represent. If disputes arise about qualifications or election results, each chamber of Congress determines the eligibility of its own members. The House and Senate can also expel a member for misconduct. In 2002, for example, the House of Representatives voted to oust Ohio Congressman James Traficant, who had been convicted earlier in the year of corruption charges.

Profile of the Membership

Because of the impact of the Voting Rights Act (VRA) and changing social and cultural values, Congress is more diverse than at any time in its history.[2] As recently as 1965, the year the VRA became law, only six African Americans and four Latinos served in Congress. In contrast, the 111th Congress, which took office in 2009, was relatively diverse. Seventeen women, two Asian Americans, three Latinos, and one African American served in the Senate. The House of Representatives included 78 women, 39 African Americans, 27 Latinos, 7 Asian Americans, 1 Native American, 2 openly gay men, and 1 lesbian. Despite the influx of women and minority members over the last few decades, more than three-fourths of the members of the 111th Congress were white males of European ancestry.

Most members of Congress are older, affluent, established members of society. Almost every member of Congress is a college graduate and nearly two-thirds of the members hold advanced college degrees. Law and public service are the most popular professions, followed by business and education. Many members of the House and Senate are personally wealthy. The most commonly cited religious affiliations are Roman Catholic, Episcopalian, Methodist, Baptist, and Presbyterian. Most members of Congress held elective office before coming to Congress. In the 111th Congress, the average age in the House was 57; it was 63 in the Senate.[3]

Compensation

Congress determines the compensation of its members. In 2009, rank-and-file members of the House and Senate received $174,000 a year, with members of the leadership earning higher salaries. Under a federal law enacted in 1989, lawmakers get an annual cost-of-living raise unless both the House and Senate vote to block it.

Congressional compensation is controversial. Many observers (including most members of Congress) believe that high pay is needed to attract good people. Although congressional salaries are more than adequate by most standards, the advocates of higher pay point out that senators and representatives earn less money than corporate executives and probably less than they could make working in private business, practicing law, or lobbying. Also, most members of Congress must maintain two residences—one in Washington, DC, and another residence in their district or state. In contrast, the opponents of increasing congressional pay argue that high salaries are elitist. How can Congress be a representative institution, they ask, if its members earn several times more money than the average American makes? Furthermore, many critics believe that high salaries are unjustified considering the inability of Congress to solve some of the nation's most pressing problems.

In addition to their salaries, members of Congress have provided themselves with a number of perks. Senator and representatives have an allowance sufficient to cover regular trips home. They can also travel abroad for free on official business. Members enjoy free parking on Capitol Hill and at Washington, DC, airports, long-distance telephone use, and postage for official correspondence—a perk known as the **franking privilege.** Members of Congress also benefit from a generous pension system.

Franking privilege Free postage provided members of Congress.

Personal Styles

Traditionally, members of Congress got things done and advanced their careers by building relationships with colleagues, deferring to senior members, and bargaining. New members of Congress, especially in the House, were expected to learn the ropes from more experienced members before speaking out on policy matters. They earned respect from their colleagues by specializing in a particular policy area rather than trying to have an impact on a broad range of issues. Members of Congress were expected to cooperate with one another, exchanging favors and engaging in **logrolling,** which is an arrangement in which two or more members of Congress agree in advance to support each other's favored legislation. The ideal lawmaker was someone who regarded the House or Senate as a career rather than a stepping stone to higher office.[4]

Logrolling An arrangement in which two or more members of Congress agree in advance to support each other's favored legislation.

In today's Congress, individual members have greater latitude than did their predecessors. Some members are skilled media entrepreneurs, using policy issues to gain media coverage so they can establish themselves as national political figures.

The Senate is filled with ambitious political leaders who dream of becoming president.

They are less interested in passing legislation than in advancing their own political careers. Other members use the media to promote their legislative agendas. Through news conferences, press releases, televised speeches on C-SPAN, and other staged media events, they influence the legislative agenda, define policy alternatives, and shape public opinion about proposed legislation.[5]

Home Styles

Most members of Congress believe that they have a responsibility to "vote their district," that is, take policy positions in accordance with the views of the majority of their constituents. Senators and representatives know that if they stray too far and too frequently from the policy preferences of the majority of their constituents, they may pay the price at the ballot box. Future election opponents will accuse them of "losing touch" with the folks back home and charge them with voting against the interests of the state or district.[6] Consequently, members of Congress go home often, stress their local ties, and spend considerable time in their districts.[7]

Political scientist Richard F. Fenno points out that members of Congress perceive more than one constituency whose support they cultivate. The Geographic Constituency includes everyone who lives within the boundaries of a state (for a senator) or congressional district (for a representative). In sheer numbers, the Geographic Constituency is the largest, but the least important constituency to members of Congress because it includes many people who do not vote or who consistently support candidates of the other party.

The Reelection Constituency is those voters who support the senator or representative at the polls in general elections. It consists of loyal party voters and swing voters, including independents and people who identify with the other party but are willing to vote for candidates of the opposing party under certain circumstances. Incumbent members of Congress focus on this constituency, especially in districts that are competitive between the two major political parties. Representatives and senators who potentially face strong general election opposition often take moderate policy positions to win the support of swing voters, who are usually less conservative/less liberal than core party voters.

The Primary Constituency includes the people who would back the incumbent against a serious challenger in a party primary. Although any senator or member of Congress could face a primary election challenge, members of Congress who represent districts that are solidly Democratic or Republican are unlikely to have serious opposition in any election other than the primary. Consequently, GOP members of Congress from safe districts often take more conservative policy positions than Republicans from competitive districts because they want to cultivate the support of Republican primary voters who tend to be more conservative than the electorate as a whole. For similar reasons, Democrats from safe districts are frequently more liberal than Democrats representing swing districts.[8] Congressional partisanship is more intense today than it was 20 or 30 years ago because most members of Congress win election from districts that are safe for candidates from their political party.[9]

Members of Congress work to shore up constituent support through **constituency service,** which is the action of members of Congress and their staffs attending to the

Constituency service The action of members of Congress and their staffs attending to the individual, particular needs of constituents.

individual, particular needs of constituents. Citizens sometimes ask senators or representatives to resolve problems with federal agencies, such as the Social Security Administration (SSA) or the U.S. Citizenship and Immigration Services (USCIS). Constituents may ask members and their staffs to supply information about federal laws or regulations. Also, local civic clubs and other organizations frequently invite members of Congress to make public appearances at functions in their districts or states and meet with various groups of constituents about problems of local concern. Studies show that constituency service boosts the standing of an incumbent member of Congress with constituents regardless of their party affiliation or political ideology.[10] Furthermore, incumbents benefit from a ripple effect in increased popularity among people who hear about services provided from friends, relatives, or neighbors.[11]

Membership Turnover

Members of Congress seeking reelection are usually successful, especially members of the House. Over the past 50 years, the reelection rate is 93 percent for House members and 80 percent for senators.[12] Members of Congress win reelection despite the general unpopularity of Congress because the voters make a distinction between the performance of their representative and the performance of Congress as an institution. Polls consistently show that the voters like their own member of Congress even when they disapprove of the actions of Congress as a whole.[13]

Despite relatively high reelection rates, Congress experiences significant turnover. In the 111th Congress, the average tenure for members of the House was 11 years; it was 13 years for members of the Senate.[14] Turnover is greater than statistics on incumbent reelection success rates suggest because many members decide not to seek reelection. Some members retire; some quit to run for higher office; and some leave Congress to pursue other opportunities, including work as lobbyists. For example, Representative Billy Tauzin of Louisiana, the former chair of the House Ways and Means Committee and the principal author of the Medicare prescription drug benefit, retired from Congress to become president of the Pharmaceutical Research and Manufacturers of America, the chief lobby group for brand-name drug companies. It was estimated that Tauzin would earn $2 million a year or more from his new job.[15]

Term limitation
The movement to restrict the number of terms public officials may serve.

Many critics of Congress favor **term limitation,** which is the movement to restrict the number of terms public officials may serve. The supporters of term limitation want to restrict the number of terms incumbents serve in order to open public service to new people with fresh ideas. Term limitation advocates also believe that career politicians grow cautious in office, constantly worrying about reelection. In contrast, officials who are prevented from holding office for more than a few years are free to adopt creative new ideas that may entail some political risk. The proponents of term limitation think that term limits will weaken the influence of special interest groups because officeholders will have less need to solicit money from interest groups to fund expensive reelection campaigns.

The opponents of term limitation argue that it is a gimmick that will cause harm rather than good. Term limits are undemocratic, they say, because they deny voters the

In 2009, the longest serving senator was 92-year-old Robert C. Byrd of West Virginia, who first took office in 1959.

chance to elect the candidates of their choice. If a majority of voters want to reelect an officeholder for a third, fourth, or even fifth term, they ask, should that not be their right? Furthermore, the opponents of term limitation worry that inexperienced officeholders will lack the knowledge and expertise to formulate effective public policy. Lacking personal knowledge of the workings of government, officials may have to rely on the advice of lobbyists and bureaucrats. Finally, the critics of term limitation warn that short-term officeholders may focus on securing future employment, and some future employers may be interest groups seeking special favors from government.[16]

Political science research on congressional careers supports some of the arguments of both the supporters and the opponents of term limitation. On one hand, research shows that long-term incumbents may indeed lose touch with the voters. Over time, incumbent members of Congress grow less attentive to the concerns of their constituents. On the other hand, the most experienced members of Congress are the most productive. Research indicates that senior members of Congress are far more involved in promoting a legislative agenda and shepherding bills through the legislative process than are junior members of Congress. In sum, term limitation may produce a Congress that is both more responsive and less effective.[17]

ORGANIZATION

Floor The full House or full Senate taking official action.

Senate president pro tempore The official presiding officer in the Senate in the vice president's absence.

Seniority Length of service in Congress.

Senate Majority Leader The head of the majority party in the Senate.

Majority Whip The Majority Leader's first assistant.

Minority Leader The head of the minority party in the House or Senate.

Minority Whip The Minority Leader's first assistant in the House or Senate.

Whips Assistant floor leaders in Congress.

Speaker of the House The presiding officer in the House of Representatives and the leader of the majority party in that chamber.

The organization of the House and Senate is based on political party.

Organization of the Floor

The "floor of the House" and "floor of the Senate" are the large rooms in which the members of each chamber assemble to do business. As a practical matter, the **floor** refers to the full House or full Senate taking official action. The organization of the floor refers to the structures that organize the flow of business that is conducted by the House or Senate as a whole.

The organization of the floor is based on party strength in each chamber. In the 111th Congress, the Democratic Party controlled both the House and the Senate. Democrats outnumbered Republicans in the House, 257 to 178. The party balance in the Senate was 57 Democrats, 41 Republicans, and 2 independents, both of whom voted with the Democrats to organize the chamber, effectively giving the Democrats a 59–41 advantage.

Although the Constitution designates the vice president as the Senate's presiding officer, the legislative role of the vice president is relatively unimportant. The vice president may not address the Senate without permission of the chamber and only votes in case of a tie, which is rare. During eight years as vice president, Dick Cheney cast eight tie-breaking votes in the Senate. More often than not, the vice president attends to other tasks, leaving the chore of presiding in the Senate to others.

The **Senate president pro tempore** is officially the presiding officer in the Senate in the vice president's absence. The Senate as a whole selects the president pro tempore, customarily electing the senator from the majority party with the greatest length of service, or **seniority,** in the chamber. The Senate president pro tempore in the 110th Congress was Democrat Robert Byrd of West Virginia. In practice, the post of Senate president pro tempore is more honorary than substantive, and the rather tedious chore of presiding in the Senate is usually left to junior members of the majority party.

Real power on the floor of the Senate (and the House) is in the hands of the political party organizations. At the beginning of each session of Congress, the Republican and Democratic members of each chamber elect party leaders. In the Senate, the head of the majority party is called the **Senate Majority Leader.** The Majority Leader's first assistant is the **Majority Whip.** A **Minority Leader** and a **Minority Whip** lead the minority party. **Whips** are assistant floor leaders in Congress. Both the Majority Whip and the Minority Whip coordinate the work of a number of assistant whips. Each party also selects a policy committee to consider party positions on legislation, a committee to appoint party members to standing committees, and a campaign committee to prepare for the next election.

The **Speaker of the House** is the presiding officer in the House of Representatives and the leader of the majority party in that chamber. The entire House membership selects the Speaker, but because almost all members vote for their party's candidate, the Speaker is invariably the leader of the majority party. As in the Senate, the Democratic and Republican members of the House meet at the beginning of each session to choose leaders. The person chosen to lead the majority party will become the Speaker, whereas the second ranking figure in the majority party becomes the **House Majority Leader.** The third ranking leader of the majority party is the Majority Whip. In the meantime, the minority party elects a Minority Leader and a Minority Whip. As in the Senate, the House whips head extensive networks of assistant whips, numbering, in the larger House, dozens of members.

The Senate Majority Leader and the Speaker of the House are the most important legislators in their respective chambers. The Senate Majority Leader and the

House Majority Leader The second ranking figure in the majority party in the House.

In 2007, Nancy Pelosi became Speaker of the House, the first woman ever to hold the position.

Speaker appoint members to special committees and influence assignments to standing committees. They refer legislation to committee and control the flow of business to the floor. These latter two powers are especially important for the Speaker, who can use them to control the timing of legislation and determine the policy options available to House members voting on the floor. Although the Speaker cannot force passage of unpopular legislation, the Speaker can usually prevent consideration of a measure that he or she opposes, even when the measure enjoys enough support to pass the full House if it were to come to a vote.

The Senate Majority Leader and the Speaker hold positions of high visibility and great prestige, both in Congress and the nation. As party leaders, they work with fellow party members in Congress to set policy goals and assemble winning coalitions. They consult widely with various party factions, working to compromise differences among party members and maintain party unity. As national political leaders, the Senate Majority Leader and Speaker publicize the achievements of Congress, promote their party's positions in the media, and react to presidential initiatives.

Because party leadership posts are elective, the Senate Majority Leader and Speaker maintain their power by helping members achieve their goals: reelection, influence in national politics, policy enactment, and election to higher office. Party leaders create political action committees (PACs) to raise and distribute campaign money to fellow party members running for reelection. By playing the campaign money game, party leaders can support their parties in Congress while building personal loyalty among party members.[18] For example, the 2006 congressional election was not just a campaign for control of Congress but also a personal struggle between Republican Dennis Hastert, the Speaker of the House, and Minority Leader Nancy Pelosi, who hoped to become Speaker in a Democratic Congress. Hastert distributed $1.1 million from his personal PAC to Republican House candidates, both incumbents and challengers, in hopes that the GOP would retain its majority in the House, whereas Pelosi gave $900,000 to Democratic congressional candidates.[19] Her goal was to help her party win a House majority and give herself the opportunity to replace Hastert as Speaker.

Leadership in Congress is both collegial and collective. It is collegial in the sense that the Senate Majority Leader and the Speaker of the House base their power on tact and persuasion rather than threats or criticism of other members. The two leaders generally do their best to satisfy the needs of rank and file party members, gathering IOUs that can be cashed in later. Leadership is collective in that top party leaders consult regularly with a broad range of party members, attempting to involve every party faction in setting party policy in the chamber. The whip networks transmit information between party leaders and members. Furthermore, on particular pieces of legislation, the Speaker of the House often appoints a group of rank-and-file party members to serve on party task forces to plan strategy for the passage of the party's program.

The Speaker and Majority Leader are political party leaders, working to advance their party's policy interests and maintain their majority. Democrats favor liberal policies; Republicans prefer conservative policies. When the Democratic Party controls Congress, the leadership promotes liberal policy alternatives while preventing the consideration of conservative bills (and vice versa when Republicans control). Although a Democratic majority in Congress cannot ensure the enactment of liberal legislation, it can usually prevent the passage of conservative measures.[20]

Consider the fate of immigration reform legislation in 2006. The measure that passed the House was a Republican bill. Republican lawmakers supported the bill overwhelmingly, with 203 voting for it compared with 12 who voted against it. Only 36 Democrats voted for the measure compared with 164 who opposed it. In the Senate, immigration reform had bipartisan support, although most Democrats voted for the bill and most Republicans voted against it. Senate Democrats supported the measure by a count of 38 to 4, whereas Republicans voted 23 in favor of the bill and 32 against it.[21] House Republican leaders refused to consider the Senate version of immigration reform in a conference committee because they did not want to advance a bill that a majority of Republican members of the House opposed.

The majority leadership wants to avoid scheduling votes on legislation that divides the base of the party. Immigration reform proved too hot to handle for Democratic congressional leaders in 2007 and 2008 because the issue divided the party base. Although many Latinos and liberal activists favor comprehensive immigration reform that provides a pathway to citizenship for immigrant families that have lived in the United States for years, many working-class white and African American Democrats are concerned about an influx of immigrant labor driving down wage rates. Democratic members of Congress preferred avoiding the issue to casting a vote that would upset an important part of their electoral base.

Members of Congress have a strong incentive to cooperate with their party leadership because their success is tied to the success of their political party, especially in the House. In the current Congress, Democrats want to maintain their majority, whereas Republicans want to become the majority. Members of the majority party chair all committees and subcommittees, and have a greater opportunity for input on the details of legislation, at least in the House where the majority party tightly controls deliberations in committee and on the floor. Furthermore, the election prospects of senators and members of the House elected from districts that are competitive between the two parties depend at least in part on the standing of their political party in the eyes of the voters.[22]

The role of the minority party leadership in the House and Senate is similar to that of the majority party leadership with some important exceptions. The Minority Leader and the Minority Whip work to define a party program in their chamber, plan strategy, and unite party members behind party positions. As with the Senate Majority Leader and the Speaker, the Senate and House Minority Leaders may become media spokespersons for their party. In practice, minority party leaders spend a good deal of time working to help their party become the majority party by recruiting candidates, raising money, and planning strategy. Fundraising ability has even become an important criterion in each congressional party's leadership selection process.[23]

Because of their party's minority status, the leadership of the minority party lacks the influence that their majority party counterparts enjoy, especially in the House. Although the Majority Leader in the Senate and the Speaker of the House may consult with the minority party leadership on bill scheduling, the authority to control the flow of business to the floor lies with the majority party leadership. Furthermore, the ability of the minority leadership in the House and Senate to influence legislative policy is limited by their party's minority status, especially in the House of

Representatives, where the rules enable a simple majority to conduct business. As long as the majority party in the House is united or nearly united, depending on the size of its majority, it can pass legislation without having to compromise with the minority party. Because the rules of the Senate allow a minority of senators or sometimes even a single senator to delay or defeat legislation, the minority party leadership plays a more substantive legislative role in the Senate than in the House. The immigration reform bill that passed the House was a Republican measure, written without Democratic input. In contrast, the Senate bill was a bipartisan compromise, supported by both Democrats and Republicans.

The style of party leadership in Congress depends to a large degree on the occupant of the White House. When the opposition party controls the White House, congressional leaders act independently from and frequently in opposition to the White House. They scrutinize presidential appointments, aggressively investigate policy missteps, and critically evaluate presidential initiatives. President Clinton had a contentious relationship with Congress after the Republican Party won control in the 1994 election, culminating in his 1998 impeachment. In contrast, Congressional leaders usually have a positive relationship when the same party controls both the legislative and executive branches of government. Republican Congressional leaders worked closely with President Bush to enact his policy proposals, especially during his first term. The Senate approved most of the president's nominees and generally sheltered the administration from investigatory scrutiny over such matters as the war in Iraq and the government's response to Hurricane Katrina. Bush had considerably less success in his dealings with Congress in his second term because his public approval rating fell. Republicans in Congress decided that it was more important to take positions designed to help with their own reelections—even if it meant failing to support their party's president. After the 2006 election, Bush faced a Congress controlled by the Democrats. Chapter 11 discusses the relationship between presidential popularity and presidential relations with Congress in detail.

Committee and Subcommittee Organization

The detailed work of Congress takes place in committees. The advantage of the committee system is that it allows Congress to divide legislative work among a number of subgroups while giving individual members the opportunity to specialize, developing expertise in particular policy areas. The disadvantage of the committee system is that the division of broad issues into smaller subissues may impede the development of comprehensive and coordinated national policy. Because Congress deals with policy problems on a piecemeal basis, it tends to offer piecemeal solutions.

Standing committee A permanent legislative committee with authority to draft legislation in a particular policy area or areas.

A **standing committee** is a permanent legislative committee with authority to draft legislation in a particular policy area or areas. The House Agriculture Committee, for example, deals with subjects related to agriculture, including rural economic conditions, crop insurance, agricultural trade, commodity futures trading, agricultural research and promotion, conservation, farm credit, welfare and food nutrition programs, and food safety inspection. The jurisdiction of the Senate Foreign Relations Committee includes matters relating to American national security policy, foreign policy, and international economic policy.

GLOBAL PERSPECTIVE

The Indian Parliament

The Indian Parliament is bicameral. The lower chamber, which is called the Lok Sabha, has 545 members chosen from districts apportioned among the Indian states on the basis of population. Rajya Sabha, the upper chamber, has 250 members elected from the states also on the basis of population, except that small states enjoy somewhat more representation than their population would merit.

Lok Sabha is the more important of the two chambers. It has exclusive authority on bills dealing with spending, taxation, and borrowing. Lok Sabha more often than not gets its way on other measures as well. When the two chambers disagree on the content of legislation, they meet in joint session and decide by majority vote. The larger size of Lok Sabha gives it the advantage.

The Indian Parliament, similar to most legislative bodies in democracies other than the United States, does not usually initiate major legislative proposals. In a parliamentary system, most legislative proposals come from the Prime Minister and the cabinet. The legislative role of Parliament is limited to scrutinizing and revising the details of legislation. Parliament rarely defeats government-sponsored legislation because Indian law mandates party discipline. Legislators who vote against their party's official position

lose their seats unless one-third or more of a party's members defect. The law then assumes that the party has split and a new party is formed.

Despite party discipline, the Indian Parliament has the ability to hold the government accountable for its actions. When Parliament is in session, the legislative day begins with an hour in which the members question cabinet ministers about government policies. The sessions allow opposition lawmakers the opportunity to criticize government policies and put cabinet ministers on the spot. Furthermore, a majority of the members of Lok Sabha can bring down the government by voting "no confidence." A no-confidence vote leads to the dissolution of Parliament and the holding of new elections.

QUESTIONS TO CONSIDER

1. In what way is the relationship between the two chambers of the Indian Parliament similar to the relationship between the U.S. House and Senate?
2. Would party discipline make the U.S. Congress more or less democratic?
3. Which legislative body plays the greater policymaking role, the U.S. Congress or the Indian Parliament? What is the basis of your answer?

Special or **select committee** A committee established for a limited time only.

In addition to standing committees, Congress has special or select committees and joint committees. A **special** or **select committee** is a committee established for a limited time only. A **joint committee** is a committee that includes members from both houses of Congress. In contrast to standing committees, joint committees and special or select committees do not usually have the legislative authority to draft legislation. They can only study, investigate, and make recommendations.

Joint committee A committee that includes members from both houses of Congress.

Committees are divided into subcommittees. Not all committees have subcommittees, and not all bills are referred to subcommittee, but in the House in particular, subcommittees have become the center of legislative work. For example, the House Ways and Means Committee—which deals with tax issues, trade, and Social Security—has six subcommittees, each of which addresses a different aspect of the committee's responsibilities.

Senators typically have more committee assignments than members of the House because the Senate is a smaller body. Senator Dianne Feinstein of California, for example, serves on four standing committees and one select committee, including the Appropriations Committee, Energy and Natural Resources Committee, Judiciary Committee, Rules and Administration Committee, and the Select Committee on

Intelligence. Feinstein is also a member of a number of subcommittees. Because senators are stretched thin, they pick and choose when to get involved in committee processes. Consequently, committee decisions in the Senate usually reflect the work of less than half the committee membership, except on especially high-profile matters such as immigration reform or a major tax bill.[24] Most members of the House serve on no more than two committees and four subcommittees. Representative Lincoln Diaz-Balart of Florida, for example, serves on one committee, The Rules Committee, and one subcommittee. Because members of the House have fewer committee assignments than their Senate counterparts, they have more time to devote to committee work and are more likely to develop policy expertise in the issues dealt with by the committees on which they serve. As a result, committees play a more important role in the legislative process in the House than they do in the Senate.

When senators and representatives are first elected, they request assignment to standing committees that they believe will help them win reelection, gain influence in national politics, and/or affect policy. Committees dealing with money qualify on all three counts and are in great demand. The money committees in the Senate are Appropriations, Budget, and Finance. In the House, the committees dealing with money are Appropriations, Budget, and Ways and Means. The other Senate committees that are considered prestigious assignments are Foreign Relations, Armed Services, and Judiciary.[25] In the House, members want to serve on the Energy and Commerce Committee because it deals with a broad range of important legislation. The Transportation and Infrastructure Committee is popular as well because members see it as a way to procure projects for their districts. Senators and representatives frequently request assignments on committees that deal with policy issues particularly relevant to their states and districts. Members of Congress from urban and financial centers are attracted to the banking committees; members from agricultural states favor membership on the agricultural committees. Finally, some members of Congress request particular committee assignments for personal reasons. For example, members of the House with prior military service may seek membership on the Armed Services Committee.[26]

Party committees in each chamber make committee assignments for members of their party. Party leaders control these committees and, in theory, could use them to reward friends and punish enemies. In practice, however, the party committees try to accommodate the preferences of members, usually giving them either their first or second choices of committee assignments. If members are unhappy with a committee assignment, they may request a transfer when openings occur on committees they prefer. Committee switching is not especially common, particularly among senior members, because members who change committees must start over on the seniority ladder of the new committee. Nonetheless, it is not unusual for members to request transfer to one of the really choice committees.

The nature of the committee assignment process has an impact on the composition of committees. Membership on the major committees mirrors the membership of Congress as a whole because senators and representatives seek to serve on the major committees without regard for ideology or constituency.[27] Consequently, legislation emerging from major committees is likely to be acceptable to a majority of members of Congress. In contrast, members of committees that deal with particular policy areas, such as agriculture and armed services, are generally composed of members whose constituencies are directly affected by the committee's work.[28] Legislation emerging from these committees tends to reflect the concerns of particularized interests, such as defense contractors and farmers, rather than broader policy perspectives.[29]

Members choose subcommittees based on seniority. When committee members change committees, die, retire, or suffer defeat at the polls, other committee members volunteer for their subcommittee assignments in order of seniority. The most senior members get their choice; the least senior members get the leftovers.

The majority party controls each committee and subcommittee. Before the 2006 election, the Republican Party was the majority party in the House and Senate. Republicans comprised a majority of the membership of each committee and subcommittee and chaired every committee and subcommittee in both chambers. In 2006, the Democrats won majorities in both houses of Congress and the roles of the parties reversed. Beginning in 2007, Democrats made up a majority of every committee and subcommittee and Democrats chaired every committee and subcommittee.

Each party has its own procedures for selecting committee chairs (for the majority party) and ranking members (for the minority party). Republican Party rules stipulate that the party committee that makes initial committee assignments nominates chairs or ranking members with confirmation by the **party caucus,** which is all of the party members of a chamber meeting as a group. The Republicans select chairs or ranking members based on party loyalty and ability to raise campaign money for party candidates, rather than using seniority as the basis for selection.[30] Each Republican member of the House is expected to contribute money to the party's campaign fund ranging from $70,000 to $600,000, depending on the member's position. Party members who fail to meet their financial obligations will be passed over for leadership positions.[31] Democrats, meanwhile, provide for the selection of committee chairs and ranking members by a secret-ballot vote of the party caucus. The Democrat with the most seniority on a particular committee usually wins the vote, except on those rare occasions when a senior member has alienated his or her colleagues. Both parties limit chairs and subcommittee chairs to six-year terms.

Party caucus All of the party members of the House or Senate meeting as a group.

THE LEGISLATIVE PROCESS

The traditional image of the legislative process is that a member introduces a bill; it is referred to committee; it goes from committee to the floor, from the floor to a conference committee; and, if it passes every step, it goes to the president. Since the early 1990s, the legislative process has not conformed to the traditional "bill-becomes-a-law" formula, especially for major pieces of legislation. Congress has adopted modifications in the traditional legislative process to increase the likelihood that it can pass major legislation. The key differences between the traditional model and the new model of legislative policymaking are the following:

Omnibus bills Complex, highly detailed legislative proposals covering one or more subjects or programs.

- Major legislation is often written in the form of **omnibus bills,** which are complex, highly detailed legislative proposals covering one or more subjects or programs. The immigration reform measure that passed the House included border security provisions, criminalization of illegal immigration status, sanctions against people who assist the undocumented, and a tighter worker verification process for employers. The Senate bill contained provisions affecting border security, a guest worker program, employee verification, and a pathway to citizenship for unauthorized residents. Congressional leaders assemble omnibus bills in order to attract as much support as possible.

- Pieces of major legislation are frequently referred to more than one standing committee. Involving several committees in the legislative process provides a measure's supporters with an opportunity to draft legislation that enjoys a broader base of support than a bill considered by one committee. Furthermore, the strategy avoids the danger of a hostile committee chair bottling up the bill in committee, which sometimes happens to measures referred to only one committee.

- The legislative leadership, especially in the House, coordinates the work of the standing committees. The leadership sets timetables to move legislation through the committee stage.

- The legislative leadership, especially in the House, fashions the details of the legislation and develops a strategy for winning passage of the measure on the floor. Even after a bill clears committee, the leadership may change its provisions to broaden its base of support and increase its chances of success.

- A conference committee, including dozens maybe even hundreds of members, works out the final compromise language of the bill. Once again, the goal is to build a broad enough coalition of support for the measure to ensure its passage.[32]

Figure 10.1 (page 264–265) outlines the basic steps of the legislative process.

Origin and Introduction

Bill A proposed law.

In 2008, members of Congress introduced 4,815 bills and resolutions—3,225 in the House and 1,590 in the Senate.[33] A **bill** is a proposed law. Except for revenue raising bills, which must begin in the House, any bill may be introduced in either chamber. A **resolution** is a legislative statement of opinion on a certain matter. Resolutions may be introduced in either chamber. A member who introduces a measure is known as its **sponsor.** Bills and resolutions may have multiple sponsors, which are known as cosponsors. Over the years, legislative measures have grown longer and more complex. Since the 1940s, the length of the average bill has increased from 2.5 pages to more than 19 pages.[34] Omnibus bills are far longer. The No Child Left Behind Act, the education reform measure enacted in 2002, was 670 pages.[35]

Resolution A legislative statement of opinion on a certain matter.

Sponsor A member who introduces a measure.

Although the formal introduction of legislation is a privilege limited to actual members of Congress, the ideas and initiative for legislation are varied. Interest groups, the president, executive branch agencies, journalists, constituents, individual members of Congress, and other political actors may advance policy proposals that are embodied in formal legislation. Executive branch agencies and major interest groups may even draft the text of a bill, turning a policy proposal into formal legislation.

Members of Congress do not always introduce measures with the expectation that they will become law, at least not in the short run. Members sometimes propose bills as symbolic gestures. In the early 1950s, legislators introduced civil rights measures, even though they knew they would not pass. Their goal was to raise civil rights issues to the public agenda in hopes of seeing their proposals become laws in the future. Members may also introduce legislation that is unlikely to pass in order to placate constituents or score political points. Sometimes the measure's sponsors may even secretly hope that the legislation fails.

Legislative activity is less today than it was 30 years ago. In the 1960s, senators and representatives introduced on average more than 50 bills and resolutions apiece during a two-year session of Congress. In contrast, the average member of Congress introduced only 9 measures in 2008.[36] The decline in legislative activity reflects a political climate that has grown skeptical of government solutions to the nation's problems. Many members of Congress, especially Republicans, won office by campaigning against government programs. Their goal is to reduce the scope of government activity rather than passing legislation to create new programs.

Committee and Subcommittee Action

Once a bill or resolution is introduced, it is assigned a number and referred to committee. A measure introduced in the House has the initials H.R. for House of Representatives, whereas Senate measures begin with the letter S. for Senate. The immigration reform measure passed by the House was H.R. 4437. (The number signifies the order in which a measure was introduced.) The sponsors of a bill also give it a popular title designed to put the measure in a favorable light. Representative James F. Sensenbrenner Jr., the House sponsor of immigration reform, called his bill the Border Protection, Antiterrorism, and Illegal Immigration Control Act. The chamber parliamentarian, working under the oversight of the Speaker of the House or the Senate Majority Leader, refers the measure to committee based on the subject covered by the bill or resolution. A bill to increase the federal cigarette tax, for

The detailed work of Congress takes place in committees.

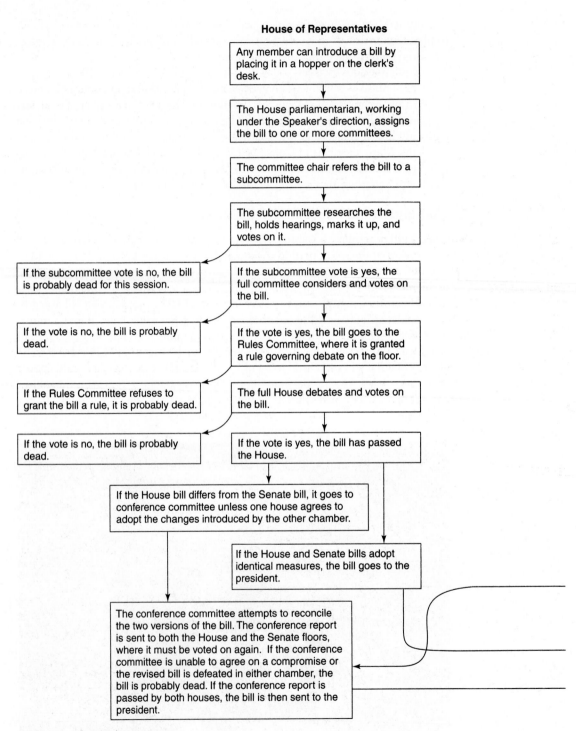

House of Representatives

Any member can introduce a bill by placing it in a hopper on the clerk's desk.

The House parliamentarian, working under the Speaker's direction, assigns the bill to one or more committees.

The committee chair refers the bill to a subcommittee.

The subcommittee researches the bill, holds hearings, marks it up, and votes on it.

If the subcommittee vote is no, the bill is probably dead for this session.

If the subcommittee vote is yes, the full committee considers and votes on the bill.

If the vote is no, the bill is probably dead.

If the vote is yes, the bill goes to the Rules Committee, where it is granted a rule governing debate on the floor.

If the Rules Committee refuses to grant the bill a rule, it is probably dead.

The full House debates and votes on the bill.

If the vote is no, the bill is probably dead.

If the vote is yes, the bill has passed the House.

If the House bill differs from the Senate bill, it goes to conference committee unless one house agrees to adopt the changes introduced by the other chamber.

If the House and Senate bills adopt identical measures, the bill goes to the president.

The conference committee attempts to reconcile the two versions of the bill. The conference report is sent to both the House and the Senate floors, where it must be voted on again. If the conference committee is unable to agree on a compromise or the revised bill is defeated in either chamber, the bill is probably dead. If the conference report is passed by both houses, the bill is then sent to the president.

FIGURE 10.1 The Legislative Process.

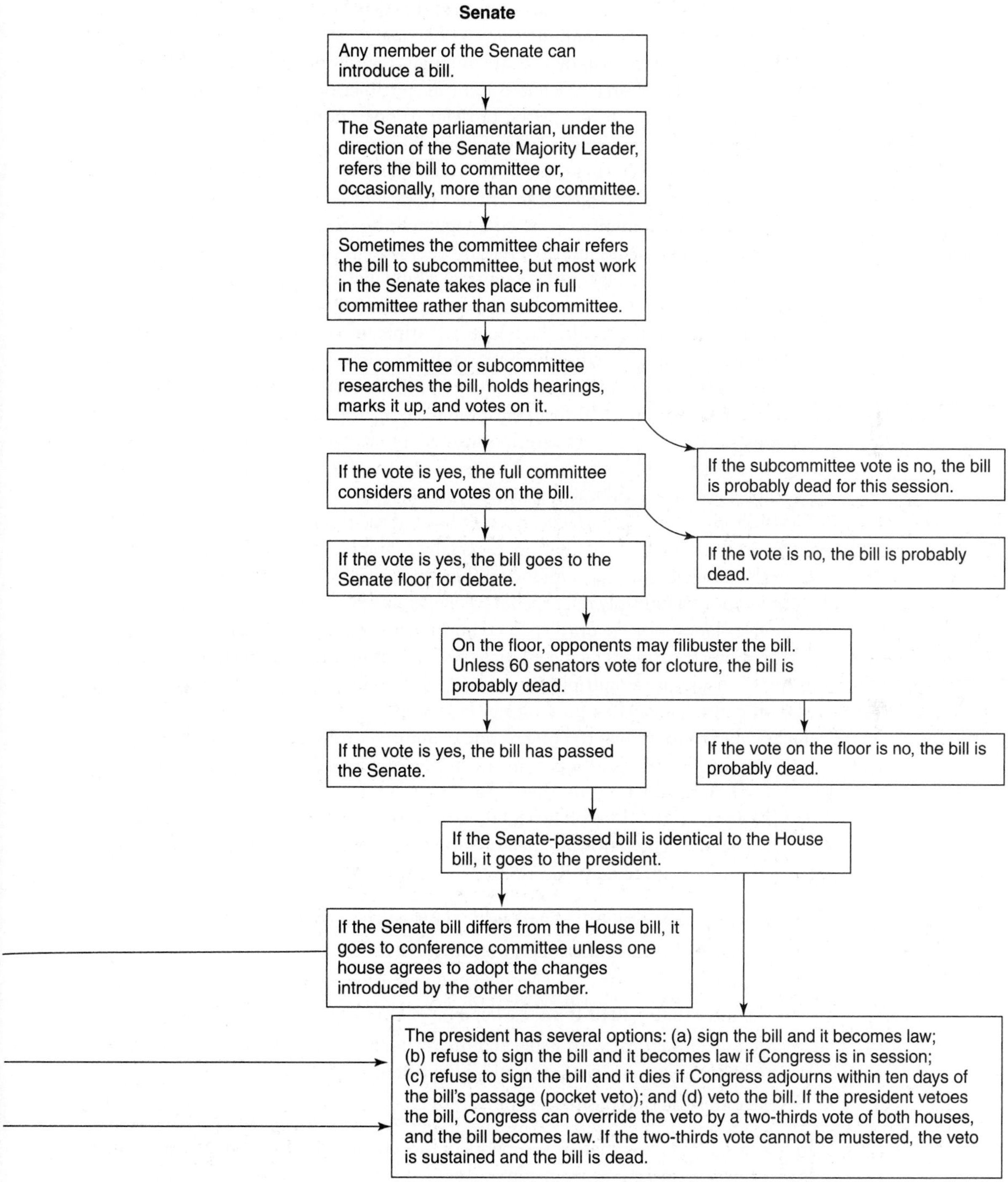

Senate

Any member of the Senate can introduce a bill.

The Senate parliamentarian, under the direction of the Senate Majority Leader, refers the bill to committee or, occasionally, more than one committee.

Sometimes the committee chair refers the bill to subcommittee, but most work in the Senate takes place in full committee rather than subcommittee.

The committee or subcommittee researches the bill, holds hearings, marks it up, and votes on it.

If the vote is yes, the full committee considers and votes on the bill.

If the subcommittee vote is no, the bill is probably dead for this session.

If the vote is yes, the bill goes to the Senate floor for debate.

If the vote is no, the bill is probably dead.

On the floor, opponents may filibuster the bill. Unless 60 senators vote for cloture, the bill is probably dead.

If the vote is yes, the bill has passed the Senate.

If the vote on the floor is no, the bill is probably dead.

If the Senate-passed bill is identical to the House bill, it goes to the president.

If the Senate bill differs from the House bill, it goes to conference committee unless one house agrees to adopt the changes introduced by the other chamber.

The president has several options: (a) sign the bill and it becomes law; (b) refuse to sign the bill and it becomes law if Congress is in session; (c) refuse to sign the bill and it dies if Congress adjourns within ten days of the bill's passage (pocket veto); and (d) veto the bill. If the president vetoes the bill, Congress can override the veto by a two-thirds vote of both houses, and the bill becomes law. If the two-thirds vote cannot be mustered, the veto is sustained and the bill is dead.

FIGURE 10.1 (*Continued*)

example, would fall under the jurisdiction of the Ways and Means Committee in the House and the Finance Committee in the Senate.

Complex issues such as healthcare, immigration reform, international trade, and homeland security often cut across committee jurisdictions. Sometimes, committees develop arrangements to cooperate or defer to one another.[37] At other times, the leadership employs **multiple referral of legislation,** which is the practice of assigning legislation to more than one committee. The Senate permits joint, sequential, and partial referrals of legislation. House rules allow only sequential and partial referrals, and one committee may be designated the committee of primary jurisdiction. The Speaker makes multiple referral decisions in the House. The Speaker may also appoint an *ad hoc* (special) committee, which may be called a task force, to consider a measure whose subject matter does not fit neatly within the jurisdiction of a single standing committee. In the Senate, multiple referral of legislation requires the unanimous agreement of the chamber. Multiple referral of legislation is more common in the House than the Senate and more likely to be used for major legislation than routine measures. Although most multiple referrals go to only two committees, complex measures may be referred to several committees. Four committees considered immigration reform in the House, including Judiciary, Homeland Security, Education and the Workforce, and Ways and Means.

Multiple referral of legislation has enhanced the power of the legislative leadership over the content of legislation, especially in the House. The Speaker can devise referral arrangements that enhance policy goals and set timetables for committee consideration of multiply referred bills. A multiply referred measure cannot continue in the legislative process until each committee dealing with it has finished its work. Furthermore, the Speaker can negotiate policy compromises among the various committees considering a multiply referred measure. In practice, multiple referral of legislation is also a means for moving legislation through the process because it enables the Speaker to intervene to prevent one committee from stalling a measure.[38]

Committees are gatekeepers in the lawmaking process, killing most of the bills and resolutions referred to them. In 2008, congressional committees reported 856 measures to the floor of 4,815 bills and resolutions introduced for a report rate of 17.8 percent. The following measures are most likely to receive detailed committee and subcommittee consideration:

- Measures that committee and subcommittee chairs personally favor.
- Measures that have the support of the legislative leadership.
- Measures that enjoy broad support in Congress as a whole.
- Measures that benefit from the backing of important interest groups.
- Measures that deal with issues that many members of Congress and a large segment of the general public consider important.
- Measures that are pushed by the White House.

In contrast, measures that lack support or are opposed by the committee or party leadership seldom emerge from committee.

Committees and subcommittees do the detailed work of Congress. Once a measure is sent to committee or subcommittee, the chair and the ranking minority

Multiple referral of legislation The practice of assigning legislation to more than one committee.

member ask their staffs to prepare separate reports on its merits. For major legislation, the committee or subcommittee chair schedules hearings to allow the measure's supporters and opponents a chance to make their case. Full committees generally conduct Senate hearings; subcommittees hold most hearings in the House.

The next step is **legislative markup.** This is the process in which legislators go over a measure line-by-line, revising, amending, or rewriting it. In the House, markup usually takes place in subcommittee. Markup in the Senate generally occurs in full committee.

The primary avenue for policymaking in committee is not formal markup itself, but informal negotiations that take place before and during markup. The most important participants in these negotiations are the committee and subcommittee chairs and the ranking minority members on the committee and subcommittee. On major legislation, the party leadership, the president, and major interest groups will probably be involved as well.[39]

Once markup is complete, the subcommittee and then the full committee vote on whether to recommend passage. If the measure is voted down at either stage or members vote to **table** it (i.e., postpone consideration), it is probably dead, at least for the session. If the measure is approved in subcommittee and committee, the next step is the floor of the full House or Senate.

The rules of the House provide a mechanism for members to bring a bill to the floor that has been tabled or defeated in committee, but the procedure is seldom used and almost never successful. A bill's supporters can compel a committee to report a measure to the floor by means of a **discharge petition,** which is a procedure whereby a majority of the members of the House of Representatives can force a committee to report a bill to the floor of the House. Since 1910, only three measures forced from committee through the use of a discharge petition eventually became law.[40] Most members of Congress are reluctant to sign a discharge petition because they do not want to undermine committee authority. Furthermore, the threat of a discharge petition is sometimes enough to stimulate a committee to act on stalled legislation.

Floor Action

In the House, the process for moving measures from committee to the floor varies, depending on the type of measure involved. The House considers noncontroversial measures of relatively minor importance through a shortcut procedure on designated special days set aside for that purpose. Budget resolutions and appropriation bills may go directly from committee to the House floor. (An **appropriation bill** is a legislative authorization to spend money for particular purposes.)

The leadership brings some major pieces of legislation to the floor either without committee consideration or with only cursory committee examination. If a measure was carefully studied in committee in the last session of Congress, the leadership may determine that no more committee work is necessary. Sometimes, the leadership wants to move quickly for political reasons. In 2005, the House leadership put legislation to provide aid for people impacted by Hurricane Katrina on a fast track, moving it directly to the floor without committee consideration.[41]

Legislative markup The process in which legislators go over a measure line-by-line, revising, amending, or rewriting it.

Table To postpone consideration of a measure during the legislative process.

Discharge petition A procedure whereby a majority of the members of the House of Representatives can force a committee to report a bill to the floor of the House.

Appropriation bill A legislative authorization to spend money for particular purposes.

House Rules Committee A standing committee that determines the rules under which a specific bill can be debated, amended, and considered on the House floor.

Most measures that clear standing committee must go to the Rules Committee before going to the floor. The **House Rules Committee** is a standing committee that determines the rules under which a specific bill can be debated, amended, and considered on the House floor. Because more measures clear committee than the full House has time to consider, the Rules Committee determines which measures go forward. Measures that are not assigned rules are not considered on the House floor and therefore have no chance of passage unless supporters can succeed in forcing the legislation out of the Rules Committee by means of a discharge petition.

When the Rules Committee refers a bill to the floor, it sets a time limit for debate and determines the ground rules for amendments. Debate in the House is defined by the rule under which a measure is considered. The Rules Committee limited debate on the immigration reform bill to two hours, divided equally between proponents organized by the chair of the Judiciary Committee and opponents organized by the committee's ranking member. The Rules Committee also sets the terms for consideration of amendments, including identifying which amendments may be offered, who may propose amendments, and the order in which amendments may be considered. A rule that opens a measure to amendment on the House floor without restriction is an **open rule.** In contrast, a **closed rule** is a rule that prohibits floor consideration of amendments on the House floor. The measure must be voted up or down without amendment. In practice, both open rules and strict closed rules are rare. Nearly two-thirds of rules are at least somewhat restrictive. For most major pieces of legislation, the Rules Committee grants restrictive rules that limit the consideration of amendments to certain specific alternatives. Restrictive rules also determine the order of consideration for amendments.[42]

Open rule A rule that opens a measure to amendment on the House floor without restriction.

Closed rule A rule that prohibits floor consideration of amendments on the House floor.

Rules are a means for structuring debate on the House floor. Rules allowing choice among comprehensive substitute bills focus debate on big choices rather than the details of legislation. Rules can also prevent a measure's opponents from forcing votes on the most unpopular provisions of a bill or offering amendments that the leadership opposes.[43] The Rules Committee is an important element of the Speaker's power. In contrast to other House committees, the Speaker personally appoints the majority party members of the Rules Committee subject to approval by the party caucus, thereby ensuring control. The Speaker uses the Rules Committee not only to determine which measures reach the floor, but also to structure the policy choices available to members on the floor.

Unanimous consent agreement (UCA) A formal understanding on procedures for conducting business in the Senate that requires the acceptance of every member of the chamber.

In the Senate, a measure typically reaches the floor through the mechanism of a **unanimous consent agreement (UCA),** which is a formal understanding on procedures for conducting business in the Senate that requires the acceptance of every member of the chamber. UCAs limit debate and determine the amendments that can be offered similar to the rules granted by the Rules Committee in the House. Except for measures that are noncontroversial, UCAs reflect negotiation between the Senate leadership and the membership that considers the needs of every member because a single senator can prevent the adoption of an agreement. A member who objects to a UCA is said to place a "hold" on the measure. Members who work through the Majority Leader's secretary can place holds anonymously, but that approach is rare because the purpose of a hold is usually to force some sort of concession, sometimes on an unrelated piece of legislation. The Majority Leader

Filibuster An attempt to defeat the measure through prolonged debate.

Nongermane amendments Amendments which are unrelated to the subject matter of the original measure.

Killer amendment An amendment designed to make a measure so unattractive that it will lack enough support to pass.

may choose to bring the measure to the floor despite the hold, but the motion to proceed may face a **filibuster,** which is an attempt to defeat the measure through prolonged debate. If that is overcome, then the bill itself may be filibustered.

Nonetheless, senators can usually get their legislation to the floor. A senator can often obtain unanimous consent by accepting policy compromises or threatening to oppose the legislation favored by the measure's opponents. A senator can also bring a measure to the floor by offering it as an amendment to another bill. Senate rules allow consideration of **nongermane amendments,** which are amendments unrelated to the subject matter of the original measure. For example, Senator James N. Imhofe of Oklahoma offered an amendment to the Senate immigration reform bill to declare English as the official language of the United States. The amendment passed along with another amendment by Senator Ken Salazar of Colorado to make English "the common and unifying language of the United States."[44] Nongermane amendments are not allowed in the House.

Senators can offer amendments strategically to weaken legislation or to raise other, unrelated issues. A **killer amendment** is an amendment designed to make a measure so unattractive that it will lack enough support to pass. Opponents of term limitation legislation, which Congress considered in 1995, offered an amendment to the measure that would count time already served in the calculation. Were it adopted, many members of Congress voting for term limits would effectively be voting themselves out office.[45] Senators sometimes propose unrelated amendments in order to promote their particular policy views or embarrass their political opponents. Former Senator Jesse Helms of North Carolina, for example, frequently offered nongermane amendments on homosexuality, pornography, abortion, and other controversial issues.

Congress has a reputation as one of the great debating bodies of the world, but it is unusual for debates to sway many votes. Floor debates are often poorly attended and many of the members who are present may be inattentive. The real work of Congress does not take place on the floor, but in committee and subcommittee, congressional offices, the cloakroom, and elsewhere around the capital. Debates allow members to read into the record the case for and against a measure and to justify their own position to their constituents. Debates serve to inform the world outside of Congress rather than sway opinion within. They also have symbolic value, demonstrating to the world that Congress respects majority and minority opinion and that it makes decisions democratically.

Floor proceedings are relatively more structured in the House than the Senate. Although disgruntled House members can sometimes delay action through parliamentary maneuvers, the Rules Committee system generally ensures that House proceedings move forward in a predictable fashion. In contrast, the rules of the Senate are designed to maximize the rights of expression of individual senators. One senator or a group of senators are often able to produce chaos on the Senate floor if they wish.

Indeed, senators sometimes take advantage of the rules to defeat legislation they oppose. Because Senate rules do not limit the amount of time a senator or the chamber as a whole can spend discussing a measure, a bill's opponents may filibuster. Under Senate rules, each senator who wishes to speak must be recognized and

The 1964 Civil Rights Bill became law after Senate supporters were able to invoke cloture, ending a 57-day filibuster.

cannot be interrupted without consent. The Senate cannot vote on a piece of legislation until every senator has finished speaking.[46]

Cloture The procedure for ending a filibuster.

The procedure for ending a filibuster is known as **cloture.** Senators wanting to halt a filibuster must announce their intentions and gather the signatures of a sixth of the Senate—16 senators—to force a vote on cloture, which, in turn, requires a three-fifths' vote of the Senate membership (60 votes) to succeed. Although Senate rules limit post-cloture debate to 30 hours, a measure's opponents often delay action even longer through parliamentary maneuvering.

Filibusters have grown more common. In the 1950s, the Senate had more the atmosphere of an exclusive social club than it does today and senators reserved the filibuster for issues of great import and emotion. From 1955 to 1960, the Senate experienced only two filibusters.[47] In contrast, recent sessions of Congress have averaged 28 filibusters each, with half of all major pieces of legislation facing a filibuster or a serious threat of a filibuster.[48] The filibuster is a potent weapon. Since 1970, the passage rate for legislation subject to filibuster has been 54 percent compared with a 74 percent passage rate for measures not filibustered.[49]

The nature of the filibuster has changed. In the 1950s and 1960s, Senators conducting a filibuster engaged in longwinded debate while Senate leaders kept the chamber in overnight marathon session in order to break the filibuster and move on with a vote. Today, classic filibusters are a thing of the past. Senators simply announce their intention to filibuster and the Senate goes on with other business while the leadership works to gather sufficient support to invoke cloture. Sometimes, Senate leaders file a cloture petition to end debate even before a filibuster materializes. The Senate invoked cloture to end the debate on immigration reform despite the absence of an organized filibuster against the measure.

 WHAT IS YOUR OPINION?

If you were a member of the Senate, would you use the filibuster to defeat legislation you opposed?

Conference Committee Action

A measure does not pass Congress until it clears both the House and Senate in identical form. If the House and Senate pass similar but not identical bills, the chamber that initially passed the measure can agree to the changes made by the other chamber or the two houses can resolve their differences by adopting a series of reconciling amendments. When the differences between the two houses are too great for easy resolution, the two chambers create a conference committee. Although Congress resorts to the conference committee process for only about 10 percent of the measures that ultimately become law, conference committees are typical for major legislation.[50]

Conferees
Members of a conference committee.

The Speaker and the Senate Majority Leader appoint the members of a conference committee (called **conferees**) from lists given to them by committee leaders. Although the Speaker and Majority Leader can appoint any member of Congress to serve on a conference committee, they almost always select members of the standing committee or committees that considered the bill, including the committee chair(s) and ranking member(s). If the Speaker and Majority Leader are concerned that the conferees may not uphold the position of the majority party, they may also appoint members who are sympathetic to the party's position.[51] Because of the increased use of multiple referrals and the increasing tendency of Congress to write omnibus bills, the size of conference committees has grown, sometimes including dozens or even hundreds of members.

A conference committee is sometimes called the third house of Congress because it writes the final version of legislation. The conferees are not bound to stick with the version of the measures passed by either the House or the Senate. The conference committee can delete provisions passed by both houses and include provisions passed by neither. In practice, the final version of major legislation produced by a conference committee reflects not just a compromise between the House and Senate, but a compromise among the party leadership in each chamber, the president, and key interest groups with a stake in the legislation.

Conference report
A revised bill produced by a conference committee.

Once a majority of each chamber's conferees voting separately agree on a compromise, the revised measure, called the **conference report,** goes back to the floor of the House and Senate. The first chamber to vote on the conference report has three options: to accept, reject, or return to conference for more negotiations. If the first chamber accepts the measure, the second chamber has two options, to adopt or reject. If both chambers accept the conference report, the measure has passed Congress and goes to the president.

Presidential Action

The Constitution gives the president several options for dealing with legislation passed by Congress. If the president signs a measure, it becomes law. If the president does not sign the measure, it becomes law anyway after 10 days unless Congress is adjourned, in which case it dies. The action of a president allowing a measure to die without signature after Congress has adjourned is known as a **pocket veto.** In practice, modern presidents rarely use the latter two options. Because Congress now stays in session nearly year-round, presidents have few opportunities for pocket vetoes. Furthermore, image-conscious presidents believe it appears more decisive either to sign a measure or veto it outright.

If the president opposes a measure passed by Congress, the president can issue a **veto,** which is an action by the chief executive refusing to approve a measure passed by the legislature. A president vetoes a bill by returning it to Congress with a statement of objections. If Congress overrides the veto by a two-thirds' vote of each house, the measure becomes law anyway. Should either house fall short of two-thirds, the veto is sustained and the measure has failed. Over the last century, presidents have vetoed about 1 percent of the measures reaching their desks, with Congress overriding only about 7 percent of the vetoes.[52]

The president must accept or reject a measure in its entirety. Congress takes advantage of the situation by passing omnibus bills hundreds or even thousands of pages long that combine provisions the president wants with measures the president would veto were they standing alone. A **rider** is a provision, unlikely to become law on its own merits, that is attached to an important measure so that it will ride through the legislative process. Appropriation bills are favorite vehicles for riders because they are must-pass legislation that presidents are reluctant to veto. For example, Congress enacted a prohibition against smoking on commercial airline flights as a rider attached to an appropriation measure.[53]

Statistics on presidential vetoes indicate that presidents are more likely to veto measures and have their vetoes overridden when the opposition party controls Congress. Since 1960, the presidents who issued the most vetoes were, in order of veto frequency, Ronald Reagan, Gerald Ford, George H. W. Bush, and Richard Nixon, all Republican presidents operating with Congresses that were controlled, in part or in whole, by Democrats. Ford, Reagan, and Nixon suffered the largest number of veto overrides.[54]

The modifications in the legislative process adopted to increase the likelihood that major legislation will become law have been effective. Although the overall success rate for bills is poor, a majority of the major pieces of legislation considered by Congress become law. In 2008, only 278 bills out of 4,815 measures introduced in the House and Senate became law, for a success rate of only 5.8 percent.[55] In contrast, major pieces of legislation fare much better. Over the last decade, 59 percent of major bills have become law.[56]

Pocket veto The action of a president allowing a measure to die without signature after Congress has adjourned.

Veto An action by the chief executive refusing to approve a measure passed by the legislature.

Rider A provision, unlikely to become law on its own merits, which is attached to an important measure so that it will ride through the legislative process.

GETTING INVOLVED

The United States is a **representative democracy,** which is a political system in which citizens elect representatives to make policy decisions on their behalf. Members of the U.S. House represent the interests of the people who live in the districts that elect them. House members recognize that if they fail to represent the wishes of their constituents satisfactorily, then they may risk reelection defeat.

Your assignment is to participate in America's representative democracy by sending an e-mail message about a current policy issue to the man or woman who represents you in the U.S. House. You can find the name and e-mail address of your U.S. representative online at www.house.gov. The following guidelines will help you write an effective letter:

- Know what you are writing about. If you do not understand the issue you address, your

message will have little impact. You may choose an issue discussed in the textbook or another topic in the news. Be sure, however, that you have researched the issue sufficiently so you can speak about it intelligently.

- Use correct grammar. E-mail messages filled with grammatical errors and misspelled words will not have a positive impact.

- Make your point clearly and succinctly. Present your opinion and give the reasons behind your position in no more than a few paragraphs. Long, rambling messages are ineffective.

Print the e-mail message and submit a copy to your instructor. Your instructor will not grade you on your point of view but will evaluate your work on the stated criteria.

CONCLUSION: CONGRESS AND PUBLIC POLICY

Representative democracy A political system in which citizens elect representatives to make policy decisions on their behalf.

Along with the presidency, Congress is the foremost policymaking institution of American national government. It participates in every stage of the policymaking process.

Agenda Building

Congress plays an important role in agenda building. Although many of the issues that Congress addresses were first raised by other political actors, such as interest groups, the media, political parties, and the president, Congress increases their visibility by holding hearings and conducting debates. In recent years, Congress has helped focus attention on such issues as immigration reform, campaign finance reform, the cost of prescription drugs, gun control, gay marriage, global warming, and Internet privacy.

Policy Formulation and Adoption

Congress formulates policy through the legislative process. Individual members, committees, subcommittees, the floor, and conference committees all participate in drafting policy proposals. The policy formulation process in Congress usually involves competition among political interests. The outcome of that process may reflect compromise among those interests or the triumph of one set of interests over other interests, depending on the relative political strength of competing groups.

Congress participates in policy adoption when it passes legislation, ratifies treaties, confirms appointments, and proposes constitutional amendments. In each of these situations, Congress shares policy adoption authority with other political actors. Legislation passed by Congress does not become law unless it is signed by the president or passed by a two-thirds' margin over a presidential veto. Treaties cannot be ratified and appointees confirmed unless they are first proposed or nominated by the president. Constitutional amendments must be ratified by three-fourths of the states.

Policy Implementation and Evaluation

Congress uses the authorization process and the budget process to influence policy implementation. Congress typically authorizes the creation of agencies or programs for a limited number of years after which the agency or program must be reauthorized. Executive branch officials, knowing that their agencies and programs face periodic reauthorization, have an incentive to conform with the wishes of Congress as they implement policy.[57] Similarly, Congress uses the budget process to influence policy implementation. Executive officials want to stay on the good side of Congress because Congress controls their budgets.

Finally, Congress evaluates policy. Congress as a whole evaluates programs when problems persist or when the media publicize scandals in administration. Standing committees provide legislative oversight over administrative agencies, conducting investigations of policy missteps. The appropriation committees scrutinize agency spending. Congress sometimes uses the feedback from policy evaluation to formulate and adopt policy revisions.

KEY TERMS

appropriation bill	impeach	rider
bicameralism	joint committee	Senate Majority Leader
bicameral legislature	killer amendment	Senate president pro tempore
bill	legislative markup	seniority
closed rule	logrolling	Speaker of the House
cloture	Majority Whip	special *or* select committee
conferees	Minority Leader	sponsor
conference committee	Minority Whip	standing committee
conference report	multiple referral of legislation	supermajority
constituency service	nongermane amendments	table
discharge petition	omnibus bills	term limitation
filibuster	open rule	unanimous consent agreement (UCA)
floor	party caucus	veto
franking privilege	pocket veto	whips
House Majority Leader	representative democracy	
House Rules Committee	resolution	

NOTES

1. Charles B. Cushman Jr., *An Introduction to the U.S. Congress* (Armonk, NY: M. E. Sharpe, 2006), p. 5.

2. Robert V. Remini, *The House: The History of the House of Representatives* (New York: HarperCollins, 2006), p. 496.

3. Mildred Amer and Jennifer E. Manning, "Membership of the 111th Congress: A Profile," Congressional Research Service, December 31, 2008, available at http://assets.opencrs.com.

4. Donald R. Matthews, *U.S. Senators and Their World* (New York: Vintage Books, 1960), pp. 116–117.

5. Burdett Loomis, *The New American Politician: Ambition, Entrepreneurship, and the Changing Face of Political Life* (New York: Basic Books, 1988), pp. 233–244.

6. Brandice Canes-Wrone, David W. Brady, and John F. Cogan, "Out of Step, Out of Office: Electoral Accountability and House Members' Voting," *American Political Science Review* 96 (March 2002): 127–140.

7. Sally Friedman, *Dilemmas of Representation: Local Politics, National Factors, and the Home Styles of Modern U.S. Congress Members* (Albany: State University of New York Press, 2007), pp. 223–225.

8. Richard F. Fenno, *Home Style* (Boston: Little, Brown, 1978), p. 18.

9. Richard G. Forgette, *Congress, Parties, and Puzzles: Politics as a Team Sport* (New York: Peter Lang, 2004), p. 174.

10. Robert A. Bernstein, "Determinants of Differences in Feelings Toward Senators Representing the Same State," *Western Political Quarterly* 45 (September 1992): 701–725.

11. George Serra, "What's in It for Me? The Impact of Congressional Casework on Incumbent Evaluation," *American Politics Quarterly* 22 (October 1994): 403–420.

12. Roger H. Davidson and Walter J. Oleszek, *Congress and Its Members*, 8th ed. (Washington, DC: CQ Press, 2004), p. 60.

13. John R. Hibbing and Christopher W. Larimer, "What the American Public Wants Congress to Be," in Lawrence C. Dodd and Bruce I. Oppenheimer, eds., *Congress Reconsidered*, 8th ed. (Washington, DC: CQ Press, 2005), p. 63.

14. Amer and Manning, "Membership of the 111th Congress: A Profile."

15. Robert Pear, "House's Author of Drug Benefit Joins Lobbyists," *New York Times*, December 16, 2004, available at www.nytimes.com.

16. Rebekah Herrick and Samuel H. Fisher III, *Representing America: The Citizen and the Professional Legislator in the House of Representatives* (Lanham, MD: Lexington Books, 2007), pp. 93–96.

17. John R. Hibbing, "Contours of the Modern Congressional Career," *American Political Science Review* 85 (June 1991): 405–428.

18. Kristin Kanthak, "Crystal Elephants and Committee Chairs: Campaign Contributions and Leadership Races in the U.S. House of Representatives," *American Politics Research* 35 (May 2007): 389–406.

19. The Center for Responsive Politics, available at www.opensecrets.org.

20. Gary W. Cox and Mathew D. McCubbins, *Setting the Agenda: Responsible Party Government in the U.S. House of Representatives* (New York: Cambridge University Press, 2005), pp. 1–9.

21. Library of Congress, available at http://thomas.loc.gov.

22. Gary W. Cox and Mathew D. McCubbins, *Legislative Leviathan: Party Government in the House*, 2nd ed. (New York: Cambridge University Press, 2007), pp. 256–257.

23. Eric S. Heberlig and Bruce A. Larson, "Party Fundraising, Descriptive Representation, and the Battle for Majority Control: Shifting Leadership Appointment Strategies in the U.S. House of Representatives, 1990–2002," *Social Science Quarterly* 88 (June 2007): 404–421.

24. Barbara Sinclair, "The New Role of U.S. Senators," in Dodd and Oppenheimer, eds., *Congress Reconsidered*, 8th ed., p. 5.

25. Laura W. Arnold, "The Distribution of Senate Committee Positions: Change or More of the Same?" *Legislative Studies Quarterly* 26 (May 2001): 227–248.

26. Scott A. Frisch and Sean Q. Kelly, *Committee Assignment Politics in the U.S. House of Representatives* (Norman: University of Oklahoma Press, 2006), pp. 328–330.

27. D. Roderick Kiewiet and Mathew D. McCubbins, *The Logic of Delegation: Congressional Parties and the Appropriations Process* (Chicago: University of Chicago Press, 1991), pp. 232–233.

28. Barry Rundquist, Jungho Rhee, Jeong-Hwa Lee, and Sharon E. Fox, "Modeling State Representation on Defense Committees in Congress, 1959–1989," *American Politics Quarterly* 25 (January 1997): 35–55.

29. Richard L. Hall and Bernard Grofman, "The Committee Assignment Process and the Conditional Nature of Committee Bias," *American Political Science Review* 84 (December 1990): 1149–1166.

30. Paul R. Brewer and Christopher J. Deering, "Musical Chairs: Interest Groups, Campaign Fund-Raising, and Selection of House Committee Chairs," in Paul S. Herrnson, Ronald G. Shaiko, and Clyde Wilcox, eds., *The Interest Group Connection: Electioneering, Lobbying, and Policymaking in Washington*, 2nd ed. (Washington, DC: CQ Press, 2005), pp. 141–146.

31. Jeff Zeleny, "Of Party Dues and Deadbeats on Capital Hill," *New York Times*, October 1, 2006, available at www.nytimes.com.

32. Barbara Sinclair, *Unorthodox Lawmaking: New Legislative Processes in the U.S. Congress*, 3rd ed. (Washington, DC: Congressional Quarterly Press, 2007), pp. 5–8.

33. *Congressional Record*, Daily Digest, "Résumé of Congressional Activity, 110th Congress," available at www.senate.gov/reference/resources/pdf/110_1.pdf.

34. Roger H. Davidson and Walter J. Oleszek, *Congress and Its Members*, 7th ed. (Washington, DC: CQ Press, 2000), p. 31.

35. Public Law 107–110, January 2002.

36. *Congressional Record*, "Résumé of Congressional Activity, 110th Congress."

37. John Baughman, *Common Ground: Committee Politics in the U.S. House of Representatives* (Stanford, CA: Stanford University Press, 2006), pp. 175–179.

38. Sinclair, *Unorthodox Lawmaking*, p. 12.

39. C. Lawrence Evans, "Participation and Policy Making in Senate Committees," *Political Science Quarterly* 106 (Fall 1991): 490.

40. Davidson and Oleszek, *Congress and Its Members*, 7th ed. p. 242.

41. Sinclair, *Unorthodox Lawmaking*, p. 19.

42. Ibid., p. 22.

43. Ibid, p. 32.

44. Library of Congress.

45. John D. Wilerson, "'Killer' Amendments in Congress," *American Political Science Review* 93 (September 1999): 535–552.

46. Gregory J. Wawro and Eric Schickler, *Filibuster: Obstruction and Lawmaking in the U.S. Senate* (Princeton, NJ: Princeton University Press, 2006), pp. 13–14.

47. Christopher J. Deering, "Leadership in the Slow Lane," *PS: Policy and Politics* (Winter 1986), pp. 37–42; Bruce I. Oppenheimer, "Changing Time Constraints on Congress: Historical Perspectives on the Use of Cloture." in Lawrence C. Dodd and Bruce I. Oppenheimer, eds., *Congress Reconsidered*, 4th ed. (Washington, DC: Congressional Quarterly Press, 1989), pp. 393–413.

48. Sinclair, *Unorthodox Lawmaking*, p. 69.

49. Barbara Sinclair, "The '60-Vote Senate:' Strategies, Process, and Outcomes," in Bruce I. Oppenheimer, ed., *U.S. Senate Exceptionalism* (Columbus: Ohio State University Press, 2002), pp. 258–259.

50. Sinclair, *Unorthodox Lawmaking*, p. 76.

51. Jeffrey Lazarus and Nathan W. Monroe, "The Speaker's Discretion: Conference Committee Appointments in the 97th through 106th Congresses," *Political Research Quarterly* 60 (December 2007): 593–606.

52. Samuel B. Hoff, "Saying No: Presidential Support and Veto Use, 1889–1989," *American Politics Quarterly* 19 (July 1991): 317.

53. Dan Morgan, "Along for the Rider," *Washington Post National Weekly Edition*, August 19–25, 2002, p. 15.

54. *Statistical Abstract of the United States 1990* (Washington, DC: Bureau of the Census, 1990), p. 255.

55. *Congressional Record*, "Résumé of Congressional Activity, 110th Congress."

56. Sinclair, *Unorthodox Lawmaking*, p. 272.

57. James H. Cox, *Reviewing Delegation: An Analysis of the Congressional Reauthorization Process* (New York: Praeger, 2004), p. 124.

Chapter 11

The Presidency

CHAPTER OUTLINE

LEARNING OUTCOMES

After studying Chapter 11, students should be able to do the following:

▸ Outline the constitutional presidency, considering qualifications and backgrounds, term of office, impeachment and removal, succession, and disability. (pp. 279–284)

▸ Trace the evolution of the office of the vice presidency. (p. 285)

▸ Identify the constitutional powers of the presidency, and describe how those powers have expanded beyond the constitutional outline of the office, considering diplomatic, military, inherent, judicial, executive, and legislative powers. (pp. 286–292)

▸ Evaluate the two presidencies thesis. (p. 293)

▸ Trace the historical development of the modern presidency. (pp. 293–295)

- Describe the organization of the White House staff and the Executive Office of the President. (pp. 295–299)
- Compare and contrast the approaches to presidential leadership taken by Barber and Greenstein. (pp. 300–301)
- Compare and contrast the perspectives on presidential power taken by Neustadt and Kernell with the perspective of scholars who focus on the unilateral tools of presidential leadership. (pp. 301–304)

- Identify the factors affecting presidential popularity. (pp. 304–306)
- Describe the impact of contextual factors on presidential influence. (pp. 306–308)
- Describe the role of the presidency in America's policy process. (pp. 308–309)
- Define the key terms listed on page 309 and explain their significance.

B arack Obama made healthcare reform a priority for his administration, but he recognized that the enactment of healthcare reform legislation would be a challenge. Some of the most powerful groups in the country have a stake in the issue, including insurance companies, physicians, hospitals, business groups, and labor unions. Any reform plan would need the support or at least neutrality of most if not all of the major groups involved to make it through Congress. Furthermore, Obama knew that the last Democratic administration to make healthcare reform a priority failed miserably. Soon after taking office, President Bill Clinton created a Task Force on National Healthcare Reform, chaired by Hillary Clinton, but the effort became the target of intense interest group opposition. Critics attacked the process for being overly secretive and the plan it produced for being overly bureaucratic and too restrictive of patient choice. The proposal died in the Senate without coming to a vote, the victim of a Republican-led filibuster.

Obama hoped to learn from the mistakes of the Clinton administration by promising an open and inclusive policymaking process. Because his campaign focused on the healthcare issue, he could claim that his election represented a mandate for reform. An **electoral mandate** is the expression of popular support for a particular policy demonstrated through the electoral process. To head off opposition, Obama mobilized his network of supporters to hold house parties to discuss healthcare reform and lobby their representatives in Congress.[1]

President Obama's effort to reform the healthcare system introduces this chapter on the presidency by drawing attention to the factors that affect the ability of the president to accomplish policy goals. Chapter 11 is the second of four chapters dealing with the institutions of American national government. The subject of Chapter 10 was the Congress of the United States. Chapters 12 and 13 focus on the federal bureaucracy and the judiciary, respectively. We begin our study of the presidency by focusing on the constitutional outline of the office.

Electoral mandate
The expression of popular support for a particular policy demonstrated through the electoral process.

THE CONSTITUTIONAL PRESIDENCY

The Constitution describes the office of the presidency in Article II.

Qualifications and Backgrounds

The Constitution declares that the president must be at least 35 years of age, a natural-born American citizen (as opposed to a naturalized citizen), and a resident of the United States for at least 14 years. Before the 2008 election, all the nation's presidents had been white males of Western European ancestry. Two sets of presidents were father and son (John and John Quincy Adams and George H. W and George W. Bush); two were grandfather and grandson (William Henry and Benjamin Harrison); and two were cousins (Theodore and Franklin D. Roosevelt). All but one, John Kennedy, have been Protestant Christians. Kennedy was Roman Catholic. Most presidents have been fairly wealthy; the majority of them have been experienced politicians. Most presidents have come from states outside the South. In recent years, however, social barriers have begun to fall: the nation has elected a Roman Catholic (Kennedy), three native Southerners (Jimmy Carter, Clinton, and George W. Bush), and a divorced person (Ronald Reagan) to the White House. The election of Barack Obama, the son of a white woman from Kansas and a black immigrant from Kenya, shattered the barriers of race and ethnicity. Furthermore, Hillary Clinton's strong

A president whose influence is diminished because the official either cannot or will not seek reelection is known as a lame duck.

Source: © ED Fischer/www.CartoonStock.com.

showing in the race for the Democratic presidential nomination suggested that gender was no longer a major barrier to the White House. The myth that anyone born in the United States could grow up to become president came closer to reality than ever before in the nation's history.

Term of Office

The president's constitutional term of office is four years. The framers of the Constitution placed no limit on the number of terms presidents could serve, believing that the desire to remain in office would compel presidents to do their best. George Washington, the nation's first chief executive, established a custom of seeking no more than two terms, which every president honored until Franklin D. Roosevelt broke tradition in the early 1940s. After Roosevelt, a Democrat, won election to a third and then a fourth term, unhappy Republicans launched a drive to amend the Constitution to limit the president to two terms. They succeeded with the ratification of the Twenty-second Amendment in 1951. The proponents of the two-term limit argued that it prevented a president from becoming too powerful. In contrast, critics believed that the two-term limit unnecessarily weakened the office of the presidency by making a second-term president a **lame duck,** which is an official whose influence is diminished because the official either cannot or will not seek reelection. The opponents of the Twenty-second Amendment also complained that it was undemocratic because it denied voters the right to reelect a president they admired.

Lame duck An official whose influence is diminished because the official either cannot or will not seek reelection.

 WHAT IS YOUR OPINION?

Should presidents be permitted to run for more than two terms?

Impeachment and Removal

Impeachment is a process in which an executive or judicial official is formally accused of an offense that could warrant removal from office. The Constitution states that the president may be impeached for "treason, bribery, or other high crimes and misdemeanors." The Founders foresaw two broad, general grounds on which a president could be impeached and removed from office: (1) Impeachment could be used against a president who abused the powers of office, thereby threatening to become a tyrant. (2) It could be employed against a president who failed to carry out the duties of the office.[2]

The actual process of impeachment and removal involves both houses of Congress. The House drafts **articles of impeachment,** which is a document listing the impeachable offenses that the House believes the president committed. Technically, *impeach* means to accuse; so when the House impeaches the president by majority vote, it is accusing the president of committing offenses that may warrant removal from office. The Senate then tries the president, with the chief justice presiding. The Senate must vote by a two-thirds' margin to remove the president from office.

Impeachment A process in which an executive or judicial official is formally accused of an offense that could warrant removal from office.

Articles of impeachment A document listing the impeachable offenses that the House believes the president committed.

Andrew Johnson's Impeachment   In 1868, Andrew Johnson became the first president to be impeached. Johnson was a former Democratic senator from Tennessee who was chosen by the Republican Party to be President Abraham Lincoln's running

The election of Barack Obama shattered the barriers of race and ethnicity that had limited the presidency to white males of Western European descent.

mate in the 1864 election. The Republicans hoped that adding Johnson to the ticket would broaden its appeal to Democrats who supported the Union during the Civil War. When Johnson became president after Lincoln's assassination, he quarreled with the Republican Congress over which branch of government would control **Reconstruction,** which was the process whereby the states that had seceded during the Civil War were reorganized and reestablished in the Union. Congress overrode Johnson's veto to pass several laws aimed at limiting the president's power. One of these measures, the Tenure of Office Act, stipulated that any official appointed by the president and confirmed by the Senate could not be removed from office until the Senate had confirmed a replacement. Johnson challenged the law by removing Secretary of War Edwin M. Stanton and appointing General Ulysses S. Grant as his interim successor. The House of Representatives responded to Johnson's challenge by voting to impeach him 126 to 47. The Senate voted 35 to 19 for conviction, just one vote short of the two-thirds' vote necessary to remove President Johnson from office.

Richard Nixon's Resignation   More than a century after Andrew Johnson survived impeachment, President Nixon resigned in the face of impeachment proceedings stemming from the Watergate scandal. The Watergate affair began in June 1972 when five men were arrested breaking into the Democratic National Committee headquarters in the Watergate office complex in Washington, DC. The burglars, employed by the Committee to Reelect the President, were hired to plant electronic eavesdropping devices in the opposition's headquarters. Their mission was part of a conspiracy formed by aides of President Nixon to manipulate the Democratic Party's presidential nomination process to assist the weakest Democratic candidate possible

Reconstruction The process whereby the states that had seceded during the Civil War were reorganized and reestablished in the Union.

and defeat any potential nominee strong enough to beat Nixon. It was many months, however, before these facts were generally known.

Once the burglars were arrested, Nixon and his aides attempted to conceal the nature of the initial conspiracy. They paid more than $300,000 in hush money to the burglars and their supervisors to keep them quiet. In the meantime, the White House played down the significance of the break-in, calling the event a third-rate burglary.

The cover-up did not begin to unravel until early 1973, when the burglars stood trial. Although they remained silent, Judge John Sirica voiced the opinion that the truth had not come out. In the meantime, two investigative reporters for the *Washington Post* newspaper, Carl Bernstein and Bob Woodward, began to uncover facts and ask questions about the affair.

By early summer 1973, the investigation was proceeding on several fronts. In the Senate, a special committee, chaired by Senator Sam Ervin, conducted televised hearings at which presidential aides told startling tales of political dirty tricks and cover-ups in the White House. "What did the president know and when did he know it?" asked Senator Howard Baker. While the hearings continued, Special Counsel Archibald Cox conducted an investigation on behalf of the Justice Department. In October, Nixon decided that Cox's probe was coming too close to the truth and he fired Cox in what came to be known as the Saturday Night Massacre. For the first time, congressional leaders publicly considered impeachment.

Nixon clung to his presidency for another nine and a half months. He called on the nation "to put Watergate behind us," but each week brought new accusations and revelations. In 1974, the House Judiciary Committee held hearings on proposed articles of impeachment against the president, eventually recommending impeachment to the full House. Meanwhile, a new special counsel, Leon Jaworski, pursued the investigation, aided immeasurably by tape recordings the president had made secretly of conversations with his aides.

Watergate came to a climax in midsummer 1974 when the U.S. Supreme Court ordered Nixon to hand over a key group of tapes to the special prosecutor. One tape, containing a conversation between the president and Chief of Staff H. R. Haldeman, proved to be the smoking gun that linked Nixon directly to the cover-up. What support Nixon still had in Congress and the Republican Party crumbled. In August, he resigned the presidency.

The Impeachment of Bill Clinton   In 1998, President Clinton became the second president to be impeached. An investigation by Special Counsel Kenneth Starr provided the basis for the case against Clinton. Starr was initially appointed to look into allegations of the president's involvement in a failed Arkansas land development called Whitewater when Clinton was governor of Arkansas. The scope of Starr's investigation subsequently expanded to include allegations that Clinton had lied under oath about an alleged sexual liaison with White House intern Monica Lewinsky and that Clinton encouraged Lewinsky to lie as well. Starr's focus on Lewinsky stemmed from a sexual harassment lawsuit filed against Clinton by Paula Corbin Jones over an incident that allegedly occurred while Clinton was governor of Arkansas. In her lawsuit, Jones charged that then-Governor Clinton engaged in illegal sexual harassment by asking her for sexual favors. Her attorneys subpoenaed both Lewinsky and Clinton in hopes of establishing a pattern of sexual misconduct by Clinton. Starr investigated the matter to ascertain whether President Clinton had lied under oath while giving a deposition in the case and whether he had illegally encouraged Lewinsky to lie under oath as well.

Starr's report to Congress included 11 specific allegations of impeachable offenses. Starr charged that Clinton committed perjury by lying under oath about having an affair during the Jones deposition and while testifying to a grand jury convened by the special counsel. He accused the president of obstructing justice by helping Lewinsky find a job after she left the White House and making false statements to his staff about his relationship to her. Finally, Starr charged Clinton with abusing his constitutional authority by lying to the public and Congress about the affair. Starr supported his allegations by filling his report with page after page of explicit details of the sexual encounters between the president and Lewinsky.

Clinton responded to the crisis by admitting to an "inappropriate relationship" with Lewinsky. Clinton said that he had made a mistake and began a series of apologies to his wife, staff, members of Congress, cabinet, and the American people. All the while, Clinton and his lawyers declared that technically he had not perjured himself by lying under oath and that he had not committed an impeachable offense. The investigation should end, they said, so the president and Congress could get on with the nation's business.

But the investigation did not end—at least not before the impeachment process played itself out. The House Judiciary Committee held hearings on the charges and recommended four articles of impeachment on a strict party-line vote, with every Republican on the committee voting for at least one of the articles and every Democrat voting against all of them. In late 1998, the House impeached Clinton by voting in favor of Article I, which accused the president of lying under oath, and Article III, which charged Clinton with obstruction of justice in the investigation of his testimony in the Jones case. The vote in the House was close, with all but five Republicans voting for at least one article of impeachment and all but five Democrats voting against all the articles. In February 1999, the Senate failed to convict the president and remove him from office. The vote was 45 to 55 in favor of Article I and 50 to 50 on Article III. All 45 Senate Democrats voted against both articles, whereas 10 Republican Senators voted against Article I and five Republicans opposed Article III.

 WHAT IS YOUR OPINION?

If you were a member of the Senate, would you have voted to remove Clinton from office? Why or why not?

Presidential Succession and Disability

The vice president succeeds a president who is removed, resigns, or dies in office. After the vice president, the line of succession passes to the Speaker of the House, president pro tempore of the Senate, secretary of state, and down through the cabinet. In American history, nine vice presidents have succeeded to the presidency, but no Speakers or Senate presidents pro tempore. Furthermore, because of the Twenty-fifth

Amendment, the order of succession probably will never extend beyond the office of vice president.

The Twenty-fifth Amendment was ratified in 1967, after President Dwight Eisenhower's heart attack and President Kennedy's assassination focused attention on the issue of presidential succession and disability. The amendment authorizes the president to fill a vacancy in the office of vice president subject to majority confirmation by both houses of Congress. This procedure was first used in 1973, when President Nixon nominated Gerald Ford to replace Vice President Spiro Agnew, who resigned under accusation of criminal wrongdoing. When Nixon himself resigned in 1974, Ford moved up to the presidency and appointed former governor of New York Nelson Rockefeller to be the new vice president.

Other provisions of the Twenty-fifth Amendment establish procedures for the vice president to become acting president should the president become disabled and incapable of performing the duties of office. The president may declare disability by written notice to the Senate president pro tempore and the Speaker of the House. The vice president then becomes acting president until the president declares in writing his or her ability to resume the responsibilities of office. If the president is unable or unwilling to declare disability, the vice president can declare the president disabled in conjunction with a majority of the cabinet. Should the vice president/cabinet and president disagree on the question of the president's disability, Congress may declare the president disabled by two-thirds' vote of each house.

Franklin D. Roosevelt was elected to four terms. Because of the Twenty-second Amendment, the president is now limited to two terms.

The Vice Presidency

The Constitution gives the vice president two duties. The vice president is president of the Senate and votes in case of a tie. The vice president also becomes president of the United States if the office becomes vacant. For most of American history, however, the vice president was the forgotten person of Washington. In 1848, Daniel Webster, a prominent political figure of the time, rejected the vice presidential nomination of his party, by saying "I do not propose to be buried until I am dead."[3] John Nance Garner, one of Franklin Roosevelt's vice presidents, once declared the job was not worth a "bucket of warm piss." Before the last half of the twentieth century, the vice president had no staff and few responsibilities. The vice president represented the nation at selected ceremonial occasions, such as the funeral of a foreign leader, but had no policy responsibilities.

Today, the vice presidency has become a more visible and important office. The death in office of President Franklin Roosevelt, Eisenhower's heart attack, Kennedy's assassination, Nixon's resignation, and the assassination attempt against Reagan all called attention to the possibility that the vice president could become president at any time. A contemporary president who kept the vice president uninformed and uninvolved in policy issues would be generally regarded as an irresponsible chief executive. Furthermore, the vice presidency has become the most common path to the office of the presidency, either through succession or election. Since 1950, five presidents (Harry Truman, Lyndon Johnson, Nixon, Ford, and the elder Bush) held office as vice president prior to becoming president. Men and women of stature are now willing to serve as vice president.

Recent presidents have actively involved their vice presidents in their administrations. President Carter used Vice President Walter Mondale as an adviser, troubleshooter, and emissary to interest groups and Congress. Mondale and every vice president since had an office in the White House, a sizable staff, and an open invitation to attend any meeting on the president's schedule. President Reagan named George H. W. Bush to chair the Task Force on Regulatory Relief and placed the vice president in charge of the war on drugs. When George H. W. Bush became president, he appointed his vice president, Dan Quayle, to head a Council on Competitiveness that reviewed proposed regulations for their impact on business and the economy. President Clinton made Vice President Al Gore the chair of the National Performance Review Commission, which was assigned the task of recommending reforms to make government more efficient and cost effective. He assigned Gore the task of debating Ross Perot on the North American Free Trade Agreement (NAFTA), which the administration favored and Perot opposed. The **North American Free Trade Agreement (NAFTA)** is an international accord among the United States, Mexico, and Canada to lower trade barriers among the three nations.[4] Although Vice President Richard Cheney was probably not a co-president, as some critics suggested, he almost certainly exercised more policy influence than any vice president in history.[5] President Bush preferred to focus on broad policy objectives and delegate authority to work out the details of policy to subordinates. Cheney developed great influence because he was detail oriented and was willing to assert himself. Many observers believed he was Bush's most important advisor on energy policy, the war in Iraq, judicial nominations, and tax policy.[6]

North American Free Trade Agreement (NAFTA) An international accord among the United States, Mexico, and Canada to lower trade barriers among the three nations.

PRESIDENTIAL POWERS

The powers of the presidency have developed through the give-and-take of the political process. Although the Constitution outlines the powers to the office in Article II, many of the provisions are not clearly defined.[7] This ambiguity of Article II has enabled presidents to expand the limits of presidential power beyond the initial understanding of the authority granted the office.[8]

Diplomatic Powers

Chief of state The official head of government.

The Constitution gives the president, as **chief of state** (the official head of government), broad diplomatic authority to conduct foreign relations. The president has the power officially to recognize the governments of other nations and to receive and appoint ambassadors. For example, the United States broke off diplomatic relations with China after the communist takeover in 1940. President Nixon began the process of normalizing relations with the People's Republic of China as the legitimate government of mainland China. President Carter completed the process, and the two nations exchanged ambassadors. The only constitutional limitation on the president's power of diplomatic recognition is that ambassadorial appointments must be approved by majority vote of the Senate.

The Constitution empowers the president to negotiate treaties with other nations, subject to a two-thirds' vote of ratification by the Senate. Since 1789, the Senate has rejected only 21 of more than 1,500 treaties submitted to it, but that figure underestimates the role of the Senate in the ratification process. Most treaties that lack sufficient support to pass the Senate are either withdrawn from consideration by the president or bottled up in committee. For example, the Law of the Sea Treaty, which is an international agreement governing the oceans, has languished in the Senate Foreign Relations Committee since 1982, even though it has been ratified by more than a hundred other nations. At least 85 treaties have been withdrawn because the Senate failed to act on them. The Senate may make its approval of a treaty conditional, depending on the acceptance of amendments, interpretations, understandings, or other reservations. The president and the other countries involved must then decide whether to accept the conditions, renegotiate the provisions, or abandon the treaty altogether.[9]

Executive agreement An international understanding between the president and foreign nations that does not require Senate ratification.

Presidents use executive agreements to expand their diplomatic authority beyond the treaty power. An **executive agreement** is an international understanding between the president and foreign nations that does not require Senate ratification. Although the Constitution says nothing about executive agreements, the Supreme Court has upheld their use based on the president's diplomatic and military powers. Executive agreements are more numerous than treaties. The United States is currently a party to nearly 900 treaties and more than 5,000 executive agreements.[10] Many executive agreements involve relatively routine matters, such as the exchange of postal service between nations. Congress has passed legislation authorizing the executive branch to make executive agreements with other countries in certain fields, such as agriculture, trade, and foreign aid. Some executive agreements also require congressional participation because they involve changes in American law.

Congress had to pass legislation authorizing NAFTA, even though it was an executive agreement, because it required changes in American trade laws.

Military Powers

The Constitution names the president commander-in-chief of the armed forces. As commander-in-chief, the president makes military policy, including decisions involving the use of force, operational strategy, and personnel. President Franklin Roosevelt, for example, chose the time and place of the Normandy invasion in World War II. Truman decided to drop the atomic bomb on Japan during World War II and fired General Douglas McArthur for publicly disagreeing with the administration's war policy during the Korean conflict. Reagan ordered the marines to invade the Caribbean nation of Grenada and directed air strikes against Libya. The first President Bush sent American forces to the Persian Gulf to roll back the Iraqi invasion of Kuwait. Clinton dispatched American forces on peacekeeping missions to Somalia and Bosnia, ordered air strikes against Iraq, and directed the U.S. Air Force to conduct an air war to protect ethnic Albanian civilians from attack by Serbian forces in the Yugoslavian province of Kosovo. President George W. Bush ordered American forces to take military action against the Taliban government in Afghanistan and the al Qaeda terrorists that it sheltered. He also ordered the American military to overthrow the government of Saddam Hussein in Iraq.

Civilian supremacy of the armed forces The concept that the armed forces should be under the direct control of civilian authorities.

The president's role as commander-in-chief embodies the doctrine of **civilian supremacy of the armed forces,** which is the concept that the armed forces should be under the direct control of civilian authorities. The doctrine of civilian supremacy is based on the belief that military decisions should be weighed in light of political considerations. The concept of civilian supremacy also reflects the view that the preservation of representative democracy depends on keeping the military out of politics. In many nations, the armed forces are a powerful political force and military men sometimes seize the reigns of government from civilian authorities. The government of Burma (also known as Myanmar), for example, is a military government, headed by generals whose power depends on the support of the armed forces rather than the votes of the nation's people. In the United States, the president, a civilian, stands at the apex of the command structure of the armed forces. The government controls the military rather than the military controlling the government.

Presidents sometimes use their power as commander-in-chief as the basis for exercising authority beyond the scope of direct military action. After Japan bombed Pearl Harbor in 1941 and the United States entered World War II, President Franklin Roosevelt issued an executive order authorizing the military to relocate all persons of Japanese ancestry from the West Coast to inland war relocation centers. More than 120,000 persons were interned, including 70,000 native-born American citizens, and the U.S. Supreme Court upheld the constitutionality of the action.[11] After the terrorist attacks of September 11, 2001, President Bush exercised his authority as commander-in-chief to order the arrest and detention of persons suspected of involvement in terrorist activity.

Congress and the president have frequently quarreled over the relative authority of the legislative and executive branches to make military policy. Although

President Bush ordered that enemy combatants captured in the war on terror be held at Guantánamo Bay, Cuba.

the president is commander-in-chief, the Constitution grants Congress sole authority to declare war. The last war in which the United States participated that was declared, however, was World War II. The president has initiated all subsequent American military actions, including the Korean War and the war in Vietnam, without benefit of a congressional declaration of war. Although Congress authorized the use of force in Iraq before the U.S. invasion, it did not issue a declaration of war.

In 1973 during the War in Vietnam, Congress responded to what it considered an infringement of its constitutional power to declare war by enacting the **War Powers Act,** which is a law limiting the president's ability to commit American armed forces to combat abroad without consultation with Congress and congressional approval.[12] The measure includes a number of important provisions:

- The president should consult with Congress "in every possible instance" before introducing American forces into situations where hostilities would be likely.
- The president must make detailed, periodic reports on the necessity and scope of the operation.
- American forces must be withdrawn after 60 days of the first reports of fighting (with a 30-day grace period to ensure safe withdrawal) unless Congress declares war or votes to authorize the presence of the American forces.
- Congress can order the withdrawal of American forces by majority vote of both houses at any time, even before the 60-day period has expired. This last provision was apparently invalidated by a 1983 Supreme Court decision that found similar measures unconstitutional.[13]

War Powers Act A law limiting the president's ability to commit American armed forces to combat abroad without consultation with Congress and congressional approval.

The War Powers Act has been a source of conflict between the president and Congress. The two branches of government have often disagreed about the measure's consultation requirement. Whereas some members of Congress believe that the law requires that the president discuss the use of force with Congress and seek advice, presidents have generally only informed congressional leaders in advance of pending military actions. Chief executives have also tried to avoid the application of the War Powers Act by denying that the military actions they ordered fell under the scope of the law. President Carter, for example, failed to consult congressional leaders before ordering an ill-fated hostage-rescue mission in Iran, arguing that rescue missions are not combat situations.

In practice, the War Powers Act is probably a less effective check on the president's military power than is public opinion. If a president's actions enjoy broad public support, as was the case with the first war in the Persian Gulf, Congress is unlikely to order a withdrawal of American forces. In contrast, the risk of adverse public reaction may deter some military initiatives or cut short others. In 1983, for example, Reagan ordered American forces withdrawn from Beirut, Lebanon, well in advance of a War Powers Act cut-off date after several hundred marines were killed in a terrorist bombing. Perhaps more significantly, the ordered withdrawal came well in advance of the 1984 presidential election.

In 2008, a commission recommended that Congress and the president scrap the War Powers Act and replace it with legislation requiring the president and congressional leaders to consult before going to war. The commission, which was headed by two former secretaries of state, Republican James A. Baker III and Democrat Warren Christopher, declared the War Powers Act "ineffective at best and unconstitutional at worst."[14] The new law the commission proposed would create a new committee of congressional leaders and relevant committee chairs, with a full-time staff that would have access to military and foreign policy intelligence information. The president would be required to consult with the new committee in advance of military action expected to take longer than a week (except in rare emergencies) and meet with it regularly during an extended conflict. Congress as a whole would be required to vote on an authorization resolution within 30 days of the initiation of hostilities. If the authorization resolution failed, any member of Congress could introduce a resolution of disapproval, which would have to pass both houses of Congress and be signed by the president to go into effect. A presidential veto would have to be overridden by a two-thirds' vote before the resolution had the force of law.[15]

? WHAT IS YOUR OPINION?

Is the president's authority as commander-in-chief too broad?

Inherent Powers

Inherent powers are those powers vested in the national government, particularly in the area of foreign and defense policy, that do not depend on any specific grant of authority by the Constitution, but rather exist because the United States is a sovereign nation. Consider the **Louisiana Purchase,** which was the acquisition from France of a vast expanse of land stretching from New Orleans north to the Dakotas. President Thomas Jefferson justified his decision to acquire the territory on the basis of inherent

Inherent powers Those powers vested in the national government, particularly in the area of foreign and defense policy, which do not depend on any specific grant of authority by the Constitution, but rather exist because the United States is a sovereign nation.

Louisiana Purchase The acquisition from France of a vast expanse of land stretching from New Orleans north to the Dakotas.

powers because the Constitution says nothing about purchasing land from another country. Similarly, Lincoln claimed extraordinary powers to defend the Union during the Civil War on the basis of inherent powers. President George W. Bush used the doctrine of inherent powers to justify the use of military tribunals to try enemy combatants captured in the War on Terror, designate U.S. citizens as enemy combatants, send terror suspects to countries that practice torture, and authorize eavesdropping on American citizens by the National Security Agency (NSA).[16]

Presidential assertions of inherent powers are almost invariably controversial because they involve an expansion of government authority and presidential power not authorized by the Constitution. Critics of the Louisiana Purchase, for example, called Jefferson a hypocrite because he had long argued that the authority of the national government was limited to powers clearly delegated by the Constitution. In recent years, critics accused President George W. Bush of not just exceeding his power but violating the Constitution. They challenged his actions in Congress and the courts.

Judicial Powers

The president plays a role in judicial policymaking. The president nominates all federal judges pending majority-vote confirmation by the Senate. The Senate usually approves nominees, but not without scrutiny, especially for Supreme Court selections. The Senate rejected two consecutive Supreme Court appointments by President Nixon before confirming his third choice. Similarly, the Senate rejected Reagan's nomination of Robert Bork to the Supreme Court.

The power of appointment gives a president the opportunity to shape the policy direction of the judicial branch of American government, especially a president who serves two terms. During his eight years in office, President Clinton appointed 374 federal judges; George W. Bush named more than 300 judges during his presidency. Clinton and Bush each appointed two Supreme Court justices.[17]

The Constitution empowers the president to grant pardons and reprieves. A **pardon** is an executive action that frees an accused or convicted person from all penalties for an offense. A **reprieve** is an executive action that delays punishment for a crime. With some exceptions, such as President Ford's pardon of former President Nixon, most presidential pardons and reprieves are not controversial.

Executive Powers

The president is the nation's **chief executive,** that is, the head of the executive branch of government. The Constitution grants the president authority to require written reports of department heads and enjoins the president to "take care that laws be faithfully executed." As head of the executive branch of government, presidents can issue executive orders to manage the federal bureaucracy. An **executive order** is a directive issued by the president to an administrative agency or executive department. Although the Constitution says nothing about executive orders, the courts have upheld their use based on law, custom, and the president's authority as head of the executive branch.

Presidents have used executive orders to enact important (and sometimes controversial) policies. President Lincoln, for example, used an executive order to issue

Pardon An executive action that frees an accused or convicted person from all penalties for an offense.

Reprieve An executive action that delays punishment for a crime.

Chief executive The head of the executive branch of government.

Executive order A directive issued by the president to an administrative agency or executive department.

the Emancipation Proclamation. President Eisenhower issued an executive order to send National Guard troops into Little Rock, Arkansas, in 1957 to protect African American youngsters attempting to attend a whites-only public high school. The first President Bush issued executive orders to prohibit abortion counseling at federally funded family planning centers. Clinton, in turn, used an executive order to reverse the Bush order. President Obama issued executive orders to prohibit the use of torture in the interrogation of prisoners held in the war on terror and to close the detention camp at Guantánamo Bay, Cuba.

The president's power to issue executive orders is not unlimited. Presidents may only issue executive orders that fall within the scope of their constitutional powers and legal authority. In 1952, for example, during the Korean War, the U.S. Supreme Court overturned an executive order by President Truman to seize the nation's steel mills and head off a strike that would have disrupted steel production and hurt the war effort. The Court declared that the president lacked the legal authority to seize private property and that the president's power as commander-in-chief did not extend to labor disputes.[18] Congress can also overturn an executive order legislatively. Because the president would likely veto a measure reversing an executive order, Congress would need to vote not only to repeal the order but then to vote again by a two-thirds' margin to override the veto.

In 1957, President Dwight Eisenhower issued an executive order to send the National Guard into Little Rock, Arkansas, to protect African American youngsters attempting to attend a whites-only public high school.

Legislative Powers

Finally, the Constitution grants the president certain tools for shaping the legislative agenda. From time to time, it says, the president shall "give to Congress information of the state of the Union, and recommend to their consideration such measures as he shall judge necessary and expedient." Traditionally, the president makes a State of the Union address each January before a joint session of Congress and a national television audience. The speech gives the president the opportunity to raise issues and frame the terms of their discussion. Although the State of the Union address allows the president the opportunity to present himself or herself as the nation's chief legislator, it may also create unrealistic public expectations. In practice, Congress approves only 43 percent of the policy initiatives included in the average State of the Union speech, either in whole or in part.[19]

The president can use the veto power to shape the content of legislation. The Constitution empowers the president to return measures to Congress along with objections. A vetoed measure can only become law if both the House and Senate vote to override by a two-thirds' margin. The veto is a powerful weapon. In more than 200 years, Congress has overridden less than 1 percent of presidential vetoes.[20] Nonetheless, political scientists consider the actual use of the veto a sign of weakness rather than strength because influential presidents can usually prevent passage of measures they oppose by threatening a veto.[21]

Presidential signing statement
A pronouncement issued by the president at the time a bill passed by Congress is signed into law.

A **presidential signing statement** is a pronouncement issued by the president at the time a bill passed by Congress is signed into law. Presidents historically have used signing statements to comment on the bill they are signing, score political points, identify areas of disagreement with the measure, and discuss its implementation. President George W. Bush went further than any of his predecessors in using signing statements to expand the powers of his office. Bush's signing statements identified more than 800 provisions in 500 measures that he signed into law that he considered unconstitutional limitations on his authority as president, and he asserted his intention to ignore the provisions or treat them as advisory. Bush declared, for example, that legislative provisions that establish qualifications for executive branch officials were advisory rather than mandatory because he believed that they unconstitutionally restricted the presidential power of appointment. He asserted his intention to withhold information from Congress and rejected legislative provisions that he believed would limit his power as commander-in-chief.

Presidential signing statements are controversial. Political scientist Phillip J. Cooper believes that President Bush used presidential signing statements as a vehicle for revising legislation without issuing a veto, which is subject to congressional override.[22] The American Bar Association (ABA) declares that Bush's use of signing statements is "contrary to the rule of law and our constitutional system of separation of powers" because the Constitution requires that the president sign legislation or veto it in its entirety.[23] In contrast, law professors Curtis A. Bradley and Eric A. Posner argue that signing statements are legal and useful because they provide a way for the president to disclose his or her views about the meaning and constitutionality of legislation.[24]

TWO PRESIDENCIES THESIS

Two Presidencies Thesis The concept that the president enjoys more influence over foreign policy than domestic policy.

The **Two Presidencies Thesis** is the concept that the president enjoys more influence over foreign policy than domestic policy. The exponents of the Two Presidencies Thesis offer several theoretical explanations for the phenomenon. As commander-in-chief of the armed forces and head of state, the president possesses clearer constitutional authority in foreign and defense policy than in most other policy areas. In the meantime, members of Congress often have less interest in and knowledge about foreign policymaking than domestic politics. Also, fewer interest groups pressure Congress on foreign policy matters than on domestic policy.[25]

Research shows that congressional support for presidential initiatives in foreign and defense policy is greater than it is for domestic policy initiatives but only during times of international crisis. After the terrorist attacks of September 11, 2001, for example, congressional leaders of both political parties rallied to support the president as commander-in-chief. Although Democrats in Congress continued to criticize the administration's domestic policies, they offered nothing but praise and support for Bush's war leadership for the six months following September 11. During normal times, however, research finds no significant difference in the level of congressional support between domestic and foreign policy issues.[26]

THE DEVELOPMENT OF THE MODERN PRESIDENCY

In the nineteenth century, the presidency was an institution on the periphery of national politics. Early presidents generally confined their initiatives to foreign affairs, leaving domestic policymaking to Congress. The nation's first chief executives did not negotiate with Congress over policy and used the veto only when they considered legislation unconstitutional. Three of the first six presidents vetoed no legislation at all. In contrast, President Reagan cast 78 vetoes in eight years; the first President Bush issued 46 vetoes in four years.[27]

Andrew Jackson and Abraham Lincoln expanded the powers of the presidency. Jackson, who served as president from 1829 to 1837, vetoed legislation on policy grounds, issuing more vetoes than the first six presidents combined. He asserted his legislative leadership by asking the voters to elect different people to Congress who would be more supportive of his policy priorities. President Lincoln, who held office during the Civil War from 1861 to 1865, used his authority as commander-in-chief to justify taking actions without congressional authorization. He declared martial law, ordered the blockade of southern ports, freed slaves in the rebelling territories, stationed troops in the South, and spent money not appropriated by Congress.

In the twentieth century, the role of the president grew as the role of the national government grew. Early twentieth-century presidents were more active than their nineteenth-century counterparts, especially Theodore Roosevelt and Woodrow Wilson. In foreign affairs, Roosevelt, who held office from 1901 to 1909, sent the navy halfway around the globe and schemed to acquire the Panama Canal. Domestically, Roosevelt attacked monopolies, crusaded for conservation, and lobbied legislation through

Congress. Wilson, who served from 1913 through 1921, was the first president to recommend a comprehensive legislative program to Congress. He was also the first president to conduct face-to-face diplomacy with foreign leaders, negotiating the League of Nations Treaty. He also made direct policy appeals to the public, campaigning across the nation in support of the ratification of the League of Nations Treaty.[28]

Most political scientists believe that the era of the modern presidency began with Franklin D. Roosevelt, who served from 1933 to 1945. FDR, as President Franklin Roosevelt was known, was first elected during the Great Depression and held office through most of World War II. Both of these events served to increase the scope of federal government activities and centralize policymaking in the executive branch. The Depression generated public pressure for the national government to act to revive the nation's economy, help those Americans hardest hit by the collapse, and regulate business and industry in an effort to prevent recurrence of the disaster. FDR responded with the **New Deal,** a legislative package of reform measures that involved the federal government more deeply in the nation's economy than ever before.

New Deal A legislative package of reform measures proposed by President Franklin Roosevelt for dealing with the Great Depression.

World War II also increased presidential power. Presidential power grows during wartime and other periods of international tension because the president has the opportunity to exercise authority as commander-in-chief. The general public and Congress tend to defer to presidential leadership in the face of international threats. Also, Congress delegates extraordinary powers to the chief executive to expedite the war effort. During World War II, Congress ceded so many powers to the presidency that scholars often refer to FDR during the war years as a constitutional dictator.

Political scientists define the modern president as a chief executive who is active and visible. The modern president often takes the lead in legislative policymaking. Roosevelt offered the New Deal, Truman proposed a set of policy initiatives labeled the Fair Deal, Kennedy offered the New Frontier, and Lyndon Johnson proposed the Great Society. President Reagan called for major tax and spending cuts. Although the chief executive was not the original author of most of these legislative proposals, the president focused attention on them and lobbied successfully for their enactment. The modern president uses executive orders to act without congressional approval. Truman issued executive orders to racially integrate the armed forces and commit troops to combat in Korea. Reagan used an executive order to direct agencies in the executive branch of government to balance the costs and benefits of proposed regulations before putting them into effect. The modern president has the support of an expanded presidential bureaucracy. The White House staff is now both larger and more involved in the policymaking process than it was before the Franklin Roosevelt administration. The modern presidency has become personalized. The media, especially television, have made the president the central figure of American government. No other political actor in the nation is better positioned to influence the policymaking process.

Political scientists Matthew Crenson and Benjamin Ginsberg identify a number of factors contributing to the emergence of the president as the chief actor in the political system. First, the United States has become a world power, thrusting foreign policy and national security issues to the top of the policy agenda. These are areas in which the president's constitutional powers are stronger than they are in domestic policy. Second, the modern presidential selection process favors the election of assertive individuals with big ideas rather than individuals chosen primarily for their loyalty to their political parties. Finally, the executive branch of the national government has grown, giving the president the means to expand influence.[29]

Political scientist Richard M. Skinner uses the term "partisan presidency" to describe the administrations of recent presidents, especially Reagan and George W. Bush. Skinner says that partisan presidents use the White House to further the interests of their political party. Rather than trying to build bipartisan coalitions, they work exclusively with the members of their own party in Congress to adopt their party's legislative agenda. President Bush, for example, worked with Republican congressional leaders during his first term to pass Republican policy proposals without Democratic input or support.[30] After Democrats won control of Congress in the 2006 election, Bush and the Republican minority in Congress found themselves on the defensive. They could prevent the enactment of Democratic Party priorities—either by use of the filibuster in the Senate or a presidential veto—but they could no longer advance Republican initiatives. Those measures that did become law reflected compromise between the White House and the Democratic leadership in Congress.

THE ORGANIZATION OF THE PRESIDENCY

The development of the modern presidency has been accompanied by a significant growth in the size and power of the presidential bureaucracy, that is, the White House staff and the Executive Office of the President. Early chief executives wrote their own speeches and even answered their own mail. They had only a few aides, whom they paid from their own funds. Thomas Jefferson, for example, had one messenger and one secretary. Eventually, Congress appropriated money for the president to hire aides and advisors, and the presidential bureaucracy grew. In the 1920s, the president had a staff of 30. By the 1950s, the number of presidential aides and advisors had grown to 250. Today, the combined staffs of the Executive Office and the White House number more than 2,000, and the president has grown to rely on them more and more.[31] The modern president spends time bargaining with Congress while dealing with the media and the public. Reelection campaigns begin almost from the first day in office. Presidents have responded to the demands of the office by hiring aides with specialized expertise.[32]

The White House Staff

The White House staff consists of personal aides, assistants, and advisors to the president, including a chief of staff, press secretary, speechwriter, appointments secretary, national security advisor, legislative liaison, counselor to the president, and various special assistants. They give the president advice on policy issues and politics, screen key appointments, manage press relations, organize the president's workday, and ensure that the president's wishes are carried out. The president selects the White House staff without Senate confirmation. As with most presidential appointees (the exceptions are federal judges and regulatory commissioners), White House staff members serve at the president's pleasure, which means that the president can remove them at will.

Political and personal loyalty is usually the foremost criterion the president uses in selecting a staff. When George W. Bush became president, he recruited his staff primarily from his father's administration, his own administration as governor of Texas, and his presidential campaign. Andrew H. Card, Jr., the White House chief of staff during Bush's first term, was Secretary of Transportation in the first Bush administration. Similarly, President Obama selected Rahm Emanuel, a member of Congress from Chicago, Illinois, Obama's political home base, to serve as his chief of staff.

Although every presidential candidate promises to keep politics out of the White House, the White House staff focuses on politics as if the last presidential campaign had never ended or the next one has already begun. Bush appointed Karl Rove, his campaign manager in the 2000 presidential election, to coordinate policy development in the White House in order to integrate policy with political strategy.[33] When Bush made public appearances to promote policy initiatives, he frequently visited a populous state where the vote was close in the 2000 presidential election, such as Michigan, Florida, and Pennsylvania. As the 2004 election approached, Bush's official travel schedule focused more and more on populous battleground states.[34]

The Executive Office of the President

Executive Office of the President
The group of White House offices and agencies that develop and implement the policies and programs of the president.

The **Executive Office of the President** is the group of White House offices and agencies that develop and implement the policies and programs of the president. Congress established the Executive Office in 1939 after a special investigative commission concluded that the responsibilities of the presidency were too great for any one individual. "The president needs help," the commission said. The legislation creating the Executive Office allowed the president to create and disband components without further congressional authorization. Consequently, the size and composition of the Executive Office changes somewhat from administration to administration. During the most recent Bush administration, the Executive Office had 17 units.[35]

The major agencies of the Executive Office are the National Security Council (NSC), Office of Management and Budget (OMB), Council of Economic Advisers (CEA), Council on Environmental Quality, Office of Science and Technology Policy, Office of the United States Trade Representative, and Domestic Policy Council. The first two are the most prominent. The **National Security Council (NSC)** is an agency in the Executive Office of the President that advises the chief executive on matters involving national security. It includes the president, vice president, secretaries of state and defense, and other officials the president may choose to include, such as the national security advisor, the head of the Joint Chiefs of Staff, and the director of the Central Intelligence Agency (CIA). Although the NSC was created primarily as an advisory body, in some administrations it has participated in policy formulation and implementation. During the G. W. Bush administration, the NSC became a separate foreign policy staff, reporting directly to the White House. During his first term, Bush put the NSC (under Condoleezza Rice) in charge of dealing with the insurgency in Iraq rather the Department of State (under Secretary of State Colin Powell). When Powell resigned at the beginning of Bush's second term, the president named Rice secretary of state.[36]

National Security Council (NSC) An agency in the Executive Office of the President that advises the chief executive on matters involving national security.

Office of Management and Budget (OMB) An agency that assists the president in preparing the budget.

The **Office of Management and Budget (OMB)** is an agency that assists the president in preparing the budget. The OMB is an important instrument of presidential control of the executive branch. It assists the president in preparing the annual budget to be submitted to Congress, screens bills drawn up by executive branch departments and agencies to ensure that they do not conflict with the president's policy goals, monitors expenditures by executive branch departments, and evaluates regulations proposed by executive agencies. As with other federal agencies, most OMB personnel below the level of executive management are career employees chosen through a merit hiring system. The president appoints the director of the OMB and other top-level agency officials pending Senate confirmation.

The Presidential Bureaucracy and Presidential Influence

The presidential bureaucracy is essential to the effective operation of the modern presidency. An efficient, knowledgeable White House staff is an important element of presidential power. Members of the staff not only advise the president on policy issues and political strategy, but they often act on behalf of the president in dealing with Congress, members of the executive branch bureaucracy, and the media. An efficient, professional staff can further the president's policy goals and create an image of presidential competence. A White House staff that is accessible to members of Congress and maintains open lines of communication will help promote the president's policies while keeping the president well enough informed to prevent surprises.[37] In contrast, an inefficient staff makes the president appear incompetent. During the first two years of the Clinton administration, a disorganized White House staff contributed to the president's penchant for putting off decisions and failing to stick to decisions once they were made. As a result, Clinton developed a reputation for indecision and inconsistency, a reputation that contributed to substantial Democratic losses in the 1994 congressional elections. Leon Panetta, whom Clinton named chief of staff in 1994, brought discipline to the White House, enabling the president to rehabilitate his image and win reelection in 1996.[38]

The tendency of newly elected presidents to select old friends and campaign aids who are unfamiliar with Washington politics to serve in the White House often undermines the president's effectiveness. The problem is made worse if the president is also inexperienced in national politics. Healthcare reform was the foremost goal of Clinton's first term in office. The president appointed a task force chaired by Hillary Clinton to hold hearings and develop a plan to be presented to Congress. Because the task force lacked broad-based representation and conducted much of its work in secret, it failed to develop a plan with enough support to pass Congress, and the effort became an embarrassing failure.

The challenge for a president is to develop a leadership style that neither delegates too little nor too much. Because a president's time, energy, and abilities are limited, the president must delegate some tasks. To be effective, a president must know which tasks can be delegated and which cannot. The president must also have a strong enough grasp of policy issues to recognize when the proposals of subordinates make sense and when they do not.[39]

GLOBAL PERSPECTIVE

The Russian Presidency

Russia elects a president by popular vote to serve a four-year term. If no candidate receives a majority in the first election, the two candidates with the most votes face each other in a runoff election a month later. Russia has no vice president. If the office of president becomes vacant, the prime minister becomes acting president for 90 days and a special election is held.

The Russian Constitution makes the president the most powerful office in the government. The president appoints the prime minister to head the cabinet and administer the government. The Duma, the lower chamber of the Russian parliament, must approve the president's choice for prime minister. If the Duma rejects the president's nominee three times, the president must either select a different prime minister or call for new parliamentary elections. The Duma can also vote "no confidence" in the prime minister. Upon a second vote of no confidence, the president must either replace the prime minister or call for new parliamentary elections. In practice, the Duma is unlikely to reject a prime minister or vote no confidence because its members would have to face reelection, whereas the president would not.

The Russian president plays a role in the legislative process somewhat similar to the role played by the American president in the legislative process. Measures passed by the parliament go to the president, who may sign or reject them. If the president rejects a bill, the parliament may vote to override the rejection by a two-thirds' vote of both chambers. If parliament cannot override the rejection, it creates a conciliation commission along with representatives of the president in an attempt to reach compromise. The president also has the power to make laws by decree. The Russian Constitution declares that presidential decrees may not contradict existing laws. Furthermore, the parliament can rescind a presidential decree by majority vote.

The presidency was the dominant institution of Russian politics during the administration of Vladimir Putin, who served from 2000 through 2008. Putin crushed his opponents and consolidated power. President Putin won reelection in 2004 with 72 percent of the vote against several unknown opponents because the government disqualified on the basis of technicalities every candidate with enough support to seriously challenge Putin. The government also took control of the news media to ensure that Putin received flattering coverage, while political opponents were either ignored or attacked. News editors who dared to exercise their independence were beaten or prosecuted for criticizing the government.*

The importance of the presidency in Russian government is now in decline, ironically, because of Putin. The Russian Constitution limits the president to two four-year terms. Rather than attempting to change the Constitution to remain as president, Putin promoted the candidacy of a handpicked successor, Dmitry Medvedev, a relatively unknown bureaucrat who won easily over token opposition. Putin then became prime minister. Many observers believed that the Russian system will evolve to resemble most parliamentary systems in which the real power is in the hands of the prime minister, whereas the president is the ceremonial head of state without significant decision-making influence.[†]

QUESTIONS TO CONSIDER

1. Is there a difference between the Russian president ruling by decree and the American president issuing executive orders?
2. Could a future American political leader execute a maneuver similar to that accomplished by Putin to stay in power despite the end of a second term in the White House?
3. What keeps the American president from taking actions similar to those taken by Putin?

---

*M. Steven Fish, *Democracy Derailed in Russia: The Failure of Open Politics* (New York: Cambridge University Press, 2005), pp. 30–80.

[†]Clifford J. Levy, "With Tight Grip on Ballot, Putin Is Forcing Foes Out," *New York Times*, October 14, 2007, available at www.nytimes.com.

Weapons of mass destruction (WMDs) Nuclear, chemical, and biological weapons that are designed to inflict widespread military and civilian casualties.

President George W. Bush's decision to go to war against Iraq was based on a flawed decision-making process within the administration. Bush ordered the overthrow of Saddam Hussein because he believed that Iraq possessed **weapons of mass destruction (WMDs),** which are nuclear, chemical, and biological weapons that are designed to inflict widespread military and civilian casualties. The United States had to act, the president declared, before Iraq gave WMDs to terrorist groups that could then use them against the United States or its allies. The conclusion that Iraq possessed WMDs, however, was wrong. The administration not only misinterpreted some of the intelligence it received, but also attempted to influence the nature of that intelligence to support its position. It sought evidence to prove that Iraq possessed WMDs while ignoring information to the contrary. Furthermore, Bush decided to go to war without deliberating with his advisors as to whether war was necessary. The White House shut out Secretary of State Colin Powell from the decision-making process and ignored warnings from the military.[40]

President George W. Bush's decision to go to war against Iraq was based on a flawed decision-making process within the administration.

THEORIES OF PRESIDENTIAL LEADERSHIP

Political scientists take different approaches to describing and explaining presidential leadership.

Presidential Character

Political scientist James David Barber believes that a president's performance in office depends on personality traits formed primarily during childhood, adolescence, and early adulthood. Barber classifies personality along two dimensions. The first dimension involves the *amount of energy* an individual brings to the office. Active presidents throw themselves into their work, immersing themselves in the details of the office, whereas passive presidents devote relatively little energy and effort to the job. The second dimension to Barber's personality classification scheme involves the president's *attitude toward the job*. Positive presidents enjoy their work. They have an optimistic, positive attitude. Negative presidents feel burdened by the weight of the office. They tend to be pessimists.

Barber uses these two dimensions to create four general types of presidential personalities: active-positive, active-negative, passive-positive, and passive-negative. According to Barber, the best type of personality for a president is active-positive. This president is self-confident, optimistic, flexible, and enjoys the job. Active-positive presidents use their office as an "engine of power." Franklin Roosevelt, for example, was a supremely self-confident man who set out to master the intricacies of his office. He was a flexible, skillful politician who truly enjoyed being president. Barber also classifies Truman, Kennedy, Ford, Carter, the first Bush, and Clinton as active-positive presidents.

Barber believes that the most dangerous chief executive is the active-negative president. This type of president puts great energy into work, but derives little pleasure from it. Barber says that active-negative presidents suffer from low self-esteem and tend to view political disputes in terms of personal success or failure. They are pessimistic, driven, and compulsive. Active-negative presidents tend to overreact to crises and continue failed policies long after it is clear they do not work, because to admit error would be to lose control. Barber classifies Richard Nixon as active-negative because he was personally insecure, combative, tough, and vindictive. He was a loner who saw himself as a righteous leader besieged by enemies. Barber says that Herbert Hoover and Lyndon Johnson were active-negative presidents as well.

Barber lists two other categories of presidential personalities, passive-positive and passive-negative. Barber identifies Eisenhower as a passive-negative president, that is, one who is involved in politics out of a sense of duty. The passive-negative president avoids conflict and uncertainty and just plain dislikes politics. Finally, the passive-positive president is indecisive and superficially optimistic. This president tends to react rather than initiate. Barber classifies Reagan as passive-positive.[41]

Scholars identify a number of weaknesses with Barber's classification scheme. It is not always clear in which category a president should be placed. President Reagan can be labeled *passive* because of his inattentiveness and willingness to allow aides to carry a good deal of his workload. Nonetheless, the Reagan administration had a substantial impact on public policy, taking important initiatives in a wide range of policy areas. Is that the record of a passive president? Some critics complain that Barber's categories are so broad as to be little help in differentiating among presidents. Barber puts Presidents Franklin Roosevelt, Carter, and the first President Bush in the same category—active-positive. How helpful is Barber's classification scheme if such different presidents fit in the same category? Historians typically rank Franklin Roosevelt among the best of the nation's presidents, whereas Carter and George H. W. Bush are considered only average. Finally, Barber's scheme ignores the political climate in which a president serves. The success or failure of a chief executive depends on a number of factors in addition to the president's personality traits.[42]

Leadership Style

Some scholars believe that the ability of a president to effectively use the powers of the office depends on leadership style. Political scientist Fred I. Greenstein takes this approach by identifying six qualities associated with effective presidential leadership.

- **Communication skills** Greenstein identifies Franklin Roosevelt, Kennedy, Reagan, and Clinton as effective public communicators. In contrast, he says that both George H. W. Bush and George W. Bush were relatively ineffective communicators because they were prone to misstatements.
- **Organizational skills** According to Greenstein, Truman, Eisenhower, Kennedy, Ford, and the elder Bush had strong organizational skills, but Lyndon Johnson, Carter, and Clinton did not. Greenstein says that George W. Bush failed to create an organizational structure that would facilitate an effective decision-making process.
- **Political skills** Greenstein says that Johnson was a skilled, determined political operator; in contrast, Carter had a poor reputation among fellow policymakers. Greenstein gives George W. Bush high marks for being politically skilled.
- **Vision** Eisenhower, Kennedy, Nixon, Reagan, and George W. Bush all had a capacity to inspire support for achieving a set of overarching goals. In the meantime, Greenstein believes that George H. W. Bush was weak in this area.
- **Cognitive skill** Both Carter and Nixon were skilled at understanding complex issues by reducing them to their component parts. Truman and Reagan were less skilled. Greenstein faults George W. Bush for a management style that relied too heavily on his staff to provide the backup for his policy actions, and that approach may have led him to error on the question of WMDs in Iraq.
- **Emotional intelligence** Greenstein says that Eisenhower, Ford, and both Bushes were emotionally mature individuals able to focus on their responsibilities without distraction. In contrast, he labels Johnson, Nixon, Carter, and Clinton as "emotionally handicapped."[43]

The Power to Persuade

Political scientist Richard Neustadt believes that presidents succeed or fail based on their skills as political bargainers and coalition builders. Although the presidency is regarded as a powerful office, Neustadt points out that presidents lack authority to command public officials other than the members of the White House staff, some executive branch appointees, and the members of the armed forces. Under America's constitutional system, the members of Congress, federal judges, and state officials do not take orders from the president. Because presidents cannot command, they must convince other political actors to cooperate with them voluntarily. The power of the president, Neustadt says, is the power to persuade.[44]

Persuasion is often difficult for the president, Neustadt notes, because the interests of other political actors do not always coincide with the concerns of the chief executive. Whereas presidents worry about their reelection by voters nationwide, members of Congress focus on winning reelection from their districts or states, whose voters are often more concerned about local problems than national issues. Former Republican Congressman Tom DeLay once gave this explanation for opposing Republican President George H. W. Bush on a particular issue: "I represent the Twenty-second District [of Texas], not George Bush."

The president cannot necessarily even count on the cooperation of the federal bureaucracy. Except for the White House staff, the heads of Executive Office agencies, and members of the cabinet, all of whom serve at the pleasure of the president, the loyalty of federal employees lies with their jobs in their own niches in the bureaucracy, not with the president's program. A chief executive who wants to reorganize the bureaucracy or cut federal programs invariably meets resistance from within the executive branch.

Consequently, Neustadt says, presidents must bargain with other political actors and groups to try to win their cooperation. Presidents are brokers, consensus builders. In this task, presidents have several assets: they have a number of appointments to make; they prepare the budget; they can help supporters raise money for reelection; and they can appeal to others on the basis of the national interest or party loyalty. To use these assets to their fullest, presidents must understand the dynamics of political power.[45]

Neustadt's approach can be used to explain the presidencies of Lyndon Johnson and Jimmy Carter. President Johnson learned as Majority Leader in the Senate how to build a political coalition to get legislation passed. In the White House, he put those skills to work and won passage for his legislative program, which was known as the **Great Society.** In contrast, President Carter never mastered the mechanics of political power. He ran for president as an outsider, someone who was not tainted by Washington politics. Once in office, Carter appeared standoffish. He had won the Democratic nomination and been elected president without having to bargain with the Washington establishment, and he thought he could govern without bargaining. He was wrong. Politics involves negotiation, give-and-take, and compromise. Carter never understood that and consequently failed to accomplish many of his goals.

Great Society The legislative program put forward by President Lyndon Johnson.

Going Public

Political scientist Samuel Kernell updates the Neustadt approach. Kernell believes that contemporary presidents often must adopt a media-oriented strategy, which he calls "going public," if they are to achieve their goals in today's political environment.

In 1981, for example, President Reagan went on television to ask citizens to contact their representatives in Congress to support his economic program. The public responded and Congress approved the president's budget proposals.

Media-oriented approaches are not new—Franklin Roosevelt was famous for his fireside chats on the radio—but the strategy has become more common. Modern communications and transportation technologies make going public relatively easy. Furthermore, today's presidential selection process tends to favor people who are better at public appeals than political bargaining. Perhaps most important, going public has become an easier and more efficient method for achieving political goals than bargaining. In the 1950s, a president pushing a policy agenda had to bargain with a handful of party leaders and committee chairs in Congress. Today, power in Congress is more fragmented, and the number of interest groups active in Washington politics has increased. As a result, it has become easier for presidents to go public than to engage in political bargaining.[46] Contemporary presidents advance their policy agendas through speeches, public appearances, political travel, and targeted outreach aimed at particular groups of voters.[47]

The George W. Bush administration illustrates both the strengths and limitations of the going public strategy. Bush effectively used the going public strategy to bring the threat of Iraq to the top of the public agenda and put pressure on Congress to approve his war policy. Public concern over Iraq made Democrats in Congress wary about opposing the president on Iraq because Saddam Hussein was a highly unpopular figure. Many Democrats believed that Saddam actually did have WMDs and was a threat to national security. Opposing Bush on Iraq could open them to the charge that they were soft on national defense. Nearly 40 percent of House Democrats and 57 percent of Senate Democrats joined nearly every Republican member of Congress in voting in favor of the resolution to authorize the use of military force in Iraq.[48] In contrast, Bush's effort to reform Social Security by allowing workers to invest some of their payroll tax payments in private accounts was a failure. Although Bush succeeded in elevating the issue to the top of the policy agenda, he failed to convince a majority of the public that private retirement accounts were a good idea. As a result, it was easy for Democrats in Congress to oppose the president on the issue and difficult for Republicans to support him. Going public is an ineffective strategy if the president's proposed initiative lacks public support.[49]

Contemporary presidents use both political bargaining and going public. Consider George W. Bush's work to win passage of his education reform initiative, the No Child Left Behind Act of 2001. On one hand, Bush used every opportunity to promote the initiative publicly. He emphasized the issue during the 2000 presidential campaign, highlighted it during his State of the Union address, and made frequent appearances to ask the public to support the reform. On the other hand, Bush worked with members of Congress to win enough votes to ensure passage, negotiating personally with Democratic Senator Edward Kennedy of Massachusetts, the chair of the Senate Health, Education, Labor, and Pension Committee. Kennedy promised to support the bill after the president agreed to drop provisions that would have used public funds to allow students to attend private schools, an education reform that Kennedy opposed.[50]

Unilateral Tools of Presidential Power

A number of political scientists believe that presidents have tools they can use to influence the policymaking process that do not depend on political bargaining or persuasion. These "power tools," as Professor Christopher S. Kelley calls them, allow the president to take unilateral action without direct congressional authorization or approval.[51] They include the following:

- **Executive orders** They enable the president to adopt a number of important policies without legislative approval.
- **Executive agreements** They give the president an important tool for conducting foreign relations that does not require Senate ratification.[52]
- **Presidential signing statements** They enable the president to define the scope and limitations of legislation passed by Congress.
- **Recess appointments** By filling vacancies during a period of time when Congress is in recess, the president can temporarily make appointments without the advice and consent of the Senate.[53]

PRESIDENTIAL POPULARITY

Presidential popularity influences presidential power. A president's personal popularity affects the position of the president as a political broker and the ability of the president to appeal to the public for policy support. A president who is politically popular can offer more benefits and inducements to other political actors for their cooperation than can an unpopular chief executive. Campaign help from a popular president is more valuable and support for legislative proposals is more effective. Similarly, a popular president can claim to speak for the national interest with greater credibility. President Johnson enjoyed considerably more political influence after his landslide reelection victory in 1964, for example, than did President Nixon in the midst of the Watergate scandal in early 1974.

A popular president enjoys more success with Congress than an unpopular chief executive. After September 11, 2001, President Bush's approval rating soared. Republican members of Congress eagerly associated themselves with the president, whereas Democrats were reluctant to oppose him. Congress passed legislation embodying the president's policy proposals dealing with taxes, the budget, government reorganization, Iraq, and the war on terror. By 2006, however, Bush's approval rating had fallen below 40 percent, and members of Congress from both parties found it easy to oppose the president's legislative agenda. Democrats attacked Bush at every opportunity while Republican members of Congress boasted of their independence from the White House.

New presidents are popular, at least for a few months. The tendency of a president to enjoy a high level of public support during the early months of an administration is known as the **honeymoon effect.** In the first few months of an administration, opposition political leaders and the press usually reserve judgment, waiting for the president to act before offering comment. Most voters, regardless of party affiliation, tell polltakers that they approve of the president's performance in

Honeymoon effect The tendency of a president to enjoy a high level of public support during the early months of an administration.

office because they have heard few complaints on which to base disapproval. Once an administration begins making controversial policy decisions, however, opposition leaders and the media begin to criticize the president's performance. As the criticism mounts, the president's popularity invariably falls, especially among people who identify with the opposition political party.[54]

Presidential approval responds to events. In domestic policy matters, presidential popularity rises with good news and falls with bad news, especially news concerning the economy. Although President Reagan was called the "Teflon President"— regardless of what went wrong, no blame stuck to him—he was an unpopular president during the recession of 1982. Only when the economy began to recover did Reagan's popular standing again exceed the 50 percent approval mark. President Clinton got off to such a slow start that the Democratic Party lost control of both houses of Congress in the 1994 mid-term elections. Subsequently, a strong economy helped the president recover in the polls and win reelection in 1996 by a comfortable margin.

Presidential popularity rises dramatically during times of international crisis because of the **rally effect,** which is the tendency of the general public to express support for the incumbent president during a time of international threat. Political scientist John Mueller defines the rally effect as "being associated with an event which (1) is international and (2) involves the United States and particularly the president directly." Mueller says that the event must be "specific, dramatic, and sharply focused."[55] Mueller found that the "public seems to react to both 'good' and 'bad' international events in about the same way"—with a burst of heightened presidential approval.[56] For example, President George W. Bush's standing in the polls soared after September 11, 2001. The percentage of Americans who told survey researchers that they approved of Bush's performance in office leaped from 51 percent in early September to 90 percent later in the month.[57] Bush's popularity level also jumped when the United States invaded Iraq and then again when Saddam Hussein was captured.

The appearance and size of a rally effect depends on how the crisis is presented to the public in terms of media coverage, comments from opposition political leaders, and statements from the White House.[58] When the nation appears threatened from abroad, the political criticism that generally accompanies presidential action is muted. The White House is able to get its interpretation of events before the public because opposition political leaders do not want to be accused of undermining the president during an international crisis. The public tends to support the president because the only messages it hears about the president's handling of the crisis are positive messages, usually conveyed by the White House itself or the president's allies in Congress.[59] Even though 9/11 was a national disaster, President Bush's approval rating soared because no one publicly raised questions about the administration's failure to foresee or prevent the terrorist attack, at least not initially. Instead, the media were filled with images of the president comforting the families of the victims and declaring that the United States would bring to justice the people responsible for the attack.[60]

The public responds differently to a domestic crisis than it does to an international crisis. Whereas opposition political leaders and the press typically withhold judgment in an international crisis, they are quick to criticize if something goes wrong domestically. Consider the reaction to Hurricane Katrina and its impact on

Rally effect The tendency of the general public to express support for the incumbent president during a time of international threat.

President Bush's standing in the polls. Within days of the hurricane's coming ashore, opposition political leaders and the news media were blasting the Bush administration for inadequately responding to the disaster. Between late August and October 2005, the president's popularity rating fell by five percentage points.[61]

A rally effect usually has only a short-term impact on presidential popularity. According to a study conducted by the Gallup organization, a president's approval rating reverts to previous levels within seven months of an international crisis unless other factors intervene, such as changing economic conditions.[62] At the beginning of an international crisis, the president enjoys near unanimous support from members of the president's political party and strong support from independents and members of the other party. As the political climate returns to normal, the press and opposition party leaders begin voicing criticism, initially about domestic policy matters and eventually about foreign affairs as well. Although members of the president's party usually continue to support the incumbent, members of the other party and independents began to register their displeasure with the president's performance, and the president's overall standing in the polls falls.[63]

Most presidents leave office less popular than they were when they first took office. New presidents are popular because of the honeymoon effect. Over time, presidents lose support because negative events and controversial decisions generate criticism that undermines their support, especially among independents and people who identify with the opposition party. Even though presidents enjoy successes as well as suffer failures, presidential approval ratings trend downward over time because negative news has a greater psychological impact than positive news. Economic downturns hurt a president's standing in the polls more than economic upswings help the president's approval ratings.[64]

THE PRESIDENCY IN CONTEXT

Many political scientists attempt to explain the role of the presidency in the policy-making process by focusing on contextual factors, such as the international environment, the state of the nation's economy, and the party balance in Congress. The terrorist attack of September 11, 2001, greatly enhanced the opportunity for the president to exert policymaking influence. Presidential power grows during wartime because a military conflict provides the president with the opportunity to exercise authority as commander-in-chief. The other branches of government generally defer to executive leadership for fear of impeding the war effort or being accused of failing to support the troops.

The party balance in Congress has a major impact on the ability of presidents to achieve their goals. President George W. Bush benefited from Republican control of the House and, after the 2002 election, the Senate as well. Congressional leaders worked closely with the White House to pass a series of tax cuts and to adopt bills dealing with education reform (No Child Left Behind) and Medicare reform (adding a prescription drug benefit). Bush issued no vetoes and rarely found it necessary to threaten a veto. Republican control of Congress also sheltered the administration from the scrutiny of aggressive investigation. The House Government Reform

GETTING INVOLVED

Why Do They Run?

Have you ever wondered why people seek political office? Do they want personal power? Do they hope to accomplish policy objectives? Are they motivated by a desire to serve the community?

Investigate the answers to these questions by interviewing an elected official in a city, county, township, school district, or special district unit of government in your area. Keep in mind that most public officials are busy, so it may be unrealistic to attempt to arrange an interview with the mayor of a large city or the county executive in a metropolitan area. Local judges, school board members, community college trustees, and city council members in small towns may prove more accessible to students. Once you decide on an official, call his or her office to introduce yourself and ask if the official is willing to set aside 15 minutes or so for an interview, either on the telephone or in person. If the official is unavailable, try another officeholder.

Before you conduct the interview, do your homework so you can make the most of the opportunity. Learn as much as you can about the office and the official. Study the questions you want to ask so you will be able to speak in a conversational tone of voice. Prepare to tape record the interview, if possible, so you will not have to worry about taking notes.

Begin the interview by thanking the official for the time. Explain that you will report to your class on what you learn. Then, conduct the interview. The following

questions can serve as a guideline. Remember, however, that these are general-purpose questions. You may want to add other questions of your own or rephrase these questions to put them in your own words.

- Is this the first elected office you have held? (If not, ask what other posts the official has held.)
- Why did you decide to seek this office?
- About how many hours a week do you spend on the job?
- Do you enjoy it?
- What do you like most about your position in local government?
- What do you like least about your position?
- Are you glad you sought this office and won? Why or why not?

Once you have completed the interview, thank the official again for the time. You will also want to write the official a thank-you letter for taking time to chat with you.

Prepare a short oral report for your class by listening to the tape of the interview, reviewing your notes, and organizing your information. Your report should include your impressions of the official, in addition to relating what the official told you in the interview. Also, prepare to discuss whether you are interested in running for office yourself.

Subpoena A legally binding order requiring an individual to appear before the committee to testify and bring requested information.

Committee failed to issue a single subpoena to the executive branch during Bush's first term. (A **subpoena** is a legally binding order requiring an individual to appear before the committee to testify and bring requested information.) In contrast, President Clinton faced a hostile Congress after Republicans won control of the House and Senate in the 1994 elections. Although Clinton did not veto a single measure in 1993 and 1994, when Democrats controlled both houses of Congress, he issued no fewer than three and as many as ten vetoes a year from 1995 to 2000, his last full year in office. The record was similar for veto threats. During the 103rd Congress (1993–1994), which the Democrats controlled, Clinton threatened the veto only four times. In contrast, he made 60 veto threats in the 104th Congress (1995–1996), which was controlled by the GOP.[65] Congress was also quick to investigate the Clinton administration, issuing more than a thousand subpoenas.[66]

The economy is the most important single factor affecting a president's personal popularity. The public blames the president for hard times and rewards the president for good times. Whereas a weak economy led to the defeat of the first President Bush in 1992, a strong economy helped President Clinton win reelection in 1996. A president also benefits from a strong economy because economic growth generates tax revenue that can be used to finance government programs or fund tax cuts.

CONCLUSION: THE PRESIDENCY AND PUBLIC POLICY

The presidency is a major participant in every stage of the policymaking process.

Agenda Building

No other figure in American politics is better positioned to influence the policy agenda than the president. Because the chief executive is always in the media spotlight, the president has a unique opportunity to direct attention to policy problems. President George W. Bush drew attention to his education reform proposal to require states to implement basic skills testing by visiting schools where similar reforms were already successfully in place. The president can discuss an issue during a State of the Union address, identify a problem during a press conference, or give a major speech to focus attention on an issue.[67] The president also has a number of spokespersons that can raise issues on behalf of the administration, including the vice president, members of the White House staff, and executive branch department heads.

Presidents have more influence in shaping the domestic policy agenda than they have at influencing the agenda in foreign affairs. World events and media coverage of those events set the foreign policy agenda; the president just reacts. George W. Bush did not run for office expecting to fight a war on terror, but after September 11, 2001, the fight against terrorism became the primary focus of his administration. In contrast to foreign policy, the president has the opportunity to operate as an issue entrepreneur in domestic policy. If an issue is not already part of ongoing media coverage or congressional hearings, a president may be able to set the agenda of the television networks and Congress. President Clinton, for example, succeeded in making health-care reform an important part of the policy agenda in his first term.[68] Furthermore, presidents can sometimes redefine issues already on the policy agenda. When George W. Bush took office, for example, education was already an important part of the nation's policy agenda. Bush succeeded in framing the issue in terms of basic skills testing.[69]

Policy Formulation and Adoption

The president is involved in the formulation and adoption of a broad range of policies. Presidents propose legislation to Congress, sometimes drafting the actual bills in the White House or the executive branch. Presidential speeches inform members of Congress of the president's policy priorities.[70] Measures that reach the president for signature often reflect a compromise negotiated between the White House and congressional leaders, especially when the opposition party controls Congress. Because the veto power gives the president a formal role in legislative policymaking, the president can influence policy formulation. As long as one-third plus one member of either the House or Senate support the president's position on an issue, congressional leaders must negotiate with the White House over the content of legislation. The measure ultimately adopted may not totally reflect the president's policy preferences, but it will likely include some features the president favors and exclude some the president opposes.[71]

The president has the authority to adopt some policies without congressional participation. Presidents make policy when they negotiate executive agreements or issue executive orders. Although Congress has the authority to cancel or repeal an executive agreement or executive order legislatively, the action would be subject to a presidential veto. Over the years, especially during time of war, presidents have exercised extraordinary policymaking power based on their authority as commander-in-chief of the armed forces.

Policy Implementation and Evaluation

As head of the executive branch, the president plays an important role in policy implementation. Congress frequently allows executive branch agencies a certain degree of discretion in implementing the nation's public policies. For example, the Environmental Protection Agency (EPA) may enforce the Clean Air Act more or less aggressively. President Carter contributed to the aggressive enforcement of environmental laws by appointing agency administrators who believed strongly in the agency's mission. Carter asked Congress for sufficient funding to support an aggressive enforcement effort. In contrast, President Reagan wanted the EPA to work more positively with the industries it regulates. He appointed critics of the EPA to head the agency and submitted budgets to Congress that cut money for enforcement activities.

The president also evaluates policies. The president can commission policy studies to identify weaknesses with current policies and then propose reforms. President George W. Bush, for example, appointed a commission to evaluate the Social Security system and recommend changes to ensure its long-term financial stability. The president also engages in policy evaluation during the budgetary process, working primarily through the OMB.

KEY TERMS

articles of impeachment

chief executive

chief of state

civilian supremacy of the armed forces

electoral mandate

executive agreement

Executive Office of the President

executive order

Great Society

honeymoon effect

impeachment

inherent powers

lame duck

Louisiana Purchase

National Security Council (NSC)

New Deal

North American Free Trade Agreement (NAFTA)

Office of Management and Budget (OMB)

pardon

presidential signing statement

rally effect

Reconstruction

reprieve

subpoena

Two Presidencies Thesis

War Powers Act

weapons of mass destruction (WMDs)

NOTES

1. Robert Pear, "At House Party on Health Care, the Diagnosis Is It's Broken," *New York Times*, December 23, 2008, available at www.nytimes.com.

2. Michael J. Gerhardt, *The Federal Impeachment Process: A Constitutional and Historical Analysis* (Princeton, NJ: Princeton University Press, 1995), p. 105.

3. Quoted in Michael Nelson, "Choosing the Vice President," *PS: Political Science and Politics*, Fall 1988, p. 859.

4. Joseph A. Pike, "The Vice Presidency: New Opportunities, Old Constraints," in Michael Nelson, ed., *The Presidency and the Political System*, 5th ed. (Washington, DC: Congressional Quarterly Press, 1998), pp. 548–554.

5. Jody C. Baumgartner, *The American Vice Presidency Reconsidered* (Westport, CT: Praeger, 2006), p. 133.

6. Barton Gellman and Jo Becker, "A 'Surrogate Chief of Staff,'" *Washington Post National Weekly Edition*, July 9–15, 2007, pp. 6–12.

7. Harold J. Krent, *Presidential Powers* (New York: New York University Press, 2005), pp. 215–216.

8. Ryan J. Barilleaux, "Venture Constitutionalism and the Enlargement of the Presidency," in Christopher S. Kelley, (ed.), *Executing the Constitution: Putting the President Back Into the Constitution* (Albany: State University of New York, 2006), pp. 40–42.

9. "Learning About the Senate: Treaties," available at www.senate.gov.

10. Ibid.

11. *Korematsu v. United States*, 323 U.S. 214 (1944).

12. Public Law 93-148 (1973).

13. *Immigration and Naturalization Service (INS) v. Chadha*, 462 U.S. 919 (1983).

14. James A. Baker III and Warren Christopher, "Put War Powers Back Where They Belong," *New York Times*, July 8, 2009, available at www.nytimes.com.

15. John M. Broder, "Report Urges Overhaul of the War Powers Law," *New York Times*, July 9, 2008, available at www.nytimes.com.

16. Louis Fisher, "The Scope of Inherent Powers," in George C. Edwards and Desmond King, eds. *The Polarized Presidency of George W. Bush*, (New York, NY: Oxford University Press, 2007), p. 53.

17. Administrative Office of the U.S. Courts, "Federal Judicial Vacancies," available at www.uscourts.gov.

18. *Youngstown Sheet and Tube Co. v. Sawyer*, 343 U.S. 579 (1952).

19. Donna R. Hoffman and Alison D. Howard, *Addressing the State of the Union: The Evolution and Impact of the President's Big Speech* (Boulder, CO: Lynne Rienner, 2006), p. 194.

20. Andrew Rudalevige, "The Executive Branch and the Legislative Process," in Joel D. Aberbach and Mark A. Peterson, eds., *The Executive Branch* (New York: Oxford University Press, 2005), p. 373.

21. Rebecca A. Deen and Laura W. Arnold, "Veto Threats as a Policy Tool: When to Threaten?" *Presidential Studies Quarterly* 32 (March 2002): 30–45.

22. Phillip J. Cooper, "George W. Bush, Edgar Allan Poe, and the Use and Abuse of Presidential Signing Statements," *Presidential Studies Quarterly* 35 (September 2005): 515–532.

23. Robert Pear, "Legal Group Faults Bush for Ignoring Parts of Bills," *New York Times*, July 24, 2006, available at www.nytimes.com.

24. Curtis A. Bradley and Eric A. Posner, "Presidential Signing Statements and Executive Power," *Constitutional Commentary* 23 (Winter 2006): 307–364.

25. Aaron Wildavsky, "The Two Presidencies," *Transaction* 4 (December 1966): 7–14.

26. Brandon C. Prins and Bryan W. Marshall, "Congressional Support of the President: A Comparison of Foreign, Defense, and Domestic Policy Decision Making During and After the Cold War," *Presidential Studies Quarterly* 31 (December 2001): 660–678.

27. Michael A. Sollenberger, *Presidential Vetoes, 1789–Present: A Summary Overview*, Congressional Research Service, available at www.house.gov.

28. Kevan M. Yenerall, "Executing the Rhetorical Presidency: William Jefferson Clinton, George. W. Bush, and the Contemporary Face of Presidential Power," in Kelly, *Executing the Constitution*, pp. 132–133.

29. Matthew Crenson and Benjamin Ginsberg, *Presidential Power: Unchecked and Unbalanced* (New York: W. W. Norton, 2007), pp. 11–13.

30. Richard M. Skinner, "The Partisan Presidency," in John C. Green and Daniel J. Coffey, eds., *The State of the Parties*, 5th ed. (Lanham, MD: Rowman & Littlefield, 2007), pp. 331–341.

31. John P. Burke, "The Institutional Presidency," in Michael Nelson, ed., *The Presidency and the Political System*, 8th ed. (Washington, DC: CQ Press, 2006), p. 386.

32. Matthew J. Dickinson and Matthew J. Lebo, "Reexamining the Growth of the Institutional Presidency, 1940–2000," *Journal of Politics* 69 (February 2007): 206–219.

33. Matthew J. Dickinson, "The Executive Office of the President: The Paradox of Politicization," in Aberbach and Peterson, eds., *The Executive Branch*, p. 154.

34. Brandon J. Doherty, "The Politics of the Permanent Campaign: Presidential Travel and the Electoral College, 1977–2004," *Presidential Studies Quarterly* 37 (December 2007): 749–773.

35. The Executive Office of the President, available at http://first.gov/Agencies/Federal/Executive/EOP.shtml.

36. Dickinson, "The Executive Office of the President," pp. 147–150.

37. Dickinson and Lebo, "Reexamining the Growth of the Institutional Presidency," pp. 206–219.

38. Paul J. Quirk, "Presidential Competence," in Nelson, *The Presidency and the Political System*, 8th ed. pp. 156–158.

39. Ibid., pp. 179–189.

40. James. P. Pfiffner, "Intelligence and Decision Making Before the War with Iraq," in Edwards and King, *The Polarized Presidency of George W. Bush*, p. 235.

41. James David Barber, *The Presidential Character*, 4th ed. (Englewood Cliffs, NJ: Prentice-Hall, 1992); "Carter and Reagan: Clues to Their Character," *U.S. News & World Report*, October 27, 1980, pp. 30–33.

42. Michael Nelson, "The Psychological Presidency," in Nelson, ed., *The Presidency and the Political System*, 8th ed., pp. 170–194.

43. Fred I. Greenstein, *The Presidential Difference: Leadership Style from FDR to George W. Bush*, 2nd ed. (Princeton, NJ: Princeton University Press, 2004), pp. 217–221; Fred I. Greenstein, "George W. Bush: The Man and His Leadership," in John C. Fortier and Norman J. Ornstein, eds., *Second-Term Blues: How George W. Bush Has Governed* (Washington, DC: American Enterprise Institute/Brookings Institution Press, 2007), pp. 61–66.

44. Quoted in Kathy Lewis, "Republicans Join Sharp Opposition to New Tax Plans," *Houston Post*, October 20, 1990, p. A-1.

45. Richard E. Neustadt, *Presidential Power: The Politics of Leadership* (New York: Wiley, 1980).

46. Samuel Kernell, *Going Public: New Strategies of Presidential Leadership*, 3rd ed. (Washington, DC: Congressional Quarterly Press, 1997).

47. Joseph A. Pike and John Anthony Maltese, *The Politics of the Presidency*, 6th ed. (Washington, DC: CQ Press, 2004), p. 118.

48. Scott B. Blinder, "Going Public, Going to Baghdad: Presidential Agenda-Setting and the Electoral Connection in Congress," in Edwards and King, eds., *The Polarized Presidency of George W. Bush*, pp. 336–344.

49. Brandice Canes-Wrone, *Who Leads Whom? Presidents, Policy, and the Public* (Chicago: University of Chicago Press, 2006), p. 185.

50. George C. Edwards III, "George W. Bush's Strategic Presidency," in George C. Edwards and Philip John Davies, *New Challenges for the American Presidency* (New York: Longman, 2004), p. 44.

51. Kelly, *Executing the Constitution*, pp. 4–5.

52. Steven A. Shull, *Policy by Other Means: Alternative Adoption by Presidents* (College Station: Texas A&M University Press, 2006), pp. 30–35.

53. Ryan C. Black, Anthony J. Madonna, Ryan J. Owens, and Michael S. Lynch, "Adding Recess Appointments to the President's 'Tool Chest' of Unilateral Powers," *Political Research Quarterly* 60 (December 2007): 645–654.

54. Raymond Tatalovich and Alan R. Gitelson, "Political Party Linkages to Presidential Popularity: Assessing the 'Coalition of Minorities' Thesis," *Journal of Politics* 52 (February 1990): 241.

55. John E. Mueller, *War, Presidents, and Public Opinion* (New York: Wiley, 1973), p. 208.

56. Ibid., p. 212.

57. Jeffrey M. Jones, "Bush's High Approval Ratings Among Most Sustained for Presidents," *Gallup Poll Monthly*, November 2001, p. 32.

58. William D. Baker and John R. O'Neal, "Patriotism or Opinion Leadership? The Nature and Origins of the Rally 'Round the Flag' Effect," *Journal of Conflict Resolution* 45 (October 2001): 661–687.

59. Richard Brody, "International Crises: A Rallying Point for the President?" *Public Opinion*, December/January 1984, pp. 41–43, 60.

60. Marc J. Hetherington and Michael Nelson, "Anatomy of a Rally Effect: George W. Bush and the War on Terrorism," *PS: Political Science and Politics*, January 2003, pp. 37–42.

61. Gallup Poll, "Presidential Job Approval in Depth," available at www.gallup.com.

62. *Gallup Poll Monthly*, June 1991, p. 27.

63. Frank Newport, "Bush Job Approval Update," Gallup News Service, July 29, 2002, available at www.gallup.com.

64. Stuart N. Soroka, "Good News and Bad News: Asymmetric Response to Economic Information," *Journal of Politics* 68 (May 2006): 372–385.

65. Barbara Sinclair, "Leading and Competing: The President and the Polarized Congress," in Edwards and Davies, *Challenges for the American Presidency*, p. 96.

66. Eric Schickler and Kathryn Pearson, "The House Leadership in an Era of Partisan Warfare," in Lawrence C. Dodd and Bruce I. Oppenheimer, eds., *Congress Reconsidered*, 8th ed. (Washington, DC: CQ Press, 2005), pp. 222–223.

67. Roger T. Larocca, *The Presidential Agenda: Sources of Executive Influence in Congress* (Columbus: Ohio University Press, 2006), pp. 5–6.

68. George C. Edwards III and B. Dan Wood, "Who Influences Whom? The President, Congress, and the Media," *American Political Science Review* 93 (June 1999): 327–344.

69. Jeffrey E. Cohen and Ken Collier, "Public Opinion: Reconceptualizing Going Public," in Steven A. Shull, *Presidential Policymaking: An End of the Century Assessment* (Armonk, NY: M. E. Sharpe, 1999), p. 43.

70. Matthew Eshbaugh-Soha, *The President's Speeches: Beyond "Going Public"* (Boulder, CO: Lynne Rienner, 2006), p. 157.

71. David W. Brady and Craig Volden, *Revolving Gridlock: Politics and Policy from Jimmy Carter to George W. Bush*, 2nd ed. (Boulder, CO: Westview Press, 2006), pp. 32–33.

Chapter 12

The Federal Bureaucracy

CHAPTER OUTLINE

Organization of the Bureaucracy
- Cabinet Departments
- Independent Executive Agencies
- Government Corporations
- Foundations and Institutes
- Independent Regulatory Commissions
- Quasi-Governmental Companies

Personnel

Rulemaking

Politics and Administration
- The President
- Congress
- Interest Groups
- Bureaucrats

Subgovernments and Issue Networks

Conclusion: The Federal Bureaucracy and Public Policy
- Agenda Building
- Policy Formulation and Adoption
- Policy Implementation and Evaluation

LEARNING OUTCOMES

After studying Chapter 12, students should be able to do the following:

▸ Describe the organization of the federal bureaucracy, discussing the cabinet departments, independent executive agencies, government corporations, foundations and institutes, independent regulatory commissions, and quasi-governmental companies. (pp. 315–321)

▸ Trace the history of federal personnel policies. (pp. 321–324)

▸ Identify the steps of the rulemaking process. (pp. 324–325)

▸ Identify the perspectives and political resources each of the following political actors has in the administrative process: the president, Congress, interest groups, and bureaucrats. (pp. 325–331)

▸ Compare and contrast the concept of subgovernments with the concept of issue networks. (pp. 331–333)

▸ Describe the role of the federal bureaucracy in the policymaking process. (pp. 333–335)

▸ Define the key terms listed on page 335 and explain their significance.

Hurricane Katrina has become a symbol of bureaucratic failure. Katrina came ashore along the Louisiana, Mississippi, and Alabama coasts in late August 2005, killing 1,400 people, flooding New Orleans, and leaving thousands of people homeless. The estimated cost of the storm's damage exceeded $100 billion.[1] Government at all levels shared blame for the catastrophe. New Orleans Mayor Ray Nagin failed to order evacuation of the city soon enough. Both the city and the state of Louisiana had no reliable plan to evacuate people in hospitals and nursing homes or to help people without transportation leave the area.

The Federal Emergency Management Agency (FEMA) endured the harshest criticism for failing to prepare for the storm and respond effectively to its devastation. While FEMA officials failed to act, thousands of people sheltered for days inside the New Orleans Superdome without adequate food, water, medical care, or security; others perched on rooftops in flooded neighborhoods.[2] Furthermore, FEMA's effort to deliver aid to people displaced by the storm was so poorly managed that it produced an extraordinary amount of waste and fraud, costing taxpayers as much as $2 billion.[3]

FEMA's failure to respond effectively to Hurricane Katrina was especially troubling because the agency is part of the new Department of Homeland Security. Katrina was a disaster that should have been foreseen. After all, New Orleans is a coastal city built below sea level in a major hurricane zone. If FEMA could not respond effectively to a hurricane, how would the agency respond to a terrorist attack, which could hit anywhere in the nation with little or no warning?

Congress and the president created the Department of Homeland Security in response to criticism that the government failed to foresee and prevent the terrorist attacks of September 11, 2001, despite clear warning signs. They hoped that a single department responsible for preventing and responding to terrorist threats would be more effective at protecting the nation than the previous bureaucratic structures. The new Department of Homeland Security placed 22 agencies within the new organization, including the Coast Guard, Transportation Security Administration, U.S. Citizenship and Immigration Service (USCIS), Customs Service, Secret Service, and FEMA.

Why did FEMA fail to respond effectively to the hurricane? The size and scope of Hurricane Katrina may have overwhelmed FEMA, which was a relatively small federal agency that focused primarily on processing disaster claims and coordinating federal help during time of crisis.[4] The ability of FEMA to respond to Katrina may also have been undermined by bureaucratic infighting following the reorganization. During the 1990s, FEMA was an independent executive agency that was highly regarded for its ability to respond effectively to natural disasters. Its director reported directly to the president. When Congress and the president decided to make FEMA part of a new department, Joe Allbaugh, the agency's director, resigned rather than report to a cabinet officer. His successor, Michael D. Brown, had no emergency management experience before joining the Bush administration. When Katrina struck, Brown was locked in a heated bureaucratic turf battle with Homeland Security Secretary Michael Chertoff, and FEMA was an agency in disarray. Three of its five operations chiefs for natural disasters and nine of ten regional director positions were occupied by temporary officials because of resignations. "People became distracted from the

Hurricane Katrina came ashore along the Louisiana, Mississippi, and Alabama coasts in late August 2005, killing 1,400 people, flooding New Orleans, and leaving thousands of people homeless.

mission," Brown explained, "because we spent so much time and energy fighting for resources and working on reorganization. It just disintegrated our capacity."[5]

The controversy over FEMA and its response to Hurricane Katrina introduces Chapter 12, which studies the role of the federal bureaucracy in the policymaking process. The chapter describes the organization of the executive branch, examines federal personnel policies, explains the rulemaking process, discusses the politics of administrative policymaking, examines the concepts of subgovernment and issue networks, and concludes with a discussion of the role of the federal bureaucracy in the policymaking process. Chapter 12 is the third of four chapters examining the institutions of American government. Chapters 10 and 11 dealt with Congress and the presidency, respectively. Chapter 13 focuses on the federal judiciary.

ORGANIZATION OF THE BUREAUCRACY

The Constitution says nothing about the organization of the executive branch. Congress and the president have created the executive departments, commissions, agencies, and bureaus of the federal bureaucracy on a piecemeal basis over the last 220 years through the legislative process. Furthermore, as the creation of the

Department of Homeland Security demonstrates, Congress and the president may reorganize the agencies of the executive branch if they see fit.

Cabinet Departments

The **cabinet departments** are major administrative units of the federal government that have responsibility for the conduct of a wide range of government operations. The 15 cabinet departments (in the order of their creation) are as follows: State, Defense, Treasury, Justice, Interior, Agriculture, Commerce, Labor, Housing and Urban Development (HUD), Transportation, Energy, Health and Human Services, Education, Veterans Affairs, and Homeland Security. The largest departments in terms of personnel are Defense and Veterans Affairs. In 2007, the Department of Defense had 674,000 civilian employees; the Department of Veterans Affairs employed 246,000 workers. In contrast, fewer than 4,100 employees worked for the Department of Education, the smallest department.[6] Each cabinet department includes a number of smaller administrative units with a variety of titles, such as bureau, agency, commission, administration, center, service, and institute. In addition to FEMA, the Department of Homeland Security includes Customs and Border Protection, Transportation Security Administration, Immigration and Customs Enforcement, U.S. Coast Guard, U.S. Secret Service, and Citizenship and Immigration Service.

With the exception of the head of the Justice Department, who is the attorney general, the people who lead the cabinet departments are called secretaries. The Secretary of Defense, for example, heads the Department of Defense. The Secretary of the Interior leads the Department of the Interior. The president appoints the heads of the cabinet departments and their chief assistants, who are called undersecretaries, deputy undersecretaries, and assistant secretaries, pending Senate confirmation.

Although the Senate confirms most presidential appointments, the approval process has grown increasingly time-consuming. The average time between presidential nomination and Senate confirmation for executive branch appointees has increased steadily from 2.35 months for the nominees of President John Kennedy[7] to 9 months for individuals nominated by President George W. Bush.[8] The Senate is more likely to reject or at least fail to confirm a nominee when one party holds the White House and the other controls the Senate. Confirmation delays have steadily increased, regardless of party control of Congress and the White House, because individual senators have more frequently been using a parliamentary procedure called a *hold* that allows an individual senator to privately delay a vote on a nomination. Holds are used as bargaining chips to extract concessions from the administration on unrelated matters or to retaliate over other issues.[9]

Presidents can sometimes avoid the confirmation process by making recess appointments. The president can temporarily fill vacancies by making appointments when the Senate is in recess. According to the Constitution, recess appointees serve until the end of the next session of the Senate. In 2005, for example, President Bush used recess appointments to fill vacancies on the Federal Election Commission (FEC) with individuals who would have been unlikely to win Senate confirmation.[10] In late 2007, Democrats kept the Senate in session over the Christmas–New Year holiday to prevent Bush from making additional recess appointments.

Presidents employ a number of criteria in selecting department heads. They look for knowledge, administrative ability, experience, loyalty, and congeniality. Some cabinet posts may be given to reward campaign assistance. Modern presidents want a cabinet that includes both men and women and that reflects the ethnic and racial diversity of the United States. Presidents also seek individuals who fit the style and image of their department and who will be acceptable to the interest groups with which their department works most closely. The secretary of the treasury, for example, is typically someone with a background in banking or finance. The secretary of agriculture is a farmer, usually from the Midwest.

Finding qualified men and women who are willing to lead cabinet departments is often a challenge. Some potential cabinet officials will not accept an appointment because the position does not pay as well as executive positions in private industry and it lacks job security. Also, some potential cabinet secretaries turn down appointments because they and their families do not want to go through a long and often intrusive confirmation process.

President's cabinet A body that includes the executive department heads and other senior officials chosen by the president, such as the U.S. ambassador to the United Nations.

The heads of the cabinet departments are all part of the **president's cabinet,** which is a body that includes the executive department heads and other senior officials chosen by the president, such as the U.S. ambassador to the United Nations. The policymaking role of the cabinet varies from president to president. President Dwight Eisenhower delegated considerable responsibilities to cabinet members. He met with his cabinet two or three times a month. In contrast, contemporary presidents seldom convene their cabinets, relying instead on the White House staff, the Executive Office of the President, and individual department heads. President Bill Clinton, for example, convened his cabinet only seven times during his first year in office.[11] The cabinet includes too many people working from too many different perspectives to be an effective policymaking body. Furthermore, the White House usually grows to distrust the cabinet. Eventually, members of the White House staff begin to suspect that department heads have grown too attached to the programs their departments administer and too friendly with the interest groups most closely associated with their departments. Most presidents pay lip service to the cabinet, but seldom consult with it and never defer to its judgment. Instead, they rely on cabinet members to run their departments in the president's interest.[12]

Inner cabinet The Secretary of State, Secretary of Defense, Secretary of the Treasury, and the Attorney General.

The traditional image of the cabinet is that its members are primarily responsible for advising the president on policy formulation and leading their departments in policy implementation. In practice, however, most executive department heads do not do much of either activity. Presidents usually turn to smaller groups of aides, advisors, and selected department heads for policy advice. Four cabinet officials—the secretary of state, secretary of defense, secretary of the treasury, and the attorney general—are known as the **inner cabinet,** because of the importance of the policy issues their departments address.[13] Full cabinet meetings tend to become forums for presidential pep talks or show-and-tell sessions for cabinet members to discuss the latest developments in their departments. As for leading their departments, many secretaries soon learn that their departments are not easily led. Also, most department heads do not have the time to concentrate on the details of administration. They are too busy dealing with Congress, doing public relations work with their department's constituents, selling the president's program, and campaigning for the president's reelection.

Independent Executive Agencies

Congress and the president have created a number of executive branch agencies that are not part of any of the 15 cabinet-level departments, hence the designation **independent executive agencies.** The Peace Corps, National Aeronautics and Space Administration (NASA), Central Intelligence Agency (CIA), Environmental Protection Agency (EPA), Social Security Administration (SSA), and the Small Business Administration (SBA) are independent executive agencies that are headed by individual administrators. The Federal Election Commission (FEC) is an independent executive agency headed by a multimember commission. The president appoints both individual agency heads and board members, pending confirmation by the Senate. The heads of independent executive agencies report directly to the president and serve at the president's pleasure. FEMA was an independent executive agency before the creation of the Department of Homeland Security.

Independent executive agencies perform a range of administrative and regulatory activities. The **Peace Corps,** for example, is an agency that administers an American foreign aid program under which volunteers travel to developing nations to teach skills and help improve living standards. The **National Aeronautics and Space Administration (NASA)** is the federal agency in charge of the space program. The **Central Intelligence Agency (CIA)** is the federal agency that gathers and evaluates foreign intelligence information in the interest of national security. The **Environmental Protection Agency (EPA)** is the federal agency responsible for enforcing the nation's environmental laws. The **Social Security Administration (SSA)** is a federal agency that operates the Social Security system. The **Small Business Administration (SBA)** is a federal agency established to make loans to small businesses and assist them in obtaining government contracts. The **Federal Election Commission (FEC)** is the agency that enforces federal campaign finance laws.

Government Corporations

Government corporations are organizationally similar to private corporations except that the government owns them rather than stockholders. Their organizational rationale is that an agency that makes a product or provides a service should be run by methods similar to those used in the private sector. For example, the **Postal Service** is a government corporation responsible for mail service. An 11-member board of governors appointed by the president to serve nine-year, overlapping terms leads the agency. The board names a postmaster general to manage the day-to-day operation of the service. In addition to the Postal Service, the list of government corporations includes the National Railroad Passenger Corporation (AMTRAK), Federal Deposit Insurance Corporation (FDIC), and the Tennessee Valley Authority (TVA). The **National Railroad Passenger Service Corporation (Amtrak)** is a federal agency that operates inter-city passenger railway traffic. The **Federal Deposit Insurance Corporation (FDIC)** is a federal agency established to insure depositors' accounts in banks and thrift institutions. The **Tennessee Valley Authority (TVA)** is a federal agency established to promote the development of the Tennessee River and its tributaries.

Social Security Administration (SSA) The federal agency that operates the Social Security system.

Small Business Administration (SBA) The federal agency established to make loans to small businesses and assist them in obtaining government contracts.

Federal Election Commission (FEC) The agency that enforces federal campaign finance laws.

Postal Service A government corporation responsible for mail service.

National Railroad Passenger Corporation (Amtrak) A federal agency that operates inter-city passenger railway traffic.

Federal Deposit Insurance Corporation (FDIC) A federal agency established to insure depositors' accounts in banks and thrift institutions.

An important principle behind government corporations is that they should be self-financing, at least to a significant degree. In the case of the Postal Service, users pay most of the cost of operation by purchasing stamps and paying service charges. Not all government corporations, however, are financially self-sufficient. Amtrak requires a subsidy from Congress to keep its trains rolling. Amtrak's critics argue that the agency should be forced to pay its own way or go out of business. If the demand for passenger rail is not sufficient to support Amtrak's operation, then the service should end. In contrast, the defenders of Amtrak believe that the agency provides an important service that should be continued. Furthermore, they point out that the government subsidizes automobile transportation by building highways and air transportation by constructing airports.

 WHAT IS YOUR OPINION?

If you were a member of Congress, would you vote in favor of government subsidies for Amtrak?

Foundations and Institutes

Foundations and institutes administer grant programs to local governments, universities, nonprofit institutions, and individuals for research in the natural and social sciences or to promote the arts. These agencies include the National Science Foundation (NSF) and the National Endowment for the Arts. The **National Science Foundation (NSF)** is a federal agency established to encourage scientific advances and improvements in science education. The **National Endowment for the Arts (NEA)** is a federal agency created to nurture cultural expression and promote appreciation of the arts. Foundations and institutes are governed by multimember boards appointed by the president with Senate concurrence from lists of nominees submitted by various scientific and educational institutions.

Independent Regulatory Commissions

An **independent regulatory commission** is an agency outside the major executive departments that is charged with the regulation of important aspects of the economy. The **Federal Trade Commission (FTC),** for example, is an agency that regulates business competition, including enforcement of laws against monopolies and the protection of consumers from deceptive trade practices. The **Federal Communications Commission (FCC)** is an agency that regulates interstate and international radio, television, telephone, telegraph, and satellite communications, as well as licensing radio and television stations. The **Securities and Exchange Commission (SEC)** is an agency that regulates the sale of stocks and bonds as well as investment and holding companies. The **Equal Employment Opportunity Commission (EEOC)** is an agency that investigates and rules on charges of employment discrimination.

Congress has attempted to insulate independent regulatory commissions from direct political pressure, especially from the White House. These agencies are headed by boards of three to seven members who are appointed by the president with Senate approval. In contrast to cabinet members and the heads of other executive departments,

Tennessee Valley Authority (TVA) A federal agency established to promote the development of the Tennessee River and its tributaries.

National Science Foundation (NSF) A federal agency established to encourage scientific advances and improvements in science education.

National Endowment for the Arts (NEA) A federal agency created to nurture cultural expression and promote appreciation of the arts.

Independent regulatory commission An agency outside the major executive departments that is charged with the regulation of important aspects of the economy.

Federal Trade Commission (FTC) An agency that regulates business competition, including enforcement of laws against monopolies and the protection of consumers from deceptive trade practices.

In 2008, Congress passed, and the president signed, legislation to commit federal funds to Fannie Mae and Freddie Mac to ensure that they would not collapse under the weight of losses incurred in the housing foreclosure crisis.

the president cannot remove regulatory commissioners. Instead, they serve fixed, staggered terms ranging from 3 to 14 years. As a result, a new president must usually wait several years before having much impact on the composition of the boards. Furthermore, the law generally requires that no more than a bare majority of board members be from the same political party.

Congress has designed independent regulatory commissions to provide closer, more flexible regulation than Congress itself can offer through **statutory law,** which is law that is written by the legislature. Congress has delegated authority to these agencies to control various business practices using broad, general language. Congress has authorized the FTC, for example, to regulate advertising in the "public convenience, interest, or necessity." It has empowered the EEOC "to prevent any person from engaging in any unlawful employment practice."

Quasi-Governmental Companies

A **quasi-governmental company** is a private, profit-seeking corporation created by Congress to serve a public purpose. For example, Congress created the Federal National Mortgage Association (Fannie Mae) and Federal Home Loan Mortgage Corporation (Freddie Mac) to increase the availability of credit to home buyers. Fannie Mae and Freddie Mac are profit-making corporations run by 18-member boards of governors appointed by the president with Senate confirmation. They are exempt

Federal Communication Commission (FCC) An agency that regulates interstate and international radio, television, telephone, telegraph, and satellite communications, as well as licensing radio and television stations.

from state and federal taxation and enjoy a line of credit at the U.S. Treasury. Because of the perception that Congress would bail them out if they got in financial trouble, Fannie Mae and Freddie Mac pay lower interest rates than they would if they were strictly private enterprises.[14] Lower rates benefit home buyers, some of whom would not be able to qualify to purchase a home at all without the lower interest rate.

In 2008, Congress passed, and the president signed, legislation to commit federal funds to Fannie Mae and Freddie Mac to ensure that they would not collapse under the weight of losses incurred in the housing foreclosure crisis. The federal government eventually took over the operation of Fannie Mac and Freddie Mac, at least temporarily, to prevent their financial failure, which would have been catastrophic for the home mortgage industry. The action kept Fannie and Freddie in business, but potentially put taxpayers on the hook for billions of dollars in bad loans.

PERSONNEL

Securities and Exchange Commission (SEC) An agency that regulates the sale of stocks and bonds as well as investment and holding companies.

Equal Employment Opportunity Commission (EEOC) An agency that investigates and rules on charges of employment discrimination.

Statutory law Law that is written by the legislature.

Quasi-governmental company A private, profit-seeking corporation created by Congress to serve a public purpose.

The size of the federal civilian bureaucracy has grown dramatically since the early days of the nation. In 1800, only about 3,000 persons worked for the U.S. government. That figure grew to 95,000 by 1881 and half a million in 1925. Today, the federal bureaucracy is the largest civilian workforce in the Western world, with 2.7 million civilian employees stationed in every state and city in the country and almost every nation in the world.[15]

As Figure 12.1 indicates, the number of federal civilian employees has generally fallen since the early 1990s. Between 1991 and 2001, the federal payroll decreased from 3.1 million to 2.7 million, a decline of nearly 13 percent. After September 11, 2001, the number of federal employees inched up. Congress passed and the president signed legislation to make airport baggage screeners federal employees, adding thousands of people to the federal payroll. Employment in other federal agencies that deal with security issues, including the Border Patrol, increased as well. The post–9/11 surge in federal employment peaked in 2003. Thereafter, the size of the federal workforce began to decline again.

Although the official size of the federal workforce has generally fallen since the early 1990s, the actual number of people employed directly and indirectly by the federal government has risen sharply over the same period of time. Political scientist Paul C. Light estimates that the true size of the federal civilian workforce is 14.6 million employees instead of the 2.7 million on the official payroll.[16] In addition to civilian employees working directly for the federal government, Light's figure includes millions of contract workers, state and local government employees working on federally funded programs, and federal grant beneficiaries at colleges and universities. The federal government pays their salaries, but their names do not appear on federal personnel rosters. Contract workers collect taxes, prepare budget documents, take notes at meetings, and perform hundreds of other governmental functions. The Department of Defense even hires private security guards to protect military bases in the United States.[17] Furthermore, Congress and the president rely on millions of state and local bureaucrats to administer federal programs, such as No Child Left Behind, Medicaid, and the Food Stamp Program.

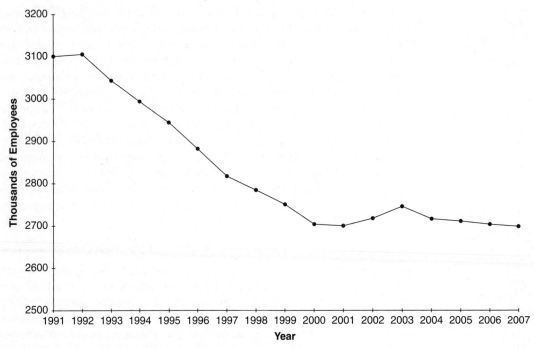

FIGURE 12.1   Federal Civilian Employment, 1991–2007.
Source: Office of Personnel Management.

Employment practices in the early days of the nation emphasized character, professional qualifications, and political compatibility with the administration in office. Under President Andrew Jackson (1829–1837), political considerations became paramount. A new president would fire many of the employees of the previous administration and replace them with friends and supporters. To the victor belonged the spoils (i.e., the prizes of victory), they said, and federal jobs were the spoils. The method of hiring government employees from among the friends, relatives, and supporters of elected officeholders was known as the **spoils system.**

When a disgruntled office seeker assassinated President James Garfield in 1881, Congress passed, and the president signed, legislation to reform the federal hiring process. The legislation created a Civil Service Commission to establish a hiring system based on competitive examinations and protect federal workers from dismissal for political reasons. Initially, the civil service system covered only about 10 percent of federal jobs, but Congress gradually expanded coverage to include more than 90 percent of federal workers.[18] In 1939, Congress enacted another reform, the **Hatch Act,** which was a measure designed to restrict the political activities of federal employees to voting and the private expression of views. The rationale behind the law was to protect government workers from being forced by their superiors to work for particular candidates.

Spoils system The method of hiring government employees from among the friends, relatives, and supporters of elected officeholders.

Hatch Act A measure designed to restrict the political activities of federal employees to voting and the private expression of views.

Although civil service ended the spoils system, it too became the target of criticism. Many observers charged that the civil service system was too inflexible to reward merit, punish poor performance, or transfer civil servants from one agency to another without having to scale a mountain of red tape. In 1978, Congress and the president responded to complaints against the civil service system by enacting a package of reforms. The legislation established a Senior Executive Service (SES) composed of approximately 8,000 top civil servants who would be eligible for substantial merit bonuses but who could be transferred, demoted, or fired more easily than other federal employees. The reform measure replaced the old Civil Service Commission with two new agencies: an Office of Personnel Management to manage the federal workforce and a Merit Systems Protection Board to hear employee grievances. The reforms also provided greater protection for **whistleblowers**—that is, workers who report wrongdoing or mismanagement—and streamlined procedures for dismissing incompetent employees.[19]

Whistleblowers Workers who report wrongdoing or mismanagement.

Congress and the president have given federal employees limited rights to organize. Federal workers won the right to form unions in 1912. Fifty years later, President John Kennedy signed an executive order giving federal workers the right to bargain collectively over a limited set of issues but not pay and benefits. **Collective bargaining** is a negotiation between an employer and a union representing employees over the terms and conditions of employment. The civil service reform legislation adopted in 1978 guaranteed federal employees the right to bargain collectively over issues other than pay and benefits, but it prohibited federal workers from striking. In 1981, President Ronald Reagan fired more than 11,000 air traffic controllers for participating in a strike organized by the Professional Air Traffic Controllers Association (PATCO).

Collective bargaining The negotiation between an employer and a union representing employees over the terms and conditions of employment.

Democratic presidents typically have a more positive relationship with federal employee organizations than do Republican presidents. Labor unions in general are allied with the Democratic Party, whereas the GOP has stronger ties to management, and public employee unions are no exception to the pattern. President Bill Clinton, for example, issued an executive order directing federal agencies to develop partnerships with the employee unions. Clinton justified the approach as a means to reform government by making it more efficient. In contrast, President George W. Bush took an adversarial approach toward employee unions. He dissolved the partnership councils created during the Clinton administration and asked Congress to change personnel policies in light of the war on terror.[20]

When Congress created the Department of Homeland Security, it gave President Bush authority to relax civil service rules to make it easier for the administration to hire, transfer, promote, cross-train, discipline, and fire employees in the new department without having to worry about union rules and civil service procedures. The president argued that the administration needed the more flexibility over personnel than the old civil service system provided in order to create a modern workforce capable of responding to the threat of international terrorism. In particular, the administration wanted to base annual salary increases on performance tied to job evaluations rather than giving every employee an annual raise based on longevity. The American Federation of Government Employees and other employee unions adamantly opposed waiving civil service rules because they feared that some managers would use the authority to reward their friends and punish their enemies without regard for the performance of the workers.[21] But the unions lost, not just for the Department of Homeland Security, but for the whole federal government. Unless Congress changes the law, the federal government will adopt a pay-for-performance system for all federal agencies in 2009, replacing the old general schedule system with its 15 GS levels and ten steps within each level. The new system will make it easier for managers to reward good work and punish poor performance while making it more difficult for unions to intervene on behalf of their members.[22] With Democrats in control of Congress and a Democrat in the White House in 2009, however, the new pay-for-performance system may never go into effect.

 WHAT IS YOUR OPINION?

Does a performance-pay system improve employee performance, or is it just a way for managers to reward their friends?

RULEMAKING

Rule A legally binding regulation.

Rulemaking The regulatory process used by government agencies to enact legally binding regulations.

Regulatory negotiation A structured process by which representatives of the interests that would be substantially affected by a rule, including employees of the regulatory agency, negotiate agreement on the terms of the rule.

Independent regulatory commissions and regulatory agencies in the executive branch do much of their work through the rulemaking process. When Congress passes regulatory legislation, it frequently delegates authority to the bureaucracy to make rules to implement the legislation. A **rule** is a legally binding regulation. **Rulemaking** is the regulatory process used by government agencies to enact legally binding regulations. The SEC, for example, makes rules governing corporate finance disclosure. On average, federal agencies produce between 4,000 and 5,000 rules a year.[23]

The rulemaking process begins with an agency giving advance notice that it is considering issuing a rule in a particular policy area. The agency publishes the text of the proposed rule in the *Federal Register* and allows a period of time at least 30 days long in which the public can comment on the proposed rule. Concerned parties, usually interest groups affected by the proposed rule, submit written comments or offer testimony at public hearings. When an agency officially adopts a rule, it is published in the *Code of Federal Regulations*.

Rules are sometimes the product of formal negotiations among government agencies and affected interest groups. **Regulatory negotiation** is a structured process by which representatives of the interests that would be substantially affected by a rule work with government officials to negotiate agreement on the terms of the rule. The federal agency considering the adoption of a rule employs a neutral third party to identify interests that would be affected by the rule. The agency interviews representatives of the interest groups, determines what issues should be considered, assesses the willingness of the interests to participate in a negotiation, and evaluates the likelihood that an agreement can be reached among the parties. The goal of a regulatory negotiation is to produce an agreement to which all parties will sign. The signed agreement stipulates that the parties participating in the negotiation will neither attempt to prevent the rule's adoption or challenge the rule in court once it is adopted.[24]

The Office of Management and Budget (OMB) is a regular participant in the rulemaking process. In 1981, President Ronald Reagan issued an executive order requiring that any executive branch agency issuing a new rule with an economic impact of $100 million or more must prepare a cost-benefit analysis and submit it to the OMB for approval. A **cost-benefit analysis** is an evaluation of a proposed policy or regulation based on a comparison of its expected benefits and anticipated costs. Reagan's order applied to executive branch agencies such as the EPA, but not to independent regulatory commissions such as the FCC. Although subsequent presidents have kept Reagan's requirement for a cost-benefit analysis of regulations, they have approached the issue from different perspectives. In Republican administrations, the OMB functions as an appeals court for business and trade groups worried about the impact of regulation on their activities. In contrast, environmentalists, consumer groups, and organized labor have more influence in the OMB review process during Democratic administrations.[25]

Congress exercises oversight of agency rules. Agencies must submit all proposed new rules to Congress, which has 60 days to overturn it through the legislative process, subject to a presidential veto and a possible override attempt. If Congress does not act within 60 days, the rule goes into effect.

Federal courts also play a role in the rulemaking process. Individuals and groups unhappy with agency decisions sometimes turn to the federal courts for relief. Courts hear challenges not just from business groups who believe that federal regulations have gone too far, but also from consumer and environmental groups who argue that regulations are not strict enough. In general, the courts have ruled that agency decisions must be supported by evidence and reasoned explanations and that the agencies must follow statutory requirements to give notice, hold hearings, and consult with parties outside the affected industries.[26]

Cost-benefit analysis An evaluation of a proposed policy or regulation based on a comparison of its expected benefits and anticipated costs.

POLITICS AND ADMINISTRATION

Bureaucratic policymaking is a complex process involving the president, Congress, interest groups, and the bureaucracy itself. Each of the participants has a perspective and a set of political resources for achieving its goals.

The President

Presidents have an important stake in the faithful and efficient implementation of federal programs, but they must work to influence the administrative process, and their success is not assured. Being chief executive does not entitle a president to command the federal bureaucracy so much as it offers the opportunity to attempt to influence policy implementation. President Jimmy Carter once ordered relevant federal agencies to develop guidelines to implement the administration's policy of discouraging industrial and commercial development in areas subject to repeated flooding. More than two years later, only 15 of 37 agencies most directly involved had written guidelines. Thirteen agencies were still working on the assignment and 12 agencies had done nothing at all![27]

Presidents face a continuous struggle to have a major impact on bureaucratic policymaking. The federal bureaucracy is too large and spread out for easy oversight from the White House, and many federal programs are administered by state and local officials or by private contractors over whom the president has little direct authority. Presidents often lack the time to manage the bureaucracy and may be uninterested in trying. It is more glamorous and politically rewarding, at least in the short run, to propose new policy initiatives than to supervise the implementation of programs already in place.

Presidents have several tools for influencing the bureaucracy. The president has the authority to name most of the top administrators in the bureaucracy, including department secretaries and undersecretaries, agency heads, and regulatory commissioners. President George W. Bush ordered each executive branch agency to create a regulatory policy office run by a presidential appointee to ensure that rules and other actions taken by the agency conformed to the president's policy priorities.[28] Except for members of the independent regulatory commissions, presidents also have the power to dismiss their appointees. The president can use the OMB to evaluate agency performance and screen rules proposed by executive branch agencies. The president proposes agency budgets and can ask Congress to reorganize the bureaucracy.

Consider the Reagan administration's efforts to reduce the regulatory activities of such agencies as the EPA, EEOC, Occupational Safety and Health Administration (OSHA), and the Office of Surface Mining. President Reagan believed that many government regulations were excessive, particularly in the areas of environmental protection, consumer rights, and workplace safety. The Reagan White House carefully screened the presidential appointees to head these agencies to ensure they were business-oriented conservatives who would be loyal to the president. For example, Reagan chose an attorney who had previously defended corporations against anti-discrimination lawsuits brought by the government to head the EEOC. Reagan selected an anti-environmentalist to run the EPA. Furthermore, Reagan used the SES to transfer or demote career civil servants the White House deemed insufficiently supportive of the president's policy goals.[29]

Reagan also attempted to limit regulatory activities by cutting agency budgets and reducing their personnel. At the president's urging, Congress reduced total EPA funding by 24 percent in 1982 alone. Between 1980 and 1983, expenditures for air pollution regulation and monitoring fell by 42 percent, and the number of personnel authorized for clean air activities declined by 31 percent.[30]

Finally, the Reagan administration used the OMB to prevent the adoption of rules by executive branch agencies that the White House considered burdensome to industry. In 1984, for example, the OMB forced the EPA to ease proposed pollution regulations for diesel vehicles.[31] Between 1981 and 1985, the OMB forced agencies to modify or withdraw 19 percent of proposed rules. Furthermore, that figure underestimated the real impact of the OMB because agencies often revised rules to make them acceptable to the White House before submitting them for OMB review.[32]

Reagan's efforts to reduce regulatory activities enjoyed mixed success. In the short run, regulatory enforcement levels in the agencies Reagan targeted declined. The EPA's air quality monitoring fell by 41 percent in 1982; its pollution abatement activities declined by 69 percent.[33] Food and Drug Administration (FDA) seizures of improperly manufactured food and drugs fell by 54 percent under Reagan.[34] Similarly, the FTC reduced its enforcement activities by about 50 percent.[35]

In at least two agencies, however, the EEOC and the EPA, Reagan's impact on regulatory enforcement proved short-lived, evaporating even before the end of Reagan's first term in office. The Reagan appointees heading the agencies were highly controversial and were eventually forced to resign amid allegations of improper or even illegal conduct. Their replacements were experienced bureaucrats who were sympathetic with the mission of the regulatory agencies they were appointed to head. Furthermore, Congress responded to the public controversy surrounding the EEOC and the EPA by conducting investigations and restoring budget cuts made in 1981 and 1982.[36]

The experience of the Reagan administration demonstrates that a determined president has sufficient power to have an impact on bureaucratic policymaking. Through the use of his appointive powers, the OMB, and his authority to propose budgets to Congress, Reagan succeeded in reducing the regulatory activities of a number of targeted agencies. To a considerable degree, however, the president's success at influencing the bureaucracy depends on the role of other political actors, including Congress, interest groups, and agency administrators. Reagan failed to achieve all of his regulatory goals because he faced a hostile environment in that the Democratic Party controlled the House of Representatives. Labor unions, environmental organizations, and consumer groups were able to delay and eventual defeat many of Reagan's regulatory reforms because they enjoyed the support of Democratic Party allies in the House. In contrast, President George W. Bush, whose regulatory policy goals were similar to those of President Reagan, succeeded at modifying the impact of federal regulation on business interests because his political party controlled both the House and Senate during most of his first six years in office. The EPA, OSHA, and other regulatory agencies sharply reduced their enforcement activities between 2001 and 2006. The EPA, for example, cut criminal prosecutions of polluters by 36 percent.[37] OSHA, meanwhile, changed its approach from issuing regulations to a voluntary compliance strategy aimed at reaching agreements with industry associations and companies to police themselves.[38]

Congress

Congress has strong legal authority to oversee the actions of the federal bureaucracy. Congress can abolish an agency, reorganize its structure, change its jurisdiction, cut its budget, audit its expenditures, investigate its performance, and overrule its decisions. In short, Congress has effective means for getting an agency's attention. The Smithsonian Institution is a national museum and educational institution chartered by Congress. When the Smithsonian's governing board failed to provide the Congress with a satisfactory justification for an exclusive deal with Showtime Network to use materials in the Smithsonian collection to make films, the House Appropriations Committee cut $15 million from the agency's budget and sought a cap on salaries for agency administrators.[39]

Some political scientists believe that congressional oversight is generally ineffective. Congress is unable to provide clear, consistent policy oversight for the bureaucracy, they say, because Congress itself lacks consensus on administrative

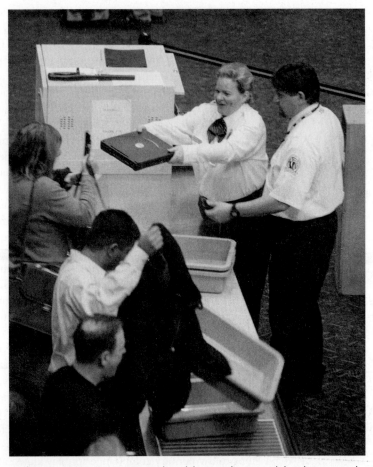

After September 11, 2001, Congress passed, and the president signed, legislation to make airport baggage screeners federal employees, adding thousands of people to the federal payroll.

Constituency service The action of members of Congress and their staffs attending to the individual, particular needs of constituents.

Fire-alarm oversight An indirect system of congressional surveillance of bureaucratic administration characterized by rules, procedures, and informal practices that enable individual citizens and organized interest groups to examine administrative decisions, charge agencies with violating legislative goals, and seek remedies from agencies, courts, and the Congress itself.

policy goals. Whereas some members of Congress will think an agency has gone too far, others will believe that it has not gone far enough. Furthermore, many political scientists believe that the increased attention of members of Congress to **constituency service** (the actions of members of Congress and their staffs attending to the individual, particular needs of constituents) has made senators and representatives more dependent on executive branch agencies for help in providing services to constituents. Members of Congress who have built mutually beneficial relationships with the bureaucracy are not going to undermine those relationships through aggressive oversight.[40]

In contrast, other political scientists believe that Congress has developed an effective method of oversight through a process that some observers call **fire-alarm oversight.** It is an indirect system of congressional surveillance of bureaucratic administration characterized by rules, procedures, and informal practices that enable individual citizens and organized interest groups to examine administrative decisions, charge agencies with violating legislative goals, and seek remedies from agencies, courts, and Congress itself. In other words, Congress exercises oversight when media reports, interest group demands, or citizen complaints call attention to a problem. Congress responded to complaints about FEMA because of the high visibility of the issue.

Interest Groups

Every agency has several or perhaps dozens of interest groups vitally concerned with the programs it administers. Broadcasters are concerned with the FCC. The airline industry, aircraft manufacturers, airline employee associations, and consumer groups have an interest in the Federal Aviation Administration (FAA). Western land interests and environmentalists monitor the activities of the Interior Department. Postal workers' unions, direct mail advertisers, publishers, and consumer groups focus on the work of the Postal Service.

Interest groups have a number of tools for influencing the bureaucracy. Groups lobby bureaucratic agencies. They also lobby Congress to pressure the bureaucracy on their behalf. Sometimes groups file lawsuits to block or reverse an agency's decisions.

Captured agencies Agencies that work to benefit the economic interests they regulate rather than serving the public interest.

Critics charge that federal agencies often become **captured agencies,** that is, agencies that work to benefit the economic interests they regulate rather than serving the public interest. The Federal Maritime Commission, for example, historically has worked closely with shippers. The Federal Power Commission has been accused of acting on behalf of the electric utility industry. Proponents of the captured-agencies thesis point to what they describe as a revolving door between industry and the bureaucracy as evidence of the comfortable relationship between the regulatory commissions and industry. Presidents appoint corporate lawyers and industry executives to serve as commissioners. When the commissioners eventually leave government, they often take jobs in the industries they once regulated.

Many political scientists believe that the captured-agencies thesis is too simplistic. Studies have found that capture is not the norm, and when it does occur, it does not always last.[41] Instead, a range of factors, including presidential appointments, congressional committees and subcommittees, judicial actions, economic conditions, and agency staffs, affect agency decisions.[42] Professor Steven P. Croley notes that government agencies do not always take the side of special interests against the public interest. The FTC, for example, adopted the National Do Not Call Registry despite the opposition of the telemarketing industry.[43] The captured-agencies thesis assumes that the political environment for each government agency consists of a single set of interest groups with a similar perspective, but that is not usually the case. The debate over the adoption of the National Do Not Call Registry involved not just an industry group, but also consumer organizations and the AARP.

Bureaucrats

Each agency has two sets of administrators—a small group of presidential appointees, typically called political appointees, and a larger group of career civil servants. Nineteen presidential appointees and 284 SES managers lead the Department of Health and Human Services. Five presidential appointees and 20 SES managers head the EEOC.[44] In contrast to presidential employees who serve no more than four or eight

GLOBAL PERSPECTIVE

The Egyptian Bureaucracy

Egypt is a developing country, struggling to overcome problems of overpopulation, poverty, illiteracy, social inequality, unemployment, and foreign debt. The nation's economy depends on foreign aid (mostly from the United States), tourism, income earned by Egyptians working abroad, and borrowing. The Egyptian economy lacks a substantial industrial base. Furthermore, rapid population growth erases whatever economic gains the nation's economy makes.

The Egyptian government assumes responsibility for feeding, educating, and employing the populace. The government owns and operates 70 percent of the nation's industry and business enterprises, including hotels, airlines, the steel industry, and utility companies.* Consequently, the government bureaucracy runs not only the government, but many business enterprises as well.

The Egyptian bureaucracy does more to impede than promote economic development. It has a huge structure with a reputation for the selective enforcement of rules, mismanagement, and corruption. It is lethargic, inflexible, and rigid. Surveys of government workers show that they hold the general public in disdain. Because the government guarantees a job

in the bureaucracy to all college graduates, the bureaucracy is overstaffed by a factor of more than three to one.[†] Anyone who wants to start a business must comply with dozens of rules and regulations and complete a sandstorm of forms. The only way for entrepreneurs to cut through the red tape is to pay a bribe to the bureaucrat overseeing the process.[‡]

Bureaucratic reform will be difficult to achieve in Egypt. To streamline the bureaucracy, the government would have to lay off millions of government workers, swelling an already high unemployment rate. High unemployment, especially among educated professionals, would threaten the political survival of the Egyptian government.

QUESTIONS TO CONSIDER

1. Does government in Egypt play a larger role in society than government in the United States?
2. In the United States, does government bureaucracy promote or hinder economic development? What is the basis of your answer?
3. Would democracy make bureaucratic reform more or less likely to take place in Egypt?

---

*Jamil E. Jreisat, *Politics Without Process: Administering Development in the Arab World* (Boulder, CO: Lynne Rienner, 1997), pp. 97–101.

[†]Monte Palmer, Ali Laila, and El Sayed Yassin, *The Egyptian Bureaucracy* (Syracuse, NY: Syracuse University Press, 1988), p. 151.

[‡]Jreisat, *Politics Without Process*, p. 110.

---

years, depending on the number of terms of the president who appoints them, SES managers are career bureaucrats who stay with a single agency for most of their careers. SES managers have interests of their own that may differ from those of the president and the political administrators appointed to run their agencies. Career SES managers typically want to preserve and enhance their positions, their programs, and their budgets. Furthermore, agencies often attract employees who are personally committed to the mission of their department. Environmentalists work for the EPA, whereas people with agricultural backgrounds seek employment with the Department of Agriculture.

Career bureaucrats have resources for defending their turf. Sometimes career employees resort to subtle, behind-the-scenes resistance to policy changes they oppose, a sort of bureaucratic guerrilla warfare. In an organization as large as the federal bureaucracy, presidential initiatives can be opposed in a number of quiet ways. Changes can be delayed. Bureaucrats may follow the letter but not the spirit of directives. Officials may "forget" to pass along orders to subordinates. News of mistakes or internal bickering can be leaked to the press.[45]

Bureaucracy finds power in alliances with important members of Congress and interest groups. Executive branch agencies are some of the most vigorous and effective lobbyists. By assisting key members of Congress with problems involving constituent complaints, agencies build friendships. Furthermore, most agencies have interest group constituencies that are willing to use their political resources on behalf of the agency. Teacher groups lobby for the Department of Education; defense contractors fight for the defense budget. Medical professionals support the Public Health Service.

Executive branch officials know that they are more likely to achieve their goals if they can find a way to connect their policy preferences with the self-interest of members of Congress. Consider NASA's successful strategy for winning congressional support for continued funding of the International Space Station (ISS). NASA distributed work on the ISS to 68 prime contractors and 35 major subcontractors in 22 states, including California, Texas, Florida, New York, Illinois, Ohio, and Pennsylvania, all states with large, politically influential congressional delegations.[46]

SUBGOVERNMENTS AND ISSUE NETWORKS

Subgovernment or iron triangle A cozy, three-sided relationship among government agencies, interest groups, and key members of Congress in which all parties benefit.

Political scientists use different concepts to explain administrative policymaking. One approach to understanding the administrative process is the concept of subgovernments or iron triangles. A **subgovernment** or **iron triangle** is a cozy, three-sided relationship among government agencies, interest groups, and key members of Congress in which all parties benefit.

- On one point of the subgovernment triangle, the bureaucracy and interest groups benefit from a special relationship. Agencies enhance the economic status of the interest group through favorable regulation or the awarding of government contracts. Interest groups return the favor by lobbying Congress on behalf of the agency.

- On the second point of the triangle, interest groups and members of Congress enjoy a mutually beneficial relationship. Interest groups assist senators and members of the House by contributing to their reelection campaigns. In return, members of Congress vote to appropriate money for programs the interest groups support.

- The third point of the triangle focuses on the interaction between agencies and members of Congress. Politically wise bureaucrats know that it is important to keep key members of Congress happy by providing all the information they request, solving problems members of Congress bring to their attention, and paying special notice to the needs of the home states and districts of key senators and representatives.

Consider the highway subgovernment. On one point of the highway triangle are interest groups that benefit from highway construction: auto manufacturers, the United Auto Workers (UAW), tire companies, asphalt and cement dealers, road contractors, long-haul trucking firms, the Teamsters Union, and oil companies. The second point is the Federal Highway Administration, which, of course, is interested in the preservation of the programs it administers. On the third point of the triangle are the congressional committees that consider highway-construction bills—the Environment and Public Works Committee in the Senate and the Committee on Transportation and Infrastructure in the House. Senators and representatives from states with extensive interstate highway systems, such as Texas, California, and Oklahoma, are also involved.

Each part of the subgovernment serves and is served by the other two. The members of Congress involved work to maintain federal support for highway construction and maintenance. The interest groups lobby Congress on behalf of highway programs, and their political action committees (PACs) contribute campaign money to members of Congress on key committees. The agency, meanwhile, makes sure that the districts and states of the members of Congress involved get their share of new highways and bridges. Also, if some town in the district wants a special favor, local officials call their representative or senator, who passes the request along to the agency. The agency is eager to please and happy to give the member of Congress the credit.

The political scientists who study subgovernments believe that a great deal of public policy is made through behind-the-scenes understandings among interest groups, key members of Congress, and the federal bureaucracy. When issues arise, the participants in the subgovernment settle the matter, with little input from political actors outside the triangle, including the president. The result is that public policy is tailored to the wishes of those groups most closely associated with the policy itself. Energy policy, they say, reflects the interests of the oil and gas industry. Highway programs are geared to match the concerns of the highway lobby.

In recent years, however, many political scientists have concluded that although subgovernments exist in American politics, their influence is less than it was during the 1940s and 1950s. Subgovernments prospered in a time when public policy was the work of a relatively small number of fairly autonomous participants: a handful of powerful committee chairs, a small number of interest groups, and a few agency administrators. Furthermore, most policy decisions were made outside public view.

Today's policy environment has changed. Power in Congress is centralized in the party leadership. Committee chairs are less influential. Interest groups are more numerous. Furthermore, new issues have arisen for which it is all but impossible to identify clearly the dominant actors, including energy, consumer protection, illegal immigration, and the environment.[47]

Political scientist Hugh Heclo believes that the concept of issue networks more accurately describes administrative policymaking today than the concept of subgovernments. An **issue network** is a group of political actors concerned with some aspect of public policy. Issue networks are fluid, with participants moving in and out. They can include technical specialists, members of Congress, journalists, the president, interest groups, bureaucrats, academic experts, and individual political activists. Powerful interest groups may be involved, but they do not control the process. Instead, policy in a particular area results from conflict among a broad range of political actors both in and out of government.[48]

Consider the fate of the Highway Trust Fund. A subgovernment once dominated federal highway policy, but that is no longer the case. During the 1970s, the number

Issue network A group of political actors that is actively involved with policymaking in a particular issue area.

of interest groups concerned with highway construction grew. Environmentalists worried about the effect of highway construction on the environment. Minority rights groups became alarmed about the impact of freeway construction on minority neighborhoods. Groups advocating energy conservation argued that government should divert money from highways to mass transit. In the meantime, congressional committees and subcommittees with jurisdiction over highway programs began to include members of Congress allied to groups opposed to highway spending. As a result, federal highway policy is now made in a more contentious, uncertain environment than before.[49] In 1991, Congress passed, and the president signed, the Intermodal Surface Transportation Efficiency Act (ISTEA), granting states considerable leeway in deciding whether to spend federal transportation money for highways or mass transit. The legislation also required that states use a certain amount of money to fund "enhancement programs," which were local transportation-related projects designed to aid a community's quality of life, such as hike and bike trails. The passage of ISTEA reflected the participation of a broad range of interests concerned with transportation policy, not just the traditional set of interest groups involved with highway funding.[50]

CONCLUSION: THE FEDERAL BUREAUCRACY AND PUBLIC POLICY

The federal bureaucracy participates in every stage of the policymaking process.

Agenda Building

Surgeon General
An official in the Public Health Service who advises the president on health issues.

The actions of federal agencies sometimes focus public attention on issues. For example, the federal bureaucracy has done more to call public attention to the health risks of tobacco than either Congress or the president. In 1964, the **Surgeon General,** an official in the Public Health Service who advises the president on health issues, released a report summarizing research showing a link between smoking and cancer. That document, which was called the *Surgeon General's Report on Smoking and Health,* was the nation's first official recognition that cigarette smoking causes cancer and other serious illnesses. Over the years, the Surgeon General has issued additional reports dealing with related issues, such as the effect of secondhand smoke and preventing tobacco use among young people. The initial report and each succeeding report received a good deal of attention, sparking a public debate about the impact of tobacco usage on the public health.

Agency reports and official statements can highlight policy issues, especially if the media and the general public perceive that agency officials are acting on the basis of their professional expertise rather than political motives. Even though Surgeons General are presidential appointees, they are held in respect because they are physicians who work in an agency dominated by health professionals. The scientific evidence presented in the various reports released by the Surgeon General put the tobacco companies on the defensive, making it difficult for them to defeat proposals to restrict tobacco advertising and require health warnings on tobacco products.

GETTING INVOLVED

Working for Uncle Sam

More than 2.7 million people work for the federal government, stationed in every state and city in the country and almost every nation in the world. Even small towns are home to a number of federal employees, working for the Post Office, Social Security Administration, and other agencies. Larger cities may contain thousands of federal government workers. Consequently, many students will have friends, relatives, or neighbors who are federal employees. If you know someone who works for the federal government, chat with him or her about federal employment and take notes so you can discuss the conversation in class. Use the following questions to guide your discussion:

- For which department or agency do you work?
- How long have you been a federal employee?

- What are the advantages of working for the federal government as opposed to a private employer?
- What are the disadvantages of working for the federal government as opposed to a private employer?
- Have you enjoyed your job with the government? Why or why not?
- Did the creation of the Department of Homeland Security affect your position? If so, how?
- Do you believe that federal employee compensation should be based on job performance?
- Would you recommend a career in the federal workforce to a college student?

WHAT IS YOUR OPINION?

Should the federal government regulate tobacco advertising?

Policy Formulation and Adoption

Federal agencies participate in policy formulation. Agency officials work directly with the White House and members of Congress during the legislative process. Agency officials may assist members of Congress in drafting legislation related to their departments. Agencies participate in the budget process by making budget requests to the president and testifying at congressional budget hearings. Officials in the executive branch advise the president on policy decisions.

Executive branch agencies do not directly adopt policy, but they participate in policy adoption by lobbying the president and Congress. Consider the role in policy adoption of the **Joint Chiefs of Staff,** which is a military advisory body that is composed of the chiefs of staff of the U.S. Army and Air Force, the Chief of Naval Operations, and sometimes the Commandant of the Marine Corps. The Joint Chiefs not only advise the president on defense policy, but they also lobby the White House and Congress on policies that concern the armed forces. When President Clinton attempted to end the policy of excluding gay men and lesbians from military service at the beginning of his first term, members of the Joint Chiefs lobbied Congress to oppose the president's initiative.

Joint Chiefs of Staff A military advisory body that is composed of the chiefs of staff of the U.S. Army and Air Force, the Chief of Naval Operations, and sometimes the Commandant of the Marine Corps.

Policy Implementation and Evaluation

The federal bureaucracy implements policy. The IRS, for example, enforces the nation's tax laws. The U.S. armed forces carry out the nation's military policies. The Department of Homeland Security implements domestic security policies. FEMA responds to natural disasters.

Congress delegates authority to federal agencies to implement policy. Sometimes Congress writes detailed legislation, giving agency administrators little enforcement discretion. At other times, Congress grants agencies broad regulatory discretion. Sometimes Congress gives agencies so much leeway that an argument can be made that the agencies are actually adopting policies themselves rather than implementing policies adopted by Congress and the president through the legislative process.

Finally, federal agencies evaluate policy. Agencies gather data, conduct research, prepare reports, and recommend policy changes. The Department of Education, for example, conducts and compiles research on the effectiveness of teacher training programs and other educational programs. The Department of Defense researches the effectiveness of weapons systems. After the Katrina disaster, Homeland Security Secretary Chertoff asked Congress to enhance the capacity of FEMA to respond to crises by adding employees and expanding its regional offices.[51]

KEY TERMS

cabinet departments

captured agencies

Central Intelligence Agency (CIA)

collective bargaining

constituency service

cost-benefit analysis

Environmental Protection Agency (EPA)

Equal Employment Opportunity Commission (EEOC)

Federal Communications Commission (FCC)

Federal Deposit Insurance Corporation (FDIC)

Federal Election Commission (FEC)

Federal Trade Commission (FTC)

fire-alarm oversight

Hatch Act

independent executive agencies

independent regulatory commission

inner cabinet

issue network

Joint Chiefs of Staff

National Aeronautics and Space Administration (NASA)

National Endowment for the Arts (NEA)

National Railroad Passenger Service Corporation (Amtrak)

National Science Foundation (NSF)

Peace Corps

Postal Service

president's cabinet

quasi-governmental company

regulatory negotiation

rule

rulemaking

Securities and Exchange Commission (SEC)

Small Business Administration (SBA)

Social Security Administration (SSA)

spoils system

statutory law

subgovernment *or* iron triangle

Surgeon General

Tennessee Valley Authority (TVA)

whistleblowers

NOTES

1. Michael Grunwald, "The Katrina Disaster Was Par for the Corps," *Washington Post National Weekly Edition*, May 22–28, 2006, p. 21.
2. Eric Lipton, "Republicans' Report on Katrina Assails Response," *New York Times*, February 13, 2006, available at www.nytimes.com.
3. Eric Lipton, "'Breathtaking' Waste and Fraud in Hurricane Aid," *New York Times*, June 27, 2006, available at www.nytimes.com.
4. Spencer S. Hsu, "Pondering FEMA's Future," *Washington Post National Weekly Edition*, February 20–26, 2006, p. 13.
5. Michael Grunwald and Susan B. Glasser, "FEMA's Failure," *Washington Post National Weekly Edition*, January 16–22, 2006, pp. 11–13.
6. "Federal Civilian Employment by Branch and Agency: 1990 to 2006," *Statistical Abstract of the United States*, available at www.census.gov.
7. G. Calvin MacKenzie, "The Real Invisible Hand: Presidential Appointees in the Administration of George W. Bush," *PS: Political Science & Politics*, March 2002, p. 28.
8. Paul C. Light, "Late for Their Appointments," *New York Times*, November 16, 2004, available at www.nytimes.com.
9. Nolan McCarty and Rose Razaghian, "Advice and Consent: Senate Responses to Executive Branch Nominations, 1885–1996," *American Journal of Political Science* 43 (October 1999): 1122–1143.
10. Ryan C. Black, Anthony J. Madonna, Ryan J. Owens, and Michael S. Lynch, "Adding Recess Appointments to the President's 'Tool Chest' of Unilateral Powers," *Political Research Quarterly* 60 (December 2007): 645–654.
11. Shirley Anne Warshaw, "The Formation and Use of the Cabinet," in Phillip G. Henderson, ed., *The Presidency Then and Now* (Lanham, MD: Rowman & Littlefield, 2000), p. 137.
12. Andrew Rudalevige, "The President and the Cabinet," in Michael Nelson, ed., *The Presidency and the Political System*, 8th ed. (Washington, DC: CQ Press, 2006), p. 533.
13. Joseph A. Pika and John Anthony Maltese, *The Politics of the Presidency*, 6th ed. (Washington, DC: CQ Press, 2004), p. 230.
14. Jonathan G. S. Koppel, *The Politics of Quasi-Government* (New York: Cambridge University Press, 2003), pp. 187–195.
15. "Federal Civilian Employment, by Branch and Agency: 1990 to 2006," *Statistical Abstract of the United States 2000*.
16. Paul C. Light, "The New True Size of Government," Robert F. Wagner Graduate School, New York University, available at http://wagner.nyu.edu.
17. Scott Shane and Ron Nixon, "In Washington, Contractors Take on Biggest Role Ever," *New York Times*, February 4, 2007, available at www.nytimes.com.
18. O. Glenn Stahl, *Public Personnel Administration*, 8th ed. (New York: Harper & Row, 1983), p. 42.
19. Joel D. Aberbach and Bert A. Rockman, "Senior Executives in a Changing Political Environment," in James P. Pfiffner and Douglas A. Brook, eds., *The Future of Merit: Twenty Years After the Civil Service Reform Act* (Washington, DC: Woodrow Wilson Center Press, 2000), pp. 81–97.
20. James R. Thompson, "Federal Labor-Management Relations Under George W. Bush: Enlightened Management or Political Retribution?" in James S. Bowman and Jonathan P. West, eds., *American Public Service: Radical Reform and the Merit System* (Boca Raton, FL: RC Press, 2007), p. 240.
21. Christopher Lee, "An Overhaul, Not a Tune-Up," *Washington Post National Weekly Edition*, June 16–22, 2003, p. 30.
22. Ann Gerhart, "Homeland Insecurity," *Washington Post National Weekly Edition*, April 4–10, 2005, pp. 6–7.
23. Cornelius M. Kerwin, *Rulemaking: How Government Agencies Write Law and Make Policy*, 3rd ed. (Washington, DC: CQ Press, 2003), p. 21.
24. Alana S. Knaster and Philip J. Harter, "The Clean Fuels Regulatory Negotiation," *Intergovernmental Perspective*, Summer 1992, pp. 20–22.
25. Terry M. Moe, "The Presidency and the Bureaucracy: The Presidential Advantage," in Michael Nelson, ed., *The Presidency and the Political System*, 6th ed. (Washington, DC: CQ Press, 2000), pp. 465–468.
26. Alan B. Morrison, "Close Reins on the Bureaucracy: Overseeing the Administrative Agencies," in Herman Schwartz, ed., *The Burger Years* (New York: Viking, 1987), pp. 191–205.
27. Ron Duhl, "Carter Issues an Order, But Is Anybody Listening?" *National Journal*, June 14, 1979, pp. 1156–1158.
28. Robert Pear, "Bush Directive Increases Sway on Regulation," *New York Times*, January 30, 2007, available at www.nytimes.com.
29. Marissa Martino Golden, *What Motivates Bureaucrats? Politics and Administration During the Reagan Years* (New York, NY: Columbia University Press, 2000), pp. 152–159.
30. B. Dan Wood, "Principals, Bureaucrats, and Responsiveness in Clean Air Enforcement," *American Political Science Review* 82 (March 1988): 218.
31. Kay Lehrman Schlozman and John T. Tierney, *Organized Interests and American Democracy* (New York: Harper & Row, 1986), p. 353.
32. Joseph Cooper and William F. West, "Presidential Power and Republican Government: The Theory and Practice of OMB Review of Agency Rules," *Journal of Politics* 50 (November 1988): 864–895.
33. Wood, "Principals, Bureaucrats, and Responsiveness in Clean Air Enforcements," pp. 222–226.
34. B. Dan Wood and Richard W. Waterman, "The Dynamics of Political Control of the Bureaucracy," *American Political Science Review* 85 (September 1991): 813.

35. Ibid., p. 811.

36. Ibid., pp. 806–807, 818–821.

37. John Solomon and Julier Eilperin, "Dwindling Pursuit of Polluters," *Washington Post National Weekly Edition*, October 8–14, 2007, p. 34.

38. Stephen Labaton, "OSHA Leaves Worker Safety in Hands of Industry," *New York Times*, April 25, 2007, available at www.nytimes.com.

39. Edward Wyatt, "House Panel Challenges Smithsonian," *New York Times*, May 11, 2006, available at www.nytimes.com.

40. Michael D. Reagan and John G. Salzone, *The New Federalism*, 2nd ed. (New York: Oxford University Press, 1981), ch. 3.

41. Schlozman and Tierney, *Organized Interests and American Democracy*, pp. 341–346.

42. Terry M. Moe, "Control and Feedback in Economic Regulation: The Case of the NLRB," *American Political Science Review* 79 (December 1985): 1094–1116; Jeffrey E. Cohen, "The Dynamics of the 'Revolving Door' on the FCC," *American Journal of Political Science* 30 (November 1986): 689–708.

43. Steven P. Croley, *Regulation and Public Interests: The Possibility of Good Regulatory Government* (Princeton, NJ: Princeton University Press, 2008), pp. 214–230.

44. Colin Campbell, "The Complex Organization of the Executive Branch: The Legacies of Competing Approaches to Administration," in Joel D. Aberbach and Mark A. Peterson, eds., *The Executive Branch* (New York: Oxford University Press, 2005), p. 254.

45. Dennis D. Riley and Bryan E. Brophy-Baermann, *Bureaucracy and the Policy Process* (Lanham, MD: Rowman & Littlefield Publishers, 2006), p. 98.

46. Jeffrey Kluger, "Space Pork," *Time*, July 24, 2000, pp. 24–26.

47. Jeffrey M. Berry, "Subgovernments, Issue Networks, and Political Conflict," in Richard A. Harris and Sidney M. Milkis, eds., *Remaking American Politics* (Boulder, CO: Westview Press, 1989), pp. 239–260.

48. Hugh Heclo, "Issue Networks and the Executive Establishment," in Anthony King, ed., *The New American Political System* (Washington, DC: American Enterprise Institute, 1978), pp. 87–124.

49. John R. Provan, "The Highway Trust Fund: Its Birth, Growth, and Survival," in Theodore W. Taylor, ed., *Federal Public Policy* (Mt. Airy, MD: Lomond Publications, 1984), pp. 221–258.

50. Jonathan Walters, "Revenge of the Highwaymen," *Governing*, September 1997, p. 13.

51. Hsu, "Pondering FEMA's Future," p. 13.

Chapter 13

The Federal Courts

LEARNING OUTCOMES

After studying Chapter 13, students should be able to do the following:

- Evaluate approaches to judicial interpretation of the Constitution and the proper role of judges. (pp. 340–341)

- Trace the history of the Supreme Court as a policymaking body. (pp. 341–345)

- Outline the organization of the judicial branch of American national government, considering judicial selection and jurisdiction for U.S. District Courts, Courts of Appeals, and the Supreme Court of the United States. (pp. 345–354)

- Describe the decision-making process of the Supreme Court, focusing on the selection of cases, opinion assignment, opinion writing, and implementation. (pp. 355–359)

- Evaluate the policy influence of the federal courts. (pp. 360–362)

- Describe the role of the federal courts in the policymaking process. (pp. 362–363)

- Define the key terms listed on page 364 and explain their significance.

In 2009, President Barack Obama made history by nominating Sonia Sotomayor to fill the Supreme Court vacancy created by the retirement of Associate Justice David Souter. Sotomayor would be the nation's first Hispanic Supreme Court justice and only the third woman. Considering the age of the remaining members of the Court, Obama might well have the opportunity to make several appointments. When Souter made his announcement, the average age on the Court was 69, with five justices older than 70 years of age. The oldest member of the Court was Associate Justice John Paul Stevens, age 89.

Obama may be able to change the policymaking direction of the Supreme Court could be critical because it is closely divided philosophically. In recent sessions, the Court has decided many cases by the narrowest of margins. In 2007, fully a third of the Court's decisions came on a vote of five to four. In 2008, the Court decided 17 percent of its cases by a five-to-four vote. In most of these closely decided cases, Justices Stevens, Souter, Stephen Breyer, and Ruth Bader Ginsburg—the so-called liberal wing of the Court—voted as a bloc. Four other justices—Chief Justice John Roberts and associates justices Antonin Scalia, Clarence Thomas, and Samuel Alito—voted together as the conservative wing of the Court. Associate Justice Anthony Kennedy was the swing vote, siding with the conservatives on some issues and the liberals on other issues.[1] Depending on which additional seats become vacant during his tenure, Obama could maintain the current philosophical balance or move the Court in a liberal direction on such issues as abortion, gun control, affirmative action, **capital punishment** (the death penalty), and gay and lesbian rights.[2]

Capital punishment The death penalty.

JUDICIAL POLICYMAKING

Judicial review The power of courts to declare unconstitutional the actions of the other branches and units of government.

Courts make policy by interpreting the law and the Constitution.[3] When courts interpret the law, they modify policies adopted by the executive and legislative branches by aggressively expanding or narrowly restricting the provisions of a law. When courts interpret the Constitution, they exercise **judicial review,** which is the power of courts to declare unconstitutional the actions of the other branches and units of government. Altogether, the Supreme Court has overturned at least one provision in more than 160 federal laws and nearly 1,300 state laws and local ordinances.[4]

Strict construction A doctrine of constitutional interpretation holding that the document should be interpreted narrowly.

Controversy rages over the leeway courts should exercise in interpreting the Constitution. **Strict construction** is a doctrine of constitutional interpretation holding that the document should be interpreted narrowly. Advocates of strict construction believe that judges should stick close to the literal meaning of the words in the Constitution and place themselves in harmony with the purpose of the framers. In contrast, **loose construction** is a doctrine of constitutional interpretation holding that the document should be interpreted broadly. Loose constructionists argue that strict construction is neither possible nor desirable. They point out that it is often difficult to ascertain original intent because no complete and accurate records exist

Loose construction A doctrine of constitutional interpretation holding that the document should be interpreted broadly.

Judicial activism The charge that judges are going beyond their authority by making the law and not just interpreting it.

Judicial restraint The concept that judges should defer to the policymaking judgment of the legislative and executive branches of government unless their actions clearly violate the law or the Constitution.

to indicate what the authors of the Constitution had in mind. Furthermore, records that are available show that the nation's founders often disagreed with one another about the Constitution's basic meaning.

A similar and related debate involves the role of judges. Conservative opponents of the Supreme Court sometimes accuse it of **judicial activism,** which is the charge that judges are going beyond their authority by making the law and not just interpreting it. For example, critics of *Roe v. Wade*, the Supreme Court's landmark abortion decision, call it an activist ruling because the U.S. Constitution does not specifically address the issue of abortion. Republican presidential candidates typically promise to nominate men and women to the Supreme Court who will practice **judicial restraint,** which is the concept that judges should defer to the policymaking judgment of the legislative and executive branches of government unless their actions clearly violate the law or the Constitution.

Many political scientists believe that the debate between judicial activism and judicial restraint is more about politics than judicial behavior. Professors Kermit Roosevelt III and Thomas M. Keck contend that the accusation of judicial activism is a convenient line of attack for people who disagree with a court ruling for whatever reason.[5] The real dispute is not between the advocates of judicial activism and judicial restraint, but between liberal and conservative activism. All judges regard the Constitution as a charter of fundamental principles that courts are pledged to uphold. The real controversy is that conservative and liberal judges disagree as to what those principles are.[6]

 WHAT IS YOUR OPINION?

If you were a member of the Supreme Court, how would you approach the job?

POLITICAL HISTORY OF THE SUPREME COURT

Throughout most of its history, the U. S. Supreme Court has been an active participant in some of the nation's most significant public policy debates. In its first decade, however, the Court was relatively unimportant. It decided only 50 cases from 1789 to 1800. Some of its members even resigned to take other, more prestigious jobs.[7]

After John Marshall was named Chief Justice, the Supreme Court's role in the policy process began to take shape. Under his leadership from 1801 to 1835, the Court claimed the power of judicial review in *Marbury v. Madison* (1803)[8] and assumed the authority to review the decisions of state courts on questions of federal law in *Martin v. Hunter's Lessee* (1816).[9] The Marshall Court also decided a number of landmark cases dealing with commercial law and the nature of the federal system. In the *Dartmouth College* case (1819), the Court held that the Constitution protected private contracts from infringement by state legislatures.[10] This decision played an important role in the nation's economic development because it assured private investors that the courts would enforce the terms of contractual agreements.

The Marshall Court ruled in favor of a strong national government in controversies concerning the relative power of the national government and the states. In *McCulloch v. Maryland* (1819), the Court struck down a Maryland tax on the national bank and gave broad scope to federal authority under the Constitution.[11] In *Gibbons v. Ogden* (1824), the Court ruled that a New York law that established a monopoly for a steamboat company was a state infringement of the constitutional power of the federal government to regulate interstate commerce.[12]

Under Chief Justice Roger Taney (1836–1864), Marshall's successor, the Supreme Court's involvement in the slavery controversy led the Court away from support for a strong national government toward a states' rights position. The doctrine of **states' rights** is an interpretation of the Constitution that favors limiting the authority of the national government while expanding the powers of the states. In the infamous *Dred Scott* decision (1857), the Supreme Court declared the Missouri Compromise unconstitutional and held that the federal government had no power to prohibit slavery in the territories.[13]

After the Civil War, the Supreme Court turned its attention to the protection of property rights, reviewing government efforts to regulate business activity. Initially, the Court was ambivalent, allowing some regulations while disallowing others. By the 1920s and early 1930s, however, the Court had grown hostile to government regulation of business. It scrutinized state and federal taxation and regulatory policies and found many of them unconstitutional under the Due Process Clauses of the Fifth and Fourteenth Amendments, which declare that neither the national government nor state governments may deprive persons of property without due process of law. The Court struck down state laws prohibiting child labor and invalidated a number of federal laws passed during the early days of the **New Deal,** which was a legislative package of reform measures proposed by President Franklin Roosevelt.

While the Supreme Court protected the property rights of business corporations, it ignored the civil rights of African Americans. Around the turn of the century, a number of states, primarily in the South, enacted **Jim Crow laws,** which were legal provisions requiring the social segregation of African Americans in separate and generally unequal facilities. In the meantime, many states, again mostly in the South, adopted fiendishly clever devices to prevent African Americans from voting. The Supreme Court responded to this situation by legitimizing racial segregation in *Plessy v. Ferguson* (1896)[14] and essentially overlooking voting rights violations.

In 1937, the Supreme Court changed course. In a remarkable turn of events, the Court began to uphold the constitutionality of New Deal legislation. No longer would the Court protect business against government regulation. Although the Supreme Court generally required that government agencies follow proper procedures in their regulatory activities, it broadly and consistently endorsed the right of government to regulate business and the nation's economy.

After 1937, the agenda of the U.S. Supreme Court focused primarily on civil liberties and civil rights. **Civil liberties** refer to the protection of the individual from the unrestricted power of government. **Civil rights** concern the protection of the individual from arbitrary or discriminatory acts by government or by individuals based on that person's group status, such as race and gender.

States' rights An interpretation of the Constitution that favors limiting the authority of the federal government while expanding the powers of the states.

New Deal A legislative package of reform measures proposed by President Franklin Roosevelt for dealing with the Great Depression.

Jim Crow laws Legal provisions requiring the social segregation of African Americans in separate and generally unequal facilities.

Civil liberties The protection of the individual from the unrestricted power of government.

Civil rights The protection of the individual from arbitrary or discriminatory acts by government or by individuals based on that person's group status, such as race or gender.

Under the leadership of Chief Justice Earl Warren (1953–1969), the Supreme Court adopted liberal policy positions on a number of civil liberties and civil rights issues. The Court strengthened the First Amendment guarantees of freedom of expression and religion, broadened the procedural rights of persons accused of crimes, and ruled decisively in favor of civil rights for African Americans and other minorities. In *Brown v. Board of Education of Topeka* (1954), the Court struck down laws requiring school segregation, overturning the *Plessy* decision.[15] In *Mapp v. Ohio* (1961), the Court extended the exclusionary rule to the states.[16] The **exclusionary rule** is the judicial doctrine stating that when the police violate an individual's constitutional rights, the evidence obtained as a result of police misconduct or error cannot be used against the defendant. In *Miranda v. Arizona*, the Court held that persons arrested for crimes must be informed of their constitutional rights before being interrogated by police officers.[17]

Exclusionary rule
The judicial doctrine stating that when the police violate an individual's constitutional rights, the evidence obtained as a result of police misconduct or error cannot be used against the defendant.

During Warren Burger's tenure as chief justice (1969–1986), the Supreme Court continued to focus primarily on civil liberties and civil rights, but its policy preferences were neither consistently liberal nor consistently conservative. In some issue areas, such as abortion rights, capital punishment, education for the children of illegal aliens, affirmative action, school busing, and gender discrimination, the Burger Court broke new ground. In *Roe v. Wade*, the Court held that states could not prohibit abortion in the first two trimesters of pregnancy.[18] In other policy areas, however, particularly on issues involving the rights of persons charged with crimes, the Burger Court limited or qualified Warren Court positions without directly reversing any of the major precedents set during the Warren years.

The Supreme Court continued to defy labels during the tenure of Chief Justice Rehnquist (1986–2005). On some policy issue, the Rehnquist Court adopted conservative positions. The Court declared that government programs designed to remedy the effects of discrimination in government contracting were unconstitutional unless the government could demonstrate a compelling interest to justify their creation.[19] The Rehnquist Court also pleased conservatives by upholding a school voucher program that allowed students to use public funds to attend religious schools. The Court ruled that the program did not violate the First Amendment's prohibition against an establishment of religion.[20] On other issues, however, the Rehnquist Court adopted liberal positions. The Court consistently blocked government efforts to include spoken prayer in school activities, ruling against clergy-led invocations and benedictions at graduation[21] as well as student-led prayers before high school football games.[22] The Rehnquist Court broke new ground on the issue of gay and lesbian rights by overturning the Texas sodomy law that prohibited sexual relations between adults of the same gender even in the privacy of the home.[23]

The Rehnquist Court addressed a number of policy controversies by taking moderate, compromise positions. The Court allowed state governments to restrict abortion rights without overturning *Roe*. Similarly, the Rehnquist Court upheld the constitutionality of the death penalty while ruling against the execution of mentally retarded murderers.[24] It struck down college admissions procedures that gave a numerical advantage to minority applicants,[25] but allowed college officials to consider race and ethnicity in order to achieve a diverse student body as long as they did not grant minority applicants a set number of points.[26]

The Rehnquist Court was more willing than any Supreme Court since the 1930s to limit federal regulatory power, especially over state governments. The Supreme Court overturned the Gun-Free School Zone Act of 1990, which was a federal law banning firearms within 1,000 feet of a school. The Court said that Congress could regulate only those economic activities that substantially affect interstate commerce and that the possession of a firearm in the vicinity of a school does not meet that criterion.[27] The Supreme Court also ruled that Congress lacks the constitutional authority to enact laws that override the **sovereign immunity** of a state government, which is the legal concept that individuals cannot sue the government without the government's permission.[28]

Sovereign immunity The legal concept that individuals cannot sue the government without the government's permission.

Ironically, the Rehnquist Court may be best remembered for a case that ended the 2000 presidential election by overturning the decision of a state supreme court. *Bush v. Gore* involved an appeal by the George W. Bush campaign of the decision of the Florida Supreme Court to order a manual recount of thousands of punch-card ballots that had not been counted by machine. Vice President Al Gore wanted a hand count because he hoped that it would give him enough additional votes to carry the state of Florida and thus win the presidency. The Gore campaign argued that a hand count was the only way to determine the true outcome of the race because it would ensure that every legal vote was counted. In contrast, the Bush campaign charged that a hand recount would introduce subjectivity into the vote count. When the Florida Supreme Court ordered a manual recount of uncounted ballots in every county in the state, the Bush campaign appealed to the U.S. Supreme Court, charging that the Florida court had violated both federal law and the U.S. Constitution.

The U.S. Supreme Court halted the recount, ensuring that Bush would be the next president. The Court ruled that the recount violated the **Equal Protection Clause,** which is a provision of the Fourteenth Amendment of the U.S. Constitution that declares that "No State shall . . . deny to any person within its jurisdiction the equal protection of the laws." Because the Florida Supreme Court had not established a uniform statewide standard for determining a legal vote, different counties could treat votes differently, thereby giving more weight to some voters than others. Although the state of Florida could fix the problem by setting a statewide standard, the U.S. Supreme Court ruled by a 5–4 margin that it was too late for them to try because the Florida Legislature had set December 12, 2000, as the last date for naming presidential electors. The Court issued its ruling at 10 P.M. on December 11, two hours before the deadline.[29]

Equal Protection Clause A provision of the Fourteenth Amendment of the U.S. Constitution that declares that "No State shall . . . deny to any person within its jurisdiction the equal protection of the laws."

The Supreme Court's decision in *Bush v. Gore* was controversial. Many Democrats accused the Court of conservative judicial activism. They charged that the Court's conservative five-judge majority, all of whom had been appointed either by President Reagan or the first President Bush, had abandoned their principles to overturn a state court so they could hand the presidency to George W. Bush.[30] In contrast, the Court's defenders argued that the Court had merely applied established judicial principles to resolve a difficult dispute, thus sparing the nation weeks of political turmoil and a possible constitutional crisis.[31]

The Supreme Court under Chief Justice Roberts has been difficult to characterize because it is closely divided philosophically. Some rulings have satisfied conservatives; others have gratified liberals. On one hand, the Court pleased conservatives

The U.S. Supreme Court halted the Florida recount in 2000, ensuring that George W. Bush would win the state and be elected president.

by striking down a District of Columbia ordinance banning handgun possession. For the first time in the history of the Court, it ruled that the Constitution guarantees an individual right of gun ownership. The vote on the Court was 5–4 with Justice Kennedy joining the four conservative-leaning justices to overturn the ordinance.[32] On the other hand, the Court satisfied liberals with its decision holding unconstitutional a Louisiana law that provided for the death penalty for a defendant convicted of sexually assaulting a child who survived the assault. In this case, Kennedy joined the Court's four liberal-leaning justices to provide a 5–4 majority limiting the death penalty to murder and treason.[33]

THE FEDERAL COURT SYSTEM

Trial The formal examination of a judicial dispute in accordance with law before a single judge.

The Constitution says relatively little about the organization of the federal court system. "The judicial Power of the United States," it declares, "shall be vested in one supreme Court, and in such inferior Courts as the Congress may from time to time ordain and establish." Over the years, Congress and the president have created the federal court system through the legislative process.

Figure 13.1 diagrams the federal court system. Trial courts make up the lowest tier of federal courts. A **trial** is the formal examination of a judicial dispute in accordance

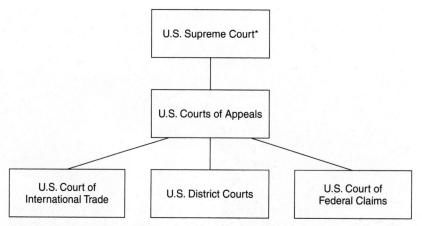

FIGURE 13.1   The U.S. Federal Courts.
*The U.S. Supreme Court also hears appeals from the state court systems.

with law before a single judge. Trials involve attorneys, witnesses, testimony, evidence, judges, and, occasionally, juries. The U.S. District Courts are the most important federal trial courts, hearing nearly all federal cases. The U.S. Court of Federal Claims and the U.S. Court of International Trade are specialized trial courts, created to deal with some of the more complex areas of federal law. The U.S. Court of Federal Claims hears disputes over federal contracts and cases involving claims for monetary damages against the U. S. government; the U.S. Court of International Trade hears cases involving international trade and customs issues.

An **appeal** is the taking of a case from a lower court to a higher court by the losing party in a lower court decision. The procedures of appeals courts differ notably from those of trial courts. In general, trial courts are concerned with questions of fact and the law as it applies to those facts. In contrast, appeals are based on issues of law and procedure. Appellate courts do not retry cases appealed to them. Instead, appellate court justices (juries do not participate in appellate proceedings) make decisions based on the law and the Constitution, the written and oral arguments presented by attorneys for the litigants in the lawsuit, and the written record of the lower-court proceedings. Also, appellate court justices usually make decisions collectively in panels of three or more judges rather than singly, as do trial court judges.

The U.S. Courts of Appeals and the U.S. Supreme Court are primarily appellate courts. The courts of appeals hear appeals from the federal trial courts and administrative agencies. The U.S. Supreme Court stands at the apex of the American court system. Although it has authority to try a limited range of cases, it is in practice an appellate court, hearing appeals from both the federal and state court systems.

District Courts

Congress has created 94 district courts, with at least one court in every state and one each in the District of Columbia, Guam, Northern Mariana Islands, Puerto Rico, and the Virgin Islands. Although only one judge presides in each courtroom, each of the districts has enough business to warrant more than one courtroom, each with its

Appeal The taking of a case from a lower court to a higher court by the losing party in a lower court decision.

own judge. The number of judges per district ranges from 1 to 28. Altogether, 678 full-time judges and more than a hundred semiretired senior judges staff the district courts. In addition, each district court has a clerk, a U.S. marshal, and one or more bankruptcy judges, probation officers, court reporters, and magistrates attached to it. The magistrates are attorneys appointed by district court judges under a merit selection system to serve eight-year terms. They conduct preliminary hearings; set bail; issue arrest warrants; and, if litigants consent, conduct certain types of trials.[34]

Jurisdiction The authority of a court to hear a case.

Jurisdiction   The term **jurisdiction** refers to the authority of a court to hear and decide a case. The jurisdiction of district courts includes both civil and criminal matters. A **civil case** is a legal dispute concerning a private conflict between two parties—individuals, corporations, or government agencies. A **criminal case** is a legal dispute dealing with an alleged violation of a penal law. More than 80 percent of district court cases are civil disputes.[35] In sheer volume, the main chores of the district courts are naturalizing new citizens and granting passport applications. District courts also have jurisdiction over bankruptcy cases filed under federal law; civil cases involving more than $75,000 in which the U.S. government is a party; and, if either litigant requests it, lawsuits in which the parties live in different states and in which more than $75,000 is at stake. In these latter types of cases, federal judges apply the laws of the applicable state rather than federal law.

Civil case A legal dispute concerning a private conflict between two parties—individuals, corporations, or government agencies.

As for criminal matters, district courts try all cases involving violations of federal law as well as criminal offenses occurring on federal territory, federal reservations, or the high seas. District judges must also rule on *habeas corpus* petitions filed by inmates in both state and federal prisons. A **writ of *habeas corpus*** is a court order requiring government authorities either to release a person held in custody or demonstrate that the person is detained in accordance with law. *Habeas corpus* petitions allege that a prisoner is held contrary to law and ask a court to inquire into the matter. An inmate's attorney may charge, for example, that a state trial court erred in admitting certain evidence, thereby violating the Fourth and Fourteenth Amendments to the U.S. Constitution. If the judge sees merit in the petitioner's complaint, the judge can direct the jailer to reply and a suit will be joined. Death row inmates often use *habeas corpus* petitions to avoid or at least delay their execution. Litigants who lose their district court cases may appeal to a U.S. Court of Appeal. In practice, less than 20 percent of district court decisions are appealed.[36]

Criminal case A legal dispute dealing with an alleged violation of a penal law.

Writ of *habeas corpus* A court order requiring government authorities either to release a person held in custody or demonstrate that the person is detained in accordance with law.

Selection of Judges   The president appoints federal judges subject to Senate confirmation by majority vote. **Senatorial courtesy,** which is the custom that senators from the president's party have a veto on judicial appointments from their states, determines the selection of most district judges. When district court vacancies occur, senators from the president's party submit names to the president, who makes the formal nomination. The president can reject a senator's recommendation, of course, but rarely does. If both of a state's senators belong to the president's political party, the senior senator makes the recommendations. When vacancies develop in states where neither senator shares the president's party affiliation, the White House usually consults state party leaders and/or members of the House for their recommendations.

Senatorial courtesy The custom that senators from the president's party have a veto on judicial appointments from their states.

The Senate Judiciary Committee evaluates district court nominees. After the committee staff conducts a background check, the committee chair schedules a hearing to allow the nominee and interested parties an opportunity to be heard. The confirmation of district court judges is usually a quiet affair, with few nominees rejected. Confirmation is not necessarily speedy, however, especially when the Senate and White House are in the hands of different political parties. Toward the end of a presidential term, the chair of the Senate Judiciary Committee and the Senate Majority Leader will sometimes delay the confirmation process in hopes that the White House changes parties and the new president can then fill pending vacancies. Even early in a term, the confirmation process takes anywhere from four months to two years or even more.[37]

Presidents typically nominate judges whose party affiliation and political philosophy are compatible with their own. Democratic presidents appoint Democratic judges; Republican presidents select Republicans. Some presidents also seek judges with particular political philosophies. In general, Republican presidents choose judges with conservative political philosophies, whereas Democratic presidents select liberal judges. Conservative judges tend to favor government interests over criminal defendants, interpret narrowly the constitutional guarantees of equal rights for women and minorities, support corporate interests against the claims of individual workers or consumers, and rule against federal government involvement in local policy issues. In contrast, liberal judges are more inclined than their conservative counterparts to favor judicial underdogs, such as consumers, workers, criminal defendants, and members of minority groups. They tend to support the federal government in federalism disputes over the relative power of the states and the national government.[38]

Federal judges hold lifetime appointments, with "good behavior," as the Constitution puts it. They may not be retired involuntarily or removed for political reasons, but they are subject to impeachment by the House and removal by the Senate. Although members of Congress occasionally threaten to impeach judges with whom they have policy disagreements, impeachment is rare and always directed against judges who are accused of misconduct. In American history, only seven federal judges have been impeached and removed from office. Most judges who get in trouble resign rather than face the humiliation of impeachment.[39]

 WHAT IS YOUR OPINION?

Do you think federal judges should be appointed for life? Why or why not?

Courts of Appeals

The U.S. Courts of Appeals (also known as circuit courts of appeals) are the primary intermediate appellate courts in the federal system. There are 13 courts of appeals, one for each of the 12 judicial circuits (or regions) and a 13th circuit called the U.S. Court of Appeals for the Federal Circuit. The latter court hears appeals in specialized cases, such as patent law, and cases appealed from the Court of International Trade and the Court of Federal Claims. The number of justices for each of the circuits ranges from 3 to 24. Altogether, 179 justices staff the courts of appeals along with another 40 senior justices.

Jurisdiction   The courts of appeals are exclusively appellate courts, usually hearing cases in panels of three justices each. They hear appeals from the U.S. District Courts, the Court of International Trade, and the Court of Federal Claims. The courts of appeals also hear appeals on the decisions of the regulatory commissions, with the rulings of the National Labor Relations Board (NLRB) producing the most appeals. The courts of appeals are generally not required to hold hearings in every case. After reading the legal briefs in a case (a **legal brief** is a written legal argument) and reviewing the trial court record, the appeals court may uphold the lower court decision without hearing formal arguments.

Legal brief A written legal argument.

When an appeals court decides to accept an appeal, the court usually schedules a hearing at which the attorneys for the two sides in the dispute present oral arguments and answer any questions posed by the justices. Appeals courts do not retry cases. Instead, they review the trial court record and consider legal arguments. After hearing oral arguments and studying legal briefs, appeals court justices discuss the case and eventually vote on a decision, with a majority vote of the justices required to decide a case. The court may **affirm** (uphold) the lower court decision, reverse it, modify it, or affirm part of the lower court ruling while reversing or modifying the rest. Frequently, an appeals court may **remand** (return) a case to the trial court for reconsideration in light of the appeals court decision. The courts of appeals have the final word on more than 95 percent of the cases they hear because the Supreme Court rarely intervenes on appeal.[40]

Affirm The action of an appeals court to uphold the decision of a lower court.

Remand The decision of an appeals court to return a case to a lower court for reconsideration in light of an appeals court decision.

Selection of Justices   The White House generally takes more care with nominations to the courts of appeals than it does with district court selections. Because the judicial circuits usually include several states, senatorial courtesy does not dictate the selection of justices on the courts of appeals.[41] Consequently, presidents are able to seek out men and women who not only share their political party affiliation but also their policy preferences.[42] When a vacancy occurs, a deputy attorney general gathers names of potential nominees, asking party leaders, senators, and members of the House for suggestions. Eventually, the deputy attorney general suggests a name or perhaps a short list of names for the president's consideration, and the president makes a choice. The Senate examines appellate court nominees more closely than it considers district court selections, especially when the opposition party controls the Senate. Furthermore, as with district court nominees, delays are not unusual. The length of confirmation delays depends on the size of the president's opposition in the Senate, the proximity of the next presidential election, and whether the nominee is a woman or minority. Appellate court nominees who are women or minority take twice as long to confirm than white males.[43] The Senate is more likely to reject nominees when the opposition party controls the Senate and in the last year of a president's term. Since 1950, the Senate has confirmed 94 percent of district and appellate court appointees when the president's party controls the Senate but only 80 percent of nominees when the opposition controls the Senate. The odds of confirmation in any event decline by 25 percent in a presidential election year.[44]

The nomination process for courts of appeals judges has become an arena for conflict between the two political parties. After Republicans won control of the Senate in 1994, Democrats accused the Judiciary Committee of blocking many Clinton judicial nominees by failing to hold hearings on them. When George W. Bush won the White House in 2000, he was able to appoint judges to fill the vacancies left at the end of Clinton's term. During Bush's first term, Democrats filibustered 10 of 52 appellate court nominees, declaring that the judicial philosophies of the 10 were so conservative that they were outside the judicial mainstream. Republicans responded to the Democrats' tactic by threatening a procedure they labeled the "constitutional option." Democrats called it the "nuclear option." The strategy involved Republican senators asking the presiding officer of the Senate, probably Vice President Dick Cheney, to rule that it was unconstitutional to filibuster judicial nominees. Because a simple majority would be sufficient to uphold the vice president's ruling, Senate Republicans—who outnumbered Democrats 55 to 45—would be able to end the Democratic filibuster and force a vote on Bush's nominations whose appointments had been blocked. Democrats responded to the Republican strategy by threatening to use various parliamentary maneuvers to shut down or at least seriously delay Senate business.[45] Eventually, a group of 14 senators, 7 Democrats and 7 Republicans, brokered a compromise to allow the confirmation of some of the filibustered judicial nominees. The compromise defused the crisis temporarily but did not resolve the issue.

The confirmation process for judicial nominees has become increasingly contentious because political parties in Congress are more ideologically polarized now than they were in the past and because the partisan balance on the bench is close. Republican members of Congress are almost all conservative, whereas their Democratic counterparts are almost all liberal. Most important votes in Congress break down along party lines, so it should be no surprise for judicial confirmation votes to become a partisan battleground as well. Furthermore, the stakes are high because of the close partisan balance on the courts. In 2003, the federal judiciary included 398 judges appointed by Republican presidents and 400 judges appointed by Democrats.[46]

Supreme Court

The Supreme Court of the United States is the highest court in the land. Its rulings take precedence over the decisions of other federal courts. On matters involving federal law and the U.S. Constitution, the decisions of the U.S. Supreme Court take precedence over state court rulings as well.

The Constitution says nothing about the size of the Supreme Court, letting Congress and the president set its size legislatively. Through the years, the size of the Court has varied from five to ten justices. The present membership of nine justices has been in effect for more than a century. In the 1930s, President Franklin Roosevelt attempted to enlarge the Court in order to appoint new justices friendly to the New Deal, but his effort was popularly attacked as a court-packing plan and defeated by Congress. Since then, no serious efforts have been made to change the Court's size.

Today's Court includes a chief justice and eight associate justices. The justices are equal and independent, similar to nine separate law firms, but the chief justice is first among them. The chief presides over the Court's public sessions and private conferences. The chief justice can call special sessions of the Court and helps administer the federal court system. The chief justice also assigns justices the responsibility of writing the Court's majority opinion in cases when the chief votes with the majority.

The chief justice is a political leader who, to be successful, must deal effectively with political pressures both inside and outside the Court. Internally, the chief attempts to influence the other members of the Court. Externally, the chief justice lobbies Congress, responding and/or reacting to attacks against the Court. One scholar rates John Marshall, Charles Evans Hughes, and Earl Warren as the best chief justices, not because they were the best legal philosophers—they were not—but because they were the best political leaders.[47] Regular sessions of the Supreme Court run from the first Monday in October until the end of June or early July. The summer months are a time for vacation and individual study by the Court's members, although the chief justice can call a special session to consider particularly pressing matters.

Original jurisdiction The set of cases a court may hear as a trial court.

Jurisdiction   Technically, the Supreme Court can be both a trial court and an appellate court. The Constitution gives the Court a limited **original jurisdiction,** which is the set of cases a court may hear as a trial court. The Supreme Court may try "cases affecting ambassadors, other public ministers and consuls, and those in which a state shall be a party," except for cases initiated against a state by the citizens of another state or nation. In practice, however, the Court does not conduct trials. The Court shares jurisdiction with the U.S. District Courts on the matters included in its original jurisdiction and leaves most of those cases for the district courts to decide. Even for the few cases of original jurisdiction that the justices consider worthwhile, the Supreme Court does not hold a trial. Instead, the Court appoints a special master to conduct a hearing to determine the facts before it decides the legal issues.

The Court's appellate jurisdiction is set by law, and through the years, Congress has made the Supreme Court of the United States the nation's highest appellate court for both the federal and the state judicial systems. In the federal system, the courts of appeals generate the largest number of appeals by far. Cases may arise from the court of military appeals and special three-judge courts, which Congress has authorized to hear redistricting cases and some civil rights cases. Cases can also be appealed to the Supreme Court from the highest court in each state, usually the state supreme court.

Congress can reduce the jurisdiction of the Supreme Court if it chooses. After the Civil War, Congress removed the authority of the Court to review the constitutionality of Reconstruction legislation. Since then, Congress has been reluctant to tamper with the jurisdiction of the federal courts on grounds that it would interfere with the independence of the judicial branch. In recent years, most attempts to limit the jurisdiction of federal courts in cases involving such controversial issues as abortion, school prayer, busing, and the rights of criminal defendants have all failed.[48]

Selection of Justices   Nominating individuals to the Supreme Court is one of the president's most important responsibilities. Certainly it is an opportunity that may not come often. President Richard Nixon was able to appoint four justices in less than six years in office, but President Carter was unable to make any appointments during his four-year term. Furthermore, each appointment has the potential to affect public policy for years to come, particularly if the Court is closely divided or the president has the chance to name a new chief justice.

The formal procedures of appointment and confirmation of Supreme Court justices are similar to those for appellate court justices except they are generally performed more carefully and receive considerably more publicity. The attorney general begins the task by compiling a list of possible nominees. The president narrows the list to a few names and the FBI conducts background checks on each.

In selecting individuals to serve on the Supreme Court, presidents look for nominees who share their political philosophy: Conservative presidents prefer conservative justices, whereas liberal presidents want liberal justices. When President Franklin Roosevelt finally had the chance to make appointments to the Supreme Court, he was careful to select nominees sympathetic to the New Deal. In contrast, President Reagan screened nominees to ensure their political conservatism.

Presidents are sometimes surprised and disappointed by the performance of their nominees on the Court. Liberal President Woodrow Wilson, for example, appointed James MacReynolds, one of the most conservative justices ever to serve on the Court. Similarly, conservative President Dwight Eisenhower chose Chief Justice Earl Warren and Associate Justice William Brennan, two of the more liberal justices ever to serve. When asked if he had made any mistakes as president, Eisenhower replied, "Yes, two, and they are both sitting on the Supreme Court."[49]

Presidents occasionally make Supreme Court appointments as rewards for political support or personal friendship. In 1952, Warren, who was then governor of California, helped Eisenhower win the Republican presidential nomination. Eisenhower owed Warren a favor and paid it back by naming him chief justice. In the 1960s, Presidents John Kennedy and Lyndon Johnson appointed old friends and political allies to the Court. Kennedy named Byron White and Johnson picked Abe Fortas.

Finally, presidents sometimes make appointments in hopes of scoring political points. Eisenhower's nomination of William Brennan before the 1956 election, for example, may have been timed to influence the Catholic vote because Brennan was Catholic. Certainly Lyndon Johnson was aware of the political significance of selecting Thurgood Marshall as the Court's first African American member. President Reagan's appointment of Sandra Day O'Connor, the first woman to serve on the Court, fulfilled a campaign promise.

The Senate scrutinizes Supreme Court nominations more closely than lower-court appointments. The Judiciary Committee staff and the staffs of individual senators carefully examine the nominee's background and past statements on policy issues. The committee conducts hearings at which the nominee, interest group spokespersons, and other concerned parties testify. The Senate as a whole then debates the nomination on the floor before voting to confirm or reject.

The confirmation process is highly political with the White House and interest groups conducting public relations campaigns in hopes of putting pressure on wavering senators to confirm or reject the president's choice.[50] For example, the nomination of Clarence Thomas by the first President Bush became a political tug-of-war between women's groups and the White House over Thomas's fitness to serve after Anita Hill, a former employee of Thomas at the Equal Employment Opportunity Commission (EEOC), accused him of sexual harassment. Thomas eventually won confirmation by a narrow margin.

The Senate confirms most Supreme Court nominees. Since 1789, the Senate has approved 122 of 151 nominations. In the twentieth century alone, the rate was 52 of 62.[51] Senators routinely vote to confirm nominees who are perceived as well qualified and whose political views are close to those of their constituents. When nominees are less well qualified or hold controversial views, the outcome of the confirmation vote depends to a large degree on the political environment.[52] Opponents of a nomination attempt to identify negative information about a nominee to justify rejection. They hope to expand the conflict over the nomination to the general public through committee hearings and the media.[53] Consider the fate of Harriet Miers, President George W. Bush's first choice to replace the retiring Sandra Day O'Connor on the Supreme Court. She asked the president to withdraw her nomination even before the Senate Judiciary Committee held hearings in the face of withering criticism from conservative commentators that she was both poorly qualified and insufficiently conservative for the job.

The Senate is most likely to reject Supreme Court nominees when the opposition party controls the Senate and/or when a nomination is made in the last year of a president's term.[54] When both of these conditions apply, the failure rate for Supreme Court nominees is 71 percent. It is 19 percent when one condition applies and only 10 percent when neither condition exists.[55] Some political scientists believe that the frequency of divided government forces the president to nominate politically moderate, cautious justices who accept a rather limited role for the federal judiciary in the political process.[56]

The backgrounds of individuals selected to serve on the Supreme Court are less diverse now than they once were. Historically, members of the Supreme Court came to the bench from a variety of backgrounds. Chief Justice Warren had been governor of California. Justice O'Connor was a member of the Arizona legislature. Justice Marshall was chief counsel for the National Association for the Advancement of Colored People (NAACP). In contrast, most justices chosen in the past 40 years have been federal judges, serving on the courts of appeal. Political scientist David A. Yalof believes that a Supreme Court dominated by appointees without political experience is less likely to defer to the judgment of elected officials on matters of constitutional and political importance than would a Court whose members had personal experience in the legislative and executive branches of government.[57]

Political scientists have examined the relationship between the backgrounds of judges and their decisions. In general, younger judges, judges who are Democrats, and judges who are Catholic or Jewish tend to support the claims of "underdog" litigants (such as women, minorities, aliens, atheists, labor union members, indigent persons, and criminal defendants) more frequently than do judges who are older, Republican, and Protestant.[58] Older judges are more likely to rule in favor of people bringing age discrimination lawsuits than are younger judges.[59]

Similar to other federal judges, members of the Supreme Court enjoy the ultimate in job security. With "good behavior," they can serve for life, and many have continued on the bench well past traditional retirement age. Associate Justice Hugo Black, for example, served until age 85; William O. Douglas stayed on the Court until he was 77, despite having a debilitating stroke. Justices can be impeached and removed from office, but Congress is unlikely to act without clear evidence of misconduct. Politics or old age and ill health are probably not reason enough for Congress to initiate impeachment proceedings. Furthermore, because of advances in medicine, life tenure means more today than it did when the Constitution was written. Between 1789 and 1970, the average justice served less than 15 years, with vacancies occurring on average every two years. Since 1970, the average justice serves more than 26 years and a vacancy occurs every three years.[60]

 WHAT IS YOUR OPINION?

Do you think that federal judges should be periodically subject to reappointment? Why or why not?

Deciding to Decide   Supreme Court justices set their own agenda. Each year, litigants appeal 7,000 to 10,000 cases to the Supreme Court, far more cases than the Court can reasonably handle. As a result, the justices screen the cases brought to them to decide which ones merit their attention.

Cases are the raw material from which the Supreme Court makes policy. An important judicial ground rule is that the Court must wait for a case to be appealed to it before it can rule. The Supreme Court does not issue advisory opinions. Although the members of the Court decide themselves what cases they will hear, their choices are limited to those cases that come to them on appeal. During the Civil War, for example, Chief Justice Taney and perhaps a majority of the members of the Supreme Court believed that the draft law was unconstitutional. They never had the opportunity to rule on the issue, however, because no case challenging the law ever reached the Court. Today, questions have been raised about the constitutionality of the limitations of the War Powers Act on the president's prerogatives as commander-in-chief, but the issue remains undecided because a case has yet to arise under the law.

The legal requirement that the Supreme Court can only rule when presented a case gives interest groups an incentive to promote and finance **test cases,** which are lawsuits initiated to challenge the constitutionality of a legislative or executive act. *Brown v. Board of Education of Topeka*, for example, was a test case initiated by the NAACP. Linda Brown was a public school student who was prohibited by state law from attending a whites-only school near her home. The NAACP recruited the Brown family to file suit and provided the legal and financial resources necessary for carrying the case through the long and expensive process of trial and appeals.

Lawyers for losing parties in lower-court proceedings begin the process of appeal to the Supreme Court by filing petitions and submitting briefs explaining why their clients' cases merit review. Appellants must pay a filing fee and submit multiple copies of the paperwork, but the Court will waive these requirements when a litigant is too poor to hire an attorney and cover the expenses of an appeal. The Court allows indigent appellants to file *in forma pauperis,* which is the process whereby an indigent litigant can file an appeal of a case to the Supreme Court without paying the usual fees. Frequently, pauper petitions come from prison inmates who study law books and prepare their own appeals. In 2006, 80 percent of the cases appealed to the Supreme Court were *in forma pauperis*.[61] The Court rejects most of these petitions, but a few make the Court's docket for full examination. When the Court decides to

Test cases Lawsuits initiated to challenge the constitutionality of a legislative or executive act.

In forma pauperis The process whereby an indigent litigant can file an appeal of a case to the Supreme Court without paying the usual fees.

Conference A closed meeting attended only by the members of the Supreme Court.

Rule of Four A decision process used by the Supreme Court to determine which cases to consider on appeal, holding that the Court will hear a case if four of the nine justices agree to the review.

Certiorari or **cert** The technical term for the Supreme Court's decision to hear arguments and make a ruling in a case.

Per curiam opinion Unsigned written opinion of a court.

Amicus curiae or **friend of the court briefs** Written legal arguments presented by parties not directly involved in the case, including interest groups and units of government.

accept a case from the *in forma pauperis* docket, it appoints an attorney to prepare and argue the case for the indigent petitioner.

The actual selection process takes place in **conference,** a closed meeting attended only by the members of the Supreme Court. The justices decide which cases to hear based on the **Rule of Four,** a decision process used by the Supreme Court to determine which cases to consider on appeal, holding that the Court will hear a case if four of the nine justices agree to the review. In practice, the Supreme Court grants *certiorari* or *cert,* for short—which is the technical term for the Supreme Court's decision to hear arguments and make a ruling in a case—to only about 1 percent of all the cases appealed to it. In its 2006 term, the Court heard arguments on only 78 of 8,857 cases appealed to it.[62]

What kinds of cases does the Supreme Court accept? The justices choose cases with legal issues of national significance that the Court has not already decided, cases involving conflicts among courts of appeals or between a lower court and the Supreme Court, and cases in which the constitutionality of a state or federal law is under attack. The Court rejects cases it considers trivial or local in scope, and cases that raise issues already decided by earlier rulings. The Court will not accept appeals from state courts unless the appellant can demonstrate that a substantial national constitutional question is involved.

In practice, the justices of the Supreme Court set their own rules for deciding which cases to accept, and they follow or violate the rules as they see fit. For years, the Court refused to consider whether legislative districts that varied considerably in population size violated the Constitution. It was a political question, the justices said, declaring that the legislative and executive branches of government should address the issue rather than the judicial branch. In 1962, however, in *Baker v. Carr*, the Court chose to overlook its political questions doctrine and rule on the dispute.[63]

Political scientists search for clues as to which cases the Court will agree to decide. In general, studies have found that the justices are more likely to accept a case when the U.S. government is the appellant, civil liberties or race-related issues are involved, a number of interest groups file supporting briefs in a case, and lower courts disagree with one another. The members of the Supreme Court also choose cases that enable them to express their policy preferences with maximum impact. During the 1950s and 1960s, the Warren Court accepted cases to extend the guarantees of the Bill of Rights to the poor and other underdog litigants in both federal and state courts. In contrast, the more conservative Burger and Rehnquist Courts often selected cases in order to adopt conservative policy positions. "Upperdogs," such as the government and business corporations, were more successful in having their appeals heard.[64]

Deciding the Case   The Supreme Court usually deals with the cases it chooses to hear in one of two ways. It decides some cases without oral arguments, issuing a ruling accompanied by an unsigned written opinion called a *per curiam* opinion that briefly explains the Court's decision. The justices may use this approach, for example, to reverse a lower court ruling that is contrary to an earlier decision of the Court.

The Court gives full treatment to the remainder of the cases it accepts. The attorneys for the litigants submit briefs arguing the merits of the case and the Court schedules oral arguments. The Court may also receive *amicus curiae* or **friend of the court briefs,**

GLOBAL PERSPECTIVE

Islamic Law in Nigeria

Nigeria is an ethnically and religiously diverse country. Its population includes several major ethnic groups (the Hausa-Fulani, Yoruba, and Igbo) as well as hundreds of smaller groups. The most important religions are Islam, Christianity, Orisha (the traditional Yoruba religion), and Animism (which is the belief that souls inhabit most bodies, including people, animals, plants, and even inanimate objects, such as stones).

After military rule ended in Nigeria in 1999 and the country established a federal system, 12 of the northern states adopted Sharia, which is Islamic law based on the Koran. Sharia addresses issues of sexual morality and alcohol consumption in addition to other crimes. Punishments under Sharia can be harsh. Adulterers may be stoned to death or flogged. Thieves may suffer the amputation of a hand. Public intoxication is punishable by flogging.

The adoption of Sharia in the northern states of Nigeria has been controversial. Even though Sharia applies only to Muslims, some aspects of it, including banning alcohol and prostitution, apply generally.

Critics declare that the use of Sharia violates the principle of separation of state and religion. Furthermore, they charge that the status of women under Sharia and its imposition of harsh punishments cast the nation in an unfavorable light. They point to the 2002 case that provoked international outrage in which a divorced Muslim woman was sentenced to death after having a child out of wedlock. Islamic courts eventually overturned the sentence on the basis of a technicality. Sharia courts have subsequently avoided high-profile controversial cases.*

QUESTIONS TO CONSIDER

1. In a country as diverse as Nigeria, is it better for different regions to follow their own legal traditions, or would it be preferable for the entire nation to have a uniform system?
2. Should a nation's laws be based on its religious traditions?
3. To what extent, if any, is American law grounded in Judeo-Christian legal traditions?

*John N. Paden, *Muslim Civic Cultures and Conflict Resolution: The Challenge of Democratic Federalism in Nigeria* (Washington, DC: Brookings Institution Press, 2005), pp. 139–174.

which are written legal arguments presented by parties not directly involved in the case, including interest groups and units of government. *Amicus* briefs offer the justices more input than they would otherwise receive and provide interest groups and other units of government an opportunity to lobby the Court. The justices sometimes use information contained in *amicus* briefs to justify their rulings.[65]

Attorneys for the litigants present oral arguments publicly to the nine justices in the courtroom of the Supreme Court building. The Court usually allows each side half an hour to make its case and answer any questions the justices may ask. The members of the Court use the oral arguments to gather information about the case and identify their policy options.[66] A few days after oral arguments, the justices meet in closed conference to discuss the case and take a tentative vote. If the chief justice sides with the Court's majority on the initial vote, the chief either writes the majority opinion or assigns another justice the task. If the chief justice does not vote with the majority, the most senior justice in the majority is responsible for opinion assigning. The **majority opinion** is the official written statement of the Supreme Court that explains and justifies its ruling and serves as a guideline for lower courts when similar legal issues arise in the future. The majority opinion is more important than the actual decision of the Court because the majority opinion establishes policy.

Majority opinion
The official written statement of the Supreme Court that explains and justifies its ruling and serves as a guideline for lower courts when similar legal issues arise in the future.

Sandra Day O'Connor, appointed by President Ronald Reagan, was the first woman to serve on the Supreme Court.

When the initial opinion assignment is made, everything is still tentative. Over the next several months, some justices may switch sides and others may threaten to change if the majority opinion is not written to their liking. The justice drafting the majority opinion searches for language to satisfy a majority of the Court's members. Inevitably, the opinion will be a negotiated document, reflecting compromise among the justices. Research indicates that justices initially in the minority are more likely to switch to the majority side than justices who initially voted with the majority are to defect. Apparently, justices change sides in hopes of influencing the wording of the majority opinion.[67]

While the majority opinion is being drafted, other justices may be preparing and circulating concurring or dissenting opinions. A **concurring opinion** is a judicial statement that agrees with the Court's ruling but disagrees with the reasoning of the majority opinion. A justice may write a concurring opinion to point out what the Court did not do in the majority opinion and identify the issues that remain open for further litigation.[68] A **dissenting opinion** is a judicial statement that disagrees with the decision of the court's majority. Justices write dissenting opinions in order to note disagreement with the Court's ruling, emphasize the limits of the majority opinion, and express the conscience of the individual justice. Only the majority opinion of the Court has legal force.

Concurring opinion A judicial statement that agrees with the Court's ruling but disagrees with the reasoning of the majority opinion.

Dissenting opinion A judicial statement that disagrees with the decision of the court's majority.

The Decision   Eventually, the positions of the justices harden or coalesce and the Supreme Court announces its decision. The announcement takes place in open court and the final versions of the majority, concurring, and dissenting opinions are published in the *United States Reports*. The Court decides cases by majority vote— 9–0, 5–4, or anything in between, assuming, of course, that the Court is fully staffed and every justice participates.

Many observers believe that the strength of a Supreme Court decision depends on the level of agreement among the justices. *Brown v. Board of Education* was decided unanimously; the death or resignation of one or two justices was not going to reverse the majority on the issue should a similar case come before the Court in the near future. Furthermore, the Court issued only one opinion, the majority opinion written by Chief Justice Warren. The decision offered no comfort to anyone looking for a weakness of will on the Court. In contrast, the Court's decision in *Furman v. Georgia* (1972) was muddled. In *Furman*, the Court ruled that the death penalty as then practiced was discriminatory and hence unconstitutional. The Court did not say, however, that the death penalty as such was unconstitutional. The ruling's weakness, perhaps fragility, came from the closeness of the vote, 5–4, and the number of opinions—four concurring and four dissenting opinions besides the majority opinion. The justices could not agree on which facts were important in the case or what goals the Court should pursue.[69]

Implementation   Political scientists Charles Johnson and Bradley Canon divide the judicial policymaking process into three stages. First, higher courts, especially the U.S. Supreme Court, develop policies. Although major policy cases make headlines, the Supreme Court frequently clarifies and elaborates on an initial decision with subsequent rulings on related issues. Second, lower courts interpret the higher court rulings. In theory, lower federal courts apply policies formulated by the U.S. Supreme Court without modification. In practice, however, Supreme Court rulings are often general, leaving room for lower courts to adapt them to the circumstances of specific cases. The third stage of Johnson and Canon's model of judicial policymaking is the implementation of court decisions by relevant government agencies and private parties.[70] State legislatures had to rewrite death penalty statutes to comply with the *Furman* ruling, for example. Local school boards had the task of developing integration plans to comply with the *Brown* decision.

Although the implementation of Supreme Court rulings is not automatic, direct disobedience is rare because Court actions enjoy considerable symbolic legitimacy. When the Supreme Court ordered President Nixon to turn over key Watergate tapes to the special prosecutor, for example, Nixon complied. Had the president made a bonfire of them, as some observers suggested, he probably would have been impeached. Instead of defiance, unpopular Supreme Court decisions are often met with delay and subtle evasion. Ten years after the *Brown* ruling, there was not a single state in the Deep South where as many as 10 percent of African American students attended school with any white youngsters.[71] Evasion of the Supreme Court's rulings against government-sponsored school prayers is widespread.[72]

Impact   Supreme Court decisions have their greatest impact when the Court issues a clear decision in a well-publicized case and its position enjoys strong support from

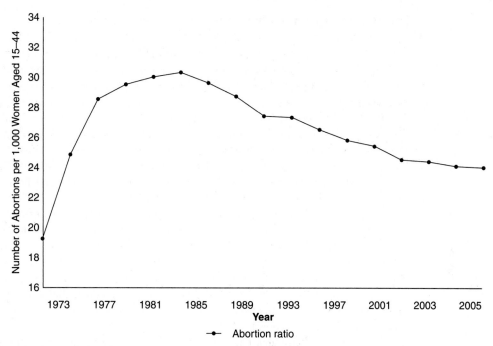

FIGURE 13.2   Abortion Ratio, 1973–2005.
Source: Alan Guttmacher Institute.

other branches and units of government, interest groups, and public opinion.[73] Figure 13.2 traces the impact of the Court's rulings on abortion. In 1973, when *Roe v. Wade* was decided, the number of abortions per 1,000 women aged 15 to 44 was 16.3. (Abortion was already legal in many states.) Four years later, the number of abortions per 1,000 women in the 15 to 44 age group had risen to 26.4 and continued climbing until 1980. During the same period, the number of adoptions was falling, apparently because legalized abortion was reducing the number of unwanted infants. In 1970, before *Roe v. Wade,* the total number of adoptions in the nation was 175,000. In 1975, after the decision, the number of adoptions had declined to 129,000.[74]

As the opponents to abortion have grown more aggressive and the Supreme Court has modified its policy position, the impact of *Roe v. Wade* has lessened. Compared with the middle 1970s, fewer physicians are performing abortions, and the number of hospitals and clinics offering abortion services has declined. Pro-life groups such as Operation Save America have not only picketed abortion clinics but also the homes of doctors who perform abortions. Some abortion clinics have been bombed and abortion providers threatened with violence. Several doctors who perform abortions have been shot and killed by abortion opponents. Furthermore, the Supreme Court has somewhat backed away from the *Roe* decision, allowing states more leeway to restrict access to abortion. Declining abortion rates may be due to other factors as well, including better access to contraceptives and pregnancy counseling and changing attitudes about family size.[75]

POWER, POLITICS, AND THE COURTS

How much influence do federal courts have in the policymaking process? How responsive are they to public concerns? On different occasions in American history, various groups and individuals have attacked the federal courts as both too powerful and too undemocratic. In the early 1930s, liberals said that the members of the Supreme Court were "nine unelected old men" who abused their power to unravel the New Deal despite strong popular support for President Roosevelt's program. In the 1960s and 1970s, conservatives complained about court rulings that gave rights to accused criminals, atheists, and political protesters, while preventing state and local governments from outlawing abortion or controlling the racial balance of local schools.

Political scientists who study the judicial branch identify a number of restrictions on the power of the federal courts. Both the Constitution and the law check judicial authority. The president appoints federal judges and the Senate confirms their appointments. In the long run, Franklin Roosevelt won his battle with the Supreme Court by waiting for justices to die or retire and then replacing them with individuals friendly to New Deal policies. Voters who believe that the Supreme Court is too liberal or too conservative can eventually reverse the Court by electing conservative/liberal presidents and senators.

If Congress and the president believe that judicial rulings are wrong, they can undo the Court's work by changing the law or the Constitution. If Congress and the president disagree with the Court's interpretation of federal law, they can rewrite the law. In 1978, for example, the Supreme Court ruled that the completion of a dam on the Little Tennessee River would violate the Endangered Species Act because it threatened a tiny fish called the snail darter.[76] The following year, Congress legislated to reverse the Court.

Statutory law Law that is written by the legislature.

Constitutional law Law that involves the interpretation and application of the Constitution.

Congress and the president cannot overrule Supreme Court decisions that are based on interpretations of the Constitution by simply passing legislation. **Statutory law,** which is law that is written by the legislature, does not supersede **constitutional law,** which is law that involves the interpretation and application of the Constitution. Amending the Constitution to overturn court rulings is a more difficult procedure than changing statutory law, of course, but it has been done. The Twenty-sixth Amendment, giving 18-year-olds the right to vote, was passed and ratified after the Supreme Court held that Congress could not legislatively lower the voting age because of constitutional restrictions.[77] Congress and the states have overturned four Supreme Court decisions by enacting constitutional amendments.[78]

The power of the federal courts is also limited by the practical nature of the judicial process. Courts are reactive institutions. They respond to policies adopted in other branches and at other levels of government, and then only when presented with a case to decide. The Supreme Court cannot rule on the constitutionality of the War Powers Act until given a case dealing with the issue.

Because the courts cannot enforce their own rulings, they must depend on the cooperation and compliance of other units of government and private parties to implement their decisions. Consider, for example, the difficulty in enforcing the Supreme Court's school prayer rulings. For years after the Court's original decision, a public high school in a suburb of Houston, Texas, used a school song that was essentially a prayer set to music. It asked God's blessing and guidance and ended with the phrase, "In Jesus' name we pray. Amen." Despite the Supreme Court's longstanding decision against government-prescribed official prayers in public school classrooms, the school was still using the song years later. Eventually, a federal judge ordered the use of the song discontinued, but the ruling came only after several offended parents brought a lawsuit to federal court. Had no one objected to the song and, just as importantly, had no one been willing to go to the expense and endure the publicity surrounding a lawsuit, the school would probably still be using the song in official functions today.

Political scientist Robert Dahl believes that the courts are not out of step with Congress and the executive branch for long. Dahl conducted a study in which he traced the fate of 23 "important" laws that had been struck down by the Supreme Court. Three-fourths of the time, Dahl found that the original policy position adopted by Congress and the president ultimately prevailed. In most instances, Congress simply passed legislation similar to the measure that had been initially invalidated. The second time around, however, the Court ruled the legislation constitutional. The role of the courts, Dahl said, is to legitimize the policy decisions made by the elected branches of government rather than to make policy on their own.[79]

In contrast, other political scientists believe that Dahl underestimated the policy influence of the courts. They note that whereas Dahl examined issues that he considered important, many so-called unimportant decisions are not unimportant at all, particularly to the groups most directly affected. Even on important matters, Dahl admits that court rulings affect the timing, effectiveness, and details of policy.[80]

The federal courts are important participants in America's policy process, but their influence depends on the political environment, the issue, and the political skills and values of the judges. One study concludes that the power of the federal courts, particularly the Supreme Court, hinges on their capacity to forge alliances with other political forces, including interest groups and the executive branch. In the 1960s, for example, the Supreme Court joined forces with civil rights groups and the White House under Presidents Kennedy and Johnson to promote the cause of African American civil rights.[81] Another study finds that federal judges are more likely to rule against presidential policy when the chief executive has lost popularity than when the president enjoys strong public support.[82]

The role of the courts varies from issue to issue. In today's policy process, the courts are most likely to defer to the other branches of government on issues involving foreign and defense policy, and economic policy. The courts are least likely to follow the lead of other branches and units of government on matters dealing with civil rights and civil liberties.

Political scientist Jeffrey Rosen believes that the courts reflect the views of a majority of Americans on most issues. Judges can nudge the country in one policy direction or another, but they are sensitive to public opinion through pressure by Congress and the president. They recognize that their policy decisions will not be accepted by the country unless those decisions are perceived as being rooted in constitutional principles rather than the personal preferences of judges. On those occasions when courts stray too far away from mainstream public opinion, they get slapped down.[83]

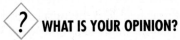 **WHAT IS YOUR OPINION?**

If you were a member of the Supreme Court, when, if ever, would you consider public opinion in making decisions?

CONCLUSION: THE COURTS AND PUBLIC POLICY

The federal courts are important participants in the policymaking process.

Agenda Building

The courts play a role in agenda building by tackling issues that might not otherwise be addressed by other levels and branches of government. For example, the U.S. Supreme Court made abortion a national issue in *Roe v. Wade*. Before *Roe*, state governments made abortion policy. Some states, such as New York, permitted abortion; other states, such as Texas, prohibited abortion except to preserve the life of the woman. After *Roe*, abortion became a national policy issue not just for the courts, who continued to hear abortion cases, but also for the president and Congress because the politics of judicial appointment and confirmation now became the politics of abortion as well. Other issues that have become part of the official policy agenda because of court decisions include legislative redistricting and school prayer.

Policy Formulation and Adoption

The courts play an important role in policy formulation and adoption. Judges formulate policy when they read legal briefs, listen to oral arguments, and negotiate rulings and opinions among themselves. Furthermore, court decisions affect policy formulation in the other branches and units of government. Members of Congress and state legislators formulating abortion policy, for example, must work within the guidelines established in *Roe* and subsequent abortion decisions or face the likelihood of having any legislation they pass being overturned in federal courts.

Courts adopt policy when they make rulings and issue opinions. When the Supreme Court issued its decision in *Brown v. Board of Education of Topeka*, for example, it adopted a policy on racial segregation of public schools. Most judicial policymaking involves civil liberties and civil rights policies. Political scientists concerned with public policies on capital punishment, government-sponsored prayer in public schools, affirmative action, and pornography regulation will spend a good deal of time reading Supreme Court opinions. In contrast, the judicial branch plays a relatively minor role in economic, regulatory, foreign, and defense policymaking.

GETTING INVOLVED

A Day in Court

Learn about the judicial branch of government by visiting a courtroom in your community. Consult the government pages of the telephone directory to locate a court near you. Large cities will be home to federal courts and state courts, whereas small towns may only have municipal courts or justice of the peace courts. Call to learn when the court is in session, and visit the court for at least an hour. Then, write an essay in which you address the following questions:

1. Which court did you visit? (Give its official title.)
2. When did you visit?
3. Who was the presiding judge?
4. How many cases did you witness?
5. Were the cases civil or criminal?
6. What issue(s) did the case(s) address?
7. How many people were in the courtroom and who were they (defendants, lawyers, jurors, law officers, etc.)?
8. Did the court run smoothly? Why do you say so?
9. Do you think the court ran fairly? Why do you say so?
10. If you could make one change in the manner in which the court was run, what would it be?
11. Did you have a good time? Discuss.

Policy Implementation and Evaluation

Americans with Disabilities Act (ADA) A federal law designed to end discrimination against persons with disabilities and eliminate barriers to their full participation in American society.

The federal courts play a role in policy implementation. Lower courts implement Supreme Court rulings by applying them to new cases as they arise. The courts also affect policy implementation when they interpret the law. Consider the implementation of the **Americans with Disabilities Act (ADA),** which is a federal law designed to end discrimination against persons with disabilities and to eliminate barriers to their full participation in American society. The law requires companies to make "reasonable accommodation" for otherwise qualified job applicants or current employees who happen to be disabled unless the business can show that the accommodation would put an "undue hardship" on its operation. When Congress wrote the law, it did not define "reasonable accommodation" and "undue hardship." As a result, the federal courts have been heavily involved with the implementation of the ADA by interpreting its meaning in the context of specific controversies.

Item veto The power of an executive to veto sections or items of a tax or appropriation measure while signing the remainder of the bill into law.

Finally, federal courts evaluate policies in light of the Constitution. In theory, at least, judges do not evaluate policies on their effectiveness or wisdom, but only on their constitutionality. In 1996, for example, Congress passed, and President Clinton signed, legislation granting the president the **item veto,** which is the power of an executive to veto sections or items of a tax or appropriation measure while signing the remainder of the bill into law. Two years later, a legal challenge to the policy reached the U.S. Supreme Court. The Court ruled that the law giving the president the item veto was unconstitutional because it legislatively made a fundamental change in the relationship between the executive and legislative branches of government. The Court held that changes of such constitutional significance must be made through the adoption of a constitutional amendment rather than through the legislative process.[84]

KEY TERMS

affirm

Americans with Disabilities
Act (ADA)

amicus curiae or friend
of the court brief

appeal

capital punishment

certiorari (cert)

civil case

civil liberties

civil rights

concurring opinion

conference

constitutional law

criminal case

dissenting opinion

Equal Protection Clause

exclusionary rule

in forma pauperis

item veto

Jim Crow laws

judicial activism

judicial restraint

judicial review

jurisdiction

legal brief

loose construction

majority opinion

New Deal

original jurisdiction

per curiam opinion

remand

Rule of Four

senatorial courtesy

sovereign immunity

states' rights

statutory law

strict construction

test cases

trial

writ of *habeas corpus*

NOTES

1. Jeffrey Rosen, "Supreme Agreement," *Time*, July 14, 2008, pp. 36–37.
2. Robert Barnes, "It 'Sits on a Knife's Edge,'" *Washington Post National Weekly Edition*, July 7-13, 2008, p. 33.
3. Richard L. Pacelle, Jr., *The Role of the Supreme Court in American Politics: The Least Dangerous Branch* (Boulder, CO: Westview, 2002), p. 35.
4. Harold W. Stanley and Richard G. Niemi, *Vital Statistics on American Politics 2001–2002* (Washington, DC: Congressional Quarterly Press, 2001), p. 288.
5. Kermit Roosevelt III, *The Myth of Judicial Activism: Making Sense of Supreme Court Decisions* (New Haven, CT: Yale University Press, 2006), p. 3.
6. Thomas M. Keck, *The Most Activist Supreme Court in History: The Road to Modern Judicial Conservatism* (Chicago: University of Chicago Press, 2004), pp. 286–289.
7. Robert A. Carp, Ronald Stidham, and Kenneth L. Manning, *Judicial Process in America*, 6th ed. (Washington, DC: Congressional Quarterly Press, 2004), p. 28.
8. *Marbury v. Madison*, 1 Cranch 137 (1803).
9. *Martin v. Hunter's Lessee*, 1 Wheaton 304 (1816).
10. *Dartmouth College v. Woodward*, 4 Wheaton 518 (1819).
11. *McCulloch v. Maryland*, 4 Wheaton 316 (1819).
12. *Gibbons v. Ogden*, 9 Wheaton 1 (1824).
13. *Dred Scott v. Sandford*, 19 Howard 393 (1857).
14. *Plessy v. Ferguson*, 163 U.S. 537 (1896).
15. *Brown v. Board of Education of Topeka*, 347 U.S. 483 (1954).
16. *Mapp v. Ohio*, 367 U.S. 643 (1961).
17. *Miranda v. Arizona*, 377 U.S. 201 (1966).
18. *Roe v. Wade*, 410 U.S. 113 (1973).
19. *City of Richmond v. J. A. Croson Co.*, 488 U.S. 469 (1989).
20. *Zelman v. Simmons-Harris*, 536 U.S. 639 (2002).
21. *Lee v. Weisman*, 505 U.S. 577 (1992).
22. *Santa Fe School District v. Doe*, 530 U.S. 290 (2000).
23. *Lawrence v. Texas*, 539 U.S. 558 (2003).
24. *Atkins v. Virginia*, 492 U.S. 302 (2002).
25. *Gratz v. Bollinger*, 539 U.S. 244 (2003).
26. *Grutter v. Bollinger*, 539 U.S. 306 (2003).
27. *United States v. Lopez*, 514 U.S. 549 (1995).
28. *Florida Prepaid Postsecondary Ed. Expense Bd. v. College Savings Bank*, 527 U.S. 666 (1999); *Alden et. al. v. Maine*, 527 U.S. 706 (1999); *Kimel v. Florida Board of Regents*, 528 U.S. 62 (2000).
29. *Bush v. Gore*, 531 U.S. 98 (2000).
30. Jeffrey Rosen, *The Most Democratic Branch: How the Courts Serve America* (New York: Oxford University Press, 2006), p. 148.
31. Elizabeth Garrett, "The Impact of *Bush v. Gore* on Future Democratic Politics," in Gerald M. Pomper and Marc D. Weiner, eds., *The Future of American Democratic Politics: Principles and Practices* (New Brunswick, NJ: Rutgers University Press, 2003), pp. 141–142.
32. *District of Columbia v. Heller*, No. 07-290 (2008).
33. *Kennedy v. Louisiana*, No. 07-343 (2008).
34. Carp, Stidham, and Manning, *Judicial Process in America*, pp. 43–44.

35. Ibid., p. 52.
36. Ibid., p. 53.
37. Karl Derouen, Jr., Jeffrey S. Peake, and Kenneth Ward, "Presidential Mandates and the Dynamics of Senate Advice and Consent, 1885–1996," *American Politics Research* 33 (January 2005): 106–131.
38. Cass R. Sunstein, David Schkade, Lisa M. Ellman, and Andres Sawicki, *Are Judges Political? An Empirical Analysis of the Federal Judiciary* (Washington, DC: Brookings Institution, 2006), pp. 147–149.
39. Ibid., p. 141.
40. Joan Biskupic, "Barely a Dent on the Bench," *Washington Post National Weekly Edition*, October 24–30, 1994, p. 31.
41. Ashlyn Kuersten and Donald Songer, "Presidential Success Through Appointments to the United States Courts of Appeal," *American Politics Research* 31 (March 2003): 119.
42. Michael W. Giles, Virginia A. Hettinger, and Todd Peppers, "Picking Federal Judges: A Note on Policy and Partisan Selection Agendas," *Political Research Quarterly* 54 (September 2001): 623–641.
43. David C. Nixon and David L. Gross, "Confirmation Delay for Vacancies on the Circuit Courts of Appeal," *American Politics Research* 29 (May 2001): 246–274.
44. Sarah A. Binder and Forrest Maltzman, "Congress and the Politics of Judicial Appointments," in Lawrence C. Dodd and Bruce I. Oppenheimer, *Congress Reconsidered*, 8th ed. (Washington, DC: CQ Press, 2205), pp. 302–305.
45. Helen Dewar and Mike Allen, "GOP May Target Use of Filibuster," *Washington Post*, December 13, 2004, p. A01.
46. Binder and Maltzman, "Congress and the Politics of Judicial Appointments," pp. 312–314.
47. Robert J. Steamer, *Chief Justice: Leadership and the Supreme Court* (Columbia: University of South Carolina Press, 1986), pp. 296–297.
48. Charles Gardner Geyh, *When Courts and Congress Collide: The Struggle for Control of America's Judicial System* (Ann Arbor: University of Michigan Press, 2006), p. 19.
49. Quoted in Henry J. Abraham, *Justices and Presidents: A Political History of Appointments to the Supreme Court* (New York: Oxford University Press, 1974), p. 246.
50. Timothy R. Johnson and Jason M. Roberts, "Presidential Capital and the Supreme Court Confirmation Process," *Journal of Politics* 66 (August 2004): 663–683.
51. Updated data, based on Lawrence Baum, *The Supreme Court* (Washington, DC: CQ Press, 1981), p. 25.
52. Charles M. Cameron, Albert D. Cover, and Jeffrey A. Segal, "Senate Voting on Supreme Court Nominees: A Neoinstitutional Model," *American Political Science Review* 84 (June 1990): 525–534.
53. Glen S. Krutz, Richard Fleisher, and Jon R. Bond, "From Abe Fortas to Zoë Baird: Why Some Presidential Nominations Fail in the Senate," *American Political Science Review* 92 (December 1998): 871–881.
54. Keith E. Whittington, "Presidents, Senates, and Failed Supreme Court Nominations," *2006 The Supreme Court Review* (Chicago: University of Chicago Press, 2006), pp. 412–422.
55. John Massaro, *Supremely Political: The Role of Ideology and Presidential Management in Unsuccessful Supreme Court Nominations* (Albany: State University of New York Press, 1990), p. 136.
56. Mark Silverstein, "Bill Clinton's Excellent Adventure: Political Development and the Modern Confirmation Process," in Howard Gillman and Cornell Clayton, eds., *The Supreme Court in American Politics: New Institutional Interpretation* (Lawrence: University of Kansas Press, 1999), p. 145.
57. David A. Yalof, "The Presidency and the Judiciary," in Michael Nelson, ed., *The Presidency and the Political System*, 8th ed. (Washington, DC: CQ Press, 2006), p. 497.
58. Henry R. Glick, *Courts, Politics, and Justice* (New York: McGraw-Hill, 1983), ch. 9.
59. Kenneth L. Manning, Bruce A. Carroll, and Robert A. Carp, "Does Age Matter? Judicial Decision Making in Age Discrimination Cases," *Social Science Quarterly* 85 (March 2004): 1–18.
60. Linda Greenhouse, "New Focus on the Effects of Life Tenure," *New York Times*, September 10, 2007, available at www.nytimes.com.
61. U.S. Supreme Court, "2007 Year-End Report on the Federal Judiciary," available at www.supremecourtus.gov.
62. Ibid.
63. *Baker v. Carr*, 369 U.S. 186 (1962).
64. Gregory A. Caldeira and John R. Wright, "Organized Interests and Agenda Setting in the U.S. Supreme Court," *American Political Science Review* 82 (December 1988): 1109–1127.
65. Lee Epstein and Jack Knight, "Mapping Out the Strategic Terrain: The Informational Role of *Amici Curiae*," in Cornell W. Clayton and Howard Gillman, eds., *Supreme Court Decision-Making, New Institutional Approaches* (Chicago: University of Chicago Press, 1999), p. 229.
66. Timothy R. Johnson, "Information, Oral Arguments, and Supreme Court Decision Making," *American Politics Research* 29 (July 2001): 331–351.
67. Forrest Maltzman and Paul J. Wahlbeck, "Strategic Policy Consideration and Voting Fluidity on the Burger Court," *American Political Science Review* 90 (September 1996): 581–592.
68. David O. Stewart, "A Chorus of Voices," *ABA Journal* (April 1991), p. 50.
69. *Furman v. Georgia*, 408 U.S. 238 (1972).
70. Charles A. Johnson and Bradley C. Canon, *Judicial Policies: Implementation and Impact* (Washington, DC: Congressional Quarterly Press, 1984), ch. 1.
71. Harrell R. Rodgers, Jr., and Charles S. Bullock III, *Law and Social Change* (New York: McGraw-Hill, 1977), p. 75.
72. H. Frank Way, Jr., "Survey Research on Judicial Decisions: The Prayer and Bible Reading Cases," *Western Political Quarterly* 21 (June 1968): 189–205.

73. Gerald N. Rosenberg, *The Hollow Hope: Can Courts Bring About Social Change?* (Chicago: University of Chicago Press, 1991), pp. 336–338.

74. *Statistical Abstract of the United States, 1991,* 111th ed. (Washington, DC: U.S. Department of Commerce, 1991), p. 71.

75. Naseem Sowti, "Fewer Abortions," *Washington Post National Weekly Edition,* July 25–31, 2006, p. 29.

76. *Tennessee Valley Authority v. Hill,* 437 U.S. 153 (1978).

77. *Oregon v. Mitchell,* 400 U.S. 112 (1970).

78. Carp, Stidham, and Manning, *Judicial Process in America,* p. 371.

79. Robert Dahl, "Decision-Making in a Democracy: The Supreme Court as a National Policy-Maker," *Journal of Public Law* 6 (Fall 1957): 279–295.

80. Johnson and Canon, *Judicial Policies,* pp. 231–232.

81. Mark Silverstein and Benjamin Ginsberg, "The Supreme Court and the New Politics of Judicial Power," *Political Science Quarterly* 102 (Fall 1987): 371–388.

82. Craig R. Ducat and Robert L. Dudley, "Federal District Judges and Presidential Power During the Postwar Era," *Journal of Politics* 51 (February 1989): 98–118.

83. Rosen, *The Most Democratic Branch,* pp. 7–8.

84. *Clinton v. City of New York,* 524 U.S. 417 (1998).

Chapter 14

Economic Policymaking

LEARNING OUTCOMES

- Assess the significance of the national debt. (p. 390)
- Describe the process through which Congress and the president make fiscal policy. (pp. 391–394)
- Discuss the role of the Federal Reserve in setting monetary policy. (pp. 393–394)

- Analyze economic policymaking using the public policy model. (pp. 394–398)
- Define the key terms listed on page 398 and explain their significance.

Recession An economic slowdown characterized by declining economic output and rising unemployment.

In late 2008, the National Bureau of Economic Research announced what most Americans had known for months: The U. S. economy was in recession and had been for a year. A **recession** is an economic slowdown characterized by declining economic output and rising unemployment. During 2008, the American economy lost 2.6 million jobs and the unemployment rate rose from 4.9 to 7.2 percent.[1] The unemployment rate rose to 8.5 percent in March 2009. Moreover, between October 2007 and November 2008, the stock market lost nearly half its value.

Most economists blame overly aggressive home mortgage lending for the recession. In the mid-1990s, banks, savings and loans, and mortgage companies began marketing low-interest adjustable rate mortgages (ARMs) to home buyers with marginal credit ratings or poor credit histories. The lenders profited nicely from the fees they charged for making the loans. They also made money when they sold these so-called "subprime" mortgages to investors, including Wall Street investment banks, such as Lehman Brothers and Bear Stearns. These firms in turn bundled the mortgages with other assets and sold them to investors worldwide as collateralized debt obligations (CDOs). The investors believed that CDOs were safe and profitable investments, but they were wrong.

The subprime mortgage industry began to unravel when interest rates increased in 2004, 2005, and 2006, at just about the same time that housing prices began to fall. With housing prices falling, some homeowners found themselves owing more money on their homes than they were worth. People with ARMs no longer had the option of refinancing to reduce their monthly payments. Some of them walked away from their homes, forcing lenders to foreclose. Consequently, many financial institutions found themselves holding properties which were not worth the amount of money loaned on them. A number of financial institutions declared bankruptcy or sold out to competitors. All of them tightened their loan practices, making it difficult for consumers to borrow money purchase homes or buy automotive vehicles. With sales off dramatically, General Motors (GM), Ford, and Chrysler, the big three of American car companies, neared bankruptcy.[2]

The U.S. government acted to shore up the economy with economic stimulus packages, financial bailouts, and interest rate cuts. Early in 2008, Congress passed, and President George W. Bush signed, legislation to give most taxpayers a $600 tax rebate in hopes that they would spend the money and thus boost the economy. The rebates, which cost the government $170 billion, helped stimulate economic growth—but only temporarily. Later in the year, with economic conditions worsening, the Bush administration loaned billions of dollars to companies to keep them from failing, including GM and Chrysler. Meanwhile, Congress authorized the U.S. Department of the Treasury to spend $700 billion to bail out the financial industry in hopes that banks and mortgage companies would begin making loans again, freeing the credit market. The Federal Reserve reduced interest rates to near zero. In early 2009, Congress passed, and President Barack Obama signed, a $787 billion stimulus package of tax cuts and spending programs designed to get the economy moving again. The administration revealed yet another plan for shoring up the financial markets. President Obama also promised that his administration would regulate the financial industry more closely to prevent a repeat of the lax lending practices that led to the financial meltdown.

Government efforts to respond to the recession of 2008–2009 introduce this chapter on economic policymaking. This is the first of a series of chapters dealing with particular areas. Each chapter describes the nature of public policy in a particular area, discusses some of the more important policy controversies, and explores how policy is made in the particular area. The subject of this chapter is economic policymaking. Civil liberties policymaking is the topic addressed in Chapter 15, whereas Chapter 16 examines civil rights policymaking. Finally, Chapter 17 focuses on foreign and defense policymaking. Each chapter in the series considers both the substance of public policy in a particular area as well as the dynamics of policymaking.

The Goals of Economic Policy

Americans disagree about the goals of economic policy.

 WHAT IS YOUR OPINION?

If you were a member of Congress, what sort of healthcare reform proposal would you support? Why?

Fund Government Services

The most basic goal of economic policy is to fund government services. In fiscal year 2008, which ran from October 1, 2007, through September 30, 2008, the federal government spent $2.9 trillion funding government programs, including various healthcare programs, Social Security, and national defense.[3] Nonetheless, Americans disagree over spending priorities and the appropriate level of funding for federal government activity. In general, liberals believe that government can play a positive role in addressing the needs of society. They favor programs to improve the nation's health, education, and welfare, such as a government program to provide healthcare coverage for individuals and families not currently covered. In contrast, conservatives believe that the role of government should be limited to the provision of basic services. They support spending for national defense and to promote economic development, but they are wary about spending for social programs, especially by the federal government, because they think that high taxes and big government suppress economic growth. They see the provision of tax credits to enable individuals to buy health insurance on the open market as a better approach to healthcare reform than a government program.

Consider the controversy over the National Endowment for the Arts (NEA), which is a government agency created to nurture cultural expression and promote appreciation of the arts. The NEA helps fund art exhibitions, drama productions, and musical performances all over the United States. Many conservative members of Congress want to end funding for the NEA. They are angry because some NEA money has gone to support controversial artistic works that they consider sacrilegious or that they believe promote homosexuality. Conservative members of Congress also question whether the federal government has a role in funding art. Why should taxpayers support art, they ask, especially art that may offend them? In contrast, liberal members of Congress defend the NEA. Government should support the arts, they declare, because it enriches the cultural life of the nation. Theatrical productions, musical performances, and art exhibits enhance local economic development by promoting tourism. Sometimes art will be controversial, but the government should not dictate to artists what their art should embody.

 WHAT IS YOUR OPINION?

Do you think that tax money should support the National Endowment for the Arts (NEA)? Why or why not?

Welfare state A government that takes responsibility for the welfare of its citizens through programs in public health, public housing, old-age pensions, unemployment compensation, and the like.

Americans also disagree about the future of the **welfare state,** which is a government that takes responsibility for the welfare of its citizens through programs in public health, public housing, old-age pensions, unemployment compensation, and the like. The most important welfare programs in the United States are pensions for the elderly, unemployment insurance for workers, agricultural support for farmers, assistance programs for the poor, and health insurance coverage for poor people and the elderly. Most of these programs were enacted during the administrations of two Democratic presidents, Franklin Roosevelt in the 1930s and Lyndon Johnson in the 1960s. Liberals want to expand the welfare state to add universal healthcare, and they support updating current programs to assist two-wage earner families in balancing the demands of work and family. In contrast, conservatives favor cutting back the welfare state to reduce the size and cost of government.[4]

Encourage/Discourage Private-Sector Activity

The Patel and Martinez families live next door to one another in a middle-class suburb of Los Angeles, California. The two families are the same size, have the same family income, and live in homes of equal value. Nonetheless, the Patel family pays more money in income tax than the Martinez family pays. The only difference between the two families is that the Patel family rents, whereas the Martinez family owns its home. Money paid for real estate taxes and home mortgage interest is tax deductible, but rent payments are not.

Congress and the president use economic policy to encourage some private-sector activities while discouraging others. By making home mortgage interest and real estate taxes deductible, the federal government promotes housing construction and home ownership. Similarly, the government uses tax breaks to encourage people

Critics of the NEA are offended by some of the art that the agency supports.

to give money to charity, save for retirement, and invest in state and local government bonds. Congress and the president also use tax policy to discourage certain activities. Increasing cigarette taxes, for example, reduces the smoking rate for teenagers. Raising gasoline taxes saves energy and decreases pollution by discouraging driving.

Subsidy A financial incentive given by government to an individual or a business interest to accomplish a public objective.

A **subsidy** is a financial incentive given by government to an individual or a business interest to accomplish a public objective. The federal government encourages people to go to college by providing students with low-interest loans. It keeps the U.S. merchant marine in business by requiring that goods shipped between American ports travel on American-flag vessels rather than less expensive foreign-registered ships. Government subsidizes farm production, cattle grazing on western lands, offshore oil production, and marketing American products and goods overseas.

The government operates a number of agricultural subsidy programs. It gives some farmers price-support loans. Farmers borrow money from the government, using their crops as collateral. The value of the crops, and hence the amount of money the farmer can borrow, is determined by a target commodity price set by the U.S. Department of Agriculture (USDA). If the market price rises above the target price, the farmer sells the crop, repays the loan, and makes a profit. Should the market price stay below the target price, the farmer is allowed to forfeit the crop to the government as full repayment for the loan. Some farmers receive direct subsidies from the government. If the market price falls below the target price, the government pays farmers the difference between the two prices, either in cash or in certificates for government-stored commodities. The government also subsidizes farmers by intervening to limit commodity production, thus driving up market prices. No one can grow peanuts, for example, without a federal license. Because the number of licenses is limited, the number of peanut growers is limited as well. New farmers cannot get into the business unless they buy or rent a license from someone who already owns one. In practice, the expense of renting a license is usually the single largest cost of doing business for peanut farmers.[5] The cost to the government of agricultural subsidies rises and falls as market prices rise and fall. In 2006, the U.S. agricultural industry benefited from government subsidies totaling more than $13 billion corn farmers were the foremost beneficiaries followed by wheat and cotton farmers.[6]

 WHAT IS YOUR OPINION?

Do you think the government should subsidize farm production?
Why or why not?

Tax incentives and subsidies are controversial. Their defenders argue that tax incentives and subsidies enable the government to accomplish worthwhile goals, such as promoting home ownership and the export of American-made goods. Farm subsidies are necessary to preserve the family farm and support the rural economy. Just because everyone may not agree with every tax break or subsidy, they say, is not good reason to discredit the approach. In contrast, the critics of tax incentives and subsidies charge that they are based more on politics than the desire to achieve worthwhile policy goals. Tax breaks and subsidies drive up taxes and product costs for ordinary Americans and consumers. Congress and the president persist in reauthorizing and funding farm programs because of the political power of agricultural interest groups. Even though consumers and taxpayers are much more numerous than farmers, they are typically indifferent to farm subsidies because the cost to the average American is only a few dollars a year. In contrast, agricultural interests have a strong incentive to fight to defend and even expand their subsidies because they receive thousands of dollars in annual benefits.[7]

Income redistribution The government taking items of value, especially money, from some groups of people and then giving items of value, either in cash or services, to other groups of people.

Redistribute Income

Income redistribution involves the government taking items of value, especially money, from some groups of people and then giving items of value, either in cash or services, to other groups of people. Those people who favor income redistribution

GLOBAL PERSPECTIVE

Healthcare in Canada

Canada provides its citizens with universal healthcare provided on the basis of need rather than ability to pay. Canada administers its healthcare program through the nation's ten provinces, which are the Canadian equivalent of states, and its three territories. Because the provinces have some leeway to design their own plans, healthcare funding and delivery varies somewhat from one part of the nation to another. Some provinces assess their citizens a monthly premium or charge a fee for each visit to a physician, whereas others fund the program from tax money. Coverage varies somewhat from province to province and waits for services are longer in some areas than others.*

Although Canadian healthcare is publicly funded, it is privately provided. Citizens seeking medical services go to private physicians or visit hospitals and clinics that are either for-profit business or nonprofits governed by boards of trustees. Many Canadians also have supplemental insurance coverage, often provided through their employers, to pay for services not covered or only partially covered by the national health system, including dental, optical, and prescription drug service.

Is the Canadian healthcare system better than its counterpart in the United States? Proponents of the Canadian system point out that life expectancy is longer in Canada than it is in the United States and that infant mortality rates are lower. Furthermore, Canada devotes a smaller share of its GDP to healthcare than does the United States. In contrast, critics of the Canadian healthcare system complain that wait times for nonemergency services are sometimes long. Canadian medicine may also be relatively slow to adopt new treatments and technologies.[†]

QUESTIONS TO CONSIDER

1. Would you prefer the Canadian healthcare system to that in the United States?
2. What individuals and groups in the United States would support moving to a system similar to the Canadian system? Which would oppose?
3. Would either the Obama or McCain healthcare proposals lead to a Canadian-style system in the United States? Why or why not?

*Health Canada, available at www.hc-sc.gc.ca.
[†]Gerard W. Boychuk, *National Health Insurance in the United States and Canada* (Washington, DC: Georgetown University Press, 2008), pp. 3–21.

believe that government has an obligation to reduce the income gap between the poorest and wealthiest income groups in the nation. They advocate the adoption of programs that provide benefits based on need and a tax structure whose burden falls most heavily on business and the wealthy. Furthermore, many scholars believe that extreme levels of income inequality are incompatible with democracy. They note that the world's democracies tend to be countries with a large middle class, whereas countries that are divided between a small group of very rich families and a huge group of the very poor typically do not have democratic governments. In contrast, the opponents of income redistribution believe that government should adopt tax systems and spending programs designed to foster economic development because, in the long run, economic development will benefit all segments of society— including low-income groups—more than programs designed to redistribute wealth. In practice, they warn, programs designed to redistribute wealth hinder economic development, hurting everyone. They believe that government has a role to ensure a level playing field in which everyone can compete fairly to get ahead, but that government should not intervene to dictate economic winners and losers.

Economic Growth with Stable Prices

Depression A severe and prolonged economic slump characterized by decreased business activity and high unemployment.

Inflation A decline in the purchasing power of the currency.

Americans also disagree about the role the government should play in promoting economic growth. Some Americans think that the federal government can play a positive role in promoting economic growth with stable prices. They believe that the government should seek to avoid depression, minimize the severity of recession, and control inflation.[8] A **depression** is a severe and prolonged economic slump characterized by decreased business activity and high unemployment. It is more severe then a recession. A recession is less severe than a depression. **Inflation** is a decline in the purchasing power of the currency. By controlling interest rates, taxes, and expenditures, they argue, government can promote a healthy economy. In contrast, other Americans believe that government does more harm than good when it attempts to manage the economy. In their view, the best government policies for promoting economic growth are low taxes, low spending, and minimal regulation.

TAX REVENUES

In 2008, the U.S. government raised $2.5 trillion in tax revenues. Figure 14.1 shows the relative importance of the major sources of tax revenue.

Individual Income Tax

Fiscal year Budget year.

As Figure 14.1 shows, the individual income tax is the largest single source of revenue for the national government, generating 45.4 percent of the nation's total tax revenue in **fiscal year** (budget year) 2008. The income tax system divides taxable income into brackets and applies a different tax rate to the portion of income falling into each bracket, with higher incomes taxed at higher rates than lower incomes. Table 14.1 shows the taxable income ranges for each bracket for couples and singles in 2008. Because the income tax brackets are adjusted annually for inflation, the

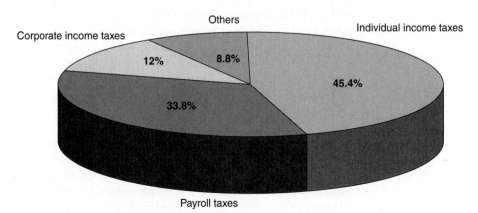

FIGURE 14.1   Sources of Tax Revenue, 2008.
Source: Office of Management and Budget, available at www.omb.gov.

TABLE 14.1   Federal Income Tax Brackets, 2008

Tax Rate	Married Couple Filing Jointly	Singles
10%	Not over $16,050	Not over $8,025
15%	$16,051–$65,100	$8,025–$32,550
25%	$65,101–$131,450	$32,551–$78,850
28%	$131,451–$200,300	$78,851–$164,550
33%	$200,301–$375,700	$164,551–$357,700
35%	Over $375,700	Over $357,700

Source: Internal Revenue Service, available at www.irs.gov.

cutoff points between brackets change somewhat from year to year. A married couple filing jointly earning $150,000 of taxable income in 2008 paid a 10 percent tax on the first $16,050 of taxable income, 15 percent on money earned from $16,051 to $65,100, 25 percent on taxable income from $65,101 through $131,450, and 28 percent on the remainder of their income. Their tax bill would have been calculated as follows:

10% × $16,050	=	$ 1,605
15% × $49,050 ($65,100 − $16,050)	=	$ 7,358
25% × $66,350 ($131,450 − $65,100)	=	$16,588
28% × $18,550 ($150,000 − $131,450)	=	$ 5,194
Total tax owed		$30,745

Tax preference A tax deduction or exclusion that allows individuals to pay less tax than they would otherwise.

Because of the bracket system, the couple's income tax bill amounted to 20 percent of their *taxable* income.

Because of tax preferences, not all income is taxable. A **tax preference** is a tax deduction or exclusion that allows individuals to pay less tax than they would otherwise. Tax preferences include tax exemptions, deductions, and credits. A **tax exemption** is the exclusion of some types of income from taxation. Veterans' benefits, pension contributions and earnings, and interest earned on state and local government bonds are exempt from the income tax. Social Security benefits are exempt for retired couples with a taxable annual income less than $32,000 a year and retired individuals who have a taxable annual income that is less than $25,000. Retirees earning more than those amounts pay income tax on 85 percent of the Social Security benefits they receive. Taxpayers are also allowed to claim personal exemptions for themselves and their dependents. In 2008, the personal exemption was $3,500 for every taxpayer and each dependent.

Tax exemption The exclusion of some types of income from taxation.

Tax deduction An expenditure that can be subtracted from a taxpayer's gross income before figuring the tax owed.

A **tax deduction** is an expenditure that can be subtracted from a taxpayer's gross income before figuring the tax owed. Taxpayers can itemize deductions for such expenditures as home mortgage interest payments, charitable contributions, and state and local real estate taxes. For example, a family that contributes $5,000 to charity reduces its taxable income by $5,000.

Tax credit An expenditure that reduces an individual's tax liability by the amount of the credit.

A **tax credit** is an expenditure that reduces an individual's tax liability by the amount of the credit. A tax credit of $500 reduces the amount of tax owed by $500.

The Hope Scholarship, for example, grants first- and second-year college students tax credits up to $1,500 to cover the cost of college tuition and fees. A family tax credit of $5,000 to purchase health insurance would reduce the family's income tax burden by $5,000.

Tax preferences have both critics and defenders. Their opponents say that tax preferences erode taxpayer confidence in the income tax. The U.S. Tax Code is 1.4 million words, filling 9,500 pages of small print, and the Internal Revenue Service (IRS) has published another 20,000 pages of regulations to explain the Tax Code.[9] Tax preparation has become a major industry. Tax preferences also reduce tax receipts. In 2007, tax preferences reduced individual and corporate income tax collections by more than $900 billion.[10] Nonetheless, every tax preference has its defenders. One person's loophole is another's sacred right. Homeowners, wage earners, the elderly, churches, schools, businesses, and many others benefit from one tax preference or another. Furthermore, the defenders of tax preferences point out that they are a mechanism that government can use to promote certain activities or assist particular groups of taxpayers. By allowing taxpayers to deduct contributions to charitable institutions, government promotes private efforts to assist the poor, promote the arts, support education, and care for the disabled. Government encourages business expansion by giving tax credits for investment expenditures.

 WHAT IS YOUR OPINION?

If you were in Congress, which tax preferences would you keep and which would you eliminate?

Payroll Taxes

As Figure 14.1 indicates, payroll taxes are the second largest source of federal tax revenue, producing 33.8 percent of total revenues in 2008. The payroll tax rate, which is levied on wages and salaries but not other sources of income, is 15.3 percent, with 7.65 percent withheld from the employee's paycheck and an equivalent 7.65 percent paid by the employer. Most workers pay more in payroll taxes than they pay in personal income taxes. A single worker earning $30,000 a year in wages, for example, paid $4,590 in payroll taxes in 2008 compared with less than $3,000 in income taxes. The payroll tax funds both the Social Security and Medicare programs, with 12.4 percent going to finance Social Security and 2.9 percent set aside for Medicare. Wage earners and their employers paid Social Security payroll taxes on the first $102,000 of an employee's annual salary in 2008. They paid the Medicare payroll tax on all wage income.

Corporate Income Taxes and Other Revenue Sources

In 2008, the national government derived 20.8 percent of its tax revenue from corporate income taxes, excise taxes, and miscellaneous revenue sources. The corporate income tax, which generated 12 percent of federal tax revenues in 2008, has four brackets—15 percent on the first $50,000 of taxable earnings, 25 percent on income between $50,000 and $75,000, 34 percent on earnings between $75,000 and $10 million, and 35 percent on income greater than $10 million. Because the 15 percent and 25 percent rates apply only to income below $75,000, most corporate profits are taxed at the higher rates. **Excise taxes** are taxes levied on the manufacture, transportation, sale, or consumption of a particular item or set of related items. The government assesses excise taxes on gasoline, alcohol, tobacco, tires, airplane tickets, and a number of other items. The government also raises revenue through customs duties, fines, penalties, and inheritance taxes.

Excise taxes Taxes levied on the manufacture, transportation, sale, or consumption of a particular item or set of related items.

Issues in Government Finance

Policymakers face a number of issues in government finance.

Gross domestic product (GDP) The total value of goods and services produced by a nation's economy in a year, excluding transactions with foreign countries.

Tax Burden   Are taxes too high? Economists believe that the best way to evaluate the size of the tax burden is to consider it in proportion to the nation's **gross domestic product (GDP),** which is the total value of goods and services produced by a nation's economy in a year. Figure 14.2 graphs both government receipts and government expenditures relative to GDP from 1996 through 2008. Receipts rose during the latter 1990s, peaking at 20.9 percent in 2000. Tax receipts fell in the early years of the twenty-first century, both because of a recession and because of tax cuts passed by Congress and signed by President Bush. In 2008, the federal tax burden stood at 17.6 percent of the nation's GDP. National, state, and local taxes combined represented 31.6 percent of GDP.[11]

Observers disagree about the weight of the nation's tax burden. Scholars who believe that the taxes are either too low or about right note that the tax burden in the United States is relatively light compared to the tax burden in many other

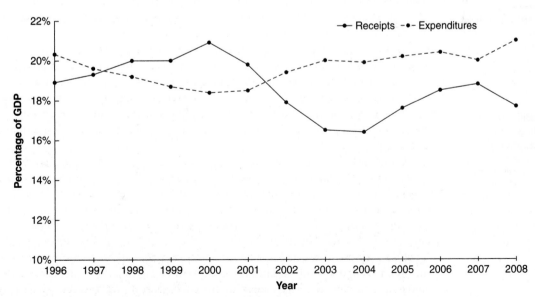

FIGURE 14.2   Receipts and Expenditures as Pct. of GDP, 1996–2008.
Source: Office of Management and Budget.

industrialized nations. Italy, Canada, France, Germany, and the United Kingdom all allocate more than 40 percent of their gross domestic products to government compared with less than 30 percent for the United States.[12] In contrast, other scholars contend that Americans are overtaxed, and they warn that high tax rates depress economic growth. In general, Republicans believe that high taxes undermine economic prosperity, whereas Democrats resist tax cuts because they want to ensure that the government has sufficient revenue to fund government services.

Tax incidence The point at which the actual cost of a tax falls.

Progressive tax A levy that taxes people earning higher incomes at a higher rate than it does individuals making less money.

Proportional tax A levy that taxes all persons at the same percentage rate, regardless of income.

Regressive tax A levy whose burden falls more heavily on lower-income groups than on wealthy taxpayers.

Ability to pay theory of taxation The approach to government finance that holds that taxes should be based on an individual's ability to pay.

Tax Incidence and Tax Fairness   The term **tax incidence** refers to the point at which the actual cost of a tax falls. Using this concept, social scientists identify three general types of taxes: progressive, proportional, and regressive. A **progressive tax** is a levy that taxes people earning higher incomes at a higher rate than it does individuals making less money. The federal income tax is a progressive tax because people earning higher incomes pay a higher tax rate than persons making less money. A **proportional tax** is a levy that taxes all persons at the same percentage rate, regardless of income, whereas a **regressive tax** is a levy whose burden falls more heavily on lower-income groups than on wealthy taxpayers. Economists generally classify sales and excise taxes as regressive taxes because lower-income persons spend a greater proportion of their earnings on items subject to taxation than do upper-income persons.

Observers disagree about the fairest tax system. The advocates of progressive taxation often defend the concept on the basis of the **ability to pay theory of taxation,** which is the approach to government finance that holds that taxes should be based on an individual's ability to pay. Well-to-do persons can better afford taxes than lower-income individuals, so they should pay more.[13] Furthermore, the advocates of income redistribution point out that a progressive tax helps narrow the income differential between the poor and the affluent.

Other experts on public finance believe that the best tax system is one that encourages economic growth. They favor sales and excise taxes because those levies discourage people from spending their money on consumer goods. They want people to save and invest their incomes. They also believe that progressive taxes such as the income tax are harmful to the economy because they reduce the amount of money middle- and upper-income individuals have available to invest in economic development.

Economists conclude that the current federal tax system is either slightly progressive or slightly regressive, depending on the set of assumptions one accepts. The personal income tax is progressive, but payroll taxes and excise taxes are regressive. Most economists believe that the corporate income tax is progressive as well because the burden of the tax falls primarily on stockholders who, as a group, are more affluent than the average American.[14] Although the payroll tax *appears* proportional, it is actually regressive because it is assessed only on wages and not on other types of income, such as dividends and interest earned on savings. Furthermore, because the amount of wage income that is subject to Social Security payroll taxes is capped, persons in the highest income groups pay a lower proportion of their wages in payroll taxes than do middle-income taxpayers.[15]

WHAT IS YOUR OPINION?

Do you think people who make more money should pay a greater proportion of their earnings in taxes than people with lower incomes?

Tax Reform

Critics of the nation's tax system offer a number of prescriptions for reform. The advocates of progressive tax systems favor increasing income tax rates on corporations and upper-income taxpayers while cutting taxes for people at the lower end of the income ladder. They also support reducing or eliminating deductions that allow upper-income persons and corporations to avoid paying taxes. In contrast, the opponents of progressive income tax systems charge that raising taxes on upper-income families and corporations would hurt the economy by discouraging savings and investment.

Instead of making the income tax more progressive, some reformers favor making it proportional. They want the United States to replace the current income tax system with a **flat tax,** which is an income tax that assesses the same percentage tax rate on all income levels above a personal exemption while allowing few if any deductions. The advocates of the flat tax prefer it to the current income tax system because it is simpler and because it would close loopholes that allow wealthy individuals to escape taxation. Moreover, people who work harder and earn more money would no longer be penalized by having a greater proportion of their earnings taken by the government in taxes.

Not everyone thinks the flat tax is a good idea. Critics charge that it would increase the tax bite on middle-income Americans while cutting taxes for the wealthy. The current income tax system is graduated in that it assesses a higher tax rate on higher incomes than on lower incomes. A flat tax that was designed to generate the same amount of revenue as the current income tax system would lower taxes on wealthy families while increasing taxes for lower- and middle-income families. Another criticism of the flat tax is that it would eliminate popular tax deductions. If homeowners cannot deduct mortgage interest and real estate taxes, the cost of owning a home would rise significantly. Charities, religious organizations, colleges, and universities would suffer because contributions to them would no longer be tax deductible. Businesses that lose tax breaks would probably pass along their additional costs to consumers.

 WHAT IS YOUR OPINION?

Would you be better off with the current income tax or with a flat tax?

Some reformers want to replace the income tax with a national **sales tax,** which is a levy assessed on the retail sale of taxable items. Because the national sales tax could be collected through the systems that the states now use to collect state and local sales taxes, the IRS could be eliminated and taxpayers would no longer have to spend time and money keeping tax records. Furthermore, a national sales tax would provide a powerful incentive for savings and investment because investment income would not be taxed. Nonetheless, the proposal for a national sales tax has its share

Flat tax An income tax that assesses the same percentage tax rate on all income levels above a personal exemption while allowing few if any deductions.

Sales tax A levy assessed on the retail sale of taxable items.

of critics. Opponents point out that a national sales tax rate would have to be set at 18 to 20 percent on top of existing state and local sales taxes in order to raise as much money as the current personal income tax. Also, the burden of the sales tax would fall most heavily on low- and middle-income wage earners because they spend a greater proportion of their earnings on retail purchases, which are taxed. In contrast, upper-income families who devote a greater share of their earnings to real estate purchases and investments in stocks and bonds, transactions that are not subject to sales taxes, would pay less than they do now.

The Bush Tax Reforms   Shortly after taking office, President George W. Bush proposed, and Congress passed, a major income tax cut that would be phased in over the next ten years. They also agreed to repeal the **estate tax,** which is a tax levied on the value of an inheritance. In subsequent years, Congress and the president accelerated the pace of the earlier tax cuts already adopted, reduced taxes on dividend income, and exempted or deferred taxes on interest income from savings.

Estate tax A tax levied on the value of an inheritance.

The Bush tax reforms reflected the president's goal of increasing savings and investment. Bush focused the bulk of his tax cuts on upper-income taxpayers because they save money. With more money available for business to expand, he reasoned, the economy would grow and everyone would be better off. Companies would hire more workers and investors would realize greater gains from investments. Even though lower-income people would not benefit directly from the tax reductions, the president argued that they would be better off in the long run because the economy would grow.[16]

Supply-side economics The economic theory that tax cuts, especially for business and the wealthy, will lead to savings and investment that will benefit everyone.

The Bush tax cuts reflected **supply-side economics,** which is the economic theory that tax cuts, especially for business and the wealthy, will lead to savings and investment that will benefit everyone. Supply-side economists believe that high tax rates discourage investment and worker productivity. Why risk your savings on investments or work harder to earn more money if much of it goes to the government? Supply-side economists advocate tax reductions in order to stimulate investment and economic growth. In fact, some supply-siders believe that economic growth generated by tax reductions will be sufficient to actually produce an increase in tax receipts.

The tax policies adopted during the Bush administration dramatically changed the nation's tax structure by shifting the federal tax burden away from taxes on dividends, capital gains, and interest income to taxes on wages and salaries. If people make money from working, they pay taxes. If they make money as investors, they do not pay taxes.

The Bush tax reforms are controversial. Although everyone favors economic growth, not everyone agrees that policies designed to increase the savings rate are the only way or even the best way to grow the economy. Bush's critics favor policies aimed at increasing consumption. The economy will grow if consumers increase their purchases of goods and services. Economists taking this approach favor increasing the minimum wage (because low-income people spend their money), cutting taxes for lower- and middle-income taxpayers, and adopting government spending programs. Many economists also warn that tax cuts that are not offset by spending reductions will eventually harm the economy because they create budget deficits.[17]

Tax Policy in the Obama Administration   President Obama's initial approach to tax policy was influenced by the severe recession underway when he entered office. In early 2009, Congress passed, and Obama signed, an economic stimulus package that included a series of tax reductions for lower- and middle-income taxpayers. Congress and the president hoped that people would spend the extra money in their paychecks and thus help jumpstart the economy. In the long run, President Obama promised to reduce taxes on lower- and middle-income wage earners by renewing some of the Bush administration tax reductions which were set to expire in 2010. In contrast, Obama promised to raise taxes on people earning more than $200,000 a year by allowing the Bush tax cuts to expire.[18]

BUDGET DEFICITS AND SURPLUSES

Budget deficit The amount by which annual budget expenditures exceed annual budget receipts.

Budget surplus The sum by which annual budget *receipts* exceed annual budget *expenditures*.

Balanced budget Budget receipts equal budget expenditures.

National debt The accumulated indebtedness of the federal government.

The terms *budget deficit*, *budget surplus*, and *balanced budget* all refer to the relationship between annual budget revenues and budget expenditures. A **budget deficit** is the amount of money by which annual budget *expenditures* exceed annual budget *receipts*, whereas a **budget surplus** is the sum by which annual budget *receipts* exceed annual budget *expenditures*. If budget receipts equal budget expenditures, the government has a **balanced budget**. Finally, the **national debt** is the accumulated indebtedness of the federal government. An annual budget deficit increases the debt by the amount of the deficit, whereas a surplus decreases the debt. In 2008, for example, federal budget receipts were $2.52 trillion compared with outlays of $2.98 trillion, for a budget deficit of $455 billion.[19] As a result, the national debt grew by $455 billion during 2008.

By graphing both budget receipts and budget outlays as a percentage of GDP, Figure 14.2 also graphs the relative size of budget deficits and surpluses between 1996 and 2008. During the 1990s, the budget deficit turned into a surplus as receipts rose and outlays fell. After several years of surplus, deficit spending returned in 2002 because of falling revenues and increased expenditures. Although rising tax collections in 2005 through 2007 helped close the deficit gap, the deficit bloomed in 2008 because of an economic slowdown that depressed tax revenues while increasing government spending. Because of the recession, budget analysts believe that the budget deficit will be substantially higher in 2009 than it was in 2008, perhaps as much as a trillion dollars higher.[20]

Changes in budget deficits and surpluses reflect the cost of war, fluctuations in the health of the nation's economy, and the policy decisions of Congress and the president. Historically, budget deficits have soared during wartime because the government borrows freely to finance the war effort. During World War II, the federal budget deficit rose to more than 30 percent of GDP. Economic conditions impact the budget by affecting both revenues and expenditures. During a recession, tax revenues fall because personal income and corporate profits are down, while welfare payments and unemployment compensation claims rise. For opposite reasons, economic booms increase government revenues, while decreasing expenditures. The mounting surpluses of the late 1990s and 2000 were largely the result of an economic boom that produced rapidly growing tax collections.

Deficits and surpluses also reflect policy decisions. During the 1980s and early 1990s, the government ran record-high budget deficits for peacetime because Congress and the president chose to spend hundreds of billions of dollars more than they were willing to levy in taxes. In the early 1980s, President Ronald Reagan proposed, and Congress agreed, to cut taxes while increasing spending for the military. Although Reagan asked Congress to reduce domestic spending, the proposed cuts were insufficient to balance the budget, and Congress did not enact many of the reductions anyway. Subsequently, the White House and Congress failed to propose, and refused to enact, spending reductions and/or tax increases sufficient to make a significant reduction in the deficit.

When 2001 began, both the OMB and the Congressional Budget Office (CBO) were projecting a decade of budget surpluses, totaling trillions of dollars. The government would be able to pay off the national debt; fully fund government programs, including Social Security and Medicare; and enact a tax cut. Within a few years, however, the decade of surpluses turned into a decade of deficits because of war, recession, and policy decisions. An economic downturn in late 2001 and early 2002 cost the Treasury a projected $1.7 trillion of revenue over the next ten years. Meanwhile, Congress and the president adopted a series of tax cuts that reduced government revenues by $5 trillion over the next decade. Government spending soared as well. Although some of the increased expenditures were earmarked to conduct the war on terror, fight wars in Afghanistan and Iraq, and provide for homeland security, the president and Congress added hundreds of billions of dollars more to the budget imbalance by increasing spending for education, transportation, healthcare, and farm subsidies.[21]

How important is a balanced budget? Economists generally agree that small deficits probably do not matter, whereas big deficits probably do. The American economy is so large that deficits (or surpluses) of $100 billion or so are probably too small to have much effect. Similarly, most economists agree that deficits that are so large that the national debt grows more rapidly than the nation's economy are dangerous because eventually the economy will be unable to support them. Funding the debt will sap the economy of resources and drive up interest rates, harming economic growth. Economists disagree about the importance of intermediate-size deficits. Some economists believe that persistent deficits will retard the nation's long-term economic growth because money that would otherwise be invested to promote economic development goes instead to finance the deficit. In contrast, other economists think that deficits have little if any impact on economic growth.[22]

Nonetheless, many economists and policy analysts believe that the nation's return to deficit spending in the early 2000s came at a bad time. In fiscal year (FY) 2008, the national government spent $232 billion on interest on the national debt.[23] The sizable budget surpluses of FY 2000 and 2001 offered the prospect that the government would pay off most or all of the national debt, cutting or eliminating the expense of paying interest from future budgets. The money saved could be used to address the looming budget crisis brought on by the aging of the baby-boom generation. With the OMB and the CBO predicting years of future deficits, the government's opportunity to shore up Social Security, Medicare, Medicaid, and other programs without substantial reductions in benefit levels, major tax increases, or significant deficit spending was probably lost for good.

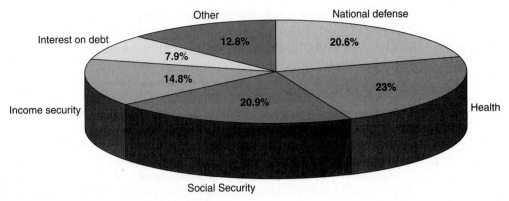

FIGURE 14.3 Federal Government Expenditures, 2008.
Source: Office of Management and Budget.

GOVERNMENT EXPENDITURES

As Figure 14.3 shows, the most important spending priorities for the federal government in 2008 were healthcare, Social Security, national defense, income security, and interest on the debt.

Healthcare

Medicare A federally funded health insurance program for the elderly.

Medicaid A federal program designed to provide health insurance coverage to low-income persons, people with disabilities, and elderly people who are impoverished.

Baby-boom generation The exceptionally large number of Americans born during the late 1940s, 1950s, and early 1960s.

Health is the largest category, accounting for 23 percent of federal government spending. Although health expenditures include money for medical research and disease control, by far the largest federal health programs are **Medicare** and **Medicaid.** In 2008, 44 million people participated in the Medicare program at a cost of $454 billion, including premiums and deductibles paid by program participants and general revenue expenditures, which, in 2008, were $185 billion.[24] Part A of Medicare is compulsory hospitalization insurance that covers the cost of inpatient care after beneficiaries pay a deductible. It is financed from premiums deducted from the Social Security checks of retirees and by a 2.9 percent payroll tax, divided evenly between workers and their employers. Medicare Part B is a voluntary medical insurance plan that covers certain physician fees and nonhospital services after beneficiaries pay a deductible. It is funded by premiums deducted from the Social Security checks of retired persons who choose to participate. In 2008, the premium was $96.40 a month for most recipients. Medicare recipients earning more than $82,000 in adjusted annual income had to pay a surcharge. In 2009, affluent recipients had to pay an amount equal to either 1.4 times, 2.6 times, or 3.2 times the standard premium, depending on their income level.[25] Medicare Part D is a prescription drug benefit offered and managed by private insurers under contract with the government. Medicare recipients who choose to participate pay a monthly premium, which averaged $25 in 2008, along with various deductibles and co-pays.[26]

The Medicare program faces a long-term financial crisis that is more serious than the Social Security shortfall. The aging of the **baby-boom generation** is a demographic time bomb for the Medicare program. Between 2010 and 2030, the Medicare rolls will more than double, adding huge costs to the system.[27] Furthermore, inflation in the healthcare industry is driving up the cost of medical care faster than wages are rising to provide tax revenues to cover the cost. The addition of the prescription drug benefit to Medicare will make the program's financial crisis more severe because the cost of prescription drugs is rising more rapidly than healthcare costs in general. The cost of the prescription drug benefit, which was $33 billion in 2006 when the program began, will rise every year. In 2015, the annual cost is expected to be nearly $140 billion.[28] The Medicare Board of Trustees estimates that program expenditures will exceed assets in five years.[29]

To preserve the financial integrity of the Medicare system, Congress and the president will have to adopt reforms involving benefit reductions, tax increases, and greater charges to recipients. The most commonly offered reform proposals are the following:

- Slow the growth of healthcare expenditures by reducing government payments to hospitals and doctors and encouraging recipients to participate in managed care programs.
- Increase the 2.9 percent payroll tax.
- Push back the age at which beneficiaries can qualify for benefits from 65 to 67.
- Increase premiums and service charges to recipients, especially to retirees who are better off financially.

Preserving the Medicare program is a political necessity, but none of the alternatives will be politically easy to adopt. The Medicare Board of Trustees estimates it would take a reduction of program expenditures of 51 percent, an increase in program revenues of 122 percent, or some combination of tax increases and benefit cuts in order to ensure the program's long-term solvency.[30] Congress and the president may have no choice but to take the necessary steps to preserve Medicare because it enjoys strong public support, not just among the elderly but also among their children who would otherwise have to help cover their parents' medical bills. Nonetheless, each of the policy options for fixing Medicare faces opposition from one or more powerful interest group, including the American Medical Association (AMA), AARP, companies that manufacture hospital equipment, hospital associations, and groups philosophically opposed to tax increases.

Medicaid is another large and rapidly growing federal healthcare program. In 2008, Medicaid served 63 million clients at a cost to the federal government of $207 billion. The poor—particularly pregnant women, mothers, and their young children—are the largest group of recipients, accounting for three-fourths of Medicaid beneficiaries. Nearly two-thirds of Medicaid spending, however, goes to the other 25 percent of recipients—the blind, disabled, and impoverished elderly—because their medical needs are greater and therefore more expensive to meet. All told, Medicaid covers the cost of healthcare for one in every three children. It pays for 40 percent of births and funds two-thirds of the nursing home care in the country.[31]

The Congressional Budget Office estimates that Medicaid costs will double over the next decade. The CBO projects that Medicaid enrollment of elderly persons will increase by an average of 2.5 percent a year over the next ten years because of the aging of the baby-boom generation. Rising Medicaid costs also reflect inflation in the healthcare industry, which has been greater than in the economy as a whole, particularly with the introduction of expensive new technologies and the introduction of expensive new prescription drugs.[32]

Social Security

Are you counting on Social Security for your retirement? Half of all Americans who are not now retired believe that Social Security will be unable to pay them a benefit when they retire.[33] Is their pessimism about the future of Social Security warranted?

Social Security A federal pension and disability insurance program funded through a payroll tax on workers and their employers.

Social Security, which is a federal pension and disability insurance program funded through a payroll tax on workers and their employers, accounted for 20.9 percent of federal expenditures in 2008. Congress created the program in 1935 to provide limited coverage to workers in industry and commerce upon their retirement at age 65. Through the years, Congress has extended the program's scope and increased its benefits. Even before the first benefit checks were mailed, Congress expanded coverage to include the aged spouse and children of a retired worker as well as the young children and spouse of a covered worker upon the worker's death. Congress subsequently added disability insurance to the package and provided for early retirement.

Congress and the president have also increased Social Security benefits, especially over the last 35 years. They raised benefits 15 percent in 1970, 10 percent in 1971, and 20 percent in 1972. Beginning in 1975, Congress and the president indexed benefits to the **Consumer Price Index (CPI),** a measure of inflation that is based on the changing cost of goods and services. In 2009, for example, Social Security recipients enjoyed a 6.2 percent cost-of-living adjustment (COLA) in their benefit checks because the CPI rose 6.2 percent in 2008. A **cost-of-living adjustment (COLA)** is a mechanism designed to regularly increase the size of a payment to compensate for the effects of inflation. In 2008, the average retired worker received a monthly Social Security check of $1,079.[34]

Consumer Price Index (CPI) A measure of inflation that is based on the changing cost of goods and services.

Cost-of-living adjustment (COLA) A mechanism designed to regularly increase the size of a payment to compensate for the effects of inflation.

The Social Security program can most accurately be described as a tax on workers to provide benefits to elderly retirees and disabled persons. Contrary to popular belief, Congress did not create Social Security as a pension/savings plan in which the government would simply refund the money retirees contributed over the years. Instead, current payroll taxes pay the benefits for current recipients. Because the initial tax rate was relatively low, current retirees draw substantially more money in Social Security benefits than they paid in payroll taxes. The average person who is retired today got back all the money he or she paid into Social Security with interest in about seven years. Because tax rates are higher today, workers who are now in their thirties will likely pay more money in taxes during their lifetimes than they will collect in benefits after they retire.

Even though payroll taxes were initially low, the Social Security trust funds maintained healthy surpluses into the early 1970s. With the baby-boom generation coming of age and more women entering the workforce than ever before, the pool of workers paying taxes into the system grew more rapidly than did the number of retirees collecting benefits. Furthermore, the system benefited from a healthy economy and rising wages.

Eventually, demographic and economic changes combined with political decisions to drive the Social Security system into near bankruptcy. Early retirement,

Millions of elderly Americans rely on Social Security and Medicare benefits.

increased longevity, and falling birthrates served to swell the ranks of Social Security beneficiaries while slowing the increase in the number of employees paying taxes. When Social Security was created, the average worker retired at age 69 and lived another eight years. Today, the average worker retires at 64 and draws retirement benefits for 19 years.[35] In the meantime, Congress and the president increased benefits and pegged future increases in Social Security payments to the inflation rate. When the economy slumped and inflation soared in the late 1970s, the Social Security system faced a financial crisis.

In 1983, Congress and the president responded to the situation by adopting a Social Security bailout plan that increased payroll taxes significantly while somewhat limiting future benefit payments. The plan provided for an increase in the retirement age by small annual increments after the year 2000 until the retirement age reaches 67. Also, the bailout legislation provided that half the benefits of upper-income recipients would be counted as taxable income for income tax purposes. In 1993, Congress increased the share of taxable Social Security for middle- and upper-income recipients from 50 to 85 percent.

The goal of the Social Security bailout plan was not only to keep the program solvent for the short-term but also to ensure its long-range stability despite unfavorable demographic trends. In 1950, 16 workers paid taxes for every person drawing benefits. In 2000, the ratio was down to three to one. By the year 2030, when the baby-boom generation will have retired, the ratio of workers to retirees will be only two to one.[36] The architects of the bailout plan hoped that the payroll tax increases would be sufficient to allow the Social Security trust funds to build up sizable surpluses that could be used to pay benefits well into the twenty-first century. In 2008, the Social Security trust funds held assets worth $2.4 trillion and were growing. During 2008, for example, the trust funds grew by $192 billion based on payroll tax revenues worth $708 billion and benefit outlays of $506 billion.[37]

Although the bailout plan has put Social Security in the black for now, the retirement of the baby-boom generation threatens the system's long-term financial viability. Benefit payments begin to exceed payroll tax revenue in 2017 and the trust funds will be exhausted by 2041. At that point, payroll taxes will generate only 78 percent of the cost of the program.[38] Because trust fund assets are held in Treasury notes, the key date for policymakers is 2017 rather than 2040. The Social Security trust funds are a record of funds transferred from one part of the government—the Social Security system—to other parts of the government. They contain no real assets. Consequently, from a practical financial perspective, it makes no difference whether the Social Security trust funds contain a paper balance of trillions of dollars or a balance of zero dollars.[39] Once the annual cost of Social Security benefits exceeds payroll tax revenues, Congress and the president will have to make up the shortfall by cutting other programs, raising taxes, borrowing, or reducing benefit rates.

A number of reformers want to go beyond tinkering with benefits and funding mechanisms to change the basic structure of Social Security. Some reformers want to make Social Security a **means-tested program,** which is a government program that provides benefits to recipients based on their financial need. Under the current system, recipients qualify for benefits based on their age and contributions, regardless of personal wealth or other income. If Social Security were a means-test program, benefit levels would also depend on the financial need of the recipients. The advantage of this approach is that it would reduce benefits without hurting low-income retirees. The disadvantage is that middle- and upper-income taxpayers might be unwilling to continue supporting the program if their benefits were reduced.

Many conservatives favor reforming Social Security through **privatization,** which is a process that involves the government contracting with private business to implement government programs. President George W. Bush proposed supplementing Social Security with a pension plan system in which workers would invest some of the money they would have contributed to Social Security in private savings accounts. Bush and other proponents of privatization believe that employees would have a better

Means-tested program A government program that provides benefits to recipients based on their financial need.

Privatization A process that involves the government contracting with private business to implement government programs.

Welfare programs Government programs that provide benefits to individuals based on their economic status.

return on an investment in stocks and bonds than they could count on from the Social Security system. The returns on the private accounts would cushion the impact of future reductions in Social Security benefits. In contrast, the critics of privatization warn that private investments carry risk. Falling stock prices could endanger retirement income. Furthermore, even if privatization succeeds in the long run, the government would have to put additional funds into the Social Security system to make up for the money diverted into private accounts. Bush's proposal got nowhere in Congress, leaving resolution of the Social Security for a future administration.

Earned Income Tax Credit (EITC) A federal program designed to give cash assistance to low-income working families by refunding some or all of the taxes they pay and, if their wages are low, giving them a payment rather than assessing a tax.

 WHAT IS YOUR OPINION?

If you were a member of Congress, what actions would you favor to ensure the long-term solvency of the Social Security program?

National Defense

National defense is the third largest category of federal government expenditures, accounting for 20.6 percent of spending in 2008. This budget category includes funding for the Department of Defense as well as nuclear-weapons-related activities of the Department of Energy and defense-related expenditures by several other agencies, such as the Coast Guard and the Federal Bureau of Investigation (FBI). Chapter 17 examines defense spending in detail.

Food Stamp Program A federal program that provides vouchers to low-income families and individuals that can be used to purchase food from grocery stores.

Income Security

Income security is the fourth largest category of federal government spending, accounting for 14.8 percent of expenditures in 2008. It encompasses a variety of domestic spending programs, including unemployment insurance, federal retirement, and, with the major exception of Medicaid, most welfare programs. Federal Civilian Retirement and Federal Military Retirement collectively represent almost half the expenditures in the category. **Welfare programs,** which are government programs that provide benefits to individuals based on their economic status, account for most of the rest.

Supplemental Security Income (SSI) A federal program that provides money to low-income people who are elderly, blind, or disabled who do not qualify for Social Security benefits.

The most important welfare programs are the Earned Income Tax Credit (EITC), Food Stamps, Supplemental Security Income (SSI), Temporary Assistance to Needy Families (TANF), and Medicaid, which was discussed earlier in the chapter. The **Earned Income Tax Credit (EITC)** is a federal program designed to give cash assistance to low-income working families by refunding some or all of the taxes they pay and, if their wages are low, giving them an additional refund. The **Food Stamp Program** is a federal program that provides vouchers to low-income families and individuals that can be used to purchase food. **Supplemental Security Income (SSI)** is a federal program that provides money to low-income people who are elderly, blind, or disabled who do not qualify for Social Security benefits. **Temporary Assistance for Needy Families (TANF)** is a federal program that provides temporary financial assistance and work opportunities to needy families.

Temporary Assistance for Needy Families (TANF) A federal program that provides temporary financial assistance and work opportunities to needy families.

Federal welfare policy changed in the mid-1990s with the adoption of welfare reform. Before 1996, the unofficial goal of the nation's welfare system was to provide welfare recipients with a minimum standard of living.[40] In 1996, Congress passed, and President Bill Clinton signed, sweeping welfare reform legislation that explicitly changed the underlying philosophy of American welfare policy. Instead of attempting to supply low-income individuals and families with cash and benefits sufficient to meet basic human needs, the goal of welfare reform was to move recipients from the welfare rolls to the workforce. The legislation limited the amount of time able-bodied adult recipients could draw benefits by placing a lifetime limit of five years on welfare assistance. Furthermore, childless adults between the ages of 18 and 50 could receive Food Stamps for no more than three months in any three-year period. Welfare reform instituted work requirements for welfare recipients. The heads of families on welfare would have to find work within two years or the family would lose benefits. It reduced the amount of federal money available for public assistance programs. Welfare reform also included a number of provisions aimed at changing the behavior of welfare recipients. To collect benefits, unmarried teenage mothers would have to live at home and stay in school. States were given the option to deny assistance to children born to welfare recipients in order to discourage welfare mothers from having additional children. The measure even offered a cash prize to the states that were most successful in reducing the number of children born outside of marriage.

 ## ? WHAT IS YOUR OPINION?

Should states cut off welfare benefits to women who have children while on welfare?

Welfare reform has shifted the focus of government assistance to the poor from cash benefits to services designed to help poor people get and keep jobs. Cash assistance now counts for less than half of all spending under TANF. Instead, states are using their welfare dollars to help meet the transportation needs of welfare recipients to get to work, address drug abuse and mental health problems, and provide child-care for single parents.[41]

Welfare reform has helped reduce the welfare rolls, but it has not eliminated poverty. As Figure 14.4 shows, the number of TANF recipients has fallen dramatically from 14.2 million in 1994 to 3.8 million in 2008. Government data show that most people leaving welfare find work and earn enough money so that they are better off than they were before.[42] Nonetheless, most of the people who have left welfare still rely heavily on public assistance, especially EITC, which is now larger than TANF, Food Stamps, or SSI.[43] Most of the people who have made their way off welfare lack the skills necessary to get jobs that pay much more than $7 or $8 an hour. As a result, they remain dependent on government assistance. The impact of welfare reform has been to change from a system that subsidized families unconditionally to one that subsidizes families in work. Although people who have left welfare are no longer totally dependent on the government for their livelihood, most of them still rely on government assistance. The new welfare debate centers on how government

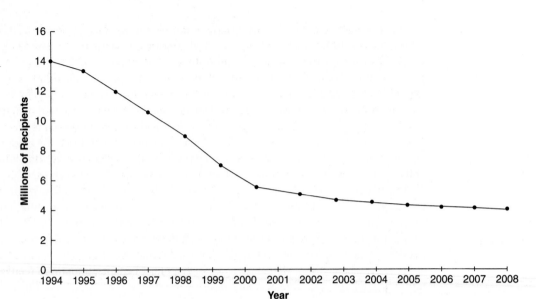

FIGURE 14.4   TANF Recipients, 1994–2008.
Source: Administration for Children and Families.

can best help the working poor, especially single-parent families headed by women, to rise above the poverty level.[44]

Interest on the Debt

Interest on the debt, which accounted for 7.9 percent of federal government expenditures in 2008, is the fifth largest spending category. When the federal budget is in deficit, the Department of the Treasury borrows money to close the gap between revenues and expenditures. Much of the money needed to cover the deficit is borrowed from surplus funds in other federal accounts, such as the Social Security Old Age and

Survivors Insurance (OASI) Trust Fund, which by law must be invested in U.S. Treasury securities. The government borrows the rest of the money from public sources, such as savings and loan institutions, corporations, insurance companies, commercial banks, state and local governments, foreign investors, foreign governments, and individual Americans. The national government does not have to pay interest on money borrowed from government accounts, but it does pay interest on debt that is held by the public. In mid-2008, the national debt stood at $9.6 trillion, including $5.4 trillion publicly held and $4.2 held in government accounts.[45] Because the federal budget deficit is growing, the share of the federal budget devoted to interest on the debt will likely increase relative to the budget as a whole for the near future.

FISCAL POLICYMAKING

Fiscal policy The use of government spending and taxation for the purpose of achieving economic goals.

Fiscal policy is the use of government spending and taxation for the purpose of achieving economic goals.

Ground Rules for Budgeting

Congress and the president must operate under certain ground rules as they formulate and adopt an annual budget.

Entitlement program A government program providing benefits to all persons qualified to receive them under law.

Entitlements   An **entitlement program** is a government program providing benefits to all persons qualified to receive them under law. Social Security, Medicare, Medicaid, unemployment compensation, Food Stamps, federal retirement programs, and most agriculture programs are entitlements. Spending for entitlement programs depends on the number of recipients collecting benefits. Anyone who qualifies for Social Security, for example, is entitled to collect benefits regardless of the budget. Consequently, the amount of money Congress and the president include in the annual budget for each entitlement program is a prediction of how much money the government will actually spend on the program rather than a policy decision about spending levels. If Congress and the president underestimate the amount of money needed, the funds will be spent anyway. Entitlement programs consume more than half of the federal budget.

Contractual Commitments   The budgetary discretion of Congress and the president is limited by contractual commitments made in previous years. Congress and the president often stretch weapons purchases over several years, contracting with the manufacturer to supply a certain number of ships or planes each year for several years. Money for the purchase must be included in each year's budget. Similarly, the federal government is legally committed to pay interest on the national debt.

Budget Agreements   Between 1990 and 2002, Congress and the president (first President George H. W. Bush and then President Clinton) prepared the annual budget on the basis of negotiated budget agreements that established spending limits for the part of the budget that is not predetermined because of entitlements or prior contractual agreements. The negotiated budget agreements set bottom-line budget limits but did not mandate spending amounts for individual budget items. The budget agreement negotiated between the president and Congress covering the period from 1990 through 2002 set strict spending caps for three spending areas—domestic, defense, and international expenditures—and prohibited shifting money among the categories.[46] As a result, the annual budget debate revolved around the distribution of a predetermined amount of money among items within the three categories. Instead of debating spending priorities between domestic and defense spending, for example, Congress and the president considered how to allocate budget resources among budget items within each category. The budget agreements also included a **PAYGO** provision, which is a pay-as-you-go budget rule that requires that any tax cut or spending increase be offset by tax increases or spending cuts elsewhere in the budget. In 2002, however, Congress and the president allowed the budget agreement to expire so they could adopt tax cuts and increase spending without adopting corresponding tax increases and budget reductions. Without the discipline of a budget agreement, federal spending increased dramatically, from 18.5 percent of GDP in 2001 to 20.7 percent in 2008.[47] Spending associated with homeland security, the war on terror, and wars in Iraq and Afghanistan drove up the cost of government, of course, but the absence of a budget agreement made it easier for Congress and the president to increase spending for education, agriculture, transportation, healthcare, and other programs. After winning control of Congress in the 2006 election, Democrats restored PAYGO, but Congress waived or circumvented the rule repeatedly rather than make tough decisions on spending and taxation.

PAYGO A pay-as-you-go budget rule that requires that any tax cut or spending increase be offset by tax increases or spending cuts elsewhere in the budget.

The Budget Process

The White House begins the process of formulating a budget in March, a year and a half before the start of the fiscal year, when the president sets economic goals and establishes overall revenue and expenditure levels. The president may map plans for spending initiatives in some areas, retrenchments in others.

Once the president has set administration priorities, the OMB sends spending guidelines to the various departments of the executive branch and directs them to prepare detailed budgets. Several months later, the agencies send the OMB their budget proposals, which are often over the original ceiling. The OMB questions the size of some of the spending requests, and the agencies respond by justifying their proposals. The head of the agency, the director of the OMB, and a member of the White House staff—and, perhaps, even the president—negotiate a final budget request for inclusion in a detailed budget proposal, which the president submits to Congress in January. The budget document, which is the size of a telephone book for a large city, includes specific spending recommendations to fund every agency of the federal government and for all federal activities.

Budget expenditures are classified as mandatory or discretionary. **Mandatory spending** refers to budgetary expenditures that are mandated by law, including entitlements and contractual commitments made in previous years. Interest on the debt is also mandatory spending because the government has no choice but to pay interest on money it has borrowed. **Discretionary spending** includes budgetary

Mandatory spending Budgetary expenditures that are mandated by law, including entitlements and contractual commitments made in previous years.

Discretionary spending Budgetary expenditures that are not mandated by law or contract, including annual funding for education, the Coast Guard, space exploration, highway construction, defense, foreign aid, and the Federal Bureau of Investigation (FBI).

expenditures that are not mandated by law or contract, including annual funding for education, the Coast Guard, space exploration, highway construction, defense, foreign aid, and the Federal Bureau of Investigation (FBI). More than 60 percent of total government expenditures are mandatory. The 2008 budget included $1.1 trillion in discretionary spending and $1.8 billion in mandatory expenditures.[48]

Appropriations process The procedure through which Congress legislatively allocates money for a particular purpose.

Discretionary expenditures must be approved through the **appropriations process,** which is the procedure through which Congress legislatively provides money for a particular purpose. Appropriation bills begin in the appropriations committees in each house although, by tradition, the House Appropriations Committee takes the lead in the process. Congress appropriates money annually. The House Appropriations Committee divides the discretionary part of the budget into 13 separate categories for assignment to its 13 subcommittees. Congress never reunites the budget into a single document; instead, it passes 13 separate appropriation bills. Spending for entitlement programs is included in the budget but does not go through the appropriations process.

Authorization process The procedure through which Congress legislatively establishes a program, defines its general purpose, devises procedures for its operation, specifies an agency to implement the program, and indicates an approximate level of funding for the program but does not actually provide money.

Spending programs must be authorized, regardless of whether they are entitlements or programs funded by discretionary spending. The **authorization process** is the procedure through which Congress legislatively establishes a program, defines its general purpose, devises procedures for its operation, specifies an agency to implement the program, and indicates an approximate level of funding for the program (but does *not* actually provide money). The standing legislative committees in each chamber, such as Agriculture and Armed Services, consider authorization bills. Congress may authorize a program for one year only or for several years. The budget timetable calls for Congress and the president to complete work on the budget by October 1, the beginning of the fiscal year. If Congress and the president have not agreed on appropriation legislation by then, Congress can either vote to continue government operations at their current funding rate or allow the government to shut down nonessential services.

Congress and the president adopt tax measures through the legislative process with the constitutional stipulation that revenue-raising bills must originate in the House. Consequently, tax legislation must pass the House before it passes the Senate. The Ways and Means Committee has jurisdiction over tax measures in the House. In the Senate, the Finance Committee considers tax bills.

MONETARY POLICYMAKING

Interest Money paid for the use of money.

Interest is money paid for the use of money. Most Americans are concerned about interest rates. Consumers pay interest on credit card debt and when they borrow money to purchase vehicles or homes. Investors earn interest on the money they save. Interest rates also affect the economy. Low interest rates encourage companies to borrow money to expand their operations. Low interest rates for automobile loans and home mortgage interest promote consumer automobile and home purchases. In contrast, high interest rates promote savings and discourage borrowing by business and consumers alike.

Many economists believe that the government can influence the performance of the nation's economy by adjusting interest rates. Increasing interest rates can cool inflation by slowing down economic activity, whereas cutting interest rates can stimulate economic growth. The government affects interest rates through its control of the money supply. **Monetary policy** is the control of the money supply for the purpose of achieving economic goals.

The **Federal Reserve Board (Fed)** is an independent regulatory commission that makes monetary policy. A seven-member board of governors, which is appointed by the president with Senate confirmation to serve fixed, overlapping terms of 14 years, heads the Fed, as the agency is often called. The president designates one member of the board as the chair to serve a four-year term, pending Senate confirmation. Alan Greenspan, who was first appointed by President Reagan, chaired the Fed from 1987 to 2006, having been re-appointed by President George H. W. Bush, President Clinton, and President George W. Bush. When Greenspan retired, President Bush appointed, and the Senate confirmed, economist Ben Bernanke as the new Fed chair.

Congress has ordered the Fed to make policy with the aim of achieving two goals: full employment and price stability. The **Federal Open Market Committee (FOMC)** is a committee of the Federal Reserve that meets eight times a year to review the economy and adjust monetary policy to achieving the goals. The FOMC is a 12-member group that includes the seven members of the Federal Reserve board; the president of the Federal Reserve Bank of New York; and 4 of the 11 other Federal Reserve Bank presidents, who serve on a rotating basis. If the FOMC determines that the demand for goods and services is growing faster than businesses can supply them, it tightens monetary supply to fight inflation. It does this by reducing the funds available to banks for loans and by raising interest rates to make businesses and individuals less willing to borrow money. In contrast, if the FOMC believes that businesses are not selling as many goods and services as they can produce and fewer people have jobs than want them, it eases monetary policy to prevent recession. It lowers interest rates by increasing the funds that banks can lend, hoping to encourage businesses and consumers to borrow to make purchases.

In 2008–2009, the Fed, under Chairman Bernanke's leadership, took extraordinary steps designed to avert the danger of the recession becoming a depression. After dropping interest rates to near zero, the Fed invoked emergency authority to lend money in hopes of jumpstarting the credit markets. The Fed made money available for auto loans, credit card loans, and home mortgages. In particular, the Fed purchased hundreds of billions of dollars in mortgage-related securities with the goal of lowering mortgage rates and encouraging home sales. Whereas critics charged that the Fed was exceeding its authority by risking billions of taxpayer dollars on questionable loans, the Fed's defenders said that its actions were necessary to save the economy.[49]

Monetary policy
The control of the money supply for the purpose of achieving economic goals.

Federal Reserve Board (Fed) An independent regulatory commission that makes monetary policy.

Federal Open Market Committee (FOMC) A committee of the Federal Reserve that meets eight times a year to review the economy and adjust monetary policy to achieving the goals.

CONCLUSION: ECONOMIC POLICYMAKING

The most important elements of the environment for economic policymaking are public opinion, the strength of the economy, and party control of the executive and legislative branches of government. Conventional wisdom holds that people "vote their pocketbooks," that is, they reelect incumbent officeholders if the economy is strong, but turn them out of office if the economy is weak. In this case, political

President George W. Bush appointed Ben Bernanke to head the Fed in 2006 after Allan Greenspan retired.

science research supports the conventional wisdom. Economic conditions have an important impact on voter choices.[50] Furthermore, many Americans are part of attentive publics for specific economic policy issues, such as Social Security, Medicare, tax reform, and agriculture policy.

The strength of the economy expands or limits the policy options available to economic policymakers. A growing economy generates revenue that can be used to fund new spending programs or provide tax cuts. Strong economic growth in the mid- and late 1990s did at least as much to eliminate the budget deficit as the policy choices of elected officials. In contrast, economic decline reduces the options available to policymakers. Although the president and Congress may want to respond to a recession by cutting taxes or increasing government programs to help the unemployed, they will not have the money to fund tax cuts or new programs unless they borrow it.

It matters which party controls Congress. Democrats generally back policies designed to assist their traditional support groups: organized labor, inner-city voters, and lower- and middle-income families. Republicans, meanwhile, steer economic policy to benefit their support groups: businesspeople and professionals, suburban voters, and middle- and upper-income families. When Congress and the presidency are in the hands of different parties, economic policy typically reflects compromise between the parties.

Agenda Building

A number of political actors participate in elevating economic issues to the official policy agenda. Candidates often highlight economic issues during election campaigns. Ross Perot made deficit reduction a major talking point when he ran for president as an independent in 1992 and 1996. Bill Clinton stressed welfare reform when he first ran for president, promising to "end welfare as we know it." George W. Bush promised to cut taxes during his presidential campaign in 2000. Barack Obama stressed health-care reform.

Interest groups frequently emphasize economic issues. The **AARP,** an interest group representing the interests of older Americans, stresses the need to preserve Social Security and Medicare. Business groups are concerned about tax issues. Farm groups, such as the American Farm Bureau, lobby for farm support programs.

AARP An interest group representing the concerns of older Americans (formerly known as the American Association of Retired Persons).

Policy Formulation and Adoption

Economic policy formulation takes place in congressional committees, executive branch agencies, and the White House. It involves officials from all levels of government as well as a wide range of interest group participants. The president and the president's staff, department heads, and the OMB prepare detailed budget proposals for submission to Congress. The appropriations committees in each house draft budget legislation; standing committees work on authorization measures. The Ways and Means Committee in the House and the Finance Committee in the Senate deal with tax measures. Conference committees iron out the final details for most appropriation bills, tax measures, and authorization bills. The Federal Reserve Board formulates monetary policy.

Individual members of Congress focus on issues important to their states and districts. Farm-belt senators and representatives pay special attention to legislation affecting agriculture. Members with defense bases or defense industries in their districts are concerned with the defense appropriation. Senators and representatives are also interested in special projects that benefit their states and districts. **Earmarks** are provisions that direct that funds be spent for particular purposes. In 2008, Congress earmarked almost $8 billion for special projects, including money for water resource development, local transportation projects, tourist attractions, and special projects for colleges and universities.[51] The opponents of earmarks charge that they are nothing more than **pork barrel spending,** which are expenditures to fund local projects that are not critically important from a national perspective are known as. John McCain promised to end earmarking when he ran for president in 2008. Other members of Congress defend earmarks, noting that they have funded many worthwhile projects, including most federal breast cancer research and the Boys & Girls Clubs of America. Moreover, the congressional leadership uses earmarks to win support for appropriation bills that might not otherwise pass.[52]

Earmarks Legislative provisions that direct that funds be spent for particular purposes.

Pork barrel spending Expenditures to fund local projects that are not critically important from a national perspective.

Interest groups also take part in policy formulation. Corporations lobby Congress to affect the impact of tax policies on their firms. Weapons manufacturers attempt to influence decisions on defense spending. AARP participates in negotiations over reform of the Medicare program and changes in Social Security.

The executive and legislative branches of American national government are primarily responsible for the adoption of fiscal policy. The judiciary plays relatively little role. Congress and the president create government programs and appropriate money to fund them. They raise funds through taxation and borrowing. In the meantime, the Fed adopts monetary policies through its rulemaking process.

Tax Breaks for College Students

The Hope Credit and Lifetime Learning Credit are tax breaks for college students. Your assignment is to research the tax rules to determine whether you or your parents can benefit from these credits. You can find information about the Hope Credit and the Lifetime Learning Credit from official publications available at the local IRS office or online at the IRS website, www.irs.gov. Research these tax breaks for college students, review your family's tax situation, and answer the following questions:

1. How do the Hope Credit and Lifetime Learning Credit programs differ?

2. Do you have to be a full-time student to benefit?

3. Are the credits available for both public and private schools or for public-school students only?

4. If parents have two children in college at the same time, can they claim a tax credit for both of them?

5. Can you claim the cost of this textbook as an educational expense? Why or why not?

6. Do you or your parents qualify for either the Hope Credit or the Lifetime Learning Credit? Why or why not?

7. If you qualify for either the Hope Credit or the Lifetime Learning Credit, how will the credit affect your tax liability? Explain.

8. Did you or your parents claim a credit last year? Will you claim it next year?

Policy Implementation and Evaluation

The implementation of economic policy involves nearly the whole of government in America. The Treasury Department, especially the IRS, is responsible for tax collection and borrowing. The Federal Reserve and its member banks implement monetary policy. Money is spent by the agencies of the executive branch and, through federal programs, by an array of state and local governments. State governments, for example, are responsible for implementing federal transportation policies, Medicaid, and most welfare programs.

Congress and the president often leave considerable discretion to officials who implement economic policies. Welfare reform initially allowed states considerable flexibility to design their welfare programs. For example, states could grant hardship exemptions to individual recipients who had exhausted their benefits or were unable to find work. In general, the legislation set goals and allowed state governments to develop their own strategies for achieving the goals. States who met the goals would receive financial rewards; states falling short of goals would suffer penalties. When Congress reauthorized welfare reform in 2006, however, it tightened the definitions of work and work-related activities, reducing state flexibility.[53]

Congress and the president sometimes overturn policy implementation decisions made by federal agencies and state officials. Consider the history of Supplemental Security Income (SSI) for disabled children. In 1972, Congress included a provision in a welfare bill stating that children would be eligible for SSI payments if they had a "medically determinable physical or mental impairment of comparable severity" to impairments that made adults eligible for SSI. Congress did not define the term *comparable severity*, leaving that task to the Social Security Administration

(SSA), which wrote regulations establishing eligibility criteria that were then enforced by state officials. After years of complaints by constituents that eligibility rules were too strict, Congress ordered states to make it easier for children to qualify for payments and the number of children receiving SSI benefits more than tripled in a little over five years. To reduce costs, Congress ordered the states to tighten the eligibility standard, reversing the position it had taken just a few years earlier.[54]

Both the executive and legislative branches of American government have mechanisms for evaluating economic policy. The OMB assesses the operation of programs within the executive branch for the president, whereas the Government Accountability Office (GAO) performs a similar role for Congress, investigating agency activities and auditing expenditures. Outside of the GAO, however, efforts at oversight are haphazard and unsystematic. Furthermore, when they do occur, they tend to focus on nickel-and-dime matters, such as expense accounts and limousine use, or on well-publicized abuses, such as cost overruns on weapons systems purchased by the Pentagon.

The George W. Bush administration adopted a new method of evaluating how efficiently agencies spend their financial resources, using a scorekeeping system based on traffic lights—a green light for success, yellow for mixed results, and red for unsatisfactory progress. The administration promised to use the system to help determine each agency's slice of the budgetary pie. In theory, the system improved government efficiency by rewarding good performance and punishing failure.[55]

KEY TERMS

AARP

ability to pay theory of taxation

appropriations process

authorization process

baby-boom generation

balanced budget

budget deficit

budget surplus

Consumer Price Index (CPI)

cost-of-living adjustment (COLA)

depression

discretionary spending

earmarks

Earned Income Tax Credit (EITC)

entitlement program

estate tax

excise taxes

Federal Open Market Committee (FOMC)

Federal Reserve Board (Fed)

fiscal policy

fiscal year

flat tax

Food Stamp Program

gross domestic product (GDP)

income redistribution

inflation

interest

mandatory spending

means-tested program

Medicaid

Medicare

monetary policy

national debt

PAYGO

pork barrel spending

privatization

progressive tax

proportional tax

recession

regressive tax

sales tax

Social Security

subsidy

Supplemental Security Income (SSI)

supply-side economics

tax credit

tax deduction

tax exemption

tax incidence

tax preference

Temporary Assistance for Needy Families (TANF)

welfare programs

welfare state

NOTES

1. Bureau of Labor Statistics, available at www.bls.gov.
2. Michael Comiskey and Pawan Madhogarhia, "Unraveling the Financial Crisis of 2008," *PS: Political Science & Politics*, April 2009, pp. 271–275.
3. Office of Management and Budget, *Fiscal Year 2009, Mid-Session Review*, available at www.omb.gov.
4. Jacob S. Hacker, "Privatizing Risk without Privatizing the Welfare State: The Hidden Politics of Social Policy Retrenchment in the United States," *American Political Science Review* 98 (May 2004): 251–256.
5. James Bovard, "The 1995 Farm Bill Follies," *Regulation*, 1995, p. 69.
6. Environmental Working Group, "Farm Subsidy Database," April 14, 2008, available at www.farm.ewg.org.
7. Randal R. Rucker and E. C. Pasour, Jr., "The Growth of U.S. Farm Programs," in Price V. Fishback, et. al., *Government & the American Economy: A New History* (Chicago: University of Chicago Press, 2007), p. 483.
8. Chris J. Dolan, John Frendreis, and Raymond Tatalovich, *The Presidency and Economic Policy* (Lanham, MD: Rowman & Littlefield, 2008), p. 3.
9. Albert B. Crenshaw, "Is a Simpler Tax Code in America's Future?" *Washington Post National Weekly Edition*, May 7–13, 2001, p. 20.
10. Office of Management and Budget, *Budget of the United States Government, Analytical Perspectives, Fiscal Year, 2007*, available at www.omb.gov.
11. Office of Management and Budget, *The Budget for Fiscal Year 2009, Historical Tables*, available at www.omb.gov.
12. U.S. Census Bureau, "Gross Public Debt, Expenditures, and Receipts by Country: 1990–2006," *The 2008 Statistical Abstract*, available at www.census.gov.
13. Anthony J. Cataldo II and Arline A. Savage, *U.S. Individual Federal Income Taxation: Historical, Contemporary, and Prospective Policy Issues* (Oxford, UK: Elsevier Science, 2001), pp. 39–40.
14. Office of Management and Budget, *Fiscal Year 2009, Mid-Session Review*.
15. Joseph A. Pechman, *Federal Tax Policy*, 5th ed. (Washington, DC: Brookings Institution, 1987), p. 5.
16. Wojciech Bieńkowski, Josef C. Brada, and Mariusz-Jan Radto, *Reaganomics Goes Global: What Can the EU, Russia, and Other Transition Countries Learn from the USA?* (New York: Palgrave MacMillan, 2006), p. 69.
17. Lori Montgomery, "The Bush Tax Cuts, Revisited," *Washington Post National Weekly Edition*, April 7–13, 2008, p. 23.
18. "The Agenda: Taxes," at www.whitehouse.gov.
19. Congressional Budget Office, available at www.cbo.gov.
20. Matthew Benjamin, "Cost of U.S. Crisis Action Grows, Along with Debt," October 10, 2008, available at www.bloomberg.com.
21. Catherine E. Rudder, "The Politics of Taxing and Spending in Congress: Ideas, Strategy, and Policy," in Lawrence C. Dodd and Bruce I. Oppenheimer, *Congress Reconsidered*, 8th ed. (Washington, DC: CQ Press, 2005), pp. 319–342.
22. Michael E. Bradley, "The Inexorable Rise of the National Debt," in Phillip John Davies, ed., *An American Quarter Century: U.S. Politics from Vietnam to Clinton* (Manchester, UK: Manchester University Press, 1995), pp. 59–61.
23. Office of Management and Budget, *Fiscal Year 2009, Mid-Session Review*.
24. Congressional Budget Office, "CBO's March 2008 Baseline: Medicare," available at www.cbo.gov.
25. Robert Pear, "Medicare Costs to Increase for Wealthier Beneficiaries," *New York Times*, September 11, 2006, available at www.nytimes.com.
26. Centers for Medicare and Medicaid Services, available at www.cms.hhs.gov.
27. Congressional Budget Office, "Budget Options," available at www.cbo.gov.
28. Edmund L. Andrews, "Sharp Increase in Tax Revenue Will Pare U.S. Deficit," *New York Times*, July 13, 2005, available at www.nytimes.com.
29. *Social Security and Medicare Boards of Trustees 2008 Annual Reports*, available at www.ssa.gov.
30. Ibid.
31. Congressional Budget Office, "Fact Sheet for CBO's March 2008 Baseline: Medicaid," available at www.cbo.gov.
32. Donald B. Marron, "Medicaid Spending Growth and Options for Controlling Costs," Testimony before the Senate Select Committee on Aging, available at www.cbo.gov.
33. "Social Security," Gallup Poll, available at www.gallup.com.
34. Social Security Administration, available at www.ssa.gov.
35. Jesse J. Holland, "Raise Retirement Age to Save Social Security?" *Business Week*, August 1, 2008, available at www.businessweek.com.
36. *Social Security and Medicare Boards of Trustees 2008 Annual Reports*.
37. Social Security Administration, Trust Fund Data, available at www.ssa.gov.
38. *Social Security and Medicare Boards of Trustees 2008 Annual Reports*.
39. June O'Neill, "The Trust Fund, the Surplus, and the Real Social Security Problem," in Michael D. Tanner, ed., *Social Security and Its Discontents: Perspectives on Choice* (Washington, DC: CATO Institute, 2004), pp. 37–38.
40. William A. Kelso, *Poverty and the Underclass: Challenging Perceptions of the Poor in America* (New York: New York University Press, 1994), p. 4.
41. Robert Pear, "Welfare Spending Shows Huge Shift from Checks to Services," *New York Times*, October 13, 2003, available at www.nytimes.com.
42. U.S. Department of Health and Human Services, Office of Family Assistance, Temporary Assistance for Needy Families, *Sixth Annual Report to Congress*, November 2004, available at www.acf.hhs.gov.

43. Congressional Budget Office, "The Budget and Economic Outlook: An Update."

44. Jonathan Walters, "Is Welfare Working?" *Governing*, February 2008, pp. 28–33.

45. Bureau of the Public Debt, available at www.treasurydirect .gov.

46. Roger H. Davidson and Walter J. Oleszek, *Congress and Its Members*, 7th ed. (Washington, DC: CQ Press, 2000), p. 372.

47. Office of Management and Budget, *Budget of the United States Government, Fiscal Year 2009*.

48. Ibid.

49. Neil Irwin, "The Revolutionary: Bernenke Reinvented the Federal Reserve after the Financial Collapse," *Washington Post National Weekly Edition*, April 13–19, 2008, pp. 6–7.

50. Alan I. Abramowitz, "Can McCain Overcome the Triple Whammy?" May 29, 2008, Larry J. Sabato's Crystal Ball 2008, available at www.centerforpolitics.org.

51. Carl Hulse, "Congress is Still Pursuing Earmarks," *New York Times*, December 20, 2007, available at www.nytimes.com.

52. Jonathan Weisman, "Bush Puts the Kibosh on Lawmakers' Pet Projects—Later," *Washington Post National Weekly Edition*, February 4–10, 2008, p. 7.

53. Sheri Steisel and Jack Tweedle, "TANF Rules Tough on States," *State Legislatures*, March 2006, p. 23.

54. Eileen Shanahan, "Devolution and the Blame Game," *Governing*, January 1996, p. 13.

55. Donald F. Kettl, "Government by Traffic Light," *Governing*, April 2002, p. 12.

Chapter 15

Civil Liberties Policymaking

CHAPTER OUTLINE

The Constitutional Basis of Civil Liberties
Policymaking
    The U.S. Constitution
    State Constitutions

Civil Liberties Issues and Policies
    Government and Religion
    Freedom of Expression
    Privacy Rights

Due Process of Law and the Rights of
the Accused
Executive Authority, Civil Liberties, and the
War on Terror

Conclusion: Civil Liberties Policymaking
    Agenda Building
    Policy Formulation and Adoption
    Policy Implementation and Evaluation

LEARNING OUTCOMES

After studying Chapter 15, students should be able
to do the following:

▸ Describe the significance of the following
landmark Supreme Court decisions: *Everson v.
Board of Ewing Township*, *Engel v. Vitale*,
Employment Division v. Smith, *Roe v. Wade*,
Lawrence v. Texas, *Miranda v. Arizona*, *Gideon v.
Wainwright*, and *Gregg v. Georgia*. (pp. 407–408,
410, 417–418, 420, and 422–423)

▸ Identify the civil liberties policy issues raised by
the detention of José Padilla. (pp. 402–403)

▸ Identify the sections of the U.S. Constitution
that have had the greatest impact on civil
liberties policymaking. (pp. 403–405)

▸ Distinguish between fundamental constitutional
rights and other rights. (pp. 404–405)

▸ Describe the relationship between government
and religion, focusing on issues related both to
the establishment of religion and the free
exercise of religion. (pp. 405–411)

▸ Compare and contrast the constitutional
status of high-value and low-value expression.
(pp. 411–412)

▸ Compare and contrast the constitutional status
of expression that is content-neutral, content-
specific, and viewpoint-specific. (pp. 411–413)

▸ Describe government policy relative to the free
expression of ideas, focusing on the following
types of expression: statements of anti-
government views, expression that might lead
to a disruption of the public order, and symbolic
expression. (pp. 413–416)

▸ Evaluate the constitutionality of government
efforts to prevent the expression of ideas.
(pp. 413–414)

▸ Assess the arguments for and against hate
crimes legislation. (pp. 414–415)

▸ Trace the development of a constitutional right
of privacy, considering both abortion rights and
gay rights. (pp. 416–418)

▶ Describe the current status of constitutional law regarding the following issues: searches and seizures, the exclusionary rule, the *Miranda* warning, double jeopardy, fair trial, and cruel and unusual punishments. (pp. 419–422)

▶ Describe the status of capital punishment in the United States. (pp. 422–424)

▶ Identify the constitutional issues raised by the Bush administration's conduct of the war on terror. (pp. 424–426)

▶ Analyze civil liberties policymaking using the public policy model. (pp. 426–428)

▶ Define the key terms listed on pages 428–429 and explain their significance.

In May 2002, José Padilla arrived in Chicago on a plane from Pakistan only to be taken into custody by federal law enforcement officials. A month later, Attorney General John Ashcroft announced that the government was holding Padilla in a naval prison off the coast of South Carolina as an "enemy combatant," allied with al Qaeda, the international terrorist organization led by Osama bin Laden. The attorney general alleged that Padilla was part of a terrorist plot to build and explode a radioactive "dirty bomb" in the United States. A dirty bomb is a conventional bomb equipped with radioactive material designed to spread over a wide area. Even though Padilla was an American citizen, Ashcroft indicated that he would be held indefinitely without access to an attorney or opportunity to defend himself in court.[1]

Attorney General Ashcroft and President George W. Bush defended the decision to hold Padilla, saying that he had trained with al Qaeda and was returning to the United States to do harm. "This guy Padilla is a bad guy," said Bush, "and he is where he needs to be, detained."[2] If the government were forced to grant Padilla a public trial, it would have to reveal the sources of its information and thereby undermine the war against terrorism. The government also argued that constitutional standards should not apply when national security is at stake. Should the government be required to prove guilt beyond a reasonable doubt before it can hold someone that may be plotting a terrorist attack?

President Bush justified his actions in detaining Padilla and the others on the basis of his executive authority as commander-in-chief. Bush declared that the president has the constitutional power to designate citizens or aliens as enemy combatants and detain them indefinitely. The president also signed an executive order allowing foreign nationals suspected of terrorism to be tried secretly by military courts that would not operate under the standards of American courts. Defendants would not necessarily have the right to an attorney of their choice or be allowed to challenge evidence used against them. The military courts could convict defendants based on a standard less than the usual standard in criminal cases and juries would not have to reach a unanimous verdict. Defendants might not even have the right of appeal.[3]

The arrest of José Padilla illustrates the dilemma of a democracy at war. How can a free society protect itself against its enemies without restricting freedoms that are a fundamental part of democracy? Administration critics charged that the decision to hold Padilla and other American citizens and permanent residents without charges and trial undermined the values that the nation purports to defend. The U.S. Constitution protects Americans from the excessive power of government. As a citizen, Padilla has a constitutional right to be charged with a crime or released. He is entitled to an attorney and enjoys the presumption of innocence. If the president can take away Padilla's rights without direct congressional authorization or any sort of judicial process, then the freedom of all Americans is threatened.

This chapter on civil liberties is another in a series of chapters that focus on particular areas of public policy. Chapter 14 examined economic policymaking. The next chapter in the series, Chapter 16, deals with civil rights. Finally, Chapter 17 considers foreign and defense policymaking.

THE CONSTITUTIONAL BASIS OF CIVIL LIBERTIES POLICYMAKING

Civil liberties The protection of the individual from the unrestricted power of government.

Civil liberties concern the protection of the individual from the unrestricted power of government. Civil liberties policymaking takes place within the context of the U.S. Constitution and, to a lesser but still important extent, state constitutions as well.

The U.S. Constitution

Bill of Rights A constitutional document guaranteeing individual rights and liberties. The U.S. Bill of Rights is the first ten amendments to the U.S. Constitution.

The Bill of Rights and the Fourteenth Amendment are the most important constitutional provisions affecting civil liberties policymaking. The **Bill of Rights,** which is contained in the first ten amendments to the Constitution, is a constitutional document guaranteeing individual rights and liberties. Initially, the Bill of Rights restricted the national government but not the states. It prohibited Congress from passing laws abridging the freedom of speech, for example, but it did not affect the actions of state and local governments.

The Due Process Clause of the Fourteenth Amendment provided the mechanism by which the U.S. Supreme Court eventually applied most of the provisions of the Bill of Rights to the states. Section 1 of the Fourteenth Amendment reads as follows: "No State shall . . . deprive any person of life, liberty, or property, without due process of law." The Supreme Court has interpreted the word *liberty* in the Due Process Clause to include most of the individual rights and liberties protected by the Bill of Rights. As a result, most of the provisions of the Bill of Rights now apply not just to the national government but to state and local governments as well. The process through which the U.S. Supreme Court interpreted the Due Process Clause of the Fourteenth Amendment of the U.S. Constitution to apply most of the provisions of the national Bill of Rights to the states is known as the **selective incorporation of the Bill of Rights against the states.** If Congress passed a law abridging freedom of speech, it would violate the First Amendment. If a state legislature enacted a similar law, it would violate both the Fourteenth and the First Amendments because the Due Process Clause of the Fourteenth Amendment applies the provisions of the First Amendment to the states.

Selective incorporation of the Bill of Rights against the states The process through which the U.S. Supreme Court interpreted the Due Process Clause of the Fourteenth Amendment of the U.S. Constitution to apply most of the provisions of the national Bill of Rights to the states.

The Supreme Court has held that the guarantees of the Bill of Rights are not absolute. Note the wording of the Due Process Clause: "No State shall . . . deprive any person of life, liberty, or property, *without due process of law*" (emphasis added). The Supreme Court has interpreted the Constitution to allow government restrictions on individual rights and liberties when government can demonstrate sufficient reason.

TABLE 15.1   Fundamental Rights

- Freedom of speech
- Freedom of press
- Freedom of assembly
- Separation of church and state
- Guarantee against unreasonable searches and seizures
- Guarantee against compulsory self-incrimination
- Right to confront witnesses
- Right to have a compulsory process for obtaining witnesses
- Right to reproduce (not be sterilized)
- Right to teach and study
- Right to travel
- Freedom of association
- Freedom of petition
- Freedom of religion
- Guarantee against taking private property without just compensation
- Guarantee against double jeopardy
- Right to counsel
- Right to a speedy trial
- Right to a trial by jury
- Right to be free from cruel and unusual punishments
- Right to privacy
- Right to vote
- Right to terminate pregnancy

Source: Milton R. Konvitz, *Fundamental Rights: History of a Constitutional Doctrine* (New Brunswick, NJ: Transaction Publishers, 2001), pp. 157–164.

Furthermore, the Bill of Rights only applies to the actions of government, not those of individuals or private employers. Consider the controversy surrounding Don Imus, the former radio talk show host of "Imus in the Morning." CBS canceled the show after Imus referred to the members of the Rutgers University women's basketball team as "nappy-headed hos." Because of the First Amendment's guarantee of freedom of expression, the government could not fine Imus or put him in jail because of his views. The Constitution did not protect him, however, from losing his job because of his statements.

The Supreme Court has determined that some rights are more important than other rights. A **fundamental right** is a constitutional right that is so important that government cannot restrict it unless it can demonstrate a compelling or overriding public interest for so doing. Table 15.1 lists the rights that the U.S. Supreme Court has identified as fundamental rights. To restrict rights that are not fundamental, government need only show that it is acting in pursuit of a legitimate public purpose. Suppose a city government prohibited both holding political rallies and drinking alcoholic beverages in a public park. Because the U.S. Supreme Court has recognized freedom of expression as a fundamental right, the city would have to show a compelling or overriding public interest in prohibiting political rallies for that policy to survive legal challenge. In contrast, because the Supreme Court has

Fundamental right A constitutional right that is so important that government cannot restrict it unless it can demonstrate a compelling or overriding public interest for so doing.

not held that drinking alcoholic beverages is a fundamental right, the city government would only need to demonstrate a legitimate public purpose to justify its policy on alcohol consumption.

State Constitutions

State constitutions affect civil liberties policymaking as well. In America's federal system of government, states must grant their residents all the rights guaranteed by the U.S. Constitution (as interpreted by the Supreme Court). If state governments so choose, they may offer their residents *more* rights than afforded in the U.S. Constitution.[4] All state constitutions include bills of rights, many of which are longer and use more expansive language than the national document. Since 1970, state supreme courts around the nation have issued hundreds of rulings in which they have granted broader rights protection under state constitutions than the U.S. Supreme Court has allowed under the U.S. Constitution.

 WHAT IS YOUR OPINION?

Do you think there will ever be a compromise solution to the issue of abortion that satisfies both sides? What would that be?

CIVIL LIBERTIES ISSUES AND POLICIES

Civil liberties policies reflect judicial response to policy initiatives taken by legislatures and executives at the state and national levels of government. Although Congress, the president, federal agencies, states, and local governments are all involved in civil liberties policymaking, the judicial branch of government, particularly the Supreme Court of the United States, establishes the limits of policy by formulating and adopting constitutional law for each policy area. **Constitutional law** is law that involves the interpretation and application of the Constitution. It is the highest form of law, superseding both **statutory law,** which is law that is written by a legislature, and **administrative law,** which refers to administrative rules adopted by regulatory agencies.

Constitutional law Law that involves the interpretation and application of the Constitution.

Statutory law Law that is written by the legislature.

Administrative law Administrative rules adopted by regulatory agencies.

Government and Religion

The First Amendment addresses the relationship between church and state with these well-known words: "Congress shall make no law respecting an establishment of religion, or prohibiting the free exercise thereof." The provision has two separate and distinct elements. On one hand, the First Amendment prohibits the establishment of religion. It concerns the degree to which the government may constitutionally support religion or promote religious belief. On the other hand, the First Amendment prohibits the government from interfering with the free exercise of religion. It addresses the extent to which government actions may constitutionally interfere with individual religious practice.

GLOBAL PERSPECTIVE

Population Policy in China

With a population of more than 1.3 billion people, China is the most populous country in the world. Because of medical advances and nutritional improvements, life expectancy in China has increased dramatically and the population has more than doubled since 1949. Chinese families have traditionally been large because Chinese couples want children to care for them when they are old. Male children are especially prized because sons traditionally live near their parents, whereas daughters marry and leave home. Chinese couples want to bear sons because their daughters-in-law will care for them in their old age, whereas their daughters will be caring for someone else.[*]

The Chinese government believes that population control is a prerequisite for economic development. Rapid population growth strains the nation's agricultural resources and contributes to the shortage of adequate housing. Substantial economic growth is necessary just to provide jobs for the growing population.

Since the 1980s, the government has implemented a one-child policy. Couples are to bear no more than one child unless they receive permission from the government based on special circumstances. Some local officials have taken drastic steps to enforce the policy, including forced abortions, sterilization for women who have too many children, and destroying the assets of families that are too large. Because of the cultural preference for male children, some families abort female children. According to Chinese demographic figures, the ratio of male to female children under the age of five in China is 117 to 100. According to the International Planned Parenthood Federation, China aborts 7 million fetuses a year, and about 70 percent are female. Chinese families apparently abandon millions of other girls to state-run orphanages.[†]

The population policy has worked more effectively in urban centers than in rural areas. In urban areas, women average only one child, whereas rural women have two or more children.[‡] Urban couples more readily comply with the policy because they are more subject to government sanctions than are people living in the countryside. Traditional cultural practices are also stronger in rural China than they are in urban centers.

QUESTIONS TO CONSIDER

1. How does China's population policy compare and contrast with America's abortion policy?
2. Would you expect a democracy to adopt a population policy similar to China's policy?
3. Do you believe that the need for economic development is sufficient to justify China's population policy?

[*]Alan Hunter and John Sexton, *Contemporary China* (London: MacMillan Press, 1999), pp. 59–60.

[†]Beth Nonte Russell, "The Mystery of the Chinese Baby Shortage," *New York Times*, January 23, 2007, available at www.nytimes.com.

[‡]Cecilia Nathansen Milwertz, *Accepting Population Control: Urban Chinese Women and the One-Child Family Policy* (Richmond Surrey, UK: Curzon Press, 1997), p. 11.

Establishment of Religion   The First Amendment prohibits government from making laws "respecting an establishment of religion." Historians agree that the authors of this provision intended to prohibit the naming of an official state church, but they disagree as to what other forms of church/state involvement constitute establishment. Some experts believe that the framers intended to build a wall of separation between church and state. The affairs of government and the affairs of religion should never intermix. In contrast, other scholars argue that the founders never envisioned so extreme an interpretation of the Establishment Clause. They believe that the authors of the Constitution favored a society in which government would accommodate the interests of religion, especially Christian religion.[5]

 WHAT IS YOUR OPINION?

Do you believe in the strict separation of government and religion, or should the government accommodate the interests of religion?

The Supreme Court has adopted a middle ground on the issue of establishment of religion, attempting to balance the concerns of groups favoring a strict separation of church and state and the values of groups calling for accommodation between government and religion.[6] Consider the controversy over state aid to parochial schools. Parents who send their children to private, church-supported schools frequently complain that they pay twice for education, once when they pay school taxes and a second time when they pay parochial school tuition. Parochial school systems save taxpayers millions of dollars. Besides, many church-related schools desperately need financial aid. On the opposite side of the issue are those individuals and groups who contend that tax money should not be used to support religious education.

The battle over public assistance to parochial schools generally begins in state legislatures and school boards but winds up in the federal courts. In 1941, the New Jersey legislature authorized school districts to subsidize the transportation of students to and from school and, if districts chose, to extend the aid to parochial school students as well. When Ewing Township did just that, a taxpayer named Everson sued, challenging the constitutionality of the action. The Supreme Court's decision in *Everson v. Board of Ewing Township* set an important precedent on the meaning of the Establishment Clause. The Court ruled that New Jersey's transportation plan was constitutional because it had a "secular legislative purpose"—safe transportation for school children—and "neither advance[d] nor inhibit[ed] religion." Thus, the Court created a standard for determining the constitutionality of state aid to parochial schools: Aid that serves a public purpose is constitutional; aid that serves a religious purpose is not.[7]

The controversy over parental choice and school vouchers is a recent manifestation of the battle over public funding for church-related schools. **Parental choice** is an educational reform aimed at improving the quality of schools by allowing parents to select the school their children will attend. The theory behind the concept is that public schools will have to improve in order to hang onto students and funding. Under a parental choice program, the state gives parents a voucher that provides a type of scholarship to be paid to the school that the parents choose for their child to attend. Some parental choice programs allow parents to select not only among public schools but also among private schools, including parochial schools. For example, the state of Ohio created a parental choice program for low-income families attending the Cleveland City School District. Students who qualified could attend the private school of their parents' choice or a public school in an adjacent district and receive tuition assistance grants from the state. Although the overwhelming majority of private schools chosen by parents for student transfer were religiously affiliated, the U.S. Supreme Court ruled the program constitutional. The Court upheld the program because it had a valid secular purpose (providing educational

Parental choice
An educational reform aimed at improving the quality of schools by allowing parents to select the school their children will attend.

assistance to poor children in a weak school system), it was neutral toward religion (parents could choose any private school or even another public school), and it provided assistance to families rather than to the schools.[8]

School prayer is perhaps the most controversial Establishment Clause issue. In *Engel v. Vitale* (1962), the Supreme Court ruled that the daily classroom recitation of a prayer written by New York's state board of regents violated the First Amendment. "[I]t is no part of the business of government to compose official prayers for any group of the American people to recite as part of a religious program carried on by the government," declared the Court. Furthermore, it was irrelevant that the prayer was voluntary and students were not forced to recite it. "When the power, prestige, and financial support of government [are] placed behind a particular religious belief," the Court said, "the indirect coercive pressure upon religious minorities to conform to the prevailing officially approved religion is plain."[9]

 WHAT IS YOUR OPINION?

Do you agree with the Supreme Court's decision in Engel v. Vitale? *Why or why not?*

The Supreme Court has consistently ruled against government efforts to introduce religious observances into the public schools. The Court struck down a Pennsylvania law requiring the reading of verses from the Bible each day in public school[10] and a Kentucky law requiring that a copy of the Ten Commandments be posted in every public school classroom in the state.[11] It invalidated an Alabama "moment of silence" set aside "for meditation or voluntary prayer"[12] and ruled against benedictions and invocations at public-school graduation ceremonies.[13]

The U.S. Supreme Court declared that the student-led invocations before football games in Santa Fe, Texas, violated the Establishment Clause of the Constitution.

Consider the school prayer controversy in Santa Fe, Texas. The school district allowed students at Santa Fe High School to vote on whether to have an "invocation" before home football games and then held a second election to select a student to deliver the prayer. The district stipulated that the invocation had to be nonsectarian and that the student could not attempt to convert other students to her religion. Two families—one Mormon and the other Catholic—sued the school district and the case reached the Supreme Court in 2000. The Court's majority ruled that the invocation was an unconstitutional infringement on the Establishment Clause, rejecting the school district's argument that the student delivering the invocation was exercising her free speech rights. "The delivery of a message such as the invocation here—on school property, at school-sponsored events, over the school's public address system, by a speaker representing the student body, under the supervision of school faculty, and pursuant to a school policy that explicitly and implicitly encourages public prayer—is not properly characterized as 'private' speech."[14]

The Supreme Court is divided over the constitutionality of public displays of religious symbols that do not specifically target impressionable youths. In 2005, the Court ruled that a six-foot-tall monument of the Ten Commandments on the grounds of the Texas Capital was constitutional while holding that the display of framed copies of the Commandments on the walls of two courthouses in Kentucky was unconstitutional. The vote in each case was 5–4. The Fraternal Order of Eagles gave the Ten Commandments monument to the state of Texas more than 40 years ago with the hope of reducing juvenile delinquency. The Court held that its display was constitutional because it was erected to achieve a valid secular purpose—reducing juvenile delinquency—rather than advancing religion.[15] In contrast, the Court ruled against the Kentucky display because it determined that the county governments in Kentucky that posted the Ten Commandments did so in order to advance a religious agenda, which was a violation of the Establishment Clause.[16]

Free Exercise of Religion   The First Amendment prohibits the adoption of laws interfering with the free exercise of religion. In practice, disputes concerning free exercise fall under two general categories. The first category involves the deliberate effort of government to restrict the activities of small, controversial religious groups. Many localities have also enacted local laws aimed at preventing Jehovah's Witnesses and other religious groups from distributing religious literature door to door. The Supreme Court has upheld these sorts of restrictions on religious practice only when the government has been able to justify its action on the basis of a compelling or overriding government interest that could not be achieved in a less restrictive fashion. Because the compelling interest test is a high standard, the Supreme Court more often than not has struck down laws and regulations aimed against particular religions or religious practices. The Court has ruled, for example, that Jehovah's Witnesses may distribute religious literature door-to-door and in public places without the permission of local authorities and without paying license taxes.[17]

The second category of disputes concerns the impact on religious practice of general laws and government procedures that are otherwise neutral with respect to religion. Prison inmates who are Muslim or Jewish, for example, demand that they be provided meals that do not violate the dietary restrictions imposed by their

The First Amendment protects the right of Jehovah's Witnesses, Mormons, and other religious believers to go door-to-door to spread word of their faith.

religious faiths. Christian Scientists often object to state and local regulations requiring that their children be immunized against disease. Amish parents protest school attendance laws. For years, the Supreme Court subjected these sorts of incidental restrictions on religious practice to the compelling government interest test. Since *Employment Division v. Smith* (1990), however, the Supreme Court has held that states can enact laws that have an incidental impact on religious freedom so long as they serve a valid state purpose and are not aimed at inhibiting any particular religion. The *Smith* case involved a decision by the state of Oregon to deny unemployment benefits to state employees who were fired because they used peyote, which is a hallucinogenic drug, in Native American religious practices. The Court upheld the firing and denial of unemployment benefits because the law under which they were dismissed served a valid state purpose, was not aimed at any particular religion, and had only an incidental impact on religious belief. It would be "courting anarchy," the Court said, to find that the Constitution carves out religious exemptions from general laws.[18]

The Supreme Court's decision in *Smith* alarmed religious leaders and civil libertarians because they feared that the new standard would make it considerably more difficult for churches and individual religious practitioners to win lawsuits challenging state and local laws restricting religious freedom. In fact, in the months after the *Smith* ruling, lower federal courts ordered autopsies on members of the Jewish and Hmong religions, both of which prohibit autopsies, and overturned a ruling giving a church an exemption to Seattle's historic preservation law. The Occupational Safety and Health and Administration (OSHA) even repealed an exemption it had granted to members of the Sikh religion (who wear turbans) from having to wear hardhats on construction sites.[19]

Congress and the president responded to the outcry over *Smith* by enacting the Religious Freedom Restoration Act (RFRA). The measure, which enjoyed the support of a broad range of religious and civil liberties groups, declared that general laws and regulations enacted by federal, state, or local governments that have the incidental effect of limiting religious freedom must meet the compelling government interest standard. In effect, the RFRA would return constitutional law to what it was before the Supreme Court's decision in the *Smith* case. The life span of the RFRA was short at least as it applies to state and local governments. In 1997, the Supreme Court ruled that the measure unconstitutionally restricted the powers of state governments.[20] The RFRA prohibits the federal government from limiting the free exercise of religion, even incidentally, without a compelling government reason, but the measure does not apply to state actions.[21]

Freedom of Expression

The First Amendment guarantees freedom of expression. "Congress shall make no law . . . abridging the freedom of speech, or of the press; or the right of the people peaceably to assemble to petition the government for a redress of grievances." Some forms of expression enjoy a greater level of constitutional protection than other forms. Table 15.2 summarizes the current status of constitutional law regarding government efforts to restrict different forms of expression. High-value expression, which includes political speech, art, and literature, enjoys the highest level of constitutional protection. The government may regulate high-value expression only when it can demonstrate that it has a compelling government interest that cannot be achieved in a less restrictive fashion. Because this standard is difficult to meet, most efforts to regulate high-value expression are unconstitutional. In contrast, low-value expression, which includes false or deceptive advertising, sexual and racial harassment, and unsolicited medical or legal advice, receives a much lower level of protection. The government can regulate low-value expression if it can demonstrate a legitimate, plausible justification.[22]

Constitutional law also distinguishes among government regulation of expression that is content-neutral, content-specific, and viewpoint-specific. Table 15.3

TABLE 15.2   Standard for Determining the Constitutionality of Government Restrictions on Expression Based on the Type of Expression

Type of Expression	Example of a Government Restriction on Expression	Standard for Determining the Constitutionality of Government Restriction
High-value expression—political speech, art, and literature	A city government removes from the public library a book that questions whether the Holocaust actually occurred after protests from Jewish organizations and other members of the community.	The government can regulate high-value expression only when it can demonstrate that it has a compelling government interest that cannot be achieved in a less restrictive fashion.
Low-value expression—false advertising, sexual or racial harassment, unsolicited medical and legal advice	The Food and Drug Administration orders a pharmaceutical company to drop advertising claims that have not been proven to the FDA's satisfaction.	The government can regulate low-value expression if it can demonstrate a legitimate, plausible justification.

TABLE 15.3   Standard for Determining the Constitutionality of Regulation of Expression Based on the Focus of the Restriction

Type of Restriction	Examples	Standard for Constitutionality
Content-neutral regulation of expression	City government prohibits all portable signs in a community; a school district's dress code excludes all clothing with written messages.	The Supreme Court uses a balancing test, weighing competing interests against one another.
Content-specific regulation of expression	City government outlaws yard signs with political messages, but allows for-sale signs and advertisements for garage sales; county government prohibits political demonstrations in a public park but permits picnics and pep rallies for sports teams.	These sorts of restrictions must be justified on the basis of a compelling government interest that cannot be satisfied through less restrictive means. Because this standard is very high, most content-specific regulations of expression are held unconstitutional.
Viewpoint-specific regulation of expression.	A state-supported university prohibits the formation of a gay and lesbian student group while allowing a broad range of other groups; city government refuses to grant a parade permit to supporters of the militia movement while allowing a similar parade organized by a veterans' organization.	Viewpoint-specific restrictions on expression are almost always unconstitutional.

sorts out the differences among these types of government restrictions. *Content-neutral* regulation of expression limits a particular form of expression without regard to its content. A local government ban on billboards would be an example of a content-neutral restriction on expression because all billboards, regardless of their message, would be outlawed. The Supreme Court determines the constitutionality of content-neutral restrictions on expression by applying a balancing act, weighing one set of competing interests against another. A *content-specific* restriction involves regulation of certain types of expression, such as a school district policy to prohibit students from wearing T-shirts with political messages while allowing shirts with nonpolitical statements on them. These types of restrictions must be justified on the basis of a compelling government interest. *Viewpoint-based* restrictions limit expression based on the point of view, such as a local government allowing political rallies organized by the American Legion and Mothers Against Drunk Driving (MADD), but prohibiting a similar rally organized by the Ku Klux Klan. Viewpoint-based restrictions of expression are almost always unconstitutional.[23]

Anti-Government Speech   Constitutional law holds that the government can restrict political expression only if it has a compelling interest that cannot be achieved by less restrictive means. In practice, the compelling interest standard is so difficult to meet that most laws limiting expression are unconstitutional. Consider the case of Clarence Brandenburg, a Ku Klux Klan leader from Ohio. Brandenburg was convicted under an Ohio law for making a speech at a Klan cross-burning rally in which he threatened the president, Congress, and the Supreme Court for suppressing the white race. The Supreme Court overturned Brandenburg's conviction, saying that the mere advocacy of lawless action was not sufficient to sustain a conviction because the state does not have a compelling interest in outlawing "mere abstract teaching." Instead, the state must prove that the "advocacy is directed to inciting or producing imminent lawless action and is likely to incite or produce such action."[24]

Table 15.4 summarizes the standard of constitutionality and the specific tests that the Supreme Court uses for each of the issue areas covered in this section. The table lists the issues involving the Free Expression Clause and gives an example of each one. It then identifies the applicable standard for judging the constitutionality of government restrictions of each type of expression and the specific test the Court uses to determine if that standard has been met.

Expression That Threatens the Public Order   Can the government punish expression that may lead to a disruption of public order? Consider the controversy generated by Paul Cohen and his jacket. In 1968, during the Vietnam War, Cohen wore a jacket into the Los Angeles County Courthouse upon which the words "F _____ rule the Draft" were clearly visible. Cohen was arrested and subsequently convicted by a local court for disturbing the peace. The judge reasoned that the jacket might provoke others to commit acts of violence and sentenced Cohen to 30 days in jail. Cohen appealed and the case eventually reached the Supreme Court, which overturned the conviction. The Court held that government cannot forbid shocking language that is not legally obscene and that is not directed at an individual listener (or reader) in such a way as to provoke violence. Otherwise, government risks the unconstitutional suppression of ideas.[25]

The Supreme Court distinguishes between expression and action. Protestors do not have a constitutional right to disrupt traffic, block sidewalks, or impede access to public places. The Supreme Court has upheld lower court orders preventing anti-abortion protesters from blocking access to abortion clinics because the government has an interest in "ensuring public safety, . . . promoting the free flow of traffic, . . . protecting property rights, and protecting a woman's freedom to seek

TABLE 15.4   Standards and Tests for Determining the Constitutionality of Government Restrictions on Expression in Various Fields of Law

Type of Expression	Example	Applicable Standard of Constitutionality for Government Restriction	Specific Test for Issue Area
Anti-government expression	Speech opposing the war in Iraq	Government restriction must be based on a compelling government interest that cannot be achieved by a less restrictive means.	The only expression that may be suppressed is expression that is directed to inciting or producing imminent lawless action and is likely to incite or produce such action.
Expression that may threaten public order	Paul Cohen's jacket	Government restrictions must be based on a compelling government interest that cannot be achieved by a less restrictive means.	The only type of objectionable language that can be constitutionally prohibited is language spoken in a face-to-face confrontation in a threatening or inciting manner that is likely to lead to an immediate breach of the peace.
Hate crimes legislation	Law provides for more severe penalties for convicted criminals whose criminal acts are motivated by racial, gender, ethnic, or sexual orientation bias.	The Supreme Court has ruled that hate crimes legislation does not inhibit expression because it is aimed at the criminal behavior rather than the expression.	There is no constitutional prohibition against the enactment of hate crimes legislation.
Commercial Speech	A city adopts a billboard ordinance to limit billboard advertising to certain areas of town.	Although the Supreme Court has held that the Constitution protects commercial speech, the level of protection is not as great as it is for political speech.	Government regulation of commercial speech must be justified by a substantial interest, the regulation must directly advance the government interest, and it is no more extensive than necessary.

Hate crimes law
A legislative measure that increases penalties for persons convicted of criminal offenses motivated by prejudice based on race, religion, national origin, gender, or sexual orientation.

pregnancy related services."[26] The Court has ruled that these are all legitimate goals that justify governmental action. Nonetheless, the government may not burden expression more than is necessary to achieve its legitimate goals. Court orders creating fixed buffers around the entrances of abortion clinics and parking lot entrances are acceptable, whereas "floating buffers" around women walking in and out of clinics are not.[27]

Hate Crimes Legislation   A **hate crimes law** is a legislative measure that increases penalties for persons convicted of criminal offenses motivated by prejudice based on race, religion, national origin, gender, or sexual orientation. Suppose a group of young white men beat up an African American man who has just moved his family

"It is a fair summary of history to say that the safeguards of liberty have been forged in controversies involving not very nice people." Justice Felix Frankfurter

into a predominantly white neighborhood. During the assault, the white men use racial slurs and warn the man to move out of the area. The white men could be charged with the crime of assault. Because they acted out of racial animosity, they could also be charged with a hate crime. In recent years, many states have adopted hate crimes legislation, enhancing penalties for persons convicted of crimes motivated by bias.

Hate crimes legislation is controversial. Critics charge that hate crimes laws infringe on freedom of expression. They also believe that hate crimes provisions inhibit expression because they rely on speech as evidence of biased motive. In contrast, the proponents of hate crimes laws claim they are justified because crimes motivated by hate inflict not only physical harm but also psychological damage on their victims. Furthermore, they argue that violent crimes aimed at groups of persons are more threatening to society than crimes against particular individuals because they increase racial and social divisions.[28]

The Supreme Court has upheld hate crimes legislation, drawing a distinction between speech and action. Although biased speech is constitutionally protected, violent behavior motivated by bias is not. "A physical assault is not by any stretch of the imagination . . . protected by the First Amendment," said the Court. Because hate crimes are perceived as inflicting "greater individual and societal harm" than ordinary crimes, states are justified in providing greater penalties for their commission.[29]

WHAT IS YOUR OPINION?

Do people who commit crimes out of prejudice deserve more severe punishment than other criminals do, or should similar crimes be punished similarly regardless of motive? Why or why not?

Symbolic Expression   Symbolic expression, such as flying the flag or burning a cross, enjoys the same constitutional protection as speech or written communication. Congress and the states can restrict symbolic expression only when they can demonstrate a compelling government interest that cannot be achieved in a less restrictive fashion. Consider the issue of flag burning. In 1989, the Supreme Court overturned a Texas flag desecration law under which Gregory Lee Johnson was convicted for burning an American flag at the 1984 Republican convention in Dallas, ruling that Johnson's action was a form of symbolic speech. "If there is any bedrock principle underlying the First Amendment," wrote Justice William Brennan in the majority opinion, "it is that the government may not prohibit the expression of an idea simply because society finds the idea itself offensive or disagreeable."[30] Congress responded to the uproar over the Court's decision by passing a federal anti-flag-burning statute, which, a year later, the Court also declared unconstitutional.[31]

? **WHAT IS YOUR OPINION?**

Do you think that the Constitution should protect people who burn the American flag from prosecution? Why or why not?

Commercial Speech   Advertising and other forms of commercial speech are constitutionally protected forms of expression, but they do not enjoy the same level of constitutional protection as political expression. The Supreme Court has established a four-pronged test for protecting commercial speech:

1. Whether the speech concerns lawful conduct.
2. Whether the government interest in banning the speech is substantial.
3. Whether the regulation directly advances the government interest.
4. Whether the regulation is no more extensive than necessary to advance the government interest.[32]

In sum, the government can regulate advertising and other forms of commercial speech only if the regulation promotes a substantial government interest and is not more extensive than necessary to serve that interest. Commercial speech that is misleading or that promotes illegal activity does not enjoy constitutional protection.[33]

Privacy Rights

Do Americans enjoy a constitutional right of privacy? Although the Constitution does not specifically mention privacy, the Supreme Court has interpreted the Due Process Clause of the Fourteenth Amendment to include a right of privacy. In 1965,

the Court struck down a seldom-enforced Connecticut law that prohibited the use of contraceptives and the dispensing of birth control information even to married couples on the grounds that its enforcement would involve government's invading "the privacy of the bedroom." The Court declared that various constitutional guarantees found in the Bill of Rights create "zones of privacy." The Third Amendment's prohibition against quartering soldiers in private homes and the Fourth Amendment's protection against unreasonable searches and seizures imply a right of privacy.[34] In contrast, conservative legal scholars believe that the Supreme Court simply invented a right of privacy that does not exist in the Constitution because a majority of the justices disagreed with the Connecticut law and wanted to find an excuse to strike it down. Although few conservatives want to defend Connecticut's statute against contraception, which some label "an uncommonly silly law," they have been outraged that the Court has used the right of privacy as the basis for major decisions involving abortion and gay rights.

WHAT IS YOUR OPINION?

Should privacy be a constitutional right? Why or why not?

The Supreme Court based *Roe v. Wade*, its landmark abortion decision, on a right of privacy. The case dealt with a challenge by an anonymous Dallas woman, "Jane Roe," to a Texas law prohibiting abortion except to save the life of a woman. The Court found the Texas statute unconstitutional, declaring that a woman's right to personal privacy under the U.S. Constitution included her decision to terminate a pregnancy. The Court said, however, that a woman's right to privacy was not absolute and must be balanced against the state's interest in protecting health, medical standards, and prenatal life.

The Supreme Court balanced these competing interests by dividing a pregnancy into trimesters. During the first trimester, state governments could not interfere with a physician's decision, reached in consultation with a pregnant woman patient, to terminate a pregnancy. In the second trimester, the state could regulate abortion but only to protect the health of a woman. In the third trimester, after the fetus had achieved viability (the ability to survive outside the womb), the Court ruled that state governments could prohibit abortion except when it was necessary to preserve the life or health of a woman.[35]

In the 30-plus years since *Roe*, the Supreme Court has upheld its original decision while allowing states leeway to regulate abortion. In 1989, the Court upheld a Missouri law limiting access to abortion. The statute prohibited the use of public employees or facilities to perform or assist an abortion except to save a woman's life and outlawed the use of public funds, employees, or facilities to encourage or counsel a woman to have an abortion not necessary to save her life. Citing recent medical advances, the Court abandoned the trimester system adopted in *Roe* by allowing Missouri to require physicians to perform medical tests to determine fetal viability beginning at 20 weeks.[36] The Court subsequently ruled that a state could regulate access to abortion as long as the regulations did not place an "undue burden" on a woman's right to choose. The Court's majority defined an undue burden as one that presented an "absolute obstacle or severe limitation" on the right to decide to have an abortion. State regulations that simply "inhibited" that right were permissible.

The Court upheld a number of restrictions on abortion, including the following:

- Women seeking abortions must be given information about fetal development and alternatives to ending their pregnancies.
- Women must wait at least 24 hours after receiving that information before having an abortion.
- Doctors must keep detailed records on each abortion performed.
- Abortion records would be subject to public disclosure.
- Unmarried girls under the age of 18 must get the permission of one of their parents or the certification of a state judge that they are mature enough to make the decision on their own.

The only provision in the law that the Court considered an undue burden was a requirement that married women notify their husbands of their plans to have an abortion.[37]

The Supreme Court's most recent application of the right of privacy involved a legal challenge to the Texas sodomy law, which criminalized private, consensual sexual conduct between two adults of the same gender. When police in Houston, Texas, arrived at the home of John Lawrence because of an unrelated call, they found Lawrence and another man, Tyron Garner, engaged in sexual intercourse. They arrested the men and charged them with violating the Texas homosexual conduct law for "engaging in deviate sexual intercourse with another person of the same sex." In *Lawrence v. Texas*, the Court ruled that the Texas law violated the Due Process Clause of the Fourteenth Amendment because it intruded into the personal and private lives of individuals without furthering a legitimate state interest.[38]

Due Process of Law and the Rights of the Accused

Several provisions of the Bill of Rights protect the rights of persons under investigation or accused of crimes, including the better part of the Fourth, Fifth, and Eighth Amendments. The key constitutional phrase is found in the Fifth Amendment and repeated in the Fourteenth Amendment: No person shall be deprived of "life, liberty, or property, without due process of law." **Due process of law** is the constitutional provision that declares that government must follow fair and regular procedures in actions that could lead to an individual's suffering loss of life, liberty, or property. Neither the national government nor the states may resort to stacked juries, coerced confessions, self-incrimination, denial of counsel, cruel and unusual punishments, or unreasonable searches and seizures.

Due process of law The constitutional principle holding that government must follow fair and regular procedures in actions that could lead to an individual's suffering loss of life, liberty, or property.

warrant An official authorization issued by a judicial officer.

Probable cause The reasonable suspicion based on evidence that a particular search will uncover contraband.

Searches and Seizures   The Fourth Amendment guarantees the "right of the people to be secure in their persons, houses, papers, and effects, against unreasonable searches and seizures . . . and no warrants shall issue, but upon probable cause . . . and particularly describing the place to be searched, and the persons or things to be seized." In general, this provision means that the police need a **warrant** (i.e., an official authorization issued by a judicial officer) for most searches of persons or property. Judges or other magistrates issue warrants after the law enforcement authorities have shown probable cause that certain items will be found. **Probable cause** is the reasonable suspicion based on evidence that a particular search will uncover contraband.

Through the years, the Supreme Court has permitted a number of exceptions to the basic warrant requirement. The police do not need a warrant, for example, to search suspects who consent to be searched or to search suspects after valid arrests. If police officers have a reasonable suspicion of criminal activity, they may stop and search suspicious individuals. The Court has ruled, for example, that the police are justified in searching an individual in a high-crime area who flees when the police appear.[39] The authorities can also search luggage in airports and may fingerprint suspects after arrests.

The Supreme Court has been more willing to authorize searches of automobiles without warrants than it has offices and homes. Consider the *Ross* case. An informant tipped off the District of Columbia police about a narcotics dealer known as Bandit who sold drugs from the trunk of his purplish maroon Chevrolet Malibu. When the police spotted a car fitting the description, they pulled it over and searched the trunk, even though they did not have a warrant. Sure enough, they found heroin and cash in the trunk. The car's driver, Albert Ross, Jr., was subsequently tried and convicted of possession of narcotics with intent to distribute. He appealed his case to the Supreme Court. Did the police search of Ross's car trunk without a warrant violate his constitutional rights? The Court said that it did not because the police had legitimately stopped the car and had probable cause to believe it contained contraband. As a result, the police could search the vehicle as thoroughly as if they had a warrant. The Court added, however, that a search "must be limited by its object," that is, the police cannot conduct a general search to see what might turn up. If authorities have probable cause to believe that illegal aliens are being transported in a van, for example, they may search the van, but they have no justification for searching the glove compartment or luggage where no illegal aliens could possibly be hiding.[40]

Exclusionary rule
The judicial doctrine stating that when the police violate an individual's constitutional rights, the evidence obtained as a result of police misconduct or error cannot be used against the defendant.

The Exclusionary Rule   The **exclusionary rule** is the judicial doctrine stating that when the police violate an individual's constitutional rights, the evidence obtained as a result of police misconduct or error cannot be used against the defendant in a criminal prosecution. In 1914, the Supreme Court established the exclusionary rule in federal prosecutions in the *Weeks* case. The police arrested Weeks at his place of business and then searched his home. Both of these actions were taken without a warrant. Papers and articles seized in the search were used in federal court against Weeks and he was convicted. He appealed his conviction, arguing that the judge should not have admitted into evidence illegally seized materials. The Supreme Court agreed.

> The tendency of those who execute the criminal laws of the country to obtain convictions by means of unlawful seizures and enforced confessions . . . should find no sanction in the judgment of the courts. . . . If letters and private documents can thus be seized and held and used in evidence against a citizen accused of an offense, the protection of the Fourth Amendment . . . might as well be stricken from the Constitution.[41]

In 1961, the Supreme Court extended the exclusionary rule to the states in the case of *Mapp v. Ohio*.[42]

The exclusionary rule is controversial. Its defenders say that is a necessary safeguard to ensure that police authorities do not intentionally violate individual rights. In contrast, critics point out that the United States is the only country to take the position that police misconduct must automatically result in the suppression of evidence. In other countries, the trial judge determines whether the misconduct is serious enough to warrant the exclusion of the evidence.[43]

In recent decades, the Supreme Court has weakened the exclusionary rule without repealing it by carving out major exceptions to its application. In 1984, the Court adopted a "good-faith" exception to the exclusionary rule requirement, allowing the use of illegally seized evidence in criminal prosecutions as long as the police acted in good faith.[44] Subsequently, the Court added a "harmless error" exception, allowing a criminal conviction to stand despite the use of illegally obtained evidence when other evidence in the case was strong enough to convict the defendant anyway.[45] In 2009, the Court ruled that evidence obtained from an unlawful arrest caused by careless record keeping rather than intentional police misconduct could be used in a prosecution.[46]

 WHAT IS YOUR OPINION?

If the police obtain evidence in an unlawful search that conclusively proves a defendant guilty, should the evidence be used to prosecute the defendant? Why or why not?

The **Miranda** *Warning*   Ernesto Miranda was an Arizona man who was arrested for kidnapping and raping a young woman. Under questioning, Miranda confessed. On appeal, Miranda challenged the use of his confession as a violation of the Fifth

Amendment's guarantee against self-incrimination because the police had not informed him of his constitutional rights to remain silent and consult an attorney.

The Supreme Court reversed Miranda's conviction. The Court's majority held that the prosecution could not use a statement against an accused person in a court of law unless the authorities observe adequate procedural safeguards to ensure that the statement was obtained "voluntarily, knowingly, and intelligently." Before questioning, accused persons must be warned that (1) they have a right to remain silent, (2) that any statements they give may be used against them, and (3) that they are entitled to the presence of an attorney, either retained or appointed.[47]

The Court's *Miranda* ruling has sparked an ongoing debate. Critics say that it makes law enforcement more difficult by preventing police from interrogating suspects quickly before they have a chance to concoct an alibi or reflect on the consequences of telling the truth.[48] In contrast, *Miranda*'s defenders call it the "poor person's Fifth Amendment." Educated, middle-class defendants do not need the *Miranda* warning—they know their rights. *Miranda* protects poor, uneducated, first-time offender from police coercion.

The Supreme Court has weakened the *Miranda* ruling without reversing it. The Court has held that in cross-examining defendants, prosecutors can use statements that do not meet the *Miranda* standard.[49] The Court has also ruled that police need not give the *Miranda* warning before questioning a suspect when the public safety is immediately and directly threatened.[50] The Court even upheld a conviction when the police refused to allow an attorney hired by a suspect's relatives to see him because the suspect had not asked to see a lawyer.[51]

Double jeopardy
The government trying a criminal defendant a second time for the same offense after an acquittal in an earlier prosecution.

Double Jeopardy   The Fifth Amendment prohibits **double jeopardy,** which involves the government trying a criminal defendant a second time for the same offense after an acquittal in an earlier prosecution. No person shall be "twice put in jeopardy of life and limb" for the same criminal offense, the amendment declares. The goal of this provision is to protect individuals from the harassment of repeated prosecutions on the same charge after an acquittal. Because of the Double Jeopardy Clause, no one who has been acquitted of an offense can be retried for the same crime even if incontrovertible evidence of the person's guilt is discovered. A person acquitted of murder, for example, could walk out of the courtroom and declare, "I did it and I got away with it!" on national television and not have to worry about being retried for murder.

The prohibition against double jeopardy is not absolute. A defendant can be tried multiple times for multiple offenses committed in a single incident.[52] An individual charged with killing a gas station attendant during a holdup, for example, can be tried first for murder and then for robbery. Furthermore, separate prosecutions by different levels of government do not constitute double jeopardy, even for the same offense.[53] Timothy McVeigh and Terry Nichols, the men charged with the deadly bombing of the Oklahoma City federal building, were tried in federal court because the offense took place on federal property and a number of federal employees were killed. Nichols was also tried for murder in the state courts of Oklahoma because the crime took place in that state. Similarly, persons who have allegedly engaged in criminal activity that has transcended state lines can be tried in each state involved.[54]

The Supreme Court has held that the Double Jeopardy Clause does not protect persons convicted of child molestation from involuntary commitment to mental hospitals after they have served their prison sentences. Consider the case of *Kansas v. Hendricks*. Leroy Hendricks was a pedophile, an adult who sexually abuses children. He had five convictions for child molestation in the state of Kansas and admitted that he could not stop trying to have sex with children. In 1994, after Hendricks finished serving his most recent sentence for child molestation, the state of Kansas transferred him to a mental health facility, where he was confined indefinitely under provisions of the state's Sexually Violent Predator Act. A state judge ruled that Hendricks was "mentally abnormal" and likely to commit additional crimes. Hendricks and his attorneys filed suit against the state, charging that his continued confinement was a sort of double jeopardy in that he was tried and punished twice for the same crime. The case eventually reached the U.S. Supreme Court, which ruled against Hendricks. The Court declared that Hendricks could be confined against his will because he was being held in a mental institution rather than a prison. Technically, he was no longer being punished.[55] Although no one was sympathetic with Hendricks, a number of observers worried about the precedent set by the case. "Today we're dealing with sexual predators," said Steven Shapiro of the ACLU. "Who is it tomorrow that we're going to label as abnormal and potentially dangerous?"[56]

 WHAT IS YOUR OPINION?

Should child molesters be kept in confinement even after they have served their criminal sentences? Why or why not?

Fair Trial   A number of provisions in the Sixth Amendment are aimed at guaranteeing that defendants receive a fair trial. The amendment promises a speedy and public trial. Although the Supreme Court has been reluctant to set timetables for trials, the federal government and many states have adopted "speedy trial laws" to ensure that justice not be long delayed. As for the public trial requirement, the Supreme Court has held that the public (and the press) may not be excluded from the courtroom except in rare circumstances.[57] Furthermore, the Court has said that states may permit the unobtrusive use of television in a courtroom if they wish.[58]

The Sixth Amendment guarantees trial by an impartial jury. Although juries are traditionally 12 persons, the Supreme Court has said that juries with as few as six people are acceptable.[59] The Court has also held that jury selection processes must ensure that the jury pool represents a cross-section of the community, holding, for example, that prosecutors may not systematically exclude racial minorities from jury service.[60]

The Sixth Amendment grants defendants the right to legal counsel. In *Gideon v. Wainwright*, the Supreme Court ruled that states must provide attorneys for indigent defendants charged with serious crimes.[61] The Court has also held that assigned counsel must meet a standard of reasonable competence.[62]

Cruel and Unusual Punishments   Should mentally retarded offenders be held fully accountable for their crimes? Daryl Renard Atkins is a murderer, convicted and sentenced to death by the state of Virginia for the robbery and slaying of a U.S. airman in 1996. Atkins is also severely retarded, at least according to his defense attorneys. Would executing Atkins violate the prohibition against cruel and unusual punishments contained in the Eighth Amendment to the U.S. Constitution? In general, the Supreme Court has interpreted this provision to mean that the punishment must fit the crime. The Court, for example, has held that a life sentence without the possibility of parole for a series of nonviolent petty offenses is cruel and unusual.[63] The Court has also ruled that it is unconstitutional to impose the death penalty on a defendant who rapes a child but does not kill the victim.[64]

No issue has generated more controversy under the Eighth Amendment than the death penalty **(capital punishment).** The supporters of capital punishment quote the Bible, "an eye for an eye, a tooth for a tooth," and declare that the death penalty is an effective deterrent to serious crime. In contrast, opponents call the death penalty barbaric and say that it is little less than legalized murder. In 1972, the opponents of capital punishment won a temporary victory in the case of *Furman v. Georgia.* By a 5–4 vote, the Supreme Court declared that the death penalty, *as then applied,* was unconstitutional because it allowed too much discretion, thereby opening the door to discriminatory practices. Getting the death penalty, the Court said, was similar to being struck by lightening.[65] Because of the *Furman* decision, death row inmates around the nation escaped execution, having their sentences commuted to life in prison. Many state legislatures responded to *Furman* by adopting new capital punishment laws designed to satisfy the Court's objections. As the states began to implement their new death penalty statutes, cases began to make their way through the court system. In 1976, the U.S. Supreme Court ruled that capital punishment was constitutional in the case of *Gregg v. Georgia,* which involved a constitutional challenge to Georgia's new death penalty statute.[66] Thirty-eight states and the federal government adopted capital punishment statutes, and 32 states carried out executions, with Texas taking the lead, carrying out more than a third of the nation's executions.[67] The federal government carried out one execution, Timothy McVeigh, the convicted Oklahoma City bomber. As Figure 15.1 shows, the number of executions increased during the 1990s, peaking at 98 in 1999.

The increased rate of executions was accompanied by increased controversy. The opponents of the death penalty charged that the process of trials and appeals was so flawed that innocent people might face execution. A study published by Columbia University law professor James S. Liebman found that two-thirds of the death sentences given by American courts between 1973 and 1995 were overturned on appeal. When death penalty cases were retried, 7 percent of defendants were found not guilty.[68] Furthermore, the critics of the death penalty argued that it was inefficient because only 5 percent of death sentences were actually carried out and then only after years of evaluation.[69] In contrast, the proponents of capital punishment defended the process, saying that it was scrupulously fair. They pointed out that people given the death penalty were entitled to an appeals process that lasts for years. According to the Bureau of Justice Statistics, the average time on death row for the convicted murderers before their executions is more than 12 years, long enough for their cases to be thoroughly examined for error.[70]

Capital punishment The death penalty.

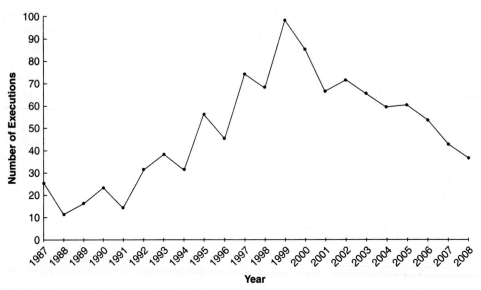

FIGURE 15.1   Executions in the United States, 1987–2008.
Source: Bureau of Justice Statistics.

The renewed debate over capital punishment has been accompanied by a de-cline in the implementation of the death penalty. As Figure 15.1 shows, the number of people executed in the United States has fallen since peaking in 1999. In some states, executive officials slowed or halted capital punishment because of concerns about efficacy. New Jersey repealed its death penalty statute, and 18 states adopted laws to prohibit the execution of mentally retarded criminals.[71]

In this context, the U.S. Supreme Court declared that the execution of defendants who are mentally retarded is a violation of the Cruel and Unusual Punishment Clause of the Eighth Amendment. The Court reversed a position it had taken in 1989 when only two states excluded mentally retarded individuals from the death penalty, arguing that a national consensus has now developed against executing the mentally retarded.[72] The Court returned the Atkins case to a trial court in Virginia to determine whether the defendant was indeed mentally retarded. Ironically, a jury found Atkins mentally competent and a judge sentenced him to death. His case is once again on appeal.

Executive Authority, Civil Liberties, and the War on Terror

Does the president have the authority to suspend the due process guarantees of the Constitution to detain individuals that the administration believes may be a threat to national security? Historically, the courts have been reluctant to limit presiden-tial power during wartime.[73] Attorney General Ashcroft pointed to the precedent set by President Franklin Roosevelt during World War II as a justification for holding Jose Padilla and others. In 1942, eight German saboteurs landed in the United States from a submarine and were quickly captured. President Roosevelt ordered them held as enemy combatants rather than prisoners of war and directed that they be tried by

GETTING INVOLVED

Talking About
Miranda

Is the *Miranda* warning a meaningful constitutional safeguard or a technical formality that has no impact on justice? Do police officers take it seriously? Do suspects understand its meaning? The class project is to research the implementation of the *Miranda* warning by interviewing one or more police officers. Some students may know police officers as friends, neighbors, or relatives. Students may also be able to interview members of the campus police at your college.

Before conducting the interviews, prepare a set of questions designed to focus on the following topics:

- **Police training.** How do police academies cover the topic of *Miranda*? Is it presented as a necessary evil or an important element of civil liberties in a free society?

- **Police supervision.** How seriously does management take the *Miranda* warning? Do police supervisors frequently review implementation procedures, or is that left to the discretion of individual officers?

- ***Miranda* implementation.** When, if ever, do officers recite the *Miranda* warning to suspects? Do they read the warning from a card or do they

have it memorized? What steps if any do officers take to ensure that suspects understand the meaning of the warning?

- ***Miranda* impact.** Do law enforcement officers believe that the *Miranda* warning has an effect on their work? Do they think the warning discourages guilty persons from confessing? Do they believe that *Miranda* plays a positive role in law enforcement by reminding innocent people of their constitutional rights? Or do they believe that the *Miranda* warning is meaningless, a waste of time to satisfy the courts that has no effect in the real world of law enforcement?

After the interviews are complete, students should organize their notes and prepare to participate in class discussion. The instructor will ask students not just about the content of the interviews and their reaction to them, but also about the *Miranda* warning in general. In particular, the instructor will invite students to discuss their assessment of the *Miranda* warning. Is it harmful or beneficial, or is it just a meaningless technicality that neither police officers nor criminal suspects take seriously?

---

a military court without many of the due process protections available in civilian courts. The U.S. Supreme Court returned from its summer vacation to review the president's action and upheld it, declaring that the saboteurs had violated the rules of war. The president, the Court said, had acted properly under his executive authority as commander-in-chief.[74]

Nonetheless, critics of the Bush administration's decision to detain American citizens without due process argue that the World War II precedent does not apply to the current situation. They point out that the saboteurs were noncitizen agents of Germany, an enemy power against which the United States was officially at war. In contrast, Padilla was an American citizen arrested on American soil for allegedly planning a terrorist act against the United States.

Although the U.S. Supreme Court did not address the Padilla case directly for technical reasons, its ruling in a similar dispute ensured that Padilla would have his day in court. In a case involving Yaser Esam Hamdi, an American citizen who was taken into custody in Afghanistan, the Court ruled that the president could not deprive Hamdi or other detainees of their right to due process. Citizens held as enemy combatants had to be given notice of the basis of their classification and a "fair opportunity to rebut the government's . . . assertions before a neutral decision-maker."[75] After the *Hamdi* decision, the government moved Padilla's case into the regular court system, charging him with raising money and recruiting operatives to fight for radical Islamic causes in several foreign countries. In 2007, a jury found Padilla guilty of conspiring to fund and support overseas terrorism. He was subsequently sentenced to 17 years and four months in prison.

The Supreme Court similarly ruled against President Bush's plan to put detainees at Guantánamo Bay, Cuba, on trial before military commissions. The Court held that Bush lacked the authority to put the Guantánamo detainees on trial because Congress had not authorized the military commissions.[76] The Court also declared that terror suspects held at Guantánamo have a constitutional right to seek their release in federal court.[77] Soon after taking office, President Barack Obama signed executive orders reversing many Bush administration policies concerning the war on terror. Obama ordered the closure of the prison at Guantanamo Bay within a year, halted trials of terror suspects pending review, and banned the use of aggressive interrogation techniques that critics have labeled torture.

CONCLUSION: CIVIL LIBERTIES POLICYMAKING

Constitutional law is the most important environmental factor affecting civil liberties policymaking. Civil liberties questions are constitutional questions. Policy debates over prayer in public schools, pornography, and capital punishment are, invariably, also debates about constitutional law. Did the founders intend for the Establishment Clause to prohibit organized spoken prayer in public schools? Is it cruel and unusual punishment under the Eighth Amendment to execute convicted murderers who are mentally retarded? The Constitution and its interpretation affect every stage of the civil liberties policy process.

Because of the constitutional nature of civil liberties policymaking, judges—especially the men and women who serve on the Supreme Court of the United States—are the most important civil liberties policymakers. Liberal judges are more likely than conservative judges to rule in favor of unpopular litigants, such as atheists, Jehovah's Witnesses, members of the Ku Klux Klan, criminal defendants, and prison inmates. During the 1960s, a liberal bloc of justices led by Chief Justice Earl Warren dominated the Supreme Court. Many of the decisions of that era, including *Engel v. Vitale* and *Miranda v. Arizona*, reflected their policy preferences. In contrast to liberal members of the judiciary, judges with conservative policy preferences tend to decide cases in favor of the police, criminal prosecutors, majority religious preferences, and traditional values. The Supreme Court today is closely divided on civil liberties issues, and many cases are decided by the narrowest margin.

Civil liberties policymaking is affected by the presence of interest groups and other organizations capable and willing to participate in the policy process. The American Civil Liberties Union (ACLU) is a frequent participant in civil liberties policymaking. Other interest groups involved with various civil liberties issues include the National Organization for Women (NOW), Planned Parenthood,

NARAL Pro-Choice America, National Rifle Association (NRA), and National Right to Life Committee.

Public opinion affects the civil liberties policymaking process. Legislatures and executives respond to public demands by enacting death penalty statutes, school prayer requirements, and other measures related to civil liberties. At times, judges seem to respond to public opinion. Historically, the Supreme Court has been more willing to support presidential actions to limit civil liberties during wartime than after the war is over.

In the long run, the policy preferences of the president affect civil liberties policymaking because the president appoints judges. Republican presidents tend to select conservative judges, whereas Democratic presidents appoint liberals. Because federal judges enjoy lifetime appointments, a president's influence on judicial policymaking will be slow to materialize but continue well after the president leaves office. In the early years of the twenty-first century, former Presidents Reagan, George H.W. Bush, and Clinton continue to affect the judicial branch of government because their appointees still serve on the Court. The survival of the *Roe* precedent depends on future presidential and senatorial elections.

Agenda Building

A number of political actors help set the agenda for civil liberties policymaking. Interest groups and other organizations are particularly important. Conservative groups call on the government to get tough on pornography and crime, and to limit access to abortion. Groups with unpopular views, such as Nazis and members of the Ku Klux Klan, stimulate debate on the First Amendment by attempting to march and demonstrate. Many of the civil liberties disputes reaching the Supreme Court are test cases initiated by groups such as the ACLU or the Jehovah's Witnesses. The latter have been responsible for more than 50 cases involving religious liberty, winning 90 percent of them.[78] A **test case** is a lawsuit initiated to assess the constitutionality of a legislative or executive act. Furthermore, interest groups ranging from the Chamber of Commerce to B'nai B'rith, a Jewish organization, join other civil liberties cases by means of the *amicus* brief. An *amicus curiae* or **friend of the court brief** is a written legal argument presented by a party not directly involved in a case.

Individuals can raise civil liberties issues to the public agenda. Many criminal justice disputes arise from appeals filed by convicted felons, such as Ernesto Miranda. Other individuals raise civil liberties issues on the basis of principle. Madalyn Murray O'Hair, for example, was famous for initiating test cases to challenge what she regarded as unconstitutional government support of religion.

Policy Formulation and Adoption

Many civil liberties policies are formulated and adopted in the executive and legislative branches of government, both at the national level and in the states. After the terrorist attacks of September 11, 2001, for example, Congress passed, and President George W. Bush signed, the USA Patriot Act, which makes it easier for federal officials to get wiretapping orders from judges to investigate terrorism, and

Test cases Lawsuits initiated to challenge the constitutionality of a legislative or executive act.

Amicus curiae or friend of the court briefs Written legal arguments presented by parties not directly involved in the case, including interest groups and units of government.

authorizes nationwide search warrants for computer information in terrorism investigations.[79] State governments adopt policies dealing with the death penalty, state aid to parochial schools, abortion, and other civil liberties issues.

The courts become involved in civil liberties policymaking only when a civil liberties policy adopted by another unit of government is challenged on constitutional grounds. The U.S. Supreme Court has addressed the issues of school prayer and school choice because of legal challenges filed against state and local policies. Court rulings then serve as guidelines for other institutions of government. The Court's decision to uphold the school voucher program in Ohio did not require state legislatures to adopt similar programs for their states; the impact of the ruling was to inform state legislatures that school voucher programs similar to the one in Ohio were constitutional. The decision was permissive in that it allowed states to adopt voucher programs, but it did not require them to adopt a program.

If the Supreme Court overturns *Roe v. Wade*, the issue of abortion will return to the states. Before *Roe*, states set their own abortion policies. Some states allowed abortion, whereas other states prohibited it except when necessary to protect the life of the woman. In *Roe*, the Supreme Court ruled that women have a constitutional right to an abortion during the first trimester. States could regulate second trimester abortions; they could prohibit late-term abortions. If the Supreme Court overturns the *Roe* precedent, some states will prohibit abortion except when the woman's life is in jeopardy, whereas others will allow most abortions. Other states will likely take a moderate approach, allowing abortion under certain circumstances but prohibiting abortions otherwise.

Policy Implementation and Evaluation

A broad range of government entities participates in the implementation of civil liberties policy. The Supreme Court's willingness to allow states to enact school voucher programs may not necessarily lead to the adoption of voucher programs, at least not in all states. Some state legislatures will adopt programs, but other legislatures will not. The Supreme Court's decision effectively moves the policymaking arena from the courthouse to the legislature, the governor's mansion, and the school district.

Scholars have completed a number of studies evaluating certain aspects of civil liberties policy. For example, research suggests that the primary impact of the *Miranda* decision has been psychological and that the ruling has had little appreciable effect on confessions and convictions.[80] Another observer concludes that *Miranda* has had no measurable impact on reducing police misconduct.[81] The Liebman study of capital punishment was designed to assess the effectiveness of the death penalty.[82]

KEY TERMS

administrative law	capital punishment	due process of law
amicus curiae or friend of the court briefs	civil liberties	exclusionary rule
	constitutional law	fundamental right
Bill of Rights	double jeopardy	hate crimes law

parental choice

probable cause

selective incorporation
of the Bill of Rights
against the states

statutory law

test cases

warrant

NOTES

1. CNN.com, "U.S. Authorities Capture 'Dirty Bomb' Suspect," June 10, 2002, available at cnn.com.

2. Quoted in Ted Bridis, "Bush Promises More Terror Arrests," June 11, 2002, available at http://foi.missouri .edu/terrorandcivillib/bushpromises.html.

3. Josh Tyrangiel, "And Justice for . . ." *Time*, November 26, 2001, pp. 66–67.

4. *Pruneyard Shopping Center v. Robins*, 447 U.S. 74 (1980).

5. Richard H. Fallon, Jr., *The Dynamic Constitution: An Introduction to American Constitutional Law* (New York: Cambridge University Press, 2004), pp. 60–61.

6. Patrick M. Garry, *Wrestling with God: The Court's Tortuous Treatment of Religion* (Washington, DC: Catholic University of America Press, 2006), pp. 70–72.

7. *Everson v. Board of Ewing Township*, 330 U.S. 1 (1947).

8. *Zelman v. Simmons-Harris*, 536 U.S. 639 (2002).

9. *Engel v. Vitale*, 370 U.S. 421 (1962).

10. *Abington School District v. Schempp*, 374 U.S. 203 (1963).

11. *Stone v. Graham*, 449 U.S. 39 (1980).

12. *Wallace v. Jaffree*, 472 U.S. 38 (1985).

13. *Lee v. Weisman*, 505 U.S. 577 (1992).

14. *Santa Fe School District v. Doe*, 530 U.S. 290 (2000).

15. *Van Orden v. Perry*, 545 U.S. 667 (2005).

16. *McCreary County v. American Civil Liberties Union*, 545 U.S. 844 (2005).

17. *Cantwell v. Connecticut*, 310 U.S. 296 (1940); and *Martin v. Struthers*, 319 U.S. 141 (1943).

18. *Employment Division, Oregon Department of Human Resources v. Smith*, 493 U.S. 378 (1990).

19. Ruth Marcus, "One Nation, Under Court Rulings," *Washington Post National Weekly Edition*, March 18–24, 1991, p. 33.

20. *City of Boerne v. Flores*, 521 U.S. 507 (1997).

21. *Gonzales v. Centro Espirita Beneficiente Uniao Do Vegetal*, 546 U.S. 418 (2006).

22. David M. O'Brien, *Constitutional Law and Politics, Vol. 2, Civil Rights and Liberties*, 5th ed. (New York: W. W. Norton, 2003), pp. 411–412.

23. Cass R. Sunstein, *Democracy and the Problem of Free Speech* (New York: Free Press, 1993), pp. 11–13.

24. *Brandenburg v. Ohio*, 395 U.S. 444 (1969).

25. *Cohen v. California*, 403 U.S. 15 (1971).

26. *Madsen v. Women's Health Center*, 512 U.S. 753 (1994).

27. *Schenck v. Pro Choice Network*, 519 U.S. 357 (1997).

28. "Hate Is Not Speech: A Constitutional Defense of Penalty Enhancement for Hate Crimes," *Harvard Law Review* 106 (April 1993): 1314–1331.

29. *Wisconsin v. Mitchell*, 508 U.S. 47 (1993).

30. *Texas v. Johnson*, 491 U.S. 397 (1989).

31. *United States v. Eichman*, 396 U.S. 310 (1990).

32. *Central Hudson Gas & Electric Corp. v. Public Service Commission of New York*, 447 U.S. 557 (1980).

33. Fallon, *The Dynamic Constitution*, p. 49.

34. *Griswold v. Connecticut*, 381 U.S. 479 (1965).

35. *Roe v. Wade*, 410 U.S. 113 (1973).

36. *Webster v. Reproductive Health Services*, 492 U.S. 490 (1989).

37. *Planned Parenthood of Southeastern Pennsylvania v. Casey*, 505 U.S. 833 (1992).

38. *Lawrence v. Texas*, 539 US 558 (2003).

39. *Illinois v. Wardlow*, 528 U.S. 119 (2000).

40. *United States v. Ross*, 456 U.S. 798 (1982).

41. *Weeks v. United States*, 232 U.S. 383 (1914).

42. *Mapp v. Ohio*, 367 U.S. 643 (1961).

43. Adam Liptak, "U.S. Alone in Rejecting All Evidence if Police Err," *New York Times*, July 19, 2008, available at www.nytimes.com.

44. *Massachusetts v. Shepherd*, 468 U.S. 981 (1984); and *United States v. Leon*, 468 U.S. 897 (1984).

45. *Arizona v. Fulminante*, 499 U.S. 270 (1991).

46. *Herring v. United States*, No. 7–513 (2009).

47. *Miranda v. Arizona*, 384 U.S. 436 (1966).

48. Gary L. Stuart, *Miranda: The Story of America's Right to Remain Silent* (Tucson: University of Arizona Press, 2004), p. 100.

49. *Harris v. New York*, 401 U.S. 222 (1971).

50. *New York v. Quarles*, 467 U.S. 649 (1984).

51. *Moran v. Burdine*, 475 U.S. 412 (1986).

52. *Cucci v. Illinois*, 356 U.S. 571 (1958).

53. *United States v. Lanza*, 260 U.S. 377 (1922).

54. *Heath v. Alabama*, 474 U.S. 82 (1985).

55. *Kansas v. Hendricks*, 521 U.S. 346 (1997).

56. Quoted in *Time*, July 7, 1997, p. 29.

57. *Globe Newspaper Co. v. Superior Court*, 457 U.S. 596 (1982).

58. *Chancler v. Florida*, 449 U.S. 560 (1981).

59. *Williams v. Florida*, 399 U.S. 78 (1970).

60. *Snyder v. Louisiana*, No. 06-10119 (2008).

61. *Gideon v. Wainwright*, 372 U.S. 335 (1963).

62. *Tollett v. Henderson*, 411 U.S. 258 (1973).

63. *Solem v. Helm*, 463 U.S. 277 (1983).

64. *Kennedy v. Louisiana*, No. 07-343 (2008).

65. *Furman v. Georgia*, 408 U.S. 238 (1972).

66. *Gregg v. Georgia*, 428 U.S. 153 (1976).

67. Bureau of Justice Statistics, "Capital Punishment Statistics," available at www.ojp.usdoj.gov.

68. James S. Liebman, *A Broken System: Error Rates in Capital Cases, 1973–1995,* available at www.thejusticeproject.org.

69. Ibid.

70. Bureau of Justice Statistics, "Capital Punishment 2005," available at www.ojp.usdoj.gov.

71. "Supreme Court Bars Executing Mentally Retarded," June 20, 2002, available at cnn.com.

72. *Atkins v. Virginia,* 536 U.S. 304 (2002).

73. Otis H. Stephens, Jr., "Presidential Power, Judicial Deference, and the Status of Detainees in an Age of Terrorism," in David B. Cohen and John W. Wells, eds., *American National Security and Civil Liberties in an Era of Terrorism* (New York: Palgrave MacMillan, 2004), p. 82.

74. *Ex parte Quirin,* 317 U.S. 1 (1942).

75. *Hamdi v. Rumsfeld,* 542 U.S. 507 (2004).

76. *Hamdan v. Rumsfeld,* 548 U.S. 557 (2006).

77. *Boumediene v. Bush,* 553 U.S. _____ (2008).

78. Henry J. Abraham and Barbara A. Perry, *Freedom and the Court,* 7th ed. (New York: Oxford University Press, 1998), p. 236.

79. Ranata Lawson Mack and Michael J. Kelly, *Equal Justice in the Balance: America's Legal Responses to the Emerging Terrorist Threat* (Ann Arbor: University of Michigan Press, 2004), p. 238.

80. Otis H. Stephens, Jr., *The Supreme Court and Confessions of Guilt* (Knoxville, TN: University of Tennessee Press, 1973).

81. Donald L. Horowitz, *The Courts and Social Policy* (Washington, DC: Brookings Institution, 1977), p. 223.

82. Liebman, *A Broken System.*

Chapter 16

Civil Rights Policymaking

LEARNING OUTCOMES

After studying Chapter 16, students should be able to do the following:

▶ Identify the significance of the following landmark Supreme Court decisions: *Plessy v. Ferguson*, *Brown v. Board of Education of Topeka*, *Parents Involved in Community Schools v. Seattle School District No. 1*, *Romer v. Evans*, *Shelley v. Kraemer*, *City of Richmond v. J. A. Croson Co.*, *Adarand Constructors v. Pena*, and *Regents of the University of California v. Bakke*. (pp. 434, 436, 439–440, 445, 450–452)

▶ Describe the constitutional basis of civil rights policymaking, considering both the U.S. Constitution and state constitutions. (pp. 432–433)

▶ Describe the approaches taken by the U.S. Supreme Court to legalize classifications based on race and ethnicity, citizenship status, gender, and sexual orientation. (pp. 433–435)

▶ Trace the history of the battle for school desegregation from *Plessy v. Ferguson* to *Parents Involved in Community Schools v. Seattle School District No. 1*. (pp. 434–441)

▶ Describe the steps taken by state governments in the South to disfranchise African Americans in the late nineteenth and early twentieth centuries. (pp. 442–443)

▶ Trace the struggle for voting rights for African Americans from the ratification of the Fifteenth Amendment to the implementation of the Voting Rights Act. (pp. 444–445)

▶ Trace the history of federal civil rights statutes. (pp. 445–448)

▶ Describe the role that state and local governments play in protecting the civil rights of their residents. (pp. 448–449)

▶ Identify the current status of sexual harassment law. (p. 449)

▶ Describe the current status of constitutional law regarding affirmative action. (pp. 450–452)

▶ Analyze civil rights policymaking using the public policy model. (pp. 453–457)

▶ Define the key terms listed on page 458 and explain their significance.

The University of Michigan Law School is one of the most prestigious law schools in the nation. Each year it receives more than 3,500 applications from which it selects a first-year class of 350 students. The law school looks for capable students with the promise of success in the classroom and in the future profession of law. It also strives to admit a mixture of students with varying backgrounds and experiences who will learn from each other. In particular, the law school attempts to ensure that its student body is racially and ethnically diverse by enrolling a critical mass of students from groups that have historically suffered discrimination—African Americans, Latinos, and Native Americans. To achieve its admissions goals, the law school rejects some academically strong applicants in favor of other applicants who add diversity to its student body. Barbara Grutter was one such student rejected by the law school. Grutter, a white woman, had a college grade point average of 3.8 and a high score on the Law School Admissions Test (LSAT). When the law school rejected her application, Grutter accused it of favoring minority applicants who were less qualified academically. She filed suit, charging that the school discriminated against her on the basis of race in violation of the Fourteenth Amendment and the Civil Rights Act of 1964.[1]

Did the University of Michigan Law School illegally discriminate against Barbara Grutter? We explore the answer to that question as we study civil rights policy in Chapter 16. This chapter is the third in a series of four chapters focusing on substantive policy areas. Chapters 14 and 15 dealt with economic and civil liberties policymaking, respectively. Chapter 17 considers foreign and defense policymaking. This chapter examines the constitutional basis for civil rights policymaking, studies the nature of civil rights policies in a number of substantive areas, and concludes by discussing the policymaking process for civil rights policies.

 WHAT IS YOUR OPINION?

How important is it for the student body of a law school to be racially and ethnically diverse?

THE CONSTITUTIONAL BASIS OF CIVIL RIGHTS POLICYMAKING

Equal Protection Clause A provision of the Fourteenth Amendment of the U.S. Constitution that declares that "No State shall . . . deny to any person within its jurisdiction the equal protection of the laws."

Both the U.S. Constitution and state constitutions affect civil rights policymaking. The most important provisions in the U.S. Constitution dealing with civil rights are the Fourteenth and Fifteenth Amendments. The Fourteenth Amendment includes the **Equal Protection Clause:** "No State shall . . . deny to any person within its jurisdiction the equal protection of the laws." The Fifteenth Amendment declares that the right to vote "shall not be denied or abridged by the United States or by any State on account of race, color, or previous condition of servitude." Both the Fourteenth and Fifteenth Amendments contain sections granting Congress authority to pass legislation to enforce their provisions.

Most state constitutions include provisions prohibiting discrimination and/or guaranteeing equal protection of the laws. In recent years, a number of state supreme courts have interpreted their state constitutions to require equitable funding for public schools; guarantee equal rights for women; and, in Massachusetts, Connecticut, and Iowa, grant marriage rights to same-sex couples. In each of these cases, state courts adopted policy positions embracing a more expansive interpretation of civil rights than were taken at the time either in the U.S. Constitution or federal law.

CIVIL RIGHTS ISSUES AND POLICIES

Civil rights The protection of the individual from arbitrary or discriminatory acts by government or by individuals based on that person's group status, such as race or gender.

Civil rights is the protection of the individual from arbitrary or discriminatory acts by government or by other individuals based on an individual's group status, such as race or gender. Whereas civil liberties issues involve individual rights, civil rights issues concern group rights. Civil liberties policy issues revolve around the rights of individuals to be free from unwarranted government restrictions on expression, religious belief, and personal liberty. Civil rights policy issues concern the relationship of the government to individuals based on their status as members of a group.

Civil rights issues are similar to civil liberties issues in that they are often constitutional issues. Although executives, legislatures, bureaucracies, interest groups, and political parties are all involved in civil rights issues, the courts, especially the Supreme Court of the United States, usually have the last word on the parameters of policymaking. Consequently, any discussion of civil rights issues focuses heavily on **constitutional law,** that is, law that involves the interpretation and application of the Constitution.

Constitutional law Law that involves the interpretation and application of the Constitution.

Equality Before the Law

Although the Fourteenth Amendment guarantees individuals equal protection under the law, the Supreme Court has never required that laws deal with everyone and everything in precisely the same fashion. By their nature, laws distinguish among groups of people, types of property, and kinds of actions. The Court has recognized that most distinctions are necessary and desirable, and hence permissible under the Constitution. Only certain types of classifications that the Court considers arbitrary and discriminatory violate the Equal Protection Clause.

Suspect classifications Distinctions among persons that must be justified on the basis of a compelling government interest.

The Supreme Court has ruled that policy distinctions among persons based on their race, ethnicity, and citizenship status are **suspect classifications,** which are distinctions among persons that must be justified on the basis of a compelling government interest. The Supreme Court has declared that it will apply "strict judicial scrutiny" to any law that distinguishes among persons based on their race and ethnicity or citizenship. **Strict judicial scrutiny** is the judicial decision rule holding that the Supreme Court will find a government policy unconstitutional unless the government can demonstrate a compelling interest justifying the action. In other words, government cannot constitutionally adopt policies that treat people differently on the basis of race or citizenship status unless it can demonstrate an overriding public interest in making that distinction. Furthermore, the government must prove that a policy that distinguishes among persons based on their race, ethnicity, or citizenship status is the least restrictive means for achieving the compelling policy objective.

Strict judicial scrutiny The judicial decision rule holding that the Supreme Court will find a government policy unconstitutional unless the government can demonstrate a compelling interest justifying the action.

The Supreme Court has chosen not to look so closely at laws that discriminate against persons on grounds other than race and ethnicity or citizenship status. It has held that government need only demonstrate some "reasonable basis" in order to justify public policies that distinguish among persons on the basis of such factors as relative wealth, physical ability, marital status, residency, or sexual orientation. As for gender, the Court has ruled that the government must offer an "exceedingly persuasive justification" that gender-based distinctions are necessary to achieve some "important governmental objective." Commentators see this standard as somewhere between "compelling government interest" and "reasonable basis."[2]

Table 16.1 summarizes the current application of the Equal Protection Clause to governmental distinctions among groups. The first column identifies a group distinction, such as race, citizenship status, and gender. The second column offers some examples of laws or government policies that distinguish among people based on their group status. The third column identifies the current judicial standard for determining the constitutionality of those policies. Finally, the last column briefly evaluates the likelihood of a policy that makes a distinction based on group status being held constitutional.

Racial Equality   Although the Equal Protection Clause of the Fourteenth Amendment was intended to protect the civil rights of freed slaves, it initially did little to shelter African Americans from discrimination. In the late nineteenth and early twentieth centuries, southern state legislatures enacted **Jim Crow laws,** which were legal provisions requiring the social segregation of African Americans in separate and generally unequal facilities. Jim Crow laws prohibited blacks from sharing schools, hospitals, hotels, restaurants, passenger railcars, and a wide range of other services and public facilities with whites.

Did Jim Crow laws violate the Equal Protection Clause? The U.S. Supreme Court addressed the question in 1896 in the famous case of *Plessy v. Ferguson.* Homer Plessy purchased a first-class ticket on the East Louisiana Railway to travel from New Orleans to Covington, Louisiana. Plessy, who is described in court papers as a man "of mixed descent, in the proportion of seven-eighths Caucasian and one-eighth African blood," took a seat in the rail car reserved for whites. He was arrested and charged with violating a state law that prohibited members of either race from occupying accommodations set aside for the other with the exception of "nurses attending the children of the other race." Plessy initially insisted that he was white, but when that argument failed, he contended that the Louisiana law violated his rights under the U.S. Constitution to equal protection. By an 8–1 vote, the U.S. Supreme Court ruled that the law was a reasonable exercise of the state's power, holding that states can require separate facilities for whites and African Americans as long as the facilities are equal. Thus, the Court adopted the policy known as **separate-but-equal,** which is the judicial doctrine holding that separate facilities for whites and African Americans satisfy the equal protection requirement of the Fourteenth Amendment. Justice John Marshall Harlan, the Court's lone dissenter in *Plessy,* called the decision "a compound of bad logic, bad history, bad sociology, and bad constitutional law . . . Our Constitution is color-blind," he said, "and neither knows nor tolerates classes among citizens."[3]

Jim Crow laws Legal provisions requiring the social segregation of African Americans in separate and generally unequal facilities.

Separate-but-equal The judicial doctrine holding that separate facilities for whites and African Americans satisfy the equal protection requirement of the Fourteenth Amendment.

TABLE 16.1   Status of Selected Groups Under the Equal Protection Clause

Type of Group Distinction	Examples of Government Policies That Make a Distinction Based on the Particular Group Status	Judicial Standard	Likely Outcome of Challenge
Race and ethnicity	State law that prohibits interracial adoption; state law that outlaws interracial marriage; practice of local district attorney to exclude African Americans from juries in cases involving African American defendants; university scholarship program that targets minority students.	Race/ethnicity is a suspect classification. Public policy distinctions based on race or ethnicity must be justified by a compelling government interest. Policies must be narrowly drawn to achieve the goal in the least restrictive fashion possible.	Public policies that disadvantage racial and ethnic minority group members are invariably unconstitutional. Policies designed to remedy the effects of past discrimination against minority group members are constitutional if they are justified by a compelling governmental interest are narrowly drawn.
Citizenship status	State law that denies the children of illegal aliens a free public education; state requirement that only American citizens can be licensed to practice medicine or law in the state; federal requirement that airport luggage screeners must be U.S. citizens.	Citizenship status is a suspect classification. Public policy distinctions based on citizenship status must be justified by a compelling government interest. Policies must be narrowly drawn to achieve the goal in the least restrictive fashion possible.	The outcome of cases involving policies distinguishing among persons based on their citizenship status depends on the Court's evaluation of the government interest involved. Some policies have been upheld, whereas others have been rejected.
Gender	Exclusion of women serving in the military from combat units; state policy that favors the mother over the father in child custody disputes; height requirement for service in local police department that excludes most women.	The Supreme Court has ruled that the government must offer an "exceedingly persuasive justification" that gender-based distinctions are necessary to achieve some "important governmental objective."	Although the Court will allow policy distinctions in some circumstances, the trend is for the Court to look very closely at public policies that treat men and women differently and to find most such distinctions unconstitutional.
Other (including sexual orientation, marital status, residency, etc.)	State law limiting adoption to married couples; health insurance for state employees that provides pregnancy services to married employees only; city ordinance requiring that city employees live within the city limits; state law prohibiting gay men and lesbians from serving as foster parents.	The government must demonstrate that the policy has a rational basis and that it is narrowly tailored to achieve some legitimate end.	Although the Supreme Court upholds most policies in this area, *Romer v. Evans* demonstrates that it will not automatically rule that every distinction is constitutional. This is a developing area of constitutional law.

The Supreme Court allowed state and local governments to determine whether racially segregated facilities were actually equal. In 1899, for example, the Court held that a Georgia school district's decision to close the only African American high school in the county did not violate the Equal Protection Clause even though two white high schools remained open.[4] In another case, the Court permitted a Mississippi school district to require a youngster of Chinese descent to attend an African American school in a neighboring district rather than a nearby whites-only school. As far as the Supreme Court was concerned, state and local officials could determine school assignments without interference from federal courts.[5]

The Supreme Court began to reassess the constitutional status of racial segregation in the late 1930s. The Court started chipping away at the *Plessy* precedent in 1938 in *Missouri ex rel Gaines v. Canada*, the beginning of a long line of test cases brought by the National Association for the Advancement of Colored People (NAACP). A **test case** is a lawsuit initiated to assess the constitutionality of a legislative or executive act. Gaines, who was an African American citizen of Missouri, applied to attend the University of Missouri law school. The state denied him admission, but offered to pay his tuition at a law school in a neighboring state where he could be accepted. Gaines sued, charging that the arrangement violated the Equal Protection Clause, and the Court agreed. Separate-but-equal had to be in the same state.[6]

The Supreme Court further undermined *Plessy* in two cases decided in 1950. In *Sweatt v. Painter*, it ruled that Texas's hasty creation of an African American law school did not satisfy the constitutional criterion of equal protection.[7] In *McLaurin v. Oklahoma State Regents*, the Court ruled against segregation within an institution. The University of Oklahoma admitted G. W. McLaurin, an African American man, to graduate school but forced him to sit in a particular seat, study in a particular carrel in the library, and eat at a particular table in the cafeteria. All of these facilities were labeled, "Reserved for Colored." The Supreme Court ordered that McLaurin be treated like other students.[8]

In 1954, the Court took the final step, unanimously overturning *Plessy* with the landmark decision known as *Brown v. Board of Education of Topeka*. The case involved a lawsuit brought by the parents of Linda Brown, an African American youngster who was denied admission to a whites-only school near her home and forced to travel across town to a school for African Americans. The Court ruled that racial segregation mandated by law denied African American students equal educational opportunity. "Segregation of white and colored children in public schools has a detrimental effect upon the colored children," wrote Chief Justice Earl Warren in the Court's majority opinion. "A sense of inferiority affects the motivation of the child to learn." In essence, the Court declared that separate-but-equal was a contradiction in terms. Once the law requires racial separation, it stamps the badge of inferiority on the minority race.[9]

The *Brown* decision may have been the most important judicial ruling of the twentieth century, but it left two important questions unanswered. One concerned the distinction between de jure and de facto segregation. **De jure segregation** means racial separation required by law, whereas **de facto segregation** is racial separation resulting from factors other than law, such as housing patterns. In *Brown*, the Court ruled that *de jure* segregation was unconstitutional, but it left the issue of *de facto*

Test cases Lawsuits initiated to challenge the constitutionality of a legislative or executive act.

De jure segregation Racial separation required by law.

De facto segregation Racial separation resulting from factors other than law, such as housing patterns.

School desegregation in Little Rock, Arkansas, in 1957.

segregation undecided. The second problem left unsettled by *Brown* was implementation. How was desegregation to be achieved and at what pace? The Court delayed its implementation decision until 1955 when it ordered the lower federal courts to oversee the transition to a nondiscriminatory system "with all deliberate speed."[10]

Implementation proved more deliberate than speedy. Although states in the Upper South made some progress toward desegregation, public officials in the Deep South responded to the *Brown* decision with delay, evasion, defiance, and massive resistance. Alabama Governor George Wallace spoke for many white Southerners: "I say segregation now, segregation tomorrow, segregation forever."[11]

For years, *Brown* was a hollow victory for civil rights forces. Congress did nothing. President Dwight Eisenhower stood silent. The president finally took action in 1957, ordering federal troops into Little Rock, Arkansas, to enforce a school desegregation order against a stubborn Governor Orval Faubus and an angry mob. Nonetheless, a decade after the *Brown* decision, only 1 percent of African American students living in the South attended public schools that were not racially segregated.[12]

The civil rights movement of the 1960s succeeded in rallying support for the cause of African American civil rights. African American protest demonstrations, vividly displayed on the television evening news, moved public opinion to support the cause. Presidents John Kennedy and Lyndon Johnson called for action, and Congress responded with the Civil Rights Act of 1964, which authorized the Department of Health, Education, and Welfare (which has since been divided to form the Department of Health and Human Services and the Department of Education) to cut off federal money to school districts practicing segregation. The department set guidelines, and some progress took place. Furthermore, the Supreme Court lost patience with the slow pace of school desegregation, declaring an end to "all deliberate speed" and ordering immediate desegregation.[13] By the 1972–1973 school year, 91 percent of African American students living in the South attended integrated schools.[14]

The Court's decision to order an end to racial segregation forced the justices to deal with the issues left unresolved by the original *Brown* case. How could integration be achieved? In *Swann v. Charlotte-Mecklenburg Board of Education* (1971), the Court unanimously held that busing, racial quotas, school pairing or grouping, and gerrymandered attendance zones could all be used to eliminate the vestiges of state-supported segregation.[15] Two years later, the Court expanded the definition of *de jure* segregation to include segregation fostered by administrative policies even in the absence of segregation laws. Consequently, the Court ordered the integration of Denver schools, not because they were segregated by force of law, but because the local school board had manipulated attendance zones to create one-race schools.[16]

Today, racial segregation no longer has a legal basis. Few issues of constitutional law are more firmly established than the principle that any law or procedural requirement compelling the physical separation of people by race or ethnicity is unconstitutional. The old Jim Crow laws are now all gone, either repealed or rendered unenforceable by court rulings.

Nonetheless, the end of legal segregation has not necessarily brought about meaningful racial integration in the public schools. Today, African American and Latino students have less contact with white students than their counterparts had in 1970, and most African American and Latino children attend schools where their racial/ethnic group is in the majority.[17] Racial segregation in the schools is growing because of a major increase in enrollment by minority students, continued migration of white families from urban neighborhoods, housing patterns that isolate racial and ethnic groups, and the end of court-ordered racial integration.[18] Neither local officials nor the courts have been willing to take steps sufficient to racially integrate inner-city schools. Although most Americans favor school desegregation in principle, busing for the purposes of achieving racial balance in schools is unpopular, even with many minority parents.

 WHAT IS YOUR OPINION?

How important is it for your children to attend schools that are racially diverse?

Furthermore, the Supreme Court is no longer willing to order state and local officials to act aggressively to achieve racial integration. In *Millikin v. Bradley* (1974), the Court ruled that a district judge in Michigan lacked authority to order student busing between Detroit's predominantly African American inner-city school district and 53 predominantly white suburban school districts. Suburban school districts could not be forced to help desegregate a city's schools unless the suburbs had been involved in illegally segregating them in the first place.[19] In *Missouri v. Jenkins* (1995), the Supreme Court overturned a district court order requiring the state of Missouri to pay for a plan to upgrade predominantly African American schools in Kansas City, Missouri. The goal of the district court order had been to improve the inner-city schools in hopes of enticing white parents who live in the suburbs to voluntarily send their children to the inner city. The Supreme Court held that local desegregation plans could not go beyond the purpose of eliminating racial discrimination. Once the lingering effects of legally enforced segregation were eradicated, it would be legal for the district to operate schools that happened to be all black or all white.[20] Finally, in *Parents Involved in Community Schools v. Seattle School District No. 1* (2007), a closely divided Supreme Court struck down a Seattle school assignment procedure that used race as a "tiebreaker" in making student assignments to high schools, even though the goal of the plan was to achieve racial integration rather than segregation.[21] Instead of using the *Brown* precedent to further efforts to achieve racial integration of public schools, the Court declared that *Brown* required school districts to follow color-blind school assignment policies.

Other Equal Protection Issues   Not all equal protection claims involve African Americans or school desegregation. The Supreme Court has declared that citizenship status is a suspect classification similar to race, justifiable only by a compelling government interest. For example, the Court has struck down state laws that prohibited noncitizen permanent residents from becoming lawyers, engineers, or notary publics and ruled that states may not deny legal residents who are not citizens the opportunity to apply for financial aid for higher education.[22] In each case, the Court ruled that the government had failed to establish that it had a compelling interest in making the distinction. In contrast, the Court has held that states do indeed have a compelling interest in excluding noncitizens from playing a role in government, either by voting, running for office, or working as police officers.

After the terrorist attacks of September 11, 2001, Congress passed, and President Bush signed, the Aviation and Transportation Security Act, which included a provision restricting employment as airport screeners to U.S. citizens. Thousands of noncitizen legal residents who had been employed as airport screeners lost their jobs because of the measure, and several of them filed suit, attacking the constitutionality of the new law. A federal district judge ruled that the provision excluding noncitizens from employment as security screeners was unconstitutional. The judge concluded that the government had a compelling interest in protecting aviation security but held that the exclusion of noncitizens from screening jobs was not the "least restrictive means" for achieving that goal.[23]

Over the years, the Supreme Court has considered a number of equal protection issues raised on the basis of gender. For nearly a century after the adoption of the Fourteenth Amendment, the Court refused to apply the Equal Protection Clause to gender discrimination. Instead, the Court accepted discrimination against women as a necessary protection for the weaker sex. In 1873, for example, the Supreme Court

States must demonstrate that laws that distinguish among individuals based on their gender have been enacted to fulfill an important government function, that they are a least restrictive method of achieving the function, and that they are not based on stereotypical notions about men and women.

upheld an Illinois law denying women the opportunity to practice law with the following explanation: "The natural and proper timidity and delicacy which belong to the female sex evidently unfit it for many of the occupations of civil life."[24]

Within the last 30 years, the Supreme Court has begun to look closely at claims of gender discrimination. Although the Court has not added gender to its list of suspect classifications, it has required that state governments prove that sex-based distinctions are necessary to achieve some "important governmental objective." The Court has also declared that the government must offer an "exceedingly persuasive justification" for gender-based distinctions if they are to be held constitutional.[25] The Court ruled, for example, that Virginia Military Institute (VMI), a state-supported military university, could not constitutionally exclude women and that the state's offer to create a separate military college for women was unacceptable. The Court held that the state of Virginia had failed to show an exceedingly persuasive justification for maintaining a male-only university.[26] Nonetheless, the Court still upholds some gender-based laws, such as Congress's decision to exclude women from having to register for military service, on the basis of traditional attitudes about the respective roles of men and women in society.[27]

In 1996, the Supreme Court issued its first equal-protection ruling favoring gay and lesbian rights in the case of *Romer v. Evans.* The legal dispute concerned a challenge to an amendment to the constitution of Colorado approved by state voters in 1992. Amendment Two, as it was known, not only repealed all local ordinances and statewide policies protecting gay men and lesbians from discrimination but also prohibited the

GLOBAL PERSPECTIVE

Women's Rights in Saudi Arabia

Women in Saudi Arabia have limited legal rights. Under Saudi law, which is based on a conservative interpretation of Islam, women are socially and legally dependent on their male guardians—their fathers at birth and their spouses upon marriage. Women cannot even have their own legal identity cards. Their names are added to their father's identity card when they are born and transferred to their husband's identity card when they marry. As a result, a woman cannot travel, purchase property, or enroll in college without the written permission of a male relative.*

The Saudi government encourages women to be stay-at-home mothers. Women must cover themselves fully in public and wear a veil. They cannot attend classes with men or work with men. Women's education is aimed at making women better wives and mothers. Women cannot study law or become pilots. Instead, they are directed toward occupations deemed suitable for their gender, such as teaching in a girls' school. Women are not allowed to vote or drive a vehicle. Women who fail to conform to societal norms are subject to harassment by the religious police. They may be arrested, imprisoned, and even caned.

Nonetheless, Saudi Arabia has a women's rights movement. Many Saudi women are aware of the status of women in other countries, including Muslim countries, because of the Internet, satellite TV, and travel abroad, and they are demanding better treatment. Young Saudi women in particular, who are better educated than most of the older women, are challenging their society's conservative interpretation of Islam. They are demanding access to education and employment opportunities.

The Saudi government has made some concessions to women's rights. Women are now permitted to stay in a hotel alone without the presence of a male relative. Even though some leading universities only admit men, women now constitute a majority of university students.[†] The Saudi government is also reportedly considering lifting the ban against women driving.[‡]

QUESTIONS TO CONSIDER

1. Is the treatment of women in Saudi Arabia a concern for people around the world, or should it be an internal matter for the Saudis alone to address?
2. Should the United States pressure Saudi Arabia to improve the status of women?
3. Do you think most women in Saudi Arabia are comfortable with their legal and social status?

*Stephen Schwartz, "Shari'a in Saudi Arabia, Today and Tomorrow," in Paul Marshall, ed., *Radical Islam's Rules: The Worldwide Spread of Extreme Shari'a Law* (Lanham, MD: Rowman & Littlefield, 2005), pp. 33–34.

[†]Mai Yamani, "Muslim Women and Human Rights in Saudi Arabia," in Eugene Cotran and Mai Yamani, eds., *The Rule of Law in the Middle East and the Islamic World: Human Rights and the Judicial Process* (London, UK: I. B. Tauris, 2000), pp. 137–145.

[‡]Damien McElroy, "Saudi Arabia to Lift Ban on Women Drivers," *Daily Telegraph*, January 21, 2008, available at www.telegraph.co.uk.

future enactment of similar measures. The Supreme Court declared that the state of Colorado would have to demonstrate that the amendment bore a rational relationship to some legitimate end in order to meet the requirements of the Equal Protection Clause. The amendment was so broadly drawn, however, that the only logical explanation for its enactment was animosity toward gay men and lesbians. The real purpose of the measure was evidently "to make homosexuals unequal to everyone else," which, the Court said, is not a legitimate goal of state government. Consequently, Amendment Two violated the Equal Protection Clause of the Fourteenth Amendment.[28]

Voting Rights and Representation

Suffrage The right to vote.

Although the right to vote is a fundamental civil right, universal adult **suffrage** (the right to vote) is a relatively recent development in the United States. The original Constitution (Article I, Section 2) allowed the states to establish voter qualifications, and initially most states limited the right to vote to adult white males who owned property. Popular pressure forced states to drop the property qualification in the early decades of the nineteenth century. Women won the right to vote with the ratification of the Nineteenth Amendment in 1920.

Disfranchisement The denial of voting rights.

The struggle for voting rights for African Americans was particularly difficult despite the Fifteenth Amendment, which declared that the right to vote could not be abridged on account of race or color. In the late nineteenth and early twentieth centuries, southern white authorities adopted an array of devices designed to prevent African Americans from exercising meaningful voting rights. Disfranchisement methods included tests of understanding, literacy tests, the white primary, grandfather clauses, and poll taxes. **Disfranchisement** is the denial of voting rights.

White primary An electoral system used in the South to prevent the participation of African Americans in the Democratic primary.

The **white primary** was an electoral system used in the South to prevent the participation of African Americans in the Democratic primary. (A **primary election** is an intraparty election held to select party candidates for the general election ballot.) Because Democrats dominated southern politics from the 1870s through the 1950s, the Democratic Party primary was by far the most important election in most southern states. By excluding African Americans from the Democratic primary, southern officials effectively prevented them from participating meaningfully in state politics. The Supreme Court invalidated the white primary in 1944.[29]

Primary election An election held to determine a party's nominees for the general election ballot.

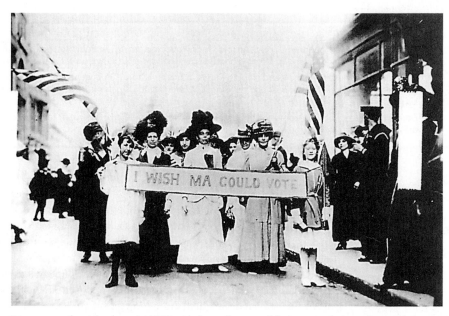

Women won the right to vote in 1920 with the ratification of the Nineteenth Amendment.

Test of understanding A legal requirement that citizens must accurately explain a passage in the United States or state constitution before they could register to vote.

Literacy test A legal requirement that citizens demonstrate an ability to read and write before they could register to vote.

Poll tax A tax levied on the right to vote.

Grandfather clause A provision that exempted those persons whose grandfathers had been eligible to vote at some earlier date from tests of understanding, literacy tests, and other difficult-to-achieve voter qualification requirements.

At-large election A method for choosing public officials in which the citizens of an entire political subdivision, such as a state, vote to select officeholders.

District election A method for choosing public officials that divides a political subdivision, such as a state, into geographic areas called districts and each district elects one official.

Tests of understanding, literacy tests, and poll taxes were often used in combination with a grandfather clause. A **test of understanding** was a legal requirement that citizens must accurately explain a passage in the U.S. or state constitution before they could register to vote. A **literacy test** was a legal requirement that citizens demonstrate an ability to read and write before they could register to vote. A **poll tax** was a tax levied on the right to vote. A **grandfather clause** was a provision that exempted those persons whose grandfathers had been eligible to vote at some earlier date from tests of understanding, literacy tests, and other difficult-to-achieve voter qualification requirements. The effect of the grandfather clause was to allow prospective white voters to escape voter requirements used to discourage or disqualify prospective African American voters.

Although the Supreme Court invalidated the grandfather clause in 1915,[30] tests of understanding, literacy tests, and poll taxes survived constitutional challenge for decades. The Court finally knocked down the use of tests of understanding in 1965, holding that they were often used to deny African Americans the right to vote.[31] In the same year, Congress passed, and the president signed, legislation that suspended the use of literacy tests throughout the South. Five years later, Congress extended the ban on literacy tests to the entire nation. The poll tax lasted until the mid-1960s. The Twenty-fourth Amendment, ratified in 1964, eliminated the use of poll taxes for elections to federal office. In 1966, the Supreme Court held that the poll tax was an unconstitutional requirement for voting in state and local elections as well.[32]

After the demise of the white primary and the poll tax, the opponents of minority voting rights developed more subtle methods to reduce the political influence of African Americans and other minority group members in American politics. Consider the role of at-large election systems. An **at-large election** is a method for choosing public officials in which every citizen of a political subdivision, such as a state, votes to select a public official. Even if 40 to 45 percent of an area's voters are African American or Latino, at-large elections could still prevent the election of any minority candidates if white citizens voted as a bloc for white candidates. In general, the election of minority candidates is more likely in a **district election,** which is a method for choosing public officials in which a political subdivision, such as a state, is divided into districts and each district elects one official.

Nonetheless, district elections do not offer absolute protection against voter discrimination because the opponents of minority voting rights can use minority-vote dilution or minority-vote packing to reduce the political influence of African American and Latino voters. **Minority-vote dilution** is the drawing of election district lines so as to thinly spread minority voters among several districts, thus reducing their electoral influence in any one district. In contrast, **minority-vote packing** is the drawing of electoral district lines so as to cluster minority voters into one district or a small number of districts, thus reducing their overall electoral influence. Although minority voters could control a handful of districts, their political influence would be restricted to those few districts.

The **Voting Rights Act (VRA)** is a federal law designed to protect the voting rights of racial and ethnic minorities. The VRA makes it illegal for state and local governments to enact and enforce election rules and procedures that diminish African American and Latino voting power. Furthermore, the VRA requires state

Minority-vote dilution The drawing of election district lines so as to thinly spread minority voters among several districts, thus reducing their electoral influence in any one district.

Minority-vote packing The drawing of electoral district lines so as to cluster minority voters into one district or a small number of districts, thus reducing their overall electoral influence.

Voting Rights Act (VRA) A federal law designed to protect the voting rights of racial and ethnic minorities.

Pre-clearance A requirement of the Voting Rights Act that state and local governments in areas with a history of voting discrimination must submit redistricting plans to the federal Department of Justice for approval *before* they can go into effect.

Majority-minority districts Legislative districts whose population was more than 50 percent African American and Latino.

and local governments in areas with a history of voting discrimination to submit redistricting plans to the federal Department of Justice for approval *before* they can go into effect. This procedure is known as **pre-clearance.** Congress and the president included the pre-clearance provision in the VRA in order to stay one step ahead of local officials who would adopt new discriminatory electoral procedures as soon as the federal courts threw out an old procedure. The pre-clearance provision of the VRA only applies to states and parts of states that have substantial racial and language minority populations with relatively low rates of voter participation.

The VRA was instrumental in the election of record numbers of African American and Latino candidates during the 1990s. Under pressure from the Justice Department, state legislatures across the nation, but especially in the South, created a number of **majority-minority districts.** These were legislative districts whose population was more than 50 percent African American and Latino. Most of these districts elected minority candidates.

The creation of majority-minority districts is controversial. Many supporters of minority rights believe that African American candidates, especially in the South, do not stand a realistic chance of winning office in majority white districts. They point to research showing that white voters are less likely to support African American candidates than white candidates with similar views and qualifications, especially dark skinned African American candidates.[33] In fact, no minority candidates won election to Congress from the South between 1898 and 1972.[34]

Critics of majority-minority districts argue their case along both philosophical and practical lines. Creating election districts on the basis of race is wrong, they say, regardless of whether the goal is electing minority or nonminority candidates. Furthermore, the practical impact of majority-minority districts is to limit the influence of minority voters to a relatively small number of districts. To draw majority-minority districts, legislatures must group minority voters in a few districts, removing them from surrounding districts. Research shows that incumbent members of Congress who lost black constituents after redistricting were less sensitive to the concerns of the African American community. In effect, the creation of majority-minority districts presented a trade-off for African Americans—more black faces in Congress, but fewer members of Congress sensitive to African American concerns.[35]

 WHAT IS YOUR OPINION?

Do you think election districts should be drawn in order to increase the likelihood that a minority candidate will win election? Why or why not?

The future of majority-minority districts is in doubt because of the rulings of the U.S. Supreme Court in *Shaw v. Reno* (1993) and *Miller v. Johnson* (1995). The cases involved constitutional challenges to redistricting plans in North Carolina and Georgia. The Court ruled that a state could not create legislative districts based on the race of district residents unless it could demonstrate a compelling government interest. Satisfying the requirements of the VRA would not be a satisfactory reason, the Court said, because Congress and the president adopted the VRA to prohibit discrimination rather than maximize the number of majority-minority districts. In sum, the Court ruled that districts drawn in order to favor racial and ethnic minorities are no more justifiable than districts created to discriminate against them.[36]

Freedom from Discrimination

Civil rights concerns the protection of the individual, not just against government action, but also against discrimination by *private* parties, such as hotels, restaurants, theaters, and business firms. Most individual rights claims against private discrimination are based on **statutory law,** which is law that is written by a legislature, rather than constitutional law.

Statutory law Law that is written by the legislature.

After the Civil War, Congress enacted two important laws designed to protect the civil rights of former slaves. The Civil Rights Act of 1866 declared that citizens "of every race and color" were entitled "to make and enforce contracts, to sue . . . , give evidence, to inherit, purchase, lease, sell, hold, and convey real and personal property."[37] The Civil Rights Act of 1875 declared that "all persons within the jurisdiction of the United States shall be entitled to the full and equal enjoyment of the accommodations . . . of inns, public conveyances on land or water, theaters, and other places of public amusement."[38]

In the *Civil Rights Cases* (1883), however, the U.S. Supreme Court found the Civil Rights Act of 1875 unconstitutional. These cases involved disputes over theaters that would not seat African Americans, hotels and restaurants that would not serve African Americans, and a train that refused to seat an African American woman in the "ladies" car. The Court held that the Fourteenth Amendment protected individuals from discrimination by government but not by private parties.[39] The Court's decision in the *Civil Rights Cases* opened the door for private individuals, businesses, and organizations to discriminate in housing, employment, and a broad range of public accommodations.

It took civil rights forces more than 80 years to overcome the precedent set in the *Civil Rights Cases.* Consider the issue of housing discrimination. Although the Supreme Court ruled in 1917 that cities could not establish exclusive residential zones for whites and blacks,[40] housing developers often achieved the same result through **racially restrictive covenants,** which were private deed restrictions that prohibited property owners from selling or leasing property to African Americans or other minorities. The NAACP finally succeeded in undercutting restrictive covenants in *Shelley v. Kraemer* (1948). The Supreme Court held that private contracts calling for discrimination could be written, but state courts could not constitutionally enforce them because enforcement would make the state a party to discrimination.[41]

Racially restrictive covenants Private deed restrictions that prohibited property owners from selling or leasing property to African Americans or other minorities.

The executive and legislative branches of government participated in the battle against housing discrimination as well. In 1962, President Kennedy issued an executive order banning discrimination in property owned, sold, or leased by the federal government. Subsequently, Title IV of the Civil Rights Act of 1964 extended nondiscrimination provisions to all public housing and urban renewal developments receiving federal assistance. The most important legislative move against housing discrimination was the Fair Housing Act of 1968, which prohibited discrimination in all transactions involving realtors.

A few weeks after the passage of the Fair Housing Act, the Supreme Court ruled that the Civil Rights Act of 1866 prohibited discrimination in all real estate transactions, including those among private individuals. The Court held that Congress in 1866 intended to ban all discrimination in the purchase or lease of property, including discrimination by private sellers. Furthermore, the Court ruled that Congress's action in prohibiting private housing discrimination was a constitutional exercise of authority granted by the Thirteenth Amendment, which prohibits slavery. "[W]hen racial discrimination herds men into ghettoes and makes their ability to buy property turn on the color of their skin, then it . . . is a relic of slavery."[42]

Civil rights forces used litigation and legislation to attack other forms of private discrimination. In the late 1950s and early 1960s, African American activists staged sit-ins at segregated dime store lunch counters and refuse to leave until served. Local police would arrest the protesters, charging them with disturbing the peace or breaking a local Jim Crow ordinance. With NAACP legal assistance, the demonstrators would appeal their conviction to the federal courts, where it would be reversed and the local segregation ordinance overturned. This case-by-case approach desegregated many public facilities, but it was slow and expensive.

Interstate Commerce Clause The constitutional provision giving Congress authority to "regulate commerce . . . among the several states."

The Civil Rights Act of 1964 was a more efficient tool for fighting discrimination. Title II of the act outlawed discrimination based on race, religion, color, sex, or national origin in hotels, restaurants, gas stations, and other public accommodations. Congress based Title II on the Interstate Commerce Clause in order to overcome the precedent set in the *Civil Rights Cases* that the Fourteenth Amendment prohibits discrimination by the government but not discrimination by private individuals and firms. The **Interstate Commerce Clause** is the constitutional provision giving Congress authority to "regulate commerce . . . among the several states." Because hotels, restaurants, gas stations, and the like serve individuals traveling from state to state, and because they purchase products that have been shipped in interstate commerce, Congress reasoned that they are part of interstate commerce and, consequently, subject to regulation by Congress. In *Heart of Atlanta Motel v. United States* and *Katzenbach v. McClung* (1964), the Supreme Court upheld the constitutionality of Congress's action.[43]

Americans with Disabilities Act (ADA) A federal law designed to end discrimination against persons with disabilities and eliminate barriers to their full participation in American society.

Employment Non-Discrimination Act (ENDA) A proposed federal law that would protect Americans from employment discrimination on the basis of sexual orientation.

Congress and the president have enacted legislation extending civil rights protection to groups based on criteria other than race, religion, color, gender, or national origin. The **Americans with Disabilities Act (ADA)** is a federal law intended to end discrimination against disabled persons and eliminate barriers to their full participation in American society. Other federal legislation prohibits age discrimination and protects families with children from housing discrimination. Title IX of the Education Amendments of 1972 is a federal law that prohibits gender discrimination in programs at educational institutions that receive federal funds. Because of Title IX, high schools, colleges, and universities have expanded athletic opportunities for women. Congress has considered but not passed the **Employment Non-Discrimination Act (ENDA),** which is a proposed federal law that would protect Americans from employment discrimination on the basis of sexual orientation.

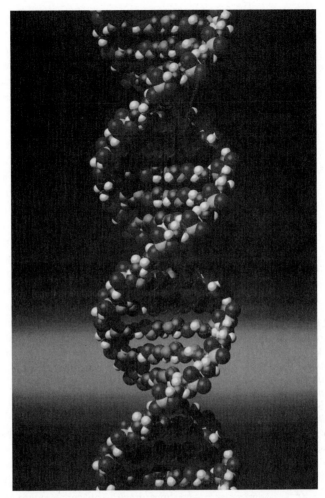

In 2008, Congress passed, and President George W. Bush signed, the Genetic Information Nondiscrimination Act. It prohibited health insurance companies from using genetic information to deny benefits or raise premiums. It also prohibited employers from using genetic information to make employment decisions.

The Civil Rights Act of 1991 dealt with hiring practices that are not overtly discriminatory but which nonetheless limit employment opportunities for women and minorities. Suppose a city government requires prospective police officers to stand at least 5 feet 5 inches tall. That requirement would disproportionately reduce the number of women eligible to apply for jobs because women are typically shorter than men. The Civil Rights Act of 1991 declared that hiring practices that have a disproportionate impact on women and minorities must be "job-related for the position in question and consistent with business necessity." The city's height requirement for police officers would be illegal unless the city could show that a height of at least 5 feet 5 inches was necessary to do the job. Furthermore, the Civil Rights Act of 1991 allowed women, minorities, and the disabled to sue for monetary damages in cases of intentional job discrimination and harassment.

In recent years, however, the Supreme Court has made it more difficult for women and minorities to win discrimination lawsuits. In 1989, for example, the Court reversed a 13-year-old precedent that interpreted the Civil Rights Act of 1866 to allow workers to sue employers for job discrimination. The Court ruled that the law only prohibited hiring discrimination but not racial harassment in the workplace and discrimination in promotions.[44] Furthermore, the Court ruled that workers who lose their jobs must specifically prove that their firing was motivated by unlawful bias. The case involved an African American man who claimed that he was demoted and then fired from his job at a prison in Missouri because of his race. The Court ruled that it was insufficient for the man to show that the reasons given by his employer for firing him were untrue. He had to prove that he was fired because of racial bias rather than personal dislike.[45]

State and local governments have also adopted policies protecting various groups from discrimination. Many state and local governments offer protection from discrimination based on race, ethnicity, gender, age, color, national origin, and disability, similar to those contained in federal law. Some state and local governments go beyond federal law, offering protection from discrimination based on sexual orientation and sexual identify (to protect transgendered persons from discrimination). A number of states have enacted legislation to allow gay men and lesbians to form **civil unions,** which are legal partnerships between two men or two women that gives the couple all the benefits, protections, and responsibilities under law as are granted to spouses in a marriage. Other states allow same-sex couples and opposite-sex couples to create a **domestic partnership,** which is a legal status similar to civil unions in that it confers rights similar to marriage. Several states recognize gay marriage.

The U.S. Supreme Court has held, however, that state and local civil rights laws must be balanced against individual rights. Consider the case of *Boy Scouts of America v. Dale* (2000). James Dale had been a scout since he was eight, earning the rank of Eagle Scout at the age of 18. Dale became an adult member of the Scouts and served as an assistant scoutmaster while he was a student at Rutgers University. After a story appeared in a local newspaper identifying Dale as the co-president of the Rutgers University Lesbian/Gay Alliance, the Boy Scouts sent him a letter revoking his membership, stating that the organization specifically forbids membership by homosexuals. Dale sued the Boy Scouts, charging that their action violated a New Jersey law prohibiting discrimination in public accommodations on the basis of sexual orientation. The U.S. Supreme Court ruled that applying the New Jersey law to the Boy Scouts would violate the organization's First Amendment right of "expressive association." The Boy Scouts claimed that opposition to homosexuality was an integral part of its organizational message. The Court decided that forcing the Scouts to include an openly gay member would unconstitutionally violate the organization's freedom of expression because it would make it difficult for the Scouts to convey their value system to members and the general public.[46]

The decision in the *Dale* case extended an earlier ruling that dealt with the exclusion of an Irish gay and lesbian organization from a privately organized St. Patrick's Day parade in Boston. The Supreme Court held that the state of Massachusetts could

Civil union A legal partnership between two men or two women that gives the couple all the benefits, protections, and responsibilities under law as are granted to spouses in a traditional marriage.

Domestic partnership A legal status similar to civil unions in that it confers rights similar to marriage.

not enforce a law prohibiting discrimination in public accommodations on the basis of sexual orientation against the parade organizers. The Court said that a parade is a form of expression. By forcing the parade organizers to include a group whose message the organizers did not wish to convey, the government would be violating the free speech rights of the parade organizers. The Court held that Massachusetts could not limit free speech unless it could demonstrate a compelling government interest that could not be achieved in a less restrictive manner.[47]

 WHAT IS YOUR OPINION?

Should gay men and lesbians enjoy the same legal protection from discrimination that women and the members of racial and ethnic minority groups have?

Sexual Harassment

The male chief executive officer (CEO) of a large organization invites a young, female employee of the organization to meet him in private. He allegedly exposes his genitals to her and asks for sexual favors. The young woman refuses. The alleged incident is a one-time-only event. The CEO does not threaten the female employee with retaliation, and, in fact, she continues her career in the organization without suffering any apparent penalty. Does the alleged event constitute sexual harassment under the law?

The legal concept of sexual harassment is based on federal laws prohibiting gender discrimination in employment.[48] The courts have held that employers who sexually harass their employees or permit sexual harassment in the workplace are guilty of illegal employment discrimination. Sexual harassment can be male–female, female–male, male–male, or female–female.[49]

The federal courts have identified two categories of sexual harassment: *quid pro quo* harassment and harassment based on a hostile environment. *Quid pro quo* harassment involves a supervisor threatening an employee with retaliation unless the employee submits to sexual advances. "You either sleep with me or you are fired," is a clear and blatant example of *quid pro quo* sexual harassment. Defining sexual harassment based on a hostile environment is more difficult. Even when no sexual demands are made, an employer may be guilty of sexual harassment if an employee is subjected to sexual conduct and comments that are pervasive and severe enough to affect the employee's job performance. A supervisor who continues to ask a subordinate for a date despite repeated rejections may be guilty of creating a hostile work environment.

Was the CEO in our example guilty of sexual harassment if, of course, the alleged incident actually occurred? A federal judge threw the case out of court, declaring that the alleged incident, even if true, did not constitute illegal sexual harassment. No threat of retaliation occurred, so the incident could not have constituted *quid pro quo* harassment. Because the alleged incident was an isolated occurrence, the judge ruled that the employee was not subjected to a hostile work environment. The woman appealed the ruling, however, and rather than risk losing on appeal, the CEO agreed to pay her a settlement of $850,000 in exchange for her dropping the lawsuit. Incidentally, the CEO of the large organization was Bill Clinton, who was then governor of Arkansas. The young female employee was Paula Jones.

Affirmative Action

Affirmative action
A program designed
to ensure equal
opportunities in
employment and
college admissions
for racial minorities
and women.

Affirmative action refers to steps taken by colleges, universities, and employers to remedy the effects of past discrimination. Affirmative action takes a number of forms. A corporation may target colleges and universities with substantial minority enrollments in hopes of increasing the number of African Americans, Latinos, and Asians in its applicant pool. A local government taking bids for the construction of a new sports stadium may stipulate that contractors make a good-faith effort to ensure that at least 25 percent of subcontracts go to firms owned by women or minorities. A federal grant program designed to provide scholarships to college students studying to become teachers may be limited to students who are members of racial and ethnic minority groups. A law school may reserve 20 percent of the places in its first-year class for African Americans and Latinos. A city government may require that 30 percent of city contracts go to firms owned by women or minorities.

Few issues in American government are more controversial than affirmative action. The proponents of race- and gender-based preferences believe they are necessary to remedy the effects of past discrimination. Colleges and universities assert that they benefit from a diverse student body. Employers value a diverse workforce. In contrast, the opponents of racial and gender preferences argue that the only fair way to determine college admissions and employment decisions is merit. It is wrong, they say, to hire or promote someone because of race or gender.

Federal government efforts to remedy the effects of discrimination began in the early 1960s. Presidents Kennedy and Johnson ordered affirmative action in federal employment and hiring by government contractors, but their orders had little practical effect until the late 1960s, when the Department of Labor began requiring government contractors to employ certain percentages of women and minorities. For the following decade, affirmative action took on a momentum all its own. For some, affirmative action meant nondiscrimination. For others, it required seeking out qualified women and minorities. For still others, affirmative action stood for hiring set percentages of women and minorities—a quota system. All the while, employers kept careful records of how many women and minority group members were part of their operations.

The election of Ronald Reagan as president in 1980 was a major setback for the proponents of affirmative action. During the Reagan administration, the Equal Employment Opportunity Commission (EEOC), under the leadership of Clarence Thomas, dismantled affirmative action programs and anything that resembled a quota system for women and minorities. In Reagan's view, civil rights laws should offer relief not to whole groups of people, but only to specific individuals who could prove that they were victims of discrimination. Hiring goals, timetables, and racial quotas, the administration argued, were reverse discrimination against whites. Reagan's most lasting impact on affirmative action was in the judicial branch of government. Reagan appointees, later reinforced by justices appointed by President George H. W. Bush, created a Supreme Court majority who shared Reagan's conservative philosophy on affirmative action issues.

In *City of Richmond v. J. A. Croson Co.* (1989) and *Adarand Constructors v. Pena* (1995), the Supreme Court put many affirmative policies in constitutional jeopardy. The *Croson* case dealt with a minority business set-aside program for municipal

Minority business set-aside A legal requirement that firms receiving government grants or contracts allocate a certain percentage of their purchases of supplies and services to businesses owned or controlled by members of minority groups.

construction contracts established by the city of Richmond, Virginia. A **minority business set-aside** is a legal requirement that firms receiving government grants or contracts allocate a certain percentage of their purchases of supplies and services to businesses owned or controlled by members of minority groups. Even though African Americans constituted half of Richmond's population, less than 1 percent of city government construction dollars had typically gone to minority-owned firms. In light of this history, the city council passed an ordinance requiring that prime contractors awarded city construction contracts over the following five years must subcontract at least 30 percent of the dollar amount of their contracts to one or more minority-business enterprises. The ordinance allowed waivers when contractors could prove that the requirements of the ordinance could not be achieved.

Richmond's minority business set-aside program soon became the target of litigation. J. A. Croson Co., a contracting company whose bid for a city project was rejected for failing to meet the minority set-aside, filed suit against the ordinance, charging that it was unconstitutional. The U.S. Supreme Court ruled that Richmond's set-aside ordinance unconstitutionally violated the Equal Protection Clause of the Fourteenth Amendment because it denied certain persons the opportunity to compete for a fixed percentage of city contracts based solely on their race.

The most significant aspect of the *Croson* decision was that the Court applied strict judicial scrutiny to race-conscious efforts to remedy the effects of past discrimination. For years, the Court had applied the standard of strict judicial scrutiny to government restrictions on measures that disadvantaged individuals based on their race or citizenship status. In *Croson*, the Court served notice that it would also apply strict scrutiny to programs designed to correct the effects of past discrimination.

The Court's majority opinion declared that although minority set-aside programs can be justified as a remedy for discrimination in some instances, the Richmond city council failed to demonstrate a specific history of discrimination in the city's construction industry sufficient to justify a race-based program of relief. The mere fact that few city construction contracts had gone to minority firms was not sufficient evidence to prove discrimination either by the city government or in the city's construction industry. Instead of comparing the number of city contracts going to minority businesses with the proportion of minority citizens in Richmond, the Court ruled that the city council should have compared contracts with the proportion of minority-owned enterprises in the city's construction industry. Perhaps Richmond had few minority-owned construction companies. Instead of racial discrimination, the lack of minority-owned businesses might have reflected differences in educational opportunities or career choices by members of minority groups.

The Court also held that Richmond's set-aside program was constitutionally unacceptable because it was not narrowly tailored to achieve any goal except "outright racial balancing." The plan gave absolute preference to minority entrepreneurs from anywhere in the country, not just the Richmond area. Furthermore, the Court said, the program made no effort to determine whether particular minority businesspersons seeking a racial preference had themselves suffered the effects of discrimination.[50]

Adarand Constructors v. Pena involved a discrimination lawsuit by Adarand Constructors, a Colorado construction company, against the U.S. Department of

Transportation (DOT). Adarand's low bid on a contract to build highway guardrails was rejected in favor of a higher bid by Gonzales Construction Company, which was certified by the DOT as a small business controlled by "socially and economically disadvantaged individuals." The DOT, which gave additional compensation to prime contractors who subcontracted with socially and economically disadvantaged companies, assumed that businesses that are 51 percent owned by individuals who are "black, Hispanic, Asian Pacific, Subcontinent Asian, and Native American" were socially and economically disadvantaged. The prime contractor for the job stipulated that Adarand would have received the bid were it not for the financial incentive given by the DOT for using a company that is certified as socially and economically disadvantaged.

The Supreme Court ordered the *Adarand* case returned to the trial court for reconsideration in light of the standard of strict judicial scrutiny. All racial classifications, whether imposed by state and local governments or the federal government, must serve a compelling government interest and must be narrowly tailored to further that interest. The goal of remedying the effects of past discrimination may be sufficient justification, the Court said, but only when a clear history of specific discrimination can be demonstrated. Statistics showing racial disparities in hiring and promotion are not sufficient to prove discrimination as long as an employer can produce evidence that employment practices resulting in a racial imbalance are justified by legitimate business necessity, such as the absence of qualified minority workers. Furthermore, any affirmative action plan designed to address the problem must be narrowly tailored to achieve that end.[51]

The Supreme Court first dealt with affirmative action in college admissions in *Regents of the University of California v. Bakke* (1978). Allan Bakke, a white male, sued the university after he was denied admission to medical school. The university had a minority admissions program in which it set aside 16 of 100 places each year for minority applicants. Because he was not allowed to compete for any of the slots reserved for minority applicants, Bakke charged that he was the victim of illegal racial discrimination and the Court agreed. The Court ordered Bakke admitted, saying that a numerical quota for minority admissions violated the Equal Protection Clause of the Fourteenth Amendment. The Court added, however, that race and ethnicity could be considered as one of several factors in admissions decisions as a "plus factor" in an individualized admissions process.[52]

The Supreme Court reaffirmed the *Bakke* precedent in the University of Michigan Law School case discussed in the introduction to this chapter. The Court ruled that the university, which is a government agency, could consider race in its admissions program because the government has a compelling interest in promoting racial and ethnic diversity in higher education. Ms. Grutter lost her case.[53] In the meantime, the Court struck down an undergraduate admissions program at the same university because it assigned applicants a set number of points if they happened to be members of an underrepresented minority group—Latinos, African Americans, or Native Americans. The Court ruled that the undergraduate admissions process violated the Constitution because, unlike the law school process, it was not narrowly tailored to achieve the goal of diversity.[54]

GETTING INVOLVED

Voices from the Past

The African American civil rights movement was one of the most important political developments of the twentieth century. Laws that once prevented African Americans from voting and attending public schools with white children were repealed or struck down by the courts. Today, more African Americans hold elective office and have joined the ranks of the middle class than ever before. Nonetheless, racism and its vestiges have not been eliminated. African Americans are disproportionately affected by unemployment and poverty. They are underrepresented in corporate boardrooms and college campuses but overrepresented in prison.

Your class project is to interview older African American adults in your community to ascertain their perspective on the impact of the civil rights movement on their lives and on the United States. Identify African Americans 50 years of age and older who are friends, relatives, acquaintances, or coworkers who will agree to participate in short interviews with members of the class. Plan and conduct interviews that cover the following topics:

- What was it like for African Americans where you lived when you were growing up? What was good and what was bad? What events do you remember?

- What are the most important changes that have taken place? Which changes are most important? Have all the changes been positive?

- What still needs to be done? What do you see as the biggest remaining barrier to full equality for African Americans?

- How do you feel about Barack Obama's presidential campaign?

- Are you optimistic or pessimistic about the future? Why?

After the interviews are complete, the instructor will lead the class in discussing what students have learned. Students will want to compare and contrast the recollections of different interview subjects who may have different perspectives, depending on their personal life experiences and points of view. The instructor will also ask students to relate the content of their interviews with the information contained in the textbook. Did some of the interview subjects mention historical events discussed in the textbook, such as the Supreme Court's decision in *Brown v. Board of Education of Topeka?* To what extent do their current concerns about the status of African American civil rights mirror the controversies discussed in the text?

CONCLUSION: CIVIL RIGHTS POLICYMAKING

The Constitution is the most important environmental factor affecting civil rights policymaking, just as it is for civil liberties. Affirmative action, school integration, voting rights, and other civil rights concerns are constitutional issues. Consequently, civil rights policies reflect the parameters of constitutional law.

The policy preferences of federal judges affect civil rights policymaking. Liberal judges are more likely than conservative judges are to rule in favor of women and members of minority groups. In contrast, conservative judges are hesitant to expand constitutional rights. The appointment of relatively more conservative justices by recent Republican presidents has created a Supreme Court majority almost as skeptical of racial, ethnic, and gender preferences as it is of racial, ethnic, and gender discrimination. Because the current Court is closely divided on a number of civil rights issues, including affirmative action, the retirement of one or two justices could have a major policy impact, depending, of course, on the judicial philosophy of their replacements.

Civil rights policymaking is affected by the presence of organized groups concerned with civil rights issues. For example, the adoption of policies favorable to gay and lesbian rights coincides with the appearance of homosexual rights organizations, such as the Human Rights Campaign. Laws protecting gay and lesbian rights are least common in the South, where conservative Christian groups opposed to gay and lesbian rights are influential.

Party control of Congress and the White House influences civil rights policy. Groups favoring women's rights, affirmative action, voting rights, and gay and lesbian rights have more influence in the Democratic Party than they do in the GOP. Presidents Reagan, George H. W. Bush, and George W. Bush, for example, appointed relatively conservative justices whose rulings on school integration, legislative redistricting, and affirmative action have been generally conservative. At the state level, Republican legislatures and governors are less likely to enact affirmative action laws and measures outlawing discrimination against gay men and lesbians than are their Democratic counterparts.

Public opinion is another important element of the environment for civil rights policymaking. Survey research shows that Americans have grown more tolerant of racial and cultural diversity. As recently as the 1940s, a majority of white Americans supported racial segregation and discrimination, both in principle and in practice. By the 1970s, support for overt discrimination had virtually vanished. Today, polls find that large majorities of Americans of all races and both genders oppose discrimination.[55] Nonetheless, whites and African Americans do not see eye-to-eye on the rate of minority progress. A recent public opinion survey found that 61 percent of African Americans say that there has been "no real progress for blacks in the last few years," compared with 31 percent of white Americans who take that position.[56]

Agenda Building

Individuals, groups, political parties, and the media all participate in setting the agenda for civil rights policymaking. Susan B. Anthony, for example, was a leader of the movement for women's suffrage. Dr. Martin Luther King, Jr., was the foremost spokesperson for civil rights for African Americans during the 1960s. Linda Brown advanced the cause of civil rights issues by participating in a lawsuit.

A number of groups help set the agenda for civil rights issues. The NAACP Legal Defense Fund, Mexican American Legal Defense and Education Fund (MALDEF), the National Organization for Women (NOW), and other groups raise civil rights issues by supporting lawsuits as test cases. Large national membership organizations—such as NOW, the NAACP, and the League of United Latin American Citizens (LULAC)—lobby elected officials at the state and national level to address their policy concerns. Groups gather signatures to put their pet policy issues on the ballot in states with the **initiative process,** which is a procedure available in some states and cities whereby citizens can propose the adoption of a policy measure by gathering a prerequisite number of signatures. Voters must then approve the measure before it can take effect. After the Supreme Court upheld the University of Michigan Law School's affirmative action program, Barbara Grutter and other opponents of racial preferences gathered signatures to put the issue on the ballot and won. In

Initiative process
A procedure available in some states and cities whereby citizens can propose the adoption of a policy measure by gathering a prerequisite number of signatures.

November 2006, Michigan voters approved an amendment to the state constitution to prohibit state agencies and institutions from operating affirmative action programs that grant preferences based on race, color, ethnicity, national origin, or gender.[57]

Political parties often promote civil rights causes. The modern Democratic Party has adopted platforms supporting school integration, affirmative action, women's rights, equal employment opportunity, and gay and lesbian rights. All of these positions reflect alliances between the party and various interest groups and blocs of voters. African American, Latino, female, and gay and lesbian voters are a major part of the base of the Democratic Party. Although the Republican Party favors equal opportunity and opposes discrimination based on race, ethnicity, or gender, the GOP is generally against affirmative action and opposes gay and lesbian rights. The Republican position reflects the views of the middle-income whites who comprise the core of GOP voters, and the conservative Christian groups that ally with the party.

The media play a role in setting the agenda for civil rights. News reports and media coverage of political demonstrations highlight issues that might otherwise receive relatively little notice. During the 1960s, for example, media coverage of political demonstrations in favor of black civil rights and the violent reaction to those demonstrations helped mobilize northern white public opinion in favor of the protesters.

Policy Formulation and Adoption

Civil rights policy formulation and adoption may involve action by the president, Congress, the bureaucracy, local governments, private individuals, corporations, and the courts. Civil rights policies often take the form of legislation or executive orders. The ADA, for example, is a federal law, passed by Congress and signed by the president. State and local governments adopt affirmative action plans, such as Richmond's minority business set-aside plan. Colleges and universities formulate and adopt admissions policies. Civil rights policies may sometimes take the form of executive orders. President Truman, for example, issued an executive order to racially integrate the armed forces.

Court decisions set the boundaries for civil rights policymaking for other branches of government. Legislatures and executives considering affirmative action policies must take into account the *Croson* and *Adarand* rulings or risk the possibility of an expensive court challenge that they will likely lose. After the *Adarand* ruling, for example, President Clinton issued new guidelines for federal affirmative action programs designed to conform to the Court's decision. According to the new guidelines, federal affirmative action programs cannot reward unqualified individuals, create quotas, or continue after their purposes have been achieved.[58]

Judicial decisions are not necessarily the last word in civil rights policymaking, especially when the courts base their rulings on the interpretation of statutory law. Congress, after all, can rewrite laws to overcome judicial objections. In 1984, for example, the Supreme Court severely restricted the impact of federal laws prohibiting discrimination on the basis of gender, race, age, or disability by institutions receiving federal funds. The Court ruled that the law prohibited discrimination only by the *direct* recipient of the money.[59] Thus, if a university's chemistry department received federal funds but its athletic department did not, the latter would not be covered. Congress responded to the Court's decision by rewriting the law (and overriding President Reagan's

In 2008, Congress passed, and President Bush signed, legislation to expand protections for people with disabilities by overturning several recent Supreme Court decisions that had narrowed the standard used to determine whether an individual was disabled.

veto in the process). Because athletic programs receive little if any federal money, most college athletic departments did not take Title IX seriously until after Congress rewrote the law. In theory, a college or university that fails to comply with Title IX in athletics could lose federal funding for student scholarships and research grants.

Policy Implementation and Evaluation

The implementation of civil rights policy falls to the executive branch of the national government, lower federal courts, state and local governments, individuals, and private businesses. Under the provisions of the VRA, for example, the Justice Department reviews changes in election laws and procedures proposed by state and local governments in covered jurisdictions. The implementation of school desegregation policy takes place under the supervision of federal district judges.

Interest groups, individuals, and their attorneys play a major role in civil rights policy implementation by suing and threatening to sue. Civil rights groups file suit, for example, to challenge legislative districts they believe violate the VRA. Individuals who think that they have been denied a job or promotion because of illegal bias can sue as well. In practice, many companies devise hiring and promotion procedures with the goal of protecting themselves against discrimination lawsuits.

Consider the implementation of Title IX. Congress voted to prohibit discrimination on the basis of gender without specifying how that prohibition would apply to college athletic programs. In fact, southern conservatives added Title IX to the measure, hoping Congress would defeat the entire bill rather than enact legislation to prohibit discrimination on the basis of gender. They were wrong; the legislation passed anyway. The details of implementation of Title IX were left to the federal bureaucracy, universities, and the courts. In practice, each university takes steps to implement Title IX based on federal court decisions, guidelines set by the Department of Education, and the resources at hand. Individuals and groups who believe that a university has failed adequately to implement the law can file suit, asking a federal court to issue an **injunction,** that is, a court order, directing the university to take additional steps to comply with the law. People can also ask a court to award financial damages.

Injunction A court order.

The evaluation of civil rights policies involves both factual analyses and analyses based on values. Consider the impact of the elimination of affirmative action in university admissions after the passage of Proposition 209 in California, which was a state ballot measure passed in 1996 that was designed to eliminate affirmative action in the state by banning preferential treatment of women and minorities in public hiring, contracting, and education. The number of African American students admitted to law school at the University of California, Berkeley, fell 81 percent. Latino admissions dropped 50 percent. Minority enrollment grew, however, at less prestigious law schools in the state.[60] The critics of Proposition 209 worry that the state's best colleges and universities will have student bodies composed almost entirely of white and Asian students. In contrast, other observers believe that ending affirmative action helps well-qualified African American and Latino students who are admitted to the best schools because no one will question whether they really belong. Minority students who are not as well prepared will benefit as well because they will not be placed in situations where they cannot effectively compete.

KEY TERMS

affirmative action

Americans with Disabilities Act (ADA)

at-large election

civil rights

civil union

constitutional law

de facto segregation

de jure segregation

disfranchisement

district election

domestic partnership

Employment Non-Discrimination Act (ENDA)

Equal Protection Clause

grandfather clause

initiative process

injunction

Interstate Commerce Clause

Jim Crow laws

literacy test

majority-minority districts

minority business set-aside

minority-vote dilution

minority-vote packing

poll tax

pre-clearance

primary election

racially restrictive covenants

separate-but-equal

statutory law

strict judicial scrutiny

suffrage

suspect classifications

test case

test of understanding

Voting Rights Act (VRA)

white primary

NOTES

1. *Grutter v. Bollinger*, 539 U.S. 306 (2003).
2. Elder Witt, *The Supreme Court and Individual Rights*, 2nd ed. (Washington, DC: Congressional Quarterly Press, 1988), pp. 223–226.
3. *Plessy v. Ferguson*, 163 U.S. 537 (1896).
4. *Cumming v. Richmond County Board of Education*, 175 U.S. 528 (1899).
5. *Gong Lum v. Rice*, 275 U.S. 78 (1927).
6. *Missouri ex rel Gaines v. Canada*, 305 U.S. 337 (1938).
7. *Sweatt v. Painter*, 399 U.S. 629 (1950).
8. *McLaurin v. Oklahoma State Regents*, 339 U.S. 637 (1950).
9. *Brown v. Board of Education of Topeka*, 347 U.S. 483 (1954).
10. *Brown v. Board of Education of Topeka*, 349 U.S. 294 (1955).
11. Quoted in Harrell R. Rodgers, Jr., and Charles S. Bullock III, *Law and Social Change* (New York: McGraw-Hill, 1972), p. 71.
12. Gerald Rosenberg, "Substituting Symbol for Substance: What Did *Brown* Really Accomplish?" *P.S. Political Science and Politics*, April 2004, p. 205.
13. *Alexander v. Holmes County Board of Education*, 396 U.S. 19 (1969).
14. Rosenberg, "Substituting Symbol for Substance," p. 206.
15. *Swann v. Charlotte-Mecklenburg Board of Education*, 402 U.S. 1 (1971).
16. *Keyes v. School District #1, Denver, Colorado*, 413 U.S. 189 (1973).
17. Greg Winter, "Schools Resegregate, Study Finds," *New York Times*, January 21, 2003, available at www.nytimes.com.
18. "School Segregation on the Rise," *Harvard Gazette News*, July 19, 2001, available at www.new.harvard.edu/gazette.
19. *Millikin v. Bradley*, 418 U.S. 717 (1974).
20. *Missouri v. Jenkins*, 515 U.S. 70 (1995).
21. *Parents Involved in Community Schools v. Seattle School District No. 1*, 551 U.S. 701 (2007).
22. *In re Griffiths*, 413 U.S. 717 (1973); *Examining Board of Engineers, Architects and Surveyors v. de Otero*, 426 U.S. 572 (1976); *Bernal v. Fainter*, 467 U.S. 216 (1984).
23. Henry Weinstein, "Airport Screener Curb Is Rejected," *Los Angeles Times*, November 16, 2002, available at www.latimes.com.
24. *Bradwell v. Illinois*, 16 Wall 130 (1873).
25. Philippa Smith, "The Virginia Military Institute Case," in Sibyl A. Schwarzenbach and Paticia Smith, eds., *Women and the Constitution: History, Interpretation, and Practice* (New York: Columbia University Press, 2003), p. 343.
26. *United States v. Virginia*, 518 U.S. 515 (1996).
27. *Rostker v. Goldberg*, 453 U.S. 57 (1981).
28. *Romer v. Evans*, 517 U.S. 620 (1996).
29. *Smith v. Allwright*, 321 U.S. 649 (1944).
30. *Guinn v. United States*, 238 U.S. 347 (1915).
31. *Louisiana v. United States*, 380 U.S. 145 (1965).
32. *Harper v. State Board of Elections*, 383 U.S. 663 (1966).
33. Nayda Terkildsen, "When White Voters Evaluate Black Candidates: Processing Implications of Candidate Skin Color, Prejudice, and Self-Monitoring," *American Journal of Political Science* 37 (November 1993): 1032–1053.

34. Charles Cameron, David Epstein, and Sharyn O'Halloran, "Do Majority-Minority Districts Maximize Substantive Black Representation in Congress?" *American Political Science Review* 90 (December 1996): 810.

35. L. Marvin Overby and Kenneth M. Cosgrove, "Unintended Consequences? Racial Redistricting and the Representation of Minority Interest," *Journal of Politics* 58 (May 1996): 540–550.

36. *Shaw v. Reno*, 509 U.S. 630 (1993); *Miller v. Johnson*, 515 U.S. 900 (1995).

37. Quoted in Alfred H. Kelley and Winfred A. Harbison, *The American Constitution: Its Origins and Development* (New York: Norton, 1970), p. 460.

38. Quoted in Witt, *The Supreme Court and Individual Rights*, p. 247.

39. *Civil Rights Cases*, 109 U.S. 3 (1883).

40. *Buchanan v. Warley*, 245 U.S. 60 (1917).

41. *Shelley v. Kraemer*, 334 U.S. 1 (1948).

42. *Jones v. Alfred H. Meyer Co.*, 392 U.S. 409 (1968).

43. *Heart of Atlanta Motel v. United States*, 379 U.S. 241; *Katzenbach v. McClung*, 379 U.S. 294 (1964).

44. *Patterson v. McLean Credit Union*, 491 U.S. 164 (1989).

45. *St. Mary's Honor Center v. Hicks*, 509 U.S. 502 (1993).

46. *Boy Scouts of America, et. al. v. Dale*, 530 U.S. 640 (2000).

47. *Hurley v. Irish-American Gay, Lesbian, and Bisexual Group of Boston*, 515 U.S. 557 (1993).

48. Augustus B. Cochran III, *Sexual Harassment and the Law* (Lawrence: University of Kansas Press, 2004), p. 114.

49. *Oncale v. Sundowner Offshore Services, Inc.*, 523 U.S. 75 (1998).

50. *City of Richmond v. J. A. Croson Co.*, 488 U.S. 469 (1989).

51. *Adarand Constructors v. Pena*, 515 U.S. 200 (1995).

52. *Regents of the University of California v. Bakke*, 438 U.S. 265 (1978).

53. *Grutter v. Bollinger*, 539 U.S. 306 (2003).

54. *Gratz v. Bollinger*, 539 U.S. 244 (2003).

55. Gallup, "Race Relations," available at www.gallup.com.

56. The Pew Center for the People and the Press, "The Black and White of Public Opinion," October 2005, available at www.people-press.org.

57. Peter Schmidt, "Michigan Overwhelmingly Adopts Ban on Affirmative-Action Preferences," *Chronicle of Higher Education*, November 17, 2006, p. A23.

58. Kenneth Jost, "After *Adarand*," *ABA Journal* (September 1995): 70–75.

59. *Grove City College v. Bell*, 465 U.S. 555 (1984).

60. *Time*, June 23, 1997, p. 34.

Chapter 17

Foreign and Defense Policymaking

CHAPTER OUTLINE

LEARNING OUTCOMES

After studying Chapter 17, students should be able to do the following:

- Describe the challenge posed to the United States by the efforts of Iran and North Korea to develop nuclear weapons. (pp. 462–463)

- Describe the international community. (pp. 464–466)

- Identify the goals of American foreign and defense policy. (pp. 466–467)

- Identify the means the United States uses to achieve its foreign and defense policy goals. (pp. 467–469)

- Trace the development of American foreign policy from the 1790s through the present. (pp. 470–477)

- Evaluate the impact of the events of September 11, 2001, on American foreign and defense policy. (p. 478)

- Compare and contrast the internationalist and unilateralist approaches to American foreign and defense policy. (pp. 478–479)

- Describe changes in the defense budget since the 1940s, and identify the factors underlying those changes. (p. 480)

461

▶ Describe the structure of America's strategic and conventional forces, and explain their role in U.S. defense strategy. (p. 481)

▶ Compare and contrast the defense strategies of deterrence and military preemption. (pp. 481–483)

▶ Analyze foreign and defense policymaking using the public policy model. (pp. 484–490)

▶ Define the key terms listed on pages 490–491 and explain their significance.

Weapons of mass destruction (WMDs) Nuclear, chemical, and biological weapons that are designed to inflict widespread military and civilian casualties.

Soon after taking office, President George W. Bush declared that Iran, Iraq, and North Korea were an "axis of evil," arming to threaten the peace of the world. Bush charged that the three nations were seeking to develop **weapons of mass destruction (WMDs),** which are nuclear, chemical, and biological weapons that are designed to inflict widespread military and civilian casualties. He warned that Iran, Iraq, and North Korea might give WMDs to terrorist groups. They might attack their neighbors or blackmail the United States. The president also made it clear that the United States would not wait to be struck before taking action. "The United States of America will not permit the world's most dangerous regimes to threaten us with the world's most destructive weapons."[1]

In March 2003, the United States went to war against Iraq to overthrow the government of Saddam Hussein and prevent Iraq from developing nuclear weapons or giving biological or chemical weapons to terrorist groups. American forces quickly defeated the Iraqis and toppled the government, but, ironically, found no weapons of mass destruction. Saddam had apparently been bluffing about his WMD program in order to deter hostile neighbors from attacking Iraq.

Iran and North Korea responded to the American invasion of Iraq by speeding up their own weapons development programs. Iran has been acquiring the raw materials, building the parts, and developing the expertise necessary to build nuclear weapons. Although the government of Iran insists that its only goal is the peaceful development of nuclear energy, the United States is skeptical because Iran is a major oil producer without the need of alternative energy sources. Furthermore, the Iranian government has generally failed to cooperate with the International Atomic Energy Agency (IAEA), denying it access to nuclear sites and refusing to answer questions about the suspected link between Iran's nuclear program and the Iranian military. North Korea is further along than Iran, testing both nuclear weapons and missiles.[2] In 2009, North Korea test fired a long-range missile that would be capable of delivering a nuclear weapon, threatening Japan and, eventually, the United States.

Rogue states Nations that threaten world peace by sponsoring international terrorism and promoting the spread of weapons of mass destruction.

The United States and its allies believe that a nuclear Iran and a nuclear North Korea would threaten world peace. President George W. Bush declared that the two countries are **rogue states,** which are nations that threaten world peace by sponsoring international terrorism and promoting the spread of weapons of mass destruction. Iran supports international terrorism by providing arms and money to Hezbollah, an Islamic organization based in Lebanon that has carried out terrorist attacks against Israel. North Korea has sold weapons and weapons technology to other nations and to terrorist organizations. American policymakers worry that Iran and North Korea, armed with nuclear weapons, would bully their neighbors, perhaps setting off regional arms races with other nations rushing to acquire nuclear weapons themselves to counter the Iranian or North Korean threat. The North Koreans or Iranians might even use a nuclear weapon against the United States or its allies. Mahmoud Almadinejad, the president of Iran, has said that Israel should be "wiped off the map."

Foreign policy
Public policy that concerns the relationship of the United States to the international political environment.

Defense policy
Public policy that concerns the armed forces of the United States.

The threat of nuclear weapons development in Iran and North Korea is a major foreign and defense policy challenge for the United States. The United States went to war against Iraq to defuse a threat that in retrospect was less serious than the threats posed by the Iranians and North Koreans. Does the United States have realistic military options for dealing with either nation now in light of the ongoing war in Iraq? Can the United States and its allies convince Iran and North Korea to abandon their nuclear ambitions through negotiations? Will the United States simply have to learn to live with a nuclear Iran and a nuclear North Korea?

These questions introduce Chapter 17, the last of a series of chapters dealing with particular policy areas. Chapters 14, 15, and 16 considered economic, civil liberties, and civil rights policymaking, respectively. Chapter 17 addresses the topic of foreign and defense policymaking. **Foreign policy** is public policy that concerns the relationship of the United States to the international political environment. **Defense policy** is public policy that concerns the armed forces of the United States.

The United States and its allies believe that a nuclear Iran/North Korea would threaten world peace.

THE INTERNATIONAL COMMUNITY

Nation-state A political community, occupying a definite territory, and having an organized government.

Postindustrial societies Nations whose economies are increasingly based on services, research, and information rather than heavy industry.

Diplomatic relations A system of official contacts between two nations in which the countries exchange ambassadors and other diplomatic personnel and operate embassies in each other's country.

United Nations (UN) An international organization founded in 1945 as a diplomatic forum to resolve conflicts among the world's nations.

International Monetary Fund (IMF) The international organization created to promote economic stability worldwide.

Since the seventeenth century, the nation-state has been the basic unit of the international community. A **nation-state** is a political community, occupying a definite territory, and having an organized government. Other nations recognize its independence and respect the right of its government to exercise authority within its boundaries free from external interference. Today, more than 190 countries comprise the world community of nations.[3]

Political scientists divide the word's nations into three groups based on their level of economic development. The United States, Canada, Japan, and the countries of Western Europe are **postindustrial societies,** or nations whose economies are increasingly based on services, research, and information rather than heavy industry. India, China, South Korea, Brazil, and a number of other countries are *modernizing industrial states* that are emerging as important economic powers. Finally, many of the countries of Asia, Africa, and Latin America are *pre-industrial states* with an average standard of living well below that found in postindustrial societies.[4]

The United States has diplomatic relations with almost all of the world's nations. The term **diplomatic relations** refers to a system of official contacts between two nations in which the countries exchange ambassadors and other diplomatic personnel and operate embassies in each other's country. North Korea, Iran, Cuba, and Libya are among the few nations with which the United States does not have formal diplomatic ties.

In addition to the governments of the world, more than a hundred transnational (or multinational) organizations are active on the international scene. The best known of these is the **United Nations (UN),** which is an international organization founded in 1945 as a diplomatic forum to resolve conflicts among the world's nations. In practice, the UN has not always been effective at maintaining the peace. The UN Security Council, which is the organization charged with maintaining peace and security among nations, has frequently been unable to act because each of its five permanent members (Russia, China, Britain, France, and the United States) has a veto on its actions. The Security Council has been unable to persuade either Iran or North Korea to give up its nuclear weapons program at least in part because the permanent members disagree on how best to approach the problem.

Some of the UN's most important accomplishments have come in the areas of disaster relief, refugee relocation, agricultural development, loans for developing nations, and health programs. The UN has several agencies that carry out these and other tasks, including the International Monetary Fund and the World Health Organization. The **International Monetary Fund (IMF)** is an international organization created to promote economic stability worldwide. It provides loans to nations facing economic crises, usually on the condition that they adopt and implement reforms designed to bring long-term economic stability. The **World Health Organization (WHO)** is an international organization created to control disease worldwide. The WHO is a world clearinghouse for medical and scientific information. It sets international standards for drugs and vaccines and, on government request, helps fight disease in any country. The WHO is in the forefront of the battle against the spread of AIDS in the developing world.

World Health Organization (WHO) An international organization created to control disease worldwide.

The UN and its affiliated agencies are funded through dues and assessments charged to member nations. The amount of each nation's contribution depends, in general, on the strength of the nation's economy. Although every nation, even small and very poor nations, must support the work of the UN financially, the United States has the largest assessment because the American economy is the world's largest. As a result, the United States is also the UN's most influential member. Nonetheless, the United States has often been highly critical of some UN procedures, especially those associated with budgeting. Congress has sometimes made payment of American dues contingent on the UN agreeing to internal reforms to improve its operations.[5]

North Atlantic Treaty Organization (NATO) A regional military alliance consisting of the United States, Canada, and most of the European democracies.

A number of other international organizations are important to American foreign and defense policies. The **North Atlantic Treaty Organization (NATO)** is a regional military alliance consisting of the United States, Canada, and most of the European democracies. The United States and its allies formed NATO after World War II to defend against the threat of a Soviet attack in Western Europe. With the collapse of the Soviet Union, NATO has expanded to include some of the nations that were once part of the Soviet bloc: Poland, Hungary, the Czech Republic, Bulgaria, Estonia, Latvia, Lithuania, Romania, Slovakia, and Slovenia. The United States, Canada, and the established democracies of Western Europe hope that the inclusion of these nations in the NATO alliance will strengthen their commitment to democratic institutions and capitalist economic structures. In the meantime, NATO has changed its military focus to take into account the changing international environment by creating a multinational force that can be deployed to operate quickly. The United States wants NATO to become a global security organization that is capable either of taking military action or providing humanitarian relief anywhere in the world.

World Trade Organization (WTO) An international organization that administers trade laws, and provides a forum for settling trade disputes among nations.

The **World Trade Organization (WTO)** is an international organization that administers trade laws and provides a forum for settling trade disputes among nations. It promotes international trade by sponsoring negotiations to reduce **tariffs,** which are taxes on imported goods, and other barriers to trade. The WTO also arbitrates disputes over trade among the 145 member nations. For example, the WTO has sponsored negotiations to allow developing countries to make generic versions of lifesaving drugs for their own use and for export to countries too poor either to make the drugs themselves or purchase them from pharmaceutical companies. Wealthy nations, led by the United States, want to sharply limit the number of diseases covered by the drugs in order to protect the intellectual property rights of pharmaceutical companies. In contrast, developing nations, such as Brazil, China, and India, argue that governments should have the right to determine which diseases constitute public health crises in their countries.[6]

Tariffs Taxes on imported goods.

Nongovernmental organizations (NGOs) International organizations committed to the promotion of a particular set of issues.

Nongovernmental organizations (NGOs) are international organizations committed to the promotion of a particular set of issues. Greenpeace, Friends of the Earth, World Wide Fund for Nature, and the Nature Conservancy are NGOs that address environmental issues. Save the Children is an NGO concerned with the welfare of children. NGOs vary in their relationship to the international community. NGOs such as the International Red Cross and Doctors Without Borders work in partnership with national governments to assist the victims of natural disasters or political turmoil. Other NGOs lobby national governments over policy issues such as the effort to ban the importation of genetically modified foods. Some NGOs encourage consumers to boycott retailers who sell goods produced under exploitative working conditions in developing countries. They organize protests at international meetings of the WTO to push for the incorporation of health and safety conditions in international trade agreements.[7] Meanwhile, with the collapse of the Soviet Union, al Qaeda and other international terrorist organizations have emerged as the principle opponents to the United States in the world.[8]

THE ENDS AND MEANS OF AMERICAN FOREIGN AND DEFENSE POLICY

The United States has consistently pursued three foreign and defense policy goals throughout its history: national security, economic prosperity, and the projection of American values abroad.[9] The foremost goal of American foreign and defense policies is national security. A basic aim of the foreign policy of any nation is to preserve its sovereignty and protect its territorial integrity. No nation wants to be overrun by a foreign power or dominated by another nation. During the **Cold War,** which was the period of international tension between the United States and the Soviet Union lasting from the late 1940s through the late 1980s, American foreign was premised on the goal of protecting the nation from communist aggression. Although the United States is today the world's foremost military power, it still has national security concerns. The terrorist attacks of September 11, 2001, demonstrated the vulnerability of the United States to terrorism. Although neither Iran nor North Korea would be able to mount a direct attack on the United States, they could threaten American interests in their regions of the world. They could also give or sell nuclear weapons to terrorist groups.

Cold War The period of international tension between the United States and the Soviet Union lasting from the late 1940s through the late 1980s.

National prosperity is another goal of American foreign and defense policy. This goal includes encouraging free markets, promoting international trade, and protecting American economic interests and investments abroad. Because the American economy is closely entwined with the global economy, it is essential to the nation's economic health that the United States has access both to foreign suppliers of goods and services and to foreign markets for American products. The nation's military involvement in the Persian Gulf, for example, has been motivated at least in part by a desire by the United States to protect access to the region's oil fields.

International trade has grown increasingly important to the economy of the United States. Trade now accounts for 28 percent of the nation's output of goods and services compared with only 11 percent in 1970. The United States exported $1.6 trillion worth of goods and services in 2007 while importing $2.3 trillion worth. The nation's most important trading partners were, in order of importance, Canada, Mexico, China, and Japan.[10]

Trade is controversial in the United States because it produces winners and losers. Consumers benefit from trade because they have the opportunity to purchase a broad range of goods at competitive prices. American manufacturers of medical instruments, farm equipment, pharmaceuticals, oil drilling equipment, and electronics benefit because they sell their products abroad. In contrast, inefficient small farmers, old steel mills, and the nation's clothing and textile manufacturers suffer because they do not compete effectively against international competition. Furthermore, some liberal groups in the United States oppose international trade because they believe it rewards international corporations that exploit low-wage workers in developing countries and leads to environmental degradation around the globe.

Recent administrations of both political parties have favored the growth of trade because they believe that the economic gains from trade outweigh the costs. President Bill Clinton won congressional support for the **North American Free Trade Agreement (NAFTA),** which was an international accord among the United States, Mexico, and Canada to lower trade barriers among the three nations, despite the opposition of a majority of the members of his own political party. The George W. Bush administration negotiated the Central America Free Trade Agreement (CAFTA) with Nicaragua, Honduras, Costa Rica, El Salvador, and Guatemala to phase out tariffs among participating nations on manufactured goods, agricultural commodities, chemicals, and construction equipment.

A final general policy goal of American foreign and defense policy is the promotion of American ideas and ideals abroad. Historically, American policymakers have justified military interventions as efforts to protect freedom and promote democracy. Many of the nation's foreign policies today are designed to further the causes of democracy, free-market capitalism, and human rights. For years, the United States has attempted to isolate Cuba economically and diplomatically in hopes of either driving the Castro regime out of power or forcing Castro to bring democracy and free-market capitalism to the island.

Spreading democracy was at the center of the foreign policy of the George W. Bush administration. When American forces failed to uncover WMDs in Iraq, President Bush offered the promotion of democracy as the new justification for the invasion. Democracies are stronger economically and more stable politically than undemocratic governments, he declared. Consequently, their residents have few incentives to join terrorist organizations. Bush also endorsed the theory of the **democratic peace,** which is the concept that democracies do not wage war against other democracies.[11]

Critics of the Bush administration warn that an emphasis on democratization is unrealistic, naïve, and counterproductive. Implanting democracy in countries without a democratic tradition may be impossible because people may be unwilling to make the compromises necessary for democracy to work. The various tribal and religious factions in Iraq fought with each other despite the introduction of democracy after the fall of Saddam. Furthermore, democracy may result in the election of regimes hostile to American interests. In much of the Arab world, including Egypt and Saudi Arabia, free elections would likely produce the selection of distinctly anti-American Islamic regimes. Finally, American pressure to democratize may alienate allies in the war on terror. The United States depends on the cooperation of undemocratic regimes in Egypt and Saudi Arabia to combat terrorism.

The United States pursues its foreign and defense policy goals through military, economic, cultural, and diplomatic means. Since the end of World War II, the armed forces of the United States have intervened militarily in Korea, Lebanon, the Dominican Republic, Indochina, Grenada, Panama, Kuwait, Afghanistan, the Serbian province of Kosovo, Iraq, and Liberia. The United States has also given military assistance in the form of arms and advisors to friendly governments fighting

North American Free Trade Agreement (NAFTA) An international accord among the United States, Mexico, and Canada to lower trade barriers among the three nations.

Democratic peace The concept that democracies do not wage war against other democracies.

against forces hostile to the interests of the United States. For example, the United States has provided military aid to the government of Columbia to assist it in its war against guerrilla forces supported by international narcotics traffickers. After September 11, 2001, the United States supplied military aid, including American advisors, to the government of the Philippines to assist in the war against insurgent forces, which may have ties to al Qaeda.

Besides the actual use of military force, the United States has pursued its policy goals by forming defense alliances and transferring military hardware to other nations. Since the end of World War II, the United States has participated in a number of defense alliances, including NATO and SEATO (the Southeast Asia Treaty Organization). America is also the world's major distributor of weapons, accounting for 32 percent of the world's arms sales to developing nations. Egypt, Israel, Saudi Arabia, South Korea, Pakistan, and Taiwan are among the major purchasers of American arms.[12] Some international arms sales are private transactions between American firms and foreign governments. Most sales, however, are government-to-government transactions in which the U.S. Department of Defense acts as a purchasing agent for a foreign government wanting to buy American-made weapons.

The United States attempts to achieve foreign policy goals through economic means, such as trade and foreign aid. Trade can be used to improve international relations. One method the United States employed to improve relations with China was to open the door to trade. In contrast, America has erected trade barriers against foreign governments it wishes to pressure or punish. The United States attempts to isolate Cuba and North Korea economically. In fact, Congress passed and President Clinton signed legislation designed to punish third countries that violate the American embargo against Cuba by trading with the island nation. The measure, which was called the Helms-Burton Act, named for former Senator Jesse Helms and Representative Dan Burton, provoked accusations of hypocrisy from Canada and Europe. Whereas the United States tries to punish Cuba economically, it disregards human rights abuses in China, a country that is a major trading partner of the United States.

The United States uses foreign aid to achieve foreign policy goals. Although the United States is the world's largest donor, its level of giving as a share of national income is among the lowest among developed nations, less than half that of European countries.[13] The size of the foreign aid budget is relatively small, less than 1 percent of the federal budget—and most of the money goes to further the nation's foreign policy aims. The top two recipients of American foreign aid are Israel and Egypt, nations that are close allies of the United States. Both countries receive more money in military aid than they do in economic assistance. Colombia is the third-ranking foreign aid recipient. The United States assists Colombia in its war against drug traffickers and terrorists. Furthermore, since September 11, 2001, the United States has increased aid to countries whose assistance America needs in the war on terror, including Jordan, Pakistan, Turkey, and postwar Afghanistan.[14] The United States has also made it clear to countries such as Yemen and the Philippines that their ability to get loans from the IMF depends on their cooperation in the war on terror. Even though the IMF is an international organization, the United States has considerable influence on its loan decisions because the United States is the IMF's largest source of funds.

WHAT IS YOUR OPINION?

Should the United States focus its foreign aid expenditures on humanitarian assistance to poor nations, or should it use aid primarily to further its own foreign policy objectives?

Foreign policy goals can sometimes be realized through cultural means, including the promotion of tourism and student exchanges, goodwill tours, and international athletic events. The process of improving relations between the United States and the China, for example, was facilitated by cultural exchanges. In fact, one of the first contacts between the two nations was the visit of an American table tennis team to China—"ping-pong diplomacy," the pundits called it. The Olympic Games, meanwhile, are not just a sporting event but also a forum for nations to make political statements. The United States boycotted the 1980 Moscow Olympics to protest the Soviet invasion of Afghanistan. The Soviet Union returned the favor in 1984 by staying home when the games were held in Los Angeles.

Diplomacy The process by which nations carry on political relations with each other.

Finally, foreign policy goals can be achieved through **diplomacy,** which is the process by which nations carry on political relations with each other. Ambassadors and other embassy officials stationed abroad provide an ongoing link between governments. The UN, which is headquartered in New York City, offers a forum in which the world's nations can make diplomatic contacts, including countries that may not have diplomatic relations with one another. Diplomacy can also be pursued through special negotiations or summit meetings among national leaders.

President George W. Bush proposed, and Congress approved, funding for a major foreign assistance initiative to combat HIV/AIDS.

THE HISTORY OF AMERICAN FOREIGN POLICY

American foreign policy is best understood within the context of its historical development.

From Isolationism to Internationalism

Isolationism The view that the United States should stay out of the affairs of other nations.

Monroe Doctrine A declaration of American foreign policy opposing any European intervention in the Western Hemisphere and affirming the American intention to refrain from interfering in European affairs.

For almost a century, the principle theme of American foreign policy toward Europe was **isolationism,** which is the view that the United States should minimize its interactions with other nations. In his farewell address in 1796, retiring President George Washington warned the nation to avoid "entangling alliances" with other countries. President James Monroe articulated the policy in his **Monroe Doctrine** of 1823, which was a declaration of American foreign policy opposing any European intervention in the Western Hemisphere and affirming the American intention to refrain from interfering in European affairs. The United States would stay out of European affairs; the Europeans must stay out of American affairs. Isolationism had its practical side. The United States was far from a world power in the early nineteenth century. Americans devoted their energies to subduing and developing North America and did not welcome European interference. The American policy of isolationism also had an aspect of arrogance in that the country wanted to avoid soiling itself by making alliances with colonial powers. Instead, the United States would serve as a moral example for them. Finally, isolationism contained an element of hypocrisy because it did not apply to American actions in the Western Hemisphere. The United States reserved for itself the right to interfere in the affairs of the nations of the Americas.

And interfere it did. America fought a war with Mexico in order to annex Mexico's northern provinces, the area that is now California, Arizona, and New Mexico. President Theodore Roosevelt intervened in Colombia to create the nation of Panama so the United States could build a canal. In the twentieth century, America intervened militarily in several Latin American nations, including Cuba, El Salvador, Nicaragua, the Dominican Republic, Grenada, and Panama. The United States was involved indirectly in the political affairs of many other countries in the hemisphere, including Chile, Honduras, Venezuela, Guatemala, Ecuador, Brazil, and Guyana.

The United States began to break out of its isolationism toward nations outside the Western Hemisphere in the 1890s. The treaty that ended the Spanish-American War awarded the United States a colonial empire extending beyond this hemisphere to Guam and the Philippines. Furthermore, America had developed trading interests around the world that it wanted to protect. Eventually, World War I thrust the United States to the forefront of international affairs.

Between the two world wars, the United States once again turned inward. Part of the explanation for the return to isolationism was that President Woodrow Wilson (1913–1921), the wartime chief executive, had oversold World War I as "the war to end all wars" and "the war to make the world safe for democracy." The idealism faded in the midst of bloody war, and the international political haggling after the war disillusioned many Americans. Another reason for the focus on domestic affairs was the Great Depression. Americans looked inward as they sought to cope with economic collapse.

By 1945, America's romance with isolationism had ended. Because of improved technology, isolationism was more difficult, if not impossible, to achieve. Modern communications and transportation had shrunk the world. More important, the United States emerged from World War II as a great power, militarily and economically. It was the only nation with nuclear weapons and the only major industrial country whose economic foundations had not been battered by war. With important military, political, and economic interests around the globe, the United States could no longer afford isolationism.

The Cold War and the Policy of Containment

The relationship between the United States and the Soviet Union was the dominant element of American foreign policy after World War II. Even though the United States and the Soviet Union had been wartime allies, the two nations began a bitter struggle for dominance in the international arena in the late 1940s. In the eyes of most Americans, the Soviets were determined to expand their control into Eastern Europe and Southeast Asia. In contrast, the Soviets regarded American actions, particularly Central Intelligence Agency (CIA) activities in Eastern Europe, as a threat to their national security.

Truman Doctrine
The foreign policy put forward by President Harry Truman calling for American support for all free peoples resisting communist aggression by internal or outside forces.

The Cold War was both an ideological and political struggle. It pitted communism against capitalism, and dictatorship against democracy. The leaders of both the United States and the Soviet Union pictured the international competition as a contest between different ways of life, one representing good and the other representing evil. The Cold War was also a bipolar (two-sided) struggle between the world's two remaining military superpowers. The other great powers of the prewar era—Germany, France, the United Kingdom, and Japan—had either been destroyed or weakened by the war. That left a political vacuum into which the war's survivors, the United States and the Soviet Union, sought to enter. As one observer phrased it, they were like two scorpions trapped in a jar. Tension and conflict were probably inevitable.

Containment The American policy of keeping the Soviet Union from expanding its sphere of control.

President Harry Truman (1946–1953) first articulated America's response to the Soviet Union and the spread of communism. The **Truman Doctrine** was the foreign policy put forward by President Harry Truman calling for American support for all free peoples resisting communist aggression by internal or outside forces. In particular, Truman asked Congress to appropriate money for military and economic aid to Greece and Turkey to strengthen them against local communist insurgencies. Congress complied with the president's request.

Balance of power
A system of political alignments in which peace and security may be maintained through an equilibrium of forces between rival groups of nations.

The Truman Doctrine was part of the strategy of **containment,** which was the American policy of keeping the Soviet Union from expanding its sphere of control. The United States adopted the policy of containment for essentially the same reason it entered World War I and World War II—to preserve the balance of power in Europe and Asia. A **balance of power** is a system of political alignments in which peace and security may be maintained through an equilibrium of forces between rival groups of nations. America's leaders recognized that any nation controlling all of Europe and Asia would command more industrial power than the United States.[15]

The United States had to intervene militarily in World War I and World War II to prevent rival powers from becoming stronger than the United States.

The policy of containment included several aspects. First, the United States gave economic assistance to nations threatened by communist subversion. The **Marshall Plan,** for example, was an American program that provided billions of dollars to the countries of Western Europe to rebuild their economies after World War II. The United States also adopted programs giving technical and economic aid to developing nations. Second, the United States devoted substantial resources to national defense, including the development of its nuclear forces. Finally, America offered military assistance to nations threatened by communism. Not only did the United States send weapons and financial aid to foreign countries, such as Greece and Turkey, but at times also committed American fighting forces abroad in countries such as Korea and Vietnam.

In the early 1950s, the Cold War entered a new phase. Before then, the struggle between the United States and the Soviet Union had been waged on the perimeters of Soviet influence—Eastern Europe, Berlin, China, Indochina, and Korea. In the 1950s, Nikita Khrushchev, an imaginative new Soviet leader, adopted a different tactic. The Soviets leapfrogged the old lines to push their cause into Cuba, Egypt, the Congo, Indonesia, and elsewhere in the developing world, well behind the American wall of containment. Furthermore, the Soviets had developed nuclear weapons and, with the launch of the *Sputnik* satellite in 1957, demonstrated that they were ahead of the United States in missile technology.

The Cuban missile crisis of 1962 was the climactic event of the Cold War. Despite launching the world's first satellite, **Sputnik,** the Soviet Union remained clearly inferior to the United States in nuclear weaponry. To close the gap, Khrushchev decided to install missiles in Cuba, just 90 miles from American soil. When the United States discovered the Soviet move, President John Kennedy responded with a naval blockade. The stage was set for a nuclear confrontation, but the Soviets backed down, withdrawing their missiles. The two nations were eyeball-to-eyeball on the brink of nuclear war, said Secretary of State Dean Rusk, and the Soviets blinked.

Détente

The Cuban missile crisis may have had a sobering effect on the leaders of the United States and the Soviet Union. In the late 1960s and early 1970s, the two superpowers entered an era of improved relations known as **détente,** which was a period of improved communications and visible efforts to relieve tensions between the two superpowers. The United States and Soviet Union increased trade and cultural relations, and exchanged scientific information in such fields as cancer research, weather forecasting, and space exploration. Some observers promoted a **convergence theory,** the view that communism and capitalism were evolving in similar ways, or converging. As communism and capitalism become more alike they would no longer be a threat to one another.[16]

Perhaps the most important aspect of détente was arms control. Both the United States and the Soviet Union found advantage in slowing the arms race. Arms control saved money and, perhaps, reduced the probability of nuclear war. It was also good domestic politics, certainly in the United States and probably in the Soviet Union as well.

Marshall Plan The American program that provided billions of dollars to the countries of Western Europe to rebuild their economies after World War II.

Sputnik The world's first satellite, launched by the Soviet Union.

Détente A period of improved communications and visible efforts to relieve tensions between the two superpowers.

Convergence theory The view that communism and capitalism were evolving in similar ways, or converging.

During the 1960s and 1970s, the United States and the Soviet Union agreed on a number of important arms-control measures. In 1963, the two superpowers and Great Britain signed a treaty prohibiting the above-ground testing of nuclear weapons. Subsequently, the United States and the Soviet Union agreed to ban nuclear weapons from the ocean floor. In 1968, they signed the **Nuclear Nonproliferation Treaty,** which is an international agreement designed to prevent the spread of nuclear weapons. Under terms of the treaty, the five nations that then possessed nuclear weapons (the United States, Soviet Union, China, France, and Great Britain) agreed not to deliver nuclear weapons or weapons technology to other nations; non-nuclear countries agreed not to seek or develop nuclear weapons. All of the world's nations are parties to the Nuclear Nonproliferation Treaty except for Cuba, Israel, India, and Pakistan. North Korea signed the treaty but subsequently withdrew after the United States accused it of having a weapons program.[17] Iran stands accused of violating the treaty. Although North Korea is no longer a party to the treaty, the international community is in general agreement that a nuclear North Korea would be a threat to world peace.

In 1969, the United States and the Soviet Union began the Strategic Arms Limitation Talks (SALT), which was a series of negotiations designed to control nuclear weapons, delivery systems, and related offensive and defensive weapons systems. In 1972, the two nations agreed to the Anti-Ballistic Missile (ABM) Treaty to limit the deployment of ABM systems, which are designed to destroy enemy missiles carrying nuclear weapons. The treaty also established a five-year moratorium on the placement of additional land- and sea-based missiles.

Ten years later, a second round of negotiations, know as SALT II, produced another arms agreement, setting limits on weapons, missiles, and long-range bombers. The SALT II treaty, however, never came to a vote in the Senate. Treaty opponents, including then presidential candidate Ronald Reagan, argued that the United States had given up too much. Furthermore, détente was ending as a result of the Soviet invasion of Afghanistan and the beginning of a substantial American military buildup.

In retrospect, détente was probably overrated by a world eager to find signs of peace in a nuclear age. Similarly, convergence theory was more wishful thinking than it was an accurate assessment of reality. The United States and the Soviet Union had vastly different historical, cultural, political, and economic backgrounds. Each nation had interests around the globe and those interests sometimes clashed. Détente was a period of better communications between the superpowers that eased tensions, but it was naive to expect détente to bring an end to international conflict.

Nuclear Nonproliferation Treaty
An international agreement designed to prevent the spread of nuclear weapons.

American Foreign Policy in the 1970s: Recognition of Limits

During the 1970s, the administrations of Presidents Richard Nixon, Gerald Ford, and Jimmy Carter attempted to adapt American foreign policy to the realities of a changing, more complex world and adjust to what they saw as the long-term decline of American economic and military power. Nixon and Henry Kissinger, who was chief foreign policy advisor to both Presidents Nixon and Ford, spoke of the end of the post-war world and emphasized what they called a realistic foreign policy, designed to

Nixon Doctrine
The corollary to the policy of containment enunciated by President Richard Nixon providing that, although the United States would help small nations threatened by communist aggression with economic and military aid, those countries must play a major role in their own defense.

control America's descent into an uncertain future. The Nixon-Ford-Kissinger foreign policy sought to maintain American interests and commitments abroad but at a reduced cost. The cornerstone of this policy was the **Nixon Doctrine,** which was a corollary to the policy of containment. Although the United States would help small nations threatened by communist aggression with economic and military aid, those countries must play a major role in their own defense.

Foreign policy during the Carter administration also reflected an understanding that the international system had changed since the 1950s. Carter's restrained response to the hostage crisis in Iran showed that the president recognized the limits of American power. The Panama Canal Treaty, which provided for the eventual return of sovereignty over the canal to the government of Panama, represented an accommodation to the concerns of Latin America.

The Carter administration's foreign policy stressed the importance of human rights. Carter declared that American trade, aid, and alliances would be based at least in part on the way other governments treated their own citizens. The policy had both an idealistic and a practical side. In the aftermath of the Vietnam War, Carter wanted to return an air of morality to American foreign policy. The United States would have a "foreign policy as good as the American people," Carter promised. From a practical standpoint, the president hoped to pressure repressive noncommunist governments to reform their policies. Carter recognized that dictatorships are politically unstable. They invite subversion, increasing opportunities for communist influence.

Carter's critics argued that the principle of human rights was too simplistic a doctrine on which to base a global foreign policy strategy. What if American security interests and human rights conflict? Would the administration sacrifice U.S. defense interests in South Korea, for example, in the name of human rights? The answer turned out to be no, leaving the Carter administration open to charges of hypocrisy. Furthermore, many observers believed that the policy reflected an arrogant attitude toward the rest of the world. It seemed that Carter had adopted the role of a missionary, helping the poor abroad and bringing American values to those who suffer in the dark.[18]

American Foreign Policy in the 1980s: A Resurgent America

When Ronald Reagan became president, he promised an end to the self-doubt and decline that had infected United States foreign policy in the 1970s. The problem, Reagan charged, lay not with America but with its leaders. Reagan spoke optimistically of a resurgent United States, which he called, quoting Abraham Lincoln, "the last, best hope of man on earth." In contrast, he branded the Soviet Union "the evil empire."

Reagan based his foreign policy on firm opposition to communism. He regarded world politics as a bipolar rivalry between the United States and the Soviet Union, and he left no doubt who the bad guys were. The Soviet leaders, Reagan declared, reserved for themselves the right "to lie, to cheat, to commit any crime." To meet the challenge, Reagan called for a resolute national will and a military buildup.

Reagan Doctrine
A corollary to the
policy of containment
enunciated by
President Reagan
calling for the United
States to offer military
aid to groups
attempting to
overthrow communist
governments
anywhere in the
world.

The centerpiece of the president's foreign policy was known as the **Reagan Doctrine,** which was a corollary to the policy of containment enunciated by President Reagan calling for the United States to offer military aid to groups attempting to overthrow communist governments anywhere in the world. Reagan offered military assistance to "liberation forces" in Nicaragua, Afghanistan, and Angola. In this fashion, Reagan aimed to increase the cost to the Soviet Union for what the president considered to be its policy of exporting revolution. Reagan hoped that the Soviets would eventually have to choose between reducing their commitments abroad and economic collapse at home. Rejecting the Carter emphasis on human rights, Reagan offered practically unconditional support to anticommunist governments, even those that were undemocratic.

During his first term in office, Reagan rejected the idea that the United States should adapt its policies to a changing international environment. Reagan asked Congress for a substantial increase in defense spending and began to flex American military muscle abroad. Reagan ordered an invasion of the Caribbean country of Grenada to overthrow a government friendly to Cuba. He directed air strikes against the North African nation of Libya in retaliation for that country's alleged support of terrorism. He ordered American naval vessels to escort Kuwaiti oil tankers through the Persian Gulf, protecting them from attacks by Iran.

By the mid-1980s, however, the key feature of American foreign policy was once again caution. In a number of crisis situations, the Reagan administration responded with restraint. The United States reacted to an apparently accidental Iraqi missile attack against the *U.S.S. Stark,* an American naval vessel, by taking no action. (In those days, the United States and Iraqi President Saddam Hussein were friends.) Similarly, the administration responded to a terrorist bombing in Beirut, Lebanon, that killed more than 200 marines by withdrawing American forces. Although the White House often talked tough, the substance of Reagan's foreign policies increasingly resembled the policies of the 1970s that Reagan had so roundly criticized. On arms control, for example, the Reagan administration generally adhered to the weapons limits set by SALT II, even though the treaty was never ratified. Furthermore, by the mid-1980s, the United States and the Soviet Union were engaged in serious negotiations aimed at arms control and arms reductions. As for the Reagan Doctrine, the administration continued to support the Contras in Nicaragua and other anticommunist forces, but it changed its policy of unconditional support for anticommunist dictators. In both the Philippines and Haiti, the administration backed local efforts to oust unpopular dictators in favor of reform-minded democratic governments.

Several factors were behind the modifications in President Reagan's foreign policy focus. First, Congress was unwilling to support all of the president's foreign policy initiatives. Congress consistently refused to give the Contras as much aid as Reagan requested. By Reagan's second term, Congress's willingness to fund the president's military buildup had evaporated. Second, public opinion did not support all aspects of Reagan's foreign policies. Although the president's vision of an America standing tall was popular, surveys found substantial opposition to American military involvement in Nicaragua and other trouble spots. Many Americans feared a confrontation with the Soviet Union. Also, polls taken in the mid-1980s showed that a majority of Americans believed the United States was spending enough money for defense. Finally, firsthand experience in dealing with the realities of international affairs forced Reagan to modify his foreign policy focus. Once in office, President Reagan found that dealing with terrorism and hostage taking was as difficult for him as it had been for President Carter.[19]

The Disintegration of the Soviet Union and the End of the Cold War

In the late 1980s, a new Soviet leader, Mikhail Gorbachev, recognized that the Soviet system was failing. Although the Soviet Union was a military superpower, its relative influence in world affairs was in decline; its economy was a shambles. Gorbachev responded to the crisis with a bold series of economic and political reforms that dramatically changed both the Soviet Union and the international political environment.

To increase production and improve the supply of consumer goods, Gorbachev launched an economic reform program known as *Perestroika*, the Russian word for "economic restructuring." Although some of Gorbachev's initiatives were traditional Soviet approaches to improving economic productivity, other aspects of *Perestroika* represented real innovations, at least by Soviet standards. Most notably, Gorbachev reduced central planning and began adding free-market features to the nation's socialist economy. Gorbachev also changed Soviet law to permit the establishment of private, profit-oriented businesses.

In addition to economic reforms, Gorbachev initiated a series of domestic political reforms known as *Glasnost*, the Russian word for "openness." He introduced reforms allowing Soviet citizens unprecedented freedom of political expression and ordered that free, competitive elections be held to choose a Congress of People's Deputies, an elected legislature that would actually play a role in the governing process. Perhaps most significant, Gorbachev pushed through changes in the Soviet Constitution to allow opposition political parties to compete against the Communist Party.

Western observers disagree about the motivation behind *Glasnost*. Some scholars think that Gorbachev decided to open the political system to participation by ordinary Russian citizens in hopes of generating public support that would help him overcome the opposition of entrenched party and state bureaucrats to *Perestroika*.[20] In contrast, other observers believe that Gorbachev initiated *Glasnost* because he concluded that in today's information age, it is unrealistic to expect that the economy can be made more competitive without opening the political system to competition as well.

Perestroika and *Glasnost* led to changes in Soviet foreign and defense policies. Gorbachev reasoned that economic reforms would not succeed unless some of the enormous human and material resources devoted to the Soviet military could be diverted to the domestic economy. To make this shift in priorities possible, Gorbachev proposed "new thinking" in foreign and defense policy to ease tensions with the West and reduce Soviet commitments abroad. Gorbachev declared that the Soviet Union would not intervene militarily in the internal affairs of other nations and ordered the withdrawal of Soviet military units from Afghanistan, where they had been fighting a protracted guerrilla war against anticommunist rebels. Gorbachev also announced significant reductions in Soviet defense spending and called for the negotiation of arms-control and arms-reduction treaties with the United States.

Changes in Soviet foreign policy led to changes in the status of Eastern Europe. For decades after the end of World War II, the Soviet Union held the nations of Eastern Europe as political satellites, intervening politically and militarily to ensure communist party rule. The primary purpose of the policy was to maintain a buffer between the Soviet Union and Western Europe, which in modern times has been the main source of invasion against Russia. Gorbachev decided, however, that the Soviet Union could no longer afford to maintain satellites. He ordered Soviet forces to withdraw from Eastern Europe and encouraged the nations of the region to adopt political and economic reforms similar to *Perestroika* and *Glasnost*.

Although the opening of the Berlin Wall may have been the single most dramatic development, nearly every nation in the region underwent major change. Without the backing of the Soviet military, one-party communist regimes in one country after another collapsed under popular pressure to be replaced by reform governments promising democratic elections, individual freedom, and fewer economic controls. In fact, most of the nations of Eastern Europe adopted more extensive economic and political reforms than were then in place in the Soviet Union.[21]

In the meantime, the Soviet Union began to break up. Many of the Republics that comprised the Soviet Union had different histories and cultures than Russia, the largest Soviet republic, and resented Russian domination. When given the opportunity for political change offered by *Glasnost* and the developments in Eastern Europe, a number of Soviet republics, including Lithuania, Estonia, Belarus, Georgia, and the Ukraine, declared their independence from Russian control. In late 1991, Russia and some of the other republics dissolved the Soviet Union. With the dissolution of the Soviet Union, leadership passed from Gorbachev to Boris Yeltsin, the president of the Russian Republic, and the heads of the other republics.

The disintegration of the Soviet Union ended the Cold War. Russia and the other Republics that once comprised the Soviet Union lacked the resources or the desire to continue the conflict with the West, focusing instead on creating new economic and political institutions. In exchange for its retreat from its external empire, Russia sought access to the global economy.[22] In particular, Yeltsin requested Western economic aid and investment.

The end of the Cold War changed the basic premise of American foreign policy. From the late 1940s until the early 1990s, the overriding purpose of U.S. foreign policy was to prevail against a perceived threat to the nation's survival presented by international communism and the Soviet Union. During the Cold War era, authoritarian communism and capitalist democracy competed for the allegiance of non-aligned countries. Regional conflicts were usually redefined in terms of the East–West rivalry. In contrast, no single theme dominates world politics in the post–Cold War era. Today's regional conflicts are generally unrelated to larger global issues. The balance of world power has also changed. The Cold War was a face-off between two military superpowers—the United States and the Soviet Union—and their allies. The collapse of the Soviet Union has left the United States as the world's single dominant military superpower.

FOREIGN POLICY

The events of September 11, 2001, provide the backdrop for American foreign policy in the post–Cold War world. American policymakers generally agree that the United States must be closely engaged in world affairs not just to protect its economic interests abroad but also to guard the American homeland against assault by terrorist groups or rogue states. Policymakers also concur that the United States should exert leadership in international affairs because it is the world's foremost military and economic power. As former secretary of state Madeleine Albright phrased it, the United States is the world's "indispensable nation" in that its participation is essential to solving the world's military, economic, and humanitarian problems.[23] Policymakers disagree, however, on how closely the United States should work with its allies and the other nations of the world.

Some policymakers believe that the United States should take an internationalist approach to achieving its foreign policy goals by working in close concert with the global community. After World War II, the United States and its allies established the UN, NATO, the IMF, and other international institutions to keep the peace, deter aggression, and promote economic development. The advocates of an internationalist approach to American foreign policy believe that the United States should work with these institutions and with its allies to address the problems of international terrorism, nuclear proliferation, and rogue states. Consider the challenges presented by nuclear weapons development in Iran and North Korea. The United States can take the lead in addressing each nation, but it needs the support of other nations if it hopes to convince either nation to forego weapons development.

In contrast, other policymakers believe that the United States should follow a unilateralist approach to achieving its foreign policy goals, acting alone if necessary. President George W. Bush justified attacking Iraq without UN support because the United States believed that Saddam Hussein had weapons of mass destruction that he could give to terrorists who could then have used them to kill tens of thousands of Americans. "When it comes to our security," said the president, "we really don't need anybody's permission."[24] The advocates of the unilateralist approach argue that the United States should cooperate with international agreements only as far as they benefit America. Because the United States has the world's most powerful military and largest economy, it can assert itself internationally. Other nations will have no choice but to accept the leadership of the United States and adapt to American preferences.[25]

Contemporary American foreign policies reflect both internationalist and unilateralist impulses, indicating, perhaps, that American policymakers are not firmly committed to either approach. On one hand, the United States has worked with the international community to combat terrorism. The United States organized an international coalition to overthrow the Taliban government in Afghanistan that had harbored the al Qaeda terrorist network and has enlisted the support of countries around the globe to track down terrorist cells. The United States has found support not just from traditional allies in Western Europe but from other countries as well, such as Yemen that had long been regarded as safe havens for terrorists. On the other hand, the United States has rejected a series of global agreements that enjoy overwhelming international support, including the Global Warming Treaty, Biological Diversity Treaty, Land Mine Ban Treaty, and the International Criminal Court. The United States refused to ratify the **Global Warming Treaty,** which is an international agreement to reduce the worldwide emissions of carbon dioxide and other greenhouse gases, because it believed that the treaty put too much of the burden for reducing emissions on the United States. It rejected the Biological Diversity Treaty because it argued that the agreement did not go far enough to protect the patent rights of bioengineering companies. The United States opposed the Land Mine Treaty because it claimed that it needs land mines to protect American troops in South Korea. The United States rejected the International Criminal Court Treaty because it did not want Americans subject to international criminal court prosecution.

Global Warming Treaty An international agreement to reduce the worldwide emissions of carbon dioxide and other greenhouse gases, because it believed that the treaty puts too much of the burden for reducing emissions on the United States.

The war against Iraq illustrated the ambivalence of American policy. The United States initially worked with the UN to force Iraq to submit to UN inspection to ensure its compliance with UN resolutions to disarm. Eventually, however, the United States grew impatient with the pace of inspection, arguing that the Iraqi government was not honestly cooperating with the process. When the UN Security Council refused to adopt a new resolution giving Iraq a short deadline for full and complete disclosure, President Bush set his own deadline and then ordered military action when the deadline was not met to the president's satisfaction.

By the end of the Bush administration, the approach of the United States in dealing with rogue states had shifted from focusing on regime change, which it applied in Iraq, to behavior change. With American forces occupied fighting ongoing insurgencies in Iraq and Afghanistan, the United States was in no position to take military action against other rogue states. Libya, a North African country associated with international terrorism, demonstrated the utility of the approach when it renounced efforts to develop WMDs in exchange for American assurances that it would not seek regime change. The United States and its European allies have been working through the IAEA to pressure Iran to abandon its nuclear program. They have threatened economic sanctions if the Iranians do not cooperate, but their leverage against Iran is diminished because Russia and China have a strong trading relationship with Iran and are reluctant to reduce those ties. Meanwhile, the Bush administration, after initially refusing to engage in direct talks with the North Koreans, agreed to participate in six-party talks (the United States, North Korea, Japan, China, Russia, and South Korea) to resolve the crisis over North Korea's nuclear program.[26] In 2007, North Korea agreed to shut down its nuclear program in return for international food aid and steps toward normalizing relations with the United States and Japan. In 2008, however, the North Korean government announced that it was going to restart its nuclear program.[27]

? WHAT IS YOUR OPINION?

If necessary, should the United States act on its own to achieve its foreign policy and defense goals, even if its allies disagree with the action?

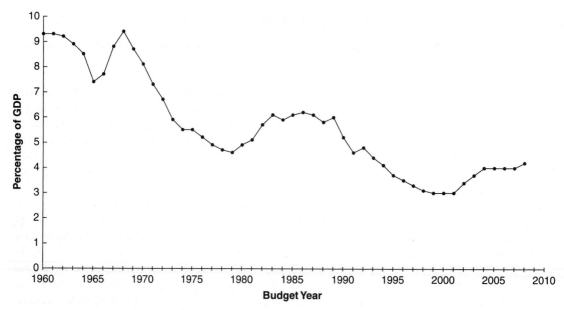

FIGURE 17.1   Defense Spending as Percentage of GDP.
Source: Office of Management and Budget.

DEFENSE POLICY

The nineteenth-century military strategist Karl von Clausewitz once described war as "diplomacy by other means." He meant that defense concerns and foreign policy issues are closely related. Foreign policy goals determine defense strategies. Military capabilities, meanwhile, influence a nation's foreign policy by expanding or limiting the options available to policymakers.

Defense Spending

Gross Domestic Product (GDP) The total value of goods and services produced by a nation's economy in a year, excluding transactions with foreign countries.

Figure 17.1 depicts United States defense spending from 1960 through 2008 as a percentage of the **Gross Domestic Product (GDP),** which is the total value of goods and services produced by a nation's economy in a year, excluding transactions with foreign countries. In general, defense spending increases during wartime and falls during peacetime. Defense expenditures peaked relative to the size of the economy during the Vietnam War in the late 1960s and then fell after the war ended. The only exception to the pattern of rising defense spending during wartime and falling defense expenditures during peacetime occurred during the early 1980s when President Reagan proposed, and Congress passed, the largest peacetime increase in military spending in the nation's history. Defense spending fell again in the 1990s after the collapse of the Soviet Union and the end of the Cold War. Since September 11, 2001, defense expenditures have increased as Congress and the president fund the war on terror as well as military operations in Afghanistan and Iraq.

Defense Forces and Strategy

America's defense strategy is based on **strategic** (nuclear) and **conventional** (non-nuclear) **forces.**

Strategic Forces   The United States has more than 10,000 nuclear weapons. More than half are currently active and deployed, ready to be carried to their targets through a variety of delivery systems. The Air Force can deliver at least 320 nuclear missiles by plane—B-52s or B-2s. The Navy has more than 2,000 nuclear missiles on submarines, with at least a third of the subs on patrol at any one time. The Army has 1,450 nuclear weapons configured for cruise missile delivery. Other missiles sit in silos located in 12 states and six European countries, ready for launch.[28]

Many defense theorists believe that nuclear weapons promoted world peace during the Cold War because no national leader acting rationally would risk initiating a nuclear holocaust. This concept was formalized in the doctrine of **mutual assured destruction (MAD),** which was the belief that the United States and the Soviet Union would be deterred from launching a nuclear assault against each other for fear of being destroyed in a general nuclear war. MAD can be explained more fully by defining first- and second-strike capability. A **first strike** is the initial offensive move of a general nuclear war, aimed at knocking out the other side's ability to retaliate. A **second strike** is a nuclear attack in response to an adversary's first strike. **First-strike capability** is the capacity of a nation to launch an initial nuclear assault sufficient to cripple an adversary's ability to retaliate. **Second-strike capability** is the capacity of a nation to absorb an initial nuclear attack and retain sufficient nuclear firepower to inflict unacceptable damage on its adversary. According to the principles of MAD, America's best defense against nuclear attack and best deterrent to nuclear war hinge on maintaining a second-strike capability.

Deterrence was the organizing principle of American defense policy during the Cold War. It was the ability of a nation to prevent an attack against itself or its allies by threat of **massive retaliation,** which is the concept that the United States will strike back against an aggressor with overwhelming force. American leaders often explained the concept of deterrence with the phrase "peace through strength." By preparing for war, the United States would ensure the peace. Weaker nations would be deterred from attacking the United States because America enjoyed military superiority. In the meantime, the United States and the Soviet Union would be deterred from attacking each other because both countries possessed nuclear arsenals capable of destroying the other. Deterrence worked to prevent nuclear war during the Cold War because both the United States and the Soviet Union believed that the other side possessed an effective second-strike capability. The Soviet Union did not dare launch an attack against the United States (and vice versa) because Soviet leaders believed that enough American nuclear forces would survive the initial Soviet strike to destroy their country.

Deterrence does not fit the post–Cold War world because of rogue states and, especially, terrorist organizations. Although deterrence continues to be an effective defense strategy against the threat of nuclear attack by Russia or China, some defense analysts believe that may be ineffective against rogue states whose leaders are sometimes prone to engage in high-risk behavior. Terrorist organizations, meanwhile, are

---

Strategic forces Nuclear forces.

Conventional forces Non-nuclear forces.

Mutual assured destruction (MAD) The belief that the United States and the Soviet Union would be deterred from launching a nuclear assault against each other for fear of being destroyed in a general nuclear war.

First strike The initial offensive move of a general nuclear war, aimed at knocking out the other side's ability to retaliate.

Second strike A nuclear attack in response to an adversary's first strike.

First-strike capability The capacity of a nation to launch an initial nuclear assault sufficient to cripple an adversary's ability to retaliate.

Second-strike capability The capacity of a nation to absorb an initial nuclear attack and retain sufficient nuclear firepower to inflict unacceptable damage on its adversary.

GLOBAL PERSPECTIVE
Nuclear Weapons in Pakistan

Pakistan became a nuclear power in 1998 when it successfully tested several nuclear weapons. International observers believe that it has now produced enough fissile material to make as many as 50 nuclear devices.* Pakistan has also purchased or developed medium-range ballistic missiles that are capable of striking cities in neighboring India.

Pakistan developed nuclear weapons to achieve military parity with India and to gain international prestige as a nuclear power. Pakistan and India are longstanding enemies, having fought three wars since 1948. The two nations remain locked in a bitter dispute over control of the border region of Kashmir. Pakistan began a nuclear program in the early 1970s to match India's nuclear program and to offset India's advantage in conventional weapons. By developing nuclear weapons, Pakistan hopes to establish itself as a regional power and to claim leadership of the Muslim world as the first Muslim nation to have the bomb.

The United States opposes Pakistan's nuclear weapons program because of the danger that the next war between Pakistan and India will be a nuclear war and because of the fear that Pakistani nuclear weapons may fall into the hands of terrorists. The government of Pakistan is unstable, and senior officials in the Pakistani military are known for being sympathetic with the former Taliban government of Afghanistan and with Osama bin Laden. The United States responded to Pakistan's nuclear tests in 1998 by imposing economic sanctions in hopes of convincing the Pakistani government that the price of nuclear weapons was too high, but Pakistan refused to change course. After September 11, 2001, the United States lifted the sanctions in exchange for Pakistani cooperation in the war against the Taliban government of Afghanistan and the fight against Osama bin Laden's terrorist network.†

QUESTIONS TO CONSIDER

1. Does Pakistan having nuclear weapons make war between Pakistan and India more likely or less likely? Explain the reasoning behind your answer.
2. Is the United States hypocritical to oppose nuclear weapons in Pakistan, considering that the United States is the world's foremost nuclear power?
3. Is a nuclear Pakistan a threat to world peace? Why or why not?

*David Albright, "Securing Pakistan's Nuclear Weapons Complex," Institute for Science and International Security," October 2001, available at www.isis-online.org/publications/terrorism/stanleypaper.html.

†Farzana Shaikh, "Pakistan's Nuclear Bomb: Beyond the Non-Proliferation Regime," *International Affairs* 78 (January 2002): 29–48.

Deterrence The ability of a nation to prevent an attack against itself or its allies by threat of massive retaliation.

Massive retaliation The concept that the United States will strike back against an aggressor with overwhelming force.

unlikely to be deterred by threat of massive retaliation because they lack a home base that the United States could attack.[29]

President George W. Bush responded to the terrorist attacks of September 11, 2001, by announcing that the United States had adopted the policy of **military preemption,** which is the defense policy that declares that the United States will attack nations or groups that represent a potential threat to the security of the United States. Under certain circumstances, military preemption could even involve the United States using nuclear weapons against a potential enemy threat. President Bush justified the policy of military preemption as follows:

> Given the goals of rogue states and terrorists, the United States can no longer solely rely on a reactive posture as we have in the past. The inability to deter a potential attacker, the immediacy of today's threats, and the magnitude of potential harm that could be

American nuclear-powered submarines roam the world's oceans armed with sea-launched ballistic missiles.

Military preemption The defense policy that declares that the United States will attack nations or groups that represent a potential threat to the security of the United States.

caused by our adversaries' choice of weapons, do not permit that option. We cannot let our enemies strike first.[30]

The American attack against Iraq to overthrow the regime of Saddam Hussein was the first application of the doctrine of military preemption. The United States went to war not because Iraq posed an immediate threat to national security, but because of the possibility that Iraq could give weapons of mass destruction to terrorists. "The people of the United States will not live at the mercy of an outlaw regime that threatens the peace with weapons of mass murder," said Bush.

The policy of military preemption is controversial, especially against rogue states. Critics question the assertion that deterrence is ineffective against rogue states. The leaders of North Korea, Iran, and other enemies of the United States are not suicidal. Overwhelming military force as effectively deters rogue states as it does other nations. Just because American policymakers may not always understand North Korean or Iranian politics does not mean that those nations or their leaders behave irrationally.[31] Saddam Hussein was an evil dictator, but was he really an immediate threat to the United States? Critics also warn that the consistent application of the doctrine of military preemption would involve the United States in perpetual war. Iran and North Korea have greater weapons capability than Iraq had. Does the United States plan to go to war against those nations just as it did Iraq? Finally, the critics of military preemption worry that other nations will use the doctrine to justify attacking their neighbors.[32]

Conventional Forces   For decades, the United States maintained a large standing army in order to defend against a possible conventional arms attack by the Soviet Union in Western Europe. More than 2 million men and women served in the U.S. armed forces through the 1980s. After the end of the Cold War, the United States scaled back its conventional forces, cutting the size of its armed forces sharply in the early 1990s. With the dissolution of the Soviet Union, the chances of great armies clashing on the scale of World War II were remote. Nonetheless, the United States kept the basic structure of a large military in tact, with 1.4 million troops in uniform. Pentagon planners believed that substantial military forces were still needed to fulfill the mission of fighting regional wars, promoting regional stability, keeping the peace, and participating in humanitarian relief efforts.

Donald Rumsfeld, the secretary of defense in the George W. Bush administration from 2001 through the end of 2006, advocated restructuring the U.S. military. He believed that the U.S. armed forces could accomplish their mission by relying on speed, mobility, and firepower rather than a large army characteristic of twentieth-century warfare.[33] Rumsfeld put his theory into action in Afghanistan, where American airpower, including an unmanned aircraft called the Predator, defeated Taliban and al Qaeda forces by using precision weapons operating at extremely long range, with targeting information gathered on the ground, in the air, and from space. American troops on the ground initially served as spotters for airpower and acted as liaison to local Afghan militia. The United States employed a similar strategy in Iraq, using highly mobile ground forces to slice through Iraqi defenses by use of overwhelming firepower, much of it delivered by air.

Rumsfeld's critics believe that the United States still needs substantial conventional forces and that, in fact, the U.S. military is too small. Although firepower and mobility enabled the United States to defeat the Taliban and the Iraqi army in short order, American forces were insufficient to stabilize either nation. As a result, the United States and its allies remained embroiled in protracted warfare against insurgent forces in both Afghanistan and Iraq years after the initial invasion. Conditions in Iraq finally began to improve when the United States adopted a surge strategy, increased troop strength in Iraq, especially in Baghdad, the nation's capital. The goal of the strategy was to establish order to buy time for Iraqi forces to develop the capacity to take over the defense of their own country while allowing the nation's political factions the opportunity to reconcile their divisions.

The United States is restructuring its conventional forces to respond to the challenge of fighting two military campaigns simultaneously, including a large-scale conflict and a prolonged irregular conflict conducted on a worldwide basis.[34] The U.S. Navy is expanding its fleet to add a number of small, fast vessels that can operate in relatively shallow coastal waters against terrorists, while maintaining 11 aircraft carriers and other major vessels to counter the growth of Chinese naval power.[35] Meanwhile, the Department of Defense is reconfiguring the Army toward dealing with rogue states and terrorist threats. The goal is to develop mobile forces capable of operating in dozens of countries at once to defeat terrorists; counter the threat of WMDs; and deter China, Russia, and India from becoming adversaries.[36]

CONCLUSION: FOREIGN AND DEFENSE POLICYMAKING

International events are the most important environmental factors affecting foreign and defense policymaking. During the Cold War, American foreign and defense policies were formulated, adopted, implemented, and evaluated in light of the perceived threat of international communism. The Cold War shaped international

GETTING INVOLVED

America in the Eyes of the World

What do people in other countries think about the United States? Do they love America or hate it? Do they fear it or respect it? Are they envious or admiring? The class project is to interview international students and other foreign nationals about the perceptions held by people in their home countries about the United States. Note that the assignment is not to ask international students *their* opinion about the United States because they may be uncomfortable expressing anything other than positive points of view. Instead, class members should ask international students about the attitudes of people back home in their country. International students who are part of the class can take the lead, interviewing their friends and helping American students understand the information they receive.

The interviews should focus on the following subject areas:

- **Culture.** How influential is American culture (television, films, music, etc.) in your country? Do people admire American culture, or does it offend them? Do they worry that American culture will overwhelm their own culture?

- **Economics.** Do people in your country believe that they benefit from the economic power of the United States, or do they think that they are hurt economically by the United States?

- **Foreign policy.** What do people in your country think about American foreign policy? Do they consider the United States to be a force for good, or do they believe the United States acts unfairly in its own interest? Do they think that the United States is a bully?

After the interviews are complete, your instructor will ask the students to discuss what they learned from the activity. In which of the three areas (culture, economics, and foreign policy) were attitudes about the United States the most positive? In which area were they the least positive? How did points of view vary from region to region? Finally, why do people from other nations think as they do about the United States?

diplomacy, alliances, defense budgets, and defense strategy. Today, the most important event for shaping American foreign and defense policy is the terrorist attack of September 11, 2001.

Survey research shows that although most Americans support an active role for the United States in world affairs, the general public is more cautious about American involvement abroad than are policy leaders in government, the media, business, and academia. For example, the general public is less supportive of foreign aid and immigration than are policy leaders. The public is also less willing than policy leaders to endorse the use of the U.S. armed forces to defend American interests abroad.[37]

Agenda Building

Events, public opinion, the media, interest groups, Congress, and the president all play a role in setting the agenda for foreign and defense policymaking. Some issues become important items on the policy agenda because of media coverage of dramatic international events, such as the bombing of Pearl Harbor, the launch of *Sputnik*, or the terrorist attacks of September 11, 2001. Events affect the agenda for foreign and defense policymaking because of their impact on elite and mass public opinion. When the Soviet Union launched the *Sputnik* satellite, for example, the American scientific and educational communities became alarmed that the United States was falling behind the Soviet Union in science education and space technology.

Many interest groups participate in foreign and defense policymaking. Dozens of corporations and their employee unions lobby on behalf of weapons systems in which they have a financial interest. Corporate and trade groups focus on trade policy, either seeking protection from foreign competition or working against restrictive trade policies that could threaten their import or export businesses. Environmental groups emphasize international environmental issues, such as global warming and resource conservation. Ethnic groups—African Americans, Mexican Americans, Cuban Americans, Greek Americans, Chinese Americans, Arab Americans, and Jewish Americans—take an interest in foreign policies affecting regions of the world that are of particular interest to them. The American Jewish community, for example, is concerned about policy toward Israel and the Arab world. Cuban Americans focus on U.S. policy toward Cuba.

Historically, the president has taken the lead in foreign and defense policy matters.[38] In 1947, for instance, the Truman administration convinced congressional leaders that U.S. aid for Greece and Turkey was essential to American security. During the 1960s and 1970s, a series of presidents and a procession of Department of State and Pentagon spokespersons worked to persuade Congress and the nation of the importance of American intervention in Vietnam. After September 11, President George W. Bush announced a new American policy of military preemption and focused the world's attention on the goal of disarming Iraq. Bush used his second inaugural address to emphasize that democratization had become the principle goal of American foreign policy.

Bipartisanship The close cooperation and general agreement between the two major political parties in dealing with foreign policy matters.

During the Cold War, presidents could generally count on bipartisan support for foreign policy issues. **Bipartisanship** is the close cooperation and general agreement between the two major political parties in dealing with foreign policy matters. Democrats and Republicans alike agreed that Soviet expansion was the primary threat to American interests and that deterrence and containment were the appropriate strategy to counter the threat. Congressional consensus on foreign policy and defense policy issues has become much less frequent since the War in Vietnam. Since 9/11, there has been consensus on the importance of eliminating al Qaeda but disagreement over how best to deal with rogue states.[39] Consider the controversy over the war in Iraq. When the president ordered the U.S. military to invade Iraq to overthrow Saddam Hussein, Congress offered support and voted to provide additional money to fund the war and help rebuild Iraq. As the situation in Iraq worsened and public opinion began to turn against the war, individual members of Congress spoke out against administration policies, and congressional committees initiated investigations of the Iraqi prisoner abuse scandal at Abu Ghraib prison and allegations that Halliburton and other private contractors had overcharged the U.S. government for work performed in Iraq. After Democrats won control of Congress in the 2006 election, congressional opposition to the war increased. Although Congress continued to fund operations, Democratic leaders spoke out against the war and attempted to enact legislation to force the Bush administration to set a timetable for withdrawing American forces.

Policy Formulation and Adoption

The president and Congress share constitutional authority to formulate and adopt foreign and defense policy. The president negotiates treaties, but the Senate must ratify them. The president has the power of diplomatic recognition, but the Senate

American troops on patrol in Iraq.

must confirm ambassadorial appointments. The president can request money for foreign aid and defense, but Congress must appropriate the funds. The president is commander-in-chief of the armed forces, but Congress declares war. Congress also has the constitutional authority to raise and support armies and a navy.

The president often initiates foreign and defense policies, with Congress acting to modify or, occasionally, reject policies formulated in the executive branch. This division of labor has developed for a number of reasons. First, the executive branch is better equipped to deal with international crises than the legislative branch. The executive branch is unitary, under the authority of a single person, the president. In contrast, Congress is a bicameral institution that often seems to speak with 535 separate voices, the sum total of members of the House and Senate. Whereas the president can respond quickly to international events and speak with one voice, Congress often reacts slowly and without unity.

Second, the president has an advantage in that secret national security information from the Central Intelligence Agency (CIA), military, Federal Bureau of Investigation (FBI), and diplomatic corps flows directly to the White House. The president can keep Congress in the dark about foreign and defense developments or can release information selectively to justify policies. President Bush justified the invasion of Iraq by declaring that the U.S. government had proof that Iraq had WMDs.

Third, the general public expects the president to lead in foreign and defense policymaking. As a rule, the public is neither well informed nor particularly attentive to foreign affairs. In times of international crisis, Americans tend to rally around the president. Presidents typically enjoy a surge of popularity for roughly a 30-day period following the visible use of military force.[40] Immediately after September 11, 2001, for example, the percentage of Americans who told survey researchers that they approved of President Bush's performance in office leaped from 51 percent in early September to 90 percent later in the month. Bush's approval rating stayed well above the 60 percent level for more than a year, significantly strengthening the president's hand on foreign and defense policy issues.[41]

Finally, the president has often had considerable influence on foreign and defense policymaking because Congress has allowed it. Many members of Congress are not interested in overall foreign policy and defense strategy. Congress as an institution is decentralized, addressing the parts of policy but rarely the big picture. Individual members focus primarily on the big issues that gain national attention, such as the war in Iraq, or on issues of primary importance to their constituents, such as Department of Defense decisions on closing military bases or the purchase of weapons systems manufactured in their states and districts.

The nature of the president's role in foreign and defense policymaking depends on the individual officeholder. Presidents with a special interest and experience in foreign policy may take personal charge of foreign and defense policymaking. Richard Nixon and George H. W. Bush, two presidents with extensive foreign policy experience and expertise, immersed themselves in the details of the nation's foreign policies. In contrast, Ronald Reagan entered office with almost no foreign policy experience and apparently little interest in the subject. He relied heavily on aides and advisors for foreign policy advice.

Some foreign and defense policies can be adopted in the executive branch alone, but most require congressional action as well. Foreign aid and defense budgets must journey through the regular appropriations process. The Senate must ratify treaties and confirm appointments. In practice, Congress more frequently modifies than blocks executive branch initiatives in foreign and defense policy. The Senate, for example, ratified the Panama Canal Treaty after tacking on 24 amendments, reservations, conditions, and understandings.

In general, Congress is more likely to support presidential initiatives in foreign and defense policy when the president's party controls Congress, when the president enjoys a relatively high approval rating, and during times of international crisis. After September 11, 2001, President George W. Bush benefited from an atmosphere of international crisis and strong public support on foreign and defense policy issues. Furthermore, the Republican Party controlled the House and the Senate during the first few months of 2000 and then again after the 2002 election. As a result, Bush won congressional support for his proposals concerning homeland security, defense spending, trade, and the invasion of Iraq. Congress also granted the president authority to negotiate trade agreements that would not be subject to congressional amendment. Even after the situation in Iraq soured and public opinion began to turn against administration policy, congressional criticism of the administration was muted until 2007 because Republican legislative leaders did not want to challenge a president from their party. After Democrats won a majority in Congress in the 2006 election, however, Bush faced a Congress hostile to his administration's foreign and defense policies, especially in Iraq.

The controversy over gay men and lesbians serving in the armed forces illustrates the dynamic political nature of foreign and defense policy formulation and adoption. When President Clinton announced shortly after taking office that he was preparing an executive order to end the Pentagon's ban on gay men and lesbians serving in the military, he was taking a principled stand against discrimination and fulfilling a campaign promise as well. Clinton argued that ending the ban was the right thing to do. Men and women who serve their country honorably, he said, should be judged on the basis of their behavior rather than their sexual orientation. Both homosexuals and heterosexuals who engage in inappropriate sexual behavior should be removed from the armed forces, he argued, but people who play by the rules should be allowed to serve without discrimination. Clinton's promise to end the ban also fulfilled a campaign promise to a key group of political supporters. Gay men and lesbians are an important voter bloc, especially in the large states of California and New York. Furthermore, gay and lesbian rights groups raised millions of dollars for the Clinton campaign during the 1992 election season.

President Clinton's proposal generated a firestorm of controversy. The **Joint Chiefs of Staff,** which is a group of military advisors composed of the chiefs of staff of the army and air force, the chief of naval operations, and sometimes the commandant of the Marine Corps, warned that allowing openly gay men and lesbians to serve in the armed forces would undermine morale and threaten unit cohesion. Although gay and lesbian rights groups and a coalition of civil rights and civil liberties organizations favored lifting the ban, they were outgunned by veterans' organizations and conservative religious groups who launched letter-writing campaigns directed at members of Congress, urging them to oppose the president on the issue.

Democratic Senator Sam Nunn, who was then the chair of the Armed Services Committee, was the most effective opponent of the president's proposal. Nunn's committee staged televised hearings on the issue, allowing critics of the president's proposal a public forum to attack the plan while giving groups and individuals who favored the president's position little opportunity to make their case. Nunn even took the committee on a fact-finding tour of an aircraft carrier, showing television reporters the close quarters where service men and women live and work.

Clinton eventually compromised on the issue because he recognized that had he signed an executive order lifting the ban, Congress would have quickly passed legislation writing the original policy into law. The compromise, which pleased few, was called the **don't ask, don't tell policy.** The military would not ask new recruits about their sexual orientation and would stop conducting investigations aimed at identifying and discharging homosexuals, but it would discharge service members who revealed their sexual orientation. Gay men and women who stayed in the closet could continue their service.

? WHAT IS YOUR OPINION?

Should gay men and lesbians be allowed to serve openly in the armed forces of the United States?

Policy Implementation and Evaluation

The executive branch is primarily responsible for the implementation of foreign policy. The Department of State, Department of Defense, and CIA are prominently involved, but many other agencies and departments play a role as well. The Department

Joint Chiefs of Staff A military advisory body that is composed of the chiefs of staff of the U.S. Army and Air Force, the Chief of Naval Operations, and sometimes the Commandant of the Marine Corps.

Don't ask, don't tell policy The official policy for dealing with gay men and lesbians in the U.S. armed forces. The military would not ask new recruits about their sexual orientation and would stop conducting investigations aimed at identifying and discharging homosexuals, but it would discharge service members who revealed their sexual orientation.

of Agriculture, for example, promotes the sale of American agricultural products abroad. The Department of Education administers student-exchange programs.

Foreign and defense policies may not always be implemented the way the president and Congress originally intended or expected. Bureaucrats sometimes have priorities of their own. Also, large bureaucracies tend to develop standard operating procedures (SOPs) that they follow in performing their tasks, regardless of whether they conform to the goals of the original policy.

The implementation of the don't ask, don't tell policy concerning gay men and lesbians in the military demonstrates that official policy changes do not always lead to changes in policy implementation, at least not the desired changes. After the adoption of the policy, the military has actually become more diligent at seeking out and discharging suspected homosexuals from the armed services. The military dismissed 1,227 people in 2001 for being gay or lesbian, far more people than were discharged for homosexuality in 1993, before the policy went into effect. The number of people forced out of the military because of their sexual orientation fell significantly in subsequent years, but most observers believed that the decline reflected the military's need to hold onto qualified personnel during wartime.[42]

The government has no systematic, ongoing mechanism for evaluating foreign and defense policies. Congress monitors expenditures, but often limits its policy oversight to high-profile issues, such as the war in Iraq, or issues that affect the home districts of members, such as the decision by the Pentagon to close a local military base. Scandals also receive considerable attention as well. Other efforts at evaluation take place in the executive branch, in academia, and by the news media.

In general, foreign and defense policies are probably more difficult to evaluate than policies in other areas. It is not always possible to determine whether policy goals have been met. In the absence of war, for example, any evaluation of the effectiveness of particular defense strategies has to be at least somewhat speculative. Another problem is that many of the details of policy implementation are secret. Only now, years after the events took place, is information available so that historians can begin intelligently to evaluate American foreign policy in the years immediately following World War II.

KEY TERMS

balance of power	diplomacy	isolationism
bipartisanship	diplomatic relations	Joint Chiefs of Staff
Cold War	don't ask, don't tell policy	Marshall Plan
containment	first strike	massive retaliation
conventional forces	first-strike capability	military preemption
convergence theory	foreign policy	Monroe Doctrine
defense policy	Global Warming Treaty	mutual assured destruction
democratic peace	Gross Domestic Product (GDP)	(MAD)
détente	International Monetary Fund	nation-state
deterrence	(IMF)	Nixon Doctrine

nongovernmental organiza-
tions (NGOs)

North American Free Trade
Agreement (NAFTA)

North Atlantic Treaty
Organization (NATO)

Nuclear Nonproliferation Treaty

postindustrial societies

Reagan Doctrine

rogue states

second strike

second-strike capability

Sputnik

strategic forces

tariffs

Truman Doctrine

United Nations (UN)

weapons of mass destruction
(WMDs)

World Health Organization
(WHO)

World Trade Organization
(WTO)

NOTES

1. George W. Bush, "State of the Union Address," January 29, 2002, available at www.whitehouse.gov.
2. Steven Lee Myers and Elaine Sciolino, "North Koreans Bar Inspectors at Nuclear Site," *New York Times*, September 25, 2008, available at www.nytimes.com.
3. Marcus Franda, *The United Nations in the Twenty-First Century: Management and Reform Processes in a Troubled Organization* (Lanham, MD: Rowman & Littlefield, 2006), p. 1.
4. Robert Cooper, *The Postmodern State and the World Order* (London, UK: Demos, 2000), p. 22.
5. Courtney B. Smith, *Politics and Process at the United Nations: The Global Dance* (Boulder, CO: Lynne Rienner, 2006), p. 28.
6. Elizabeth Becker, "Trade Talks Fail to Agree on Drugs for Poor Nations," *New York Times*, December 21, 2002, available at www.nytimes.com.
7. Jonathan P. Doh and Hildy Teegan, *Globalization and NGOs: Transforming Business, Government, and Society* (Westport, CT: Praeger, 2003), pp. 3–9, 206–219.
8. Michael E. Brown, ed., *Grave New World: Security Challenges in the 21st Century* (Washington, DC: Georgetown University Press, 2003), p. 307.
9. Terry L. Deibel, *Foreign Affairs Strategy: Logic for American Statecraft* (New York: Cambridge University Press, 2007), p. 271.
10. "United States Foreign Trade Highlights," International Trade Administration, U.S. Department of Commerce, available at www.ita.doc.gov.
11. Marvin Zonis, "The 'Democracy Doctrine' of President George W. Bush," in Stanley A. Renshon and Peter Suedfeld, eds., *Understanding the Bush Doctrine: Psychology and Strategy in an Age of Terrorism* (New York: Routledge, 2007), p. 232.
12. Congressional Research Report, *Conventional Arms Transfers to Developing Nations, 1999–2006*, September 26, 2007, available at http://opencrs.com.
13. Celia W. Dugger, "U.S. Challenged to Increase Aid to Africa," *New York Times*, June 5, 2005, available at www.nytimes.com.
14. Budget of the United States Government, Fiscal Year 2009, available at www.omb.gov.
15. George F. Kennan, *American Diplomacy 1900–1950* (New York: New American Library, 1951), p. 10.
16. Philip J. Allen, ed., *Pitirim A. Sorokin in Review* (Durham, NC: Duke University Press, 1963).
17. "Treaty on the Non-proliferation of Nuclear Weapons," available at www.un.org.
18. Stanley Hoffman, "Requiem," *Foreign Policy* 42 (Spring 1981): 3–26.
19. Robert J. Lieber, "*Eagle* Revisited: A Reconsideration of the Reagan Era in U.S. Foreign Policy," *Washington Quarterly*, Summer 1989, pp. 115–126.
20. Robert G. Kaiser, "The End of the Soviet Empire: Failure on a Historic Scale," *Washington Post National Weekly Edition*, January 1–7, 1990, pp. 23–24.
21. Coil D. Blacker, "The New United States-Soviet Détente," *Current History* 88 (October 1989): 321–325, 357–359.
22. Robert E. Hunter, "Starting at Zero: U.S. Foreign Policy for the 1990s," *Washington Quarterly* 15 (Winter 1992): 35.
23. Robert J. Lieber, *Eagle Rules? Foreign Policy and American Primacy in the Twenty-First Century* (Upper Saddle River, NJ: Pearson, 2002), pp. 5–6.
24. Quoted in G. John Ikenberry, "Is American Multilateralism in Decline?" *Perspectives on Politics* 1 (September 2003): 534.
25. Stanley A. Renshon, "The Bush Doctrine Reconsidered," in Renshon and Suedfeld, eds., *Understanding the Bush Doctrine*, p. 2.
26. Robert S. Litwak, *Regime Change: U.S. Strategy Through the Prism of 9/11* (Baltimore, MD: Johns Hopkins University Press, 2007), pp. 2–10.
27. Steven Lee Myers and Elaine Sciolino, "North Koreans Bar Inspectors at Nuclear Site," *New York Times*, September 25, 2008, available at www.nytimes.com.
28. Isaiah Wilson III, "What Weapons Do They Have and What Can They Do?" *PS: Political Science & Politics*, July 2007, p. 473.
29. Willie Curtis, "Illusionary Promises and Strategic Reality: Rethinking the Implications of Strategic Deterrence in a

Post 9/11 World," in Renshon and Suedfeld, eds., *Understanding the Bush Doctrine*, pp. 133–143.

30. George W. Bush, "The National Security Strategy of the United States of America," available at www.whitehouse.gov.

31. Steven Mufson, "Rogue States: A Real Threat?" *Washington Post National Weekly Edition*, June 12, 2000, p. 15.

32. John Dumbrell, "The Bush Doctrine," in George C. Edwards III and Philip John Davies, eds., *New Challenges for the American Presidency* (New York: Longman, 2004), pp. 232–234.

33. Thomas E. Ricks, "A New Way of War," *Washington Post National Weekly Edition*, December 10–16, 2001, p. 6.

34. Renshon, "The Bush Doctrine Considered," p. 5.

35. David S. Cloud, "Navy to Expand Fleet with New Enemies in Mind," *New York Times*, December 5, 2005, available at www.nytimes.com.

36. Ann Scott Tyson, "A Road Map for Resources," *Washington Post National Weekly Edition*, February 13–19, 2006, p. 29.

37. Richard Morin, "A Gap in Worldviews," *Washington Post National Weekly Edition*, April 19, 1999, p. 34.

38. Cecil V. Crabb, Jr., Glenn J. Antizzo, and Leila E. Serieddine, *Congress and the Foreign Policy Process* (Baton Rouge: Louisiana State University Press, 2000), p. 189.

39. Litwak, *Regime Change*, p. 48.

40. Richard J. Stoll, "The Sound of the Guns," *American Politics Quarterly* 15 (April 1987): 223–237.

41. Jeffrey M. Jones, "Bush's High Approval Ratings Among Most Sustained for Presidents," *Gallup Poll Monthly*, November 2001, p. 32.

42. Thom Shanker and Patrick Healy, "A New Push to Roll Back 'Don't Ask, Don't Tell,'" *New York Times*, November 30, 2007, available at www.nytimes.com.

Chapter 18

The People, Economy, and Political Culture of Texas

CHAPTER OUTLINE

LEARNING OUTCOMES

After studying Chapter 18, students should be able to do the following:

▶ Explain the relationship among education, economic growth, and demographic change in Texas. (p. 494)

▶ Compare and contrast the population growth rate in Texas with population growth nationwide. (p. 495)

▶ Assess the effect of illegal immigration on the state. (pp. 496, 508–509)

▶ Describe recent population growth in Texas, considering the growth rate and the effect of that growth on the racial/ethnic makeup of the state. (pp. 496–499)

▶ Trace the development of the state's economy from the days of King Cotton to the present era of high-technology development. (pp. 499–502)

▶ Compare household income, poverty rates, and health insurance coverage in Texas with similar statistics in other states. (pp. 502–504)

▶ Describe the political culture of Texas, considering the approaches of Elazar and the team of Rice and Sundberg. (pp. 504–507)

▶ Explain the relationship between changes in the state's demographic, economic, and cultural environment and policy change. (pp. 507–510)

▶ Define the key terms listed on page 510 and explain their significance.

Education is the key to the future of Texas. In 2006, the average annual income of adults 25 years of age and older with a bachelor's degree was $82,827 compared with $38,137 for adults with only a high school education. High school dropouts, meanwhile, earned just $26,297 a year.[1] Educated citizens pay more in taxes than people without degrees because they earn more money. Moreover, high school dropouts cost the state more than $3,000 a year apiece because they are more likely than their educated counterparts to collect unemployment, receive welfare benefits, or go to prison.[2]

Unfortunately, Texas lags behind other states in educational attainment. Texas has the lowest high school graduation rate in the nation. In 2005, 78.2 percent of Texans 25 years of age and older had graduated from high school compared with a national high school graduation rate of 85.2 percent. Texas also trailed the national average in the proportion of adults holding bachelor's degrees, 25.5 percent to 28.2 percent.[3] Today, only 4.9 percent of Texas residents are enrolled in higher education compared with 6.1 percent of the residents of California, 6 percent in Illinois, and 5.6 percent in New York. To make matters worse, the rate of college enrollment in Texas is dropping. State officials estimate that the proportion of Texans attending college will fall to 4.6 percent or less by 2015.[4]

The fastest growing segment of the Texas population is also the least well educated. Latino and African American Texans as a group are less well educated and have lower incomes than whites and Asian Americans. In 2005, Latinos and African Americans made up 55 percent of the state's population but comprised only 36 percent of college and university enrollment.[5] Furthermore, the high school dropout rates for Latino and African American youngsters are higher (43 percent and 38 percent, respectively) than they are for white students (20 percent).[6] Population experts project that the state's population will be 46 percent Latino and 10 percent African American by the year 2030. If the educational, occupational, and income status of Hispanic and African American Texans does not improve significantly, a majority of the state's working-age population will be poorly educated, low-income minority residents. As a result, personal income per capita (per person) in Texas will decline from $19,663 in 2000 to $18,708 in 2020.[7] Business and industry will be reluctant to relocate to the state, tax collections will fall, and the state budget will be strapped trying to provide social services for a large population of low-income residents.[8]

The complex relationship among race and ethnicity, income and education, and public policy illustrates the importance of demographic, economic, and cultural factors to policymaking in Texas. This chapter examines some of the more significant factors shaping the environment for policymaking in Texas. The first section of the chapter profiles the people of Texas, considering the size of the state's population, population growth, population diversity, and the geographic distribution of the state's people. The second section examines the state's economy, looking at economic trends, personal income, and poverty. The final section of the chapter deals with the subject of political culture.

THE PEOPLE OF TEXAS

The population of Texas is one of the largest and most diverse of any state in the nation.

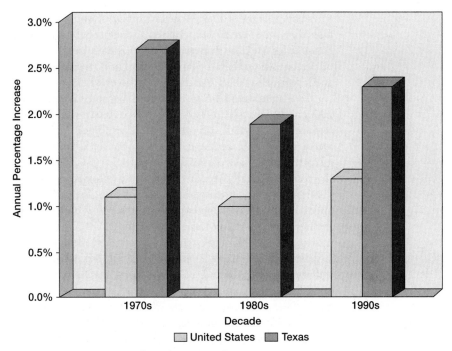

FIGURE 18.1   Average Annual Population Growth Rate.
Source: U.S. Census Bureau.

Population Size and Growth

Texas is the nation's second most populous state. In July 2006, the U.S. Census Bureau estimated that the population of Texas was 23.5 million. Only California, with 36.5 million people, had a larger population.[9]

Figure 18.1 traces the growth of the state's population decade by decade from the 1970s through the 1990s and compares the population growth rate of Texas with the growth rate for the United States as a whole. As the figure shows, the state's population expanded the most rapidly between 1970 and 1980, growing at an annual rate of 2.7 percent. The state's population growth rate fell to just less than 2 percent a year in the 1980s before rebounding to grow at a rate of 2.3 percent a year in the 1990s. In each of the three decades covered in the figure, the population of the **Lone Star State,** which is a nickname for Texas, increased at a more rapid pace than did the population of the nation as a whole. Furthermore, the U.S. Census Bureau estimates that the population of Texas has continued to increase at a relatively rapid rate. Between April 1, 2000, and July 1, 2006, the population of Texas grew by 12.7 percent compared with a national growth rate of 6.4 percent.[10]

Both natural population increase and immigration contribute to population growth in Texas. **Natural population increase** is the extent to which live births exceed deaths. The birthrate in Texas is the second highest in the nation. In 2004, the birthrate in Texas was 17.1 new babies for every 1,000 people. Only Utah had a higher birthrate.[11] Because the state's population is relatively young (a median age of 32.3 compared with

Lone Star State
Nickname for Texas.

Natural population increase The extent to which live births exceed deaths.

a national average of 35.3),[12] the proportion of women of childbearing age is relatively high. The state's ethnic composition also contributes to rapid population growth. The birthrate for Mexican American women, particularly recent immigrants, is more than 50 percent higher than the birthrates for Latino women who are not of Mexican origin and for women who are African American or white.[13]

The state's population also grows because of immigration. Between April 1, 2000, and July 1, 2006, Texas recorded a net gain of 1.3 million residents from international and domestic immigration combined. The state experienced a net increase of 801,576 residents from international immigration and added another 451,910 people from domestic immigration.[14] Many international immigrants enter the country illegally. According to a study conducted by the Pew Hispanic Center, 1.4 million undocumented residents lived in Texas in 2004; only California had a larger number of undocumented residents. Fifty-seven percent of the undocumented immigrants were from Mexico, with another 24 percent from other Latin American countries. Although undocumented workers work in all sectors of the economy, the largest numbers are employed in service industry jobs; construction and mining; installation and repair; and sales and administrative support.[15]

Illegal immigration is controversial. Critics charge that undocumented workers take jobs from American citizens while overcrowding schools and hospital emergency rooms. They add to traffic congestion and contribute to the crime problem. In contrast, immigration advocates contend that the United States benefits from immigration, even illegal immigration. They argue that undocumented workers fill jobs that citizens do not want and that they pay more in taxes than they receive in government services.

The Texas Comptroller of Public Accounts recently released a report assessing the costs and benefits of illegal immigration in Texas. On one hand, the report finds that undocumented workers add to the state's economy and pay more money in state taxes than they receive in services. Illegal immigrant workers and their families boost the Texas economy by $17.7 billion a year through their purchases of goods and service. They also pay more taxes to state government than they receive in state services—$1.58 billion in sales, excise, and motor vehicle taxes paid compared with $1.16 billion in state services for education, healthcare, emergency medical services, and incarceration. On the other hand, illegal immigrants are a drain on local governments because of the expense to local governments to provide healthcare services and law enforcement. The report found that illegal immigrants pay $513 million a year in local sales and property taxes while receiving $1.44 billion in local services.[16]

Because of immigration, Texas has a large and diverse foreign-born population. Texas has 3.3 million foreign-born residents, 15 percent of the state's population.[17] The foreign-born population of Texas is younger, poorer, and less well educated than are the state's native-born residents. More than three-fourths of the state's foreign-born residents are not American citizens.[18]

Rapid population growth presents both opportunities and challenges for policy-makers. On one hand, population growth has led to greater representation for Texas in Congress, a bigger share of federal grant money, and an enlarged tax base. Because the number of seats in the U.S. House of Representatives each state receives is based on its population, relatively rapid population growth in the Lone Star State translates into more representation in Congress. Texas gained 3 House seats after the 1990 Census and

Education is key to the future of Texas, especially of the state's growing Latino and African American populations.

2 more after the 2000 Census, giving the state 32 seats in the U.S. House. Population growth means an increase in federal financial aid because funding for many grant programs is based on population. Furthermore, population growth has generally meant a larger tax base for state and local governments. With more consumers to buy products, sales tax receipts have risen. On the other hand, population growth also presents policy challenges. Rapid population growth has placed a considerable strain on public services in Texas. More people mean more automobiles on city streets and freeways, more garbage to be collected and disposed of, more children to be educated, and more subdivisions for local law enforcement agencies to police.

Population Diversity

The population of Texas is quite diverse. In fact, a majority of Texans (50.2 percent) are members of racial and ethnic minority groups. The U.S. Census Bureau estimates that the population of Texas in 2004 was 50 percent white, 35 percent Latino, 12 percent African American, and 3 percent Asian American.[19] Although most Latino residents of Texas are Mexican American, the state's Hispanic population includes significant numbers of people who trace their ancestries to Cuba, El Salvador, or other Latin American countries. Similarly, the state's Asian population includes 27 different nationalities, the largest of which are Vietnamese, Chinese, Indian, Filipino, Korean, and Japanese.[20]

Foreign-Born Residents

The 2000 Census found that Texas has a large and growing population of foreign-born residents. Go to the website of the U.S. Census Bureau: **www.census.gov**. Scroll to the bottom of the page to the area labeled "Special Topics" and look for the link to the online version of the *Statistical Abstract of the United States*, which is an excellent reference source. Point your mouse to the population section and click on the link to "Foreign Born and Native Populations." Study the table and answer the following questions:

1. In 2000, what percentage of Texas residents were born abroad? How does that percentage compare with the national average?
2. What percentage of the foreign-born population in Texas entered the country during the 1990s? How does that percentage compare with the national average?
3. Why does Texas have a larger foreign-born population than most other states?
4. What are some of the public policy issues that are affected by Texas having a relatively large foreign-born population?

Texas's ethnic communities are distributed unevenly across the state. Most African Americans live in the rural areas and small towns of East Texas, along the Gulf Coast, and in the state's metropolitan areas. Houston and Dallas are home to a third of the state's African American population. Although Latinos live in every part of the state, they are more numerous in South and West Texas, especially along the Mexican border. San Antonio, El Paso, Corpus Christi, Brownsville, McAllen, and Laredo all have Hispanic majorities.[21] Asians are clustered in the Gulf Coast region, whereas many Texans of German and Czech descent live in the Hill Country in Central Texas. More than 90 percent of the state's foreign-born residents, regardless of racial/ethnic origin, live in metropolitan areas.[22]

Population Distribution

The population of Texas is not evenly distributed across the state. The most populous regions are Central, South, North, and East Texas and the Gulf Coast region. The most rapidly growing areas of the state are the San Antonio–Austin corridor in Central Texas, the Dallas–Fort Worth region in North Texas, the Houston area in Southeast Texas, and the strip along the border with Mexico. In contrast, the Panhandle region in Northwest Texas and far West Texas (with the exception of the border area near El Paso) are sparsely populated and growing slowly, if at all. Many of the rural counties in West Central Texas and the Panhandle lost population during the 1990s.[23]

Texas is an urban state, with 85 percent of its population living in metropolitan areas. Table 18.1 identifies the largest cities in the state, showing their population in 2006 and their rate of population growth since the 2000 Census. Three Texas cities—Houston, San Antonio, and Dallas—are among the ten largest cities in the United States. Houston is the fourth largest, San Antonio the seventh, and Dallas the ninth. Many Texas cities are also growing rapidly. As Table 18.1 shows, Fort Worth, Plano, San Antonio, and Arlington grew by 10 percent or more between

TABLE 18.1   Population and Growth Rates for Texas Cities, 2000–2006

City	2000 Population	2006 Population	Pct. Change, 2000–2006
Houston	1,953,631	2,144,491	9.8%
San Antonio	1,144,646	1,296,682	13.3
Dallas	1,188,580	1,232,940	3.7
Austin	656,562	709,893	8.1
Fort Worth	534,694	653,320	22.1
El Paso	563,662	609,415	8.1
Arlington	332,969	367,197	10.3
Corpus Christi	277,454	285,267	2.8
Plano	222,030	255,009	14.9
Garland	215,768	217,963	1.0

Source: U.S. Census Bureau, available at www.census.gov.

2000 and 2006. Nineteen Texas cities were among the top 100 fastest growing cities in the United States during that time period. Five Texas cities (McKinney, Brownsville, Laredo, Grand Prairie, and Fort Worth) grew by more than 20 percent between 2000 and 2006.[24]

Much of the growth in metropolitan areas occurred in the suburbs. During the 1990s, eight of the ten most rapidly growing counties in Texas were suburban counties. Collin County, which is north of Dallas, grew by 86 percent. Montgomery County and Fort Bend County, which are part of the Greater Houston metropolitan area, grew by 61 percent and 57 percent, respectively.[25]

The state's rural areas are growing slowly or, in some cases, losing population. Less than 10 percent of the 3.9 million residents added to the state's population during the 1990s lived in rural areas. The two most important industries for rural Texas, agriculture and oil, have changed to require fewer workers than before. Consequently, many rural areas have been losing population. During the 1990s, more than a third of Texas's rural counties lost population, whereas every metropolitan county grew.[26]

 WHAT IS YOUR OPINION?

If you could afford to live anywhere, would you prefer to live in the city, the suburbs, or the countryside?

THE TEXAS ECONOMY

The economy is a key part of the policymaking environment in Texas.

An Economy in Transition

For most of Texas history, the state's economy was based on the sale of agricultural commodities and raw materials. In the nineteenth century, cotton and cattle formed the basis of economic activity. Unfortunately for the state, neither product provided the necessary foundation for a manufacturing boom. Texas exported most of its ginned cotton for clothing production to other states or countries. Meanwhile, cattle ranchers drove their herds to railheads in Kansas for shipment to stockyards in the Midwest.

In 1901, oil was discovered at Spindletop near Beaumont. Subsequently, oil and gas deposits were found throughout the state and Texas became the nation's leading producer of oil and gas. In contrast to other commodities, oil spawned huge processing industries, including pipelines and refineries. The growth of petroleum-related businesses helped move the majority of Texans into urban areas by the 1950s.

Having an economy built on agriculture and oil had a major impact on the state's development. In the nineteenth century, Texas's economic health depended on the prices of cotton and cattle. For much of the twentieth century, the state's economy rose and fell in line with oil prices. Because commodity prices tend to fluctuate widely, Texas's economic history was one of booms and busts as prices for Texan products soared or collapsed. The state's economy boomed in the 1970s and early 1980s, for example, as oil prices rose to around $40 a barrel but then sagged in the mid-1980s as the price of oil dipped to less than half its earlier level.

The nature of the state's economy has contributed to a relatively lopsided distribution of income. Texas has been a rich state, but most Texans have not been wealthy. Although agriculture and oil were sources of significant wealth for the state's major landowners and big oil producers, more Texans were farmworkers and oil-field roughnecks than large landowners or oil producers. Workers in these industries historically were poorly organized and poorly paid, at least in comparison with

East Texas oil fields in 1903.

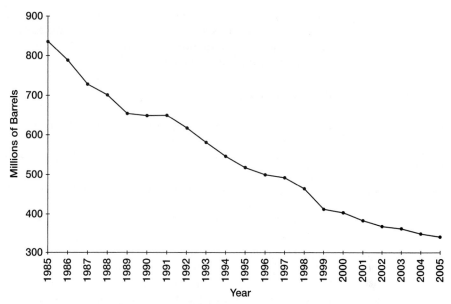

FIGURE 18.2   Texas Oil Production, 1985–2005.
Source: Texas Railroad Commission.

workers in the auto assembly plants or steel mills of northern states. Because people employed in industrial plants work together in close proximity, it is easier for them to organize and form unions to demand higher wages and better working conditions than farmworkers and oil-field roughnecks who are dispersed, working outdoors.

The Texas economy is changing. As Figure 18.2 demonstrates, Texas oil production has been falling sharply and fairly steadily for years and continues to decline. Natural gas production has fallen as well. In 2007, the oil and gas business provided only 1.8 percent of the state's nonfarm payroll, down from 7.3 percent in the early 1980s.[27] As oil and gas production has fallen, so have severance tax revenues. (A **severance tax** is a tax imposed on the extraction of natural resources, such as oil, coal, or gas.) Since the early 1970s, the proportion of state revenues generated by severance taxes on oil and gas production has declined from more than 20 percent to less than 5 percent in 2006.[28]

Declining oil and gas production and stagnant farm prices have forced state leaders, both in government and in private enterprise, to take steps to diversify the Texas economy. Although agriculture and petroleum are still important features of the state's economic picture, other industries are playing a greater role. Today, the state's economy is more diverse than ever before, resembling the national economy.

The economic changes that are taking place in the state affect Texas's workforce. The most rapidly growing components of the state's economy involve healthcare and **high-technology industries,** which are industries based on the latest in modern technology, such as telecommunications and robotics. These fields employ workers with technical knowledge and a capacity to learn new skills as technology changes. Texans who meet these criteria have a bright economic future. In 2007,

Severance tax A tax imposed on the extraction of natural resources, such as oil, coal, or gas.

High-technology industries Industries that are based on the latest in modern technology.

medical professionals, engineers, and computer programmers in Texas enjoyed annual salaries in excess of $70,000.[29] In contrast, unskilled workers were lucky to find jobs that paid much more than **minimum wage,** which is the lowest hourly wage that an employer can pay covered workers.

Wealth, Poverty, and Economic Growth

Texas is a big state with a big economy. In 2006, the Texas **gross state product (GSP),** which is the total value of goods and services produced in a state in a year, stood at $1.09 trillion.[30] Only California and New York had larger economies than Texas.[31] If Texas were an independent nation, it would have the eighth biggest economy in the world, larger even than Mexico, Brazil, Russia, India, Canada, Spain, and the Netherlands.[32]

The Texas economy has been growing at a more rapid pace than the national economy. Figure 18.3 compares the annual growth rate of the Texas economy with the rate of economic growth for the entire nation from 1990 through 2004. As the figure indicates, Texas economic performance generally parallels that of the national economy. Both economies experienced periods of relatively slow economic growth in the early 1990s and then again in 2001–2003. In the meantime, both the national economy and the state economy enjoyed several years of brisk economic expansion in the mid- to late 1990s. The figure also shows that the Texas economy grew more rapidly than the national economy throughout the period. The economic slumps were not as deep in Texas, whereas the economic booms were more robust.

Nonetheless, Texas is a relatively poor state, at least in terms of individual and family income. The median annual household income in Texas for 2003–2005 was

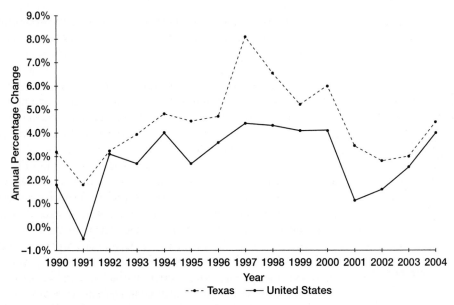

FIGURE 18.3   Changes in Economic Activity, 1990–2004.
Source: Texas Comptroller of Public Accounts.

$41,959 compared with a national figure of $46,037. Texas ranked 37th among the 50 states.[33]

Household income varies with race and ethnicity. The median income for white families nationwide in 2005 was $48,554 compared with $35,967 for Latino households and $30,858 for African American households.[34] Professor Stephen Klineberg, a Rice University sociologist, attributes the income disparity among ethnic and racial groups to a historic lack of access to quality education for African Americans and Latinos. Because the economy is changing, relatively few jobs are now available for people with weak job skills. "The good jobs that used to pay good money for unskilled or semiskilled work are much harder to find these days," he explains.[35] As we discussed in the introduction to this chapter, the future economic health of Texas hinges on the socioeconomic progress of its large and growing minority populations, especially the Latino and African American populations, and that progress depends on education.

The income differential among the rich, the poor, and those in the middle in Texas is relatively large. According to a report jointly published by the Center on Budget and Policy Priorities and the Economic Policy Institute, the top fifth of Texas families have an annual income of $118,971, whereas the middle fifth of Texas families earn $41,015 a year. The average annual income for the bottom fifth of families is $14,724. The income gap between the top and the middle is greater in Texas than in any other state, whereas the gap between the top and the bottom is second only to that in the state of New York.[36] Analysts attribute the income gap to Texas having a large population of poorly educated people, including many immigrants from Mexico, who are unable to find good-paying jobs.[37]

 WHAT IS YOUR OPINION?

Should the government adopt policies designed to narrow the wealth and income gaps between the poorest and wealthiest segments of the populations?

Poverty line The amount of money an individual or family needs to purchase basic necessities, such as food, clothing, healthcare, shelter, and transportation.

The poverty rate is relatively high in Texas. The government measures poverty on the basis of subsistence. By the official government definition, the **poverty line** is the amount of money an individual or a family needs to purchase basic necessities, such as food, clothing, healthcare, shelter, and transportation. The actual dollar amount varies with family size and rises with inflation. In 2005, the poverty line stood at $19,350 for a family of four.[38] The poverty rate in Texas was 17.6 percent compared with a rate of 12.6 percent for the United States as a whole. Texas ranked fifth among the 50 states in the percentage of people living in poverty.[39]

Poverty is concentrated among racial minorities, single-parent families headed by women, and the very young. In 2005, the national poverty rate for whites was 10.6 percent. It was 24.9 percent for African Americans, 21.8 percent for Latinos, and 11.1 percent for Asians and Pacific Islanders. Nearly 18 percent of the nation's children under age 18 lived in poor families, whereas 31 percent of families headed by women with no husband present earned incomes below the poverty line.[40]

Texas has the highest percentage of residents without health insurance in the nation. Nearly 24 percent of Texas adults lack health insurance coverage compared with a national average of 15 percent. Texas also trails the national average in the percentage of children without health insurance coverage, 19 percent in Texas compared with a national average of 9.3 percent.[41] Most Texans without insurance are employed in low-wage jobs that do not provide health coverage. They and their families must do without healthcare, pay for health services out of pocket, or go to hospital emergency rooms.[42] Texas has the second lowest percentage of immunized children, 75 percent, just above Nevada, which has an immunization rate of 71 percent.[43] It also has the highest teen birthrate in the nation.[44]

These sorts of data on health insurance, poverty rates, and income distribution trigger lively policy debates. Some policy analysts believe that the government should adopt policies designed to improve the lives of ordinary Texans. They favor government-sponsored health insurance programs, increased spending for education, and legislation to raise the state minimum wage. In contrast, other policy analysts argue that government programs hurt poor families by damaging the economy and thus limiting job growth. The best way to improve conditions for low- and middle-income people, they say, is to allow the market to work.

The state's high teen birthrate has sparked debate about sex education in the state. A number of observers believe that the high teenage birthrate is an indication that the state's abstinence-only approach to sex education is a failure. School districts in Texas are not required to teach sex education at all, but if they do, they must present abstinence as the preferred choice for unmarried persons of school age. If a school district chooses to teach about contraception, it must allow parents to remove their children from the class and it must teach that contraception methods have failure rates. Critics of the state's sex education policy favor a balanced approach that combines information about contraception with an emphasis on abstinence. They believe that students need to know about birth control because abstinence-only is not realistic for everyone. Meanwhile, the defenders of the state's sex education policy stress that abstinence is the only foolproof way to prevent pregnancy. They oppose teaching youngsters about contraception because they do not want to give the impression that the state condones premarital sex.[45]

 WHAT IS YOUR OPINION?

Is abstinence-only education the correct approach in Texas?

POLITICAL CULTURE

Political culture
The widely held, deeply rooted political values of a society.

Political culture refers to the widely held, deeply rooted political values of a society. Professor Daniel Elazar identifies three strains of political culture found in the United States: individualistic, moralistic, and traditionalistic.[46] The **individualistic political culture** is an approach to government and politics that emphasizes private initiative with a minimum of government interference. This political culture stresses the importance of the individual and private initiative. In this view of society, the role of government should be limited to protecting individual rights and

NATIONAL PERSPECTIVE   Legal Prostitution in Nevada

Nevada is the only state in the nation with legal prostitution. State law allows every county except Clark County (where Las Vegas is located) to license and regulate brothel prostitution. Street prostitution is illegal throughout the state. Eleven Nevada counties permit licensed brothels in certain areas. As of January 2004, 30 legal brothels employed 300 prostitutes in the state.* Prostitutes must use condoms during sex acts, and state law requires weekly checks for certain sexually transmitted diseases and monthly HIV tests.

Prostitutes are independent contractors, living and working for several weeks at a time in a brothel. They seldom leave the premises and cannot have nonpaying guests during their contract period. The brothel typically collects half the fee charged by the prostitutes for their room and board. Both the brothel owner and the prostitutes pay taxes to the government.

The Nevada legislature frequently debates whether to outlaw prostitution. Casino operators and business groups favor banning brothel prostitution in order to improve the state's image, whereas religious groups oppose prostitution on moral grounds. In contrast, the Brothel Owners' Association argues that the issue should be left to local government and that it is

safer for prostitution to be legal and regulated rather than illegal and unregulated. Lawmakers from rural areas typically oppose efforts to outlaw the brothels because they provide income to poor counties.

Public opinion in Nevada is split on the issue. Newcomers to Nevada generally favor outlawing prostitution, whereas long-time residents endorse the status quo. In the meantime, politicians typically play both sides of the issue—they say they are against prostitution but believe that the counties, rather than the state legislature, should decide the issue.

QUESTIONS TO CONSIDER

1. If you were in the Nevada legislature, would you vote to outlaw the brothels? Why or why not?
2. Which political culture do you think is dominant in Nevada—moralistic, individualistic, or traditionalistic? What is the basis of your answer?
3. Do you think the Texas legislature will ever seriously consider legalizing brothel prostitution? Why or why not?

*"Prostitution in Nevada," available at www.answers.com.

Individualistic political culture
An approach to government and politics that emphasizes private initiative with a minimum of government interference.

ensuring that social and political relationships are based on merit rather than tradition, family ties, or personal connections. Elazar says that individualistic political culture developed from the eighteenth- and nineteenth-century business centers in New York, Philadelphia, and Baltimore and spread westward through the central part of the nation. Immigrants from areas dominated by the individualistic political culture settled in the northern and central parts of Texas in the mid-nineteenth century.

The **moralistic political culture** is an approach to government and politics in which people expect government to intervene in the social and economic affairs of the state, promoting the public welfare and advancing the public good. Participation in political affairs is regarded as one's civic duty. Elazar says the moralistic political culture developed from Puritanism (a religious reform movement) and New England town meetings and spread westward through the northern part of the nation and down the West Coast. Texas has received relatively little immigration from areas where the moralistic political culture was important.

Moralistic political culture An approach to government and politics in which people expect government to intervene in the social and economic affairs of the state, promoting the public welfare and advancing the public good.

Traditionalistic political culture An approach to government and politics that sees the role of government as the preservation of tradition and the existing social order.

Civic culture A political culture that is conducive to the development of an efficient, effective government that meets the needs of its citizens in a timely and professional manner.

The **traditionalistic political culture** is an approach to government and politics that sees the role of government as the preservation of tradition and the existing social order. Government leadership is in the hands of an established social elite, and the level of participation by ordinary citizens in the policymaking process is relatively low. The role of government is to protect and preserve the existing social order. Elazar says that the traditional form of political culture developed from the plantation society of the South and spread westward through the southern states. Many immigrants from areas where the traditionalistic political culture was strong settled in East Texas.

Elazar believes that the political culture of Texas is a hybrid, including both traditionalistic and individualistic elements, and he identifies some aspects of state politics that reflect these two strains of political culture. Texas's traditionalistic political culture, Elazar says, is represented in the state's long history as a one-party state, low levels of voter turnout, and social and economic conservatism. Elazar identifies the state's strong support for private business, opposition to big government, and faith in individual initiative as reflections of Texas's individualistic political culture.

Political scientists Tom W. Rice and Alexander F. Sundberg take a different approach to political culture. They focus on the concept of **civic culture,** which is a political culture that is conducive to the development of an efficient, effective government that meets the needs of its citizens in a timely and professional manner. States with a civic culture have innovative and effective governments, they say, whereas states in which the culture is less civic have governments that are less responsive to citizen demands.

Rice and Sundberg identify four elements of a civic culture:

- **Civic engagement** Citizens participate in the policymaking process in order to promote the public good.
- **Political equality** Citizens view each other as political equals with the same rights and obligations.
- **Solidarity, trust, and tolerance** Citizens feel a strong sense of fellowship with one another, tolerating a wide range of ideas and lifestyles.
- **Social structure of cooperation** Citizens are joiners, belonging to a rich array of groups, from recreational sports teams to religious organizations.

Texas is 43rd among the 50 states in its level of civic culture. Rice and Sundberg found that most of the civic states are in the North, running from New England to the Northwest. In contrast, most southern states are low in civic culture.[47]

Political culture is a useful concept for students of public policy because it leads them to focus on a state's history and development as important factors influencing politics and policy. Scholars who study the American states recognize variations in political behavior and beliefs among different regions of the country that can be explained on the basis of political culture. The concepts developed by Elazar and the team of Rice and Sundberg are useful tools for understanding policy differences among states that cannot be explained simply on the basis of socioeconomic factors.

GETTING INVOLVED

Volunteering

Everyone should do volunteer work, especially college students. Volunteering is a way to give back to the community for the kindnesses of others. People who volunteer develop an attachment to their community by learning about the problems in their area and helping solve them. Furthermore, volunteer work is a rewarding experience.

Your community has many fine organizations that welcome volunteers, including hospitals, schools, nursing homes, and animal shelters. Your college may have a service-learning program that matches volunteers with organizations needing help. Contact the organization of your choice and find out the procedures for volunteering. Even if you are able to put in only a few hours between semesters or on an occasional weekend, you will benefit from the experience.

It's your community—get involved!

CONCLUSION: THE SOCIOECONOMIC CONTEXT OF POLICYMAKING

The demographic, economic, and cultural environments affect every stage of the policymaking process.

Agenda Building

Because Texas is an urban state, issues such as mass transportation, air quality, crime, and inner-city development more frequently appear on the official policy agenda than they would in a predominantly rural state. Population growth in the suburbs increases the influence of voices calling for lower property taxes, strong local schools, and highway construction to relieve traffic congestion. Similarly, the state's large racial and ethnic minority groups raise matters of particular concern, including issues of political representation and opportunity in employment and access to higher education. Texas's status as a border state ensures that immigration and trade issues frequently appear on the policy agenda.

Policy Formulation and Adoption

The demographic, economic, and cultural environments impact policy formulation. Political culture limits the range of alternatives to a policy problem. The political culture of Texas presupposes a minimal role for government. The state's economy affects policy formulation as well. Economic growth generates tax revenues that can be used to expand government services or finance tax reductions. In contrast, an economic slump forces legislators and the governor to cut programs or increase taxes.

Environmental factors affect policy adoption. Although Latinos and African Americans comprise a substantial proportion of the state's residents, they lack economic power and, consequently, their political influence is less than their numerical representation in the state's population. As a result, state and local governments usually adopt policies that more closely reflect the desires of the white population than they do those of racial and ethnic minority groups. Similarly, the weakness of

LET'S DEBATE

Is Illegal Immigration Good or Bad for Texas?

Overview: On January 26, 2005, the University of North Texas (UNT) chapter of the Young Conservatives of Texas held a controversial "Catch the Illegal Immigrant Game." To highlight the issue of illegal immigration in Texas and to spark debate over President Bush's guest worker proposal, UNT students were encouraged to "capture" chapter members wearing bright orange shirts bearing the words "illegal immigrant." Once "caught," chapter members would offer candy bars and information regarding Bush's illegal immigration policy. This protest caught the attention of North Texas media and sparked passionate and heated debate from UNT to University of Texas at Austin discussion boards. Those on both sides of the issue offered substantive arguments to support their positions, as the debate centered on whether to give illegal immigrants some sort of amnesty or legal protection, or whether to further seal the Texas–Mexico border and deport illegal immigrants. Political commentators argue that concern over illegal immigration may be of the larger issues in the next several state and national election cycles, and electoral success may hinge on what side of the issue candidates for office embrace.

According to the Pew Hispanic Center, approximately 1.4 million illegal immigrants reside in Texas (this is roughly 14 percent of the national total). Texas itself has an estimated total population of nearly 22.5 million. How do these numbers affect native Texans? Illegal immigration is a contentious issue for a number of reasons. First, many Texans view illegal immigrants as lawbreakers and as a result do not wish to further encourage lawbreaking through immigration by giving "illegals" taxpayer-funded support. For example, research indicates that in 2004 Texas spent roughly $3.9 billion (out of a budget of $35 billion) to educate the children of undocumented immigrants. Governor Rick Perry enacted legislation that allows undocumented students to receive in-state tuition rates (this law is currently being challenged in federal circuit court as discriminatory against out-of-state students). Second, undocumented aliens consume additional state-funded public services and resources. Many argue that illegal immigrants not only use public healthcare (the effect of which takes away scant funds from needy Texans), but also redirect law enforcement assets to border areas, thus denying Texans across the state the full force of police protection.

Those who wish to provide illegal immigrants with amnesty or legal protection, however, argue that by assimilating this demographic not only does Texas benefit by enriching its culture and heritage, but Texas's economy and politics also benefit because most undocumented aliens are hardworking and wish to participate in the political culture in which they live. Furthermore, as Mexico's former President Vicente Fox points out, illegal workers provide certain services (e.g., spending hours in the blazing Texas sun picking produce) that many Texans would not do. Is former President Fox correct in his assessment, or are Texas natives correct that illegal immigration lowers the quality of life for both native-born and legal immigrants and encourages a culture of lawbreaking?

Arguments for Amnesty or Legal Protection for Illegal Immigrants

❏ **America has a tradition of welcoming immigrants fleeing economic hardship and political oppression.** Many scholars argue that the strength of the American experience is the ability to absorb different cultures and values and transform them into a unique political society. Illegal immigrants flock to the United States to pursue economic prosperity and enjoy political freedom, and this, in turn, can strengthen social and political bonds between native citizens and immigrants.

❏ **Illegal immigrants provide necessary unskilled labor.** According to the Hudson Institute and the Hispanic Chamber of Commerce (and former Mexican President Vicente Fox), illegal immigrants do work that most native citizens will not do; thus, their labor adds significantly to the stability and growth of the state and national economy. Current research provides scant evidence that illegal immigrants displace poorly skilled native workers.

❏ **Illegal immigrants pay taxes and user fees and spend income in local economies.** The *New York Times* reports that approximately 7 million illegal aliens pay in nearly $7 *billion* in Social Security taxes annually and that most illegal immigrants will not receive these benefits, which contribute to government coffers. Furthermore, illegal immigrants spend income in many poverty-stricken areas of Texas, helping support local economics.

Arguments Against Amnesty or Legal Protection for Illegal Immigrants

❏ **Illegal immigration is responsible for unique criminal activity.** The Federal Reserve Bank of Dallas–El Paso's research shows that, in border counties, there has been a significant increase in violent crime that has been linked to increased illegal immigration. The report also states that this is likely due to increased activity in drug smuggling and human trafficking. News organizations report on many stories each year in which illegal immigrants are found dead in trafficking vehicles.

❏ **Illegal immigration may negatively affect state and national political institutions.** Research by the Center for Immigration Studies determined that illegal immigration may skew decennial apportionment. The report found that illegal immigration in some states may have caused three other states to lose a House seat in the 2000 Census, although these three states had an *increase* in population. Illegal immigration may distort representation as commanded by the U.S. Constitution.

❏ **Illegal immigration may help foster a culture opposed to American political values and political culture.** Harvard political scientist Samuel Huntington argues that condoning Hispanic illegal immigration encourages increasing social and political segregation and alienation. The use of multiple languages and cultural viewpoints unsupported by a common civic education and political origin can create competing sources of identity—with detrimental effects for social cohesion.

QUESTIONS

1. Can undocumented immigrants truly be integrated into Texas political culture? Or do the loyalties and allegiances of the aliens reside in their home countries and, as a result, foster divisiveness?

2. Isn't it a question of fairness to allow those who pay taxes and provide necessary unskilled labor to enjoy some public benefits, as a gesture of acknowledgment for their efforts? Could it be an issue of compassion?

SELECT READINGS

1. Robert Lee Maril, *Patrolling Chaos—the U.S. Border Patrol in Deep South Texas* (Lubbock, TX: Texas Tech University Press, 2004).

2. Barry Edmonston and Ronald Lee, *Local Fiscal Effects of Illegal Immigration: Report of a Workshop* (Washington, DC: National Academy Press, 1996).

SELECT WEBSITES

1. **www.cis.org/index.cgi**
   Website for the Center for Immigration Studies, a think tank dedicated to a "pro-immigrant, low immigration" policy domain.

2. **www.dallasfed.org/research/border/tbearrenius.html**
   Federal Reserve Bank of Dallas study that examines the relationship between illegal immigration and the cost of border enforcement in the U.S. Southwest.

organized labor and consumer interests in Texas ensures that the state adopts policies that more closely mirror the concerns of business owners and corporate managers than they do either labor or consumer interests.

Policy Implementation and Evaluation

Demographic, economic, and cultural factors influence policy implementation. Because of the state's geographic size and diversity, policy implementation sometimes varies from place to place. As we discussed in the introductory chapter, counties implement the state's capital punishment law differently because of disparities in resources. Large counties can afford to pursue the death penalty aggressively, whereas small counties lack the financial resources to prosecute more than a handful of capital punishment cases. Similarly, small rural school districts implement state educational policies differently than do large urban districts.

Environmental factors also influence policy evaluation. Because Texas is a large and diverse state, it has a significant number of individuals and groups whose policy perspectives do not always coincide. Consequently, policy evaluation is more contentious than it would be in a more homogeneous state. Individuals and groups who lost out in the policy formulation and adoption stages evaluate a policy harshly, whereas those interests who initially supported the policy defend it.

Changes in the policymaking environment often lead to policy change. The number of political actors that are influential in the policy process has increased as the state's economic base has broadened. Oil and gas interests are still important but are no longer dominant. Population change has also produced a change in the policy process. Newcomers to the state sometimes have different perspectives than those of native Texans. Historically, white immigrants from other states have been more likely to identify with the Republican Party than have been native white Texans.[48]

Studying Texas's social structure, economy, and political culture is important for students of Texas government because these factors provide the context for policymaking. They determine the types of political issues that make the official policy agenda, establish the boundaries of acceptable policy options available to public officials during the policy formulation and adoption stages, set the ground rules for policy implementation, and establish standards for evaluating policies. Finally, changes in the state's population, economy, and political culture will lead to changes in public policies. As we discussed in the introductory section of this chapter, education is critical to the state's economic future, especially the education of its large and growing minority populations.

KEY TERMS

civic culture	Lone Star State	political culture
gross state product (GSP)	minimum wage	poverty line
high-technology industries	moralistic political culture	severance tax
individualistic political culture	natural population increase	traditionalistic political culture

NOTES

1. U.S. Census Bureau, "Money Income of People—Selected Characteristics by Current Income Level: 2006," *The 2009 Statistical Abstract*, available at www.census.gov.
2. "Dropouts Cost State $3,168 a Year per Student." *El Paso Times*, February 13, 2007, available at www.elpasotimes. com.
3. U.S. Census Bureau, "Educational Attainment of the Population 25 Years and over: 2005," available at www.census.gov.
4. Michael Arnone, "Texas Falls Behind in Plan to Enroll More Minority Students," *Chronicle of Higher Education*, January 17, 2003, A23.
5. Texas Higher Education Coordinating Board, "Closing the Gaps by 2015: 2006 Progress Report," available at www.thecb.state.tx.us.
6. McNelly Torres, "High Schools Losing 1/3rd of Their Students," *San Antonio Express News*, March 7, 2005, available at www.mysanantonio.com.

7. Patrick McGee, "College Ethnic Gaps May Hit Economy, Report Says," *Fort Worth Star-Telegram*, November 9, 2005, available at www.dfw.com.

8. Martin Basaldua, "Closing the Gaps: Texas Higher Education Plan," Texas Higher Education Coordinating Board, 2000, available at www.thecb.state.tx.us.

9. U.S. Census Bureau, "Annual Estimates for the Population of the United States and States, and for Puerto Rico: April 1, 2000 to July 1, 2006," available at www.census.gov.

10. U.S. Census Bureau, "Cumulative Estimates of Population Change for the United States, Regions, States and Puerto Rico and Region and State Ranking: April 1, 2000 to July 1, 2006," available at www.census.gov.

11. National Center for Health Statistics, "Births, Birth Rates, and Fertility Rates by State, 2004," available at www.cdc.gov.

12. U.S. Census Bureau, "Profile of General Demographic Characteristics for Texas: 2000," available at www.census.gov.

13. U.S. Census Bureau, *Fertility of American Women: June 2004*, available at www.census.gov.

14. U.S. Census Bureau, "Cumulative Estimates of the Components of Population Change for the United States, Regions, and States: April 1, 2000 to July 1, 2006," available at www.census.gov.

15. Pew Hispanic Center, quoted in Scott Huddleston, "Texas Now 2nd to California in Undocumented Residents," *San Antonio Express-News*, June 15, 2005, available at www.mysanantonio.com.

16. Texas Comptroller of Public Accounts, *Undocumented Immigrants in Texas: A Financial Analysis of the Impact to the State Budget and Economy*, December 2006, available at www.window.state.tx.us.

17. U.S. Census Bureau, "Native and Foreign Born Population by Place of Birth and State: 2004," *The 2007 Statistical Abstract*, available at www.census.gov.

18. U.S. Census Bureau, *Profile of the Foreign-Born Population in the United States: 2000*, available at www.census.gov.

19. U.S. Census Bureau, "Texas Becomes Nation's Newest 'Majority-Minority' State," August 11, 2005, available at www.census.gov.

20. *Fiscal Notes*, November 1997, p. 3.

21. U.S. Census Bureau, "Percent of Population by Race and Hispanic or Latino Origin, for States, Puerto Rico, and Places of 100,000 or More Population: 2000," available at www.census.gov.

22. U.S. Census Bureau, *Profile of the Foreign-Born Population in the United States: 2000*.

23. Texas State Data Center and Office of the State Demographer, "Texas Population Growth in Texas Counties, 1850–2040," available at http://txsdc.tamu.edu/maps/thematic/popgrowth.php.

24. U.S. Census Bureau, available at www.census.gov.

25. "Texas Population Growth in Texas Counties, 1850–2040."

26. U.S. Census Bureau, *Census 2000 Geographic Definitions*, revised November 16, 2000, available at www.census.gov.

27. Texas Workforce Commission, *Texas Labor Market Review*, January 2007, available at www.tracer2.com.

28. Texas Comptroller of Public Accounts, "Texas Net Revenue by Source, 2006," available at www.window.state.tx.us/.

29. Texas Workforce Solutions, "Wage Information Network," available at www.texasindustryprofiles.com.

30. Texas Comptroller of Public Accounts, "Texas Economic Update, Fall 2004" available at www.window.state.tx.us.

31. U.S. Census Bureau, "Gross State Product in Current and Real (2000) Dollars by State: 1990 to 2005," *The 2007 Statistical Abstract*, available at www.census.gov.

32. U.S. Census Bureau, "Gross National Income by Country: 1990 and 2004," *The 2007 Statistical Abstract*, available at www.census.gov.

33. U.S. Census Bureau, *Income, Poverty, and Health Insurance in the United States, 2005*, available at www.census.gov.

34. Ibid.

35. David Plesa, "Racial Income Gap Widens," *Houston Post*, April 16, 1993, p. A-1.

36. Center on Budget and Policy Priorities, "Income Inequality Grew Across the Country Over the Past Two Decades," available at www.cbpb.org.

37. Asher Price and Claire Osborn, "Texas Leads Nation in Upper and Middle Income Gap," *Austin American-Statesman*, January 28, 2006, available at www.statesman.com.

38. U.S. Department of Health and Human Services, "The 2005 HHS Poverty Guidelines," available at www.hhs.gov.

39. U.S. Census Bureau, *Annual Demographic Survey*, available at www.census.gov.

40. Ibid.

41. National Center for Health Statistics, "National Health Interview Survey," available at www.cdc.gov.

42. Carlos Guerra, "Private Group's Count Reveals Many More Uninsured Texans," *San Antonio Express News*, June 17, 2004, available at www.mysanantonio.com.

43. Corrie MacLaggan, "Report: Texas Ranks in Bottom 10 States for Percentage of Children in Poverty," *Austin American-Statesman*, June 27, 2006, available at www.statesman.com.

44. Melanie Markley, "Texas Ranked No. 1 in Teen Birth Rate," *Houston Chronicle*, July 25, 2007, available at www.chron.com.

45. Robert T. Garrett, "Texas Teens Lead Nation in Birth Rate," *Dallas Morning News*, November 5, 2007, available at www.dallasnews.com.

46. Daniel Elazar, *American Federalism: A View from the States*, 2nd ed. (New York: Crowell, 1972), pp. 84–126.

47. Tom W. Rice and Alexander F. Sundberg, "Civic Culture and Government Performance in the American States," *Publius: The Journal of Federalism* 27 (Winter 1997): 99–114.

48. Poll conducted by the University of Houston Center for Public Policy, quoted in *Houston Chronicle*, September 19, 1990, p. 1A.

Chapter 19

The Texas Constitution

CHAPTER OUTLINE

LEARNING OUTCOMES

After studying Chapter 19, students should be able to do the following:

- Describe the role of the Texas Constitution in the controversy over education finance. (pp. 514–515)

- Compare and contrast state constitutions with the U.S. Constitution. (pp. 515–518)

- Trace the historical background of the Texas Constitution. (pp. 518–519)

- Identify the goals of the majority of delegates at the state constitutional convention of 1875, and describe the impact of those goals on the document they drafted. (pp. 520–522)

- Describe the principal features of the Texas Constitution. (pp. 522–524)

- Outline the process whereby the Texas Constitution can be amended, and evaluate the significance of the changes that have been made through amendment. (pp. 524–527)

- Describe the means through which constitutions can change other than formal amendment, and assess the relative importance of those means of change for the Texas Constitution. (pp. 527–528)

- Summarize the main criticisms of the Texas Constitution, and trace the history of constitutional revision in the state. (pp. 528–530)

- Describe the role played by Texas courts and the Texas Constitution in the protection of individual rights. (pp. 531–532)

- Assess the impact of the Texas Constitution on each stage of the policymaking process. (pp. 532–533)

- Define the key terms listed on page 535 and explain their significance.

The issue of education finance has been near the top of the official policy agenda in the Lone Star State longer than most Texans can remember. Public education is critically important not just to the state's 4.5 million public school students but also to thousands of teachers and other school employees, as well as to the communities in which they live. Moreover, education is expensive, the single largest expenditure for state and local government in Texas. In 2004, the average Texan paid nearly $1,700 in taxes to support public education.[1]

The state's education funding system is controversial because of its reliance on the **property tax,** which is a tax levied on the value of real property, such as land and buildings. Communities with substantial business property, industry, and wealthy neighborhoods can generate a significant amount of tax money for schools, even with a relatively low tax rate. In contrast, less affluent communities can raise relatively little money, even with a high tax rate. Consequently, wealthy districts can afford new school buildings, state-of-the-art science and computer labs, high teacher pay, and low student-teacher ratios, whereas poor districts cannot.

The controversy over school funding came to a head in 1989 with *Edgewood v. Kirby,* which was a lawsuit filed by a number of poor school districts, including the Edgewood Independent School District (ISD) in San Antonio, against the state's system of education finance. The Texas Supreme Court held that the school finance system violated the Texas Constitution because it failed to treat all persons equally and because it was inefficient. The court ordered the Texas legislature to change the system to ensure that school districts that levied the same tax rate would have roughly the same amount of tax revenue available for local use.[2] Eventually, the legislature settled on a plan capping local property tax rates at $1.50 per $100 of property valuation and forcing wealthy districts to transfer some of their revenue to poor districts. Some commentators referred to the system as the **Robin Hood Plan** because it took money from the rich and gave it to the poor.

Despite the passage of the Robin Hood Plan, legal challenges to the Texas school finance system continued. Several wealthy districts filed suit against the system, charging that the state property tax cap that limits their ability to raise local money to support their schools amounted to an unconstitutional state property tax. They argued that the state spending and tax caps made it impossible for them to obtain the necessary funds to operate quality schools. In the meantime, poor school districts filed a new suit attacking the system over the issue of funding adequacy. They noted that, although the Texas Constitution provides for an efficient state school system, school funding was too low for the system to be efficient. They, too, believed that they lacked the money to provide a quality education for their students.

In 2005, the Texas Supreme Court once again declared the Texas system of school finance unconstitutional in a case entitled *Neeley v. West Orange-Cove Consolidated ISD.* The court held that the state's property tax cap coupled with extensive state mandates to school districts had effectively created an unconstitutional state property tax. It disagreed, however, that the state education funding level was unconstitutionally inadequate, at least not yet. The court ordered the legislature and the governor to adopt a new funding system that would not violate the state constitution and set a deadline of June 1, 2006.[3]

Property tax A tax levied on the value of a real property, such as land and buildings.

Edgewood v. Kirby A lawsuit filed by a number of poor school districts, including the Edgewood Independent School District (ISD) in San Antonio, against the state's system of education finance.

Robin Hood Plan A reform of the state's school finance system designed to increase funding for poor school districts by redistributing money from wealthy districts.

Governor Rick Perry and the legislature eventually agreed on a school finance reform measure that they hoped would satisfy the Texas Supreme Court. The measure required school districts to reduce their property tax rates from $1.50 per $100 valuation in 2006 to $1.33 in 2007 and $1.00 in 2008. Districts would have the option to increase their property tax rates somewhat if they wanted to raise additional money. By giving districts some discretion in their tax rates, the governor and the legislature hoped to satisfy the Supreme Court's objections to the state funding system. To pay for the property tax reduction, the state increased the cigarette tax by $1.00 a pack, created a state business tax, and required that people selling used cars pay sales tax on at least 80 percent of the Blue Book value of the vehicle.

The controversy over education finance illustrates the relevance of the Texas Constitution to the policymaking process. Although school finance has been a perennial issue on the state's policy agenda, the legislature has generally failed to address the issue seriously except when it has been under court order. *Edgewood v. Kirby* forced the state to close the funding gap between wealthy districts and poor districts. The state achieved that goal by somewhat increasing funding for poor districts and by limiting the amount of money available to wealthy districts. *Neeley v. West Orange-Cove Consolidated ISD* forced the state to increase the state funding available to school districts to enable them to lower local property taxes below the state-mandated tax cap.

This chapter examines the Texas Constitution as an important element of the policymaking environment in the Lone Star State. The chapter begins with a discussion of the role of state constitutions in general. It explores the background of the Texas Constitution, describes the constitutional convention of 1875, and presents an overview of the document. The chapter discusses constitutional change and the role the Texas Constitution plays in protecting individual rights. Finally, the chapter examines the impact of the Texas Constitution on the policymaking process.

Constitution
A fundamental law by which a state or nation is organized and governed.

STATE CONSTITUTIONS

Bicameral legislature
A legislative body with two chambers.

A **constitution** is the fundamental law by which a state or nation is organized and governed. The U.S. Constitution is the fundamental law of the United States. It establishes the framework of government, assigns the powers and duties of governmental bodies, and defines the relationship between the people and their government. Similarly, a state constitution is the fundamental law for a state. The U.S. Constitution and the state constitutions together provide the total framework for government within the United States.

Separation of powers The division of political authority among legislative, executive, and judicial branches of government.

State constitutions resemble the U.S. Constitution in some respects but differ in others. The framers of the U.S. Constitution based the document on the principle of separation of powers, with a strong chief executive, a **bicameral legislature** (which is a legislative body with two chambers), and a judiciary appointed for life. Although every state constitution provides for the **separation of powers** (which is the division of political authority among the legislative, executive, and judicial

GETTING INVOLVED

Joining a Student Club or Organization

If you join a student organization, you will enjoy college more and probably earn better grades as well. Joining a club will give you the chance to make new friends with similar interests and become acquainted with a faculty advisor outside the classroom setting. Because you will be better connected to the school, you will be more likely to stay in college and finish your education.

Colleges and universities typically offer a range of student clubs and organizations. Students at your school may participate in such organizations as an international student association, Campus Crusade for Christ, chess club, Young Democrats, Young Republicans, choir, gay/lesbian/bisexual student association, black student union, bridge club, Muslim student association, computer science club, Jewish life organization, Latino student association, karate club, pre-medical society, Catholic Student Union, math club, and Asian student association. The student life office at your college will have a list of student groups active on your campus. It's your college—get involved!

Plural executive
The division of executive power among several elected officials.

Unicameral legislature A legislative body with one chamber.

Representative democracy or republic A political system in which citizens elect representatives to make policy decisions on their behalf.

Direct democracy A political system in which the citizens vote directly on matters of public concern.

Initiative process A procedure whereby citizens can propose the adoption of a policy measure by gathering a prerequisite number of signatures. Voters must then approve the measure before it can take effect.

branches of government), many state documents differ from the national constitution in important details. A number of state constitutions, including the Texas Constitution, give their governor fewer official powers than the U.S. Constitution grants the president. Indeed, the constitutions of Texas and several other states weaken their governors through means of the **plural executive,** which is the division of executive power among several elected officials. Most state constitutions, including the Texas Constitution, provide for the the election of judges. One state, Nebraska, has a **unicameral legislature,** which is a legislative body with one chamber.

Some state constitutions reflect a different approach to democracy than the U.S. Constitution embodies. The U.S. Constitution creates a **representative democracy,** or a **republic,** which is a political system in which citizens elect representatives to make policy decisions on their behalf. The framers of the U.S. Constitution believed that elected representatives were needed to act as a buffer between the people and government policies. In contrast, some state constitutions include certain elements of **direct democracy,** which is a political system in which the citizens vote directly on matters of public concern. Almost half the states (but not Texas) provide for the **initiative process,** which is a procedure whereby citizens can propose the adoption of a policy measure by gathering a prerequisite number of signatures. Voters must then approve the measure before it can take effect. State officials then place the measure on the ballot for approval by the voters. Citizens can use the initiative process either to adopt measures or to repeal legislation enacted through the legislative process. Voters in California, Oregon, and other states with the initiative process have used it to make policy decisions concerning such issues as state tax rates, bilingual education, gay and lesbian rights, insurance rates, term limits for elected officials, and the provision of public services to illegal immigrants.

In contrast to the U.S. Constitution, state constitutions have a quality of impermanence to them. Although the present state constitution of Massachusetts was written in 1780, only six state constitutions now in effect were drafted before 1850. The average state constitution lasts for 70 years.[4] About a fourth of the states have adopted new constitutions since World War II. Furthermore, most states have changed constitutions several times. Louisiana, for example, has had 11 constitutions; Georgia has had 10.[5]

Most state constitutions have more amendments than the U.S. Constitution, which has only 27. The average state constitution has been amended nearly a hundred times. The Constitution of South Carolina has been changed formally more than 450 times. The Alabama Constitution has more than 700 amendments.[6]

Finally, state constitutions are on average four times longer than the U.S. Constitution. The Alabama Constitution, at 310,000 words, is the longest constitution in the nation, compared with only 7,400 words in the U.S. Constitution. The Texas Constitution is 93,000 words.[7] The length of state constitutions reflects the broader scope of state policy responsibilities compared with those of the national government. State constitutions deal with some matters not discussed at all in the U.S. Constitution, such as the structures, functions, and finances of local governments. State constitutions consider other issues, such as elections and land management, in greater detail than they are covered in the national document.

The state capitol building in Austin.

Statutory law Law made by a legislature.

Constitutional law Law that involves the interpretation and application of the constitution.

State constitutions also generally include numerous miscellaneous provisions that might be called "super legislation." These measures are the same quality and type as **statutory law** (law made by a legislature) but for historical or political reasons are upgraded to **constitutional law,** which is law that involves the interpretation and application of the constitution.[8] The South Dakota Constitution, for example, provides for state hail insurance; the Oklahoma Constitution requires that home economics be taught in public schools.[9]

BACKGROUND OF THE TEXAS CONSTITUTION

Jacksonian democracy The philosophy (associated with President Andrew Jackson) that the right to vote should be extended to all adult male citizens and that all government offices of any importance should be filled by election.

Suffrage The right to vote.

Long ballot An election system that provides for the election of nearly every public official of any significance.

Radical Republicans Members of the Republican Party who wanted sweeping social change to take place in the South after the Civil War.

Texans adopted their first state constitution in 1845, when the Lone Star State joined the Union. As with most other state constitutions written in the first half of the nineteenth century, the Texas Constitution of 1845 was patterned after the U.S. Constitution. Following the national model, it created a government with legislative, executive, and judicial branches. Similar to the U.S. Constitution, the Texas Constitution of 1845 was a document of broad, general principles that allowed state government leeway to deal with policy problems as they arose. The voters would select the governor, lieutenant governor, and members of the legislature. The governor would appoint other state executive officials and members of the state judiciary.

In 1850, Texas amended the state constitution to provide for the election rather than appointment of state judges and most executive officeholders. The change reflected the principle of **Jacksonian democracy,** which was the philosophy (associated with President Andrew Jackson) that the right to vote should be extended to all adult male citizens and that all government offices of any importance should be filled by election. The advocates of Jacksonian democracy believed that government is made responsive to the people through broad-based **suffrage,** which is the right to vote, and the **long ballot,** which is an election system that provides for the election of nearly every public official of any significance.

When Texas joined the Confederacy in 1861, the state changed its constitution. The new document pledged the state's allegiance to the Confederacy and included a strong prohibition against the abolition of slavery. Otherwise, the Constitution of 1861 closely resembled its predecessor.

In 1866, with the war lost, Texas rewrote its constitution once again in hopes of rejoining the Union under President Andrew Johnson's reconstruction plan. This new constitution repealed secession, repudiated the war debt, and recognized the supremacy of the U.S. Constitution. The document abolished slavery but fell short of granting full equality to former slaves. African Americans could not testify in court cases unless other African Americans were involved and were denied the right to vote. In most other respects, though, the Constitution of 1866 simply reenacted provisions of the 1845 document.

The Texas Constitution of 1866 was short-lived. By the time of its adoption, the Radical Republican majority in Congress had taken control of Reconstruction from President Johnson. The **Radical Republicans** were members of the Republican Party who wanted sweeping social change to take place in the South after the Civil War.

Congress passed legislation over President Johnson's veto declaring that Texas and the other states of the Confederacy could not reenter the Union until they granted African Americans the right to vote, ratified the Thirteenth and Fourteenth Amendments to the U.S. Constitution, and drafted new state constitutions acceptable to Congress.

Because Union troops occupied Texas, the state had little choice but to accept the demands. Ninety Texans, representing a broad range of political factions, gathered in convention in June 1868 to draft another state constitution. The convention was a stormy one, with the delegates unable to agree on a document. In 1869, the military commander of Texas intervened to order the bits and pieces the convention had been working on gathered into a single document. The U.S. Congress accepted this new constitution and Texas was readmitted to the Union in 1870.

The Texas Constitution of 1869 created an active state government. Reverting to the procedure established in the original state constitution of 1845, it provided for the gubernatorial appointment rather than election of judges and most executive branch officials. It established annual sessions of the legislature and authorized increased salaries for state officials. The constitution also included a compulsory school attendance law and provided for state supervision of education.

For most white, ex-Confederate Texans, the Constitution of 1869 represented defeat and humiliation. Many Texans regarded the document not as a Texas constitution at all but a document imposed on them by outside forces. Radical Republican Governor E. J. Davis held office under this constitution and the two were closely linked in the minds of the ex-Confederate Texans who considered Davis arrogant and corrupt. In particular, Democrats criticized the Davis administration for excessive spending, taxation, and borrowing.

Defenders of the Davis administration argued that the policies adopted by the governor and the Republican legislature were an appropriate effort to help the state recover from the Civil War. Under Davis, the state undertook programs to promote railroad construction, build an extensive network of roads, and construct a free public school system. Furthermore, Democratic Governor Richard Coke and the Democratic majority in the legislature who succeeded the Republicans in office were no more successful at dealing with the state's financial problems than their predecessors. The state budget deficit was higher in 1875 and 1876 under Coke than it had been in 1872 and 1873 under Davis.[10] A **budget deficit** is the amount of money by which annual budget expenditures exceed annual budget receipts.

Budget deficit The amount of money by which annual budget expenditures exceed annual budget receipts.

Nonetheless, the association of the Texas Constitution of 1869 with Reconstruction guaranteed strong Democratic support for a new document. When Democrats regained control of state government in 1872 and 1873, their first priority was to draft a new constitution for Texas. Governor Coke and Democratic legislative leaders initially proposed that a new constitution be written by the state legislature. When legislators deadlocked over a new document, however, the governor and the Democratic leaders had no choice but to call for the election of delegates to a state constitutional convention.

 **WHAT IS YOUR OPINION?**

Do you agree with the political philosophy underlying the concept of Jacksonian democracy?

CONSTITUTIONAL CONVENTION OF 1875

In the fall of 1875, 83 Texans gathered in Austin to draft a new constitution for the state. Although a number of Republicans, including several African Americans, served as convention delegates, a majority of the delegates were white Democrats. Farmers, ex-Confederate officers, and lawyers were all well represented at the convention. The largest organized group of delegates was the Texas Patrons of Husbandry, better known as the **Grange,** an organization of farmers. Indeed, "retrenchment and reform," the Grangers' slogan, became the watchword of the convention.

Grange An organization of farmers.

The Grangers' slogan embodied two basic goals: to restrict the size and scope of state government and to control the excesses of big business. Most of the delegates at the convention wanted to restrain a state government that they believed was too large and expensive. To accomplish this task, the delegates abandoned one constitutional tradition while reinstating another. On one hand, the authors of the new constitution turned away from the pattern initially established in the Texas Constitution of 1845 of a general document phrased in broad terms, favoring instead a restrictive constitution of great length and detail. On the other hand, the delegates returned to the tradition of Jacksonian democracy, reinstating the long ballot and shortening the terms of office for elected officials.[11]

The convention restricted the authority of every branch and unit of Texas government. The new constitution weakened the office of governor by cutting the governor's salary and reducing the term of office from four to two years. It restricted the governor's power of appointment by creating a plural executive, which divided executive power among several elected officials, including a lieutenant governor, an attorney general, a comptroller, a treasurer, and a land commissioner. Executive officials elected independently from the governor would owe no allegiance to the governor. Indeed, they might be political rivals. The governor could appoint a number of lesser officials, but they would have little incentive to follow the governor's lead because the governor had no power to remove them before the end of their terms.

The constitution's framers limited the power of the legislature by cutting its meeting time and restricting the scope of its policymaking authority. They limited regular sessions of the legislature to 140 calendar days, every other year. They reduced legislative salaries and required that the legislature adopt a balanced budget unless four-fifths of the membership agreed to deficit spending. Furthermore, by including long, detailed sections on education, finance, railroad regulation, and the like in the constitution, the framers forced legislators to propose constitutional amendments if they wanted to adopt policy changes in many areas.

The authors of Texas's new constitution employed several devices for reducing the power of the judicial branch of state government. They divided the state's court system into two segments, limiting the types of cases individual courts would be authorized to hear. In the best tradition of Jacksonian democracy, they provided for the election of judges to relatively brief terms. The framers also reduced judicial discretion by writing a long, detailed constitution that left relatively little room for judicial interpretation.

Nor did the framers of the Texas Constitution overlook local government. They specified the forms local governments must take and restricted local authority to levy taxes, provide services, adopt regulations, and go into debt. In many instances, local officials would have to ask the state legislature for permission to adopt even relatively minor policies. Changing local political structures would frequently necessitate a constitutional amendment.

Another major goal of the Granger-dominated convention was to control the excesses of big business. Consider the constitutional provisions dealing with banking. Many of the convention delegates were small farmers, used to living on the financial edge. They distrusted big, impersonal banks, which might be inclined to foreclose during hard times, preferring instead smaller, locally owned banks whose managers would be more understanding. Consequently, the convention prohibited **branch banking,** which is a business practice whereby a single, large bank conducts business from several locations. This provision ensured that banks would be locally owned rather than branches of large banks headquartered in Dallas or Houston.

The constitution's deference to local values is reflected in its provisions dealing with liquor regulation as well. Although the constitution empowered the legislature to regulate the manufacture, packaging, sale, possession, and transportation of alcoholic beverages, it left the decision to legalize the sale of alcoholic beverages to local voters. **Local-option elections** (also known as **wet–dry** elections) are held to determine whether an area legalizes the sale of alcoholic beverages. The voters living in

Branch banking
A business practice whereby a single, large bank conducts business from several locations.

Local-option (wet–dry) elections Elections held to determine whether an area legalizes the sale of alcoholic beverages.

Because the Texas Constitution prohibited branch banking, the legislature and the voters had to adopt a constitutional amendment to allow ATM machines.

a city, a county, or even an area as small as a justice of the peace precinct may vote to keep their area dry—that is, to prohibit the sale of alcoholic beverages. Once an area goes dry, it cannot go wet unless the voters approve. Of the 254 counties in Texas, 51 are totally dry and 39 are entirely wet. The other 164 counties are partially wet, which means that they include some areas where alcohol cannot be sold.[12]

The delegates at the constitutional convention believed in the old adage that a family's home is its castle, and they set about to protect it. They provided that a family **homestead** (i.e., legal residence) could not be taken in payment of debt except for delinquent taxes and mortgage payments on a loan taken out to purchase the home itself. The framers added a measure to the constitution requiring that both spouses must give written consent before the homestead could be sold. The constitution also prohibited the garnishment of wages for payment of debt. (A modern constitutional amendment provides an exception—garnishment for the enforcement of court-ordered child support or spousal maintenance.)

It was not uncommon in the 1870s for states to adopt restrictive constitutions. Although the Texas Constitution written in 1875 reflected the political concerns of rural-oriented Texans, the document was not far out of step with other state constitutions adopted in the late nineteenth century. Many states provided for the election of judges and a broad range of executive branch officials. Short terms of office for governors and judges were common. Furthermore, Texans were not the only Americans who distrusted public officials and worried about the corrupting influences of big banks, corporations, and railroads.[13]

The delegates finished their work in less than three months and, in early 1876, the voters approved the new constitution by a margin of 2–1. With amendments, the Constitution of 1876 remains today the fundamental law of the state of Texas.

Homestead Legal residence.

OVERVIEW OF THE TEXAS CONSTITUTION

To students familiar with the U.S. Constitution, the most striking feature of the Texas Constitution is its length. At 93,000 words, the Texas Constitution is one of the longest state constitutions in the nation. It can be found in most reference libraries, in the *Texas Almanac*, and online.

The Texas Constitution includes a number of features in common with the U.S. Constitution: a bill of rights, the separation of powers with checks and balances, and the creation of a bicameral legislature. A **bill of rights** is a constitutional document guaranteeing individual rights and liberties. As with other provisions of the Texas Constitution, the Texas Bill of Rights is long, considerably longer than its counterpart in the national constitution. The Texas document contains 29 sections and includes most of the guarantees found in the national Bill of Rights, such as the protection of free speech and a free press, the guarantee of the right of trial by jury, and a safeguard against "unreasonable searches and seizures."

The Texas Bill of Rights does more than merely restate the guarantees found in the U.S. Constitution. The Texas document phrases the protection of rights positively rather

Bill of rights A constitutional document guaranteeing individual rights and liberties.

The Freedom of Worship
Provision of the Texas Constitution

Both the U.S. Constitution and the Texas Constitution include provisions dealing with religious liberty. Article I, Section 6, of the Texas Constitution is the state's Freedom of Worship Provision. It can be found online at the following Internet address: **www.capitol.state.tx.us/txconst/toc.html**. Read it from the perspective of comparing and contrasting it with the First Amendment of the U.S. Constitution, which can be found at the following website: **www.house.gov/Constitution/Constitution.html**. Complete the assignment by answering the following questions:

1. "Congress shall make no law respecting an establishment of religion." This provision from the First Amendment of the U.S. Constitution is known as the Establishment Clause. Does Article I, Section 6, of the Texas Constitution include equivalent language? What passage or passages in the Texas document are comparable to the Establishment Clause of the U.S. Constitution?

2. "Congress shall make no law . . . prohibiting the free exercise [of religion.]" This provision from the First Amendment of the U.S. Constitution is known as the Free Exercise Clause. Does Article I, Section 6, of the Texas Constitution include equivalent language? What passage or passages in the Texas document are comparable to the Free Exercise Clause of the U.S. Constitution?

3. The framers of the Texas Constitution were familiar with the wording of the U.S. Constitution and could have chosen simply to duplicate it in the Texas document. Why do you think they decided to take a different approach?

4. Do you think the wording of the Texas document provides individuals with greater protection for religious liberty than the First Amendment of the U.S. Constitution? Why or why not?

5. Suppose a Texas resident believed that a unit of state or local government had violated her freedom of religion. She filed suit in federal court under the U.S. Constitution but lost her case. Could she also seek relief in a Texas court based on the Texas Constitution? Explain the basis of your answer.

6. Would it be possible for the Texas resident in question 5 to win her case in Texas court even though she lost in federal court? Why or why not?

than negatively. Consider the issue of freedom of expression. The First Amendment to the U.S. Constitution prohibits the abridgement of free expression: "Congress shall make no law . . . abridging the freedom of speech, or of the press." In contrast, the Texas Bill of Rights guarantees free expression: "Every person shall be at liberty to speak, write or publish his opinions on any subject . . . and no law shall ever be passed curtailing the liberty of speech or of the press" [Art. 1, Sect. 8]. Professor James C. Harrington believes that the provision in the Texas Constitution is potentially a stronger guarantee of free expression than the First Amendment to the U.S. Constitution. Whereas the U.S. Bill of Rights identifies rights the national government *may not infringe upon*, the Texas Bill of Rights lists rights state government *must protect*.[14]

The Texas Constitution protects the individual right of gun ownership. The Second Amendment to the U.S. Constitution declares that "the right of the people to keep and bear Arms shall not be infringed," but it couches that provision in the context of a state militia. Consequently, the federal courts have consistently held that the Second Amendment does not grant a federal constitutional right to own or carry weapons. In contrast, Article I, Section 23, of the Texas Constitution states that a citizen has the "right to keep and bear arms in the lawful defense of himself." Although the legislature can regulate "the wearing of arms, with a view to prevent crime," gun owners enjoy greater protection under the Texas Constitution than they do under the U.S. Constitution.

Furthermore, the Texas Bill of Rights includes a number of measures not found in the national Bill of Rights. Whereas the U.S. Constitution provides for the right to a jury trial only if defendants face more than six months in jail, the Texas Constitution guarantees the right to trial by jury for persons charged with any offense, even minor traffic violations. The Texas Constitution also contains two guarantees of equal rights more explicit and detailed than any comparable measure included in the U.S. Constitution. Both provisions are found in Article I, Section 3. The first measure is fairly broad: "All free men . . . have equal rights." The second guarantee, which was added in 1972, is known as the **Texas Equal Rights Amendment (ERA).** It is a provision in the Texas Constitution that states the following: "Equality under the law shall not be denied or abridged because of sex, race, color, creed, or national origin" (Art. I, Sect. 3a.).

The Texas Constitution establishes a separation of powers system with checks and balances. Similar to the national government, Texas state government has three branches: an executive branch headed by the governor; a bicameral legislature, including the Texas House of Representatives and the Texas Senate; and a judicial branch. **Checks and balances** is the overlapping of the powers of the branches of government, so that public officials limit the authority of one another. The governor's appointments, for example, must be confirmed by a two-thirds' vote of the Texas Senate. Legislation must pass both the House and the Senate before it has passed the Texas legislature. The governor can veto bills passed by the legislature, but the legislature can override the veto by a two-thirds' vote of each house.

The Texas Constitution includes features not found in the U.S. Constitution. Some of these provisions involve policy matters of primary concern to state government. One section, for example, deals with voter qualifications and elections. Other sections outline the structures and responsibilities of local governments. Much of the length and detail of the Texas Constitution, though, can be attributed to the inclusion of long sections dealing with substantive policy areas. The framers of the constitution devoted thousands of words to such matters as railroad regulation, education, welfare, and taxation. Subsequent amendments have added thousands of words.

Texas Equal Rights Amendment (ERA) A provision in the Texas Constitution that states the following: "Equality under the law shall not be denied or abridged because of sex, race, color, creed, or national origin."

Checks and balances The overlapping of the powers of the branches of government so that public officials limit the authority of one another.

CONSTITUTIONAL CHANGE

Constitutions change by means of formal amendment, practical experience, and judicial interpretation. The U.S. Constitution is a relatively brief document of general principles. Although it has been amended 27 times, scholars believe that practical experience and judicial interpretation have been more important means of constitutional change than written amendments. State constitutions are usually longer and more detailed than the national document, providing less opportunity for constitutional growth through practical experience and judicial interpretation. State constitutional change generally occurs through the means of written amendments. This is certainly true for the Texas Constitution.

Change Through Amendment

Constitutional amendment A formal, written change or addition to the nation's governing document.

A **constitutional amendment** is a formal, written change or addition to the state's governing document. The detailed style of the Texas Constitution has led to numerous amendments as each successive generation of Texans has attempted to adapt its features to changing times. Some amendments have been trivial, such as an amendment to allow city governments to donate surplus firefighting equipment to rural volunteer fire departments. Other amendments have dealt with weighty policy matters, such as an amendment authorizing the legislature to cap noneconomic damages for pain and suffering awarded in lawsuits. The voters approved both amendments in 2003.

Through the years, amendments have produced several major changes in the Texas Constitution. The legislature and the voters have amended the constitution to strengthen the authority of state officials, especially the governor. Amendments have increased the term of office of the governor and the state's other elected executive officials from two years to four years and have empowered the governor to remove his or her own appointees, pending Senate approval. The constitution has also been amended to give the governor limited **budget execution authority,** which is the power to cut agency spending or transfer money between agencies during the period when the legislature is not in session.

Budget execution authority The power to cut agency spending or transfer money between agencies during the period when the legislature is not in session.

The legislature and the voters have amended the Texas Constitution to enable state government to promote economic development. Amendments have eliminated the constitutional prohibition against branch banking, allowed local governments to give tax breaks to businesses relocating to Texas, and provided money for the development and conservation of the state's water resources. Other amendments have provided funds for highway construction, student loans, and college expansion.

General obligation bonds Certificates of indebtedness that must be repaid from general revenues.

The legislature and the voters have periodically approved amendments to enable the state to go into debt by issuing **general obligation bonds,** which are certificates of indebtedness that must be repaid from general revenues. Borrowing enables the state to spread the cost of major projects, such as prison construction and water development, over a period of time. Because the Texas Constitution prohibits the state from incurring debt that must be repaid from general revenues, the legislature has had to propose constitutional amendments to authorize borrowing. In 2007, the bonded indebtedness of the state of Texas was $14 billion, with the state paying $513 million a year in principal and interest out of general revenues.[15] Voters authorized an additional $9.75 billion of debt in 2007 by approving constitutional amendments to allow the state to borrow money for cancer research, transportation, parks, water projects, college student loans, and other items.

The process of amending the Texas Constitution is fairly straightforward. An amendment must first be proposed by a two-thirds' vote of each house of the legislature. Then, it must be approved by a majority of the voters in an election. Through 2007, the voters had approved 456 amendments to the Texas Constitution out of 632 proposed by the legislature.[16]

The amendment process is time-consuming and the electorate apathetic. Even in the most favorable circumstances, the interval between the formulation of a proposed amendment and its ultimate approval or rejection by the voters is measured in years. Furthermore, elections to ratify constitutional amendments generate relatively little voter interest. As Figure 19.1 indicates, the number of Texas voters who decided the fate of the 22 proposed constitutional amendments on the ballot in 2005 was considerably less than the number of Texans who participated in the 2004 presidential election or the 2006 governor's election.

Nearly every state allows its citizens to vote on constitutional amendments, and defenders of the process say that the people should have a voice in the adoption of changes in their state's fundamental law. They frame the issue in terms of democracy. Although the legislature can propose constitutional change, the voters should have the final word on whether changes are adopted.

In contrast, critics argue that most citizens are not well enough informed to make reasonable judgments about the details of state constitutional law. For example, Texas voters have twice rejected efforts to repeal a provision in the Texas Constitution requiring companies that seek investment from the Texas Growth Fund to disclose whether they do business with the white-minority governments of South Africa and Namibia. With the introduction of democratic, black-majority-rule governments in those countries, the original rationale for the requirement no longer applies. Even though there is no organized opposition to repeal the measure, the voters, apparently confused by the issue, have failed twice to ratify amendments repealing the provision.

The Texas legislature sometimes words amendments with an eye toward deceiving the voters. The Texas Constitution requires that the state publish a summary and a brief explanation of proposed constitutional amendments in newspapers at least twice before Election Day. In 1989, the summary for one proposed amendment clearly explained that the amendment would increase the pay for members of the Texas legislature from $7,200 to $23,358 a year. It would raise the salaries of the Speaker of the House and the lieutenant governor even more. On the ballot, however, the description of the measure began as follows: "The constitutional amendment to *limit* the

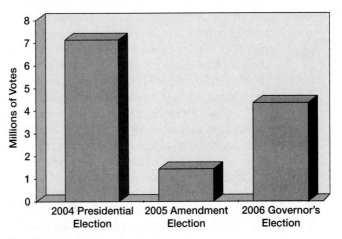

FIGURE 19.1   Voter Turnout.
Source: Texas Secretary of State.

salary. . . ." Poorly informed voters might well have voted to raise legislative salaries while believing they were doing the opposite. In this instance, at least, the legislature's effort at deception failed because the amendment was defeated.

The legislature even manipulates the timing of amendment ratification elections to influence their outcome. In 2003, the legislature passed a constitutional amendment to clarify that the legislature had the constitutional authority to limit the amount of noneconomic damages that a jury could award in a personal injury lawsuit. The legislature adopted the amendment to head off legal challenges against laws limiting the right of individuals to sue over faulty products, personal injuries, or medical malpractice. Instead of scheduling the ratification election for November, when amendment ratification elections are typically held, the legislature set the vote for a Saturday in September. Critics charged that legislative leaders reasoned that the amendment would be more likely to pass if it were held in a low-turnout special election in September than it would in November when a Houston city election would bring large numbers of minority voters to the polls who might vote against it. The plan apparently worked because the amendment passed.

Change Through Practice and Experience

Not all constitutional changes result from the adoption of formal amendments. Many of the fundamental features of American national government have developed through practice and experience. Consider the military powers of the president. The U.S. Constitution declares that the president is the commander-in-chief of the armed forces. To determine what this important constitutional power really entails, however, one must look to its practical application by actual presidents, such as Lincoln during the Civil War or Franklin Roosevelt during World War II. When President George W. Bush commanded the American armed forces to attack Iraq to overthrow the regime of Saddam Hussein, for example, no one seriously questioned the president's constitutional authority to order the military into combat, despite the lack of a congressional declaration of war, because previous presidents had taken similar action.

Because of its detail and specificity, the Texas Constitution has not grown as much through practice and experience as the U.S. Constitution, but some informal changes have occurred. For example, the office of lieutenant governor of Texas as outlined in the state constitution resembles that of the vice president of the United States, which, historically, has been a relatively weak office. In practice, however, the lieutenant governor has become one of the most important policy leaders in the state, far more important in state government than the vice president has been on the national scene. This is an important development in the fundamental structures of Texas government that resulted not from formal amendment but through the informal processes of practice and experience.

Change Through Judicial Interpretation

Many scholars believe that the most important mechanism through which the U.S. Constitution has changed has been judicial interpretation. Federal court rulings have defined constitutional principles in such key policy areas as school integration, voting rights, freedom of expression, freedom of religion, and the rights of persons accused of crimes. Because of the more detailed nature of state constitutions, judicial interpretation has historically been a less significant means for constitutional change at the state level than it has been at the national level. Today, however, this situation may be changing. State courts have begun to play an increasingly important policymaking role through the interpretation of state constitutions, especially in the area of state funding for public education.

 WHAT IS YOUR OPINION?

Are state constitutional amendment elections so complicated that ordinary citizens cannot make intelligent choices?

Constitutional Revision

Dedicated funds
Constitutional or statutory provisions that set aside revenue for particular purposes.

Dedicated Highway Fund
A constitutionally earmarked account containing money set aside for building, maintaining, and policing state highways.

Permanent University Fund (PUF) Money constitutionally set aside as an endowment to finance construction, maintenance, and some other activities at the University of Texas, Texas A&M University, and other institutions in those two university systems.

Constitutional revision The process of drafting a new constitution.

Many critics of the Texas Constitution believe that Texas should have a new state constitution. The League of Women Voters, the Texas Bar Association, some public officials, and many political scientists (including most textbook authors) contend that the document is so long and detailed, and so often amended, that most citizens (and even many public officials) do not understand it. A simpler, more straightforward document, they say, would increase respect for and understanding of state government.

The most telling criticism of the Texas Constitution is that it hinders the formulation, adoption, and implementation of sound public policy. During the 1980s and early 1990s, and then again in 2003, the legislature was forced to deal with serious budget shortfalls, necessitating spending cuts, tax increases, or a combination of the two. The legislature's ability to set spending priorities, however, was limited by constitutionally **dedicated funds,** which are constitutional or statutory provisions that set aside revenue for particular purposes. For example, the **Dedicated Highway Fund** is a constitutionally earmarked account containing money set aside for building, maintaining, and policing state highways. The **Permanent University Fund (PUF)** is money constitutionally set aside as an endowment to finance construction, maintenance, and some other activities at the University of Texas, Texas A&M University, and other institutions in those two university systems. In preparing the budget, legislators did not have the option of cutting highway funds to avoid a tax increase or diverting construction money from the University of Texas and Texas A&M University systems to other colleges and universities because the constitution would not allow it. Instead, the legislature had to raise taxes and fees and/or look for budget cuts in areas not protected by constitutionally dedicated funds.

Critics of the Texas Constitution charge that it is loaded with provisions that hinder the operation of efficient government. The governor has insufficient power, they say, to manage the state bureaucracy, the legislature meets too briefly and infrequently to resolve the state's policy problems, and the election of judges makes for a judiciary excessively dependent on interest-group campaign contributions. The critics believe that many of the problems facing the state will not be resolved until the Texas Constitution is significantly revised or rewritten entirely.

The most recent efforts at **constitutional revision,** which is the process of drafting a new constitution, have failed. In 1972, Texas voters approved a constitutional

The Dedicated Highway Fund is a constitutionally earmarked account containing money set aside for building, maintaining, and policing state highways.

amendment to call a state constitutional convention with members of the legislature serving as convention delegates. The ground rules for the convention required a two-thirds' vote of approval for a new constitution, but two-thirds of the legislator-delegates could not agree on a new document. Three years later, the legislature tried to make the best of the situation. After dropping the most controversial items, the legislature divided the rest of the document into a series of amendments to submit to the voters. If the voters approved all of the amendments, the state would effectively have a new constitution.

The campaign for the new constitution was hard fought, with state officials, interest groups, local officeholders, and a host of others getting involved. The proponents, including many state officials, newspaper editorial writers, and scholars, argued that the revision would produce a more efficient and effective state government. In response, the opponents, including many local officials and a number of interest groups, warned that the new constitution would increase the power of state government too much and might well lead to the adoption of a state income tax. In the end, the opponents of the new constitution won big as voters rejected all of the amendments by an overwhelming margin.

In the late 1990s, two respected members of the legislature once again raised the issue of constitutional revision. They proposed a new constitution of only 19,000 words that would be a more general statement of fundamental law than the document it would replace. Their proposed constitution would strengthen the powers of the governor, reorganize the executive branch to reduce the number of elected officials, replace the election of judges with a merit selection process, and reorganize the judicial branch of government. The idea never came to a vote in the legislature, however, because most legislators wanted to avoid having to address controversial issues.

NATIONAL PERSPECTIVE

Gay Marriage in Massachusetts

Gay couples have been able to marry legally in Massachusetts since May 2004. Gay marriage is the result of a ruling by the Massachusetts Supreme Judicial Court (SJC) holding that the state cannot discriminate against same-sex couples when it issues marriage licenses. The SJC, which is the state's highest court, acted in response to a lawsuit filed by seven same-sex couples. The court ruled that the state lacked a rational basis for denying the couples a marriage license simply based on their desire to marry a person of the same gender. "The Massachusetts Constitution affirms the dignity and equality of all individuals," declared the court. "It forbids the creation of second class citizens."*

The opponents of the decision immediately began an effort to amend the Massachusetts Constitution to overturn the SJC's ruling. The most commonly used procedure for amending the state constitution begins with the legislature passing an amendment by majority vote in two consecutive legislative sessions. The amendment then goes to the voters for approval. In 2004, the Massachusetts legislature voted 105–92 in favor of a state constitutional amendment that would ban gay marriage and establish civil unions. A **civil union** is a legal partnership between two men or two women giving the couple all the benefits, protections, and responsibilities under law as are granted to spouses in a marriage. A year later, however, the legislature rejected the amendment by a lopsided 157–39 vote. Over the preceding year, 6,600 same-sex couples had married uneventfully and the elected officials who supported gay marriage had generally won reelection. In short, the sky had not fallen. A legislator who initially opposed gay marriage but changed his mind to support it explained his decision as follows: "When I look in the eyes of the children living with these couples, I decided that I don't feel at this time that same-sex marriage has hurt the [state] in any way. In fact I would say that in my view it has had a good effect for the children in these families."[†]

With the failure of the constitutional amendment in the legislature, the opponents of gay marriage turned to the initiative process. An organization called VoteonMarriage.org gathered more than 150,000 signatures to put on the ballot a constitutional amendment to limit future marriages to one man and one woman. (The measure would not annul the same-sex marriages that had already been performed.) The procedure for approving the voter-initiated amendment requires that it receive the votes of at least 50 lawmakers in two consecutive legislative sessions, then voter approval in a referendum. The measure won the votes of 61 legislators in early 2007, but it received only 45 votes in the next session held later in the year. Massachusetts opponents of gay marriage would have to start all over if they hoped to amend the state constitution.[‡]

Gay marriage opponents outside of Massachusetts, including President George W. Bush, have proposed an amendment to the U.S. Constitution that would declare that marriage in the United States is limited to the union of a man and a woman. The amendment would overrule any action taken at the state level, including the decision of the SJC. The procedure for amending the U.S. Constitution involves the U.S. House and U.S. Senate voting to propose an amendment by a two-thirds' vote. Three-fourths of the states must agree to ratify the amendment. In 2004 and 2006, the marriage amendment fell well short of the two-thirds' margin needed in both the House and the Senate.

QUESTIONS TO CONSIDER

1. The process for amending the Massachusetts Constitution is different from the process for amending the Texas Constitution. Which process do you prefer? Why?
2. Which level of government should decide the issue of gay marriage—the national government or the states? What is the basis of your answer?
3. Do you think gay men and women should be able to marry legally in Texas?

---

*Goodridge et al. v. Department of Public Health, SJC-08860 (2003).

[†]Pam Belluck, "Massachusetts Rejects Bill to Eliminate Gay Marriage," New York Times, September 15, 2005, available at www.nytimes.com.

[‡]Pam Belluck, "Massachusetts Gay Marriage to Remain Legal," New York Times, June 15, 2007, available at www.nytimes.com.

INDIVIDUAL RIGHTS AND THE TEXAS CONSTITUTION

Civil union A legal partnership between two men or two women that gives the couple all the benefits, protections, and responsibilities under law as are granted to spouses in a traditional marriage.

Historically, people who believe that their rights have been violated have turned to the federal courts for relief under the U.S. Constitution. During the 1950s and 1960s, in particular, the U.S. Supreme Court acted to protect individuals from racial discrimination, guarantee freedom of expression, and expand the rights of people who were accused of crimes. In *Brown v. Board of Education of Topeka* (1954), for example, the U.S. Supreme Court ruled that state laws that required racial segregation in the public schools violated the U.S. Constitution.[17]

Over the past 40 years, state courts have increasingly become a forum for disputes over individual rights lawsuits filed under the provisions of state constitutions. In America's federal system of government, states must grant their residents all the rights guaranteed by the U.S. Constitution (as interpreted by the Supreme Court). If state governments so choose, however, they may offer their residents *more* rights than afforded in the U.S. Constitution.[18] Since 1970, state courts around the nation have issued hundreds of rulings providing broader rights than those recognized by the U.S. Supreme Court. The areas in which state courts have been most active are abortion rights, criminal procedure, church/state relations, and gender discrimination.[19]

Equal protection of the law The legal principle that state laws may not arbitrarily discriminate against persons.

In Texas, state courts have relied on the Texas Constitution to expand individual rights in several policy areas involving **equal protection of the law,** which is the legal principle that state laws may not arbitrarily discriminate against persons. The Texas Supreme Court has held that "similarly situated individuals must be treated equally under [state law] . . . unless there is a rational basis for not doing so."[20] In *Edgewood v. Kirby,* for example, the Texas Supreme Court ruled that the state's system of financing public education violated the Texas Constitution because it resulted in unequal treatment for schoolchildren residing in different school districts.[21]

The emergence of the Texas Constitution as an instrument for the protection of individual rights is a relatively recent development. Whether it is a lasting development will depend on the state's judges and the voters who elect them. Will the justices serving on the state's two highest courts, the Texas Supreme Court and the Texas Court of Criminal Appeals, dare to make controversial decisions, considering that they must stand periodically for reelection? Election-minded justices may be eager to rule in favor of schoolchildren and property taxpayers, but will they be just as willing to uphold the rights of gay men and lesbians, atheists, persons accused of crimes, or other individuals and groups who may not be popular with the average Texas voter? Because voters are generally uninformed about judges, a single, highly publicized case can have a major import on a judge's electoral fortunes. Research shows that as Election Day approaches judges bring their rulings in line with public opinion.[22]

Consider the legal challenge to the state's homosexual conduct law. In 1998, Harris County sheriff deputies, responding to a false tip about an armed intruder, entered a home and discovered John G. Lawrence and Tyron Garner having sex. The deputies arrested the men on charges of "deviant homosexual conduct." Lawrence and Garner pled "no contest" to the charges, so they could challenge the constitutionality of the law on appeal. Subsequently, a three-judge appeals panel ruled on a 2–1 vote that the state's sodomy law violated the Texas ERA because it singled out gay men and lesbians. The judges held that the state had no rational basis for punishing gay male and lesbian couples for behavior that is legal for heterosexual couples.

Conservative opponents of the court's decision to overturn the sodomy law focused their criticism on the two judges who issued the ruling. The chairman of the Harris County Republican Party circulated a letter demanding that the judges who voted to strike down the law either reverse their ruling or resign from office. The Texas Republican Party called on the voters to defeat the two judges at the next election. Although the judges who issued the initial ruling held their ground, the other members of the appellate court apparently caved in to the pressure. In an unusual move, all nine members of the appeals court agreed to reconsider the decision of the three-judge panel. They voted 7–2 to reverse the decision of the three-judge panel and reinstate the law.

In 2003, the U.S. Supreme Court ruled that the Texas homosexual conduct law violated the U.S. Constitution. After Lawrence and Garner lost in state court, they turned to the federal court system. "[Lawrence and Garner] are entitled to respect for their private lives," declared the Court. "The State cannot demean their existence or control their destiny by making their private sexual conduct a crime."[23]

CONCLUSION: THE CONSTITUTIONAL CONTEXT OF POLICYMAKING IN TEXAS

The Texas Constitution is an important part of the policymaking environment for state and local government in Texas.

Agenda Building

Some issues appear on the state's official policy agenda because of the Texas Constitution or because of its interpretation by state courts. Although the controversy over public school finance was long simmering, it was not until the Texas Supreme Court ruled in the *Edgewood* case that the system violated the Texas Constitution that the legislature and governor were forced to address the issue. The *West Orange-Cove* case forced them to deal with state funding and local property tax rates.

Policy Formulation and Adoption

The state constitution affects policy formulation by limiting the options available to policymakers. It sets a framework within which policymakers must work. *Edgewood v. Kirby* forced the legislature not only to address school funding issues but also to consider and eventually adopt a solution that the legislature would have been unlikely to consider seriously otherwise. The legislature and the governor adopted the Robin Hood Plan because they believed that the Texas Supreme Court was unlikely to accept a lesser solution as constitutional. *Neeley v. West Orange-Cove Consolidated ISD* forced the legislature and the governor to increase state education funding to enable local school districts to reduce property tax rates below the state tax cap.

The Texas Constitution establishes the ground rules for policy adoption. Legislation must pass both houses of the Texas legislature and be signed into law by the governor. If the governor vetoes a measure, the constitution provides that it dies unless passed again by a two-thirds' margin in both chambers of the legislature.

Policy Implementation and Evaluation

The Texas Constitution fragments policy implementation by dividing administrative responsibilities among dozens of elected or appointed executive officials, boards, commissions, and agencies. Neither the governor nor any other state executive official has the authority to oversee or coordinate policy implementation. Elected officials answerable only to the voters administer tax collection, oil and gas regulation, land management, and agriculture policy. Appointed boards administer the state's prison system, regulate utility companies, and license professionals ranging from medical doctors to hair stylists.

The Texas Constitution ensures that policy evaluation is haphazard and uncoordinated. With relatively little administrative authority, the governor has few incentives and no real power to conduct systematic evaluation studies or put their recommendations into practice. Although the legislature has the authority to evaluate policy and the power to use feedback from the evaluation to make policy changes, short, biennial sessions make evaluation difficult. In practice, the legislature and other state offices have created evaluation mechanisms, but their effectiveness is reduced because of structural limitations imposed by the Constitution.

LET'S DEBATE

Gay Marriage

Overview: On November 8, 2005, Texans went to the polls in unusually high numbers to amend the state constitution to declare that marriage is solely a union between one man and one woman. With the ratification of Proposition 2, Texas thus became the 19th state to pass a constitutional measure either banning same-sex marriage or defining marriage as a heterosexual institution. Since the amendment overwhelmingly passed with 76 percent of the vote (with only one county, Travis County, voting against the measure), and voters in 11 states in the 2004 General Election also overwhelmingly affirmed the traditional meaning of marriage rights, the issue of same-sex marriage was not at the forefront of the American culture wars, and not just the American or Texas culture wars. European nations, such as Great Britain, Belgium, and Spain, as well as Canada, have recently given legal sanction to same-sex unions. Why has this issue attained such prominence? Why, according to the National Conference of State Legislatures, and the majority of American states choosing to affirm either constitutionally or in law the traditional status of marriage rights?

Many political commentators point to the activities of various state judiciaries in overturning or declaring unconstitutional particular state law. In 1933, the Hawaiian Supreme Court declared the state government could not deny gay couples the right to marry, and this decision prompted the state's citizens to amend their constitution to give the government legal authority to define marriage as a heterosexual institution. Three years later, Congress passed the Defense of Marriage Act (DOMA), which gave states the right not to recognize homosexual marriages sanctioned by other states. Though still a prominent issue, the debate over gay unions accelerated after the Massachusetts Supreme Court declared unconstitutional a state law that defined marriage as being between a man and a woman. After the Massachusetts Supreme Court decision, more than 35 states (including Texas) introduced legislation or constitutional amendments in regard to this issue. Is this a matter of civil rights or one of state sovereignty? Is it a matter of maintaining traditional institutions or one of bigotry?

continued on next page

Proponents of Proposition 2 argue the amendment is both an issue of state sovereignty and an issue of maintaining traditional institutions. Opponents argue that marriage is a human right and claim that the same-sex marriage movement can be likened to the civil rights movement during the last century. There is no doubt the debate over the issue is a part of the larger Texas and national culture wars as the state tries to adapt to dramatically changing social norms while preserving traditional institutions. Proponents assert that some institutions are a mater of tradition and religion and not of rights, and Proposition 2 establishes that fact. Barring an unfavorable U.S. Supreme Court decision, advocates of same-sex unions are preparing for a long battle to change public opinion and eventually change state laws and constitutions. What should those who favor expansive marriage rights do to realize their vision? What is the best way to preserve traditional institutions? Is there a compromise that can satisfy both sides of the issue?

Arguments for Keeping the Amendment

❏ **Citizens of Texas, rather than the courts, should define marriage.** There has been a trend for state judiciaries to overturn duly promulgated law written to be consonant with state constitutions. It is up to citizens to determine certain rights through elected representatives, and a constitutional amendment prevents the judiciary from denying the wishes of the people acting through constitutional institutions.

❏ **Same-sex couples are not prevented from living their chosen lifestyles.** The amendment does not prevent gay couples from living and sharing their lives together. They may live together in any manner they choose as long as it is within the bounds of law (as we all must do), and they are free to love in their own fashion. The amendment merely does not give state sanction to this lifestyle.

❏ **The sanctity of traditional marriage should not be violated.** Heterosexuals, too, should be allowed to have their own unique institutions, which are understood to provide family strength and provide a safe environment for children. The amendment simply defines *marriage* as a union between one man and one woman and gives heterosexual married couples constitutional protection. This guarantees that heterosexuals have legal sanction for their traditionally unique social institution.

Arguments Against Keeping the Amendment

❏ **The amendment does not truly provide social stability.** There are many incidences of child abuse, spousal abuse, divorce, neglect, and financial malfeasance in heterosexual marriages. There are good couples and bad couples, good parents and bad parents, in both communities. State law and policy should address all problems that destroy the social fabric, so all citizens have the necessary state support to better their lives.

❏ **The amendment may infringe on future rights of homosexuals.** Texas law already bans gay marriage, and this amendment may prohibit the Texas government in the future from writing law to reflect changing social mores. For example, it has only been in the past 40 years that the U.S. Supreme Court invalidated laws prohibiting interracial marriage, so it is imperative that the legislature have the flexibility to adjust to changing notions of family structures as a result of an evolving understanding of rights.

❏ **The amendment's language is too broad.** The phrasing of the amendment can be construed in such a way as to invalidate common-law marriages and nullify legal contracts, such as living wills and powers of attorney. All citizens should receive equal protection of contracts, and, as long as the law is obeyed, legal contracts between consenting citizens should be held inviolable.

QUESTIONS

1. Is same-sex marriage a matter of human rights?
2. Do traditional marriages really support family structures and ensure the well-being of children? What about the high rates of divorce and abuse found in the heterosexual community?

SELECT READINGS

1. Mark Strasser, *On Same-Sex Marriage, Civil Unions, and the Rule of Law: Constitutional Interpretation at a Crossroads* (Westport, CT: Greenwood, 2002).
2. Lynn Wardle et al., *Marriage and Same-Sex Unions: A Debate* (Westport, CT: Praeger, 2003).

SELECT WEBSITES

1. **www.southernpoliticalreport.com/stories/November%202005/11-4/texas.htm**
   Straightforward analysis of the politics surrounding Proposition 2 by the Southern Political Report.
2. **www.dfw.com/mld/startelegram/news/state/13120523.htm**
   The *Star-Telegram's* analysis of the Proposition 2 vote.

KEY TERMS

bicameral legislature
bill of rights
branch banking
budget deficit
budget execution authority
checks and balances
civil union
constitution
constitutional amendment
constitutional law
constitutional revision
dedicated funds
Dedicated Highway Fund

direct democracy
Edgewood v. Kirby
equal protection of the law
general obligation bonds
Grange
homestead
initiative process
Jacksonian democracy
local-option (wet–dry) elections
long ballot
Permanent University Fund (PUF)
plural executive

property tax
Radical Republicans
representative democracy *or* republic
Robin Hood Plan
separation of powers
statutory law
suffrage
Texas Equal Rights Amendment (ERA)
unicameral legislature

NOTES

1. "K–12 Education Finances," *Governing State and Local Source Book, 2006*, p. 15.
2. *Edgewood v. Kirby*, 777 S.W.2d 391 (1989).
3. *Neeley v. West Orange-Cove Consolidated ISD*, 176 S.W. 3d 746 (2005).
4. Christopher W. Hammons, "Was James Madison Wrong? Rethinking the American Preference for Short, Framework-Oriented Constitutions," *American Political Science Review* 93 (December 1999): 837.
5. Lawrence W. Friedman, "An Historical Perspective on State Constitutions," *Intergovernmental Perspective* (Spring 1987): 9–13.
6. Data collected by Janice May, quoted in David C. Saffell and Harry Basehart, *State and Local Government: Politics and Public Policies*, 8th ed. (New York: McGraw-Hill, 2005), pp. 24–26.
7. Ibid.
8. Friedman, "An Historical Perspective on State Constitutions," pp. 9–13.
9. Hammons, "Was James Madison Wrong?" p. 840.
10. John Walker Mauer, *Southern State Constitutions in the 1870s: A Case Study of Texas*, Ph.D. thesis, Rice University, Houston, Texas, 1983, p. 152.
11. Ibid.

12. Glenda Taylor, "Going Wet," *Kerrville Daily Times*, February 12, 2005, available at www.dailytimes.com.

13. Friedman, "An Historical Perspective on State Constitutions," pp. 9–13.

14. James C. Harrington, "The Texas Bill of Rights and Civil Liberties," *Texas Tech Law Review* 1487 (1986).

15. Comptroller of Public Accounts, "General Obligation Bonds and Revenue Bonds Payable from General Revenue," available at www.cpa.state.tx.us/treasops/bondapp.html.

16. Legislative Reference Library of Texas, "Constitutional Amendments," available at www.lrl.state.tx.us/legis/constAmends/lrlhome.cfm.

17. *Brown v. Board of Education of Topeka*, 347 U.S. 483 (1954).

18. *Pruneyard Shopping Center v. Robins*, 447 U.S. 74 (1980).

19. Jim Kincaid and Robert F. Williams, "The New Judicial Federalism: The States Lead in Rights Protection," in Thad L. Beyle, ed., *State Government: CQ's Guide to Current Issues and Activities 1993–94* (Chapel Hill: University of North Carolina Press, 1993), p. 183.

20. *Whitworth v. Bynum*, 699 S.W.2d 194 (1985).

21. *Edgewood v. Kirby*.

22. Gregory A. Huber and Sanford C. Gordon, "Accountability and Coercion: Is Justice Blind When It Runs for Office?" *American Journal of Political Science* 48 (April 2004): 247–263.

23. *Lawrence v. Texas*, 539 US 558 (2003).

Chapter 20

The Federal Context of Texas Policymaking

CHAPTER OUTLINE

LEARNING OUTCOMES

After studying Chapter 20, students should be able to do the following:

▶ Describe the federal system, discussing the relative positions of the federal government and the states. (pp. 538–541)

▶ Assess the impact of the U.S. Constitution and federal courts on policymaking in Texas, discussing *Brown v. Board of Education of Topeka, Ruiz v. Estelle,* and *Roe v. Wade.* (pp. 541–544)

▶ Evaluate the effect of federal law on policymaking in Texas, considering in particular the role of federal preemption and federal mandates. (pp. 544–547)

▶ Describe the process through which federal grant programs are adopted and implemented. (pp. 547–548)

▶ Distinguish among the various kinds of grant programs: categorical grants, block grants, entitlements programs, project grants, and formula grants. (pp. 548–550)

▶ Identify and discuss the various types of conditions that the federal government places on the receipt of federal funds. (pp. 550–552)

▶ Evaluate the importance of federal programs to state and local governments in Texas. (pp. 552–553)

▶ Assess the impact of the federal system on each stage of the policymaking process in Texas. (pp. 553–555)

▶ Define the key terms listed on page 557 and explain their significance.

Getting a driver's license or a license renewal will soon become more complicated and maybe more expensive as well. In 2005, Congress passed, and President George W. Bush signed, the Real ID Act to prevent potential terrorists or illegal immigrants from fraudulently obtaining official state identification. The Real ID Act, which goes into effect in December 2008, establishes national standards for state-issued driver's licenses and identification cards for nondrivers. To get or renew a license, applicants must provide state officials with the following:

- A photo ID with their full legal name and date of birth.
- Documentation of their date of birth, such as a birth certificate.
- Documentation of legal status and Social Security number, such as a visa, naturalization papers, or an original Social Security number card.
- Documentation showing their name and the address of their principal residence.

States are required to verify the authenticity of every document and store the information they gather in a database linked to the databases of other states.[1]

State officials nationwide are worried that the requirements of the Real ID Act will overwhelm their capacity to issue driver's licenses. The Texas Department of Public Safety (DPS) will be inundated with paperwork. State residents, who will be required to apply in person for license renewals every five years, will likely face long lines and increased cost. If the state passes along the expense of complying with the Real ID Act to consumers, the cost of a license renewal could exceed $100.[2]

Nonetheless, states have no choice but to comply with the law. States that fail to create databases and link them to other states will lose federal funding. Moreover, state residents who do not have an ID that meets federal standards by May 2013 will be unable to board an airplane, enter a federal building, get a job, or do banking business.

The controversy over the Real ID Act illustrates the importance of the federal system for policymaking in American government. The chapter identifies the role of state and local governments in the federal system of American government. It explores the impact of the U.S. Constitution and federal courts on state and local governments by examining three important cases in constitutional law. The chapter studies the influence of federal law on state and local policymaking, considering federal preemption of state authority and federal mandates. The chapter describes federal grant programs and examines their influence on the state and local policymaking process. The chapter concludes with a discussion of the impact of the federal government and the federal system on policymaking in Texas.

Federal system or federation A political system that divides power between a central government, with authority over the whole nation, and a series of state governments.

ROLE OF THE STATES IN THE FEDERAL SYSTEM

Policymaking in Texas takes place within the context of America's federal system of government. A **federal system,** or **federation,** is a political system that divides power between a central government, with authority over the whole nation, and a series of state governments. In a federal system, both the national government and the states

Sovereignty The authority of a state to exercise legitimate powers within its boundaries, free from external interference.

National Supremacy Clause A constitutional provision that declares that the Constitution, the laws made under it, and the treaties of the United States are the supreme law of the land.

Local governments Subunits of states.

Blame avoidance The effort on the part of government officials to assign responsibility for policy failures to someone else.

Budget deficit The amount of money by which annual budget expenditures exceed annual budget receipts.

Medicaid A federal program designed to provide health insurance coverage to low-income persons, people with disabilities, and elderly people who are impoverished.

enjoy **sovereignty,** which is the authority of a state to exercise legitimate powers within its boundaries, free from external interference. The national government and the states derive their authority not from one another but from the U.S. Constitution. Both levels of government act directly on the people through their officials and laws, both are supreme within their proper sphere of authority, and both must consent to constitutional change.

The national government is constitutionally the dominant partner in the federal system. Article VI of the U.S. Constitution includes a passage known as the **National Supremacy Clause,** which is a constitutional provision that declares that the U.S. Constitution, the laws made under it, and the treaties of the United States are the supreme law of the land. In short, the National Supremacy Clause states that the legitimate exercise of national power supersedes state action when the two conflict.

Nonetheless, state and **local governments,** which are subunits of states, enjoy considerable policymaking authority. States and localities provide their residents with a wide range of services. The major budget items for state and local governments in Texas and around the nation are education, healthcare, public safety, and transportation. State and local governments build and repair roads, put out fires, educate young people, spray mosquitoes, vaccinate children, provide parks and recreation facilities, police neighborhoods, operate hospitals, provide water and sewer service, collect garbage, and provide healthcare services for low-income and disabled people.

State and local governments regulate a wide range of industries, including insurance, finance, oil and gas, and utilities. State governments require business owners to obtain licenses and follow state guidelines in operating their establishments. They license a wide range of professions, including doctors, lawyers, realtors, accountants, nurses, and hair stylists. Cities regulate land use, establish construction codes, and inspect food vendors.

States and localities levy taxes. The most important tax sources for state and local governments nationwide are sales, property, excise, and income taxes. All of these taxes, except the income tax, are important in Texas. Texas is one of only a handful of states that do not levy a personal income tax.

In many policy areas, state governments rather than the federal government have taken the policymaking lead. Partisan wrangling and budget deficits have hamstrung Congress and the president, preventing them from addressing many of the nation's pressing domestic policy problems. **Blame avoidance,** which is the effort on the part of government officials to assign responsibility for policy failures to someone else, has taken precedence over problem solving. Congress and the president have also lacked the resources to address domestic policy problems because of budget deficits. (A **budget deficit** is the amount of money by which annual budget expenditures exceed annual budget receipts.)

Whereas Congress and the president have been unable to agree on a national health system, for example, many state governments have pieced together a health insurance system for low-income families using Medicaid and the Children's Health Insurance Program (CHIP). **Medicaid** is a federal program designed to provide health insurance coverage to low-income persons, people with disabilities, and

NATIONAL PERSPECTIVE

Drilling for Oil in Alaska

The petroleum industry is more important to Alaska than it is to Texas. In 2007, taxes and royalties on oil and gas production accounted for nearly 70 percent of state revenue in Alaska. Because of petroleum revenue, individual Alaskans enjoy the lowest state taxes in the nation, with no personal income tax and a relatively low sales tax.*

The state of Alaska and the federal government are locked in controversy over extending oil development in the state. One of the most promising areas for future oil development in the United States is located on Alaska's North Shore in the Arctic National Wildlife Refuge (ANWR). Oil industry executives and most elected officials in Alaska believe that the ANWR oil fields can be developed without causing serious harm to the Arctic environment. A majority of Alaska residents, including many native Alaskans who live in the affected area, support drilling as well. In contrast, environmentalists contend that oil exploration in the ANWR would threaten the fragile ecology of the region.

The future of oil development in the ANWR depends on the federal government. When Congress created the ANWR in 1980, it designated the coastal plain for eventual development. In 1995, Congress included a provision in a budget measure to open the coastal plain for oil drilling, but it died when President Bill Clinton vetoed the bill. The prospects for future oil development in the ANWR improved substantially in 2000 with the election of George W. Bush, a Texas oilman, to the presidency. Bush supports opening the ANWR for oil drilling and has made that position the centerpiece of his administration's energy policy. Although both the U.S. House of Representatives and the Senate have voted in favor of drilling at different times, they have yet to agree on a single piece of legislation that would permit oil exploration in the region. Furthermore, the election of a Democratic House and Senate in the 2006 election reduced the chances that Congress will agree to oil exploration in the ANWR in the near future.

QUESTIONS TO CONSIDER

1. Do you favor or oppose oil exploration in the ANWR? Why?
2. Why do you think most elected officials in Alaska favor oil development in the ANWR?
3. Who should decide whether to drill in the ANWR—the state government of Alaska or the federal government?

*Alaska State Budget, available at www.gov.state.ak.us.

Children's Health Insurance Program (CHIP)
A federal program designed to provide health insurance to children from low-income families whose parents are not poor enough to qualify for Medicaid.

elderly people who are impoverished. The **Children's Health Insurance Program (CHIP)** is a federal program designed to provide health insurance to children from low-income families whose parents are not poor enough to qualify for Medicaid. States have extended Medicaid to cover working families above the poverty line who cannot afford health insurance, adults with disabilities who cannot get insurance, women with breast cancer or cervical cancer, and people with HIV.[3] They have expanded CHIP coverage to include millions of children in working families that earn too much to qualify for Medicaid but cannot afford private health insurance.

State governments have also taken the lead in addressing the problem of **global warming,** which is the gradual warming of the atmosphere that is reportedly caused by industrial pollutants and the burning of fossil fuels. California and ten other states have adopted regulations that go beyond federal requirements limiting the amount of carbon dioxide and other gases that can be emitted from vehicle tailpipes. The California plan is particularly ambitious, calling for a 25 percent reduction in carbon dioxide emissions by 2020.[4] A number of states have adopted energy efficiency requirements for lightbulbs and household appliances. Seven states have agreed on a regional plan to restrict power plant emissions.[5]

STATES, THE COURTS, AND THE CONSTITUTION

Global warming The gradual warming of the Earth's atmosphere reportedly caused by the burning of fossil fuels and industrial pollutants.

The U.S. Constitution is the supreme law of the land. It takes legal precedence over state constitutions, state laws, state administrative procedures, and the actions of local government. State and local officials pledge to uphold the U.S. Constitution and most of them take that responsibility quite seriously. When the legislature considers changes in the state's capital punishment law, for example, the debate frequently centers on the likelihood that any proposed revision will survive a constitutional challenge. Individuals and groups who believe that the policies of state and local government violate the U.S. Constitution may file suit in federal court, asking the court to intervene. We can illustrate the importance of federal court rulings on policymaking in Texas by examining three historic cases: *Brown v. Board of Education of Topeka*, *Ruiz v. Estelle*, and *Roe v. Wade*.

School Desegregation

National Association for the Advancement of Colored People (NAACP) An interest group organized to represent the interests of African Americans.

Brown v. Board of Education of Topeka (1954) dealt with the constitutionality of state laws requiring racially segregated schools. The Brown family, residents of Topeka, Kansas, wanted their daughter Linda to attend a public school near their home. The law of the state of Kansas required separate schools for white and African American youngsters. Because the school near the Brown home was for whites only, Linda, who was African American, would have to travel across town to another school. With the legal support of the **National Association for the Advancement of Colored People (NAACP),** which is an interest group organized to represent the interests of African Americans, the Browns filed suit against the state. They charged that the law requiring a racially segregated public school system violated the **Equal Protection Clause,** which is the constitutional provision found in the Fourteenth Amendment of the U.S. Constitution that declares "No State shall . . . deny to any person within its jurisdiction the equal protection of the laws."

Equal Protection Clause The constitutional provision found in the Fourteenth Amendment of the U.S. Constitution that declares that "No State shall . . . deny to any person within its jurisdiction the equal protection of the laws."

The U.S. Supreme Court ruled that the state law was unconstitutional because it denied equal educational opportunities to African American students. "Segregation of white and colored children in public schools has a detrimental effect upon the colored children," wrote Chief Justice Earl Warren in the Court's opinion. "A sense of inferiority affects the motivation of the child to learn."[6]

Dual school system Separate sets of schools for white and African American youngsters.

Brown v. Board of Education of Topeka ultimately had a profound impact on policymaking in Texas. Even though the case involved a state law in Kansas, the precedent set by the Supreme Court in its ruling applied to all similar statutes throughout the United States. As was true for most southern states, Texas had a **dual school system**—that is, separate sets of schools for white and African American youngsters. Because of the *Brown* case, the state was eventually forced to dismantle its dual school system and adopt policies aimed at achieving racial integration of public schools.

PRISON OVERCROWDING

Ruiz v. Estelle (1972) addressed the issue of living conditions in the Texas Department of Corrections (TDC). In 1972, a group of prison inmates filed suit in federal court, claiming that living and working conditions in Texas prisons constituted "cruel and unusual punishment," forbidden by the Eighth Amendment to the U.S. Constitution. They charged that the state's prison system was severely overcrowded, the prison staff was too small to maintain security, working conditions were unsafe, disciplinary procedures were severe and arbitrary, and medical care was inadequate.

In 1980, federal District Judge William Wayne Justice ruled against the state of Texas, ordering sweeping changes in the Texas prison system. Although an appeals court later overturned part of Judge Justice's ruling, it upheld the key points of his decision. Eventually, the state settled the suit by agreeing to limit the inmate population to 95 percent of prison capacity, to separate hard-core offenders from inmates convicted of nonviolent crimes, to improve the guard-to-inmate ratio, and to upgrade inmate medical treatment.[7]

Linda Brown and her family were the plaintiffs in the *Brown v. Board of Education of Topeka* case, in which state laws requiring racial segregation in public schools were ruled to be unconstitutional.

Parole The conditional release of convicted offenders from prison to serve the remainder of their sentences in the community under supervision.

The *Ruiz* case forced Texas to limit its prison population. Initially, the state responded with early release, turning offenders out on **parole,** which is the conditional release of convicted offenders from prison to serve the remainder of their sentences in the community under supervision. In the long run, the state complied with the court's decision to reduce overcrowding by dramatically increasing the capacity of its prison system.

Abortion

Roe v. Wade (1973) dealt with the issue of abortion. "Jane Roe," an anonymous woman living in Dallas, challenged the constitutionality of a Texas law prohibiting abortion except to save the life of a woman. The U.S. Supreme Court found the Texas statute unconstitutional, saying that a woman's right to personal privacy under the U.S. Constitution included her decision to terminate a pregnancy within six months of inception.

The Supreme Court explained the ruling by dividing a pregnancy into three trimesters. During the first trimester (a three-month period), state governments could not interfere with a physician's decision, reached in consultation with a pregnant patient, to terminate a pregnancy. In the second trimester, a state could regulate abortion only to protect the health of the woman. In the third trimester, after the fetus has achieved viability (the ability to survive outside the womb), the Court ruled that states could choose to prohibit abortion except when necessary to preserve the life or health of the woman.[8]

In subsequent cases, the Supreme Court modified its ruling in *Roe v. Wade* to allow states greater leeway to limit abortion rights. Although the Court reaffirmed a woman's right to choose to abort a fetus before viability, it ruled that a state could regulate access to abortion as long as the regulations did not place an "undue burden" on a woman's right to choose. The Court's majority defined an undue burden

GETTING INVOLVED

Contacting Your Representative in Washington, DC

In America's federal system of government, individuals are citizens of the United States and citizens of the state in which they live. If you live in the Lone Star State, you are both an American citizen and a citizen of Texas. You receive services, pay taxes, and are subject to the laws and regulations of both the national government and the state of Texas.

American citizens have the constitutional right to participate in the policymaking process for both the national government and their state government. They may vote in both national and state elections and contact their elected representatives at both levels of government to make their policy preferences known.

The names, postal addresses, and e-mail addresses of the people who represent you in Congress are available online. The website for the U.S. Senate is www.senate.gov. The website for the U.S. House is www.house.gov. Each site has an interactive window that enables you to identify the name of your representatives. You can also find contact information. Write or e-mail your U.S. senators and U.S. representative, expressing your point of view on Real ID, No Child Left Behind, drilling in the ANWR, or any other federal or national issue about which you have an opinion.

It's your country—get involved!

as one that presented an "absolute obstacle or severe limitation" on the right to decide to have an abortion. State regulations that simply "inhibited" that right were permissible.[9]

The Texas legislature and the governor have taken advantage of the Supreme Court's flexibility on state abortion regulation by adopting the following measures:

- **Parental consent for minors** A physician may not perform an abortion on an unmarried girl younger than 18 without the written permission of a parent or guardian. The consent requirement can be waived if a judge determines that involving a parent could put the minor at risk of physical or emotional abuse or that the girl seeking an abortion is sufficiently mature to make the decision herself.

- **Twenty-four-hour waiting period** Before performing an abortion, a physician must provide a pregnant patient with a state-created packet that includes information on the health risks associated with abortion, alternatives to terminating a pregnancy, and color images of fetal development. The woman must then wait 24 hours before having the abortion.

- **Late-term abortion prohibition** A physician may not perform an abortion on a woman who has carried a fetus more than 26 weeks unless the woman's life is in jeopardy or the fetus has serious brain damage.

Roe v. Wade and other court cases dealing with abortion rights affected Texas law by restricting the state's ability to adopt policies controlling access to abortion. Before *Roe*, the state was free to adopt any policy ranging from legalization of abortion in most circumstances to the prohibition of abortion in almost all circumstances. Because of *Roe*, abortion is now legal in every state, including Texas, whether legislators and governors like it or not. In 2005, Texas physicians performed 74,399 abortions.[10]

The data indicate that the Texas parental consent requirement may be reducing the number of abortions performed on minors. After Texas began enforcing the consent requirement, the abortion rate for 15-year-olds fell by 11 percent. It fell by 20 percent among 16-year-olds and 16 percent among 17-year-olds. Ironically, the second-trimester abortion rate increased for 18-year-olds who became pregnant within six months of their eighteenth birthday, suggesting that some 17-year-olds were waiting to seek abortion services until they were no longer covered by the parental consent requirement.[11]

 WHAT IS YOUR OPINION?

Do you agree with the Texas law that forces a minor to have the written permission of a parent before she can have an abortion? Why or why not?

STATES AND FEDERAL LAW

Federal laws apply to state and local governments as long as Congress acts within the scope of its powers under the U.S. Constitution. Article I, Section 8, of the Constitution grants Congress authority to legislate in a range of policy areas, including trade, immigration, patent and copyright law, and national defense. In practice, Congress has made frequent use of the Interstate Commerce Clause as a basis for legislation affecting the states. The **Interstate Commerce Clause** is the constitutional provision giving Congress the authority to "regulate commerce . . . among the several states." Congress has used this constitutional provision as a basis for legislation dealing with such diverse subjects as cable television regulation, agricultural price supports, and racial discrimination.

The federal laws and regulations that have the greatest impact on state and local policymaking take the form of federal preemption and federal mandates. Federal preemption *prevents* states from adopting their own policies in selected policy areas, whereas federal mandates *require* certain state policy actions.

Federal Preemption

The federal government prevents state and local governments from making policy in some policy areas. An act of Congress adopting regulatory policies that overrule state policies in a particular regulatory area is known as a **federal preemption of state authority.** Congress has passed more than a hundred laws preempting state regulation, including preemption of state policies dealing with cellular phone rates, nuclear power safety, pension plans, and trucking rates.[12]

Preemption is controversial. The proponents of preemption believe that uniform national regulatory standards are preferable to state-by-state regulation. In contrast, critics of preemption contend that congressional efforts to override state authority violate states' rights principles that hold that state legislators know best what policies are most appropriate for their states.

Ironically, business interests, which often oppose regulation in general, typically support the federal preemption of state regulations. Firms doing business nationwide would rather adapt to a uniform national policy than conform to 50 different state regulations. As one state official put it, "A lot of . . . companies feel it is easier to work with Congress than 50 state legislatures."[13] Business interests would also prefer that Congress adopt a relatively mild nationwide regulatory standard than deal with tough regulations at the state level.

Federal Mandates

A **federal mandate** is a legal requirement placed on a state or local government by the national government requiring certain policy actions. The **Americans with Disabilities Act (ADA),** which is a federal law intended to end discrimination against persons with disabilities and to eliminate barriers preventing their full participation in American society, imposes a broad range of federal mandates. The ADA mandates that, when a new building goes up or an old building undergoes a major renovation, it must be made accessible to people with disabilities, and accommodations must be made for employees with disabilities. Because of the ADA, colleges and universities typically provide special assistance to students with disabilities, such as sign language interpreters for students who have hearing impairments and additional time to take exams for students with learning disabilities.

Interstate Commerce Clause The constitutional provision giving Congress authority to "regulate commerce . . . among the several states."

Federal preemption of state authority An act of Congress adopting regulatory policies that overrule state policies in a particular regulatory area.

Federal mandate A legal requirement placed on a state or local government by the national government requiring certain policy actions.

Americans with Disabilities Act (ADA) A federal law intended to end discrimination against disabled persons and eliminate barriers preventing their full participation in American society, imposes a broad range of federal mandates.

The ADA requires that public buildings be accessible to persons with disabilities.

No Child Left Behind Act
A federal law that requires state governments and local school districts to institute basic skills testing as a condition for receiving federal aid.

State and local government officials often resent federal mandates because they are sometimes so detailed that they force states to abandon their own policy innovations in favor of a one-size-fits-all federal prescription. Consider the **No Child Left Behind Act,** which is a federal law that requires state governments and local school districts to institute basic skills testing as a condition for receiving federal aid. The measure, which was named for a slogan used by the George W. Bush presidential campaign in 2000, forced states to administer tests in mathematics and language arts for students in grades 3 through 8 by the 2005–2006 school year. Schools must conduct science tests in grades 3 through 5, 6 through 9, and 10 through 12 by 2007–2008. The results of the tests must be used to assess school performance and track the progress of individual students.[14] In 2006, 624 Texas schools failed to show "adequate yearly progress" toward having all students pass state achievement tests in reading and math and graduate on time by 2014. A total of 186 Texas schools failed to meet the federal standard for the second year in a row, meaning that their students were eligible to transfer to better-performing campuses.[15] Poor-performing schools that fail to improve will eventually face the loss of federal aid money. State officials argue that No Child Left Behind is so complex that school officials will be forced to spend all of their time and money testing and tracking students rather than implementing the educational reforms they think will work best. Many professional educators also believe that the goal of having all students pass skill tests and graduate on time by 2014 is unrealistic.[16]

State officials also complain about cost shifting from the federal government to the states. The war on terror, for example, has become a major drain on the finances of state and local government. Because the nation's cities, power plants, bridges, refineries, and monuments are potential targets for terrorists, state and local authorities have been forced to increase security. They have also had to invest millions of dollars in training and equipment for police officers, firefighters, and other emergency responders, so that they will be ready in case of an attack. State officials believe that the cost of homeland security should be borne by the national government because national security has historically been a federal function. Nonetheless, the federal government has shifted most of the cost of homeland security to the states.

The National Conference of State Legislatures (NCSL) estimates that federal mandates cost the states $27 billion in 2007.[17] The most expensive programs for the states were the Disabilities Education Act, No Child Left Behind, prescription drug costs for people eligible for Medicaid or Medicare, the Help America Vote Act, federal environmental protection requirements, and the cost to states of incarcerating illegal immigrants.[18] The federal government projects the cost to states of implementing the Real ID Act at $23 billion spread over several years.[19]

FEDERAL GRANT PROGRAMS

Federal grant program A program through which the national government gives money to state and local governments to spend in accordance with set standards and conditions.

A **federal grant program** is a program through which the national government gives money to state and local governments to spend in accordance with set standards and conditions. In 2006, the federal government distributed $434 billion in federal grant money to state and local governments, 16.3 percent of the federal budget.[20] Nearly 90 percent of the funds went directly to state governments rather than localities, although much of that money was passed on by the state to local agencies for health and human services, housing and urban development, transportation, and education.[21] Between 2000 and 2006, for example, the federal government awarded $20 billion in grant money to the Texas Education Agency (TEA), which passed along most of the money to local school districts to support various programs.[22]

Program Adoption

Congress and the president adopt federal grant programs through the legislative process. Both houses of Congress must agree to establish a program and the president must either sign the legislation or allow it to become law without signature. If the president vetoes the measure, it can become law only if Congress votes to override the veto by a two-thirds' margin in each house.

Federal programs must be authorized and funds appropriated for their operation. The **authorization process** is the procedure through which Congress legislatively establishes a program, defines its general purpose, devises procedures for its operation,

Authorization process The procedure through which Congress legislatively establishes a program, defines its general purpose, devises procedures for its operation, specifies an agency implementation, and indicates an approximate level of funding.

specifies an agency for implementation, and indicates an approximate level of funding. The authorization process does not actually allocate money for the program. Congress sometimes specifies that programs be reauthorized periodically. The **appropriation process** is the procedure through which Congress legislatively provides money for a particular purpose. The appropriation process takes place annually.

The adoption of the Help America Vote Act of 2002 illustrates the distinction between authorization and appropriation. Congress passed, and President George W. Bush signed, the measure to reform state election systems after the debacle of the Florida presidential election controversy in 2000. The law requires states to maintain a database of registered voters, provide voting systems with minimum error rates, set voter identification requirements, provide access for people with disabilities, and draft procedures for resolving voter complaints.[23] Although the measure authorized $4 billion to cover the cost of new voting machines and other improvements, Congress failed to include the money in the annual appropriation bill, leaving the states to bear the cost of the measure on their own.[24]

Types of Federal Programs

Federal programs come in a variety of forms.

Categorical and Block Grants   A **categorical grant program** is a federal grant-in-aid program that provides funds to state and local governments for a fairly narrow, specific purpose, such as removing asbestos from school buildings or acquiring land

Appropriation process The procedure through which Congress legislatively provides money for a particular purpose.

Categorical grant program A federal grant-in-aid program that provides funds to state and local governments for a fairly narrow, specific purpose, such as removing asbestos from school buildings or acquiring land for outdoor recreation.

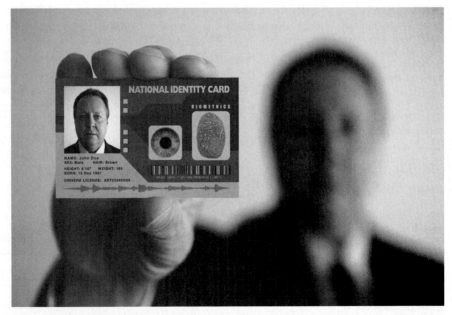

The Real ID Act establishes national standards for state-issued driver's licenses and identification cards for nondrivers.

for outdoor recreation. In this type of program, Congress allows state and local officials little discretion as to how money is spent. Categorical grants comprise 97 percent of all federal grants, accounting for 79 percent of federal grant money to state and local governments.[25]

A **block grant program** is a federal grant-in-aid program that provides money for a program in a broad, general policy area, such as elementary and secondary education or transportation. State and local governments have more discretion in spending block grant funds than they have for categorical grant money. For example, **Temporary Assistance for Needy Families (TANF)** is a federal block grant program that provides temporary financial assistance and work opportunities to needy families. The goal of the program is to move welfare families into the workforce. States have considerable leeway in designing their own programs, but if they fall short of federally mandated goals, such as the requirement that half of single parents receiving benefits must participate in a work activity program, they lose some federal funding.

Over time, Congress tends to attach conditions to the receipt of block grant funds, thus reducing the flexibility of state and local officials. When Congress and the president created the Surface Transportation Program in 1991, for example, they gave states a lump sum of money to spend on highways and other transportation projects in accordance with statewide objectives. Subsequently, Congress and the president have added restrictions, requiring that 10 percent of the funds be used to improve the safety of state highways and that 10 percent be spent on "transportation enhancement" activities, such as hike and bike trails.[26]

Policymakers disagree about the relative merits of categorical and block grants. The proponents of categorical grants argue that they enable Congress to identify particular policy problems and ensure that the money that Congress provides targets those problems. Categorical grants, they say, allow Congress to set national goals and apply national standards to achieve those goals. If local officials are given too much discretion, they may use grant money to reward campaign supporters or pay back political debts. In contrast, the proponents of block grants contend that state and local officeholders know better what their residents want and need than do officials in Washington, DC. Block grants enable the officials closest to the people to direct the federal dollars to where they will do the most good.

 WHAT IS YOUR OPINION?

If you were a member of Congress, would you prefer block grants or categorical grants?

Entitlement Programs   Some federal programs, including Medicaid, the School Lunch Program, and Unemployment Compensation, are **entitlement programs,** which are government programs providing benefits to all persons qualified to receive them under law. Congress sets eligibility standards based on such factors as age, income, and disability. Individuals who meet the criteria are entitled to receive the benefits.

Spending for entitlement programs does not go through the appropriation process. The amount of money the federal government spends each year on Medicaid

Block grant program A federal grant-in-aid program that provides money for a program in a broad, general policy area, such as elementary and secondary education, or transportation.

Temporary Assistance for Needy Families (TANF) A federal block grant program that provides temporary financial assistance and work opportunities to needy families.

Entitlement programs Government programs providing benefits to all persons qualified to receive them under law.

and other entitlement programs depends on the number of eligible recipients who apply for benefits and the cost of providing those benefits. If Congress and the president want to reduce (or increase) spending for an entitlement program, they must pass legislation to change the program.

Entitlement programs are controversial. The proponents of entitlement programs say that they represent a national commitment to address certain important policy issues, including healthcare for the poor and for people with disabilities (Medicaid), nutritious lunches for low-income school children (the School Lunch Program), and income security for unemployed workers (Unemployment Compensation). Program recipients do not have to depend on Congress and the president to appropriate money each year for their benefits because they are entitled to them by law. In contrast, the critics of entitlement programs charge that they are budget busters. Spending for entitlement programs goes up each year automatically as the number of beneficiaries rises and the cost of providing services increases, regardless of the budgetary situation. For example, state governments are hard pressed to keep up with the rapidly rising costs of the Medicaid program.

Project grant program A grant program that requires state and local governments to compete for available federal money.

Project and Formula Grants   Federal grants differ in the criteria by which funding is awarded. A **project grant program** is a grant program that requires state and local governments to compete for available federal money. State and local governments present detailed grant applications, which federal agencies evaluate in order to make funding decisions. The Department of Education, for example, administers project grants dealing with a range of educational initiatives, such as teacher training, math and science education, and preparation of students for the demands of today's workforce. Public schools, colleges, and universities make application to the agency, which then decides which grant proposals merit funding.

Formula grant program A grant program that awards funding on the basis of a formula established by Congress.

A **formula grant program** is a grant program that awards funding on the basis of a formula established by Congress. In contrast to project grants, formula grants provide money for every state and/or locality that qualifies under the formula. The Clean Fuels Formula Grant Program, administered by the Department of Transportation, allocates money to transit authorities to assist in the purchase and use of low-emissions buses and related equipment. The program awards funds based on a formula that includes area population, the size of the bus fleet, the number of bus passenger miles, and the severity of the area's air pollution problem.[27]

Grant Conditions

Matching funds requirement A legislative provision that the national government will provide grant money for a particular activity only on condition that the state or local government involved supply a certain percentage of the total money required for the project or program.

Federal grants usually come with conditions. A **matching funds requirement** is a legislative provision that the national government will provide grant money for a particular activity only on the condition that the state or local government involved supply a certain percentage of the total money required for the project or program. For example, if the total cost of a sewage treatment plant in Laredo is $20 million, the national government may supply $16 million (80 percent) while requiring the city to match the federal money with $4 million of local funds (20 percent). Even federal programs that do not require financial participation by state and local governments often require contributions in-kind. The national government covers

Food Stamp Program A federal program that provides vouchers to low-income families and individuals that can be used to purchase food.

the entire cost of the **Food Stamp Program,** which is a federal program that provides vouchers to low-income families and individuals that can be used to purchase food, but state governments must administer its operation.

Congress imposes legislative mandates on the recipients of federal funds. Some mandates apply to grant recipients in general. These include provisions in the area of equal rights, equal access for people with disabilities, environmental protection, historic preservation, and union wage rates for construction workers on federally funded projects. Furthermore, many individual programs have particular strings attached. For example, in order to receive money from the Violent Crime Control and Enforcement Act of 1994 to construct, expand, and operate correctional facilities, states had to adopt "truth in sentencing" laws that accurately showed the amount of time persons convicted of crimes would spend behind bars. States had to ensure that violent criminals served at least 85 percent of their prison sentences. The federal government also required states to impose stiff penalties for criminal offenders and adopt programs to protect the rights of crime victims.[28]

The School Lunch Program is a federal program that provides free or inexpensive lunches to children from poor families.

Congress sometimes uses federal grant money to compel states to adopt policies favored in Washington, although not necessarily in state capitals. In the 1970s and 1980s, Congress threatened states with the loss of federal highway grant money unless they adopted the 55-miles-per-hour speed limit and raised their minimum legal drinking age to 21. Although Congress has dropped the speed limit requirement, it now requires that states ban open containers and revoke the driver's licenses of repeat DUI offenders. If states fail to comply with the open container ban and driver's license revocation rule, the federal government transfers a portion of their highway construction money into a fund that can be used only for highway safety.

Congress initially took an incentive approach to setting a national blood-alcohol content standard of 0.08 for determining whether a driver is legally intoxicated. Although some states already followed the 0.08 standard, most states, including Texas, had set the drunk-driving level at a blood-alcohol content of 0.10. Instead of penalizing states that failed to adopt the 0.08 standard with the loss of federal money, Congress established a fund to pay a cash bonus to states that voluntarily adopted the tougher blood-alcohol standard. Two years later, however, Congress decided that the incentive plan was not working well enough, so it adopted legislation mandating the loss of highway funds for states that failed to adopt the 0.08 standard. Although most states (including Texas) complied with the federal requirement rather than risk the loss of highway funding, state officials complained about Congress forcing its policy preferences on the states. "If states want 0.08, that's fine," said an Iowa legislator, "[but] if Congress says you have to have it, they've [sic] overstepped their bounds."[29]

States that fail to follow federal rules risk the loss of federal funds. In 2005, for example, the U.S. Department of Education fined Texas for violating the requirements of No Child Left Behind. The Department of Education punished Texas because the state exceeded the cap on how many students with learning disabilities could be exempted from regular testing. The federal government allows states to exempt 1 percent of their students from taking the regular test because of learning disabilities. Texas exempted about 9 percent of its students. As a result, Texas test scores were higher than they would have been otherwise, allowing more schools to meet the achievement goals established by No Child Left Behind.[30]

Federal Money and Texas

State and local governments in Texas receive billions of dollars in federal funds annually. Federal aid accounts for 18 percent of combined state and local revenue in the state, with federal grants providing money to the state for healthcare and nutrition for low-income families, highway construction, and homeland security and emergency preparedness.[31] The state's school districts receive federal grant funds for special education, bilingual education, and the School Lunch Program. Federal money flows to Texas cities for such activities as sewage treatment plant construction, parkland acquisition, neighborhood revitalization, and airport construction. In 2005, for example, Congress passed, and President Bush signed, legislation to allocate $286.4 billion to the states from the federal Highway Trust Fund for the period covering 2004 through 2009. Texas received more than $14 billion in highway funds, as well as $669 million designated for priority highway and transit projects in the state.[32]

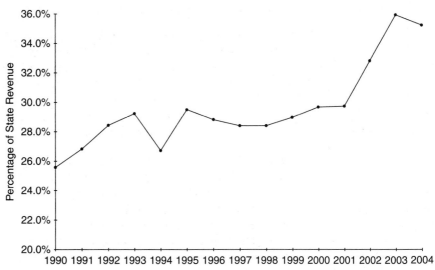

FIGURE 20.1   Federal Funds as Percentage of State Revenue.
Source: Texas Comptroller of Public Accounts.

**Pork barrel
spending**
Expenditures to fund
local projects that are
not critically
important from a
national perspective.

Furthermore, Congress includes billions of dollars worth of special projects for states and localities in the annual appropriation bill. Critics call these projects **pork barrel spending,** which are expenditures to fund local projects that are not critically important from a national perspective. The 2006 appropriation bill contained $403 million in special projects for Texas, including a million dollars to fund a flywheel bus and truck program at the University of Texas at Austin and a quarter million dollars to renovate the Globe Theater in Odessa.[33]

Figure 20.1 documents the growth in federal aid to state government in Texas between 1990 and 2004. The relative importance of federal funding to state government in Texas grew from 1990 through 2003, increasing from less than 26 percent in 1990 to 36 percent in 2003. Since then, the relative importance of federal money has somewhat declined. Growth in the Medicaid program accounted for more than 40 percent of the increase in federal grant funds during the period, but it was not the only federal program to grow. Funding for three-fourths of federal programs increased during the 1990s, including money for programs dealing with natural resources and the environment, transportation, community and regional development, income security, and education and training.[34]

CONCLUSION: THE FEDERAL SYSTEM AND THE POLICY PROCESS

The federal system affects every stage of the policymaking process in Texas.

Agenda Building

The federal government frequently raises issues that must be addressed by state and local government in Texas. *Brown v. Board of Education of Topeka* and subsequent

federal court cases dealing with school desegregation forced the state and its school
districts to desegregate the public schools. Prison reform became a major item on the
state's official policy agenda only after *Ruiz v. Estelle*. The federal Clean Air Act requires Texas to address air pollution problems. Texas must revise its procedures for issuing driver's licenses because of the Real ID Act. It is unlikely that any of these
issues would have become part of the official policy agenda in Texas when they did
and in the form they did were it not for federal action.

Policy Formulation and Adoption

The federal system affects policy formulation. The consideration of policy options by
state and local officials often depends on the availability of federal funds and the limitations imposed by federal guidelines. About a fourth of the total state budget is written
to conform to federal mandates, to provide matching funds for federal programs, or to
comply with federal court orders.[35] Furthermore, state and local policymakers typically
design policies dealing with health, welfare, law enforcement, education, job training,
prison management, and other areas with the goal of increasing federal funding.

The federal government influences state policy adoption. Most states, including
Texas, raised their drinking ages to 21 and lowered their speed limits to 55 mph because Congress threatened them with the loss of federal highway grant money,
should they do otherwise. Texas adopted a testing program for automobile emissions
in order to comply with federal clean air requirements.

Policy Implementation and Evaluation

The federal system affects policy implementation. When a state or local government accepts federal funds, it must agree to follow federal guidelines in program
implementation, such as filing an environmental impact statement for construction

projects, paying union wage scale to contract workers, and ensuring accessibility for persons with disabilities. Because most major policy areas in Texas (including education, transportation, and healthcare) involve at least some federal money, federal regulations have a major impact on policy implementation. Because of the Real ID Act, Texas is changing its driver's licensing procedures.

State and local governments implement many federal programs. Congress sets program goals, establishes guidelines, and then charges the states with implementation. State governments enjoy the leeway to implement the programs as they see fit within the guidelines set by the federal government. Consider the federal Clean Air Act. The law requires Texas to reduce pollution to meet federal air quality standards, but the federal government does not specify the steps Texas must take to achieve the goal. Texas has leeway to develop a plan to meet local needs as long as the plan reduces pollution enough to meet the standard.

Finally, the federal system influences policy evaluation. Federal officials act as policy evaluators, determining whether grant proposals merit continued funding or if state policies are constitutional. Furthermore, state policymakers often judge policies on the number of federal dollars they are able to bring to the state or whether the policies can pass muster when challenged in federal court.

LET'S DEBATE

Does Texas Law Restrict Access to Abortion Too Much or Not Enough?

Overview: Texas has been at the forefront of the nation's abortion wars. In 1973, Jane Roe sued the state to challenge the constitutionality of its abortion laws, and the result of her suit was the landmark U.S. Supreme Court ruling *Roe v. Wade*. This *Roe* decision sparked a furious national and state debate while creating deep political divisions over the issue of abortion rights. Immediately, many states, including Texas, began to consider legislation to circumvent the ruling. Since *Roe*, the Supreme Court has retrenched on expansive abortion rights. For example, the Court has upheld state legislation that both prohibits the use of public facilities to perform abortions and mandates a required 24-hour "reflection" period before the performance of the abortion procedure. The Court has also upheld regulations prohibiting healthcare providers from receiving federal funds from referring or counseling patients on abortion rights. With each new decision, many states adjust their abortion law accordingly.

Abortion plays a large part in Texas politics. Both pro-life and pro-choice groups vigorously lobby the state legislature with the hope of changing abortion regulations, and over the years it is the pro-life lobby that has prevailed. Since *Roe*, Texas law has been brought slowly into conformity with the policy preferences of the pro-life, yet the majority of Texas citizens either consider themselves pro-choice or are agnostic on the issue. According to a 2005 Survey USA poll, 52 percent of all Texans consider themselves pro-choice, and national polls also reflect this split. Detailed research by the American Enterprise Institute shows that attitudes regarding abortion have been stable over time, with public opinion hovering around the 50 percent mark. The research shows that, during the 30 years since *Roe*, the majority generally favors those with pro-choice views. Why, then, if a majority favors relatively free abortion access, have Texas lawmakers seen fit to act in the fashion of those states with a majority of pro-life citizens?

continued on next page

No one can read the minds of legislators, but a 2005 Gallup/CNN/*USA Today* poll shows that a majority of Americans, even those who are pro-choice, tend to favor legislation that mandates provisions such as parental notification and consent and the notification of husbands prior to the abortion procedure. Additionally, many major Texas abortion regulations are not a result of direct legislation. For example, the ban on third-trimester abortions and parental notification provisions were amendments to the 2005 Board of Medical Examiners Sunset Bill, and the defunding of state clinics was the result of a rider to the state's 2003 budget bill. Nevertheless, proponents of either side of the issue are sure of the justness of their cause, and any reconciliation or compromise on this issue seems unlikely anytime soon.

Arguments That Texas Abortion Law Is Becoming More Restrictive

❏ **2003's Prental Projection Act may allow for the legal redefinition of a fetus.** This act defines a fetus as a victim in the event of a violent crime. It is plausible that future judicial interpretation could construe the language of this act to further redefine a fetus to be an unborn child—it is then only a small step to legally define a fetus as a human being and further restrict abortion access.

❏ **The state's Woman's Right to Know Act unduly restricts abortion access.** The Woman's Right to Know Act mandates that a woman seeking an abortion get counseling (some of this counseling regarding the connection between abortion and breast cancer may be based on dubious science) and then wait 24 hours to "reflect" on her choice. This has the effect of prolonging an already emotionally painful process and could prevent a woman from exercising her choice rights and acting in her own perceived best interest.

❏ **Abortion regulations passed during the Texas legislature's 2005 session further restrict abortion access.** During the 79th Legislative Session, the state placed increased restrictions on the ability of a woman to have a third-trimester abortion—the legislation narrowed the definition of severe physical impairment and removed the mental health exception. Additionally, the state mandated parental-consent notification for pregnant minors and penalizes physicians who perform the procedure. As of 2006, Texas abortion law is becoming increasingly restrictive.

Arguments That Texas Abortion Law Is Not Restrictive

❏ **Abortion regulations enacted during the 2005 legislative session are reasonable.** The legislation simply prohibits the abortion of a viable fetus in the third trimester unless a mother's life is in danger. After all, babies born during the third trimester have a 50 percent chance of survival. Parental notification is not unreasonable for nonemergency situations because Texas hospitals require parental notification and consent to perform medical procedures on unemancipated minors. Why should abortion be any different?

❏ **No right is absolute.** Texas abortion law is simply responding and conforming to evolving abortion case law. The Texas legislature represents the will of its constituents, and the citizens of Texas are free to change abortion law by electing legislators who share their views. The state's elected representatives are merely adjusting the definition of abortion rights to conform to evolving standards set forth by the U.S. Supreme Court.

❏ **Defunding state support of abortion is fair.** Rider 8, enacted in 2003, prohibits the state from funding entities that perform or refer abortions. If having an abortion is a "personal choice," and in most cases is considered an "elective procedure," why should others have to pay for it? This type of regulation does not restrict access but enforces accountability for those who choose to have an abortion.

QUESTIONS

1. Is the issue of abortion one of civil rights? If it is, shouldn't the state follow the nation's lead in expanding and broadening our civil rights and liberties?
2. Is the issue of abortion one of human life? If an unborn baby can live outside its mother's womb after six months' gestation, shouldn't it be afforded protection?

SELECT READINGS

1. Robert Baird and Stuart E. Rosenbawm, eds., *The Ethics of Abortion: Pro-Life vs. Pro-Choice* (Amherst, NY: Prometheus Books, 2001).
2. Cynthia Gorney, *Articles of Faith: A Frontline History of the Abortion Wars* (New York: Simon and Schuster, 2000).

SELECT WEBSITES

1. **www.plannedparenthood.org/pp2/tcr/ ;jsessionid=11B9A2A7D80AB67B3B39B861F32F8916** Website for the Texas Region's Planned Parenthood Chapter.
2. **www.texasrighttolife.com/home_3.php** Website for Texas Right to Life—Texas's oldest and only statewide pro-life organization.

KEY TERMS

Americans with Disabilities Act (ADA)
appropriation process
authorization process
blame avoidance
block grant program
budget deficit
categorical grant program
Children's Health Insurance Program (CHIP)
dual school system
entitlement programs
Equal Protection Clause

federal grant program
federal mandate
federal preemption of state authority
federal system *or* federation
Food Stamp Program
formula grant program
global warming
Interstate Commerce Clause
local governments
matching funds requirement
Medicaid

National Association for the Advancement of Colored People (NAACP)
National Supremacy Clause
No Child Left Behind Act
parole
pork barrel spending
project grant program
sovereignty
Temporary Assistance for Needy Families (TANF)

NOTES

1. Public Law 109–13.
2. State Senator Leticia Van de Putte, Media Advisory, available at www.vandeputte.sentate.state.tx.us.
3. Trinity D. Tomsic, "Managing Medicaid in Tough Times," *State Legislatures,* June 2002, pp. 13–17.
4. Jad Jouawad and Jeremy W. Peters, "California Plan to Cut Gases Splits Industry," *New York Times,* September 1, 2006, available at www.nytimes.com.
5. Justin Blum, "Stepping In Where Uncle Sam Refuses to Tread," *Washington Post National Weekly Edition,* January 30–February 5, 2006, p. 18.
6. *Brown v. Board of Education of Topeka,* 347 U.S. 483 (1954).
7. *Ruiz v. Estelle,* 503 F. Supp 1265 (S.D. Tex 1980); 679 F 2d 115 (5th Cir. 1982).
8. *Roe v. Wade,* 410 U.S. 113 (1973).
9. *Planned Parenthood of Southeastern Pennsylvania v. Casey,* 505 U.S. 833 (1992).
10. Texas Department of State Health Services, *Vital Statistics 2005 Annual Report,* available at www.dshs.state.tx.us.
11. Theodore Joyce, Robert Kaestner, and Silvie Colman, "Changes in Abortions and Births and the Texas Parental Notification Law," *New England Journal of Medicine* 354 (March 2006): 1031–1038.
12. Joseph F. Zimmerman, "The Nature and Political Significance of Preemption," *PS: Political Science & Politics,* July 2005, p. 361.
13. Idaho Attorney General Jim Jones, quoted in Martha M. Hamilton, "On Second Thought, We'd Prefer the Feds on Our Backs," *Washington Post National Weekly Edition,* December 14, 1987, p. 32.
14. Public Law 107–110.
15. Jennifer Radcliffe, "State Progress Report Fails Three Area School Districts," *Houston Chronicle,* August 18, 2006, available at www.chron.com.

16. Sam Dillon, "Schools Slow in Closing Gaps Between Races," *New York Times*, November 20, 2006, available at www.nytimes.com.

17. National Conference of State Legislatures, "Mandate Monitor," January 2007, available at www.ncsl.org.

18. Molly Stauffer and Carl Tubbesing, "The Mandate Monster," *State Legislatures*, May 2004, pp. 22–23.

19. Suzanne Gamboa, "Senators Call for Real ID Overhaul," *Dallas Morning News*, March 27, 2007, available at www.dallasnews.com.

20. Office of Management and Budget, "Summary Comparison of Total Outlays for Grants to State and Local Governments: 1940–2012," *The Budget for Fiscal Year 2008, Historical Tables*, available at www.omb.gov.

21. "Federal Aid to States and Localities," *Governing State and Local Source Book, 2006*, p. 32.

22. Bennett Goth, "Texas Near the Top for Raking in Federal Dollars," *Houston Chronicle*, October 9, 2007, available at www.chron.com.

23. Public Law 107-252.

24. Alan Greenblatt, "Squeezing the Federal Turnip," *Governing*, March 2003, p. 29.

25. Robert J. Dilger, "The Study of American Federalism at the Turn of the Century," *State and Local Government Review* 32 (Spring 2000): p. 103.

26. Transportation Equity Act for the Twenty-first Century, available at www.fhwa.dot.gov.

27. Department of Transportation, "Fact Sheet: Clean Fuels Formula Grant Program," available at www.fhwa.dot.gov/tea21/factsheets/clnfuel.htm.

28. Public Law 103–322.

29. Anya Sostek, "Slow to Toe the DUI Line," *Governing*, May 2003, p. 42.

30. Sam Dillon, "Texas Officials Shrug Off Fine over Bush Law," *New York Times*, April 26, 2005, available at www.nytimes.com.

31. "Federal Aid to States and Localities," *Governing State and Local Source Book, 2006*, p. 32.

32. Gary Martin, "Texas Bringing Home $669 Million for Road Projects," *San Antonio Express News*, July 30, 2005, available at www.mysanantonio.com.

33. Samantha Levine, "Texas Ranks 4th in Amount of 'Pork-Barrel' Spending," *Houston Chronicle*, April 6, 2006, p. A5.

34. Dilger, "The Study of American Federalism at the Turn of the Century," p. 100.

35. House Research Organization, *Writing the State Budget*, 80th *Legislature*, February, 2007, available at www.hro.house.state.tx.us.

Chapter 21
Political Participation in Texas

CHAPTER OUTLINE

LEARNING OUTCOMES

After studying Chapter 21, students should be able to do the following:

▸ Trace the history of voting rights in Texas, explaining the significance of the poll tax, white primary, and *Smith v. Allwright* in the struggle for minority voting rights in Texas. (pp. 560–564)

▸ Identify the various means by which individuals can participate in the policymaking process. (pp. 564–568)

▸ Compare voter participation rates in Texas with participation rates in other states. (p. 568)

▸ Explain why participation rates in Texas are relatively low compared with other states. (pp. 568–570)

▸ Describe variations in participation rates based on income, age, race/ethnicity, and gender. (p. 571)

▸ Compare and contrast the Texas electorate with the state's total population in terms of income, education, and age. (pp. 571–574)

▸ Describe the role of participation in the policymaking process. (pp. 574–576)

▸ Define the key terms listed on pages 578–579 and explain their significance.

M ost Texans do not vote. In 2006, only 26 percent of the voting age population participated in the state's gubernatorial election despite a ballot full of well-known and colorful candidates. Voters could choose from among Republican Governor Rick Perry, who was seeking reelection; Democrat Chris Bell, a former member of Congress; Comptroller Carole Keeton Strayhorn, a Republican running as an independent; humorist and novelist Kinky Friedman, running as an independent; and Libertarian James Weaver. Perry won with just 39 percent of the vote. (The candidate with the most votes wins a general election even if that candidate falls short of a majority.) Perry's total represented a meager 13 percent of registered voters and a tiny 10 percent of the voting age population.[1]

This is the first of four chapters dealing with participation in the policymaking process in Texas. Each chapter considers who participates in the policymaking process, how participation takes place, and what effect participation has on policy. This chapter examines individual participation, focusing primarily on voting and voting rights. The chapter considers why voter turnout is low in Texas and the impact of that on the policymaking process. Chapter 22 looks at interest groups, Chapter 23 considers political parties, and Chapter 24 deals with elections.

VOTING RIGHTS AND MINORITY PARTICIPATION

Only white males enjoyed the right to vote when Texas joined the Union in 1845. Much of the subsequent history of the state is the story of the efforts of women and the members of racial and ethnic minority groups to gain the right to vote and participate meaningfully in Texas politics.

Women's Suffrage

In the nineteenth century, politics was a man's world, not just in Texas but in the entire United States. The women's rights movement began in the North in the 1840s as an offshoot of the abolition movement, which was a political reform effort in early nineteenth-century America whose goal was the elimination of slavery. In Texas, the weakness of the abolition movement hindered the cause of women's rights. The drive for women's **suffrage**—that is, the right to vote—did not begin to pick up steam in the state until 1903 with the founding of the Texas Woman Suffrage Association. In 1915, the state legislature narrowly rejected an amendment to the Texas Constitution calling for women's suffrage. Three years later, the legislature approved a law allowing women to vote in primary elections. Finally, in 1919, the U.S. Congress proposed a constitutional amendment granting women the right to vote nationwide. Texas was the first state in the South to ratify the Nineteenth Amendment, which became law in 1920, giving women in Texas and all across America the right to vote.[2]

Suffrage The right to vote.

Minority Voting Rights

Winning the right to vote and having that vote counted was a more elusive goal for Texans of African and Hispanic descent than it was for women.

African American Enfranchisement After the Civil War Before the Civil War, nearly all African Americans who lived in Texas were slaves; none could vote or hold public office. The war ended slavery, but the state's white political establishment refused to enfranchise former slaves. (**Franchise** is the right to vote; to **enfranchise** means to grant the right to vote.) The Texas Constitution of 1866, written under President Andrew Johnson's Reconstruction plan, denied African Americans the right to vote and hold public office. The U.S. Congress, however, refused to accept the Johnson plan for Reconstruction. In 1867, Congress passed legislation over Johnson's veto that placed the South under military rule and forced southern states to grant African Americans the right to vote.

Franchise The right to vote.

Enfranchise To grant the right to vote.

African Americans registered to vote for the first time in Texas in 1867. The following year, they cast ballots in an election to select delegates to a state constitutional convention. Of the 90 delegates chosen, 9 were African American men, all of whom were Republicans. In 1869, African American voters helped elect E. J. Davis governor. In the same election, 11 African Americans won seats in the state legislature.

After the early 1870s, Texas politics began to return to the pattern in place before the Civil War. The Democratic Party regained control of the legislature in the 1872 election and recaptured the governor's mansion a year later. Meanwhile, some white Texans organized chapters of the Ku Klux Klan to threaten and intimidate African American leaders. The Klan sometimes resorted to violence to assert white control.

Nonetheless, African Americans continued to participate in Texas politics. Six African Americans were among the delegates elected to the constitutional convention of 1875. Furthermore, with the exception of the legislature elected in 1887, all legislatures chosen from 1868 through 1894 included African American members. All told, 41 African Americans served in the Texas legislature between 1868 and 1900.[3]

Minority Disfranchisement In the early twentieth century, the white establishment in Texas restricted the voting rights of minorities in order to maintain political power. After Reconstruction, Texas was a one-party state. The Democratic Party, which was controlled by wealthy economic interests, held virtually every elective office in the state. **Disfranchisement,** the denial of voting rights, was the response of the political establishment to the attempt of the Populist Party to win power by uniting lower-income voters of all races against the wealthy economic interests that controlled state politics. Conservative political leaders in Texas (and throughout the South) used racial issues to divide the working class along racial lines. They hoped to ensure their long-term control of state government by disfranchising African Americans (as well as many poor whites and Latinos).[4]

Disfranchisement The denial of voting rights.

The poll tax and the white primary were the main instruments of disfranchisement. The **poll tax,** which was a tax that prospective voters had to pay in order to register to vote, kept low-income people of all races from voting. In 1902, the Texas legislature proposed and the voters passed a state constitutional amendment requiring a poll tax of $1.50 or $1.75 a year (depending on the county), not an insignificant sum in early twentieth-century Texas. (In today's value, the poll tax would be $30 or $35.) Before the implementation of the poll tax, more than 60 percent of voting-age Texans typically participated in presidential elections. In contrast,

Poll tax A tax that prospective voters had to pay in order to register to vote.

election turnout dipped to 30 percent of voting age adults in 1904 after the poll tax went into effect.[5]

White primary An election system that prohibited African Americans from voting in Democratic primary elections, ensuring that white voters would control the Democratic Party.

The **white primary,** which was an election system that prohibited African Americans from voting in Democratic primary elections, ensured that white voters would control the Democratic Party. In 1903, the state Democratic Party executive committee suggested that all county party committees exclude African Americans from party primary elections. A **primary election** is an intraparty election during which a party's candidates for the general election are chosen. By the 1920s, most counties with significant African American populations were using the white primary and in 1924 the Texas legislature adopted the procedure statewide. Because the Democratic Party dominated Texas politics in those days, the Democratic primary was the most important election in the state. Whoever won the primary election invariably won the general election. Consequently, the exclusion of African Americans from participation in the Democratic primary barred them not only from influence in Democratic Party politics but also from meaningful participation in Texas politics in general.

Primary election An intraparty election during which a party's candidates for the general election are chosen.

Boss Control in South Texas   Although the white primary did not keep Latinos from the ballot box, political bosses often controlled their votes. In heavily Hispanic South Texas, in particular, ranch owners (some of whom were Latino) controlled both local economies and local politics. The boss would pay the poll tax for his workers (most of which were Latino) and then instruct them how to vote. With their jobs depending on it, the workers had little choice but to do as they were told.

Many Texans know the story of George Parr, the so-called Duke of Duval County, which is located in South Texas just west of Corpus Christi. For years, Parr

Texans once had to pay a poll tax in order to register to vote.

ran Duval County as his own political kingdom. The most famous example of Parr's influence came in 1948 when a young member of Congress named Lyndon B. Johnson ran for the U.S. Senate against former governor Coke Stevenson. Parr supported Johnson, but the day after the election it appeared that Stevenson had won the statewide vote by a razor-thin margin. One ballot box remained uncounted, however, Box 13 in neighboring Jim Wells County, where Parr's influence extended. Johnson won Box 13 almost unanimously and "Landslide Lyndon" became an 87-vote winner. Remarkably, 200 voters at Box 13 arrived to cast their ballots in alphabetical order. The affair still inspires deathbed confessions.[6]

The Struggle for Minority Voting Rights   African Americans in Texas turned to the federal courts for help in regaining the right to vote. Lawrence A. Nixon, an El Paso physician, challenged the constitutionality of the Texas White Primary Law in federal court. In 1927, the U.S. Supreme Court unanimously struck down the law as a "direct and obvious infringement" of the Equal Protection Clause of the Fourteenth Amendment to the U.S. Constitution.[7]

The Texas legislature responded to the ruling by repealing the White Primary Law and replacing it with a statute allowing the executive committee of each political party to "prescribe the qualifications of its own members." The executive committee of the state Democratic Party then declared that only whites could vote in Democratic primary elections. Dr. Nixon again carried the fight to the U.S. Supreme Court and once again the Court invalidated the Texas law. The vote on the Court was close, however, 5–4.[8]

Next, the legislature repealed all laws dealing with primary elections, and the Texas Democratic Party declared itself a private organization whose membership was exclusively white. Only party members could vote in Democratic primary elections. African Americans again turned to the federal courts, with Richard R. Grovey, a Houston barbershop owner, filing suit. This time, however, the courts refused to help. In 1935, the U.S. Supreme Court unanimously upheld the white primary on grounds that the state of Texas was not involved. The Court ruled that the Fourteenth Amendment did not apply to the Democratic Party because the party was a private organization.[9]

The white primary survived until 1944 when the U.S. Supreme Court decided *Smith v. Allwright*, reversing its earlier ruling. This case involved a suit brought by Lonnie Smith, a Houston dentist who was an African American community leader and political activist. The Court ruled eight to one that the Democratic Party acted as an agent of the state when it conducted primary elections. Consequently, the Court declared, the exclusion of African Americans from the Democratic primary was an unconstitutional violation of the Fifteenth Amendment to the U.S. Constitution, which grants African Americans the right to vote.[10]

The white primary was history, but other forms of voting discrimination persisted. In Fort Bend County, for example, white officials arranged a whites-only pre-primary called the Jaybird primary. White voters would cast their ballots for the winner of the Jaybird primary in the regular Democratic primary, thus minimizing the impact of the African American vote. The U.S. Supreme Court overturned this procedure in 1953.[11]

The poll tax was the next to fall. In 1962, the U.S. Congress proposed a constitutional amendment to prohibit poll taxes in elections for the presidency or Congress. When it was ratified as the Twenty-fourth Amendment in 1964, the Texas poll tax could be collected only for state and local elections. Two years later, the U.S. Supreme Court struck that down as well as a violation of the Equal Protection Clause of the Fourteenth Amendment.[12] The poll tax was now just as dead as the white primary.

The Texas legislature and the governor responded to the loss of the poll tax by establishing the most difficult and restrictive system of voter registration in the nation. Prospective voters had to register between October 1 and January 31 each year. Anyone who lacked the foresight to sign up three months before the spring primaries and nine months before the November general election was out of luck. In practice, this system worked against poor persons of all races. It survived until 1971, when, as with so many other Texas election procedures, it was struck down by the federal courts.[13]

PARTICIPATION IN TEXAS POLITICS

Democracy A system of government in which the people hold ultimate political power.

A **democracy** is a system of government in which the people hold ultimate political power. Most political scientists believe that a successful democracy depends on citizen participation in the policymaking process.

Forms of Participation

Individual Texans can participate in the policy process in a number of ways: voting, campaigning, joining political groups, contacting public officials, and participating in protest demonstrations and unconventional political acts.

Voting   To vote in Texas, individuals must be 18 years of age as of the next election, American citizens (either native-born or naturalized), and residents of Texas. Newcomers need not wait to establish residency; anyone who has a Texas home address is eligible to vote, including students who may be living in the state temporarily to attend college. Persons who have been declared mentally incapacitated by the final judgment of a court of law are disqualified from voting. Individuals who have been convicted of serious crimes (felonies) lose the right to vote as well, at least temporarily. Convicted criminals in Texas are eligible to vote again after they have fully completed their sentences, including time served on probation or parole. (**Probation** is the suspension of a sentence, permitting the defendant to remain free under court supervision, whereas **parole** is the conditional release of convicted offenders from prison to serve the remainder of their sentences in the community under supervision.)

Probation The suspension of a sentence, permitting the defendant to remain free under court supervision.

Parole The conditional release of convicted offenders from prison to serve the remainder of their sentences in the community under supervision.

Individuals must register before they can vote. Registration becomes effective 30 days after an application is received, so prospective voters must apply at least a month before the election in which they want to cast a ballot. Either the county tax assessor-collector's office or, in smaller counties, the county clerk or an election administrator handles voter registration. Voter registration applications are readily available in driver's license offices, libraries, and other government offices and public places. They are printed in both English and Spanish; are easy to complete; and require only a person's name, gender, birth date, address, court of naturalization

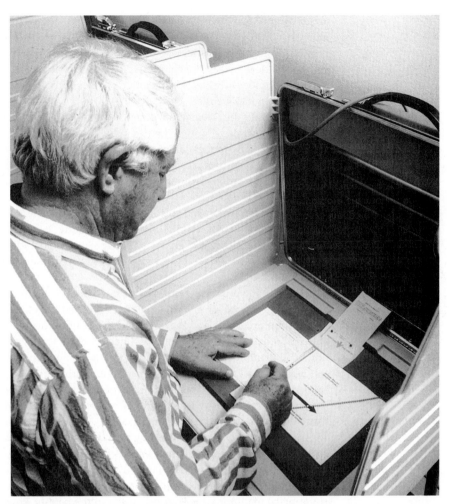

In 2002, the number of voters aged 65 or older outnumbered younger voters below the age of 30 by a 2–1 margin.

(if applicable), and signature. Voter registration applications are available online as well at the following Internet address: www.sos.state.tx.us/elections/forms/vr17.pdf.

Voter registration is permanent as long as voters keep their addresses current with county election officials. People who change addresses within the same county may return to their old polling place to vote for 90 days after their move. Every two years, however, county election officials mail out new voter registration certificates and purge the voter rolls of the names of people who are no longer at their listed addresses. Consequently, people who move must take the initiative to report changes of address in order to remain registered. Texans who relocate from one county to another must register again in their new county of residence. People who lose their voter certificates can request replacements from county election officials.

Voters cast their ballots in election precincts near their homes. An **election precinct** is a voting district. Rural counties may have only a handful of precincts, but

Election precinct
An election district.

urban counties have hundreds. Harris County, the state's most populous county, has more than 900 election precincts. Precinct polling places are typically located in public buildings, such as schools or fire stations. Newspapers usually print a list of polling locations a day or so before an election. Prospective voters can also learn the polling place for their election precinct by telephoning the county clerk's office or checking a county website.

Republicans and Democrats disagree on voting procedures. Under current law, citizens are allowed to vote when they present their voter registration cards to an election worker. Republican members of the Texas legislature want to change the law to require prospective voters to present either a photo identification card or two forms of identification without a photo, such as a bank statement, library card, or fishing license. Republicans say the identification requirement is necessary to prevent voter fraud. Democrats, meanwhile, declare that the real goal of the Republicans is to discourage ethnic minorities, elderly people, and the poor from participating because these groups typically vote Democratic. Voter impersonation is not a problem in Texas. At any rate, they say, someone wanting to commit voter fraud could easily purchase a forged picture ID.

Texans can vote early if they wish. State law once limited early voting (formerly called absentee voting) to individuals who planned to be out of town on the day of the election or at least *said* they planned to be out of town—some people voted absentee in order to avoid Election Day lines. In 1987, the legislature revised the election code to allow people to vote early without having to give an explanation, and many Texans now take advantage of no-excuse early voting. The period for early voting begins 17 days before an election and ends 4 days before. Locations for early voting may be limited to the county clerk's office at the courthouse or a handful of branch offices located throughout the county.

It is also possible to vote early by mail. Individuals who expect to be out of the county on the day of the election and during the early voting period may write the county clerk's office and request a mail ballot. People age 65 and older and those who are disabled or ill may vote by mail as well. Students away at school have the option of voting by mail or registering and voting in the county where they attend classes. Nearly 40 percent of the people who participated in the November 2006 general election for governor voted early.[14]

Early voting affects both the composition of the electorate and the strategy of election campaigns. Research shows that early voting increases election turnout by less physically active older adults who might have difficulty getting to the polls on Election Day.[15] With so many people casting their ballots early, early voting has turned Election Day into an election period, forcing candidates to advertise earlier and perhaps longer than they did before early voting.[16] Candidates can also take advantage of early voting by organizing early get-out-the-vote drives. Because state law requires election officials to keep a running list of who has voted early and who has not, campaigns can concentrate on getting people to the polls who are most likely to be their supporters.

Campaigning   People take part in politics by working on election campaigns. Although this is the age of television campaigns and the Internet, volunteers still have a place in election campaigns. Underfinanced campaigns can often compensate for a lack of money with well-organized volunteer efforts. Many local election contests rely almost exclusively on volunteers. Even well-funded campaigns can put volunteers to good use in contacting prospective voters and encouraging them to go to the polls.

Campaigns ask volunteers to do work that demands energy and attention to detail. Volunteers often help with mass mailings. Although campaign professionals believe that direct mail is an effective means for getting a candidate's message across, sending letters and campaign literature to thousands of potential voters is a huge job. Computers can do the work, but that approach is expensive. Consequently, many campaigns use volunteers to flare envelopes, fold literature, stuff the literature into envelopes, seal the envelopes, affix address labels, and bundle the envelopes for mailing.

Some of the most important volunteer work involves staffing telephone banks. Campaigns spend thousands of dollars having dozens of phones installed a few weeks before the election. They either hire workers or recruit volunteers to call registered voters from lists that can be obtained from the county tax office. When volunteers call potential voters, they identify themselves as workers on the campaign of Candidate A and then ask, "Can Candidate A count on your support in the upcoming election?" The goal is to identify supporters and undecided voters. On Election Day, campaign volunteers call supporters and remind them to vote. Meanwhile, other volunteers mail literature to people who claimed to be undecided.

There is almost no end to the work volunteers perform in an election campaign. They assemble yard signs and distribute them to the candidate's supporters. They answer office telephones and deliver soft drinks and snacks to other volunteers. (One of the cardinal rules of a successful campaign is to feed the volunteers.) On Election Day, volunteers drive people who lack transportation to the polls and pass out campaign literature outside polling places.

Some Texans participate in political campaigns by giving money to support the political party and the candidates they favor. Money is critical to electoral success. Although the best-funded candidates do not always win, poorly funded candidates almost always lose. Candidates can raise the money they need to compete successfully by soliciting small contributions from thousands of individuals or huge sums of money from a few contributors. Wealthy individuals can become major players in Texas politics by giving generously to candidates they favor. In 2006, Houston homebuilder Bob Perry of Perry Homes gave more than $7 million to various candidates for statewide office and the legislature. San Antonio businessman James Lieninger gave $5.5 million. Houston attorney John O'Quinn gave more than $1 million to one candidate, Chris Bell, the Democratic nominee for governor.[17]

Other Forms of Participation   Voting and campaigning are not the only ways individuals take part in politics. People participate by working through a group. One person casting a single ballot or working alone for a candidate is not as effective as a group of people working together. Many Texans make their voices heard by taking part in such political organizations as the National Rifle Association (NRA), Mothers Against Drunk Driving (MADD), and the League of United Latin American Citizens (LULAC). The **National Rifle Association (NRA)** is an interest group organized to defend the rights of gun owners and defeat efforts at gun control. **Mothers Against Drunk Driving (MADD)** is an interest group that supports the

National Rifle Association (NRA) An interest group organized to defend the rights of gun owners and defeat efforts at gun control.

Mothers Against Drunk Driving (MADD) An interest group that supports the reform of laws dealing with drunk driving.

reform of laws dealing with drunk driving. The **League of United Latin American Citizens (LULAC)** is a Latino interest group.

People participate in the policy process by contacting government officials. Citizens may send e-mail messages to their state legislators or telephone city council members. Individuals may speak before the board of trustees of the local school district or community college.

Some Americans participate in politics by engaging in protest demonstrations, rallies, and marches. In recent years, Texans have engaged in demonstrations to influence government policy on issues such as immigration and the war in Iraq. Americans have a constitutional right to express their political views and that includes the right to protest publicly. As long as protestors do not break the law (by blocking traffic, for example), they are acting legally within the spirit and the letter of the U.S. Constitution.

Finally, some people go beyond peaceful protest to engage in acts of political violence, including the bombing of abortion clinics and the destruction of property. Although political violence will draw attention to a cause, it is often counterproductive because it provokes a backlash. Most mainstream anti-abortion groups, for example, dissociate themselves from individuals who advocate violence against abortion providers because they believe that violence undermines their cause with mainstream voters. Furthermore, people who commit violent acts or destroy property may face criminal prosecution as ordinary criminals.

Participation Rates in Texas

As noted in the introduction to this chapter, most adult Texans do not vote, even in high-profile elections. Figure 21.1 summarizes participation in the 2006 statewide election in Texas. As the figure indicates, 16.6 million Texans were old enough to vote in 2006. Of that number, 13.1 million, 79 percent of the voting age population, were registered to vote. Voter turnout, meanwhile, was 4.4 million, 27 percent of voting age adults. Turnout in lower-profile contests is less than it is in gubernatorial or presidential races. Voter participation in the 2005 constitutional amendment election was only 14 percent of the voting age population.[18]

Compared with other states, the level of political participation in Texas is relatively low, at least in terms of voter turnout. Although voting is not the *only* form of participation, it is the most common form and the most easily measured. Figure 21.2 shows that less than 50 percent of the state's voting-age adult population has turned out to vote in every presidential election since 1980. Furthermore, voter turnout in Texas is consistently below the national average. In 2004, the voter turnout rate in Texas was the fourth lowest in the nation.[19]

Political scientists identify several factors that may account for the relatively low rate of political participation in the state. High levels of participation are associated with older, better-educated populations with relatively high incomes. Compared with other states, income levels in Texas are lower, the age distribution is younger, and levels of educational achievement are below average. All of these factors are related to lower levels of political participation.

The weakness of political parties and labor unions in Texas may be associated with relatively low levels of voter turnout. Strong parties and unions are able to educate citizens about politics and motivate them to participate politically.[20] They

NATIONAL PERSPECTIVE

Mail Voting in Oregon

Oregon conducts all of its primary and general elections by mail. Election officials mail ballots to registered voters from 18 to 14 days prior to the election. A voter marks the ballot in blue or black ink and places it in an unmarked envelope; the voter then places the first envelope in a second envelope. The voter signs the outer envelope and either mails it or drops it off at the county election office. Voters have until the day of the election to return their ballots.*

Oregon election officials believe that mail balloting has increased voter participation. In 1996, approximately 1.4 million Oregon voters cast ballots for president the old-fashioned way, in person and by traditional absentee ballot. The figure represented 71 percent of the state's registered voters. In contrast, the 2004 presidential election turnout was 1.8 million, 86 percent of registered voters.[†]

Mail balloting is popular with Oregon voters. Nearly three-fourths of the state's voters tell survey researchers that they prefer voting by mail to traditional in-person voting. Younger adults and voters over the age of 50 are the biggest supporters of the new system. They like mail balloting not only because it is convenient but also because it gives them time to discuss races with their friends and family before deciding how to vote.[‡]

Research on the impact of mail voting in Oregon finds that it has increased participation without affecting the partisan profile of the electorate. Women, young people, persons with disabilities, and homemakers report that they are more likely to take part in elections with mail voting than they were using traditional voting methods because they find the new system more convenient. The reform has had no apparent effect on the party balance in the electorate or on candidate preferences.[§]

QUESTIONS TO CONSIDER

1. Do you see any disadvantages to voting by mail?
2. Would you like to vote by mail rather than in person?
3. Do you think Texas and other states will adopt a mail voting system like the Oregon procedure?

---

*Don Hamilton, "The Oregon Voting Revolution," *The American Prospect,* May 2006, pp. A3–A7.
[†]Oregon Secretary of State, available at www.sos.state.or.us.
[‡]Dave Scott, "Ways to Turn Out Voters," *State Government News,* February 2000, pp. 18–19.
[§]Priscilla L. Southwell, "Five Years Later: A Re-Assessment of Oregon's Vote by Mail Electoral Process," *PS: Political Science & Politics* (January 2004): 89–93.

recruit voters. Political parties in Texas are generally less organized than parties in many other states. Furthermore, labor unions in Texas are weaker than unions in the Northeast and Midwest.

The relatively high percentage of recent immigrants to Texas may help account for the state's low participation rates. In general, newcomers to an area need a few years to settle into their new communities before becoming active in state and local political affairs. People vote because they are concerned about their communities, and new residents take time to identify with their new communities.[21] Newcomers to an area must also take the time to register to vote. Furthermore, many of the state's immigrants are not yet American citizens and therefore are ineligible to vote.

Finally, some political scientists believe that election frequency and ballot complexity reduce election turnout.[22] Considering the frequency of elections in Texas and the length and complexity of the ballot (22 constitutional amendments in 2003!), it would be understandable if many of the state's voters suffer burnout.

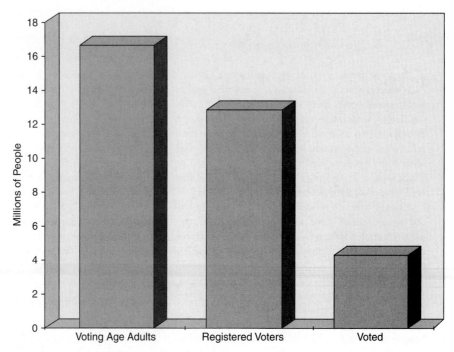

FIGURE 21.1   Participation in the 2006 Election.
Source: Texas Secretary of State.

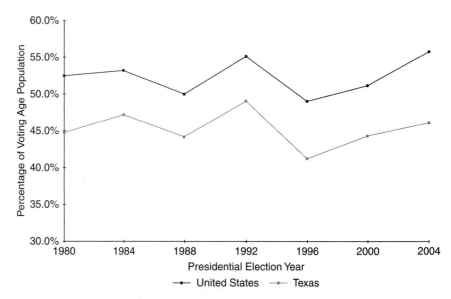

FIGURE 21.2   Voter Turnout, United States and Texas.
Source: U.S. Census Bureau, Texas Secretary of State.

Patterns of Participation

Participation rates vary among individuals based on income, age, and race/ethnicity. Middle- and upper-income groups participate at a higher rate than lower-income groups. According to **exit polls,** which are surveys based on random samples of voters leaving the polling place, 56 percent of Texas voters in 2004 had annual household incomes in excess of $50,000. More than a quarter of the Texas electorate earned more than $75,000 a year.[23] In contrast, the average household income in the state was less than $41,000.[24]

The relationship between income and participation also holds true for forms of participation other than voting. A survey of local party activists in Texas and other southern states found that a majority of the activists of both political parties had family incomes well above average.[25] Lower-income people are also considerably less likely to make campaign contributions than are the wealthy.[26] Obviously, relatively few Texans can afford to give as much money to candidates as can Bob Perry, James Leininger, and other wealthy contributors.

Political participation increases with age until advanced age and ill health force the elderly to slow down.[27] National surveys show that voter participation rates among younger adults are 20 or 30 percentage points lower than those for older citizens.[28] Young people have fewer resources and are less interested in the policy process than are older adults. As adults mature, their incomes increase and their skills develop. Older adults establish roots in their communities that increase their interest in and awareness of the political process.

The overall participation rates for blacks and whites are similar, whereas the participation rates for Latinos are substantially lower than they are for other racial and ethnic groups. According to the U.S. Census Bureau, the population of Texas is 50 percent white, 35 percent Latino, 12 percent African American, and 3 percent Asian.[29] In contrast, the 2004 electorate in Texas was 63 percent white, 23 percent Latino, 12 percent African American, 1 percent Asian, and 2 percent "other."[30] Whites are significantly overrepresented at the ballot box, whereas Latinos are dramatically underrepresented.

Racial/ethnic patterns of participation reflect the importance of recruitment to political participation.[31] Political scientists would anticipate that participation rates for African American and Latino citizens would be lower than those for whites because of income and age differences. As a group, minority citizens are less affluent and younger than whites of European descent. Participation rates for African Americans somewhat exceed expectations because of the effectiveness of organizations in the African American community, such as churches and political groups, at stimulating participation. In contrast, participation rates for Latino Texans reflect the relative weakness of Latino political organizations at turning out the vote. Also, many of the state's Latino residents are not citizens or are younger than 18 years of age.

Men and women are equally likely to vote, but men are more likely than women to engage in other forms of political participation. Women comprised 54 percent of the Texas electorate in 2004, reflecting the gender distribution of the state's adult population.[32] Women and men are also equally likely to participate in election campaigns. In contrast, women are less likely than men to contribute money to political campaigns, to contact public officials, and to join political organizations.[33]

Latinos, African Americans, and Asian Americans combined made up 36 percent of the Texas electorate in 2004.

Participation and Representation

Political scientists Robert A. Jackson, Robert D. Brown, and Gerald C. Wright have published research comparing the population of each state with those people who vote. To what degree, they ask, does the electorate resemble the adult population of the state in terms of income, education, and age? Jackson, Brown, and Wright use a 100-point scale to show the results of their study. If the state's electorate has the same proportion of poor people as its population, the income score for that state is 100. A score of 75 indicates that the state's electorate includes only 75 percent as many low-income people as the state's population.

Table 21.1 compares the scale scores for Texas with the national mean for the 50 states. Voters as a group are wealthier, better educated, and older than the state's adult population. This is true not only in the Lone Star State but also in other states.

TABLE 21.1   Representation Based on Income, Education, and Age

Population Characteristic	Texas	Mean of 50 States
Income	50	67
Education	46	58
Age	43	47

Data Source: Robert A. Jackson, Robert D. Brown, and Gerald C. Wright, "Representation, Turnout, and the Electoral Representativeness of U.S. State Electorates," *American Politics Quarterly* 26 (July 1998): 259–287.

INTERNET RESEARCH   **Tracking Election Turnout**

The Texas electorate is shifting from the state's big cities to the suburbs. Students can research turnout patterns using data available at the website of the Texas Secretary of State: **www.sos.state.tx.us/**. Point your mouse at the "Elections and Voter Information" link. Scroll down to "election returns" and click. Then, select the link "Voter Registration Figures—County History." Your assignment is to research voter turnout figures in the presidential election years of 1992 and 2004 for five Texas counties—the two largest counties in the state (Harris and Dallas) and three of the state's more rapidly growing suburban counties (Collin, Montgomery, and Fort Bend). Use the data to complete the following table:

County	Voter Turnout in 1992 (No. of Voters)	Voter Turnout in 2004 (No. of Voters)	Pct. Increase 2004 over 1992
Harris Co.			
Dallas Co.			
Collin Co.			
Montgomery Co.			
Fort Bend Co.			

Figure the percentage increase by subtracting the voter turnout in 1992 from turnout in 2004 to find the number of additional voters in the latter year. Then divide that number by turnout in 1992 to find the percentage increase between 1992 and 2004. Once you have completed the table, answer the following questions:

1. Did voting participation increase more rapidly in the urban counties (Harris and Dallas) or the suburban counties (Collin, Montgomery, and Fort Bend) between 1992 and 2004?
2. Does the growth of voter turnout in suburban counties reflect recent population growth patterns in the state?
3. Would you expect the residents of suburban counties to have different policy preferences than the residents of urban areas? On what sorts of issues would they differ?

The Texas electorate, however, is less representative of the state population than the average state electorate, especially in terms of income and education. The proportion of poor people in the electorate in Texas is only 50 percent as large as it is in the state's adult population. The comparable figure for the average state is 67 percent. In sum, the poor are underrepresented among voters in all states, but they are more underrepresented in Texas than in the average state.[34]

The underrepresentation of Texans who are poor is the legacy of the state's long history of public policies designed to limit the right to vote to middle-class and upper-income white people. The white primary, poll tax, and restrictive voter registration requirements all discouraged or prevented poor Texans from registering to vote. Although federal intervention has forced the state to expand its electoral system to broad-based participation, the legacy of exclusion still affects voter turnout today. Parents who could not vote were unable to serve as participation role models for their children. Adult Texans who grew up in households with adults who could not vote are less likely to participate politically than are citizens who were raised in families that participated in the political process.

Lupe Valdez was elected Dallas County Sheriff in 2004. As the state's electorate has grown more diverse, the number of Latino and African American officeholders has increased.

The disparity between voters and the electorate affects public policy. The electorate in Texas is significantly more conservative than the population as a whole. Because elected officials respond to the policy preferences of voters rather than nonvoters, the result is that public policies in Texas are more conservative than they would be if the electorate mirrored the state's population.[35]

CONCLUSION: PARTICIPATION AND POLICYMAKING

Abraham Lincoln, the great American president of the Civil War era, described democracy as government of the people, by the people, and for the people. Political scientists would probably qualify Lincoln's characterization to add that democracy is a government of, by, and for those people who participate. People who cannot participate in the policymaking process or who choose not to participate have no influence.

For decades, political participation in Texas was restricted to a narrow segment of society. The white primary coupled with boss control in South Texas limited meaningful participation to whites. The poll tax ensured that middle- and upper-income voters would dominate elections. Minority citizens and low-income residents of all races had relatively little input into the state's policymaking process.

Federal intervention and demographic change have transformed the face of political participation in Texas. Court rulings, a constitutional amendment, and federal laws have knocked out the white primary, the poll tax, and other devices designed to restrict participation. Meanwhile, the potential electorate has expanded dramatically as the state's population has grown more diverse. African American, Latino, and Asian voters combined represented more than a third of the Texas electorate in 2004, and their numbers are certain to grow as the Latino and Asian populations grow older and obtain citizenship status, and as elderly white citizens die. The Texas electorate in 2020 will be dramatically different in terms of race and ethnicity from the Texas electorate today.

Although whites are no longer the demographic majority in Texas, they remain the political majority because of the state's participation patterns. Since the 2000 Census, whites have slipped below the 50 percent mark. Latinos, the most rapidly growing ethnic group in the state, currently constitute 35 percent of the population and will likely become the state's largest population group well before mid-century. Nonetheless, whites still dominate Texas politics. Even though Latinos constitute more than a third of the state's population, they make up just a fifth of its registered voters.[36] Every executive official running statewide and a majority of the members of the Texas legislature won office with the strong support of white voters, especially older middle- and upper-income whites living in the suburbs.

Agenda Building

The state's major demographic groups have different policy preferences. As a group, Latinos and African Americans are younger, less well educated, and less affluent than the state's white population. Latinos are three times more likely to lack health insurance than whites; African Americans are two times more likely to lack insurance.[37] African Americans and Latinos are less likely than whites to live in inner-city areas and less likely to reside in the suburbs. They are more likely to rely on public assistance. Almost all of their children attend public school. The policy issues most important to the state's Latino and African American residents are funding for public education, access to higher education, healthcare, public transportation, and inner-city redevelopment. In contrast, older middle- and upper-income white Texans who live in the suburbs are most concerned with rising property taxes, retirement security, highways, and economic development in general.

Policy Formulation and Adoption

Recession An economic slowdown characterized by declining economic output and rising unemployment.

Public policy in Texas reflects the policy preferences of the state's electoral majority. In 2003, for example, state government faced a significant budget shortfall because of a **recession,** which is an economic slowdown characterized by declining economic output and rising unemployment. The state's chief budget officer estimated that tax revenues would fall more than $10 billion short of the funds necessary to maintain state services at their current levels. The governor and legislature chose to address the shortfall by cutting spending, even though public services in Texas were already among the most poorly funded in the nation. They cut funding for school textbooks, higher education, and healthcare for children in low-income families. All of the cuts disproportionately affected low-income Latino and African American families. Similarly, in 2005, when the governor and legislature debated school funding, they focused on cutting school property taxes rather than increasing state funding for public education. Their focus on property tax relief reflected the policy preferences of well-to-do white suburbanites and business owners rather than low-income Latino and African

GETTING INVOLVED

Become a Volunteer Deputy Voter Registrar

You can do more to influence the policymaking process than registering to vote and casting your own ballot. By becoming a volunteer deputy voter registrar, you can register other people to vote—your friends, family, and fellow students; members of your religious group; and even strangers walking through a shopping mall. If you are 18 years old and have never been convicted of failing to deliver a voter application to a voter registrar, you are qualified to become a deputy voter registrar. Visit the voter registrar in your county (whose location can be found online at www.sos.state.tx.us/elections/voter/votregduties.shtml) and ask to become a deputy registrar. The clerk will give you voting application materials,

swear you in as an official deputy voter registrar, issue you a certificate of appointment, and give you a receipt book. You may then distribute and collect a voter registration application from any resident of the county who is eligible to vote. You may also accept updated registration information from registered voters who have changed addresses. Once you have collected completed voter registration applications, you must deliver them to the voter registrar within five days of receiving them. A conscientious deputy voter registrar can register hundreds of potential voters, more than enough to change the outcome of a close local election.

It's your government—get involved!

American Texans whose children attended public schools. In 2007, strong economic growth created a sizable budget surplus, a near mirror image of the shortfall of 2003. Nonetheless, instead of using the surplus to address the state's needs for better healthcare and education, the governor and the legislature left billions of dollars unspent in anticipation that the money would be needed later to fund future property tax reductions. Once again, the state's budget priorities reflected the policy priorities of middle- and upper-income whites rather than those of low-income minority residents.

Policy Implementation and Evaluation

Individual Texans play relatively little direct role in policy implementation. People support the efforts of police to enforce the law by reporting offenses to law officers and assisting in criminal investigations. Individuals may also file lawsuits to challenge the way state agencies implement policy.

Individuals play a larger role in policy evaluation than they do in policy implementation. Political scientists believe that citizens often base their voting choice on their evaluation of the effectiveness of public policies. The concept that voters choose candidates based on their perception of an incumbent candidate's past performance in office or the performance of the incumbent party is known as **retrospective voting.** If citizens are pleased with the performance of the government, they vote to reelect incumbent officeholders. (An **incumbent** is a current officeholder.) If they are unhappy with governmental performance, they vote against incumbent officials.

The changing face of the Texas electorate has changed the tone of policy evaluation. For decades, the only voices that counted in Texas politics were the voices of middle- and upper-income whites. As the electorate has expanded, evaluation has changed. The rapid growth of the state's minority population ensures that African American, Latino, and Asian interests will have more policymaking influence in the twenty-first century than they did in the twentieth century.

Retrospective voting The concept that voters choose candidates based on their perception of an incumbent candidate's past performance in office or the performance of the incumbent party.

Incumbent Current officeholder.

LET'S DEBATE

Would the Adoption of the Initiative Process Enhance the Quality of Democracy in the State?

Overview: In 1978, the passage of California's Proposition 13 sent a jolt through both state capitols and the nation's political class. With a sluggish economy and high inflation, average California homeowners, reeling from the state's notoriously high property taxes, overwhelmingly voted for "The People's Initiative to Limit Property Taxation," an initiative to lower and limit state property taxes. The passage of Proposition 13 demonstrated to the nation the power of direct democracy, and, as a result, it helped launch the current "direct democracy" movement. Since 1978, states with the initiative and referendum process (called I&R states) have dramatically increased the number of ballot initiatives offered to their citizens. Proponents of I&R maintain that the process gives average citizens the means to affect government directly by allowing them to create and vote on law and policy they deem substantial and important. This gives them a real and tangible stake in the political process—after all, isn't this the essence of a truly democratic government?

Initiative and referendum mechanisms have their origin in the Progressive Movement from the turn of the nineteenth and twentieth centuries. The first state to inaugurate an I&R mechanism was South Dakota in 1898, and 18 other states soon followed suit (currently 24 states have some form of I&R mechanism in place). In 1913, Texas enacted legislation allowing for I&R in home-rule cities, but Texas voters rejected a proposed I&R constitutional amendment in 1914. The initiative and referendum process was pursued in the state's 1974 constitutional convention, but the state's direct democracy movement really began to accelerate after the passage of California's Proposition 13. A 1998 Rasmussen Research poll showed that 74 percent of Texas residents would like to see an I&R mechanism put in place. Why is it that Texas has not been able to amend I&R provisions to its constitution?

Detractors of initiative and referendum argue that the process does not truly facilitate quality democratic policies. They argue that the mass public will have neither the time nor the inclination to study and deliberate on proposed initiatives—they point to the generally dismal turnout for Texas elections as proof of an apathetic citizenry. Why should the important business of lawmaking and government be entrusted to those whose interests lie elsewhere? Critics maintain that, if Texans are truly unhappy with their government, all they have to do is show up at the ballot box and "throw (vote) the bums out." The same critics also point out that states with numerous initiatives are currently trying to reform their respective systems, as voters are realizing that policy-by-initiative is uniquely susceptible to the law of unintended consequences—not to mention that their voters are also becoming disenchanted with long and confusing ballots and too many elections.

Arguments That Initiative and Referendum Enhance Democratic Practices

❑ **Initiative elections can help circumvent an unresponsive state government.** Supporters of initiative elections say they are a great means to implement new laws, policy, and constitutional amendments that legislators are unable or unwilling to implement. For example, citizens in California, Colorado, and Oklahoma used the initiative process to impose term limits on state legislators and, in 2005, voters in Washington State approved a measure that requires performance audits of government agencies. Initiatives are used as a "check" on legislators to hold them accountable to their constituents.

❑ **Initiative elections allow for the expansion of democratic processes.** The initiative process gives average citizens the ability to participate in the law and the policymaking process. One of the promises of republican government is that ordinary citizens have the ability to influence government and guide the policies that affect their lives, and the initiative and referendum process provides this. In addition to using I&R to control state tax and spending policy, citizens of I&R states have also directed their governments on how to conduct social policy. For example, voters in Washington State approved an initiative to ban smoking inside public facilities, and voters in Maine rejected a call to repeal their law prohibiting discrimination based on sexual orientation.

continued on next page

❏ **Initiative elections help voters counter the effects of interest-group activity.** The influence of interest groups and their expenditures on state and local government are undeniable. For example, the Center for Public Integrity reports that, in 2003, interest groups in Texas spent approximately $140 million lobbying state representatives. It is safe to assume that this money would not be spent if it were not effective. I&R mechanisms will allow Texans to counteract some of the more unsavory effects of Texas's strong lobbies.

Arguments That Initiative and Referendum Hinder Democratic Practices

❏ **Initiative elections impede effective government.** Many times, initiatives prevent legislatures from developing consistent and coherent policy. For example, initiatives that restrict legislatures from raising certain revenue may effectively prevent legislators from adequately budgeting to meet changing needs and priorities. Take, for instance, California's Proposition 13. Many policy researchers believe that, because the government was denied this revenue stream, California legislators have not been able to sufficiently fund state social services and educational establishments.

❏ **Passage of initiatives may lead to undesirable consequences.** Many drafters of initiatives do not have the requisite legal or political expertise to craft legislation skillfully. Legislators tend to make better laws when they have access to a professional staff for both the research and drafting of legislation. Citizens do not have the necessary experience to understand the relationship between a given initiative and existing statutes and policy. This can result in implementation problems and poor and confused law.

❏ **Initiatives may be antidemocratic.** Paradoxically, initiatives may actually be antimajoritarian and *not* representative of a state's political culture. In states with historically low voter turnout (such as Texas), only a small number of minorities and interest groups are politically active and pursue their own narrow interests; if effective, this can result in minority tyranny. Additionally, many initiatives amend state constitutions and, as a consequence, poorly crafted initiatives can become fundamental law. Initiatives may be hard to repeal due to the general difficulty in amending state constitutions.

QUESTIONS

1. Is it reasonable to expect that an initiative and referendum process in Texas would improve the quality of Texas's democratic politics? If so, why? If not, why not?
2. Do I&R mechanisms give citizens a "check" on their government and interest groups, or are these instruments simply tools for interested minorities?

SELECT READINGS

1. David D. Schmidt, *Citizen Lawmakers: The Ballot Initiative Revolution* (Philadelphia: Temple University Press, 1991).
2. Richard J. Ellis, *Democratic Delusions: The Initiative Process in the United States* (Lawrence: University Press of Kansas, 2002).

SELECT WEBSITES

1. **www.initiativefortexas.org**
Website for Initiative for Texas, a nonpartisan advocacy group for amending the state constitution to include the right of initiative.

2. **www.landrinstitute.org**
Website for the Initiative and Referendum Institute, a nonpartisan research organization dedicated to studying the initiative and referendum process.

KEY TERMS

democracy	enfranchise	incumbent
disfranchisement	exit polls	League of United Latin
election precinct	franchise	American Citizens (LULAC)

Mothers Against Drunk Driving (MADD)

National Rifle Association (NRA)

parole

poll tax

primary election

probation

recession

retrospective voting

suffrage

white primary

NOTES

1. Texas Secretary of State, available at www.sos.state.tx.us.
2. Elizabeth A. Taylor, "The Woman Suffrage Movement in Texas," *Journal of Southern History* 17 (May 1951): 194–215.
3. Merline Pitre, *Through Many Dangers, Toils and Snares: Black Leadership in Texas, 1868–1900* (Austin: Eakin Press, 1985).
4. V. O. Key, Jr., *Southern Politics in State and Nation* (New York: Alfred A. Knopf, 1949).
5. *Historical Statistics of the United States* (Washington, DC: U.S. Government Printing Office, 1975), pp. 1071–1072.
6. Dudley Lynch, *Duke of Duval* (Waco: Texian Press, 1978).
7. *Nixon v. Herndon*, 273 U.S. 536 (1927).
8. *Nixon v. Condon*, 286 U.S. 73 (1932).
9. *Grovey v. Townsend*, 295 U.S. 45 (1935).
10. *Smith v. Allwright*, 321 U.S. 649 (1944).
11. *Terry v. Adams*, 345 U.S. 461 (1953).
12. *United States v. Texas*, 384 U.S. 155 (1966).
13. *Beare v. Smith*, 321 F. Supp. 1100 (1971).
14. Texas Secretary of State, available at www.sos.state.tx.us.
15. William Lyons and John M. Scheb II, "Early Voting and the Timing of the Vote: Unanticipated Consequences of Electoral Reform," *State and Local Government Review* 31 (Spring 1999): 148.
16. Paul Gronke, Eva Galanes-Rosenbaum, and Peter A. Miller, "Early Voting and Voter Turnout," *PS: Political Science & Politics* 40 (October 2007): 639–645.
17. Texans for Public Justice, "Texas' 2006 Election Cycle '$100,000 Club,'" available at www.tpj.org.
18. Texas Secretary of State, "Turnout and Voter Registration Figures (1992–2007)," available at www.sos.state.tx.us.
19. Laurie Kellman, "Minnesota Led the Way in '04 Election Turnout," *Houston Chronicle*, January 23, 2005, p. A10.
20. G. Bingham Powell, Jr., "American Voter Turnout in Comparative Perspective," *American Political Science Review* 80 (March 1986): 17–43; Benjamin Radcliff and Patricia Davis, "Labor Organization and Electoral Participation in Industrial Democracies," *American Journal of Political Science* 44 (April 2000): 132–141.
21. André Blais, *To Vote or Not to Vote?* (Pittsburgh: University of Pittsburgh Press, 2000), p. 13.
22. Richard W. Boyd, "Election Calendars and Voter Turnout," *American Politics Quarterly* 14 (January–April 1986): 89–104.
23. "Exit Polls for Texas," available at www.cnn.com/elections/2004.
24. U.S. Census Bureau, *Income, Poverty, and Health Insurance in the United States, 2003*, available at www.census.gov.
25. Charles D. Hadley and Lewis Bowman, eds., *Party Activists in Southern Politics* (Knoxville: University of Tennessee Press, 1998), p. 6.
26. Sidney Verba, Kay Lehman Schlozman, and Henry E. Brady, *Voice and Equality: Civic Volunteerism in American Politics* (Cambridge, MA: Harvard University Press, 1995), p. 190.
27. M. Kent Jennings and Gregory B. Markus, "Political Involvement in the Later Years: A Longitudinal Survey," *American Journal of Political Science* 32 (May 1988): 302–316.
28. U.S. Census Bureau, "Reported Voting and Registration, by Race, Hispanic Origin, Sex, and Age, for the United States, November 2004," available at www.census.gov.
29. U.S. Census Bureau, "Texas Becomes Nation's Newest 'Majority-Minority' State," August 11, 2005, available at www.census.gov.
30. "Exit Polls for Texas."
31. Henry E. Brady, Sidney Verba, and Kay Lehman Schlozman, "Beyond SES: A Resource Model of Political Participation," *American Political Science Review* 89 (June 1995): 271–294.
32. "Exit Polls for Texas."
33. Verba, Schlozman, and Brady, *Voice and Equality: Civic Volunteerism in American Politics*, p. 255.
34. Robert A. Jackson, Robert D. Brown, and Gerald C. Wright, "Representation, Turnout, and the Electoral Representativeness of U.S. State Electorates," *American Politics Quarterly* 26 (July 1998): 259–287.
35. John D. Griffin and Brian Newman, "Are Voters Better Represented?" *Journal of Politics* 67 (November 2005): 1214.
36. R. G. Ratcliffe, "Once-Courted Latino Vote Suddenly Forgotten," *San Antonio Express-News*, September 4, 2006, available at www.mysanantonio.com.
37. Texas Health Institute, "Access to Health Insurance for the Uninsured," December 1, 2006, available at www.texashealthinstitute.org.

Chapter 22

Interest Groups in Texas

CHAPTER OUTLINE

LEARNING OUTCOMES

After studying Chapter 22, students should be able to do the following:

- Describe the key issues underlying the debate over medical malpractice insurance reform and identify the interest groups involved on either side of the controversy. (pp. 582–583)

- Identify the various types of interest groups active in Texas politics and evaluate their relative influence on the policymaking process. (pp. 583–593)

- Identify the basic political goals for each of the following types of interest groups: business groups and trade associations; professional associations; organized labor; agricultural groups; racial and ethnic minority groups; religious groups; and citizen, advocacy, and cause groups. (pp. 583–593)

- Describe the tactics that interest groups employ to achieve their goals. (pp. 593–599)

- Evaluate the scheme devised by Thomas and Hrebenar for classifying the influence of interest groups in the state policymaking process. (pp. 599–601)

- Describe the role that interest groups play in the state's policymaking process. (pp. 601–602)

- Define the key terms listed on pages 604–605 and explain their significance.

Texas Medical Association (TMA)
A professional organization of physicians.

Punitive damages
Monetary awards given in a lawsuit to punish a defendant for a particularly evil, malicious, or fraudulent act.

Texas Trial Lawyers Association (TTLA)
An organization of attorneys who represent plaintiffs in personal injury lawsuits.

Interest group An organization of people who join together voluntarily on the basis of some interest they share for the purpose of influencing policy.

Tort reform The revision of state laws to limit the ability of plaintiffs in personal injury lawsuits to recover damages in court.

Texas doctors have complained about the high cost of medical malpractice insurance for years. Between 1987 and 2002, malpractice insurance premiums rose by 400 percent in Texas.[1] Some physicians, especially doctors with high-risk specializations, such as obstetrics, claimed that they could no longer afford to remain in practice. According to the American Medical Association (AMA), the annual cost of malpractice insurance for a Texas physician ranged from $10,000 to $117,000 a year in 2003, depending on the specialization.[2]

The **Texas Medical Association (TMA),** a professional organization of physicians, advocated a cap on the amount of money a jury could award in noneconomic damages. Economic damages awarded in a medical malpractice lawsuit include lost wages and the cost of medical care. Noneconomic damages include money to compensate for disfigurement, loss of companionship, pain, suffering, and **punitive damages,** which are monetary awards given in a lawsuit to punish a defendant for a particularly evil, malicious, or fraudulent act. The TMA noted that the California legislature capped noneconomic damages in medical malpractice cases at $250,000 in 1975. In subsequent years, medical malpractice premiums in California rose by only 167 percent compared with an increase of 500 percent in the rest of the country.[3]

The **Texas Trial Lawyers Association (TTLA),** which is an organization of attorneys who represent plaintiffs in personal injury lawsuits, blamed bad doctors and a weak stock market, rather than excessive jury awards, for rising medical malpractice premiums. The TTLA noted that data provided by the insurance companies showed that noneconomic damages awarded by juries in medical malpractice cases had actually been falling. In 1988, Texas juries awarded $60 million in noneconomic damages and $88 million in economic damages. In 2000, jury awards for noneconomic damages stood at $40 million, whereas economic awards had risen to $298 million.[4] The TTLA contended that malpractice awards had been climbing because the Texas State Board of Medical Examiners had neglected to purge the profession of the small number of bad doctors who were guilty of malpractice. Between 1997 and 2002, the Board of Medical Examiners failed to revoke the license of a single physician for committing medical errors.[5] Furthermore, the TTLA believed that insurance companies were increasing premiums to make up for poor investments. When the stock market is doing well, insurance companies make enough money on investments to keep their premiums low. When the market is weak, as it was in the early years of this decade, insurance companies increase premiums to make up for their investment losses.[6]

The battle over medical malpractice insurance reform features some of the most powerful interest groups in Texas politics. An **interest group** is an organization of people who join together voluntarily on the basis of an interest they share for the purpose of influencing policy. Although the TMA and the TTLA are the main combatants, other groups are involved as well. Business groups and trade associations support the efforts of the TMA because they want the legislature to limit lawsuits in general, not just medical malpractice lawsuits. The revision of state laws to limit the ability of plaintiffs in personal injury lawsuits to recover damages in court is known as **tort reform.** Meanwhile, consumer groups, such as Public Citizen and Texas Watch, join forces with the TTLA to oppose medical malpractice reform in particular and tort reform in general because they want to defeat legislation that will make it more difficult for injured consumers to file suit and recover damages.

Interest groups are important participants in the policymaking process. Groups on either side of the medical malpractice insurance controversy attempted to influence the policymaking process by contributing to the election campaigns of candidates for governor, the legislature, and judicial office. They conducted public relations campaigns to sway public opinion and lobbied lawmakers and other officials to formulate, adopt, and implement the policies they favored. Finally, groups attempted to influence policy evaluation by interpreting the impact of policies in a light favorable to their interests.

This chapter is the second in a series of four chapters examining the political environment for policymaking. Chapter 21 discussed political participation in Texas. Chapters 23 and 24 will focus on political parties and elections. This chapter studies the role of interest groups in the policymaking process. It identifies the major interest groups active in the state, discusses the strategies and tactics interest groups employ to achieve their goals, and evaluates the impact of groups on the policymaking process.

 WHAT IS YOUR OPINION?

Do you favor capping the amount of money that juries can award for noneconomic damages in medical malpractice cases?

INTEREST GROUPS IN TEXAS POLITICS

Most Texans have an interest in the policies of state and local government in Texas, but not all Texans have organized to promote and defend their interests. Compare and contrast the position of college students with that of the people who manage large energy companies, such as Reliant Energy and TXU Energy. Both groups have an interest in state and local government. Public policies dealing with college funding, university admissions, course transfer, tuition, and the availability of scholarships and financial aid affect college students. In the meantime, energy company executives have an interest in electricity deregulation, property taxes, and government regulations dealing with environmental pollution, electric power transmission, and workplace safety. College students and energy company executives are not equally well organized. College students have little, if any, interest-group representation. Although student organizations exist at many of the state's colleges and universities, their primary focus is not political. In contrast, energy company executives are organized both by firm and by industry group. They are widely regarded as being among the most influential voices in state and local government.

We begin our study of interest groups by identifying the most important organized interests in Texas politics. Who are the interests, how well are they organized, what do they want from state and local government, and how effective are they at achieving their goals?

Business Groups and Trade Associations

Business groups and trade associations are the most powerful interest groups in Texas politics. Other groups may be influential at particular levels of government, on certain issues, and at certain points in the policy process, but business interests are important everywhere, from the county courthouse to the governor's mansion. Whereas other interests focus on one issue or a narrow range of issues, business voices are heard on virtually every major policy issue, whether education finance, insurance regulation, medical malpractice insurance reform, water development, immigration, or transportation.

Business interests pursue their political goals both as individual firms and through trade associations. Bank of America, Reliant Energy, AT&T, State Farm Insurance, and other large business enterprises are major players in state politics. Business groups also work through **trade associations,** which are organizations representing the interests of firms and professionals in the same general field. The Texas Association of Builders, for example, is a trade association representing the interests of building contractors. The Mid-Continent Oil and Gas Association is a trade association that speaks for the interests of the major oil producers. The Insurance Council of Texas is a trade association representing insurance companies. The **Texas Association of Business (TAB)** is a trade association for business firms ranging from giant corporations to small neighborhood business establishments. The TAB, which includes local chambers of commerce in its organizational structure, is perhaps the single most powerful interest group in the state.

Business groups and trade associations are effective because they are organized, well financed, and skilled in advocating their positions. Businesspeople usually know what they want from government and have the financial and organizational resources to pursue their goals aggressively. Furthermore, business groups as a whole enjoy a relatively favorable public image. Although the alcohol, gambling, and tobacco industries have public relations problems, most Texans have a favorable image of business in general, especially small business.

Business groups and trade associations generally agree on the need to maintain a **good business climate,** which is a political environment in which business would prosper. Businesspeople believe that tort reform is an important element of a good business climate because it reduces the premium costs to business of insurance against lawsuit judgments. In general, a good business environment includes low tax rates on business, laws that restrict union influence, and regulation favorable to business growth. Business interests also support education to train the skilled, well-educated workforce needed for high-technology development.

When business groups and trade associations are united, they usually get what they want in Texas. The battle over tort reform illustrates the power of business interests united behind a particular policy objective. During the 1990s, the Texas legislature passed and the governor signed legislation enacting the following tort reform measures:

- **Frivolous lawsuits** The legislature and the governor adopted legislation allowing judges to punish plaintiffs for filing lawsuits that the court determined to be without merit. (A **plaintiff** is the party initiating a civil suit.) The judge could fine the plaintiff or order the plaintiff to pay the attorney's fees for the defendant.

Trade associations Organizations representing the interests of firms and professionals in the same general field.

Texas Association of Business (TAB) A trade association for business firms ranging from giant corporations to small neighborhood business establishments.

Good business climate A political environment in which business would prosper.

Plaintiff The party initiating a civil suit.

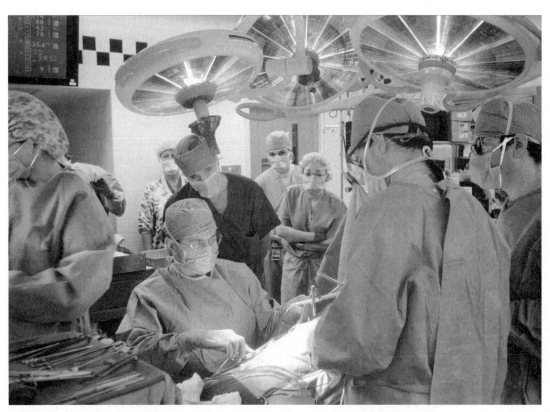

Texas physicians complained that the high cost of medical malpractice was driving them out of business.

- **Punitive damages** The legislature and the governor made it more difficult for plaintiffs to recover punitive damages. They also capped the amount of punitive damages that could be awarded to twice the economic damages suffered by the plaintiff, such as medical bills and lost wages, plus no more than $750,000 for pain and suffering.

- **Forum shopping** The legislature and the governor limited the locations in which a plaintiff could file a personal injury lawsuit to the county of the principal office of the defendant, the site where the injury occurred, and the residence of the defendant.

- **Joint and several liability reform** The legislature and the governor limited the applicability of **joint and several liability,** which is the legal requirement that a defendant with "deep pockets" held partially liable for a plaintiff's injury must pay the full damage award for those defendants unable to pay. In most personal injury lawsuits, a defendant cannot be held 100 percent responsible for a judgment unless the defendant is deemed at least 50 percent responsible for the injury.[7]

- **Lawsuit immunity** The legislature and the governor passed legislation sheltering some potential defendants from liability suits, including medical providers who volunteer their help to charitable organizations. The state also prevents city governments from filing product liability lawsuits against firearms manufacturers.

Joint and several liability The legal requirement that a defendant with "deep pockets" held partially liable for a plaintiff's injury must pay the full damage award for those defendants unable to pay.

In 2003, the legislature and governor reacted to the crisis over medical malpractice insurance by adopting an additional set of tort reform measures:

- **Caps on noneconomic damages in medical malpractice suits** Patients injured by medical malpractice can recover no more than $250,000 in noneconomic damages from a physician or another healthcare provider. If a hospital, clinic, or nursing home is also found liable, the patient can recover a maximum $250,000 each from two other parties for a total cap of $750,000.
- **Protection against product liability suits** The manufacturers of defective products are shielded from liability if they followed federal standards or regulatory requirements.
- **Joint and several liability** Juries may allocate fault among all responsible parties, including parties with no financial assets. In cases involving automobile accidents, when apportioning liability juries may also be informed whether the injured party was wearing a seatbelt or was in a car seat.

The legislature and the governor adopted additional tort reform measures in 2005. They passed a measure that limited the number of lawsuits for asbestos- and silica-related exposure, allowing only people with serious illness to file suit. They added another measure to prohibit lawsuits against restaurants and food makers for obesity-related health problems.

Business groups also enjoy considerable influence with the judicial branch of Texas government, which is responsible for implementing tort reform legislation. Business interests that lose personal injury lawsuits or consumer fraud cases are more than twice as likely to win on appeal as are individual consumers who appeal.[8] Business groups are especially successful before the Texas Supreme Court. According to a study conducted by Texas Watch Foundation, a consumer research and education organization, corporate and governmental defendants won 70 percent of the cases decided by the Texas Supreme Court between 1997 and 2006.[9]

Business interests are more influential in Texas politics than they are in national politics because they have fewer competitors in Texas than they do at the national level or in many other states. Organized labor, consumer groups, environmental organizations, and other groups that often oppose business interests on various policy issues are relatively weak in the Lone Star State. The best that the organizations opposed to tort reform have been able to accomplish, for example, has been to limit the extent of their defeat. The TTLA, the major organization against tort reform, enjoys considerable financial resources, but it has been outspent and outorganized by business interests.

Nonetheless, business interests do not get everything they want in Texas because they are not always united. The eightieth regular session of the legislature, which met in 2007, featured a heavyweight battle between liquor wholesalers and package liquor stores over the way liquor is sold in the state. Under current Texas law, liquor manufacturers sell to liquor wholesalers, who sell to retail package stores, which in turn sell to consumers. Some of the package stores have special permits to sell liquor to bars and restaurants that sell liquor by the drink. The liquor wholesalers wanted the legislature to change state law to require bars and restaurants to purchase their alcohol supply directly from wholesale distributors. The Texas Restaurant Association, a trade association for the restaurant industry, supported the change because it hoped that it could save money by cutting out the middlemen and purchasing liquor directly from wholesalers. In contrast, the Texas Package Stores Association, a trade association for package store owners, fought the proposal, claiming it would actually drive up costs for consumers by reducing competition because only two firms, Republic Beverage Co. and Glazer's Distributing, control nearly all the wholesale distribution business in the state. Furthermore, hundreds of package stores would likely be forced out of business, leaving thousands of their employees out of work.[10]

Business interests in unrelated fields sometimes clash as well. Downtown business interests and suburban retailers fight over the location of civic centers and sports facilities, Sunday-closing laws, and urban mass transit. Downtown interests prefer economic development policies aimed at attracting office-space occupants and retail customers to the central business district, such as the construction of new downtown sports and theater complexes. In contrast, suburban interests favor policies that promote suburban development, such as highway construction and flood control.

Professional Associations

Professional associations are politically influential because of the relatively high socioeconomic status of their members. Doctors, dentists, lawyers, realtors, and other professionals generally have the financial resources to make their voices heard. Furthermore, they enjoy an added advantage in that many elected officials come from the ranks of professionals, especially lawyers. Public officials who happen to be lawyers, for example, are more likely to understand and sympathize with the policy perspectives of attorneys than are officials who lack legal training.

Professional associations concern themselves with public policies that affect their members. Doctors and lawyers battle one another over medical damage award caps in malpractice lawsuits. Real estate professionals are primarily concerned with public policies affecting real estate transactions, such as home equity lending and professional licensure.

Organized Labor

Right-to-work law A statute prohibiting a union shop.

Union shop or **closed shop** A workplace in which every employee must be a member of a union.

Organized labor is relatively weak in Texas. State laws make it difficult for unions to organize workers and easy for business to use nonunion labor. Texas is a "right-to-work" state. A **right-to-work law** is a statute prohibiting a union shop. A **union shop,** or **closed shop,** is a workplace in which every employee must be a member of a union. In states without right-to-work laws, the employees in a particular workplace may vote whether to create a union shop. If a majority of the workers agree, everyone employed in the plant must join the union and pay union dues. Union membership becomes mandatory. In a right-to-work state, union organizers are forced to recruit members individually.

Nationally, labor unions are strongest in the large, industrialized states of the Northeast and Midwest. In 2006, almost a fourth of the workforce in New York belonged to unions; the unionization rate in Michigan was nearly 20 percent. In contrast, organized labor is not nearly as well established in the states of the South and Southwest. Only 5 percent of Texas workers belonged to unions in 2006, less than

INTERNET RESEARCH   **Profile of an Interest Group**

Many of the state's interest groups have websites that publicize mission statements, issue positions, news, and contact information.

- Lone Star Chapter of the Sierra Club (environmental group): **http://texas.sierraclub.org/**
- Texas Right to Life Committee (anti-abortion group): **www.texasrighttolife.com/**
- Public Citizen (consumer rights and environmental group): **www.citizen.org/texas/**
- Texas Public Interest Research Group (public interest advocacy group founded by students): **www.texpirg.org/**
- Children's Defense Fund of Texas (advocacy group for children): **www.cdftexas.org/**
- Texas Eagle Forum (interest group focusing on traditional values): **http://texaseagle.org/**
- NARAL Pro-Choice Texas (pro-choice group): **www.prochoicetexas.org/**
- Texas Freedom Network (interest group focusing on opposition to religious conservatives): **www.tfn.org/**
- Texas Civil Liberties Union (interest group focusing on civil liberties issues): **www.aclutx.org/**
- Texas League of United Latin American Citizens (Latino rights organization): **www.txlulac.org**
- League of Women Voters of Texas (nonpartisan group focusing on voter education): **www.lwvtexas.org/**
- Texas State Conference of NAACP Branches (African American rights organization): **www.texasnaacp.org/**
- Common Cause Texas (nonpartisan group focusing on campaign finance reform and ethics in government): **www.commoncause.org**
- Texas Watch (consumer group): **www.texaswatch.org**
- Texas State Rifle Association (group supporting the rights of gun owners): **www.tsra.com/**
- The Metropolitan Organization (faith-based nonpartisan organization focusing on civic education): **http://tmohouston.net/**
- Texas Christian Coalition (conservative Christian group): **www.ccoatx.com/**
- Gay and lesbian political groups (various cities): **http://dv-8.com/resources/us/local/tx.html**
- National Organization for Women chapters in Texas (women's rights organizations): **www.nowtexas.org/**

Browse the website of one of the groups, and answer the following questions:

1. What issues does the group stress in its website?
2. Does it appear that the group is more interested in raising money, recruiting volunteers, or influencing public policy?
3. Would you describe the group's website as organized and informative? Why or why not?

half the national unionization rate of 12 percent. Texas ranked 46th among the 50 states in the level of unionization.[11]

Labor unions in Texas are too small and too poorly organized to compete effectively against business groups in state politics. In 2006, labor interests contributed $5.1 million to candidates for various legislative and executive offices compared with $57 million given by business interests.[12]

In Texas, labor unions are strongest in the state's more heavily industrialized areas, such as the Texas Gulf Coast and the Dallas–Fort Worth area. Organized labor has political influence in Houston, Dallas, and Fort Worth, and labor unions may be the single most important political force in Pasadena, Deer Park, and the Golden Triangle area of Beaumont, Port Arthur, and Orange. Unions also have influence within the organization of the state Democratic Party.

American Federation of Labor-Congress of Industrial Organizations (AFL-CIO) A national association of labor unions.

Most Texas unions belong to the **American Federation of Labor-Congress of Industrial Organizations (AFL-CIO),** which is a national association of labor unions. The Texas AFL-CIO represents 230,000 workers and includes Texas affiliates of the Communications Workers of America; International Brotherhood of Electrical Workers; Fire Fighters; American Federation of Government Employees; National Association of Letter Carriers; International Association of Machinists; Oil, Chemical, and Atomic Workers Union; American Federation of State, County, and Municipal Employees (AFSCME); and Texas Federation of Teachers. The fastest growing unions are those representing service-sector workers and government employees.[13] In Houston, for example, the Service Employees International Union (SEIU) and AFSCME have been aggressively organizing janitors, city hall workers, security guards, and medical workers.

Minimum wage The lowest hourly wage that an employer can pay covered workers.

Private-sector unions are concerned with employee compensation, working conditions, job availability, job training, and state laws affecting the ability of unions to organize. The AFL-CIO supports increasing the state minimum wage, which covers farmworkers and other employees not covered by the federal minimum wage. The **minimum wage** is the lowest hourly wage that an employer can pay covered workers. Unions also favor public education, job training, and other social programs that benefit working-class families.

Public employee organizations are similar to private-sector unions in that they want higher wages, secure jobs, salaries based on seniority rather than merit, attractive fringe benefits, and good working conditions. Teachers' organizations, for example, favor increased state spending for education and pay raises for teachers, but they oppose merit pay. Fire and police unions are concerned with state civil service rules for municipal fire and police employees. Public employee organizations also address issues related to the professional concerns of their members. Teachers' groups, for example, participate in policy debates over school funding, basic skills testing, and the ratio of students to teachers. Police organizations take positions on proposals to revise the state's criminal laws. Employees of the Texas Department of Corrections oppose efforts to privatize the state's prison system.

Agricultural Groups

Agricultural interests have long been powerful in Texas politics. In the nineteenth century, the most influential political voices in the state were those of major landowners, and the rural population was large enough to overwhelm the city vote in statewide elections. Even after Texas became an urban, industrial state, rural interests continued to exercise disproportionate power. Rural areas were overrepresented in the legislature and farm groups were politically skillful.

Urbanization has weakened rural interests in Texas, but farm groups retain influence. Farmers and ranchers are politically astute, organized, and knowledgeable about how to exert influence in state politics. A great deal of agriculture in Texas has become agribusiness, run by corporations that possess all the political skills and advantages of big business in general. Also, many of the policy goals of agricultural interests have long since been achieved and entrenched in law or the state constitution. As a result, agricultural interest groups have the advantage of defending ground already won rather than pushing for new policies.

Agriculture is a tenuous business, and farmers are well aware that government actions can frequently determine whether they make a profit or go broke. Taxes are an area of concern. Farmers on the outskirts of metropolitan areas, for example, can be hurt by rising property taxes. As the big city sprawls in their direction, the value of their land goes up, but so do their property taxes. Their crops, though, are worth no more. Farm groups have lobbied successfully to have farmland taxed on its value as farmland, not on its value as the site of a future subdivision. Agricultural interests have also won tax breaks on the purchase of farm machinery, seed grain, and fertilizer.

Agricultural groups have other interests as well. They are concerned with state laws and regulations affecting agriculture, such as livestock quarantine requirements and restrictions on the use of pesticides. They support generous state funding for agricultural research conducted at Texas A&M University. Water development and conservation are important for agricultural interests needing water for their livestock and irrigation for their crops.

Nonetheless, agricultural groups in Texas are not always united. The concerns of the family farm and agribusiness do not always coincide. Many government programs that benefit the corporate farm have hurt the small farmer. Regional disputes also flare. West Texas agricultural interests once advocated a plan for pumping water from East Texas to their part of the state. Farm and ranch interests in East Texas eventually killed the plan, fearing it would damage agriculture in their region.

Racial and Ethnic Minority Groups

Racial and ethnic minority groups enjoy some political influence in Texas. The two best-known minority rights organizations in the state are affiliates of well-known national organizations. The Texas **League of United Latin American Citizens (LULAC)** is a Latino interest group, whereas the Texas chapter of the **National Association for the Advancement of Colored People (NAACP)** is an interest group organized to represent the interests of African Americans.

Minority groups are interested in the enforcement of laws protecting the voting rights of minority citizens, the election and appointment of minority Texans to state and local office, college and university admission policies, public services for low-income residents of the state, and inner-city development. In recent sessions of the legislature, Latino and African American members have pushed for the passage of legislation concerning hate crimes and racial profiling. **Hate crimes legislation** refers to legislative measures that increase penalties for persons convicted of criminal offenses motivated by prejudice based on race, religion, national origin, gender, or sexual orientation. **Racial profiling** is the practice of a police officer targeting individuals as suspected criminals on the basis of their race or ethnicity. Most Latino and African American legislators also support funding for public education and

League of United Latin American Citizens (LULAC) A Latino interest group.

National Association for the Advancement of Colored People (NAACP) An interest group organized to represent the interests of African Americans.

Hate crimes legislation Legislative measures that increase penalties for persons convicted of criminal offenses motivated by prejudice based on race, religion, national origin, gender, or sexual orientation.

Racial profiling The practice of a police officer targeting individuals as suspected criminals on the basis of their race or ethnicity.

GETTING INVOLVED

Joining a Group

People who want to influence policy in a particular issue area should join a group. The Internet Research feature on page 588 includes the websites of a number of interest groups active in Texas politics. Each of these groups is a membership organization in that it invites the participation of ordinary citizens.

Contact the group whose values and viewpoints most nearly conform to your own and find out how you can join the group and contribute to its work. Add your name to the group's mailing list, give money to the organization, attend meetings, and volunteer.

It's your government—get involved!

Children's Health Insurance Program (CHIP) A federal program designed to provide health insurance to children from low-income families whose parents are not poor enough to qualify for Medicaid.

healthcare programs targeting low-income residents, such as the **Children's Health Insurance Program (CHIP),** which is a federal program designed to provide health insurance to children from low-income families whose parents are not poor enough to qualify for Medicaid.

Racial and ethnic minority groups are considerably more influential in Texas politics today than they were in the early 1960s. More African American and Latino Texans are registered to vote than ever before. In 2004, Latino, African American, and Asian Texans constituted more than a third of the statewide vote.[14] No serious candidate for statewide or municipal office in the state's big cities can afford to ignore African American and Hispanic concerns. Latino and African American legislators have also become an important voting bloc in the state legislature.

Nonetheless, racial and ethnic minority groups are not as powerful as the more established interest groups in the state. Racial and ethnic minority groups are sometimes divided among themselves and are almost always short of funds. Many minority residents are not registered to vote; others stay home on Election Day. Furthermore, African American and Hispanic voters do not necessarily follow the political lead of groups such as LULAC and the NAACP.

Religious Groups

Churches and other religious institutions provide the foundation for a number of political organizations. Roman Catholic and Protestant churches in poor and minority areas have helped organize political groups to support healthcare, education, and neighborhood improvement for the state's poor people. These organizations include Communities Organized for Public Service (COPS) in San Antonio, Interfaith Alliance in the Rio Grande Valley, the Metropolitan Organization (TMO) in Houston, and the El Paso Inter-religious Sponsoring Organization (EPISO). They favor expanding CHIP coverage, increasing funding for public education, and protecting the rights of immigrant workers.

Religious right Individuals who hold conservative views because of their religious beliefs.

The most active and probably most influential religiously oriented political groups are associated with the **religious right,** who are individuals who hold conservative social views because of their religious beliefs. The Christian Coalition, Eagle Forum, and American Family Association are national organizations with branches in Texas. Conservative religious organizations oppose abortion, pornography, stem cell research, gay marriage, and the teaching of evolution in public schools.

CALVIN AND HOBBES

Source: Calvin and Hobbes copyright © 1999 Watterson. Distributed by Universal Press Syndicate. Reprinted with permission. All rights reserved.

Citizen groups
Organizations created to support government policies that they believe will benefit the public at large.

Advocacy groups
Organizations created to seek benefits on behalf of persons who are unable to represent their own interests.

Cause groups
Organizations whose members care intensely about a single issue or a group of related issues.

Texas Right to Life Committee An organization that opposes abortion.

National Abortion and Reproductive Rights Action League (NARAL Pro-Choice Texas) An organization that favors abortion rights.

They favor sexual abstinence before marriage, prayer in schools, home schooling, and family values in general. Some conservative religious groups also take positions on issues that do not have an obvious family values connection, such as tax rates, immigration, and the United Nations.

Conservative Christian groups are an important part of the base of the Texas Republican Party, and that alliance has enabled them to win some important legislative victories. In recent sessions, the Texas legislature passed a constitutional amendment to outlaw gay marriage, adopted a measure to require couples to attend premarital counseling or pay higher marriage license fees, and blocked an executive order by Governor Rick Perry to require school girls to be vaccinated against the human papilloma virus. The legislature has also adopted a number of restrictions on access to abortion, including a parental consent requirement for minors.[15]

Citizen, Advocacy, and Cause Groups

Citizen groups are organizations created to support government policies that they believe will benefit the public at large. For example, Common Cause and Texans for Public Justice are organizations that work for campaign finance reform, ethics regulations for public officials, and other good government causes. Texas Public Interest Research Group (Tex-PIRG) and Texas Watch are consumer rights organizations.

Advocacy groups are organizations created to seek benefits on behalf of persons who are unable to represent their own interests. The Children's Defense Fund, for example, is an organization that attempts to promote the welfare of children. The Texas AIDS Network represents the interests of people with HIV/AIDS.

Cause groups are organizations whose members care intensely about a single issue or a group of related issues. The **Texas Right to Life Committee,** for example, opposes abortion, whereas the Texas chapter of the **National Abortion and Reproductive Rights Action League,** which is known as **NARAL Pro-Choice Texas,** favors abortion rights. The **Sierra Club** is an environmental organization. Other cause groups include the **National Rifle Association (NRA), National Organization for Women (NOW),** and **AARP.** The NRA is an interest group organized to

Sierra Club Environmental organization.

National Rifle Association (NRA) An interest group organized to defend the rights of gun owners and defeat efforts at gun control.

National Organization for Women (NOW) A group that promotes women's rights.

defend the rights of gun owners and defeat efforts at gun control. NOW is a group that promotes women's rights. AARP, which was once the American Association of Retired Persons but now just goes by the acronym, is an interest group representing the concerns of older Americans.

Citizen, advocacy, and cause groups vary in political influence, depending on the strength of their organization, the strength of the opposition, and the popularity of their cause. **Mothers Against Drunk Driving (MADD),** which is an interest group that supports the reform of laws dealing with drunk driving, has been able to overcome the opposition of the liquor industry and DWI defense attorneys because it is well organized and its cause enjoys considerable popular support. In contrast, the Sierra Club and other environmental organizations have been relatively unsuccessful. Even though the environment is a popular cause, environmental organizations in Texas have been no match against the political influence of the oil and gas industry or electric utilities.

INTEREST GROUP TACTICS

AARP An interest group representing the concerns of older Americans.

Mothers Against Drunk Driving (MADD) An interest group that supports the reform of laws dealing with drunk driving.

Political action committees (PACs) Organizations created to raise and distribute money in political campaigns.

Interest groups employ a variety of tactics in an effort to achieve their goals.

Electioneering

Interest groups attempt to influence public policy by participating in the electoral process. Groups with a large membership and/or influence beyond their ranks try to affect election outcomes by endorsing favored candidates and delivering a bloc vote on their behalf. Unions, racial and ethnic minority groups, and some citizen groups regularly use this strategy. In 2006, for example, the Texas Right to Life Committee endorsed Republican Governor Perry for governor, whereas the Texas AFL-CIO threw its support behind Chris Bell, the Democratic Party nominee for governor. The Texas State Teachers Association and the Texas Federation of Teachers both endorsed Carole Keeton Strayhorn.

The most effective tool interest groups have for affecting election outcomes is money. Interest groups contribute to candidates they support through their **political action committees (PACs),** which are organizations created to raise and distribute money in political campaigns. People associated with the interest group, such as union members and business executives, contribute money to the group's PAC, which in turn gives money to candidates for office. Executives with Reliant Energy, for example, contribute to the Reliant Energy PAC. Texas physicians give money to the TMA PAC, and trial lawyers contribute to the TTLA PAC.

Texas does not limit the amount of money individuals or PACs can contribute in election campaigns, and some interest groups take advantage of the opportunity to give large amounts of money to the candidates of their choice. Groups involved in the tort reform debate were particularly generous during the 2003–2004 election cycle. Figure 22.1 graphs the amount of campaign contributions given by three of the major financial players in the battle over medical malpractice reform—TMA

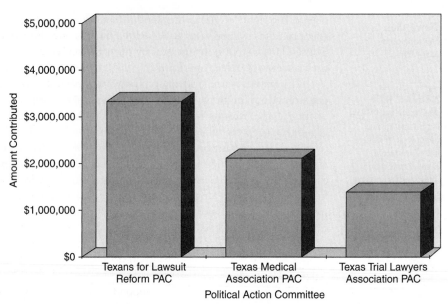

FIGURE 22.1   Campaign Contributions, 2003–2004.
Source: National Insititute of Money in State Politics.

PAC, TTLA PAC, and Texans for Lawsuit Reform (TLR) PAC, which is a PAC organized by business interests that support tort reform. As the figure shows, the two PACs supporting tort reform significantly outspent the trial lawyers' PAC.

Interest groups consider several factors in determining which candidates to support. Groups back candidates who are sympathetic with their policy preferences. The TMA PAC and TLR PAC support candidates favoring tort reform, mostly Republicans, whereas the TTLA PAC gives its money to tort reform opponents, mostly Democrats. Interest groups also consider the likelihood of a candidate's winning the election because groups want to back winners. Interest-group leaders would rather give to a strong candidate who is only somewhat supportive of their group than throw their money away on an almost certain loser who is completely behind the group's goals. Consequently, interest groups typically contribute more generously to incumbents than to challengers because they know that an **incumbent**—that is, a current officeholder—is more likely to win than is a challenger. Finally, interest groups prefer giving to incumbent officeholders who hold important policymaking positions, such as the members of the key policymaking committees in the legislature. Elected officials who hold important posts, such as the chairs of key committees in the legislature, are in a better position to return favors than are officeholders who have little power.

The political contribution pattern of large corporations illustrates the strategy that many groups follow in making campaign contributions. In 2007, the 46 Texas companies listed in the Fortune 500, which is a list of the 500 largest corporations in the United States compiled by *Fortune* magazine, made 73 percent of their campaign contributions to Republican House and Senate candidates in Texas. They gave the

Incumbent Current officeholder.

other 27 percent of their contributions to Democrats. Even though business groups typically favor Republicans because of philosphical reasons, the state's largest corporations still give some money to Democratic officeholders, especially Democrats who hold influential positions in Congress and the Texas legislature. Congressman Gene Green of Houston was the leading Democratic recipient of corporate campaign contributions in 2007 because he serves on the House Energy and Commerce Committee, an important committee to Texas oil interests, and has generally been a friend of the energy industry in the U.S. House.[16]

The political money game can be hazardous to the health of an interest group that winds up on the losing side of an election contest. Consider the experience of the Texas Automobile Dealers Association (TADA). Automobile dealers are businesspeople who are traditionally allied with the Republican Party. In 2001, however, Governor Perry angered the automobile dealers by vetoing both of their top legislative priorities. One measure would have allowed dealers to increase the documentary fee they charge on new car sales from $50 to $75; the other would have allowed dealers to sell "gap insurance" to cover the shortfall when an outstanding loan exceeds the value of a new car that is totaled.[17] The car dealers retaliated against the governor by throwing their support to his Democratic opponent in the 2002 election. When Perry won anyway, the automobile dealers moved quickly to try to repair relations with the governor by contributing $50,000 to the Perry campaign, matching the amount they had earlier given to his unsuccessful Democratic opponent.[18] Giving campaign contributions to a candidate after an election that the candidate has already won is known as **catching the late train.** The group also hired a former top aide to Governor Perry as a lobbyist.

Catching the late train The practice of giving campaign contributions to a candidate after an election is over and the candidate has won.

Lobbying

Lobbying is the communication of information by a representative of an interest group to a government official for the purpose of influencing a policy decision. Nearly 1,700 registered lobbyists represent group interests in Texas.[19] Although some interests hire a single lobbyist to represent them, big companies often employ a small army of high-priced lobbyists. SBC Communications, which now calls itself AT&T, spent as much as $6.8 million on 112 lobby contracts during the 2005 regular session of the legislature. SBC was well armed because it wanted the legislature to approve a measure to allow telephone companies to get into the cable TV market. The bill would also give phone companies more freedom to set local rates. Although the legislature failed to act on the proposal during the regular session, it passed the measure SBC favored in a subsequent special session and the governor signed it into law.[20]

Lobbying The communication of information by a representative of an interest group to a government official for the purpose of influencing a policy decision.

The traditional approach of lobbyists in Texas was called **social lobbying,** which is the attempt of lobbyists to influence public policy by cultivating personal, social relationships with policymakers. Cynics referred to the practice as "booze, bribes, and babes." Lobbyists would ply their trade by meeting legislators and executive branch officials at a local barbecue restaurant for an evening of ribs, beer, and storytelling.[21]

Social lobbying The attempt of lobbyists to influence public policy by cultivating personal, social relationships with policymakers.

Lobbyists are now more professional because government officials are more sophisticated. Professional lobbyists are skilled technicians, knowledgeable both in how to approach public officials and in the subject matter vital to their groups. The basic

NATIONAL PERSPECTIVE

Campaign Contribution Limits in Minnesota

Minnesota law limits the amount of money interest groups can contribute to candidates for legislative or executive office. During an election year, PACs and individuals can give no more than $500 to a candidate for governor or the state legislature, $200 to a candidate for attorney general, and $100 to a candidate for other statewide offices. In other years, contribution limits are lower—$100 per candidate.*

Minnesota's strict campaign finance law limits the amount of money available to candidates. In 2006, total campaign spending in Minnesota was $39 million, $17.70 for every voter who took part in the election. In contrast, candidates in Texas spent $179 million, $40.68 per voter.†

Minnesota's contribution limit influences the dynamics of election contests. Jesse Ventura, the former professional wrestler, won election as governor of Minnesota in 1998 as the candidate of the Reform Party, which is the political party founded by Dallas billionaire Ross Perot. Ventura defeated two well-known opponents, Republican Norm Coleman and Democrat Hubert Humphrey III, despite raising barely $1 million. The contribution limit helped Ventura because it prevented either of his opponents from raising more than $2.5 million.‡ In mid-October, when polls showed Humphrey and Coleman neck and neck, with Ventura running third, the two major party candidates decided to focus their campaigns on defeating each other while ignoring Ventura. As Election Day approached, the polls showed Ventura moving up, but neither Humphrey nor Coleman had enough money to buy television time for attack ads to stem Ventura's momentum. Were it not for the contribution limits, Coleman and Humphrey could have raised millions of dollars more in campaign contributions from interest groups that could have been used to cut Ventura down to size. Without significant interest-group support, Ventura would have lacked the money to respond to the attacks and would almost certainly have lost the election.§

QUESTIONS TO CONSIDER

1. Do strict contribution and expenditure limits contribute to the quality of democracy? Why or why not?
2. Do you think it is likely that the Texas legislature will adopt campaign finance limits? Why or why not?
3. Who would benefit from campaign contribution limits in Texas? Who would be harmed by contribution limits?

*Minnesota Secretary of State, available online at www.sos.state.mn.us.

†National Institute on Money in State Politics, available at www.followthemoney.org.

‡National Institute on Money in State Politics, available at www.followthemoney.org.

§Stephen I. Frank and Seven C. Wagner, *"We Shocked the World": A Case Study of Jesse Ventura's Election as Governor of Minnesota* (Orlando, FL: Harcourt College, 1999).

stock in trade of the skilled lobbyist is information. In fact, interest groups are sometimes the main source of information on a piece of legislation. "We have 140 days to deal with thousands of bills," said one state senator. "The lobbyists are providers of information about those issues. I don't know how we could operate without them."[22] Even though today's lobbyists are more professional than their predecessors, social lobbying continues to be a big part of the way they do business. In 2005, lobbyists showered $2.87 million worth of food, entertainment, and gifts on the 181 members of the Texas legislature.[23] In contrast to the national government and 22 other states, Texas places no limit on the amount of money interest groups and lobbyists can contribute to political campaigns or can spend on meals and entertainment for public officials.[24]

The most effective lobbyists build personal relationships with members of the legislature. Consider the case of Bill Miller, a founder of Hillco Partners, one of the state's most successful lobbying firms. Over the years, Miller has developed a close relationship with Speaker of the House Tom Craddick. In 2004, Miller helped arrange a private meeting with the pope for Craddick, who is a devout Catholic. Miller went along on the trip.[25] Many lobbyists are former members of the legislature or former staff members hired by interest groups to lobby their former colleagues over policy issues that they had worked on together in a previous legislative session. Unlike many states, Texas law allows former members of the legislature and employees of the executive branch to begin work as lobbyists the day after they resign their government positions.

Research shows that the most successful lobbying efforts are those that are supported by contributions during election season and reinforced by contacts from constituents.[26] Texas liquor wholesalers laid the groundwork for their effort to convince the legislature to change the state's liquor laws by contributing generously to the political campaigns of the governor, the lieutenant governor, the speaker of the House, and key legislative leaders. Liquor wholesalers gave $100,000 each to Governor Perry and Speaker Tom Craddick. They contributed $75,000 to Lieutenant Governor David Dewhurst, $40,000 to the chair of the Senate Business and Commerce Committee, and thousands of dollars more to dozens of other legislators. Altogether, the liquor wholesalers gave nearly $1.7 million in campaign contributions to state leaders in the months leading up to the opening of the 2007 session of the Texas legislature.[27]

Although legislators all deny that campaign contributions influence their votes, most will admit that groups that give generously to political campaigns enjoy access to lawmakers that other interests do not share. **Legislative access** is an open door through which an interest group hopes to influence the details of policy. Lobbyists for interest groups that contribute heavily to political campaigns usually have the opportunity to make their case to lawmakers. Legislators return their calls, invite them into their offices, and respond to them more quickly than they do for ordinary citizens who are not major campaign contributors.

Interest groups back their legislative lobbyists by mobilizing group members in the home districts of legislators to contact their representatives. The TMA, for example, asks its physician members to personally contact public officials who happen to be their patients. Even though the doctors who make the contacts with policymakers are not professional lobbyists, they are particularly effective because they already have a personal relationship with the public official.

Legislative access
An open door through which an interest group hopes to influence the details of policy.

Public Relations Campaigns

Interest groups attempt to influence policy by building public support for their points of view. They recognize that public officials, especially elected officials, are unlikely to jeopardize their political future by publicly supporting an unpopular cause, regardless of PAC money and lobbying. Interest groups understand that their lobbying efforts will be more effective if policymakers know that group goals enjoy public support.

The groups supporting tort reform have conducted a sophisticated public relations campaign to win support for their point of view. They have purchased billboards and run television and radio advertisements against what they call "lawsuit abuse." They have also used radio talk shows and other media to publicize examples of what they consider unreasonable jury judgments, such as the story of a woman who sued McDonald's restaurant chain after hot coffee spilled in her lap. According to a survey conducted in 2003 by the Scripps Howard Texas Poll, the public relations campaign of the tort reform supporters has been effective. By a 57 percent to 33 percent margin, Texans favored a $250,000 cap on noneconomic damages in medical malpractice lawsuits.[28]

Groups without substantial membership or financial resources sometimes employ public relations as their primary strategy for influencing public policy. For example, consumer groups, such as Texas Watch, produce research reports on consumer-related issues, such as tort reform and utility rates. They publish the reports on their websites and hold press conferences to call attention to their findings and recommendations.

Litigation

Sometimes interest groups use litigation (i.e., lawsuits) to achieve their goals. The NAACP and Mexican American Legal Defense and Education Fund (MALDEF) have gone to court many times to argue cases involving school desegregation, education finance, and voting rights. MALDEF, for example, provided legal support to the poor school districts that sued the state over its education funding system in the case of *Edgewood v. Kirby*.[29]

Although litigation has been an important political tool for interest groups, it has its limitations. Court action is both time-consuming and expensive. Not all groups can afford it. Also, litigation is reactive. Lawsuits are inevitably filed in response to policy actions with which a group disagrees. Court actions can sometimes succeed in overturning policies already in place, but they are usually an ineffective means for initiating policies.

Protest Demonstrations

Groups that cannot afford public relations experts and advertising campaigns attempt to influence public opinion by means of protest demonstrations. Civil rights groups used this technique in the 1960s. Today, it is occasionally employed by a variety of groups pursuing many different goals, ranging from antinuclear groups opposing the construction of a nuclear power plant to antipornography crusaders picketing convenience stores that sell *Playboy* magazine. In general, protest demonstrations are a tactic used by groups unable to achieve their goals through other means. Sometimes the protest catches the attention of the general public and pressure is brought to bear on behalf of the protesting group. In most cases, though, protests have only a marginal impact on public policy.

Political demonstrations sometimes backfire. Immigrant rights supporters lost ground when high school–aged demonstrators waived Mexican flags rather than American flags. In Houston, meanwhile, protestors organized by the SEIU had to pay fines as large as $2,000 and spend several days in jail after illegally blocking intersections in support of a union strike against janitorial companies.[30]

Political Violence

Occasionally, frustrated groups go beyond peaceful protest to violent, illegal activities. During the 1960s, some groups opposed to the war in Vietnam took over college administration buildings or burned Reserve Officer Training Corps (ROTC) offices on campus. The Ku Klux Klan has also been linked to violence in the state. Although political violence usually produces a violent response from the political establishment, violence can occasionally succeed in calling the public's attention to an issue that might otherwise be ignored.

 WHAT IS YOUR OPINION?

Is violence on behalf of a political cause ever justified?

Alliances

Interest groups find power in alliances with other interest groups and political parties. The battle over medical malpractice reform in particular and tort reform in general pitted two powerful interest group–political party alliances against one another. The TMA, business groups as a whole (especially insurance companies and construction companies), and the Republican Party lined up in favor of tort reform, whereas trial lawyers, consumer groups, and the Democratic Party were opposed. The tort reformers got most of what they wanted out of the legislature because their interest-group alliance was better funded and better organized than were their opponents. Furthermore, the Republican Party had won electoral control of all three branches of state government, including both chambers of the Texas legislature.

Groups also build alliances with other interests, sometimes even with groups that are usual opponents. SBC Communications lined up support not just from fellow telecommunications companies, such as Verizon Communication, but also from the Communications Workers of America, the union representing thousands of the company's rank-and-file workers. When groups that are not normally aligned lobby on behalf of the same issue, it gets the attention of lawmakers.[31]

CONCLUSION: INTEREST GROUPS AND POLICYMAKING

Interest groups are important participants in a state's policymaking process. Political scientists Clive S. Thomas and Ronald J. Hrebenar classify states as to the relative influence of groups in state politics. They identify the following types of states:

- **Dominant states** The policymaking influence of interest groups in these states is overwhelming and consistent. Thomas and Hrebenar put five states in this category: Alabama, Florida, Montana, Nevada, and West Virginia.
- **Complementary states** In these states, groups either must work with or, alternatively, are constrained by other elements of the state's political system, such

Immigrant rights supporters lost ground when high school–aged demonstrators waived Mexican flags rather than American flags.

as its political culture or a strong executive branch. Sixteen states fall into this category: Colorado, Connecticut, Delaware, Hawaii, Indiana, Maine, Massachusetts, New Hampshire, New Jersey, New York, North Carolina, North Dakota, Pennsylvania, Rhode Island, Vermont, and Wisconsin.

- **Subordinate states** Interest groups are subordinate to other elements of the state's political climate. No state falls into this category.
- **Dominant/complementary states** The states that are in this category alternate between the dominant and complementary classifications. This category includes 26 states: Alaska, Arizona, Arkansas, California, Georgia, Idaho, Illinois, Iowa, Kansas, Kentucky, Louisiana, Maryland, Mississippi, Missouri, Nebraska, New Mexico, Ohio, Oklahoma, Oregon, South Carolina, Tennessee, Texas, Utah, Virginia, Washington, and Wyoming.
- **Complementary/subordinate** The states in this category alternate between the complementary and subordinate classifications. This group includes three states: Michigan, Minnesota, and South Dakota.

Thomas and Hrebenar classify Texas as a dominant/complementary state. The Lone Star State alternates between periods when the influence of interest groups is overwhelming and times when groups are constrained by other elements of the state's political system. In Texas, the governor and legislative leaders are powerful enough to limit the influence of interest groups if they wish. Nonetheless, the governor and legislative leaders do not always choose to restrain the power of groups because they may support the goals the groups are trying to achieve. Furthermore, the state's executive and legislative officials are not involved in every policy issue and in every detail of the issues in which they do participate.[32]

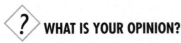 **WHAT IS YOUR OPINION?**

Do interest groups have too much influence in Texas?

Agenda Building

Interest groups participate in every stage of the policymaking process. Groups attempt to set the policy agenda and define the way issues on the agenda are perceived. Medical malpractice reform became part of the official agenda in Texas because of the efforts of the TMA, the TLR, and other groups advocating changes in the state's tort laws. The proponents of tort reform campaigned to define the issue in terms of lawsuit abuse by publicizing instances of frivolous lawsuits and excessive jury awards. In contrast, the TTLA and consumer groups defended the civil justice system by arguing that most jury awards are reasonable and that excessive awards are almost always overturned or reduced on appeal. The TTLA attempted to define the issue in terms of consumer rights by pointing to examples of patients seriously injured by grossly incompetent physicians.

Policy Formulation and Adoption

Interest groups play a prominent role in policy formulation. Groups formulate policy proposals by drafting measures that can then be introduced as legislation by sympathetic members of the legislature or local governing bodies. Groups also attempt to influence the details of policy proposals being considered by legislative bodies and government agencies. The medical malpractice reform proposals considered by the 2003 session of the legislature were written in close consultation with the TMA and other tort reform proponents. In the meantime, tort reform opponents, recognizing that they lacked the votes to defeat the measures outright, attempted to modify the details of the legislation to minimize its impact.

Interest groups affect policy adoption both by influencing the identity of elected officials and by lobbying policymakers. The proponents of tort reform were in a good position to accomplish many of their goals in 2003 because their candidate for governor and most of the legislative candidates they backed had won. The lobbying battle was not over whether tort reform would pass because the votes were already in place. Instead, the fight was over the exact shape of the legislation.

Policy Implementation and Evaluation

Interest groups influence policy implementation through electioneering and lobbying. In Texas, many of the executive and judicial branch officials who carry out policies are elected. For example, a majority of the members of the Texas Supreme Court, the state's highest court for civil disputes, has won election with the support of tort reform advocates. Furthermore, groups interested in policy implementation frequently lobby state agencies and local officials in charge of carrying out policies just as they lobby legislators.

Interest groups participate in policy evaluation as well, hoping to shape policy feedback in accordance with their particular points of view. The TMA, the TLR, and other proponents of tort reform argue that the medical malpractice legislation adopted in 2003 is working. In Harris County, they note, medical malpractice lawsuits dropped 41 percent from their pre-2003 averages.[33] Medical malpractice insurance rates have fallen and the number of physicians in high-risk specializations such as obstetrics/gynecology, neurosurgery, and orthopedics has risen.[34] Between 2003 and 2007, the Texas Medical Board licenced 10,878 new physicians compared to 8,391 in the previous four years.[35] The American Medical Association even removed Texas from the list of states experiencing a medical liability crisis.[36] In contrast, consumer groups, trial lawyers, and other opponents of the malpractice lawsuit reform argue that the new law hurts consumers without helping doctors. Medical malpractice lawsuit filings are down, they declare, because medical malpractice cases are expensive to investigate and the award caps have discouraged attorneys from filing lawsuits even in meritorious cases. The $250,000 ceiling on noneconomic damages effectively slams the courthouse door in the face of nursing home residents, children, and stay-at-home mothers and others who cannot demonstrate economic damages such as lost wages. Lawyers will not take nursing home negligence cases or medical malpractice cases involving children and stay-at-home mothers, regardless of their merits, because the most they can recover is $250,000 in noneconomic damages. The new law is also hurting lawyers, both attorneys who filed medical malpractice lawsuits and attorneys who defended against them. The ABA reports that many medical malpractice lawyers are either leaving the state or pursuing other specializations.[37]

By and large, interest group participation in Texas politics has a conservative impact on public policy because the most powerful interest groups in the state typically promote conservative policy preferences. Business groups and trade associations favor low overall tax rates with a tax structure dependent on consumer taxes, limited government services, and government regulations designed to foster business development. In contrast, the interest groups that counterbalance business forces in other states and at the national level, especially organized labor, consumer organizations, and environmental groups, are relatively weak in Texas. Only about 30 of 1,700 registered lobbyists work for consumer and environmental groups; most of the rest represent business interests.[38] Until the balance of power among Texas interest groups changes, public policy is unlikely to change.

LET'S DEBATE

Would Public Funding of Elections Enhance the Quality of Democracy in the State?

Overview: Most political commentators agree that one of the principal problems in American state and national politics is the corrupting influence of money in the electoral process, and Texas is not immune from this problem. Compared with other states, Texas has strong, effective, and entrenched lobbies, and many observers of the Texas political scene believe the money spent by lobbies on Texas elections is harmful to the quality of the state's democratic politics. It is reasonable to assume that candidates who receive campaign contributions have an "interest" in ensuring that campaign contributors' voices are heard and affairs are addressed. But if elected officials spend their time concerned with the relationships to their contributors, what does this mean for the interests of the average Texan who is not financially engaged in politics? The Clean Elections (or Clean Money) movement to have publicly funded state and local elections proposes an answer.

The Clean Elections (CE) movement gained momentum in the mid-1990s as a reaction to the various campaign finance scandals at both the state and national levels. The goal of the CE movement is to create across the states a regime of publicly funded electoral systems in which average citizens can use public money to run for elective public service. CE politics will increase the number of citizens who will run for office and, as a result, there will be a greater diversity of views and interests represented in government. It is now widely believed that, under the current campaign financing system, there are fewer competitive elections because it takes a significant amount of funding to run a viable campaign. It is believed that the current system benefits and institutionalizes incumbents, since they have access to the wealth necessary for modern campaigns, and this limits the number of challengers for representative office.

Although only seven states have a CE system in place, Maine and Arizona have been the models for the clean money movement. In both states, the majority of state legislators are "clean" and, in Arizona, Governor Janet Napolitano won using public financing. In December 2005, Connecticut enacted its CE system as a reaction to the major campaign finance scandal that brought down Governor John G. Rowland. The CE movement is relatively new in state politics, and its contribution to the quality of democratic politics is still an open question. Opponents claim that CE systems are more expensive government-run programs, and they are subject to the red tape, inefficiency, and corruption that is found in many bureaucracies. Some believe that CE electoral systems can have a dampening effect on free and competitive elections and, therefore, should be banned.

Arguments for Public Funding of Elections

❏ **Public funding of elections expands the candidate pool and voter choice.** Public financing of elections would give interested and qualified Texans of average means the opportunity to commit to public service. By giving public funding the qualified citizens, CE laws remove the financial barrier that prohibits many from running for office. As the Maine experience shows, once the financial burden of campaigning is removed, the number of citizens who run for office significantly increases, and the result is that voters have a diverse and wide range of candidate choice.

❏ **Public funding of elections allows for independent politics.** CE candidates who win office are not tied to the lobbying interests that contribute to a candidate's campaign. A touchstone of the theory underlying CE law is that, when a candidate accepts public funding, he or she loses or diminishes the expectations lobbies have of those to whom they give campaign contributions. Officeholders end their reliance on interest group contributions and are able to engage in politics unencumbered by the demands of campaign contributors.

❏ **CE regimes help realize the goal of political equality.** A hallmark of effective democratic governance is the ability of all qualified citizens to run for elective office. Under the current system, those who have access to personal wealth or are well networked with moneyed interests have the means to campaign for office. The result is an upper-class bias in both the

continued on next page

candidates and in the law and policy they make. The consequence of CE laws is to promote equality of access to political office and foster equality in law and policy.

Arguments Against Public Funding of Elections

❏ **Publicly funded elections are coercive and violate political freedom.** Publicly funded elections compel citizens to support, through their tax dollars, candidates and positions they do not endorse or find objectionable. This is coercion because citizens are forced by law to participate in a system in which political liberty also means the freedom not to participate. Interested Texans have other means, such as volunteering and working for political parties, as well as their own individual initiative, through which to lay the groundwork for a run for office.

❏ **CE candidates are not immune to corruption.** Just because candidates forgo interest group contributions does not make them virtuous. For instance, in the nine years Maine has had its CE system, its ethics commission has found CE candidates who've spent public money on personal rent, meals, travel, and auto repair. They've also investigated candidates who cannot account for campaign expenditures (one candidate kept receipts in a jar on a desk that "looked like an advertisement for attention deficit disorder"). There is no guarantee that publicly funded campaigns will mitigate corruption in office.

❏ **Though flawed, the current system encourages true pluralist democratic politics.** The genius of the American political system is that interested parties and groups have the ability to compete for office. Our founders believed that federal and state governments would reflect the myriad of economic and political interests found in the United States, and that these interests would seek representation by placing candidates in office. The check on corruption would come from the political negotiation and compromise by the multitude of competing interests. CE regimes would not only stifle pluralist competition but also would limit the quality of law and policy forged by necessary accommodation.

QUESTIONS

1. Would CE improve the quality of Texas politics and electoral competition? Why or why not?
2. Do publicly financed elections limit corruption in office and prevent free democratic practice? What is the best way to limit political corruption?

SELECT READINGS

1. Gerald Lubenow, *A User's Guide to Campaign Finance Reform* (Lanham, MD: Rowman & Littlefield, 2001).
2. Bradly Smith, *Unfree Speech: The Folly of Campaign Finance Reform* (Princeton, NJ: Princeton University Press, 2001).

SELECT WEBSITES

1. **www.publicampaign.org/**
   Website of public financing advocacy group for state and local elections.

2. **www.democracymatters.org/**
   Website for Democracy Matters, a university student organization dedicated to limiting money in politics and other pro-democracy reforms.

KEY TERMS

AARP

advocacy groups

American Federation of Labor-Congress of Industrial Organizations (AFL-CIO)

catching the late train

cause groups

Children's Health Insurance Program (CHIP)

citizen groups

good business climate

hate crimes legislation

incumbent

interest group

joint and several liability

League of United Latin American Citizens (LULAC)

legislative access

lobbying

minimum wage

Mothers Against Drunk
Driving (MADD)

National Abortion and Reproductive Rights Action League
(NARAL Pro-Choice Texas)

National Association for the
Advancement of Colored
People (NAACP)

National Organization for
Women (NOW)

National Rifle Association
(NRA)

plaintiff

political action
committees (PACs)

punitive damages

racial profiling

religious right

right-to-work law

Sierra Club

social lobbying

Texas Association of
Business (TAB)

Texas Medical
Association (TMA)

Texas Right to Life
Committee

Texas Trial Lawyers
Association (TTLA)

tort reform

trade associations

union shop *or* closed shop

NOTES

1. Guillermo X. Garcia, "Group Says Tort Reform Won't Fix Medical Crisis," *San Antonio Express News*, April 17, 2003, available at www.mysanantonio.com.
2. "States Said to Be in Trouble," *USA Today*, April 27, 2003, available at www.usatoday.com.
3. Gary Boulard, "The Doctors' Big Squeeze," *State Legislatures*, December 2002, p. 26.
4. David Pasztor, "Malpractice Pain Awards Haven't Risen, Study Finds," *Austin American Statesman*, March 18, 2003, available at www.statesman.com.
5. Doug J. Swanson, "Patients' Deaths Haven't Moved State Board to Act," *Dallas Morning News*, July 28, 2002, available at www.dallasnews.com.
6. Alan Greenblatt, "Medical Mayhem," *Governing*, April 2003, p. 36.
7. Texas Department of Insurance, "Tort Reform Statutes," available at www.tdi.state.tx.us.
8. Janet Elliott, "Defendants Fare Better on Appeal, Study Finds," *Houston Chronicle*, Nov. 6, 2003, p. 27A.
9. Texas Watch Foundation, *A Decade of Watching and Waiting*, March 2007, available at www.texaswatch.org.
10. Mark Lisheron, "Liquor Stores Shaken, Stirred, by Distributors' Plan," *Austin American-Statesman*, February 5, 2007, available at www.statesman.com.
11. Bureau of Labor Statistics, "Union Affiliation of Employed Wage and Salary Workers by State," available at www.bls.gov.
12. Texas for Public Justice, "Texas PACs.: 2006 Cycle Spending," available at www.tpj.org.
13. Texas AFL-CIO, available at www.texasaflcio.org.
14. "Exit Polls for Texas," available at www.cnn.com/elections/2004.
15. Emily Ramshaw, "Christian Right Faring Well at Capitol," *Dallas Morning News*, May 16, 2007, available at www.dallasnews.com.
16. Richard S. Dunham and Kathrine Schmidt, "Texas' Top Corporations Stay Loyal to GOP," *Houston Chronicle*, November 26, 2007, available at www.chron.com.
17. Terry Box and Pete Slover, "Car Dealers Make U-Turn to Sanchez," *Dallas Morning News*, July 18, 2002, available at www.morningnews.com.
18. National Institute on Money in Politics, available at www.followthemoney.com.
19. Texas Ethics Commission, available at www.ethics.state.tx.us.
20. Sanford Nowlin, "Swarming Capitol Paid Off for SBC," *San Antonio Express-News*, April 13, 2006, available at www.mysanantonio.com.
21. Keith E. Hamm and Charles W. Wiggins, "Texas: The Transformation from Personal to Informational Lobbying," in Ronald J. Hrebenar and Clive S. Thomas, eds., *Interest Group Politics in the Southern States* (Tuscaloosa: University of Alabama Press, 1992), p. 163.
22. Brent Manley, "Texas Lobbyists' Big Bucks Get Bigger," *Houston Post*, March 18, 1984, pp. 1A, 18A.
23. Lisa Sandberg and Kelly Guckian, "Lobbyists' Money Talks—Softly, But It's Heard," *San Antonio Express-News*, April 12, 2006, available at www.mysanantonio.com.
24. Ibid.
25. Ibid.
26. John R. Wright, "Contributions, Lobbying, and Committee Voting in the U.S. House of Representatives," *American Political Science Review* 84 (June 1990): 417–438.
27. Robert T. Garrett, "Liquor Wholesalers Ply Legislators with Cash," *Dallas Morning News*, January 23, 2007, available at www.dallasnews.com.
28. Janet Elliott, "Most Texans Favor Cap in Medical Malpractice," *Houston Chronicle*, May 17, 2003, p. 36A.
29. *Edgewood v. Kirby*, 777 S.W.2d 391 (1989).

30. L. M. Sixel, "Union Protesters Pay Price in City," *Houston Chronicle*, March 25, 2007, pp. D1–D4.

31. Nowlin, "Swarming Capitol Paid Off for SBC."

32. Clive S. Thomas and Ronald J. Hrebenar, "Interest Groups in the States," in Virginia Gray and Russell L. Hanson, eds., *Politics in the American States*, 8th ed. (Washington, DC: CQ Press, 2004), p. 122.

33. Dave Mann and Jake Bernstein, "Craddickism," *Texas Observer*, December 15, 2006, p. 13.

34. Travis E. Polling, "Lawsuit Limit May Be Just What the Doctor Ordered," *San Antonio Express-News*, February 26, 2006, available at www.mysanantonio.com.

35. Ralph Blumenthal, "More Doctors in Texas After Malpractice Caps," *New York Times*, October 5, 2007, available at www.nytimes.com.

36. Janet Elliott, "AMA Takes Texas off Its Liability Crisis List," *Houston Chronicle*, May 16, 2005, available at www.houstonchronicle.com.

37. Terry Carter, "Tort Reform Texas Style," *ABA Journal*, October 2006, p. 33.

38. Sandberg and Guckian, "Lobbyists' Money Talks—Softly, But It's Heard."

Chapter 23

Political Parties in Texas

CHAPTER OUTLINE

LEARNING OUTCOMES

After studying Chapter 23, students should be able to do the following:

▸ Describe the party system in the United States and Texas. (pp. 608–609)

▸ Describe the party organization of the two major parties at the national and state levels. (pp. 610–613)

▸ Trace the history of political party competition in Texas from the late nineteenth century through the present. (pp. 613–617)

▸ Compare and contrast the Texas Democratic and Republican Parties today in terms of voter support and offices held. (pp. 617–618)

▸ Identify the groups of voters who generally support each of the major political parties in

terms of income, race and ethnicity, region, and place of residence. (pp. 619–620)

▸ Identify the interest groups allied with each of the state's major political parties. (p. 620)

▸ Compare and contrast the issue orientation of the state's two major political parties. (pp. 621–625)

▸ Evaluate the policy impact of the emergence of the GOP as the state's dominant political party. (pp. 625–626)

▸ Identify the factors affecting the future of party politics in Texas, and assess the challenge facing both major parties in the state. (pp. 627–628)

▸ Describe the role of political parties in the state's policymaking process. (pp. 629–630)

▸ Define the key terms listed on page 632 and explain their significance.

Dallas County became Democratic in 2006. The Democratic Party ended two decades of Republican dominance by winning every contested countywide office on the ballot, including county judge, district attorney, and 42 judicial positions. The Democrats won because of good timing and demographic change. In the short run, Dallas Democrats benefited from a strong national tide running in their favor caused by the unpopularity of President George W. Bush. In the long run, demographic changes worked to the Democrats' advantage. Between 2000 and mid-year 2005, Dallas County lost 130,000 white residents while gaining 175,000 Latinos. More than 60 percent of county residents were either African American or Latino.[1] Because most whites vote Republican and most Latinos vote Democratic, the Democrats benefited from the population shift.

What, if anything, does the Democratic victory in Dallas County in 2006 portend for the future of party politics in the state? Demographers estimate that Latinos will become the majority ethnic group in Texas by 2035. By 2040, the Texas population will be a quarter white and 60 percent Latino.[2] Does population change mean that Texas will inevitably become a Democratic state? This chapter addresses that and other questions as it examines political parties in Texas.

This chapter on political parties is the third in a series of four chapters examining the political environment for policymaking. Chapter 21 discussed political participation in Texas, whereas Chapter 22 dealt with interest groups. Chapter 24 will focus on elections. This chapter begins by describing the party system in Texas and the United States. It traces the state's party history and examines party organization at the national and state levels. The chapter compares the state's major parties in terms of strength, base of support, interest group alliances, and issue positions. It examines the impact of partisan change on public policy in the state and explores the challenges facing both major parties. The chapter concludes by discussing the role of political parties in the policymaking process.

THE PARTY SYSTEM

Political party A group of individuals who join together to seek public office in order to influence public policy.

A **political party** is a group of individuals who join together to seek public office in order to influence public policy. Parties are similar to interest groups in that both types of political organizations attempt to affect the policymaking process and both are interested in election outcomes. The difference is that political parties attempt to win control of the machinery of government by nominating candidates for elected office to run under the party label and, if they are successful, they identify with the party while in office. The Republican Party, Democratic Party, Texas Association of Business (TAB), and Texas Trial Lawyers Association (TTLA) all participate in the election process and attempt to influence public policy, but only the Republicans and the Democrats actually put forward candidates for office under their organizational name. They are political parties, whereas the other two organizations are interest groups.

Two-party system The division of voter loyalties between two major political parties, resulting in the near exclusion of minor parties from seriously competing for a share of political power.

Throughout most of its history, the United States has had a **two-party system,** which is the division of voter loyalties between two major political parties, resulting in the near exclusion of minor parties from seriously competing for a share of political power. Since the Civil War era, the Democrats and the Republicans have been the two dominant parties in American national politics. The Libertarian, Green,

NATIONAL PERSPECTIVE

Minor Parties in New York

Voters in New York choose from among candidates for the two major parties and several minor parties. State law allows a political party to receive a place on the official ballot if its supporters can collect 20,000 petition signatures. The party holds its ballot slot as long as its candidate for governor receives at least 50,000 votes. Since 1970, the New York ballot has consistently included candidates for the Conservative, Liberal, and Right to Life Parties in addition to the Democrats and Republicans. In recent years, the ballot in New York has also included the Independence, Green, and Working Families Parties.

Minor parties in New York have been successful at holding their places on the ballot because of the state's cross-endorsement rule. An individual can run for office as the candidate of more than one party. In 2006, for example, Hillary Rodham Clinton ran for reelection to the U.S. Senate as the candidate of both the Democratic Party and the Independence Party, whereas her chief opponent, John Spencer, was the candidate of both the Republican Party and the Conservative Party. People who want to vote for a minor party candidate who is cross-endorsed by a major party do not have to worry about throwing their votes away because the candidate receives the sum total of votes cast for that candidate, whether they came from minor party or major party voters.

New York's minor parties are more interested in influencing policy than electing candidates. The Liberal Party's primary goal is to make the state's Democratic Party more liberal. Most of the Liberal Party's endorsed candidates are Democrats but, if party leaders believe that the Democratic candidate is not sufficiently liberal, the party can run its own candidate or make no endorsement in the race, thereby taking votes away from the Democratic candidate. Sometimes the Liberal Party will even endorse a moderate Republican. Similarly, the Conservative Party works to push the Republican Party in a conservative direction by withholding support from GOP nominees who are not conservative enough for Conservative Party tastes.

The New York Right to Life Party focuses on a single issue, opposition to abortion. It selects its candidates based solely on their position on the issue of abortion. The Right to Life Party occasionally cross-endorses one of the major party candidates, usually the Republican candidate. Most of the time, however, the Right to Life Party nominates its own candidate and uses the campaign as an opportunity to discuss opposition to abortion.

QUESTIONS TO CONSIDER

1. Would you like for Texas to have election laws, similar to those in New York, that allow minor parties to cross-endorse major party candidates?

2. If you lived in New York, would you consider minor party endorsements in deciding which candidate to support?

3. Would you ever consider voting for a minor party candidate who was not also endorsed by a major party, knowing that the candidate had no realistic chance of winning? Why or why not?

and Reform Parties are minor parties that have tried to have an impact in Texas politics. Except for the election of a small number of Libertarian candidates at the local level, minor party candidates have had little success in the Lone Star State. After the 2006 election, every member of the Texas legislature and every member of the congressional delegation from Texas was either Republican or Democrat.

Despite a national two-party system, many states have experienced periods of one-party dominance. The most significant example of one-party control took place in the South after the end of the Civil War era. The Democratic Party dominated southern politics for nearly a century. Political conflicts still occurred in the South, but they took place within the Democratic Party between factions divided over issues or personalities. A **party faction** is an identifiable subgroup within a political party.

Party faction An identifiable subgroup within a political party.

PARTY ORGANIZATION

The Democratic and Republican Parties have both national and state party structures.

National Party Organization

A national committee and a national committee chair head the national party organization. The national committee consists of a committeeman and committeewoman from each state and the District of Columbia, chosen by their state or the district party organization. The national committee elects the national chair. When the party controls the White House, the national chair is usually the choice of the president.

Independent expenditures
Money spent in support of a candidate but not coordinated with the candidate's campaign.

The national party organizations support party candidates at the state level primarily with **independent expenditures,** which is money spent in support of a candidate but not coordinated with the candidate's campaign. Although parties can contribute a limited amount of money directly to candidates, they can make unlimited independent expenditures. Parties also back candidates by providing them with polling data and conducting get-out-the-vote efforts. Furthermore, individuals interested in running for state or national office can attend candidate training sessions sponsored by the national party organizations, at which they learn how to build a campaign organization, raise money, deal with the media, identify issues, and present themselves to voters.

Texas Party Organization

Political parties in Texas have both temporary and permanent party organizations. Figure 23.1 depicts the various structures.

Temporary Party Organization   The temporary party organization of each party assembles for a few hours or days in general election years (even-numbered years—2006, 2008, etc.) to allow rank-and-file party supporters a chance to participate in the party's decision-making process. On the evening of the March primary after the polls have closed, Texans have the opportunity to attend precinct conventions, usually in the same location as the polling place, with Republicans gathering in one area and Democrats in another. Citizens who voted in the primary election are eligible to participate in the precinct convention of the party in whose primary they voted. The turnout at precinct conventions is usually light, especially in nonpresidential years. The main business of precinct conventions is to elect delegates to the county or state senatorial district conventions, which are held on the second Saturday after the primary. In large urban counties with more than one state senatorial district (Harris, Dallas, Bexar, and Tarrant Counties), delegates elected at precinct conventions attend state senatorial district conventions. In other counties, they attend a county convention. The number of delegates an election precinct may send to the county or district convention depends on the size of the vote in that precinct for the party's candidate in the last governor's election.

The county and district conventions are larger and more formally organized than precinct conventions, and they generally last longer, sometimes a full day. The convention usually includes speeches by party leaders and officeholders, and the

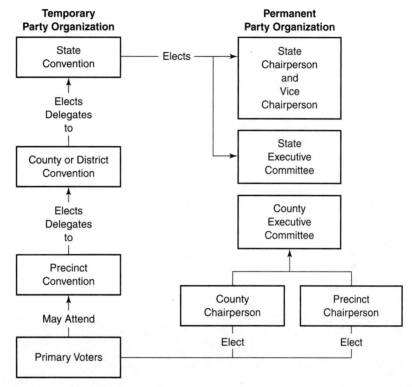

FIGURE 23.1   Texas Party Structures.

delegates will likely debate and vote on a number of resolutions. Once again, the main business of the meeting is to select delegates to the next highest level—in this case, the state convention. The number of delegates each county or district convention sends to the state convention depends on the size of the vote for the party's candidate in the last governor's election in the county or district.

The Republican and Democratic Parties hold their state conventions in June. This meeting is the largest, most formal, and longest of all, generally lasting most of a weekend. The state convention certifies party nominees for the fall general election, adopts a state **party platform** (which is a statement of party principles and issue positions), elects the state party chairperson and vice chairperson, chooses members of the state executive committee, and selects individuals to serve on the national party executive committee. The state convention also gives the party the opportunity to showcase itself and its candidates for the upcoming general election.

In presidential election years, the state party convention selects delegates to the national party convention. State law provides that delegates to the national party conventions be pledged to support presidential candidates in rough proportion to the candidates' strength in the spring presidential preference primary. In addition to selecting delegates to the national party convention, each state party convention also names a slate of potential presidential electors to cast the electoral college votes for Texas, should the party's presidential candidate carry the state in the November

Party platform A statement of party principles and issue positions.

Electoral college
The system established in the U.S. Constitution for the selection of the president and vice president of the United States.

general election. The **electoral college** is the system established in the U.S. Constitution for the selection of the president and vice president of the United States.

Permanent Party Organization   Each party has a permanent party organization, which operates year-round. At the base of the permanent party organization are the precinct chairpersons, elected by party voters in each of the state's precincts, except in those areas where one party is so weak that no one can be found to accept the job. Precinct chairpersons conduct primary elections by staffing the polling place on Election Day. They may also work to organize the precinct for their party.

The county executive committee is the next highest level of permanent party organization. It includes all the precinct chairpersons in the county and the county chairperson, who is elected by party voters countywide. The county executive committee receives filing petitions and fees from primary election candidates for countywide offices and is responsible for placing candidate names on the ballot. The county executive committee also arranges for county and district conventions.

The state executive committee is the highest level of party organization in the state. It includes the party chair and vice-chair and a committeeman and committeewoman representing each of the 31 state senatorial districts. The State

Delegates cheer Governor Rick Perry at the Texas Republican State Party convention.

Democratic Executive Committee (SDEC) includes a party treasurer as well. The main duties of the SDEC and the State Republican Executive Committee (SREC) are to certify statewide candidates for the March primary, arrange state party conventions, raise money for party candidates, and, in general, promote the party. In particular, state party chairs serve as media spokespersons for their party.

HISTORY OF THE TEXAS PARTY SYSTEM

Grand Old Party (GOP) Nickname for the Republican Party.

Solid South The usual Democratic sweep of southern state electoral votes in presidential election years between the end of the Civil War era and the current party era.

Conservatism The political view that seeks to preserve the political, economic, and social institutions of society against abrupt change. Conservatives generally oppose most government economic regulation and heavy government spending while favoring low taxes and traditional values.

The Civil War and Reconstruction produced the one-party Democratic South. Most native white southerners hated the Republican Party because of its association with the Union during the Civil War era. In Texas, the **Grand Old Party (GOP),** as the Republican Party was known, could count on the loyalty of African Americans, German Americans living in the Hill Country who had opposed secession before the Civil War, and few others. With the Republican Party in disrepute, the Democrats were the dominant party not only in Texas but also throughout the South, so much so, in fact, that political commentators coined the term **Solid South** to refer to the usual Democratic sweep of southern state electoral votes in presidential election years. In Texas, Democrats won nearly every statewide race, most seats in Congress and the state legislature, and the overwhelming majority of local and judicial contests, frequently without Republican opposition.

Large landowners and industrialists controlled the Democratic Party of the late nineteenth and early twentieth centuries. The public policies they favored reflected a political philosophy of **conservatism,** which is the political view that seeks to preserve the political, economic, and social institutions of society against abrupt change. Conservatives generally oppose most government economic regulation and heavy government spending while favoring low taxes and traditional values.

By the 1930s, an identifiable liberal faction had emerged to challenge conservative dominance of the Democratic Party. **Liberalism** is the political view that seeks to change the political, economic, or social institutions of society to foster the development of the individual. Liberals believe that the government can (and should) advance social progress by promoting political equality, social justice, and economic prosperity. Liberals usually favor government regulation and high levels of government spending for social programs. Liberals value social and cultural diversity and defend the right of individual adult choice on issues such as access to abortion. Liberal Democrats in the Lone Star State supported Democratic President Franklin Roosevelt and his **New Deal program,** which was the name of Roosevelt's legislative program for countering the Great Depression. Liberal Democrats called for a more active role for state government in the fields of education, job training, healthcare, and public assistance to the poor. To pay for these programs, liberal Democrats proposed higher taxes on business and industry, as well as on people earning substantial incomes. Liberal Democrats in Texas called for the elimination of the white primary and the poll tax. They supported an end to discrimination against African Americans and Latinos.

The liberal wing of the Texas Democratic Party achieved some political success during the 1930s as the Great Depression caused many Texans to question the wisdom

INTERNET RESEARCH

Political Parties in Texas

The Texas Democratic, Green, Libertarian, Reform, and Republican Parties all have homepages. Learn more about the state's political parties by checking out their websites.

Democratic Party: **www.txdemocrats.org**

Texas Green Party: **www.txgreens.org/**

Texas Libertarian Party: **www.tx.lp.org/**

Texas Reform Party: **www.texasreformparty.org/**

Texas Republican Party: **www.texasgop.org**

Review each of the websites, and answer the following questions:

1. Which website is the most visually attractive? Why?

2. Which website is the least visually attractive? Why?

3. Pick out one website and write a short review, discussing its main features, strong points, and weaknesses.

Liberalism The political view that seeks to change the political, economic, or social institutions of society to foster the development of the individual. Liberals believe that the government can (and should) advance social progress by promoting political equality, social justice, and economic prosperity. Liberals usually favor government regulation and high levels of government spending for social programs. Liberals value social and cultural diversity and defend the right of individual adult choice on issues such as access to abortion.

New Deal program The name of President Franklin Roosevelt's legislative program for countering the Great Depression.

of the state's conservative public policies. The high point for the liberals was the election of James Allred as governor in 1935 and 1937. During the Allred administration, the legislature and the governor enacted several liberal programs designed to combat the Great Depression. Support for the liberal Democrats came primarily from a loose coalition of unemployed persons, working-class whites, labor union members, Jews, university people, some professionals, Latinos, and African Americans, which were beginning a wholesale change of allegiance from the GOP to the party of Franklin Roosevelt.

The conservative Democrats reestablished themselves as the dominant wing of the Democratic Party during the 1940s. With the depression over, the economic issues raised by liberal Democrats were less effective. Conservative Democrats claimed that the return of economic prosperity proved the correctness of their philosophy. Another advantage for conservatives was that they enjoyed easier access to the financial resources needed to wage a modern political campaign in a large and rapidly growing state than did the liberal Democrats. Furthermore, working-class and minority voters who made up the core of support for the liberal Democrats were less likely to vote than the middle- and upper-income white supporters of the conservative Democrats.

The period running from the early 1950s through the late 1970s was a time of transition for party politics in the Lone Star State. By the 1950s, the liberal wing of the Texas Democratic Party had become a formidable political force. Although conservative Democrats still held the upper hand, liberal challengers had to be taken seriously. Liberal Democrats scored a major breakthrough in 1957 when Ralph Yarborough, a liberal Democrat, won a special election to the U.S. Senate. He held the seat through 1970. Liberal Democrats also captured a few seats in Congress, won a number of positions in the state legislature, and ran credible races for the party's gubernatorial nomination.

Liberal Democrats gained strength because the electorate was changing. The legal barriers that had kept many African Americans, Latinos, and poor whites from the polls were coming down, primarily because of the intervention of the federal courts and the U.S. Congress. The liberal wing of the party also benefited from the defection of some conservative voters to the GOP. A poll taken in the mid-1960s found that 37 percent of Texans who said they were once conservative Democrats had left the party, to become either Republicans (23 percent) or independents (14 percent).[3] The exodus of conservative voters from the Democratic Party made it easier for liberal candidates to win Democratic primary elections.

In the meantime, the Texas Republican Party was coming to life. The presidential candidacy of General Dwight D. Eisenhower in 1952 brought a flood of new faces into the Republican camp, many of which were former Democrats. Furthermore, many conservative Democrats, including Governor Allan Shivers, deserted their party's presidential nominee, Governor Adlai Stevenson of Illinois, to openly support the Republican presidential candidate. Eisenhower carried the state in both 1952 and 1956.

Texas Republicans built their party throughout the 1960s and 1970s. They elected candidates to the U.S. Congress and the Texas legislature and won a number of local races, particularly in urban areas. Perhaps their most important victory came in 1961, when Republican John Tower, a young college professor at Midwestern State University in Wichita Falls, won a special election to serve the remainder of Lyndon Johnson's U.S. Senate term after Johnson resigned to become vice president. Tower won reelection in 1966, 1972, and 1978.

Surveys of party identification among voters traced the Republican surge. For decades, the most common political animal in the Lone Star State was the Yellow Dog Democrat. This was a Texan, it was said, who would vote for a yellow dog, were it the Democratic candidate. In other words, a **Yellow Dog Democrat** was a loyal Democratic Party voter. In 1952, 66 percent of Texans called themselves Democrats, whereas only 6 percent declared allegiance to the Republican Party. Twenty years later, the margin was a bit closer, 57 percent to 14 percent.[4] By 1984, however, Democrats had outnumbered Republicans by only 33 percent to 28 percent.[5]

What accounts for the rise of the GOP as a significant electoral force in Texas? First, the legacy of the Civil War finally began to diminish in importance, especially for younger Texans. Surveys showed that younger voters were more likely to identify with the GOP than were older people.[6] Second, many conservative white Democrats became disenchanted with what they saw as an increasingly liberal national Democratic Party. Whereas some conservative southern Democrats openly defected to GOP ranks, other conservatives remained nominal Democrats but supported Republicans in statewide and national races whenever the Democratic nominee seemed too liberal for their taste. Finally, the Texas Republican Party benefited from the migration of white-collar workers from outside the South. Many of these Republican newcomers identified with the GOP in their old states and simply took their party loyalties with them to their new homes in Texas.

The 1978 election signaled the emergence of a competitive two-party system in Texas. The spring primary produced the most significant development for the Democrats when Attorney General John Hill, a liberal Democrat, defeated incumbent Governor Dolph Briscoe, a conservative. Hill's victory demonstrated that liberal Democrats could compete with conservative Democrats on an equal footing. The determining political event in 1978 for the GOP came in the fall general election, when Bill Clements defeated Hill to become the first Republican governor in more than a century. The election of Clements demonstrated that well-funded Republican

Yellow Dog Democrat A loyal Democratic Party voter.

The suburbs have become Republican strongholds.

candidates could win statewide elections in Texas, especially against Democrats from the liberal wing of the party.

From 1978 to 1994, Texas party politics was more competitive than ever before. The GOP enjoyed an advantage at the top of the ballot, winning most races for governor and U.S. senator. The Republican presidential nominee carried the state every time during the period. In contrast, Democrats were considerably more successful in contests below the top of the ballot. Throughout the period, Democrats won most statewide executive offices below the level of governor, enjoyed majorities in the Texas House and Texas Senate, elected most of the state's judges, and held most county offices.

The Republican Party became the clear majority party in the state in 1994, when Republican gubernatorial nominee George W. Bush defeated incumbent Democratic Governor Ann Richards and the GOP won a majority of seats in the Texas Senate. No Democrat has won a statewide election for any office since 1994. The Democrats lost their last hold on power at the state level in 2002, when the GOP captured a majority of seats in the Texas House. Although Democrats clung to office at the county level in many areas of the state, especially in South Texas, the GOP made significant inroads into the state's urban centers, capturing every local office and judgeship elected countywide in Harris, Dallas, and Tarrant Counties. Since 2002, the Democratic Party has begun to make a comeback, picking up a number of seats in the Texas House and making gains at the local level, especially in Dallas County.

Figure 23.2 documents the changing fortunes of the state's political parties by charting their strength in the Texas House of Representatives. Between 1981 and 2001, the Republican delegation in the Texas House more than doubled, increasing from

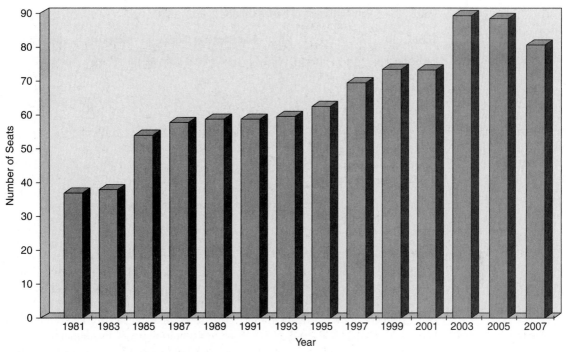

FIGURE 23.2 Republican Strength in the Texas House.
Source: Texas House, www.capital.state.tx.us.

35 to 72 members. The Republican Party fell short of a majority in the 150-member chamber until 2002, when the GOP captured 88 seats in the House. Since reaching low ebb in 2002, the Democrats have begun a comeback, adding 1 seat in 2004 and 6 more in 2006. The eightieth legislature, which met in regular session in 2007, included 81 Republicans and 69 Democrats in the Texas House.

THE PARTY BALANCE

Republicans outnumber Democrats in Texas. Political scientists determine party identification by asking survey respondents if they consider themselves Democrats, Republicans, or independents. Researchers typically follow up on their initial question by asking those people who declare a party identification if they consider themselves strong Democrats/Republicans or weak Democrats/Republicans. They also ask the people who say they are independents if they lean toward one party or another. In 2006, surveys showed that 50 percent of Texans considered themselves Republicans or leaned toward the Republican Party compared with 42 percent who identified with or leaned toward the Democratic Party. Texas ranked as the fourth most Republican state in the nation, after Utah, Idaho, and Nebraska. Nationally, Democrats held a 50 percent to 40 percent edge over the GOP in party identification.[7]

TABLE 23.1   Party Affiliation of Elected Officials in Texas, 2007

Office	Total Number of Officials	Democrats	Republicans
U.S. Senate	2	0	2
U.S. House	32	13	19
State Executives*	6	0	6
Texas Senate	31	11	20
Texas House	150	69	81
Texas Supreme Court	9	0	9
Texas Court of Criminal Appeals	9	0	9
Texas Railroad Commission	3	0	3
Texas State Board of Education	15	5	10

*Governor, lieutenant governor, attorney general, comptroller, agriculture commissioner, and land commissioner.

Table 23.1 compares the electoral strength of the Texas Republican and Democratic Parties. After the 2006 election, the three highest-profile elective officeholders in the state were Republicans: Rick Perry was governor, whereas Kay Bailey Hutchison and John Cornyn represented Texas in the U.S. Senate. The Republican Party held 19 of 32 seats in the U.S. House of Representatives. Every member of the Texas Railroad Commission, Texas Supreme Court, and Texas Court of Criminal Appeals was Republican. A majority of the members of both houses of the Texas legislature and the Texas Board of Education were Republican as well. The Republican Party also held a majority of county offices and district judgeships in most large urban and suburban counties, with the exception of El Paso County and, since 2006, Dallas County. Bexar County is competitive.

An analysis of the 2002, 2004, and 2006 election returns suggests that the baseline Republican vote statewide is around 57 percent of the electorate. Contests for the Texas Court of Criminal Appeals are a good measure of party strength because the individual candidates are not well known and seldom raise enough money to mount the media-based campaign necessary to build name recognition. Without information about the individual candidates, voters typically base their choices on party affiliation. When the Democratic Party dominated Texas politics, Democrats routinely swept races for the Court of Criminal Appeals. For more than a decade, however, the GOP has won every race for the Texas Court of Criminal Appeals. In 2002, 2004, and 2006, the Republican candidates for the five Court of Criminal Appeals races on the ballot (three in 2002, one in 2004, and one in 2006) won 57 percent to 58 percent of the vote.[8]

The Texas Republican Party is better funded and better organized than the Texas Democratic Party. In 2006, the Texas Republican Party and its allied campaign organization raised $6.8 million to support its campaign activities. In contrast, the Texas Democratic Party and its allied committees took in $3 million.[9] The fundraising disparity between the two parties is greater between elections. In 2005, the Texas Democratic Party struggled to make payroll for its office staff, whereas the state GOP enjoyed ample funds to support its organization.[10]

VOTING PATTERNS

Voting patterns in Texas reflect differences in income, race and ethnicity, region, and place of residence.

Income

Voting patterns reflect income, with higher-income citizens supporting Republican candidates and lower-income voters backing Democrats. Exit polls taken during the 2004 presidential election showed a clear relationship between income and voter choice. Democrat John Kerry led Republican George W. Bush by a 54 percent to 46 percent margin among voters with incomes between $15,000 and $30,000 a year. With each succeeding income bracket, however, Kerry lost support and Bush gained. Among Texas voters making between $100,000 and $150,000 a year, Bush trounced Kerry by a margin of 75 percent to 25 percent.[11]

Race and Ethnicity

Voting patterns vary based on race and ethnicity. Minority voters, especially African Americans, support the Democrats. In 2004, exit polls showed that African Americans in Texas backed Kerry over Bush by a lopsided margin, 83 percent for Kerry to 16 percent for Bush. The Latino vote tends to be Democratic as well, but the margin between the two parties is closer.[12] Political analysts estimate that just over 60 percent of Latino voters in Texas voted for Democratic candidates for Congress in 2006.[13] In contrast, the white vote in Texas is heavily Republican. In 2004, 72 percent of white voters backed Bush compared with only 28 percent who supported Kerry.[14]

Region

Historically, Texas voting patterns have had a regional flavor. East Texas and South Texas, especially the counties along the Mexican border, have been Democratic strongholds. West Texas, the Panhandle region, and Central Texas, excluding the city of Austin, have been areas of Republican strength. The party balance in other regions of the state has been relatively close.

As the Republican Party has gained strength in Texas, regional voting patterns have shifted. The border region along the Rio Grande remains firmly in the Democratic camp, but East Texas is changing. Democrats still hold most local offices in East Texas, but Republican candidates for statewide and national office often run strong in the region.

Place of Residence

The GOP is strongest in the suburbs, whereas Democrats run best in the inner city. In the meantime, the rural areas of the state, which were once solidly Democratic, are now trending Republican, at least for national and statewide office. Democrats hold inner-city congressional districts in Houston, Dallas, San Antonio, Austin, and

El Paso, whereas Republicans have won most of the state's predominantly suburban congressional districts. The state's most rapidly growing suburban counties (Collin and Denton Counties in the Dallas–Fort Worth area and Fort Bend and Montgomery Counties in the Houston area) are Republican strongholds.

INTEREST GROUP–POLITICAL PARTY ALLIANCES

Political parties and interest groups form informal alliances. Interest groups assist political parties by providing campaign funds and organizational support to party candidates. Groups endorse candidates and distribute campaign literature to group members and people who would likely sympathize with the group's goals. Interest groups may also provide lobbying support for policies the party favors. In turn, political parties reward their interest-group allies by adopting policies that benefit them.

Table 23.2 lists the interest groups generally associated with the Texas Democratic and Republican Parties. Although the list of groups allied with the Democratic Party is longer than the list associated with the GOP, the groups in the Democratic column are not necessarily more effective politically. With the exception of trial lawyers, who support the Democrats, the groups allied with the Republican Party have more money to devote to political action than do the groups who support the Democratic Party. Many of the groups allied with the Democrats, such as teachers' organizations and labor unions, have a large membership base, which can be tapped for volunteer campaign support. Their numbers are somewhat offset, however, by the dedication of anti-abortion activists and conservative religious groups supporting the Republican Party.

Although political parties and interest groups form alliances, groups are not wholly owned subsidiaries of parties. Not all African Americans, Latinos, and gay men and lesbians support the Democratic Party by any means; some are Republican. The Log Cabin Republicans, for example, is an organization of gay and lesbian Republicans. Furthermore, groups and group members may not agree with a political party on every issue or endorse all of its candidates.

TABLE 23.2   Political Party and Interest Group Alliances

Groups Allied with the Democratic Party	Groups Allied with the Republican Party
• Organized labor	• Business groups and trade associations
• Environmental organizations	• Most professional organizations, including doctors and realtors
• Consumer groups	• Farm groups
• African American rights organizations	• Religious conservatives
• Latino rights groups	• National Rifle Association
• Gay and lesbian rights organizations	• Pro-life groups
• Teachers' groups	• Tort reform organizations
• Pro-choice groups	
• Trial lawyers	
• Women's rights groups	

Many of the delegates at state Republican Party conventions have been associated with the Christian Coalition or other conservative religious organizations.

ISSUE ORIENTATION

Trans-Texas Corridor A proposed network of transportation corridors a quarter mile wide and 370 miles long running from Brownsville to Oklahoma that would include toll roads, railways, and utility lines.

Texas Assessment of Knowledge and Skills (TAKS) A state-mandated basic skills test designed to measure student progress and school performance.

The two major political parties in Texas agree on the fundamental principles of America's political and economic systems. Neither party wants to secede from the Union, rejoin Mexico, or establish a monarchy. Both Democrats and Republicans favor good schools, safe streets, healthy families, and a sound economy. The two parties disagree on some of the details of policy, particularly on the role of government in society.

Table 23.3 compares the 2006 platforms of the state's two major political parties on selected issues. As the table shows, the two parties agree on some matters. Both the Democrats and the Republicans favor the election of state judges. Both parties oppose the **Trans-Texas Corridor,** which is a proposed network of transportation corridors, a quarter mile wide and 370 miles long running from Brownsville to Oklahoma, that would include toll roads, railways, and utility lines. Both parties also express reservations about the **Texas Assessment of Knowledge and Skills (TAKS)** program, although neither party platform identified TAKS by name. The TAKS is a state-mandated basic skills test designed to measure student progress and school performance. High school students have to pass the test before they can graduate. The Democratic platform advocates the use of a more complete evaluation system of students rather than just one test, whereas the GOP platform deplores the amount of time devoted to test preparation rather than teaching basic skills.

TABLE 23.3   Texas Democratic and Republican Party Platforms, 2006, Selected Issues

Issue	Democratic Platform Position	Republican Platform Position
State taxes	Opposes any further increase in the sales tax, calls for a constitutional amendment to ban sales taxes on food and prescription medicine.	Opposes the adoption of a state income tax "even to pay for education"; supports abolishing property taxes
School finance	Declares that the state should establish a funding system sufficient to offer an exemplary education to all students	Urges state to focus funding on academics rather than nonacademic activities; opposes tax increases to fund schools
School choice	Opposes any form of private school voucher program	Favors giving parents state funding vouchers and then letting them choose from among public, private, or parochial schools contingent on the passage of a state constitutional amendment exempting private and parochial schools from state regulation
Bilingual education	Supports multi-language instruction that allows English-speaking children to learn a second language; rejects effort to destroy bilingual education	Calls for the termination of bilingual education programs
Basic skills testing	Calls for improving the accountability system by relying on a more complete evaluation than just one standardized test score	Deplores the amount of time devoted to test preparation to the detriment of basic academic instruction
Higher education	Supports the provision of two years of public college or postsecondary technical education tuition free for all who complete high school; favors expanding Texas grant program	Advocates a single standard of college and university admission based on merit and ability without regard for class standing or the school students attended
Illegal immigration	Calls for allocation of resources to police the border effectively; supports enforcement of laws against employers who knowingly hire illegal workers at substandard wages; endorses legislation to create path to citizenship for undocumented workers living in the United States	Declares that all necessary means should be used to control the border, including building a physical barrier; opposes any form of amnesty for illegal immigrants and calls for their deportation to their home countries

Children's Health Insurance Program (CHIP) A federal program designed to provide health insurance to children from low-income families whose parents are not poor enough to qualify for Medicaid.

Privatization The process that involves the government contracting with private business to implement government programs.

Hate crimes legislation Legislative measures that increase penalties for persons convicted of criminal offenses motivated by prejudice based on race, religion, national origin, gender, or sexual orientation.

Tort reform The revision of state laws to limit the ability of plaintiffs in personal injury lawsuits to recover damages in court.

Joint and several liability The legal requirement that a defendant with "deep pockets" held partially liable for a plaintiff's injury must pay the full damage award for those defendants unable to pay.

TABLE 23.3   Continued

Issue	Democratic Platform Position	Republican Platform Position
Children's Health Insurance Program (CHIP), which is a federal program designed to provide health insurance to children from low-income families whose parents are not poor enough to qualify for Medicaid	Favors expansion of the program to cover all uninsured children in the state	Supports private-sector solutions to healthcare problems
Privatization, which is the process that involves the government contracting with private business to implement government programs	Opposes privatization of social services and prisons	Supports the privatization of most government services
Transportation	Opposes the Trans-Texas Corridor	Opposes the Trans-Texas Corridor
Hate crimes legislation, legislative measures that increase penalties for persons convicted of criminal offenses motivated by prejudice based on race, religion, national origin, gender, or sexual orientation	Calls for strong enforcement of the state hate crimes act	Calls for repeal of the hate crimes act
Tort reform, which is the revision of state laws to limit the ability of plaintiffs in personal injury lawsuits to recover damages in court	Proposes the reversal of "unjust provisions" of the tort reform legislation passed in 2003 "that have proven harmful by denying Texans who have suffered severe harm fair and open courts and the ability to redress their grievances"	Strongly supports "common-sense" continuation of tort reform; favors elimination of **joint and several liability,** which is the legal requirement that a defendant with "deep pockets" held partially liable for a plaintiff's injury must pay the full damage award for those defendants unable to pay
Capital punishment, which is the death penalty	Proposes a moratorium on executions pending a study of the Texas death penalty system	Declares that capital punishment, when "properly applied," is a legitimate form of punishment and a deterrent for serious crime; wants to extend the death penalty to convictions of forcible rape

(continued)

TABLE 23.3   Continued

Capital punishment The death penalty.

Issue	Democratic Platform Position	Republican Platform Position
Judicial selection	Supports the election of state judges as well as meaningful judicial campaign finance reform	Supports the election of state judges
Role of religion	Supports religious freedom and the separation of church and state	Affirms that the United States is a Christian nation; declares that the separation of church and state is a myth
Minimum wage	Supports increasing the federal minimum wage	Calls for the repeal of the minimum wage
Abortion	Declares that women should decide when and whether to bear children "in consultation with their family, their physician, and their God . . . rather than having these personal decisions made by politicians"	Declares that the unborn child has an individual fundamental right to life that cannot be infringed; supports a constitutional amendment to ban abortion
Divorce	Has no position	Calls for the repeal of no-fault divorce laws
Campaign finance reform	Supports government funding of general election campaigns; favors limiting campaign contributions and expenditures	Opposes campaign finance reforms other than full disclosure of contributions
Election reform	No one should be denied the right to vote because of language barriers or confusing voting systems	Supports requiring the reregistration of voters every four years; prospective voters should produce state or federal photo IDs
Gay and lesbian rights	Endorses a federal law to prohibit employment discrimination based on sexual orientation; declares that it is "wrong to write discrimination into the Constitution of the United States or the Texas Constitution"	Calls for the enactment of a constitutional amendment to protect traditional marriage; opposes laws granting civil rights protection to gay men and lesbians; declares that homosexuals should not be allowed to adopt, have custody of children, or have unsupervised visitation with minor children

On other platform issues, the Democrats and Republicans take positions that are clearly different. Whereas the Democrats support a woman's right to choose, the GOP platform calls for the adoption of a constitutional amendment to outlaw abortion. The Democrats endorse **bilingual education,** which is the teaching of academic subjects in both English and a student's native language, usually Spanish; the Republicans reject it. The Democrats advocate campaign finance reform to limit campaign contributions and candidate spending; the Republicans reject all campaign finance reform proposals except for full disclosure of the sources of campaign contributions. Democrats propose increasing the **minimum wage,** which is the lowest hourly wage that an employer can pay covered workers; Republicans want to repeal it altogether. The Democrats favor creating a path to citizenship for undocumented workers, whereas the Republicans demand their deportation.

The party platforms show that the two parties have different perspectives on the role of government. The Democrats believe that government should play a role in addressing social problems. The Democratic platform supports adequate funding for public education, Medicaid, and the Children's Health Insurance Program (CHIP). The Democrats favor government regulation designed to protect the environment and help low-income wage earners. On social issues, Democrats support abortion rights and favor the adoption of a federal law to protect gay men and lesbians from job discrimination. In contrast, the Republicans believe that government's primary role is to support traditional family values rather than solve social problems. The GOP platform proposes the repeal of the property tax, which is the major source of tax revenue for local governments in Texas. The Republicans propose reducing or eliminating a broad range of state spending programs. The Republicans believe that government should strengthen traditional marriage by making divorce more difficult, outlawing same-sex marriage, and prohibiting homosexuals from adopting or having custody of children.

Bilingual education The teaching of academic subjects in both English and a student's native language, usually Spanish.

Minimum wage The lowest hourly wage that an employer can pay covered workers.

 WHAT IS YOUR OPINION?

Which party's platform more closely matches your political views—the Democratic or the Republican?

THE IMPACT OF PARTISAN CHANGE

Texas has undergone a political transformation. In less than 30 years, Texas has gone from a state in which Democrats captured almost every elective office to one in which the Republican Party controls all three branches of state government as well as many local offices. Has the dramatic change in the state's partisan balance been accompanied by a similarly remarkable change in policy?

The simple answer is no. Public policies in Texas have always reflected the state's individualistic–traditionalist political culture regardless of the political party in control of state government. The **individualistic political culture** is an approach to government and politics that emphasizes private initiative with a minimum of government interference. The **traditionalistic political culture** is

Individualistic political culture An approach to government and politics that emphasizes private initiative with a minimum of government interference.

Traditionalistic political culture
An approach to government and politics that sees the role of government as the preservation of tradition and the existing social order.

an approach to government and politics that sees the role of government as the preservation of tradition and the existing social order. Historically, Texas has boasted low tax rates, poorly funded public services, minimal regulation of private business activity, and social policies designed to embrace and promote traditional Christian values. By and large, the new Republican leaders of state government have adopted policy initiatives consistent with the basic approach to state government taken by generations of Democratic officeholders in years past.

Consider the policy decisions of the legislature and governor since the GOP came to power. When faced with a major budget shortfall in 2003, the legislature and governor balanced the budget without raising taxes, primarily by cutting state spending. In 2007, a strong economy produced a sizable surplus, but the legislature chose to leave billions of dollars unspent to fund future property tax cuts rather than using the money for education, healthcare, and other priorities. As for social issues, the legislature passed and the governor signed a bill outlawing same-sex marriage; they made abortion more difficult by imposing a 24-hour waiting period for women seeking to end a pregnancy. The legislature and the governor also adopted a package of tort reform measures.

Each of the legislature's actions reflected the conservative philosophy of the majority Republican Party, but none of them was a dramatic departure from policies enacted by previous Democratic legislatures and Democratic governors. The legislature and governor reduced state spending in 2003 in order to avoid a tax increase, but the programs they cut were already poorly funded. The Democrats who once controlled the state presided over a government that was the least generous in the nation in terms of funding public services. In 2000, Texas ranked 50th in state government spending per capita.[15] Texas government has never been especially friendly to gay and lesbian rights or supportive of abortion rights. The enactment of a ban on same-sex marriage in 2003 was more symbolic than substantive because Texas law already defined marriage as a union between a man and a woman. Texas was one of a handful of states that criminalized private, consensual sexual conduct among adults of the same gender. The Texas legislature has never passed pro-choice legislation, regardless of the party in control. Furthermore, the tort reforms adopted in 2003 only added to an extensive list of lawsuit restrictions enacted in the 1990s when Democrats still ran the legislature.

GETTING INVOLVED

Volunteer to Support Your Political Party

Political parties are a means for individuals to influence the policymaking process. The Internet Research feature found on page 614 includes the websites of the five most important political parties in Texas politics. Each party website includes information on how Texans can contact the party and get involved in its work. Contact the party of your choice and offer to help. Volunteers support their party by registering voters, helping out in the local office, raising money, and researching issues. People who get involved with their party may eventually win the opportunity to attend the county, state, or national convention. Some may even decide to run for office and may be elected.

It's your country—get involved!

In 2006, Craig Watkins won election as Dallas County district attorney, the first Democrat to hold the office in 20 years and the first African American ever.

THE FUTURE OF PARTY POLITICS IN TEXAS

The 2006 election gave Democrats hope that they would soon be able to challenge Republican dominance of state government. The Democrats gained several seats in the Texas House of Representatives and did well in county and judicial contests in some urban areas—most prominently, Dallas County, where Democrats won every contested race. With the state's minority population growing and white citizens no longer a majority, the future of the Democratic Party seemed promising.

Nonetheless, demographic change alone will not be sufficient to return the Democratic Party to power statewide anytime soon. Although minority residents represent a majority of the state's population, they do not make up a majority of the electorate. In 2004, the Texas electorate was 63 percent white, 23 percent Latino, 12 percent African American, 1 percent Asian, and 2 percent "other."[16] More than a third of Latinos in Texas are not old enough to vote, and a fourth of adult Latino residents are not citizens and thus cannot vote.[17] Every election, the proportion of ballots cast by minority residents grows, but it will be many years before African Americans and Latinos constitute a majority of statewide voters.

The challenge for Democratic candidates is to do better with white voters, especially white voters living outside the inner city. In the 2006 governor's election, Democrat Chris Bell outpolled Republican Governor Perry in the state's six largest counties (Bexar, Dallas, El Paso, Harris, Tarrant, and Travis) by 688,000 to 671,000 votes. Nonetheless, Bell lost to Perry statewide 1.7 million to 1.3 million in a four-way race that included two independents, Comptroller Carole Keeton Strayhorn and novelist/entertainer Kinky Friedman, who finished third and fourth. Bell lost the election because he trailed badly in suburban counties. For example, Perry led Bell in Collin County, which is just north of Dallas, by 68,000 to 32,000. The vote in Montgomery County, which is north of Houston, was 41,000 for Perry to 12,000 for Bell.[18] No Democratic candidate for statewide office can hope to win unless he or she does better in the state's rapidly growing suburbs than did Bell. Demographic change will eventually make the suburbs more hospitable territory for Democrats, but in the meantime Democrats need to get more white votes if they hope to compete statewide.

The challenge for the Texas Republican Party, meanwhile, is to adapt to demographic change. The Republican base is shrinking. Unless GOP candidates can do better with minority voters, especially Latino voters, they will continue to lose elections in urban centers and will sooner or later lose their statewide majority. The Democrats swept county races in Dallas County in 2006. They may be one or two elections away from winning county races in Harris County as well.

Republican leaders recognize the need to extend their party's appeal to minority voters. Republican governors Clements, Bush, and Perry appointed Latinos and African Americans to high-profile positions as secretary of state and to vacancies on the Texas Railroad Commission and the Texas Supreme Court. Bush campaigned hard to win Latino votes, speaking Spanish in campaign appearances and in radio campaign ads. Republicans also hope to attract Latino support by stressing social issues, such as their opposition to abortion and gay marriage.

The dilemma for Republican leaders is that the party's base, especially those voters most likely to participate in Republican primary elections, favors some policy positions that will be a hard sell for minority voters. The 2006 Texas Republican Party platform calls for repealing the minimum wage, terminating bilingual education programs, making American English the state's official language, and deporting undocumented workers. The platform opposes raising any state taxes and fees, even to pay for education, and supports abolishing the property tax, which funds schools and other local governments. Those issue positions appeal to conservative suburban whites but are unlikely to attract the votes of very many African American or Latino voters.[19] Republican officeholders who try to broaden the party's appeal by taking moderate positions on immigration or the CHIP program may be vulnerable to defeat by more conservative challengers in the Republican primary. In 2006, conservative activists challenged a number of Republican legislators in the GOP primary for not following the party line on taxes and education issues, such as **school choice,** which is an educational reform movement that would allow parents to choose the elementary or secondary school their children will attend. Chapter 24 examines the Republican primary battle in depth.

School choice An educational reform movement that would allow parents to choose the elementary or secondary school their children will attend.

CONCLUSION: POLITICAL PARTIES AND POLICYMAKING

For years, political parties hardly mattered in Texas politics because Texas was a one-party state. Now that Texas has become a two-party state, parties do matter, but they do not dominate the policymaking process. In the legislature and the executive branch, party affiliation probably has less impact on policy than other factors, such as the ideology of individual officeholders, the wishes of the legislators' constituents, and interest group pressure.

Political scientists use the concept of issue networks to describe policymaking in America. An **issue network** is a group of political actors that is concerned with some aspect of public policy. They may include technical specialists, journalists, legislators, the governor, other state executive officials, interest groups, bureaucrats, academic experts, individual political activists, and political parties. In Texas, political parties play a role in the policymaking process, but their influence is tempered by the participation of other political actors.

Issue network A group of political actors that is concerned with some aspect of public policy.

Agenda Building

Texas political parties play a role in agenda building but usually to advance issues that are already part of the policy agenda because of the actions of the courts, the federal government, or interest groups. Both major parties in Texas have long addressed the issue of education finance in their party platforms, for example, but they did not raise the issue. Education finance has been part of the policy agenda in Texas because of the work of interest groups, school districts, and the courts. Political parties seldom raise issues on their own. Instead, they identify issues that are already important to key segments of the population, such as property tax rates and healthcare availability, and offer policy proposals for addressing those issues that are designed to appeal to their core supporters or to independents not closely aligned with either major party. Republicans, for example, offer policy proposals for reducing property taxes because that is an important issue to the suburban homeowners who comprise an important part of the Republican base. Democrats, meanwhile, propose increasing CHIP coverage, an important issue for low-income voters who typically vote Democratic.

Policy Formulation and Adoption

Parties participate in policy formulation and adoption. Parties and party candidates propose solutions to policy problems. Once in office, party leaders may work together to adopt policies reflecting their party's position. Governor Perry and the Republican legislative leadership worked together to pass tort reform in 2003. The governor declared that tort reform was a major goal during his 2002 election campaign and he asked the legislature to act. Republican leaders in both chambers helped push through a tort reform legislation and then Perry signed it into law.

Policy Implementation and Evaluation

Political parties play a role in policy implementation. Most of the officials who head the units of government responsible for policy implementation are either elected under the party label or appointed by elected officials who ran for office under the party name. They may use their position to further their party's policy objectives. Some of the Republican members of the State Board of Education (SBOE), for example, have worked to shape the school curriculum and to adopt textbooks that reflect the socially conservative views of the GOP platform.

Party leaders evaluate public policies. The party out of power typically attacks the work of the governing party, whereas the incumbent party defends its position. In recent years, Texas Democrats have blasted the Republican-controlled legislature for being more interested in holding the line on taxes than improving education, raising teacher pay, and extending health insurance coverage to children living in low-income families. In the meantime, Republican leaders have declared that Texas has prospered economically because they have held the line on taxes and state spending.

LET'S DEBATE

Do Religious Conservatives Have Too Much Influence in the Texas Republican Party?

Overview: On June 5, 2005, using the filled church gymnasium of Fort Worth's Calvary Christian Academy as a backdrop and in a ceremony filled with religious references and imagery, Governor Rick Perry enacted into law abortion bills that limit late-term abortions and require parental notification for minors. At this gathering he also signed a ceremonial resolution defining marriage as a union between one man and one woman. Religious conservatives within the Texas Republican Party (also known as the Grand Old Party, or GOP) advocated forcefully for these measures. Outside of the ceremony, there were approximately 350 protesters, some carrying signs admonishing Texans to keep religion out of politics, and others carrying signs decrying the influence of the Texas GOP on state social policy. With the elevation of the outspoken Christian Governor George W. Bush to the presidency, the political spotlight has been fixed on the influence of religious conservatives in the Texas Republican Party. Many observers of the Texas political scene have noted the link between religious conservatives and the Texas GOP, but is this a cause for worry, or much ado about nothing?

The Texas Republican Party represents many different interests other than those of religious conservatives (economic interests, tax policy, limited government, etc.) but it is fair to say that Republican social policy is largely informed by Christian tradition. In the Texas GOP's 2004 platform there is a pledge to "exert influence to restore the original intent of the First Amendment . . . and dispel the myth of the separation of Church and State," as well as an affirmation that the "United States is a Christian nation and the public acknowledgement of God is undeniable in our history. . . . Our nation was founded on fundamental Judeo-Christian principles based on the Holy Bible." Additionally, a plank in the platform "urges school administrators and officials to inform . . . students of their First Amendment rights to pray and engage in religious speech . . . on school property without government interference." There can be no doubt that the Texas Republican platform embodies both strong conservative and Christian values. With the Republican takeover of the Texas House in 2002, the GOP now controls the Texas legislative, executive, and the majority of state elective offices, and as the state's majority party, the GOP would be remiss in not trying to enact the policy preferences of its constituents.

It is the nature of our democratic practice that the majority should enact policy as long as it is constitutional and within the rule of law. The religious right's effect on Texas Republican politics and social policy may be influenced by a traditional understanding of constitutionalism. That is, the Texas GOP adheres to a strong state's rights understanding of modern republicanism in that state government should reflect the political culture of the people it governs. It should come as no surprise that Texas culture and politics, as part of the American "Bible Belt," would be influenced by this powerful religious current.

Arguments for the Belief That Religious Conservatives Have Too Much Influence in the Texas Republican Party

❑ **The goals of the Texas GOP violate the principle of separation of church and state.** The history of both the United States and Texas has in part been one of an evolving understanding of basic rights, and a cornerstone of political liberty is the principle of the separation of church and state. Today, there is more religious diversity and pluralism, and the fact that the GOP platform seeks to impose its views on others who may not share its vision may violate the principle of religious and political separation.

❑ **Certain policies supported by religious conservatives are not supported by the majority of Texans.** How is it fair that an active and vocal minority of Texans is able to dictate policy that runs contrary to the changing political culture of Texas? Polling research shows that the majority of Texans are pro-choice and support most pro-choice policies within limits. Furthermore, national polls show that a significant majority supports some form of stem cell research to advance the cause of medical science and the quality of human life. Why should an insular minority determine scientific policy?

❑ **Conservative Christians do not have the monopoly on religious practice and biblical interpretation.** A fundamental assumption of conservative Christian politics is that government should enshrine its particular understanding of Christianity in the state's legal code and policy. This assumes their understanding of Christianity is superior to that of other Christian beliefs. As the progressive Texas Freedom Network points out, there are numerous interpretations of biblical ethics and scripture, so how can one Christian group claim to speak with the authority for all?

Arguments Against the Belief That Religious Conservatives Have Too Much Influence in the Texas Republican Party

❑ **Religious citizens, like all citizens, have the right to engage in political activity.** The case against the political activity of religious conservatives is overstated. Nowhere in the U.S. or Texas Constitution does it state that citizens of faith may not act politically. One of the hallmarks of American and Texas democracy is that citizens have the right to political association to

further their understanding of what constitutes the good life. Those who disagree with the religious constituency of the Texas GOP are free to oppose them in open public discourse as well as in the electoral arena.

❑ **Texas has always been a conservative and religious state. It is the nature of representative government to reflect the political culture of the state.** As previously noted, the Texas Republican Party adheres to the view that the American federal system gives each state the authority to determine its moral culture and determine social policy. The genius of the federal principle is that the states are free to represent the wishes and politics of their citizens within constitutional boundaries. Just as citizens of Nevada are free to allow the morality of prostitution and gambling, Texans are free to put religiously moral limits on social behavior.

❑ **The Texas Republican Party represents the wishes of its constituents.** Party politics is about representation, and the policy preferences of the Texas GOP are a direct-result of its members' activities. The Republican Party of Texas provides a home and political forum for those who believe government and law should reflect traditional Christian values. Those who are opposed to the policies of the Texas GOP can offer the public different policy alternatives, and the most favored policy can be determined at the ballot box.

QUESTIONS

1. Do religious conservatives have too much influence in the Texas GOP? Why or why not?
2. What is the right balance between the practice of both religious faith and democratic politics?

SELECT READINGS

1. Michael Lind, *Made in Texas: George W. Bush and the Takeover of American Politics* (New York: Basic Books, 2002).
2. Jim Wallis, *God's Politics: Why the Right Gets It Wrong and the Left Doesn't Get It* (San Francisco: Harper, 2005).

SELECT WEBSITES

1. **www.texasgop.org/site/PageServer**
   Website of the Texas Republican Party.

2. **www.txdemocrats.org**
   Website of the Texas Democratic Party.

KEY TERMS

bilingual education

capital punishment

Children's Health Insurance Program (CHIP)

conservatism

electoral college

Grand Old Party (GOP)

hate crimes legislation

independent expenditures

individualistic political culture

issue network

joint and several liability

liberalism

minimum wage

New Deal program

party faction

party platform

political party

privatization

school choice

Solid South

Texas Assessment of Knowledge and Skills (TAKS)

tort reform

traditionalistic political culture

Trans-Texas Corridor

two-party system

Yellow Dog Democrat

NOTES

1. U. S. Census Bureau, available at www.census.gov.
2. Texas State Data Center and Office of the State Demographer, available at http://txsdc.utsa.edu.
3. James A. Dyer, Arnold Vedlitz, and David B. Hill, "New Voters, Switchers, and Political Party Realignment in Texas," *Western Political Quarterly* 41 (March 1988): 156.
4. Clay Robison, "Texas GOP Beats Dems in Key Areas," *Houston Chronicle*, November 28, 1989, p. 16A.
5. *Texas Weekly*, July 15, 1991, p. 5
6. "The Two Souths," *National Journal*, September 20, 1986, pp. 2218–2220.
7. Jeffrey M. Jones, "Democratic Edge in Partisanship in 2006 Evident at the National and State Levels," January 30, 2007, available at www.gallup.com.
8. Texas Secretary of State, available at www.sos.state.tx.us.
9. "State at a Glance: Texas 2006," available at www.follow themoney.org.
10. John Moritz, "State Democrats Short on Funds," *Fort Worth Star-Telegram*, July 14, 2005, available at www.dfw.com.
11. Exit poll data, available from www.cnn.com/elections/2004.
12. Ibid.
13. Greg Jefferson, "Hispanics' Demo Shift Is Debated," *San Antonio Express-News*, December 16, 2006, available at www.mysanantonio.com.
14. Exit poll data.
15. "State Governments—Expenditures and Debt by State: 2000," *Statistical Abstract of the United States 2002*, available at www.census.gov.
16. Exit poll data.
17. R. G. Ratcliffe, "Once-Courted Latino Vote Suddenly Forgotten," *San Antonio Express-News*, September 4, 2006, available at www.mysanantonio.com.
18. Texas Secretary of State, available at www.sos.state.tx.us.
19. Jonathan Gurwitz, "The Troubled Texas GOP," *Wall Street Journal*, July 8, 2007, available at www.wsj.com.

Chapter 24

Texas Elections

CHAPTER OUTLINE

LEARNING OUTCOMES

After studying Chapter 24, students should be able to do the following:

▸ Describe the long ballot in Texas, and evaluate its advantages and disadvantages. (pp. 635–636)

▸ Identify and describe the various types of elections held in Texas. (pp. 636–642)

▸ Describe the process through which Texans participate in the presidential nomination process. (pp. 639–640)

▸ Identify the officials in Texas who are elected at large and those who are elected by districts. (p. 642)

▸ Discuss the impact of one person, one vote on legislative redistricting. (pp. 643–644)

▸ Describe the impact of the Voting Rights Act on legislative redistricting. (pp. 644–645)

▸ Assess the role of politics on redistricting, focusing on the battle over redistricting following the 2000 Census and the off-cycle redistricting struggle in 2003. (pp. 645–650)

▸ Describe the effort to reform the redistricting process in Texas and other states and assess its likelihood of success. (p. 651)

▶ Evaluate the role of money in Texas elections— where it originates, how it is spent, and the difference it makes. (pp. 651–654)

▶ Describe campaigns for major office in Texas. (pp. 654–656)

▶ Describe the role that each of the following plays in voter choice: political party

identification, issues, incumbency, campaigns, candidate image, retrospective and prospective voting, and national factors. (pp. 656–659)

▶ Evaluate the role of elections in the policymaking process. (pp. 659–661)

▶ Define the key terms listed on page 663 and explain their significance.

Republicans in name only (RINOs) Legislators who call themselves Republicans but vote with the Democrats.

School choice An educational reform movement that would allow parents to choose the elementary or secondary school their children will attend.

Some of the most important election contests in 2006 took place not in the November general election but in the spring Republican Party primary. Conservative activists challenged a group of incumbent Republican House members for not supporting the legislative leadership on school funding and educational reform issues. They accused the legislators of being **Republicans in name only (RINOs),** which is the accusation that the legislators called themselves Republicans but voted with the Democrats.

San Antonio businessman James Leininger provided the money for the challenge. Leininger is a proponent of **school choice,** which is an educational reform movement that would allow parents to choose the elementary or secondary school their children will attend. Under a parental choice program, the state would give parents a voucher, which would provide a type of scholarship to be paid to the school that the parents select for their children. In theory, school choice leads to an improvement in educational quality because schools compete for students. If low-quality public schools did not upgrade the quality of their educational programs, students would go elsewhere and the schools would have to shut down for lack of funding. After legislation creating a pilot school choice voucher program narrowly lost in the 2005 session of the Texas legislature, Leininger set out to defeat five Republican House members who voted against the bill. He recruited five pro-voucher candidates and provided them with hundreds of thousands of dollars to challenge the targeted legislators in the Republican primary. Leininger also paid for campaign mailers and advertisements to support the candidates he favored.[1]

While conservative activists were busy organizing to defeat legislators who opposed school vouchers, the education community was working to support candidates on the other side of the issue. A group of parents, teachers, and school administrators created the Texas Parent PAC to back legislators who supported increased school funding and defeat lawmakers who voted for school choice. The people who organized the Texas Parent PAC opposed school choice because they worried that vouchers would enable middle-class parents to transfer their children to private schools, leaving the children of poor families behind in public schools with even less funding. Public schools would get worse, they said, not better. The Texas Parent PAC both raised money and recruited volunteers to help with campaigns. In addition to supporting the legislators targeted by Leininger, the Texas Parent PAC backed challengers to members of the legislature who voted for the voucher program. In particular, the PAC recruited former school board member Diane Patrick to challenge Representative Kent Grusendorf of Arlington, the chair of the House Public Education Committee and the author of the education bill that included the school choice program.[2]

When the votes were counted, James Leininger had lost and the Texas Parent PAC had won. Three of the five legislators Leininger targeted in the primary survived the challenge. Meanwhile, most of the candidates endorsed by the Texas Parent PAC won, including Patrick, who handily defeated Representative Grusendorf. Because of the election, the legislature that met in 2007 had eight fewer members who supported school choice than did the legislature that had met in 2005.[3]

This chapter on elections is the last in a set of four chapters examining the political environment for policymaking. Chapter 21 dealt with participation, whereas Chapter 22 addressed the topic of interest groups in Texas. Chapter 23 focused on political parties.

THE LONG BALLOT

Long ballot An election system that provides for the election of nearly every public official of any significance.

Texas has the **long ballot,** which is an election system that provides for the election of nearly every public official of any significance. A conscientious Texas voter who never misses an election has the opportunity to cast a ballot for each of the following public officials:

- The president and vice president.
- Two U.S. senators.
- One member of the U.S. House of Representatives.
- The governor of Texas and five other state executive officials.
- Three railroad commissioners.
- One member of the state board of education.
- One state senator.
- One state representative.
- Nine members of the Texas Supreme Court.
- Nine members of the Texas Court of Criminal Appeals.
- At least 2 and perhaps as many as 60 or more state appellate and district court judges.
- Numerous local officials, including county executives, county judges, city officials, and members of school district boards of trustees.

The ballot is especially long in the state's urban counties, where a large number of state district court judges must stand for election. In 2006, Dallas County voters faced a ballot with more than 60 contested races.

The long ballot is not unusual in America, but few states vote on as many officials as Texas. Only four states elect more statewide executive officeholders than Texas; three states select only a governor statewide.[4] Considering the number of candidates and constitutional amendments facing Texas voters, the Lone Star State may well have the longest, most complicated election ballot in the nation.

The long ballot is controversial. Its defenders believe that the electoral process is the best way to ensure that public officials remain accountable to the people. If citizens grow unhappy with some aspect of state government, they can simply vote the responsible officials out of office. In contrast, critics of the long ballot argue that most Texans lack the information necessary to make intelligent voting choices on many down-ballot races. Not knowing the qualifications of the candidates, voters may cast ballots for persons with familiar or catchy names who may be unqualified for the offices they seek.

 WHAT IS YOUR OPINION?

Is the ballot too long for Texas voters to be able to make informed choices?

TYPES OF ELECTIONS

Texans have the opportunity to cast ballots in different types of elections held at various times throughout the year.

General Elections

General election
A statewide election to fill national and state offices, which is held on the first Tuesday after the first Monday in November of even-numbered years.

A **general election** is a statewide election to fill national and state offices, held on the first Tuesday after the first Monday in November of even-numbered years. In recent years, the Texas statewide general election ballot has included candidates for the Republican Party, Democratic Party, and Libertarian Party. Independents and candidates affiliated with other political parties, such as the Green Party, must gather signatures equivalent to 1 percent of all the votes cast for governor in the last general election to qualify for the ballot. In 2006, Carole Keeton Strayhorn and Kinky Freidman each had to collect the signatures of 45,540 registered voters who had not participated in the March primary during a 60-day period in order to qualify for the general election ballot. Only Texas and North Carolina make it so difficult for independents and third-party candidates to get on the ballot.[5] A party can hold its ballot slot as long as one of its candidates receives at least 5 percent of the statewide vote in at least one race.

Split ticket voting
Citizens casting their ballots for candidates of two or more parties for different offices during the same election.

State law allows either split ticket or straight ticket voting. **Split ticket voting** refers to citizens casting their ballots for candidates of two or more parties for different offices during the same election. **Straight ticket voting** involves citizens casting their ballots only for the candidates of one party. The general election ballot includes a straight ticket box to allow voters to cast straight ticket ballots by marking a single box rather than having to vote individually on all of a party's candidates.

Straight ticket voting Citizens casting their ballots only for the candidates of one party.

The candidate with the most votes wins the general election, regardless of whether that candidate has a majority (more than 50 percent) of the ballots cast. There are no runoffs. The 2006 governor's race featured four major candidates—Republican Rick Perry, Democrat Chris Bell, Strayhorn, and Friedman. The outcome of the election was as follows:

Perry	39 percent
Bell	30 percent
Strayhorn	18 percent
Friedman	12 percent

Under the state's election laws, Perry won the election, despite having taken less than a majority of the total votes cast because the candidate with the most votes wins the general election.

Primary Elections

Although minor parties may select their general election candidates at a state convention, Texas law requires that major parties choose their candidates in a **primary election,** which is an intraparty election at which a party's candidates for the general election are chosen. Democrats compete against other Democrats, Republicans against Republicans. In Texas, primary elections take place on the first Tuesday in March of even-numbered years.

The two basic kinds of primary election methods are the closed primary and the open primary. A **closed primary** is an election system that limits primary election participation to registered party members. Many party leaders favor the closed primary because they believe that it prevents the supporters of the opposition party from influencing the selection of candidates for their party. Why should Democrats be allowed to help select Republican nominees and vice versa? In contrast, an **open primary** is an election system that allows voters to pick the party primary of their choice without disclosing their party affiliation. Some party leaders

Primary election
An intraparty election during which a party's candidates for the general election are chosen.

Closed primary
An election system that limits primary election participation to registered party members.

Open primary An election system that allows voters to pick the party primary of their choice without disclosing their party affiliation.

Texas voters choose among candidates for dozens of offices.

favor the open primary because they believe that it will produce nominees who can appeal to independent voters and supporters of the other party more than the closed primary can. Candidates with broad appeal are more likely to win the general election than are candidates who can attract only the votes of other Democrats or Republicans.

The Texas primary system is a cross between an open primary and a closed primary. In contrast to the practice in many states, Texas does not require that citizens disclose their party affiliation when they register to vote. On primary election day, however, voters must publicly choose the party in whose primary they wish to participate. They cannot vote in both primaries. Once a voter declares a choice, the election judge stamps the voter registration card with the following phrase: "Voted in the Republican (Democratic) primary."

Primary election participation has changed as the fortunes of the state's two major political parties have changed. From the 1870s until the middle of the twentieth century, most of the state's voters participated in the Democratic primary. A majority of Texans identified with the Democratic Party, and the Democratic primary had the more hotly contested races. In recent years, participation in the Republican primary has risen as the Grand Old Party (GOP) has gained strength and the Republican primary has featured interesting and important races for president, governor, and senator.

Figure 24.1 compares Democratic and Republican primary election turnout in statewide (nonpresidential) election years from 1978 to 2006. In 1978, Democratic primary voters outnumbered GOP primary participants by a better than 10–1 margin. Subsequently, the Democratic primary electorate shrank while the number of people voting in the Republican primary increased. In 2006, Republican primary voters outnumbered Democratic primary voters.

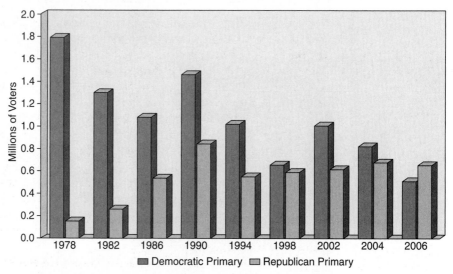

FIGURE 24.1   Primary Turnout, 1978–2006.
Source: Texas Secretary of State.

The state has come full cycle from the days when the winner of the Democratic primary inevitably became the officeholder because of the weakness of the opposition party. For years, the Democratic primary was the most important election in Texas for statewide offices because the winner of the Democratic primary inevitably won the general election contest. Today, statewide races are now settled in the Republican primary rather than the general election.

To win a primary election, a candidate must receive a majority of the votes cast (50 percent plus one vote). If no one receives a majority in a multicandidate race, the two highest finishers meet in a runoff. Suppose that Joe Nava, Elizabeth Jackson, and Lee Chen are running for the Democratic nomination for the office of county sheriff and the vote totals are as follows:

Nava	4,102
Jackson	2,888
Chen	2,009

Nava and Jackson would face one another in the primary runoff because neither received a majority of the votes cast. Chen is eliminated because he finished third.

A **runoff primary election** is an election between the two top finishers in a primary election when no candidate received a majority of the vote in the initial primary. In Texas, the primary runoff takes place on the second Tuesday in April, a little more than a month after the initial primary. People who voted in the March primary may only vote in the same party's runoff election. They cannot switch parties for the runoff. Citizens who failed to vote in March can vote in either party's runoff primary. The winner of the runoff is the party's official nominee for the fall general election.

The Presidential Delegate Selection Process

Every four years, Texans have the opportunity to participate in the process through which the Democratic and Republican Parties choose their presidential candidates by selecting delegates to attend the national conventions of the two major parties. The procedure for selecting delegates to national party conventions varies from state to state. About two-thirds of the states select delegates by means of a **presidential preference primary election,** which is an election in which party voters cast ballots for the presidential candidate they favor and in so doing help determine the number of convention delegates that candidate will receive. Other states choose national convention delegates by the **caucus method of delegate selection,** which is a procedure for choosing national party convention delegates that involves party voters participating in a series of precinct and district or county political meetings. The process begins with party members attending precinct conventions, where they elect delegates to district meetings. The district meetings in turn select delegates to the state convention. Finally, the state party convention chooses national convention delegates.

In Texas, the state Republican Party chooses delegates to the national party convention through a presidential preference primary. To receive any delegates, a presidential candidate has to win at least 20 percent of the vote in one or more

Runoff primary election An election between the two top finishers in a primary election when no candidate received a majority of the vote in the initial primary.

Presidential preference primary election An election in which party voters cast ballots for the presidential candidate they favor and in so doing help determine the number of convention delegates that candidate will receive.

Caucus method of delegate selection A procedure for choosing national party convention delegates that involves party voters participating in a series of precinct and district or county political meetings.

U.S. congressional districts. Any candidate who gets a majority of the vote in a congressional district claims all of that district's delegates. A candidate who gets more than 20 percent but less than a majority receives a share of the delegates allotted to that district.

The Texas Democratic Party selects national convention delegates through a system that combines the primary and the caucus methods. More than half the state's Democratic delegates are awarded to presidential candidates in rough proportion to the percentage of votes they receive in a presidential preference primary as long as a candidate qualifies by winning at least 15 percent of the statewide vote. Candidates also win delegates based on the results of a caucus process. Finally, the party reserves a number of delegate positions for **superdelegates,** which are Democratic officeholders and party officials who attend the national party convention as delegates who are not officially pledged to support any candidate.

Superdelegates Democratic officeholders and party officials who attend the national party convention as delegates who are not officially pledged to support any candidate.

The Texas legislature has periodically tinkered with the timing of the spring primary in hopes of increasing the state's influence in the presidential selection process. In 1987, the legislature moved the spring primary date from May to March. Despite its size, Texas had enjoyed relatively little influence in presidential nomination contests because each party's presidential nomination was long decided by the time Texas got around to selecting its convention delegates. The legislature hoped that, by moving the state's presidential delegate selection process up a couple of months, presidential candidates would be forced to campaign in the Lone Star State and appeal to Texas voters. The scheme failed, however, because other states moved their primaries and caucuses as well. In 2003, the Texas legislature tried once again to increase the state's role in the presidential selection process by moving the primary up another week, from the second to the first Tuesday in March. The plan was unsuccessful in 2004 because the party nominations were settled before Texans went to the polls. In 2007, some legislators and party leaders proposed moving the 2008 presidential preference primary up to early February in hopes of regaining influence in the nomination process, but the proposal failed to pass the legislature.

Local Elections

Under state law, local elections for city, school district, and special district officials must be held on either the second Saturday in May or the first Tuesday after the first Monday in November. Local governments usually conduct their elections in odd-numbered years, so that they will not coincide with general elections for president, senator, and governor. Most city governments choose officials by majority vote, with a runoff election if no one candidate receives a majority in a multicandidate field. Most school districts choose the members of their boards of trustees by plurality vote—the candidate who receives the most votes wins, regardless of whether it is a majority. The state constitution *requires* majority election for terms of office greater than two years. State law allows cities and school districts to cancel elections if all candidates are running unopposed and no other issues are on the ballot.

Nonpartisan elections Election contests in which the names of the candidates appear on the ballot but not their party affiliations.

Most local races in Texas are **nonpartisan elections,** which are election contests in which the names of the candidates, but not their party affiliations, appear on the ballot. The supporters of nonpartisan elections argue that the elimination of political parties from local elections reduces corruption. Furthermore, they say that nonpartisan

NATIONAL PERSPECTIVE

The Open Primary in Louisiana

Louisiana has a unique primary system. Every candidate competes for votes in an open primary, regardless of party affiliation. If 1 candidate wins a majority of the vote, that candidate is elected. Otherwise, the 2 top finishers face each other in a runoff election, regardless of party affiliation. In theory, the runoff could involve 2 Democrats, 2 Republicans, or 1 candidate from each party. In 2003, for example, 17 candidates competed in the open primary for governor, including 3 Republicans, 9 Democrats, and 5 independents. The 2 top candidates, Democrat Kathleen Babineaux Blanco and Republican Bobby Jindal, met in a runoff, which Blanco won.

Democratic Governor Edwin Edwards invented the open primary and got the state's Democratic-controlled legislature to adopt it as a device to slow the rise of the state's Republican Party. To win office, Democrats had to survive a bruising Democratic primary election and then defeat a Republican opponent in the general election who had usually won the Republican primary without strong opposition. Edwards figured that the open primary would erase the Republican advantage by forcing all the candidates into the same set of elections.

Although the open primary has not prevented Republicans from making substantial inroads into Louisiana politics, it probably was responsible for Edwards winning a fourth nonconsecutive term as governor in 1991. The three main contenders, Edwards, Republican state legislator David Duke, and incumbent Republican Governor Buddy Roemer, carried considerable political baggage into the race. Many Louisiana voters thought that Edwards was a crook because he had spent most of his career fighting off corruption charges. (They were apparently right about Edwards because the former governor is currently serving a ten-year prison sentence for racketeering.) Duke was notorious as a former Nazi sympathizer and leader of the Ku Klux Klan. Finally, Roemer had angered many voters because he broke his promise not to raise taxes. Most experts on Louisiana politics believed that Roemer would have been able to defeat either Edwards or Duke in a runoff, but he finished third. (Raising taxes was apparently a worse political liability than either charges of corruption or ties to the Ku Klux Klan!) Edwards easily defeated Duke in the runoff and became governor of Louisiana once again.

QUESTIONS TO CONSIDER

1. What are the advantages of an open primary system, such as the one in Louisiana?
2. What are the disadvantages of an open primary?
3. Would you like to see Texas adopt an open primary system? Why or why not?

elections free local politics from state and national political controversies. In contrast, critics of nonpartisan elections believe they work to the advantage of upper-income groups because they reduce the amount of information available to voters about candidates. In partisan elections, the single most important piece of information voters have about candidates is the party label. In nonpartisan elections, voters do not know the party attachments of the candidates. They must study the positions of the candidates if they are going to vote in their own best interest. Upper-income persons are in a better position to determine which candidates best represent their interests because they are better able to learn about candidates than low-income people are.

Scholarly research largely supports the critics of nonpartisan elections. Turnout for nonpartisan elections is generally lower than turnout for partisan elections. Without party labels on the ballot to guide their choice, some potential voters stay home because they are unable to distinguish among the candidates. Furthermore, some people who do cast ballots base their voting decisions on such factors as incumbency, gender, and the perceived ethnicity of the candidates based on their names.[6]

Special Elections

Special election
An election called at a time outside the normal election calendar.

A **special election** is an election called at a time outside the normal election calendar. Special elections may be used to approve local bond issues or to fill unexpected vacancies in the legislature or the state's congressional delegation. Vacancies in executive and judicial offices are generally filled by gubernatorial appointment. When a vacancy occurs, the governor calls a special election. Special elections are nonpartisan, although party organizations often get involved. A candidate must receive a majority of the votes cast (50 percent plus one) to win a special election. Otherwise, the two leading candidates meet in a runoff.

Noncandidate Elections

Bond A certificate of indebtedness issued to investors who loan money for interest income; in lay terms, a bond is an IOU.

Texas voters have the opportunity to participate in a number of noncandidate elections, including bond elections, recall elections, and referenda. A **bond** is a certificate of indebtedness issued to investors who loan money for interest income; in lay terms, a bond is an IOU. A **bond election** is an election for the purpose of obtaining voter approval for a local government going into debt. Approval for state government indebtedness is obtained through the adoption of a constitutional amendment.

Bond election An election for the purpose of obtaining voter approval for a local government going into debt.

Recall is a procedure allowing voters to remove elected officials from office before the expiration of their terms. If enough signatures can be gathered on petitions, disgruntled citizens can force a recall election to remove the targeted official, and voters decide whether to keep the officeholder or declare the office vacant. The vacancy is then filled in a special election. In 2003, California voters recalled Governor Gray Davis and replaced him with Hollywood actor Arnold Schwarzenegger, but that sort of action could not happen in the Lone Star State because state officials are not subject to recall. In Texas, the power of recall is limited to the citizens of some city governments.

Recall A procedure allowing voters to remove elected officials from office before the expiration of their terms

Initiative process
A procedure whereby citizens can propose the adoption of a policy measure by gathering a prerequisite number of signatures. Voters must then approve the measure before it can take effect.

Many cities (but not the state government) provide for the **initiative process,** which is a procedure whereby citizens can propose legislation by gathering a certain number of signatures on a petition. Election officials then place the measure on the ballot for approval by the voters. Some cities also allow citizens to repeal ordinances passed by the city council through a similar process. In some municipalities, city officials may place nonbinding referenda on the ballot. Furthermore, the executive committees of the state Republican and Democratic Parties sometimes include nonbinding referendum proposals on their spring primary ballots.

Texans vote on other measures as well. Voters must approve amendments to the state constitution. The legislature usually places amendments on the November ballot—usually in odd-numbered years, so that they will not share the ballot with a general election. Voters must also approve the establishment and dissolution of special districts, such as hospital districts or municipal utility districts. Finally, **local-option elections** are held to determine whether an area will legalize the sale of alcoholic beverages.

Local-option elections Elections held to determine whether an area legalizes the sale of alcoholic beverages.

 WHAT IS YOUR OPINION?

Does Texas have too many elections?

ELECTION DISTRICTS

At-large election
A method for choosing public officials in which every citizen of a political subdivision, such as a state or county, votes to select a public official.

Texas voters select public officials in a combination of at-large and district elections. An **at-large election** is a method for choosing public officials in which every citizen of a political subdivision, such as a state or county, votes to select a public official. The president and vice president, two U.S. senators, the governor, the lieutenant governor, the comptroller of public accounts, the land commissioner, the attorney general, the agricultural commissioner, three railroad commissioners, nine justices of the Texas Supreme Court, and nine justices of the Texas Court of Criminal Appeals are all elected in at-large, statewide elections. Furthermore, a number of local officials, including county and district judges, sheriffs, city mayors, city council members, and school district trustees, are elected in local at-large elections.

District election A method for choosing public officials in which a political subdivision, such as a state or county, is divided into districts and each district elects one official.

A **district election** is a method for choosing public officials in which a political subdivision, such as a state or county, is divided into districts and each district elects one official. Members of the Texas legislature, U.S. Congress, and State Board of Education (SBOE) are elected from districts. For example, the 150 members of the Texas House of Representatives are elected 1 each from 150 state representative districts. The state's 31 state senators are chosen from 31 state senatorial districts. A number of local officials, including county commissioners, city council members in some cities, and the members of boards of trustees in some school districts, are also elected from single-member districts.

REDISTRICTING

Redistricting The process of redrawing the boundaries of legislative districts.

Election districts must be redrawn every ten years to adjust for changes in population. The process of redrawing the boundaries of legislative districts is known as **redistricting.** The Texas legislature is responsible for redrawing Texas House districts, Texas Senate districts, U.S. congressional districts, and the districts for the State Board of Education (SBOE). Local governing bodies, such as city councils and commissioners courts, redraw the districts of local officials. The national census, which is taken every ten years, provides the population data for redistricting.

One Person, One Vote

One person, one vote The judicial ruling that the Equal Protection Clause of the Fourteenth Amendment to the U.S. Constitution requires that legislative districts be apportioned on the basis of population.

State legislatures have not always been conscientious about redistricting. During the first half of the twentieth century, the legislatures of a number of states, including Texas, failed to redistrict despite dramatic population movement from rural to urban areas because rural legislators did not want to relinquish control. As a result, the population sizes of legislative districts sometimes varied dramatically. In 1961, the ratio between the most populous and the least populous U.S. congressional district in Texas was 4.4 to 1. The ratio was 8 to 1 for state senate districts and 2 to 1 for state house districts.[7]

The U.S. Supreme Court addressed this issue in a series of cases that established the doctrine of **one person, one vote,** which was the judicial ruling that the Equal Protection Clause of the Fourteenth Amendment to the U.S. Constitution requires that legislative districts be apportioned on the basis of population.[8] If one legislative district has substantially more people than another district, then the people living in the less populous district have more political influence than do the residents of the larger district. Suppose an urban district has ten times more people than a rural district. The people in the rural district have ten times the influence in the election of a legislator or a member of Congress. Compared with the citizens living in the large urban district, the voters in the smaller rural district effectively have ten votes. The Supreme Court ruled that the Constitution requires that citizens have equal political influence regardless of where they live. "One person, one vote," ruled the Court, not "one person, 10 votes." District boundaries would have to be drawn to ensure nearly equal population size. Although the Court allowed some leeway in state legislative and local district size, it required that U.S. congressional districts have almost exactly the same number of people. In 2002, for example, a federal court overturned Pennsylvania's redistricting plan because two U.S. House districts varied in size by 19 people—646,361 compared with 646,380![9]

The Supreme Court's one person, one vote decisions had a significant impact on policymaking in Texas. Because of the Court's rulings, urban areas gained representation, whereas rural interests lost ground. The legislative delegation for Harris County, the state's most populous county, increased from 1 state senator and 12 members of the House to 4 senators and 19 House members.[10] African Americans, Latinos, and Republicans, all groups that are more numerous in urban areas than rural, increased their representation in legislative bodies. Urban problems, such as education, transportation, race relations, crime, and healthcare, won a more prominent place on the state's policy agenda.[11]

The Voting Rights Act

Voting Rights Act (VRA) A federal law designed to protect the voting rights of racial and ethnic minorities.

The **Voting Rights Act (VRA)** is a federal law designed to protect the voting rights of racial and ethnic minorities. The VRA makes it illegal for state and local governments to enact and enforce election rules and procedures that diminish African American and Latino voting power. Furthermore, the preclearance provision of the VRA requires that state and local governments in areas with a history of voting discrimination submit redistricting plans to the U.S. Department of Justice for approval *before* they can go into effect. Congress and the president included the preclearance provision in the VRA in order to stay one step ahead of local officials who would adopt new discriminatory electoral procedures as soon as the federal courts threw out an old procedure. The preclearance provision of the VRA applies only to states and parts of states that have substantial racial and language minority populations with relatively low rates of voter participation. Texas is covered, along with all or part of 15 other states: Alaska, Alabama, Arizona, California, Florida, Georgia, Louisiana, Michigan, Mississippi, New Hampshire, New York, North Carolina, South Carolina, South Dakota, and Virginia.

In the late 1980s and early 1990s, the Justice Department in the first Bush administration interpreted amendments to the VRA adopted in 1982 to require that state legislatures go beyond nondiscrimination to drawing districts designed to maximize minority representation. If a legislature *could* draw a district that would likely elect an African American or Latino candidate, then the legislature *must* draw the district. In other words, state legislatures would have to maximize the number of legislative districts with populations that were more than 50 percent minority.[12]

Why would a Republican administration choose to implement the VRA to increase African American and Latino representation in Congress and state legislatures? After all, most minority lawmakers are Democrats. The reason was simple: The policy also helped the Republican Party gain legislative seats.[13] To construct majority African American and Latino districts, state legislatures redrew district lines to shift minority voters away from adjacent districts into new districts designed to elect minority officeholders. Because most African American and Latino voters are Democrats, the redistricting reduced Democratic voting strength in surrounding districts, threatening the political survival of some white Democratic members of Congress. The Georgia congressional delegation, for example, went from one African American Democrat, eight white Democrats, and one white Republican before redistricting in 1991 to three African American Democrats and eight white Republicans after the 1994 election. Nationwide, the creation of minority districts after the 1990 census helped white Republicans pick up about ten seats in Congress, defeating white Democrats who were stripped of some of their minority voter support.[14]

In the mid-1990s, the U.S. Supreme Court overruled the Justice Department's interpretation of the VRA. Responding to legal challenges filed against minority districts created in Louisiana, Georgia, and other southern states, the Court declared that state governments cannot use race as the predominant, overriding factor in drawing district lines unless they have a "compelling" reason. The goal of maximizing the number of minority districts was not sufficient to justify race-based redistricting, the Court said, because Congress enacted the VRA to prevent discrimination rather than maximize the number of districts that would elect African American and Latino candidates.[15]

 WHAT IS YOUR OPINION?

Should state legislatures consider race and ethnicity in drawing legislative districts?

The role of the VRA in the redistricting process changed considerably during the 1990s. At the beginning of the decade, the VRA forced legislatures to focus on race and ethnicity during redistricting, and legislatures throughout the South created minority districts whenever possible. By the end of the decade, however, the U.S. Supreme Court had made it clear that legislatures could not use race and ethnicity as the primary basis for redistricting unless they had a compelling reason. State legislatures could not regress; that is, they could not legally create legislative districts that would diminish the political influence of minority voters, but neither did they have to increase the number of minority districts.

The Politics of Redistricting

Gerrymandering
The drawing of legislative district lines for political advantage.

Redistricting is a highly political process. Legislative districts can be drawn to the advantage of one political party over another or one candidate over another. The drawing of legislative district lines for political advantage is known as **gerrymandering.** In the 1991 redistricting, for example, Democratic State Senator (now U.S. Representative) Eddie Bernice Johnson of Dallas used her position as chair of the Texas

More than 50 Democratic legislators spent several days in Ardmore, Oklahoma, in May 2003 in hopes of defeating a congressional redistricting plan that would favor the Republicans.

Senate redistricting committee to enhance her own chances of winning a seat in Congress. The congressional district she created not only included much of her old state Senate district but also excluded the residences of potential opponents.[16]

Gerrymandering can affect election outcomes. After redistricting in 1980, the political parties that drew the lines usually won more seats than they did before redistricting and almost always held the seats created for them throughout the decade. Furthermore, they generally won a higher percentage of seats than votes.[17] On average, a political party with complete control of the redistricting process can gerrymander legislative districts to allow the party's candidates to win 54 percent of legislative seats while capturing only 50 percent of the total vote.[18]

Democrats controlled the redistricting process in Texas following the 1990 Census because they held a majority of seats in both chambers of the Texas legislature and Democrat Ann Richards was governor. Republicans accused the Democrats of using their power to create congressional and legislative districts that were unfair to Republican candidates. In 1992, Democratic candidates for the U.S. House won 21 of the state's 30 congressional seats, even though they received only 50 percent of the votes cast. Two years later, Republican congressional candidates carried the popular vote 56 percent to 42 percent, but Democrats still won 19 of 30 seats.

Similarly, Democrats captured 17 of the 30 seats at stake in 1996, despite once again losing the popular vote, this time by 54 percent to 44 percent.[19]

The political landscape in Texas after the 2000 Census was considerably different than it was ten years earlier because neither party enjoyed clear control of the redistricting process. Although Democrats still held a majority of seats in the Texas House, Republicans enjoyed a 16 to 15 advantage in the Texas Senate, and Governor Rick Perry was a Republican. The result was a legislative stalemate. The 2001 session of the Texas legislature ended without passage of a redistricting plan for either the two houses of the legislature or the Congress.

When the legislature and the governor failed to adopt redistricting plans, the responsibility for drawing new district lines for the Texas legislature fell to the **Legislative Redistricting Board (LRB),** which is an agency composed of the speaker, lieutenant governor, comptroller, land commissioner, and attorney general that draws the boundaries of Texas House and Texas Senate seats when the legislature is unable to agree on a redistricting plan. In 2001, Republicans held four of the five seats on the LRB. Lieutenant Governor Bill Ratliff, Attorney General John Cornyn, Comptroller Carole Keeton Rylander, and Land Commissioner David Dewhurst were all Republicans. Speaker Pete Laney was the sole Democrat on the panel.

The LRB considered two alternative redistricting schemes. Speaker Laney and Lieutenant Governor Ratliff proposed a plan that was designed to protect incumbent legislators of both parties. The two legislative leaders were more interested in protecting their friends and colleagues in the legislature than they were in advancing the cause of either political party. The problem for Laney and Ratliff was that the LRB makes decisions by majority vote and none of the other members of the LRB would agree to support their plan.

In the meantime, Attorney General Cornyn presented an alternative plan aimed at increasing Republican strength in the legislature at the expense of incumbent legislators of both parties. Based on voting history, Republicans would win control of the Texas House under Cornyn's proposal and increase their majority in the Texas Senate.[20] To improve Republican chances to win seats, Cornyn ignored the interests of incumbents, even Republican incumbents. His plan would force 39 members of the House, including 27 Democrats, to run in the same districts.[21] Many other incumbent members of the legislature were put in new districts from which it would be difficult to win reelection.

Rylander and Dewhurst joined Cornyn to provide a 3–2 majority for the Cornyn plan, making it the official redistricting plan for the Texas House and Texas Senate. With some minor modifications imposed by a federal court, the districts drawn by the LRB elected the members of the Texas House and Texas Senate in 2002. As predicted, the plan enabled the GOP to win a majority of seats in the Texas House for the first time in more than a century and to increase the Republican majority in the Texas Senate.

Whereas the Republicans were pleased with the results of legislative redistricting, the Democrats were relieved at the outcome of congressional redistricting. Because the LRB has jurisdiction only over redistricting the legislature, a federal court drew the lines for the state's congressional districts. The court redrew the state's existing 30 congressional districts in such a fashion that incumbent members of

Legislative Redistricting Board (LRB) An agency composed of the speaker, lieutenant governor, comptroller, land commissioner, and attorney general that draws the boundaries of Texas House and Senate seats when the legislature is unable to agree on a redistricting plan.

Congress from both parties would likely win reelection. It then put one of the state's 2 new congressional districts in Central Texas and the other in the Dallas suburbs. Although Republicans easily captured the 2 new congressional districts, the Democrats clung to a 17–15 majority in the state's congressional delegation because Democratic incumbents were able to retain their seats.

The Republican Party attempted to increase its strength in the U.S. House of Representatives by revisiting the issue of redistricting in 2003. Republican Congressman Tom DeLay of Sugar Land, Texas, the House Majority Leader, presented the GOP leadership in the Texas House with a congressional redistricting plan that could produce a congressional delegation from the Lone Star State of 22 Republicans and 10 Democrats. When Tom Craddick, the Speaker of the Texas House, pushed for a vote on the plan in the closing days of the legislative session, more than 50 Democratic members of the Texas House of Representatives secretly traveled to Ardmore, Oklahoma, where they would be outside the jurisdiction of Texas law enforcement officials who had been sent to find them and take them back to Austin. The strategy for the Democrats was to prevent the House from having a quorum, which is the number of members that must be present for the chamber to conduct official business. Because the rules of the House set a quorum at two-thirds of the 150-member body, the absence of more than 50 Democratic legislators blocked the redistricting bill, at least for the time being. Once the deadline for passing legislation expired in the House, the Democrats returned to the state and the legislature resumed its business.

DeLay's redistricting proposal was highly controversial. Republicans said that redrawing the state's congressional district lines to increase the number of Republicans in Congress was fair because Texas is a Republican state. In 2002, Democrats won 17 of the state's 32 U.S. House seats, even though 57 percent of Texas voters supported Republicans for Congress. If most Texans vote Republican, DeLay said, most Texas members of Congress should be Republican as well. In contrast, Democrats pointed out that redistricting anytime other than the session after the census is both unusual and unnecessary. They accused DeLay of a power grab aimed at preserving Republican control of the U.S. House of Representatives. Democrats hold a majority of the state's congressional delegation, they said, because Texas voters in a number of districts split their tickets to vote Republican for statewide office while backing Democrats for Congress.

Shortly after the end of the 2003 regular session of the legislature, Governor Perry called a 30-day special session to consider congressional redistricting. The House quickly passed a redistricting plan and sent the measure to the Senate, where it ran into trouble. Many Senate Republicans disagreed with the plan put forward by the House. To maximize the number of Republicans in Congress, the House plan linked most of rural and small-town Texas to suburban areas, which reliably vote Republican. Republican senators from East Texas and West Texas opposed the plan because their communities would be placed in congressional districts dominated by the suburbs of Dallas or Houston. Meanwhile, the Senate Democrats held together to block consideration of the plan on the floor of the Senate. The longstanding practice in the Texas Senate is to require a two-thirds' vote before a measure can be considered on the floor. With 11 Senate Democrats refusing to agree to debate, the redistricting bill failed. The first special session ended without accomplishing anything.

As the first special session ended, the Republican leadership set a trap for the Democrats. Lieutenant Governor Dewhurst declared that he would not honor the two-thirds' rule in a second special session, therefore ensuring that the Republican majority would be able to vote a redistricting plan out of the Senate. While Democrats caucused in the capital, Governor Perry called a second special session and Dewhurst ordered the doors locked to trap the Democrats inside. Unfortunately for Dewhurst and Perry, the Democrats got word of the scheme just in time and slipped out a side door. They drove to the airport and flew to Albuquerque, New Mexico, out of the reach of Texas authorities. With 11 Democrats in Albuquerque, the Senate lacked the quorum necessary to conduct official business. The second special session accomplished nothing.

Before Governor Perry could call a third special session, the Senate Democrats in Albuquerque broke ranks. Senator Whitmire returned to Texas, declaring that he and his fellow Democrats had made their point and that he would be on the Senate floor when the governor called the next special session, ensuring a quorum. Although the other Democrats were furious with Whitmire, they had no choice but to end their boycott and return to Texas.

Whitmire's return did not mean a quick end to the redistricting battle because House and Senate Republicans could not agree on a new map. After several weeks of wrangling, Congressman DeLay flew to Texas to broker an agreement. The House and Senate passed and Governor Perry signed a redistricting plan that many observers believed would increase the number of Republicans in the U.S. House from 15 to at least 20 and maybe 22.

The predictions proved true. The GOP picked up 1 seat in the House even before the next election when Democratic Congressman Ralph Hall of East Texas switched parties. The Republicans added 5 more seats in the 2004 election, defeating every targeted Democratic incumbent, except for Congressman Chet Edwards of West Texas, who barely hung on to his seat with 51 percent of the vote. In 2005, the state's congressional delegation included 21 Republicans and 11 Democrats.[22]

In late 2005, the U.S. Supreme Court agreed to hear a legal challenge to the Texas mid-cycle redistricting. The case presented the Court with several intriguing issues:

- Did the Texas redistricting plan violate the VRA? Minority rights groups charged that the plan diminished the political influence of Latino and African American Texans.

- Is mid-cycle redistricting unconstitutional? The U.S. Constitution requires redistricting every ten years after the Census, but Texas redistricted twice after the 2000 Census, once in 2001 and then again in 2003 after the Republicans took control of both chambers of the legislature.

- Did Texas violate the one-person, one-vote rule by using 2000 Census data to redistrict in 2003? Because the state used the 2000 Census figures, the districts did not reflect population changes that had taken place in the three years since the data were collected.

- Was the Texas redistricting so political that it constituted an unconstitutional gerrymander? Although the Supreme Court has never overturned a redistricting scheme because of gerrymandering, it has declared that partisan gerrymandering is unconstitutional if it can be demonstrated that the "electoral system is arranged in such a manner that will consistently degrade a . . . group of voters' influence on the political process as a whole."[23]

INTERNET RESEARCH

Legislative Districts and State House Elections

The Texas House of Representatives has 150 members elected from 150 districts called state house districts. The districts are numbered from 1 to 150, with each district electing one person to the Texas House. In 2007, for example, Veronica Gonzalez represented District 41, which is located in McAllen.

Students of Texas government can learn a good deal about legislative districts and elections from online resources, especially those located at the website of the Texas legislature: **www.capitol.state.tx.us**. Answer the following questions based on the information in the textbook and your research online:

1. In which state house district is your home located? (Go to the website of the Texas legislature and find the link "Who represents me?" Click on the link and enter your complete address. The district type is "House.")

2. Who represents the district in which you live?

3. The website displays a map of the district. Describe where it is located by making reference to major streets, neighborhoods, bodies of water, or other landmarks.

4. Write a paragraph in which you describe the district's population. Is it urban or rural? Is its population older or younger than the state average? Is its population better educated or less well educated than the state average? Is the average income in the district above or below the state average? Is the population predominantly white, black, Latino, or mixed? (All of this information can be found at the website. Click on the tab at the top of the page labeled "District Information." Indicate that the district type is "Texas House" and enter the number for the district in which you live. Use the pull-down menu to display tables containing the data needed to answer the preceding questions.)

5. Based on your description of the district, would you expect it to vote typically Republican or Democrat or would you anticipate it to be a swing district? Explain the basis for your answer. (Before you attempt to answer this question, you may wish to review the information in Chapter 23 that describes the voter base for each of the two major political parties.)

6. Is your analysis on the party leanings of the district correct? Use the drop-down menu to review the district election report. It displays the vote breakdown in the district for state, county, and district elections. Do the figures indicate that the district trends Republican or Democratic? Discuss the information you considered in reaching your conclusion.

With one exception, the Supreme Court upheld the Texas redistricting plan. The Court ruled that the plan was not an impermissible partisan gerrymander, that mid-cycle redistricting was acceptable under the Constitution, and that the state was justified in using 2000 Census data. The Court did, however, find that the Texas plan violated the VRA by removing 100,000 Latino residents from the Twenty-third Congressional District in Southwest Texas. The Republican leaders who drew up the plan wanted to shore up electoral support for Republican Congressman Henry Bonilla. Even though Bonilla is Latino himself, most Latino residents of the district vote Democratic. The Supreme Court ordered a lower federal court to redraw the boundaries of the district and adjacent districts to correct the violation of the VRA.[24] Bonilla was subsequently defeated for reelection by Democrat Ciro Rodriguez.

Reforming the Redistricting Process

Critics believe that the modern redistricting process undermines the quality of democracy in the United States. The redistricting process typically produces legislative districts that are safe for one party or the other, depriving voters of the opportunity to participate in competitive elections for Congress or state legislatures. If elected officials do not have to worry about a serious electoral challenge, critics warn, they have little incentive to represent the interests of their constituents.

State legislators have always tried to create districts that would be safe for their party. Democrats want to draw Democratic districts, whereas Republicans prefer to create Republican districts. No one in the legislature has an incentive to design a competitive district. Computer technology has enabled legislators to accomplish their goals more efficiently than ever before. As a result, relatively few legislative seats are competitive between the two parties.

The critics of redistricting also believe that it produces legislators who represent the extremes of the political spectrum. Legislators who are chosen from districts that are stacked for one political party tend to represent the extremes of that party because those are the people who participate in primary elections. Republican primary voters are somewhat more conservative than Republicans in general and much more conservative than the electorate as a whole. Democratic primary voters, meanwhile, are somewhat more liberal than Democrats in general and much more liberal than the electorate as a whole. In competitive districts, candidates recognize the value of appealing to a broad spectrum of voters because they understand that they must win not just the primary election but the general election as well. Primary voters also have an incentive to select more moderate candidates because they have a better chance of winning the general election than do candidates whose views are more extreme. Legislative bodies dominated by members representing the extremes of either party may have difficulty reaching compromise on complex policy issues, instead dissolving into partisan gridlock.

Reformers want to change the redistricting process to make it less political. In Iowa, for example, a bipartisan redistricting commission creates a redistricting plan, which the legislature must accept or reject but not amend. If the legislature rejects the plan, the commission tries a second and even a third time. If the legislature fails to approve any of the commission's plans, a court redistricts for the state. After the 2000 Census, four of the state's five U.S. congressional districts were fairly evenly divided between the two parties. The other district was heavily Republican. After the 2006 election, the Iowa congressional delegation included three Democrats and two Republicans. A bill designed to change the redistricting process in Texas to resemble the Iowa system was introduced in a recent session of the legislature, but it has gotten nowhere.

MONEY

Election campaigns are expensive. The total cost of the campaigns for governor, other statewide executive offices, and the legislature in 2006 was nearly $180 million.[25] Candidates running competitive races for the Texas House of Representatives typically spend $600,000 or more. The cost of a Texas Senate seat in rural areas is a million dollars; it can be as high as $2 or $3 million in urban areas.[26] Local contests in large metropolitan areas are expensive as well. Candidates for mayor in the state's major cities often spend well in excess of a million dollars on their campaigns.

Candidates need money to hire a campaign staff, cover overhead expenses, and purchase advertising. They hire consultants to plan strategy, pollsters to assess public reaction to candidates and issues, media consultants to develop an advertising campaign, field organizers to get out the vote, opposition research experts to dig for dirt on opponents, and fundraisers to find the cash to pay for it all. Other money goes for campaign literature, office space, postage, telephones, polling, and consulting fees. The largest single item in the big-time campaign budget is media, especially television. A week's worth of television advertising that covers all of the state's major markets costs about $1 million.[27]

Advertising costs vary by medium and market size. The average charge for running a 30-second television ad during the late-night news in Dallas is about $5,000. A 60-second radio spot during drive time in a major market is much less expensive, only around $600, but the audience for radio is only a fraction of what television reaches.[28] Candidates for statewide office buy advertising on both radio and television throughout the state if they have the money available. In contrast, candidates for local office or the legislature may focus their efforts on less expensive approaches, such as radio, cable television, billboards, and direct mail.

Candidates who are wealthy can bankroll their own campaigns. In 2002, David Dewhurst invested $24.2 million in his successful campaign for lieutenant governor, counting both contributions and personal loans.[29] Candidates who loan money to their campaigns can often raise money after the election to cover their loans, especially if they have won the election. State law caps the amount of reimbursement for personal loans to $500,000 for candidates for governor and $250,000 for candidates for other statewide offices. Because the law puts no limit on reimbursement for third-party loans personally guaranteed by candidates, none of Dewhurst's loans were subject to the cap.[30]

 ## WHAT IS YOUR OPINION?

Should wealthy individuals be allowed to finance their own political campaigns?

Campaign money comes from a relatively small number of contributors. In 2006, 140 wealthy individuals donated more than $100,000 apiece to political action committees (PACs) and candidates, totaling more than a fourth of the total money raised during the campaign. Bob Perry, a Houston homebuilder, was the top donor, contributing $7.1 million, mostly to Republican candidates and campaign committees. Other multimillion-dollar donors included James Leininger and Fred Baron, a trial lawyer. Leininger supported Republicans, whereas Baron funded Democrats.[31]

Most of the individuals and groups who give money to candidates for office have a financial stake in the operation of state government. For example, Bob Perry and other members of the Texas Association of Builders favored legislation to shelter homebuilders from lawsuits filed by homebuyers. In 2003, the Texas legislature and the governor delivered for Perry by creating the Texas Residential Construction

Commission (TRCC). The nine-member commission, which includes four builders, establishes building standards for home construction. Disgruntled homeowners must complete the agency's dispute resolution process before they can file a lawsuit against the builder. Even if the TRCC rules in favor of the homeowner, it has no power to force the builder to make repairs. The critics of the TRCC charge that it protects builders by exhausting complaining homeowners emotionally and financially before they can file a lawsuit over defective workmanship.[32]

Most states restrict the amount of money individuals and groups can contribute to candidates for office, but not Texas. Two-thirds of the states limit campaign contributions and one-third provide public funding for campaigns in exchange for voluntary spending limits.[33] In contrast, Texas law places no limits on campaign contributions or campaign expenditures for candidates for executive or legislative office. Contribution and expenditure limits on judicial races are voluntary. In short, candidates for executive and legislative office in Texas can raise an unlimited amount of money from individuals or political action committees as long as they report the names, occupations, and employers of people who give them $500 or more in campaign contributions. Labor unions and corporations may not contribute directly to candidates for office, although they can fund nonpartisan voter registration drives and get-out-the-vote campaigns.

In 2005, a Travis County grand jury indicted Majority Leader DeLay and two associates for violating the state's campaign finance laws in connection with the 2002 election when the Republican Party took over the Texas House and set the stage for redistricting. Ronnie Earl, the Travis County district attorney, brought the grand jury evidence that DeLay and the other men had raised $190,000 in corporate contributions over and above administrative expenses and then gave that amount of money to an arm of the Republican National Committee, along with a list of seven Republican candidates for the Texas House and the amounts each of those candidates should get. Those seven checks totaled $190,000. The action, if it were proved true, would violate the state prohibition of using corporate money for campaign purposes. The specific charges against DeLay and the other two defendants were money laundering and conspiracy to violate state laws. In the face of the allegations, DeLay dropped his reelection bid in 2006 and resigned his seat in Congress. Ironically, Democrat Nick Lampson, a former member of Congress who lost his race for reelection after the 2003 redistricting, captured DeLay's old seat in the House, defeating a Republican candidate who was forced to run a write-in campaign.[34]

Money is indispensable to major campaign efforts. In general, candidates who spend the most money get the most votes.[35] Money is especially important for challengers and first-term incumbents who usually are not as well known as long-term officeholders.[36] Raising money early in the campaign is particularly important because it gives candidates credibility with potential contributors, making it easier to raise money later in the campaign season.[37] Candidates who amass campaign war chests often scare away potential serious challengers.

 WHAT IS YOUR OPINION?

Would you support using taxpayer money to finance election campaigns in order to reduce the role of private contributions?

Nonetheless, money does not guarantee victory. Democrat Tony Sanchez burned more than $60 million of his family's fortune in his campaign for governor in 2002 and got barely 40 percent of the vote. Furthermore, studies suggest that a law of diminishing returns may apply to campaign spending.[38] The marginal difference between spending $15 million and spending $13 million is not nearly as great as that between spending $2 million and spending $4 million. After all, if the average Texas voter sees a candidate's commercial 15 times, will it make much difference to see it once or twice more?

The relationship between money and electoral success is complex. Although it is true that well-funded candidates are usually successful, it is perhaps more accurate to say that successful candidates are well funded. Major campaign contributors give money to candidates they believe are likely to win because they hope to gain access to elected officials. Money makes strong candidates stronger; the lack of money makes weak candidates weaker. In 1998, for example, Governor George W. Bush raised more than $25 million for his reelection campaign, even though no one believed that his main opponent, Democrat Gary Mauro, had a serious chance of winning the election.[39] Individuals and groups gave generously to Governor Bush because he was almost a sure bet for reelection. Bush was also someone prominently mentioned as a likely presidential candidate in 2000. Major money players were eager to write big checks to the Bush campaign in hopes of gaining influence not just with the governor of Texas but also with someone who might become president of the United States.

CAMPAIGNS

Political campaign An attempt to get information to voters that will persuade them to elect a candidate or not elect an opponent.

A **political campaign** is an attempt to get information to voters that will persuade them to elect a candidate or not elect an opponent. Campaigns educate voters about issues and candidates and increase interest in the election campaign. The more familiar citizens are with the candidates, the more likely they are to vote.[40]

Political campaigns vary in their size and intensity. Many local contests are modest affairs. The candidates, their families, and a few friends shake some hands, knock on a few doors, put up some signs, create a website, and perhaps raise enough money to buy an ad in the local newspaper. The contest may be hard fought, but the stakes are not high enough to support a major-league campaign effort. Not so, however, with statewide races, local elections in big cities, and contests for Congress and the state legislature. These elections feature professional campaign consultants, well-oiled organizations, and big money.

Big-time campaigns are long, drawn-out affairs, beginning years before voters go to the polls. Candidates spend the early months of a race raising money, building the organization, and planning strategy. Candidates who successfully raise money and create a professional organization well before Election Day establish a reputation as serious candidates. In contrast, candidates who fail to raise money and build an organization early in the political season will probably never seriously contend.

An important goal for many campaigns is to improve the candidate's name recognition, especially if a candidate is a challenger who is not already well known. Races for low-profile offices may never move beyond the name-recognition stage.

Why is Tony Sanchez smiling? He spent more than $60 million of his family fortune running for governor in 2002 but barely got 40 percent of the vote.

It helps if voters are already familiar with the candidate, or at least the candidate's name. A man named Bruce Wettman once ran for state district judge in Harris County by posting billboards picturing his name written on an umbrella; the strategy must have worked because he won easily.

Sometimes candidates borrow name recognition from better-known namesakes. In 1990, a San Antonio attorney named Gene Kelly won the Democratic nomination for a seat on the Texas Supreme Court despite spending almost no money on the race. Primary voters apparently associated Kelly with the famous entertainer of the same name. "If I had been Fred Astaire, I might have won," joked Kelly's defeated opponent. Kelly's luck ran out in the general election when he lost to Republican nominee John Cornyn, who spent heavily on media advertising that attacked Kelly as unqualified. Ten years later, Kelly repeated his primary success by winning the Democratic nomination for the U.S. Senate to oppose Senator Kay Bailey Hutchison. Once again, Kelly failed to mount a serious general election campaign and Hutchison easily won reelection.

Besides building name recognition, campaigns attempt to create a favorable image for the candidate. In the fall of 1989, advertising firms hired by Clayton Williams ran a series of political commercials that turned Williams from a virtually unknown candidate into the frontrunner for the Republican nomination for governor. Riding on horseback, wearing a white hat, and bathed in golden light, Williams promised to get tough on illegal drugs by teaching teenagers who use drugs "the joys of bustin' rocks."

Campaigns also attempt to create unfavorable impressions of their opponents. In 2002, for example, Governor Perry ran radio and television ads that attempted to link Sanchez to the 1985 murder of Enrique "Kiki" Camarena, a federal narcotics officer, because the gang responsible for the murder had earlier done banking business with a savings and loan owned by Sanchez. The ads featured a pair of former drug agents who advised voters to "just say no to Tony Sanchez." Research on negative campaigning finds that challengers are more likely to use it than are incumbents; Republicans are more inclined to go negative than Democrats. Negative campaigns by challengers are somewhat effective, especially if they are based on policy rather than personality. Going negative may backfire on incumbents unless they are attacked first. Negative campaigning stimulates election turnout among party loyalists but depresses it among independents.[41]

The last but perhaps most important task for each campaign is to get supporters to the polls. The most popular candidate will not win if his or her supporters stay home on Election Day. Well-organized campaigns identify likely voters and remind them to vote. The campaign distributes early voting materials and telephones likely supporters to urge them to cast their ballots. Getting out the vote is usually more important for Democrats than Republicans. GOP voters tend to be better educated and more affluent than are Democratic voters and thus more likely to participate in elections. Turning out likely Democratic voters, especially African Americans and Latinos, often requires an organized effort.

THE VOTERS DECIDE

Why do voters decide as they do? Political scientists identify a number of factors influencing voter choice.

Incumbency

Incumbent Current officeholder.

In most election contests, an **incumbent** (current officeholder) enjoys a distinct advantage over a challenger. Nationwide, incumbent members of the U.S. Congress win reelection at a rate that typically exceeds 90 percent,[42] and incumbent state legislators seeking reelection do nearly as well. The success rate for incumbent governors running for reelection is greater than 80 percent.[43] Furthermore, the advantages of incumbency are apparently growing. A study of legislative elections held in the South finds that the number of incumbents winning reelection has increased and a substantial number of incumbents win without facing opposition in either the party primary or the general election. Many potential candidates decide not to run against an incumbent because they believe the incumbent will be difficult to beat.[44]

Incumbent success rates are based on several factors. Incumbents have more name recognition than most challengers and they are usually able to raise more money than their opponents can. Incumbent officeholders can often use their positions to generate favorable publicity for themselves through press releases, whereas most challengers, especially in down-ballot races, struggle to generate a meaningful amount of press coverage. Incumbents can make friends by providing services to individual constituents or groups of constituents. Incumbents also benefit from districting schemes that stack most legislative districts for one party or the other.

Political Party Identification

Political party identification is closely related to voter choice.[45] Democrats vote for Democratic candidates; Republicans back Republicans. On average, 75 percent of voters cast their ballots for the candidate of the party with which they identify.[46] In 2004, 87 percent of Democratic voters in Texas supported Democrat John Kerry for president, whereas 97 percent of the Republicans cast their ballots for George W. Bush.[47] Nonetheless, party identification is a complex phenomenon. People identify with one party because they agree with its issue positions, have confidence in its leaders, or feel comfortable with groups associated with the party. When citizens decide to vote for Candidate A because Candidate A is a Democrat (or Republican), their choice is more than blind allegiance to a party label but is also a response to the perceived issue positions and image of the party.

Issues and Ideology

A significant number of voters, perhaps as high as 30 percent, hold ambivalent partisan attitudes. They agree with Democrats on some issues, Republicans on other issues. On still other issues, they may be torn, embracing core elements of both sides of a debate. On the issue of abortion, for example, they may be opposed to a woman deciding to

Campaign volunteers staff phone banks to get out the vote for their candidate.

end a pregnancy but still uncomfortable with government involvement in such a personal decision. People who lack a clear party allegiance will vote on grounds other than partisanship. Well-informed voters will evaluate candidates on their issue stands or political ideology. Less-informed voters will consider other factors, such as the state of the economy, voting for incumbents in good times and against them in bad times.[48]

Campaigns

Campaigns matter because they make it easier for voters to obtain information about candidates and issues. Candidates attempt to raise the visibility of issues that benefit them and weaken their opponents.[49] In the 2006 race for governor, for example, Governor Perry positioned himself as a successful governor willing and able to address important issues. He took credit for cutting property taxes and promised to take action to improve border security. In contrast, Chris Bell, the Democratic candidate, accused the governor of failing to lead to improve education and healthcare. He endorsed a pay raise for teachers and promised to cut the red tape that was preventing hundreds of thousands of youngsters in low-income families from qualifying for the Children's Health Insurance Program (CHIP). In the meantime, Carole Keeton Strayhorn and Kinky Friedman, the two independents in the race, declared that they would be constructive alternatives to the politics-as-usual approach of the major party candidates. Strayhorn promised to provide two years of free college education to the state's high school graduates, whereas Friedman said that Texas should legalize casino gambling because the revenues would enable the state to better fund education while cutting taxes.

Candidate Image

Voter perceptions of the personal images of candidates influence candidate choice. This does not mean that most voters are primarily concerned with a candidate's age, hairstyle, and wardrobe, at least not explicitly. Instead, they focus on qualities related to performance in office. One recent study of presidential voting concludes that voters evaluate candidates on the basis on their model of what a president should be like. This study found that voters regard competence, integrity, and reliability as qualities they desire in a president. On Election Day, voters pick the candidate they believe best matches the qualities the office requires.[50] Although political scientists have yet to conduct similar studies on state and local elections, it is reasonable to expect that voters approach state and local election voting decisions in a similar fashion.

Retrospective and Prospective Voting

Retrospective voting The concept that voters choose candidates based on their perception of an incumbent candidate's past performance in office or the performance of the incumbent party.

Citizens make voting decisions based on their evaluations of the past and expectations for the future. **Retrospective voting** is the concept that voters choose candidates based on their perception of an incumbent candidate's past performance in office or the performance of the incumbent party. If voters perceive that things are going well, incumbent officeholders and their party usually get the credit. In contrast, they get the blame if voters believe that the state or country is on the wrong track.[51] Political science research indicates that the state of the nation's economy is a key element of voters' evaluations of incumbent performance. As economic

GETTING INVOLVED   Campaigning

People who volunteer to work in an election campaign can have more of an impact on the outcome than they would by just voting. An individual controls one vote and it is rare for a single vote to swing the outcome of an election. In contrast, a hardworking campaign volunteer can affect enough votes to make the difference in a close election, especially a low-profile down-ballot race or a local election contest.

Select a candidate to support and contact the candidate's campaign to inquire about volunteering. All major campaigns and some candidates for local office have websites with contact information for prospective volunteers. Every well-organized campaign will have a telephone number. Contact directory assistance to get the number of the campaign office, call, and volunteer your services. Not only will you have the chance to make a difference in the outcome of the race but your instructor may also give you extra credit for your volunteer work.

It's your government—get involved!

---

conditions worsen, citizens are more likely to vote against the incumbent party, and vice versa.[52] Similarly, research shows that voters evaluate governors on the state unemployment rate compared with the national average.[53] Voter evaluations have a prospective as well as a retrospective component. **Prospective voting** is the concept that voters evaluate the incumbent officeholder and the incumbent's party based on their expectations of future developments. One study finds, for example, that voter expectations of economic performance have a strong influence on voter choice.[54]

Prospective voting The concept that voters evaluate the incumbent officeholder and the incumbent's party based on their expectations of future developments.

National Factors

National factors can affect voting decisions in Texas. Presidential popularity and economic conditions can influence the outcome of races in nonpresidential election years.[55] Texas candidates can also be helped by popular national figures. In a presidential election year, for example, a popular presidential candidate can sometimes provide coattails to boost candidates of the same party in other races. The **coattail effect** is a political phenomenon in which a strong candidate for one office gives a boost to fellow party members on the same ballot seeking other offices. A study of presidential coattails in U.S. Senate elections estimates that a 10 percent gain in a party's presidential vote in a state adds about 2 percentage points to the vote for its Senate candidate.[56]

Coattail effect A political phenomenon in which a strong candidate for one office gives a boost to fellow party members on the same ballot seeking other offices.

CONCLUSION: ELECTIONS AND POLICYMAKING

Elections have a significant impact on the policymaking process.

Agenda Building

Election campaigns focus public attention on particular issues. Candidates and parties who raise issues during a campaign often address those issues once in office. The candidates supported by the Texas Parent PAC opposed school choice and supported a teacher pay raise. Because they won and the candidates backed by James Leininger lost, school choice voucher programs fell off the agenda of the Texas legislature. After the defeat of several school choice proponents in the 2006 Republican primary, including the chair of the House Public Education Committee, most legislators wanted to drop the issue.

Policy Formulation and Adoption

Electoral mandate
The expression of popular support for a particular policy demonstrated through the electoral process.

Political scientists use the concept of electoral mandate to discuss the relationship between elections and public policy. An **electoral mandate** is the expression of popular support for a particular policy demonstrated through the electoral process. The concept of electoral mandate reflects the democratic ideal that elections enable citizens to shape the course of public policy as voters select candidates who endorse policies that the voters favor. On Election Day, voters judge officeholders on how well they followed through with their policy promises. In theory at least, the electoral system makes government responsive to the people.

In America, the relationship between elections and specific public policies is indirect at best because elections are fought over many issues. The 2006 election in Texas addressed a range of issues—taxes, school choice, education finance, transportation, border security, funding for CHIP, and more. Although some races focused on a single issue or a set of related issues, most races involved disagreements over a range of issues.

Voter choice is based on more than just issues. Party affiliation, perceptions of the candidates' personal qualities and image, and voter assessments of past and future performance, especially economic performance, affect voter decisions. Most candidates win because of a range of factors, rather than one or a small set of high-profile issues.

Election constituencies overlap. Whereas the president is chosen nationally through the Electoral College, senators and governors are elected in statewide elections; members of the U.S. House and state legislatures are chosen from districts. One group of voters, desiring one set of policy outcomes, selects the governor; other groups of voters, preferring other policy outcomes, elect members of the legislature.

Furthermore, the constitutional system tempers the short-term impact of electoral change. Because of separation of powers with checks and balances, as well as the federal system, no newly elected governor or group of legislators can achieve dramatic change without the cooperation of other political actors. Elections are one factor affecting the course of public policy, but they are not the only factor.

Policy Implementation and Evaluation

Elections have an indirect influence on policy adoption. Public officials may interpret an election outcome as an indication that the voters want the government to implement a policy more or less aggressively. Consider the impact of the Republican primary election on the fate of school choice in the Texas legislature. In 2005, the Texas House barely defeated a proposal to create a pilot school choice program in the state's largest school districts. In contrast, the legislature voted overwhelmingly in 2007 to prohibit the expenditure of tax money to support a voucher program. The success of the candidates supported by the Texas Parent PAC and the failure of the candidates backed by Leininger sent a clear signal to legislators that school choice was a losing issue for them.

Elections are a means for citizens to evaluate the policy performance of government officials. The concept of retrospective voting is that citizens base their election decisions on their evaluation of the performance of incumbent officials. Indeed, the history of elections in America is one of the voters tossing officials out of office when they believe that government policies have failed and reelecting incumbents when times are good.

LET'S DEBATE

Should a Nonpartisan Commission, Rather Than the Legislature, Draw Legislative District Boundaries?

Overview: Due to the majoritarian principle, which is a tenet of American democratic politics, the party in power generally directs the policy and law Americans and Texans must live under. However, most Americans and Texans assume this principle means that elected officials (and the parties they represent) are chosen in free and contested elections. Nevertheless, most national and many state electoral contests are not competitive at all. Much of the problem, according to scholars and elected officials, is that in the American system elected officials decide electoral rules and determine geographic and demographic districts. It is generally understood that elected officials will create districts that will both ensure their reelection and enhance the power of their political party—at the expense of free electoral competition and voter choice.

Congressional and legislative redistricting has taken on new urgency during the last two decades. Political analysts note that, with the Republican takeover of both the majority of state legislatures (including Texas) and Congress, the new parity between parties has fostered not only polarization but an increased frenzied competition for a very limited number of legislative seats on the national and state levels. This competition has caused the parties to engage in unseemly politics. For example, the Democratic Party spent millions of dollars to oppose redistricting reform in California (where they have a majority of both state and national legislators) and, in the same election cycle, the Republican Party spent millions of dollars in Ohio to defeat redistricting reform (where *they* have a majority of state and national legislators). Both parties pay lip service to reform, yet, for all the discussion of change, many state legislatures still seek unique ways to gerrymander for partisan and incumbent advantage. Making redistricting new in 2004, the states of Texas and Colorado attempted to enact mid-decade redistricting plans to circumvent judicial rulings. Texas was successful (thus far) and Colorado's plan was declared in violation of that state's constitution. What, if anything, can be done to foster free and competitive elections?

A possible answer may be in the establishment of nonpartisan commissions to redraw district lines after each constitutionally mandated census. The idea is that legislators will draw lines to benefit themselves and their parties, but a nonpartisan commission will create districts based on constitutional law and principles of equity. The consequences should be more electoral competition and accountability on incumbents, with the result being better law and policy. Currently, 12 states have unelected bipartisan commissions that redraw state and congressional districts, but not all voters may desire this type of change. Though most of the current redistricting commissions owe their existence to voter initiatives, voters in California and Ohio recently rejected electoral reform (the effect of party activity, however, may have had an impact). Is redistricting reform necessary for contemporary Texas politics?

Arguments for the Creation of a Nonpartisan Redistricting Commission

❏ **A nonpartisan commission can help enhance electoral competition.** Legislative redistricting results in less electoral competition. As history has shown, incumbents generally redistrict to protect their seats. Through the current process (enhanced by new technology), there has been a dramatic decline in competitive seats, and this has the effect of limiting voter

(continued)

choice. It limits diversity of views by preventing those with new and innovative governing and policy proposals from being elected to office.

❏ **Nonpartisan elections will help foster incumbent accountability.** If incumbents are not guaranteed reelection due to safe, gerrymandered districts, they will be forced to be attentive to constituents' needs and policy preferences. Incumbents will be compelled to address issues and policies put forth by challengers, and they will be compelled to defend actions and stances taken while in office.

❏ **Nonpartisan commissions will prevent national parties and their leaders from interfering with states' redistricting rights.** A disturbing development is the increasing involvement of parties and party leaders in the state redistricting process. Former House Majority Leader Tom DeLay was instrumental in orchestrating a mid-decade redistricting in Texas, and both national parties were instrumental in helping prevent redistricting reform in California and Ohio. Nonpartisan commissions can prevent states from succumbing to outside influence by denying voice to the national parties and their leaders.

Arguments Against the Creation of a Nonpartisan Redistricting Commission

❏ **Research shows most commissions are not free from partisan bias.** The University of Southern California Policy Institute has found that most state redistricting commissions are not free from political bias. Many of the commissioners are appointed by legislatures (and their respective parties) or are legislators themselves and have a vested interest in maintaining the status quo. Independent commissions are no guarantee against partisan gerrymandering.

❏ **Nonpartisan commissions are not an answer to noncompetitive elections and voter apathy.** If the problem with partisan redistricting is the lack of competitive elections and voter choice, the answer is not to add yet another political institution but to increase voter awareness and political participation.

Increased voter knowledge and concern has demonstrated that voters will unseat entrenched incumbents. For example, in the 1994 U.S. House election 34 incumbents were defeated (including the sitting Speaker of the House), and a 54-seat swing changed partisan control. The electorate has enough sense about it to vote for change when necessary.

❏ **It is the proper place of judicial review to determine equity in redistricting.** An independent, unelected judiciary may be the answer to partisan gerrymandering. The question for Texans is not whether to have a redistricting commission but whether to amend the state constitution to create a truly independent judiciary. Once an unelected judiciary is in place, the exercise of judicial review should help push the legislature to create truly competitive legislative and congressional districts.

QUESTIONS

1. Is the solution to entrenched incumbency to create an independent redistricting commission? Why or why not?
2. What is the best way to create competitive legislative and congressional districts? Are political parties part of the problem?

SELECT READINGS

1. Peter Galderisi, *Redistricting in the New Millennium* (Lanham, MD: Lexington Books, 2005).
2. Mark Rush, *Does Redistricting Make a Difference? Partisan Representation and Electoral Behavior* (Lanham, MD: Lexington Books, 2001).

SELECT WEBSITES

1. **www.tlc.state.tx.us/redist/redist.htm**
   State of Texas redistricting resource website.
2. **www.ncsl.org/programs/legman/elect/redist.htm**
   National Conference of State Legislatures redistricting resource website.

KEY TERMS

at-large election
bond
bond election
caucus method of
delegate selection
closed primary
coattail effect
district election
electoral mandate
general election
gerrymandering
incumbent
initiative process

Legislative Redistricting
Board (LRB)
local-option elections
long ballot
nonpartisan elections
one person, one vote
open primary
political campaign
presidential preference
primary election
primary election
prospective voting
recall

redistricting
Republicans in name only
(RINOs)
retrospective voting
runoff primary election
school choice
special election
split ticket voting
straight ticket voting
superdelegates
Voting Rights Act (VRA)

NOTES

1. "V for Vouchers," *Texas Observer*, March 24, 2006, p. 3.
2. Dave Mann, "Wrath of the Soccer Moms," *Texas Observer*, March 24, 2006, pp. 6–9, 18–20.
3. Gary Scharrer, "Voucher Advocate Has Little to Show for His Donations," *San Antonio Express-News*, November 12, 2006, available at www.mysanantonio.com.
4. Thad L. Beyle, ed., *State Government: CQ's Guide to Current Issues and Activities 1985–86* (Washington, DC: Congressional Quarterly Press, 1985), p. 93.
5. Christy Hoppe, "Independents' 1st Hurdle: Getting on the Ballot," *Dallas Morning News*, February 6, 2005, available at www.dallasnews.com.
6. Marsha Matson and Terri Susan Fine, "Gender, Ethnicity, and Ballot Information: Ballot Cues in Low-Information Elections," *State Politics and Policy Quarterly* 6 (Spring 2006): 49–72.
7. Steve Bickerstaff, "State Legislative and Congressional Reapportionment in Texas: A Historical Perspective," *Public Affairs Comment* 37 (Winter 1991): 2.
8. *Wesberry v. Sanders*, 376 U.S. 1 (1964) and *Reynolds v. Sims*, 377 U.S. 533 (1964).
9. *Vieth v. Commonwealth of Pennsylvania*, 195 F. Supp. 2d 672 (M.D. Pa. 2002).
10. Victor L. Mote, "The Geographical Consequences of Politics in the United States and Texas," in Kent L. Tedin, Donald S. Lutz, and Edward P. Fuchs, *Perspectives on Texas and American Politics*, 4th ed. (Dubuque, IA: Kendall/Hunt, 1994), p. 10.
11. Mathew D. McCubbins and Thomas Schwartz, "Congress, the Courts, and Public Policy: Consequences of the One Man, One Vote Rule," *American Journal of Political Science* 32 (May 1988): 388–415.
12. Mark Monmonier, *Bushmanders and Bullwinkles: How Politicians Manipulate Electronic Maps and Census Data to Win Elections* (Chicago: University of Chicago Press, 2001), p. 62.
13. David Lublin and D. Stephen Voss, "Racial Redistricting and Realignment in Southern State Legislatures," *American Journal of Political Science* 44 (October 2000): 792–810.
14. David T. Canon, *Race, Redistricting, and Representation: The Unintended Consequences of Black Majority Districts* (Chicago: University of Chicago Press, 1999), p. 257.
15. *Shaw v. Reno*, 509 U.S. 630 (1993) and *Miller v. Johnson*, 515 U.S. 900 (1995).
16. *Texas Government Newsletter*, July 11, 1994, p. 1.
17. Peverill Squire, "The Partisan Consequences of Congressional Redistricting," *American Politics Quarterly* 23 (April 1995): 229–240.
18. Richard G. Niemi and Simon Jackman, "Bias and Responsiveness in State Legislative Districting," *Legislative Studies Quarterly* 16 (May 1991): 183–202.
19. Michael Barone and Grant Ujifusa, *The Almanac of American Politics 1998* (Washington, DC: National Journal, 1997), p. 1339.
20. Sam Attlesey, "Panel OKs Map Favoring GOP," *Dallas Morning News*, November 29, 2001, available at www.dallasnews.com.

21. *Capitol Update*, December 14, 2001, p. 1.

22. Seth C. McKee, Jeremy M. Teigen, and Mathieu Turgeon, "The Partisan Impact of Congressional Redistricting: The Case of Texas, 2001–2003," *Social Science Quarterly* 87 (June 2006): 308–317.

23. *Davis v. Bandemer*, 478 U.S. 109 (1986).

24. *League of United Latin American Citizens v. Perry*, 547 U.S. _____ (2006).

25. National Institute on Money in State Politics, available at www.followthemoney.org.

26. Sam Kinch Jr., *Too Much Money Is Not Enough: Big Money and Political Power in Texas* (Austin, TX: Campaign for People, 2000), pp. 5–6.

27. W. Gardner Selby, "Perry, Strayhorn Poised to Blast Off TV Ads," *Austin American-Statesman*, September 3, 2006, available at www.statesman.com.

28. *Texas Weekly*, August 15, 2005, available at www.texas weekly.com.

29. R. G. Ratcliffe, "GOP Winners' Coffers Fattened After Election," *Houston Chronicle*, January 16, 2003, available at www.houstonchronicle.com.

30. *Capitol Update*, December 13, 2002, p. 1.

31. Texans for Public Justice, "Texas' 2006 Election Cycle '$100,000 Club,'" available at www.tpj.org.

32. Paula Lavigne, "Home Buyers Wary of Agency," *Dallas Morning News*, January 24, 2005, available at www.dallas news.com.

33. Malcolm E. Jewell and Sarah M. Morehouse, *Political Parties and Elections in American States*, 4th ed. (Washington, DC: CQ Press, 2001), pp. 67–69.

34. Steve Bickerstaff, *Lines in the Sand: Congressional Redistricting in Texas and the Downfall of Tom DeLay* (Austin: University of Texas Press, 2007), pp. 370–390.

35. Randall W. Partin, "Assessing the Impact of Campaign Spending in Governors' Races," *Political Research Quarterly* 55 (March 2002): 213–233.

36. Kedron Bardwell, "Not All Money Is Equal: The Differential Effect of Spending by Incumbents and Challengers in Gubernatorial Primaries," *State Politics and Policy Quarterly* 3 (Fall 2003): 294–308.

37. Robert Siersack, Paul S. Herrnson, and Clyde Wilcox, "Seeds for Success: Early Money in Congressional Elections," *Legislative Studies Quarterly* 18 (November 1993): 535–551.

38. Anthony Gierzynski and David A. Breaux, "Money and the Party Vote in State House Elections," *Legislative Studies Quarterly* 18 (November 1993): 515–533.

39. The National Institute on Money in State Politics, available at www.followthemoney.org.

40. Paul Freedman, Michael Franz, and Kenneth Goldstein, "Campaign Advertising and Democratic Citizenship," *American Journal of Political Science* 48 (October 2004): 723–741.

41. Richard R. Lau and Gerald M. Pomper, *Negative Campaigning: An Analysis of U.S. Senate Elections* (Lanham, MD: Rowman & Littlefield, 2004), pp. 30–88.

42. John H. Aldrich, "Political Parties in a Critical Era," *American Politics Quarterly* 27 (January 1999): 24.

43. Jewell and Morehouse, *Political Parties and Elections in America*, pp. 183, 202.

44. Thomas A. Kazee, "Ambition and Candidacy: Running as a Strategic Calculation," in Thomas A. Kazee, ed., *Who Runs for Congress: Ambition, Context, and Candidate Emergence* (Washington, DC: Congressional Quarterly, 1994), pp. 175–176.

45. Warren E. Miller, "Party Identification, Realignment, and Party Voting: Back to the Basics," *American Political Science Review* 85 (June 1991): 557–568.

46. John R. Petrocik, "Reporting Campaigns: Reforming the Press," in James A. Thurber and Candice J. Nelson, eds., *Campaigns and Elections American Style* (Boulder, CO: Westview, 1995), p. 128.

47. Exit poll data, available at www.cnn.com/elections/2004.

48. Scott J. Basinger and Howard Lavine, "Ambivalence, Information, and Electoral Choice," *American Political Science Review* 99 (May 2005): 169–184.

49. James N. Druckman, Lawrence R. Jacobs, and Eric Ostermeier, "Candidate Strategies to Prime Issues and Image," *Journal of Politics* 66 (November 2004): 1180–1202.

50. Arthur H. Miller, Martin P. Wattenberg, and Oksana Malachuk, "Schematic Assessments of Presidential Candidates," *American Political Science Review* 80 (June 1986): 521–540.

51. Dennis M. Simon, Charles W. Ostrom, Jr., and Robin F. Marra, "The President, Referendum Voting, and Subnational Elections in the United States," *American Political Science Review* 85 (December 1991): 1177–1192.

52. Michael S. Lewis-Beck, *Economics and Elections: The Major Western Democracies* (Ann Arbor: University of Michigan Press, 1988), pp. 155–156.

53. Jeffrey E. Cohen and James D. King, "Relative Unemployment and Gubernatorial Popularity," *Journal of Politics* 66 (November 2004): 1180–1202.

54. Brad Lockerbie, "Prospective Voting in Presidential Elections, 1956–1988," *American Politics Quarterly* 20 (July 1992): 308–325.

55. Thomas M. Holbrook-Provow, "National Factors in Gubernatorial Elections," *American Politics Quarterly* 15 (October 1987): 471–483; and Alan I. Abramowitz, "Economic Conditions, Presidential Popularity, and Voting Behavior in Mid-term Congressional Elections," *Journal of Politics* 47 (February 1985): 31–43.

56. James E. Campbell and Joe A. Sumners, "Presidential Coattails in Senate Elections," *American Political Science Review* 84 (June 1990): 513–524.

Chapter 25

The Texas Legislature

CHAPTER OUTLINE

LEARNING OUTCOMES

After studying Chapter 25, students should be able to do the following:

▸ Describe the battle over the position of speaker of the House during the 80th session of the Texas legislature. (pp. 666–667)

▸ Compare and contrast the Texas House and Texas Senate. (pp. 667–668)

▸ Describe the impact of bicameralism, biennial sessions, and limited session length on legislative policymaking in Texas. (pp. 667–670)

▸ List the formal qualifications for membership in the Texas legislature and describe the changes that have taken place in the composition of the legislature since the early 1960s. (p. 671)

▸ Evaluate the attractiveness of a seat in the Texas legislature, considering salary and nonsalary compensation as well as turnover rates. (pp. 672–673)

▸ Assess the impact of term limits on state legislatures. (pp. 673–675)

▶ Describe the organization of the Texas legislature, focusing on leadership selection, the powers and responsibilities of legislative leaders, the committee system, and legislative assistance. (pp. 676–679)

▶ Trace the steps of the legislative process, including introduction, committee action, floor action, conference committee action, and action by the governor. (pp. 679–684)

▶ Evaluate the impact of the following factors on the legislative process: legislative leadership, interest groups, constituency, political parties, and political ideology. (pp. 685–690)

▶ Describe the role of the legislature in the policymaking process. (pp. 690–691)

▶ Define the key terms listed on page 693 and explain their significance.

The 80th session of the Texas legislature, which met in 2007, began and ended with a fight over who would be speaker. The speaker of the House is one of the three most powerful figures in state government, along with the governor and lieutenant governor. In contrast to the other two officials, the speaker is not chosen by the voters in a statewide election. Instead, the 150 members of the Texas House of Representatives select a speaker from among their membership by majority vote. State representatives who hope to become speaker gather signed pledges of support from other House members in hopes of obtaining majority backing well ahead of the actual vote. Because representatives do not want to be on the speaker's bad side, members quickly climb on the bandwagon as soon as it becomes clear that one candidate has the edge. Usually, one candidate wraps up the race early, months or even years ahead of the vote.

Challenges to incumbent speakers are rare because of the risk involved. Voting for speaker is done publicly rather than by secret ballot, so members who vote against the speaker may fear retaliation. Anyone who challenges a speaker and falls short will almost certainly be assigned to relatively unimportant committees. Any legislation an unsuccessful challenger proposes may suffer from inaction. Members who back a losing candidate for speaker will likely have little influence in the chamber.

The challenge to Speaker Craddick in 2007 reflected widespread unhappiness with his leadership style. The opponents of Craddick, including some Republicans and most Democrats, accused the speaker of being dictatorial, concentrating power in his office rather than sharing it with committee chairs. Many members were particularly unhappy with the speaker for forcing votes during the 2005 session of the legislature on controversial issues, such as school choice, that had no chance of passing the Texas Senate and thus becoming law. As we discussed in Chapter 24, school choice became an issue during the 2006 legislative election and it helped defeat incumbents on both sides of the controversy.

Several members of the House announced their intention to run for speaker in late 2006 and began gathering support. By the time the legislature convened in early 2007, the opposition had coalesced around a single candidate, Republican Jim Pitts of Waxahachie. No one knew for sure whether Pitts had enough support to dethrone Craddick until a test vote on a procedural motion for a secret ballot went in favor of Craddick by an 80–68 count. Pitts dropped his challenge and Craddick was reelected speaker. The actual vote was 121–27.

Opposition to the speaker simmered throughout the session. Craddick's opponents, including both Democrats and Republicans, did their best to demonstrate the speaker's weakness. They used parliamentary maneuvers to delay the legislative process and called for frequent votes to challenge the speaker's rulings. They accused Craddick of using his position to block legislation backed by his opponents and of plotting to fund challengers against them in the next election. As the session wore on, some of the members who had backed Craddick in January began to distance themselves from the speaker, complaining that Craddick had neither made peace with his opponents nor successfully asserted his authority to run the House. Near the end of the session, Craddick's opponents decided to offer a motion to declare the office of speaker vacant and force the selection of a new speaker. Several members declared their intention to seek the position. Speaker Craddick, however, refused to allow the motion and the vote. After replacing the House parliamentarians for disagreeing with him, Craddick declared that he alone had the authority to decide which members would be recognized on the floor for the purpose of offering motions and that the entire membership of the House could not vote to override his rulings unless he allowed the vote. The session ended in rancor, but with Craddick holding on to his position.[1]

The end of the session did not end the fight over who would serve as speaker. Within days of the close of the session, seven state representatives, including several members who had been part of the Craddick leadership team during the just-completed session, announced their intention to run for speaker in 2009; Craddick declared that he would seek reelection to the post as well.[2] With the legislative session over, the battle for speaker shifted to the electoral arena. Some conservative Republican activists who admired Craddick because of his efforts to pass legislation they favor labeled the late-session effort to replace Craddick as an attempted mutiny. They accused Craddick's Republican opponents of being RINOs, Republicans in name only, and they promised to try to defeat them in the 2008 Republican primary.

This chapter on the legislature is the first of a series of five chapters dealing with the policymaking institutions of Texas government. The next chapter, Chapter 26, focuses on the executive branch of Texas government; Chapter 27 studies the judicial branch. Chapters 28 and 29 examine local government. Chapter 28 considers city government, and Chapter 29 discusses the other units of local government in the state—counties, school districts, and special districts.

STRUCTURE

The Texas Constitution provides for a bicameral legislature to meet in biennial regular sessions of 140 days in length. The legislative sessions are numbered consecutively, dating from the 1840s, when Texas became a state. The 80th legislature was elected in 2006 and met in regular session in 2007. The legislature that meets in regular session in 2009 will be the 81st legislature.

Bicameralism

Bicameral legislature
A legislative body with two chambers.

Texas has a **bicameral** (two-chamber) **legislature** consisting of a House of Representatives and a Senate. The House has 150 members elected from districts to serve two-year terms, whereas the Senate consists of 31 senators elected from districts to serve four-year terms. Senate terms overlap, with about half the senators standing for reelection every two years. The exception to this pattern occurs in the first election after redistricting, when the entire Senate must stand for election. In 2002, all 31 Senate seats were up for election under new district lines drawn after the 2000 Census. The newly elected senators then drew lots to determine whether they would have to run for election again in 2004 or 2006.

The Texas Constitution assigns each legislative chamber certain powers and responsibilities. The Senate has sole authority to confirm or reject the governor's appointments by a two-thirds' vote. Only the House may initiate legislation to raise taxes, although both chambers must agree before any tax bill can pass. The House alone, by majority vote, has the power of **impeachment,** which is a formal accusation against an executive or judicial officeholder. The Senate tries the impeached official, with a two-thirds' vote needed for conviction and removal from office.

Impeachment
A formal accusation against an executive or judicial officeholder.

The constitution requires that the two legislative chambers share certain responsibilities. Both the House and the Senate must concur before any measure can pass the legislature. Both must vote by a two-thirds' margin to propose constitutional amendments. Also, two-thirds of the members of each chamber must agree to override a governor's veto.

The Texas House and Texas Senate often approach policy issues differently because of structural differences in the two legislative chambers. Compare, for example, Texas House and Senate districts. Each House member represents approximately 139,000 people, whereas the population of each state Senate district is 673,000. Because state Senate districts are roughly five times larger than House districts, they will probably be more diverse than the smaller House districts. Needing to please a more diverse constituency, senators may prove more moderate than House members, whose districts are more homogeneous. In Texas, the two legislative chambers also differ in the length of the terms of office of members. House members must stand for election every two years, whereas senators serve four-year terms. As a result, senators can evaluate policy issues from a longer-range perspective than House members, whose next reelection campaign is always just around the corner.

Bicameralism has supporters and critics. Its defenders believe that bicameralism allows one house to correct the mistakes of the other. In contrast, the critics of bicameralism believe that a single-house legislature is more economical and efficient. Every state has a bicameral legislature except Nebraska, which has a **unicameral** (one-chamber) **legislature.** Nebraska adopted a state constitutional amendment in 1937 to create a unicameral legislature whose members would be chosen in **nonpartisan elections,** which are contests in which the names of the candidates, but not their party affiliations, appear on the ballot. The 49 members of the Nebraska legislature serve four-year overlapping terms.

Unicameral legislature
A legislative body with one chamber.

Nonpartisan elections
Election contests in which the names of the candidates appear on the ballot but not their party affiliations.

The conventional wisdom is that bicameralism has a conservative effect on the policymaking process because two chambers must approve a measure before it can clear the legislature. Nonetheless, Professor James R. Rogers believes that bicameralism is as likely to increase legislative output as to decrease it because both chambers can initiate legislation as well as reject it. Furthermore, he says, the historical evidence from legislative bodies that have switched from unicameral to bicameral or vice versa fails to support the conventional view.[3]

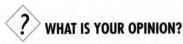 **WHAT IS YOUR OPINION?**

Should Texas replace its bicameral legislature with a unicameral legislature?

Session Frequency

The Texas Constitution provides that the legislature meet in regular session every other year, in odd calendar years (2007, 2009, etc.), with sessions beginning on the second Tuesday in January. In the late nineteenth century, when the Texas Constitution was written, biennial legislative sessions were standard practice in most American states. As recently as 1960, 32 states still had biennial sessions. Today, Texas is one of only 6 states (Arkansas, Montana, Nevada, North Dakota, Oregon, and Texas) whose legislatures do not meet in regular session every year. The Arizona legislature, for example, meets every year for 100 days. The California legislature is in session nearly year-round every year.[4] The Texas Constitution empowers the governor to call special sessions of the legislature, which may last for a maximum of 30 calendar days. Although most state legislatures may call themselves into special session, the Texas legislature has no such power.

Annual legislative sessions are near the top of the list of constitutional reforms proposed by those who would like to see a more streamlined state government. Reformers believe that the affairs of state government are too complex to handle in biennial sessions. Budget issues are particularly difficult to address in biennial sessions because the legislature can neither anticipate state spending needs nor estimate tax revenues over so long a period. The most popular proposal for annual sessions would maintain the current 140-day session in odd-numbered years and add a shorter, 60-day session in even years. The 140-day sessions would write a one-year budget and deal with general legislative concerns. Sixty-day sessions would be limited to writing a budget, plus any additional matters the governor wished to submit for legislative consideration.

Nonetheless, biennial legislative sessions have their defenders. Give the legislature more time, they say, and Texas will have more laws, more regulations, more spending, and more taxes. Although observers often blame biennial sessions for legislative logjams at the end of a session, research shows that legislatures that have annual sessions have worse logjams than legislatures with biennial sessions.[5] For example, the New York legislature, which meets annually, has been ridiculed for years because of its inability to pass a budget on time. Furthermore, the citizens of Texas have expressed their support for biennial sessions every time they have had a chance to vote on the issue. In 1930, 1949, 1958, 1969, 1973, and 1975, voters rejected constitutional amendments that would have provided for annual legislative sessions.

Session Length

Constitutional reformers would also like to increase the length of legislative sessions in the Lone Star State. With sessions limited to 140 calendar days, the legislature may not have time to do the state's business. The legislature often falls behind and has to act on a flood of bills in the last few weeks of the session before time runs out. On the last day of the 1995 session, for example, the Senate acted on 72 bills and resolutions in a span of only 90 minutes.[6]

Speaker Tom Craddick fought off challenges to his leadership at the beginning and the end of the 2007 session of the Texas legislature.

Defenders of the 140-day session point out that legislative session limits are common among the states and a useful device for forcing legislators to get down to business. Political scientist Malcolm Jewell believes that session limits force lawmakers to make decisions because they establish a defined endpoint, a looming deadline, for wrapping up business. "When there's no limit," he says, "it drags on. They [legislators] postpone compromise to the last minute; they bargain; they play games."[7]

Research shows that the legislative workload in Texas is not as congested as conventional wisdom suggests. Legislative activity in Texas tends to concentrate at certain times, such as the deadline for submitting bills and the end of the session, but lawmakers work on legislation throughout the session. Although 80 percent of the votes for the final passage of bills come in the last two weeks of the session, most of the measures passed have been under legislative consideration for months.[8] Furthermore, the Texas House and Texas Senate have adopted rules to prevent a last-minute rush of legislative activity.

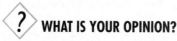 **WHAT IS YOUR OPINION?**

Should the Texas legislature meet in annual sessions?

MEMBERSHIP

In 2007, the combined membership of the Texas House and Texas Senate included 36 women, 35 Latinos, 16 African Americans, and 1 Asian American of 181 members. Although the Texas legislature is a more diverse body than at any time in its history, it is not a cross-section of the state's population. As Figure 25.1 indicates, Latinos, African Americans, and women were all underrepresented in the 80th legislature, whereas whites were overrepresented. Times are changing, though, and the number of African Americans, Latinos, and women in the legislature continues to increase. Greater racial tolerance may lead to the election of more minority candidates to public office. The number of women in the legislature may increase also as social attitudes change. Women continue to hold a minority of legislative seats because they are less likely than men to think about running or to consider themselves qualified to hold office. They are also less likely than men to be encouraged to run for office. As attitudes change, the number of women in the legislature will increase.[9]

Compensation

The official salary for members of the legislature, whether they serve in the House or the Senate, is set by the Texas Constitution at $600 a month, or $7,200 a year. Compared with other states, this figure is low. Legislative pay in Texas is lowest

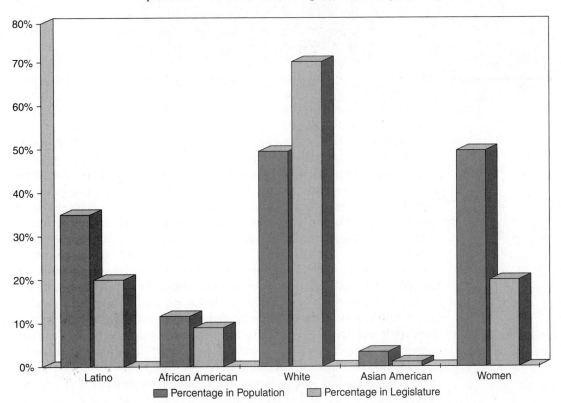

FIGURE 25.1   Representation in the 80th Legislature.

among the ten largest states.[10] Several states have full-time, professional legislatures and pay their lawmakers accordingly. Legislators in California, for example, earn $110,880 a year. Even most states whose legislatures meet for limited periods pay their lawmakers more than Texas pays its legislators. Members of the Oklahoma legislature receive $38,400 a year. The pay for lawmakers in Louisiana is $16,800 a year. Florida legislators earn $29,916 annually.[11]

Should legislators be paid more? The proponents of higher legislative salaries believe that better pay would allow a wide cross-section of Texans to seek office, not just people who are independently wealthy or have careers that permit them time off to attend legislative sessions. Furthermore, higher salaries would help keep legislators independent of interest groups. In contrast, defenders of the current salary structure argue that low salaries ensure the continuation of a citizen-legislature whose members are relatively immune from outside pressures. Because lawmakers are not dependent on legislative salaries, they are more willing to take political chances to do the right thing than they would if their salaries were higher.

Nonsalary compensation for Texas legislators is relatively generous. When the legislature is in session, lawmakers receive a daily expense allowance of $139. The allowance enables legislators to increase their earnings by $19,460 for each regular session and $4,170 for each 30-day special session. Furthermore, legislators have provided themselves with one of the most generous pension plans in the nation. When State Senator Gonzalo Barrientos retired in January 2007 after serving 32 years in the legislature, he immediately began collecting an annual pension of $92,000. Members who serve a minimum of 8 years can qualify for a pension of $23,000 a year at age 60. Members serving 12 or more years can begin collecting at 50 years of age. For each year of legislative service, a member receives an annual pension equal to 2.3 percent of the salary of a state district judge, which was $125,000 in 2007. State lawmakers also receive full healthcare benefits, both as active members and in retirement.[12]

Many legislators use excess campaign funds to supplement their incomes and enrich their families. A 2004 study conducted by Campaigns for People found that Texas senators spent only 40 percent of their campaign contributions actually running for office. They spent the rest of the money on office and living expenses.[13] State law allows legislators to deposit leftover campaign funds into officeholder accounts that can be used to pay for whatever expenses the lawmaker wants to cover. Although legislators use money from their officeholder accounts to help cover the cost of operating a legislative office, some lawmakers divert money for personal and family expenses. Speaker Craddick pays his daughter Christi a salary of more than $100,000 a year to manage his Stars over Texas Political Action Committee.[14] Members use campaign funds to purchase transportation, pay living expenses, and pay rent in Austin. During the 2007 legislative session, for example, State Senator Jeff Wentworth used $20,000 in campaign funds to rent a Lexus to drive back and forth between his home in San Antonio and the state capitol in Austin.[15] State law prevents lawmakers from using campaign funds to buy real estate, but it does not prevent them from paying rent on homes that are in the names of their spouses, who then use the money to finance the mortgage.[16]

Legislative Turnover

Legislative turnover refers to the replacement of individual members of a legislature from one session to the next. Legislative turnover peaks in the first election after redistricting because the redistricting process changes the geography of legislative districts. Some legislators retire rather than attempt reelection from new, less hospitable districts, whereas others are defeated for reelection. The 78th legislature, which was the first legislature elected from lines drawn after the 2000 Census, included 43 new members—5 senators and 38 members of the House. In contrast, legislative turnover declines as redistricting approaches. Incumbents become entrenched and potential challengers often choose to wait until after redistricting before deciding whether to run. The 80th legislature, which was elected in 2006, included 29 new faces out of 181 members. Legislative turnover rates in Texas are below the national average. During the 1990s, the percentage of new House members in each session was 17 percent; it was 16 percent for the Texas Senate. The comparable figures for state houses and state senates nationwide were 25 percent and 23 percent, respectively.[17]

Legislative turnover in Texas is generally more often the result of voluntary retirement than election defeat. For example, 17 of the 29 first-term legislators in the 80th session of the legislature replaced members who retired or resigned to run for higher office.[18] Some members leave because they know they cannot win reelection, whereas others quit out of frustration. They complain about low pay, poor staff support, little public appreciation for their efforts, the hectic pace of legislative sessions, and pressure from interest groups and constituents. House members, in particular, often grow cynical about their ability to accomplish their goals. Not all reasons for leaving are negative. Some legislators attempt to move up the political ladder by running for higher office. Others choose to leave because their law practice has picked up or they receive a business offer they cannot refuse. Some resign to become well-paid lobbyists. Although many states impose a waiting period between the time legislators leave office and the time they can become lobbyists, usually a year, Texas has no such limitation. Members can begin working for interest groups as registered lobbyists the day they leave office, and many do. Seventy former legislators are registered lobbyists in Texas, more than in any other state.[19] Moreover, lobbyists earn considerably higher incomes than legislators. The average lobbyist in Texas has contracts worth up to half a million dollars a year.[20]

Term Limits

Term limitation is the movement to restrict the number of terms public officials may serve. Fifteen states limit the terms of state legislators. The limits for members of the House range from 6 to 12 years. They vary from 8 to 12 years for state senators. The legislature enacted term limits in only one of the states that have legislative term limits.[21] In every other state, the voters adopted term limitation through the **initiative process,** which is a procedure whereby citizens can propose the adoption of a policy measure by gathering a prerequisite number of signatures. State officials then place the measure on the ballot for approval by the voters. Because Texas does not have initiative, most observers think it is unlikely that the

---

Legislative turnover
The replacement of individual members of a legislature from one session to the next.

Term limitation
The movement to restrict the number of terms public officials may serve.

Initiative process
A procedure whereby citizens can propose the adoption of a policy measure by gathering a prerequisite number of signatures. Voters must then approve the measure before it can take effect.

The membership of the Texas legislature is more diverse today than at any time in its history.

state will adopt term limitation. Although polls show that term limits are popular with the voters, many members of the legislature are unwilling to vote themselves out of a job.

The advocates of term limits believe that they will improve the capacity of the legislature to do work. They offer the following arguments on behalf of term limitation:

- Members who are not career-oriented can focus on solving the state's problems rather than entrenching themselves in office.
- By forcing veteran lawmakers from office, term limits give new people with fresh ideas an opportunity to have an impact on public policy.
- Term limits reduce the power of interest groups by forcing their favorite law-makers from office.

In contrast, the opponents of term limitation are convinced that term limits make legislatures less effective. The following are some of the arguments they offer against term limitation:

- Legislators with valuable experience and expertise will be forced from office.
- Bureaucrats and lobbyists will be more powerful because it will be easier for them to outwit inexperienced lawmakers than it was for the veteran legislators who were forced to retire.
- Legislators will concern themselves only with short-run problems because they serve for limited periods of time.

NATIONAL PERSPECTIVE

Repealing Term Limits in Idaho

In 1994, Idaho voters adopted the most sweeping term-limits law in the country. The measure, which received nearly 60 percent of the vote, restricted the terms of every elected state official from the governor down to county commissioners and school board members. It limited most state and local officials to 8 years in office over any 15-year period; county commissioners and school board members could serve no more than 6 years out of 11. Because the term-limit clock did not begin ticking until 1996, term limits would not apply to officials in major offices until 2004; it would not impact local officeholders until 2002.

Opposition to term limits grew as the date for their implementation approached. The Republican Party, which is the majority party in Idaho, declared its opposition to term limits because many of its officials, including the legislative leadership, would be forced from office. Party leaders worked behind the scenes to convince Republican legislators to vote to repeal term limits. Local officials and business leaders in rural areas opposed term limits as well because of their potential impact on local government. In sparsely populated rural areas, relatively few people may be willing to serve in low-pay or no-pay positions as county officials and school board members. If long-term incumbents were forced from office by term limits, perhaps no one would be willing to take their places.

In 2002, Idaho became the first state to repeal term limits. (Utah became the second in 2003.) Early in the year, the Idaho legislature voted for repeal, overriding the governor's veto. Term-limit supporters gathered sufficient signatures to put the issue on the ballot to give the voters the chance to "repeal the repeal" in the November 2002 election. By the narrow margin of 1,889 votes out of more than 400,000 ballots cast, Idahoans approved the legislature's action and sustained the repeal of term limits, with rural voters providing the margin of victory.*

QUESTIONS TO CONSIDER

1. When the idea of legislative term limits was introduced more than a decade ago, Republicans supported the concept. Now, however, they oppose term limits, at least in Idaho. Why do you think many Republicans switched sides?
2. Do you think that Idaho voters would support term limits if local governments were exempted?
3. For which level of government are term limits the most appropriate (if any)?

*Daniel A. Smith, "Overturning Term Limits: The Legislature's Own Private Idaho?" *P.S. Political Science and Politics,* April 2003, pp. 215–220.

In practice, term limits have been neither as beneficial as their advocates have hoped nor as harmful as their opponents have warned. On the positive side, state legislators who are term limited place a greater emphasis on the needs of the state as a whole relative to the interests of the districts they represent. Term-limited legislators are less focused on obtaining special benefits for their districts than are other legislators. On the negative side, term limits strengthen the governor and possibly legislative staffers while weakening legislative leaders. Because term-limited legislators are relatively inexperienced, they have not developed the personal relationships that form the basis for legislative compromise and cooperation. Consequently, influence slips away from the legislature toward other political actors, especially executive branch officials and legislative staffers.[22] Furthermore, rather than focusing on legislative business, many term-limited legislators concentrate on lining up their next job as elected officials in local government or as lobbyists.[23]

ORGANIZATION

Modern legislatures choose leaders, establish committees, and hire staff assistance in order to facilitate their work.

Leadership

The lieutenant governor and speaker of the House are the presiding officers and foremost political leaders of the Texas legislature. As we discussed in the introduction to this chapter, the speaker, who presides in the House, is a state representative who is selected by the members of the House to serve as speaker. The lieutenant governor, who presides in the Senate, is elected statewide for a four-year term in the same general election year in which the governor is chosen. In contrast to the president and vice president of the United States, the governor and lieutenant governor do not run as a formal ticket. Voters cast ballots for the two offices separately and may choose individuals from different political parties. In 1994, when Republican George W. Bush was initially elected governor, Bob Bullock, a Democrat, was reelected lieutenant governor.

If the office of lieutenant governor becomes vacant, the Senate chooses a successor. When Bush resigned as governor to move to the White House in 2001, Lieutenant Governor Rick Perry moved up to become governor, leaving the office of lieutenant governor vacant. The 31 members of the Texas Senate selected fellow senator Bill Ratliff to replace Perry by majority vote. Ratliff served the remainder of Perry's term as lieutenant governor without resigning his Senate seat. He chose not to stand for election as lieutenant governor in 2002, preferring to run for reelection to the Senate.

The speaker and lieutenant governor are two of the most powerful public officials in the state, exercising extraordinary authority in their respective chambers. The speaker and lieutenant governor control many of the legislative procedures of the House and Senate. They assign bills to committee, and once committees have done their work the speaker and lieutenant governor have considerable influence over which bills are scheduled for debate. As presiding officers in their respective chambers, the speaker and lieutenant governor recognize members for debate, rule on points of order, and interpret rules.

The speaker and lieutenant governor rarely participate directly in the official deliberations of their respective chambers. As an elected member of the House, the speaker is entitled to participate in debate and vote on every issue before the chamber. In practice, though, the speaker seldom engages in floor discussions and votes only on those matters for which he or she wishes to register strong support. With the exception of Ratliff, who was a state senator, the lieutenant governor is technically not a member of the Senate and may vote only to break a tie.

The speaker and lieutenant governor serve on and make appointments to some of the state's most important policymaking bodies, including the Legislative Budget Board (LBB) and the Legislative Redistricting Board (LRB). The **Legislative Budget Board (LBB)** is an agency created by the legislature to study state revenue and budgetary needs between legislative sessions and prepare budget and appropriation bills to submit to the legislature. The **Legislative Redistricting Board (LRB),** which is composed of the speaker, lieutenant governor, comptroller, land commissioner, and attorney general, is responsible for redrawing the boundaries of

Legislative Budget Board (LBB)
An agency created by the legislature to study state revenue and budgetary needs between legislative sessions and prepare budget and appropriations bills to submit to the legislature.

Legislative Redistricting Board (LRB)
An agency composed of the speaker, lieutenant governor, comptroller, land commissioner, and attorney general that draws the boundaries of Texas House and Senate seats when the legislature is unable to agree on a redistricting plan.

Texas House and Senate seats when the legislature is unable to agree on a redistricting plan.

Finally, the speaker and lieutenant governor exercise considerable control over committee membership. They appoint legislative committee chairs, vice chairs, subcommittee chairs, most committee members, and some subcommittee members. After the effort to oust the speaker at the beginning of the eightieth session of the legislature failed, Craddick used his powers of appointment to punish enemies and reward friends. He demoted the 5 committee chairs from the previous session who voted against him on the key procedural vote. None of the 68 members on the wrong side of that vote served as a committee chair in 2007. In contrast, Craddick rewarded 10 of the 15 Democrats who broke with the majority of their party to support him on the key procedural vote by making them committee chairs.[24]

Although the lieutenant governor and the speaker have extraordinary powers, they seldom act in an arbitrary or dictatorial fashion. For the most part, the powers of the speaker and lieutenant governor are not spelled out in the state constitution, and as recently as the 1930s their authority extended little beyond presiding. The powers of the leadership have grown because of changes in House and Senate rules adopted by majority vote in each chamber that could just as easily be withdrawn. The offices of speaker and lieutenant governor have acquired and maintained such broad authority because the people who have held the posts have generally exercised power in a fashion that a majority of legislators approve. Speaker Craddick faced a serious leadership challenge in 2007 because a sizable number of House members believed that he had abused his power.

The speaker and lieutenant governor base their authority in their ability to keep most members of the legislature happy. Both the speaker and the lieutenant governor are in a position to bestow favors on their friends. These favors can be as small as giving a legislator a larger office or as great as appointing a member to chair a prestigious committee. In either case, the lawmaker owes a favor, which the speaker or lieutenant governor can cash when the time is right. If enough members are unhappy with the speaker or lieutenant governor, they can face trouble from the membership, as Speaker Craddick discovered. House members have the authority to change leadership, at least at the beginning of a session. Senators cannot replace the lieutenant governor, but they can strip the lieutenant governor of authority.

The leadership of the speaker and lieutenant governor is collective rather than individual. Each official heads a leadership team made up of supporters in the chamber. This is especially true in the House, where the speaker must first win the backing of a majority of members of the chamber. Both the speaker and the lieutenant governor have a corps of supporters in the chamber that makes up their leadership team. The members of the leadership team advise the speaker or lieutenant governor and work to organize the full chamber to support the leadership's position. The speaker and lieutenant governor reward their team leaders by appointing them to chair the most important committees.[25]

Committees

Standing committee
A permanent committee established to handle legislation in a certain field.

Some of the legislature's most important work takes place in committee. A **standing committee** is a permanent committee established to handle legislation in a certain field. The Texas House had 41 committees in 2007, ranging in size from 5 to

29 members. The most common size for House committees was 9 members. The Texas Senate had 15 committees, ranging from 5 to 15 members.

Committees are important because they enable members to divide the legislative workload. More than 5,000 bills may be introduced in a regular session, far too many for each member to consider in depth. Committees allow small groups of legislators to examine a bill in detail and then report their evaluation to the full chamber. Committees also permit members to specialize in particular policy areas. Most committees deal with particular substantive policy areas, such as higher education, criminal justice, or agriculture.

Legislators usually have strong preferences regarding committee assignments. In the House, the most coveted committee assignments are the Appropriations, State Affairs, and Ways and Means Committees. The committees of choice in the Senate are the Finance, State Affairs, and Jurisprudence Committees. The committees dealing with business interests (Business and Industry in the House, Business and Commerce in the Senate) are popular as well. Legislators may also prefer a particular committee assignment because of personal preference or constituency interest. A state representative from Houston or Dallas, for example, may favor service on the Urban Affairs Committee.

House and Senate rules limit the number of standing committees on which legislators may serve to three. Senators are restricted to membership on no more than two of the three most influential committees: Finance, State Affairs, and Jurisprudence. No House member may serve on more than two of the following three committees: Ways and Means, Appropriations, and State Affairs. No legislator may chair more than one committee.

State senators typically serve on more committees than do state representatives. Because the Senate has only 31 members, individual members typically serve on three or four committees. In 2007, for example, State Senator Rodney Ellis of Houston chaired the Government Organization Committee and served on the Criminal Justice, State Affairs, and Transportation and Homeland Security Committees. Because the House is larger, with 150 members, individual representatives have more opportunity to specialize on committee assignments. In 2007, most House members served on only one or two committees. Representative Anna Mowery of Fort Worth, for example, chaired the Land and Resource Management Committee and served on the Public Education Committee.

The lieutenant governor and speaker make most committee assignments. In the Senate, the lieutenant governor appoints all committee chairs, vice chairs, and committee members at the beginning of each legislative session. The only restriction on the lieutenant governor's assignment power is that three members of each committee with ten or fewer members, and four members of each committee with more than ten members, must be senators who served on the committee during the last regular session.

In the House, the speaker appoints committee chairs, vice chairs, and all of the members of the Appropriations Committee and the Calendars Committee. The speaker also names at least half of the members of each of the other standing committees. House rules allow representatives, in order of seniority, to select one committee assignment, provided that the committee is not already half

Seniority
The length of continuous service a member has with a legislative body.

Interim committee
A committee established to study a particular policy issue between legislative sessions, such as higher education or public school finance.

Select, or **special, committee**
A committee that is established for a limited period of time to address a specific problem.

staffed. **Seniority** refers to the length of continuous service a member has with a legislative body.

An **interim committee** is a committee established to study a particular policy issue between legislative sessions, such as higher education or public school finance. Frequently, an interim committee is also a **select,** or **special, committee,** which is a committee that is established for a limited period of time to address a specific problem. Interim committees may include private citizens as well as legislators. The speaker, lieutenant governor, and governor may appoint interim committees. Legislative leaders use interim committees as a way to compensate for biennial legislative sessions of limited duration. Because interim committees have more time to study issues and formulate policies than do standing committees, they can lay the groundwork for legislation before the regular session begins.

Legislative Assistance

Staff assistance is important to the Texas legislature because legislators are essentially part-time employees who are asked to perform a monumental legislative task in a limited period of time. Legislative staff members improve the quantity and quality of information available to legislators, bring insight to issues, and help solve con-stituent problems. Texas legislators have sufficient funds to employee staff assistance in Austin and their home districts.

The legislature provides members with some institutional assistance as well. Be-fore each session, the Legislative Council conducts a brief orientation for new legis-lators. During sessions, the staff of the Legislative Council helps members draft bills and assists committees. The Legislative Reference Library fulfills routine requests for research assistance. The House Research Organization (HRO) and Senate Research Center (SRC) research issues, help draft legislation, and prepare technical analyses of bills pending in the legislature. The HRO and SRC also publish daily floor reports explaining and presenting arguments for and against proposed legislation. Standing committees have permanent staffs as well, ranging in size from 1 to 15 staff members in the Senate and from 1 to 6 in the House.[26]

THE LEGISLATIVE PROCESS

The legislative process in the Texas legislature resembles that of the U.S. Congress, but with important differences that affect policy.

Introduction

Bill
A proposed law.

Each legislative session, members introduce thousands of bills and hundreds of reso-lutions. A **bill** is a proposed law, such as a measure to prohibit small children from riding in the open bed of a pickup truck. A **resolution** is a legislative statement of opinion on a certain matter, such as a measure congratulating a Texas sports team for winning a championship. An amendment to the Texas Constitution takes the form of a **joint resolution,** which is a resolution that must be passed by a two-thirds' vote of each chamber.

Resolution
A legislative statement of opinion on a certain matter, such as a measure congratulating a Texas sports team for winning a championship.

Joint resolution
A resolution that must be passed by a two-thirds' vote of each chamber.

Introducing bills and resolutions into the legislative process is fairly straightforward. Members of the House or Senate may officially introduce legislation by filing copies in their own chamber with the secretary of the Senate or the chief clerk of the House during a period that begins on the first Monday after the November general election. After the first 60 days of a session, members can introduce only local bills or measures declared an emergency by the governor unless they obtain the approval of four-fifths of the members of their chamber. Once a bill is introduced, the secretary of the Senate or the chief clerk of the House assigns the measure a number, indicating the chamber of origin and order of introduction. HB 45, for example, indicates that the measure is the 45th bill introduced in the House during the session. SR 102 is the 102nd resolution introduced in the Senate.

Committee Action

The lieutenant governor and the speaker, in consultation with the chamber parliamentarian, assign newly introduced measures to committee. With important exceptions, the legislative leadership matches a bill with the committee that specializes in the subject matter it addresses. The exception to the general practice of matching legislation to the committee that deals with its subject matter involves the House Committee on State Affairs and the Senate Committee on State Affairs, which are general-purpose committees to which the speaker and lieutenant governor regularly assign major pieces of legislation regardless of their subject matter.

Mark up
The process in which legislators go over a piece of legislation line by line, revising, amending, or rewriting it.

Fiscal note
An analysis of a legislative measure indicating its cost to state government, if any.

Committees do the detailed work of the legislative process. They begin their consideration of proposed legislation by holding public hearings. After the hearings are complete, the committee meets for **mark up,** which is the process in which legislators go over a piece of legislation line by line, revising, amending, or rewriting it. Major legislation is almost always rewritten in committee, with the final product reflecting a compromise among the various groups and interests involved. Eventually, committee members vote whether to recommend the revised measure to the entire House or Senate for passage. If a majority on the committee votes in the affirmative, the measure leaves committee with a favorable report. The report includes the revised text of the measure, a detailed analysis of the bill, and a **fiscal note,** which is an analysis of a legislative measure indicating its cost to state government, if any. If the majority on the committee votes against the measure, the legislation is probably dead.

Floor Action

Appropriation bill
A legislative authorization to spend money for particular purposes; they are usually assigned to the emergency calendar as well.

The procedure by which legislation moves from committee to the floor differs in the two chambers of the Texas legislature. In the House, measures recommended favorably by a standing committee go to the Calendars Committee for assignment to a House calendar, which sets the order of priority for considering legislation. In 2007, the House calendars were, in order of priority, the following:

- **Emergency calendar** This calendar is reserved for legislation declared an emergency by the governor and other measures deemed by the Calendars Committee to merit immediate attention. Tax bills and the **appropriation bill,** which is a legislative authorization to spend money for particular purposes, are usually assigned to the emergency calendar as well.

The detailed work of the legislature takes place in committees.

- **Major state calendar** This calendar includes measures of statewide effect that do not merit emergency designation.
- **Constitutional amendment calendar** This calendar is for proposed amendments to the Texas Constitution or ratification of amendments to the U.S. Constitution.
- **General state calendar** This calendar is for bills of statewide impact, but of secondary significance.
- **Local, consent, and resolution calendar** This calendar includes bills and resolutions that are not controversial, as well as **local bills,** which are proposed laws that affect only a single unit of local government.
- **Resolutions calendar** This calendar is reserved for resolutions.
- **Congratulatory and memorial resolutions calendar** This calendar contains resolutions congratulating people, places, and organizations for various accomplishments or honoring individuals who have died.

Local bills
Proposed laws that affect only a single unit of local government.

Although House rules provide for the consideration of measures in order of priority as set by the calendar system, the House may vote by a two-thirds' margin to consider a measure outside the sequence established by the calendar system. On Mondays, which are known as Calendar Mondays, members can suspend the rules by a simple majority vote. House members may also suspend the rules on other days to sandwich time for items on the last three calendars between other measures.

The House calendar system becomes more important as a legislative session wears on. During the early months of a session, relatively few bills pass committee for assignment to a calendar and the House typically considers every measure before ending its legislative day. Toward the end of the session, however, the legislative pace quickens and the number of measures on the calendar grows. By the end of the session, measures placed on low-priority calendars risk failure for lack of action.

In the Senate, suspending the rules to consider legislation out of order is standard practice. Although Senate rules require that bills emerging from committee be placed on a single calendar for consideration in order, the procedure is almost never followed. The first bill reported out of committee at the beginning of a session is invariably a "blocking bill," introduced not to be passed but to rest atop the Senate calendar, blocking consideration of other measures. In 2007, the blocking bill SB 259 proposed the creation of a county park beautification and improvement program. Except for local bills and other noncontroversial measures, which are scheduled for debate by the Senate Committee on Administration, bills require a two-thirds' vote to be considered on the floor of the Senate. An important feature of this practice is that 11 senators (one-third plus 1) can block Senate action on a bill they oppose. Consequently, measures without the support of at least two-thirds of the members of the Senate do not even come to a vote in that chamber.

The two-thirds' rule provided a moment of drama in the 80th legislative session. The bill in question would have required prospective voters to present either a photo identification card or two forms of identification without a photo, such as a bank statement, library card, or fishing license. Lieutenant Governor Dewhurst and every Republican in the Senate backed the so-called Voter ID bill, arguing that it was needed to prevent voter fraud. Every Democrat, meanwhile, opposed the bill, declaring that the real purpose of the measure was to discourage ethnic minorities, elderly people, and the poor from voting because those groups typically vote Democrat. As long as all 11 Democratic members of the Senate were present and voting, the bill had no chance to pass because the Republicans lacked the two-thirds' vote needed to bring it to the floor. At one point, it appeared that Dewhurst would be able to bring the Voter ID bill to the floor because Democratic Senator Carlos Uresti of San Antonio was absent with the flu, but Uresti walked into the chamber just in time to cast his vote. Subsequently, another Democratic senator, Mario Gallegos of Houston, recovering from a liver transplant, risked his health by resting in a hospital bed just outside the floor of the Senate, so that he could be wheeled in if necessary to cast a vote to block the bill. The measure failed.

Once a bill reaches the floor of either chamber, members debate its merits and perhaps offer amendments. Because House rules limit debate, the measure eventually comes to a vote unless the session ends before action can be taken. In the Senate, members may speak as long as they please, and occasionally senators attempt to defeat a bill through prolonged debate, a practice known as a **filibuster.** Because debate can be ended by majority vote, the filibuster is not the weapon in the Texas Senate that it is in the U.S. Senate, where 60 of 100 votes are needed to shut off debate.

Filibuster
An attempt to defeat a bill through prolonged debate.

Both the Senate and House set deadlines for the consideration of measures several days in advance of the constitutional end of the session. Senate rules declare that no bill can be considered unless it is reported from committee at least 15 days before final adjournment. No votes can be taken on the last day of the session except to correct errors. The House has comparable rules.

Ordinary legislation passes the House and Senate by majority vote of those members present and voting. If all 150 House members participate, 76 votes constitute a majority. In the Senate, 16 of 31 senators are a majority if every senator participates. Constitutional amendments require a two-thirds' vote of each chamber. Members of the House vote electronically and a scoreboard displays each vote. In the smaller Senate, the clerk calls the roll and members shout their preference. Citizens who are interested in how their representatives voted on a particular measure can find the information online at the website of the Texas legislature (www.capitol.state.tx.us/). The names of members voting for or against a measure are printed in the journal for each chamber. The website provides a link to the journal page showing the vote breakdown on particular pieces of legislation.

Conference Committee Action

A measure has not cleared the legislature until it has passed both the House and the Senate in identical form. Sometimes legislation passes one chamber and then goes to the other for consideration. At other times, legislators introduce similar or identical measures simultaneously in the House and Senate. Legislation that passes one house of the legislature may be rewritten in the other chamber, either during committee mark up or on the floor. By the time a measure that has passed the House has made its way through the Senate (or vice versa), it may differ considerably from the measure originally passed by the other chamber.

What happens when the House and Senate pass similar, but not identical, measures? Frequently, the chamber that initially passed the legislation agrees to the changes adopted by the other chamber. When agreement cannot be reached, and this is often true with major pieces of legislation, the House and Senate form a conference committee to work out differences. A **conference committee** is a special committee created to negotiate differences on similar pieces of legislation passed by the House and Senate. Separate conference committees are formed to deal with each bill in dispute. In the Texas legislature, conference committees include five members from each chamber, appointed by the presiding officers. A majority of conference members from each house must concur before the conference committee has finished its work.

Conference committee
A special committee created to negotiate differences on similar pieces of legislation passed by the House and Senate.

Once conference committee members have reached an agreement, the conference committee returns it to the floor of the House and the Senate for another vote. Each chamber has the option of voting the legislation up or down or returning it to conference committee for further negotiation. The House and Senate may not amend the measure at this point; legislators must accept or reject the piece of legislation in its entirety.

All told, the legislature passes about a fourth of the measures introduced during a session. In the 2007 regular session, the legislature approved 1,480 bills of 6,190 measures that were introduced, for a passage rate of 24 percent.[27] Many of the measures that passed were local bills or other noncontroversial pieces of legislation.

Action by the Governor

Once a bill passes the legislature, it goes to the governor, who has three options. First, the governor may do nothing. If the legislature remains in session, the bill becomes law after 10 days. If the measure reaches the governor's desk within 10 days of adjournment, it becomes law 20 days after the legislative session has ended.

Begin by identifying the people who represent you in the Texas legislature at the following website: **www.capitol.state.tx.us/**. Look for the link "Who Represents Me" on the left column panel. Click on the link and enter your complete address. Take note of the name of your Texas state representative and your Texas state senator. Click on the name of either legislator to go to his or her personal website. The website includes a good deal of information about the legislator, including a link to the bills he or she authored in the last session of the legislature. Click on that link and answer the following questions:

1. What are the names of the people who represent you in the Texas House and the Texas Senate?

2. Select a bill to research that was authored by either your Texas state senator or your Texas state representative in the last legislative session. What is the number of the bill? Who was its author?

3. Click on the bill number and you will be taken to a page that includes links to detailed information about the bill, including the bill's complete text. When was the bill introduced?

4. What would the measure do if it became law? (Write in your own words. Do not copy the brief description at the website.)

5. Did the measure become law? If not, at what stage of the legislative process was it halted?

6. Had you been a member of the legislature, would you have voted for the bill? Why or why not?

Veto
An action by the chief executive of a state or nation refusing to approve a bill passed by the legislature.

Line-item veto
The power of the governor to veto sections or items of an appropriation bill while signing the remainder of the bill into law.

Governors generally use this option for bills about which they have mixed feelings. Although they are willing for the measures to become law, they do not want to go on record in favor of them. Second, the governor can sign the bill into law. Governors often sign politically popular bills with great fanfare, staging televised bill-signing ceremonies. Finally, the governor can issue a **veto,** which is an action by the chief executive of a state or nation refusing to approve a bill passed by the legislature. In 2007, Governor Perry vetoed 53 bills. Except for appropriation bills, the governor must choose to veto all of a bill or none of it. For appropriation bills, the governor has the **line-item veto,** which is the power of the governor to veto sections or items of an appropriation bill while signing the remainder of the bill into law. In 2007, Governor Perry used the line-item veto to cut $650 million from the state budget of $152 billion.[28]

If the legislature is still in session, it can override the governor's veto by a two-thirds' vote of each chamber and the bill becomes law despite the governor's opposition. Nonetheless, overrides are rare in Texas. Because most bills that clear the legislature pass in the last two weeks of the session, the governor can wait until the legislature has adjourned before casting a veto and the veto stands unchallenged.

Laws take effect at different times. The Texas Constitution declares that all laws except the appropriation bill go into effect 90 days after the legislature adjourns unless the legislature by a two-thirds' vote stipulates another date. The appropriation bill takes effect on October 1, the beginning of the state budget year. Sometimes the legislature specifies that a measure take effect immediately upon signature of the governor. At other times the legislature directs that legislation go into effect on September 1.

LEGISLATIVE POLICYMAKING

A number of factors affect the legislative process in Texas.

Legislative Leadership

The speaker of the House and the lieutenant governor are the most powerful figures in the Texas legislature. They appoint members of their leadership team to chair committees and stack key standing committees and conference committees with members who share their political perspectives. They have the power to reward their friends in the legislature and punish their enemies. Their support greatly enhances any measure's chances for passage; their opposition almost certainly dooms a bill to defeat.

The centralization of legislative power in the hands of the leadership offers both advantages and disadvantages for the policymaking process in the legislature. On one hand, the centralization of legislative power enables the legislature to act on a fair amount of legislation in a relatively short period of time. Leaders with power are in position to make things happen. On the other hand, the disadvantage of a centralized power structure is that members who are not part of the leadership team may be left out of the legislative policymaking process. Texas is a diverse state, but that diversity has not always been represented in the outcomes of the legislative process. Historically, the poor, minorities, organized labor, consumers, and other groups not part of the conservative legislative majority have often had little impact on the outcome of policy debates.

Nonetheless, it would be a mistake to regard the speaker and lieutenant governor as legislative dictators. Their considerable powers have been freely given to them by the members of the legislature and could as easily be withdrawn by majority vote of the membership by simply changing the rules of the House or the rules of the Senate. Historically, the most effective legislative leaders have exercised their authority in a fashion that most members consider fair. The members of the legislature want the opportunity to pass legislation important to their constituents. They also want to avoid, whenever possible, having to cast a vote on a controversial issues that could be used against them in the next election.

Speaker Craddick faced a challenge in 2007 because many members believed that he neglected their needs in order to advance his policy agenda. They faulted the speaker for failing to share power with the membership, especially the committee chairs, and they resented having to vote on controversial issues that would likely fail in the Senate, anyway. Craddick lost more support during the session because of the continuing conflict over his leadership. Some of Craddick's former supporters apparently decided that the House would be unable to function smoothly again until it had new leadership.

Interest Groups

Legislative access
An open door
through which an
interest group hopes
to influence the
details of policy.

Interest groups lay the groundwork for influencing the legislative process by contributing money to candidates. Groups give money to legislative candidates because they want **legislative access,** which is an open door through which an interest group hopes to influence the details of policy. Consequently, interest groups target their contributions to the legislature's most powerful members, including the leadership and members of important committees. The speaker, lieutenant governor, and key committee chairs are able to raise huge amounts of money because they hold positions of influence. In January 2007, Speaker Craddick had $4.1 million of cash on hand in his campaign account, even though he had not faced a serious opponent for reelection in decades.[29] The speaker's considerable fundraising ability was itself a source of power because he could transfer the money to members of the House who supported him to help them win reelection. If Craddick wished, he could also use his money to fund primary election opponents for members who opposed his leadership.

Lobbying
The communication of information by a representative of an interest group to a government official for the purpose of influencing a policy decision.

Interest groups attempt to affect the legislative process through **lobbying,** which is the communication of information by a representative of an interest group to a government official for the purpose of influencing a policy decision. Some lobbyists represent a single firm or organization, whereas others contract to lobby on behalf of several clients. In 2007, for example, former state senator David Sibley was a registered lobbyist for 42 interests. Sibley's clients included AT&T, Cingular Wireless, the City of Harlingen, El Paso Electric Co., State Farm Insurance, and the Wholesale Beer Distributors.[30]

Interest groups are often able to achieve their policy goals by working behind the scenes away from the public spotlight. Consider the debate (which never happened) over illegal immigration in the 80th session of the legislature. Conservative legislators filed more than 60 bills addressing the issue of illegal immigration, including measures that would have denied citizenship to the children of undocumented workers, taxed the money that immigrants send back to their home countries, and penalized employers who hire undocumented workers. Only one of the bills passed—a noncontroversial measure that prohibited employers with a history of hiring undocumented workers from getting state grants and tax breaks.[31] Most anti-immigrant measures failed to make it out of committee because of the opposition of the Texas Association of Business, many of whose members rely heavily on immigrant labor.[32]

Constituency

To what extent do the actions of legislators reflect the wishes of their constituents? The traditional model of representation is that candidates make promises during the election campaign and then keep (or fail to keep) those promises once in office. In this approach to representation, citizens hold legislators accountable for keeping their promises. A second model of representation contends that lawmakers do what they think their constituents will approve at the next election. This approach to representation recognizes that legislators may sometimes address issues that were not discussed during the last election. It also implies that voters worry more about performance than promises. A third model of representation holds that legislators use common sense and good judgment to do what is best for their constituents and the state as a whole. Finally, another model of representation suggests that lawmakers sometimes represent constituents outside their districts, such as campaign contributors. From this perspective, big money campaign contributors may have as much or more influence over legislative decision making as do the voters. In practice, legislative behavior mixes several forms of representation, depending on the issue.[33]

Insurance industry lobbyists at work in the Texas capitol.

The most ambitious study of constituency influence in the Texas legislature is an examination of the congruence between the votes of legislators and constituents on two proposed state constitutional amendments in 1967. One amendment involved repeal of the statewide prohibition against the sale of mixed drinks in restaurants, whereas the other would have required annual sessions of the legislature. Both amendments cleared the legislature by the required two-thirds' margin but only the liquor-sale amendment won voter approval. The study compared the votes of individual legislators on each of the measures with the votes of their constituents. It found 85 percent congruence between legislators and their districts on the liquor-by-the-drink amendment, but only 45 percent agreement on the amendment to provide for annual legislative sessions. The authors of the study concluded that issue salience might have been the key factor accounting for this difference. Legislators are more likely to vote with the views of their constituents on issues of high visibility than on lower-visibility issues. The fight over liquor by the drink was hot and heavy, but the discussion about annual legislative sessions was relatively subdued. As a result, legislators were better able to identify the preferences of their constituents on liquor by the drink and probably were more fearful of electoral retaliation if they did not vote with the position of their constituents on the issue.[34]

Some of the most important constituency-based legislative divisions in the Texas legislature reflect whether a district is predominantly inner city, suburban, or rural. Inner-city residents worry about crime, public school quality, neighborhood restoration, and opportunities for minorities. Suburban voters are concerned about property taxes, crime, annexation, and neighborhood preservation. Rural residents focus on agricultural issues, natural-resource development, and property rights. Consider the controversy over the **top 10 percent rule,** which is a state law that grants automatic college admission to public high school graduates who finish in the top 10 percent of their class. The legislature passed the measure in hopes of increasing minority enrollment at the state's two flagship state universities—the University of Texas at Austin and Texas A&M University at College Station. University officials would like for the legislature to modify the rule, so that they can have more flexibility in admissions. In 2006, the University of Texas at Austin admitted 71 percent of its freshman class through the top 10 percent rule. The legislature has defeated efforts to change the rule, however, because of the opposition of both minority legislators who see it as a symbol of racial integration and white legislators from small towns whose constituents also benefit from the provision.[35]

Top 10 percent rule
A state law that grants automatic college admission to public high school graduates who finish in the top 10 percent of their class.

Political Parties

For most of the state's history, Texas had a **nonpartisan legislature,** which is a legislative body in which political parties play little or no role. Nearly every legislator was a Democrat. As recently as 1970, only two Republicans served in Senate, whereas ten Republicans sat in the House. Neither the Democrats nor the Republicans in the Texas legislature organized formally, nor did they elect party leaders or meet regularly as party groups. Even as the Republican contingent in the legislature grew, partisanship generally remained in the background. The speaker and lieutenant governor included both Republicans and Democrats in their leadership teams and appointed legislators of both parties to chair important committees. In 2001, for example, Republican Lieutenant Governor Bill Ratliff appointed a Democrat, Rodney Ellis of Houston, to chair the important Finance Committee, whereas Democratic House Speaker Pete Laney named a Republican, Delwin Jones of Lubbock, to chair the critical Redistricting Committee.

Nonpartisan legislature
A legislative body in which political parties play little or no role.

In contrast, the U.S. Congress is a **partisan legislature,** which is a legislative body in which political parties play a defining role. The members of Congress organize along party lines. The political parties choose committee leaders and floor leaders, with the majority party holding every leadership position both on the floor and in committee. The party leadership acts to advance the party's agenda, and the voting on most pieces of major legislation breaks down along party lines, with a majority of Democrats voting on one side of the issue and a majority of Republicans voting on the other side. Interest group allies and party activists outside of Congress work with the congressional leadership to promote the party's agenda on major issues.

Partisan legislature
A legislative body in which political parties play a defining role.

The 78th legislature, which met in 2003, marked the beginning of a turn toward a more partisan legislature, especially in the Texas House. The redistricting plan adopted by the LRB after the 2000 Census produced legislative districts that were clearly tilted to the advantage of one party or the other. Consequently, most legislators owed their election to primary voters, forcing Democrats to appeal to their liberal base while Republicans targeted their conservative base.[36]

The speaker fight that consumed the 80th session of the legislature was an episode in the transition from a nonpartisan legislature to a partisan legislature. Craddick won election as speaker after a partisan takeover of the House engineered by Republican Congressman Tom DeLay. Craddick has used his power to promote Republican issue positions on a series of controversial issues, including congressional redistricting; reduced spending for the Children's Health Insurance (CHIP) program; a constitutional amendment to outlaw gay marriage; voter ID legislation; and **school choice,** which is an educational reform movement that would allow parents to choose the elementary or secondary school their children will attend. Democrats opposed the speaker on each of these issues but lost on party-line votes. Although most Republican members of the House embraced the party's position on these issues, some members resented being pressured by the speaker to support the party position on some issues that would be controversial in their districts. As discussed in Chapter 24, a number of Republican legislators from suburban districts found themselves under attack in the 2006 election, either in the Republican primary or from Democrats in the general election, because of votes they took on CHIP, education finance, or school choice.

The fight over Speaker Craddick's leadership has taken place because the Texas legislature is in transition. A nonpartisan legislature would never have elected a partisan infighter, such as Tom Craddick, as speaker, choosing instead someone who would seek legislative consensus without much regard for party concerns. Speaker Laney, Craddick's predecessor, was regarded by members from both political parties as fair and relatively nonpartisan. He protected the membership whenever possible from having to take controversial votes and supported the reelection of incumbents of both parties. In contrast, the speaker's role in a partisan legislature is that of a party leader. Partisan leaders promote their party's policy agenda and work to build the size of their party's majority in the chamber, including working to defeat incumbent legislators from the other party. They may even support the defeat of incumbent members of their own political party who are not sufficiently committed to the party's policy agenda.

The future of the legislature depends on the outcome of the 2008 election. Craddick held on to his job in January with the support of 65 Republicans and 15 Democrats over the opposition of 54 Democrats and 14 Republicans. The Democrats who backed Craddick believed that Craddick would probably win and that they would be in a better position if they signed onto the winning side. They were right because Craddick rewarded them with good committee assignments and in some cases committee chairmanships. In contrast, the Republicans who opposed Craddick wanted a less partisan speaker who would share power broadly. Craddick reacted to their opposition by appointing none of the 14 to positions of leadership in the 80th legislature. At the end of the session, party activists and interest-group allies for both parties began gearing up to defeat party defectors. Craddick and his allies outside the legislature targeted for defeat the Republican members of the House who had joined with the Democrats to attempt to oust the speaker. In the meantime, Democratic activists targeted the Democratic members of the House who were part of his leadership team. If Republican primary voters reject Republican legislators who opposed Craddick and Democratic primary voters defeat the Democrats who sided with the speaker, the Texas House will become a much more partisan body than it has ever been in the past. Otherwise,

School choice
An educational reform movement that would allow parents to choose the elementary or secondary school their children will attend.

Liberalism
The political view that seeks to change the political, economic, or social institutions of society to foster the development of the individual. Liberals believe that the government can (and should) advance social progress by promoting political equality, social justice, and economic prosperity. Liberals usually favor government regulation and high levels of government spending for social programs. Liberals value social and cultural diversity and defend the right of individual adult choice on issues such as access to abortion.

GETTING INVOLVED

Contacting Your State Legislators

Two people represent you in the Texas legislature—a state senator and a state representative. You can learn their names and find their e-mail addresses online at the following URL: www.capitol.state.tx.us/. Every session, the legislature deals with issues that affect ordinary citizens in general and college students in particular, including university tuition, college admission requirements, and higher education funding. Write your state legislators about these and other issues. Find out where they stand and let them know how you feel. They represent you, so they need to hear what you have to say.

It's your state—get involved!

Craddick is likely to be replaced by a less partisan speaker who will try to return the body to a time when political parties played a secondary role in the legislative process.

Political Ideology

Political ideology (liberalism/conservatism) influences the legislative process. **Liberalism** is the political view that seeks to change the political, economic, or social institutions of society to foster the development and well-being of the individual. Liberals believe that government should foster social progress by promoting social justice, political equality, and economic prosperity. Liberals usually favor government regulation and high levels of spending for social programs. On social issues, such as abortion, liberals tend to support the right of adult free choice against government interference. In contrast, **conservatism** is the political view that seeks to preserve the political, economic, and social institutions of society against abrupt change. Conservatives generally oppose most government economic regulation and heavy government spending while favoring low taxes and traditional values.

Historically, conservatives have dominated the Texas legislature and legislative policies have reflected their political values. The legislature has enacted regulatory and tax policies designed to promote business expansion while adopting social welfare policies that stress personal responsibility. Few states spend less money on welfare than Texas. The legislature has been tough on crime, building the nation's largest prison system. The legislature has also created the nation's most prolific capital punishment system, executing more convicted murderers than any other state.

Conservatism
The political view that seeks to preserve the political, economic, and social institutions of society against abrupt change. Conservatives generally oppose most government economic regulation and heavy government spending while favoring low taxes and traditional values.

CONCLUSION: THE LEGISLATURE AND THE POLICYMAKING PROCESS

The legislature is the central policymaking institution of state government.

Agenda Building

External forces and institutional responsibilities set the agenda for the legislature. Interest groups, the media, political parties, the federal government, local governments, public opinion, election campaigns, and state officials in other branches of government all raise issues for legislative consideration. The legislature addresses some issues because they are part of its institutional responsibilities. Every session, the legislature must pass an appropriation bill, forcing the body to debate issues of taxing and spending. Every ten years, the legislature must address redistricting.

Policy Formulation and Adoption

The legislature formulates policy by drafting legislation and proposing constitutional amendments. Individual members of the House and Senate introduce measures that may be revised during committee mark up, amended on the floor of each chamber, and then rewritten in conference committee. The policy formulation process in the legislature usually involves competition among political interests. The outcome of that process may reflect compromise among interests or the triumph of one set of interests over other interests, depending on the relative political strength of competing groups.

Although the legislature is the most important institution for policy adoption in state government, it shares power with other bodies. The veto gives the governor a major role in policy adoption for all ordinary legislative policies, including the budget, on which the governor has the line-item veto. Voters participate in the policy adoption process for policies formulated as constitutional amendments. The courts, both state and federal, adopt policies in certain areas, such as education finance, sometimes overriding legislative policy. Furthermore, the legislature has delegated the authority to adopt some policies to state agencies and local governments. The Public Utility Commission (PUC), for example, adopts policies regarding electric and telephone rates. City governments, counties, school districts, and special districts adopt policies concerning local public services, regulations, and taxes within parameters set by the state legislature and the state constitution.

Policy Implementation and Evaluation

The legislature plays an indirect, informal role in policy implementation. Individual legislators may contact the heads of state agencies concerning the implementation of a policy. Because agency heads want to stay on the good side of legislators, they respond positively to most requests.

Legislative oversight
The process through which the legislature evaluates the implementation of public policy by executive branch agencies.

Finally, the legislature evaluates policy. **Legislative oversight** is the process through which the legislature evaluates the implementation of public policy by executive branch agencies. The legislature as a whole evaluates programs when problems persist or when the media publicize scandals in administration. Standing committees provide legislative oversight over administrative agencies. The House Committee on Higher Education, for example, reviews the operation of the state college and university system. The Health and Human Services Committee in the Senate oversees the Texas Health and Human Services Commission. We examine legislative oversight in more detail in the next chapter.

Should the Texas Legislature Meet in Regular Session Every Year?

Overview: Over the past 25 years, there have been numerous calls to reform the Texas legislature and electoral politics. Many advocate that the state constitution should be amended to establish initiative and recall elections, create a redistricting commission, allow for publicly funded elections, and institute annual legislative sessions. Over the past 50 years, there has been significant reform, with many states implementing variations of these proposals. A significant number of states have implemented regular annual sessions. In 1960, 19 states had annual sessions, and in 2001 Kentucky became the 44th state to establish annual sittings of its legislature. According to the *Oregonian,* the main problem confronting state legislatures is that government is growing too large, too complex, and too expensive to be handled adequately by biennial sessions. Texas is one of the 6 remaining states to keep the institution of biennial elections.

Why should Texas consider annual legislative sessions? Texas is the second most populous state, and the U.S. Census Bureau is projecting significant population growth through 2025 and beyond. According to the Texas comptroller, if Texas stood alone as its own nation, its increasingly diversifying economy would rank as the eighth largest economy *globally.* Also, immigration rates (both legal and illegal) are increasing along with the uncertainty of both the war on terror and globalization. It is prudent to have a continually informed and active legislature to meet these challenges. The institution of annual sittings would foster the creation of an expert and experienced support staff capable of helping legislators meet demands as they arise, and the Texas legislature would join the majority of states that are reforming their governments to meet the new burdens of a changing political culture.

It may be, however, that Texas's political culture would not abide annual sessions. Texans take pride in their reputation for rugged individualism and self-sufficiency, and the state government reflects these beliefs. Texans historically have rejected a large and active government. When the legislature is not sitting, it is not making law and regulations and not stripping away or impinging on the natural liberty of Texans. Isn't it the nature of lawmakers to make law, and isn't it the nature of law to restrict the actions of citizens? It could be argued that Texas's economic well-being and growth are due to a limited government and a relative lack of economic regulation. Within the past 50 years, the state has sent *three* Texans to the U.S. presidency. The arguments for both annual and biennial sittings have merit, and it may be that historical, social, and technological change will force the issue of reform.

Arguments for Having Annual Legislative Sessions

❑ **Annual sessions are necessary for today's political world.** Annual sessions are essential for confronting the complex social and political demands made on contemporary legislatures. The duties and responsibilities of the Texas legislature have become such that it cannot adequately handle its commitments or obligations to the state and its needs on a biennial basis. With an annual sitting, the legislature has the flexibility to address change and respond to problems as they arise without the need to call for special sessions.

❑ **Annual sessions would allow for continuity in policy.** An advantage of annual sessions is that there is continuity and timeliness in law and policymaking. Legislators do not need to "go back" two years to relearn policy and then attempt to adapt it to

the social and political changes that may have happened between sessions. Legislators would then gain experience and expertise in policy domains and policymaking. The result would be better law and policy.

❑ **Annual sessions would encourage better governance.** Annual sessions would allow for enhanced constituent service and improved oversight over the state executive, judiciary, bureaucracy, and subgovernmental units. The legislature cannot operate well in fits and starts, and relatively continuous legislative oversight will ensure accountability in government and easily enable the enforcement of legislative policies.

Arguments Against Having Annual Legislative Sessions

❑ **Biennial sessions embody the principle of truly limited government and prevent the**

concentration of political power. When the legislature is not in session, the people are governing and making policy themselves at the local level. Biennial sessions provide a safeguard against profligate lawmaking and unnecessary policymaking. They also prevent the creation of an entrenched political class providing a safeguard against the inevitable concentration of power in government, which usually results in limitations on individual liberty.

❑ **Biennial sessions are more cost-effective.** Annual sessions tend to increase legislative costs over time. To maintain the legislative support, staff, and bureaucracy necessary to support annual sessions, state expenditures must increase. Because annual sessions address more issues than biennial sessions, one can expect increased regulation by state bureaucracies and agencies, resulting in increased taxes and fees.

❑ **Biennial sessions encourage better lawmaking.** Unlike professional legislators, Texas legislators work in their chosen profession or career. Because they spend a significant amount of time between sessions engaged in their occupation, legislators have increased contact with the public and have a better understanding of the needs and concerns of the state. They are able to preserve close relationships with constituents and maintain intimate contact with their districts, allowing the desires and wishes of their constituents to find their way into law and policy.

QUESTIONS

1. What are the advantages of annual legislative sessions? Disadvantages?
2. Do Texas's biennial legislative sessions reflect Texas's political culture? Is this an advantage for the state's political life? Why or why not?

SELECT READINGS

1. Sam Kinch Jr. and Anne Marie Kilday, *Too Much Money Is Not Enough: Political Power and Big Money in Texas* (Austin, TX: Campaigns for People, 2001).
2. Billy Lee Brammer, *The Gay Place* (Austin: University of Texas Press, 1961, 1995).

SELECT WEBSITES

1. **www.capitol.state.tx.us**
   Website of the Texas legislature.

2. **www.texaslegislatureobserved.com**
   The *Texas Observer*'s blog coverage of the Texas legislature's 79th session.

KEY TERMS

appropriation bill
bicameral legislature
bill
conference committee
conservatism
filibuster
fiscal note
impeachment
initiative process
interim committee
joint resolution
legislative access

Legislative Budget Board (LBB)
legislative oversight
Legislative Redistricting Board (LRB)
legislative turnover
liberalism
line-item veto
lobbying
local bills
mark up
nonpartisan elections
nonpartisan legislature

partisan legislature
resolution
school choice
select, *or* special, committee
seniority
standing committee
term limitation
top 10 percent rule
unicameral legislature
veto

NOTES

1. Laylan Copelin, "Behind the Scenes, Fight over Speakership Was Full of Surprises," *Austin American-Statesman*, June 10, 2007, available at www.statesman.com.
2. *Capitol Update*, June 14, 2007, pp. 2–3.
3. James R. Rogers, "The Impact of Bicameralism on Legislative Production," *Legislative Studies Quarterly* 28 (November 2003): 509–528.
4. "Texas Legislature Should Meet Every Year," *El Paso Times*, May 22, 2007, available at www.elpasotimes.com.
5. Harvey J. Tucker, "Legislative Logjams: A Comparative State Analysis," *Western Political Quarterly* 38 (September 1985): 432–446.
6. Ross Ramsey and Kathy Walt, "Fast to the Finish Line," *Houston Chronicle*, May 30, 1995, pp. 13A, 15A.
7. Quoted in Ellen Perlman, "The Gold-Plated Legislature," *Governing*, February 1998, p. 40.
8. Harvey J. Tucker, "Legislative Workload Congestion in Texas," *Journal of Politics* 49 (May 1987): 565–578.
9. Barbara Palmer and Dennis Simon, *Breaking the Political Glass Ceiling: Women and Congressional Elections* (New York: Routledge, 2006), p. 195.
10. W. Gardner Seldy, "Another Special Session Gives Rise Legislative Pay Chatter," *Austin American-Statesman*, April 11, 2006, available at www.statesman.com.
11. Empire Center for New York State Policy, "Legislative Salaries per State," available at www.empirecenter.org.
12. Jay Root, "But the Perks Sure Are Nice," *Fort Worth Star-Telegram*, February 4, 2007, available at www.dfw.com.
13. Quoted in Emily Ramshaw, "Do Campaign Funds Bankroll a Cushy Lifestyle?" *Dallas Morning News*, December 17, 2006, available at www.dallasnews.com.
14. Bob Campbell, "Business, Professional Groups Give Craddick $1.9 Million," *Midland Reporter-Telegram*, February 6, 2007, available at www.mywesttexas.com.
15. R. G. Ratcliffe, "Spending Cycle Lives on After Campaigns," *Houston Chronicle*, July 30, 2007, available at www.chron.com.
16. Jay Root, "Why Are Some Legislators Paying Rent to Spouses?" *Fort Worth Star-Telegram*, February 22, 2007, available at www.dfw.com.
17. Gary F. Moncrief, Richard G. Niemi, and Lynda W. Powell, "Time, Term Limits, and Turnover: Trends in Membership Stability in U.S. State Legislatures," *Legislative Studies Quarterly* 29 (August 2004): 365.
18. *Texas Weekly*, January 9, 2006, available at www.texasweekly.com.
19. "Revolving-Door Service," *Governing*, January 2007, p. 18.
20. Karen Brooks, "Texas No. 1 in Legislators-Turned-Lobbyists," *Dallas Morning News*, October 13, 2006, available at www.dallasnews.com.
21. U.S. Term Limits, "State Legislative Term Limits," available at www.termlimits.org.
22. John M. Carey, Richard G. Niemi, and Lynda W. Powell, *Term Limits in the State Legislatures* (Ann Arbor: University of Michigan Press, 2000), pp. 123–127.
23. Lan Greenblatt, "Term Limits Aren't Working," *Governing*, April 2005, pp. 13–14.
24. *Texas Weekly*, February 2, 2007, available at www.texasweekly.com.
25. *Texas Government Newsletter*, January 26, 1987, p. 2.
26. Johanna M. Donlin and Brian J. Weberg, *Legislative Staff Services: Profiles of the 50 States and Territories* (Washington, DC: National Conference of State Legislatures, 1999), p. 167.
27. Texas Legislature Online, "Legislative Reports for the 80th Legislature," available at www.capitol.state.tx.us.
28. Office of the Governor, "Bills Vetoed by Governor Perry, 80th Legislature," available at www.governor.state.tx.us.
29. Texas Ethics Commission, "January Semi-Annual Report," January 2007, available at www.ethics.state.tx.us.
30. Texas Ethics Commission, "Lobby Lists," available at www.ethics.state.tx.us.
31. Brandi Grissom, "Immigration Not Addressed Much by Legislature," *El Paso Times*, June 25, 2007, available at www.elpasotimes.com.
32. Megan Headley, "Northward Ho!" *Texas Observer*, March 23, 2007, pp. 12–13.
33. Jane Mansbridge, "Rethinking Representation," *American Political Science Review* 97 (November 2003): 515–528.
34. William C. Adams and Paul H. Ferber, "Measuring Legislator-Constituency Congruence: Liquor, Legislators and Linkage," *Journal of Politics* 42 (February 1980): 202–208.
35. Polly Ross Hughes and Matthew Tresaugue, "Small-Town GOP Behind Survival of Top 10% Rule," *Houston Chronicle*, May 30, 2007, pp. B1–B2.
36. Bill Bishop, "A Steady Slide Towards a More Partisan Union," *Austin American-Statesman*, May 30, 2004, available at www.statesman.com.

Chapter 26

The Executive Branch in Texas

CHAPTER OUTLINE

LEARNING OUTCOMES

After studying Chapter 26, students should be able to do the following:

▸ Evaluate Governor Perry's effort to expand the powers of his office through the use of executive orders. (pp. 696–697)

▸ Describe the background and socioeconomic characteristics of the typical governor of Texas, and evaluate how closely recent officeholders have fit the image. (pp. 697–698)

▸ Outline the constitutional/legal office of governor, including formal qualifications, length of term, removal, compensation, and staff assistance. (p. 698)

▸ Describe the powers and responsibilities of the office of governor, focusing on legislative

powers, appointive powers, judicial powers, budgetary powers, law enforcement and military powers, ceremonial powers, political party leadership, and administrative authority. (pp. 699–706)

▸ Evaluate the power of the office of governor of Texas in comparison with governors of other states and in light of scholarly efforts to measure gubernatorial power. (p. 706)

▸ Compare and contrast the experiences of Governor George W. Bush and Governor Perry with the Texas legislature. (pp. 706–708)

▸ Describe the role of the governor in the policymaking process. (pp. 708–709)

▸ List the powers and responsibilities of each of the following elected executive officials:

lieutenant governor, attorney general, comptroller of public accounts, commissioner of agriculture, and commissioner of the General Land Office. (pp. 709–713)

▶ Describe the powers and responsibilities of the Texas secretary of state, Texas Railroad Commission, and State Board of Education. (pp. 714–716)

▶ Describe the organization of the appointed boards and commissions. (pp. 716–719)

▶ Assess the arguments for and against privatization. (pp. 719–720)

▶ Evaluate the tools available to the legislature and the governor for overseeing the state's administrative bureaucracy. (pp. 720–722)

▶ Describe the role of the executive branch in the state's policymaking process. (pp. 722–723)

▶ Assess the impact of the plural executive on administrative policymaking in Texas. (pp. 724–725)

▶ Define the key terms listed on page 725 and explain their significance.

Governor Rick Perry believes that the best way to fight cervical cancer is to require young girls to be vaccinated against the virus that causes it. In early 2007, the governor issued an executive order to require that all Texas girls entering the sixth grade be vaccinated against the human papillomavirus (HPV), which is the major cause of a sexually transmitted virus that leads to cervical cancer. The state would pick up the cost of the vaccination for children from low-income families.

Perry defended his action as the right thing to do. Nearly 4,000 women nationwide die of cervical cancer every year, 400 of them in Texas. The vaccine prevents almost all strains of HPV, as well as 90 percent of genital warts.[1] "The HPV vaccine provides us with an incredible opportunity to effectively target and prevent cervical cancer," Perry declared. "Requiring young girls to get vaccinated before they come into contact with HPV is responsible health and fiscal policy that has the potential to significantly reduce cases of cervical cancer and mitigate future medical costs."[2]

Perry's order was controversial. Conservatives complained that the governor had usurped the role of parents. Lieutenant Governor David Dewhurst phrased the argument as follows: "I think while the HPV vaccine can play a very important role in preventing cervical cancer, I don't think government should ever presume to know better than the parents."[3] Some social conservatives also worried that the order would undermine their effort to teach young people to abstain from sex before marriage by making premarital sex seem less risky.

Other critics accused the governor of exceeding his authority under the Texas Constitution. An **executive order** is a directive issued by the governor to an administrative agency or executive department. Although Governor Perry and his predecessors in office have issued executive orders before, most of them have been dealt with routine matters, such as a disaster declaration or directive to fly the flag at half-staff to honor the dead. The Texas Constitution does not give the governor authority to tell state agencies what to do, at least not in so many words. Furthermore, many constitutional experts doubt that the power to issue executive orders can be read into the constitution, considering the restrictive nature of the document. If the governor wanted to require HPV vaccinations for schoolgirls, they say, he should have asked the legislature to address the issue.[4]

Executive order
A directive issued by the governor to an administrative agency or executive department.

The legislature did address the issue, but not in the fashion that Governor Perry wanted. It passed legislation reversing the governor's order and mandating that no HPV vaccine could be ordered for schoolchildren in the next four years. The measure also prohibited the state from paying for the vaccine for low-income families. The vote in the House was 118–23; it was 30–1 in the Senate. Rather than suffer a certain veto override, Perry allowed the bill to become law without his signature. "A debate which affects real lives has been hijacked by politics and posturing," said the governor. "I have never seen so much misinformation spread about a vital public health issue."[5]

The controversy over Governor Perry's executive order to require HPV vaccinations for schoolgirls introduces the study of the role of the governor in the policymaking process. This chapter focuses on the executive branch of state government. The first part examines the office of governor. It considers the qualifications and background of the state's chief executive. The chapter identifies the powers and responsibilities of the governor and assesses the strength of the office in Texas compared with governors in other states. The chapter then studies the role of the governor in the policymaking process. The second part of the chapter describes the various agencies and departments that constitute the executive branch of state government. It discusses the elected executive officials other than the governor, appointed executive officials, elected boards and commissions, and appointed boards and commissions. The chapter discusses the tools available to the governor and legislature for overseeing administrative agencies and assesses their effectiveness. Finally, the chapter concludes with a discussion of the role of the executive branch of state government in the policymaking process.

This chapter is the second in a series of five chapters dealing with the policymaking institutions of state and local government. The first three chapters in the series—Chapters 25, 26, and 27—examine the legislative, executive, and judicial branches of state government, respectively. The final two chapters in the series focus on units of local government. Chapter 28 discusses city government, whereas Chapter 29 studies counties, school districts, and special districts.

THE GOVERNOR

The governor is the chief executive officer of the state with important powers to influence the policymaking process.

Qualifications and Background

The Texas Constitution declares that the governor must be an American citizen, a resident of Texas for five years preceding election, and at least 30 years of age. In practice, most of the state's chief executives have come from narrow social circles. All governors have been white, Anglo-Saxon Protestants. Only two (Miriam Ferguson and Ann Richards) were women. Most governors have been well-to-do, middle-aged lawyers or business executives with prior experience in public affairs. They have also had fairly common, easy-to-pronounce names, such as Perry, Bush, Richards, White, Clements, Briscoe, Smith, and Connally.

Although most recent governors have conformed fairly closely to the traditional image, the election of Ann Richards showed that Texas voters are willing to consider candidates who do not fit the mold in all respects. Not only was Richards a woman, but her political career was based on her own efforts rather than those of her husband. Richards was a divorcee who was a schoolteacher before winning election as a county commissioner in Travis County (which includes the city of Austin). In 1982, Richards was elected state treasurer, holding that post until her election as governor in 1990.

Term of Office, Selection, and Removal

The governor's term of office is four years, increased from two years by a constitutional amendment adopted in 1972. Today, only 2 of the 50 states elect their governors for two years instead of four.[6] Elections for governor and other elective state executive officials are held in even-numbered years, timed so that they will not coincide with national presidential elections (e.g., 2006, 2010). The Texas Constitution sets no limit on the number of terms a governor may serve. Rick Perry, who assumed office when George W. Bush resigned in 2001 to become president, will hold the record for longest service if he completes the term he began in January 2007.

Impeachment
A formal accusation against an executive or judicial officeholder.

A governor can be removed from office before a term is ended through the process of impeachment and removal by the legislature. **Impeachment** is the formal process through which the House accuses an executive or judicial branch official of misconduct serious enough to warrant removal from office. The House votes to impeach the governor by majority vote. The Senate conducts a trial and may vote to remove by a two-thirds' margin. In 1917, the House impeached Governor James Ferguson and the Senate removed him from office over the alleged misuse of public funds.[7] Ferguson is the only governor to be impeached in the history of the state. Many of the state's voters apparently did not share the legislature's opinion of Ferguson because they twice elected his wife, Miriam Ferguson, to serve as the state's chief executive.

Staff Support

The governor has a full-time professional staff of 137 people with a two-year office budget of $17 million, including the governor's salary of $115,345. In addition, programs assigned to the governor's office employ 136 full-time staff members with a two-year budget of $669 million.[8] The governor appoints staff members without need of Senate confirmation and they serve at the governor's pleasure. The governor has a chief of staff, a general counsel, and a press secretary. The governor's office also includes administrative units dealing with legislative matters, communications, budgeting and planning, and criminal justice. The size of the governor's staff has grown over the years because state government is larger and more complex, and today's governor has become a more visible and active participant in the state policy process. Furthermore, federal grant programs often require gubernatorial participation in and coordination of program planning and implementation.[9]

GETTING INVOLVED

Forming a Study Group

A study group is an excellent way for students to learn and retain course material. Studying in a group is more efficient than individual study because the collective knowledge of the group almost always exceeds the knowledge of even the best prepared student in the class. Consequently, students are less likely to be stumped for an answer to a question and have to waste time looking it up. Study groups are also more fun than studying alone and they motivate students to succeed.

Take the initiative to organize a study group for this course. Identify students who seem serious about their education based on their class attendance and participation and schedule a group study session at a mutually agreed time and place. Coffee shops are a traditional hangout for students preparing for exams. Use the materials in the study guide or the various learning resources in the textbook (review questions, key terms, etc.) to organize your session. It's your education—get involved!

Powers and Responsibilities

Although the Texas Constitution grants the governor authority to act in a broad range of policy areas, most of the governor's powers are coupled with limitations.

Legislative Powers   The strongest constitutional powers of the governor are those used for influencing the legislature. The Texas Constitution requires that the governor deliver a message to the legislature at the beginning of each legislative session on the condition of the state. The State of the State address, which is comparable to the State of the Union speech the president makes to Congress, enables the governor to focus attention on issues the governor considers the state's most serious policy needs and offer proposals to meet those needs. The governor can send messages to the legislature at other times as well, both formally and informally. Of course, any legislative measure that the governor proposes must be introduced by a member of the legislature and passed by the Texas House and Texas Senate before it can become a law. The governor can also influence legislative priorities by declaring certain pieces of legislation emergency measures. In the House, emergency measures receive priority attention on the floor. Furthermore, members of the legislature can introduce legislation after the deadline for bill filing if the governor designates the measure as emergency legislation.

> **Veto**
> An action by the chief executive of a state or nation refusing to approve a bill passed by the legislature.

The governor has the power of the **veto,** which is an action by the chief executive of a state or nation refusing to approve a measure passed by the legislature. If the governor objects to a bill passed by the legislature, the governor has 10 days to act unless the legislature adjourns during that time. In that case, the governor has 20 days from adjournment in which to decide to issue a veto. Governor Perry vetoed 53 bills in 2007.

> **Line-item veto**
> The power of the governor to veto sections or items of an appropriation bill while signing the remainder of the bill into law.

The governor also enjoys the power of the **line-item veto,** which is the authority of the governor to veto sections or items of an appropriation bill while signing the remainder of the bill into law. Keep in mind that the power of the governor to issue the line-item veto is limited to the **appropriation bill,** which is a legislative authorization to spend money for particular purposes. In 2007, Governor Perry used the

> **Appropriation bill**
> A legislative authorization to spend money for particular purposes; they are usually assigned to the emergency calendar as well.

line-item veto to cut $650 million from the state budget of $152 billion.[10] On other pieces of legislation, the governor's options are limited to either accepting or rejecting the measure in its entirety.

The Texas legislature can override the governor's veto by a two-thirds' vote of each chamber, voting separately. Nationwide, state legislatures override about 10 percent of gubernatorial vetoes.[11] Since Texas became a state, the legislature has successfully overridden only 52 of more than 1,600 gubernatorial vetoes (not counting item vetoes), for an override rate of 3 percent. Furthermore, since 1941 the legislature has overridden only one veto—a veto cast by Governor Bill Clements in 1979 of a local bill exempting Comal County from the state's game laws.

Why has the legislature so seldom reversed the governor's vetoes? Two-thirds' majorities are difficult to attain, of course. More important, most gubernatorial vetoes in Texas come after adjournment when overriding is impossible. Because much of the legislation introduced during a regular session does not pass until the session's final days, the governor can simply wait until adjournment to issue a veto. With the legislature gone home, a veto stands unchallenged. Although a number of state constitutions allow the legislature to call itself back into session to consider overriding vetoes, the Texas Constitution does not.

A final legislative power the governor enjoys is the authority to call special sessions. The state constitution empowers the governor to convene the legislature in special sessions that may last no longer than 30 days. The Texas Constitution places no limit on the number of special sessions a governor can call. Between May 2003 and January 2007, Governor Perry called seven special sessions to deal with either legislative redistricting or school finance and property tax rates. The constitution declares that in a special session the "legislature may consider only those matters that the governor specifies in the call or subsequently presents to the legislature." The governor can use the power to set the agenda for special sessions as a bargaining tool in negotiations with legislators. In exchange for support on other matters, the governor can offer to expand the call to include issues of particular interest to individual legislators or groups of lawmakers.

Appointive Powers   The governor has extensive powers of appointment. The governor is responsible for staffing positions on more than 200 state administrative boards and commissions that set policy for state agencies under their authority. Furthermore, the Texas Constitution empowers the governor to fill vacancies in many otherwise elective positions, including district and appellate judgeships, should openings occur between elections. A governor makes about 3,000 appointments during a four-year term.[12]

The power of appointment gives the governor the opportunity to influence policy and score political points. As the state's population has grown more diverse, governors of both political parties have sought a diverse set of appointees. Governor Richards named more women and minorities to office than any governor in the history of the state. Forty-one percent of her appointees were women, 32 percent Latino, and 12 percent African American. Governor Bush and Governor Perry continued to diversify state government. Nine percent of Bush's appointees were African American, 13 percent Latino, and 37 percent women. During Perry's first

After the 2007 legislative session, Governor Rick Perry vetoed 53 bills.

four years in office, his list of appointments was 11 percent African American, 16 percent Latino, and 36 percent women.[13]

The appointive powers of the governor are limited. Because most administrative board members serve six-year overlapping terms, new governors must work with an administrative structure that was put in place by a predecessor. Although new governors can fill about a third of administrative positions when they first assume office, they do not have the opportunity to name their own people to a majority of posts for another two years.

The governor has little official removal power. The Texas Constitution gives governors the authority to remove their *own* appointees (but not those of a predecessor) with a two-thirds' vote of approval by the state Senate, but this limited procedure has not been used. An incoming governor cannot force the resignation of holdover administrators.

State law allows the governor to appoint a conservator to take over a wayward agency, but the governor can act only on the recommendation of the Legislative Audit Commission based on a finding that the agency is guilty of gross fiscal mismanagement. In 2007, the procedure was used to take control of the Texas Youth Commission (TYC), which is the state agency responsible for housing juveniles convicted of criminal offenses. The legislature and the governor acted after media reports that TYC officials ignored signs that administrators at a West Texas juvenile prison were sexually abusing inmates.[14]

The governor's appointive powers are often restricted by technical, legal requirements. Consider the make-up of the Texas Racing Commission, which oversees the operation of parimutuel wagering on horse and dog racing in the state. The legislature reserved two of the eight positions on the commission for the state comptroller and the chair of the Texas Public Safety Commission. The governor can appoint the other six members, but only within certain, strict guidelines. Two members of the commission must be experienced in horse racing and two others must be experienced at racing greyhounds. The other two commission members must be veterinarians, one specializing in large animals and the other in small animals. Furthermore, the legislature specified that all members of the commission be residents of Texas for at least ten years and file detailed financial statements. Persons with a financial interest in a racetrack or who are closely related to someone with such as interest would be ineligible to serve.

Finally, the governor's appointees must be confirmed by a two-thirds' vote of the Texas Senate. In contrast, presidential appointees require only a majority vote of approval in the U.S. Senate. Furthermore, the tradition of senatorial courtesy ensures that the governor's appointees must pass political inspection by their home-area senator or face rejection. **Senatorial courtesy** is a custom of the Texas Senate that allows individual senators a veto over nominees who live in their districts. By tradition, senators will vote against a nominee if the senator from the district in which the nominee lives declares opposition to the nomination.

Judicial Powers   The Texas Constitution gives the governor some authority in the judicial process. On the recommendation of the Board of Pardons and Paroles, the governor may grant reprieves, commutations, and pardons. A **reprieve** is the postponement of the implementation of punishment for a criminal offense; a **commutation** is the reduction of punishment for a criminal offense. A **pardon** is the exemption from punishment for a criminal offense. In a **capital punishment** (death penalty) case, the governor has authority to grant one 30-day reprieve independently, without recommendation by Pardons and Paroles, thus postponing a condemned person's execution.

Probably the most effective tool the governor has for influencing judicial policy is the power of appointment. Texas state judges are elected but, when appellate and district judges die, retire, or resign during the midst of a term, the state constitution empowers the governor to appoint a new judge to serve until the next election. In 2006, 48 percent of the state's appellate judges and 43 percent of district judges had initially taken office through gubernatorial appointment rather than election.[15]

Senatorial courtesy
A custom of the Texas Senate that allows individual senators a veto over nominees who live in their districts.

Reprieve
A postponement of the implementation of punishment for a criminal offense.

Commutation
A reduction of punishment for a criminal offense.

Pardon
The exemption from punishment for a criminal offense.

Capital punishment
The death penalty.

Budgetary Powers The president of the United States and the governors of 47 states enjoy budget-making authority, preparing a budget to submit to the legislative branch.[16] Although the final budget is invariably a negotiated document between the legislative and executive branches of government, the chief executive has the advantage of proposing the initial document. Consequently, the budget debate in the legislature at least begins with the governor's budgetary priorities and policy proposals.

The governor of Texas has no such advantage. Although the Texas Constitution requires the governor to submit budget proposals to the legislature, the Legislative Budget Board (LBB) prepares a budget as well, and its ideas generally carry more weight. The **Legislative Budget Board (LBB)** is an agency created by the legislature to study state revenue and budgetary needs between legislative sessions and prepare budget and appropriation bills to submit to the legislature. As the legislature debates the budget, the point of departure is not the governor's budget but, rather, the budget proposed by the LBB. As a result, the governor begins on the defensive.

The most important power the governor of Texas has for influencing budget priorities is the line-item veto. In contrast to the president, whose only option on an appropriation bill is to accept or reject the measure in its entirety, most state governors can selectively eliminate items while signing the rest into law. This veto and the threat of its use allow a politically skilled governor the opportunity to exercise considerable influence over the final budget document.

Budget execution authority refers to the power to cut agency spending or transfer money between agencies during the period when the legislature is not in session. Much can happen in the two-year interval between legislative sessions. Because of unforeseen events, such as a hurricane striking the coast or declining welfare rolls, some budget categories may run short of money, whereas others may have excess cash. Budget execution authority is the power to transfer funds among accounts between legislative sessions. The Texas Constitution allows either the governor or the LBB to propose a reduction in spending or a shift in state funds. Both the governor and the LBB must concur on proposed spending reductions or money transfers before they can take place.

Law Enforcement and Military Powers The governor has some peripheral authority in law enforcement. The governor appoints the three-member board that heads the Department of Public Safety and is empowered to assume command of the Texas Rangers, should circumstances warrant, which is rare. The governor is also commander-in-chief of the Texas National Guard, which the governor can call out to assist in situations beyond the control of local law enforcement agencies, such as a natural disaster or civil disorder. In 2005, for example, Governor Perry called several units of the Texas State Guard to active duty to help with people evacuated to Texas from Louisiana after Hurricane Katrina. Guard units subsequently helped with disaster relief in Texas after Hurricane Rita struck the upper Texas coast. Governor Perry has also ordered several hundred National Guard troops to deploy along the border to assist local police and federal agents in securing the border against drug smuggling and illegal immigration.

Ceremonial Powers In addition to official powers, the governor is the ceremonial leader of the state. The governor greets foreign leaders, speaks at local chamber of commerce luncheons, issues proclamations on state holidays, and shakes hands with

Legislative Budget Board (LBB)
An agency created by the legislature to study state revenue and budgetary needs between legislative sessions and prepare budget and appropriations bills to submit to the legislature.

Budget execution authority
The power to cut agency spending or transfer money between agencies during the period when the legislature is not in session.

visiting scout troops. Although some observers may view these sorts of activities as somewhat trivial, they allow the governor the opportunity to give the appearance of leadership, which can be helpful for a governor attempting to influence the policy process. Leadership depends on the perceptions of the public and other political leaders as much as it depends on official powers.

Governors sometimes use their leadership position to recruit out-of-state companies to relocate to the state. Governor Perry, for example, helped convince Toyota to select San Antonio as the site of a new auto-assembly plant. The legislature did its part by approving the expenditure of state funds to build rail tracks to connect the plant to major rail lines. State and local governments are also paid to train 2,000 full-time workers for the plant.[17]

Political Party Leadership   The governor is the unofficial leader of his or her political party in the state. The governor sometimes speaks out on partisan controversies and usually campaigns for the party's candidates in state and national elections. Furthermore, as the most visible elected official in a large state, the governor of Texas is often a national political figure. Governor Richards was a prominent figure in Democratic national politics. Her successor, Governor Bush, was elected president of the United States in 2000.

Administrative Powers   The governor of Texas is probably weakest in the area of administration because of the **plural executive,** which is the division of executive power among several elected officials. Because the land commissioner, attorney

Plural executive
The division of executive power among several elected officials.

Governor Ann Richards, who died in 2006, was a prominent figure in national Democratic Party politics.

general, comptroller, lieutenant governor, and commissioner of agriculture are all elected, they answer not to the governor but to the voters. Elected executive officials may not share the governor's party affiliation and may be political rivals, even when they have the same political party affiliation. Comptroller Carole Keeton Strayhorn, for example, challenged Governor Perry for reelection in 2006. Both Strayhorn and Perry were Republicans, although Strayhorn chose to run for governor as an independent.

Nonetheless, a determined governor, especially one who serves more than one term in office, can have an influence over state agencies. By the end of one four-year term, a governor has appointed two-thirds of administrative officials. After six years in office, the governor has had the opportunity to staff the entire executive branch except for those agencies with elected administrators. Many of these officials, especially administrators serving in the most important agencies, are political allies of the governor. They are inclined to listen to the governor's point of view on policy matters and take direction from the governor if the governor wishes to be assertive. Even if the governor cannot force an official out of office, few appointed administrators can withstand the pressure if the governor calls for resignation. For example, every member of the troubled TYC resigned in the face of demands from the governor and legislative leaders to step down.

Governor Perry has struggled to assert influence over the executive branch of state government. He asked the legislature for authority to appoint agency heads, but it turned him down. It also turned down his request to appoint the heads of all the governing boards. Perry then acted on his own to create the Governor's Management Council, which includes the heads of the state's 11 largest agencies and representatives of small and medium-size agencies. The purpose of the council, which the governor chairs, is to coordinate the operation of the executive branch.[18]

Perry has also tried to expand his authority to issue executive orders. Historically, Texas governors have used executive orders to create task forces or advisory groups or simply to express an opinion on a policy issue. Governors have not used executive orders to make policy.[19] In contrast, Perry has used executive orders as a tool for achieving his policy goals. In addition to the executive order to require school girls to be vaccinated against HPV, the governor has issued several other high-profile executive orders. In 2005, Perry ordered the Texas Education Agency (TEA) to change the state reporting system for school districts to require that districts spend at least 65 percent of their funds on classroom instruction. Education Commissioner Shirley Neeley indicated that the agency would implement the governor's order.[20] The governor also directed the TEA to create a limited merit pay plan for teachers using $10 million in federal grant money that would financially reward teachers in the 100 campuses that had the most improvement in student performance.[21] In addition to the orders dealing with education, Governor Perry issued an executive order to the State Office of Administrative Hearings, directing it to speed up the permitting process to allow utility companies to build coal-fired power plants in the state.

Governor Perry's effort to expand the powers of his office through executive orders has met considerable resistance from the legislature and the courts. As we discussed in the introduction to this chapter, the legislature shot down the governor's effort to mandate HPV vaccinations and a state district judge ruled that Perry exceeded his constitutional authority by ordering faster consideration of power plant permits. Even Texas Attorney General Greg Abbott weighed in on the matter, at least unofficially. Although the attorney general did not issue a formal opinion, he did indicate to members of the legislature that the governor cannot authorize an agency to do something through an executive order that the agency does not have authority to do and that, in any event, the agency is not obligated to carry out the executive order. In other words, executive orders are advisory opinions without legal weight.[22]

Measuring Gubernatorial Powers

Observers have long held that the constitutional/legal powers of the governor of Texas are among the weakest in the nation. Political scientist Thad Beyle has created an index to measure the official powers of state governors based on the following factors: the number of separately elected officials in the state, the number of years the governor serves and whether the governor can be reelected, the governor's powers of appointment, the governor's power over the state budget, the extent of the governor's veto power, and the governor's authority to reorganize the bureaucracy. Professor Beyle gives the governor of Texas a score of 3.2 on a 5-point scale, placing the powers of the Texas governor in the bottom third among the 50 states. The average score is 3.5. The Texas governor scores well on the length of term and opportunity for reelection measure, the veto, and the governor's power to reorganize the bureaucracy. The Texas chief executive scores low on the other measures.

Formal, official powers are an incomplete measure of a governor's authority. Beyle augments his index of official powers with an index measuring each governor's personal power. This index includes the size of the governor's margin of victory in the last election, whether the governor has previously served in lower office and is on an upward career track, whether the governor is early or late in a term, whether the governor can run for reelection, and the governor's standing in public opinion polls. A newly elected governor who won office by a large margin who is perceived as a rising political star is in a better position to be influential than is an unpopular governor nearing the end of a term who is perceived as heading toward retirement.[23]

Other aspects of gubernatorial leadership, such as communication skills and leadership ability, are also critical to a governor's success in office. Professor Martha Wagner Weinberg believes that the official powers of the governor or the number of orders the governor can give has relatively little impact on the success of the governor as a policy leader. Instead, a governor's influence hinges on how the governor chooses to spend time, what resources the governor can bring to achieve goals, whose advice the governor takes, and whose pleas for support the governor heeds.[24]

The experience of Governor Bush in dealing with the legislature illustrates the ability of a governor to use unofficial, informal powers to achieve policy influence. In 1995, when Bush first took office, he targeted four policy areas—public education, juvenile justice, welfare, and tort reform. The legislature enacted major reforms in each of these areas. With the exception of welfare policy, the legislature adopted policies that closely reflected the policy preferences of the governor.

Governor Bush succeeded in 1995 because he set limited goals for himself and communicated regularly with legislators. Bush targeted policy areas already high on the official policy agenda because of media attention, the efforts of interest groups, and the recent election campaign. He staked out policy positions on the issues that already enjoyed a good deal of support in the legislature and were popular with the electorate. Bush and his staff communicated directly with individual members of the House and Senate, and the governor spoke regularly with Speaker of the House Pete Laney and Lieutenant Governor Bob Bullock.

In 1997, Governor Bush used his political skills to survive the defeat of his primary legislative goal and emerge from the session with his reputation as a leader intact. At the beginning of the session, Bush proposed a sweeping reform of the state's tax system. The governor asked the legislature to reduce local school property taxes by $6 billion over the next two years and replace the lost revenues by broadening the sales tax base and increasing taxes on business. The Texas House passed a modified version of Bush's plan, but it died in the Texas Senate. Ironically, the main opposition to Bush's proposal came from Republican legislators who did not want to go on record voting in favor of a tax increase on business. Instead of accepting defeat, Governor Bush scaled back his goals and asked for a $1 billion property tax cut to be funded out of a budget surplus left over from the previous budget cycle. The legislature agreed and the governor declared victory, even though the final product was considerably less than what he had initially requested.

The chief goals of Governor Bush in the 1999 session of the legislature were to pass a tax cut bill and avoid controversies that could damage his planned campaign for the presidency. The legislature passed a tax cut, enabling Bush to run for the White House as a governor who signed tax cut legislation in two consecutive legislative sessions. Bush also succeeded in avoiding controversy by persuading the Texas Senate to kill **hate crimes legislation,** which is a legislative measure that increases penalties for persons convicted of criminal offenses motivated by prejudice based on race, religion, national origin, gender, or sexual orientation. On one hand, Bush did not want to sign the measure because of the opposition of conservative Republicans who disagreed with the concept of hate crimes legislation in general and opposed the inclusion of sexual orientation in particular. On the other hand, Bush did not want to veto the hate crimes bill because Democrats would use the veto against him in his presidential campaign. Texas was the site of several well-publicized hate crimes, and a veto would have made Bush appear insensitive to the concerns of minority populations.

Governor Perry's relationship with the Texas legislature has contrasted sharply with that of his predecessor. In 2007, for example, Perry announced a set of priorities at the beginning of the 80th legislative session. The governor asked the legislature to sell the Texas Lottery to private investors and use the proceeds to create endowments to fund cancer research and public education. He proposed a 5 percent cap on property tax appraisal growth and called on the legislature to reduce property taxes by $2.5 billion. He asked the legislature for additional money for border security. Perry also demanded that the legislature change the way it funds higher education by breaking out spending into more detailed line items.[25] The change would make spending priorities more transparent to the public, but it would also make it easier for the governor to veto individual line items.

Hate crimes legislation
Legislative measures that increase penalties for persons convicted of criminal offenses motivated by prejudice based on race, religion, national origin, gender, or sexual orientation.

The legislature enacted relatively few of the governor's priorities. Although the legislature increased funding for border security and proposed a constitutional amendment to create a cancer research fund, it took no action on the governor's proposal to sell the lottery. The legislature failed to pass a cap on property tax appraisal growth and refused to enact the proposed property tax cut, preferring instead to save surplus cash to fund property tax reductions already enacted. The legislature refused to change the way it funds higher education. It also overturned the governor's order to require HPV vaccinations for Texas schoolgirls and adopted a partial moratorium on toll road construction, another of the governor's priority initiatives.

Governor Perry was in a weaker position in 2007 than Governor Bush had been during his tenure in office. Whereas Bush was widely regarded as an up-and-coming political figure, perhaps even a future president, Perry was seen as a politician in decline. Perry won reelection in 2006 with less than 40 percent of the vote against a multicandidate field, and speculation was already building as to potential candidates for governor in 2010. Many observers believed that Lieutenant Governor Dewhurst had his eye on the office and would thus have little incentive to help Perry enact his agenda.

Governor Perry was also less skilled in dealing with the legislature than his predecessor. Perry failed to establish personal relationships with individual legislators, as Bush had done. By and large, Perry ignored the legislative process until bills reached his desk. Consequently, the governor had little influence on the details of legislation. Furthermore, Perry's numerous vetoes angered legislators and other officials who were blindsided by the governor's opposition. When the legislature failed to change the way it funds higher education, Governor Perry responded by vetoing hundreds of millions of dollars in line-item funding for colleges and universities. Community colleges were the biggest losers. Perry knocked out more than $150 million the legislature had appropriated to pay health insurance benefits for community college employees, an expenditure that is mandated by state law. In his veto message, Perry accused community colleges of falsifying their budget requests in order to increase their appropriation. Community college leaders and legislators were caught completely by surprise by the governor's action and outraged by the accusation for which the governor provided no proof. The action left community colleges scrambling to close a substantial funding gap, by cutting programs, raising local taxes, or increasing student tuition.[26]

The Governor of Texas and the Policymaking Process

Theodore Roosevelt once said that the presidency was a "bully pulpit." By that phrase, he meant that the office provided its occupants with an excellent platform for making their views widely known. In today's age of modern communications, the phrase "big microphone" might be a more appropriate metaphor.

Similar to the president, the governor is well positioned to influence the official policy agenda. Texas governors are required by the state constitution to make recommendations to the legislature and are empowered to call the legislature into special session for the sole purpose of considering gubernatorial proposals. The governor is the most visible public official in the state and today's mass media provide the governor ample opportunity to get messages across to the people.

The governor's powers to affect policy formulation and adoption are considerable as well. The governor presents a budget to the legislature and may offer policy initiatives on any subject. As the legislature debates policy proposals, the governor can be an effective lobbyist. The governor's veto power, especially the item veto for appropriation measures, puts the governor in a powerful position to bargain on behalf of his or her program. At the very least, the veto virtually ensures that the governor can defeat legislation he or she opposes.

The governor is weakest in the areas of policy implementation and evaluation. In Texas, public policies are implemented by departments headed by elected executives or appointed boards, all of which are largely independent of direct gubernatorial control. Although the state constitution calls the governor the state's "chief executive," it offers the governor little power to fulfill that role. Furthermore, the governor has no formal mechanism for policy evaluation. Instead, the governor must rely on policy analyses conducted by others, including legislative committees, the LBB, the comptroller, the Sunset Advisory Commission, and the press.

Although scholars have frequently described the office of governor of Texas as politically weak, the governor has sufficient power to play an important policy-making role. Governors who set realistic policy goals can often achieve them if they are willing to use the resources at their disposal. Governor Bush demonstrated that a politically skillful governor could have influence on at least a range of policy issues. The governor lacks the official powers to coordinate policy implementation effectively, but he or she has ample tools to be a successful leader in agenda setting, policy formulation, and policy adoption.

THE EXECUTIVE BUREAUCRACY

The executive bureaucracy of Texas government includes more than 150 boards, agencies, offices, departments, committees, councils, and commissions. Some parts of the bureaucracy, such as the Office of the Attorney General and the Railroad Commission, are constitutionally established. The legislature and the governor have created the rest of the state bureaucracy through the legislative process. The executive branch of state government employs 358,400 people.[27]

The executive bureaucracy in Texas is decentralized. No one official is in charge of the entire structure. Agencies directed by elected executives or elected boards are virtually independent of direction by the governor or other state officials. They respond to the voters, not other officials. Agencies directed by appointed boards operate with a good deal of autonomy as well.

Jacksonian democracy
The philosophy (associated with President Andrew Jackson) that the right to vote should be extended to all adult male citizens and that all government offices of any importance should be filled by election.

Bureaucratic fragmentation in Texas is a legacy of Jacksonian democracy and the post-Reconstruction distrust of central authority. **Jacksonian democracy** is the view (associated with President Andrew Jackson) that the right to vote should be extended to all adult male citizens and that all government offices of any importance should be filled by election. The influence of Jacksonian democracy in the South led to the creation of the plural executive, in which state executive power was divided among several elected executive branch officials. The framers of the Texas Constitution distrusted central control of government because of their experience with it during Reconstruction. They created a decentralized executive branch to guard against the excessive concentration of power in any one person or department.

Elected Executive Officials

In addition to the governor, voters elect five other state executive officials: the lieutenant governor, attorney general, comptroller of public accounts, commissioner of agriculture, and commissioner of the General Land Office. These officials are elected simultaneously with the governor to serve four-year terms. Only four states elect more executive officials than Texas. Every state elects a governor, and a majority of states also elect an attorney general, a lieutenant governor, and a treasurer. Only about a fourth of the states elect agriculture commissioners or comptrollers and only a tenth elect land commissioners.[28]

Lieutenant Governor   The lieutenant governor is first in line of succession to the governor's office, should the governor die, resign, or be removed from office. When Governor George W. Bush resigned to become president, Lieutenant Governor Perry moved up to the office of governor. The lieutenant governor also becomes temporary governor whenever the governor is absent from the state. In practice, the foremost responsibilities of the office lie in the state Senate, where the lieutenant governor presides, votes in case of a tie, appoints members of standing and conference committees, helps determine the order of business on the floor, and enforces Senate rules. In addition, the lieutenant governor is a member of several boards and councils, including the LBB and the Legislative Redistricting Board. The **Legislative Redistricting Board (LRB)** is an agency composed of the speaker, lieutenant governor, comptroller, land commissioner, and attorney general; it is responsible for redrawing the boundaries of Texas House and Texas Senate seats when the legislature is unable to agree on a redistricting plan. These responsibilities make the lieutenant governor one of the most visible and important figures in state government. When the legislature is in town, the lieutenant governor is arguably the most powerful official in the state, more powerful even than the governor.

Legislative Redistricting Board (LRB)
An agency composed of the speaker, lieutenant governor, comptroller, land commissioner, and attorney general that draws the boundaries of Texas House and Senate seats when the legislature is unable to agree on a redistricting plan.

 WHAT IS YOUR OPINION?

Who is more powerful, the governor or lieutenant governor?

Attorney General   Sometimes candidates for attorney general broadcast political advertisements touting their law-and-order credentials and their determination to get tough on crime. Although these kinds of campaign pitches may be politically effective, they are factually misleading. Other than representing Texas in lawsuits challenging the constitutionality of state criminal laws, the attorney general has relatively little to do with fighting crime. That job is primarily the responsibility of city and county law enforcement agencies and county district attorneys.

The attorney general is the state's lawyer, representing state government and its various components in court. In recent years, the attorney general's office has defended the state in federal court against lawsuits over bilingual education, prison overcrowding, the death penalty, and congressional redistricting. The attorney general has broad authority to initiate legal action on behalf of the state. In the late 1990s, for example, Texas Attorney General Dan Morales filed a lawsuit against the tobacco industry to recover the cost of smoking-related illnesses covered by the Medicaid program. Before the case could go to trial, the tobacco industry and the attorney general agreed on a $17.3 billion settlement to be paid out over the next 25 years. The industry also agreed to remove all tobacco billboards in Texas, as well as tobacco advertising on buses, bus stops, taxis, and taxi stands.[29]

The attorney general gives legal advice to state and local officials and agencies in the form of opinions. An **attorney general's opinion** is a written interpretation of existing law. The attorney general issues opinions in response to a written request from certain state officials who are authorized by law to ask for an opinion. In 2007, for example, Attorney General Gregg Abbott responded to a request from State Senator Jane Nelson (R., Lewisville) by issuing an opinion holding that cities can legally pass ordinances prohibiting registered sex offenders from living near schools, parks, or other locations where children typically congregate. State law requires sex offenders to register with authorities but it does not limit where they can live.[30] An attorney general's opinion is not binding on the court system, but in the absence of a court ruling it stands as the highest existing interpretation of law or the Texas Constitution.

Comptroller of Public Accounts   The comptroller is the state's chief tax administrator and accountant. The comptroller monitors compliance with state tax laws and collects taxes on behalf of the state. Texans who operate retail businesses work closely with the

Attorney general's opinion
A written interpretation of existing law.

Attorney General Abbott issued an opinion holding that cities can legally pass ordinances prohibiting registered sex offenders from living near schools, parks, or other locations where children typically congregate.

comptroller's office to collect the state sales tax from their customers and remit tax receipts to the state. If a retailer fails to pass along sales tax receipts to the state, the comptroller has the power to shut it down and sell off its assets to pay back taxes.

The comptroller is also the state's banker, receiving funds, assuming responsibility for their safekeeping, and paying the state's bills. When tax revenues flow in more rapidly than the state expends funds, the comptroller deposits the money in interest-bearing accounts to generate additional revenue for the state. When the rate of revenue collection lags behind the rate of expenditure, the comptroller borrows money on a short-term basis to ensure that the state will have enough cash on hand to pay its bills.

The comptroller's most publicized task involves the state budget. The Texas Constitution requires the comptroller to estimate state revenues for the next biennium at the beginning of each legislative session. The comptroller may update the revenue estimate during a session to take account of revisions in state tax laws and changing economic conditions. The constitution specifies that no appropriation bill may become law without the comptroller's certification that it falls within the revenue estimate unless the legislature votes by a four-fifths margin to adopt an unbalanced budget.

Commissioner of Agriculture   The commissioner of agriculture administers all statutes relating to agriculture and enforces the state's weights and measures law. The agency inspects and regulates a variety of items, including seeds, gasoline pumps, meat market scales, flower and plant nurseries, and the use of pesticides. The commissioner of agriculture promotes the sale of Texas agricultural products. The agency also administers the **school lunch program,** which is a federal program that provides free or reduced-cost lunches to children from poor families.

School lunch program
A federal program that provides free or reduced-cost lunches to children from poor families.

Commissioner of the General Land Office   The treaty of annexation that added Texas to the Union in 1845 allowed the Lone Star State to retain its state lands. Although much of that land was eventually sold, the state still owns at least the mineral rights on more than 20 million acres. The land commissioner is responsible for managing the land, leasing it for mineral exploration and production and for agricultural purposes. In 2006, state lands generated $860 million, more than 1 percent of total state revenue.[31] That money goes into the **Permanent School Fund (PSF),** which is a fund established in the Texas Constitution as an endowment to finance public elementary and secondary education. The Texas Board of Education invests the money in the PSF to generate investment income known as the Available School Fund (ASF), which is distributed annually to Texas school districts on a per-student basis under laws passed by the legislature. The land commissioner also manages the Veterans' Land Program, which provides low-interest loans to the state's military veterans to purchase land.

Permanent School Fund (PSF)
A fund established in the Texas Constitution as an endowment to finance public elementary and secondary education.

Appointed Executives

One measure of a governor's power over administration is the number of officials he or she can appoint. In Texas, the most important executive officials are elected, leaving only a handful of executive positions to be filled by the governor, subject, of course, to two-thirds' Senate confirmation. The most significant of these officials is the Texas secretary of state, who is the state's chief election officer, responsible for the uniform application, implementation, and interpretation of election laws. On election night, the office of the secretary of state gathers election returns from around the state, compiles them, and releases running vote totals to the press. Later, the office tabulates and releases final, official returns. In addition to its electoral responsibilities, the secretary of state's office serves as a depository of various agreements, reports, and records of state agencies. The governor also appoints the head of the Texas Education Agency (TEA), the executive commissioner of the Texas Health and Human Services Commission, and the adjutant general (who heads the Texas National Guard).

INTERNET RESEARCH   Profile of a State Agency

Your assignment is to research an agency of state government. The agency assigned to you depends on the last digit of your Social Security number. If, for example, your Social Security number is 346-70-1379, your assignment is number 9:

0. Racing Commission
1. Department of Parks and Wildlife
2. Board of Pardons and Paroles
3. Commission on Environmental Quality
4. Department of Public Safety
5. Department of Insurance
6. Department of Criminal Justice
7. Alcoholic Beverage Commission
8. Funeral Service Commission
9. State Board of Athletic Trainers

You can find out a good deal about the agency online. Begin your research at the following website: **www2 .tsl.state.tx.us/trail/agencies.jsp**

Once you have read about the agency and reviewed its homepage, answer the following questions:

1. Your textbook classifies state agencies. In which category would you place the agency you have been assigned?

2. What is the title of the person (or persons) who heads the agency? What is that person's name?

3. How is the head of the agency chosen? Does the agency head serve a fixed term?

4. What does the agency do? (Answer in your own words. Do not copy the agency's mission statement.)

5. What (if any) are the major administrative units of the agency?

6. What current issues or events are affecting the agency?

7. What power does the legislature have to influence the operation of the agency?

8. What power does the governor have to influence the operation of the agency?

9. Give an example of an interest group that would be concerned with the activities of the agency.

10. How do the activities of this agency affect ordinary citizens?

Elected Boards and Commissions

The Railroad Commission and the State Board of Education (SBOE) are executive agencies headed by elected boards.

The Railroad Commission   The Texas Railroad Commission was originally established to enforce state laws concerning railroads. Today, the Railroad Commission regulates the Texas oil and gas industry, gas utilities, pipeline safety, the surface mining of coal, and safety in the liquefied petroleum gas industry. Ironically, the Railroad Commission no longer regulates railroads, which are now under the jurisdiction of the Texas Department of Transportation. The Railroad Commission is composed of three members elected for six-year overlapping terms. In practice, most commission members initially assume office through gubernatorial appointment. When a commission member resigns before the end of a six-year term, the governor names a replacement subject to a two-thirds' confirmation vote by the Texas Senate. Appointed railroad commissioners must face the voters at the next general election, but their initial appointment gives them a significant advantage in name recognition and fundraising capability.

The Railroad Commission's regulatory policies fall into three broad categories. First, the commission is a conservation agency. To prevent the waste of natural resources, the commission establishes what is called an allowable for each oil and gas well in the state. The **allowable** is the maximum permissible rate of production for oil and gas wells in Texas as set by the Railroad Commission. This rate, which is determined by technical engineering and geological considerations, maximizes current production without jeopardizing long-term output. The Railroad Commission also regulates the drilling, storage, and pipeline transmission of oil and gas to protect the natural environment.

Second, the commission historically has prorated oil production to conform to market demand. Every month, the commission establishes a percentage of allowable that each well may produce. For example, if a well's allowable were 100 barrels a day and the commission prorated production to 80 percent of allowable, the well could pump only 80 barrels a day for that month. From the 1930s to the 1970s, the Railroad Commission used this method to limit the supply of oil to an amount sufficient to fill market demand *at the current price.* If a new oilfield came on line, the commission prevented oversupply by reducing the percentage allowable for wells across Texas. Because Texas oil was such a big proportion of the national and world oil supply, the commission effectively controlled oil supplies and, consequently, oil prices worldwide. Since the early 1970s, the worldwide demand for petroleum has been so great that the Railroad Commission no longer prorates oil production below the 100 percent allowable.

Third, the Railroad Commission has protected the rights of producers and royalty owners, particularly smaller operators. In the early years, the commission established rules on well spacing, transportation, and oil production quotas that generally benefited small producers at the expense of major oil companies. More recently, however, hostile court decisions and personnel changes have led the commission to adopt more evenhanded rules.[32]

Allowable
The maximum permissible rate of production for oil and gas wells in Texas as set by the Railroad Commission.

The Railroad Commission regulates the Texas oil industry.

State Board of Education (SBOE)   The SBOE coordinates education activities and services below the college level. A 15-member elected board heads the agency. Each member of the board runs for election from a district to serve a four-year term. The terms of the board members are staggered, with roughly half the members facing the voters each general election year. The SBOE oversees the investment of the money in the Permanent School Fund to generate income for the Available School Fund. It sets standards for teacher certification and school accreditation. The SBOE also approves curricula and selects textbooks for use in the state's public schools.

The textbook approval process has been the board's most publicized and controversial activity. For years, conservative political activists dominated the textbook selection process by attacking books for what they considered to be threats to traditional family values. The SBOE once required that high school biology texts carry a disclaimer that evolution was just a theory and told publishers to delete all references to venereal disease in textbooks for junior high school students.

In 1995, the legislature passed and Governor Bush signed legislation to limit the ability of the SBOE to order textbooks rewritten to reflect political values. The measure restricted SBOE oversight to ensuring that textbooks cover at least 50 percent of the state's curriculum standards, contain no factual errors, and meet physical manufacturing specifications. Textbooks that satisfied these minimum standards would be available for possible adoption by local school districts.

Nonetheless, the battle over textbooks has not subsided. Conservative groups, such as the Texas Public Policy Foundation, argue that the inclusion of political bias or the omission of certain information in a textbook constitutes factual inaccuracy. They also base their textbook critiques on a provision in the Texas Education Code that declares that texts should "present positive aspects of the United States and its heritage." In the face of the conservative criticism, publishing companies have rewritten textbooks to tone down references to pollution, equivocate about the threat of global warming, avoid discussions of sexuality, limit references to evolution, and remove critical discussions of American society.[33] Liberal groups, such as the Texas Freedom Network, worry that self-censorship by publishers trying to meet conservative objections and satisfy the SBOE will impact the quality of education not just in Texas but nationwide. Because Texas represents a substantial share of the national textbook market, publishers sell textbooks developed for the Texas market nationwide.

 WHAT IS YOUR OPINION?

Should textbooks reflect the political values of a majority of Texans?

Appointed Commissions

Appointed commissions comprise a substantial part of the executive branch of state government. An unpaid board of 3, 6, 9, or 18 members heads most of the commissions (which may also be called a department, a board, a council, or an authority). The governor appoints board members with two-thirds' Senate approval to serve fixed, overlapping terms of six years. Boards meet periodically to set policy. An executive director, who is either appointed by the governor or hired by the board, depending on the agency, manages the professional staff, which does the day-to-day work of the agency. The nine-member board of the Texas Department of Parks and Wildlife, for example, hires an executive director who heads a professional staff that carries out the work of the agency.

Agencies perform such a wide variety of functions that they are a challenge to classify. Nonetheless, it is possible to group many of the agencies by form or function.

Administrative Departments   The executive branch of Texas government includes a number of administrative departments, which are responsible for implementing policy and carrying out basic state functions. The Texas Department of Criminal Justice operates the state prison system. The General Land Office manages state lands. The Texas Department of Agriculture implements state agricultural policy. The Lottery Commission operates the state lottery. The Texas Department of Transportation is responsible for the financing, construction, regulation, and use of highways, rail stations, airports, and other facilities of public transportation. Other state administrative departments include Parks and Wildlife, Health Services, and Public Safety.

College and University Boards   Appointed boards of regents oversee each of the state's public colleges and university systems. University boards consist of nine members appointed by the governor with Senate concurrence to serve overlapping six-year terms. University regents are considered prestige appointments, eagerly sought by well-to-do alumni and often awarded to the governor's major financial backers during the last election campaign. The members of the board of regents of the University of Texas and the Texas A&M University systems in particular read like a "Who's Who" of major political supporters of recent governors. For example, Texas Tech University regent Larry Anders has contributed more than $220,000 to Governor Perry's political campaigns. Other major Perry contributors who were appointed to university boards include University of Texas regent Robert Rowling ($207,000) and Texas A&M regent Erle Nye ($131,000).[34] In general, the board of regents sets basic university policy while leaving daily management to professional administrators on campus.

Licensing Boards   A number of boards and commissions are responsible for licensing and regulating various professions. Some of these include the Department of Licensing and Regulation, Advisory Board of Athletic Trainers, Board of Chiropractic Examiners, Polygraph Examiners Board, and Funeral Service Commission. State law generally requires that licensing boards include members of the professions they are charged with regulating, as well as lay members. The Funeral Service Commission, for example, includes morticians and cemetery owners.

Regulatory Boards   Other state agencies regulate various areas of business and industry. The Public Utility Commission (PUC) regulates telephone and electric utilities. The Texas Department of Insurance (TDI) licenses and regulates insurance companies. The Finance Commission regulates banks and savings and loan institutions. The Texas Alcoholic Beverage Commission regulates the manufacture, transportation, and sale of alcoholic beverages in the state. The Texas Racing Commission oversees horse and dog racing.

Rules
Legally binding regulations adopted by a regulatory agency.

State regulatory agencies make **rules,** which are legally binding regulations adopted by a regulatory agency. Whenever the PUC sets telephone rates, for example, it does so through **rulemaking,** which is a regulatory process used by government agencies to enact legally binding regulations. In Texas, the formal rulemaking process has several steps. When a board or commission considers the adoption of a rule, it must first publish the text of that rule in the *Texas Register*. Interested parties may then file comments on the rule. State law requires regulatory agencies to hold public hearings if as many as 25 people request one. After a hearing (if one is held), the board votes to adopt or reject the proposed rule. If the rule is adopted, it goes into effect no sooner than 20 days after the agency files two certified copies with the Texas secretary of state.

Rulemaking
A regulatory process used by government agencies to enact legally binding regulations.

The rulemaking process in Texas often involves only a minimal amount of public input. Although some regulatory agency actions, such as the adoption of new telephone rates, receive a great deal of media attention, most rulemaking decisions escape notice of all but those parties most directly involved with the particular

NATIONAL PERSPECTIVE

California Addresses Global Warming

California has taken the lead in the effort to address **global warming,** which is the gradual warming of the Earth's atmosphere reportedly caused by the burning of fossil fuels and industrial pollutants. In 2006, the California legislature passed, and Governor Arnold Schwarzenegger signed, legislation to reduce carbon dioxide emissions by 25 percent by 2020. The measure included incentives for alternative energy production and penalties for companies that failed to meet the standard. The legislation calling for a reduction in carbon dioxide emissions was only the most recent attempt by the state to control harmful emissions. California has adopted legislation requiring automobile manufacturers to reduce automobile tailpipe emissions and to mandate that 20 percent of energy sold in the state come from renewable sources, such as wind and geothermal. The state also requires that homebuilders offer buyers the option to have roofs with tiles that convert sunlight into energy.

California political leaders decided to take action to curb greenhouse gas emissions because the federal government has failed to respond to the problem. California is so big that it produces 2.5 percent of the world's total emissions of carbon dioxide. Among the 50 states, only Texas produces more. The California economy is so large that energy companies, automobile manufacturers, appliance manufacturers, and others cannot afford to ignore the California requirements.[*] Furthermore, California officials hoped that other states would follow California's lead and some have done just that. A number of states have adopted energy efficiency requirements for lightbulbs and household appliances. Seven states have also agreed on a regional plan to restrict power plant emissions.[†]

Nonetheless, critics warn that the state is taking a huge gamble that it can cut emissions without wrecking the state's economy. Because of the new regulations, California consumers may well have to pay more for energy than consumers in other states and they may face an energy shortage. The new regulations may also place California companies at a competitive disadvantage against firms based in other states without similar environmental regulations.[‡]

QUESTIONS TO CONSIDER

1. Are you worried about the impact of global warming in your lifetime?
2. Would you be willing to pay more for energy in order to curb emissions that cause global warming?
3. Do you think Texas will follow California's lead on the issue of global warming?

[*]Jad Mouadwad and Jeremy W. Peters, "California Plan to Cut Gases Splits Industry," *New York Times,* September 1, 2006, available at www.nytimes.com.

[†]Justin Blum, "Stepping In Where Uncle Sam Refuses to Tread," *Washington Post National Weekly Edition,* January 30–February 5, 2006, p. 18.

[‡]Felicity Barringer, "In Gamble, California Tries to Curb Greenhouse Gases," *New York Times,* September 15, 2006, available at www.nytimes.com.

Global warming
The gradual warming of the Earth's atmosphere reportedly caused by the burning of fossil fuels and industrial pollutants.

agency's action. In practice, most proposed rules generate little comment and public hearings are rare.[35]

Agencies have no inherent constitutional power to make rules. Instead, the legislature delegates authority to agencies to make regulations to implement legislative policy. If the legislature is unhappy with an agency's actions, it can enact legislation to restrict or even eliminate the agency's rulemaking authority.

Social Service Agencies   The legislature has created a number of agencies to facilitate the receipt of federal funds and promote the interests of particular groups in society. The Governor's Committee on People with Disabilities advises state government on disability issues. Other social service agencies include the Texas Department on Aging and Disability Services, Diabetes Council, Council for Developmental Disabilities, and Cancer Council. Appointed boards head social service agencies. Board members are appointed by the governor pending Senate confirmation to serve fixed terms.

Promotional and Preservation Agencies Several state agencies are charged with either promoting economic development or preserving the state's historical heritage. The Texas Film Commission seeks to attract major motion picture and video production to the state. The Texas Historical Commission works to preserve the state's architectural, archeological, and cultural landmarks.

Privatization

Privatization
The process that involves the government contracting with private business to implement government programs.

Not all public services are delivered by state agencies. Texas is a national leader in **privatization,** which is the process that involves the government contracting with private business to implement government programs. Thousands of the state's prison inmates are housed in private correction facilities rather than state prisons. Private agencies manage the state's foster care system. Furthermore, Texans traveling from Brownsville in far South Texas to the Oklahoma border may eventually have the opportunity to drive the Trans-Texas Corridor, a privately built highway, rail, and pipeline corridor financed by tolls rather than tax money.[36]

Privatization is controversial. The advocates of privatization believe that it saves taxpayers money because private companies operate more efficiently than government bureaucracies. Privatization also enables the government to gear up or gear down rapidly because private companies do not have to deal with government personnel policies that make it difficult to hire and fire workers. In contrast, the critics of privatization argue that private companies may cut corners at the expense of public service because they are less interested in serving the public than they are in making a profit. They also worry that elected officials may award contracts to campaign contributors and political cronies rather than to the companies best qualified to deliver government services.

The state's effort to privatize some aspects of the welfare programs administered by the Texas Health and Human Services Commission (HHSC) has stumbled. In 2003, the Texas legislature decided that the state could save hundreds of millions of dollars by outsourcing most of the customer service functions of the HHSC. Instead of going to a welfare office to meet in person with a case worker, needy Texans would contact a call center to sign up for Medicaid, Food Stamps, the Children's Health Insurance Program (CHIP), and other programs. In theory, privatization would save money by allowing the state to close hundreds of government offices, lay off thousands of state workers, and replace them with four call centers staffed by lower-paid, privately employed workers hired by the Texas Access Alliance. In practice, the privatization effort was a disaster. Calls were dropped, applications were lost, technology malfunctioned, and thousands of people who qualified for benefits were turned away. The state canceled the contract in 2007 and began hiring state workers to staff the call centers. Instead of saving money, the privatization effort will cost the state more than $30 million as it tries to pick up the pieces and fix the problems caused by the failed experiment.[37] Despite the setback, the state has not given up on privatization. It has hired another company, Maximus, to handle operation of the call centers.

ADMINISTRATIVE OVERSIGHT

State agencies mostly run themselves with relatively little oversight from the legislature or the governor. Agencies headed by elected executives or commissions are almost immune from legislative or gubernatorial control. The legislature determines their budget and can change the laws under which they operate, but they are generally free to set policy with no obligation to coordinate their activities with the governor or other agencies. The ballot box provides some accountability. Because the elected officials who head the agencies must periodically face the voters, they have an incentive to ensure that the agencies they head avoid scandal and at least appear to be well run.

The agencies led by appointed boards and commissions are even more independent than agencies headed by elected executives. The multimember boards that typically head these agencies are composed of laypeople selected on the basis of their political ties to the governor rather than their policy expertise. They meet several times a year for a few hours to set basic policy for the agency. In practice, boards typically defer to the leadership of the professional staff.

The legislature and the governor struggle to oversee the state bureaucracy.

Legislative Oversight

In theory, the legislature has ultimate authority over most administrative agencies. It can restructure or eliminate a state agency if it chooses or adopt legislation directing an agency to take or refrain from taking particular actions. In practice, however, the legislature sometimes struggles to exert control because of its brief, infrequent sessions. Consequently, the legislature has adopted a number of procedures to provide ongoing oversight and administrative control, including sunset review, committee oversight, and LBB supervision.

Sunset review is the periodic evaluation of state agencies by the legislature to determine whether they should be reauthorized. Approximately 130 state agencies are subject to sunset review. Each agency undergoes sunset review every 12 years, with 20 to 30 agencies facing review each legislative session. The list of state agencies facing sunset review in 2009 includes the Texas Department of Agriculture, Credit Union Commission, Texas Department of Insurance, Texas Department of Parks and Wildlife, Polygraph Examiners Board, Texas Department of Public Safety, and Texas Racing Commission.[38]

The sunset review process involves the agency facing review, the Sunset Advisory Commission, the legislature, and, to a lesser degree, the governor. The Sunset Advisory Commission includes five members of the House, five members of the Senate, and two citizens. The Speaker of the House appoints the House members and one citizen representative, whereas the lieutenant governor names the state senators and the other citizen representative.

Sunset review
The periodic evaluation of state agencies by the legislature to determine whether they should be reauthorized.

Both the agency under review and the staff of the Sunset Advisory Commission evaluate the agency's operation and performance. The agency conducts a self-study while the Commission staff prepares an independent evaluation. Commission members review the two documents and hold hearings at which agency officials, interest-group spokespersons, and interested parties present testimony. After the hearings are complete, the commission recommends whether the agency should be kept as it is, reformed, or abolished. These steps take place before the legislature meets in regular session.

Once the legislative session convenes, lawmakers consider the Sunset Advisory Commission's recommendations and decide the agency's fate. The key feature of the process is that the legislature must reauthorize each agency under review. The reauthorization legislation then goes to the governor for signature or veto. If the legislature fails to act or the governor vetoes the reauthorization measure, the agency dies: The sun sets on it. Since the legislature began the sunset process in 1979, it has eliminated 52 agencies and consolidated 12 others.[39] In practice, the legislature reauthorizes most state agencies while mandating reforms in their procedures. The legislature has added public representation to governing boards, provided for more public input into agency decision making, imposed conflict-of-interest restrictions on board members, and mandated closer legislative review of agency expenditures.

In addition to the sunset process, the legislature uses the committee system and the Legislative Budget Board (LBB) to oversee the executive bureaucracy. During legislative sessions, standing committees may evaluate agency operations and hold hearings to investigate agency performance. Interim committees may oversee agency operations between sessions. An **interim committee** is a committee that is established to study a particular policy issue between legislative sessions. The LBB influences agency operations through its role in budget execution. Between legislative sessions, the LBB may propose moving funds from one budget category to another, pending the governor's approval. In practice, budget execution authority gives the LBB power to act as a board of directors for the state bureaucracy. The LBB sets goals for agencies, reviews whether the goals are met, and fine-tunes the budget between legislative sessions to reward (or punish) agencies based on their support of LBB goals.

Interim committee
A committee established to study a particular policy issue between legislative sessions, such as higher education or public school finance.

Gubernatorial Oversight

The legal/constitutional powers of the governor of Texas for influencing administrative policymaking are relatively weak. Although the line-item veto (and the threat of its use) can be an effective weapon at times, the governor's powers over administration are otherwise limited. The heads of a number of state agencies are independently elected and thus immune from direct gubernatorial control. The governor appoints the members of most state boards but, because members serve fixed, multiyear terms, a new governor does not usually get to name a majority of the members of any particular agency for several years. Furthermore, board members are not legally obliged to consult with the governor on policy matters or necessarily follow the governor's lead.

Barbers and barbershops are regulated by the Texas Department of Licensing and Regulation.

Over time, a governor can influence the administrative bureaucracy through the appointment process. A governor can shape an agency's policy perspectives by appointing men and women to agency boards who share a particular point of view. Governor Bush and Governor Perry both tended to name business-oriented conservatives to serve on most boards, especially boards that directly impact business interests. For example, Governor Perry appointed businessman John R. Krugh, a senior vice president with Perry Homes, one of the state's largest homebuilders, to serve on the Residential Construction Commission. The legislature created the commission to develop home-building performance standards and establish a dispute resolution process that disgruntled purchasers would have to complete before they could file a lawsuit. Bob Perry, the chief executive officer of Perry Homes (and no relation to the governor), is Rick Perry's most generous campaign contributor.[40]

CONCLUSION: THE EXECUTIVE BRANCH AND THE POLICYMAKING PROCESS

The governor and the various agencies and departments of the executive branch of Texas government play an important role in the policy process.

Agenda Building

Executive branch officials help set the policy agenda. The governor enjoys the public visibility to focus public attention on an issue. Governor Perry increased awareness of the danger of cervical cancer when he issued the executive order requiring HPV vaccinations for schoolgirls. Other executive officials can take action that put items on the official policy agenda as well. Attorney General Morales's lawsuit against the tobacco industry pushed the issue of industry liability for state health costs to the forefront of the policy agenda.

Policy Formulation and Adoption

The officials and departments of the executive branch participate in policy formulation. Executive branch officials and their staffs testify before legislative committees and advise individual legislators on how best to address policy problems. Furthermore, the governor and other state executives participate in policy formulation by supporting one particular policy approach over alternatives. In 2007, for example, Governor Perry asked the legislature to use part of the budget surplus to provide additional property tax relief rather than save the money or use it to fund public services.

The executive branch plays a key role in policy adoption. The comptroller limits government spending by providing the legislature with an official estimate of state revenues. The governor may sign, veto, or allow measures passed by the legislature to become law without signature. A number of state agencies also adopt policy through the rulemaking process. The Railroad Commission, for example, makes state energy policy. The Texas Department of Transportation sets transportation policy.

Policy Implementation and Evaluation

Executive branch agencies and departments implement policy. The comptroller's office collects taxes. The Department of Agriculture enforces state laws dealing with agriculture. The Texas Department of Parks and Wildlife carries out state policy concerning game laws, conservation, and parks management. The Texas Commission on Environmental Quality implements the state's environmental laws.

Finally, the executive branch evaluates policy. State agencies, departments, and bureaus regularly compile data on the operation of state programs and occasionally conduct formal evaluation reports. The comptroller, in particular, gathers data and conducts performance reviews of state agencies. Executive branch officials, legislators, political activists, and the media sometimes use the data and reports as feedback to promote new agendas and policy initiatives.

LET'S DEBATE

Should Texas Have a Cabinet System Rather Than the Plural Executive?

Overview: The current Texas executive is unique in that it was born out of the Texas Reconstruction and the controversial administration of Governor E. J. Davis (the majority of Texans believed that Davis usurped and abused his authority). The solution to executive abuse was determined at the Texas Constitutional Convention of 1875. The convention resulted in the creation of a weak governor position that must share significant authority with other executive offices. This created institutional competition that would act as a further check to any pretensions to power. The limited authority and diffuse power of the Texas executive branch mirror the state political culture's deep mistrust of political authority. The trajectory of history, however, has created a Texas political world in which the state is fully integrated into national politics and is integral to the national economy. Texas has developed a cosmopolitan and savvy political culture, and isn't it time the state's executive institutions reflect this culture?

Over the past 50 years, state governments have responded to calls to reform not only their legislative and electoral institutions but their executive institutions as well. Texas is no exception. Between 1972 and 1992, the 50 states reduced the number of elected executive officials from 772 to 446, a reduction of 42 percent. According to a report commissioned by Oklahoma, moving to a more unified executive institution allows for more efficient executive management of government and political institutions. A cabinet system is streamlined and responds better to the needs of the state, because there is "hands on" and personal coordination among the governor, cabinet officers, state agencies, and the two other branches of government. Critics say the fractured nature of plural executives weakens a governor's authority and slows down decision making, and this is considered an impediment to efficient execution of policy. A more efficient executive encourages better government and fosters accountability.

Proponents of the current system believe that although the Texas governor is relatively weak compared with other governors, he or she still exerts profound influence over the operation of the state government. Not only can the governor call special sessions when necessary, but also he or she has the authority to appoint the heads of important state agencies, such as the secretary of state and the Health and Human Services commissioner (who commands an annual budget of $19 billion). Through these appointments, the governor is able to place his or her stamp on policy initiatives and direct state political institutions. It is also argued that a plural executive fosters accountability by holding elected executives answerable to voters for any corruption or harmful policy enterprises. As these positions are elective, officials must heed the desires and maintain the well-being of the Texans who placed them in office.

Arguments for a Unified Executive with a Cabinet

❑ **The Texas plural executive encourages poor government.** Elected executive officials in Texas are generally protective of their jurisdictions, authority, and privileges. These officials are elected independently of the governor, and, since they are responsible to their bureaucratic constituencies, they result in regulations and policies that are fragmented and lack the coordination necessary to produce effective governance. A cabinet system will minimize friction when regulations and policies conflict by providing a unified executive environment.

❑ **The Texas plural executive conceals official accountability.** When most Texans seek accountability

in the executive, they naturally place blame on the most visible executive office—the governor. The governor may have little say in the policy of other executive offices, and executive officials may point to the activities of other offices to deflect blame for policy failures. Reducing the number of elected officials will make the governor solely accountable to Texans for the management of the state's executive branch.

❑ **The Texas plural executive lacks political cohesion.** Different executives pursue different political agendas. Each executive maintains his or her individual campaign and political machinery supported by a particular political base. This can also cause conflicting policy goals (especially when executives are from different parties). For example, Governor Rick Perry and Texas Comptroller of Public Accounts Carole

Strayhorn have engaged in pointed public debate regarding state and Republican policy and goals, such as school finance reform and tax policy. If elected officials cannot get along, how can there be cohesive political and policy objectives?

Arguments Against a Unified Executive with a Cabinet

❑ **The Texas plural executive prevents abuse of power in the executive.** A plural office prevents the consolidation of executive power in a single person. It is difficult to guarantee that the governor will always be a person of upright character with the best interests of the state in mind, and it is reasonable to assume that eventually (as has been the case in Texas history) a corrupt and self-seeking person will inhabit the office. The institution of the plural executive, through its diffusion of power, is a check on the abuse of executive authority.

❑ **The Texas plural executive provides increased accountability.** Many argue that a plural executive lessens executive accountability; however, the opposite may be true. By having a multiple executive, the electorate can vote out those whose performance or character is disagreeable: If one opposes an official's policies or dislikes his or her politics, voters are free to remove that official from office while retaining those executive officials whom they support. For example, in the election for Texas attorney general in 1998, the previous state attorney general, Dan Morales, did not run for reelection due to his ethically dubious activities. His questionable dealings as state attorney general were his and his alone, so the voters did not have to consider turning out the entire executive office as a result of Morales's untoward behavior.

❑ **The Texas plural executive increases executive expertise.** A multiple executive gives elected officials the capability to concentrate and gain expertise in one area of policy or governance. The attorney general can focus on the state's law enforcement institutions; the comptroller of public accounts can concentrate on tax collection. Not only do plural offices foster expertise, but also the diversity of offices facilitates policy innovation and experimentation due to the decentralized nature of the executive.

QUESTIONS

1. Does the Texas plural executive facilitate good government and prevent corruption? Why or why not?
2. What are the advantages of a unified cabinet executive? What are the disadvantages?

SELECT READINGS

1. Michael Lauderdale, *Reinventing Texas Government* (Austin: University of Texas Press, 1999).
2. Jameson W. Doig and Erwin Hargrove, eds., *Leadership and Innovation: Entrepreneurs in Government* (Baltimore, MD: The Johns Hopkins University Press, 1990).

SELECT WEBSITES

1. **www.governor.state.tx.us**
   Website of the Texas governor.
2. **www.statelocalgov.net/ state-tx.htm#Executive%20Branch**
   Web resource for the Texas executive and bureaucracy.

KEY TERMS

allowable	impeachment	plural executive
appropriation bill	interim committee	privatization
attorney general's opinion	Jacksonian democracy	reprieve
budget execution authority	Legislative Budget Board (LBB)	rulemaking
capital punishment	Legislative Redistricting Board (LRB)	rules
commutation		school lunch program
executive order	line-item veto	senatorial courtesy
global warming	pardon	sunset review
hate crimes legislation	Permanent School Fund (PSF)	veto

NOTES

1. Emily Ramshaw, "HPV Is Fueling a Familiar Fight," *Dallas Morning News*, February 18, 2007, available at www.dallasnews.com.

2. Quoted in Corrie MacLaggan, "Governor Requires HPV Vaccine for Sixth-Grade Girls," *Austin American-Statesman*, February 3, 2007, available at www.statesman.com.

3. Quoted in Corrie MacLaggan, "Perry's HPV Vaccine Order Draws Backlash from GOP," *Austin American-Statesman*, February 6, 2007, available at www.statesman.com.

4. Christy Hoppe, "Does Perry Really Have the Power?" *Dallas Morning News*, February 23, 2007, available at www.dallasnews.com.

5. Quoted in Christy Hoppe, "Legislature Defeats HPV Mandate, Perry," *Dallas Morning News*, May 9, 2007, available at www.dallasnews.com.

6. David M. Hedge, *Governance and the Changing American States* (Boulder, CO: Westview, 1998), p. 93.

7. Jack Keever, "Impeachment Winds Stir Memories of Ferguson," *Houston Post*, July 5, 1987, p. 8A.

8. "The Imperial Governor," *Texas Observer*, April 20, 2007, p. 3.

9. Susan A. MacManus, "Playing a New Game: Governors and the Job Training Partnership Act (JTPA)," *American Politics Quarterly* 14 (July 1986): 131–149.

10. Office of the Governor, "Bills Vetoed by Governor Perry, 80th Legislature," available at www.governor.state.tx.us.

11. David C. Saffell, *State and Local Government: Politics and Public Policies*, 4th ed. (New York: McGraw-Hill, 1990), p. 154.

12. Governor's Appointment Office, available at www.governor.state.tx.us.

13. Kelly Shannon, "27% of Perry Appointees are Minorities," *Houston Chronicle*, November 28, 2003, p. 1A.

14. Clay Robinson, "No Shortage of Blame for TYC's Woes," *Houston Chronicle*, March 5, 2007, available at www.chron.com.

15. "Profile of Appellate and Trial Judges," *Texas Judicial System Annual Report—Fiscal Year 2006*, available at www.courts.state.tx.us/publicinfo/.

16. Glen Abney and Thomas P. Lauth, "The Executive Budget in the States: Normative Idea and Empirical Observation," *Policy Studies Journal* 17 (Summer 1989): 829–862.

17. "Perry Signs Toyota Rail Legislation," *San Antonio Business Journal*, April 11, 2003, available at www.bizjournals.com/sanantonio.

18. Mike Ward, "A Quiet Revolution in Governor's Office," *Austin American-Statesman*, January 18, 2005, available at www.statesman.com.

19. Kelly Shannon, "Perry Says He's Not Overstepping His Bounds," *Bryan–College Station Eagle*, February 25, 2007, available at www.theeagle.com.

20. "You're Doing What?" *Fort Worth Star-Telegram*, August 24, 2005, available at www.dfw.com.

21. Janet Elliott, "Gov. Perry Institutes Teacher Merit Pay," *Houston Chronicle*, November 3, 2005, p. A1.

22. *Texas Weekly*, March 19, 2007, available at www.texasweekly.com.

23. Thad Beyle, "Gubernatorial Power: The Institutional Power Ratings of the 50 Governors of the United States, 2005 Updates," available at www.unc.edu~beyle/gubnewpwr.html.

24. Martha Wagner Weinberg, "Gubernatorial Style in Managing the State," in David C. Saffell and Terry Gilbreth, eds., *Subnational Politics: Readings in State and Local Government* (Reading, MA: Addison-Wesley, 1982), pp. 137–156.

25. Governor Rick Perry, "State-of-the-State Address," February 6, 2007, available at www.governor.state.tx.us.

26. Ralph K. M. Haurwitz, "Perry Signs Budget, Blasts Higher Education Funding," *Austin American Statesman*, June 16, 2007, available at www.statesman.com.

27. "State Government Employees," *Governing State and Local Source Book* 2006, p. 47.

28. Council of State Governments, *The Book of the States, 1984–85* (Lexington, KY: Council of State Governments, 1984), pp. 72–73.

29. *Texas Weekly*, February 2, 1998, p. 6.

30. Opinion #GA-0526, available at www.oag.state.tx.us.

31. Comptroller of Public Accounts, "Texas Net Revenue by Source—Fiscal 2006," available at www.window.state.tx.us.

32. David F. Prindle, *Petroleum, Politics, and the Texas Railroad Commission* (Austin: University of Texas Press, 1981), ch. 1.

33. Alexander Stille, "Textbook Publishers Learn to Avoid Messing with Texas," *New York Times*, June 29, 2002, available at www.nytimes.com.

34. Texans for Public Justice, "Governor Perry's Patronage," available at www.tpj.org.

35. Edwin S. Davis, "Rule Making Activity of Selected Texas Regulatory Agencies," *Texas Journal of Political Studies* 8 (Fall/Winter 1985–86): 26–36.

36. Jim Vertuno, "Giant Toll Network Is Perry's Vision," *Houston Chronicle*, December 24, 2004, available at www.houstonchronicle.com.

37. Jonathan Walters, "The Struggle to Streamline," *Governing*, September 2007, pp. 45–48.

38. Sunset Advisory Commission, available at www.sunset.state.tx.us.

39. Sunset Advisory Commission, "Guide to the Sunset Process," January 2006, available at www.sunset.state.tx.us.

40. Janet Elliott, "Perry Homes Executive Named to Commission," *Houston Chronicle*, September 30, 2003, p. 15A.

Chapter 27

The Judicial Branch in Texas

CHAPTER OUTLINE

Types of Legal Disputes
    Criminal Cases
    Civil Disputes

Court Procedures

The Texas Court System
    Local Courts
    District Courts
    Appellate Courts

Judges

Judicial Selection
    Is Justice for Sale in Texas?
    Do Voters Know the Candidates?

Is the Texas Judiciary Representative of the State's Population?

Is Partisan Politics Incompatible with Judicial Impartiality?

Reforming the Judicial Selection Process

Judicial Retirement and Removal

Visiting Judges

Conclusion: The Judicial Branch and the Policymaking Process
    Agenda Building
    Policy Formulation and Adoption
    Policy Implementation and Evaluation

LEARNING OUTCOMES

After studying Chapter 27, students should be able to do the following:

▸ Distinguish between criminal and civil cases and among the types of disputes within each classification. (pp. 728–730)

▸ Compare and contrast trial court and appellate court procedures. (pp. 730–732)

▸ Outline the organization of the judicial branch of Texas government, identifying the various courts and describing the types of cases they hear. (pp. 732–739)

▸ List the terms of office, method of selection, and qualifications for judges in Texas. (pp. 739–740)

▸ Describe the process of judicial selection in Texas, evaluating the arguments for and against the state's system of selecting judges. (pp. 740–743, 751–753)

▸ Identify and assess the various proposals for reforming the judicial selection process in the state. (pp. 743–746)

▸ Describe the process of judicial retirement and removal. (pp. 746–747)

▸ Describe the role of the judicial branch in the state's policymaking process. (pp. 748–751)

▸ Define the key terms listed on page 753 and explain their significance.

Medicaid A federal program designed to provide health insurance coverage to low-income persons, people with disabilities, and elderly people who are impoverished.

Should the government cover the cost of medically necessary abortions for low-income women? **Medicaid** is a federal program designed to provide health insurance coverage to the poor, persons with disabilities, and elderly Americans who are impoverished. Although the U.S. Supreme Court has long held that women have the constitutional right to terminate a pregnancy until the fetus has achieved viability, Congress has prohibited the use of federal Medicaid money to pay for an abortion except when the life of the women is at stake or in the case of rape or incest. States may choose to include abortion services in their Medicaid programs and fund them with state money, but Texas has not made that choice. Poor women in Texas who are advised by a physician to terminate a pregnancy because of a medical condition, such as epilepsy, cancer, or asthma, must either cover the $400–$500 cost themselves or carry the pregnancy to term.

Texas Equal Rights Amendment (ERA) A provision in the Texas Constitution that states the following: "Equality under the law shall not be denied or abridged because of sex, race, color, creed, or national origin."

Abortion rights advocates filed suit in Texas court against the state's refusal to cover medically necessary abortions in its Medicaid program, charging that the policy amounted to illegal sex discrimination. They based their lawsuit on the **Texas Equal Rights Amendment (ERA),** which is a provision in the Texas Constitution that states the following: "Equality under the law shall not be denied or abridged because of sex, race, color, creed, or national origin." Although the Texas Medicaid program covers all medically necessary procedures for men, they argued, it does not fund all medically necessary procedures for women because it does not cover abortion services.

The Texas Supreme Court rejected the argument. The purpose of the policy, the court said, was not to discriminate against women but to promote childbirth. Because Texas has a legitimate interest in favoring childbirth over abortion, the state is not constitutionally required to fund medically necessary abortions.[1]

The judicial branch is an important part of the policymaking process. The courts are primarily involved in policy implementation through the administration of justice. They try criminal defendants and hear lawsuits among private parties. As the lawsuit over the state's refusal to cover medically necessary abortions in its Medicaid program demonstrates, Texas courts sometimes participate in policy adoption. In this example, the Texas Supreme Court confirmed a policy decision made by the legislative and executive branches of government.

This chapter is the third in a series of five chapters examining the policymaking units of state and local government in Texas. Chapter 25 focused on the Texas legislature and Chapter 26 examined the executive branch. The next two chapters deal with the units of local government. Chapter 28 studies city government. Chapter 29 considers counties, school districts, and special districts.

TYPES OF LEGAL DISPUTES

The courts administer justice by settling criminal and civil disputes.

Criminal case A legal dispute dealing with an alleged violation of a penal law.

Criminal Cases

A **criminal case** is a legal dispute dealing with an alleged violation of a penal law. A **criminal defendant** is the party charged with a criminal offense, whereas the **prosecutor** is the attorney who tries a criminal case on behalf of the government.

Criminal defendant The party charged with a criminal offense.

Prosecutor The attorney who tries a criminal case on behalf of the government.

Burden of proof The legal obligation of one party in a lawsuit to prove its position to a court.

Misdemeanor A relatively minor criminal offense, such as a traffic violation.

Felony A serious criminal offense, such as murder, sexual assault, or burglary.

Capital punishment The death penalty.

Civil case A legal dispute concerning a private conflict between two or more parties—individuals, corporations, or government agencies.

Plaintiff The party initiating a civil suit.

The role of the court in a criminal case is to guide and referee the dispute. Ultimately, a judge or jury rules on the defendant's guilt or innocence and, if the verdict is guilty, assesses punishment.

 WHAT IS YOUR OPINION?

Should the Texas Mediacid program cover the cost of medically necessary abortions for low-income women?

The **burden of proof** is the legal obligation of one party in a lawsuit to prove its position to a court. The prosecutor has the burden of proof in a criminal case. In other words, the prosecutor must show that the defendant is guilty; the defendant need not demonstrate innocence. Texas law requires that the government prove the defendant's guilt "beyond a reasonable doubt." Unless the evidence clearly points to the defendant's guilt, the law requires that the defendant be found not guilty.

The penal code classifies criminal cases according to their severity. A **misdemeanor** is a relatively minor criminal offense, such as a traffic violation. Texas law classifies misdemeanor offenses as Class A, B, or C. Class A misdemeanors are the most serious, Class C the least serious. Class A misdemeanors can be punishable by a fine not to exceed $3,000 and/or a jail term of a year or less. In contrast, the maximum punishment for a Class C misdemeanor is a fine of $500.

A **felony** is a serious criminal offense, such as murder, sexual assault, or burglary. Texas law divides felony offenses into five categories—capital and first-, second-, third-,

The Texas Supreme Court ruled that the Texas Constitution does not require the state to cover medically necessary abortions for poor women in its Medicaid program.

Civil defendant
The responding party in a civil suit.

and fourth-degree (state jail) felonies—with fourth-degree being the least serious category of offenses. Convicted felons may be fined heavily and sentenced to as many as 99 years in prison. In Texas and 37 other states, convicted capital murderers may be sentenced to death. The death penalty is known as **capital punishment.**

Civil Disputes

Courts also settle civil disputes. A **civil case** is a legal dispute concerning a private conflict between two or more parties—individuals, corporations, or government agencies. In this type of legal dispute, the party initiating the lawsuit is called the **plaintiff;** the **civil defendant** is the responding party. The plaintiff feels wronged by the defendant and files suit to ask a court to award monetary damages or order the defendant to remedy the wrong.

Property case A civil suit over the ownership of real estate or personal possessions, such as land, jewlery, or an automobile.

The burden of proof in civil cases is on the plaintiff, but it is not as heavy as it is in criminal disputes. With the exception of lawsuits filed to terminate parental rights, the plaintiff is required to prove the case "by a preponderance of the evidence." For the plaintiff's side to win a lawsuit, it need only demonstrate that the weight of evidence in the case is slightly more in its favor. If a judge or jury believes that the evidence is evenly balanced between the plaintiff and the defendant, the defendant prevails because the plaintiff has the burden of proof. A lawsuit to terminate parental rights is a civil action filed by Child Protective Services to ask a court to end a parent–child relationship. The plaintiff has the burden of proof to show by clear and convincing evidence that an individual's parental rights should be terminated because he or she is not a fit parent.

Probate case A civil suit dealing with the disposition of the property of a deceased individual.

Civil disputes include property, probate, domestic-relations, contract, and tort cases. A **property case** is a civil suit over the ownership of real estate or personal possessions, such as land, jewelry, or an automobile. A **probate case** is a civil suit dealing with the disposition of the property of a deceased individual. A **domestic-relations case** is a civil suit based on the law involving the relationship between husband and wife, as well as between parents and children, such as divorce and child custody cases. A **contract case** is a civil suit dealing with disputes over written or implied legal agreements, such as a suit over a faulty roof repair job. Finally, a **tort case** is a civil suit involving personal injury or damage to property, such as a lawsuit stemming from an automobile accident.

Domestic-relations case A civil suit based on the law involving the relationships between husband and wife, and between parents and children, such as divorce and child custody cases.

Contract case A civil suit dealing with disputes over written or implied legal agreements, such as a suit over a faulty roof repair job.

COURT PROCEDURES

Tort case A civil suit involving personal injury or damage to property, such as a lawsuit stemming from an automobile accident.

The typical image of a court at work is that of a trial with judge, jury, witnesses, and evidence. The parties in the lawsuit, the **litigants,** are represented by counsel engaging in an **adversary proceeding,** which is a legal procedure in which each side presents evidence and arguments to bolster its position while rebutting evidence that might support the other side. Theoretically, the process helps the judge or jury determine the facts in the case.

In practice, most legal disputes are settled not by trials but through a process of negotiation and compromise between the parties involved. In civil cases, litigants

Litigants The parties in a lawsuit.

Adversary proceeding A legal procedure in which each side presents evidence and arguments to bolster its position while rebutting evidence that might support the other side.

Plea bargain A procedure in which a defendant agrees to plead guilty in order to receive punishment less than the maximum for an offense.

Trial The formal examination of a civil or criminal action in accordance with law before a single judge who has jurisdiction to hear the dispute.

Appeal The taking of a case from a lower court to a higher court by the losing party in a lower-court decision.

Reversible error A mistake committed by a trial court that is serious enough to warrant a new trial because the mistake could have affected the outcome of the original trial.

usually decide that it is quicker and less costly to settle out of court than to go through the trial process. They agree on a settlement either before the case goes to trial or during the early stages of the trial. Similarly, most criminal cases are resolved through a **plea bargain,** which is a procedure in which a defendant agrees to plead guilty in order to receive punishment less than the maximum for an offense. On occasion, defendants may plead guilty to lesser offenses than the crime with which they were originally charged.

Judicial procedures are divided into trials and appeals. A **trial** is the formal examination of a civil or criminal action in accordance with law before a single judge who has jurisdiction to hear the dispute. Trials involve attorneys, witnesses, testimony, evidence, judges, and occasionally juries. In civil cases, the verdict determines which party in the lawsuit prevails. A criminal verdict decides whether the defendant is guilty or not guilty as charged. In general, the outcome of a trial can be appealed to a higher court for review.

Criminal defendants have a constitutional right to trial by jury. The U.S. Supreme Court has held that the U.S. Constitution obliges state governments to offer jury trials to persons charged with felony offenses.[2] The Texas Constitution goes further, granting accused persons the right to trial by jury in *all* cases, misdemeanor and felony, although defendants may waive the right to a jury trial and be tried by a judge alone. Litigants in civil cases have the option of having their case heard by a judge alone or by a jury.

Prospective trial jurors are selected from county voter registration rolls and lists of persons holding Texas driver's licenses and Department of Public Safety (DPS) identification cards. Jurors must be American citizens. Persons who are convicted felons or are under felony indictment are ineligible to serve on a jury. Some groups of people are exempt from jury service if they wish, including full-time students, individuals over 70 years of age, and persons with custody of small children whose absence would leave the children without proper supervision.

An **appeal** is the taking of a case from a lower court to a higher court by the losing party in a lower-court decision. Civil litigants argue that the trial court failed to follow proper procedures or incorrectly applied the law. They hope that an appellate court will reverse or at least temper the decision of the trial court. Parties who lose tort cases, for example, may ask an appellate court to reduce the amount of damages awarded. Criminal defendants who appeal their convictions contend that the trial court committed **reversible error,** which is a mistake committed by a trial court that is serious enough to warrant a new trial because the mistake could have affected the outcome of the original trial. In contrast, **harmless error** is a mistake committed by a trial court that is not serious enough to warrant a new trial because it could not have affected the outcome of the original trial. The right to appeal criminal court decisions extends only to the defendant; the prosecution does not have the right to appeal an acquittal. The constitutional principle that an individual may not be tried a second time by the same unit of government for a single offense if acquitted in the first trial is known as the prohibition against **double jeopardy.**

The procedures of appeals courts differ notably from those of trial courts. In general, trial courts are concerned with questions of fact and the law as it applies to those facts. In contrast, appeals are based on issues of law and procedure. Appellate courts do not retry cases appealed to them. Instead, appeals court justices (juries do not

Harmless error A mistake committed by a trial court that is not serious enough to warrant a new trial because it could not have affected the outcome of the original trial.

Double jeopardy The constitutional principle that an individual may not be tried a second time by the same unit of government for a single offense if acquitted in the first trial.

participate in appellate proceedings) make decisions based on the law and the constitution, the written and oral arguments presented by attorneys for the litigants in the lawsuit, and the written record of the lower-court proceedings. Also, appellate court justices usually make decisions collectively in panels of three or more judges rather than singly, as do trial court judges. Appeals court decisions are themselves subject to appeal. Both the prosecution and the defendant have the right to appeal the decisions of appellate courts in criminal cases. The constitutional protection against double jeopardy applies only to trial proceedings.

Appeals courts may uphold, reverse, or modify lower-court decisions. An appeals court may direct a trial court to reconsider a case in light of the appellate court's ruling on certain legal issues. If an appeals court overturns a criminal conviction, the defendant does not necessarily go free. The district attorney who initially prosecuted the case has the option either to retry the case or to release the defendant. In practice, many defendants are retried, convicted, and sentenced once again. Ignacio Cuevas, for example, was tried three times for capital murder, convicted three times, and sentenced to death three times. Twice the Texas Court of Criminal Appeals overturned Cuevas's conviction, but not a third time. Cuevas was executed.

THE TEXAS COURT SYSTEM

The Texas court system has three levels:

- **Local courts** Municipal courts, justice of the peace (JP) courts, and county courts hear relatively minor civil cases and misdemeanor criminal disputes.
- **District courts** State district courts are the general trial courts of the state, hearing major civil disputes and trying felony criminal cases.
- **Appellate courts** The Texas Courts of Appeals, Texas Court of Criminal Appeals, and Texas Supreme Court constitute the state's appellate court system.

Local Courts

Municipal, JP, and county courts are local courts operated by cities and county governments.

Municipal Courts   The Texas legislature has created municipal courts in every incorporated city in the state. Municipal courts operate in 914 cities, staffed by 1,396 judges.[3] Smaller cities have one municipal court with a single judge; larger cities operate several courtrooms, each with its own judge.

City ordinances Laws enacted by the governing body of a municipality.

Most municipal court cases involve relatively minor criminal matters. Municipal courts have exclusive jurisdiction over cases involving violations of **city ordinances,** which are laws enacted by the governing body of a municipality. In general, persons convicted of violating city ordinances may be fined no more than $500, although violators of ordinances relating to litter, fire safety, zoning, public health, and sanitation may be fined as much as $2,000. Municipal courts share jurisdiction with justice of the peace courts in misdemeanor cases involving violations of Class C misdemeanors within city limits. The maximum fine for a Class C misdemeanor is $500. Municipal courts also have the power to award limited civil monetary penalties in cases involving dangerous dogs.

Traffic ticket cases account for more than 80 percent of the workload of municipal courts. Sixty percent of municipal court defendants plead guilty and pay a relatively small fine. Almost all of the defendants requesting a trial either before a judge alone or with a jury are found guilty as well. Under state law, municipal court proceedings in all but a handful of the state's largest cities (including Houston, Dallas, Fort Worth, San Antonio, and Austin) are not recorded. Consequently, municipal court defendants in most cities are entitled to a new trial called trial *de novo*, usually in county court, if they appeal a conviction. In cities whose municipal courts are courts of record, the appeal is done by the record only and is not a trial *de novo*. Nonetheless, less than 1 percent of municipal court defendants found guilty appeal their conviction.[4] Few defendants appeal because the cost of hiring an attorney to handle the appeal usually exceeds the amount of the fine.

Magistrates
Judicial officers.

Municipal court judges serve as **magistrates** (judicial officers) for the state in a range of proceedings involving both misdemeanor and felony offenses. They may issue search and arrest warrants, set bail for criminal defendants, and hold preliminary hearings. Municipal court judges may also conduct driver's license suspension hearings and emergency mental commitment hearings.

Justice of the Peace (JP) Courts   The Texas Constitution requires each county to operate at least one JP court and allows larger counties to have as many as 16. In 2006, 825 JP courts operated statewide. JP courts hear both criminal and civil cases, with criminal disputes comprising more than 90 percent of their caseloads. Most criminal cases heard in JP court involve Class C misdemeanor traffic offenses, with the rest concerning nontraffic Class C misdemeanors, such as game law violations, public intoxication, disorderly conduct, and some thefts. Justice of the peace courts have a civil jurisdiction. Individuals with civil disputes valued at no more than $10,000 can file suit in JP court and present their case to the justice of the peace without aid of an attorney. JP courts also conduct civil proceedings dealing with mortgage foreclosures, property liens, and forcible entry and detainer suits. A **property lien** is a

Property lien A financial claim against property for payment of debt.

SHOE

INDICTED, CONVICTED, REVERSED ON APPEAL...

TALK SHOWS, BOOK DEAL, MADE-FOR-TV MOVIE, YUP...

ALL THE ELEMENTS OF A MODERN SUCCESS STORY.

Source: © Tribune Media Services, Inc. All rights reserved. Reprinted with permission.

Forcible entry and detainer suit
An effort by a landlord to evict a tenant (usually for failure to pay rent).

financial claim against property for payment of debt. A **forcible entry and detainer suit** is an effort by a landlord to evict a tenant (usually for failure to pay rent).

JP court proceedings, similar to most municipal court proceedings, are not recorded. As a result, a person who files an appeal of a JP court decision is entitled to a new trial, generally in county court. In practice, most cases appealed from JP courts are settled by plea bargains or dismissed by county court judges. Appeals of justice court decisions are rare, involving less than 1 percent of the cases disposed by trial in a JP court.[5]

Similar to municipal court judges, justices of the peace are state magistrates. They may issue search and arrest warrants in both misdemeanor and felony cases, set bail for criminal defendants, and conduct preliminary hearings. They also hold driver's license suspension hearings and conduct emergency mental commitment hearings.

County Courts   Each of the state's 254 counties has a constitutional county court, so called because it is required by the Texas Constitution. These courts have both criminal and civil jurisdiction. County courts try criminal cases involving violations of Class A and Class B misdemeanors. In practice, criminal cases constitute 80 percent of the cases heard by county courts, with theft, worthless checks, and driving while intoxicated or under the influence of drugs (DWI/DUID) the most common offenses. County courts also try Class C misdemeanor cases appealed from JP or municipal courts.

The civil jurisdiction of the constitutional county courts extends to disputes in which the amount of money at stake is between $200 and $5,000, although these courts may also hear cases involving lesser amounts that are appealed from JP court. The constitutional county courts share their civil jurisdiction with both JP and district courts. An individual suing for $1,000, for example, can legally file in JP, district, or county court. Suits over debts, personal injury or damage, and divorce are the most commonly heard civil cases in constitutional county courts.

In addition to their basic civil and criminal jurisdictions, the constitutional county courts fulfill a number of other functions. They probate uncontested wills, appoint guardians for minors, and conduct mental health competency/commitment hearings. The decisions of county courts on mental competency and probate may be appealed to district courts, but all other appeals from county court are taken to the courts of appeals.

The Texas legislature has created 218 additional county courts known as statutory county courts (because they are established by statute) and 17 statutory probate courts to supplement the constitutional county courts. These courts, which are sometimes also called county courts at law, operate primarily in urban areas where the caseload of the constitutional county court is overwhelming, and the county judge, who presides in the constitutional county court, is busy with the affairs of county government. Some statutory county courts concentrate on civil matters and some handle only criminal cases. The legislature allows many of the statutory county courts to hear civil cases involving as much as $100,000. Appeals from the statutory county courts proceed in the same manner as appeals from constitutional county courts.[6]

District Courts

Texas has 432 district courts. Each court serves a specific geographic area, which, in rural areas, may encompass several counties. In urban counties, the legislature has created multiple courts, many of which specialize in particular areas of the law. Harris

County alone has nearly 60 district courts, including civil, criminal, family, and juvenile district courts.

District courts are the basic trial courts of the state of Texas. They hear all felony cases and have jurisdiction in civil matters involving $200 or more, sharing jurisdiction on smaller sums with JP and county courts. Civil cases comprise more than 70 percent of the caseload for district courts. Family law disputes, including divorce and child custody cases, are the civil matters most frequently handled by district courts. Personal injury cases, tax cases, and disputes over debts are important as well. The most frequently heard criminal cases are felony drug offenses, thefts, assaults, and burglary.[7] District courts may also issue a number of **legal writs,** which are written orders issued by a court directing the performance of an act or prohibiting some act. The constitutional challenge to the state's Medicaid program involved a district court suit filed by abortion rights advocates. They asked the judge to issue a legal writ to permanently prevent the state from enforcing its policy against funding medically necessary abortions because the policy violated the Texas ERA. Appeals from district court decisions are taken to the courts of appeals, except capital murder cases in which the death penalty is assessed. These cases are appealed directly and automatically to the Texas Court of Criminal Appeals. After the district court ruled against the plaintiffs in the abortion funding case, they appealed to the Third Court of Appeals.

Appellate Courts

The courts of appeals, Texas Court of Criminal Appeals, and Texas Supreme Court constitute the state's appellate court system, considering appeals filed by litigants who lose in lower courts. With the exception of capital murder cases in which the death penalty has been assessed, appellate courts need not hold hearings in every case. After reading **legal briefs,** which are written legal arguments, and reviewing the trial court record, appeals court justices may simply **affirm** (uphold) the lower-court ruling without holding a hearing to consider formal arguments. In practice, appellate courts reject the overwhelming majority of appeals based solely on the legal briefs filed in the case.

When an appeals court decides to accept a case on appeal, the court generally schedules a hearing at which attorneys for the two sides in the dispute present oral arguments and answer questions posed by the justices. Appeals courts do not retry cases. Instead, they review the trial court record and consider legal arguments raised by the attorneys in the case. After hearing oral arguments and studying legal briefs, appeals court justices discuss the case and eventually vote on a decision, with a majority vote of the justices required to decide a case. The court may affirm the lower-court decision, reverse it, modify it, or affirm part of the lower-court ruling while reversing or modifying the rest. Frequently, an appeals court will **remand** (return) a case to the trial court for reconsideration in light of the appeals court decision.

When the court announces its decision, it may issue a **majority,** or **deciding, opinion,** which is the official written statement of a court that explains and justifies its ruling and serves as a guideline for lower courts when similar legal issues arise in

Legal writs Written orders issued by a court directing the performance of an act or prohibiting some act.

Legal briefs Written legal arguments.

Affirm Uphold.

Remand An appellate court returning a case to a trial court for further consideration.

Majority, or **deciding, opinion** An official written statement of a court that explains and justifies its ruling and serves as a guideline for lower courts when similar legal issues arise in the future.

The plaintiff has the burden of proof in a civil trial.

Dissenting opinion A written judicial statement that disagrees with the decision of the court's majority.

the future. Associate Supreme Court Justice Harriett O'Neill wrote the opinion of the court in the Medicaid abortion funding case. In addition to the court's majority opinion, members of an appellate court may release dissenting or concurring opinions. A **dissenting opinion** is a written judicial statement that disagrees with the decision of the court's majority. It presents the viewpoint of one or more justices who disagree with the court's decision. A **concurring opinion** is a written judicial statement that agrees with the court ruling but disagrees with the reasoning of the majority. Justices who voted in favor of the court's decision for reasons other than those stated in the majority opinion may file concurring opinions. No justices wrote dissenting or concurring opinions in the Medicaid abortion funding case.

Concurring opinion A written judicial statement that agrees with the court's ruling but disagrees with the reasoning of the majority.

Courts of Appeals   Texas has 14 courts of appeals, each serving a specific geographic area called a court of appeals district. The Third Court of Appeals, which sits in Austin, heard the appeal of the challenge to the state's ban on Medicaid funding for medically necessary abortions. The number of justices in each court varies from 3 to 13, depending on the workload. Altogether, 80 justices staff the 14 courts of appeals. The justices on each court hear cases in panels of at least three justices, with decisions made by majority vote. A panel of the Third Court of Appeals voted 2–1 in favor of the plaintiffs in the abortion funding case.

Each of the courts of appeals has jurisdiction on appeals from trial courts located in its district. The courts of appeals hear both civil and criminal appeals, except death penalty appeals, which are considered by the Texas Court of Criminal Appeals. The courts of appeals dealt with nearly 12,000 cases in 2006, with criminal cases outnumbering civil cases by a narrow margin. The courts of appeals reversed the decision of the trial court in whole or in part in 6 percent of the cases it heard.[8] The rulings of the courts of appeals may be appealed either to the Texas Court of Criminal Appeals for criminal matters or to the Texas Supreme Court for civil cases. After the Third Court of Appeals ruled against it in the Medicaid abortion funding case, the state appealed to the Texas Supreme Court.

Texas Court of Criminal Appeals   Texas is one of two states (Oklahoma is the other) with two supreme courts—the Texas Supreme Court for civil disputes and the Texas Court of Criminal Appeals for criminal matters. The Texas Court of Criminal Appeals, which meets in Austin, is the court of last resort for all criminal cases in the state. It has nine judges, one presiding judge and eight additional judges. They sit *en banc* (as a group), with all nine judges hearing a case. As in other appellate courts, the judges of the Texas Court of Criminal Appeals decide cases by majority vote. Decisions of the Texas Court of Criminal Appeals may be appealed to the U.S. Supreme Court when they involve matters of federal law or the U.S. Constitution. The Texas Court of Criminal Appeals is the highest court on issues of state criminal law and the state constitution. The U.S. Supreme Court will not accept appeals on state matters unless they involve federal issues.

The Texas Court of Criminal Appeals considers appeals brought from the Courts of Appeals and death penalty cases appealed directly from district courts. In 2006, the Texas Court of Criminal Appeals disposed of more than 2,000 cases, including 26 death penalty appeals. Although the court is required to review death penalty cases, other appeals are discretionary—the justices have the option to review the lower-court decision or to allow it to stand without review. In 2006, the Texas Court of Criminal Appeals agreed to consider about 7 percent of the cases appealed to it. The court reversed the decision of the lower court in 23 percent of the cases it reviewed.[9]

The Texas Court of Criminal Appeals is empowered to issue a number of writs. The most important of these is the **writ of *habeas corpus,*** which is a court order requiring a government official to show cause why a person is being held in custody. Persons serving sentences in the state's prisons who believe that their rights have been violated may petition the Texas Court of Criminal Appeals for a writ of habeas corpus as a means of reopening their case. If the court grants the petition, the state must respond to the prisoner's charges in court. In 2006, the Texas Court of Criminal Appeals granted 220 writs of *habeas corpus* out of 6,381 petitions filed.[10]

writ of *habeas corpus* A court order requiring a government official to show cause why a person is being held in custody.

Texas Supreme Court   The Texas Supreme Court, which sits in Austin, has nine members—one chief justice and eight associate justices—who decide cases by majority vote *en banc*. The Texas Supreme Court decided the Medicaid abortion funding case by an 8–0 vote, with one justice not participating. The Texas Supreme

INTERNET RESEARCH

Shirley Neeley v. West Orange-Cove Consolidated Independent School District

In 2004, State District Judge John Dietz declared the Texas school finance system unconstitutional because it failed to provide enough money to ensure that students receive an adequate education as required by the Texas Constitution. The judge also ruled that the state's property tax cap amounted to an unconstitutional statewide property tax because school districts were effectively required to tax at the maximum rate. Dietz ordered the state to devise a new system for funding public education that would satisfy the requirements of the Texas Constitution, and the state appealed the decision to the Texas Supreme Court. (Because Judge Dietz ruled on the constitutionality of a state law, the case could be appealed directly to the Texas Supreme Court rather than having to go through the courts of appeals.)

Students can research the case online at the website of the Texas Supreme Court: **www.supreme.courts.state .tx.us/**. Point the mouse to the "Case Information" link in the panel on the right and then click on "Case Search." In the style box, type in the word *Neeley* and the computer will take you to an information page with multiple links. Review the information and click on some of the links to read about the case. In particular, look for the opinion of the court. Use the information you find online (and your good judgment) to answer the following questions:

1. When the case was filed, it was styled (or titled) *West Orange-Cove Consolidated ISD v. Neeley*. On appeal to the Texas Supreme Court, the litigant names are reversed and the case has become *Neeley v. West Orange-Cove Consolidated ISD*. Why has the title of the case changed? (This is not a question you can answer from online research, at least not directly. Reason through the answer based on the progression of the case through the court system.)

2. In what trial court did the case originate? Identify the court by number and by judge.

3. Who is Shirley Neeley, and why is her name attached to the case? (You may need to do an Internet search to answer this question, using a search engine, such as **www.google.com**.)

4. When did the Texas Supreme Court issue its decision?

5. Who wrote the opinion of the court?

6. What was the vote on the court?

7. Did every member of the court participate in the decision? If not, why not?

8. In your own words, what did the Texas Supreme Court decide in the case? Did the Supreme Court agree with Judge Dietz or overrule his decision?

Court is the civil court of highest authority on matters of state law, although losers in cases decided by the Texas Supreme Court may appeal to the U.S. Supreme Court *if* they can demonstrate that an issue under federal law or the U.S. Constitution is involved. The U.S. Supreme Court will not review state court interpretations of state law or the state constitution. The Texas Supreme Court was probably the end of the line for the plaintiffs in the Medicaid abortion funding case because they based their argument on the Texas ERA, a provision of the Texas Constitution.

The Texas Supreme Court hears civil matters only. Most of its cases come from the Courts of Appeals, although appeals may be taken directly to the Texas Supreme Court whenever any state court rules on the validity of a state law or an administrative action under the Texas Constitution. The court is also empowered to issue writs of *mandamus* to compel public officials to fulfill their duties and/or follow the law. A **writ of *mandamus*** is a court order directing a public official to perform a specific act or duty. In 2006, the court acted on a total of 2,940 matters.[11]

writ of mandamus A court order directing a public official to perform a specific act or duty.

The Texas Supreme Court reviews lower-court decisions on a discretionary basis—the justices choose which cases they will consider. In 2006, the Texas Supreme Court granted review to 13 percent of the cases appealed to it. If the court refuses to grant review, then the lower-court decision stands. The Texas Supreme Court reversed the decision of the lower court in whole or in part in 90 percent of the cases it agreed to hear.[12]

In addition to its judicial functions, the Texas Supreme Court plays an important role in administering the judicial branch of state government. It sets the rules of administration and civil procedure for the state court system (as long as those rules do not conflict with state law). It has authority to approve law schools in the state and appoints the Board of Law Examiners, which administers the bar exam to prospective attorneys. The court also has final authority over the involuntary retirement or removal of all judges in the state.

JUDGES

Table 27.1 summarizes the length of term, method of selection, and qualifications for the more than 3,100 judges who staff Texas courts. As the table shows, the term of office for Texas judges ranges from two to six years. Although municipal court judges in some cities serve two-year terms, most trial court judges are elected for four years. Appellate court judges serve six-year terms.

Partisan election An election contest in which both the names and the party affiliations of candidates appear on the ballot.

Except for some municipal court judges who are appointed, Texas judges are chosen by **partisan election,** which is an election contest in which both the names of the candidates and their party affiliations appear on the ballot. Elected municipal court judges run citywide, generally in nonpartisan city elections. Justices of the peace are elected from JP precincts. Counties with a population of 18,000 to 30,000 people have two to five JP precincts; larger counties have between four and eight JP precincts. Each JP precinct elects either one or two justices of the peace, depending on the size of the county. County court judges are elected countywide. District court judges and courts of appeals justices run from districts ranging in size from countywide for district courts in metropolitan areas to geographically large, multicounty districts for courts of appeals and district court judges in rural areas. Judges on the Texas Court of Criminal Appeals and the Texas Supreme Court are elected statewide.

The qualifications of judges in Texas depend on the court. The requirements to serve as a municipal court judge vary from city to city, with many municipalities requiring prospective judges to be experienced attorneys. The qualifications of JPs and constitutional county court judges are set in the state constitution. Justices of the peace and constitutional county court judges must be qualified voters, but they need not be attorneys and most have not even attended law school. Although the Texas Constitution requires that constitutional county court judges "shall be well-informed in the law of the state," it gives no standard for measuring that requirement. Less

TABLE 27.1   Texas Judges

Court	Length of Term	Method of Selection	Qualifications
Municipal courts	Two or four years, depending on the city	Election or appointment, depending on the city	Set by city government
Justice of the peace courts	Four years	Partisan election from precincts	Qualified voter
Constitutional county courts	Four years	Partisan election countywide	"Well-informed in the law of the state"
Statutory county courts	Four years	Partisan election countywide	Licensed to practice law; other qualifications vary
District courts	Four years	Partisan election countywide or from multicounty districts, with vacancies filled by gubernatorial appointment	Citizen, resident of district for two years, licensed to practice law in Texas, and a practicing attorney or judge for four years
Courts of appeals	Six-year overlapping terms	Partisan election from a court of appeals district, with vacancies filled by gubernatorial appointment	Citizen, 35 years of age, practicing attorney or judge of a court of record for 10 years
Texas Court of Criminal Appeals	Six-year overlapping terms	Partisan election statewide, with vacancies filled by gubernatorial appointment	Citizen, 35 years of age, practicing attorney or judge of a court of record for 10 years
Texas Supreme Court	Six-year overlapping terms	Partisan election statewide, with vacancies filled by gubernatorial appointment	Citizen, 35 years of age, practicing attorney or judge of a court of record for 10 years

than 20 percent of the state's county court judges and JPs are lawyers.[13] State law does require, however, that individuals who are elected as judges but who are not attorneys complete a course in legal training before they can serve. The qualifications of statutory county court judges vary, with many courts requiring two to five years of experience as a practicing attorney.

The Texas Constitution establishes the requirements for judges serving on district and appellate courts. District court judges must be citizens and residents of the district for two years. They must be licensed to practice law in Texas and have at least four years experience as a practicing attorney or a judge in a court of record. Appellate court judges are required to be citizens at least 35 years of age and must be practicing lawyers or judges in a court of record for at least ten years.

JUDICIAL SELECTION

Texas and eight other states elect judges on the partisan ballot.[14] Except for municipal court judges, Texas judges are chosen in a fashion that is formally the same as that for electing officials to the legislative and executive branches of government. People who want to become judges run in either the Democratic or the Republican primary, with the primary election winners representing their party on the general election ballot. The candidate with the most votes in November becomes judge.

Despite the formality of an election system, a substantial number of the state's district and appellate judges first reach the bench through appointment. The Texas Constitution empowers the governor (with Senate confirmation) to staff newly created courts at the appellate and district levels and fill judicial vacancies on those courts caused by deaths, retirements, or resignations. In 2006, 48 percent of the state's appellate judges and 43 percent of district judges had initially taken office through gubernatorial appointment rather than election.[15] When a vacancy occurs on a county or JP court, the commissioners court of that county fills the vacancy. Although appointed judges must face the voters at the next election, they enjoy the advantage of incumbency.

Is Justice for Sale in Texas?

Critics of the judicial selection system in Texas believe that money plays too prominent a role in the process. Sitting judges and candidates for judicial office raise and spend money in amounts comparable to candidates for other down-ballot statewide and local offices. Successful candidates for the Texas Supreme Court must raise and spend $1 million or more. Even candidates for district judgeships may raise and spend sums well in excess of $30,000 on their campaigns.

Although Texas law limits campaign expenditures in judicial elections, the limits are ineffective. Candidates for statewide judicial office may spend no more than $2 million for each election. Candidates seeking seats on the courts of appeals or district court judgeships have lower spending limits. In practice, however, the spending limits are too high to have a meaningful impact on judicial elections. Supreme Court candidates, for example, can raise $2 million for the primary election, $2 million more for the primary runoff (if there is one), and another $2 million for the general election. The limits are voluntary. Furthermore, candidates who pledge to adhere to the spending limits are not bound if an opponent exceeds the limits.[16]

Candidates for judicial office in Texas collect campaign contributions from individuals and groups who have a stake in the outcome of cases. In 2006, five incumbent Supreme Court justices ran for reelection, but only one, Don Willett, faced a Democratic opponent. Willet raised nearly $1.8 million for his successful reelection effort, with more than half the money coming from law firms and their lobbyists. Vinson & Elkins, Locke Liddell and Sapp, Fulbright & Jaworski, and Andrews & Kurth were prominent law firms making major investments in Willet's campaign. Frequent litigants also gave generously. Oil and gas interests, pharmaceutical companies, homebuilders, and health professionals were among Willet's major contributors.[17]

The critics of Texas's judicial selection system believe that campaign contributions have undermined the integrity of the state's court system. Consider the legal battle between Bob and Jane Cull of Mansfield and Perry Homes. The Culls sued Perry Homes in 2000, asking a court to order the homebuilder to correct fundamental defects in their $250,000 home. Before the case went to trial, the Culls moved to have the dispute settled by an independent arbiter because they wanted to avoid a long legal battle. The arbiter directed Perry Homes to pay the Culls $800,000,

Punitive damages
Monetary awards given in a lawsuit to punish a defendant for a particularly evil, malicious, or fraudulent act.

including the cost of the house, legal fees, and **punitive damages,** which are monetary awards given in a lawsuit to punish a defendant for a particularly evil, malicious, or fraudulent act. Perry Homes refused to pay, arguing that the Culls had waived their right to arbitration by filing suit. The arbiter, a district court, and a court of appeals all disagreed with that position. Perry Homes then filed an appeal with the Texas Supreme Court, which agreed to hear the appeal. Bob Perry, the owner of Perry Homes, has contributed more than $340,000 to the nine justices serving on the court, giving at least the appearance that the court will be biased in his favor.[18]

 WHAT IS YOUR OPINION?

Should judicial candidates and sitting judges be prevented from accepting campaign contributions from potential litigants?

Do Voters Know the Candidates?

Critics believe that many voters are unable to intelligently evaluate the qualifications of judicial candidates. This problem has worsened, they say, as the number of judgeships has increased. In November 2006, for example, the election ballot in Dallas County included more than 40 contested judicial races. Many Dallas County voters apparently based their voting decision on the one piece of information they knew about the candidates, their party affiliation, because every Democratic judicial candidate defeated every Republican judicial candidate on the ballot. Partisan sweeps for one party or the other have taken place in judicial races in most of the state's large urban counties over the last 20 years.

The election of Steve Mansfield in 1994 to the Texas Court of Criminal Appeals suggests that voters are often uninformed about judicial candidates even in statewide judicial races. Mansfield admitted having lied in his campaign literature about his place of birth, legal experience, and political background. Nonetheless, the message apparently did not reach many of the voters because they chose Republican Mansfield over incumbent Democratic Judge Chuck Campbell. After the election, the press discovered that Mansfield had been charged with the use of marijuana in Massachusetts and the unauthorized practice of law in Florida.[19]

Is the Texas Judiciary Representative of the State's Population?

Critics of Texas's system of judicial selection note that it has produced a judiciary that does not reflect the ethnic and racial diversity of the state's population. As Figure 27.1 shows, whites are overrepresented on the Texas bench, whereas Latinos, African Americans, and people of other ethnicities are underrepresented. Nearly 70 percent of Texas judges are men and the average age is mid-50s.[20]

Is Partisan Politics Incompatible with Judicial Impartiality?

Can a Republican defendant receive a fair trial from a Democratic judge (and vice versa)? Before going to trial for violating state campaign finance regulations, Republican Congressman Tom DeLay asked that the Travis County district judge

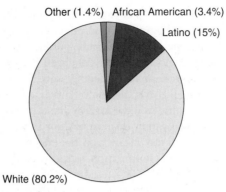

FIGURE 27.1 Profile of Texas Judges.
Source: Office of Court Administration.

assigned to hear the case be removed because the judge was a Democrat who had contributed money to groups that oppose DeLay. After a court granted DeLay's request to change judges, the district attorney responded by challenging the impartiality of the administrative judge appointed to name a new trial judge because the administrative judge had ties to a fundraising group associated with DeLay. When that judge withdrew from the case, the chief justice of the Texas Supreme Court ended the fight over judges by appointing a Democratic judge from San Antonio to hear the case. The new judge was acceptable to both sides because of his reputation for fairness and his relative dissociation from partisan politics.

Every judge in Texas is either a Republican or a Democrat. If partisan figures, such as Tom DeLay, face trial or if court cases deal with high-profile political issues, such as school finance or abortion, the judges hearing the disputes and deciding the issues will be Democrats or Republicans, elected in the same fashion as executive branch officials or members of the legislature. As long as Texas elects judges on the partisan ballot, at least some people will believe that party politics will determine the outcomes of cases rather than the law and the constitution.

Reforming the Judicial Selection Process

Reformers offer a number of options for changing the state's method for choosing judges. Some reformers propose that the state adopt the so-called Merit Selection (or Missouri Plan) system of judicial selection, which originated in the state of Missouri in 1941. **Merit Selection, or the Missouri Plan,** is a method for selecting judges that combines gubernatorial appointment with voter approval in a retention election. Eighteen states use Merit Selection to fill a significant number of judgeships.[21]

 WHAT IS YOUR OPINION?

How important is it that Texas judges reflect the racial and ethnic diversity of the state?

Merit Selection (or the Missouri Plan) A method for selecting judges that combines gubernatorial appointment with voter approval in a retention election.

Former Chief Justice John Hill offered the most detailed proposal for implementing Merit Selection in Texas. Under Hill's plan, the governor, lieutenant governor, speaker of the House, president of the state Bar Association, and chairs of the state Democratic and Republican Parties would each choose one or more individuals to serve on a 15-member nominating commission. These 15 individuals would include 9 lawyers and 6 nonlawyers who would serve six-year staggered terms. When an opening would occur on one of the state's appellate or trial courts, the commission would draw up a list of three to five qualified persons from which the governor would fill the vacancy on the bench. The governor's choice would be subject to a two-thirds' confirmation vote by the state Senate. The newly appointed judge would face the voters in a retention (or confirmation) election in the next general election. The ballot would read as follows: "Should Judge _____ be retained in office?" If a majority of voters approved, the judge would continue in office for a full term before facing another retention election. Judges failing to win majority support at a retention election would lose their seats. Replacements would be selected through the initial procedure of nomination by commission and gubernatorial appointment. Merit Selection can be used to choose all or part of a state's judges. Hill proposed separate nominating commissions for appellate and trial courts. He would also permit individual counties to opt out of the plan and continue electing local trial judges if they wished. Other proposals would limit Merit Selection to appellate justices.

The proponents of Merit Selection believe that it is an ideal compromise between a system of appointing judges and the election method. Although the governor is able to select the state's judges under Merit Selection, the bipartisan nominating commission limits the governor's choices to qualified individuals rather than political cronies. Retention (or confirmation) elections allow voters to participate in the process while removing judicial selection from party politics.

Not all Texans favor Merit Selection. Critics note that research shows no appreciable difference between the qualifications of judges chosen through Merit Selection and those of judges selected through other methods.[22] Furthermore, retention elections are generally meaningless in that voters almost never turn incumbent judges out of office.[23]

The strongest attack on Merit Selection is that it is an elitist system that produces a judiciary unrepresentative of the state's population. Critics say that Merit Selection takes control of judicial selection away from the people and gives it to lawyers who will ensure that judgeships go to attorneys from the best families who went to the most prestigious law schools and now work for the most prominent law firms.[24] Merit Selection, critics warn, leads to the appointment of judges simply because they are technically well qualified, without regard to their basic values, philosophy, or life experience. William Garrett, a voting rights attorney for the **League of United Latin American Citizens (LULAC),** a Latino interest group, goes so far as to argue that Merit Selection is racist:

> Merit selection is a scheme by those in power to stay in power. What you end up with is this elitist club. The idea of merit selection brought up at this point is rooted in racism: It was fine to elect judges so long as they were white, but as soon as it became possible for blacks and Hispanics to get elected, they want to stop elections. Why the hell weren't they crying about it in 1955 or '65? It's only now . . . that they're complaining.[25]

League of United Latin American Citizens (LULAC) A Latino interest group.

In Texas, judges campaign for election just like members of the legislative and executive branches of government.

District election A method for choosing public officials in which a political subdivision, such as a state or county, is divided into districts and each district elects one official.

Many minority rights advocates prefer the election of district judges from relatively small subcounty districts, perhaps even single-member districts. A **district election** is a method for choosing public officials in which a political subdivision, such as a state or county, is divided into districts, with each district electing one official. The proponents of district elections believe they increase representation for ethnic/racial minorities, make judges more responsive to citizens, and lessen the importance of money in judicial elections. In contrast, opponents of district elections warn that judges chosen from relatively small districts might be partial to litigants from their districts. Furthermore, they point out that many minority judges who now hold office would be defeated under a district system because they live in upper-income neighborhoods that would be unlikely to elect African American or Latino judicial candidates.

? WHAT IS YOUR OPINION?

Should the current system of judicial selection be replaced?

Other proposed reforms of the judicial selection process in Texas involve ballot modifications. Some reformers believe that judges should be chosen through

Nonpartisan elections Election contests in which the names of the candidates appear on the ballot but not their party affiliations.

Straight ticket voting Citizens casting their ballots only for the candidates of one party.

nonpartisan elections, which are elections in which candidates run without party labels. Others reformers propose preventing voters from casting a straight ticket ballot for judicial races. **Straight ticket voting** refers to citizens casting their ballots only for the candidates of one party. The advocates of these ballot reforms argue that they reduce the likelihood of partisan sweeps, such as the Democratic sweep in Dallas County in 2006. Furthermore, some research indicates that African American and Latino judicial candidates lose not because of their race but because they usually run as Democrats in counties that are leaning Republican.[26] If party labels are removed from the ballot or straight ticket voting is made more difficult, minority candidates may have more success. In contrast, other observers point out that these limited reforms do little to lessen the role of money in judicial elections and do nothing to solve the problem of poorly informed voters. In fact, nonpartisan elections reduce the amount of information readily available to voters about the candidates because they remove party labels from the ballot.

Not all Texans oppose the current system of electing judges. Many political leaders, elected officials, and judges (including many of the justices on the state Supreme Court) favor retaining the current system of partisan election of judges. Texans who want to preserve the state's current system of judicial selection argue that election is the democratic way for choosing public officials. Elected judges are more likely to reflect the will of the community than appointed judges. Furthermore, most of the criticisms made against the election of judges could also be made against the election of legislators and executive branch officials. The best way to improve the judicial election process (and the election process in general) is better voter education.

Judicial Retirement and Removal

Judges leave the bench for a variety of reasons. Some die, some are defeated for reelection, and some retire. State law requires district and appellate judges to retire at age 75. Judges who reach retirement age before the end of a term can finish that term before retiring. Judges can qualify for an increased pension if they retire before reaching 70.

Judges may be disciplined and removed from office for incompetence or unethical conduct. The Texas Constitution empowers the Commission on Judicial Conduct, a body composed of judges, lawyers, and laypersons, to investigate complaints against judges and recommend discipline. The commission may take any of the following disciplinary actions:

- An admonition is the least serious sanction the commission can impose. It consists of a letter to a judge suggesting that a given action was inappropriate or that another action might have been better. Admonitions may be either private or public.
- A warning is stronger than an admonition. It may be issued privately or publicly.
- A reprimand is more serious than either an admonition or a warning. The Commission on Judicial Conduct issues a reprimand, either publicly or privately, when it believes a judge has committed serious misconduct.
- Recommendation to remove from office is the strongest action the commission may take. When this happens, the chief justice of the Texas Supreme Court

NATIONAL PERSPECTIVE

Drug Courts in Florida

Over the past decade, states around the nation have been creating a new type of court called a problem-solving court to deal with criminal offenses such as drug use and possession, prostitution, shoplifting, and domestic violence. In contrast to a traditional court, which focuses on facts and legal issues, a **problem-solving court** is a judicial body that attempts to change the future behavior of litigants and promote the welfare of the community. The goal of a problem-solving court is not just to punish offenders but also to prevent future harm.*

The oldest problem-solving court in the nation is the drug court of Dade County (Miami), Florida. The Florida legislature created the drug court in 1989 because of the ineffectiveness of traditional judicial approaches to drug crime. The legislature hoped that the drug court would achieve better results for victims, defendants, and the community than traditional courts had achieved. The drug court sentences addicted defendants to long-term drug treatment instead of prison. The judge monitors the defendant's drug treatment and responds to progress or failure with a system of rewards or punishments, including short-term jail sentences. If a defendant completes treatment successfully, the judge reduces the charges or even dismisses the case altogether.

Research shows that the Florida drug court is effective. Defendants who go through drug court are less likely to be rearrested than are defendants whose cases are heard by a traditional court. Drug court defendants are also more likely to complete treatment than are defendants who enter drug rehabilitation voluntarily.[†]

Drug courts are now in use in 35 states, including Texas.[‡] In 2001, the Texas legislature passed and the governor signed a measure requiring counties of more than 550,000 people to set up drug courts and meet minimum enrollment figures in treatment programs. Texas officials hope not only to reduce drug offenses but also to save the state money because it is less expensive to sentence drug defendants to drug rehabilitation than it is to send them to prison.[§]

QUESTIONS TO CONSIDER

1. Are drug courts soft on crime?
2. Would you favor the use of a problem-solving court for other sorts of crimes, such as robbery and assault? Why or why not?
3. Are you for or against using drug courts in Texas?

---

*Jeffrey A. Butts, "Introduction: Problem-Solving Courts," *Law & Policy* 23 (April 2001): 121–124.

†Greg Berman and John Feinblatt, "Problem-Solving Courts: A Brief Primer," *Law & Policy* 23 (April 2001): 125–132.

‡Mark Thompson, "Hug-a-Thug Pays Off," *State Legislatures*, September 2006, p. 30.

§Pam Wagner, "Drug Courts on Trial," *Fiscal Notes*, June 2002, pp. 8–9.

---

selects a seven-judge panel chosen by lot from justices sitting on the various courts of appeals. The panel reviews the report and makes a recommendation to the Supreme Court, which may then remove the offending judge from office.

Address from office A procedure for removing judicial officials that is initiated by the governor and requires a two-thirds' vote by the legislature.

In addition to removal by the Supreme Court, Texas judges may be removed through the impeachment process or by a procedure known as address from office. Judges may be impeached by majority vote in the state House and removed by a two-thirds' vote of the Senate. **Address from office** is a procedure for removing judicial officials that is initiated by the governor and requires a two-thirds' vote by the legislature. Neither impeachment nor address from office is used with any frequency. Judges in trouble usually choose to resign rather than undergo the public humiliation of removal.

Problem-solving court A judicial body that attempts to change the future behavior of litigants and promote the welfare of the community.

Visiting Judges

Retirement or election defeat does not necessarily spell the end of a Texas judge's career on the bench. Many judges who have retired or been defeated for reelection continue working as visiting judges, the judicial equivalent of temporary workers. Visiting judges are especially in demand in the state's rapidly growing urban areas where the number of district courts has not increased rapidly enough to keep pace with growing caseloads. Visiting judges now hear about a fourth of district court cases in the state and participate in a tenth of appellate court decisions.[27]

The visiting judge system is controversial. The defenders of the practice declare that temporary judges are needed to keep up with crowded court dockets. Unless the legislature is willing to create dozens of new courts with their own full-time judges, the only alternative to visiting judges is a hopelessly overloaded court system. In contrast, critics charge that visiting judges are unaccountable to the voters, especially visiting judges who were defeated for reelection.

CONCLUSION: THE JUDICIAL BRANCH AND THE POLICYMAKING PROCESS

Tort reform The revision of state laws to limit the ability of plaintiffs in personal injury lawsuits to recover damages in court.

The judicial branch of Texas government plays an important role in the policymaking process in a broad range of policy areas. The courts have been prominent participants in death penalty appeals and tort reform because both of these issues involve access to the courts. (**Tort reform** refers to the revision of state laws to limit the ability of plaintiffs in personal injury lawsuits to recover damages in court.) State policy in both of these areas reflects the interplay of legislative action and judicial decisions.

The courts participate in other policy areas because of their role in interpreting state law and the Texas Constitution. Parties unhappy with the outcome of the policy process in the executive and legislative branches of government often turn to the courts for relief. Abortion rights advocates, critical of the state's refusal to fund medically necessary abortions in its Medicaid program, sued the state, asking the courts to overturn the policy on the basis of the Texas Constitution.

Agenda Building

Litigants set the agenda of the state's courts by filing cases that raise policy issues. Abortion rights activists raised the issue of Medicaid abortion funding by filing suit against the current state policy. School districts have gone to court on numerous occasions to attack the state's school funding system. In each instance, plaintiffs turned to the courts because they had failed to achieve their policy goals in the legislative and executive branches. The Texas Supreme Court's decision in *Edgewood v. Kirby* in 1989 set the agenda for the legislature and the governor by forcing them to devise a school funding system that would be constitutional.[28] Although legislators had been debating the school funding system for years, the legislature and the governor had only taken half-steps toward funding equalization. The *Edgewood* decision forced the legislature and the governor to adopt a major overhaul of the school finance system. More than a decade later, school districts were back in court, once again suing

GETTING INVOLVED

Volunteer to Become a Court-Appointed Special Advocate

A court-appointed special advocate is a trained volunteer appointed by a juvenile or family court judge to represent the interests of children who appear before the court. A majority of cases involving an advocate concern children who are removed from their homes because of abuse or neglect. The advocate meets with the child, the child's parents, prospective foster parents, social service caseworkers, and other people involved in the child's life to determine what course of action is in the best interest of the child. The advocate makes recommendations to the court and assists the child in making a transition to a new living situation.

Although the court-appointed special advocacy program is extremely rewarding, it requires a major time commitment and should not be taken lightly. Volunteers must be at least 21 years old, mature enough to handle difficult situations, and willing to complete a 30-hour training course. They must have their own transportation and be willing to commit to a year or more of volunteer work to see a case through to its resolution.

You can learn more about the Texas child advocacy program at the following website: www.texas casa.org/. The website discusses the program and provides contact information for potential volunteers in most of the state's counties. Contact the local organization in your community and inquire about participating in the program. It is your opportunity to play a positive role in the life of a child who needs help.

It's your community—get involved!

over the state's school funding system. This time, the suit, *West Orange-Cove Consolidated ISD v. Neeley,* was about state funding levels and local property tax rates. The school districts bringing the lawsuit argued that the amount of money the state provided for public education was too low for the system to be efficient, a requirement of the Texas Constitution. They also charged that the state property tax cap of $1.50 was effectively a state income tax because most districts had to levy a tax at or near the cap in order to meet state education requirements. The Texas Supreme Court agreed with the latter argument and ordered the state to reform the state funding mechanism to reduce dependence on local property taxes.[29]

The *Edgewood* and *West-Orange-Cove* cases are the exception rather than the rule. Relatively few state court rulings in Texas have raised major issues that were subsequently addressed by the other branches of state government. To some degree, this situation reflects the style of the Texas Constitution. The detailed nature of the state constitution leaves relatively little room for judicial interpretation. Furthermore, Texas judges may be reluctant to raise policy issues that have not been addressed by the other branches of government because they must periodically face the voters. Unlike federal judges who are appointed for life, state judges in Texas serve no more than six years before they must stand for election. Finally, Texas judges may have little incentive to raise policy issues because their policy values are similar to those of executive and legislative branch officials. Most Texas judges are conservative Republicans, and so are most of the members of the Texas legislature and the executive branch of state government. Few observers were surprised by the Texas Supreme Court's ruling on the constitutionality of the state's Medicaid abortion funding policy in light of the stridently anti-abortion position of the Texas Republican Party. Any Republican Supreme Court justice who ruled in favor of Medicaid funding for medically necessary abortions would almost certainly face a pro-life opponent in the Republican primary.

Policy Formulation and Adoption

The judicial branch of Texas government participates in policy formulation and adoption in selected policy areas. Consider the role of the Texas Supreme Court in reforming the school finance system. The majority opinion in *Edgewood* gave legislators some guidance on how the school finance system should be revised in order for it to satisfy the Texas Constitution. Subsequently, the court rejected legislative efforts to fix the problem until finally approving a solution that included the transfer of funds from wealthy school districts to poor school districts, the so-called Robin Hood Plan. Although the Supreme Court did not formulate and adopt the policy itself, it set the parameters for the other branches of government.

Tort reform is another policy area that bears the imprint of the judicial branch. In the early 1980s, the Texas Supreme Court issued a series of rulings that expanded the opportunities for individuals to recover damages from insurance companies and other business defendants in personal injury lawsuits. In 1986, for example, the court ruled that the relatives of a man killed by a drunken driver could sue the restaurant that served alcohol to the intoxicated driver.[30] Subsequently, the legislature and the governor adopted tort reform measures to limit access to the courts and reduce damage awards to plaintiffs in personal injury cases. Although courts in a number of states overturned tort reform laws as unconstitutional, the Texas Supreme Court embraced tort reform by interpreting state laws to limit the ability of plaintiffs to file suit and recover damages in civil cases.[31]

Judicial review
The authority of courts to declare unconstitutional the actions of the other branches and units of government.

Courts participate in policy adoption by exercising the power of **judicial review**, which is the authority of courts to declare unconstitutional the actions of the other branches and units of government. If a court believes that a state law, a regulatory rule, a city ordinance, or another policy of state or local government violates the constitution, the court declares it unconstitutional. An unconstitutional policy is null and void.

The scope of a court's authority to exercise judicial review depends on the level of the court. Although Texas district courts may declare policies unconstitutional, the impact of their rulings is limited to the case at hand. In 1998, for example, a district court in El Paso declared unconstitutional a state law prohibiting the sale of automobiles on consecutive Saturdays and Sundays.[32] The ruling affected only the case before the court and had no impact statewide. A decision by the courts of appeals is binding only on the particular courts of appeals district. The Texas Supreme Court and the Texas Court of Criminal Appeals are the only state courts whose decisions have statewide applicability.

Texas courts rule on both the Texas and U.S. Constitution. *Edgewood v. Kirby*, for example, was based on the Texas Constitution. On issues of state constitutional law, the Texas Supreme Court is the final authority for civil issues, whereas the Texas Court of Criminal Appeals is the court of last resort for criminal matters. The only recourse for litigants who lose on state constitutional grounds in either of the state's highest appellate courts is either to ask the court to rehear the case or to lobby the legislature to propose a constitutional amendment.

The state's courts also base their rulings on the U.S. Constitution. In 1996, for example, the Texas Supreme Court held that a police officer's constitutional rights had not been violated when the city of Sherman denied him a promotion because he had had an affair with the wife of another officer. The court declared that neither the Texas Constitution nor the Constitution of the United States includes a right to privacy that encompasses adultery.[33] The police officer could not file an appeal of the court's interpretation of the Texas Constitution because the Texas Supreme Court is the final authority on issues of state constitutional law. He could, however, file an appeal of the court's interpretation of the U.S. Constitution to the U.S. Supreme Court. Although Texas courts may base their rulings on the U.S. Constitution, their decisions may be appealed to the federal courts.

Policy Implementation and Evaluation

The judicial branch of Texas government plays a key role in implementing the state's criminal and civil justice systems. The state courts enforce the criminal law by hearing cases filed against people accused of violating the law. They apply the civil law by settling disputes among litigants over personal injuries, property, domestic relations, and other matters. Although the importance of most court decisions is limited to the case at hand, the courts occasionally make decisions that have a significant impact on the implementation of the law. In 1997, for example, the Texas Court of Criminal Appeals ruled that convicted child molesters were eligible for the prison early release program. When the legislature wrote the law, it inadvertently left the crime of indecency with a child off the list of crimes for which offenders were ineligible for early release. The Texas Court of Criminal Appeals declared that the state had no choice but to implement the law as it was written.[34]

The judicial branch plays a limited role in policy evaluation. In contrast to legislative committees and executive branch agencies, courts do not conduct performance audits of state agencies or issue reports on the effectiveness of government programs. Courts do, however, evaluate government programs on the basis of their consistency with the constitution. *Edgewood v. Kirby* represented an evaluation of the state's school finance system.

LET'S DEBATE

Should State Judges Be Elected or Appointed?

Overview: As with the legislative and executive branches, there have been numerous calls in the states for judicial reform, and the one reform cited most often is the appeal to eliminate partisan elections for judges. Currently, only Texas, Louisiana, Alabama, and West Virginia choose their trial and appellate judges through partisan elections; most other states have modified or reformed their judicial systems within the last 40 years. A *Houston Chronicle* poll of the Houston Bar Association showed that 81 percent of the Houston metro area's lawyers believe the method of Texas judicial selection should be changed, with nearly half desiring that Texas move to some form of Merit Selection institution. The Texas judiciary has been the subject of high-profile journalistic investigation (notably, the *60 Minutes* exposé "Justice for Sale," in which it was alleged that trial lawyers who donated to Texas judicial campaigns won two-thirds of their cases before the state Supreme Court), and the Texas courts have been held as an example of the judicial "corruption" that is an "inevitable" result of partisan elections. The idea behind reform is to remove the influence of interest groups and campaign contributions from judicial selection.

continued on next page

If the previous paragraph is true, what are the alternatives to partisan elections? A number of reforms have been proposed, with some arguing that you can both satisfy the demands of electoral accountability and limit interest-group influence by having publicly funded elections. The most emulated reform, however, is a type of merit-based appointment system in which appointed judges face voters in uncontested, nonpartisan retention elections. This is based on reform known as the Missouri Plan, and there are currently 39 states with some form of merit-based system and retention elections. A merit-based appointment procedure uses some sort of nonpartisan commission to evaluate the qualifications and desirability of potential justices. By appointing justices from a pool chosen by a nonpartisan commission, judges will be removed from the disagreeable politics and perception of being "bought" by interest groups that are part of election campaigns. Electoral accountability is ensured by retention elections in which voters shortly ratify or reject the government's choice.

Most of all, it is the judicial branch that needs the public to believe it is impartial and fair because even the *perception* of impropriety or corruption in the judiciary diminishes the effectiveness of the rule of law. Those who advocate direct election of judges and those who advocate reform are both concerned with the disinterested and unbiased administration of justice. It can be fairly argued that the American and Texas electorate are concerned with the current operation of state judiciaries. For example, an argument for Proposition 2 (the new amendment to the Texas Constitution, which defines marriage as being between "one man" and "one woman") was to place the definition of marriage out of reach of the state's justices. What is the best way to ensure an unbiased judiciary and, at the same time, hold justices accountable to the democratic process?

Arguments for Elected Judges

❏ **Elected judges are accountable to the people.** The signature feature of democratic practice is that ultimate political authority resides within the body of the people, and it is the people who have the final say (through their representatives or otherwise) regarding the type and form of law and policy under which they wish to live. An elected judiciary is crucial to the realization of this democratic norm. Research indicates that, though voters may be "ignorant," the electorate uses partisan cues when voting, with the result that citizens can select judges who best represent the state's political culture. The voters can then hold judges accountable for their actions on the bench by voting them out of office.

❏ **The election of judges helps ensure a judiciary independent from the executive and legislative branches of government.** Though there are checks on the judiciary from the other two branches, elected judges generally do not hold their positions due to direct legislative or executive action. Most justices serve at the pleasure of Texas voters, and this provides an institutional safeguard to judicial independence. Judges are thereby not beholden to the governor or legislature for their offices and are thus freer to exercise judicial independence. Elected justices lack the direct political bonds to members of legislative and executive institutions; as a result, they can adjudicate accordingly.

❏ **Merit Selection is just as political in nature as partisan elections.** Moving to a merit appointment process would only change the political arena. Lobbyists and interest groups will merely seek to influence the appointment process. Texas Appellate Justice Tom James writes that, when there is a gubernatorial appointment for a vacant seat, interest groups control the process through their relationships with the incumbent governor and the Texas Senate. The reality is that interested parties will always find a way to affect political office, and elections provide a means to remove incompetent or corrupt justices.

Arguments for Judicial Reform

❏ **A merit-based appointment system would remove interest-group influence on the judiciary.** The theory behind an elected judiciary rests on solid principles, but the truth is that, in modern political campaigns, those pursuing office need significant funding. Former Chief Justice John Hill argues that increasingly expensive campaigns are financed by lawyers who practice before the bar and by interest groups representing business and industry, and the result is a bench that effectively represents and elevates the interest of contributors over others. The result is diminished public confidence in the impartiality and fairness of the Texas judiciary.

❏ **Judges should spend their time adjudicating, not seeking campaign funds and/or running for office.** Merit Selection and appointment release judge from having to consume significant time raising funds, meeting voters, and spending time on the campaign trail. The nature of the judiciary demands that judges spend their time studying complex, detailed, and technical law and precedents, thus increasing a judge's competence, capability, and, most important, fairness. Running for office diminishes a justice's ability to have the requisite time for such study and research.

❏ **An impartial judiciary must be protected from the influence of public opinion.** An elective judiciary impairs judicial impartiality. In order to ensure fairness, judges must be impartial and resolve disputes based on law and evidence, not on statements made in an electoral campaign. Individuals running for office must give voters a reason to place them in office, which means outlining a political agenda or giving a statement of policy. What is a judge to do if confronted with a case or controversy that contradicts what the public now expects? Elections force justices to give credence to the public opinion that elevated them to judicial office.

QUESTIONS

1. Do merit-based appointment systems based on the Missouri Plan model ensure judicial impartiality and democratic accountability?

2. Do partisan elections allow voters to elect those justices who reflect the state's political culture? Shouldn't the judiciary abide by the majority's political philosophy?

SELECT READINGS

1. Anthony Champagne, *Judicial Politics in Texas: Partisanship, Money, and Politics in State Courts* (New York: Peter Lang, 2004).
2. Philip Dubois, *From Ballot to Bench: Judicial Elections and the Quest for Accountability* (Austin: University of Texas Press, 1980).

SELECT WEBSITES

1. **www.state.tx.us/category.jsp?language=eng&category-Id=6.3**
   Website resource for the Texas judicial system.

2. **www.ajs.org/js/TX_elections.htm.**
   American Judicature Society's website regarding the status of Texas judicial reform.

KEY TERMS

address from office

adversary proceeding

affirm

appeal

burden of proof

capital punishment

city ordinances

civil case

civil defendant

concurring opinion

contract case

criminal case

criminal defendant

dissenting opinion

district election

domestic-relations case

double jeopardy

felony

forcible entry and detainer suit

harmless error

judicial review

League of United Latin American Citizens (LULAC)

legal briefs

legal writs

litigants

magistrates

majority, or deciding, opinion

Medicaid

Merit Selection *or* the Missouri Plan

misdemeanor

nonpartisan elections

partisan election

plaintiff

plea bargain

probate case

problem-solving court

property case

property lien

prosecutor

punitive damages

remand

reversible error

straight ticket voting

Texas Equal Rights Amendment (ERA)

tort case

tort reform

trial

writ of *habeas corpus*

writ of *mandamus*

NOTES

1. *Bell v. Low Income Women of Texas*, Texas Supreme Court, No. 01-0061 (December 2002).
2. *Duncan v. Louisiana*, 391 U.S. 145 (1968).
3. "Court Structure of Texas," *Annual Report of the Texas Judicial System*, Fiscal Year 2006, available at www.courts.state.tx.us.
4. "Activity Report for Municipal Courts," *Annual Report of the Texas Judicial System*, Fiscal Year 2006.
5. "Activity Report for Justice Courts," *Annual Report of the Texas Judicial System*, Fiscal Year 2006.
6. "Court Structure of Texas."
7. "District Courts: Summary Activity by Case Type," *Annual Report of the Texas Judicial System*, Fiscal Year 2006.
8. "Activity for the Fiscal Year Ended August 31, 2006," *Annual Report of the Texas Judicial System*, Fiscal Year 2006.
9. "Court of Criminal Appeals Activity: FY 2006," *Annual Report of the Texas Judicial System*, Fiscal Year 2006.
10. Ibid.
11. "Supreme Court Activity: FY 2002–2006," *Annual Report of the Texas Judicial System*, Fiscal Year 2006.
12. Ibid.
13. "Profile of Appellate and Trial Judges," *Annual Report of the Texas Judicial System*, Fiscal Year 2006.
14. Charles Mahtesian, "Bench Press," *Governing*, August 1998, p. 20.
15. "Profile of Appellate and Trial Judges."
16. Sam Kinch Jr., *Too Much Money Is Not Enough: Big Money and Political Power in Texas* (Austin: Campaign for People, 2000), p. 14.
17. National Institute on Money in State Politics, available at www.followthemoney.org.
18. Wayne Slater, "Couple's Dream Home a 10-Year Legal Nightmare," *Dallas Morning News*, January 21, 2007, available at www.dallasnews.com.
19. *Texas Weekly*, December 12, 1994, p. 4.
20. "Profile of Appellate and Trial Judges."
21. Kenyon D. Bunch and Gregory Casey, "Political Controversy on Missouri's Supreme Court: The Case of Merit vs. Politics," *State and Local Government Review* 22 (Winter 1990): 5–16.
22. Craig F. Emmert and Henry R. Glick, "The Selection of State Supreme Court Justices," *American Politics Quarterly* 16 (October 1988): 445–465.
23. Robert C. Luskin, Christoper N. Bratcher, Christopher B. Jordan, and Kris S. Seago, "How Minority Judges Fare in Retention Elections," *Judicature* 71 (1994): 316–321.
24. Amy Johnson, "Court Reform? The Case Against the Appointment of Judges," *Texas Observer*, February 6, 1987, pp. 8–10.
25. Quoted in Brett Campbell, "Courting Inequality," *Texas Observer*, March 9, 1990, p. 17.
26. Delbert A. Taebel, "On the Way to Midland: Race or Partisanship? A Research Note on Comparative Voting in Urban Counties in Judicial Elections," *Texas Journal of Political Studies* 12 (Fall/Winter 1989/90): 5–23.
27. Mark Smith, "Business Good for Visiting Judges," *Houston Chronicle*, September 20, 1998, p. 23A.
28. *Edgewood v. Kirby*, 777 S.W.2d 391 (1989).
29. House Research Organization, *Court Rules School Finance System Unconstitutional*, February 21, 2005, available at www.capitol.state.tx.us/hrofr/focus/dietz79-6.pdf.
30. *Poole v. El Chico Corp.*, 713 S.W.2nd 959 Tex. (1986).
31. Sarah Whitmire, "Torts Pit Lawmakers vs. Courts," *State Government News*, February 2000, pp. 14–17.
32. *Texas Weekly*, September 14, 1998, p. 5.
33. Peggy Fikac, "Court Concludes Right to Privacy Doesn't Apply to Adultery," *Houston Chronicle*, July 9, 1996, p. 15A.
34. "Many Child Molesters May Walk Free Under Appeals Court Ruling," *Houston Chronicle*, November 28, 1997, p.43A.

Chapter 28

City Government in Texas

CHAPTER OUTLINE

Legal Status of Texas Cities
    Incorporation
    General-Law and Home-Rule Cities

Forms of City Government
    Mayor-Council Form
    Council-Manager Form
    Hybrid Structures

Election Systems

Public Policies in Texas Cities
    Budgetary Policy
    Annexation and Suburban Development
    Land Use Regulation

City Politics in Texas

Conclusion: City Government and Policymaking

LEARNING OUTCOMES

After studying Chapter 28, students should be able to do the following:

▸ Assess the effectiveness of the effort by Farmers Branch to address the issue of illegal immigration. (p. 756)

▸ Distinguish between general-law and home-rule cities. (pp. 757–759)

▸ Compare and contrast the various forms of city government. (pp. 759–764)

▸ Evaluate the various types of city election systems, tracing the history of their use in Texas. (pp. 764–767)

▸ Compare and contrast developmental, redistributive, and allocational policies, giving examples of each type of policy. (pp. 768–769)

▸ Identify the major expenditure items and revenue sources for city governments in Texas. (pp. 769–770)

▸ Explain how property taxes are assessed and collected. (pp. 770–771)

▸ Assess the arguments for and against tax increment financing, tax abatements, and enterprise zones. (pp. 772–773)

▸ Describe annexation policies. (pp. 773–776)

▸ Describe land use policies in Texas cities. (pp. 776–777)

▸ Compare and contrast zoning with deed restrictions. (pp. 777–778)

▸ Compare and contrast the elite approach to describing urban politics with the pluralist approach. (pp. 779–781)

▸ Describe the evolution of big-city politics in the state since the 1950s. (p. 781)

▸ Define the key terms listed on page 784 and explain their significance.

Farmers Branch has become a focus in the debate over illegal immigration. Frustrated with the inability of the U.S. Congress to pass immigration reform legislation, the Farmers Branch city council adopted a set of ordinances addressing the problem. First, the city council declared English the official language of Farmers Branch. It removed signs in Spanish posted in the public library, stopped printing the holiday trash pickup schedule in Spanish, and no longer allowed people exercising at the city recreation center to watch Spanish-language television channels while they worked out. The city continued to print documents in Spanish if health and safety was involved.[1] Second, the city authorized the police department to participate in a federal program to train officers to verify the residency status of people held in police custody. People identified as illegal immigrants could then be turned over to federal immigration officials. Finally, the city required apartment owners and managers to ensure that prospective tenants were in the country legally before renting to them. Landlords who failed to verify residency status or who rented to illegal immigrants would face fines.[2]

City officials and many of the city's residents blamed illegal immigration for the decline of their city's neighborhoods. Since 1970, Farmers Branch, which is located in northwest Dallas County, had grown from a predominantly white community with a declining population to a city of 28,000 people that was 37 percent Latino.[3] Residents worried about overcrowded schools with teachers having to spend much of their time teaching English to Spanish-speaking youngsters. They complained about multiple families living in single-family homes surrounded by vehicles blocking streets and sidewalks.

In contrast, advocates for immigrant rights and some city residents believed that the Farmers Branch ordinances were a mistake, especially the ordinance directing apartment owners and managers to verify the residency status of prospective tenants. Apartment managers are not trained to evaluate residency documents, they warned, and may engage in racial discrimination against Latinos who are citizens or legal residents. Furthermore, critics worried that the city would be forced to spend hundreds of thousands of dollars defending against the inevitable lawsuits filed against the ordinances.[4]

The critics were right about the lawsuits. The Mexican American Legal Defense and Education Fund (MALDEF) and the American Civil Liberties Union (ACLU) filed suit in federal court on behalf of Latino residents and apartment owners. The lawsuit charged that the city lacked the legal authority to enact the ordinances and asked the judge to block their enforcement. U.S. District Judge Sam Lindsey agreed. He issued an order to block enforcement of the apartment ordinance because the city ordinance conflicted with federal immigration law.[5]

This chapter is the fourth of five chapters examining the policymaking institutions of state and local government. Chapters 25, 26, and 27 considered the legislative, executive, and judicial branches of state government, respectively, whereas Chapter 29 focuses on counties, school districts, and special districts. This chapter deals with the role of cities in the policymaking process. It examines the legal status of Texas cities and describes their political structures and election systems. The chapter discusses three areas of urban policymaking: budgetary policy, annexation and suburban development, and land use regulation. The chapter also examines big-city politics in Texas.

LEGAL STATUS OF TEXAS CITIES

City ordinances
Laws enacted by the governing body of a municipality.

City governments in Texas have broad authority to provide public services, enact regulations, and levy taxes. Texas cities may provide hospitals, libraries, parks, paved streets, police protection, airports, water and sewer service, health clinics, and fire protection for their residents. They may adopt **city ordinances,** which are laws enacted by the governing body of a municipality to regulate such matters as building construction, land use practices, and driving habits. Cities fund their operations by levying property taxes, sales taxes, and a variety of other taxes, fees, and service charges.

Nonetheless, cities and other units of local government are subordinate units of government, subject to the constitutions and laws of the United States and the state of Texas. Federal laws take precedence over city ordinances and regulations. Judge Lindsay blocked enforcement of the Farmers Branch ordinance, for example, because he ruled that it conflicted with federal law. Cities are dependent on state constitutions and state laws for their creation, organization, and authority. State law controls such matters as city tax rates and exemptions; wages, hours, benefits, and promotion policies for city employees; and annexation procedures.

The Texas legislature and the governor frequently adopt legislation designed to define and limit the policymaking authority of city government. For example, Texas is one of 40 states that prohibit cities from suing the firearms industry.[6] A number of cities in other states have sued gun manufacturers to hold them accountable for manufacturing guns with inadequate safety features that would prevent unauthorized and unintentional shootings, as well as for negligent distribution and marketing practices that contribute to the illegal gun market. The legislature and the governor have also adopted legislation prohibiting city governments from establishing their own **minimum wage,** which is the lowest hourly wage that an employer can pay covered workers.

Minimum wage
The lowest hourly wage that an employer can pay covered workers.

Interest groups and even individual citizens who are unhappy with the decisions of a city government can ask the legislature to intervene. Moreover, the legislature and the governor have grown increasingly willing to override the policy decisions of city governments because of a shift in partisanship. Even though most city elections are officially nonpartisan (party labels are not on the ballot), most officials in the state's major cities are Democrats. In contrast, the Republican Party now controls both chambers of the Texas legislature and the governorship. On issues that pit city governments against interests usually aligned with the Republican Party, such as suburban residents and developers, the legislature and the governor more often than not intervene against the city.

Incorporated municipality A city under the laws of the state.

Unincorporated area Territory not part of a legal city.

Incorporation

State law sets the requirements and procedures under which an unincorporated urban area in Texas may become an **incorporated municipality,** which is a city under the laws of the state. An **unincorporated area,** which is territory not part of a legal city, must have a population of at least 200 people to form a municipality. It must also be outside the legal jurisdiction of other incorporated municipalities unless it receives permission to incorporate from the established city. The proponents of

City charter The basic law of a city that defines its powers, responsibilities, and organization.

General-law city A municipality that is limited to those governmental structures and powers specifically granted by state law.

Dillon's rule The legal principle that a city can exercise only those powers expressly allowed by state law.

Home-rule city A municipality that can take any actions not prohibited by state or federal law or the constitutions of the United States or the state of Texas.

Annexation The authority of a city to increase its geographic size by extending its boundaries to take in adjacent unincorporated areas.

Recall A procedure allowing voters to remove elected officials from office before the expiration of their terms.

incorporation begin the process by collecting signatures on an incorporation petition. After they have gathered the required number of names, perhaps as many as 10 percent of the registered voters in the prospective municipality, they present their petition to the county judge, who calls an election in which the area's voters may choose either to incorporate or to remain unincorporated. The residents of an incorporated city can follow the same procedure if they wish to disincorporate. The voters of a newly incorporated municipality must also approve a **city charter,** which is the basic law of a city that defines its powers, responsibilities, and organization. Changes in a city charter must receive voter approval as well.

General-Law and Home-Rule Cities

Texas cities are classified as either general-law or home-rule cities. A **general-law city** is a municipality that is limited to those governmental structures and powers specifically granted by state law. Municipalities with fewer than 5,000 people must be general-law cities.

General-law cities are bound by **Dillon's rule,** which is the legal principle that a city can exercise only those powers expressly allowed by state law. Dillon's rule is named after Judge J. F. Dillon, a member of the Iowa Supreme Court, who wrote an opinion in 1868 concerning the legal status of cities. Dillon concluded that municipalities owe their origins to and derive their power from the state legislature. Therefore, they are totally dependent on and subservient to the legislature. Courts in Texas and in other states have followed Dillon's rule in defining the authority of general-law cities. If a general law city wants to offer a service or adopt a structure of government not provided in state law, it must first obtain specific authorization from the legislature.

In 1913, the Texas legislature proposed and the voters approved an amendment to the state constitution to allow a municipality with 5,000 or more people to become a **home-rule city,** which is a municipality that can take any actions not prohibited by state or federal law or the constitutions of the United States or the state of Texas. In contrast to general-law cities, home-rule cities are not burdened by the limitations of Dillon's rule. A home-rule city can do anything that qualifies as a "public purpose" that does not violate the Texas Constitution or the laws of the state. Compared with general-law cities, home-rule cities enjoy more freedom in the following areas:

- **Organizational structure** Home-rule cities can adopt any structure of municipal government they choose, whereas general-law cities are limited to a narrow range of options.
- **Annexation** Home-rule cities can annex without the approval of the people living in the annexed area. General-law cities cannot annex unless the residents of the targeted area vote to accept annexation. (**Annexation** is the authority of a city to increase its geographic size by extending its boundaries to take in adjacent unincorporated areas.)
- **Ordinance-making authority** Home-rule cities have broader authority to adopt ordinances than do general-law municipalities.
- **Election processes** Home-rule cities may include both recall and the initiative process in their charters. More than 90 percent of home-rule cities allow citizens the power of **recall,** which is a procedure for allowing voters to remove elected

Initiative process
A procedure whereby citizens can propose the adoption of a policy measure by gathering a prerequisite number of signatures. Voters must then approve the measure before it can take effect.

officials from office before the expiration of their terms. Eighty-five percent of home-rule cities have the **initiative process,** which is a procedure available in some states and cities whereby citizens can propose the adoption of a policy measure by gathering a prerequisite number of signatures. Voters must then approve the measure before it can take effect.[7] Opponents of the Farmers Branch ordinances used the initiative process to force a vote to overturn the measure requiring landlords to verify residency status, but the voters upheld the ordinance by a two-thirds' margin.[8]

Nearly 300 Texas cities are home rule, including all of the state's big cities. Only 19 cities larger than 5,000 people have chosen to remain general law cities. If a home-rule city falls below the 5,000-population threshold, it maintains its home rule status.[9]

The legislature has the power to pass laws limiting home rule authority. For example, the legislature has established uniform election dates, limiting most local elections to either the second Saturday in May or the first Tuesday after the first Monday in November. Although the Texas Constitution prevents the legislature from passing local laws regulating the affairs of individual cities, the legislature gets around the restriction by enacting **population bracket laws,** which are state laws designed to target particular cities based on their population. Houston and Austin are the most frequent targets of population bracket legislation. For example, the legislature could pass a measure that applied to all Texas cities with a population larger than 1.9 million. It so happens that only one city meets that criterion—Houston. If the legislature wanted to target Austin, it could adopt a bill aimed at cities with populations between 650,000 and 660,000 in 2000. That description applies only to Austin.

Population bracket laws State laws designed to target particular cities based on their population.

FORMS OF CITY GOVERNMENT

The mayor-council and council-manager forms of city government are the basic structures of municipal government in Texas.

Mayor-Council Form

Mayor-council form of city government A structure of municipal government in which the voters elect a mayor as the chief executive officer of the city and a council that serves as a legislative body.

The **mayor-council form of city government** is a structure of municipal government in which the voters elect a mayor as the chief executive officer of the city and a council that serves as a legislative body. In the mayor-council form of city government, the mayor and council together make policy for the city. They are responsible for raising and spending city revenue, passing local ordinances, and supervising the city's administrative departments.

Being mayor or serving on city council is a full-time job in big cities using the mayor-council form of government, but not in small towns. In Houston, for example, the mayor runs the city government full-time and earns a salary of $187,500 a year. Although most members of the Houston city council have other jobs, they, too, spend many hours a week on city business, making $50,000 a year. In contrast, mayors and council members in small towns using the mayor-council form of city government usually earn only a small salary for a job that normally takes just a few hours a week.

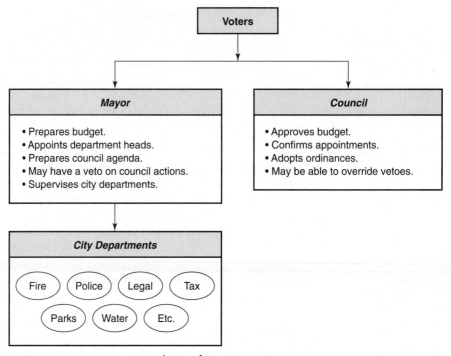

FIGURE 28.1   Strong Mayor-Council Form of City Government.

Cities using the mayor-council form of city government differ in the amount of power the mayor enjoys. Figures 28.1 and 28.2 diagram the strong mayor and weak mayor variations of the mayor-council form of city government. In the strong mayor variation (Figure 28.1), the mayor is the foremost figure in city government, acting as both a political leader and the city's chief administrative officer. The mayor prepares the budget, enjoys a veto over council actions (with or without possibility of a council override), hires and fires department heads, and essentially runs city government. Although the city council must approve (and thus may reject) many of the mayor's actions, politically skillful mayors can usually win approval of most of their initiatives and appointments. Council members elected from districts will want to stay in the mayor's favor because the mayor oversees the provision of public services to their districts. Furthermore, the mayor and the mayor's financial backers may get involved in council races to elect individuals to council who will be part of the "mayor's team" and to defeat the mayor's opponents on the council. Bob Lanier, who was mayor of Houston in the 1990s, lost only three council votes during his six years in office.[10] Former Houston City Council Member Vince Ryan described the strong mayor system in Houston as "King Kong and the 14 chimps" because of the relative imbalance of power between the mayor and the 14 council members.[11]

The advocates of the strong mayor variation of the mayor-council form of city government believe that the system provides for efficient city government because it concentrates power and responsibility for policy leadership and policy implementation in the hands of a single elected official, the mayor. The mayor can take the lead

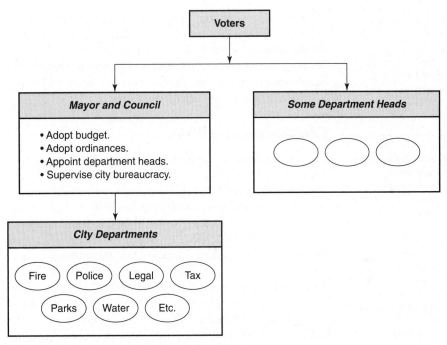

FIGURE 28.2   Weak Mayor-Council Form of City Government.

in agenda setting, policy formulation, policy adoption, and policy implementation. The voters can then evaluate the mayor on performance. In contrast, the critics of the mayor-council form of city government contend that the strong mayor variation gives the mayor too much power. They worry that the mayor will build a personal empire and become a political boss. Although the voters elect council members to represent neighborhoods and communities, they have relatively little influence on major policy decisions in the strong mayor variation. Instead, council members focus on the most mundane details of urban policy implementation, such as abandoned houses, overgrown vacant lots, potholes, and stray dogs.[12]

In contrast to the strong mayor system, the weak mayor variation of the mayor-council form of city government (Figure 28.2) fragments political authority by forcing the mayor to share power with council and other elected officials, including a tax assessor, a treasurer, and even a police chief. The mayor and council together appoint administrative officials, supervise city administration, and adopt the budget. The proponents of the weak mayor system contend that it prevents the mayor from becoming too powerful by creating a check-and-balance system. Critics of the weak mayor variation say that it invites corruption and dilutes accountability because it fails to assign policymaking authority to any single official.

The mayor-council system is the traditional form of city government in America, and it is still found in all of the nation's cities with a population greater than a million, except for Dallas, El Paso, San Antonio, and Phoenix.[13] The mayor-council form is also the most common form of city government among general-law municipalities in Texas. Most general-law cities prefer the mayor-council form because it is less expensive to operate than the council-manager form, which would require the city to hire a full-time city manager. In contrast, only 38 of the state's home-rule cities use the mayor-council form of city government.[14] Houston is the only big city in Texas to use the mayor-council form. The state's other large cities, including Dallas, San Antonio, Fort Worth, Austin, Corpus Christi, and most recently El Paso, have adopted the council-manager form instead.

Council-Manager Form

Council-manager form of city government A structure of municipal government in which the city council/mayor appoints a professional administrator called a city manager to act as the chief executive officer of the municipality.

The **council-manager form of city government** is a structure of municipal government in which the city council/mayor appoints a professional administrator, called a city manager, to act as the chief executive officer of the municipality. In this form of city government, the power of the mayor is limited to performing ceremonial duties and presiding at council meetings. In fact, in some smaller council-manager cities, voters do not directly choose a mayor at all. Instead, the office may go to the at-large council member receiving the most votes. Alternatively, the council may choose one of its members to serve as mayor. In such cases, the mayor's ability to act as a policy leader depends on personal leadership skills rather than official powers.

City manager A professional administrator hired by city council in the council-manager form of city government to manage the day-to-day affairs of city government.

The major difference between the mayor-council and council-manager forms of city government concerns the implementation of policy. In both systems, the mayor and council make basic policy decisions but, in the council-manager form, policy implementation is the responsibility of a professional administrator hired by the city council—a **city manager.** Figure 28.3 diagrams this form of city government. The city manager is the chief administrative officer of the city and is generally responsible for hiring and firing department heads, preparing the budget, and overseeing policy administration. In council-manager cities, the mayor and council members are usually considered part-time officials and are paid accordingly. In Fort Worth, for example, the mayor and council members each receive $75 for every week they attend one or more official meetings. In contrast, the Fort Worth city manager earns $186,513 a year.[15]

The council-manager form is the most common type of city government among the state's home rule cities. Its advocates believe that it is an efficient system that keeps politics out of administration and administrators out of politics. They argue that a professional city manager can provide more efficient policy administration than a mayor with no administrative experience. Nonetheless, most political scientists believe that city managers inevitably become involved in politics, even in the sense of participating extensively in policy formulation and adoption. Furthermore, policy implementation is inherently political because it determines how the power of government is exercised. City managers act politically when they make recommendations to elected officials and seek to develop support for their positions among public officials and interest groups influential in city politics.[16]

? WHAT IS YOUR OPINION?

If you were one of the founders of a new city in Texas, what form of city government would you favor for the new city? Why?

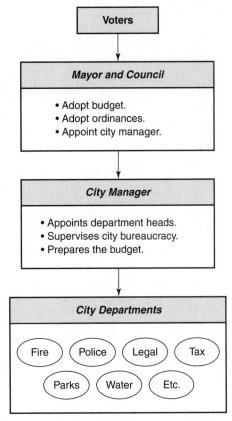

FIGURE 28.3   Council-Manager Form of City Government.

Critics of the council-manager form of city government argue that it may work fine for mid-size, uncomplicated cities, but not for larger cities. They believe that big cities with diverse populations need the policy leadership of a strong mayor. The city manager system is designed to ensure the efficient implementation of policy. What happens, they ask, when city residents and the city council are deeply divided over policy alternatives? Neither the city manager nor the mayor in the council-manager form of government has the political strength to forge a consensus among competing political forces.[17] Critics of city government in Dallas, for example, charge that the city suffers from a council that is divided along ethnic, ideological, and geographic lines and that the mayor has too little power to provide leadership.[18] Nonetheless, Dallas voters turned down a proposal to scrap the council-manager system and replace it with the mayor-council form of city government. Mayor Laura Miller argued that the reform would provide for a more efficient city government, but city council members countered that it would give the mayor too much power without checks and balances.

Hybrid Structures

In practice, the structures of city government seldom match the classic mayor-council or council-manager form of municipal government. Many mayor-council cities have added chief administrative officers or deputy mayors who function much as city managers do. Furthermore, many council-manager cities have increased the power of the mayor to provide greater accountability.[19]

ELECTION SYSTEMS

At-large election
A method for choosing public officials in which every citizen of a political subdivision, such as a state or county, votes to select a public official.

District election A method for choosing public officials in which a political subdivision, such as a state or county, is divided into districts and each district elects one official.

Cumulative voting system An election system that allows individual voters to cast more than one ballot in the simultaneous election of several officials.

The most popular system for choosing council members in Texas is the **at-large election** system, which is a method for choosing public officials in which every citizen of a political subdivision, such as a state or county, votes to select a public official. As Table 28.1 indicates, 131 cities use a place system. Candidates must declare for particular seats (or places) on council and voters then select among the candidates for each council seat. Thirty-six cities elect council members at-large without the use of a place system. On Election Day, voters select as many candidates as seats on council. If the city has five council members, for example, a voter chooses five candidates from among the list of people running for council.

In contrast to the at-large election method, a **district election** is a method for choosing public officials in which a political subdivision, such as a state or city, is divided into districts, with each district electing one official. Seventy-four cities use district election systems. El Paso, for example, elects eight council members from districts.

Not all Texas cities use either at-large or district election systems. Forty-eight cities have a combination of at-large and district seats. The Houston city council, for example, has 14 members—9 members chosen from districts and 5 elected at-large. Finally, one Texas home-rule city has a **cumulative voting system,** which is an election system that allows individual voters to cast more than one ballot in the simultaneous election of several officials. The difference between at-large and cumulative voting is that the cumulative system allows voters to cast all of their votes for a single candidate.

TABLE 28.1   Methods of Council Election in Texas Home-Rule Cities

Method of Election	No. of Cities Using System
At-large election by place	131
At-large election	36
District election	74
Combination of district and at-large seats	48
Cumulative voting	1
Total	**290**

Source: Terrell Blodget, "Municipal Home Rule Charters in Texas," *Public Affairs Comment* 41 (1996), p. 4.

Both district and at-large election systems have their proponents. Supporters of district elections believe that they make government more responsive to citizens and increase participation. District elections reduce the role of money in city politics, they say, because candidates need less money to campaign in a district than they would to run a campaign citywide. Furthermore, the advocates of district elections argue that they produce a council that more closely reflects the racial and ethnic diversity of the city because they enable geographically concentrated minorities to elect group members to public office.

In contrast, defenders of at-large elections believe that council members chosen at large consider policy issues from a broader perspective than do district council members. Whereas district representatives focus on the particular concerns of their districts, at-large council members must consider what is best for the city as a whole. Furthermore, the supporters of at-large elections believe that citywide campaigns produce better-quality officials than do district elections.

Historically, district (or ward) election systems were associated with big-city **political machines,** which were entrenched political organizations headed by a boss or small group of leaders who held power through patronage, control over nominations, and bribery. **Political patronage** is the power of an officeholder to award favors, such as government jobs, to political allies. In the late nineteenth century, machine politicians in New York City, St. Louis, Cleveland, Chicago, and other big cities won election from districts with the support of geographically concentrated white ethnic minorities, especially Italian, Irish, and Polish Americans.

Well-to-do white Anglo-Saxon business groups who opposed the political machines attacked district elections as corrupt, proposing instead the adoption of nonpartisan at-large council election systems. **Nonpartisan elections** are elections in which candidates run without party labels. The business leaders packaged their proposal as a "good government" reform but, in fact, it was designed to favor the interests of affluent business groups who would have more money to fund candidates for citywide seats than would the working-class ethnic minority groups who supported the political machine.

Although most large industrialized cities, including Chicago, St. Louis, and Cleveland, did not adopt nonpartisan at-large election systems, many of the new cities in the South and West did, including most cities in Texas. Dallas, for example, created a nine-member city council, with each member elected at-large. Houston's eight-member council was chosen at-large as well.

The adoption of at-large council elections in Texas cities limited the political influence of ethnic and racial minorities, primarily African Americans and Latinos. Under the at-large council system in Dallas, no African Americans and only one Latino won election to council, and the successful Latino candidate was a North Dallas businessman who was endorsed and financed by wealthy white business groups.[20] Similarly, the only minority candidate elected to the Houston city council under that city's at-large election system was an African American real estate investor who had the support of downtown business interests.

The **Voting Rights Act (VRA),** which is federal law designed to protect the voting rights of racial and ethnic minorities, provided a means for minority rights groups to attack election systems they considered discriminatory. The act allows

Political machines Entrenched political organizations headed by a boss or small group of leaders who held power through such techniques as patronage, control over nominations, and bribery.

Political patronage The power of an officeholder to award favors, such as government jobs, to political allies.

Nonpartisan elections Election contests in which the names of the candidates appear on the ballot but not their party affiliations.

Voting Rights Act (VRA) A federal law designed to protect the voting rights of racial and ethnic minorities.

NATIONAL PERSPECTIVE

Municipal Elections in New York City

Voters in New York City elect the mayor, the city council, and other city officials in a partisan election system similar to the state's method of electing a governor and members of the state legislature. Candidates compete in a primary election for the right to represent their party on the general-election ballot— Democrats against other Democrats, Republicans against Republicans. The candidates with the most votes in each party's primary election face off in the general election and the person with the most votes wins the office.

New York Mayor Michael Bloomberg attempted to replace party primaries with a nonpartisan election system. Bloomberg argued that the current system excludes a third of the city's electorate from the first round of voting because they are not registered as either Democrats or Republicans. New York uses the **closed primary,** which is an election system that limits primary election participation to registered party members. Only Democrats can vote in the Democratic primary, whereas only Republicans can participate in the Republican primary. Independents and people registered as supporters of other parties cannot vote until the general election. Bloomberg wanted to open the primary to participation by candidates and voters without regard for their party affiliation. The top two candidates in the primary would then face one another in a general election, regardless of their party affiliation. All voters would be able to participate in both rounds of voting.

Most party leaders in New York City campaigned against Bloomberg's proposed reform. They said that party labels help voters choose intelligently among candidates because party affiliation often indicates a candidate's political alliances and policy preferences. Some party leaders also argued that nonpartisan elections would reduce the opportunities of African American and Latino candidates to win office. Because most minority voters are Democrats, African American and Latino candidates frequently win Democratic primary contests for municipal office and then win election as the Democratic candidate in the general election. The elimination of party primary elections would diminish the impact of minority votes in the first round of voting. Finally, many critics of the mayor's proposal declared that it was nothing more than a political ploy to help the mayor win reelection. Bloomberg, a lifelong Democrat, ran for mayor in 2001 as a Republican and won after spending $75 million of his personal fortune on the campaign. Critics charged that the mayor asked the city to adopt a nonpartisan election system because he wanted to avoid the possibility of having to face a Republican primary in 2005 against a candidate with a longer history as a member of the party. In the end, the voters rejected Bloomberg's proposal by a large margin, and New York City continues to hold partisan municipal elections. The voters did not reject Bloomberg, however, who easily won reelection.

QUESTIONS TO CONSIDER

1. Are nonpartisan elections unfair to minorities? Why or why not?
2. Would elections for governor and the legislature be improved if they were nonpartisan instead of party contests?
3. How much effect do election systems have on the outcomes of elections?

Closed primary
An election system that limits primary election participation to registered party members.

voters to file lawsuits in federal court challenging local election laws and procedures they believe discriminate against minority voters.[21] In 2007, three Latino residents of Farmers Branch filed a VRA lawsuit to force the city to stop at-large council elections and adopt a district election system. Even though Latinos constitute nearly 40 percent of Farmers Branch residents, whites hold all five council seats. The mayor is white as well.[22]

In the late 1970s and early 1980s, minority rights groups used the VRA to force Dallas, Houston, San Antonio, El Paso, Fort Worth, and other cities in the state to abandon at-large election systems. Some cities, such as San Antonio, El Paso, and Fort Worth, began electing all council members from districts; other cities adopted mixed systems that combined district seats with at-large positions. Dallas adopted a system with eight district seats and two at-large positions, with the mayor elected at-large. In 1991, the City of Dallas settled a VRA lawsuit by changing its city election to provide for a 14-member council, all chosen from districts, with only the mayor elected at-large.[23]

The introduction of district election systems led to the selection of city councils in most of the state's big cities that were more ethnically and racially diverse than ever before. In the first election after the implementation of single-member districts, Houston voters chose three African Americans and one Latino to serve on council. In San Antonio, Latinos and African Americans together won a majority on that city's ten-member council. A study of ten Texas cities found that the change from at-large to district election systems led to increases in the number of Latino council candidates, Latinos elected to office, and Latino council members living in Latino neighborhoods.[24]

 WHAT IS YOUR OPINION?

What sort of city election system is the best—district, at-large, or mixed?

The Austin city council meets to consider city business.

PUBLIC POLICIES IN TEXAS CITIES

Developmental urban policies
Local programs that enhance the economic position of a community in its competition with other communities.

Redistributive urban policies
Local programs that benefit low-income residents of an area.

Allocational urban policies
Local programs that are more or less neutral in their impact on the local economy.

Political scientist Paul E. Peterson divides urban public policies into three categories: developmental, redistributive, and allocational. **Developmental urban policies** are local programs that enhance the economic position of a community in its competition with other communities. They strengthen the local economy, expand the tax base, and generate additional tax revenues for the city. New sports stadiums, highway expansion, and civic centers are examples of projects that would be part of a developmental urban policy because they could be justified as an investment in the economic vitality of their community.

Redistributive urban policies are local programs that benefit the low-income residents of an area. These include such programs as the provision of low-income housing and food assistance to poor families. Although redistributive programs may be desirable from a humanitarian point of view, Peterson says that they retard economic development. Consider the provision of city health clinics for low-income families. City-funded health clinics may discourage businesses and middle-income taxpayers from relocating to the city because they will have to pay more in taxes for this service than they will receive in benefits. Health clinics may encourage the migration of low-income families to the city to take advantage of the service, especially if neighboring ("competing") cities choose not to provide their residents health clinics, instead keeping their tax rates low.

Allocational urban policies are local programs that are more or less neutral in their impact on the local economy. The best examples of allocational policies are urban housekeeping programs, such as police and fire protection, garbage pickup, and routine street maintenance. Allocational programs are neither developmental nor redistributive because all members of the community benefit from them without regard for economic status.[25]

Economic factors influence the adoption of urban public policies. Cities concentrate on developmental and allocational programs in order to enhance their tax bases and protect the local economy. Research shows that levels of municipal services and tax rates tend to be lower in cities bordered by other municipalities than they are in cities that are relatively isolated. The study concludes that city officials are forced to keep taxes down and, of course, services low because businesses and middle-income taxpayers have the option of moving to a neighboring municipality with lower tax rates.[26]

City governments frequently adopt developmental policies that entail building entertainment centers, such as sports stadiums and convention centers designed to attract visitors from out of town and the suburbs. Houston, Dallas, San Antonio, and Arlington have all used tax money to built new sports arenas to keep or attract professional sports teams. Although city officials promise that expensive new sports and entertainment facilities generate tax revenue and increase employment, research indicates that most projects never pay for themselves. Economists note that most people have fixed entertainment budgets. People who spend money at new sports stadiums would have spent the money on entertainment elsewhere in the city if the stadium had not been built. Furthermore, new stadiums do little to revitalize neighborhoods. New stadiums may be symbols of mayoral leadership, but they seldom contribute to economic development.[27]

INTERNET RESEARCH   Profile of a City Government

What are the issues on the agenda of big-city governments in Texas today? The homepages of the state's largest cities can be found at the following Internet addresses:

Austin: **www.ci.austin.tx.us/**

Dallas: **www.dallascityhall.com**

El Paso: **www.ci.el-paso.tx.us/**

Fort Worth: **www.fortworthgov.org/**

Houston: **www.houstontx.gov/**

San Antonio: **www.ci.sat.tx.us/**

Identify the city nearest you, study its website, and answer the following questions:

1. What form of government does the city have?

2. Who is the mayor of the city?

3. How many members does the city council have? Are they elected from districts or at-large?

4. What is the city's property tax rate?

5. What would be the annual tax bill for a piece of business property valued at $500,000?

Political factors also play an important role in urban policymaking. Developmental and allocational policies are often characterized by conflict as political forces compete over policy alternatives. In Houston, for example, two sets of business groups opposed one another over the location of a new convention center, whether it would be built east or west of the downtown business district. Similarly, neighborhoods fought over the timing of the construction of new decentralized police command stations, with each region of town wanting its command station built first.

City officials must balance economic concerns with political demands. Groups representing the interests of disadvantaged constituents in the state's big cities call for the adoption of redistributive programs. They demand home rehabilitation loans, low-interest mortgage loans, small business loans, technical assistance to new businesses, public housing, affirmative action, public transportation in low-income areas, and hiring goals for women and minorities. Research shows that cities become more responsive to the concerns of minority residents as minorities increase their elected representation in city government. One study finds that, after city councils experience an increase in minority representation, city governments hire more minorities, award more contracts to minority-owned businesses, and enact programs favored by minority groups.[28]

Budgetary Policy

The state's largest cities are big enterprises with annual budgets greater than a billion dollars. In fiscal (budget) year 2007, for example, the general-fund budget for the City of Houston was $1.8 billion.[29] The state's largest cities offer their residents a broad range of services, including police protection, street repair, garbage pickup, libraries, recreational facilities, health clinics, fire protection, emergency medical services (EMS), water and sewer service, airports, sidewalks, and street lighting. In contrast, small towns may provide only a limited number of basic services. Public safety—police, fire, and municipal courts—is typically the largest item in all city budgets because it is labor-intensive.

Texas cities generate revenue from property taxes, sales taxes, franchise fees, and other sources. Figure 28.4 shows the relative importance of the various revenue sources for the City of Houston in 2008. As the figure shows, property and sales taxes combined accounted for 76 percent of city revenue. Franchise fees represented 12 percent of revenues, with a variety of other sources supplying the remaining 12 percent.

Property tax A tax levied on the value of real property, such as land and buildings.

The **property tax,** which is also known as the *ad valorem* property tax, is a levy assessed on real property, such as houses, land, business inventory, and industrial plants. State law sets a maximum property tax rate of $1.50 per $100 of valuation for general-law cities and $2.50 per $100 for home-rule cities. In practice, the property tax rates in most cities are well below the maximum. In 2006, the property tax rate for Dallas was $0.7292. It was $0.645 for Houston, $0.57854 for San Antonio, $0.86 for Fort Worth, and $0.4126 for Austin.[30]

Homestead exemption A property tax reduction granted homeowners on their principal residence.

City governments may grant property tax breaks, called exemptions, to certain categories of taxpayers, such as homeowners, elderly residents, and disabled veterans. Fort Worth, for example, grants exemptions for homeowners, senior citizens, persons with disabilities, property that is a historic site, and transitional housing for indigent persons. The most common exemption is the **homestead exemption,** which is a property tax reduction granted to homeowners on their principal residence. State law stipulates that property tax exemptions must be at least $5,000 but not more than 20 percent of property value (unless that figure is less than $5,000).

Figuring a property tax bill is relatively easy. Assume, for example, that a home is assessed at $150,000, the city tax rate is $0.60 per $100 valuation, and the city

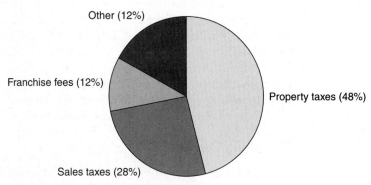

FIGURE 28.4   General Fund Revenues, Houston 2008.
Source: City of Houston, Fiscal Year 2004 Budget.

grants a $5,000 homestead exemption. The homeowner's annual property tax bill to the city would be figured as follows:

$150,000	Assessed value
−$5,000	Homestead exemption
$145,000	Taxable value
×.60 per $100	Municipal tax rate
$870	Municipal tax due

A property owner's tax bill depends on both the tax rate and the valuation of the property. Property taxes go up (and down), of course, when the local government raises (or lowers) tax rates. Taxes also change when property values change. Texas is not one of the 22 states that have **truth in taxation laws,** which are laws that block local governments from raising the total amount of property taxes they collect from one year to the next when assessed values go up. When property values increase in these states, local officials have to vote to increase their total tax revenues and advertise their action in the newspaper. Otherwise, the tax rate falls automatically to compensate for rising property values.[31] In contrast, local governments in Texas benefit from rising property values without elected officials having to go on record in favor of raising additional revenue. Over the last decade, many Texas property owners have experienced a sharp rise in their property taxes because the value of their property has increased.

The sales tax is the other major tax source for municipal government in Texas. A **sales tax** is a levy on the retail sale of taxable items. State law allows cities to piggyback an extra 1 percent onto the state's general sales tax rate of 6.25 percent. All of the state's larger cities and many smaller towns take advantage of the sales tax option. Cities without transit authorities may seek voter approval to levy a ½ percent additional sales tax to reduce city or county property taxes or help fund law enforcement. Cities of 56,000 or more population that do not want to swap property taxes for sales taxes can ask voter approval for a ¼ percent sales tax to use for mass transit.

In addition to property and sales taxes, city governments in Texas raise revenue from franchise fees, licenses, permits, fines, and various other sources. Telephone, gas, cable TV, and electric utility companies pay annual franchise fees to city governments for the right to use public rights of way to string wires or lay cable. Cities generate revenue from service charges, such as fees for water and sewer service. Fines for traffic infractions and violations of city ordinances provide cities with revenues as well. Cities raise money from hotel and motel occupancy taxes, rental car taxes, and burglar and fire alarm fees. Federal grant programs offer assistance to municipalities to build sewage treatment plants, acquire parkland, construct airports, treat drug addiction, rehabilitate economically depressed neighborhoods, and provide housing to low-income families.

City governments borrow money by issuing bonds to cover the cost of capital improvements, such as the construction of buildings, airports, roads, and utility plants. A **bond** is a certificate of indebtedness. A **capital expenditure** is the purchase by government of a permanent, fixed asset, such as a new city hall or highway

Truth in taxation laws Laws that block local governments from raising the total amount of property taxes they collect from one year to the next when assessed values go up.

Sales tax A levy on the retail sale of taxable items.

Bond A certificate of indebtedness issued to investors who loan money for interest income; in lay terms, a bond is an IOU.

Capital expenditure The purchase by government of a permanent, fixed asset, such as a new city hall or highway overpass.

overpass. City governments levy property taxes to pay back the money they borrow plus interest. In 2004, for example, the property tax rate for the City of Houston was $0.45927 for general purposes and $0.18573 for debt service.[32]

Budgetary policies in urban Texas have historically been allocational and developmental. Police and fire protection, sanitation, and street maintenance—the largest expenditure items for municipal government in the state—are allocational programs. Other allocational expenditures include money for libraries, parkland acquisition, and traffic management. In the meantime, capital expenditures for street construction, sewer trunk line replacement, and new police and fire stations are developmental because they provide infrastructure improvements essential to economic growth.

City governments use tax incentives to promote economic growth, including tax increment financing, tax abatements, and enterprise zones. **Tax increment financing** is a program in which a local government promises to earmark increased property tax revenues generated by development in a designated area, called a tax increment financing district, to fund improvements in the area, such as roads, parks, sidewalks, and street lighting. A city hopes to encourage private investment by promising that any additional tax revenues generated from higher property values resulting from private development in the district will be spent by the city in the area under development. **Tax abatement** is a program that exempts property owners from local property taxes on new construction and improvements in a designated tax abatement district for a set period of time. San Antonio, for example, recently granted the Sino Swearingen Aircraft Corporation a series of tax abatements to lure the company into agreeing to manufacture a new business jet in San Antonio, a decision that would bring 850 new jobs to the city.[33] **Enterprise zones** are part of a state program that allows local governments to designate certain areas, called enterprise zones, in which private investors can receive property tax abatements, local sales tax rebates (refunds), and government-backed low-interest loans.

Local officials argue that tax incentives are an important economic development tool. They believe that tax breaks may make the difference between a company deciding to build a plant in Texas or locating it in another state. When businesses establish new facilities in the state, they create new jobs that fuel economic growth because their employees purchase goods and services from established businesses. Local governments benefit as well because the increased economic activity generates added tax revenues, which may be sufficient to make up for the revenues lost by the tax incentives.

 WHAT IS YOUR OPINION?

Should city governments use tax increment financing, tax abatements, and enterprise zones to promote economic development?

The critics of tax incentives charge that they are unnecessary and unfair. Tax breaks are unnecessary, they say, because business managers seldom, if ever, base their relocation decisions on taxes. Businesses decide to expand or relocate based primarily on such factors as transportation and the availability of an educated workforce. Critics charge that tax breaks for new firms are unfair because they shift the cost of

Tax increment financing A program in which a local government promises to earmark increased property tax revenues generated by development in a designated area called a tax increment financing district to fund improvements in the area, such as roads, parks, sidewalks, and street lighting.

Tax abatement A program that exempts property owners from local property taxes on new construction and improvements in a designated tax abatement district for a set period of time.

Enterprise zones A state program that allows local governments to designate certain areas called enterprise zones in which private investors can receive property tax abatements, local sales tax rebates (refunds), and government-backed low-interest loans.

government to other taxpayers, including homeowners and established businesses. Businesspeople, in particular, strongly oppose the use of tax incentives to attract potential competitors.

Furthermore, research shows that the developmental policies of city government have little, if any, impact on the location decisions of investors and business managers. One study of the factors influencing the location of manufacturing plants in Texas found that local taxes had little effect on plant location decisions. The research discovered that the availability of skilled labor and the presence of strong colleges and universities were important to **high-technology industries,** which are industries based on the latest in modern technology. Some of the other factors important to economic development were the presence of port facilities and the concentration in the area of firms in a similar line of work.[34] Some scholars believe that local officials grant tax incentives because of the political pressure to create jobs.[35] Tax incentive programs give the *appearance* that local officials are doing something to help the economy, even if they have little real impact on economic development. Businesses that accept economic development money typically exaggerate the number of jobs they plan to create and actually expand more slowly than companies that do not accept government subsidies.[36]

High-technology industries
Industries that are based on the latest in modern technology.

Annexation and Suburban Development

Traditionally, cities annex to protect their tax bases. Big cities across America have been caught in a financial squeeze as revenues have fallen while demand for services has risen. For decades, the tax bases of the nation's largest cities have declined. Middle-class taxpayers and business establishments have moved to the suburbs in search of safer streets, better schools, and more desirable housing. In contrast, poor people, seriously ill persons who do not have health insurance, and people without places to live have moved into the city to take advantage of health clinics, shelters, and other social services not available in the suburbs. Texas cities have used their power to annex to maintain their tax bases and financial health.

Another reason for annexation is the desire of city officials to prevent encirclement by other incorporated municipalities. Because state law prohibits cities from annexing other cities without their consent, a big city surrounded by smaller incorporated municipalities cannot grow. Many cities located in the Northeast and Midwest find themselves in just such a position. Dallas allowed itself to become ringed by small towns during the early years of its development. In 1976, Dallas broke out of its encirclement by convincing the town of Renner to agree to become part of Dallas. Since the Renner annexation, Dallas has pushed its city limits to the north into Collin and Denton Counties. Other Texas cities have avoided a similar predicament by annexing adjacent unincorporated areas before they could incorporate and by annexing the land around neighboring small towns to prevent their expansion. In Harris County, for example, the municipalities of Bellaire and West University Place are completely surrounded by Houston.

Finally, cities annex in order to reap the political benefits of a larger population. Federal grant money is often awarded on the basis of formulas that include population. The more people living within a city, the more federal grant money it receives. Because legislative districts are drawn on the basis of population size, increased population also leads to additional representation in Congress and the Texas legislature.

State law permits a city to increase its total land area by as much as 10 percent in any one year. A city that does not annex its full allotment in a year may carry the remaining amount forward to be used in later years, as long as the city does not increase its geographic size by more than 30 percent in any one year. A city of 100 square miles, for example, could add another 10 square miles to its land area this year. Because state law allows municipalities to carry forward unused annexation authority, the city of 100 square miles could wait a few years and then annex up to 30 square miles.

A city government typically annexes an entire **utility district,** which is a special district that provides utilities, such as water and sewer service, to residents living in unincorporated urban areas. When a city annexes a subdivision, it annexes the utility district that services the subdivision, rather than the development itself. The annexing city takes over the operation of the utility district, similar to a large corporation taking over a small business. The city takes possession of the utility district's physical assets, such as its water and sewer facilities, and assumes its financial assets and liabilities. The city brings police, fire, solid waste, and emergency medical services (EMS) to the area while contracting with a private company to operate the old utility district's water and sewer system.

Utility district
A special district that provides utilities such as water and sewer service to residents living in unincorporated urban areas.

Most city governments provide garbage collection services for their residents.

Historically, Texas cities have annexed aggressively. Between 1950 and 1980, Houston added more than 370 square miles, Dallas more than 230, San Antonio nearly 200, El Paso more than 200, Fort Worth nearly 150, Corpus Christi more than 150, and Austin more than 80. During the 1970s alone, Texas cities annexed 1,472 square miles containing 456,000 people. That is an area bigger than Rhode Island and a population almost as large as Wyoming.[37]

Since the early 1980s, the pace of annexation by Texas cities has slowed. The annexations of the 1970s produced a political backlash from newly annexed residents who were determined to do their best to vote incumbent mayors and council members out of office. Subsequently, local officeholders grew cautious about adding more angry constituents to their cities. Furthermore, the Texas legislature and the governor have responded to complaints from people living in unincorporated areas near major cities by adopting legislation forcing cities to better accommodate the interests of suburban residents living in unincorporated areas.

In 1999, the legislature passed and the governor signed a measure overhauling annexation policy to require that cities adopt an annexation plan that specifically identifies the areas to be annexed and details how the city will provide those areas with services. The county government may appoint a panel of citizens to negotiate with the city on behalf of area residents. The city cannot complete the actual annexation until the third anniversary of the adoption of the annexation plan, and then it must act within 31 days or lose the opportunity to annex the identified areas for five years. The city must provide police, fire, EMS, solid waste, street repair, water and sewer, and park maintenance services immediately. It has 2½ years to provide full services comparable to those offered to other city residents. If a majority of residents in the newly annexed area believe that the city has failed to provide them with full services, they may petition the city to be disannexed. If the city fails to act, residents may file suit in district court to ask a judge to order disannexation.

 ## WHAT IS YOUR OPINION?

Do you favor changing state law to require that the people in an area to be annexed approve before the annexation can take place?

The legislation also gave cities and utility districts the authority to negotiate Strategic Partnership Agreements (SPAs) to provide for limited-purpose annexation. The utility district gives the city permission to collect sales taxes at retail businesses within the district, but not property taxes. In exchange, the city provides the district with some city services, such as police and fire service, and a portion of the sales tax revenue collected within its borders. The city also pledges to postpone annexing the district during the period of the partnership.[38] Both units of government benefit from the additional tax revenues, whereas utility district residents avoid annexation, at least in the short run. Houston has moved more aggressively than other cities in the state to negotiate partnership agreements with surrounding utility districts, signing more than 100 agreements by mid-2006. In fact, SPAs have become so popular that some utility districts have approached the city about establishing partnerships in order to share in the sales tax revenue and stave off the possibility of annexation.[39]

Houston and The Woodlands signed an agreement in 2007 that would enable the suburban community to eventually incorporate in exchange for a share of local sales tax revenues that would be deposited in a special fund to be used for regional development.[40]

In addition to reforming annexation procedures, the legislature and the governor have revised state laws dealing with **extraterritorial jurisdiction (ETJ),** which is the authority of a city to require conformity with city ordinances and regulations affecting streets, parks, alleys, utility easements, sanitary sewers, and the like in a ring of land extending from ½ to 5 miles beyond the city-limits line. The width of an ETJ depends on the population of the city. Within the extraterritorial area, no new cities may be incorporated without the consent of the existing city. The ETJ is not part of the city; its residents do not pay property or sales taxes to city government and receive no services.

The original purpose of extraterritoriality was to enable a city to control development within the ETJ, thus preparing it for future annexation. When the city eventually annexed subdivisions in the ETJ, they would already conform to city building standards. If the ETJs of two cities overlapped, the cities generally apportioned the area between them.

In 2001, the legislature passed and the governor signed legislation requiring cities and counties to create a single office for dealing with development in the ETJ; it would be run by the city, the county, or cooperatively by both units of local government. The legislature acted in response to complaints from developers that they were sometimes caught between conflicting county and city regulations. In practice, most cities and counties have created a joint office, with a city office the next most popular option.[41]

Land Use Regulation

Historically, land use policies in Texas cities have been developmental. Instead of regulating land use, municipalities in the Lone Star State have promoted private development through street construction and the provision of streetlights, drainage, and water and sewer services in undeveloped areas. In the process, city governments have left decisions about land use policy to private interests—developers, investors, builders, realtors, and architects.

Land use policy in Texas cities is undergoing a transformation. The introduction of single-member districts has increased the political strength of neighborhood groups concerned about quality-of-life issues, such as traffic congestion, air pollution, and neighborhood revitalization. Neighborhood groups in low-income areas have demanded that city government focus on land use policies affecting their neighborhoods, such as low-cost housing and urban redevelopment.

Building and Housing Codes   Building and housing codes are established by city ordinance to set minimum standards for the construction and maintenance of buildings. **Building codes** are municipal ordinances that set minimum standards for the types of materials used in construction, building design, and construction methods employed in all buildings within the city. Building permits are required for all construction covered by the code. **Housing codes** are local ordinances requiring all

Extraterritorial jurisdiction (ETJ)
The authority of a city to require conformity with city ordinances and regulations affecting streets, parks, alleys, utility easements, sanitary sewers, and the like in a ring of land extending from one half to five miles beyond the city-limits line.

Building codes
Municipal ordinances that set minimum standards for the types of materials used in construction, building design, and construction methods employed in all buildings within the city.

Housing codes
Local ordinances requiring all dwelling places in a city to meet certain standards of upkeep and structural integrity.

dwelling places in a city to meet certain standards of upkeep and structural integrity. City officials enforce the housing codes by making systematic inspections and investigating complaints. Property owners are responsible for structural integrity. Owners and occupants share the responsibility for upkeep. Violators of building codes and housing codes may be fined.

Building and housing codes are designed to promote the health, safety, and welfare of the community, but the results often fall short of the ideal. Critics say that codes are frequently outdated and inconsistent across cities. They believe that enforcement is often lax and too frequently accompanied by graft. The opponents of building codes also charge that they increase building costs, thus encouraging construction outside a city's ETJ, beyond the reach of city authority. Furthermore, the opponents of building and housing codes argue that property owners sometimes fail to repair old, run down structures because improvements would place them under the building codes, thus forcing owners to undertake more expensive work than they desire and can afford.

Compared with cities in other states, Texas municipalities have been slow to establish code standards. Many Texas cities did not adopt building codes until after 1954, when the federal government made them a condition for obtaining federal funds for public housing, FHA, and urban renewal programs. Houston did not even adopt fire codes until the 1970s.

Zoning and Planning   The governmental designation of tracts of land for industrial, commercial, or residential use is known as **zoning.** In 1927, the Texas legislature authorized municipalities to adopt zoning ordinances to restrict the use of privately owned land. Subsequently, many Texas cities adopted local zoning ordinances.

Zoning
The governmental designation of tracts of land for industrial, commercial, or residential use.

How does zoning work? Once a city decides it wishes to control land use within its boundaries, it creates a zoning commission. The commission studies land use in the area and makes recommendations concerning appropriate uses of land and the location of commercial and residential districts. After public hearings, the city council considers the proposal and adopts a zoning ordinance based on the commission's recommendation. After the ordinance goes into effect, property owners may not build any structure or put property to any use that conflicts with the zoning ordinance applicable to their district.

Proponents of zoning and other types of land use regulation believe that they help create an orderly city. They say that zoning enables city government to separate districts for residential, commercial, and industrial uses, thus preventing nuisances from developing in residential areas, such as strip shopping centers and trailer parks. Careful planning, they argue, can prevent street congestion, the overcrowding of land, and the overconcentration of population by allowing city officials to plan adequately for the provision of transportation, water, sewage, schools, parks, drainage, and other public requirements.

Opponents of zoning and other types of land use restrictions believe that city planning is inefficient and potentially corrupt because it substitutes the judgment of government bureaucrats for free-enterprise development. Without government controls, they say, cities develop and change in accordance with the dictates of the marketplace. Zoning shifts the basis for deciding how land will be used from economics to politics. As a result, land use decisions become political, with decisions made on the basis of which developers have made the largest campaign contributions.

Urban land use policies reflect political conflict between the owners of developed land and the owners of undeveloped property. Homeowners and commercial property owners favor the imposition of strict land use controls to manage further development in their neighborhoods in order to maintain and enhance their property values. In contrast, persons who own undeveloped tracts of land prefer few land use restrictions, so that they can develop their property unhindered. Throughout much of the twentieth century, developers held the upper hand politically in big-city Texas and used their influence to limit land use controls. Over the last decade or so, however, the political balance has changed in most of the state's large cities. As cities have matured and development has slowed, the owners of developed land have gained political influence. Furthermore, the introduction of single-member districts has enhanced the political influence of neighborhood civic associations concerned about property values.

 WHAT IS YOUR OPINION?

Are you in favor of zoning?

Deed restrictions
Private contractual agreements that limit what residential property owners can do with their houses and land. Almost every modern residential subdivision in the state has deed restrictions.

Deed Restrictions   The opponents of zoning sometimes argue that deed restrictions are preferable to government regulation. **Deed restrictions** are private contractual agreements that limit what residential property owners can do with their houses and land. Almost every modern residential subdivision in the state has deed restrictions. Developers and sometimes the mortgage company draw up deed restrictions to spell out in detail what lot owners may or may not do. Deed restrictions differ from zoning in that they are the result of voluntary contractual agreements between private parties, whereas zoning involves the enactment of city ordinances.

Deed restrictions typically allow owners to use their property only for specified purposes. They force property owners to observe certain standards and refrain from altering their property without the written approval of the neighborhood civic association's architectural control committee. Deed restrictions cover such issues as where residents can park their vehicles, the color they can paint their homes, and the type of shingles they can put on their roofs. If someone violates the restrictions, the civic association can get a court order commanding the offender to stop the violation. Property owners who disobey a court order can be fined or jailed for contempt of court. Deed restrictions that are not enforced may terminate or become unenforceable. This is most likely to occur, of course, in older neighborhoods.

Deed restrictions accomplish some but not all of the goals of zoning. At its best, zoning represents an attempt by government to ensure orderly development. In contrast, deed restrictions provide piecemeal zoning by private developers without resort to a comprehensive plan. People who live in the suburbs benefit, whereas the residents of older neighborhoods without zoning must live with changes wrought by market forces.

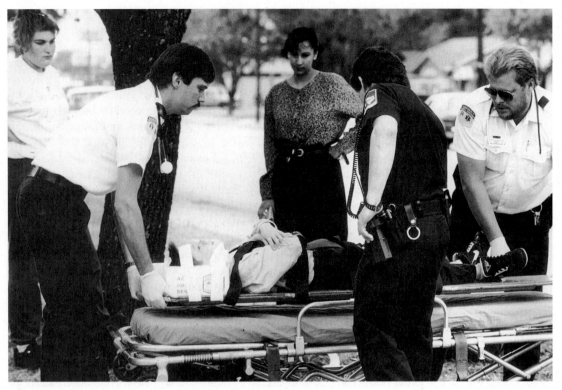

Emergency medical services are also provided by city governments.

GETTING INVOLVED

Contacting City Officials

City governments deal with issues that are close to home—police and fire protection, street repair, garbage pickup, water and sewer service, EMS, parks, libraries, airports, animal control, and local taxes. You can find the name and contact information for the mayor and council members of your city at its homepage, which can be found at the following website: www.statelocalgov.net/state-tx.cfm. Contact the people who represent you at city hall and let them know how you feel about city services, taxes, and regulations.

It's your city—get involved!

CITY POLITICS IN TEXAS

Before the mid-1970s, a small group of business people controlled political power in big-city Texas. **Elite theory** (or **elitism**) is the view that political power is held by a small group of people who dominate politics by controlling economic resources. Growth-oriented business leaders in each of the state's major cities used their economic power to dominate the local policymaking process. In Houston, the elite were

Elite theory, or **elitism** The view that political power is held by a small group of people who dominate politics by controlling economic resources.

Boosters People who promote local economic development.

Environmental Protection Agency (EPA) The federal agency responsible for enforcing the nation's environmental laws.

Subsidence The sinking of the surface of the land caused by the too-rapid extraction of subsurface water.

Communities Organized for Public Service (COPS) A predominantly Latino neighborhood reform organization in San Antonio.

a small group of business leaders called the 8-F Crowd because of their practice of meeting informally in Suite 8-F of a downtown hotel. The members of the 8-F Crowd were all wealthy businessmen with interests in real estate, construction, oil and gas, banking, law, and insurance.[42]

The overriding goal of the business groups who dominated city politics was economic growth and development. They were **boosters** (people who promote local economic development) who believed that whatever was good for business was also good for their city. The business leaders favored low tax rates, rapid annexation, and few restrictions on land use. When the occasion arose, they did what was necessary to boost their cities. During the 1930s, for example, Dallas business leaders convinced the legislature to make their city the site for the official celebration of the Texas Centennial, even though Dallas did not exist during the Texas Revolution. In Houston, business leaders promoted the construction of the Ship Channel and the creation of the Johnson Spacecraft Center (JSC).

Business leaders frequently exerted their influence through the vehicle of nonpartisan "good government" groups, such as the Citizens' Charter Association (CCA) in Dallas, Good Government League (GGL) in San Antonio, Seventh Street in Fort Worth, Citizens for Better Government in Abilene, and Citizens' Committee for Good Government in Wichita Falls. These groups recruited slates of candidates sympathetic with their goals and backed them financially in the at-large nonpartisan elections that were then the norm in most Texas cities. In San Antonio, the GGL won 85 of 97 contested council races between 1955 and 1975. In Dallas, the CCA captured 181 of 211 seats between 1931 and 1975.[43]

Most of the candidates supported by business groups were white businessmen. In Fort Worth, no African Americans were elected to city council before 1967; no Latinos won election before 1977. In fact, most Fort Worth council members lived within blocks of one another on the city's affluent southwest side.[44] In Houston, no women, no Latinos, and only one African American were elected to council before 1981.

Texas cities grew rapidly, but the growth came with social costs. Texas cities developed serious air and water pollution problems. The **Environmental Protection Agency (EPA),** the federal agency responsible for enforcing the nation's environmental laws, identified four major areas of the state that had failed to meet federal air quality standards for ozone: Dallas–Fort Worth, Houston–Galveston, Beaumont–Port Arthur, and El Paso. In the meantime, air quality in Austin, San Antonio, and Tyler barely met the standard.[45] Texas cities also suffered from traffic congestion, overcrowded schools, and flooding brought on by **subsidence,** which is the sinking of the surface of the land caused by the too-rapid extraction of subsurface water.

The costs of rapid development mobilized opposition to the growth-oriented business groups that had long dominated city politics. The business community split between the industries that benefited from development and those that were more concerned with quality-of-life issues. Real estate developers, construction contractors, and other firms that depend on development favored continuing growth-oriented public policies. In contrast, the tourist industry and high-technology firms that employed middle-class professionals were more concerned with the quality of urban life. Neighborhood groups and minority interests demanded that city governments respond to their needs. For example, **Communities Organized for Public Service**

(COPS), a predominantly Latino neighborhood reform organization in San Antonio, demanded better city services for low-income communities.[46]

By the mid-1970s, the rules of the political game had changed sufficiently to allow the new forces to have an impact on the policy process. The elimination of the poll tax and the liberalization of Texas's once highly restrictive voter registration procedures opened the door to greater political participation by African Americans and Latinos. Furthermore, the extension of the VRA in 1975 to include Texas led to the introduction of single-member districts in most of the state's largest cities, including Houston, Dallas, San Antonio, El Paso, Lubbock, Corpus Christi, and Waco.

The new voter registration procedures and single-member district elections enabled minority and neighborhood groups to gain a real share of political power in big-city Texas. More African Americans and Latinos won city council seats than ever before, and some Asian Americans won seats on councils as well. The number of women serving on city councils increased and both Houston and Dallas elected city council members who were openly gay or lesbian. African Americans, Latinos, and women served as mayor in the state's major cities.[47]

The nature of business groups in big-city Texas also changed. During the 1950s, each city's business establishment was dominated by a fairly small group of strong-willed, fiercely independent, wealthy entrepreneurs, such as Eric Jonsson in Dallas and George Brown in Houston. By the 1980s, the business community in big-city Texas had grown too diverse for any one individual or small group of individuals to speak on its behalf. Furthermore, the days of the individual entrepreneur were past, as management teams now ran the state's major corporations. Before local managers could agree to support a development project, they would have to obtain approval from a corporate board of directors based in New York, San Francisco, or Tokyo.

Contemporary urban politics in Texas can best be described as pluralist. **Pluralist theory** (or **pluralism**) is the view that diverse groups of elites with differing interests compete with one another to control policy in various issue areas. In big-city Texas today, different groups are active on different issues, but no one group is able to dominate policymaking across issue areas. Business groups may control policymaking in one issue area, whereas neighborhood or minority rights groups may have more influence in another issue area.

Political scientists use the term *deracialization* to describe contemporary urban politics. **Deracialization** is the attempt of political candidates to deemphasize racially divisive themes in order to garner crossover support from voters of other races/ethnicities while receiving the overwhelming majority of support from voters of the candidate's own racial/ethnic group. To be successful, candidates running for citywide office in the state's major cities know that they have to attract voters from more than one racial/ethnic group because no one group has an electoral majority. They promote images of themselves that other racial/ethnic groups will perceive as nonthreatening and avoid issues that divide voters along racial/ethnic lines, such as bilingual education, affirmative action, and immigration. In the meantime, they work aggressively to mobilize their own base of support.[48] For example, Lee P. Brown, who served three terms as the first African American mayor of Houston, campaigned on such nonracial issues as mobility and economic development. Although Brown took almost all the black vote, he would not have won had he not also had some support from white, Latino, and Asian voters.[49]

Pluralist theory, or pluralism The view that diverse groups of elites with differing interests compete with one another to control policy in various issue areas.

Deracialization The attempt of political candidates to deemphasize racially divisive themes in order to garner crossover support from voters of other races/ethnicities while also receiving the overwhelming majority of support from voters of the candidate's own racial/ethnic group.

CONCLUSION: CITY GOVERNMENT AND POLICYMAKING

We discuss the role of city government in the policymaking process in the conclusion of the next chapter as part of a general discussion of local government in Texas.

LET'S DEBATE

Should Cities Use Tax Money to Build Sports Stadiums?

Overview: Over the past 30 years, change in the political economy of professional sports has been profound. With dramatically rising player salaries, the prestige attached to sports franchises, and the transformation of professional sports into more of an entertainment industry (the "ESPNization" of sports), professional sports charters have become big business—and, with big business, there is usually misunderstood and unsavory politics. The primary political problem involves (1) citizen groups opposed to increased tax rates and government subsidies for private business, as well as changes in or the possible destruction of the character of local communities, and (2) those local businesses and the sports franchise itself, which stand to benefit from the economic development and activity that surround new stadiums and franchise activity. These businesses argue that the community as a whole benefits from the economic activity generated by professional sports, and this increases the quality of life for all. Those opposed to stadium development cite the dislocation of homeowners and renters; more important, they do not believe that private business, such as sports franchises, should be subsidized with taxpayer dollars.

In the past 11 years, Texans in the three largest metro areas (Dallas–Fort Worth, Houston, and San Antonio) have seen the building of two professional baseball stadiums, two professional basketball centers (one of which also houses the NHL's Dallas Stars), and one professional football stadium (Reliant Stadium in Houston). In November 2004, Arlington voters approved a tax increase to help fund a $650 million stadium complex for the Dallas Cowboys (on the same day, voters in Kansas City and St. Louis rejected similar measures to fund new stadiums). This complex will include large shopping and entertainment districts dedicated to Cowboy and NFL themes. In each of the previous cases, controversy swirled around the financing for the construction of each park and its infrastructure. In some cases, the votes were close (approval for Dallas's American Airlines Center was by 1,600 votes, and it took two elections for voters to authorize tax increases to build Houston's $175 million Toyota Center, which was entirely publicly financed). Is it true that professional sports centers add value to communities in such a way that they should be financed by taxpayers?

Scholars from the left-leaning Brookings Institution to the right-leaning Cato Institute argue that there is scant evidence to show that professional sports franchises improve the economies of their home cities. Evidence could be interpreted in such a way as to indicate that, in some cases, personal income may actually *decrease* once the effect of increased taxes and the cost of public utilities are taken into account. The jury is still out on this topic. In Texas, most of the tax increases to fund stadiums are from sales taxes and hotel and car rental taxes—taxes affecting individuals, industries, and business that are only tangentially related to franchise activity. Why should taxpayers, hotels, and car rental agencies be singled out? The answer is that sports franchises encourage tourism and the economic activity the sports economy brings, but the tourism industry replies that the significant bulk of tourism in Texas is nonsports-related, and increased taxes may have the effect of discouraging tourism. Fans and civically minded Texans who understand sports culture, however, argue that thee are intangible benefits to the sports industry that cannot be quantified, and they say that the cost is justified because sports teams foster civic cohesion and unity. Who can put a price on civic comity?

Arguments for Taxpayer Funding of Sports Complexes

❏ **Professional sports complexes provide long-term benefits to local communities.** Researchers point out that voters and elected officials should not focus on the immediate economic impact of building a new stadium; rather, interested parties should look to long-term advantages. These advantages include new and improved infrastructure (new roads, sewage and electrical plants, etc.), urban renewal (improving the local neighborhood in which the stadium will be built), and long-term revenue for locally operated businesses.

❏ **Sports franchises foster community pride and awareness.** Sports are a part of human history and can be considered a part of human nature. The love of sports and the excitement sport brings cut across demographic and partisan lines and can unify a community in many different ways. A goal of politics is to fairly promote those institutions that provide social bonding. Studies indicate that there are numerous, unquantifiable advantages to those cities that support professional sports franchises and their stadiums.

❏ **Sports teams and new stadiums add an intangible quality to home cities.** Sports stadiums demonstrate a political commitment to the economic and social well-being of the home city. New stadiums are usually integral to community revitalization or the creation of entertainment and arts districts, and the building of new sports facilities helps fulfill this major policy agenda of franchise cities. The realization of development and community goals adds significantly to a city's quality of life in ways that can't be measured.

Arguments Against Taxpayer Funding of Sports Complexes

❏ **There is no guarantee that new stadiums spur economic development.** Considerable research indicates a negligible to small positive impact on economic development; the effect may be so insignificant that other development projects, such as revitalizing and turning a warehouse district into an arts center, may provide greater economic growth. There is no guarantee that a sports franchise and its understood benefits will remain in a city, as the move of the Houston Oilers to Tennessee demonstrates.

❏ **Taxpayers should not subsidize private business.** The Cato Institute reports that the changing sports economy over the past 30 years has effectively increased the revenues of franchise owners and players at the taxpayers' expense. The prestige attached to professional sports has caused politicians and local governments to offer incentives, such as publicly funded stadiums, complexes, and infrastructure, that were at one time financed with private investments. Business entails risk and franchise owners should not receive market protection at the taxpayers' expense.

❏ **Taxpayers may simply not want a stadium complex in their neighborhood.** Citizen groups opposed to new franchise complexes are at a disadvantage. Franchise owners can spend millions in advocacy while being admitted to local politics in a way generally not accessible to average individual citizens. Local citizen associations are typically at an organizational and institutional disadvantage and have to compete not only with franchise owners but also with fans (who can be a large and boisterous bunch). These citizen groups know that in 25 years things may not progress as advertised.

QUESTIONS

1. Do sports stadiums aid local economies and help with community revitalization? Why or why not?
2. Should taxpayers subsidize or otherwise support new stadiums? Isn't the nature of private business to find its own investors and take its own risk?

SELECT READINGS

1. Kevin Delaney, *Public Dollars, Private Stadiums: The Battle over Building Sports Stadiums* (New Brunswick, NJ: Rutgers University Press, 2003).
2. Roger Noll, *Sports, Jobs, and Taxes: The Economic Impact of Sports Teams and Stadiums* (Washington, DC: Brookings Institution Press 1997).

SELECT WEBSITES

1. **www.dallasnews.com/sharedcontent/dws/news/local-news/cowboysstadium/vitindex.html**
Dallas Morning News's website chronicle of the Dallas Cowboys' quest for a new stadium.

2. **en.Wikipedia.org/wiki/SBC_Center**
Wikipedia site dedicated to the development of San Antonio's SBC Center, the new home of the San Antonio Spurs basketball franchise.

KEY TERMS

allocational urban policies

annexation

at-large election

bond

boosters

building codes

capital expenditure

city charter

city manager

city ordinances

closed primary

Communities Organized for Public Service (COPS)

council-manager form of city government

cumulative voting system

deed restrictions

deracialization

developmental urban policies

Dillon's rule

district election

elite theory *or* elitism

enterprise zones

Environmental Protection Agency (EPA)

extraterritorial jurisdiction (ETJ)

general-law city

high-technology industries

home-rule city

homestead exemption

housing codes

incorporated municipality

initiative process

mayor-council form of city government

minimum wage

nonpartisan elections

pluralist theory *or* pluralism

political machines

political patronage

population bracket laws

property tax

recall

redistributive urban policies

sales tax

subsidence

tax abatement

tax increment financing

truth in taxation laws

unincorporated area

utility district

Voting Rights Act (VRA)

zoning

NOTES

1. Stephanie Sandoval, "FB Making It Official, Dropping Most Spanish," *Dallas Morning News,* December 8, 2006, available at www.dallasnews.com.
2. Anabelle Garay, "Farmers Branch Approves Sweeping Measures Against Illegal Immigrants," *Austin American-Statesman,* November 14, 2006, available at www.statesman.com.
3. Ibid.
4. Stephanie Sandoval, "Groups Decry FB Law," *Dallas Morning News,* November 15, 2006, available at www.dallasnews.com.
5. Thomas Korosec, "Illegal Immigrant Law in Farmers Branch Blocked," *Houston Chronicle,* May 22, 2007, available at www.chron.com.
6. David R. Berman, *Local Government and the States: Autonomy, Politics, and Policy* (Armonk, NY: M. E. Sharpe, 2003), p. 84.
7. Terrell Blodget, "Municipal Home-Rule Charters in Texas," *Public Affairs Comment* 41 (1996), p. 2.
8. "Texas Town Approves Ban on Renting to Illegal Migrants," *Washington Post,* May 13, 2007, p. A02.
9. Ibid.
10. Rachel Graves, "In Need of Repairs," *Houston Chronicle,* July 8, 2001, p. 23A.
11. Quoted in T. J. Milling, "'King Kong, 14 Chimps,'" *Houston Chronicle,* October 8, 1995, p. 38A.
12. Rob Gurwitt, "Are City Councils a Relic of the Past?" *Governing,* April 2003, pp. 20–24.
13. Emily Ramshaw, "Strong Mayor Foes Are Diverse," *Dallas Morning News,* January 8, 2005, available at www.dallasnews.com.
14. Blodget, "Municipal Home-Rule Charters in Texas," p. 3.
15. Wayne Lee Gay, "The Salary Survey," *Fort Worth Star-Telegram,* September 12, 2002, available at www.dfw.com.
16. Alan Ehrenhalt, "The City Manager Myth," *Governing,* September 1990, pp. 41–46.
17. Rob Gurwitt, "The Lure of the Strong Mayor," *Governing,* July 1993, pp. 36–41.
18. Rob Gurwitt, "Nobody in Charge," *Governing,* September 1997, p. 24.
19. H. George Friederickson, Gary A. Johnson, and Curtis H. Wood, *The Adapted City: Institutional Dynamics and Structural Change* (Armonk, NY: M. E. Sharpe, 2004), pp. 163–167.
20. Steven R. Reed, "Dallas: A City at a Crucial Crossroads," *Houston Chronicle,* December 3, 1990, p. 11A.
21. Joshua G. Behr, *Race, Ethnicity, and the Politics of City Redistricting* (Albany: State University of New York Press, 2000), pp. 97–114.

22. Korosec, "Illegal Immigrant Law in Farmers Branch Blocked."

23. Ruth P. Morgan, *Governance by Decree: The Impact of the Voting Rights Act in Dallas* (Lawrence: University of Kansas Press, 2004), pp. 270–273.

24. Jerry L. Polinard, Robert D. Wrinkle, and Tomás Longoria, Jr., "The Impact of District Elections on the Mexican American Community: The Electoral Perspective," *Social Science Quarterly* 72 (September 1991): 608–614.

25. Paul E. Peterson, *City Limits* (Chicago: University of Chicago Press, 1981), ch. 3.

26. Kenneth K. Wong, "Economic Constraint and Political Choice in Urban Policymaking," *American Journal of Political Science* 32 (February 1988): 1–18.

27. Josh Goodman, "Skybox Skeptics," *Governing*, March 2006, pp. 41–43.

28. *Texas Town and City*, March 1990, pp. 17–35.

29. City of Houston, "Fiscal Year 2007 Operating Budget," available at www.houstontx.gov.

30. Various municipal websites.

31. Alan Greenblatt, "The Loathsome Local Levy," *Governing*, October 2001, p. 36.

32. "Summary of Outstanding General Obligation Debt," Fiscal Year 2008 Budget, City of Houston, www.houstontx.gov/budget/.

33. Sean M. Wood, "Jet Maker to Bring 850 New Jobs to S.A.," *San Antonio Express-News*, June 30, 2006, available at www.mysanantonio.com.

34. Helen F. Ladd and John Yinger, *America's Ailing Cities: Fiscal Health and the Design of Urban Policy* (Baltimore, MD: Johns Hopkins University Press, 1989), pp. 287–293.

35. David Brunori, "Principles of Tax Policy and Targeted Tax Incentives," *State and Local Government Review* 29 (Winter 1997): 59.

36. Todd M. Gabe and David S. Kraybill, "The Effect of State Economic Development Incentives on Employment Growth of Establishments," *Journal of Regional Science* 42 (November 2002): 703–730.

37. Arnold P. Fleischmann, "Balancing New Skylines," *Texas Humanist* 6 (January/February 1984): 28–31.

38. Terry Kliewer, "Anxiety over Annexation," *Houston Chronicle*, July 15, 2002, pp. A13–A14.

39. Josh Goodman, "The Tax Grab Game," *Governing*, April 2007, p. 48.

40. Carolyn Feibel and Renee C. Lee, "Council Approves Woodlands Deal," *Houston Chronicle*, October 25, 2007, pp. B1, B4.

41. Jeremy Schwartz, "Cities, Counties Grapple with New Law," *Austin American-Statesman*, April 29, 2002, available at www.statesman.com.

42. Robert D. Thomas and Richard W. Murray, *Progrowth Politics: Change and Governance in Houston* (Berkeley, CA: Institute of Government Studies Press, 1991), p. 13.1

43. Chandler Davidson and Luis Ricardo Fraga, "Slating Groups as Parties in a 'Nonpartisan' Setting," *Western Political Quarterly* 41 (June 1988): 373–390.

44. Judy Fitzgerald and Melanie Miller, "Fort Worth," in Robert Stewart, ed., *Local Government Election Systems*, Vol. II (Austin: Lyndon B. Johnson School of Public Affairs, 1984), pp. 12–21.

45. Texas Commission on Environmental Quality, "The Quest for Clean Air," available at www.tceq.state.tx.us.

46. Dennis R. Judd and Todd Swanstrom, *City Politics: Private Power and Public Policy*, 2nd ed. (New York: Longman, 1998), pp. 280–283.

47. Karen M. Kaufmann, *The Urban Voter: Group Conflict and Mayoral Voting Behavior in American Cities* (Ann Arbor: University of Michigan Press, 2004), pp. 197–205.

48. Huey L. Perry, ed., *Race, Politics, and Governance in the United States* (Gainesville: University of Florida Press, 1996), pp. 1–7.

49. Matthew McKeever, "Interethnic Politics in the Consensus City," in Michael Jones-Correa, ed., *Governing American Cities: Interethnic Coalitions, Competition, and Conflict* (New York: Russell Sage Foundation, 2001), p. 230.

Chapter 29

Texas Counties, School Districts, and Special Districts

CHAPTER OUTLINE

County Government
Legal Status
Responsibilities
Organization
Finances
Issues in County Government
County Politics

School Districts
Public School Administration
Education Finance

Issues in Education Policy
School Performance

Special Districts
Reasons for Special Districts
Creation, Organization, and Operation
Funding
Evaluation of Special Districts

Conclusion: Local Government
and Public Policy

LEARNING OUTCOMES

After studying Chapter 29, students should be able to do the following:

▸ Describe the legal/constitutional status of county government. (p. 789)

▸ Identify the responsibilities of county government. (pp. 790–791)

▸ Outline the structures of county government, identifying the most important county officials and describing the duties of their offices. (pp. 791–794)

▸ Identify the most important revenue sources and expenditure categories for county government. (pp. 794–796)

▸ Compare and contrast county government in rural areas with county government in urban centers. (pp. 796–797)

▸ Discuss the most important issues facing county government. (pp. 797–800)

▸ Describe the organization of independent school districts, discussing the roles of boards of trustees and school superintendents. (pp. 800–801)

▸ Identify the funding sources for public education in Texas and discuss the ongoing controversy over education funding in the state. (pp. 801–805)

- Discuss each of the following educational policy issues: charter schools, school choice, class size, merit pay, bilingual education, and basic skills testing. (pp. 805–810, 816–817)

- Evaluate school performance in Texas compared with other states. (pp. 810–811)

- Identify the role special districts play in the provision of local government services. (pp. 811–813)

- Describe the creation, organization, and operation of the various types of special districts in Texas. (p. 813)

- Identify the funding sources for special districts. (pp. 813–814)

- Evaluate the benefits and liabilities of special districts. (p. 814)

- Assess the role of cities, counties, school districts, and special districts in the policymaking process. (pp. 814–815)

- Define the key terms listed on page 817 and explain their significance.

Texas Assessment of Knowledge and Skills (TAKS)
A state-mandated basic skills test designed to measure student progress and school performance.

Nearly one of six public high school seniors, more than 40,000 students, failed to graduate in 2007 because they did not pass the **Texas Assessment of Knowledge and Skills (TAKS)** graduation test.[1] The TAKS is a state-mandated basic skills test designed to measure student progress and school performance. TAKS testing begins in the third grade and continues through high school. Ninth-grade students take TAKS tests in reading and math. Tenth and eleventh graders test in English, math, science, and social sciences. Eleventh graders must pass all four subjects to earn a diploma, regardless of their course grades. Students who fail in the eleventh grade have several more opportunities to pass the test in their senior year and even during the summer after graduation. Students who fail to pass the graduation TAKS can still participate in their high school's graduation ceremony, but they receive a certificate of attendance rather than a diploma, unless they can eventually pass the test.

The proponents of basic skills tests, such as TAKS, believe that testing improves public education by holding students, teachers, and school administrators accountable. Students in elementary and middle school must pass TAKS before they can be promoted to higher grades. High school students must pass TAKS in order to graduate. Teachers may face reassignment and school administrators may lose their jobs if their students do poorly on the test. In contrast, the critics of basic skills testing argue that tests actually undermine educational quality because they force schools to focus on the test rather than student learning. Schools neglect other subjects for weeks before the test is given so they can prepare. Much of their work focuses not on basic skills but on test-taking techniques. Instead of learning to read, write, and do math, students learn how to take multiple-choice exams.

The Texas legislature and the governor adopted legislation in 2007 to replace high school TAKS testing with end-of-course exams. Students in the 9th, 10th, and 11th grades will take end-of-course exams in English, math, science, and social sciences each year for a total of 12 tests. Students will have to average passing scores in the four subjects in order to earn their high school diplomas. The new law will not affect the 40,000 students who failed to graduate because of TAKS in 2007, however, because it does not take effect until the 2011–2012 freshman class. TAKS testing in grades 3 through 8 remains unchanged.[2]

The controversy over basic skills testing illustrates the sorts of issues facing local governments in Texas. Local issues are important issues. The quality of education is critical to students, parents, and business leaders who need an educated workforce to grow their companies. Local issues are often controversial. The debate over basic skills testing involves students, teachers, parents, school administrators, and businesspersons. The controversy over basic skills testing also demonstrates that local issues are not just local in scope. The Texas legislature and the governor adopted TAKS, and the Texas Education Agency (TEA) and school districts implement the tests. President George W. Bush, who was governor of Texas from 1995 until he resigned to move to the White House in 2001, made basic skills testing the centerpiece of his education reform plan for the nation. The **No Child Left Behind Act,** which is a federal law that requires state governments and local school districts to institute basic skills testing as a condition for receiving federal aid, is modeled on basic skills testing in Texas.

This is the last in a series of chapters dealing with the institutions of state and local government in Texas. Chapters 25, 26, and 27 dealt with the legislative, executive, and judicial branches of state government, respectively. Chapter 28 focused on city government. This chapter considers county, school district, and special district government.

No Child Left Behind Act
A federal law that requires state governments and local school districts to institute basic skills testing as a condition for receiving federal aid.

◇? WHAT IS YOUR OPINION?

Has TAKS testing improved the quality of public education in Texas?

COUNTY GOVERNMENT

Texas has 254 counties, ranging in population size from Harris County, with more than 3.4 million people in 2000, to tiny Loving County, with a population of only 67.[3] Some counties are dominated by large cities, such as Harris (Houston), Bexar (San Antonio), Travis (Austin), Tarrant (Fort Worth), El Paso, and Dallas Counties. Other counties are predominantly rural, with only a few small towns and no large cities.

General law units of local government Units of local government that are limited to those structures and powers specifically granted by state law.

Legal Status

Texas Counties are **general law units of local government**—that is, units of local government that are limited to those structures and powers specifically granted by state law. In contrast to Texas cities and the counties in most other states, Texas counties may not adopt home rule status, which would allow them greater discretion in choosing governmental structures, functions, and tax systems. **Home rule** refers to the authority of a unit of local government to take actions not prohibited by the laws or constitutions of the United States or the state. If county officials want to respond to local problems by taking an action not specifically allowed by state law, they must first obtain authorization from the Texas legislature.

Home rule The authority of a unit of local government to take actions not prohibited by the laws or constitutions of the United States or the state of Texas.

Edwards County Courthouse in Rocksprings, Texas.

Responsibilities

County governments in Texas play a dual role of implementing state policies and providing services to residents.

- **Law enforcement** Counties enforce state laws. The county sheriff's office is the primary law enforcement agency for Texans living in unincorporated areas. Counties also operate county jails, which house people who are awaiting trial and persons convicted of misdemeanor offenses.

- **Courts** Counties operate justice of the peace, county, and district courts. With the exception of cases tried in municipal court, every state trial that takes place in Texas, both criminal and civil, is held in a court operated by county government.

- **Health** Counties enforce the state's health laws and provide healthcare services for indigent residents. Under Texas law, counties are required to pay for the healthcare costs of residents at or below 21 percent of the federal poverty level if those residents do not qualify for other healthcare programs. In 2004, Texas counties reported spending nearly $5.6 million on the County Indigent Care program.[4]

- **Records** County governments collect and maintain records of births, deaths, marriages, divorces, and deeds.

- **Tax collection** County governments collect a number of taxes and fees on behalf of the state, including charges for license plates and certificates-of-title for motor vehicles.
- **Elections** County governments register voters and conduct both primary and general elections for the state.
- **Roads and bridges** Counties build and maintain roads and bridges.
- **Other services** State law allows counties to provide a range of additional services. Some counties operate airports or seaports. Counties may also provide their residents with libraries, parks, and recreational facilities. In Houston, for example, Harris County owns and operates Reliant Stadium, the home of the Houston Texans National Football League team.

Organization

Figure 29.1 is the organizational chart of county government in Texas. In many respects, county government is a miniature version of state government because no single official is in charge. Instead, executive functions are divided among a sizable number of elected and appointed officials.

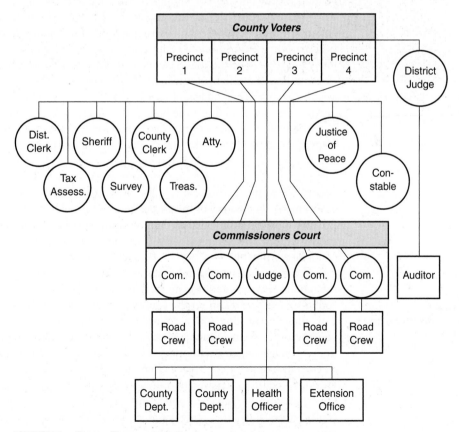

FIGURE 29.1   County Government in Texas.

Commissioners court The board of directors for county government composed of four county commissioners and the county judge.

Partisan election An election contest in which both the names and the party affiliations of candidates appear on the ballot.

Commissioners Court   The **commissioners court** is the board of directors for county government; it is composed of four county commissioners and the county judge. The members are chosen in partisan elections held concurrently with the biennial statewide general elections. A **partisan election** is an election contest in which both the names and the party affiliation of candidates appear on the ballot. County voters elect the four commissioners, one each from four districts, called county commissioners' precincts, to serve four-year staggered terms. They elect the county judge countywide to serve a four-year term as well.

Individual commissioners essentially run county government within their precincts. In most counties, the commissioners oversee road repair and construction in their precincts. In fact, roadwork is such an important part of the job of county commissioners in rural counties that residents often refer to them as road commissioners. The commissioners control large road budgets and pick contractors to do county work. Meanwhile, they hire their own crews to do routine maintenance on county roads and in county facilities, such as parks and recreation centers. In Harris County, the state's largest county, the four commissioners' budgets range in size from $40 million to $80 million. They employ full-time staffs of 280 to 380 workers, depending on the geographic size of the precincts.[5] The commissioners also select vendors for the purchase of equipment and supplies.

The responsibilities of the county judge vary, depending on the size of the county. In rural counties, the county judge is the presiding judge in the constitutional county court. In urban counties, the county judge devotes most, if not all, of his or her time to county business and leaves the work of trying cases to the county courts at law. In smaller counties, those with fewer than 225,000 people, the judge is also the county's chief budget officer. In larger counties, an auditor appointed by the district court judge(s) drafts the budget and oversees county finances.

The powers of the county judge more closely resemble those of a mayor in the council-manager form of city government than a mayor in the mayor-council form of city government with the strong mayor variation. The county judge presides in commissioners court but has only one vote and no veto. As the most visible figure in county government, the county judge often serves as the spokesperson for county government. The ability of the county judge to provide policy leadership, however, depends more on political skill than official power because the judge lacks the authority to run the commissioners court and has no executive power to manage county government.

Ordinance A law enacted by the governing body of a unit of local government.

The commissioners court has limited authority because its structure and most of the functions it may perform are established by law and the state constitution. The commissioners court can set the county property tax rate, but it does not have general ordinance-making power. An **ordinance** is a law enacted by the governing body of a unit of local government. Most of the power of the commissioners court comes from its budget-making authority and its power to choose from among the optional services available for county government to provide to county residents. The commissioners court is empowered to adopt the county budget. This authority gives it an important tool to influence policy in county departments not directly under the court's supervision. Also, state law gives the commissioners court authority to determine whether the county will offer residents such local programs/services as parks, libraries, airports, hospitals, and recreation facilities. In counties that choose to implement these optional programs, the commissioners court appoints administrators to head them. These appointed officials may include a county agricultural agent, home demonstration agent, fire marshal, county health officer, county welfare officer, medical examiner, librarian, county engineer, and, in more populous counties, county purchasing agent.

Other Elected County Officials   The county courthouse contains numerous elected officials in addition to the members of the commissioners court. These officials are chosen in partisan elections to serve staggered four-year terms. All but justices of the peace and constables are elected countywide.

After the county judge, the most visible official is the county sheriff, who is the chief law enforcement officer for the county. The sheriff's department has jurisdiction over the entire county but, in urban areas, city governments and the county usually agree on a division of responsibilities. City police departments patrol within their cities, whereas the sheriff enforces the law in unincorporated areas. The sheriff also operates the county jail, which holds prisoners awaiting trial for felony offenses and people serving sentences for misdemeanor convictions. In urban counties, in particular, managing the jail consumes a significant proportion of the sheriff department's budget and personnel. Finally, the sheriff assists county courts and state district courts within the county by serving arrest warrants and subpoenas, as well as providing deputies to serve as bailiffs. A **subpoena** is a legal order compelling the attendance of a person at an official proceeding, such as a trial.

Subpoena A legal order compelling the attendance of a person at an official proceeding, such as a trial.

Larger counties elect both a district attorney and a county attorney. In smaller counties and in Bexar County (San Antonio), the district attorney performs both roles. In counties with both officials, the district attorney's office prosecutes felony criminal cases in state district courts. The county attorney advises the commissioners court and other county officials on legal issues and represents the county in court, mostly in lawsuits to collect delinquent property taxes. The county attorney's office also prosecutes misdemeanor cases in JP and county court, except in Harris County, where the district attorney prosecutes both felony and misdemeanor cases.

Two other offices whose titles frequently confuse voters are those of county clerk and district clerk. The county clerk records legal documents, such as deeds, mortgages, and contracts, and keeps vital statistics on births, deaths, marriages, and divorces. The county clerk is also the county election official. He or she conducts early voting, instructs precinct election workers, certifies election returns, and forwards election results to the office of the Texas secretary of state. In a few counties, the county clerk registers voters. The district clerk, meanwhile, maintains legal records for the district courts. In small counties, the county clerk performs the functions of the district clerk.

Justices of the peace (JPs) try Class C misdemeanor cases and hear small-claims civil suits. Depending on its population, a county may be divided into as many as eight JP precincts, with each precinct electing one or two JPs. In addition to their judicial duties, JPs in small counties may assume the responsibilities of the county clerk. The JP may also serve as county coroner (although few justices of the peace have medical backgrounds).

Each county elects as many constables as it has justices of the peace. Although constables are certified law enforcement officers, their primary chore in most counties is to assist the JP court(s) by serving legal papers, such as subpoenas and warrants. Constables also handle evictions, execute judgments, and provide bailiffs for the justice courts. In some urban counties, particularly Harris County, constables provide for-hire law enforcement services to subdivisions in unincorporated areas through contract deputy programs.

The tax assessor-collector is the county's chief tax official. The tax assessor collects the county's property taxes, collects fees for automobile license plates, and issues certificates-of-title for motor vehicles. Despite the title of the office, the tax assessor-collector no longer assesses the value of county property for tax purposes. The legislature has assigned that duty to a county tax appraisal district in each county. In small counties, those with fewer than 10,000 people, the sheriff performs the duties of the tax assessor.

In most counties, the tax assessor-collector directs voter registration. This duty is a holdover from the era of the **poll tax,** which was a tax that prospective voters had to pay in order to register to vote. State law allows the commissioners court to transfer voter registration and/or election administration duties to another official, and a number of urban counties have assigned those responsibilities to the county clerk or to an appointed election administrator.

Poll tax A tax that prospective voters had to pay in order to register to vote.

The county treasurer is responsible for receiving funds and making authorized expenditures. In recent years, the state legislature has proposed and voters have passed constitutional amendments to allow several counties to abolish the office of county treasurer and transfer its duties to the auditor, who is appointed by the district judge(s) in the county.

Two counties, Harris and Dallas, still have county departments of education. These agencies are governed by five-member boards of trustees, with one trustee elected countywide and the other four trustees chosen from the four commissioners court precincts. Historically, county departments of education coordinated relations among the common school districts within the county. Common school districts have now been replaced by independent school districts, and in 1978 the legislature abolished all county education departments except those in Harris and Dallas Counties, which successfully argued that they provided important services to county residents. Critics charge that these agencies are expensive bureaucracies whose services can and should be provided by independent school districts.

Finances

Property taxes are the main source of tax revenue for county government. The county tax rate is limited to $0.80 per $100 of valuation, although state law allows county voters to approve as much as $0.15 more for road and bridge operations and up to $0.30 more to build and maintain farm-to-market (FM) roads. In practice, most county governments set their tax rates well below the allowed maximum. Table 29.1 compares the property tax rates of the six largest counties in Texas.

County governments can expand their taxing authority by creating separate but closely allied special districts to provide such costly services as healthcare, flood

The county jail holds prisoners awaiting trial for felony offenses and people serving sentences for misdemeanor convictions.

TABLE 29.1   Tax Rates in Selected Counties, 2006

County	Tax Rate per $100 Valuation
Bexar (San Antonio)	$0.314147
Dallas	$0.2139
El Paso	$0.39139
Harris (Houston)	$0.40239
Tarrant (Fort Worth)	$0.2715
Travis (Austin)	$0.4499

Source: Various county appraisal district websites.

control, and toll road construction and maintenance. In Harris County, for example, the commissioners court controls three special districts—the Harris County Flood Control District, Hospital District, and Port of Houston Authority. If the property tax rates for these districts were added to the Harris County tax rate, it would jump from $0.40239 to $0.64251. Although that figure would still be well below the state-approved maximum rate for counties, members of the commissioners court find it politically beneficial to spread taxes and occasional tax increases among special districts with their own separate boards of directors, rather than consolidate them under the taxing authority of county government.

Property taxes are not the only revenue source for county governments. Counties that do not have transit authorities or incorporated cities within their boundaries can levy sales taxes. Other revenue sources for county governments include fees for motor vehicle licenses, service charges, and federal aid.

The relative importance of county expenditures varies considerably among counties. Road and bridge construction and maintenance is a major budget item for all counties, but it is particularly prominent in geographically large counties. Rural, sparsely populated counties do little more than maintain the roads, enforce the law, operate a county court, and carry out the basic administrative functions of county government, such as recording deeds and registering voters. In contrast, county governments in metropolitan areas provide a wide range of services, especially if the county has a large population living in unincorporated areas. Although the largest single item in the budget for Harris County is road and bridge construction and maintenance, Harris County government and its related special districts also spend millions of dollars for law enforcement, jail operation, indigent healthcare, the operation of county and district courts, flood control, and parks.

Legislative budget decisions sometimes impact county government. In 2001, the Texas legislature passed and the governor signed legislation requiring counties to establish indigent defense plans to ensure that indigent criminal defendants receive competent legal representation. Although the legislature provided for some funding, county governments were forced to cover more than 90 percent of the cost of the program.[6] Similarly, legislative cuts in the Children's Health Insurance Program increased healthcare costs for counties. The **Children's Health Insurance Program (CHIP)** is a federal program designed to provide health insurance to children from low-income families whose parents are not poor enough to qualify for Medicaid. In 2003, legislative cuts in the program left several hundred thousand youngsters from low-income families without health insurance. Without CHIP coverage, their parents often took their ill children to county hospital emergency rooms, forcing county governments to pick up the cost of their healthcare.[7]

Children's Health Insurance Program (CHIP) A federal program designed to provide health insurance to children from low-income families whose parents are not poor enough to qualify for Medicaid.

Issues in County Government

County government has both staunch defenders and harsh critics. The proponents of county government declare that counties are the unit of local government that is closest and most responsive to the people. Counties provide basic government services that citizens want and need. In contrast, critics charge that county government is a relic of the nineteenth century. They believe that county government is inefficient and often corrupt.

To a substantial degree, the validity of the criticism against county government depends on the size of the county. For the most part, county government functions satisfactorily in rural and small-town Texas. In rural areas, counties are the primary units of local government. Citizens are aware of county services and know county officials well. In contrast, county governments are almost invisible governments in urban Texas, despite employing thousands of persons and spending millions of dollars. Counties operate with little accountability because the media and most citizens are focused primarily on other units and levels of government.

The Long Ballot and Responsibility of the Voters   The critics of county government believe that the long ballot makes it difficult for county voters intelligently to choose qualified officeholders, at least in urban areas. The **long ballot** is an election system that provides for the election of nearly every public official of any significance. County elections coincide with state and national primary and general elections held in even-numbered years. Considering all the other races on the ballot in those years, especially in urban counties, many voters may be uninformed about the relative merits of candidates for county clerk, district clerk, or many other county offices. For that matter, most urban voters probably cannot even distinguish between the county clerk and the district clerk.

The theory of democracy is that elections make public officials responsive to the citizens. Public officials do what the voters want because, if they do not, they face defeat at the ballot box. Democracy does not work or at least does not work well if the voters are unaware of public officials. Furthermore, elected officials have no incentive to serve the public if the public is unaware of their work. The danger is that public officials who are not likely to be held accountable to the voters will act instead to further their own personal interests and the interests of the individuals and groups who support them politically.

The critics of county government would like to reform the system to make county officials more accountable, at least in urban areas. Reformers would like to reduce the number of elected county officials, either consolidating positions into a smaller number of offices or providing for the appointment of officials by a single county executive who would be accountable to the voters. Reformers would also like to minimize the role of organized interests in county policymaking.

Long ballot An election system that provides for the election of nearly every public official of any significance.

 WHAT IS YOUR OPINION?

Are too many county officials elected for voters to keep track of the offices and the candidates?

Hiring, Purchasing, Contracting, and Conflict of Interest   **Conflict of interest** refers to a situation in which the personal interests of a public official may clash with that official's professional responsibilities. For example, a public official faces a conflict of interest in determining whether to award a government contract to a firm owned by family members, as opposed to a company whose management has no personal connection to the official. Public policy analysts generally believe that government works better when public officials avoid decisions in which their personal interests are at stake.

The critics of county government believe that county operations make conflict of interest inevitable. In general, county commissioners and elected department heads hire and fire employees as they see fit. County governments lack a merit-hiring

Conflict of interest A situation in which the personal interests of a public official may clash with that official's professional responsibilities.

system and county employees do not enjoy civil service protection. Critics say that county officials often hire and fire employees for political reasons. Furthermore, county employees have an incentive to become campaign workers for their bosses at election time, perhaps even on county time.

Another problem is the absence of centralized purchasing in most counties. Each department contracts for goods and services on its own, often without the benefit of competitive bids. At a minimum, this practice prevents the county from taking advantage of quantity discounts. More seriously, it increases opportunities for corruption by county officials who may be tempted to do business with their friends and political supporters.

The contracting process presents similar problems. County governments contract for services from engineers, accountants, surveyors, architects, and attorneys. Most of these services are provided in connection with road construction projects. Although rural counties are small businesses, urban counties are big businesses. In 2007, general fund expenditures for Harris County totaled $1.2 billion.[8]

Because state law prohibits competitive bidding, individual commissioners decide which firms receive the contracts for work in their precincts, whereas the commissioners court as a whole awards contracts for the entire county. In practice, the firms who win the contracts are also the major election campaign supporters of the members of the commissioners court. Between 2003 and 2007, for example, the five members of the commissioners court in Harris Count raised more than $10 million in campaign contributions, with most of the money coming from contractors, engineering firms, law firms, and architects that receive millions of dollars in no-bid contracts from the county. The single largest campaign donor, James Dannenbaum of Dannenbaum Engineering, contributed $160,000, while receiving $6.6 million in county contracts.[9]

The contracting process is highly controversial. County commissioners declare that they select the firms best able to provide the services to their constituents. Political contributions have no impact on their decisions, they say, because state law makes it illegal for public officials to accept campaign contributions or anything else of value in return for a contract. In contrast, critics charge that the contracting process is inherently corrupt. Furthermore, they say, the system helps insulate county commissioners from electoral accountability. County commissioners receive so much campaign money from firms doing business with the county that incumbent commissioners are virtually impossible to defeat for reelection, at least in urban areas.

Some counties use a unit road system, which is a centralized system for maintaining county roads and bridges under the authority of the county engineer. The proponents of the unit road system argue that it allows county government to operate more efficiently and less politically. In contrast, county commissioners, who would suffer a loss of political influence under a unit road system, contend that it would weaken local control of road and bridge maintenance.

Decentralization and Accountability   Critics believe that the decentralization of county government makes it difficult for county officials to fulfill the responsibilities of their offices and impossible for voters to evaluate their performance accurately. In many instances, the people who raise revenue and write the budget—the commissioners court—have no direct control over the people who administer county programs—the elected department heads. The sheriff, for example, is the county's chief law enforcement official but does not directly control the budget for law enforcement. If county residents are unhappy with the operation of the county jail, whom do they blame—the commissioners court for not putting enough money in the budget or the sheriff for being a poor administrator?

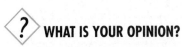 **WHAT IS YOUR OPINION?**

Is county government too decentralized to operate efficiently?

Structural Inflexibility and the Twenty-First Century   Is county government able to respond to contemporary policy problems, especially in urban areas? Anyone driving through an urban county can easily distinguish where a city's jurisdiction ends and the county jurisdiction begins by the proliferation of roadside vendors, fireworks stands, outsized billboards, portable signs, and automobile junkyards. Cities can pass ordinances to regulate such matters, but counties cannot. Some reformers favor granting county government ordinance-making power, especially county governments in urban areas. If counties could make ordinances, they could better address issues of development in unincorporated areas, such as land use, flood control, environmental protection, and neighborhood integrity. In contrast, the opponents of ordinance-making power for county government are against allowing yet another unit of government the power to regulate people's lives.

County Politics

The nature of county politics depends on the county. In rural and small-town Texas, county government is high profile because counties are the primary units of local government. The population is small enough that public officials and county residents often know one another personally. Officials in some counties hold office for decades without facing electoral challenge, sometimes because they are personally popular and sometimes because no one else wants the job. In other counties, political factions form, often on the basis of personalities, and compete for control, usually in the Democratic Party primary. (Despite the growth of the Republican Party in state politics, most rural county courthouses remain Democratic.) The issues of county government in rural Texas are relatively minor but, nonetheless, important to the people involved. Fixing potholes and paving country roads may not be the most important policy issues facing government in Texas, but they are important issues to the people who live in the region.

In urban areas, county governments are big business but low profile. Most residents of the state's big cities are unaware of county issues and ignorant of county government. The local media typically ignore county issues, preferring instead to cover crime, automobile accidents, and natural disasters. When local media outlets do cover local government, they typically focus on city government and, occasionally, school district politics, but they seldom address county issues.

County government in urban areas is important, especially to selected segments of the population. People without health insurance rely on county health clinics and charity hospitals for healthcare. Residents of unincorporated areas depend on the county sheriff for police protection. Land developers benefit from road construction that provides access to their property. Engineers, contractors, attorneys, surveyors, and other professionals do substantial business with county government.

SCHOOL DISTRICTS

Many Texans consider school districts the most important unit of local government. Public education is the single largest budget expenditure for state and local government in Texas. In fact, many homeowners pay more money in school property taxes than they do in county and city property taxes combined. School districts are major employers, and school activities, especially high school football, are the focus of social life in many communities. Good schools are the foundation for economic growth in a community and the instrument for training young people for success in college and the workforce.

Public School Administration

Independent school districts (ISDs) Units of local government that provide public education services to district residents from kindergarten through the twelfth grade.

Independent school districts (ISDs) are units of local government that provide public education services to district residents from kindergarten through the 12th grade. The state has more than a thousand school districts, ranging in size from the Houston ISD, with 210,000 students, to several hundred districts that have fewer than 500 students. In 2006–2007, more than 4.5 million students attended public schools in Texas.[10]

The governing body for ISDs is the board of trustees, generally composed of seven members (although some of the larger districts have nine members). Trustees may be elected either at-large or from districts to serve terms of two, three, four, or six years. Terms of two years are the most common. School trustee elections, which are nonpartisan, are usually held at times that do not coincide with statewide spring primaries and general elections. **Nonpartisan elections** are elections in which candidates run without party labels. In many urban areas, city elections and school trustee elections take place on the same day, usually the second Saturday in May in odd-numbered years.

Nonpartisan elections Election contests in which the names of the candidates, but not their party affiliations, appear on the ballot.

The board of trustees is a body of ordinary citizens that meets periodically to set policy for the district. The members of the board of trustees receive no salary for their services; they are laypeople rather than professional educators. The board approves the budget, sets the property tax rate, and arranges financial audits. It makes personnel decisions, involving such matters as setting the salary schedule and approving personnel contracts. Other board decisions concern the letting of contracts for the expansion and repair of the district's physical plant.

Perhaps the board's most important decision is the hiring of a superintendent. The superintendent is a professional school administrator who manages the day-to-day operation of the district and ensures that the board's policy decisions are implemented effectively. Research shows that board members tend to defer to the superintendent on

More than 4.5 million students attend public schools in Texas.

the basic outline of education policy.[11] Nonetheless, board members, especially in urban districts, frequently make political demands on a superintendent regarding contracts, jobs, and responses to the needs of particular ethnic groups or constituencies. In large urban districts, boards of trustees are sometimes split along racial and ethnic lines, as well as between members representing inner-city areas and members from the suburbs. Consequently, superintendents of urban districts may find themselves caught in the crossfire of a divided board. Nationwide, the average tenure for urban superintendents is less than three years.[12] Texas is no exception to the pattern of conflict between school boards and superintendents. The Dallas ISD, for example, had five superintendents between 1996 and 2000.[13]

Education Finance

The federal government, state government, and local taxpayers fund public education in Texas. Figure 29.2 shows the relative importance of the three revenue sources for school districts. In 2005–2006, the average ISD received 53 percent of its funds from local tax sources, 36 percent from the state, and 11 percent in federal grant money.

The relative importance of funding sources varies dramatically among school districts. Figure 29.3 compares funding sources for two large, big-city school districts, Houston Independent School District (HISD) and El Paso Independent School

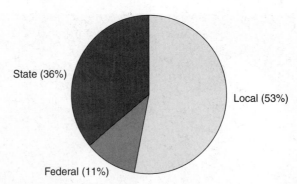

FIGURE 29.2   Education Funding Sources, 2003.
Source: Texas Education Agency.

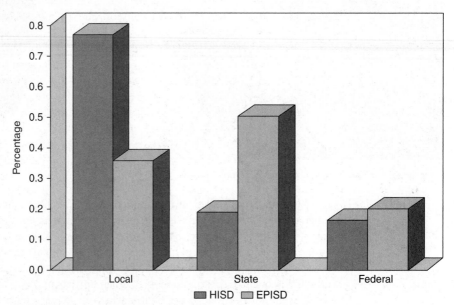

FIGURE 29.3   Funding Comparison, Houston and El Paso.
Source: Texas Education Agency.

Federal grant program A program through which the national government gives money to state and local governments to spend in accordance with set standards and conditions.

School lunch program A federal program that provides free or reduced-cost lunches to children from poor families.

District (EPISD). The HISD raises most of its money from local property taxes, whereas the EPISD gets more of its funding from the state than from any other source. Both districts receive some money from the federal government.

District funding reflects differences in the way the money is raised or awarded. The federal government gives money to school districts through a **federal grant program,** which is a program through which the national government gives money to state and local governments to spend in accordance with set standards and conditions. Federal grant money targets economically disadvantaged students and students with disabilities. Federal dollars also support the **school lunch program,** which is a federal program that provides free or inexpensive lunches to children from poor families. The amount of federal money a school district receives depends on such factors as the number of district students who are economically disadvantaged or who have limited English-language proficiency. Both the HISD and the EPISD qualify for substantial amounts of federal money under those criteria because a large proportion of their students are poor, have limited English language proficiency, or need special education. In contrast to the HISD and EPISD, school districts that serve an affluent population, such as the Highland Park ISD in Dallas, receive almost no federal grant money.

Foundation School Program
The basic funding program for public education in the state of Texas.

The **Foundation School Program** is the basic funding program for public education in the state of Texas. The legislature establishes certain minimum standards that school districts must meet in such areas as teacher compensation and student transportation. The actual amount of money a district receives depends on district wealth, local property tax rates, and a host of other factors. Wealthy districts, such as Highland Park ISD, receive relatively little state money, whereas poor districts, such as the Edgewood ISD in San Antonio, receive most of their money from the state. Because the El Paso ISD is relatively poorer than the Houston ISD, it receives a greater share of its funding from the state than does the HISD.

The state distributes other money to school districts from the Available School Fund. In the 1850s, the legislature set aside a large block of state land to create a trust fund for public education. Income from the sale and lease of that land and from royalties earned from oil and gas production on it goes into the **Permanent School Fund (PSF),** which is a fund constitutionally established as an endowment to finance public elementary and secondary education. The PSF principal of $24 billion cannot be spent.[14] Instead, it must be invested to earn interest and dividends, which go into the Available School Fund (ASF). The ASF is also supported by one-fourth of the taxes collected on motor fuels and natural resources. The state distributes ASF money to school districts based on the number of students in average daily attendance.

Permanent School Fund (PSF) A fund established in the Texas Constitution as an endowment to finance public elementary and secondary education.

Public education in Texas is also funded through local property taxes. School districts use local tax money to participate in the Foundation School Program and for "local enrichment"—that is, to pay for services that go beyond the state-mandated minimum standards. Local money pays for building and maintaining school facilities as well and to pay off debt incurred when schools and other district facilities were built.

School tax rates tend to be higher than the property tax rates assessed by counties and cities. A school district's property tax rate includes a maintenance and operations (M&O) rate, as well as an interest and sinking fund (I&S) rate. The M&O rate applies to the district's general operating expenses whereas the I&S rate is used to pay off the district's bond debt. Before 2006, the legislature limited the M&O rate to $1.50 per $100 valuation. It capped the I&S rate at $0.50 for debt incurred since 1992 plus whatever rate was needed to pay off debts incurred before 1992.[15] In 2006, the legislature passed and the governor signed a measure that reduced the maximum M&O rate to $1.33 in 2006 and $1.00 in 2007. Local school boards could add another 4 cents to the rate for local enrichment. If local school districts wanted to raise more money, they could increase their M&O tax rate as high as $1.17 with voter approval. In 2007, 118 districts asked for voter approval to raise their tax caps above the $1.04 ceiling. Voters in 92 districts approved the increase, whereas voters in the other 26 rejected it.[16] The cap for the I&S rate remained unchanged.[17]

School districts grant property tax breaks to homeowners and people over 65 years of age. The Texas Constitution provides for a $15,000 homestead exemption, reducing the taxable value of a home for school tax purposes. Most school districts grant additional exemptions for persons with disabilities and people over 65 years of age. Furthermore, a homeowner's school property taxes are frozen at age 65. Regardless of increases in tax rates, elderly Texans are assessed the same tax rate they were charged on their current home when they reached their 65th birthday.

The state's system of financing public education has long been controversial because districts with wealthy property tax bases can raise more money than districts that are less affluent, even with lower property tax rates. The Glen Rose ISD in Somervell County benefits from having a nuclear power plant in its taxing district. As a result, the taxable value of property located in the Glen Rose ISD is more than a million dollars per student. With a relatively modest tax rate of $1.218, Glen Rose ISD generates $8,931 a year per student. In contrast, Crystal City ISD in Zavala County includes no refineries or power plants within its boundaries. The taxable value of property in Crystal City ISD is only $86,733 per student. Even with a relatively hefty property tax rate of $1.65, Crystal City ISD raises just $1,131 per pupil. Left to its own financial resources, the Glen Rose ISD would have substantially more money to spend to provide a quality education to its 1,680 students than Crystal City ISD would have to support the education of its 1,993 students.[18]

In 1989, the Texas Supreme Court ruled in the case of *Edgewood ISD v. Kirby* that the state's system of financing public education violated the Texas Constitution. The court ordered the legislature to create a system whereby districts with the same tax rate would have roughly the same amount of money to spend per student.[19] The court focused on equality of tax revenues rather than equality of expenditures. It ordered the state to adopt a system of school funding that ensured that districts would generate similar revenue per student at similar levels of tax effort. If Glen Rose ISD and Crystal City ISD had the same property tax rate, then they would be able to raise the same amount of money per student. The court did not require expenditure equality because it did not force districts to have the same tax rate. The citizens of Crystal City ISD (or Glen Rose ISD) could choose to fund their schools more (or less) generously by adopting a higher (or lower) tax rate than most other districts.

Robin Hood Plan
A reform of the state's school finance system designed to increase funding for poor school districts by redistributing money from wealthy districts.

The legislature responded to *Edgewood v. Kirby* by adopting the **Robin Hood Plan,** which was a reform of the state's school finance system designed to increase funding for poor school districts by redistributing money from wealthy districts. Districts that are able to generate more property tax revenue per student than allowed have several choices, but most wealthy districts have complied with the law by either sending money to the state or transferring it to one of the state's poor school districts. In 2006–2007, Glen Rose sent the state $8.5 million out of local property tax revenue of $21.5 million.[20]

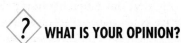 **WHAT IS YOUR OPINION?**

Is the Robin Hood school-finance reform plan fair?

TABLE 29.2   Financial Information, the Highland Park ISD and Edgewood ISD, 2005

Financial Criteria	Highland Park ISD	Edgewood ISD
Taxable value per student	$1,391,442	$60,709
Property tax rate per $100	$1.53	$1.50
Percentage total revenue from the state	12 percent	77 percent
Instructional expenditures per pupil	$6,407	$6,923
Equity transfers (funds returned to the state)	$69,806,685	$0

Source: Texas Education Agency, *www.tea.state.tx.us.*

Because of the Robin Hood Plan, poor districts have more money to spend, whereas wealthy districts have less money. Table 29.2 compares the Highland Park ISD in Dallas, one of the state's wealthiest school districts, with the Edgewood ISD in San Antonio, one of the state's poorest school districts and the lead plaintiff in *Edgewood v. Kirby.* The Highland Park ISD has more than 20 times the taxable value per student than the Edgewood ISD—$1,391,442 per student to just $60,709 per student in the Edgewood ISD. Nonetheless, the Edgewood ISD is able to spend more money per pupil on instruction than is the Highland Park ISD, $6,923 per student for Edgewood compared with $6,407 for Highland Park, primarily because of differences in state funding and the Robin Hood Plan. In 2005, Edgewood received 77 percent of its revenue from the state, whereas the Highland Park ISD got only 12 percent of its money from the state. Furthermore, the Highland Park ISD had to reduce its local revenue by transferring nearly $70 million to the state.

Education finance remains controversial. Many parents and school officials in poor districts believe that funding equality is not enough because the needs of their students are great. Although the state has achieved funding equality, they believe that it has not achieved funding adequacy. In their view, the state needs to increase education funding substantially and target the students most at risk for failure. Parents and school administrators in property-rich school districts argue that the Robin Hood Plan prevents them from providing a quality education for the youngsters living in their districts. If wealthy districts raise local taxes to improve their schools, most of the money goes to the state.

Issues in Education Policy

Education issues are an important part of the official policy agenda of the state of Texas. We discuss five of the more prominent contemporary educational issues: charter schools, school choice, class size, merit pay, bilingual education, and basic skills testing.

Charter school A publicly funded but privately managed school that operates under the terms of a formal contract or charter with the state.

Charter Schools A **charter school** is a publicly funded but privately managed school that operates under the terms of a formal contract, or charter, with the state. Parents, teachers, private companies, and nonprofit organizations may petition the state for a charter to create a school. The charter spells out the school's educational programs, targets the student population the school intends to serve, defines the school's management style, and identifies its educational goals. Each charter school

INTERNET RESEARCH   **Comparing School Districts**

The largest school districts in the state are the Aldine ISD (Harris County), Arlington ISD, Austin ISD, Cypress-Fairbanks ISD (Harris County), Dallas ISD, El Paso ISD, Fort Bend ISD, Fort Worth ISD, Garland ISD, Houston ISD, North East ISD (Bexar), Northside ISD (Bexar County), and San Antonio ISD. Each of these districts has 50,000 or more students. Your assignment is to select two of the state's largest school districts, and write an essay in which you compare and contrast the two districts. You can find a great deal of data about the state's school districts by reviewing the Texas Education Agency school report cards, which can be found at the following Internet address: **www.tea.state.tx.us/perfreport/aeis/2006/district.srch.html**. Indicate that you wish to search by district name, and then type the name of the district for which you want to find data. The website includes a good deal of information.

Your essay should cover the following topics:

- **A demographic profile of each district.** How do the two districts compare in terms of size? What is each district's racial/ethnic profile? What proportion of each district's student body has special needs?

- **A funding profile of each district.** How do the districts compare in terms of tax base? What are their tax rates? How much revenue does each district raise per student? How much state aid does each district receive?

- **A profile of each district's teachers.** How experienced are the two faculties? Does each district have a diverse group of faculty? How well paid are each district's teachers?

- **A performance evaluation.** How well do the students of each district perform on TAKS and other tests? What is each district's accountability rating?

Conclude your essay with a discussion of the strengths and weaknesses of each district. Consider whether it is possible to determine which district is more effective. Keep in mind that the challenges facing the two districts are not the same and the resources available may not be identical, either.

is independent in that it is not part of an independent school district and parents from any district may voluntarily choose to send their children to a particular charter. Charter schools may not discriminate on the basis of race, ethnicity, gender, disability, or educational need, but they may refuse to accept a student who has a history of misbehavior. A charter school may not charge tuition or levy taxes. The state funds charter schools through the Foundation School Program, awarding the same amount of money per student that it gives to traditional public schools. It provides no funding for facilities. In 2006, 71,000 students attended one of the state's 313 charter campuses at a cost to the state of $536 million.[21]

Charter schools are exempt from most state education regulations. They must conform to health and safety codes and teach the state-mandated curriculum, but they do not have to follow state regulations concerning class sizes, teacher qualifications, and the school calendar. Nonetheless, the state evaluates charter schools on the same basis as other schools, including TAKS, and on the basis of the goals the schools set for themselves. If a charter school performs poorly and fails to meet its goals, it risks losing its charter and having to close its doors.

Charter schools are controversial. Their supporters believe that each charter school is an opportunity for educational innovation. Teachers can better do their jobs when freed of red tape, they say. Moreover, the competition from charter schools will force public schools to perform better. In contrast, the critics of charter schools argue that they are a back-door method for funneling public money from the public schools to private schools. State funds should be used to improve the existing schools, rather than support an unproven educational experiment.

The performance of charter schools in Texas has been uneven. Although some charter schools, mostly small, college-preparatory schools, have excelled, other charter schools have failed to make the grade because of poor test scores, financial mismanagement, or both. In 2006, charter schools were four times as likely as traditional campuses to earn the lowest TAKS rating.[22] Furthermore, charter school students throughout the nation lag behind similar students who attend public schools.[23]

School choice An educational reform movement that would allow parents to choose the elementary or secondary school their children will attend.

School Choice   The educational reform movement that would allow parents to choose the elementary or secondary school their children will attend is known as **school choice.** Under a parental choice program, the state would give parents a voucher that would provide a type of scholarship to be paid to the school that the parents select for their child to attend. Some proponents of parental choice would allow parents to choose not only from among public schools but also from among private schools.

School choice is controversial. The proponents of school choice believe that competition for funding would force schools to improve. If low-quality public schools did not upgrade the quality of their educational programs, they would have to shut down for lack of funding. In contrast, the opponents of school choice question whether lack of competition is the main problem with public schools, believing instead that poverty, lack of parental involvement, and inadequate funding are the primary causes of poor school performance. They fear that vouchers would enable middle-class parents to take their children from public schools, leaving the children of poor families behind in public schools with even less funding. Public schools would get worse, they say, not better.

The Texas legislature has created a limited program of school choice. The parents of students in schools that are rated "Low Performing" in two of the last three years can transfer their children to any other public school that will agree to receive them, including charter schools. In 2007, students attending 284 low performing schools had the option to transfer to other public schools within the same district. Students in low performing schools are also eligible for free tutoring. In practice, however, few parents and students take advantage of their opportunities. In 2006, for example, 19,000 students in the Houston ISD were eligible to transfer or to receive free tutoring. Only 122 chose to transfer and 1,185 accepted the free tutoring.[24]

 WHAT IS YOUR OPINION?

If you were a parent of a student in a low-performing public school, would you transfer your child to another school?

Class Size   Does size matter? Some advocates of education reform believe that the key to improving education is to have smaller classes. The concept is fairly simple: Teachers can do a better job if they have fewer students in a class. In recent years, some state legislatures have mandated smaller class sizes, especially in the early grades. Texas law caps the size of classes in kindergarten through the fourth grade at 22 students, although districts may request a waiver if a school is struggling with rapid growth or lacks facilities. In general, however, if a class exceeds 22 students, the district must hire another teacher and split the class or assign students to another class to ensure that no class exceeds the cap.[25]

Critics argue that the movement to reduce class size may not be a good use of resources. Reducing class size is an expensive reform because it requires school districts to hire additional teachers. Furthermore, research on the effect of smaller class sizes is unclear. Studies show that class sizes must drop to 15–17 to make much difference, and even then smaller classes seem to make a difference only in student performance in the lowest grades. Critics of the smaller-class movement believe that the money could be better spent on teacher training.

Merit Pay   Some education reformers believe that teachers who work hard and produce positive results should be rewarded financially for their good performance. Merit pay gives all teachers an incentive to work hard and encourages the best teachers to remain on the job, rather than leaving the field for higher-paying jobs. In contrast, most teachers' unions and other critics of merit pay complain that merit pay is too often based on simplistic measures of performance that fail to grasp the essence of good teaching. Instead of incentive bonuses, the opponents of merit pay favor raising teacher salaries across the board.[26]

Texas has begun a merit pay program. In 2005, Governor Perry found $10 million to launch a pilot project. The legislature expanded the program in 2006, targeting high-performing schools that have a high percentage of low-income children. More than a thousand schools qualified in 2006 and 2007. Teachers working in those schools could qualify for bonuses of $3,000 to $10,000 if their students performed well on TAKS.[27] In 2007, the legislature and the governor appropriated $148 million for merit pay and expanded the program to allow all of the state's school districts to participate. The state recommended that districts give a $3,000 bonus to teachers who qualified. More than half the state's school districts declined to participate in the program, however, because the TEA required districts to provide a 15 percent match in local funds to qualify for the money.[28]

Bilingual education The teaching of academic subjects in both English and a student's native language, usually Spanish.

Bilingual Education   **Bilingual education** is the teaching of academic subjects in both English and the student's native language, usually Spanish. About a sixth of the state's 4.5 million public school children have limited proficiency in the English language,

GETTING INVOLVED   Helping a Child Learn

Nothing is more rewarding than helping a child learn. Most school districts have tutoring programs, in which volunteers assist students trying to learn to read or understand mathematics. Call your local school district (the number is in the telephone book) and volunteer to tutor.

It's your community—get involved!

NATIONAL PERSPECTIVE

School Choice in Cleveland, Ohio

In 1995, the Ohio legislature created a pilot school choice program targeting parents and children attending the Cleveland City School District, which is an urban school district of 75,000 students located in Cleveland, Ohio. The program provided tuition assistance to enable parents to enroll their children in alternative schools. Parents could select private schools located within district boundaries or send their children to adjacent public schools that chose to participate in the program. The amount of tuition assistance parents received depended on family income. For example, the state covered 90 percent of private school tuition for children living in families earning less than 200 percent of the poverty level.

The Ohio legislature targeted the Cleveland City School District because of its poor performance. A federal judge had put the entire district under state supervision because it had failed to meet even 1 of the 18 state standards of minimal performance. Two-thirds of Cleveland high school students dropped out or failed before graduation. A fourth of seniors failed to graduate. Furthermore, few district graduates could read, write, or do math at a level comparable to other high school graduates. The legislators who adopted the school choice program hoped that it would allow some youngsters to escape to better schools. They also hoped that competition would force the Cleveland City School District to improve its performance.

The Cleveland voucher program was particularly controversial because it allowed parents to select religious schools as well as secular private schools.

Critics charged that the program violated the **Establishment Clause,** which is a provision in the First Amendment to the U.S. Constitution that says that Congress shall make no law respecting an establishment of religion. The Establishment Clause is the basis for the doctrine of separation of church and state. Opponents of school choice in Cleveland argued that the program created an unconstitutional entanglement between the government and religion because it used public money to support religious education. Even though the overwhelming majority of private schools chosen by parents for student transfer were religiously affiliated, the U.S. Supreme Court ruled the program constitutional. The Court upheld the program because it had a valid secular purpose (providing educational assistance to poor children in a weak school system), it was neutral toward religion (parents could choose any private school or even another public school), and it provided assistance to families rather than to the schools.*

QUESTIONS TO CONSIDER

1. If you were the parent of a youngster attending the Cleveland City School District, would you take advantage of the school choice program?
2. Would money be better spent improving the Cleveland public school than used to allow students to transfer to private schools?
3. Is it wrong for the government to provide tuition assistance to students attending religious schools?

*Zelman v. Simmons-Harris, 536 U.S. 639 (2002).

Establishment Clause A provision in the First Amendment to the U.S. Constitution that says that Congress shall make no law respecting an establishment of religion.

including 30 percent in the Dallas ISD, 28 percent in the Houston ISD, and 30 percent in the El Paso ISD.[29] Spanish is far and away the most common language spoken by Texas children who have limited English-language ability, although Texas youngsters speak more than 50 languages at home.[30]

Bilingual education is a controversial education policy issue. The advocates of bilingual education believe that it enables students whose primary language is not English to learn academic subjects in their own language while they work on their English. Otherwise, they would fall behind, grow frustrated with school, and potentially drop out. Students enrolled in bilingual education programs typically take several years to learn to read, write, and speak English well enough to enter mainstream classes. In contrast, the opponents of bilingual education argue that it retards the English language development of non-English-speaking students. They believe that students with limited English-language proficiency are better served by a period of intensive English instruction, after which they enter regular academic classes.

Texas schools use a mixture of bilingual education and English-language immersion programs. The legislature has neither mandated bilingual education nor prohibited its use. Instead, each district decides how it can best meet the educational needs of students with limited English-language proficiency.

Basic Skills Testing   Texas is the model for the No Child Left Behind Act. Under the law, state governments and local school districts must institute basic skills testing in reading and math for students in grades three through eight as a condition for receiving federal aid. The results of the tests must be used to assess school performance and track the progress of individual students. Poor-performing schools that fail to improve will eventually lose federal aid money.

The Texas Education Agency (TEA) uses TAKS scores along with annual dropout rates and four-year high school graduation rates to rate schools and school districts as exemplary, recognized, academically acceptable, or academically unacceptable. In 2006–2007, 637 schools statewide earned exemplary status compared with 301 that were rated academically unacceptable. Most schools fell in the academically acceptable category.[31]

School Performance

Independent assessments of the performance of Texas schools indicate that the state's students are less well prepared for college and the workforce than students in many other states. Consider the performance of Texas students on the SAT, which is a standardized exam taken by students planning to apply for admission to a university. In 2006, the composite SAT score for Texas students was 1,481 compared with a national average of 1,511.[32]

Texas suffers from a relatively high dropout rate. The Texas Higher Education Coordinating Board tracked the progress of 266,578 seventh graders in 1992 to see what happened to them. Only 58 percent graduated from high school, with just 13 percent earning degrees or certificates from a college or university within six years of getting out of high school.[33] Latino and African American youngsters are considerably more likely to drop out of high school than are white students. The dropout rate for Latino and African American high school students is 45 percent and 40 percent, respectively, compared with a dropout rate of 20 percent for whites.[34] Because of the state's high dropout rate, the proportion of Texas residents without high school diplomas is expected to rise 11 percentage points, to 30 percent—by 2040.[35]

Texas does an average job at best in preparing students for college. Half the students entering public colleges and universities in the state are unprepared for college-level work in math, reading, or writing and therefore must take at least one remedial course. Colleges and universities spend more than $90 million a year teaching college students the basic skills that they did not learn in high school.[36] Moreover, students who enter college unprepared for college work are much less likely to graduate than are students who have college-level skills. Just 16 percent of students who require remediation earn a degree or certificate in six years compared with 47 percent of college-ready students.[37]

SPECIAL DISTRICTS

Special district A unit of local government created to perform specific functions.

Subsidence The sinking of the surface of the land caused by the too-rapid extraction of subsurface water.

A **special district** is a unit of local government created to perform specific functions. Soil and water conservation districts, for example, work to prevent soil erosion and preserve water resources. Levee improvement districts build and maintain levees. Coastal subsidence districts regulate the use of subsurface water resources in order to minimize **subsidence,** which is the sinking of the surface of the land caused by the too-rapid extraction of subsurface water. Mosquito control districts spray for mosquitoes to control annoying pests and reduce the danger of encephalitis and other diseases spread by mosquitoes.

Special districts provide important governmental services to millions of Texans. A **utility district** is a special district that provides utilities, such as water and sewer service, to residents living in unincorporated urban areas. Texas has more than 1,100 utility districts, going by such names as Fresh Water Supply Districts (FWSDs), Water Control and Improvement Districts (WCIDs), and Municipal Utility Districts (MUDs), which are the most numerous. In addition to water and sewer services, utility

The Texas Education Agency uses test scores and other factors to rate schools as exemplary, recognized, academically acceptable, or academically unacceptable.

Utility district A special district that provides utilities such as water and sewer service to residents living in unincorporated urban areas.

Hospital district A special district that provides emergency medical services, indigent healthcare, and community health services.

districts may also provide their residents with solid waste collection, fire protection, drainage, parks, and recreation facilities. A **hospital district** is a special district that provides emergency medical services, indigent healthcare, and community health services. The Harris County Hospital District, for example, is the primary medical provider for nearly a million residents in Harris County who do not have health insurance. Its operating budget exceeds $1 billion a year.[38] Community/junior college districts enroll more students in higher education than do the state's public universities. Flood control districts are responsible for flood control in many areas of the state.

Reasons for Special Districts

Special districts are created to provide services that other units of local government cannot or will not provide. For example, state law specifies a maximum property tax rate for counties and cities. Local governments can overcome the property tax ceiling by creating special districts with their own taxing authority. Harris County has a flood control district, hospital district, and port authority. Although these districts are separate units of government with their own taxing authority, the Harris County Commissioners Court controls them. Transit authorities and port authorities are other big-budget special districts whose operations could not easily be financed within the budget constraints of existing city and county governments.

Sometimes special districts are an advantageous approach to solving problems that transcend the boundaries of existing units of local government. Flooding is seldom confined to a single county or city. A countywide or area wide flood control district offers a regional approach to a regional problem. Similarly, transportation problems may affect several cities and counties. In each of these cases, it is often easier to create a special district that includes the whole area affected by the problem than it is to coordinate the efforts of existing governments.

Other motivations for the establishment of special districts include political expediency and financial gain. At times, existing units of local government refuse to provide certain services because of the opposition of individual officeholders. Special districts can be an effective means of outflanking that opposition. Some problems, such as flood control or mass transit, may become so difficult or controversial that local officials may choose to ignore them. The creation of a special district allows officials to pass the buck while taking credit for having taken the problem "out of politics."

Utility districts enable developers to build subdivisions in rural areas, outside of the coverage of municipal water and sewer services. The utility district borrows money to build water and sewer systems for the development. Homeowners pay off the debt over time through service charges and property taxes. By using a utility district to defer the construction cost of a water and sewer system, developers are able to reduce their upfront construction expenditures, and consumers can buy new homes less expensively than if the utility costs were built into the purchase price.[39]

In Denton County, for example, developer Realty Capital Belmont Corp. is using two freshwater supply districts to help fund a 4,000-home development near Argyle and Northlake. In 2006, the developer parked three mobile homes on the property and rented them to employees. The renters filed the necessary paperwork to establish residency and then requested an election to create two freshwater supply districts. In 2007, the seven registered voters living in the three mobile homes cast their ballots to approve the creation of the districts, which would borrow money to pay for roads, water pipes, and a sewer treatment system. The development's future homeowners will pay off the debt with a property tax whose rate could be as high as $1 per $100 of valuation.[40]

Creation, Organization, and Operation

Special districts are created through a variety of procedures. Hospital districts require the adoption of a constitutional amendment. The State Soil and Water Conservation Board creates soil and water conservation districts. The legislature, the Texas Commission on Environmental Quality (TCEQ), or a county commissioners court can establish utility districts. Utility districts that are to be located in a city's extraterritorial jurisdiction must first be approved by that city. The Texas legislature authorizes community/junior college districts, transit authorities, port authorities, and sports authorities.

Most districts require voter approval of area residents before they begin operations. After the legislature authorizes the creation of a utility district, for example, the measure goes on the ballot for approval by voters living within the boundaries of the proposed district. At the same election, voters may also be asked to grant the district authority to sell bonds (that is, to borrow money) and to tax. Utility districts generally issue bonds to finance the construction of sewage treatment plants. Flood control districts use them to pay for drainage improvements. Airport authorities use bond money to build runways and terminals. Sports authorities issue bonds to finance the construction of stadiums for football and baseball and arenas for hockey and basketball.

A board of directors, usually consisting of five members, is the governing body for most special districts. The board may be either appointed or elected. District voters elect most water district and community/junior college boards. City mayors appoint housing authority boards. The governor names the directors of river authorities. County commissioners courts select hospital, noxious weed control, and rural fire prevention district boards. In most cases, district board members are unsalaried. They set basic policy but leave the day-to-day operation of the district to a professional staff. Perhaps the most important task for the board of trustees of a community/junior college district, for example, is to hire a chancellor or president to manage the daily affairs of the college.

Funding

Special districts receive funding from a variety of sources. Many districts levy taxes. Utility districts, port authorities, hospital districts, flood control districts, and community/junior college districts all levy property taxes. Suburban utility districts often assess higher property tax rates than do nearby incorporated municipalities. The funding for sports authorities may come from sales taxes, hotel/motel occupancy taxes, property taxes, or taxes on rental cars. Transit authorities levy sales taxes.

Special districts raise revenues from service charges. Utility districts charge residents for water and sewer usage and for garbage pickup. Students in community/junior college districts pay tuition and fees for the classes they take. Transit authorities raise revenues from ticket charges. Toll road authorities collect tolls from drivers. Funding for coastal subsidence districts comes from fees charged for permits to drill water wells. Finally, special districts receive funding from other units of government. Federal mass transit aid supports the state's transit authorities. Community/junior college districts benefit from state funding and federal grant money. Hospital districts receive both federal and state funding to support their programs, including funding from the two huge federal healthcare programs, Medicare and Medicaid.

Evaluation of Special Districts

Special districts have both defenders and critics. Their supporters argue that they provide services that otherwise would not be available. In contrast, critics identify several problem areas. First, special districts often operate in the shadows, with little state supervision and even less public participation. For example, fewer than a dozen voters may participate in utility district authorization elections. Second, special districts generally operate less efficiently than general-purpose units of local government, such as cities and counties.[41] Small districts, particularly utility districts, can be uneconomical. Their operations are often run amateurishly and they are too small to take advantage of economies of scale. The average cost of waste disposal for utility districts is more than twice that incurred by large cities, such as Houston or Dallas.[42] Finally, the multiplicity of special districts in Texas complicates the problems of urban government. For example, many observers believe that utility districts are a major cause of land subsidence in the Houston–Galveston area because of their extensive use of subsurface water resources.

CONCLUSION: LOCAL GOVERNMENT AND PUBLIC POLICY

An influential book on urban policymaking in America is titled *City Limits*.[43] The author's point is that forces beyond local control are primarily responsible for shaping urban-development policy. The same can be said about local policymaking in general. Counties, school districts, special districts, and cities must operate within constraints imposed by the federal and state governments and by the economic environment.

The federal government shapes local policymaking through conditions attached to the provision of federal funds. Every unit of local government receiving federal money—and that includes nearly every city, county, and school district and many special districts—must conform to federal guidelines on nondiscrimination, equal access for the disabled, environmental protection, historic preservation, wage rates for construction projects, and buy-American requirements. Schools and other public buildings must be accessible to the disabled. Flood control districts and transit authorities are required to prepare environmental impact statements before beginning projects.

Federal court orders place other limits on localities. In 1980, Federal District Judge William Wayne Justice ordered Texas public schools to provide bilingual education in all school grades. A federal appeals court subsequently modified Justice's ruling, instead accepting a program that provided for bilingual education for kindergarten through the elementary grades in school districts with 20 or more students with English-language deficiencies in the same grade. School districts would have to provide bilingual classes or intensive English training in junior high school, and intensive English in high school.[44] Other federal court orders have required county jails to reduce overcrowding and have forced school districts to integrate racially. A federal judge prevented Farmers Branch from enforcing its city ordinance requiring apartment owners to verify the residency status of their tenants.

State government also limits policymaking at the local level. State laws and regulations determine the structures of local government and the scope of local authority. In some areas, state laws are restrictive and specific. Counties, for example, must seek constitutional amendments in order to modify their structures of government. Because counties lack ordinance-making authority, they must receive legislative approval to take such relatively trivial actions as prohibiting the use of fireworks or raising the speed limit on a county road.

Political scientists who study local governments believe that economic factors have considerable influence over local policymaking. Studies have found that the level of municipal expenditures correlates closely with a city's average per capita income. Wealthier cities spend more for public services than do poorer cities.[45] The same can be said for many other units of local government, such as counties and special districts. School district spending is less dependent on local financial resources because of the impact of state school funding reforms.

Nonetheless, it is misleading to suggest that local policymaking is completely determined by outside forces. The relationship between local governments and state and federal authorities is not a one-way street, with localities always on the receiving end of instructions from the state and national capitals. Local governments lobby Austin and Washington, DC, frequently with good effect. After all, representatives elected to the state legislature and to Congress are elected locally from districts that include cities, counties, school districts, and other units of local government. A member of Congress or the Texas legislature chosen from a district located in Dallas, for example, will likely be responsive to the concerns of Dallas County, the City of Dallas, the Dallas ISD, the Dallas Area Transit Authority (DART), Dallas County Community College, and other school districts and special districts in the area.

In sum, local governments are limited governments. They are at the bottom of the legal structures of American government and, accordingly, must conform to the rules and regulations established by higher levels of government. The policy options of local officials are further constrained by their area's level of economic development. Still, local officials have room to make meaningful policy decisions within the boundaries established by outside forces.

LET'S DEBATE

Do Basic Skills Tests, Such as TAAS and TAKS, Help or Harm Public Education?

Overview: To address an unacceptable and worrisome decline in educational attainment and proficiency in America's primary and secondary educational establishments, the federal government passed the No Child Left Behind Act (NCLB) in January 2002. The NCLB requires states to create and administer educational skills evaluations to measure increases in student improvement, while holding school districts accountable for student success or failure. State performance can be compared to the Department of Education's National Assessment of Educational Progress's (NAEP) baseline. The NAEP is a national project that evaluates the quality of education in each of the 50 states. Texas ranks from average to poor in student educational attainment. Brookings Institution research shows that Texas exam results consistently fall short of NAEP benchmarks, and 83 percent of all eighth graders met the Texas Assessment of Knowledge and Skills (TAKS) reading standards, whereas only 26 percent of the same eighth graders met NAEP reading proficiency. In October 2005, the National Academy of Sciences warned that, unless the American people addressed the issue of education, U.S. leadership in technological development and its economic and national security may be at risk.

Standardized exams are at the focus of the education wars and, as a result, educators and parents have divided into two opposing camps in regard to educational testing. One view argues that standardized testing does not take into account a student's life experience, creativity, and critical thinking skills, and the effect of requiring standardized testing is to force educators to "teach to the test," which means neglecting to teach other valuable learning skills and curriculum. This view argues that the result is to ignore other important aspects of the educational experience, as testing cannot take into account the nonquantifiable aspects of a student's education. Others, however, argue that uniform testing is the only means to gain clear insight into the level of student attainment, and truly good instructors teach the curriculum in such a way that students have a broad and deep education *and* do well on state exams. Proponents of exams believe the solution is not to eliminate or "dumb down" the exams but to hold the educational establishment accountable for declining educational attainment and quality.

When compared to the NAEP, Harvard University's policy expert Paul Peterson maintains that if the states received report cards on the knowledge level of primary and secondary students, the state of Texas would receive an *F*. But this does not take into account Texas's measured improvement in its educational establishment over the last decade. Due to the innovative, comprehensive nature of the pre-TAKS exam (the Texas Assessment of Academic Skills, or TAAS), the Texas educational establishment has been the subject of several high-profile studies. Though the two main studies present contradictory findings, there can be little doubt that Texas has improved the quality of its schools over the past ten years and serious questions remain as to how much and why. Nevertheless, it may be that the state's testing regime has provided educators and Texans a tool by which to judge and improve the quality of Texas schools.

Arguments for Requiring Basic Skills Tests

❏ **Standardized exams do not claim to measure the full extent of educational attainment.** The TAKS test is not meant to be a comprehensive skills exam. Its purpose is to determine the minimal level of *basic* skills necessary to proceed to the next instructional phase. Higher-order learning, such as critical thinking skills and analysis, depends on the mastery of basic skills. It is wrong to assume that average fifth and eighth graders are capable of advanced skills without knowing basic math, grammar, history, and geography.

❏ **Basic skills tests are crucial to knowing educational proficiency.** How else can a student's progress be measured? The salient fact of the matter is that standardized exams are good indicators of educational progress and student achievement. For example, exams let educators discern if students know "why there are seasons" or if a student is capable of summarizing a three-paragraph reading sample. TAKS can let administrators know where a school is proficient or weak in its presentation of curriculum.

❏ **Publishing district standardized test scores forces accountability.** Research by Stanford

University's Hoover Institution indicates that, after passage of NCLB, releasing a district's examination scores may put pressure on poor schools to improve their academic performance. Standardized exams provide a measure by which educators and parents can judge the effectiveness and quality of a given school, thus holding poor schools accountable while motivating those schools to improve the quality of their performance.

Arguments Against Requiring Basic Skills Tests

❏ **Basic skills tests do not enhance educational attainment.** Research and testing already show that too many students are not proficient in math, reading, grammar, history, geography, and so on. The answer is not more testing—the answer is to improve the quality of the curriculum, teachers, and overall educational environment. Testing has its uses, but, to improve educational proficiency, the focus should be on curricula and the competency of both teachers and administrators.

❏ **TAKS requirements force school districts to "teach to the test."** Rather than teaching analytical and creative thinking, teachers are forced by exam requirements to have students "cram" for the test without actually learning the material, thus undermining the primary goal of a true education. Educators need to provide a quality education without having to worry about how annual testing will affect their students, schools, and careers.

❏ **Standardized exams divert educational resources and funding.** Giving standardized exams is expensive and diverts time from other academic pursuits. The funding used for exams can be diverted to improve school infrastructure, provide technology, and improve curriculum development. The result should be an improvement in the overall academic environment and improved student performance. Preparing students for exams is time-intensive and detracts from the limited time teachers have to teach the curriculum.

QUESTIONS

1. Does TAKS provide a true measure of a student's educational level? Why or why not?
2. Should state-mandated exams take into account a student's life experience and creativity? If so, how can this be done?

SELECT READINGS

1. Richard Phelps, *Kill the Messenger: The War on Standardized Testing* (Piscataway, NJ: Transaction, 2003).
2. R. Murray Thomas, *High Stakes Testing: Coping with Collateral Damage* (Mahwah, NJ: Lawrence Erlbaum, 2005).

SELECT WEBSITES

1. **www.ted.state.tx.us**
   Website of the Texas Education Agency.
2. **www.waller.isd.esc4.net/curriculum/taks.htm**
   The Waller ISD's summary of the TAKS and its requirements.

KEY TERMS

bilingual education

charter school

Children's Health Insurance Program (CHIP)

commissioners court

conflict of interest

Establishment Clause

federal grant program

Foundation School Program

general law units of local government

home rule

hospital district

independent school districts (ISDs)

long ballot

No Child Left Behind Act

nonpartisan elections

ordinance

partisan election

Permanent School Fund (PSF)

poll tax

Robin Hood Plan

school choice

school lunch program

special district

subpoena

subsidence

Texas Assessment of Knowledge and Skills (TAKS)

utility district

NOTES

1. Terrence Stutz, "16% Fail TAKS Graduation Test," *Dallas Morning News*, May 12, 2007, available at www.dallasnews.com.

2. Jenny LaCoste-Caputo, "TAKS on Its Way Out, But It's Not History Yet," *San Antonio Express-News*, August 17, 2007, available at www.mysanantonio.com.

3. U.S. Bureau of the Census, available at www.census.gov.

4. Texas Comptroller of Public Accounts, "Limited Coverage," *Fiscal Notes*, February 2006, p. 1.

5. Rick Casey, "Why Run for Judge If You're King," *Houston Chronicle*, July 8, 2005, p. B1.

6. Equal Justice Center, "Texas Indigent Defense Spending," available at www.equaljusticecenter.org.

7. Glenn Evans, "Counties Concerned over Too Much Control Coming out of Austin," *Longview News-Journal*, April 4, 2004, available at www.news-journal.com.

8. Harris County, FY 2006–2007 Budget, available at www.co.harris.tx.us.

9. Chase David, "Few Rivals But Plenty of Donors," *Houston Chronicle*, November 24, 2007, pp. A1, A9.

10. Texas Education Agency, available at www.tea.state.tx.us.

11. John M. Bolland and Kent D. Redfield, "The Limits of Citizen Participation in Local Education: A Cognitive Interpretation," *Journal of Politics* 50 (November 1988): 1033–1046.

12. Rebecca Winters, "A Job for a Super Hero?" *Time*, February 7, 2000, p. 70.

13. Jim Henderson, "Dallas School Trustees Left Holding Bag Again," *Houston Chronicle*, July 9, 2000, pp. 1A, 21A.

14. Office of the Permanent School Fund, *Texas Permanent School Fund, Annual Report, Fiscal Year Ending August 31, 2006*, available at www.tea.state.tx.us.

15. *Financing Public Education in Texas*, 2nd ed., available at www.lbb.state.tx.us.

16. Gary Scharrer, "States Voting Trend Promotes Top Education," *Houston Chronicle*, November 9, 2004, available at www.chron.com.

17. House Research Organization, Focus Report, "Schools and Taxes: A Summary of Legislation of the 2006 Special Session," available at www.hro.house.state.tx.us.

18. Texas Education Agency, available at www.tea.state.tx.us.

19. *Edgewood v. Kirby*, 777 S.W.2d 391 (1989).

20. Legislative Budget Board, "Selected Variables by School District Fiscal Year 2007," available at www.lbb.state.tx.us.

21. Jeanne Russell and Jenny LaCoste-Caputo, "Just How Well Have Charter Schools Worked?" *San Antonio Express News*, January 28, 2007, available at www.mysanantonio.com.

22. Ericka Mellon, Polly Ross Hughes, and Jennifer Radcliffe, "HISD Campuses Rated Unacceptable Cut by Nearly Half," *Houston Chronicle*, August 2, 2007, pp. A1, A9.

23. Diana Jean Schemo, "A Second Report Shows Charter School Students Not Performing as Well as Other Students," *New York Times*, December 16, 2004, available at www.nytimes.com.

24. Jennifer Radcliffe and Ericka Mellon, "More HISD Schools Miss Federal Mark," *Houston Chronicle*, August 16, 2007, pp. A1, A8.

25. Terrence Stutz, "Lawmakers May Modify Class Size Cap," *Dallas Morning News*, April 4, 2004, available at www.dallasnews.com.

26. Alan Greenblatt, "Merit Pay Moves Forward," *Governing*, January 2007, p. 51.

27. Terrence Stutz, "1,132 Schools Qualify for Merit Pay," *Dallas Morning News*, April 14, 2007, available at www.dallasnews.com.

28. Terrence Stutz, "Most School Districts Reject Texas' New Merit Pay Plan," *Dallas Morning News*, November 15, 2007, available at www.dallasnews.com.

29. Texas Education Agency, "2006 District AEIS+ Report," available at www.tea.state.tx.us.

30. Alan Bernstein, "Bilingual Debate Has Texas Twang," *Houston Chronicle*, May 25, 1998, pp. 1A, 16A.

31. Mellon, Hughes, and Radcliffe, "HISD Campuses Rated Unacceptable Cut by Nearly Half," p. A9.

32. Jennifer Radcliffe, "HISD Post SAT Gains for Second Year in a Row," *Houston Chronicle*, September 1, 2007, available at www.chron.com.

33. *Texas Weekly*, November 29, 2004.

34. Michele Angel, "Gap Widens Between Hispanic and Anglo Dropout Rates," *Rio Grande Guardian*, November 1, 2007, available at www.riograndeguardian.com.

35. Raven L. Hill and Laura Heinauer, "Texas' Dropout Problem Probably Worse than Reported," *Austin American-Statesman*, May 27, 2007, available at www.statesman.com.

36. Melanie Markley, "Scores on TAAS Rose as SATs Fell," *Houston Chronicle*, June 6, 2004, p. A35.

37. Ralph K. M. Haurwitz and Laura Heinauer, "Half of Students Entering Public Colleges Need Remedial Courses," *Austin American-Statesman*, May 15, 2005, available at www.statesman.com.

38. Harris County Hospital District, "The Faces of Change: 2007 Annual Report," available at www.hchdonline.com.

39. Paula Lavigne, "Will Sprouting of MUDs Make Mess?" *Dallas Morning News*, October 26, 2003, available at www.dallasnews.com.

40. Dan X. McGraw, "Special Districts Get Voter Approval," *Denton Record-Chronicle*, November 12, 2007, available at www.dentonrc.com.

41. Kathryn A. Foster, *The Political Economy of Special-Purpose Government* (Washington, DC: Georgetown University Press, 1997), pp. 174–183.

42. David W. Tees, "A Fresh Look at Special Districts in Texas," in *Governmental Organization and Authority in Metropolitan Areas* (Arlington: Texas Urban Development Commission, 1971), p. 50; and Virginia Marion Perrenod, *Special Districts, Special Purposes* (College Station: Texas A&M University Press, 1984), p. 76.

43. Paul E. Peterson, *City Limits* (Chicago: University of Chicago Press, 1981).

44. *Houston Post*, July 13, 1982, pp. 1A, 9A.

45. Peterson, pp. 50–64.

Chapter 30

State Budget Policy in Texas

CHAPTER OUTLINE

Revenues
- Taxes
- Nontax Sources of Revenue
- Issues in State Finance
- Policy Options

Expenditures
- Healthcare
- Elementary and Secondary Education
- Higher Education

Welfare

Transportation

The Budget Process

Conclusion: Budgetary Policymaking
- The Environment for Budgetary Policymaking
- Agenda Building
- Policy Formulation and Adoption
- Policy Implementation and Evaluation

LEARNING OUTCOMES

After studying Chapter 30, students should be able to do the following:

- Describe the Trans-Texas Corridor. (p. 820)
- Identify the most important revenue sources for the state of Texas, including both tax and nontax sources, and trace changes in the relative importance of those sources over the past 20 years. (pp. 820–828)
- Compare and contrast the tax structure of Texas with the tax structures in other states. (p. 828)
- Evaluate the tax system in Texas in terms of fairness and elasticity. (pp. 828–831)
- Identify and evaluate the various policy options proposed for reforming the state's revenue structure. (pp. 831–833)
- Identify the most important spending priorities for the state of Texas, and trace changes in the

relative importance of those priorities over the past 20 years. (pp. 833–835)
- Describe the Medicaid and CHIP programs. (pp. 835–838)
- Describe the funding systems for public education and for higher education. (pp. 838–842)
- Evaluate the impact of welfare reform in Texas. (p. 842)
- Describe the system for funding transportation in the state. (pp. 843–844)
- Trace the steps in the state budgetary process. (pp. 844–848)
- Analyze the budgetary process using the policymaking model. (pp. 849–853)
- Define the key terms listed on page 855 and explain their significance.

The **Trans-Texas Corridor** is a proposed network of transportation corridors, a quarter mile wide and 370 miles long running from Brownsville to Oklahoma, that would include toll roads, railways, and utility lines. Over the next 50 years, the state of Texas plans to grant rights-of-way as much as a quarter mile wide to private developers, who will construct a network of transportation corridors. Each corridor will contain separate lanes for automobiles, trucks, and rail lines, as well as additional space for pipelines and utility lines. The private developers would recoup their investment by charging tolls to drivers and other users of the corridor. The first project, Highway 130 between Brownsville and the Oklahoma border parallel to Interstate 35, has already begun and could open as soon as 2013. Cintra Zachry, the private firm hired by the state to plan the project, estimates that it or another private builder will pay the state $2 billion to build the project. Construction costs for the project are estimated at $8.8 billion. Over the next 50 years, the contractor will make back its investment from drivers who willingly pay a toll in order to avoid the overcrowded I-35. Cars and small trucks will initially pay about 15 cents per mile; truckers will pay 58.5 cents per mile. Other projects, including a freight rail line from North Texas to Laredo, high-speed rail lines, and a road section from San Antonio to Laredo will not open until 2016 or later.[1]

The Trans-Texas Corridor is controversial. Its supporters, including Governor Rick Perry, see it as an innovative solution to the state's transportation needs because private developers, rather than taxpayers, bear the cost and the risk. The people who eventually foot the bill for the project are the people who drive the roads or consumers who purchase goods transported in the corridor. In contrast, critics charge that the Trans-Texas Corridor is a boondoggle that will benefit private developers and harm the public interest. Environmentalists warn that it will consume vast stretches of open land and harm sensitive ecosystems. In the meantime, property rights advocates oppose the project because private landowners will be forced to sell their land to private developers.[2]

The debate over the Trans-Texas Corridor illustrates the nature of the budgetary policymaking process. Budgetary policymaking involves deciding what societal needs to address and where to find the funds to address them. The chapter begins with a section examining state revenues and then turns to a discussion of expenditures. The chapter turns to a review of the budgetary process before concluding with an overview of the budgetary policymaking. This is the first of two chapters dealing with the nature of public policy in particular policy areas. Chapter 30 addresses budgetary policymaking, whereas Chapter 31 focuses on criminal justice.

REVENUES

During the 2006 **fiscal year** (i.e., budget year), the state of Texas generated $72.4 billion in revenue from all sources, including both taxes and nontax sources of revenue. Table 30.1 identifies the various sources of state revenue and indicates their relative importance. Because the table includes data for fiscal years 1986, 1996, and 2006, it also shows changes in the relative importance of each revenue source across time.

TABLE 30.1   State Revenues by Source, Fiscal Years 1986, 1996, and 2006

Tax Sources of State Revenue as a Percentage of Total Revenue			
Source	1986	1996	2006
General sales tax	24.2%	26.7%	25.2%
Severance taxes on oil and gas production	8.7	2.0	4.4
Motor vehicle sales and rental	4.8	4.9	4.2
Motor fuels tax	5.7	5.7	4.1
Franchise tax	5.0	4.0	3.6
Taxes on alcohol and tobacco products	4.0	2.4	1.7
Insurance company tax	2.3	1.5	1.7
Utility taxes	1.1	0.6	0.7
Other taxes	1.5	1.0	1.4
Total taxes	**57.3**	**48.8**	**46.3**

Nontax Sources of State Revenue as a Percentage of Total Revenue			
Source	1986	1996	2006
Federal funds	23.0%	28.8%	34.1%
Licenses and fees	6.9	9.5	8.3
Interest and investment income	6.2	5.1	2.7
Net lottery proceeds	—	4.2	2.2
Land income	4.6	0.6	1.2
Other nontax revenue	2.0	3.0	5.2
Total nontax sources of revenue	**42.7**	**51.2**	**53.7**
Total net revenue (tax and nontax sources combined)	**100%** ($17.9 billion)	**100%** ($40.5 billion)	**100%** ($72.4 billion)

Source: Texas Comptroller of Public Accounts, "Revenue by Source," various years, available at *www.cpa.state.tx.us.*

Taxes

The state of Texas raises 46 percent of its total revenue from taxes. The general sales tax is by far the most important state tax source, generating substantially more money than any other tax. The other major state taxes include severance taxes on oil and natural gas production, a tax on motor vehicle sales and rental, a motor fuels tax, and a franchise tax.

The relative importance of taxes to the state's revenue picture has declined over the past 20 years. As Table 30.1 indicates, the proportion of state revenue generated by taxes fell from more than 57 percent in 1986 to 46 percent in 2006. The trend does not reflect a decline in tax revenues. The legislature and the governor have increased various tax rates, and most tax revenues have also increased because of economic growth. Taxes have declined as a source of state revenue relative to total revenues because of the rapid growth of nontax sources of revenue, especially federal funds. Since 1986, federal funds have increased from nearly 23 percent of state revenues to 34 percent. Most of the growth in federal funds has been through the **Medicaid** program, which is

Medicaid A federal program designed to provide health insurance coverage to low-income persons, people with disabilities, and elderly people who are impoverished.

a federal program designed to provide health insurance coverage to the poor, people with disabilities, and elderly Americans who are impoverished.

Sales tax A levy on the retail sale of taxable items.

General Sales Tax   A **sales tax** is a levy on the retail sale of taxable items. Texas has a relatively high sales tax rate. In 2004, the average Texan paid $1,320 in sales taxes, the fifteenth highest sales tax bite in the nation.[3] The state levies a sales tax of 6.25 percent on the retail purchase of taxable items. Cities and other units of local government may add as much as 2 percent more to the state tax rate, bringing the total sales tax in many areas of the state to 8.25 percent.

Not all sales are subject to taxation. Although restaurant meals are taxable, food purchased at a grocery store is tax exempt (except for ready-to-eat items). The sale of most agricultural items is tax exempt, including the sale of agricultural machinery and parts, fertilizer, feed for animals, and seed. Drugs and medicine are exempt as well, whether sold over the counter or by prescription. Only some services are taxable. The list of taxable services includes charges for laundry, dry cleaning, cable television service, credit reporting, data processing, debt collection, landscaping, security, telecommunications, car repair, and janitorial services. The sales tax does not apply, however, to charges and fees for many other services, including legal retainers, accounting services, builder and contractor fees, real estate commissions, brokerage fees, and healthcare charges.

The growth of Internet sales is undermining the state sales tax base. State governments cannot legally compel an Internet or mail order retailer to collect its sales tax unless the retailer has a physical presence in the state. Sears, for example, charges sales tax on purchases made by Texas consumers because Sears has stores throughout the state, but L.L. Bean, an Internet and mail order retailer based in Maine, does not because it has no outlets based in the Lone Star State. By 2011, Texas may lose as much as 10 percent of its total expected sales tax collection to Internet sales.[4]

Severance tax A tax imposed on the extraction of natural resources, such as oil, coal, or gas.

Severance Taxes on Oil and Natural Gas Production   A tax levied on natural resources at the time they are taken from the land or water is known as a **severance tax.** The most important severance taxes in Texas are levied on the production of oil and natural gas. The state collects a 4.6 percent tax on the value of oil produced and 7.5 percent on natural gas, rates that are comparable to those charged by other energy-producing states. Texas also levies severance taxes on the production of cement and the extraction of sulfur. The importance of severance taxes has diminished over the last 20 years. In 1986, severance taxes on oil and gas generated 8.7 percent of state tax revenues. Although oil and gas prices jumped to record levels in recent years, severance taxes are a relatively minor part of the state's tax picture because of the longstanding decline in oil and gas production in the state.

Excise tax A tax levied on the manufacture, transportation, sale, or consumption of a particular item or set of related items.

Excise Taxes   An **excise tax** is a tax levied on the manufacture, transportation, sale, or consumption of a particular item or set of related items. It is a selective sales tax. Texas state government levies excise taxes on motor vehicle sales and rentals, motor fuels, alcohol, and tobacco. In 2006, the state's various excise taxes collectively generated 10 percent of state revenue, a figure that has not changed appreciably in the last 20 years. Excise taxes of alcohol and tobacco products are called sin taxes.

Sin tax A levy on
an activity that some
people consider
morally
objectionable, such
as smoking or
drinking.

A **sin tax** is a levy on an activity that some people consider morally objectionable, such as smoking or drinking. Sin taxes are designed not just to raise revenue but also to discourage the behavior. In 2006, for example, the legislature increased the state's cigarette tax by $1 a pack, to $1.41, moving the Texas tax rate up to the top third among states nationwide. The goal of the tax increase was both to raise revenue to use to fund school property tax cuts and to discourage smoking. The measure is apparently achieving both goals because tobacco tax revenues are up and smoking is down.[5]

 WHAT IS YOUR OPINION?

Should the government increase taxes on tobacco products and alcohol to discourage smoking and drinking?

Franchise tax
A tax on businesses
chartered or
organized in Texas
and doing business
in the state.

Franchise Tax   A **franchise tax** is a tax on businesses chartered or organized in Texas and doing business in the state. It is the primary tax assessed by state government on business, but it is not the *only* tax businesses pay because local governments also levy property taxes on business property, such as land, warehouses, manufacturing plants, stores, inventory, and office buildings. In 2006, the legislature increased the franchise tax rate and expanded its coverage in order to replace the revenue lost by cutting school property taxes. The new franchise tax, which goes into effect in 2008, is expected to raise considerably more revenue than the older franchise tax.

Texans pay one of the highest sales taxes in the nation.

Other Taxes   In addition to the general sales tax, excise taxes, corporation franchise tax, and severance taxes on oil and gas production, the state of Texas collects a number of other levies. These other taxes include an insurance company tax, utility taxes, and an inheritance tax. No one of these taxes accounts for as much as 2 percent of the state's total revenue, but collectively they are an important part of the state's revenue picture.

The state's tax revenue sources also include taxes on **pari-mutuel wagering,** which is a system for gambling on horse and dog racing. The total amount of money wagered on a horse or dog race is pooled and then divided among those who bet on one of the top three finishers, minus percentages that go to the owners of the winning animals, track management, and government. In 1987, the legislature authorized pari-mutuel gambling on horse and dog racing pending voter approval in a statewide referendum, which passed by a good margin. The legislature permitted the construction of major horse tracks in the Dallas, Houston, San Antonio, and Fort Worth areas, with smaller tracks allowed in other counties pending local voter approval. The legislature permitted the construction of greyhound racetracks in only three counties—Galveston, Nueces (Corpus Christi), and Cameron (Brownsville). Although some observers predicted that taxes on pari-mutuel wagering would eventually produce as much as $100 million a year, the payoff for the state has been insignificant. In 2004, pari-mutuel wagering generated $4.4 million in state revenue, well less than 0.10 percent of total state revenues.[6]

Pari-mutuel wagering A system for gambling on horse and dog racing.

 WHAT IS YOUR OPINION?

Should the state of Texas allow gambling on dog and horse racing?

Nontax Sources of Revenue

Nontax sources of revenue account for a majority of total state revenues.

Federal Funds   The federal government is a major funding source for state government in Texas, accounting for more than a third of state revenues. Medicaid is the largest single source of federal financial aid to state government. Federal money also supports highway construction, a number of welfare programs, and a broad range of other state activities.

Licenses and Fees   Texas state government raises money through the sale of licenses and the collection of fees. Texans who wish to drive motor vehicles, operate a business, practice a profession, go hunting and fishing, attend a state university, or sell alcoholic beverages must purchase licenses or pay a fee for the privilege. In 2006, licenses and fees accounted for 8.3 percent of state revenue.

Texas Teacher Retirement System (TRS) Trust Fund A pension fund for the state's public school teachers.

Interest and Investment Income   The state of Texas holds billions of dollars in cash and securities that generate dividend and interest income from investment. The largest pool of money is the **Texas Teacher Retirement System (TRS) Trust Fund,** which is a pension fund for the state's public school teachers. The TRS Trust Fund

Taxes on pari-mutuel wagering have so far generated relatively little revenue for the state.

Employees Retirement System (ERS) Trust Fund A pension fund for state employees.

held $112 billion in assets at the end of 2006. Similarly, the **Employees Retirement System (ERS) Trust Fund** is a pension fund for state employees. It was worth $28 billion in 2006.[7] The TRS and ERS trust funds provide retirement, disability, and death or survivor benefits to their members.

Although the TRS and ERS trust funds seem flush with cash, they lack sufficient assets to cover future liabilities. The TRS Trust Fund is $13.9 billion short of having enough money to cover promised retirement benefits for current and future retirees, whereas the ERS Trust Fund is $1.1 billion short. The legislature has begun to address the problem by increasing state contributions to the TRS Trust Fund and by making it difficult for teachers and state employees to take early retirement.[8]

Permanent School Fund (PSF) A fund established in the Texas Constitution as an endowment to finance public elementary and secondary education.

The Permanent School Fund (PSF) and the Permanent University Fund (PUF) support education. The **Permanent School Fund (PSF)** is a fund established in the Texas Constitution as an endowment to finance public elementary and secondary education. At the end of 2006, the market value of PSF bonds and securities stood at $27 billion. The **Permanent University Fund (PUF)** is a fund established in the Texas Constitution as an endowment to finance construction, maintenance, and some other activities at the University of Texas and Texas A&M University. The value of the PUF in 2006 was $14 billion.[9] The state's interest and investment income varies, depending on the investment climate. In 2006, interest and investment income accounted for 2.7 percent of state revenue.

Permanent University Fund (PUF) Money constitutionally set aside as an endowment to finance construction, maintenance, and some other activities at the University of Texas, Texas A&M University, and other institutions in those two university systems.

Land Income   The state of Texas owns more than 20 million acres of land that produce revenue for the state from leases for agricultural use and for oil and gas production. The PSF and PUF hold the largest blocks of land—13 million acres and 2.1 million acres, respectively.[10] Income from land held by the PSF and PUF is invested in stocks, bonds, and other securities, which, in turn, generate interest and investment income. In 2006, land income accounted for 1.2 percent of state revenue.

Lottery Revenue   Since the Texas Lottery began operation in 1992, it has generated more than $14 billion for the state.[11] Although that is a great deal of money, it is a relatively small part of the state's total revenue picture. Lottery revenues accounted for just 2.2 percent of state revenues in 2006. Furthermore, most of the money the lottery generates goes not for education but for marketing, vendor commissions, and prizes. Figure 30.1 shows the distribution of money spent on the lottery. A bit more than half of the money that Texans pay for lottery tickets goes for prizes. After subtracting money for administration and for compensation to retailers for selling lottery tickets, the state realizes 27 percent in revenue of every dollar spent on the lottery.

General Fund The state treasury account that supports state programs and services without restriction.

Lottery proceeds go into the Foundation School Program. When the lottery was created, the legislature funneled lottery earnings into the **General Fund,** which is the state treasury account that supports state programs and services without restriction. In 1997, the legislature amended the law to dedicate lottery proceeds to public education. Because the legislature reduced education spending by a sum equal to the amount of anticipated lottery proceeds, the dedication had no impact on the total amount of money spent for education in Texas. Furthermore, research indicates that states that adopt lotteries to fund education tend to decrease funding for education compared with states without lotteries.[12]

The history of lotteries nationwide is that they start strong but then decline as the novelty wears off. States attempt to slow or reverse the decline by introducing new or different games and by manipulating how jackpots pile up.[13] Texas is no exception to the pattern. In 1998, Texas Lottery sales dropped after the legislature reduced prizes in order to increase the amount of money going to the state. The Lottery Commission reacted to the situation by making it more difficult to win.

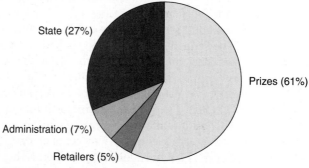

FIGURE 30.1   Distribution of Lottery Proceeds.
Source: Texas Lottery Commission.

Instead of having to pick six numbers correctly from 1 to 50, players had to pick six numbers from 1 to 54. The odds of winning increased from 15.8 million to 1 to 25.8 million to 1. By making it more difficult to win, the state hoped to increase the size of the jackpots, which would entice more people to spend money on lottery tickets. The strategy worked for a while because lottery sales increased temporarily. When ticket sales slumped again, the state made it even more difficult to win by adding a Bonus Ball, reducing the odds of winning to 47.7 million to 1.[14]

 WHAT IS YOUR OPINION?

Is it morally wrong for the government to use gambling to raise money?

In 2003, the legislature passed and the governor signed legislation authorizing the state's participation in a multi-state lottery in hopes of generating additional gambling revenue. The Lottery Commission decided to participate in Mega Millions, a game that is offered in a number of states. Mega Millions has been attractive to bettors in other states because the long odds of winning, 135 million to 1, have produced some giant jackpots, including a payout of more than $360 million.[15]

Other Nontax Revenue   The "other nontax revenue" category in Table 30.1 groups a number of miscellaneous revenue sources, which in 2006 collectively generated 5.2 percent of total state revenue. For example, the category includes employee benefit contributions, which is money withheld from the paychecks of state workers to cover health insurance for their families and other benefits. Although the money is technically revenue to the state, the funds are earmarked for employee benefits.

The category also contains revenue from the tobacco lawsuit settlement. In 1996, Texas brought suit against eight large tobacco companies, their public relations

The Texas Lottery generates 2.2 percent of total state revenues.

TABLE 30.2   Government Finance in Texas and the United States, FY 2006

Measure	Texas	National Average	Texas's National Rank
State and local revenue per capita	$6,842	$8,292	42
State and local revenue as a percentage of personal income	20.7 percent	23.8 percent	42
Personal income taxes per capita	0	$733	—
State and local sales taxes per capita	$1,320	$1,228	15
State and local property taxes per capita	$1,254	$1,084	13
State and local fees and other charges per capita	$1,407	$1,545	35
Federal aid to states and localities per capita	$1,232	$1,450	40

Source: *Governing*, State and Local Source Book 2006, pp. 30–37.

companies, and their research firms, accusing them of violating state and federal law by marketing tobacco products to children and adjusting the nicotine levels in tobacco to cause mass addiction. The suit asked for money to cover the state's share of the healthcare costs of Medicaid recipients suffering from smoking-related illnesses. Rather than go to trial, the tobacco industry agreed to a $17.3 billion settlement to be paid out over 25 years.[16]

Issues in State Finance

Texas policymakers face a number of issues in government finance.

State Revenue Adequacy   Do state and local governments in Texas generate enough money to meet the needs of the state's large and rapidly growing population? Liberals believe that state and local governments generate insufficient revenue to address pressing state needs in education, healthcare, and transportation. In contrast, conservatives favor limiting the capacity of government to raise revenue because they believe that small government promotes economic growth.

Table 30.2 presents data comparing and contrasting government revenue in Texas with the national average. The table includes both tax revenues and nontax sources of revenue, including fees, service charges, and federal aid money. As the table shows, state and local governments in Texas receive less revenue from taxes and other sources than does the average state. In 2006, total state and local revenue **per capita** (per person) in Texas was $6,842 compared with a national average of $8,292. Texas ranked 42nd among the 50 states. On average, government revenue in Texas represented 20.7 percent of personal income compared with a national average of 23.8 percent.

Per capita Per person.

State and local governments in Texas generate less revenue per capita than do their counterparts in other states, primarily because Texas is one of only seven states (Alaska, Florida, Nevada, South Dakota, Washington, and Wyoming are the others) without a personal income tax. The average state income tax generates $733 per capita annually compared with nothing in Texas. Most other state and local taxes in Texas are relatively high. As Table 30.2 indicates, Texas has the 15th highest sales tax burden in the nation and the 13th heaviest property tax burden.

Tax incidence The point at which the actual cost of a tax falls.

Tax Incidence   The term **tax incidence** refers to the point at which the actual cost of a tax falls. When social scientists and policymakers consider the incidence of a tax, they are focusing on who actually pays the tax. Sometimes the people who write the check to the government are not the only people who bear the burden of a tax. Consider the franchise tax. Although businesses pay the tax, the actual expense of the tax is borne by people—stockholders who earn smaller dividends, customers who pay higher prices for the company's products, or employees who receive lower wages. Taxes on alcohol and tobacco fall not only on those people who drink and smoke but also on tobacco and liquor companies because higher prices caused by the tax will reduce consumer demand for their products. Tobacco companies oppose efforts to increase cigarette taxes not because they want to shelter their customers from higher prices but because they know that fewer people will smoke if cigarettes cost more.

Progressive tax A levy whose burden weighs more heavily on persons earning higher incomes than it does on individuals making less money.

Proportional tax A levy that weighs equally on all persons, regardless of their income.

Regressive tax A levy whose burden weighs more heavily on low-income groups than wealthy taxpayers.

Social scientists use the terms *progressive, proportional,* and *regressive* to discuss the impact of taxation on different income groups. A **progressive tax** is a levy whose burden weighs more heavily on persons earning higher incomes than it does on individuals making less money. A luxury tax on expensive yachts and jewelry is an example of a progressive tax. If we assume that members of the upper-income groups are the primary people who purchase luxury items, then the tax would obviously represent a greater proportion of the incomes of wealthier individuals than it would the incomes of low-income people. A **proportional tax** is a levy that weighs equally on all persons, regardless of their income. An income tax that charged everyone the same percentage amount without deductions or exemptions would be a proportional tax because each income group would pay the same percentage of its earnings in tax. A **regressive tax** is a levy whose burden weighs more heavily on low-income groups than wealthy taxpayers. Economists generally classify sales and excise taxes as regressive because lower-income persons spend a greater proportion of their earnings on items subject to taxation than do upper-income persons. People in upper-income groups pay more in sales and excise taxes because they purchase more taxable items and the items they purchase tend to be more expensive. Sales and excise taxes are regressive because lower-income individuals spend a greater proportion of their incomes on taxable items than do members of middle- and upper-income groups.[17]

 WHAT IS YOUR OPINION?

Do you favor reforming the tax system in Texas to make it more progressive?

The Texas tax structure is regressive because of its heavy reliance on property, sales, and excise taxes. A family earning $12,100 a year pays 14.2 percent of its income in state and local taxes. In contrast, a family with an annual income of $177,800 pays just 5.1 percent of its income in taxes. All of the major taxes in Texas are regressive, but some are more regressive than others. The property tax is the least regressive; the gasoline tax is the most regressive. Texas has the fifth most regressive tax system of the 50 states.[18]

Even the lottery falls more heavily on lower-income groups. Texans earning less than $20,000 a year spend on average nearly twice as much on the lottery as those people who earn $50,000 to $59,000—$76.50 compared with $39.24 a month. Ironically, considering that the lottery helps fund education, high school dropouts spend more than three times as much on the lottery as Texans with college degrees—$173.17 a month compared with $48.61 a month.[19] Furthermore, the state's most expensive lottery tickets, those costing $10, $20, $25, $30, and $50 a game, sell better on a per capita basis in the state's lowest-income areas than they do in the wealthiest neighborhoods.[20]

Ability-to-pay theory of taxation The approach to government finance that holds that taxes should be based on an individual's financial resources.

Tax Fairness   Although everyone agrees that taxes should be fair, observers define fairness in different ways. Some people favor a tax system based on the **ability-to-pay theory of taxation,** which is the approach to government finance that holds that taxes should be based on an individual's financial resources. They argue that people who earn relatively high incomes should pay more in taxes because well-to-do persons can better afford to pay taxes than can people who make less money. The advocates of the ability-to-pay theory of taxation are critical of the tax system in the state of Texas because it is regressive. They favor the adoption of progressive taxes, such as the personal income tax.

In contrast, some experts on public finance favor a tax system that encourages economic growth. They think that government should keep taxes low, especially taxes on business, in order to encourage investment and business expansion. The advocates of growth-oriented tax systems believe that progressive taxes, such as the personal income tax, are harmful because they reduce the amount of money that middle- and upper-income individuals have to invest in economic development. They also oppose high property taxes because of their impact on business. Instead, they prefer the use of consumer taxes, such as sales and excise taxes. The supporters of growth-oriented tax structures give the Texas tax system mixed reviews. Although they applaud the absence of an individual income tax, they worry that local property taxes are so high that they discourage business expansion.

 WHAT IS YOUR OPINION?

What sort of tax system is the best? Why?

Tax elasticity The extent to which tax revenues increase as personal income rises.

Tax Elasticity   The term **tax elasticity** refers to the extent to which tax revenues increase as personal income rises. It is a measure of the ability of tax revenues to keep up with economic growth. If tax revenues increase in pace with economic growth, then the government has the funds to address the increased demand for services generated by growth, such as new schools and additional roads. If tax revenues fail to keep up with growth, then state government will lack the resources necessary to meet the demand for services unless the government raises tax rates. The Texas tax system is relatively inelastic.

- The general sales tax is somewhat elastic because retail sales generally increase as personal income rises. Nonetheless, the sales tax is not perfectly elastic because not all goods and services are taxable. As average income rises, people may purchase goods and services that are not taxable, such as stocks, bonds, real estate, accounting services, and legal services. Furthermore, the growth of sales over the Internet is lessening the elasticity of the sales tax.

- Excise taxes on gasoline, alcohol, and tobacco products are inelastic because sales of those products do not necessarily rise as incomes increase. In fact, gasoline tax revenues may fall as income rises because people may trade in their old vehicles for newer-model cars that get better gasoline mileage.
- Severance taxes are inelastic as well. Rising personal income is unrelated to oil and gas production.
- The franchise tax may be elastic if business growth keeps up with the growth in personal income.
- Property taxes are only mildly elastic because property values do not necessarily rise as rapidly as personal income.

Many economists believe that the state's relatively inelastic tax system will be increasingly unable to meet the needs of state government. Texas can no longer count on raising substantial tax revenues from severance taxes on oil and gas production because of falling production. Furthermore, the healthiest, most rapidly growing sectors of the state's economy are largely exempt from the general sales tax. The sales tax does not cover many service industries, including accounting, legal, medical, and brokerage services. Personal income growth from salaries and investment gains escapes direct taxation as well because Texas does not have a personal income tax.

Policy Options

Critics of the Texas tax system offer a number of policy options designed to make the state's tax structure more equitable, efficient, or productive.

A Personal Income Tax   Most discussions of tax reform in Texas include an examination of the wisdom of a personal income tax. Income tax advocates argue that the state's tax system, which relies heavily on consumer taxes, is incapable of generating sufficient revenue to meet the growing demand for state services. Although some segments of the state's economy are taxed heavily, other sectors of the economy escape taxation almost entirely. As a result, the legislature periodically faces a budget shortfall because the cost of healthcare, public education, criminal justice, higher education, highway construction, and other state services has gone up faster than the revenues have grown to pay for them. Income tax supporters believe that a personal income tax would more accurately mirror growth in the economy, thus producing more revenue for state government.[21]

Tax reformers believe that a personal income tax would be a fairer way to raise revenue than the state's current tax system. The state of Kansas levies a personal income tax with three brackets ranging from 3.5 percent to 6.45 percent of adjusted gross income minus exemptions and deductions. A family of four pays no tax on an income of $24,400. Were Texas to adopt an income tax based on the Kansas model, it would generate $16.4 billion a year.[22] The adoption of an income tax would also make the state's tax system less regressive.

Income tax opponents question its fairness. Because of loopholes and deductions, they say, wealthy individuals have often avoided paying federal income taxes, leaving the tax burden on the backs of middle- and lower-income people. Who would guarantee that a state income tax would be implemented fairly? Most important, the opponents of a state income tax believe that the real goal of its supporters is to raise revenue to pay for a bigger, more intrusive state government. Instead of replacing or reducing the state sales tax or local property taxes, they predict that a personal income tax would merely supplement other taxes. In the long run, they warn, the adoption of a state income tax would lead to higher taxes for *all* Texans, not just the wealthy.

Conservative economists argue that taxes retard economic growth—the more taxes the government collects, the slower the rate of economic growth. Income taxes are particularly harmful because they discourage people from making the sorts of investments on which business growth depends. High taxes also retard population growth because people would choose to live and do business in states with lower tax rates.[23]

The Texas Constitution prohibits the legislative adoption of a personal income tax without voter approval. The constitution declares that no personal income tax can take effect unless enacted through the legislative process and then approved by the voters in a referendum election. Furthermore, revenues generated by the tax can be used only for education and for reducing local property taxes for schools.

A Broadened Sales Tax Base   Another proposal for reforming the state tax system is to enlarge the sales tax base to include more services than are currently taxed. Although the legislature broadened the tax base somewhat in the 1980s, many services, including most of the services provided by architects, lawyers, interior designers, advertising agents, insurance companies, investment counselors, accountants, brokers, and physicians, remain untaxed. Eliminating exemptions for all services would have added another $5.2 billion in sales tax revenue in 2007.[24] The advocates of a widened tax base believe that it would spread the sales tax burden more fairly than it is now. It would also make the tax system more elastic because the service sector is one of the most rapidly growing elements of the state economy. In contrast, critics charge that broadening the sales tax base is just another means of increasing the tax burden on consumers. Regardless of the rhetoric, taxes on services are taxes on people who use the services. Businesses will inevitably pass the tax along to the consumers who purchase their services. Furthermore, extending the sales tax to cover services that are not taxed in other states might make Texas firms less competitive nationwide.

Expanded Legalized Gambling   Some states rely far more heavily on revenues generated by legalized gambling than does Texas. Revenues from taxes on casino gambling, slot machines at racetracks, and lotteries account for more than 10 percent of state revenue in Nevada, South Dakota, Rhode Island, Louisiana, and Oregon. Nevada is by far the state most dependent on gambling revenue, with taxes on games of chance exceeding 40 percent of state revenue.[25] In contrast, gambling proceeds account for less than 3 percent of state revenues in Texas.

Gambling is controversial. The proponents of legalized gambling believe that the legalization of casino gambling or the introduction of slot machines (called video lottery terminals) at racetracks would produce $1.5 billion in additional state revenue, which could be used to fund education and lower property taxes.[26] Gambling is a voluntary tax, they argue; no one pays unless he or she chooses to play. Legalized gambling creates jobs and attracts visitors with money to the state. It also provides a local alternative for Texans who have been traveling to neighboring states to visit casinos. In contrast, the opponents of legalized gambling argue that it creates a morally corrupting climate that is associated with social problems, such as crime, bankruptcy, and gambling addiction. Furthermore, the introduction of casinos and other gambling establishments into an area hurts small businesses because people spend their money gambling rather than purchasing goods and services.[27]

The fate of proposals to expand organized gambling in Texas is uncertain. Although many legislators would prefer an expansion of gambling to a tax increase, opposition to casino gambling and slot machines is substantial. Furthermore, any measure to expand legalized gambling would have to come in the form of a constitutional amendment, requiring a two-thirds' vote of the Texas House and Texas Senate, as well as voter approval, a significantly higher hurdle than required for the passage of ordinary legislation.

Selling of Assets   Some state and local governments have sold assets in order to raise money to fund public services. The city of Chicago, for example, sold four downtown parking garages to Morgan Stanley, an investment bank, for more than $500 million. Indiana leased the Indiana Toll Road to private investors for nearly $4 billion. In recent years, pension funds, banks, and other investors have decided that toll roads, lotteries, airports, and other government assets are good long-term investments because they produce steady revenue streams.[28] State and local governments then use the money to finance government operations without having to raise taxes. In 2007, Governor Perry proposed selling the Texas Lottery to private investors, but the legislature failed to act on his proposal. The Trans-Texas Corridor is a similar arrangement, except that the private investors use their resources to build the project rather than purchase government assets that are already in place.

Tax Relief to Low-Income Families   Some states have enacted special tax exemptions and credits for low-income individuals, so that their state tax systems are less regressive. Thirty-one states allow property owners a partial rebate on their property taxes if the taxes exceed a certain percentage of income (as certified on IRS tax forms).[29] Iowa, for example, grants property tax relief to those people who are eligible (mostly senior citizens and persons with disabilities) on a sliding scale based on income. New Mexico and Kansas give a sales tax rebate to low-income people.[30]

In Texas, the legislature and the governor have created a sales tax holiday for the third weekend in August. For three days, consumers can purchase clothing and footwear costing less than $100 without paying the state sales tax. Most local governments drop their sales tax as well, although they are not required to participate in the tax holiday.

EXPENDITURES

Biennium The state's two-year budget program.

The state budget for 2008–2009 was $152.4 billion. Because the Texas legislature meets in regular session only once every two years, the legislature and the governor appropriate money for a two-year budget period, which is known as the **biennium.** The 80th legislature, which met in regular session in 2007, approved spending $76.9 billion in 2008 and $75.5 billion in 2009.[31]

Table 30.3 identifies the most important items in the state budget and compares spending priorities in 1986, 1996, and 2006. The largest expenditure categories for state government are health and human services, education, transportation, and public safety and corrections. In 2006, those four categories accounted for 87 percent of total state spending. Since 1986, the share of state spending going for health and human services has nearly doubled. The proportion of the budget for public safety and corrections has increased as well. In contrast, the relative importance of education to the budget has declined.

Table 30.4 compares and contrasts Texas with other states in terms of state and local government spending. Government expenditures in Texas are below the national average, but not at the very bottom. Texas is 41st among the 50 states both

TABLE 30.3   State Expenditures for Selected Government Functions, 1986, 1996, and 2006

Expenditure	1986	1996	2006
Health and human services	19.2%	34.3%	37%
Education	48.8	37.3	33.7
Transportation	13.5	8.5	10.6
Public safety and corrections	3.9	5.8	6.1
General government administration	5.6	3.6	3.5
Natural resources/recreational services	1.0	1.7	2.4
Other	8.0	8.8	10.2
Total expenditures	**100%**	**100%**	**100%**
	($17.7 billion)	**($39.7 billion)**	**($68.9 billion)**

Source: Texas Comptroller of Public Accounts, "Texas Revenue History by Function," various years, available at www.cpa.state.tx.us.

TABLE 30.4   State and Local Government Spending, Texas and the United States, FY 2006

Criterion	Texas	National Average	Texas Rank Among the States
Total state and local government expenditures per capita	$6,447	$7,713	41
State and local government expenditures as a percentage of personal income	19.5%	22.1%	41
Elementary and secondary education expenditures per capita	$1,692	$1,608	10
Higher education expenditures per capita	$622	$589	23
Welfare expenditures per capita	$810	$1,142	48
Health and hospital expenditures per capita	$458	$544	23
Highway expenditures per capita	$374	$402	36
Parks and recreation expenditures per capita	$66	$104	39
Environmental expenditures per capita	$199	$270	42
Fire protection expenditures per capita	$75	$96	32
Police protection expenditures per capita	$191	$237	28
Corrections expenditures per capita	$182	$192	20

Source: Governing, State and Local Source Book 2006, various pages.

in total government spending per capita and in terms of spending as a percentage of personal income.

Few public services in Texas are well funded, at least in comparison with their funding levels in other states. State and local government expenditures per capita for welfare, highways, parks and recreation, the environment, fire protection, and police protection are all below the national average. Higher education and health and hospital expenditures are near the national average. The only expenditure categories in which Texas is above the national average are per capita expenditures for elementary and secondary education and for corrections (prisons). Furthermore, the high rank for education expenditures is misleading because it reflects the size of the state's population of school-age children rather than a generous commitment to funding education. Per capita expenditures for education are relatively high in Texas because the state has a comparatively large population of school-age children. School-age children represent 19.2 percent of the population of Texas compared with only 16.3 percent of the population nationwide. Only Alaska and Utah have larger percentages of school-age youngsters than Texas. In fact, on a per-student basis, funding for elementary and secondary education in the Lone Star State lags behind the national average, $7,140 per student compared with a national average of $8,554 per student. Texas ranks 38th of the 50 states.[32]

Texans disagree about the appropriate level of government expenditures. Conservatives favor limited government with low tax rates and low levels of government expenditures. They believe that low tax rates promote economic growth because they leave money in the hands of individual investors and business owners who generate business activity and create jobs. Although government expenditures stimulate economic activity as well, private spending is more economically efficient because of the profit motive. Whereas private employers have an incentive to reduce payrolls and cut costs in order to increase profit margins, government bureaucrats want to enlarge their staffs and increase their budgets. Conservatives want to limit the growth in state taxes and spending to ensure continued economic prosperity.

In contrast, liberals argue that the state's low-tax, low-spend philosophy fails to address basic social problems. They believe that economic prosperity is built on the basis of an educated workforce whose basic needs are met. Liberals note that the Lone Star State has the lowest high school graduation rate in the country and it trails the national average in the proportion of adults holding bachelor's degrees.[33] The poverty rate in Texas is 17.6 percent compared with a rate of 12.6 percent for the nation as a whole.[34] Texas has the highest percentage of residents without health insurance in the country, and the state leads the nation in the percentage of children without health insurance coverage as well.[35] Texas liberals advocate tax increases to fund enhanced public services to improve the quality of life for the state's large and diverse population.

Healthcare

Medicaid and the Children's Health Insurance Program (CHIP) are the state's major health programs.

NATIONAL PERSPECTIVE — Universal Healthcare in Massachusetts

Massachusetts is implementing a healthcare program aimed at providing universal health insurance coverage. The plan, which was passed by the legislature and signed into law by Governor Mitt Romney in 2006, uses a series of penalties and incentives to close the insurance gap. People who can afford health insurance are required to purchase it much the same way drivers in Texas and most other states are required to have automobile liability insurance. Individuals who fail to get health insurance will initially lose their personal exemption on the state income tax, which was worth $219 in 2007. In subsequent years, they would face a penalty up to half the cost of a monthly insurance premium for each month they remained uninsured. Businesses with at least ten employees would be required to provide them with health insurance coverage or face a fine as well. The government subsidizes the cost of health insurance for lower-income people based on a sliding scale. A single person earning $40,000 a year would be expected to pay no more than 9 percent of his or her income, about $300 a month, whereas a person making $25,000 a year would be expected to

pay a smaller percentage, a little more than 3 percent of his or her income, or $70 a month.*

The goal of the Massachusetts plan is to insure the 550,000 state residents, about 10 percent of the state's population, who lack health insurance.† The cost to the state is estimated to be $1.2 billion over three years, but only $125 million of that would be new money not already being spent for state healthcare programs. Other costs would be born by businesses forced to provide health insurance coverage to their employees and individual state residents who would now have to purchase insurance themselves.‡

QUESTIONS TO CONSIDER

1. Who should be responsible for providing individual health insurance coverage—the individual, private employers, or the government?
2. Is it right for the government to force healthy young people who don't think they need health insurance to purchase coverage?
3. Would you expect the Texas legislature to adopt a similar program? Why or why not?

---

* Pam Belluck, "Massachusetts Offers Details on Health Coverage," *New York Times*, April 12, 2007, available at www.nytimes.com.
† Pam Belluck, "Massachusetts Sets Health Plan for Nearly All," *New York Times*, April 5, 2006, available at www.nytimes.com.
‡ Ibid.

Medicaid   The Texas Medicaid program provides medical services to 2.8 million residents of the state who are poor or disabled. It covers such services as inpatient and outpatient hospital care, health screening, dental care, hearing evaluations, physician services, family-planning services, laboratory fees, X-ray work, and prescription drugs. Although two-thirds of the state's Medicaid recipients are children from low-income families, most Medicaid expenditures go to provide services for the blind, persons with disabilities, and impoverished elderly people because their medical needs are greater and therefore more expensive to meet.[36]

Medicaid is a **federal grant program,** which is a program through which the national government gives money to state and local governments for expenditure in accordance with set standards and conditions. Congress created the Medicaid program and set guidelines for its implementation, whereas the states administer it. Medicaid is now the nation's largest healthcare program, bigger even than the

Federal grant program A program through which the national government gives money to state and local governments to spend in accordance with set standards and conditions.

Medicare A federally funded health insurance program for the elderly.

Medicare program, which is a federally funded healthcare program for the elderly. Medicaid covers the cost of two-thirds of nursing home residents and a third of all births.[37] The states and the federal government share the cost of Medicaid, with the size of the state share depending on the state's personal income. The federal government covers 61 percent of the cost of the Texas Medicaid program, with the state paying the other 39 percent.

Medicaid is a large and rapidly growing component of state spending. Medicaid funding accounted for nearly 27 percent of state spending in 2007, up from 20.5 percent in 1996.[38] Medicaid expenditures have increased because the cost of healthcare services has been going up and the number of recipients has been growing. Prescription drug costs, in particular, have been increasing rapidly, as have long-term care costs for the elderly and people with disabilities. In the meantime, Medicaid rolls have been rising because the U.S. Congress has expanded the program to cover more people. Medicaid is an **entitlement program,** which is a government program providing benefits to all persons qualified to receive them under law. Texas cannot limit the enrollment of people who qualify for services and must pay its share of the cost of those services.

Entitlement programs Government programs providing benefits to all persons qualified to receive them under law.

State governments nationwide are struggling to cover Medicaid costs. During the early years of the 2000s, Medicaid spending rose by 10 percent or more each year, much faster than the growth in government revenues.[39] If states cannot control the

People who do not have health insurance coverage often turn to hospital emergency rooms for healthcare.

growth in Medicaid spending, they will have difficulty covering the cost of education, transportation, homeland security, and other budget priorities. The federal government has given states authority to experiment with their Medicaid programs in hopes of controlling costs. Florida, for example, limits the cost of Medicaid benefits by requiring recipients to enroll in a managed care program and paying the provider based on each individual's medical condition and historic use of healthcare.[40]

Children's Health Insurance Program (CHIP)
A federal program designed to provide health insurance to children from low-income families whose parents are not poor enough to qualify for Medicaid.

Matching funds requirement A legislative provision that the national government will provide grant money for a particular activity only on condition that the state or local government involved supply a certain percentage of the total money required for the project or program.

Foundation School Program
The basic funding program for public education in the state of Texas.

Robin Hood Plan
A reform of the state's school finance system designed to increase funding for poor school districts by redistributing money from wealthy districts.

Children's Health Insurance Program (CHIP)   The **Children's Health Insurance Program (CHIP)** is a federal program designed to provide health insurance to children from low-income families whose parents are not poor enough to qualify for Medicaid. The Texas CHIP provides health insurance to children and young adults under the age of 19 whose family income does not exceed twice the poverty level, which was $41,300 for a family of four in 2007.[41] CHIP is relatively cost-effective for the states because the federal government picks up 75 percent of the cost, leaving only 25 percent to the states. Furthermore, CHIP saves the government money because it reduces emergency care costs. Families with health insurance have fewer visits to hospital emergency rooms. One billion dollars in CHIP spending over a decade saves $4.4 billion in reduced emergency care, hospital stays, and charity care. CHIP also reduces school absences.[42]

Texas has consistently failed to take advantage of all the CHIP money available. Between 1998 and 2003, Texas passed up more than $600 million in federal funds because it failed to meet the federal **matching funds requirement,** which is a legislative provision that the national government will provide grant money for a particular activity only on condition that the state or local government involved supplies a certain percentage of the total money required for the project or program. The state passed up another $550 million in federal funds during the 2004–2005 biennium because the legislature and the governor cut CHIP funding, so that they could balance the budget without raising taxes. As Figure 30.2 shows, CHIP enrollment dropped from more than 500,000 in 2003 to less than 350,000 in 2005, 2006, and 2007.

Elementary and Secondary Education

As we discussed in Chapter 29, state government distributes money to independent school districts through the **Foundation School Program,** which is the basic funding program for public education in the state of Texas. The amount of money each district receives depends on a complex set of formulas that account for the variable costs of educating different types of students. For example, students with learning disabilities or with limited English proficiency are more expensive to educate than other students. The amount of state funding each district receives also depends on the **Robin Hood Plan,** which is a reform of the state's school finance system designed to increase funding for poor school districts by redistributing money from wealthy districts. The state guarantees that a district will generate a set amount of money per student for each penny of property tax it assesses. The state provides additional aid to districts that are relatively poor in order to bring them up to the guaranteed yield while forcing wealthy school districts to remit money to the state for redistribution to relatively poor districts.[43]

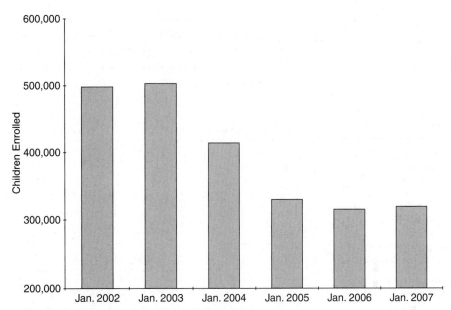

FIGURE 30.2   CHIP Enrollment in Texas, 2002–2007.
Source: Texas Health and Human Services Commission.

Between 1986 and 2006, the relative importance of public education in the state budget picture declined. As Table 30.3 shows, public education's share of state spending fell from nearly 50 percent in 1986 to a little more than a third in 2006. In part, the change in the relative position of education in the budget reflected the dramatic growth in the Medicaid program. Even though the state spent more money on education than ever before, its relative importance shrank because of the explosion in Medicaid expenditures. The decline in the budget share devoted to public education also reflected the failure of state funding to keep pace with the rising cost of public education.

The education finance reforms adopted in 2006 will increase the state's share of education spending. As we discussed in Chapter 29, the legislature cut school property tax rates and increased state funding to make up the difference. To cover the increased state share, the legislature expanded the franchise tax and increased the cigarette tax. It also changed the method for reporting sales taxes on private used car purchases to increase state revenue. The net result of the reforms will be an increase in state funding for schools but not to increase the total amount of money available for public education. In fact, many budget experts believe that the new taxes adopted by the legislature will fail to make up for the money lost in local property tax revenues, forcing future legislatures to increase taxes again, reduce spending on education, or cut other areas of the budget.[44]

Higher Education

More than a million students attend 1 of the state's 35 public universities, 3 colleges, 50 community college districts, 9 health-related campuses, and 4 technical colleges.

Only California has more publicly supported colleges and universities than Texas, and only California has more students enrolled. The University of Texas at Austin is the largest center of higher education in the state, registering nearly 50,000 students. Enrollment at Texas A&M University exceeds 45,000 students.[45] More students attend community colleges in Texas than attend universities. Community college enrollment has been growing steadily for years, but until recently the number of students attending universities has been falling. Furthermore, Latino and African American students are more likely to attend community colleges than universities.[46]

Higher education governance in Texas is a hodgepodge. Eleven boards of regents appointed by the governor with state Senate confirmation oversee management of the state's colleges and universities. The Board of Regents of the University of Texas and the Texas A&M University Board of Regents manage large university systems with campuses located throughout the state. In contrast, Midwestern State University has its own board of regents, even though it has only one campus (in Wichita Falls) and only somewhat more than 6,000 students. Each community college district has its own, locally elected board of trustees.

Higher education funding in Texas is near the national average. In 2006, Texas spent $622 per capita on higher education compared with a national average of $589.[47] The relative importance of higher education spending in state budgets nationwide has been declining, primarily because the growth of Medicaid has been overwhelming most other budget categories. State funding for higher education in Texas declined between 2003–2004 and 2004–2005 by 1.7 percent.[48] Furthermore, the legislature has failed to adopt and implement a funding plan for developing the state's college and university system. In 2001, for example, the legislature authorized

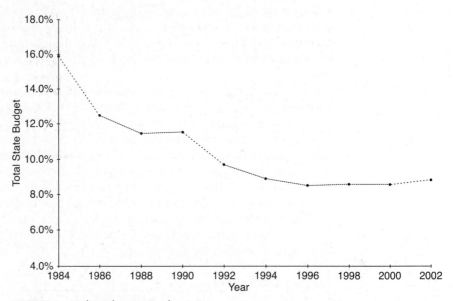

FIGURE 30.3   Higher Education Funding in Texas.
Source: Legislative Budget Board.

the creation of a pharmacy school at Texas A&M University–Kingsville with a $14.5 million building. The state built a facility, but the legislature neglected to appropriate money to operate it until it adopted the budget for the 2008–2009 biennium.[49]

Colleges and universities in Texas receive funding from a number of sources in addition to the state. Money to support community/junior colleges comes from state funding, student tuition and fees, and local tax support. The state provides 44 percent of the average community college's budget, with local property taxes (30 percent) and student tuition and fees (26 percent) supplying most of the rest. Meanwhile, financial support for the state's universities comes from state appropriations, student tuition and fees, research grants, and private donations.[50] Ironically, less than half the operating budgets of large state universities in Texas from the state. State funds now account for only 33 percent of the budget of the University of Houston, for example, with tuition and fees, federal grant money, and private contributions making up the rest.[51]

As the relative importance of state funding for higher education has declined (see Figure 30.3), tuition and fees have soared and community colleges have raised their tax rates. Between fall 2002 and spring 2006, universities increased their tuition and fees by 49 percent, from an average of $1,658 for 15 semester credit hours in 2002 to $2,470 in 2006.[52] Higher education in Texas used to be a bargain compared with its cost in other states, but tuition and fees at public four-year colleges and universities in Texas now exceed the national average.[53] State education leaders worry that the rising cost of a higher education will prevent many low-income Texas students from earning college degrees. Community college districts, meanwhile, have not only raised their tuition but have increased their tax rates as well.

The University of Texas (UT) at Austin and Texas A&M University at College Station benefit from the Permanent University Fund (PUF). In 1876, the framers of the Texas Constitution set aside a million acres of grassland in West Texas to finance "a university of the first class," including "an agricultural and mechanical branch." A few years later, the legislature added another 1.1 million acres. Income from mineral development on the land and agricultural leasing goes into a Permanent University Fund similar to the Permanent School Fund. The PUF may not be spent but is invested to earn dividends and interest. These earnings constitute the Available University Fund (AUF) to be distributed two-thirds to the University of Texas and one-third to Texas A&M University. The PUF money is used to guarantee bonds for capital improvements at schools in the UT and A&M University Systems. Funds from the AUF cover debt service, including payments on principal and interest. Surplus AUF funds can be used at the University of Texas in Austin, Texas A&M in College Station, and Prairie View A&M for "excellence programs," including scholarships, library improvements, and lab equipment.

In 1984, Texas voters approved an amendment to the Texas Constitution establishing a dedicated fund for construction and other purposes at state-supported colleges and universities outside the University of Texas and Texas A&M systems. This fund, which is called the Higher Education Assistance Fund (HEAF), is financed by an annual legislative appropriation of $175 million. Institutions that are not covered by the PUF can use HEAF money to acquire land; to construct, repair, and rehabilitate buildings; and to purchase capital equipment and library materials. The 1984 amendment also established an endowed fund, similar to the PUF, that is financed by a $50 million a year appropriation. Once the new fund, which is called the Higher Education Fund (HEF), reaches $2 billion, its annual income will go to non-PUF schools.

Welfare

The philosophy underlying the nation's welfare system has changed. Before 1996, the unofficial goal of welfare policy was to provide recipients with a minimal standard of living.[54] Low-income families and individuals who met the eligibility requirements could qualify for various federal programs providing healthcare, food vouchers, and cash. In 1996, Congress passed and President Bill Clinton signed sweeping welfare reform legislation that explicitly changed the underlying philosophy of government policy from welfare to work. Instead of attempting to supply low-income individuals and families with cash and in-kind benefits sufficient to meet basic human needs, the new goal of welfare reform was to move recipients from the welfare rolls to the workforce. Able-bodied welfare recipients would have to find work and/or participate in job training programs in order to receive welfare assistance. Furthermore, the government placed lifetime limits on the amount of time welfare recipients could collect benefits before having to leave the welfare rolls forever.

Temporary Assistance for Needy Families (TANF) A federal block grant program that provides temporary financial assistance and work opportunities to needy families.

Food Stamp Program A federal program that provides vouchers to low-income families and individuals that can be used to purchase food.

 WHAT IS YOUR OPINION?

Do you agree with placing lifetime limits on the amount of time an individual can collect welfare benefits?

The welfare reform legislation created **Temporary Assistance for Needy Families (TANF),** which is a federal program that provides temporary financial assistance and work opportunities to needy families. Low-income families and individuals who meet eligibility requirements receive cash and qualify for Medicaid and food stamp benefits. The **Food Stamp Program** is a federal program that provides vouchers to low-income families and individuals that can be used to purchase food from grocery stores. To maintain eligibility, recipients must comply with a Personal Responsibility Agreement (PRA). The PRA requires recipients to agree not to quit

 GETTING INVOLVED

Appealing a Property Appraisal

The amount of property tax homeowners owe depends on the tax rate and the appraised value of their property. Although property owners can do little about the tax rate, they can appeal their appraisal if they believe that it is inaccurate or unfair. If you think that your assessment is too high based on the value of similar property in the area, you should file a written protest with your county appraisal district. Contact your county appraisal district (the telephone number will be in the government pages of the telephone book) to determine the procedure in your county for appeal. In general, you will need to prove that the assessed value for your property is incorrect. As evidence, you can present the sales contract for your property if it was recently purchased, an independent appraisal, or lower appraisals for comparable pieces of property.

It's your government—get involved!

a job voluntarily, to stay free of alcohol or illegal drug use, to participate in parenting skills if referred, to obtain medical screenings for their children, and to ensure that their children are immunized and attending school. People who fail to comply with their PRA may suffer loss of benefits.

Welfare benefits in Texas are among the least generous in the nation. In 2006, Texas ranked 48th in welfare spending per capita, $810, compared to a national average of $1,142.[55] The average TANF recipient in Texas is a 30-year-old African American or Latino woman caring for one or two children under the age of 11. She has neither a high school education nor job training and does not have reliable transportation. Her only income is a TANF grant of $223 a month or less.[56]

Welfare reform has helped reduce the welfare rolls, but it has not eliminated poverty. Although the number of people in Texas receiving a TANF check has fallen by 73 percent since welfare reform became law, the poverty rate in the state has increased. Today, fewer than 5 percent of the state's 4 million poor children and adults receive checks. The state has succeeded in moving thousands of single mothers into the workforce, but their average wage is only $7.19 an hour, not enough to lift them out of poverty.[57]

Transportation

The Texas Good Roads Amendment has been the foundation of Texas transportation funding for more than 60 years. In 1946, the legislature proposed and the voters ratified an amendment to the Texas Constitution creating the **Dedicated Highway Fund,** which is a constitutionally earmarked account containing money set aside for building, maintaining, and policing state highways. The amendment specified that three-fourths of the motor fuels and lubricants tax be set aside for the construction, policing, and maintenance of state highways.[58] Vehicle license fees support road construction as well. A subsequent amendment to the Texas Constitution allowed the Texas Department of Transportation (TxDOT) to issue bonds secured by future revenue to raise money to support highway construction and expansion. In 2006, state funds accounted for a little more than half of the state's $8.9 billion transportation spending, with most of the rest coming from federal matching funds.[59]

The Dedicated Highway Fund is no longer sufficient to fund all of the state's transportation needs. Texas ranks 36th among the states in highway spending per capita, $374 per person compared with a national average of $402.[60] The figure is notably low, especially considering that Texas has more highway mileage than any other state. According to the TxDOT, gas tax money and federal funds combined are sufficient to fund only 35 percent to 40 percent of the transportation projects requested by local officials. This backlog of uncompleted projects contributes to pollution and congestion in metropolitan areas and undermines economic growth.[61] Although gasoline tax revenues have been rising because the number of cars on the road has been increasing steadily, gasoline tax revenues have not kept up with the cost of highway construction, especially the cost of building freeways in urban centers. Because automobile engines are more fuel efficient, they use less gasoline per mile driven than they did in 1991, when the legislature and governor set the current gasoline tax rate of $0.20 a gallon.[62]

Dedicated Highway Fund A constitutionally earmarked account containing money set aside for building, maintaining, and policing state highways.

State officials are turning to toll roads to address the state's transportation needs. The advantage of toll roads is that they provide funding without raising taxes, an action that legislators and the governor have been unwilling to do, especially considering that TxDOT officials estimate it would take a 17-cent-a-gallon increase in gasoline taxes to meet the state's highway needs.[63] Unlike the gasoline tax, toll revenues do not have to be shared with the Texas Education Agency (TEA). Nonetheless, public opposition to toll roads has been building, especially to toll roads built by private companies that may not be accountable to the public interest. Texas residents also complain about proposals to convert formerly free roads into toll roads.

 WHAT IS YOUR OPINION?

Are toll roads or higher gasoline taxes the better option for funding the state's transportation needs?

THE BUDGET PROCESS

Performance-based budgeting
A system of budget preparation and evaluation in which policymakers identify specific policy goals, set performance targets for agencies, and measure results.

The state of Texas uses **performance-based budgeting,** which is a system of budget preparation and evaluation in which policymakers identify specific policy goals, set performance targets for agencies, and measure results. The governor begins the budget process in the spring of the year before the legislature meets by defining the mission of state government, setting goals, and identifying priorities. Each state agency develops a strategic plan for accomplishing one or more of the goals. A strategic plan defines the mission of the agency, states its philosophy, and presents a strategy for achieving the goal. The agency also creates a budget to support its strategic plan. Agencies submit their strategic plans and budgets to the governor and the Legislative Budget Board in June, July, and August. The **Legislative Budget Board (LBB)** is an agency created by the legislature to study state revenue and budgetary needs between legislative sessions and prepare budget and appropriation bills to submit to the legislature. Agencies must submit budget requests by the beginning of August.

Legislative Budget Board (LBB) An agency created by the legislature to study state revenue and budgetary needs between legislative sessions and prepare budget and appropriation bills to submit to the legislature.

The philosophy behind performance-based budgeting is that agency budgets are tied to measurable goals. Agencies establish goals, identify quantitative measures to assess progress, and prepare a budget designed to support their efforts. In 2007, for example, the performance measures used by the Texas Higher Education Coordinating Board (THECB) included the number of community college students who transfer to a university and the percentage of new full-time degree-seeking students who graduate within six years.[64] The state rewards managers who achieve their goals by giving them more discretion in the use of funds or allowing them to carry over part of a budget surplus from one budget period to the next.

Professor Thomas Anton identifies three "rules of the budget game" that government agencies follow in making budget requests:

1. Agencies ask for more money than they received the year before and more money than they expect to get, so that they will have room to cut their budget requests later.

The state has embarked on a policy of solving its transportation gridlock problem by aggressively building roads and using tolls to pay at least for a big chunk of them.

2. Agencies insert some items into their budgets that are obvious targets for spending cuts, in hopes that the items they really want included in the budget will survive the cuts.

3. When agencies want large amounts of additional money, they present the requests as extensions of existing programs because it is easier to justify expanding a current program than it is to begin a new initiative.[65]

We could add a fourth rule: When asked to recommend spending reductions, agencies propose cutting programs that are politically popular. Once when the LBB asked the state bureaucracy to prepare budget requests that could be funded without a tax increase, agencies proposed cutting 23,000 poor children from welfare rolls, kicking 12,000 elderly Texans out of nursing homes, and leaving newly built prisons stand unopened.[66] Agency heads wanted to convince state budget makers that it was wiser politically to look elsewhere for budget cuts than to trim their particular piece of the budget pie.

After agencies submit their budgets, the LBB and the governor's staff hold hearings, at which agency administrators explain and defend their requests. During the last few months of the year, the LBB drafts an **appropriation bill,** which is a legislative authorization to spend money for particular purposes. Legislators introduce the LBB draft in the House and Senate as the basis for legislative deliberations on the budget for the upcoming biennium. The governor usually submits budget recommendations as well, but because the legislative leadership—the speaker and

Appropriation bill A legislative authorization to spend money for particular purposes; they are usually assigned to the emergency calendar as well.

lieutenant governor—control the LBB, its budget serves as the starting point for the legislature, rather than the proposals offered by the governor.

The Texas Constitution, similar to most other state constitutions, prohibits the adoption of a budget that is in deficit. A **budget deficit** is the amount by which budget expenditures exceed budget receipts. The state comptroller estimates state revenues for the upcoming biennium at the beginning of each legislative session. The comptroller may issue periodic updates during the session to reflect changing economic conditions or revisions in tax laws. Any spending bill the legislature approves must fall within the comptroller's revenue projections unless the legislature votes by a four-fifths' majority to run a deficit, which, of course, is unlikely.

The Texas Constitution also caps state spending to the rate of economic growth. At the beginning of a legislative session, the comptroller projects the rate of economic growth in the state for the next two-year period. The rate of growth in state spending may be no greater than the projected rate of economic growth unless a majority of legislators agree that an emergency exists that warrants additional spending. The limit does not affect the expenditure of federal funds or money generated through dedicated funds.

Most spending decisions are predetermined by federal requirements, court orders, or dedicated funds. The U.S. Congress stipulates that most federal dollars fund particular activities, such as highway construction, healthcare for low-income families and children, and vocational education. To participate in federal programs, the state must satisfy a matching funds requirement. The national government will provide grant money for a particular activity only on condition that the state or local government involved supplies a certain percentage of the total money required for the project or program.

The state must also spend money to respond to court orders issued by both federal and state courts. The legislature has appropriated billions of dollars in response to court rulings concerning state hospitals, prisons, public education, and access to higher education in South Texas. The legislature spent hundreds of millions of dollars to expand educational opportunities in South Texas, for example, because of a lawsuit charging that state higher education funding unconstitutionally discriminated against Latinos living along the border with Mexico. The Texas Supreme Court eventually ruled in favor of the state, at least in part because of the efforts of the legislature to upgrade and expand higher education in South Texas.

The legislature's budgetary discretion is also limited by **dedicated funds,** which are constitutional or statutory provisions that set aside revenue for particular purposes. The Dedicated Highway Fund and the PUF are examples of dedicated funds. The state has more than a hundred dedicated funds setting aside money for highways, parks, university construction, public schools, retirement funds, and other purposes. Constitutional or statutory dedications accounted for 45 percent of general revenue appropriations in the 2006–2007 budget.[67] The advocates of dedicated funds contend that they enable the state to make long-term commitments to goals. Earmarking revenue is also a means of generating public support for a tax increase because it makes budgeting comprehensible to ordinary people and gives the public confidence that tax money will be used as promised. In contrast, critics believe

Budget deficit The amount of money by which annual budget expenditures exceed annual budget receipts.

Dedicated funds Constitutional or statutory provisions that set aside revenue for particular purposes.

that earmarking contributes to state budget crises by limiting legislative discretion. Dedicated funds deny legislators the option of cutting certain programs, such as the highway construction budget, in order to avoid a tax increase or to find money for other priorities, such as public education or prison construction. Furthermore, dedicated funds, especially those contained in the state constitution, restrict the ability of the legislature to modify budget priorities to reflect the changing needs of the state.

The budget must pass the legislature in a fashion similar to other bills. In the Senate, the Finance Committee deals with both appropriation and tax bills, making recommendations to the Senate floor. In the House, the Appropriations Committee drafts the budget, whereas the Ways and Means Committee deals with tax measures. In most instances, the final details of the state appropriation bill and most tax packages have to be ironed out by a House-Senate **conference committee,** which is a special committee created to negotiate differences on similar pieces of legislation passed by the House and Senate. Once legislation receives final legislative approval, it goes to the governor.

On appropriation bills, the governor of Texas (and the governors of most states) has the **line-item veto,** which is the governor's power to veto sections or items of an appropriation bill while signing the remainder of the bill into law. Although the line-item veto (and the threat of its use) is a potentially potent weapon for influencing the state budget, research shows that it has a relatively small impact on total state spending.[68] In 2007, Governor Perry used the line-item veto to cut $650 million from the state budget of $152 billion, less than 1 percent of total spending.[69] In practice, the legislature has limited the governor's ability to knock out objectionable items by lumping millions of dollars of expenditures together in a single line item. In 1941, for example, the appropriation for the University of Texas at Austin included 1,528 line items.[70] Today, the legislature funds each institution of higher education through a single line item or lump-sum appropriation. Governor Perry has criticized this approach to budgeting because it limits his ability to impact the budget process.

Political scientists who study budgeting have developed models to understand the process. The most common approach is the **incremental model of budgeting,** which is a theoretical effort to explain the budget process on the basis of small (incremental) changes in budget categories from one budget period to the next. Scholars who favor this approach to understanding the budget process believe that agency heads, legislators, and governors all regard an agency's current budget share as its base. Increases or decreases in that base must be justified, whereas maintaining current levels need not be. Consequently, changes in individual budget items tend to be small. Another explanation for incremental budgeting is that an agency's current budget reflects its political strength relative to the strength of other agencies competing for money. Because the relative political influence of various claimants on the state budget is unlikely to change dramatically from one budget period to the next, budget figures are unlikely to change dramatically, either.[71]

Although incremental budgeting may be the norm, not all budget changes are incremental. Between 1986 and 2006, for example, the share of the budget devoted

Conference committee A special committee created to negotiate differences on similar pieces of legislation passed by the House and Senate.

Line-item veto The power of the governor to veto sections or items of an appropriation bill while signing the remainder of the bill into law.

Incremental model of budgeting A theoretical effort to explain the budget process on the basis of small (incremental) changes in budget categories from one budget period to the next.

to health and human services nearly doubled, increasing from 19.2 percent to 37 percent of state spending. Spending for public safety and corrections rose from 3.9 percent of the budget in 1986 to 6.1 percent in 2006, a 56 percent increase. Exceptions to incremental budgeting frequently result from a coalescing of political forces sufficient to force a change in longstanding budget priorities. The rise in spending on public safety and corrections reflected the legislature's response to public pressure to do something about rising crime rates. Spending for health and human services increased because of the growth in Medicaid spending.

Budget execution authority The power to cut agency spending or transfer money between agencies during the period when the legislature is not in session.

The governor and the LBB share **budget execution authority,** which is the power to cut agency spending or transfer money between agencies during the period when the legislature is not in session. Between legislative sessions, either the LBB or the governor may propose reductions or shifts in state spending. If the LBB proposes a change, the governor must approve the transfer before it can take effect, and vice versa.

INTERNET RESEARCH   The Texas Sales Tax

The sales tax is the most important source of state revenue. Research the Texas sales tax by studying your textbook and the following online reference sources:

www.window.state.tx.us/taxinfo/sales/index.html

www.cppp.org/files/7/POP%20284%20taxincidence.pdf

www.texaspolicy.com/pdf/2006-03-testimony-bs.pdf

Once you have completed your research, answer the following questions. Be sure to write in your own words and be sure to use correct English grammar.

1. What is a sales tax?

2. What is the sales tax rate set by the state of Texas?

3. Compared with other states, is the sales tax rate in Texas relatively high, relatively low, or about average?

4. What is the sales tax charged on the retail sale of taxable items sold in the city where you live?

5. Is the sale tax rate in the city where you live the same tax rate applied to all purchases of taxable items sold throughout the state? Why or why not?

6. Are all purchases subject to the sales tax? Give at least two examples of items whose sale is not taxed.

7. How does the Texas Public Policy Foundation (TPPF) regard the sales tax? Would it favor the adoption of a state income tax in order to reduce the sales tax rate? Why or why not?

8. How does the Center for Public Policy Priorities regard the sales tax? Would it favor the adoption of a state income tax in order to reduce the sales tax rate? Why or why not?

CONCLUSION: BUDGETARY POLICYMAKING

The public policy approach offers a useful mechanism for analyzing budgetary policymaking in Texas.

The Environment for Budgetary Policymaking

Environmental and political factors provide the context for budgetary policymaking. Economic development is the single most important factor for explaining state budgetary policies. States with greater levels of personal income have higher tax rates and higher levels of spending for transportation, education, healthcare, criminal justice, and welfare than do states with lower levels of personal income. In short, wealthy states tax their residents more heavily and provide more generous levels of public services than do poor states.[72] Budgetary policies in Texas are consistent with the state's status as a relatively poor state. Compared with other states, tax rates in the Lone Star State are low and spending programs are poorly funded.

States adopt budgetary policies to respond to competition from other states. States offer tax breaks and other subsidies to businesses to encourage them to relocate to the state. In Texas, the legislature has created a multi-million-dollar fund that the governor can use to lure companies to the state, either by providing them with cash subsidies or benefits, such as job training for workers or improved transportation to plant sites. Citgo Petroleum, BP Chemical, Home Depot, Sematech, and Tyson Foods have all benefited from state subsidies.[73] In the meantime, state governments hesitate to increase welfare benefits because they do not want to become welfare magnets, attracting low-income people from other states. Although states attempt to attract companies that create jobs and generate economic activity, they want to repel low-income people who would be a drain on public services.[74]

Short-term economic factors affect budgetary policymaking as well. Economic expansion improves the state's budget picture by fueling the growth of sales tax and excise tax revenues. In the late 1990s, the economy boomed and state officials were able to cut taxes and increase spending at the same time. In contrast, state tax revenues decline during a **recession,** which is an economic slowdown characterized by declining economic output and rising unemployment. The recession of 2002 helped produce a budget shortfall of nearly $10 billion in 2003. The economy subsequently recovered and the legislature restored some of the cuts in 2005. The budgetary picture was considerably brighter in 2007. Because of a strong economy, the legislature began the budget process with billions of dollars of surplus money, which could be spent, saved, or returned to the taxpayers in the form of tax reductions.

Recession An econimic slowdown characterized by declining economic output and rising unemployment.

 WHAT IS YOUR OPINION?

Do you favor a small state government that provides relatively modest services but holds down taxes or a larger state government that provides more services but costs more?

Political culture
The widely held, deeply rooted political values of a society.

Individualistic political culture
An approach to government and politics that emphasizes private initiative with a minimum of government interference.

Texas's budgetary policies of relatively low tax rates coupled with poorly funded public services reflect the state's political culture, interest-group environment, and political party balance. **Political culture** is the widely held, deeply rooted political values of a society. Texas's low-tax/low-spend budgetary philosophy is consistent with the state's **individualistic political culture,** which is an approach to government and politics that emphasizes private initiative with a minimum of government interference. Many Texans believe in small government. When given a choice between higher taxes with more government services and lower taxes with fewer services, they prefer the latter.

The interest-group configuration in Texas is consistent with a low-tax/low-spend government. Interest groups that would favor higher taxes to support better-funded public services, such as labor unions, consumer groups, and racial and ethnic minority organizations, are relatively weak in the Lone Star State. In contrast, business organizations, which typically prefer lower tax rates and less generously funded services, are especially strong in Texas. In particular, business interests favor low welfare benefits and strict limits on the amount of time an individual can collect benefits. Low welfare spending not only saves money and helps hold down tax rates, but also help to hold down wage rates by pushing welfare recipients into the job market and making them more willing to accept low-paying jobs.[75]

The current party balance also supports the state's low-tax/low-spend budgetary policies. The Republican Party, which now controls all three branches of state government, advocates limited government. When faced with a substantial budget shortfall in 2003, Republican leaders in the legislature and the executive branch favored cutting services rather than raising taxes to balance the budget. In 2007, Republican leaders chose to save most of the state's budget surplus, so that it could be used to pay for future property tax reductions rather than increase spending for health, education, and welfare. The Democratic Party, which tends to favor a more active government, has limited influence in the state's policymaking process.

Demographic change may eventually affect the environment for budgetary policymaking in Texas. The Latino population is young and growing rapidly, whereas the white population is aging. Population growth will invariably lead to political influence. Because Latinos as a group are more likely to be poor, they are more dependent on public services for healthcare, education, transportation, job training, and welfare than is the white population. As the political influence of Latino voters grows, the state may adopt budgetary policies that shift the tax burden away from consumers and low-income families while increasing spending for government services.

Agenda Building

Budgetary issues are always near the forefront of the state's official policy agenda because of the biennial budget cycle. Adopting a balanced budget that will meet the needs of the state is typically the overriding issue of each legislative session. Whether legislators will have sufficient funds to enact new initiatives or consider a tax cut or whether they will have to cut programs and raise taxes depends on economic conditions. Boom times produce budget surpluses that can be spent, whereas a recession causes a shortfall that must be addressed.

Public officials and interest groups raise budgetary issues because they hope to see their concerns included in the state's official policy agenda. Public school administrators want the legislature to reform school finance to increase state funding for education. Business interests favor the use of tax breaks and government subsidies to promote business expansion. Medical professionals advocate an increase in the state cigarette tax in hopes of discouraging young people from taking up the smoking habit.

Budgetary issues sometimes arise because of external pressures. Texas absorbed hundreds of thousands of evacuees after Hurricane Katrina. Although the federal government picked up some of the cost of food, housing, healthcare, transportation, and other living expenses, state and local governments had to pick up many of the costs. School districts, in particular, faced millions of dollars of unexpected expenses to cover the cost of educating thousands of children from Louisiana. Court decisions can also force budgetary issues on state government. The legislature and governor have had to address school finance in numerous regular and special sessions because of court rulings in *Edgewood v. Kirby* and *Neeley v. West Orange-Cove Consolidated ISD*.

Policy Formulation and Adoption

A broad range of political actors participate in budgetary policy formulation. State agencies make budget proposals and lobby for their adoption. For example, the THECB lobbies for increased funding for higher education. The agency's strategy is to focus on the gap in educational attainment between whites and the state's two largest minority populations, African Americans and Latinos. THECB officials, joined by allies in higher education and minority rights organizations, argue that closing the educational gap is essential to the future of the state. To achieve that goal, they declare, the state must fund higher education more generously.

The members of the legislative leadership are the key players in drafting a budget and formulating tax policy. The speaker and lieutenant governor control the LBB, which prepares the initial budget document. Their closest political allies chair the House and Senate committees that formulate the details of budget policy. The speaker and the lieutenant governor control the conference committee that prepares the final budget document.

The role of the governor in formulating budgetary policy depends on the interest and the skills of the state's chief executive. In 2003, Governor Perry made clear his opposition to raising taxes, calling instead for the legislature to cut spending to eliminate the budget shortfall. Nonetheless, the governor did not want to become deeply involved in the budget process. When given the opportunity to submit a balanced budget without new taxes at the beginning of the 2003 legislative session, Perry offered a document filled with zeros. Perry explained that his budget symbolized the importance of carefully examining every budgetary item to set priorities and make cuts; his critics accused him of zero leadership.

The federal government has a significant impact on policy formulation in Texas because of federal programs. Some of the most important items in the budget rely heavily on federal funds, including welfare, healthcare, transportation, and public education. Federal money, however, comes with strings attached. To ensure the continued flow of federal dollars, state budgetary policies must conform to federal guidelines. They must also appropriate billions of dollars in state money as matching funds.

The legislature and the governor adopt budgetary policies through the legislative process. The appropriation bill and tax bills must be passed by majority vote of both the Texas House and the Texas Senate. The governor must sign them or allow them to become law without signature. If the governor issues a veto, it can be overridden by a two-thirds vote of both chambers of the legislature. In practice, gubernatorial vetoes of tax and spending bills are seldom, if ever, overridden because the legislature invariably gets them to the governor's desk late in the session and the governor allows the legislature to go home before issuing vetoes.

The Texas Constitution establishes special rules for budgetary policymaking that create an atmosphere of budgetary caution. The constitution stipulates that the legislature adopt a balanced budget unless lawmakers agree by a four-fifths majority to run a deficit. The constitution also demands that state spending grow no more rapidly than economic growth unless both chambers vote in favor of greater spending. These two provisions create a bias in favor of spending restraint. The clear message of the Texas Constitution is that public officials should focus on limiting the growth of government rather than providing enough spending to meet the needs of the state and its people.

The governor plays a special role in budgetary policymaking because of the line-item veto. On most legislative measures, including tax bills, the governor faces a take-it-or-leave-it choice. The governor can sign the bill, allow it to become law without signature, or veto it. On appropriation measures, however, the governor can pick out individual provisions to veto while allowing the rest to become law. As a result, the governor can play a more active role in budgetary policymaking than in other sorts of policy issues.

Policy Implementation and Evaluation

Private companies, local governments, and state agencies implement budgetary policies. Retail business establishments collect sales taxes and many excise taxes on behalf of the state. State law requires that retailers obtain a sales tax permit from the comptroller, collect taxes on the retail purchase of taxable items, keep records, and remit tax receipts to the state. In return for acting as the state's tax collector, retail establishments can keep a small portion of the money they collect as compensation for their work.

Local governments play a role in administering the state's programs. Most of the state's spending for education goes to independent school districts, which provide educational services for kindergarten through high school. Community/junior colleges implement higher education policies, whereas hospital districts participate in the implementation of the state's healthcare policies. County governments collect a number of taxes and fees on behalf of the state, including charges for license plates and certificates-of-title for motor vehicles.

State agencies implement budgetary policies as well. The comptroller is the state's chief tax collector, sometimes collecting taxes directly and sometimes working through intermediaries, such as retail merchants. The Texas Department of Corrections

(TDC) administers the state's correctional programs. The Health and Human Services Commission implements welfare policies. The Texas Department of State Health Services operates mental health facilities. The state's public universities provide higher education services to the state's residents.

Performance-based budgeting ensures that state agencies evaluate at least some aspects of their programs. Agencies set goals, plan strategies, and identify measures to determine whether they are achieving their goals. Each year they produce a report showing their progress at achieving their goals.

The comptroller, LBB, and legislative committees evaluate state programs as well. The websites of the comptroller (www.cpa.state.tx.us) and the LBB (www.lbb .state.tx.us) include a number of reports evaluating the state tax system and various programs, such as the state's health programs and the Foundation School Program. Legislative committees evaluate state agencies and programs under their jurisdiction. The legislature also evaluates agencies and programs through **sunset review,** which is the periodic evaluation of state agencies by the legislature to determine whether they should be reauthorized.

Sunset review The periodic evaluation of state agencies by the legislature to determine whether they should be reauthorized.

LET'S DEBATE

Is the Texas Tax System Fair or Unfair?

Overview: According to the U.S. Census Bureau, Texas has one of the lowest per capita tax burdens in the United States. According to the Washington, DC, think tank Tax Foundation, when federal taxes are included, Texas ranked 22nd in per capita total tax burden as of 2005. Additionally, Texas has neither a state income tax nor a corporate income tax, making it one of the most business-friendly states in the nation. Many who argue the need for state tax reform point to the fact that Texas has relatively high sales and property taxes; even so, Texas ranks 14th in per capita sales tax collection and 11th in per capita property tax collections. As far as certain excise taxes go, the Texas gas tax of $0.20 ranks 29th nationally, and the state's cigarette tax of $0.41 ranks 26th in the nation. Texans are not comparatively overtaxed and enjoy a low-tax structure that reflects the history and development of the state's political culture. Texans are, after all, Americans, and the United States owes its existence in part to a tax revolt and an abhorrence of high taxes; all Texans benefit from the state's tax regime.

Although Texas is considered to have lower taxes than most states, it ranks fifth in the nation for having regressive taxes. The Texas-based Center for Public Policy Priorities finds that the state's tax system is unfair to the poor, and even those taxes paid only by businesses, such as the state's corporate franchise and natural gas taxes, are passed on as costs to Texas consumers and families. Common Cause reports that many companies avoid the state's business franchise tax by incorporating out of state while operating in the state as partnerships, which are not subject to the tax. As a result, the state loses revenue and is forced to find it elsewhere.

Moreover, most lower-wage-earning Texans spend roughly three-fourths of their income on necessary items subject to the sales tax, whereas more affluent Texans devote one-fourth or less of their income to items liable to sales taxes. This inequity is further exacerbated by the fact that many business and professional services needed and purchased by more prosperous citizens are currently not taxed. If lower-income Texans have their necessities taxed, why shouldn't the wealthy bear the same burden?

How should Texas reconcile its generally low tax burden with its recognized effect on the state's poorer citizens? Those who believe the tax system is generally fair contend that Texas's business-friendly atmosphere

continued on next page

and tax regime benefit all Texans. As the economy prospers and as corporations move subsidiaries to Texas because of low taxes, businesses will need to compete for employees by raising wages and benefits, and this profits those in the lower socioeconomic strata by increasing their earnings and improving their quality of life. Others counter that the economy is cyclical and that economic downturns are simply a part of life. Reliance on sales and property taxes increases burdens on the poor during recessions because declining revenues force the state to curtail services and benefits used primarily by lower-income citizens, further exacerbating their condition. The fairness of the state's tax system depends on one's perspective, but most agree that a just tax regime spreads the tax burden among all citizens equally, and this should be a primary policy goal.

Arguments That the Texas Tax System Is Unfair

❑ **Texans with the lowest wages pay the highest percentages of their incomes in taxes.** The Texas tax system is unfair because of the state's reliance on sales and property taxes to generate significant revenue. Sales taxes are regressive and unduly affect lower-wage-earning Texans rather than the affluent. Texans earning less than $15,000 pay 11 percent of their income in state and local taxes, whereas those earning over $175,000 pay 5.1 percent of their income in state and local taxes. The state's tax code should be modified to increase tax fairness, so that the tax burden can be borne equally.

❑ **Texas sales and property taxes impose a barrier to improving the state's quality of life.** Not only are the sales and excise taxes regressive, but Texas property taxes can be an additional burden to lower-income households as well. Renters are forced to support higher property taxes through increased rent that they cannot deduct on their federal income taxes as landowners can. High property taxes can prevent lower-income Texans from realizing dreams of home ownership. By lowering property tax rates, more Texans would be able to afford mortgage payments and begin to build equity and invest in their future.

❑ **The current school finance system places an undue burden on homeowners and Texans.** It is generally recognized that Texas's school finance system is dysfunctional. Because of skyrocketing educational expenses, the fact that Texas schools are primarily funded with property taxes, and limitations in the state constitution, there has been a dramatic increase in property taxes over the last decade, with property tax rates at or near the state-mandated cap. The result is pressure on the state to seek alternative funding, which means a search for new and/or increased taxes. Proposed increases in certain sales taxes and user fees would increase regressive taxation.

Arguments That the Texas Tax System Is Fair

❑ **Texas does not have a personal or corporate income tax.** Texas is one of only seven states that do not have personal income tax and one of only five that do not levy a corporate income tax. This allows all Texans and incorporated Texas businesses—including the smallest corporations run out of a living room—to reap monetary reward for their efforts and labor. It does not penalize business owners for assuming risk and allows individuals to keep more of their hard-earned income.

❑ **States without an income tax have lower tax burdens.** Research indicates that those states without income taxes have lower tax burdens. Citizens in those states with income taxes have seen their tax burden increase over time. As a result of a steady stream of revenue provided by income taxes, these states have seen an increase in the size and scope of their respective governments. With increased size and authority come increased operating costs, and with increased operating costs come increased taxes. No tax system can be perfectly fair, and all Texans enjoy some of the lowest tax burdens in the nation.

❑ **Lower-income Texans can receive federal tax benefits that wealthier Texans cannot.** The lower classes in Texas can receive the Earned Income Tax Credit, the Child Tax Credit, and the Child and Dependent Care Credit. These credits are federal programs that can substantially alleviate the plight of low-income Texans. As far as federal taxes go, Texas is considered a "donor" state—that is, Texas provides more revenue to the federal government than it receives in federal funding, and the state tax structure should account for this fact by emphasizing these policies to Texans.

QUESTIONS

1. Is the Texas tax system just or unjust? Why or why not?
2. Do Texans really benefit from low tax rates? If not, what can be done?

SELECT READINGS

1. Eric Stein, *2006 Guidebook to Texas Taxes* (Riverwoods, IL: CCH Inc., 2005).
2. Judith Stallmann, *Our Taxes: Comparing Texas with Other States* (Stillwater: Oklahoma State University, 1997).

SELECT WEBSITES

1. **www.window.state.tx.us/m23taxes.html**
   Texas comptroller's tax website.
2. **www.senate.state.tx.us/75r/senate/commit/c540/downloads/Texas_Taxes.pdf**
   Website of the Texas Senate's comprehensive report on Texas taxes.

KEY TERMS

ability-to-pay theory of taxation
appropriation bill
biennium
budget deficit
budget execution authority
Children's Health Insurance Program (CHIP)
conference committee
dedicated funds
Dedicated Highway Fund
Employees Retirement System (ERS) Trust Fund
entitlement programs
excise tax
federal grant program
fiscal year
Food Stamp Program

Foundation School Program
franchise tax
General Fund
incremental model of budgeting
individualistic political culture
Legislative Budget Board (LBB)
line-item veto
matching funds requirement
Medicaid
Medicare
pari-mutuel wagering
per capita
performance-based budgeting
Permanent School Fund (PSF)
Permanent University Fund (PUF)
political culture

progressive tax
proportional tax
recession
regressive tax
Robin Hood Plan
sales tax
severance tax
sin tax
sunset review
tax elasticity
tax incidence
Temporary Assistance for Needy Families (TANF)
Texas Teacher Retirement System (TRS) Trust Fund
Trans-Texas Corridor

NOTES

1. Tony Hartzel, "Corridor Toll Road May Cost $8.8 B," *Dallas Morning News*, September 28, 2006, available at www.dallasnews.com.
2. Cathy Booth Thomas, "A Big, Fat Texas Boondoggle?" *Time*, December 6, 2004, pp. 40–42.
3. "Sales Tax Revenue," *Governing*, State and Local Source Book 2006, p. 35.
4. Penelope Lemov, "The Untaxables," *Governing*, July 2002, p. 36.
5. "Cigarette Tax Increase Pushes Revenue Up, But Sales Are Down," *Dallas Morning News*, March 10, 2007, available at www.dallasnews.com.
6. Texas Racing Commission, *Year 2006 Annual Report*, available at www.txrc.state.tx.us.

7. Texas Comptroller of Public Accounts, "State of Texas 2006 Annual Cash Report," available at www.cpa.state.tx.us.

8. "Abbott Calls for Stricter Oversight of Texas Public Pensions," *Austin American-Statesman*, June 26, 2007, available at www.statesman.com.

9. Texas Comptroller of Public Accounts, "State of Texas 2006 Annual Cash Report."

10. "Solid Ground for Education," *Fiscal Notes*, May 1996, pp. 12–13.

11. Texas Lottery Commission, available at www.txlottery.org.

12. Donald E. Miller and Patrick A. Pierce, "Lotteries for Education: Windfall or Hoax?" *State and Local Government Review* 29 (Winter 1997): 34–42.

13. Ellen Perlman, "Losing Numbers," *Governing*, September 2001, pp. 46–47.

14. "Lotto Texas Jackpot Gets Longer Odds," *Houston Chronicle*, March 27, 2003, available at www.houstonchronicle.com.

15. Mega Millions, available at www.megamillions.com.

16. David W. Winder and James T. LaPlant, "State Lawsuits Against 'Big Tobacco': A Test of Diffusion Theory," *State and Local Government Review* 32 (Spring 2000): 132–141.

17. "The Nature of Tax Incidence," Comptroller of Public Accounts, available at www.cpa.state.tx.us.

18. Dick Lavine, "Who Pays Texas Taxes?" Center for Public Policy Priorities, March 20, 2007, available at www.cppp.org.

19. Ken Rodriguez, " 'Pro-Education' Lottery Quietly Fleeces the Poor, Not-So-Educated," *San Antonio Express-News*, September 29, 2006, available at www.mysanantonio.com.

20. Lisa Sandberg and Julie Domel, "So Who's Buying the $50 Scratch-Offs?" *San Antonio Express News*, June 11, 2007, available at www.mysanantonio.com.

21. Dave Mann, "The Best Idea They Won't Talk About," *Texas Observer*, April 21, 2006, pp. 6–7, 18.

22. Dick Lavine, "The Best Choice for a Prosperous Texas," Center for Public Policy Priorities, March 1, 2005, available at www.cppp.org.

23. Richard Vedder, "Taxing Texans," Texas Public Policy Foundation, available at www.texaspolicy.com.

24. Texas Comptroller of Public Accounts, "Tax Exemptions and Tax Incidence 2007," available at www.window.state.tx.us.

25. Fox Butterfield, "As Gambling Grows, States Depend on Their Cut," *New York Times*, March 31, 2005, available at www.nytimes.com.

26. Ben Wear, "Taxes 101," *Austin American-Statesman*, May 2, 2004, available at www.statesman.com.

27. Ian Pulsipher, "Counting on Gambling," *State Legislatures*, February 2005, pp. 24–26.

28. Christopher Swope, "Unloading Assets," *Governing*, January 2007, pp. 36–40.

29. *Texas Weekly*, December 23, 1996, p. 3.

30. Steven D. Gold, "Taxing the Poor," *State Legislatures*, April 1987, pp. 24–27.

31. "General Appropriation Act for the 2008–2009 Biennium," available at www.lbb.tx.us.

32. *Governing*, State and Local Source Book 2006, p. 17.

33. U.S. Census Bureau, "Educational Attainment of the Population 25 Years and over: 2005," available at www.census.gov.

34. U.S. Census Bureau, *Annual Demographic Survey*, available at www.census.gov.

35. National Center for Health Statistics, "National Health Interview Survey," available at www.cdc.gov.

36. "Texas Medicaid in Perspective," January 2007, Texas Health and Human Services Commission, available at www.hhsc.state.tx.us.

37. Donald F. Kettl, "Looking for a Real Crisis: Try Medicaid," *Governing*, April 2005, p. 20.

38. "Texas Medicaid in Perspective."

39. Ibid.

40. Robert Pear, "U.S. Gives Florida a Sweeping Right to Curb Medicaid," *New York Times*, October 20, 2005, available at www.nytimes.com.

41. *Capitol Update*, September 20, 2007, available at www.txdirectory.com.

42. Hy Gia Park and Leah Oliver, "Is CHIP Shipshape?" *State Legislatures*, May 2004, pp. 16–18.

43. House Research Organization, "State Finance Report," April 4, 2005, available at www.capitol.state.tx.us.

44. Jason Embry, "Bills for Schools May Slow Spending," *Austin American-Statesman*, May 14, 2006, available at www.statesman.com.

45. Texas Higher Education Coordinating Board, "Texas Higher Education Data," available at www.thecb.state.tx.us.

46. Texas Higher Education Coordinating Board, "Closing the Gaps Progress Report 2007," available at www.thecb.state.tx.us.

47. *Governing*, State and Local Source Book 2006, p. 14.

48. "State Appropriations: How the States Rank," *Chronicle of Higher Education*, December 17, 2004, p. A29.

49. Ralph K. M. Haurwitz and Laura Heinauer, "State Has Goals, Lacks Specifics for Colleges," *Austin American-Statesman*, August 28, 2005, available at www.statesman.com.

50. Texas Higher Education Coordinating Board, "Facts on Higher Education," available at www.thecb.state.tx.us.

51. Matthew Tresaugue, "UH Revs up the Money Engine," *Houston Chronicle*, November 25, 2007, p. B5.

52. Texas Higher Education Coordinating Board, "Tuition and Fees Data," available at www.thecb.state.tx.us.

53. Holly K, Hacker, "Report Shows College Costs More in Texas," *Dallas Morning News*, October 23, 2007, available at www.dallasnews.com.

54. William A. Kelso, *Poverty and the Underclass: Challenging Perceptions of the Poor in America* (New York: New York University Press, 1994), p. 4.

55. *Governing*, State and Local Source Book 2006, p. 84.

56. Texas Health and Human Services Commission, "Temporary Assistance for Needy Families," available at www.hhsc.state.tx.us.

57. Janet Elliott and Terri Langford, "The Cost of Cutting Welfare," *Houston Chronicle*, January 28, 2007, available at www.chron.com.

58. Article 8, Section 7a, Texas Constitution.
59. Texas Department of Transportation, available at www.dot.state.tx.us.
60. *Governing*, State and Local Source Book 2006, p. 74.
61. Robert Jones, "On the Road Again," *Fiscal Notes*, June 2002, p. 5.
62. Matt Sundeen, "State's Shift Gears," *State Legislatures*, December 2006, pp. 22–24.
63. Ben Wear, "State: No Tolls Would Mean 17-Cent Gas Tax," *Austin American-Statesman*, September 12, 2006, available at www.statesman.com.
64. Legislative Budget Board, "Performance Measures for Higher Education," available at www.lbb.state.tx.us.
65. Thomas J. Anton, *The Politics of State Expenditures in Illinois* (Urbana: University of Illinois Press, 1966).
66. Mary Lenz, "$52 Billion State Budget Clears Board," *Houston Post*, December 15, 1990, p. A-1.
67. House Research Organization, "Writing the State Budget, 80th Legislature," available at www.capitol.state.tx.us/hrofr/.
68. James W. Enderaby and Michael J. Towle, "Effects of Constitutional and Political Controls on State Expenditures," *Publius: The Journal of Federalism* 27 (Winter 1997): 83–98.
69. Office of the Governor, "Bills Vetoed by Governor Perry, 80th Legislature," available at www.governor.state.tx.us.
70. Pat Thompson and Steven P. Boyd, "Use of the Item Veto in Texas, 1940–1990," *State and Local Government Review* 26 (Winter 1994): 38–45.
71. Aaron Wildavsky, *The Politics of the Budgetary Process* (Boston: Little, Brown, 1964); David Lowery, Thomas Konda, and James Garand, "Spending in the States: A Test of Six Models," *Western Political Quarterly* 37 (March 1984): 48–66.
72. Thomas R. Dye, *Politics, Economics, and the Public* (Chicago: Rand McNally, 1966).
73. Paul Sweeney, "Texas: The Corporate Welfare State," *Texas Observer*, April 15, 2005, pp. 6–9, 28.
74. Michael A. Bailey and Mark Carl Rom, "A Wider Race? Interstate Competition Across Health and Welfare Programs," *Journal of Politics* 66 (May 2004): 326–347.
75. Carl Klasner, Xiaotong Mao, and Stan Buchanan, "Business Internet Group Power and Temporary Assistance to Needy Families," *Social Science Quarterly* 88 (March 2007): 104–119.

Chapter 31

Criminal Justice in Texas

CHAPTER OUTLINE

Crime Statistics
    Measuring Crime
    The Crime Rate
    Trends
    Victims and Criminals

Criminal Prosecution Process
    Arrest
    Pretrial Actions
    Trials
    Sentencing

Capital Punishment

Juvenile Justice

Corrections
    County Jails
    State Jails
    State Prisons
    Prison Release
    Recidivism

Conclusion: Criminal Justice Policymaking
    Agenda Building
    Policy Formulation and Adoption
    Policy Implementation and Evaluation

LEARNING OUTCOMES

After studying Chapter 31, students should be able to do the following:

- Identify the methods used to measure the incidence of crime, and evaluate the benefits and liabilities of each approach. (pp. 860–861)

- Describe the incidence of crime in the United States as a whole and the state of Texas, comparing the crime rate in Texas with the national crime rate and assessing recent trends. (pp. 861–863)

- Identify the groups of people most likely to be victims of crime, as well as those most likely to commit crimes. (pp. 863–864)

- Trace the steps of the criminal prosecution process, describing arrest, pretrial actions, trials, and sentencing. (pp. 864–869)

- Describe capital punishment in Texas. (pp. 869–872)

- Describe the way the state of Texas deals with juvenile offenders. (pp. 872–873)

- Identify the categories of prisoners held in county jails, state jails, and state prisons. (pp. 873–874)

- Assess the impact of *Ruiz v. Estelle* on the Texas prison system. (pp. 875–876)

- Evaluate the role of parole and good time as prison management tools. (p. 876)

- Analyze criminal justice policymaking using the policy model. (pp. 877–878)

- Define the key terms listed on page 880 and explain their significance.

In 2007, the Texas legislature toughened the punishment for child sexual predators by adopting "Ashley's Law," which is named after a nine-year-old Florida girl who was kidnapped and killed by a registered sex offender who lived nearby. Persons convicted of a violent sex crime against a child younger than 14 would be given a mandatory 25-year prison sentence and up to life in prison without possibility of parole. Repeat offenders would be given life in prison without parole. Anyone convicted of the sexual assault of a victim five years of age or younger would be subject to a possible death sentence. Lieutenant Governor David Dewhurst, the foremost proponent of Ashley's Law, believes that it will deter potential offenders. It will also demonstrate society's revulsion against sexual predators.

The opponents of Dewhurst's proposal fear that Ashley's Law could have unintended consequences. Considering that most sexual assaults occur within the family, the threat of life without parole or **capital punishment** (the death penalty) could have the opposite of the intended effect by decreasing the reporting of child sexual abuse to the police. Prosecutors might be less willing to file charges, and judges and juries less willing to convict, because of the harshness of the penalty. Some offenders, already facing the death penalty for child sexual assault, might kill their victims to eliminate witnesses. Finally, Ashley's Law might be unconstitutional. Even though 26 states have adopted similar measures, the federal courts have not ruled on the constitutionality of applying the death penalty to an offender convicted of something other than murder or attempted murder.[1]

Capital punishment
The death penalty.

CRIME STATISTICS

Crime is a major policy issue in Texas. Many Texans fear becoming victims of crime, local newscasts feature stories of grisly murders, and politicians run for office promising to get tough on crime. How serious is crime in Texas? Is the crime rate going up or down? Which groups of people are more likely to be victims of crime? Who are the criminals?

 WHAT IS YOUR OPINION?

Should child sexual predators be subject to the death penalty?

Measuring Crime

Uniform Crime Reports (UCR)
A record of offenses known to police compiled by the Federal Bureau of Investigation (FBI) from reports submitted by local law enforcement agencies.

The U.S. Department of Justice uses two complementary measures to assess the incidence of crime in America: the Uniform Crime Reports (UCR) and the National Crime Victim Survey (NCVS). The **Uniform Crime Reports (UCR)** is a record of offenses known to police compiled by the Federal Bureau of Investigation (FBI) from reports submitted by local law enforcement agencies. The UCR includes four violent crimes—murder, forcible rape, robbery, and aggravated assault—and four property crimes—burglary, larceny/theft, motor vehicle theft, and arson. The advantage of the UCR is that it provides crime data for every state and city in the nation, allowing researchers to compare crime rates. The disadvantage of the UCR is that it underestimates the incidence of crime because it only counts offenses known to the police. Some offenses, such as forcible rape, often go unreported because victims may feel ashamed or endangered. Other crimes, such as theft and burglary, may not be reported because victims have little confidence that the police will apprehend the offenders and recover stolen property. Some victims of crime, such as drug dealers or illegal aliens, may not report offenses because they want to avoid contact with the police.

The **National Crime Victim Survey (NCVS)** is a measure of the incidence of crime in the United States based on interviews with people in more than 50,000 households. It estimates the crime rate on the basis of the number of people in the sample who claim to have been victims of crime during the previous year. Although most social scientists regard the NCVS as a better measure of crime than the UCR, it, too, has shortcomings because it relies on individuals' accurately and honestly reporting crimes to an interviewer. Furthermore, the FBI does not break down NCVS data by states and cities because the sample size would be too small.

National Crime Victim Survey (NCVS)
A measure of the incidence of crime in the United States based on interviews with people in more than 50,000 households.

The Crime Rate

Crime affects many Americans. According to the UCR, the crime rate for the United States in 2005 was 3,926 offenses per 100,000 people, giving the average American 1 chance in 25 of being the victim of a serious crime. Property crimes occur more frequently than violent crimes. In 2005, the violent crime rate was 469 per 100,000 in population compared with a property crime rate of 3,430. Of the eight categories of crime counted by the UCR, larceny/theft was the most frequent, murder the least frequent.[2] The incidence of crime in Texas is higher than the national average. The rate of reported crime in Texas in 2005 was 4,857—24 percent higher than the national average. The odds of being a victim of a serious crime in Texas were 1 in 21.[3]

Trends

Figure 31.1 graphs the ups and downs of the crime rate in the United States from 1990 through 2005. As the figure indicates, the crime rate dropped sharply during the 1990s. It rose briefly in 2001 and then began to fall again, but at a slower pace of decline than during the 1990s.

Criminologists offer a number of possible explanations for the recent changes in the crime rate:

- **Prison expansion** Between 1990 and 2004, the number of people behind bars in the United States nearly doubled, increasing from 773,919 in 1990 to 1,468,601 in 2004.[4] Keeping criminals off the streets holds down the crime rate.

- **A strong economy** Some people who are unemployed commit crimes to pay the bills. When the economy is strong, people can support themselves and their families through honest work. The declining crime rate throughout the 1990s coincided with a long period of economic growth. The economy slumped in 2000–2001 and the crime rate rose briefly. Subsequently, the economy recovered and the crime rate began falling once again.

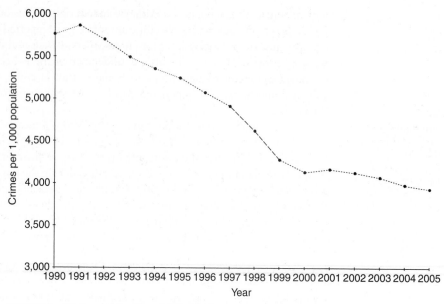

FIGURE 31.1   National Crime Rate, 1990–2005.

- **Better police work** Some experts attribute the falling crime rate to better police work, including the introduction of community policing and the implementation of zero tolerance policies in high-crime areas. **Community policing** is an approach to law enforcement that seeks to reduce crime by increasing the interaction and cooperation between local law enforcement agencies and the people and neighborhoods they serve. The goal of a zero tolerance, meanwhile, is to get lawbreakers off the street by any legitimate means. New York and a number of other cities have aggressively enforced the law in high-crime areas, arresting people not just for serious crimes but also for petty offenses, such as public intoxication, urination in public, traffic-law infractions, and vagrancy.

- **An aging population** Many criminologists believe that the best explanation for variations in the crime rate is the changing age distribution of the nation's population. Because young men are the population group most likely to commit crimes, the crime rate varies with the size of that population. Between 1980 and 2000, the number of young men age 15 to 24 in the population fell from 21.4 million to 20.1 million. In recent years, the population of young males has begun increasing and the crime rate has fallen more slowly.[5]

Although crime rates are falling, many Americans do not feel safe. On 12 occasions between 1990 and 2006, the Gallup Poll asked national samples of Americans the following question: "Is there more crime in your area than there was a year ago or less?" People answering "more crime" outnumbered people saying "less crime" in 8 of the 12 surveys.[6]

Criminologists identify a number of reasons for the disparity between falling crime rates and the public's apprehension about crime. Police departments continue

Community policing
An approach to law enforcement that seeks to reduce crime by increasing the interaction and cooperation between local law enforcement agencies and the people and neighborhoods they serve.

to warn about the dangers of crime, even when crime rates are falling because that is their job and their budgets depend on public support for law enforcement. Politicians focus on crime to win votes. The media spotlight crime, especially violent crime, to attract viewers and readers. The adage "if it bleeds, it leads" has become the catch phrase for local television news.

Victims and Criminals

Who are the victims of crime? All of us are threatened, but some groups of people are more frequent victims of crime. The incidence of crime in urban areas is more than twice as high as in rural areas and is significantly higher than in the suburbs. Low-income persons are more likely to be victims of violent crime than are middle- and upper-income individuals, who, in turn, are more likely to be victims of property crime. Young people are more frequently victimized than are older persons. Except for the crime of forcible rape, men are more likely to be crime victims than are women. Offenses occur more often against racial and ethnic minority groups than against whites. Renters are more likely to become crime victims than are homeowners.[7]

Most criminals are young, poorly educated men. A majority of the people arrested for property crimes and 45 percent of individuals arrested for violent crimes are under the age of 25. Three-fourths are men.[8] Criminals and victims often know one another. A majority of violent crimes occur between people who know one another.[9] Furthermore, murder typically stays within racial groups. According to official data, 83 percent of white murder victims nationwide are killed by whites, whereas 91 percent of black murder victims are killed by blacks.[10]

The incidence of crime in Texas is higher than the national average.

Victims of violent crime in Texas may receive up to $75,000 in financial assistance from the Texas Crime Victims' Compensation fund. This program makes money available to people who are "innocent victims of violent crimes" to cover the loss of earnings, funeral expenses, medical expenses, and the care of minor children. It does not provide compensation for stolen property. The fund is designed to pay expenses not covered by other sources, such as insurance, sick leave, workers' compensation, or Social Security. The fund is financed through fines paid by convicted felons. To receive compensation, a crime victim must report the crime to police within 72 hours, cooperate with law enforcement officials (crime participants are excluded), and file a claim with the Crime Victims' Compensation Division in the attorney general's office within 180 days.[11]

CRIMINAL PROSECUTION PROCESS

The criminal prosecution process begins with an arrest and proceeds through pretrial actions, trial, and sentencing.

Arrest

The criminal prosecution process begins with an arrest. Police officers arrest suspects when, in their professional judgment, they believe that a crime has been committed and there is probable cause that the suspects are guilty of the crime. **Probable cause** is the reasonable belief that a crime has been committed and that a particular suspect is the likely perpetrator of that crime.

Probable cause
The reasonable belief that a crime has been committed and that a particular suspect is the likely perpetrator of that crime.

Law enforcement authorities exercise discretion in deciding whether to make an arrest, especially for relatively minor offenses. A police officer may or may not stop a driver traveling at 7 miles per hour over the speed limit. A city police officer may warn a pet owner for violating the local leash ordinance, rather than issuing a citation.

Law enforcement authorities do not solve every serious crime reported to them. The **clearance rate** is the proportion of crimes known to authorities for which an arrest is made. The clearance rate varies, depending on the offense. It is highest for violent crimes against persons, such as murder, aggravated assault, and robbery. It is lowest for nonviolent crimes against property, such as larceny/theft, motor vehicle theft, and burglary. Victims of violent crimes are often able to identify offenders, whereas property crimes usually occur without witnesses. Furthermore, law enforcement authorities concentrate their resources on violent crime.

Clearance rate
The proportion of crimes known to authorities for which an arrest is made.

Pretrial Actions

After making an arrest, a police officer takes the suspect to a police station or substation to be booked. **Booking** is an administrative procedure in which law enforcement personnel document a suspect's arrest. While the suspect is fingerprinted and photographed and the paperwork is completed, officials search the records for outstanding arrest warrants against the suspect for other offenses.

Booking
An administrative procedure in which law enforcement personnel document a suspect's arrest.

An assistant district attorney determines whether to press charges. Sometimes people arrested for relatively minor offenses, such as public intoxication or gambling, are not charged. The assistant district attorney may also order a suspect released because of insufficient evidence.

If charges are filed, suspects are brought before a judge for **arraignment,** which is a judicial proceeding at which a suspect is formally charged with a crime and asked to enter a plea. The judge tells the accused persons of the charges they face and informs them of their constitutional rights. Criminal suspects have the right to remain silent and to know that anything they say may be used against them. They have the right to discontinue an interview at any time. They also have the right to an attorney and, if they cannot afford to hire a lawyer, they have the right to an attorney appointed by the state. This procedure is known as the **Miranda warning,** which is the judicial stipulation that a criminal defendant's confession cannot be admitted into evidence unless police first inform the defendant of the constitutional right to remain silent and to consult an attorney. Otherwise, any confessions suspects give may not be admitted as evidence at their trials.[12]

At the arraignment, the accused may plead not guilty, guilty, or *nolo contendere*, which is Latin for "no contest." **Nolo contendere** is a plea indicating a defendant's decision not to contest a criminal charge. As far as a criminal case is concerned, a plea of *nolo contendere* is the legal equivalent of a guilty plea. At this stage of the criminal prosecution process, most defendants plead not guilty, including many defendants who will eventually plead guilty.

The arraigning judge also sets bail. **Bail** is money or securities posted by accused persons to guarantee their appearance at later proceedings. In general, the amount of bail is based on the seriousness of the criminal offense and the likelihood of the accused returning for trial. If the offense is relatively minor or if the accused has deep roots in the community (a family, job, home, etc.), the judge may release the defendant on personal recognizance (that is, without bail) or at low bail. In contrast, the judge will set a high bond for serious offenses or when there is a strong likelihood that the accused will flee to escape prosecution. In extreme circumstances, the judge may refuse to set bail altogether, requiring the accused to remain in jail until trial. Suspects who make bail are released pending the outcome of their case. In contrast, accused persons without enough money to cover bail must either wait in the county jail or hire a private bail bond company to put up the money for a nonrefundable fee, usually 10 to 15 percent of the bond. If suspects flee, they forfeit their bail and the judge issues a warrant for their arrest. Bail jumping is a crime.

The Texas Constitution requires a grand-jury indictment in all felony cases unless the defendant waives that right. An **indictment** is a formal accusation charging an individual with the commission of a crime. A **grand jury** is a body of 12 citizens that hears evidence presented by the prosecuting attorney and decide whether to indict an accused person. Texas has two methods for selecting the members of a grand jury. In the first method, a state district criminal court judge appoints 3 to 5 people to serve as jury commissioners. The commissioners, meeting in private, compile a list of 15 to 20 potential grand jurors and present the list to the judge, who selects 12 people to serve as members of a grand jury. In the second method, grand jurors are selected at random from voter registration and driver's license lists, the same

Arraignment
A judicial proceeding at which a suspect is formally charged with a crime and asked to enter a plea.

Miranda warning
The judicial stipulation that a criminal defendant's confession cannot be admitted into evidence unless police first inform the defendant of the constitutional right to remain silent and to consult an attorney.

Nolo contendere
A plea indicating a defendant's decision not to contest a criminal charge.

Bail
Money or securities posted by accused persons to guarantee their appearance at later proceedings.

Indictment
A formal accusation charging an individual with the commission of a crime.

Grand jury
A body of 12 citizens that hears evidence presented by the prosecuting attorney and decides whether to indict an accused person.

pool from which trial jurors are chosen. Grand juries typically meet once or twice a week for a three-month term.

The grand jury works in secret, investigating criminal matters and hearing evidence brought to it by the district attorney. At least 9 of the 12 jurors must agree in order to issue an indictment, also known as a **true bill,** against a defendant. In theory, the grand jury is a screening device that protects innocent persons from unwarranted prosecution by requiring the prosecutor to marshal sufficient evidence to convince a grand jury that there is probable cause of the guilt of the accused. Nonetheless, some observers believe that, in contemporary criminal justice systems, grand juries usually act as rubber stamps for the prosecutor. The grand jury hears only the district attorney's view of the case because the defendant does not have the right to present evidence to the grand jury or challenge the information presented by the prosecutor.

Not all states use the grand jury system. Many states allow prosecutors to file felony charges directly in the form of an "information." A judge or a **magistrate** (a judicial official) conducts a hearing to determine if the evidence is sufficient to take the case to trial. Both the prosecutor and the defendant have the opportunity to present evidence to the judge or magistrate, who decides whether the evidence is sufficient to take the case to trial.

The U.S. Supreme Court has ruled that criminal defendants are constitutionally entitled to be represented by an attorney, regardless of their financial status.[13] Texas law empowers district judges to determine whether a defendant is unable to afford an attorney. In practice, judges often assume that a criminal defendant who can afford to make bond has sufficient financial resources to hire an attorney. If the judge determines that a defendant is indigent, the judge assigns the defendant an attorney, who is paid by the county for representing the defendant both at the trial stage and, if necessary, through one round of appeals. Indigent defendants who wish to continue the appeals process must obtain private legal assistance or file legal papers themselves. Ten Texas counties, including El Paso and Dallas counties, have public defender offices that employ attorneys full-time to represent indigent defendants. The advocates of the public defender system believe that it provides indigent defendants with better legal representation at less cost to the government.[14] In counties without a public defender office, district judges appoint lawyers in private practice to represent indigent criminal defendants in return for a fee paid by the county government.

Trials

Accused persons have a constitutional right to trial by jury. The U.S. Supreme Court has held that the U.S. Constitution obliges state governments to offer jury trials to persons charged with felony offenses.[15] A **felony** is a serious criminal offense, such as murder, sexual assault, or burglary. The Texas Constitution goes further, granting accused persons the right to trial by jury in *all* cases, misdemeanor and felony. A **misdemeanor** is a less serious offense than a felony. If defendants choose, they may waive the right to a jury trial and be tried by a judge alone.

Prospective trial jurors are selected from county voter registration rolls and lists of persons holding Texas driver's licenses and Department of Public Safety (DPS) identification cards. Only American citizens may serve on juries. Persons who are

True bill
An indictment issued by a grand jury.

Magistrates
Judicial officers.

Felony
A serious criminal offense, such as murder, sexual assault, or burglary.

Misdemeanor
A relatively minor criminal offense, such as a traffic violation.

Accused persons without enough money to cover bail must either wait in the county jail or hire a private bail bond company to put up the money for a nonrefundable fee.

Adversary proceeding
A legal procedure in which each side presents evidence and arguments to bolster its position while rebutting evidence that might support the other side.

Burden of proof
The legal obligation of one party in a lawsuit to prove its position to a court.

Plea bargain
A procedure in which a defendant agrees to plead guilty in order to receive punishment less than the maximum for an offense.

convicted felons or under felony indictment are ineligible to serve on a jury. Some groups of people are exempt from jury service if they wish, including full-time students, individuals over 70 years of age, and persons with custody of small children whose absence would leave the children without proper supervision. A 6-person jury hears misdemeanor cases, whereas a felony case jury consists of 12 persons.

A criminal trial is an **adversary proceeding**—that is, a legal procedure in which each side may present evidence and arguments to bolster its position, while rebutting evidence that might support the other side. An assistant district attorney prosecutes the case by presenting evidence and testimony in an effort to prove the defendant's guilt. The defense attorney, meanwhile, cross-examines the prosecution's witnesses to undermine the case against the defendant. After the prosecution has presented its side, the defense has a chance to offer evidence and testimony to show that the defendant is not guilty.

The **burden of proof,** which is the legal obligation of one party in a lawsuit to prove its position to a court, is on the prosecutor, who must demonstrate the defendant's guilt beyond a reasonable doubt. At least in theory, the defendant need not prove innocence. The judge conducts the trial, ruling on points of law and procedure. The jury or the judge, if the defendant has waived the right to a jury trial, decides guilt or innocence. The defendant is free to go if acquitted. If the verdict is guilty, punishment must be assessed.

Relatively few individuals indicted for serious crimes ever have a full-blown trial. As Table 31.1 indicates, 72.2 percent of the 154,851 felony cases disposed of by state district courts in 2006 involved the defendant pleading guilty. Most guilty pleas are the result of a **plea bargain,** which is a procedure in which a defendant

TABLE 31.1   Disposition of Felony Cases in State District Courts, 2006

Disposition	Number of Cases	Percentage
Pled guilty or *nolo contendere*	111,809	72.2%
Tried and convicted	3,787	2.4
Tried and acquitted	954	0.6
Directed acquittal ordered by judge	31	—
Dismissed	38,270	24.7
Total	154,851	100

Source: Office of Court Administration, *Texas Judicial System Annual Report Fiscal Year 2006*, available at www.courts.state.tx.us.

agrees to plead guilty in order to receive punishment less than the maximum for an offense. Prosecutors plea bargain because courts are overcrowded—plea bargaining saves money and valuable court time. Also, a plea bargain ensures a conviction. Defendants plea bargain because they fear a harsher punishment or a conviction on a more serious charge.

Most criminal cases that make it to a courtroom conclude with a conviction, through either plea bargaining or a guilty verdict. As Table 31.1 indicates, less than 1 percent of the felony cases heard in Texas in 2006 resulted in the defendant's acquittal. Most defendants pled guilty. Of those who actually went to trial, most were convicted. Furthermore, only about 2 percent of the total number of cases involved jury trials.[16]

 WHAT IS YOUR OPINION?

Do plea bargains advance the cause of justice?

Sentencing

Except for Class C misdemeanor cases, sentencing is a distinct second phase of the trial proceeding in Texas. Both prosecution and defense may present evidence and arguments on behalf of a stiffer or lighter sentence. In jury trials, the defendant may select either the jury or the judge to determine the sentence. In trials without juries, the judge sets the punishment.

Under Texas law, possible sentences vary, depending on the severity of the crime. For misdemeanor offenses, punishment can include a fine and a period of confinement not exceeding a year in jail. For felonies, the fine can be as high as $10,000 and imprisonment, which can range from 180 days to 99 years in prison. Persons convicted of capital murder may be given the death penalty.

With a few exceptions, Texas law permits the judge or jury to grant **probation,** which is the suspension of a sentence, permitting the defendant to remain free under court supervision. Instead of going to prison or jail, convicted persons live and work in the community under the supervision of a county probation officer. In granting probation, judges may require convicted defendants to hold jobs, support their families, make restitution for their crimes, and stay out of trouble with the law. Should individuals violate the terms of their probation, it may be revoked, and they will be

Probation
The suspension of a sentence, permitting the defendant to remain free under court supervision.

The Texas Constitution guarantees all criminal defendants the right to trial by jury.

Deferred adjudication
A type of probation that can be granted by a judge to a defendant who pleads guilty or *nolo contendere* to certain relatively less serious offenses.

forced to serve time in the county jail or a state prison. Texas has more than twice as many probationers (431,000 in 2006) than it has prison inmates.[17]

Persons who plead guilty to relatively minor offenses may be given **deferred adjudication,** which is a type of probation that can be granted by a judge to a defendant who pleads guilty or *nolo contendere* to certain, relatively less serious offenses. The court defers the judicial proceeding *without* entering the guilty plea in the defendant's record. If the defendant successfully completes the probation, the charges are dismissed and the defendant does not have a conviction on the record, although the defendant will have to file a petition of nondisclosure with a court in order to seal the record of the deferred adjudication from the general public. If the defendant violates probation, the case is resumed and the defendant can be convicted and sentenced as if the probation had never taken place. In 2006, state district courts granted deferred adjudication in more than 43,000 cases, 37 percent of the total number of convictions.[18]

CAPITAL PUNISHMENT

The Texas legislature enacted the state's first capital punishment law in 1923. The first executions took place on February 24, 1924, when 5 young African American men were electrocuted for murder. Between 1924 and 1964, 503 men and 3 women were sentenced to death in Texas; 361 of the men eventually died in the electric chair. Of those put to death, 229 were African American men, 108 were white men, 23 were Latino men, and 1 was an American Indian man. None of the 3 women sentenced to death was executed.[19]

In 1972, the U.S. Supreme Court ruled, in the case of *Furman v. Georgia*, that the death penalty as it was then applied was unconstitutional because it allowed too much discretion to judges and juries, thereby opening the door to discriminatory practices. Getting the death penalty, the Court said, was similar to being struck by lightning.[20] The Court did *not*, however, rule that capital punishment in and of itself was unconstitutional, at least not for the crime of murder.

After the *Furman* decision, many state legislatures adopted new capital punishment laws designed to meet the Supreme Court's objections by reducing discretion in the implementation of the death penalty. The Texas legislature passed a new death-penalty statute in 1973, which, with subsequent amendments, defined capital murder to include the following crimes:

- Murdering a peace officer or firefighter who is acting in the lawful discharge of an official duty and who the person knows is a police officer or firefighter
- Intentionally committing a murder in the course of committing or attempting to commit kidnapping, burglary, robbery, aggravated sexual assault, or arson
- Committing a murder for pay or promise to pay or employing another person to commit murder
- Committing a murder while escaping or attempting to escape from a penal institution
- Murdering a prison employee while incarcerated
- Committing a gang-related murder while incarcerated
- Committing a murder to obstruct justice or in retaliation against a witness in a criminal case
- Committing serial or mass murder
- Murdering a child

The punishment for capital murder is either life imprisonment without possibility of parole or the death penalty. To determine a verdict, the judge or jury must answer three questions:

1. Was the conduct of the defendant that caused the death of the victim committed deliberately and with the reasonable expectation that the victim's death would ensue?
2. Is it probable that the defendant would commit additional criminal acts of violence that would constitute a continuing threat to society?
3. Is there anything in the circumstances of the offense and the defendant's character and background that would warrant a sentence of life imprisonment rather than a death sentence?

Parole
The conditional release of convicted offenders from prison to serve the remainder of their sentences in the community under supervision.

The sentence is death if the jury or judge answers yes, yes, and no. Otherwise, the defendant receives life in prison without **parole,** which is the conditional release of convicted offenders from prison to serve the remainder of their sentences in the community under supervision.

In 1977, the legislature amended the state's capital punishment law to retire "Old Sparky," as the electric chair was nicknamed, and replace it with lethal injection as the means of execution. The law provides that a medically trained individual, whose identity is not revealed, inserts an intravenous catheter into the condemned person's arm. After giving the prisoner the opportunity to make a last statement, the warden orders the introduction of the lethal solution into the catheter. The individual injecting the fatal fluid is visibly separated from the execution chamber by a wall and locked door. A physician makes the final death pronouncement but has no function in the execution. The law allows family members of the convicted murderer and the family of the murder victim to witness the execution.

Because of appeals and other legal delays, no one was executed in Texas from July 1964 until December 1982, when Charlie Brooks Jr., an African American man convicted of murdering a Fort Worth auto mechanic, died of lethal injection. Between 1982 and January 2008, Texas carried out 405 executions, substantially more than any other state.[21] Today, death row in Livingston houses 362 men and 9 women.[22]

Capital punishment remains controversial. The opponents of the death penalty charge that the process of trials and appeals is so flawed that innocent people may face execution. A study published by Columbia University law professor James S. Liebman found that two-thirds of the death sentences given by American courts between 1973 and 1995 were overturned on appeal. When death penalty cases were retried, 7 percent of the defendants were found not guilty.[23] Furthermore, the critics of the death penalty argue that it is inefficient because only 5 percent of death sentences are actually carried out and only then after years of appeal.[24] In contrast, the proponents of capital punishment defend the process, saying that it is scrupulously fair. They point out that people given the death penalty are entitled to an appeals process that lasts for years. In Texas, the interval between sentencing and execution for convicted murders is 10.4 years, more than enough time for their cases to be thoroughly examined for error.[25]

NATIONAL PERSPECTIVE

Civil Commitment of Sexually Violent Criminals in Kansas

Kansas has adopted a civil commitment procedure to hold sexually violent criminals behind bars after they have completed their prison sentences. In 1994, the Kansas legislature passed and the governor signed the Kansas Sexually Violent Predator Act to provide for the involuntary confinement of sexually violent predators beyond the completion of their prison sentences. Under the law, a sexually violent predator is defined as a person convicted or charged with a sexually violent offense who suffers from a "mental abnormality" or "personality disorder" that makes the person likely to engage in repeat acts of sexual violence. Once pedophiles and other sexually violent offenders finish their prison sentences, they must be released unless the state can prove to a judge or jury that they meet the criteria to be declared a sexually violent predator. Persons held under the statute are not released until a court certifies that their mental condition has changed and that they no longer qualify as sexually violent predators.

Civil commitment for sexual predators is controversial. The defenders of the procedure argue that it is necessary to protect the community from individuals who are likely to commit horrific crimes. The recidivism rate for sexual offenders is quite high. In contrast, critics contend that the procedure is an

continued on next page

unconstitutional mechanism for continuing to punish people who have already served their criminal sentences. They believe the Kansas law violates the Double Jeopardy Clause of the Constitution, which protects people from being tried twice for the same offense.

The U.S. Supreme Court upheld the constitutionality of the Kansas Sexually Violent Predator Act in *Kansas v. Hendricks.* In a narrow 5–4 decision, the Court compared the civil commitment of sexual predators with the civil commitment of mentally ill persons who are a danger to themselves or others. The Court ruled that the Kansas law does not violate the Double Jeopardy Clause because it is not a criminal penalty. It also ruled that the state is not required to offer treatment for persons held under the statute.*

Nineteen states have adopted civil commitment laws similar to the Kansas statute. In practice, few persons have ever been released because they are no longer considered a threat to offend. Out of 3,000 sexual offenders held in civil commitment facilities nationwide, only 115 have been sent home, most because of technical legal reasons. The program is also expensive to operate, especially as the inmates in custody age and require specialized medical care. From 2001 to 2005, the cost of civil commitment in Kansas increased from $1.2 million a year to $6.9 million.[†]

QUESTIONS TO CONSIDER

1. Should Texas adopt a civil commitment procedure to hold criminally violent sexual offenders in custody after they have completed their prison sentences, similar to the Kansas law?
2. Is it ever safe to release persons convicted of sexually violent crimes from custody?
3. Is civil commitment for violent sexual offenders preferable to longer prison sentences or even the death penalty?

Kansas v. Hendricks, 521 U.S. 346 (1997).

[†]Monica Davey and Abby Goodnough, "Doubts Rise as States Hold Sex Offenders After Prison," *New York Times,* March 4, 2007, available at www.nytimes.com.

JUVENILE JUSTICE

The juvenile crime rate has been falling faster than the overall crime rate. In the mid-1990s, juvenile offenders committed about a quarter of all criminal offenses nationwide. By 2005, the percentage of arrestees under the age of 18 had fallen to 15 percent.[26] In fact, the recent decline in the crime rate can be attributed almost entirely to a decrease in juvenile crime. Between 1996 and 2005, the juvenile crime rate fell by 25 percent, whereas the adult crime rate was unchanged.[27]

Texas deals with some juvenile offenders as if they were adults. Juveniles as young as 14 who are charged with serious crimes may be certified to be tried as adults. Judges decide whether to certify a juvenile as an adult depending on the severity of the crime and the maturity of the youngster. Juveniles below the age of 14 or older juveniles who are not certified as adults are dealt with by the juvenile court system.

Juvenile courts are different from adult courts. Cases tried in juvenile court are heard under the family law code, which is a civil law code rather than criminal law. Juvenile court judges hold hearings to determine if an accused juvenile has engaged in delinquent conduct. The district or county attorney represents the state and must prove the case beyond a reasonable doubt. The juvenile has rights similar to those of adult defendants, including the right to an attorney and the right to cross-examine witnesses. Similar to adult court proceedings, many juvenile court proceedings are settled through plea bargains. If a juvenile is determined to be delinquent or in need of supervision, the court holds a disposition hearing to determine how the youngster should be handled. The court considers both the safety of the community and the best interests of the child.

Juvenile courts enjoy considerable leeway in deciding how to handle youthful defendants. The court can suspend the driver's license of a juvenile offender, order the juvenile to pay restitution to the crime victim, and require the juvenile and the juvenile's parents to perform community service. The court can also order a juvenile to be sent to a community rehabilitation facility or an alternative school. Repeat offenders or juveniles guilty of serious criminal offenses may be held in a state facility operated by the Texas Youth Commission (TYC). Juveniles guilty of certain violent offenses may be transferred to adult prison when they are between ages 16 and 21.

CORRECTIONS

The Texas prison system houses more than 170,000 inmates, making it the largest prison system in the United States, even larger than the prison system in California, a state whose population is 60 percent larger than that of the Lone Star State. The Texas prison system is more than twice as big as the prison system in New York, even though New York's population is only 12 percent smaller than the Texas population. The incarceration rate in Texas is 703 prison inmates per 100,000 people compared with a national rate of 488 per 100,000. Texas has the second highest incarceration rate in the country, after Louisiana.[28]

County Jails

Except for a few small counties, each of the state's 254 counties has a county jail, built by county tax dollars and staffed by the office of the county sheriff. Jails house people accused of felony and misdemeanor criminal offenses who have not made bail, convicted felons who are awaiting transfer to the Texas Department of Criminal Justice (TDCJ), people charged with federal criminal offenses who are awaiting transfer to a federal facility, and persons convicted of misdemeanor offenses who are serving relatively short sentences. Counties with excess capacity rent space to counties with overcrowded jails. The average daily population of Texas jails in 2006 was 69,800, a figure representing 84 percent of total jail capacity.[29]

State Jails

In 1993, the Texas legislature authorized the creation of a state jail system with an eventual capacity of 22,000 to divert certain nonviolent offenders from the state prison system. State jails house persons convicted of a new category of crime, fourth-degree (state jail) felonies. Fourth-degree felonies include forgery, fraud, relatively minor theft, possession or delivery of small amounts of certain illegal drugs, car theft (under $20,000 value), burglary of a building that is not a home, and other nonviolent crimes. Persons convicted of fourth-degree felonies can be given as much as five

Texas has the largest prison system in the country.

years' probation or be sentenced to serve as much as two years in a state jail. State jails are designed to keep inexperienced criminals away from hard-core criminals, get them off drugs, and help them finish high school equivalency courses. While in state jails, inmates can receive chemical abuse therapy, job training, and family counseling. State jail inmates serve flat time sentences, with no early release for good behavior. In 2005, 16 state jail facilities housed nearly 15,000 offenders.[30]

State Prisons

For years, the Texas prison system was widely regarded as one of the most austere in the nation. More than 90 percent of state prisoners were held in maximum-security prisons, where they were prohibited any physical contact with visitors. Inmates were even forbidden from talking with one another in dining areas. Critics called Texas prisons both brutal and brutalizing. But other observers praised the Texas prison system for its efficiency and effectiveness—the best in the country, they said. Inmates were required to work and attend school. Escapes were rare, the reported rate of inmate violence low, and prison riots unheard of. And all of this was achieved at a cost per inmate that was the lowest in the nation.[31]

In 1972, a group of prisoners filed suit in federal court, claiming that living and working conditions in Texas prisons constituted "cruel and unusual punishment," forbidden by the Eighth Amendment to the U.S. Constitution. The suit, *Ruiz v. Estelle*, charged that the state's prison system was severely overcrowded, the prison staff was too small to maintain security, working conditions were unsafe, disciplinary procedures were severe and arbitrary, and medical care was inadequate. In particular, the suit attacked the building tender system, in which inmate guards were given authority over their cellblocks to keep them clean and safe. Texas prison officials defended the system for its effectiveness, saying that inmate building tenders were nothing more than glorified janitors. In contrast, critics claimed that inmate guards were dictators who controlled their cellblocks through brute force while guards looked the other way.

In 1980, U.S. District Judge William Wayne Justice ruled against the state of Texas, ordering sweeping changes in the Texas prison system. Although an appeals court later overturned part of Judge Justice's ruling, it agreed with the key points of his decision. Eventually, the state settled the suit by agreeing to limit inmate population to 95 percent of prison capacity, separate hard-core offenders from inmates convicted of nonviolent crimes, improve the guard-to-inmate ratio, upgrade inmate medical treatment, and eliminate the building tender system.[32]

While the state struggled to deal with the impact of *Ruiz v. Estelle*, poor planning by the legislature and the governor made the problem of prison overcrowding considerably worse. During the 1970s and 1980s, the governor and legislature responded to public concerns about crime by getting tough. The legislature passed dozens of anticrime bills, upgrading the seriousness of certain offenses and increasing prison time for offenders. Texas judges and juries began sentencing more people to prison to serve longer terms. The legislature also required that persons convicted of **aggravated offenses** (violent crimes) or crimes using a deadly weapon serve at least a third of a sentence before becoming eligible for parole. As a result, the prison system stacked up with inmates who could not be paroled. In the meantime, the legislature failed to expand prison capacity sufficiently to accommodate the increase in the number of inmates. During the entire decade of the 1970s, the state built only one prison unit, with a mere 600 beds. Although the state added 13,000 more beds in the early 1980s, the increase in capacity failed to keep up with the growth of admissions. Prison capacity rose by 50 percent, but admissions increased 113 percent.[33]

In the late 1980s, the legislature, the governor, and the voters authorized a massive prison construction program to hold the state's rapidly growing prison population. The legislature proposed and the voters approved constitutional amendments to borrow money to build new prison units. Meanwhile, the legislature and the governor appropriated funds to operate the new prison units and begin the long-term process of paying for their construction. Between 1984 and 2005, the share of state spending devoted to public safety and corrections increased from 3.8 percent of total spending to 5.1 percent.[34]

The state's prison expansion plans also included the privatization of operations and management at some facilities. **Privatization** is the process that involves the government contracting with private business to implement government programs.

Aggravated offenses
Violent crimes.

Privatization
The process that involves the government contracting with private business to implement government programs.

In 2005, Texas housed more than 15,000 inmates at privately managed facilities, about 9 percent of its inmate population.[35] The proponents of privatization contend that it saves money, and research indicates that the cost of housing prisoners in privately run facilities is about 10 percent less than it is in state-run facilities. In contrast, the critics of prison privatization argue that the savings are illusory because they result from the use of poorly trained, underpaid personnel who pose a security risk.[36]

Although spending for corrections is one of the few budget categories in which Texas exceeds the national average, the Texas prison system is not especially well funded. Despite having the largest prison system in the country, Texas is 20th in per capita spending on corrections. California, with a prison population slightly smaller than the Texas inmate population, has a corrections budget more than twice as large.[37]

The Texas prison system is once again near capacity. To make room for incoming inmates, prison officials have begun renting space in county jails and increasing the parole rate.[38] Most state policymakers want to address the current overcrowding problem with strategies other than adding new prisons because they are expensive to build and operate. A new 2,250-bed prison unit costs nearly $200 million to build and $36.5 million a year to operate when it is full.[39] The Legislative Budget Board (LBB) estimates that the state will need an additional 7,300 prison beds by 2009 and 11,200 more beds by 2011 unless the state increases the use of alternatives to incarceration, including probation and parole.[40]

Prison Release

Prisoners leave the prison system through parole or by completing their sentences. In theory, parole is a mechanism for reintegrating offenders into the community because it allows the state to release prisoners to the community conditionally, under supervision. In general, parolees must not associate with known criminals, possess firearms, or drink to excess. They are required to report regularly to a parole officer and inform that official of a change of residence or a change of jobs. Parole is also cheaper than prison. The cost of parole supervision is $3.51 a day for each offender compared with $42.54 for each day in prison.[41]

Good time
A prison policy that credits inmates with time off for good behavior.

Under state law, most prisoners are eligible for parole after serving one-fourth of their sentence or 15 years, whichever is less. The state determines the amount of time served for inmates convicted of nonviolent offenses by adding together the actual days spent behind bars with good time earned. **Good time** is a prison policy that credits inmates with time off for good behavior. Prisoners can earn a maximum of 75 days' good time for every 30 days actually served if they attend school, work in prison, and generally behave themselves. Violent offenders serve flat time without the opportunity to earn good time. Furthermore, persons found guilty of violent crimes or who used a deadly weapon in the course of committing an offense must serve at least half of their sentence before becoming eligible for parole. In theory, both parole and good time are prison management tools because they give inmates an incentive to cooperate with prison officials. Prisoners who attend classes, develop work skills, and stay out of trouble behind bars earn the opportunity for parole. If parolees fail to live up to the conditions of their release, they can be returned to prison.

WHAT IS YOUR OPINION?

*Should prison inmates be released early from prison because
of good behavior?*

Recidivism
The tendency of
offenders released
from prison to commit
additional crimes
and be returned
behind bars.

Recidivism

Many inmates released from prison get in trouble again. **Recidivism** is the tendency
of offenders released from prison to commit additional crimes and be returned behind bars. In Texas, 28 percent of inmates released from prison are rearrested for a
serious crime within three years of their release.[42]

CONCLUSION: CRIMINAL JUSTICE POLICYMAKING

The most important elements of the policymaking environment for criminal justice
policymaking are public opinion, federal court rulings, and the budgetary outlook.
The general public has strong views about crime. Elected officials all want to be seen
as tough on crime. Indeed, some critics of Lieutenant Governor Dewhurst suggested
that his proposal to make child predators eligible for the death penalty was designed
to enhance his image in anticipation of a run for governor in 2010. Whereas public
opinion in Texas generally supports a "lock' em up and throw away the key" philosophy, federal court rulings and the state budget impose constraints on policymakers.
Federal court rulings establish the ground rules for the criminal justice process and
determine the range of punishments that are constitutionally acceptable. Meanwhile, the state's budget outlook determines the resources policymakers will have
available to address criminal justice issues.

Agenda Building

A number of political actors set the agenda for criminal justice policymaking. Federal
court decisions sometimes force the legislature and the governor to address policy
issues. Recent decisions of the U.S. Supreme Court on the constitutionality of
imposing the death penalty on offenders who were juveniles at the time of their crime[43]
or against the mentally retarded[44] have forced the state to revise its capital punishment
statute. The legislature and the governor had to address the issue of prison reform
because of *Ruiz v. Estelle*, a U.S. district court decision. Media reports of horrific crimes
or the possibility that the state has sent an innocent person to prison or even death row
set the agenda as well. The legislature and the governor focused on overhauling the
operation of the Texas Youth Commission after the media revealed allegations of
sexual abuse by staff members against juvenile offenders held in TYC custody.

Policy Formulation and Adoption

The legislature, governor, and some interest groups participate in criminal justice
policy formulation. Legislators formulate policy with input from the governor and a
number of interest groups that focus on criminal justice issues, such as Mothers

Against Drunk Driving (MADD), public employee groups representing police officers and corrections employees, death penalty opponents, and victims' rights organizations. MADD lobbies in favor of tougher DWI laws. Unions representing prison employees fought against prison privatization and succeeded in limiting the practice to newly built prisons, rather than privatizing existing units, thus saving the jobs of their members.

The legislature and the governor adopt criminal justice policies through the legislative process. Criminal justice bills must pass the Texas House and Texas Senate and then go to the governor for signature. If the governor vetoes a measure, it dies unless both the House and the Senate vote to override the veto by a two-thirds' vote.

Policy Implementation and Evaluation

State and local law enforcement, district attorneys, the court system, and the Texas Department of Criminal Justice (TDCJ) implement criminal justice policies. Police officers implement criminal justice policies by arresting suspects. District attorneys decide whether to prosecute and courts conduct trials. Ordinary citizens participate in policy implementation by serving on juries. The TDCJ houses prisoners serving their sentences, whereas the Board of Pardons and Paroles determines whether to grant parole.

A number of state and federal agencies evaluate criminal justice policies. The Federal Bureau of Investigation (FBI), Federal Bureau of Justice Statistics, Texas Commission on Jail Standards, and Legislative Budget Board (LBB) all gather criminal justice statistics. The LBB, comptroller, and Texas Sunset Commission prepare analytical reports evaluating the operation of the TDCJ. The legislature and the governor then use these reports as the basis for proposing legislation designed to reform criminal justice policies.

LET'S DEBATE   Offender and Ex-Offender Voting Rights

Overview: Should Texas's prisoners, parolees, and probationers be allowed to vote? In the hotly contested 2000 general election, the media spotlight lay on Florida and its electoral law and system; in 2004, allegations of voter fraud in Ohio kept political attention on franchise regulation. When national interests and partisan competition are currently at a fever pitch, it's only natural that the simmering issue of whether felons and ex-offenders should be given the right to vote is elevated as a state and national policy issue. Voter's rights advocates such as The Sentencing Project and the American Civil Liberties Union argue that state disenfranchisement laws have the effect of discriminating by race and socioeconomic status. They argue that disenfranchisement laws have their origin in post–Civil War prejudice and racism, and their consequence is to disproportionately harm the political efficacy of Black American males and America's poor, especially in the South and in Texas. States' non-notification policies for restored ex-offender electoral rights also have the effect of disenfranchisement. Others, such as those who advocate New Federalism, argue that states have the constitutional authority to prevent those who break the law from voting for those who make the law; why should those who disregard the law have a hand in making it? They argue that states themselves are liberalizing voting laws to be consonant with public mores, and that state action, as directed by the Constitution, is the proper venue for this area of political change.

As of 2007, four states (Maine, Massachusetts, Utah, and Vermont) do not deprive their prison populations and ex-felons voting rights, and two states (Virginia and Kentucky) permanently deny their ex-felons the franchise. The rest of the states have what political scientist Alec Ewald calls a "crazy quilt" of disenfranchisement law; in some states, the right-to-vote is determined at the county level, which further exacerbates the quest for uniformity in, and the expansion of, voting rights. Over the decades, Texas has steadily liberalized franchise restrictions for its ex-offender population. In 1983, a felony conviction resulted in lifetime disenfranchisement; in 2007, only those offenders who were incarcerated, on parole, under supervision, or on probation are disenfranchised.

In 1997 Governor George Bush signed into law legislation that removed the two-year post-sentence waiting period, thereby restoring voting rights to 317,000 Texans in time for the 1998 Texas gubernatorial and national midterm elections. As noted, under current Texas law, the right to vote is immediately restored to those who have completed their sentence, parole, probation, or supervision, yet the state does not have any notification requirements to inform ex-offenders of reinstated franchise rights. Voting rights advocates argue that non-notification requirements have the practical effect of denying the franchise to those who have restored privileges, and in Texas, this could presently affect nearly 350,000 parolees and probationers. In May 2007, Governor Rick Perry vetoed HB 770, which would have compelled the Texas Department of Criminal Justice to notify ex-offenders of restored rights. His veto message states that "when an individual is released from prison . . . it is imperative that they take personal responsibility for all aspects of their life, including their right to vote," and that the State does not compel notice of rights to law-abiding new voters, nor does it prohibit political parties or private organizations from registering those not on voting rolls, nor "from organizing voter registration drives among released convicts." It seems the State of Texas falls squarely in line with the current movement to liberalize franchise rules while demanding responsibility of its ex-offender population.

Arguments Against Allowing Disenfranchisement Law

❑ **A healthy democracy allows all its citizens the right to vote.** A part of American history is the quest to guarantee all citizens political equality by expanding the franchise. Though errant, those incarcerated and penalized have to live by the economic, social, and foreign policy pursued and enacted by government. It follows that since they have to live by these very moral decisions, they should have a say in how government is conducted. The global trend is moving toward the principle of a broadly expansive franchise, and the United States should join in this general democratic movement.

❑ **Disenfranchisement law disproportionately impacts racial minorities.** Studies by Human Rights Watch and the Right to Vote Campaign show that minority populations, especially African American populations, are disproportionately impacted by these laws. In some states, such as Florida, nearly one in three African American men is disenfranchised. By removing these electoral barriers, minority populations can use the vote to help eliminate those historical and structural barriers that reinforce discrimination. It is time to remove those barriers that may have been put in place to prevent American citizens from voting.

❑ **Research indicates that voting may actually reduce recidivism.** On February 7, 2005, the *New York Times* reported that having the franchise may prompt offenders to become engaged in the "civic mainstream" and as a result become more responsible and involved citizens. "Data indicates," reports the *Times*, "offenders who vote are less likely to return to jail," and that this right is so essential that other democracies "take the ballot box right to the prisons." It may be that restoring the franchise may not only help rehabilitation, but it may also induce these citizens to become more civic-minded.

Arguments for Allowing Disenfranchisement Law

❑ **Article 1, section 2 of the Constitution gives the states the right to determine voter qualifications.** Supreme Court Justice Joseph Story tells us that due to the difference of viewpoints in the Constitutional Convention, it was decided that state legislatures

continued on next page

are the proper venue for determining voter qualifications, since it would allow for "some not unimportant diversities" that would protect diverse state political cultures. It is a state's citizens who determine—within the confines of the Constitution, of course—which among them are to be entrusted with the franchise privilege, and the federal principle thus allows for the various differences in opinion in regard to whom should be permitted to vote.

❑ **Disenfranchisement is consonant with American republican tradition.** The franchise is not an absolute right. Even advocates of felon enfranchisement concede the United States's electoral heritage stems from Greek and Roman republican tradition, which denied political life to those whose criminal actions caused harm to the common good. Because the state represents the interest of its citizens, they should have a say in how political rights are distributed. If one doesn't want to lose political rights, it is argued, then one should not deliberately harm a fellow citizen.

❑ **Disenfranchisement is consonant with American liberal tradition.** Disenfranchisement is also a part of American natural rights tradition. John Locke argued that whoever violates another's right to life, liberty, and property forfeits his or her own right to the same. By expressing contempt for society and its laws, it is fitting that the offender be denied the right to choose those who make legislation. Why should those who do not respect the law have a hand in making it?

QUESTIONS

1. Should Texas further liberalize its franchise law for offenders and ex-offenders? Why or why not?
2. Is it the responsibility of ex-offenders to register to vote, or should there be state notification of restored rights?

SELECT READINGS

1. Jeff Manza and Chris Uggen, *Locked Out: Felon Disenfranchisement and American Democracy*, 2006.
2. Elizabeth Hull, *The Disenfranchisement of Ex-felons*, 2006.

SELECT WEBSITES

1. **http://www.aclu.org/votingrights/exoffenders/statelegispolicy2007.html**
   American Civil Liberties Union advocacy website, which updates state activity in regard to offender disenfranchisement legislation.

2. **http://www.constitutioncenter.org/education/ForEducators/Viewpoints/FelonDisenfranchisementIsConstitutional,AndJustified.shtml**
   Constitution Center editorial on the constitutionality of and constitutional provisions that support felon disenfranchisement law.

KEY TERMS

adversary proceeding	felony	parole
aggravated offenses	good time	plea bargain
arraignment	grand jury	privatization
bail	indictment	probable cause
booking	magistrates	probation
burden of proof	Miranda warning	recidivism
capital punishment	misdemeanor	true bill
clearance rate	National Crime Victim Survey (NCVS)	Uniform Crime Reports (UCR)
community policing		
deferred adjudication	*nolo contendere*	

NOTES

1. W. Gardner Selby, "House Passes Child Predator Legislation," *Austin American-Statesman*, May 19, 2007, available at www.statesman.com.
2. Federal Bureau of Investigation, Uniform Crime Reports, available at www.fbi.gov.
3. Texas Department of Public Safety, "Annual Report of 2005 UCR Data Collection: Crime in Texas 2005 Overview," available at www.txdps.state.tx.us.
4. "Prisoners Under Jurisdiction of Federal or State Correctional Authorities—Summary by State: 1990–2004," U.S. Census Bureau, *2007 Statistical Abstract*, available at www.census.gov.
5. "Resident Population by Age and Sex: 1980 to 2005," U.S. Census Bureau, *2007 Statistical Abstract*, available at www.census.gov.
6. "Crime," Gallup Poll, available at www.gallup.com.
7. "Victimization Rates, by Type of Crime and Characteristics of the Victim: 2003," U.S. Census Bureau, *2007 Statistical Abstract*, available at www.census.gov.
8. Federal Bureau of Investigation, "Arrests of Persons 15, 18, 21, and 25 Years of Age, 2005," *Crime in the United States 2005*, available at www.fbi.gov.
9. "Victim-Offender Relationship in Crimes of Violence, by Characteristics of the Criminal Incident," U.S. Census Bureau, *2007 Statistical Abstract*, available at www.census.gov.
10. Federal Bureau of Investigation, "Murder Victim/Offender Relationship by Race and Sex, 2005," *Crime in the United States 2005*, available at www.fbi.gov.
11. Texas Crime Victims' Compensation Fund, available at www.oag.state.tx.us.
12. *Miranda v. Arizona*, 384 U.S. 436 (1966).
13. *Gideon v. Wainwright*, 372 U.S. 335 (1963).
14. Office of Court Administration, "Evidence for the Feasibility of Public Defender Offices in Texas," available at www.courts.state.tx.us.
15. *Duncan v. Louisiana*, 391 U.S. 145 (1968).
16. Office of Court Administration, *Texas Judicial System Annual Report Fiscal Year 2006*, available at www.courts.state.tx.us.
17. "Summary of Sunset Commission Recommendations," Texas Sunset Commission, February 2007, available at www.sunset.state.tx.us.
18. Ibid.
19. U.S. Law Enforcement Assistance Administration, *Prisoners in State and Federal Institutions on December 31, 1977*, National Prisoner Statistics Bulletin, SD-NPS-PSF-5 (Washington, DC: U.S. Government Printing Office, 1979); Texas Judicial Council, "Capital Murder Study," in *Forty-seventh Annual Report 1975* (Austin: Texas Judicial Council, 1976), pp. 89–94; and Rupert C. Koeniger, "Capital Punishment in Texas, 1927–1968," *Crime and Delinquency* 15 (January 1968): 132–141.
20. *Furman v. Georgia*, 408 U.S. 238 (1972).
21. "Executions," Texas Department of Criminal Justice, available at www.tdcj.state.tx.us.
22. "Offenders on Death Row," Texas Department of Criminal Justice, available at www.tdcj.state.tx.us.
23. James S. Leibman, *A Broken System: Error Rates in Capital Cases, 1973–1995*, available at www.thejusticeproject.org.
24. Ibid.
25. "Execution Statistics," Texas Department of Criminal Justice, available at www.tdcj.state.tx.us.
26. Federal Bureau of Investigation, "Arrests of Persons Under 15, 18, 21, and 25 Years of Age," *Crime in the United States 2005*, available at www.fbi.gov.
27. Federal Bureau of Investigation, "Ten-Year Arrest Trends 1996–2005," *Crime in the United States 2005*, available at www.fbi.gov.
28. "State Prison Population," *Governing State and Local Source Book, 2006*, p. 67.
29. Texas Commission on Jail Standards, "Jail Population Report," available at www.tcjs.state.tx.us.
30. Texas Department of Criminal Justice, *Annual Review 2005*, available at www.tdcj.state.tx.us.
31. John J. DiIulio, Jr., "Judicial Intervention: Lessons from the Past," in Timothy J. Flanagan, James W. Marquart, and Kenneth G. Adams, eds., *Incarcerating Criminals: Prisons and Jails in Social and Organizational Context* (New York: Oxford University Press, 1998), pp. 81–93.
32. *Ruiz v. Estelle*, 503 F. Supp 1265 (S.D. Tex 1980); 679 F 2d 115 (5th Cir. 1982).
33. Dianna Hunt, "Justice Delayed: Our State's Criminal Crisis," *Houston Chronicle*, December 2, 1990, p. 24A.
34. Texas Comptroller of Public Accounts, "Texas Expenditure History by Function, 1978–2005," available at www.window.state.tx.us.
35. Bureau of Justice Statistics, "Prison and Jail Inmates at Midyear 2005," available at www.ojp.usdoj.gov.
36. Douglas McDonald and Carl Patten, Jr., "Governments' Management of Private Prisons," National Institute of Justice, available at www.ncjrs.gov.
37. "Corrections Spending," *Governing State and Local Source Book, 2006*, p. 66.
38. "More Prisoners Being Released Early, Report Says," *Dallas Morning News*, June 28, 2004, available at www.dallasnews.com.
39. Sheila Hotchkin, "No Escaping Prison Woes," *San Antonio Express-News*, July 10, 2005, available at www.mysanantonio.com.

40. Legislative Budget Board, "Adult and Juvenile Correctional Population Projections, 2007–2012," available at www.lbb.state.tx.us.

41. Legislative Budget Board, "Criminal Justice Uniform Cost Report Tables," available at www.lbb.state.tx.us.

42. Kathy Walt, "Study Links Lower Recidivism Rates to Longer Jail Terms," *Houston Chronicle*, July 2, 1998, p. 29A.

43. *Roper v. Simmons*, 543 U.S. 551 (2005).

44. *Atkins v. Virginia*, 536 U.S. 304 (2002).

The Declaration of Independence

In Congress, July 4, 1776

The unanimous Declaration of the thirteen united States of America.

When in the Course of human events, it becomes necessary for one people to dissolve the political bands which have connected them with another, and to assume among the Powers of the earth, the separate and equal station to which the Laws of Nature and of Nature's God entitle them, a decent respect to the opinions of mankind requires that they should declare the causes which impel them to the separation.

We hold these truths to be self-evident, that all men are created equal, that they are endowed by their Creator with certain unalienable Rights, that among these are Life, Liberty and the pursuit of Happiness. That to secure these rights, Governments are instituted among Men, deriving their just powers from the consent of the governed. That whenever any Form of Government becomes destructive of these ends, it is the Right of the People to alter or to abolish it, and to institute new Government, laying its foundation on such principles and organizing its powers in such form, as to them shall seem most likely to effect their Safety and Happiness. Prudence, indeed, will dictate that Governments long established should not be changed for light and transient causes; and accordingly all experience hath shown, that mankind are more disposed to suffer, while evils are sufferable, than to right themselves by abolishing the forms to which they are accustomed. But when a long train of abuses and usurpations, pursuing invariably the same Object evinces a design to reduce them under absolute Despotism, it is their right, it is their duty, to throw off such Government, and to provide new Guards for their future security.—Such has been the patient sufferance of these Colonies; and such is now the necessity which constrains them to alter their former Systems of Government. The history of the present King of Great Britain is a history of repeated injuries and usurpations, all having in direct object the establishment of an absolute Tyranny over these States. To prove this, let Facts be submitted to a candid world.

He has refused his Assent to Laws, the most wholesome and necessary for the public good.

He has forbidden his Governors to pass Laws of immediate and pressing importance, unless suspended in their operation till his Assent should be obtained; and when so suspended, he has utterly neglected to attend to them.

He has refused to pass other Laws for the accommodation of large districts of people, unless those people would relinquish the right of Representation in the Legislature, a right inestimable to them and formidable to tyrants only.

He has called together legislative bodies at places unusual, uncomfortable, and distant from the depository of their Public Records, for the sole purpose of fatiguing them into compliance with his measures.

He has dissolved Representative Houses repeatedly, for opposing with manly firmness his invasions on the rights of the people.

He has refused for a long time, after such dissolutions, to cause others to be elected; whereby the Legislative Powers, incapable of Annihilation, have returned to the People at large for their exercise; the State remaining in the mean time exposed to all the dangers of invasion from without, and convulsions within.

He has endeavoured to prevent the population of these States; for that purpose obstructing the Laws for Naturalization of Foreigners; refusing to pass others to encourage their migrations hither, and raising the conditions of new Appropriations of Lands.

He has obstructed the Administration of Justice, by refusing his Assent to Laws for establishing Judiciary Powers.

He has made Judges dependent on his Will alone, for the tenure of their offices, and the amount and payment of their salaries.

He has erected a multitude of New Offices, and sent hither swarms of Officers to harass our people, and eat out their substance.

He has kept among us, in times of peace, Standing Armies without the Consent of our legislatures.

He has affected to render the Military independent of and superior to the Civil Power.

He has combined with others to subject us to a jurisdiction foreign to our constitution, and unacknowledged by our laws; giving his Assent to their acts of pretended Legislation:

For quartering large bodies of armed troops among us:

For protecting them, by a mock Trial, from Punishment for any Murders which they should commit on the inhabitants of these States:

For cutting off our Trade with all parts of the world:

For imposing taxes on us without our Consent;

For depriving us in many cases, of the benefits of Trial by Jury:

For transporting us beyond Seas to be tried for pretended offences:

For abolishing the free System of English Laws in a neighbouring Province, establishing therein an Arbitrary government, and enlarging its Boundaries so as to render it at once an example and fit instrument for introducing the same absolute rule into these Colonies:

For taking away our Charters, abolishing our most valuable Laws, and altering fundamentally the Forms of our Governments:

For suspending our own Legislature, and declaring themselves invested with Power to legislate for us in all cases whatsoever.

He has abdicated Government here, by declaring us out of his Protection and waging War against us.

He has plundered our seas, ravaged our Coasts, burnt our towns, and destroyed the lives of our people.

He is at this time transporting large armies of foreign mercenaries to compleat the works of death, desolation and tyranny, already begun with circumstances of Cruelty & perfidy scarcely paralleled in the most barbarous ages, and totally unworthy the Head of a civilized nation.

He has constrained our fellow Citizens taken Captive on the high Seas to bear Arms against their Country, to become the executioners of their friends and Brethren, or to fall themselves by their Hands.

He has excited domestic insurrections amongst us, and has endeavoured to bring on the inhabitants of our frontiers, the merciless Indian Savages, whose known rule of warfare, is an undistinguished destruction of all ages, sexes and conditions.

In every stage of these Oppressions We have Petitioned for Redress in the most humble terms: Our repeated Petitions have been answered only by repeated injury. A Prince, whose character is thus marked by every act which may define a Tyrant, is unfit to be the ruler of a free people.

Nor have we been wanting in attentions to our British brethren. We have warned them from time to time of attempts by their legislature to extend an unwarrantable jurisdiction over us. We have reminded them of the circumstances of our emigration and settlement here. We have appealed to their native justice and magnanimity, and we have conjured them by the ties of our common kindred to disavow these usurpations which, would inevitably interrupt our connections and correspondence. They too have been deaf to the voice of justice and of consanguinity. We must, therefore, acquiesce in the necessity, which denounces our Separation, and hold them, as we hold the rest of mankind, Enemies in War, in Peace Friends.

We, therefore, the Representatives of the United States of America, in General Congress, Assembled, appealing to the Supreme Judge of the world for the rectitude of our intentions, do, in the Name, and by authority of the good People of these Colonies, solemnly publish and declare, That these United Colonies are, and of Right ought to be Free and Independent States; that they are Absolved from all Allegiance to the British Crown, and that all political connection between them and the State of Great Britain, is and ought to be totally dissolved; and that as Free and Independent States, they have full Power to levy War, conclude Peace, contract Alliances, establish Commerce, and to do all other Acts and Things which Independent States may of right do. And for the support of this Declaration, with a firm reliance of the Protection of Divine Providence, we mutually pledge to each other our Lives, our Fortunes and our sacred Honor.

The Constitution of the United States of America

We the people of the United States, in Order to form a more perfect Union, establish justice, insure domestic Tranquility, provide for the common defence, promote the general Welfare, and secure the Blessings of Liberty to ourselves and our Posterity, do ordain and establish this Constitution for the United States of America.

Article I

Section 1.

All legislative Powers herein granted shall be vested in a Congress of the United States, which shall consist of a Senate and House of Representatives.

Section 2.

The House of Representatives shall be composed of Members chosen every second Year by the People of the several States, and the Electors in each State shall have the Qualifications requisite for Electors of the most numerous Branch of the State Legislature.

No person shall be a Representative who shall not have attained to the Age of twenty five Years, and been seven Years a Citizen of the United States, and who shall not, when elected, be an Inhabitant of that State in which he shall be chosen.

Representatives and direct Taxes shall be apportioned among the several States which may be included within this Union, according to their respective Numbers, which shall be determined by adding to the whole Number of free Persons, including those bound to Service for a Term of Years, and excluding Indians not taxed, three fifths of all other Persons.* The actual Enumeration shall be made within three years after the first Meeting of the Congress of the United States, and within every subsequent Term of ten Years, in such Manner as they shall by Law direct. The Number of Representatives shall not exceed one for every thirty Thousand, but each State shall have at Least one Representative; and until such enumeration shall be made, the State of New Hampshire shall be entitled to chuse three, Massachusetts eight, Rhode-Island and Providence Plantations one, Connecticut five, New-York six, New Jersey four, Pennsylvania eight, Delaware one, Maryland six, Virginia ten, North Carolina five, South Carolina five, and Georgia three.

When vacancies happen in the Representation from any State, the Executive Authority thereof shall issue Writs of Election to fill such Vacancies.

The House of Representatives shall chuse their Speaker and other Officers; and shall have the sole Power of Impeachment.

Section 3.

The Senate of the United States shall be composed of two Senators from each State, chosen by the Legislature thereof, for six Years; and each Senator shall have one Vote.

Immediately after they shall be assembled in Consequence of the first Election, they shall be divided as equally as many be into three Classes. The Seats of the Senators of the first Class shall be vacated at the Expiration of the second Year, of the second Class at the Expiration of the fourth Year, and of the third Class at the Expiration of the sixth Year, so that one third may be chosen every second Year; and if Vacancies happen by Resignation, or otherwise, during the Recess of the Legislature of any State, the Executive thereof may make temporary Appointments until the next Meeting of the Legislature, which shall then fill such Vacancies.†

No Person shall be a Senator who shall not have attained to the Age of thirty Years, and been nine Years a Citizen of the United States, and who shall not, when elected, be an Inhabitant of that State in which he shall be chosen.

The Vice President of the United States shall be President of the Senate, but shall have no Vote, unless they be equally divided.

---

*"Other Persons" being black slaves. Modified by Amendment XIV, Section 2.

†Provisions changed by Amendment XVII.

The Senate shall chuse their other Officers, and also a President pro tempore, in the Absence of the Vice President, or when he shall exercise the Office of the President of the United States.

The Senate shall have the sole Power to try all impeachments. When sitting for that Purpose, they shall be on Oath or Affirmation. When the President of the United States is tried, the Chief Justice shall preside: And no person shall be convicted without the Concurrence of two thirds of the Members present.

Judgment in Cases of Impeachment shall not extend further than to removal from Office, and disqualification to hold and enjoy any Office of honor, Trust or Profit under the United States; but the Party convicted shall nevertheless be liable and subject to Indictment, Trial, Judgment and Punishment, according to Law.

Section 4.

The Times, Places and Manner of holding Elections for Senators and Representatives, shall be prescribed in each State by the Legislature thereof; but the Congress may at any time by Law make or alter such Regulations, except as to the Places of chusing Senators.

The Congress shall assemble at least once in every Year, and such Meeting shall be on the first Monday in December, unless they shall by Law appoint a different Day.*

Section 5.

Each House shall be the Judge of the Elections, Returns and Qualifications of its own Members, and a Majority of each shall constitute a Quorum to do Business; but a smaller number may adjourn from day to day, and may be authorized to compel the Attendance of absent Members, in such Manner, and under such Penalties as each House may provide.

Each House may determine the Rules of its Proceedings, punish its Members for disorderly Behaviour, and, with the Concurrence of two thirds, expel a Member.

Each House shall keep a Journal of its Proceedings, and from time to time publish the same, excepting such Parts as may in their Judgment require Secrecy; and the Yeas and Nays of the Members of either House on any question shall, at the Desire of one fifth of those Present, be entered on the Journal.

Neither House, during the Session of Congress, shall, without the Consent of the other, adjourn for more than three days, nor to any other Place than that in which the two Houses shall be sitting.

Section 6.

The Senators and Representatives shall receive a Compensation for their Services, to be ascertained by Law, and paid out of the Treasury of the United States. They shall in all Cases, except Treason, Felony and Breach of the Peace, be privileged from arrest during their Attendance at the Session of their respective Houses, and in going to and returning from the same; and for any Speech or Debate in either House, they shall not be questioned in any other Place.

*Provisions changed by Amendment XX, Section 2.

No Senator or Representative shall, during the Time for which he was elected, be appointed to any civil Office under the Authority of the United States, which shall have been created, or the Emoluments whereof shall have been encreased, during such time; and no Person holding any Office under the United States shall be a Member of either House during his Continuance in Office.

Section 7.

All Bills for raising Revenue shall originate in the House of Representatives; but the Senate may propose or concur with Amendments as on other Bills.

Every Bill which shall have passed the House of Representatives and the Senate, shall, before it become a Law, be presented to the President of the United States; If he approve he shall sign it, but if not he shall return it, with his Objections, to that House in which it shall have originated, who shall enter the Objections at large on their Journal, and proceed to reconsider it. If after such Reconsideration two thirds of that House shall agree to pass the Bill, it shall be sent, together with the Objections, to the other House, by which it shall likewise be reconsidered, and if approved by two thirds of that House, it shall become a Law. But in all such Cases the Votes of both Houses shall be determined by Yeas and Nays, and the Names of the Persons voting for and against the Bill shall be entered on the Journal of each House respectively. If any Bill shall not be returned by the President within ten Days (Sundays excepted) after it shall have been presented to him, the Same shall be a Law, in like Manner as if he had signed it, unless the Congress by their Adjournment prevent its Return, in which Case it shall not be a Law.

Every Order, Resolution, or Vote to which the Concurrence of the Senate and House of Representatives may be necessary (except on a question of Adjournment) shall be presented to the President of the United States; and before the Same shall take Effect, shall be approved by him, or being disapproved by him, shall be repassed by two thirds of the Senate and House of Representatives, according to the Rules and Limitations prescribed in the Case of a Bill.

Section 8.

The Congress shall have Power To lay and collect Taxes, Duties, Imposts and Excises, to pay the Debts and provide for the common Defence and general Welfare of the United States; but all Duties, Imposts and Excises shall be uniform throughout the United States;

To borrow Money on the credit of the United States;

To regulate Commerce with foreign Nations, and among the several States, and with the Indian Tribes;

To establish a uniform Rule of Naturalization, and uniform Laws on the subject of Bankruptcies throughout the United States;

To coin Money, regulate the Value thereof, and of foreign Coin, and fix the Standard of Weights and Measures;

To provide for the Punishment of counterfeiting the Securities and current Coin of the United States;

To establish Post offices and post Roads;

To promote the Progress of Science and useful Arts, by securing for limited Times to Authors and Inventors the exclusive Right to their respective Writings and Discoveries;

To constitute Tribunals inferior to the supreme Court;

To define and punish Piracies and Felonies committed on the high Seas, and Offences against the Law of Nations;

To declare War, grant Letters of Marque and Reprisal, and make Rules concerning Captures on Land and Water;

To raise and support Armies, but no Appropriation of Money to that Use shall be for a longer Term than two Years;

To provide and maintain a Navy;

To make Rules for the Government and Regulation of the land and naval Forces;

To provide for calling forth the Militia to execute the Laws of the Union, suppress Insurrections and repel Invasions;

To provide for organizing, arming, and disciplining, the Militia, and for governing such Part of them as may be employed in the Service of the United States, reserving to the States respectively, the Appointment of the Officers, and the Authority of training the Militia according to the discipline prescribed by Congress;

To exercise exclusive Legislation in all Cases whatsoever, over such District (not exceeding ten Miles square) as may, by Cession of particular States, and the Acceptance of Congress, become the Seat of Government of the United States, and to exercise like Authority over all Places purchased by the Consent of the Legislature of the State in which the Same shall be, for the Erection of Forts, Magazines, Arsenals, dock-Yards, and other needful Buildings;—And

To make all Laws which shall be necessary and proper for carrying into Execution the foregoing Powers, and all other Powers vested by this Constitution in the Government of the United States, or in any Department or Officer thereof.

Section 9.

The Migration or Importation of such Persons as any of the States now existing shall think proper to admit, shall not be prohibited by the Congress prior to the Year one thousand eight hundred and eight, but a Tax, or duty may be imposed on such Importation, not exceeding ten dollars for each Person.

The privilege of the Writ of Habeas Corpus shall not be suspended, unless when in Cases of Rebellion or Invasion the public Safety may require it.

No Bill of Attainder or ex post facto Law shall be passed.

No Capitation, or other direct, Tax shall be laid, unless in Proportion to the Census or Enumeration herein before directed to be taken.

No Tax or Duty shall be laid on Articles exported from any State.

No Preference shall be given by any Regulation of Commerce or Revenue to the Ports of one State over those of another; nor shall Vessels bound to, or from, one State, be obliged to enter, clear, or pay Duties in another.

No Money shall be drawn from the Treasury, but in Consequence of Appropriations made by Law; and a regular Statement and Account of the Receipts and Expenditures of all public Money shall be published from time to time.

No Title of Nobility shall be granted by the United States: And no Person holding any Office of Profit or Trust under them, shall, without the Consent of the Congress, accept of any present, Emolument, Office, or Title, of any kind whatever, from any King, Prince, or foreign State.

Section 10.

No State shall enter into any Treaty, Alliance, or Confederation; grant Letters of Marque and Reprisal; coin Money; emit Bills of Credit; make any Thing but gold and silver Coin a Tender in Payment of Debts; pass any Bill of Attainder, ex post facto Law, or Law impairing the Obligation of Contracts, or grant any Title of Nobility.

No State shall, without the Consent of the Congress, lay any Imposts or Duties on Imports or Exports, except what may be absolutely necessary for executing its inspection Laws: and the net Produce of all Duties and Imposts, laid by any State on Imports or Exports, shall be for the Use of the Treasury of the United States; and all such Laws shall be subject to the Revision and Control of the Congress.

No State shall, without the Consent of Congress, lay any Duty of Tonnage, keep Troops, or Ships of War in time of Peace, enter into any Agreement or Compact with another State, or with a foreign Power, or engage in War, unless actually invaded, or in such imminent Danger as will not admit of delay.

Article II

Section 1.

The executive Power shall be vested in a President of the United States of America. He shall hold his Office during the Term of four Years, and, together with the Vice President, chosen for the same Term, be elected, as follows:

Each State shall appoint, in such Manner as the Legislature thereof may direct, a Number of Electors, equal to the whole Number of Senators and Representatives to which the State may be entitled in the Congress; but no Senator or Representative, or Person holding an Office of Trust or Profit under the United States, shall be appointed an Elector.

The Electors shall meet in their respective States, and vote by Ballot for two Persons, of whom one at least shall not be an Inhabitant of the same State with themselves. And they shall make a List of all the Persons voted for, and of the Number of Votes for each; which List they shall sign and certify, and transmit sealed to the Seat of the Government of the United States, directed to the President of the Senate. The President of the Senate shall, in the Presence of the Senate and House of Representatives, open all the Certificates, and the Votes shall then be counted. The Person having the greatest Number of Votes shall be the President, if such Number be a Majority of the whole Number of Electors appointed; and if there be more than one who have such Majority, and have an equal Number of Votes, then the House of Representatives shall immediately chuse by Ballot one of them for President; and if no Person have a Majority, then from the five highest on the List the said House shall in like Manner chuse the President. But in chusing the President, the Votes shall be taken by States, the Representation from each State having one Vote; a quorum for this Purpose shall consist of a Member or Members from two thirds of the States, and a Majority of all the States shall be necessary to a Choice. In every Case, after the Choice of the President, the Person having the greatest Number of Votes of the Electors shall be the Vice President. But if there should remain two or more who have equal Votes, the Senate shall chuse from them by Ballot the Vice President.*

The Congress may determine the Time of chusing the Electors, and the Day on which they shall give their Votes; which Day shall be the same throughout the United States.

No Person except a natural born Citizen, or a Citizen of the United States, at the time of the Adoption of this Constitution, shall be eligible to the Office of President; neither shall any Person be eligible to that Office who shall not have attained to the Age of thirty five Years, and been fourteen Years a Resident within the United States.

In Case of the Removal of the President from Office, or of his Death, Resignation, or Inability to discharge the Powers and Duties of the said Office, the Same shall devolve on the Vice President, and the Congress may by Law provide for the Case of Removal, Death, Resignation or Inability, both of the President and Vice President, declaring what Officer shall then act as President, and such Officer shall act accordingly, until the Disability be removed, or a President shall be elected.

The President shall, at stated Times, receive for his Services, a Compensation, which shall neither be encreased nor diminished during the Period for which he shall have been elected, and he shall not receive within that Period any other Emolument from the United States, or any of them.

Before he enter on the Execution of his Office, he shall take the following Oath or Affirmation:—"I do solemnly swear (or affirm) that I will faithfully execute the Office of President of the United States, and will to the best of my Ability, preserve, protect and defend the Constitution of the United States."

Section 2.

The President shall be Commander in Chief of the Army and Navy of the United States, and of the Militia of the several States, when called into the actual Service of the United States; he may require the Opinion, in writing, of the principal Officer in each of the executive Departments, upon any Subject relating to the Duties of their respective Offices, and he shall have Power to grant Reprieves and Pardons for Offences against the United States, except in Cases of Impeachment.

He shall have Power, by and with the Advice and Consent of the Senate, to make Treaties, provided two thirds of the

Senators present concur; and he shall nominate, and by and with the Advice and Consent of the Senate, shall appoint Ambassadors, other public Ministers and Consuls, Judges of the supreme Court, and all other Officers of the United States, whose Appointments are not herein otherwise provided for, and which shall be established by Law: but the Congress may by Law vest the Appointment of such inferior Officers, as they think proper in the President alone, in the Courts of Law, or in the Heads of Departments.

The President shall have Power to fill up all Vacancies that may happen during the Recess of the Senate, by granting Commissions which shall expire at the end of their next Session.

Section 3.

He shall from time to time give to the Congress Information of the State of the Union, and recommend to their Consideration such Measures as he shall judge necessary and expedient; he may, on extraordinary occasions, convene both Houses, or either of them, and in Case of Disagreement between them, with Respect to the Time of Adjournment, he may adjourn them to such Time as he shall think proper; he shall receive Ambassadors and other public Ministers; he shall take Care that the Laws be faithfully executed, and shall Commission all the Officers of the United States.

Section 4.

The President, Vice President and all civil Officers of the United States, shall be removed from Office on Impeachment for, and Conviction of, Treason, Bribery, or other high Crimes and Misdemeanors.

Article III

Section 1.

The judicial Power of the United States, shall be vested in one supreme Court, and in such inferior Courts as the Congress may from time to time ordain and establish. The Judges, both of the supreme and inferior Courts, shall hold their Offices during good Behaviour, and shall, at stated Times, receive for their Services, a Compensation, which shall not be diminished during their Continuance in Office.

Section 2.

The judicial Power shall extend to all Cases in Law and Equity, arising under this Constitution, the Laws of the United States, and Treaties made, or which shall be made, under their Authority;—to all Cases affecting Ambassadors, other public Ministers and Consuls;—to all cases of admiralty and maritime Jurisdiction;—to Controversies to which the United States shall be a Party;—to Controversies between two or more States;—between a State and Citizens of another State;—between Citizens of different States;—between Citizens of the same State claiming Lands under

*Provisions superseded by Amendment XII.

Grants of different States, and between a State, or the Citizens thereof, and foreign States, Citizens or Subjects.*

In all Cases affecting Ambassadors, other public Ministers and Consuls, and those in which a State shall be Party, the supreme Court shall have original Jurisdiction. In all the other Cases before mentioned, the supreme Court shall have appellate Jurisdiction, both as to Law and Fact, with such Exceptions, and under such Regulations as the Congress shall make.

The Trial of all Crimes, except in Cases of Impeachment, shall be by Jury; and such Trial shall be held in the State where the said Crimes shall have been committed, but when not committed within any State, the Trial shall be at such Place or Places as the Congress may by law have directed.

Section 3.

Treason against the United States, shall consist only in levying War against them, or in adhering to their Enemies, giving them Aid and Comfort. No person shall be convicted of Treason unless on the Testimony of two Witnesses to the same overt Act, or on Confession in open Court.

The Congress shall have Power to declare the Punishment of Treason, but no Attainder of Treason shall work Corruption of Blood, or Forfeiture except during the Life of the Person attained.

Article IV

Section 1.

Full Faith and Credit shall be given in each State to the public Acts, Records, and judicial Proceedings of every other State. And the Congress may by general Laws prescribe the Manner in which such Acts, Records and Proceedings shall be proved, and the Effect thereof.

Section 2.

The Citizens of each State shall be entitled to all Privileges and Immunities of Citizens in the several States.

A Person charged in any State with Treason, Felony, or other Crime, who shall flee from Justice, and be found in another State, shall on Demand of the executive Authority of the State from which he fled, be delivered up, to be removed to the State having Jurisdiction of the Crime.

No Person held to Service or Labour in one State, under the Laws thereof, escaping into another, shall, in Consequence of any Law or Regulation therein, be discharged from such Service or Labour, but shall be delivered up on Claim of the Party to whom such Service or Labour may be due.

Section 3.

New States may be admitted by the Congress into this Union; but no new State shall be formed or erected within the Jurisdiction of any other State; nor any State be formed by the Junction of two or more States, or Parts of States, without the Consent of the Legislatures of the States concerned as well as of the Congress.

The Congress shall have Power to dispose of and make all needful Rules and Regulations respecting the Territory or other Property belonging to the United States; and nothing in this Constitution shall be so construed as to Prejudice any Claims of the United States, or of any particular State.

Section 4.

The United States shall guarantee to every State in this Union a Republican Form of Government, and shall protect each of them against Invasion; and on Application of the Legislature, or of the Executive (when the Legislature cannot be convened) against domestic Violence.

Article V

The Congress, whenever two thirds of both Houses shall deem it necessary, shall propose Amendments to this Constitution, or, on the Application of the Legislatures of two thirds of the several States, shall call a Convention for proposing Amendments, which, in either Case, shall be valid to all Intents and Purposes, as Part of this Constitution, when ratified by the Legislatures of three fourths of the several states, or by Conventions in three fourths thereof, as the one or the other Mode of Ratification may be proposed by the Congress; Provided that no Amendment which may be made prior to the Year One thousand eight hundred and eight shall in any Manner affect the first and fourth Clauses in the Ninth Section of the first Article; and that no State, without its Consent, shall be deprived of its equal Suffrage in the Senate.

Article VI

All Debts contracted and Engagements entered into, before the Adoption of this Constitution, shall be as valid against the United States under this Constitution, as under the Confederation.

This Constitution, and the Laws of the United States which shall be made in Pursuance thereof; and all Treaties made, or which shall be made, under the Authority of the United States, shall be the supreme Law of the Land; and the Judges in every State shall be bound thereby, any Thing in the Constitution or Laws of any State to the Contrary notwithstanding.

The Senators and Representatives before mentioned, and the Members of the several State Legislatures and all executive and judicial Officers, both of the United States and of the several States, shall be bound by Oath or Affirmation to support this Constitution; but no religious Test shall ever be required as a Qualification to any Office or public Trust under the United States.

*Clause changed by Amendment XI.

Article VII

The Ratification of the Conventions of nine States shall be sufficient for the Establishment of this Constitution between the States so ratifying the Same.

Done in Convention by the Unanimous Consent of the States present the Seventeenth Day of September in the Year of our Lord one thousand seven hundred and Eighty seven and of the Independence of the United States of America the Twelfth.*
In Witness whereof We have hereunto subscribed our Names.

*The Consttitution was submitted on September 17, 1787, by the Constitutional Convention, was ratified by the conventions of several states at various dates up to May 29, 1790, and became effective on March 4, 1789.

Amendments to the Constitution

(The First Ten Amendments Form the Bill of Rights)

Amendment I [1791]

Congress shall make no law respecting an establishment of religion, or prohibiting the free exercise thereof; or abridging the freedom of speech, or of the press, or the right of the people peaceably to assemble, and to petition the Government for a redress of grievances.

Amendment II [1791]

A well regulated Militia being necessary to the security of a free State, the right of the people to keep and bear Arms, shall not be infringed.

Amendment III [1791]

No Soldier shall, in time of peace, be quartered in any house, without the consent of the Owner, nor in time of war, but in a manner to be prescribed by law.

Amendment IV [1791]

The right of the people to be secure in their persons, houses, papers, and effects, against unreasonable searches and seizures, shall not be violated, and no Warrants shall issue, but upon probable cause, supported by Oath or affirmation, and particularly describing the place to be searched, and the persons or things to be seized.

Amendment V [1791]

No person shall be held to answer for a capital or otherwise infamous crime, unless on a presentment or indictment of a Grand Jury, except in cases arising in the land or naval forces, or in the Militia, when in actual service in time of War or public danger; nor shall any person be subject for the same offence to be twice put in jeopardy of life or limb; nor shall be compelled in any criminal case to be a witness against himself, nor be deprived of life, liberty, or property, without due process of law; nor shall private property be taken for public use, without just compensation.

Amendment VI [1791]

In all criminal prosecutions, the accused shall enjoy the right to a speedy and public trial, by an impartial jury of the State and district wherein the crime shall have been committed, which district shall have been previously ascertained by law, and to be informed of the nature and cause of the accusation; to be confronted with the witnesses against him; to have compulsory process for obtaining witnesses in his favor, and to have the Assistance of Counsel for his defence.

Amendment VII [1791]

In Suits at common law, where the value in controversy shall exceed twenty dollars, the right of trial by jury shall be preserved, and no fact tried by a jury, shall be otherwise reexamined in any court of the United States, than according to the rules of the common law.

Amendment VIII [1791]

Excessive bail shall not be required, nor excessive fines imposed, nor cruel and unusual punishments inflicted.

Amendment IX [1791]

The enumeration in the Constitution, of certain rights, shall not be construed to deny or disparage others retained by the people.

Amendment X [1791]

The powers not delegated to the United States by the Constitution, nor prohibited by it to the States, are reserved to the States respectively, or to the people.

Amendment XI [1798]

The Judicial power of the United States shall not be construed to extend to any suit in law or equity, commenced or prosecuted against one of the United States by Citizens of another State, or by Citizens of Subjects of any Foreign State.

Amendment XII [1804]

The Electors shall meet in their respective states and vote by ballot for President and Vice-President, one of whom, at least, shall not be an inhabitant of the same state with themselves; they shall name in their ballots the person voted for as President, and in distinct ballots the person voted for as Vice-President, and they shall make distinct lists of all persons voted for as President, and of all persons voted for as Vice-President, and of the number of votes for each, which lists they shall sign and certify, and transmit sealed to the seat of the government of the United States, directed to the President of the Senate;— The President of the Senate shall, in the presence of the Senate and House of Representatives, open all the certificates and the votes shall then be counted;—The person having the greatest number of votes for President, shall be the President, if such number be a majority of the whole number of Electors appointed; and if no person have such majority, then from the persons having the highest numbers not exceeding three on the list of those voted for as President, the House of Representatives shall choose immediately, by ballot, the President. But in choosing the President, the votes shall be taken by states, the representation from each state having one vote; a quorum for this purpose shall consist of a member or members from two-thirds of the states, and a majority of all the states shall be necessary to a choice. And if the House of Representatives shall not choose a President whenever the right of choice shall devolve upon them, before the fourth day of March next following, then the Vice-President shall act as President, as in the case of the death or other constitutional disability of the President.—The person having the greatest number of votes as Vice-President, shall be the Vice-President, if such number be a majority of the whole number of Electors appointed, and if no person have a majority, then from the two highest numbers on the list, the Senate shall choose the Vice-President; a quorum for the purpose shall consist of two-thirds of the whole number of Senators, and a majority of the whole number shall be necessary to a choice. But no person constitutionally ineligible to the office of President shall be eligible to that of Vice-President of the United States.

Amendment XIII [1865]

Section 1.

Neither slavery nor involuntary servitude, except as a punishment for crime whereof the party shall have been duly convicted, shall exist within the United States, or any place subject to their jurisdiction.

Section 2.

Congress shall have power to enforce this article by appropriate legislation.

Amendment XIV [1868]

Section 1.

All persons born or naturalized in the United States, and subject to the jurisdiction thereof, are citizens of the United States and the State wherein they reside. No State shall make or enforce any law which shall abridge the privileges or immunities of citizens of the United States; nor shall any State deprive any person of life, liberty, or property, without due process of law; nor deny to any person within its jurisdiction the equal protection of the laws.

Section 2.

Representatives shall be apportioned among the several States according to their respective numbers, counting the whole number of persons in each State, excluding Indians not taxed. But when the right to vote at any election for the choice of electors for President and Vice President of the United States, Representatives in Congress, the Executive and Judicial officers of a State, or the members of the Legislature thereof, is denied to any of the male inhabitants of such State being twenty-one years of age, and citizens of the United States or in any way abridged, except for participation in rebellion or other crime, the basis of representation therein shall be reduced in the proportion which the number of such male citizens shall bear to the whole number of male citizens twenty-one years of age in such State.

Section 3.

No person shall be a Senator or Representative in Congress, or elector of President and Vice President, or hold any office, civil or military, under the United States or under any State, who, having previously taken an oath, as a member of Congress, or as an officer of the United States, or as a member of any State legislature or as an executive or judicial officer of any State to support the Constitution of the United States, shall have engaged in insurrection or rebellion against the same, or given aid or comfort to the enemies thereof. But Congress may by a vote of two-thirds of each House, remove such disability.

Section 4.

The validity of the public debt of the United States, authorized by law, including debts incurred for payment of pensions and bounties for services in suppressing insurrection or rebellion, shall not be questioned. But neither the United States nor any State shall assume or pay any debt or obligation incurred in aid of insurrection or rebellion against the United States, or any claim for the loss or emancipation of any slave; but all such debts, obligations and claims shall be held illegal and void.

Section 5.

The Congress shall have the power to enforce, by appropriate legislation, the provisions of this article.

Amendment XV [1870]

Section 1.

The right of citizens of the United States to vote shall not be denied or abridged by the United States or by any State on account of race, color, or previous condition of servitude.

Section 2.

The Congress shall have power to enforce this article by appropriate legislation.

Amendment XVI [1913]

The Congress shall have power to lay and collect taxes on incomes, from whatever source derived, without apportionment among the several States, and without regard to any census or enumeration.

Amendment XVII [1913]

The Senate of the United States shall be composed of two Senators from each State, elected by the people thereof, for six years; and each Senator shall have one vote. The electors in each State shall have the qualifications requisite for electors of the most numerous branch of the State legislatures.

When vacancies happen in the representation of any State in the Senate, the executive authority of such State shall issue writs of election to fill such vacancies: *Provided*, That the legislature of any State may empower the executive thereof to make temporary appointments until the people fill the vacancies by election as the legislature may direct.

This amendment shall not be so construed as to affect the election or term of any Senator chosen before it becomes valid as part of the Constitution.

Amendment XVIII [1919]

Section 1.

After one year from the ratification of this article the manufacture, sale, or transportation of intoxicating liquors within, the importation thereof into, or the exportation thereof from the United States and all territory subject to the jurisdiction thereof for beverage purposes is hereby prohibited.

Section 2.

The Congress and the several States shall have concurrent power to enforce this article by appropriate legislation.

Section 3.

This article shall be inoperative unless it shall have been ratified as an amendment to the Constitution by the legislatures of the several States, as provided in the Constitution, within seven years from the date of the submission hereof to the States by the Congress.

Amendment XIX [1920]

The right of citizens of the United States to vote shall not be denied or abridged by the United States or by any State on account of sex.

Congress shall have power to enforce this article by appropriate legislation.

Amendment XX [1933]

Section 1.

The terms of the President and Vice President shall end at noon on the 20th day of January, and the terms of Senators and Representatives at noon on the 3d day of January, of the years in which such terms would have ended if this article had not been ratified; and the terms of their successors shall then begin.

Section 2.

The Congress shall assemble at least once in every year, and such meeting shall begin at noon on the 3d day of January, unless they shall by law appoint a different day.

Section 3.

If, at the time fixed for the beginning of the term of the President, the President elect shall have died, the Vice President elect shall become President. If a President shall not have been chosen before the time fixed for the beginning of his term, or if the President elect shall have failed to qualify, then the Vice President elect shall act as President until a President shall have qualified; and the Congress may by law provide for the case wherein neither a President elect nor a Vice President elect shall have qualified, declaring who shall then act as President, or the manner in which one who is to act shall be selected, and such person shall act accordingly until a President or Vice President shall have qualified.

Section 4.

The Congress may by law provide for the case of the death of any of the persons from whom the House of Representatives may choose a President whenever the right of choice shall have devolved upon them, and for the case of the death of any of the persons from whom the Senate may choose a Vice-President whenever the right of choice shall have devolved upon them.

Section 5.

Sections 1 and 2 shall take effect on the 15th day of October following the ratification of this article.

Section 6.

This article shall be inoperative unless it shall have been ratified as an amendment to the Constitution by the legislatures of three-fourths of the several States within seven years from the date of its submission.

Amendment XXI [1933]

Section 1.

The eighteenth article of amendment to the Constitution of the United States is hereby repealed.

Section 2.

The transportation or importation into any State, Territory, or possession of the United States for delivery or use therein of intoxicating liquors, in violation of the laws thereof, is hereby prohibited.

Section 3.

This article shall be inoperative unless it shall have been ratified as an amendment to the Constitution by conventions in the several States, as provided in the Constitution, within seven years from the date of the submission hereof to the States by the Congress.

Amendment XXII [1951]

Section 1.

No person shall be elected to the office of the President more than twice, and no person who has held the office of President, or acted as President, for more than two years of a term to which some other person was elected President shall be elected to the office of the President more than once. But this Article shall not apply to any person holding the office of President when this Article was proposed by the Congress, and shall not prevent any person who may be holding the office of President or acting as President, during the term within which this Article becomes operative from holding the office of President or acting as President during the remainder of such term.

Amendment XXIII [1961]

Section 1.

The District constituting the seat of Government of the United States shall appoint in such manner as the Congress may direct:
 A number of electors of President and Vice President equal to the whole number of Senators and Representatives in Congress to which the District would be entitled if it were a State, but in no event more than the least populous State; they shall be in addition to those appointed by the States, but they shall be considered, for the purposes of the election of President and Vice President, to be electors appointed by a State; and they

shall meet in the District and perform such duties as provided by the twelfth article of Amendment.

Section 2.

The Congress shall have power to enforce this article by appropriate legislation.

Amendment XXIV [1964]

Section 1.

The right of citizens of the United States to vote in any primary or other election for President or Vice President, for electors for President or Vice President, or for Senator or Representative in Congress, shall not be denied or abridged by the United States or any State by reason of failure to pay any poll tax or other tax.

Section 2.

The Congress shall have the power to enforce this article by appropriate legislation.

Amendment XXV [1967]

Section 1.

In case of the removal of the President from office or his death or resignation, the Vice President shall become President.

Section 2.

Whenever there is a vacancy in the office of the Vice President, the President shall nominate a Vice President who shall take the office upon confirmation by a majority vote of both houses of Congress.

Section 3.

Whenever the President transmits to the President pro tempore of the Senate and the Speaker of the House of Representatives his written declaration that he is unable to discharge the powers and duties of his office, and until he transmits to them a written declaration to the contrary, such powers and duties shall be discharged by the Vice President as Acting President.

Section 4.

Whenever the Vice President and a majority of either the principal officers of the executive departments or of such other body as Congress may by law provide, transmit to the President pro tempore of the Senate and the Speaker of the House of Representatives their written declaration that the President is unable to discharge the powers and duties of his office, the Vice President shall immediately assume the powers and duties of the office as Acting President.

Thereafter, when the President transmits to the President pro tempore of the Senate and the Speaker of the House of Representatives his written declaration that no inability exists, he shall resume the powers and duties of his office unless the Vice President and a majority of either the principal officers of the executive department or of such other body as Congress may by law provide, transmit within four days to the President pro tempore of the Senate and the Speaker of the House of Representatives their written declaration that the President is unable to discharge the powers and duties of his office. Thereupon Congress shall decide the issue, assembling within 48 hours for that purpose if not in session. If the Congress, within 21 days after receipt of the latter written declaration, or, if Congress is not in session, within 21 days after Congress is required to assemble, determines by two-thirds vote of both houses that the President is unable to discharge the powers and duties of his office, the Vice President shall continue to discharge the same as Acting President; otherwise, the President shall resume the powers and duties of his office.

Amendment XXVI [1971]

Section 1.

The right of citizens of the United States, who are 18 years of age or older, to vote shall not be denied or abridged by the United States or any state on account of age.

Section 2.

The Congress shall have the power to enforce this article by appropriate legislation.

Amendment XXVII [1992]

No law varying the compensation for the service of Senators and Representatives shall take effect until an election of Representatives shall have intervened.

Choosing the President

Election Year	Elected to Office			
	President	Party	Vice President	Party
1789	George Washington		John Adams	Parties not yet established
1792	George Washington		John Adams	Federalist
1796	John Adams	Federalist	Thomas Jefferson	Democratic-Republican
1800	Thomas Jefferson	Democratic-Republican	Aaron Burr	Democratic-Republican
1804	Thomas Jefferson	Democratic-Republican	George Clinton	Democratic-Republican
1808	James Madison	Democratic-Republican	George Clinton	Democratic-Republican
1812	James Madison	Democratic-Republican	Elbridge Gerry	Democratic-Republican
1816	James Monroe	Democratic-Republican	Daniel D. Tompkins	Democratic-Republican
1820	James Monroe	Democratic-Republican	Daniel D. Tompkins	Democratic-Republican
1824	John Quincy Adams Elected by House of Representatives because no candidate received a majority of electoral votes.	National Republican	John C. Calhoun	Democratic
1828	Andrew Jackson	Democratic	John C. Calhoun	Democratic
1832	Andrew Jackson	Democratic	Martin Van Buren	Democratic

Major Opponents		Electoral Vote		Popular Vote
For President	Party			
		Washington	69	Electors selected by state legislatures
		Adams	34	
George Clinton	Democratic-Republican	Washington	132	Electors selected by state legislatures
		Adams	77	
		Clinton	50	
Thomas Pinckney	Federalist	Adams	71	Electors selected by state legislatures
Aaron Burr	Democratic-Republican	Jefferson	68	
		Pinckney	59	
John Adams	Federalist	Jefferson	73	Electors selected by state legislatures
Charles Cotesworth Pinckney	Federalist	Adams	65	
Charles Cotesworth Pinckney	Federalist	Jefferson	162	Electors selected by state legislatures
		Pinckney	14	
Charles Cotesworth Pinckney	Federalist	Madison	122	Electors selected by state legislatures
George Clinton	Eastern Republican	Pinckney	47	
De Witt Clinton	Democratic-Republican (antiwar faction) and Federalist	Madison	128	Electors selected by state legislatures
		Clinton	89	
Rufus King	Federalist	Monroe	183	Electors selected by state legislatures
		King	34	
		Monroe	231	Electors selected by state legislatures
		John Quincy Adams	1	
Andrew Jackson	Democratic	Adams	84	113,122
Henry Clay	Democratic-Republican	Jackson	99	151,271
William H. Crawford	Democratic-Republican	Clay	37	47,531
		Crawford	41	40,856
John Quincy Adams	National Republican	Jackson	178	642,553
		Adams	83	500,897
Henry Clay	National Republican	Jackson	219	701,780
William Wirt	Anti-Masonic	Clay	49	482,205
		Wirt	7	100,715
		Floyd	11	Delegates chosen by South Carolina legislature

Election Year	Elected to Office			
	President	Party	Vice President	Party
1836	Martin Van Buren	Democratic	Richard M. Johnson First and only vice president elected by Senate (1837), having failed to receive a majority of electoral votes.	Democratic
1840	William Henry Harrison Died in 1841; succeeded by John Tyler.	Whig	John Tyler Assumed presidency in 1841; vice president's office was left vacant.	Whig
1844	James K. Polk	Democratic	George M. Dallas	Democratic
1848	Zachary Taylor Died in 1850; succeeded by Millard Fillmore.	Whig	Millard Fillmore Assumed presidency in 1850; vice president's office was left vacant.	Whig
1852	Franklin Pierce	Democratic	William R. King	Democratic
1856	James Buchanan	Democratic	John C. Breckenridge	Democratic
1860	Abraham Lincoln	Republican	Hannibal Hamlin	Republican
1864	Abraham Lincoln Died in 1865; succeeded by Andrew Johnson.	National Union/Republican	Andrew Johnson Assumed presidency in 1865; vice president's office was left vacant.	National Union/Republican
1868	Ulysses S. Grant	Republican	Schuyler Colfax	Republican
1872	Ulysses S. Grant	Republican	Henry Wilson	Republican

Major Opponents		Electoral Vote		Popular Vote
For President	Party			
Daniel Webster Hugh L. White William Henry Harrison	Whig Whig Anti-Masonic	Van Buren Harrison White Webster Mangum	170 73 26 14 11	764,176 550,816 146,107 41,201 Delegates chosen by South Carolina legislature
Martin Van Buren James G. Birney	Democratic Liberty	Harrison Van Buren	234 60	1,274,624 1,127,781
Henry Clay James G. Birney	Whig Liberty	Polk Clay Birney	170 105 —	1,338,464 1,300,097 62,300
Lewis Cass Martin Van Buren	Democratic Free-Soil	Taylor Cass Van Buren	163 127 —	1,360,967 1,222,342 291,263
Winfield Scott John P. Hale	Whig Free-Soil	Pierce Scott Hale	254 42 —	1,601,117 1,385,453 155,825
John C. Fremont Millard Fillmore	Republican American (Know-Nothing)	Buchanan Fremont Fillmore	174 114 8	1,832,955 1,339,932 871,731
John Bell Stephen A. Douglas John C. Breckinridge	Constitutional Union Democratic Democratic	Lincoln Breckinridge Douglas Bell	180 72 12 39	1,865,593 848,356 1,382,713 592,906
George B. McClennan	Democratic	Lincoln McClennan Eleven secessionist states did not participate.	212 21	2,218,388 1,812,807
Horatio Seymour	Democratic	Grant Seymour Texas, Mississippi, and Virginia did not participate.	286 80	3,598,235 2,706,829
Horace Greeley Charles O'Connor James Black	Democratic and Liberal Republican Democratic Temperance	Grant Greeley Greeley died before the Electoral College met. His electoral votes were divided among the four minor candidates.	286 80	3,598,235 2,834,761

Election Year	Elected to Office			
	President	Party	Vice President	Party
1876	Rutherford B. Hayes Contested result settled by special election commission in favor of Hayes.	Republican	William A. Wheeler	Republican
1880	James A. Garfield Died in 1881; succeeded by Chester A. Arthur.	Republican	Chester A. Arthur Assumed presidency in 1881; vice president's office was left vacant	Republican
1884	Grover Cleveland	Democratic	Thomas A. Hendricks	Democratic
1888	Benjamin Harrison	Republican	Levi P. Morton	Republican
1892	Grover Cleveland	Democratic	Adlai Stevenson	Democratic
1896	William McKinley	Republican	Garret A. Hobart	Republican
1900	William McKinley Died in 1901; succeeded by Theodore Roosevelt.	Republican	Theodore Roosevelt Assumed presidency in 1901; vice president's office was left vacant	Republican
1904	Theodore Roosevelt	Republican	Charles W. Fairbanks	Republican
1908	William Howard Taft	Republican	James S. Sherman	Republican
1912	Woodrow Wilson	Democratic	Thomas R. Marshall	Democratic

Major Opponents		Electoral Vote		Popular Vote
For President	Party			
Samuel J. Tilden	Democratic	Hayes	185	4,034,311
Peter Cooper	Greenback	Tilden	184	4,288,546
Green Clay Smith	Prohibition	Cooper	—	75,973
Winfield S. Hancock	Democratic	Garfield	214	4,446,158
James B. Weaver	Greenback	Hancock	155	4,444,260
Neal Dow	Prohibition	Weaver	—	305,997
James G. Blaine	Republican	Cleveland	219	4,874,621
John P. St. John	Prohibition	Blaine	182	4,848,936
Benjamin F. Butler	Greenback	Butler	—	175,096
		St. John	—	147,482
Grover Cleveland	Democratic	Harrison	233	5,447,129
Clinton B. Fisk	Prohibition	Cleveland	168	5,537,857
Alson J. Streeter	Union Labor			
Benjamin Harrison	Republican	Cleveland	277	5,555,426
James B. Weaver	Populist	Harrison	145	5,182,600
John Bidwell	Prohibition	Weaver	22	1,029,846
William Jennings Bryan	Democratic, Populist, and National Silver Republican	McKinley	271	7,102,246
		Bryan	176	6,492,559
Joshua Levering	Prohibition			
John M. Palmer	National Democratic			
William Jennings Bryan	Democratic and Fusion Populist	McKinley	292	7,218,039
		Bryan	155	6,358,345
Wharton Barker	Anti-Fusion Populist	Woolley	—	209,004
Eugene V. Debs	Social Democratic	Debs	—	86,935
John G. Woolley	Prohibition			
Alton B. Parker	Democratic	Roosevelt	336	7,626,593
Eugene V. Debs	Socialist	Parker	140	5,082,898
Silas C. Swallow	Prohibition	Debs	—	402,489
		Swallow	—	258,596
William Jennings Bryan	Democratic	Taft	321	7,676,258
Eugene V. Debs	Socialist	Bryan	162	6,406,801
Eugene W. Chafin	Prohibition	Debs	—	420,380
		Chafin	—	252,821
William Howard Taft	Republican	Wilson	435	6,296,547
Theodore Roosevelt	Progressive (Bull Moose)	Roosevelt	88	4,118,571
Eugene V. Debs	Socialist	Taft	8	3,486,720
Eugene W. Chafin	Prohibition			

Election Year	Elected to Office			
	President	Party	Vice President	Party
1916	Woodrow Wilson	Democratic	Thomas R. Marshall	Democratic
1920	Warren G. Harding Died in 1923; succeeded by Calvin Coolidge	Republican	Calvin Coolidge Assumed presidency in 1923; vice president's office was left vacant	Republican
1924	Calvin Coolidge	Republican	Charles G. Dawes	Republican
1928	Herbert C. Hoover	Republican	Charles Curtis	Republican
1932	Franklin D. Roosevelt	Democratic	John N. Garner	Democratic
1936	Franklin D. Roosevelt	Democratic	John N. Garner	Democratic
1940	Franklin D. Roosevelt	Democratic	Henry A. Wallace	Democratic
1944	Franklin D. Roosevelt Died in 1945; succeeded by Harry S. Truman	Democratic	Harry S. Truman Assumed presidency in 1945; vice president's office was left vacant	Democratic
1948	Harry S. Truman	Democratic	Alben W. Barkley	Democratic
1952	Dwight D. Eisenhower	Republican	Richard M. Nixon	Republican
1956	Dwight D. Eisenhower	Republican	Richard M. Nixon	Republican
1960	John F. Kennedy Died in 1963; succeeded by Lyndon B. Johnson	Democratic	Lyndon B. Johnson Assumed presidency in 1963; vice president's office was left vacant	Democratic
1964	Lyndon B. Johnson	Democratic	Hubert H. Humphrey	Democratic
1968	Richard M. Nixon	Republican	Spiro T. Agnew	Republican

Major Opponents		Electoral Vote		Popular Vote
For President	Party			
Charles E. Hughes Allen L. Benson J. Frank Hanly Charles W. Fairbanks	Republican Socialist Prohibition Republican	Wilson Hughes	277 254	9,127,695 8,533,507
James M. Cox Eugene V. Debs	Democratic Socialist	Harding Cox Debs	404 127 —	16,133,314 9,140,884 913,664
John W. Davis Robert M. LaFollette	Democratic Progressive	Coolidge Davis LaFollette	382 136 13	15,717,553 8,386,169 4,184,050
Alfred E. Smith Norman Thomas	Democratic Socialist	Hoover Smith	444 87	21,391,993 15,016,169
Herbert C. Hoover Norman Thomas	Republican Socialist	Roosevelt Hoover	472 59	22,809,638 15,758,901
Alfred M. Landon William Lemke	Republican Union	Roosevelt Landon	523 8	27,752,869 16,674,665
Wendell L. Wilkie	Republican	Roosevelt Wilkie	449 82	27,263,448 22,336,260
Thomas E. Dewey	Republican	Roosevelt Dewey	432 99	25,611,936 22,013,372
Thomas E. Dewey J. Strom Thurmond Henry A. Wallace	Republican States' Rights Democratic Progressive	Truman Dewey Thurmond Wallace	303 189 39 —	24,105,182 21,970,065 1,169,063 1,157,326
Adlai E. Stevenson	Democratic	Eisenhower Stevenson	442 89	33,936,137 27,314,649
Adlai E. Stevenson	Democratic	Eisenhower Stevenson	457 73	35,585,245 26,030,172
Richard M. Nixon	Republican	Kennedy Nixon Byrd (Ind. Dem.)	303 219 15 —	34,227,096 34,108,546
Barry M. Goldwater	Republican	Johnson Goldwater	486 52	43,126,584 27,177,838
Hubert H. Humphrey George C. Wallace	Democratic American Independent	Nixon Humphrey Wallace	301 191 46	31,770,237 31,270,533 9,906,141

Election Year	Elected to Office			
	President	Party	Vice President	Party
1972	Richard M. Nixon Resigned in 1974; succeeded by Gerald R. Ford	Republican	Spiro T. Agnew Resigned in 1974; replaced by Gerald R. Ford, who was in turn replaced by Nelson Rockefeller	Republican
1976	Jimmy Carter	Democratic	Walter Mondale	Democratic
1980	Ronald Reagan	Republican	George Bush	Republican
1984	Ronald Reagan	Republican	George Bush	Republican
1988	George H. Bush	Republican	J. Danforth Quayle	Republican
1992	Bill Clinton	Democratic	Albert Gore, Jr.	Democratic
1996	Bill Clinton	Democratic	Albert Gore, Jr.	Democratic
2000	George W. Bush	Republican	Richard Cheney	Republican
2004	George W. Bush	Republican	Richard Cheney	Republican
2008	Barack Obama	Democratic	Joseph Biden	Democratic

Major Opponents		Electoral Vote		Popular Vote
For President	Party			
George S. McGovern	Democratic	Nixon	520	46,740,323
		McGovern	17	28,901,598
		Hospers (Va.)	1	—
Gerald R. Ford	Republican	Carter	297	40,830,763
Eugene McCarthy	Independent	Ford	240	39,147,793
		McCarthy	—	756,631
Jimmy Carter	Democratic	Reagan	489	43,899,248
John B. Anderson	Independent	Carter	49	35,481,435
Ed Clark	Libertarian	Anderson	—	5,719,437
Walter Mondale	Democratic	Reagan	525	54,451,521
David Bergland	Libertarian	Mondale	13	37,565,334
Michael Dukakis	Democratic	Bush	426	47,946,422
		Dukakis	112	41,016,429
George Bush	Republican	Clinton	370	44,908,233
H. Ross Perot	Independent	Bush	168	39,102,282
		Perot	—	19,217,213
Robert Dole	Republican	Clinton	379	45,590,703
H. Ross Perot	Independent	Dole	159	37,816,307
		Perot	—	7,866,284
Al Gore	Democratic	Bush	271	50,456,141
Ralph Nader	Green	Gore	266	50,996,039
Patrick Buchanan	Reform	Nader	—	2,882,807
		Buchanan	—	448,868
John Kerry	Democratic	Bush	286	62,028,194
Ralph Nader	Green	Kerry	252	59,027,612
Michael Badnarik	Libertarian	Nader	—	460,650
		Badnarik	—	396,888
John McCain	Republican	Obama	365	69,456,897
Ralph Nader	Green	McCain	173	59,934,814
		Nader	—	

Glossary

527 Committees: Organizations created by individuals and groups to influence the outcomes of elections by raising and spending money that candidates and political parties raise and spend legally.

AARP: An interest group representing the concerns of older Americans (formerly known as the American Association of Retired Persons).

Ability to pay theory of taxation: The approach to government finance that holds that taxes should be based on an individual's ability to pay.

Absolute monarchy: A country ruled by one person, usually a king or queen.

Access: The opportunity to communicate directly with legislators and other government officials in hopes of influencing the details of policy.

Address from office: A procedure for removing judicial officials that is initiated by the governor and requires a two-thirds' vote by the legislature.

Administrative law: Administrative rules adopted by regulatory agencies.

Adversary proceeding: A legal procedure in which each side presents evidence and arguments to bolster its position while rebutting evidence that might support the other side.

Advocacy groups: Organizations created to seek benefits on behalf of groups of persons who are in some way incapacitated or otherwise unable to represent their own interests.

Affirm: The action of an appeals court to uphold the decision of a lower court.

Affirmative action: A program designed to ensure equal opportunities in employment and college admissions for racial minorities and women.

Agenda building: The process through which issues become matters of public concern and government action.

Agents of socialization: Those factors that contribute to political socialization by shaping formal and informal learning.

Aggravated offenses: Violent crimes.

Air war: Campaign activities that involve the media, including television, radio, and the Internet.

Allocational urban policies: Local programs that are more or less neutral in their impact on the local economy.

Allowable: The maximum permissible rate of production for oil and gas wells in Texas as set by the Railroad Commission.

American Bar Association (ABA): An interest group representing the concerns of lawyers.

American Civil Liberties Union (ACLU): A group organized to protect the rights of individuals as outlined in the U.S. Constitution.

American Federation of Labor-Congress of Industrial Organizations (AFL-CIO): A labor union federation.

American Indian Movement (AIM): A group representing the views of Native Americans.

American Medical Association (AMA): An interest group representing the concerns of physicians.

Americans with Disabilities Act (ADA): A federal law designed to end discrimination against persons with disabilities and eliminate barriers to their full participation in American society.

Amicus curiae or friend of the court briefs: Written legal arguments presented by parties not directly involved in the case, including interest groups and units of government.

Annexation: The authority of a city to increase its geographic size by extending its boundaries to take in adjacent unincorporated areas.

Anticlericalism: A movement that opposes the institutional power of religion and the involvement of the church in all aspects of public and political life.

Antifederalists: Americans opposed to the ratification of the new Constitution because they thought it gave too much power to the national government.

Appeal: The taking of a case from a lower court to a higher court by the losing party in a lower-court decision.

Apportionment: The allocation of legislative seats among the states.

Appropriation bill: A legislative authorization to spend money for particular purposes.

Appropriation process: The procedure through which Congress legislatively provides money for a particular purpose.

Arraignment: A judicial proceeding at which a suspect is formally charged with a crime and asked to enter a plea.

Articles of impeachment: A document listing the impeachable offenses that the House believes the president committed.

At-large election: A method for choosing public officials in which the citizens of an entire political subdivision, such as a state, vote to select officeholders.

Attack journalism: An approach to news reporting in which journalists take an adversarial attitude toward candidates and elected officials.

Attorney general's opinion: A written interpretation of existing law.

Authorization process: The procedure through which Congress legislatively establishes a program, defines its general purpose, devises procedures for its operation, specifies an agency to implement the program, and indicates an approximate level of funding for the program but does not actually provide money.

Baby-boom generation: The exceptionally large number of Americans born during the late 1940s, 1950s, and early 1960s.

Bail: Money or securities posted by accused persons to guarantee their appearance at later proceedings.

Balance of power: A system of political alignments in which peace and security may be maintained through an equilibrium of forces between rival groups of nations.

Balance the ticket: An attempt to select a vice presidential candidate who will appeal to different groups of voters than the presidential nominee.

Balanced budget: Budget receipts equal budget expenditures.

Base voters: Rock-solid Republicans or hardcore Democrats, firmly committed to voting for their party's nominee.

Battleground states: Swing states in which the relative strength of the two major party presidential candidates is close enough so that either candidate could conceivably carry the state.

Biased question: A survey question that produces results tilted to one side or another.

Biased sample: A sample that tends to produce results that do not reflect the true characteristics of the universe because it is unrepresentative of the universe.

Bicameral legislature: A legislative body with two chambers.

Bicameralism: The division of the legislative branch of government into two chambers.

Biennium: The state's two-year budget program.

Bilingual education: The teaching of academic subjects in both English and a student's native language, usually Spanish.

Bill: A proposed law.

Bill of attainder: A law declaring a person or a group of persons guilty of a crime and providing for punishment without benefit of a judicial proceeding.

Bill of rights: A constitutional document guaranteeing individual rights and liberties.

Bill of Rights: The U.S. Bill of Rights is the first ten amendments to the U.S. Constitution.

Bipartisan Campaign Reform Act (BCRA): A campaign finance reform law designed to limit the political influence of big money campaign contributors.

Bipartisanship: The close cooperation and general agreement between the two major political parties in dealing with foreign policy matters.

Blame avoidance: The effort on the part of government officials to assign responsibility for policy failures to someone else.

Blanket primary: A primary election system that allows voters to select candidates without regard for party affiliation.

Block grant program: A federal grant program that provides money for a program in a broad, general policy area, such as childcare or job training.

Blue states: States that voted for Democratic presidential candidates in recent presidential elections, symbolized by the color blue on the electoral college map.

Bond: A certificate of indebtedness issued to investors who loan money for interest income; in lay terms, a bond is an IOU.

Bond election: An election for the purpose of obtaining voter approval for a local government going into debt.

Booking: An administrative procedure in which law enforcement personnel document a suspect's arrest.

Boosters: People who promote local economic development.

Brady Act: A federal gun control law that requires a background check on an unlicensed purchaser of a firearm in order to determine whether the individual can legally own a weapon.

Branch banking: A business practice whereby a single, large bank conducts business from several locations.

Broadcast media: Television, radio, and the Internet.

Budget deficit: The amount by which annual budget expenditures exceed annual budget receipts.

Budget execution authority: The power to cut agency spending or transfer money between agencies during the period when the legislature is not in session.

Budget surplus: The sum by which annual budget receipts exceed annual budget expenditures.

Building codes: Municipal ordinances that set minimum standards for the types of materials used in construction, building design, and construction methods employed in all buildings within the city.

Bundling: A procedure in which an interest group gathers checks from individual supporters made out to the campaigns of targeted candidates.

Burden of proof: The legal obligation of one party in a lawsuit to prove its position to a court.

Cabinet departments: Major administrative units of the federal government that have responsibility for the conduct of a wide range of government operations.

Capital expenditure: The purchase by government of a permanent, fixed asset, such as a new city hall or highway overpass.

Capital punishment: The death penalty.

Capitalism: An economic system characterized by individual and corporate ownership of the means of production, and a market economy based on the supply and demand of goods and services.

Captured agencies: Agencies that work to benefit the economic interests they regulate rather than serving the public interest.

Catching the late train: The practice of giving campaign contributions to a candidate after an election is over and the candidate has won.

Categorical grant program: A federal grant program that provides funds to state and local governments for a narrowly defined purpose.

Caucus method of delegate selection: A procedure for choosing national party convention delegates that involves party voters participating in a series of precinct and district or county political meetings.

Cause groups: Organizations whose members care intensely about a single issue or small group of related issues.

Central Intelligence Agency (CIA): The federal agency that gathers and evaluates foreign intelligence information in the interest of the national security.

Certiorari or cert: The technical term for the Supreme Court's decision to hear arguments and make a ruling in a case.

Chamber of Commerce: A business federation representing the interests of more than 3 million businesses of all sizes, sectors, and regions.

Charter school: A publicly funded but privately managed school that operates under the terms of a formal contract, or charter, with the state.

Checks and balances: The overlapping of the powers of the branches of government designed to ensure that public officials limit the authority of one another.

Chief executive: The head of the executive branch of government.

Chief of state: The official head of government.

Children's Health Insurance Program (CHIP): A federal program designed to provide health insurance to children from low-income families whose parents are not poor enough to qualify for Medicaid.

Citizen groups: Organizations created to support government policies that they believe will benefit the public at large.

City charter: The basic law of a city that defines its powers, responsibilities, and organization.

City manager: A professional administrator hired by city council in the council-manager form of city government to manage the day-to-day affairs of city government.

City ordinances: Laws enacted by the governing body of a municipality.

Civic culture: A political culture that is conducive to the development of an efficient, effective government that meets the needs of its citizens in a timely and professional manner.

Civil case: A legal dispute concerning a private conflict between two parties—individuals, corporations, or government agencies.

Civil defendant: The responding party in a civil suit.

Civil liberties: The protection of the individual from the unrestricted power of government.

Civil rights: The protection of the individual from arbitrary or discriminatory acts by government or by individuals based on that person's group status, such as race or gender.

Civil union: A legal partnership between two men or two women that gives the couple all the benefits, protections, and responsibilities under law as are granted to spouses in a traditional marriage.

Civilian supremacy of the armed forces: The concept that the armed forces should be under the direct control of civilian authorities.

Class action lawsuits: Lawsuits brought by one or more people on behalf of themselves and others who are similarly situated.

Clearance rate: The proportion of crimes known to authorities for which an arrest is made.

Closed primary: An election system that limits primary election participation to registered party members.

Closed rule: A rule that prohibits floor consideration of amendments on the House floor.

Cloture: The procedure for ending a filibuster.

Club for Growth: A cause group that favors a low-tax and limited government agenda.

Coattail effect: A political phenomenon in which a strong candidate for one office gives a boost to fellow party members on the same ballot seeking other offices.

Cold War: The period of international tension between the United States and the Soviet Union lasting from the late 1940s through the late 1980s.

Collective bargaining: The negotiation between an employer and a union representing employees over the terms and conditions of employment.

Commerce Clause: The constitutional provision giving Congress authority to "regulate commerce . . . among the several states."

Commissioners court: The board of directors for county government composed of four county commissioners and the county judge.

Common Cause: A group organized to work for campaign finance reform and other good-government causes.

Communities Organized for Public Service (COPS): A predominantly Latino neighborhood reform organization in San Antonio.

Community policing: An approach to law enforcement that seeks to reduce crime by increasing the interaction and cooperation between local law enforcement agencies and the people and neighborhoods they serve.

Commutation: A reduction of punishment for a criminal offense.

Compulsory voting: The legal requirement that citizens participate in national elections.

Concurrent powers: Those powers of government that are jointly exercised by the national government and state governments.

Concurring opinion: A judicial statement that agrees with the Court's ruling but disagrees with the reasoning of the majority opinion.

Confederation: A league of nearly independent states, similar to the United Nations today.

Conferees: Members of a conference committee.

Conference: A closed meeting attended only by the members of the Supreme Court.

Conference committee: A special committee created to negotiate differences on similar pieces of legislation passed by the House and Senate.

Conference report: A revised bill produced by a conference committee.

Conflict of interest: A situation in which the personal interests of a public official may clash with that official's professional responsibilities.

Conservatism: The political philosophy that government power undermines the development of the individual and diminishes society as a whole.

Constituency: The district from which an officeholder is elected.

Constituency service: The action of members of Congress and their staffs attending to the individual, particular needs of constituents.

Constituents: The people an officeholder represents.

Constitution: A fundamental law by which a state or nation is organized and governed.

Constitutional amendment: A formal, written change or addition to the nation's governing document.

Constitutional law: Law that involves the interpretation and application of the Constitution.

Constitutional monarchy: A country in which the powers of the ruler are limited to those granted under the Constitution and the laws of the nation.

Constitutional revision: The process of drafting a new constitution.

Consumer Price Index (CPI): A measure of inflation that is based on the changing cost of goods and services.

Containment: The American policy of keeping the Soviet Union from expanding its sphere of control.

Contract case: A civil suit dealing with disputes over written or implied legal agreements, such as a suit over a faulty roof repair job.

Conventional forces: Non-nuclear forces.

Convergence theory: The view that communism and capitalism were evolving in similar ways, or converging.

Corporation for Public Broadcasting: A government agency chartered and funded by the U.S. government with the goal of promoting public broadcasting.

Cost-benefit analysis: An evaluation of a proposed policy or regulation based on a comparison of its expected benefits and anticipated costs.

Cost-of-living adjustment (COLA): A mechanism designed to regularly increase the size of a payment to compensate for the effects of inflation.

Council-manager form of city government: A structure of municipal government in which the city council/mayor appoints a professional administrator called a city manager to act as the chief executive officer of the municipality.

Criminal case: A legal dispute dealing with an alleged violation of a penal law.

Criminal defendant: The party charged with a criminal offense.

Cumulative voting system: An election system that allows individual voters to cast more than one ballot in the simultaneous election of several officials.

De facto segregation: Racial separation resulting from factors other than law, such as housing patterns.

De jure segregation: Racial separation required by law.

Dedicated funds: Constitutional or statutory provisions that set aside revenue for particular purposes.

Dedicated Highway Fund: A constitutionally earmarked account containing money set aside for building, maintaining, and policing state highways.

Deed adjudication: A type of probation that can be granted by a judge to a defendant who pleads guilty or *nolo contendere* to certain, relatively less serious offenses.

Deed restrictions: Private contractual agreements that limit what residential property owners can do with their houses and land. Almost every modern residential subdivision in the state has deed restrictions.

Defense of Marriage Act: The federal law stipulating that each state may choose either to recognize or not recognize same-sex marriages performed in other states.

Defense policy: Public policy that concerns the armed forces of the United States.

Deferred adjudication: A type of probation that can be granted by a judge to a defendant who pleads guilty or *nolo contendere* to certain, relatively less serious offenses.

Delegated or enumerated powers: The powers explicitly granted to the national government by the Constitution.

Democracy: A system of government in which the people hold ultimate political power.

Democratic peace: The concept that democracies do not wage war against other democracies.

Depression: A severe and prolonged economic slump characterized by decreased business activity and high unemployment.

Deracialization: The attempt of political candidates to deemphasize racially divisive themes in order to garner crossover support from voters of other races/ethnicities while receiving the overwhelming majority of support from voters of the candidate's own racial/ethnic group.

Détente: A period of improved communications and visible efforts to relieve tensions between the two superpowers.

Deterrence: The ability of a nation to prevent an attack against itself or its allies by threat of massive retaliation.

Developing countries: Nations with relatively low levels of per capita income.

Developmental urban policies: Local programs that enhance the economic position of a community in its competition with other communities.

Dillon's rule: The legal principle that a city can exercise only those powers expressly allowed by state law.

Diplomacy: The process by which nations carry on political relations with each other.

Diplomatic relations: A system of official contacts between two nations in which the countries exchange ambassadors and other diplomatic personnel and operate embassies in each other's country.

Direct democracy: A political system in which the citizens vote directly on matters of public concern.

Discharge petition: A procedure whereby a majority of the members of the House of Representatives can force a committee to report a bill to the floor of the House.

Discretionary spending: Budgetary expenditures that are not mandated by law or contract, including annual funding for education, the Coast Guard, space exploration, highway construction, defense, foreign aid, and the Federal Bureau of Investigation (FBI).

Disfranchisement: The denial of voting rights.

Dissenting opinion: A judicial statement that disagrees with the decision of the court's majority.

District election: A method for choosing public officials in which a political subdivision, such as a state or county, is divided into districts and each district elects one official.

Divided government: The phenomenon of one political party controlling the legislative branch of government while the other holds the executive branch.

Doctrine of natural rights: The belief that individual rights transcend the power of government.

Domestic partnership: A legal status similar to civil unions in that it confers rights similar to marriage.

Domestic-relations case: A civil suit based on the law involving the relationships between husband and wife, and between parents and children, such as divorce and child custody cases.

Don't ask, don't tell policy: The official policy for dealing with gay men and lesbians in the U.S. armed forces. The military would not ask new recruits about their sexual orientation and would stop conducting investigations aimed at identifying and discharging homosexuals, but it would discharge service members who revealed their sexual orientation.

Double jeopardy: The government trying a criminal defendant a second time for the same offense after an acquittal in an earlier prosecution.

Dual school system: Separate sets of schools for white and African American youngsters.

Due Process Clause: The constitutional provision that declares that no state shall "deprive any person of life, liberty, or property, without due process of law."

Due process of law: The constitutional principle holding that government must follow fair and regular procedures in actions that could lead to an individual's suffering loss of life, liberty, or property.

Earmarks: Legislative provision that direct that funds be spent for particular purposes.

Earned Income Tax Credit (EITC): A federal program designed to give cash assistance to low-income working families by refunding some or all of the taxes they pay and, if their wages are low, giving them a payment rather than assessing a tax.

Edgewood v. Kirby: A lawsuit filed by a number of poor school districts, including the Edgewood Independent School District (ISD) in San Antonio, against the state's system of education finance.

Election campaign: An attempt to get information to voters that will persuade them to elect a candidate or not elect an opponent.

Election precinct: An election district.

Electoral college: The system established in the Constitution for indirect election of the president and vice president.

Electoral mandate: The expression of popular support for a particular policy demonstrated through the electoral process.

Electors: Individuals selected in each state to officially cast that state's electoral votes.

Elite theory, or elitism: The view that political power is held by a small group of people who dominate politics by controlling economic resources.

EMILY's List: A PAC whose goal is the election of pro-choice Democratic women to office.

Empirical analysis: A method of study that relies on experience and scientific observation.

Employees Retirement System (ERS) Trust Fund: A pension fund for state employees.

Employment Non-Discrimination Act (ENDA): A proposed federal law that would protect Americans from employment discrimination on the basis of sexual orientation.

Enfranchise: To grant the right to vote.

Enterprise zones: A state program that allows local governments to designate certain areas, called enterprise zones, in which private investors can receive property tax abatements, local sales tax rebates (refunds), and government-backed low-interest loans.

Entitlement program: A government program providing benefits to all persons qualified to receive them under law.

Environmental Protection Agency (EPA): The federal agency responsible for enforcing the nation's environmental laws.

Equal Employment Opportunity Commission (EEOC): An agency that investigates and rules on charges of employment discrimination.

Equal Protection Clause: A provision of the Fourteenth Amendment of the U.S. Constitution that declares that "No State shall . . . deny to any person within its jurisdiction the equal protection of the laws."

Equal protection of the law: The legal principle that state laws may not arbitrarily discriminate against persons.

Equal Rights Amendment (ERA): A proposed amendment guaranteeing equality before the law, regardless of sex.

Equal-time rule: An FCC regulation requiring broadcasters to provide an equivalent opportunity to opposing political candidates competing for the same office.

Establishment Clause: A provision in the First Amendment to the U.S. Constitution that says that Congress shall make no law respecting an establishment of religion.

Estate tax: A tax levied on the value of an inheritance.

Excise tax: A tax levied on the manufacture, transportation, sale, or consumption of a particular item or set of related items.

Exclusionary rule: The judicial doctrine stating that when the police violate an individual's constitutional rights, the evidence obtained as a result of police misconduct or error cannot be used against the defendant.

Executive agreement: An international understanding between the president and foreign nations that does not require Senate ratification.

Executive Office of the President: The group of White House offices and agencies that develop and implement the policies and programs of the president.

Executive order: A directive issued by the governor to an administrative agency or executive department.

Executive power: The power to enforce laws.

Exit polls: Surveys based on random samples of voters leaving a polling place.

***Ex post facto* law:** A retroactive criminal statute that operates to the disadvantage of accused persons.

External political efficacy: The assessment of an individual of the responsiveness of government to his or her concerns.

Extradition: The return from one state to another of a person accused of a crime.

Extraterritorial jurisdiction (ETJ): The authority of a city to require conformity with city ordinances and regulations affecting streets, parks, alleys, utility easements, sanitary sewers, and the like in a ring of land extending from ½ to 5 miles beyond the city-limits line.

Factions: Special interests who seek their own good at the expense of the common good.

Fairness Doctrine: An FCC regulation requiring broadcasters to present controversial issues of public importance and to present them in an honest, equal, and balanced manner.

Federal Communication Commission (FCC): An agency that regulates interstate and international radio, television, telephone, telegraph, and satellite communications, as well as licensing radio and television stations.

Federal Deposit Insurance Corporation (FDIC): A federal agency established to insure depositors' accounts in banks and thrift institutions.

Federal Election Commission (FEC): The agency that enforces federal campaign finance laws.

Federal grant program: A program through which the national government gives money to state and local governments to spend in accordance with set standards and conditions.

Federal mandate: A legal requirement placed on a state or local government by the national government requiring certain policy actions.

Federal Open Market Committee (FOMC): A committee of the Federal Reserve that meets eight times a year to review the economy and adjust monetary policy to achieving the goals.

Federal preemption of state authority: An act of Congress adopting regulatory policies that overrule state policies in a particular regulatory area.

Federal Reserve Board (Fed): An independent regulatory commission that makes monetary policy.

Federal Trade Commission (FTC): An agency that regulates business competition, including enforcement of laws against monopolies and the protection of consumers from deceptive trade practices.

Federalist Papers: A series of essays written by James Madison, Alexander Hamilton, and John Jay advocating the ratification of the Constitution.

Federalists: Americans who supported the ratification of the Constitution.

Federation or **federal system:** A political system that divides power between a central government, with authority over the whole nation, and a series of state governments.

Feedback: The impact of policy evaluation on the policy process.

Felony: A serious criminal offense, such as murder, sexual assault, or burglary.

Filibuster: An attempt to defeat a bill through prolonged debate.

Fire-alarm oversight: An indirect system of congressional surveillance of bureaucratic administration characterized by rules, procedures, and informal practices that enable individual citizens and organized interest groups to examine administrative decisions; charge agencies with violating legislative goals; and seek remedies from agencies, courts, and the Congress itself.

First strike: The initial offensive move of a general nuclear war, aimed at knocking out the other side's ability to retaliate.

First-strike capability: The capacity of a nation to launch an initial nuclear assault sufficient to cripple an adversary's ability to retaliate.

Fiscal note: An analysis of a legislative measure indicating its cost to state government, if any.

Fiscal policy: The use of government spending and taxation for the purpose of achieving economic goals.

Fiscal year: Budget year.

Flat tax: An income tax that assesses the same percentage tax rate on all income levels above a personal exemption while allowing few if any deductions

Floor: The full House or full Senate taking official action.

Food Stamp Program: A federal program that provides vouchers to low-income families and individuals that can be used to purchase food from grocery stores.

Forcible entry and detainer suit: An effort by a landlord to evict a tenant (usually for failure to pay rent).

Foreign policy: Public policy that concerns the relationship of the United States to the international political environment.

Formula grant program: A grant program that awards funding on the basis of a formula established by Congress.

Foundation School Program: The basic funding program for public education in the state of Texas.

Framing: The process by which a communication source, such as a news organization, defines and constructs a political issue or public controversy.

Franchise: The right to vote.

Franchise tax: A tax on businesses chartered or organized in Texas and doing business in the state.

Franking privilege: Free postage provided members of Congress.

Free-rider barrier to group membership: The concept that individuals will have little incentive to join a group and contribute resources to it if the group's benefits go to members and nonmembers alike.

Friendly Incumbent Rule: A policy whereby an interest group will back any incumbent who is generally supportive of the group's policy preferences, without regard for the party or policy views of the challenger.

Frostbelt: The northeastern and midwestern regions of the United States.

Full Faith and Credit Clause: The constitutional provision requiring that states recognize the official acts of other states, such as marriages, divorces, adoptions, court orders, and other legal decisions.

Fundamental right: A constitutional right that is so important that government cannot restrict it unless it can demonstrate a compelling or overriding public interest for so doing.

Gender gap: Differences in party identification and political attitudes between men and women.

General election: An election to fill state and national offices held in November of even-numbered years.

General Fund: The state treasury account that supports state programs and services without restriction.

General-law city: A municipality that is limited to those governmental structures and powers specifically granted by state law.

General-law units of local government: Units of local government that are limited to those structures and powers specifically granted by state law.

General obligation bonds: Certificates of indebtedness that must be repaid from general revenues.

Gerrymandering: The drawing of legislative district lines for political advantage.

Global economy: The integration of national economies into a world economic system in which companies compete worldwide for suppliers and markets.

Global warming: The gradual warming of the earth's atmosphere reportedly caused by the burning of fossil fuels and industrial pollutants.

Global Warming Treaty: An international agreement to reduce the worldwide emissions of carbon dioxide and other greenhouse gases, because it believed that the treaty puts too much of the burden for reducing emissions on the United States.

Good business climate: A political environment in which business would prosper.

Good time: A prison policy that credits inmates with time off for good behavior.

Governing party: The political party or party coalition holding the reins of government in a democracy.

Government: The institution with authority to set policy for society.

Grand jury: A body of 12 citizens that hears evidence presented by the prosecuting attorney and decides whether to indict an accused person.

Grand Old Party (GOP): Nickname for the Republican Party.

Grandfather clause: A provision that exempted those persons whose grandfathers had been eligible to vote at some earlier date from tests of understanding, literacy tests, and other difficult-to-achieve voter qualification requirements.

Grange: An organization of farmers.

Great Society: The legislative program put forward by President Lyndon Johnson.

Gross domestic product (GDP): The total value of goods and services produced by a nation's economy in a year, excluding transactions with foreign countries.

Gross state product (GSP): The total value of goods and services produced in a state in a year.

Ground war: Campaign activities featuring direct contact between campaign workers and citizens, such as door-to-door canvassing and personal telephone contacts.

Hard money: Funds that are raised subject to federal campaign contribution and expenditure limitations.

Harmless error: A mistake committed by a trial court that is not serious enough to warrant a new trial because it could not have affected the outcome of the original trial.

Hatch Act: A measure designed to restrict the political activities of federal employees to voting and the private expression of views.

Hate crimes law: A legislative measure that increases penalties for persons convicted of criminal offenses motivated by prejudice based on race, religion, national origin, gender, or sexual orientation.

Hate crimes legislation: Legislative measures that increase penalties for persons convicted of criminal offenses motivated by prejudice based on race, religion, national origin, gender, or sexual orientation.

High-technology industries: Industries that are based on the latest in modern technology.

Home rule: The authority of a unit of local government to take actions not prohibited by the laws or constitutions of the United States or the state.

Home-rule city: A municipality that can take any actions not prohibited by state or federal law or the constitutions of the United States and the state of Texas.

Homestead: Legal residence.

Homestead exemption: A property tax reduction granted to homeowners on their principal residence.

Honeymoon effect: The tendency of a president to enjoy a high level of public support during the early months of an administration.

Hospital district: A special district that provides emergency medical services, indigent healthcare, and community health services.

House Majority Leader: The second-ranking figure in the majority party in the House.

House Rules Committee: A standing committee that determines the rules under which a specific bill can be debated, amended, and considered on the House floor.

Housing codes: Local ordinances requiring all dwelling places in a city to meet certain standards of upkeep and structural integrity.

Human Rights Campaign (HRC): An organization formed to promote gay and lesbian rights.

Impeach: The act of formally accusing an official of the executive or judicial branches of an impeachable offense.

Impeachment: A formal accusation against an executive or judicial officeholder.

Implied powers: Those powers of Congress not explicitly mentioned in the Constitution, but derived by implication from the delegated powers.

In forma pauperis: The process whereby an indigent litigant can file an appeal of a case to the Supreme Court without paying the usual fees.

Income redistribution: The government taking items of value, especially money, from some groups of people and then giving items of value, either in cash or services, to other groups of people.

Incorporated municipality: A city under the laws of the state.

Incremental model of budgeting: A theoretical effort to explain the budget process on the basis of small (incremental) changes in budget categories from one budget period to the next.

Incremental model of policy formulation: An approach to policy formulation that assumes that policymakers, working with imperfect information, continually adjust policies in pursuit of policy goals that are subject to periodic readjustment.

Incumbent: Current officeholder.

Independent executive agencies: Executive branch agencies that are not part of any of the 15 cabinet-level departments.

Independent expenditures: Money spent in support of a candidate but not coordinated with the candidate's campaign.

Independent regulatory commission: An agency outside the major executive departments that is charged with the regulation of important aspects of the economy.

Independent school districts (ISDs): Units of local government that provide public education services to district residents from kindergarten through the twelfth grade.

Indictment: A formal accusation charging an individual with the commission of a crime.

Individualistic political culture: An approach to government and politics that emphasizes private initiative with a minimum of government interference.

Inflation: A decline in the purchasing power of the currency.

Inherent powers: Those powers vested in the national government, particularly in the area of foreign and defense policy, which do not depend on any specific grant of authority by the Constitution, but rather exist because the United States is a sovereign nation.

Initiative process: A procedure available in some states and cities whereby citizens can propose the adoption of a policy measure by gathering a prerequisite number of signatures.

Injunction: A court order.

Inner cabinet: The Secretary of State, Secretary of Defense, Secretary of the Treasury, and the Attorney General.

Interest group: An organization of people who join together voluntarily on the basis of some shared interest for the purpose of influencing policy.

Interest: Money paid for the use of money.

Interim committee: A committee established to study a particular policy issue between legislative sessions, such as higher education or public school finance.

Internal political efficacy: The assessment by an individual of his or her personal ability to influence the policymaking process.

International Monetary Fund (IMF): The international organization created to promote economic stability worldwide.

Interstate Commerce Clause: The constitutional provision giving Congress authority to "regulate commerce . . . among the several states."

Isolationism: The view that the United States should stay out of the affairs of other nations.

Issue network: A group of political actors that is actively involved with policymaking in a particular issue area.

Item veto: The power of an executive to veto sections or items of a tax or appropriation measure while signing the remainder of the bill into law.

Jacksonian democracy: The philosophy (associated with President Andrew Jackson) that the right to vote should be extended to all adult male citizens and that all government offices of any importance should be filled by election.

Jim Crow laws: Legal provisions requiring the social segregation of African Americans in separate and generally unequal facilities.

Joint and several liability: The legal requirement that a defendant with "deep pockets" held partially liable for a plaintiff's injury must pay the full damage award for those defendants unable to pay.

Joint Chiefs of Staff: A military advisory body that is composed of the chiefs of staff of the U.S. Army and Air Force, the Chief of Naval Operations, and sometimes the Commandant of the Marine Corps.

Joint committee: A committee that includes members from both houses of Congress.

Joint resolution: A resolution that must be passed by a two-thirds' vote of each chamber.

Judicial activism: The charge that judges are going beyond their authority by making the law and not just interpreting it.

Judicial power: The power to interpret laws.

Judicial restraint: The concept that judges should defer to the policymaking judgment of the legislative and executive branches of government unless their actions clearly violate the law or the Constitution.

Judicial review: The authority of courts to declare unconstitutional the actions of the other branches and units of government.

Jurisdiction: The authority of a court to hear a case.

Killer amendment: An amendment designed to make a measure so unattractive that it will lack enough support to pass.

Lame duck: An official whose influence is diminished because the official either cannot or will not seek reelection.

Latent opinion: What public opinion would be at election time if a political opponent made a public official's position on the issue the target of a campaign attack.

League of United Latin American Citizens (LULAC): A Latino interest group.

Left wing: Liberal.

Legal brief: A written legal argument.

Legal writs: Written orders issued by a court directing the performance of an act or prohibiting some act.

Legislative access: An open door through which an interest group hopes to influence the details of policy.

Legislative Budget Board (LBB): An agency created by the legislature to study state revenue and budgetary needs between legislative sessions and prepare budget and appropriation bills to submit to the legislature.

Legislative markup: The process in which legislators go over a measure line-by-line, revising, amending, or rewriting it.

Legislative oversight: The process through which the legislature evaluates the implementation of public policy by executive branch agencies.

Legislative power: The power to make laws.

Legislative Redistricting Board (LBB): An agency composed of the speaker, lieutenant governor, comptroller, land commissioner, and attorney general that draws the boundaries of Texas House and Senate seats when the legislature is unable to agree on a redistricting plan.

Legislative turnover: The replacement of individual members of a legislature from one session to the next.

Libel: False written statements which lower a person's reputation or expose a person to hatred, contempt, or ridicule.

Liberalism: The political philosophy that favors the use of government power to foster the development of the individual and promote the welfare of society.

Limited government: The constitutional principle that government does not have unrestricted authority over individuals.

Line-item veto: The power of the governor to veto sections or items of an appropriation bill while signing the remainder of the bill into law.

Literacy test: A legal requirement that citizens demonstrate an ability to read and write before they could register to vote.

Litigants: The parties in a lawsuit.

Lobbying: The communication of information by a representative of an interest group to a government official for the purpose of influencing a policy decision.

Local bills: Proposed laws that affect only a single unit of local government.

Local governments: Subunits of states.

Local-option (wet–dry) elections: Elections held to determine whether an area legalizes the sale of alcoholic beverages.

Logrolling: An arrangement in which two or more members of Congress agree in advance to support each other's favored legislation.

Lone Star State: Nickname for Texas.

Long ballot: An election system that provides for the election of nearly every public official of any significance.

Loose construction: A doctrine of constitutional interpretation holding that the document should be interpreted broadly.

Louisiana Purchase: The acquisition from France of a vast expanse of land stretching from New Orleans north to the Dakotas.

Magistrates: Judicial officers.

Majority opinion: The official written statement of the Supreme Court that explains and justifies its ruling and serves as a guideline for lower courts when similar legal issues arise in the future.

Majority Whip: The Majority Leader's first assistant.

Majority, or deciding, opinion: An official written statement of a court that explains and justifies its ruling and serves as a guideline for lower courts when similar legal issues arise in the future.

Majority-minority districts: Legislative districts whose population was more than 50 percent African American and Latino.

Mandatory spending: Budgetary expenditures that are mandated by law, including entitlements and contractual commitments made in previous years.

Margin of error (or sample error): A statistical term that refers to the accuracy of a survey.

Mark up: The process in which legislators go over a piece of legislation line-by-line, revising, amending, or rewriting it.

Marshall Plan: The American program that provided billions of dollars to the countries of Western Europe to rebuild their economies after World War II.

Massive retaliation: The concept that the United States will strike back against an aggressor with overwhelming force.

Matching funds requirement: A legislative provision that the national government will provide grant money for a particular activity only on the condition that the state or local government involved supply a certain percentage of the total money required for the project or program.

Mayor-council form of city government: A structure of municipal government in which the voters elect a mayor as the chief executive officer of the city and a council that serves as a legislative body.

Means-tested program: A government program that provides benefits to recipients based on their financial need.

Medicaid: A federal program designed to provide health insurance coverage to low-income persons, people with disabilities, and elderly people who are impoverished.

Medicare: A federally funded health insurance program for the elderly.

Merit selection, or the Missouri Plan: A method for selecting judges that combines gubernatorial appointment with voter approval in a retention election.

Mid-cycle redistricting: The practice of redrawing legislative districts outside the regular redistricting cycle in order to gain political advantage.

Military preemption: The defense policy that declares that the United States will attack nations or groups that represent a potential threat to the security of the United States.

Minimum wage: The lowest hourly wage that an employer can legally pay covered workers.

Minority business set-aside: A legal requirement that firms receiving government grants or contracts allocate a certain percentage of their purchases of supplies and services to businesses owned or controlled by members of minority groups.

Minority Leader: The head of the minority party in the House or Senate.

Minority-vote dilution: The drawing of election district lines so as to thinly spread minority voters among several districts, thus reducing their electoral influence in any one district.

Minority-vote packing: The drawing of electoral district lines so as to cluster minority voters into one district or a small number of districts, thus reducing their overall electoral influence.

Minority Whip: The Minority Leader's first assistant in the House or Senate.

Miranda warning: The judicial stipulation that a criminal defendant's confession cannot be admitted into evidence unless police first inform the defendant of the constitutional right to remain silent and to consult an attorney.

Misdemeanor: A relatively minor criminal offense, such as a traffic violation.

Monetary policy: The control of the money supply for the purpose of achieving economic goals.

Monroe Doctrine: A declaration of American foreign policy opposing any European intervention in the Western Hemisphere and affirming the American intention to refrain from interfering in European affairs.

Moralistic political culture: An approach to government and politics in which people expect government to intervene in the social and economic affairs of the state, promoting the public welfare and advancing the public good.

Mother's Against Drunk Driving (MADD): An interest group that supports the reform of laws dealing with drunk driving.

Moveon.org: An advocacy group that raises money for Democratic candidates.

Multiparty system: The division of voter loyalties among three or more major political parties.

Multiple referral of legislation: The practice of assigning legislation to more than one committee.

Mutual assured destruction (MAD): The belief that the United States and the Soviet Union would be deterred from launching a nuclear assault against each other for fear of being destroyed in a general nuclear war.

National Abortion and Reproductive Rights Action League, or NARAL Pro-Choice Texas: An organization that favors abortion rights.

National Abortion Rights Action League (NARAL Pro-Choice America): An organization that favors abortion rights.

National Aeronautics and Space Administration (NASA): The federal agency in charge of the space program.

National Association for the Advancement of Colored People (NAACP): An interest group organized to represent the concerns of African Americans.

National Crime Victim Survey (NCVS): A measure of the incidence of crime in the United States based on interviews with people in more than 50,000 households.

National debt: The accumulated indebtedness of the federal government.

National Endowment for the Arts (NEA): A federal agency created to nurture cultural expression and promote appreciation of the arts.

National Organization for Women (NOW): A group organized to promote women's rights.

National Public Radio (NPR): A nonprofit membership organization of radio stations.

National Railroad Passenger Corporation (Amtrak): A federal agency that operates intercity passenger railway traffic.

National Rifle Association (NRA): An interest group organized to defend the rights of gun owners and defeat efforts at gun control.

National Right to Life Committee: An organization opposed to abortion.

National Science Foundation (NSF): A federal agency established to encourage scientific advances and improvements in science education.

National Security Council (NSC): An agency in the Executive Office of the President that advises the chief executive on matters involving national security.

National Supremacy Clause: A constitutional provision that declares that the Constitution, the laws made under it, and the treaties of the United States are the supreme law of the land.

National Voter Registration Act (NVRA): A federal law designed to make it easier for citizens to register to vote by requiring states to allow mail registration and provide an opportunity for people to register when applying for or renewing driver's licenses or when visiting federal, state, or local agencies, such as welfare offices.

Nation-state: A political community, occupying a definite territory, and having an organized government.

Natural population increase: The extent to which live births exceed deaths.

Necessary and Proper Clause or Elastic Clause: The Constitutional provision found in Article I, Section 8, that declares that "[Congress shall have the power] to make all laws which shall be necessary and proper for carrying into execution the foregoing powers, and all other powers vested by this Constitution in the government of the United States, or in any department or office thereof." It is the basis for much of the legislation passed by Congress because it gives Congress the means to exercise its delegated authority.

New Deal: A legislative package of reform measures proposed by President Franklin Roosevelt for dealing with the Great Depression.

New Deal program: The name of President Franklin Roosevelt's legislative program for countering the Great Depression.

New media: A term used to refer to alternative media sources, such as the Internet, cable television, and satellite radio.

Nixon Doctrine: The corollary to the policy of containment enunciated by President Richard Nixon providing that, although the United States would help small nations threatened by communist aggression with economic and military aid, those countries must play a major role in their own defense.

No Child Left Behind (NCLB): A federal law that requires state governments and local school districts to institute basic skills testing in reading and mathematics for students in grades three through eight, and use the results to assess school performance.

Nolo contendere: A plea indicating a defendant's decision not to contest a criminal charge.

Nongermane amendments: Amendments that are unrelated to the subject matter of the original measure.

Nongovernmental organizations (NGOs): International organizations committed to the promotion of a particular set of issues.

Nonpartisan elections: Election contests in which the names of the candidates, but not their party affiliations, appear on the ballot.

Nonpartisan legislature: A legislative body in which political parties play little or no role.

Normative analysis: A method of study that is based on certain values.

North American Free Trade Agreement (NAFTA): An international accord among the United States, Mexico, and Canada to lower trade barriers among the three nations.

North Atlantic Treaty Organization (NATO): A regional military alliance consisting of the United States, Canada, and most of the European democracies.

Nuclear Nonproliferation Treaty: An international agreement designed to prevent the spread of nuclear weapons.

Objective journalism: A style of news reporting that focuses on facts rather than opinion, and presents all sides of controversial issues.

Office of Management and Budget (OMB): An agency that assists the president in preparing the budget.

Official policy agenda: Those problems that government officials actively consider how to resolve.

Omnibus bills: Complex, highly detailed legislative proposals covering one or more subjects or programs.

One person, one vote: The judicial ruling that the Equal Protection Clause of the Fourteenth Amendment to the U.S. Constitution requires that legislative districts be apportioned on the basis of population.

Open primary: An election system that allows voters to pick the party primary of their choice without regard to their party affiliation.

Open rule: A rule that opens a measure to amendment on the House floor without restriction.

Opposition party: The political party out of power in a democracy.

Ordinance: A law enacted by the governing body of a unit of local government.

Original jurisdiction: The set of cases a court may hear as a trial court.

Pardon: An executive action that frees an accused or convicted person from all penalties for an offense.

Parental choice: An educational reform aimed at improving the quality of schools by allowing parents to select the school their children will attend.

Pari-mutuel wagering: A system for gambling on horse and dog racing.

Parliament: The British legislature.

Parliamentary system: A system of government in which political power is concentrated in a legislative body and a cabinet headed by a prime minister.

Parole: The conditional release of convicted offenders from prison to serve the remainder of their sentences in the community under supervision.

Partisan election: An election contest in which both the names and the party affiliations of candidates appear on the ballot.

Partisan legislature: A legislative body in which political parties play a defining role.

Party caucus: All of the party members of the House or Senate meeting as a group.

Party era: A period of time characterized by a degree of uniformity in the nature of political party competition.

Party faction: An identifiable subgroup within a political party.

Party platform: A statement of party principles and issue positions.

Party realignment: A change in the underlying party loyalties of voters that ends one party era and begins another.

PAYGO: A pay-as-you-go budget rule that requires that any tax cut or spending increase be offset by tax increases or spending cuts elsewhere in the budget.

Peace Corps: An agency that administers an American foreign aid program under which volunteers travel to developing nations to teach skills and help improve living standards.

Per capita: Per person.

***Per curiam* opinion:** Unsigned written opinion of a court.

Performance-based budgeting: A system of budget preparation and evaluation in which policymakers identify specific policy goals, set performance targets for agencies, and measure results.

Permanent School Fund (PSF): A fund established in the Texas Constitution as an endowment to finance public elementary and secondary education.

Permanent University Fund (PUF): Money constitutionally set aside as an endowment to finance construction, maintenance, and some other activities at the University of Texas, Texas A&M University, and other institutions in those two university systems.

Plaintiff: The party initiating a civil suit.

Plea bargain: A procedure in which a defendant agrees to plead guilty in order to receive punishment less than the maximum for an offense.

Plural executive: The division of executive power among several elected officials.

Pluralist theory, *or* pluralism: The view that diverse groups of elites with differing interests compete with one another to control policy in various issue areas.

Plurality election system: A method for choosing public officials that awards office to the candidate with the most votes, favors a two-party system.

Pocket veto: The action of a president allowing a measure to die without signature after Congress has adjourned.

Policy adoption: The official decision of a government body to accept a particular policy and put it into effect.

Policy cycle: The passage of an issue through the policy process from agenda building through policy evaluation.

Policy evaluation: The assessment of policy.

Policy formulation: The development of strategies for dealing with the problems on the official policy agenda.

Policy implementation: The stage of the policy process in which policies are carried out.

Policy outcomes: The situations that arise as a result of the impact of policy in operation.

Policy outputs: Actual government policies.

Political action committee (PAC): An organization created to raise and distribute money in election campaigns.

Policymaking environment: The complex of factors outside of government that has an impact, either directly or indirectly, on the policymaking process.

Political campaign: An attempt to get information to voters that will persuade them to elect a candidate or not elect an opponent.

Political culture: The widely held, deeply rooted political values of a society.

Political efficacy: The extent to which individuals believe they can influence the policymaking process.

Political elites: Persons that exercise a major influence on the policymaking process.

Political left: Liberalism.

Political legitimacy: The popular acceptance of a government and its officials as rightful authorities in the exercise of power.

Political machines: Entrenched political organizations headed by a boss or small group of leaders who held power through such techniques as patronage, control over nominations, and bribery.

Political participation: An activity that has the intent or effect of influencing government action.

Political party: A group of individuals who join together to seek government office in order to make public policy.

Political patronage: The power of an officeholder to award favors, such as government jobs, to political allies.

Political right: Conservatism.

Political socialization: The process whereby individuals acquire political knowledge, attitudes, and beliefs.

Politics: The process that determines who shall occupy the roles of leadership in government and how the power of government shall be exercised.

Poll tax: A tax levied on the right to vote.

Population bracket laws: State laws designed to target particular cities based on their population.

Pork barrel spending: Expenditures to fund local projects that are not critically important from a national perspective.

Postal Service: A government corporation responsible for mail service.

Postindustrial societies: Nations whose economies are increasingly based on services, research, and information rather than heavy industry.

Poverty line: The amount of money an individual or a family needs to purchase basic necessities, such as food, clothing, healthcare, shelter, and transportation.

Poverty threshold: The amount of money an individual or family needs to purchase basic necessities, such as food, clothing, health care, shelter, and transportation.

Power of the purse: The authority to raise and spend money.

Pre-clearance: A requirement of the Voting Rights Act that state and local governments in areas with a history of voting discrimination must submit redistricting plans to the federal Department of Justice for approval *before* they can go into effect.

President's cabinet: A body that includes the executive department heads and other senior officials chosen by the president, such as the U.S. ambassador to the United Nations.

Presidential preference primary election: An election in which party voters cast ballots for the presidential candidate they favor and in so doing help determine the number of convention delegates that candidate will receive.

Presidential signing statement: A pronouncement issued by the president at the time a bill passed by Congress is signed into law.

Primary election: An election held to determine a party's nominees for the general election ballot.

Print media: Newspapers and magazines.

Prior restraint: Government action to prevent the publication or broadcast of objectionable material.

Privatization: A process that involves the government contracting with private business to implement government programs.

Privileges and Immunities Clause: The constitutional provision prohibiting state governments from discriminating against the citizens of other states.

Probable cause: The reasonable belief that a crime has been committed and that a particular suspect is the likely perpetrator of that crime.

Probate case: A civil suit dealing with the disposition of the property of a deceased individual.

Probation: The suspension of a sentence, permitting the defendant to remain free under court supervision.

Problem-solving court: A judicial body that attempts to change the future behavior of litigants and promote the welfare of the community.

Progressive tax: A levy that taxes people earning higher incomes at a higher rate than it does individuals making less money.

Project grant program: A grant program that requires state and local governments to compete for available federal money.

Property case: A civil suit over the ownership of real estate or personal possessions, such as land, jewelry, or an automobile.

Property lien: A financial claim against property for payment of debt.

Property tax: A tax levied on the value of real property, such as land and buildings.

Proportional representation (PR): An election system that awards legislative seats to each party approximately equal to its popular voting strength.

Proportional tax: A levy that taxes all persons at the same percentage rate, regardless of income.

Prosecutor: The attorney who tries a criminal case on behalf of the government.

Prospective voting: The concept that voters evaluate the incumbent officeholder and the incumbent's party based on their expectations of future developments.

Public Broadcasting Service (PBS): A nonprofit private corporation that is jointly owned by hundreds of member television stations throughout the United States.

Public policy: The response, or lack of response, of government decision-makers to an issue.

Public policy approach: A comprehensive method for studying the process through which issues come to the attention of government decision makers, and through which policies are formulated, adopted, implemented, and evaluated.

Punitive damages: Monetary awards given in a lawsuit to punish a defendant for a particularly evil, malicious, or fraudulent act.

Quasi-governmental company: A private, profit-seeking corporation created by Congress to serve a public purpose.

Racial profiling: The practice of a police officer targeting individuals as suspected criminals on the basis of their race or ethnicity.

Racially restrictive covenants: Private deed restrictions that prohibited property owners from selling or leasing property to African Americans or other minorities.

Radical Republicans: Members of the Republican Party who wanted sweeping social change to take place in the South after the Civil War.

Rally effect: The tendency of the general public to express support for the incumbent president during a time of international threat.

Random sample: A sample in which each member of a universe has an equal likelihood of being included.

Rational comprehensive model of policy formulation: An approach to policy formulation that assumes that policymakers establish goals, identify policy alternatives, estimate the costs and benefits of the alternatives, and then select the policy alternative that produces the greatest net benefit.

Reagan Doctrine: A corollary to the policy of containment enunciated by President Ronald Reagan calling for the United States to offer military aid to groups attempting to overthrow communist governments anywhere in the world.

Reapportionment: The reallocation of legislative seats.

Recall: A procedure allowing voters to remove elected officials from office before the expiration of their terms.

Recession: An economic slowdown characterized by declining economic output and rising unemployment.

Recidivism: The tendency of offenders released from prison to commit additional crimes and be returned behind bars.

Reconstruction: The process whereby the states that had seceded during the Civil War were reorganized and reestablished in the Union.

Red states: States that voted for Republican George W. Bush for president in 2000 and 2004 symbolized by the color red on the electoral college map.

Redistributive urban policies: Local programs that benefit low-income residents of an area.

Redistricting: The process of redrawing the boundaries of legislative districts.

Regressive tax: A levy whose burden falls more heavily on lower-income groups than on wealthy taxpayers.

Regulatory negotiation: A structured process by which representatives of the interests that would be substantially affected by a rule, including employees of the regulatory agency, negotiate agreement on the terms of the rule.

Religious left: Individuals who hold liberal views because of their religious beliefs.

Religious right: Individuals who hold conservative social views because of their religious beliefs.

Remand: An appellate court returning a case to a trial court for further consideration.

Representative democracy, or **republic:** A political system in which citizens elect representatives to make policy decisions on their behalf.

Reprieve: A postponement of the implementation of punishment for a criminal offense.

Republic: A representative democracy in which citizens elect representatives to make policy decisions on their behalf.

Republicans in name only (RINOs): Legislators who call themselves Republicans but vote with the Democrats.

Reserved or residual powers: The powers of government left to the states.

Resolution: A legislative statement of opinion on a certain matter.

Retrospective voting: The concept that voters choose candidates based on their perception of an incumbent candidate's past performance in office or the performance of the incumbent party.

Reversible error: A mistake committed by a trial court that is serious enough to warrant a new trial because the mistake could have affected the outcome of the original trial.

Rider: A provision, unlikely to become law on its own merits, which is attached to an important measure so that it will ride through the legislative process.

Right-to-work laws: Statutes that prohibit union membership as a condition of employment.

Right wing: Conservatism.

Robin Hood Plan: A reform of the state's school finance system designed to increase funding for poor school districts by redistributing money from wealthy districts.

Rogue states: Nations that threaten world peace by sponsoring international terrorism and promoting the spread of weapons of mass destruction.

Rose garden strategy: A campaign approach in which an incumbent president attempts to appear presidential rather than political.

Rule: A legally binding regulation.

Rule of Four: A decision process used by the Supreme Court to determine which cases to consider on appeal, holding that the Court will hear a case if four of the nine justices agree to the review.

Rule of law: The constitutional principle that holds that the discretion of public officials in dealing with individuals is limited by the law.

Rulemaking: A regulatory process used by government agencies to enact legally binding regulations.

Rules: Legally binding regulations adopted by a regulatory agency.

Runoff: An election between the two candidates receiving the most votes when no candidate got a majority in an initial election.

Runoff primary election: An election between the two top finishers in a primary election when no candidate received a majority of the vote in the initial primary.

Sales tax: A levy assessed on the retail sale of taxable items.

Sample: A subset of a universe.

School choice: An educational reform movement that would allow parents to choose the elementary or secondary school their children will attend.

School lunch program: A federal program that provides free or reduced-cost lunches to children from poor families.

Second strike: A nuclear attack in response to an adversary's first strike.

Second-strike capability: The capacity of a nation to absorb an initial nuclear attack and retain sufficient nuclear firepower to inflict unacceptable damage on its adversary.

Securities and Exchange Commission (SEC): An agency that regulates the sale of stocks and bonds as well as investment and holding companies.

Select, *or* **special, committee:** A committee that is established for a limited period of time to address a specific problem.

Selective incorporation of the Bill of Rights against the states: The process through which the U.S. Supreme Court interpreted the Due Process Clause of the Fourteenth Amendment of the U.S. Constitution to apply most of the provisions of the national Bill of Rights to the states.

Senate Majority Leader: The head of the majority party in the Senate.

Senate president pro tempore: The official presiding officer in the Senate in the vice president's absence.

Senatorial Courtesy: At the national level, senatorial courtesy is the custom that senators from the president's party have a veto on judicial appointments from their states. In Texas, senatorial courtesy is a custom of the Texas Senate that allows individual senators a veto over nominees who live in their districts.

Seniority: Length of service in a legislative body.

Separate-but-equal: The judicial doctrine holding that separate facilities for whites and African Americans satisfy the equal protection requirement of the Fourteenth Amendment.

Separation of powers: The division of political authority among legislative, executive, and judicial branches of government.

Severance tax: A tax imposed on the extraction of natural resources, such as oil, coal, or gas.

Shield law: A statute that protects journalists from being forced to disclose confidential information in a legal proceeding.

Sierra Club: An environmental organization.

Signaling role: A term that refers to the accepted responsibility of the media to alert the public to important developments as they happen.

Sin tax: A levy on an activity that some people consider morally objectionable, such as smoking or drinking.

Slander: False spoken statements which lower a person's reputation or expose a person to hatred, contempt, or ridicule.

Small Business Administration (SBA): The federal agency established to make loans to small businesses and assist them in obtaining government contracts.

Social lobbying: The attempt of lobbyists to influence public policy by cultivating personal, social relationships with policymakers.

Social Security: A federal pension and disability insurance program funded through a payroll tax on workers and their employers.

Social Security Administration (SSA): The federal agency that operates the Social Security system.

Soft money: The name given to funds that are raised by political parties that are not subject to federal campaign finance regulations.

Solid South: The usual Democratic sweep of southern state electoral votes in presidential election years between the end of the Civil War era and the current party era.

Sound bite: A short phrase taken from a candidate's speech by the news media for use on newscasts.

Sovereign immunity: The legal concept that individuals cannot sue the government without the government's permission.

Sovereignty: The authority of a state to exercise its legitimate powers within its boundaries, free from external interference.

Speaker of the House: The presiding officer in the House of Representatives and the leader of the majority party in that chamber.

Special district: A unit of local government created to perform specific functions.

Special election: An election called at a time outside the normal election calendar.

Special *or* select committee: A committee established for a limited time only.

Split ticket voting: Voters casting their ballots for the candidates of two or more political parties.

Spoils system: The method of hiring government employees from among the friends, relatives, and supporters of elected officeholders.

Sponsor: A member who introduces a measure.

Sputnik: The world's first satellite, launched by the Soviet Union.

Standard of living: A term that refers to the goods and services affordable by and available to the residents of a nation.

Standing committee: A permanent committee established to handle legislation in a certain field.

States' rights: An interpretation of the Constitution that favors limiting the authority of the federal government while expanding the powers of the states.

Statutory law: Law made by a legislature.

Straight ticket ballot: Voters selecting the entire slate of candidates of one party only.

Straight ticket voting: Citizens casting their ballots only for the candidates of one party.

Strategic forces: Nuclear forces.

Strict construction: A doctrine of constitutional interpretation holding that the document should be interpreted narrowly.

Strict judicial scrutiny: The judicial decision rule holding that the Supreme Court will find a government policy unconstitutional unless the government can demonstrate a compelling interest justifying the action.

Subgovernment *or* iron triangle: A cozy, three-sided relationship among government agencies, interest groups, and key members of Congress in which all parties benefit.

Subpoena: A legal order compelling the attendance of a person at an official proceeding, such as a trial.

Subsidence: The sinking of the surface of the land caused by the too-rapid extraction of subsurface water.

Subsidy: A financial incentive given by government to an individual or a business interest to accomplish a public objective.

Suffrage: The right to vote.

Sunbelt: The southern and western regions of the United States.

Sunset review: The periodic evaluation of state agencies by the legislature to determine whether they should be reauthorized.

Superdelegates: Democratic officeholders and party officials who attend the national party convention as delegates who are not officially pledged to support any candidate.

Supermajority: A voting margin which is greater than a simple majority.

Supplemental Security Income (SSI): A federal program that provides money to low-income people who are elderly, blind, or disabled who do not qualify for Social Security benefits.

Supply-side economics: The economic theory that tax cuts, especially for business and the wealthy, will lead to savings and investment that will benefit everyone.

Surgeon General: An official in the Public Health Service who advises the president on health issues.

Survey research: The measurement of public opinion.

Suspect classifications: Distinctions among persons that must be justified on the basis of a compelling government interest.

Swing voters: Citizens who vote for either the Democratic or the Republican party.

Table: To postpone consideration of a measure during the legislative process.

Tariffs: Taxes on imported goods.

Tax abatement: A program that exempts property owners from local property taxes on new construction and improvements in a designated tax abatement district for a set period of time.

Tax credit: An expenditure that reduces an individual's tax liability by the amount of the credit.

Tax deduction: An expenditure that can be subtracted from a taxpayer's gross income before figuring the tax owed.

Tax elasticity: The extent to which tax revenues increase as personal income rises.

Tax exemption: The exclusion of some types of income from taxation.

Tax incidence: The point at which the actual cost of a tax falls.

Tax increment financing: A program in which a local government promises to earmark increased property tax revenues generated by development in a designated area called a tax increment financing district to fund improvements in the area, such as roads, parks, sidewalks, and street lighting.

Tax preference: A tax deduction or exclusion that allows individuals to pay less tax than they would otherwise.

Temporary Assistance for Needy Families (TANF): A federal block grant program that provides temporary financial assistance and work opportunities to needy families.

Tennessee Valley Authority (TVA): A federal agency established to promote the development of the Tennessee River and its tributaries.

Term limitation: The movement to restrict the number of terms public officials may serve.

Test cases: Lawsuits initiated to challenge the constitutionality of a legislative or executive act.

Test of understanding: A legal requirement that citizens must accurately explain a passage in the United States or state constitution before they could register to vote.

Texas Assessment of Knowledge and Skills (TAKS): A state-mandated basic skills test designed to measure student progress and school performance.

Texas Association of Business (TAB): A trade association for business firms ranging from giant corporations to small neighborhood business establishments.

Texas Equal Rights Amendment (ERA): A provision in the Texas Constitution that states the following: "Equality under the law shall not be denied or abridged because of sex, race, color, creed, or national origin."

Texas Medical Association (TMA): A professional organization of physicians.

Texas Right to Life Committee: An organization that opposes abortion.

Texas Teacher Retirement System (TRS) Trust Fund: A pension fund for the state's public school teachers.

Texas Trial Lawyers Association (TTLA): An organization of attorneys who represent plaintiffs in personal injury lawsuits; it blames bad doctors and a weak stock market, rather than excessive jury awards, for rising medical malpractice premiums.

Third party: A minor party in a two-party system.

Top 10 percent rule: A state law that grants automatic college admission to public high school graduates who finish in the top 10 percent of their class.

Tort case: A civil suit involving personal injury or damage to property, such as a lawsuit stemming from an automobile accident.

Tort reform: The revision of state laws to limit the ability of plaintiffs in personal injury lawsuits to recover damages in court.

Trade associations: Organizations representing the interests of firms and professionals in the same general field.

Traditionalistic political culture: An approach to government and politics that sees the role of government as the preservation of tradition and the existing social order.

Trans-Texas Corridor: A proposed network of transportation corridors a quarter mile wide and 370 miles long running from Brownsville to Oklahoma that would include toll roads, railways, and utility lines.

Trial: The formal examination of a civil or criminal action in accordance with law before a single judge who has jurisdiction to hear the dispute.

True bill: An indictment issued by a grand jury.

Truman Doctrine: The foreign policy put forward by President Harry Truman calling for American support for all free peoples resisting communist aggression by internal or outside forces.

Truth in taxation laws: Laws that block local governments from raising the total amount of property taxes they collect from one year to the next when assessed values go up.

Two-party system: The division of voter loyalties between two major political parties.

Two Presidencies Thesis: The concept that the president enjoys more influence over foreign policy than domestic policy.

Tyranny of the majority: The abuse of the minority by the majority.

Unanimous consent agreement (UCA): A formal understanding on procedures for conducting business in the Senate that requires the acceptance of every member of the chamber.

Unfunded mandate: A requirement imposed by Congress on state or local governments without providing federal funding to cover its cost.

Unicameral legislature: A legislative body with one chamber.

Uniform Crime Reports (UCR): A record of offenses known to police compiled by the Federal Bureau of Investigation (FBI) from reports submitted by local law enforcement agencies.

Unincorporated area: Territory not part of a legal city.

Union shop, *or* **closed shop:** A workplace in which every employee must be a member of a union.

Unitary government: A governmental system in which political authority is concentrated in a single national government.

United Nations (UN): An international organization founded in 1945 as a diplomatic forum to resolve conflicts among the world's nations.

Universe: The population survey researchers wish to study.

Utility district: A special district that provides utilities, such as water and sewer service, to residents living in unincorporated urban areas.

Veto: An action by the chief executive of a state or nation refusing to approve a bill passed by the legislature.

Voter mobilization: The process of motivating citizens to vote.

Voting age population (VAP): The number of U.S. residents who are 18 years of age or older.

Voting eligible population (VEP): The number of U.S. residents who are legally qualified to vote.

Voting Rights Act (VRA): A federal law designed to protect the voting rights of racial and ethnic minorities.

War Powers Act: A law limiting the president's ability to commit American armed forces to combat abroad without consultation with Congress and congressional approval.

Warrant: An official authorization issued by a judicial officer.

Weapons of mass destruction (WMDs): Nuclear, chemical, and biological weapons that are designed to inflict widespread military and civilian casualties.

Weblog or blog: An online personal journal or newsletter that is regularly updated.

Welfare programs: Government programs that provide benefits to individuals based on their economic status.

Welfare state: A government that takes responsibility for the welfare of its citizens through programs in public health, public housing, old-age pensions, unemployment compensation, and the like.

Whips: Assistant floor leaders in Congress.

Whistleblowers: Workers who report wrongdoing or mismanagement.

White primary: An election system that prohibited African Americans from voting in Democratic primary elections, ensuring that white voters would control the Democratic Party.

World Health Organization (WHO): An international organization created to control disease worldwide.

World Trade Organization (WTO): An international organization that administers trade laws, and provides a forum for settling trade disputes among nations.

Writ of *habeas corpus*: A court order requiring government authorities either to release a person held in custody or demonstrate that the person is detained in accordance with law.

Writ of *mandamus*: A court order directing a public official to perform a specific act or duty.

Yellow Dog Democrat: A loyal Democratic Party voter.

YouTube: A video sharing Internet website where users can upload, view, and share video clips.

Zone of acquiescence: The range of policy options acceptable to the public on a particular issue.

Zoning: The governmental designation of tracts of land for industrial, commercial, or residential use.

Photo Credits

Index

PRACTICE TESTS

Introduction: Government, Politics, and the Policymaking Process

Circle the correct answer.

1. Which of the following is *not* a provision of the Americans with Disabilities Act (ADA)?

    (A) Employers are required to hire any disabled person who applies for a job as long as that person meets the minimum qualifications.
    (B) Private businesses that are open to the public must be accessible to people with disabilities.
    (C) Employers must make "reasonable accommodations" for disabled employees who are otherwise qualified for their jobs.
    (D) Employers may not discriminate against disabled persons in hiring and promotions.

2. The total value of goods and services produced by a nation's economy in a year, excluding transactions with foreign countries, is the definition for which of the following terms?

    (A) Americans with Disabilities Act (ADA)
    (B) Empirical analysis
    (C) Gross domestic product (GDP)
    (D) Feedback

3. The institution with authority to set policy for society is known as which of the following?

    (A) Politics
    (B) Political science
    (C) Government
    (D) Congress

4. Congress, the president, the Federal Communications Commission, and the Supreme Court are all part of which of the following institutions?

    (A) Politics
    (B) Policymaking environment
    (C) Government
    (D) Feedback

5. The way in which decisions for a society are made and considered binding most of the time by most of the people is a definition of which of the following?

    (A) Politics
    (B) Political science
    (C) Government
    (D) Public policy

6. Which of the following terms is defined as the response, or lack of response, of government decision-makers to an issue?

    (A) Politics
    (B) Government
    (C) Political science
    (D) Public policy

7. A city council refuses to adopt an ordinance (local law) designed to regulate smoking in public places. Is this decision an example of a public policy?

    (A) No. Public policies require the adoption of a policy and the city council rejected the policy proposal.
    (B) No. This proposal would have violated the ADA.
    (C) Yes. This is an example of a public policy because it would have regulated public places.
    (D) Yes. A public policy is the response, or lack of response, of government decision-makers to an issue.

8. Is the ADA an example of a public policy?

    (A) Yes, because it is the response of government decision-makers to the issue of discrimination against people with disabilities.
    (B) Yes, because it was not done secretly.
    (C) Yes, because it affects a lot of people.
    (D) No, because it does not involve an election.

9. Which of the following is *not* an example of a public policy?

    (A) The refusal of the United States government to grant diplomatic recognition to the nation of Cuba.
    (B) The decision of CBS *News* to name Katie Couric as the anchor of its network evening news.
    (C) The decision of Federal Communications Commission (FCC) to adopt a rule concerning the joint ownership of a newspaper, television, and radio station in the same market.
    (D) The decision of the Senate to confirm a presidential appointment to the Fifth Circuit Court of Appeals.

10. The factors outside of government that affect, either directly or indirectly, the policymaking process are known as which of the following terms?

    (A) Agenda building
    (B) Policymaking environment
    (C) The public policymaking process
    (D) Politics

11. Which of the following is part of the policymaking environment?

    (A) Political parties
    (B) Interest groups
    (C) Public opinion
    (D) All of the above

12. The process through which problems become matters of public concern and government action is a definition for which of the following terms?

    (A) Policy adoption
    (B) Policy implementation
    (C) Agenda building
    (D) Policy formulation

13. Which of the following is a good example of agenda building?

(A) The president meets with advisors to discuss how best to respond to North Korea testing a nuclear weapon.
(B) The Supreme Court rules that the execution of convicted murderers who are mentally retarded violates the U.S. Constitution.
(C) A group of concerned scientists publishes a report on the problem of global warming.
(D) An economist publishes a study showing the impact of minimum wage laws on the unemployment rate of low-skilled workers.

14. The development of strategies for dealing with the problems on the official policy agenda is a definition for which of the following?

(A) Policy formulation
(B) Policy adoption
(C) Policy implementation
(D) Policy evaluation

15. A congressional committee meets to discuss the details of proposed legislation to improve automobile mileage standards. The action best illustrates which of the following stages of the policymaking process?

(A) Agenda building
(B) Policy formulation
(C) Policy adoption
(D) Policy evaluation

16. A group of political actors that is actively involved with policymaking in a particular issue area is known as which of the following?

(A) Interest group
(B) Issue network
(C) Feedback
(D) Political party

17. The official decision of a government body to accept a particular policy and put it into effect is a definition for which of the following?

(A) Policy evaluation
(B) Policy formulation
(C) Policy implementation
(D) Policy adoption

18. The president issues an executive order imposing U.S. sanctions on Sudan, a North African country whose government is accused of human rights violations. This act illustrates which stage of the policymaking process?

(A) Agenda setting
(B) Policy adoption
(C) Policy evaluation
(D) Policy implementation

19. The stage of the policy process in which policies are carried out is a definition for which of the following?

(A) Agenda setting
(B) Policy adoption
(C) Policy evaluation
(D) Policy implementation

20. The president signs legislation establishing a process for trying individuals accused of plotting terror attacks against the United States. This action best illustrates which of the following stages of the policymaking process?

(A) Agenda setting
(B) Policy adoption
(C) Policy formulation
(D) Policy implementation

21. Medicare beneficiaries register for prescription drug benefits. This action illustrates which of the following?

(A) Agenda setting
(B) Policy adoption
(C) Policy evaluation
(D) Policy implementation

22. In which stage of the policymaking process are policies assessed to determine their impact and effectiveness?

(A) Agenda setting
(B) Policy adoption
(C) Policy evaluation
(D) Policy implementation

23. Which of the following is the best example of a normative policy analysis?

(A) An economic analysis of the impact of increasing the minimum wage on unemployment rates for low-skilled workers.
(B) A public opinion survey measuring popular support for the death penalty.
(C) A graph showing the proportion of the share of the federal budget going to military spending over the past 30 years.
(D) An essay posted online that attacks the ethics of a candidate for president.

24. Which of the following is the best example of an empirical analysis?

(A) An economic assessment of the impact of immigration policy on the United States.
(B) A radio talk host attacks Congress for failing to pass immigration reform.
(C) A presidential candidate declares that a national sales tax would be fairer than the current tax system.
(D) A newspaper editorial argues in favor of a balanced budget.

25. Congress changes the Medicare prescription drug benefit program in response to complaints about coverage. This event best illustrates which of the following?

(A) Feedback
(B) Issue networks
(C) Normative analysis
(D) Empirical analysis

Chapter 1: A Changing America in a Changing World

Circle the correct answer.

1. Why is the population of older Americans growing?

   (A) The immigration rate is increasing.
   (B) The large baby-boom generation is nearing retirement age.
   (C) The birthrate is increasing.
   (D) All of the above

2. Which of the following terms is defined as "the widely held, deeply rooted political values of a society?"

   (A) Policymaking environment
   (B) Political culture
   (C) Democracy
   (D) Capitalism

3. A system of government in which ultimate political authority is vested in the people is the definition of which of the following terms?

   (A) Policymaking environment
   (B) Political culture
   (C) Democracy
   (D) Capitalism

4. According to Robert A. Dahl, which of the following is a criterion of democracy?

   (A) Candidates have the opportunity to conduct political campaigns in order to win public support.
   (B) All businesses and industry are privately owned.
   (C) All citizens enjoy a minimum standard of living, including access to healthcare.
   (D) All of the above

5. According to Robert A. Dahl's criteria of democracy, which of the following nations would *not* be considered a democracy?

   (A) In Country A, the government controls the news media and ensures that information damaging to the government is suppressed.
   (B) In Country B, the government owns and operates the airlines and the railroads.
   (C) In Country C, the income gap between the wealthiest and poorest sectors of society is huge.
   (D) All of the above

6. Why do political scientists consider Saudi Arabia to be an absolute monarchy?

   (A) Saudi Arabia is ruled by one person—King Abdullah.
   (B) Religion is very important in Saudi Arabia.
   (C) Women do not have the right to vote in Saudi Arabia.
   (D) The Saudi economy is dominated by the oil industry.

7. Which of the following is characteristic of a democracy?

   (A) People have the right to criticize the government.
   (B) People have the right to join unions and other interest groups.
   (C) People have the right to run against current officeholders.
   (D) All of the above

8. An economic system characterized by individual and corporate ownership of the means of production and a market economy based on the supply and demand of goods and services is a definition of which of the following?

   (A) Constitutional monarchy
   (B) Capitalism
   (C) Democracy
   (D) Absolute monarchy

9. Which of the following nations spends the most on its military?

   (A) United States
   (B) China
   (C) Russia
   (D) India

10. Which of the following nations has the largest economy?

    (A) United States
    (B) China
    (C) Russia
    (D) India

11. Which of the following statements is true about the baby-boom generation?

    (A) The baby-boom generation is smaller than preceding or succeeding generations.
    (B) The baby-boom generation retired just before 2000.
    (C) The baby-boom generation was born during the late 1940s, 1950s, and early 1960s.
    (D) None of the above

12. Which of the following statements is true about population growth in the 1990s?

    (A) The population growth rate increased during the decade largely because of immigration.
    (B) The population growth rate increased during the decade largely because the birthrate increased.
    (C) The population growth rate fell during the decade because the baby-boom generation began to die off.
    (D) The population growth rate fell during the decade because the birthrate declined.

13. Which of the following countries is *not* an important source of recent immigration to the United States?

    (A) Mexico
    (B) China
    (C) Great Britain
    (D) India

14. Why does Professor Dowell Myers believe that the United States should welcome immigration?

    (A) Immigrants take jobs that native-born Americans will not take.
    (B) Immigrants as a group are better educated and more skilled than native-born Americans.
    (C) Immigrants will help balance an otherwise top-heavy age structure in the population.
    (D) Immigrants help make the population of the United States more diverse.

15. Which racial/ethnic group grew the most rapidly during the 1990s?

    (A) Latinos
    (B) Whites
    (C) African Americans
    (D) Asian Americans

16. After the 2000 Census, California gained seats in the U.S. House of Representatives. Knowing that fact, which of the following statements must therefore be true?

    (A) California is the most populous state in the nation.
    (B) The population of California increased at a faster rate in the 1990s than did the population of the United States as a whole.
    (C) California is in the Sunbelt.
    (D) All of the above

17. The integration of national economies into a world economic system in which companies compete worldwide for suppliers and markets is the definition for which of the following terms?

    (A) Capitalism
    (B) Gross domestic product
    (C) Democracy
    (D) Global economy

18. Which of the following countries was not part of the North America Free Trade Agreement (NAFTA)?

    (A) United States
    (B) Mexico
    (C) Canada
    (D) El Salvador

19. How have low-skilled workers been affected by the global economy?

    (A) They have been harmed because global competition has led to price increases for many of the products that they purchase.
    (B) They have been harmed because American companies cannot afford to pay high wages to low-skill workers and still compete effectively against foreign competitors with lower wage costs.
    (C) They have been helped because the number of good jobs available to low-skill workers has increased.
    (D) All of the above

20. Which of the following statements is true about income distribution in the United States?

    (A) Since 1980, the proportion of national income received by the wealthiest fifth of the population has increased.
    (B) Since 1980, the proportion of income received by the poorest fifth of the population has fallen.
    (C) The income gap between the wealthiest and poorest families has been increasing.
    (D) All of the above

21. Median household income in the United States is highest for which of the following groups?

    (A) Asian Americans
    (B) Whites
    (C) African Americans
    (D) Latinos

22. Which of the following statements is true?

    (A) Household income is higher in the South than it is in any other region.
    (B) On average, women earn more than men.
    (C) The average income for people living in metropolitan areas is lower than it is for people living outside metropolitan areas.
    (D) None of the above

23. How is the official poverty threshold determined?

    (A) The poverty threshold is set at 30 percent of average household income. Anyone earning less than 30 percent of the average is considered poor.
    (B) The official poverty rate was set in 1950 at $8,000 and changes each year based on the inflation rate.
    (C) The poverty threshold is based on the amount of money an individual or family needs to purchase basic necessities.
    (D) People declare whether they are poor based on their perception of their ability to buy the things they need.

24. The poverty rate is highest for which of the following racial/ethnic groups?

    (A) Asian Americans
    (B) Whites
    (C) African Americans
    (D) Latinos

25. Which of the following statements is true about poverty in America?

    (A) Nearly half of African Americans and Latinos live in poverty.
    (B) Nearly a third of all Americans have incomes below the official poverty level.
    (C) More than a fourth of families headed by women are below the official poverty level.
    (D) All of the above

Chapter 2: The American Constitution

Circle the correct answer.

1. The fundamental law by which a state or nation is organized and governed, and to which ordinary legislation must conform, is the definition of which of the following?

   (A) Bicameralism
   (B) Separation of powers
   (C) Constitution
   (D) Federalism

2. What does "power of the purse" mean?

   (A) It is the control of the finances of government.
   (B) It is the control of the armed forces.
   (C) It is the control of foreign relations.
   (D) It is the control of the power to appoint public officials.

3. Which of the following was *not* a criticism of the Articles of Confederation?

   (A) The Articles were too difficult to amend.
   (B) The Articles gave too much power to the president.
   (C) The Articles failed to give the national government adequate authority to raise revenue.
   (D) The Articles failed to give the national government adequate authority to regulate commerce.

4. The political thought of John Locke had the most influence over which of the following documents?

   (A) Articles of Confederation
   (B) Declaration of Independence
   (C) Constitution of 1787
   (D) Fourteenth Amendment

5. Which of the following can be defined as a political system in which the citizens vote directly on matters of public concern?

   (A) Representative democracy
   (B) Direct democracy
   (C) Republic
   (D) Confederation

6. Suppose that the majority of the people of a particular political district adhere to the same religion. The majority uses its control of government to adopt policies that limit public office to members of that religion and they seriously disadvantage people who do not share their belief. The framers of the Constitution would use which of the following terms or phrases to describe that situation?

   (A) Tyranny of the majority
   (B) Representative democracy
   (C) Direct democracy
   (D) Separation of powers with checks and balances

7. Which of the following can be defined as a political system in which citizens elect representatives to make policy decisions on their behalf?

   (A) Federalism
   (B) Direct democracy
   (C) Unitary government
   (D) Representative democracy

8. Congress passes a law that criminalizes past actions that were taken before the law was passed. This law would be an example of which of the following?

   (A) Ex post facto law
   (B) Bill of attainder
   (C) *Habeas corpus*
   (D) Separation of powers

9. The Constitution guarantees accused persons the right to a speedy, public trial by an impartial jury, the right to confront witnesses, and the right to legal counsel. These provisions embody which of the following constitutional principles?

   (A) Separation of powers
   (B) Tyranny of the majority
   (C) Checks and balances
   (D) Due process of law

10. The constitutional principle that government does not have unrestricted authority over individuals is the definition for which of the following terms?

    (A) Limited government
    (B) Due process of law
    (C) Separation of powers
    (D) Bicameralism

11. The first ten amendments to the Constitution are known as which of the following?

    (A) Declaration of Independence
    (B) Articles of Confederation
    (C) Bill of Rights
    (D) Bill of attainder

12. Do the provisions of the Bill of Rights apply to state governments?

    (A) No. The Bill of Rights applies only to the actions of the federal government.
    (B) Yes. The Supreme Court has ruled that the entire Bill of Rights applies to state governments as well as the national government.
    (C) Yes. The Supreme Court has ruled that the Bill of Rights applies to the states but not to the national government.
    (D) Yes, for the most part. The Supreme Court has ruled that most of the provisions of the Bill of Rights apply to the states.

13. The selective incorporation of the Bill of Rights to the states is based on which of the following constitutional provisions?

    (A) The Due Process Clause of the Fourteenth Amendment.
    (B) The Equal Protection Clause of the Fourteenth Amendment
    (C) The Privileges and Immunities Clause of the Fourteenth Amendment
    (D) The Thirteenth Amendment

14. The political thought of Baron de Montesquieu is associated most closely with which of the following constitutional principles?

    (A) Bill of Rights
    (B) Separation of powers
    (C) Federalism
    (D) Due process of law

15. According to James Madison, what constitutional principle was designed to prevent the concentration of power in the hands of one government official or set of officials?

    (A) Separation of powers with checks and balances
    (B) Federalist Papers
    (C) Tyranny of the majority
    (D) Bill of Rights

16. The president nominates Person A to the U.S. Supreme Court, but the Senate rejects the nomination. This scenario is an example of which of the following?

    (A) Federalism
    (B) Bicameralism
    (C) Checks and balances
    (D) Tyranny of the majority

17. A political system that divides power between a central government, with authority over the whole nation, and a series of state governments is known as which of the following?

    (A) Unitary government
    (B) Confederation
    (C) Federal system
    (D) Authoritarian government

18. The state of California has tougher automobile emissions standards than the national government. This situation reflects which of the following constitutional principles?

    (A) Representative democracy
    (B) Bicameralism
    (C) Separation of powers with checks and balances
    (D) Federalism

19. Why did the framers of the Constitution create a bicameral legislative branch?

    (A) They wanted to ensure that the executive branch would be the dominant branch of government.
    (B) They wanted to prevent the legislative branch from becoming too powerful.
    (C) They wanted to prevent the judicial branch from becoming too powerful.
    (D) They wanted to strengthen the legislative branch.

20. Which of the following statements is true of the British parliamentary system?

    (A) It is undemocratic because it does not have separation of powers.

    (B) The House of Lords and the House of Commons are equally powerful.
    (C) The prime minister is chosen by majority vote of the House of Commons.
    (D) All of the above

21. Which of the following is a means through which the Constitution changes?

    (A) Practice and experience
    (B) Constitutional amendment
    (C) Judicial interpretation
    (D) All of the above

22. Which of the following is *not* a step in the process of amending the Constitution?

    (A) The House votes to propose the amendment by a two-thirds' vote.
    (B) The Senate votes to propose the amendment by a two-thirds' vote.
    (C) The president signs the proposed amendment.
    (D) Three-fourths of the states ratify the proposed amendment.

23. What was the significance of *Marbury v. Madison*?

    (A) It was the first case in which the U.S. Supreme Court declared an act of Congress unconstitutional.
    (B) The U.S. Supreme Court ruled that racial segregation was constitutional.
    (C) The U.S. Supreme Court ruled that state laws requiring racially segregated schools were unconstitutional.
    (D) The U.S. Supreme Court ruled that federal law takes precedence over state law.

24. Suppose the U.S. Supreme Court rules that a law passed by Congress and signed by the president violates the Constitution. What is the status of the law?

    (A) The law is suspended until Congress has another chance to vote on the measure. Congress can override the Supreme Court's decision by a two-thirds vote.
    (B) The law is null and void unless the president vetoes the decision. If the president vetoes the ruling, the law is reinstated.
    (C) The law is null and void.
    (D) The law remains in effect unless Congress repeals it. Supreme Court decisions are advisory.

25. How does the U.S. Constitution affect the policymaking process?

    (A) Change often comes slowly because the Constitution fragments political power.
    (B) Public policies often reflect compromise among various interests and groups.
    (C) Drastic policy changes are unlikely to occur.
    (D) All of the above

Chapter 3: The Federal System

Circle the correct answer.

1. Which of the following is the foremost goal of the No Child Left Behind Act (NCLB)?

   (A) To ensure that students with disabilities have access to educational opportunities.
   (B) To ensure that all public schools are racially integrated.
   (C) To make public school systems accountable for the progress of all students.
   (D) To provide free or reduced rate meals for school children from low-income families.

2. A political system that divides power between a central government with authority over the whole nation and a series of state governments is known as which of the following?

   (A) Federal system of government
   (B) Confederation
   (C) Unitary government
   (D) Republic

3. Article I, Section 8, of the U.S. Constitution declares that Congress has the authority to coin money. Coining money is an example of which of the following?

   (A) Delegated powers
   (B) Implied powers
   (C) Checks and balances
   (D) Concurrent powers

4. Which of the following is true about Congress?

   (A) The Constitution vests legislative power in Congress.
   (B) Congress has the power of the purse.
   (C) The Constitution delegates certain powers to Congress in Article I, Section 8.
   (D) All of the above

5. Which of the following statements is accurate about the powers of Congress?

   (A) Congress can exercise any power it wishes to exercise because it is a sovereign body.
   (B) Congress can exercise any power except those powers prohibited by the U.S. Constitution.
   (C) Congress can exercise only those powers delegated to it by the U.S. Constitution or implied through the application of the Necessary and Proper Clause.
   (D) Congress can exercise only those powers given to it in the Bill of Rights.

6. In Article I, Section 8, the Constitution grants Congress authority to "regulate commerce among the several states." Congress passes legislation establishing regulations for interstate trucking, including safety standards for trucks and drivers. Which of the following constitutional provisions or principles gives Congress the authority to set standards for trucks and truck drivers?

   (A) National Supremacy Clause
   (B) Implied powers

   (C) Concurrent powers
   (D) Equal Protection Clause

7. The Elastic Clause is another name for which of the following constitutional provisions?

   (A) National Supreme Clause
   (B) Equal Protection Clause
   (C) Necessary and Proper Clause
   (D) Commerce Clause

8. The Constitution delegates which of the following powers to the president?

   (A) The power to regulate commerce among the states.
   (B) The power to command the armed forces.
   (C) The power to declare war.
   (D) All of the above

9. Which of the following branches of government has the most extensive list of delegated powers?

   (A) Judicial branch
   (B) Legislative branch
   (C) Executive branch
   (D) State governments

10. Suppose Congress passes a law that conflicts with the state constitution of Georgia. Which takes precedence—the U.S. law or the Georgia Constitution?

    (A) The Georgia Constitution because of the Tenth Amendment.
    (B) The Georgia Constitution because all constitutions take precedence over all laws.
    (C) The U.S. law because of the delegated powers.
    (D) The U.S. law because of the National Supremacy Clause.

11. Mr. and Mrs. Brown are residents of Louisiana. They fly to Nevada and get divorced. Are they legally divorced in the eyes of the state of Louisiana? Why or why not?

    (A) They are not divorced. Because they were married in Louisiana, they must get divorced in Louisiana.
    (B) They are not divorced because the Defense of Marriage Act declares that states are not required to recognize divorces granted in other states.
    (C) They are divorced because the Privileges and Immunities Clause requires states to honor the official actions of other states.
    (D) They are divorced because the Full Faith and Credit Clause forces states to honor the official actions of other states.

12. A person wanted for a crime in New York flees to Florida, where he is arrested. The procedure for returning the accused person to New York to face criminal charges is known as which of the following?

    (A) Full Faith and Credit
    (B) Privileges and Immunities
    (C) Extradition
    (D) Delegated powers

13. The Tenth Amendment is the constitutional basis for which of the following?

   (A) Reserved powers
   (B) Delegated powers
   (C) Implied powers
   (D) Concurrent powers

14. Both state governments and the national government have the constitutional authority to tax and spend. Therefore, the power to tax and spend is an example of which of the following?

   (A) Reserved powers
   (B) Delegated powers
   (C) Implied powers
   (D) Concurrent powers

15. Which of the following statements would be most likely to come from an advocate of a strong national government as opposed to a supporter of states' rights?

   (A) National control makes for better public policies.
   (B) The Constitution is a compact among the states, and the powers of the national government should be narrowly interpreted.
   (C) The powers of the national government should be closely limited to the delegated powers.
   (D) All of the above

16. Would states' rights advocates favor or oppose the NCLB?

   (A) They would favor the law because it provides federal money to support state education programs.
   (B) They would favor the law because a Republican president was behind the adoption of the measure.
   (C) They would oppose the law because it increased federal involvement in education policy, which is traditionally an area of state responsibility.
   (D) They would oppose the law because it didn't provide enough money to support public education.

17. Which of the following was part of the Supreme Court's ruling in *McCulloch v. Maryland*?

   (A) The Supreme Court ruled that Congress lacked the constitutional authority to charter a bank.
   (B) The Supreme Court ruled that the powers of Congress were strictly limited to the delegated powers.
   (C) The Supreme Court upheld the Maryland tax on the bank.
   (D) None of the above

18. Which of the following constitutional provisions has played the most prominent role in the modern expansion of federal government authority?

   (A) Equal Protection Clause
   (B) Full Faith and Credit Clause
   (C) Privileges and Immunities Clause
   (D) Commerce Clause

19. Which of the following is *not* part of the authorization process?

   (A) It establishes a program.
   (B) It appropriates money for the program.
   (C) It specifies an agency to implement the program.
   (D) It defines the purpose of the program.

20. A federal grant program that provides funds to state and local governments for a fairly narrow, specific purpose is known as which of the following?

   (A) Block grant
   (B) Formula grant
   (C) Categorical grant
   (D) Program grant

21. A federal grant program that provides money for a program in a broad, general policy area, such as childcare or job training, is known as which of the following?

   (A) Block grant
   (B) Formula grant
   (C) Categorical grant
   (D) Program grant

22. A grant program that requires state and local governments to compete for available federal money is known as which of the following?

   (A) Block grant
   (B) Formula grant
   (C) Categorical grant
   (D) Program grant

23. A grant program that awards funding on the basis of a formula established by Congress is known as which of the following?

   (A) Block grant
   (B) Formula grant
   (C) Categorical grant
   (D) Program grant

24. To qualify for a federal grant, a unit of local government is required to spend a certain amount of its own money on the activity supported by the grant. This is an example of which of the following?

   (A) Matching funds requirement
   (B) Federal preemption of state authority
   (C) Appropriations process
   (D) Formula grant program

25. NCLB requires that states meet certain goals in order to continue receiving federal funds. This requirement is an example of which of the following?

   (A) Federal mandate
   (B) Matching funds requirement
   (C) Federal preemption of state authority
   (D) Project grant

Circle the correct answer.

1. Which of the following statements about the socialization process is *not* true?

   (A) Political socialization ends when individuals reach their early 20s.
   (B) Young children typically identify with the same political party as their parents.
   (C) Schools historically have taught the children of immigrants to be patriotic Americans and they continue to play that role today.
   (D) Personal involvement in religious organizations is associated with political participation.

2. Which of the following agents of socialization plays the most important role in shaping the party identification of youngsters?

   (A) Family
   (B) School
   (C) Peers
   (D) Media

3. A team of political scientists wants to measure the attitudes of college students toward politics and government. The universe for the study would be which of the following?

   (A) The group of individuals who are actually interviewed for the study.
   (B) All college-age adults.
   (C) All college students.
   (D) All Americans.

4. A professionally administered survey has a margin of error of ±3 percentage points. Assume that the sample was properly drawn and carefully conducted. How often will a sample differ from the universe by more than 3 percentage points merely on the basis of chance?

   (A) Never. If the sample is truly random, it will never differ by more than the margin of error.
   (B) One time in 20. Even a perfectly drawn sample will by chance be outside the margin of error 5 percent of the time.
   (C) Three percent of the time. The margin of error indicates the error factor built into a survey.
   (D) One time in five. A well-conducted survey will be wrong 20 percent of the time.

5. A public opinion poll taken a month before the election has a margin of error of 3 percentage points. The poll shows Candidate A ahead of Candidate B 46 percent to 44 percent with the rest undecided. What is the best analysis of the result of the poll?

   (A) Candidate A is ahead by at least 2 percentage points but may actually be ahead by 5 percentage points.
   (B) Candidate A is ahead, but it is impossible to know by how much.
   (C) Candidate B is actually ahead because Candidate A did not reach the 50 percent support level.
   (D) The candidates are in a statistical tie because the difference in their support is within the margin of error.

6. A major Internet provider regularly conducts online polls about current issues, such as stem cell research, the war in Iraq, and immigration reform. Sometimes tens of thousands of people participate. Would the results of these polls be accurate?

   (A) Yes. The sample size is large and everyone has a chance to participate.
   (B) No. The sample size is too small.
   (C) No. The sample size is too large.
   (D) Probably not. It is unlikely that the sample is a representative sample of the universe.

7. Why did the *Literary Digest* poll fail to correctly predict the outcome of the 1936 presidential election?

   (A) The sample size was too small.
   (B) The sample size was too large.
   (C) The sample was biased because it included only people with telephones and automobiles.
   (D) The questions were biased because they were slanted in favor of the Republican candidate.

8. On which of the following questions would you expect a survey to find the highest level of public support?

   (A) Gay men and lesbians should have equal employment rights and opportunities with all other Americans.
   (B) Gay men and lesbians should have the right to be employed as elementary school teachers.
   (C) Gay men and lesbians should have the right to be employed as clergymen.
   (D) Gay men and lesbians should have the right to be employed as physicians.

9. Which of the following groups would you expect to express the highest level of support for civil liberties?

   (A) Low-income people
   (B) Political elites, that is, people who exercise influence on the policy process
   (C) People who seldom if ever vote
   (D) Recent immigrants

10. What impact has the adoption of registered partners in Denmark had on Danish society?

    (A) Most gay men and lesbians have formed registered partnerships.
    (B) The marriage rate has fallen dramatically.
    (C) The divorce rate has increased significantly.
    (D) None of the above

11. The popular acceptance of a government and its officials as rightful authorities in the exercise of power is a good definition of which of the following?

    (A) Political efficacy
    (B) Political tolerance
    (C) Political legitimacy
    (D) Opinion leaders

12. Which of the following would likely be a result of a low level of political legitimacy in a society?

(A) Election turnout would be high.
(B) Most people would voluntarily obey laws and regulations.
(C) People wanting to bring about political change would turn to the electoral system rather than violence.
(D) None of the above

13. The extent to which individuals believe they can influence the policymaking process is a definition of which of the following?

(A) Political efficacy
(B) Political legitimacy
(C) Political trust
(D) Public opinion

14. Which of the following statements reflects a high level of internal political efficacy?

(A) "I don't believe that government officials care what I think."
(B) "I have a good understanding of how government works."
(C) "I think that most of the people running the government are crooks."
(D) "Sometimes politics and government seem so complicated that a person like me can't really understand what's going on."

15. The assessment of an individual of the responsiveness of government to his or her concerns is a definition of which of the following:

(A) Political trust
(B) External political efficacy
(C) Internal political efficacy
(D) Political legitimacy

16. Which of the following positions would most likely be taken by a conservative?

(A) "Government has a responsibility to ensure that all Americans have access to affordable healthcare."
(B) "Government should act aggressively to adopt regulations to slow global warming."
(C) "Government has a responsibility to protect the unborn by limiting access to abortion."
(D) "Government should address the problem of homelessness by providing more public housing."

17. Which of the following statements reflects a liberal ideology?

(A) The government that governs least governs best.
(B) Government regulations often do more harm than good.
(C) The government has no business telling women that they must carry a fetus to term.
(D) Churches and private charities do a better job than the government at solving social problems.

18. Which of the following terms is not synonymous with the other terms in the list?

(A) Political left
(B) Conservative
(C) Right wing
(D) Political right

19. Which of the following statements about political ideology is true?

(A) More people label themselves conservative than identify themselves as liberal.
(B) Most people hold conservative views on some issues, liberal views on other issues.
(C) Some issues, such as foreign policy issues, are not easily defined along liberal/conservative lines.
(D) All of the above

20. Which of the following statements about political ideology is true?

(A) Southerners as a group are more conservative than people in other regions of the country.
(B) Lower-income people are more conservative on social welfare issues than are middle- and upper-income people.
(C) African Americans and Latinos are more conservative than whites on economic issues.
(D) All of the above

21. Which of the following statements about the gender gap is correct?

(A) Women are more likely than men to vote Republican.
(B) Women are more likely than men to support abortion rights.
(C) Women are more likely than men to favor increased defense spending.
(D) Women are more likely than men to favor government programs to provide healthcare and education and to protect the environment.

22. How would Professor James Stimson explain the relationship between public opinion and the policymaking process?

(A) Elected officials can adopt whatever policies they want because most Americans are too uninformed about politics and government to know or care.
(B) Policymakers must follow public opinion closely or risk being voted out of office.
(C) Public opinion sets limits on policymakers, what Stimson calls zones of acquiescence, but within those limits policymakers are free to adopt policies of their choosing.
(D) The public does not care what policies officials adopt, but if the policies turn out badly, then they punish the officials who adopted them by voting them out of office.

Chapter 5: Political Participation

Circle the correct answer.

1. Which of the following is the most common form of political participation?

    (A) Contributing money to candidates
    (B) Joining an interest group
    (C) Contacting an elected official
    (D) Voting

2. In which of the following elections would you expect turnout to be the highest as a proportion of eligible voters?

    (A) Local election for mayor
    (B) Election for governor
    (C) Election for senator
    (D) Presidential election

3. For which election will turnout be higher as a proportion of eligible voters—a presidential election or a local election for mayor?

    (A) The presidential election because interest will be greater for that contest.
    (B) The presidential election because more people are eligible to vote for president than are eligible to vote for mayor.
    (C) The local election for mayor because local officials have a more direct impact on the lives of ordinary people.
    (D) Turnout will be the same for each type of election.

4. Which of the following is a form of political participation?

    (A) Writing a letter to a local official about a problem.
    (B) Giving money to a candidate for a school board election.
    (C) Putting up a yard sign to support a candidate for the state legislature.
    (D) All of the above

5. Which of the following is a reasonable explanation of why more people vote than volunteer to work in a political campaign?

    (A) Voting requires less time and effort than volunteer work.
    (B) Voting has a greater impact on the outcome of an election than volunteer work.
    (C) Most political campaigns don't want volunteer help because they prefer to rely on professional campaign consultants.
    (D) None of the above

6. Is political efficacy related to political participation?

    (A) No. People vote out of civic duty regardless of other factors.

    (B) Yes. People who think they can impact government policies are more likely to participate than are other people.
    (C) Yes. People who express a high level of trust in public officials are more likely to vote than people who do not trust the government to do what is right.
    (D) No. One vote seldom affects the outcome of an election.

7. The process of motivating people to vote is known as which of the following?

    (A) Political efficacy
    (B) Political participation
    (C) Voter mobilization
    (D) Straight ticket voting

8. Which of the following play(s) a positive role in voter mobilization?

    (A) Political parties
    (B) Interest groups
    (C) Individual contacts
    (D) All of the above

9. Would you expect the voter turnout rate to be higher for people earning $80,000 a year or those making $30,000 a year?

    (A) Turnout would be greater for the higher-income group.
    (B) Turnout would be greater for the lower-income group.
    (C) Turnout would be the same for both groups.
    (D) Turnout would be greater for the higher-income group in all elections but presidential elections, where the turnout rate would be the same.

10. What is the relationship between age and political participation?

    (A) Participation rates fall as people age.
    (B) Participation rates increase as people age.
    (C) Participation rates increase as people age until individuals reach old age and then participation rates turn downward.
    (D) Participation increases through middle age and then gradually declines throughout the last half of the individual lifespan.

11. For which of the following age groups would you expect the voting participation rate to be the lowest?

    (A) People in their 20s
    (B) People in their 30s
    (C) People in their 40s
    (D) People in their 50s

12. Voter turnout is usually greater for whites and Asian Americans than it is for Latinos and African Americans. Which of the following statements accurately explains different participation rates for different racial/ethnic groups?

(A) The outcome of elections does not affect the lives of African Americans and Latinos as much as it does whites and Asian Americans.
(B) African Americans and Latinos as a group do not care about government and politics.
(C) The income and educational levels of African Americans and Latinos are lower than they are for whites and Asian Americans.
(D) All of the above

13. Which of the following groups is the least represented in all areas of political participation compared with the other groups?

(A) Latinos
(B) Whites
(C) African Americans
(D) The groups participate at roughly the same rate.

14. Which of the following statements accurately explains why Latino voter participation rates are lower than they are for other groups?

(A) As a group, Latinos are not as well educated as whites and Asian Americans.
(B) As a group, Latinos earn lower incomes than whites and Asians.
(C) A higher percentage of Latinos are not citizens than for other racial/ethnic groups.
(D) All of the above

15. Which of the following groups is most seriously affected by state laws that disqualify individuals with serious criminal offenses from voting?

(A) White women
(B) Latino males
(C) African American males
(D) White males

16. Compared with men, women are more likely to do which of the following?

(A) Vote
(B) Give money to candidates
(C) Join a political group
(D) There are no differences in participation rates between men and women.

17. Which of the following statements is true about nonvoters?

(A) The primary reason people do not vote is that they are not registered to vote.
(B) Nonvoting results from a broad range of reasons.

(C) Almost all nonvoters are poorly educated people with relatively low incomes.
(D) All of the above

18. Why is the voting age population (VAP) an imperfect database to measure voter participation?

(A) The census has a fairly accurate count of the population, but measures of the population by age group are imprecise.
(B) Voter turnout numbers are often inaccurate.
(C) The VAP includes large numbers of people who are not eligible to vote, including noncitizens and people who are incarcerated.
(D) All of the above

19. Which of the following statements best describes recent trends in voter turnout?

(A) Voter turnout in presidential elections has increased in each of the last three presidential elections.
(B) Voter turnout in presidential elections has been falling consistently since the early 1960s.
(C) Voter turnout in presidential elections has been rising consistently since the early 1960s.
(D) Voter turnout in presidential elections has fallen in each of the last three presidential elections.

20. How does voter turnout in the United States compare with turnout in other western democracies?

(A) Turnout in the United States is relatively low.
(B) Turnout in the United States is relatively high.
(C) Turnout in the United States is average.
(D) Turnout in the United States is relatively high for national elections, but low for state elections.

21. What impact did the National Voter Registration Act have on participation?

(A) It failed to increase registration rates or voter turnout.
(B) It succeeded in increasing both voter registration rates and voter turnout.
(C) It succeeded in increasing voter registration rates, but had no impact on voter turnout.
(D) It failed to increase voter registration rates, but it increased voter turnout by spreading awareness of election issues.

22. Which of the following statements about political participation is true?

(A) Democrats always benefit from high voter turnout.
(B) Political activists are more liberal than the population as a whole on economic issues.
(C) Interest groups and political parties typically promote the interests of the working class.
(D) None of the above

Chapter 6: The Media

Circle the correct answer.

1. Which of the following media outlets is owned by the U.S. government?

   (A) New York Times
   (B) CBS Evening News
   (C) National Public Radio
   (D) None of the above

2. Which of the following is a set of radio stations?

   (A) NPR
   (B) PBS
   (C) Corporation for Public Broadcasting
   (D) None of the above

3. Which of the following is a set of television stations?

   (A) NPR
   (B) PBS
   (C) Corporation for Public Broadcasting
   (D) None of the above

4. Clear Channel Communications is most closely associated with which of the following?

   (A) Newspapers
   (B) Internet
   (C) Radio stations
   (D) Cable television

5. Cross-media ownership refers to which of the following?

   (A) A corporation owning several different types of media outlets.
   (B) A corporation owning a chain of television stations in more than one city.
   (C) A corporation owning multiple radio stations in the same city.
   (D) A newspaper jointly owned by several corporations.

6. Which of the following have been suffering from a loss of viewers or readers?

   (A) Daily newspapers
   (B) Network evening news shows
   (C) Newsmagazines
   (D) All of the above

7. Which of the following would be characterized as "new media"?

   (A) Washington Post
   (B) CBS television
   (C) Chicago Tribune
   (D) None of the above

8. A blog would be characterized as which of the following?

   (A) Print media
   (B) Attack journalism

   (C) New media
   (D) All of the above

9. Which of the following is *not* part of the legal definition of obscenity?

   (A) The material depicts violent behavior.
   (B) The work taken as a whole lacks serious literary, artistic, political, or scientific value.
   (C) The material is such that the average person, applying contemporary standards, would find that the work taken as a whole appeals to prurient interest.
   (D) The material depicts sexual conduct.

10. *Salomé* is an opera that is considered a masterpiece. It is regularly performed in opera houses throughout the world. The opera includes sexually suggestive dancing and suggestions of incest. In the climactic scene, Salomé dances seductively with the severed head of John the Baptist. Is the opera legally obscene?

    (A) Yes. Overtly sexual expression and violence are legally obscene.
    (B) No. The First Amendment guarantees freedom of expression.
    (C) It depends on the local standards where the opera is performed.
    (D) No. The opera is a serious work of art.

11. What is libel?

    (A) Sexually explicit conduct that violates community standards.
    (B) False written statements that lower a person's reputation or expose a person to hatred, contempt, or ridicule.
    (C) False spoken statements that lower a person's reputation or expose a person to hatred, contempt, or ridicule.
    (D) None of the above

12. The mayor and an ordinary citizen at a public forum get into a shouting match. Each individual calls the other a crook and a druggie. Each person sues the other for defamation. Which of the two individuals would be most likely to win the lawsuit and why?

    (A) The mayor has the best chance of winning because elected officials enjoy special protection under the Constitution.
    (B) The citizen has the best chance of winning because public figures have a more difficult time winning defamation lawsuits than do ordinary citizens.
    (C) The two individuals have an equal chance of winning their lawsuit.
    (D) Neither individual will win because the Constitution protects freedom of speech.

13. What is slander?

   (A) Sexually explicit conduct that violates community standards.
   (B) False written statements that lower a person's reputation or expose a person to hatred, contempt, or ridicule.
   (C) False spoken statements that lower a person's reputation or expose a person to hatred, contempt, or ridicule.
   (D) None of the above

14. Government action to prevent the publication or broadcast of objectionable material is known as which of the following?

   (A) Slander
   (B) Libel
   (C) Prior restraint
   (D) Attack journalism

15. Which of the following agencies has the authority to regulate the broadcast media that use the public airwaves?

   (A) Corporation for Public Broadcasting
   (B) National Public Radio
   (C) Public Broadcasting Service
   (D) Federal Communication Commission

16. Which of the following media outlets is *not* regulated by the FCC?

   (A) UHF television
   (B) Cable television
   (C) AM radio
   (D) FM radio

17. An FCC regulation requiring broadcasters to provide an equivalent opportunity to opposing political candidates competing for the same office is a definition of which of the following terms?

   (A) Objective journalism
   (B) Equal-time rule
   (C) Fairness Doctrine
   (D) Attack journalism

18. A major newspaper carries a series of articles discussing the backgrounds and issue orientations of all the major candidates running for the presidency. The paper's decision to cover all of the candidates and not just its favorite candidate can be explained by which of the following?

   (A) The Fairness Doctrine requires that all candidates be covered.
   (B) The equal-time rule requires that all candidates be covered.
   (C) The newspaper is voluntarily practicing objective journalism.
   (D) The newspaper is defending itself from a possible defamation lawsuit.

19. A television network carries a press conference by the president who is running for reelection. Will the network be required to give the challenger an equal amount of coverage?

   (A) No. The equal-time rule exempts news coverage.
   (B) Yes. The Fairness Doctrine requires it.
   (C) Yes. The equal-time rule requires it.
   (D) No. The television networks are not subject to FCC regulation.

20. What is the purpose of a shield law?

   (A) To protect journalists from being sued for defamation
   (B) To protect journalists from being forced to disclose confidential information in a legal proceeding
   (C) To protect journalists from being charged with violating FCC indecency standards.
   (D) None of the above

21. Arbitron ratings are the basis for setting advertising rates for which of the following media outlets?

   (A) Radio
   (B) Television
   (C) Newspapers
   (D) Internet

22. Nielson ratings are the basis for setting advertising rates for which of the following media outlets?

   (A) Radio
   (B) Television
   (C) Newspapers
   (D) Internet

23. "Read my lips: No new taxes." This is an example of which of the following?

   (A) Objective journalism
   (B) Attack journalism
   (C) Equal-time rule
   (D) Sound bite

24. Which of the following has research on bias in the network evening news discovered?

   (A) The network evening news treats Democratic candidates more favorably than it does Republicans.
   (B) The network evening news treats Republican candidates more favorably than it does Democrats.
   (C) The network evening news treats all candidates equally.
   (D) The network evening news typically favors incumbent presidents running for reelection regardless of political party.

25. The media have the greatest impact in which of the following stages of the policymaking process?

   (A) Agenda setting
   (B) Policy formulation
   (C) Policy adoption
   (D) Policy implementation

Circle the correct answer.

1. "I don't see any point in joining the neighborhood civic association. My $20 annual dues aren't enough to make much difference. At any rate, I will benefit from the association's activities whether I am a member or not." This statement reflects which of the following concepts?

   (A) Friendly Incumbent Rule
   (B) Free-rider barrier to group membership
   (C) Material incentives to group membership
   (D) Purposive incentives to group membership

2. Eric Holst joined the American Legion because he enjoys hanging out at the legion hall with his buddies. This action illustrates which of the following concepts?

   (A) Free-rider barrier to group membership
   (B) Material incentive for joining a group
   (C) Purposive incentive for joining a group
   (D) Solidary incentive for joining a group

3. Which of the following is an example of a purposive incentive for joining an interest group?

   (A) Lee Wong joins Greenpeace because he feels strongly about protecting the environment.
   (B) John Bradley joins the NRA because he wants to enroll his sons in NRA gun safety classes.
   (C) Luisa Gonzalez joins the American Federation of Teachers because many of her fellow teachers belong and she enjoys spending time with her friends.
   (D) None of the above

4. Which of the following organizations is a business federation representing the interests of businesses of all sizes, sectors, and regions?

   (A) National Federation of Independent Businesses
   (B) AFL-CIO
   (C) U.S. Chamber of Commerce
   (D) NAACP

5. Which of the following organizations would be most likely to favor legislation to make it more difficult to file class action lawsuits?

   (A) Chamber of Commerce
   (B) AFL-CIO
   (C) ABA
   (D) AARP

6. Which of the following organizations would be most likely to favor the repeal of state right-to-work laws?

   (A) Chamber of Commerce
   (B) AFL-CIO
   (C) Club for Growth
   (D) LULAC

7. Which of the following statements is true about organized labor?

   (A) The percentage of the workforce that belongs to labor unions has been in decline for years.

   (B) Wal-Mart, the nation's largest employer, has successfully resisted unionization efforts.
   (C) Organized labor is stronger in the Frostbelt, weaker in the Sunbelt.
   (D) All of the above

8. Which of the following organizations would be most likely to favor increasing the minimum wage?

   (A) Chamber of Commerce
   (B) American Farm Bureau
   (C) AFL-CIO
   (D) AARP

9. Which of the following organizations would be most likely to favor affirmative action in college and university admissions?

   (A) NAACP
   (B) AFL-CIO
   (C) AARP
   (D) Sierra Club

10. Which of the following pairs of organizations would be most likely to be on the opposite sides of the issue of abortion?

   (A) Right to Life and NARAL
   (B) Chamber of Commerce and the AFL-CIO
   (C) Club for Growth and the NRA
   (D) Sierra Club and NOW

11. Which of the following organizations would be most likely to celebrate Earth Day?

   (A) Sierra Club
   (B) Human Rights Campaign
   (C) NARAL
   (D) Common Cause

12. Which of the following organizations would be most likely to endorse a Democratic candidate for president in the next election?

   (A) Right to Life
   (B) Chamber of Commerce
   (C) NRA
   (D) NARAL

13. What are political action committees (PACs)?

   (A) They are organizations representing the interests of firms and professionals in the same general field.
   (B) They are organizations whose members care intensely about a single issue or small group of related issues.
   (C) They are organizations created to raise and distribute money in election campaigns.
   (D) They are organizations created to seek benefits on behalf of groups of persons who are in some way incapacitated or otherwise unable to represent their own interests.

14. PACs associated with which of the following types of interest groups raise the most money?

(A) Business groups
(B) Labor groups
(C) Racial/ethnic groups
(D) Agricultural groups

15. PACs associated with which of the following tend to give most of their campaign contributions to incumbent members of Congress of both political parties?

(A) Business groups
(B) Labor unions
(C) NRA
(D) Cause groups

16. Which of the following candidates would you expect to benefit the most from PAC contributions?

(A) A Republican challenger
(B) A Democratic challenger
(C) A candidate from either party running for an open seat
(D) An incumbent from either party running for reelection

17. A PAC representing Interest Group A contributed to Congressman B's reelection campaign even though the congressman sides with the interest group's issue positions only about 60 percent of the time. The PAC is acting in accordance with which of the following principles?

(A) Friendly Incumbent Rule
(B) Free-rider barrier to group membership
(C) Bundling
(D) Material incentive to group membership

18. An interest group that engages in bundling is doing which of the following?

(A) Lobbying more than one member of Congress at the same time.
(B) Joining forces with other interest groups to lobby on behalf of the same cause.
(C) Gathering checks from individual supporters made out to particular candidates and giving those checks to the candidate in a bundle.
(D) Giving money to more than one candidate for the same office.

19. An organization created by individuals and groups to influence the outcomes of elections by raising and spending money that candidates and political parties cannot legally raise is known by which of the following names?

(A) Political action committee
(B) Interest group
(C) Political party
(D) 527 committee

20. Which of the following statements about lobbying and lobbyists is true?

(A) Groups lobby the legislative branch of government but not the executive branch.
(B) Interest group lobbyists frequently focus on the details of legislation rather than votes on final passage.
(C) Former members of Congress are prohibited by law from becoming lobbyists.
(D) None of the above

21. What is the best assessment of the relationship between campaign contributions and interest group lobbying?

(A) Money buys votes. Members of Congress vote for the causes supported by the groups that give them the most money.
(B) Money buys access. Members of Congress are willing to meet with lobbyists representing groups that provide them with campaign contributions.
(C) Money and lobbying are unrelated. Members of Congress are open to consider all views regardless of political contributions.
(D) Because of campaign finance regulations, interest groups are prohibited from contributing money to help members of Congress run for reelection.

22. Which of the following statements is true about the use of protest demonstrations as a political strategy?

(A) Protest demonstrations are a tactic used by groups unable to achieve their goals through other means.
(B) Business and trade groups are more likely to use protect demonstrations than are other organizations.
(C) Protests are among the more effective approaches interest groups have for achieving their goals.
(D) All of the above

23. Which of the following organizations specializes in the use of litigation to achieve its goals?

(A) Chamber of Commerce
(B) American Bar Association
(C) ACLU
(D) NRA

24. Which of the following types of interest groups is typically allied with the Republican Party?

(A) Organized labor
(B) Environmental organizations
(C) African American rights groups
(D) Anti-tax groups

25. Which of the following types of interest groups is typically allied with the Democratic Party?

(A) Business groups
(B) Abortion rights organizations
(C) Conservative Christian organizations
(D) None of the above

Circle the correct answer.

1. Which of the following terms is best defined as a group of individuals who join together to seek government office in order to make public policy?

   (A) Interest group
   (B) Political action committee
   (C) Issue network
   (D) Political party

2. The Green, Reform, and Libertarian Parties are examples of which of the following?

   (A) Interest groups
   (B) Party eras
   (C) Third parties
   (D) Political action committees

3. Which of the following is *not* a reason why the United States has a two-party system rather than a multiparty system?

   (A) The plurality election system awards office to the candidate with the most votes, leaving candidates who finished a strong second or third with nothing.
   (B) The Electoral College awards electoral votes only to candidates who win the most votes in each state.
   (C) The United States is not deeply divided along social and political lines.
   (D) Federal law limits the number of parties on the ballot to two.

4. An election system that awards office to the candidate with the most votes is known by which of the following terms?

   (A) Proportional representation
   (B) Party realignment
   (C) Plurality election system
   (D) Two-party system

5. Which of the following statements is true about Israel but is *not* true about the United States?

   (A) If a political party gets 10 percent of the vote, it will get 10 percent of the seats in the national legislature.
   (B) Candidates for the national legislature run from geographical areas called districts.
   (C) Nearly all of the members of the national legislature are members of one of two major political parties.
   (D) Voters may be reluctant to vote for a smaller party because they do not want to "throw their vote away" on a party that has no chance to gain representation.

6. Which of the following statements is true about political parties and elections in Israel?

   (A) Candidates are chosen in primaries to run from districts.
   (B) Voters cast their ballots primarily for political parties rather than for individual candidates.

   (C) Israel has a two-party system similar to the party system in the United States.
   (D) All of the above

7. Which of the following statements is true about party fundraising?

   (A) The Democratic Party has historically raised more money than the Republican Party.
   (B) The Republican Party closed the fundraising gap with the Democrats in 2006 and especially 2008.
   (C) The Republican Party has caught up with the Democrats because of Internet fundraising.
   (D) None of the above

8. The Grand Old Party (GOP) refers to which of the following?

   (A) Libertarian Party
   (B) Green Party
   (C) Democratic Party
   (D) Republican Party

9. Which of the following is a period of time characterized by a degree of uniformity in the nature of political party competition?

   (A) Plurality election system
   (B) Party realignment
   (C) Party era
   (D) Proportional representation

10. A change in the underlying party loyalties of voters that ends one party era and begins another is known by which of the following terms?

    (A) Plurality election system
    (B) Party realignment
    (C) Proportional representation
    (D) Divided government

11. Which of the following statements about party identification is accurate?

    (A) Since 2004, the proportion of Democrats in the population has increased by at least 5 percentage points.
    (B) Since 2004, the proportion of independents in the population has decreased by at least 5 percentage points.
    (C) Since 2004, the proportion of Republicans in the population has decreased by at least 5 percentage points.
    (D) None of the above

12. Which of the following statements about independents is accurate?

    (A) Most independents are men.
    (B) As a group, independents are more religious than are Democrats and Republicans.
    (C) Most independents are so disinterested in politics that they are not registered to vote.
    (D) None of the above

13. Among which of the following income groups, would you expect the Republican candidate for president to do best in the next presidential election?

    (A) People making less than $30,000 a year.
    (B) People making between $30,000 and $60,000 a year.
    (C) People making between $100,000 and $150,000 a year.
    (D) People making more than $200,000 a year.

14. Which of the following groups would be *least* likely to give a majority of its votes to the Democratic candidate for president in the next election?

    (A) Asian Americans
    (B) African Americans
    (C) Whites
    (D) Latinos

15. The Republican Party has been losing vote share among Latinos because of which of the following issues?

    (A) Gun control
    (B) Immigration reform
    (C) Gay marriage
    (D) Abortion

16. Which of the following statements is true about the groups that support each of the two major political parties?

    (A) Men are more likely than women to vote Democratic.
    (B) The more education one has the more likely that person is to vote Republican.
    (C) White voters are more likely than nonwhite voters to support Republican candidates.
    (D) None of the above

17. Which of the following statements is true about voter preferences?

    (A) Gay and lesbian voters tend to vote Republican.
    (B) Married voters tend to vote Democratic.
    (C) Women are more likely to vote Republican than are men.
    (D) None of the above

18. The Republican Party is strongest in which of the following regions?

    (A) South
    (B) West Coast
    (C) Midwest
    (D) Northeast

19. Which of the following groups tends to vote Democratic?

    (A) People who call themselves conservative
    (B) Gays and lesbians
    (C) People living in small towns and rural areas
    (D) Men

20. Which of the following groups tend to vote Republican?

    (A) People who attend religious services on a weekly basis
    (B) Women
    (C) People living in inner-city areas
    (D) Jews

21. Which of the following groups would be the most supportive of Democratic candidates?

    (A) Catholics
    (B) White evangelical Protestants
    (C) Jews
    (D) Members of mainline Protestant denominations

22. The Republican Party takes which of the following issue positions?

    (A) Opposition to all tax increases
    (B) Opposition to abortion
    (C) Opposition to gay marriage
    (D) All of the above

23. The Democratic Party favors which of the following issue positions?

    (A) Support for Israel
    (B) Reducing the federal budget deficit
    (C) Expanding the Children's Health Insurance Program (CHIP)
    (D) All of the above

24. The Democratic Party favors which of the following issue positions?

    (A) Legislation to limit damage awards in medical malpractice lawsuits
    (B) Increasing the minimum wage
    (C) Energy exploration in the Arctic National Wildlife Preserve
    (D) All of the above

25. Political Party A controls both houses of Congress while Political Party B holds the presidency. This situation is an example of which of the following?

    (A) Divided government
    (B) Responsible parties
    (C) Proportional representation
    (D) Realignment

Chapter 9: Elections

Circle the correct answer.

1. Luisa Cangelosi voted for the Republican candidate for president, the Democratic candidate for the U.S. Senate, and the Democratic candidate for the U.S. House. Ms. Cangelosi did which of the following?

   (A) Violated the Voting Rights Act
   (B) Voted in a presidential preference primary
   (C) Voted a split ticket
   (D) Voted in a primary election

2. State A limits primary voting to people who are registered party members. State A has which of the following?

   (A) A closed primary
   (B) An open primary
   (C) A blanket primary
   (D) A presidential preference primary

3. Which of the following elections is *not* conducted statewide in most states?

   (A) Election for governor
   (B) Election for U.S. House
   (C) Election for U.S. Senate
   (D) Election for president

4. How often does reapportionment take place?

   (A) Every ten years after the U.S. Census
   (B) Every four years to coincide with the presidential election
   (C) Whenever population changes by more than 10 percent
   (D) None of the above

5. *Baker v. Carr* (1962) and *Wesberry v. Sanders* (1964) dealt with which of the following issues?

   (A) Gerrymandering
   (B) Reapportionment
   (C) Campaign finance laws
   (D) Voting Rights Act

6. Why did state legislatures, especially in the South, increase the number of congressional districts that would likely elect African Americans to Congress after the 1990 Census?

   (A) Most state legislatures were controlled by the Democratic Party, and the Democrats wanted to increase minority representation in Congress.
   (B) The population of African Americans increased rapidly in the 1980s.
   (C) The legislatures were attempting to comply with the Voting Rights Act (VRA).
   (D) All of the above

7. Which of the following statements about the Voting Rights Act (VRA) is true?

   (A) The VRA prohibits gerrymandering.
   (B) The pre-clearance provision of the VRA does not apply to the entire country.
   (C) The VRA only protects the voting rights of African Americans.
   (D) All of the above

8. Which of the following statements is true about the role of money in political campaigns?

   (A) The candidate who spends the most money always wins.
   (B) Advertising, especially television advertising, is the single largest expenditure in most campaign budgets.
   (C) Candidates who provide most of their own campaign money usually win because they do not have to spend time fundraising.
   (D) All of the above

9. America Coming Together, MoveOn, and Swift Boat Veterans for Truth were examples of which of the following?

   (A) Interest groups
   (B) PACs
   (C) 527 committees
   (D) Political parties

10. Federal funds are used to partially finance campaigns for which of the following offices?

    (A) President
    (B) U.S. House
    (C) U.S. Senate
    (D) All federal offices, including Congress and the president

11. A newspaper reports that the incumbent president running for reelection is using a "rose garden strategy." What is a rose garden strategy?

    (A) The president stresses domestic issues, such as the economy.
    (B) The president focuses on the positive.
    (C) The president runs an aggressive campaign, attacking the qualifications of the opposing candidate.
    (D) The president tries to appear presidential rather than political.

12. Which of the following statements about negative campaigning is true?

    (A) Negative campaigning is relatively new in American politics.
    (B) Political scientists agree that negative campaigning decreases voter turnout.
    (C) Political scientists agree that negative campaigning almost never works.
    (D) None of the above

13. Which of the following reasons helps explain why incumbent members of Congress typically win reelection?

    (A) They usually have more money than their challengers.
    (B) They are usually better known than their challengers.
    (C) Many congressional districts are safe for one party or the other.
    (D) All of the above

14. Which of the following officially selected John McCain as the 2008 presidential nominee of the Republican Party?

    (A) Delegates at the 2008 Republican National Convention by majority vote
    (B) Electors from each state voting in the electoral college
    (C) Voters nationwide in an open primary
    (D) Voters nationwide in a closed primary

15. How were the delegates to the 2008 Democratic National Convention chosen?

    (A) They were chosen by the Congress.
    (B) They were chosen by the electoral college.
    (C) They were chosen by each state party, either through a presidential preference primary or a party caucus.
    (D) They were chosen in a national primary election.

16. Which of the following plays the most important role in selecting the presidential nominees of the Democratic and Republican parties?

    (A) Party activists and party voters.
    (B) Party bosses.
    (C) Each party's congressional delegation
    (D) Independent voters

17. Why is doing well in the Iowa Caucus and the New Hampshire Primary important for candidates seeking their party's nomination for president?

    (A) Candidates who do well in both states benefit from large numbers of convention delegates.
    (B) Candidates who do well in both states benefit from a large amount of favorable publicity.
    (C) Candidates who do well in both states benefit from a large number of electoral votes.
    (D) All of the above

18. Which of the following statements about presidential electors is true?

    (A) They choose the party's presidential nominee at the national party convention.
    (B) They are elected officials, including members of Congress and state legislatures.
    (C) They are chosen by the state parties, potentially to cast their state's electoral votes.
    (D) They select the president by a two-thirds vote.

19. Alabama elects seven members of the House. How many electoral votes does Alabama have?

    (A) Seven
    (B) Eight
    (C) Nine
    (D) Eleven

20. Assume for the purpose of this question that a Democrat, a Republican, and a major independent candidate are running for president. In California, the Democrat gets 45 percent of the vote, the Republican gets 40 percent, and the independent receives the rest. How many of California's electoral votes will the Democratic candidate receive?

    (A) All of them
    (B) 45 percent of them
    (C) None of them
    (D) It depends on the outcome of the runoff between the Democrat and the Republican, the two top finishers.

21. Under which of the following circumstances would Candidate A win the 2012 presidential election?

    (A) Candidate A wins a majority of the popular vote nationwide.
    (B) Candidate A carries more states than any other candidate.
    (C) Candidate A wins a plurality of the popular vote nationwide.
    (D) Candidate A wins a majority of the electoral vote.

22. To which of the following states would you expect the two presidential campaigns to devote the least attention during the next general election campaign?

    (A) Ohio
    (B) Florida
    (C) Arkansas
    (D) Pennsylvania

23. Which of the following is considered a Red State?

    (A) New York
    (B) California
    (C) Texas
    (D) Illinois

24. Which of the following statements is an expression of retrospective voting?

    (A) I voted for Candidate A because I like her promises and think she will do a good job in office.
    (B) I voted for Candidate B because he is a Republican and I am a Republican.
    (C) I voted for Candidate C because I agree with her on the issues.
    (D) I voted for Candidate D because I like the way things are going and he is the incumbent.

25. Person A tells survey researchers that she is a committed Democrat who decided to vote for the Democratic nominee for president well before the party's national convention. Person A is an example of which of the following?

    (A) Base voter
    (B) Swing voter
    (C) Retrospective voter
    (D) Independent voter

Chapter 10: Congress

Circle the correct answer.

1. What happens if the House and Senate pass different versions of a bill to address a particular policy issue but cannot agree on compromise legislation?

   (A) The president creates a conference commission to negotiate a compromise.
   (B) The measure fails because nothing passes Congress unless both the House and Senate pass it in identical form.
   (C) The Supreme Court determines which measure becomes law.
   (D) The House bill goes to the president for signature.

2. Which of the following statements about the constitutional roles of the House and Senate is correct?

   (A) Legislation to raise taxes must originate in the House.
   (B) The Senate is solely responsible for ratifying constitutional amendments by a two-thirds vote.
   (C) The Senate is solely responsible for confirming presidential appointments by a two-thirds vote.
   (D) The House is solely responsible for confirming a presidential nomination to fill a vacancy in the office of vice president.

3. Which of the following statements better describes the House than it does the Senate?

   (A) It makes decisions strictly by majority vote.
   (B) It has a tradition as a great debating society where members enjoy broad freedom to voice their points of view.
   (C) It is an individualistic body where one member has considerable influence on the legislative process.
   (D) All of the above

4. Which of the following statements better describes the Senate than the House?

   (A) Every member stands for reelection every two years.
   (B) A minority of members has the power to bring legislative business to a halt in the chamber.
   (C) Members of this chamber sometimes run for seats in the other chamber.
   (D) None of the above

5. The office of Congresswoman Martinez helps a district resident resolve a problem with the Social Security Administration. The action is an example of which of the following?

   (A) Filibuster
   (B) Logrolling
   (C) Party-line vote
   (D) Constituency service

6. According to the Constitution, which of the following presides in the U.S. Senate?

   (A) Speaker of the House
   (B) Senate president pro tempore
   (C) Senate Majority Leader
   (D) Vice president

7. In practice, which of the following officials is the most important leader in the U.S. Senate?

   (A) Speaker of the House
   (B) Senate president pro tempore
   (C) Senate Majority Leader
   (D) Vice president

8. Which of the following officials is the most important leader in the U.S. House?

   (A) Speaker of the House
   (B) Senate president pro tempore
   (C) Senate Majority Leader
   (D) Vice president

9. How is the Senate Majority Leader selected?

   (A) By vote of the members of the majority party in the Senate.
   (B) By popular vote in a national election.
   (C) By the president.
   (D) He or she is the longest serving member of the majority party in the Senate.

10. What happens when the two chambers of the Indian Parliament disagree on the content of legislation?

    (A) They form a conference committee to resolve the conflict.
    (B) The prime minister resolves the conflict.
    (C) New elections are held to select a new parliament.
    (D) The two chambers meet in joint session and decide the issue by majority vote.

11. What was the party affiliation of the chair of the House Ways and Means Committee in 2008?

    (A) The chair could have been a Democrat or Republican, depending on which member of the committee had the most seniority.
    (B) The chair would be a Republican because the president was Republican.
    (C) The chair would be a Democrat because Democrats won a majority in the House in the 2006 election.
    (D) The chair could be a Democrat or a Republican, depending on which member of the committee won a vote of the committee membership.

12. In the current Congress (elected in 2008), which of the following individuals is a Republican?

    (A) Senate Minority Leader.
    (B) Speaker of the House
    (C) Chair of the House Committee on Appropriations.
    (D) Each official could be either Republican or Democrat.

13. Why do major legislative measures often take the form of omnibus bills, which are complex, highly detailed legislative proposals covering one or more subjects or programs?

   (A) Complex problems require complex solutions.
   (B) Government is so big that legislation must deal with a broad range of policy areas.
   (C) Congress is in session only part of the year and omnibus bills enable it to get more done in a short period of time.
   (D) Congressional leaders assemble omnibus bills to attract as much support as possible.

14. Which of the following individuals has the authority to introduce a bill in the U.S. Senate?

   (A) A senator
   (B) A member of the House
   (C) The president
   (D) All of the above

15. How does multiple referral of legislation affect the power of the leadership?

   (A) It diminishes the power of the leadership because the fate of a bill is in the hands of two or more committee chairs, giving the chairs more power than they would otherwise have.
   (B) It has no effect on the power of the leadership, but it delays passage of legislation by increasing the steps of the legislative process.
   (C) It diminishes the power of the leadership because a conference committee has to resolve differences among the committees.
   (D) It enhances the power of the leadership because the leadership can devise referral arrangements that enhance policy goals and set timetables for committee consideration of multiply referred bills.

16. The detailed work of Congress takes place at which point in the legislative process?

   (A) On the floor
   (B) In committee
   (C) In conference committee
   (D) In the Rules Committee

17. Legislative markup occurs at which stage of the legislative process?

   (A) On the floor
   (B) In committee

   (C) In conference committee
   (D) In the Rules Committee

18. What is the purpose of a discharge petition?

   (A) It is the process that is used to end a filibuster.
   (B) It is a demand that a member of Congress be expelled for misconduct.
   (C) It is a procedure used to force a committee to report a bill to the floor of the House.
   (D) It is the beginning of the impeachment process.

19. What is the purpose of a closed rule?

   (A) It prohibits consideration of amendments to a bill on the floor of the House.
   (B) It is a procedure for ending a filibuster.
   (C) It is a means of coordinating the work of committees when a bill is multiply referred.
   (D) It is a procedure used to force a committee to report a bill to the floor of the House.

20. An amendment designed to make a measure so unattractive that it will lack enough support to pass is known as which of the following?

   (A) Discharge petition
   (B) Nongermane amendment
   (C) Killer amendment
   (D) Cloture petition

21. The Senate is considering a controversial measure. How many votes will the measure's supporters need to ensure passage in the chamber?

   (A) 51. Legislation passes by majority vote.
   (B) 67. It takes a two-thirds vote to pass bills in the Senate.
   (C) 60. It takes 60 votes to invoke cloture and overcome a filibuster.
   (D) 40. It takes 40 votes to invoke cloture.

22. Congress passes a bill that the president generally favors with the exception of one provision. What are the president's options?

   (A) The president can ask a conference committee to rewrite the bill.
   (B) The president can ask the Supreme Court to revise the bill.
   (C) The president can veto the offensive provision while signing the rest into law.
   (D) The president can sign or veto the bill in its entirety.

Circle the correct answer.

1. After winning reelection in 2004, President George W. Bush was a lame duck. What does that phrase mean?

   (A) President Bush was unpopular.
   (B) President Bush was ineligible to run for reelection.
   (C) President Bush had to deal with a Congress controlled by the opposition party.
   (D) President Bush was facing impeachment charges.

2. Which of the following is *not* part of the impeachment process?

   (A) The House drafts articles of impeachment.
   (B) The House votes to impeach the president by majority vote.
   (C) The Chief Justice presides over an impeachment trial in the Senate.
   (D) The Senate votes to remove the president by majority vote.

3. Which of the following presidents was impeached and removed from office?

   (A) Andrew Johnson
   (B) Richard Nixon
   (C) Bill Clinton
   (D) None of the above

4. What happens if the vice president resigns or dies in office?

   (A) The Speaker of the House becomes vice president.
   (B) The president appoints another vice president subject to confirmation by the House and Senate.
   (C) The Senate president pro temp becomes vice president.
   (D) The office remains vacant until the next election.

5. Which of the following statements about the vice presidency is true?

   (A) The vice president votes in the Senate only to break a tie.
   (B) The policymaking influence of the vice president today is significantly greater than it was 50 years ago.
   (C) In case of presidential disability, the vice president can become acting president.
   (D) All of the above

6. Who is the chief of state of American government?

   (A) The Senate president pro tempore
   (B) The president
   (C) The Speaker of the House
   (D) The Chief Justice of the United States

7. The United States does not currently have diplomatic relations with Cuba. What would be the process for the United States officially to recognize the government of Cuba?

   (A) Official recognition would be granted through the legislative process. Congress would pass legislation subject to a presidential veto.
   (B) The process of recognition would require a popular vote of the American people.
   (C) The president grants diplomatic recognition.
   (D) Congress grants diplomatic recognition.

8. What is the difference between an executive agreement and a treaty?

   (A) Executive agreements do not require Senate ratification.
   (B) Treaties are more numerous than executive agreements.
   (C) The president negotiates treaties, but members of Congress negotiate executive agreements.
   (D) None of the above

9. The Constitution gives the president all but which one of the following powers?

   (A) To negotiate treaties
   (B) To appoint ambassadors
   (C) To declare war
   (D) To fill judicial vacancies

10. Which of the following is an example of a check and balance on the powers of the presidency?

    (A) The Senate must ratify treaties.
    (B) The Senate must confirm judicial appointments.
    (C) The Senate must confirm ambassadorial appointments.
    (D) All of the above

11. Which of the following statements about the War Powers Act is true?

    (A) It only applies to officially declared wars.
    (B) It requires the president to consult with Congress whenever possible before committing American forces to combat.
    (C) It has proved an effective check on the president's authority as commander-in-chief.
    (D) None of the above

12. What constitutional authority does the president have over the Supreme Court?

    (A) The president can fill vacancies by appointment subject to Senate confirmation.
    (B) The president can veto Supreme Court rulings subject to possible override by the Court.
    (C) The president can initiate removal proceedings against justices.
    (D) None of the above

13. Which of the following statements about executive orders is true?

    (A) The president can issue executive orders without congressional approval.
    (B) Congress can override an executive order legislatively, subject to possible presidential veto.
    (C) The Supreme Court can overturn an executive order on constitutional grounds.
    (D) All of the above

14. Suppose that President Barack Obama disagrees with an executive order issued by President George W. Bush. What can he do?

    (A) President Obama can issue an executive order reversing Bush's executive order.
    (B) President Obama can ask Congress to repeal the Bush executive order.
    (C) President Obama can ask the Supreme Court to overturn the Bush order.
    (D) Nothing.

15. Which of the following constitutional actions can a president take if Congress passes legislation the president opposes?

    (A) Nothing.
    (B) The president can veto the measure subject to a possible override.
    (C) The president can rewrite the legislation subject to a possible override.
    (D) The president can refuse to enforce the legislation.

16. A pronouncement issued by the president at the time a bill passed by Congress is signed into law is known as which of the following?

    (A) A veto statement
    (B) The State of the Union address
    (C) A presidential signing statement
    (D) An executive order

17. Many political scientists believe that the era of the modern presidency began with the administration of which of the following presidents?

    (A) Franklin Roosevelt
    (B) Theodore Roosevelt
    (C) Abraham Lincoln
    (D) Woodrow Wilson

18. Which of the following presidential appointments does *not* require Senate confirmation?

    (A) A cabinet secretary
    (B) A federal judge
    (C) An ambassador
    (D) A member of the White House staff

19. Which of the following agencies is part of the Executive Office of the President?

    (A) Office of Management and Budget (OMB)
    (B) Department of Justice
    (C) Federal Communication Commission (FCC)
    (D) All of the above

20. Which of the following political scientists analyzes presidential performance based on the personality traits of the president?

    (A) Samuel Kernell
    (B) Richard Neustadt
    (C) Fred I. Greenstein
    (D) James David Barber

21. Which of the following political scientists analyzes presidential performance based on leadership style?

    (A) Samuel Kernell
    (B) Richard Neustadt
    (C) Fred I. Greenstein
    (D) James David Barber

22. Which of the following political scientists analyzes presidential performance based on the chief executive's skill as a political bargainer and coalition builder?

    (A) Samuel Kernell
    (B) Richard Neustadt
    (C) Fred I. Greenstein
    (D) James David Barber

23. Which of the following is an example of a unilateral tool of presidential power that does not require congressional approval?

    (A) Executive agreements
    (B) Recess appointments
    (C) Signing statements
    (D) All of the above

24. When a president first takes office, public opinion polls typically indicate that the president enjoys a high approval rating. Which of the following terms describes this phenomenon?

    (A) Two-presidencies thesis
    (B) Coattail effect
    (C) Honeymoon effect
    (D) Rally effect

25. President George W. Bush's approval rating soared after September 11, 2001. Which of the following terms would political scientists use to describe that phenomenon?

    (A) Two-presidencies thesis
    (B) Coattail effect
    (C) Honeymoon effect
    (D) Rally effect

Chapter 12: The Federal Bureaucracy

Circle the correct answer.

1. What federal agency was responsible for responding to Hurricane Katrina?

   (A) Federal Emergency Management Agency (FEMA)
   (B) Army Corps of Engineers
   (C) Salvation Army
   (D) Office of Management and Budget

2. What sort of agency is FEMA?

   (A) Independent executive agency
   (B) Part of the Department of Interior
   (C) Part of the Department of Homeland Security
   (D) Independent Regulatory Commission

3. How did the Department of Defense, Federal Communication Commission, Postal Service, and other federal agencies come into existence?

   (A) The president created them by executive order.
   (B) The Constitution established them.
   (C) They were established by court order.
   (D) Congress and the president created them through the legislative process.

4. Which of the following is *not* a cabinet department?

   (A) Environmental Protection Agency (EPA)
   (B) Department of Homeland Security
   (C) Department of Defense
   (D) Department of Justice

5. Which of the following cabinet departments has the largest number of civilian employees?

   (A) Department of Homeland Security
   (B) Department of Defense
   (C) Department of Education
   (D) Department of Justice

6. The attorney general heads which of the following departments?

   (A) Department of Homeland Security
   (B) Department of Defense
   (C) Department of State
   (D) Department of Justice

7. Which of the following is *not* part of the inner cabinet?

   (A) Secretary of State
   (B) Secretary of Homeland Security
   (C) Secretary of Defense
   (D) Attorney General

8. Which of the following is *not* an example of an independent executive agency?

   (A) Peace Corps
   (B) CIA
   (C) FEMA
   (D) NASA

9. A college student who wanted to assist people in developing countries would volunteer for which of the following agencies?

   (A) Peace Corps
   (B) CIA
   (C) FEMA
   (D) NASA

10. Which of the following is *not* an example of a government corporation?

    (A) Amtrak
    (B) CIA
    (C) Postal Service
    (D) FDIC

11. Which of the following agencies is expected to be self-financing?

    (A) FEMA
    (B) EPA
    (C) FDIC
    (D) Peace Corps

12. Which of the following agencies regulates business competition, including enforcement of laws against monopolies and the protection of consumers from deceptive trade practices?

    (A) FCC
    (B) FTC
    (C) SEC
    (D) EPA

13. Which of the following agencies regulates interstate and international radio and television, telephone, telegraph, and satellite communications, as well as licensing radio and television stations?

    (A) FCC
    (B) FTC
    (C) SEC
    (D) EPA

14. The president has the authority to remove all but which one of the following government officials?

    (A) Attorney General
    (B) FEMA director
    (C) SEC commissioner
    (D) Secretary of Transportation

15. Which of the following agencies is an example of a quasi-government company?

    (A) Postal Service
    (B) FEMA
    (C) Amtrak
    (D) Fannie Mae

16. The spoils system involved which of the following?

    (A) Hiring friends, relatives, and political supporters to work for the government.
    (B) Giving government contracts to companies owned by friends, relatives, and political supporters.
    (C) Contracting out with private companies to implement government programs.
    (D) Forbidding government employees from engaging in political activities.

17. Which of the following rights do federal employees enjoy?

    (A) The right to form unions.
    (B) The right to vote for candidates of their choice.
    (C) The right to bargain collectively over issues other than pay and benefits.
    (D) All of the above

18. Are private companies legally obligated to follow rules adopted by regulatory agencies?

    (A) No. Only Congress has the authority to enact legally binding regulations.
    (B) Yes, but only if the rules are ratified by Congress.
    (C) Yes. Rules are legally binding.
    (D) No, although many businesses follow them voluntarily.

19. Suppose the Department of Labor adopts a rule that a majority of the members of Congress oppose. What steps if any can Congress take to reverse the rule?

    (A) Congress lacks the authority to overturn the rule.
    (B) Congress can pass legislation to reverse the rule, but it would either require presidential approval or Congress would have to vote to override a veto.
    (C) Congress can ask the Supreme Court to overturn the rule.
    (D) Congress can do nothing, but the president can veto the rule.

20. Suppose the president disagrees with the policy initiatives of a federal agency. What can the president do to exert control?

    (A) The president can ask Congress to cut the agency's budget.
    (B) The president can appoint administrators to head the agency that agree with the president's policy position.
    (C) The president can ask Congress to reorganize the agency.
    (D) All of the above

21. Suppose that a majority of the members of Congress disagree with the policy initiatives of a federal agency. What actions can Congress take to exert control?

    (A) Congress can cut the agency's budget.
    (B) Congress can change the legislation under which the agency operates.
    (C) Congress can reorganize the agency or merge it with another agency.
    (D) All of the above

22. Which of the following is an example of fire-alarm oversight?

    (A) Congress conducts periodic review of an agency's operation.
    (B) The president conducts periodic review of an agency's operation.
    (C) Congress responds to complaints about an agency's performance.
    (D) All of the above

23. An agency that is accused of working too closely with the interest groups it is supposed to be regulating is known as which of the following?

    (A) Issue network
    (B) Captured agency
    (C) Independent regulatory commission
    (D) Iron triangle

24. Which of the following political actors is *not* part of a subgovernment or iron triangle?

    (A) President
    (B) Congress
    (C) Interest group
    (D) Government agency

25. Which of the following is a group of political actors that is concerned with some aspect of public policy?

    (A) Issue network
    (B) Captured agency
    (C) Independent regulatory commission
    (D) Iron triangle

Circle the correct answer.

1. The power of the courts to declare unconstitutional the actions of the other branches and units of government is known as which of the following?

   (A) Loose construction
   (B) Judicial review
   (C) Strict construction
   (D) Civil liberties

2. Which of the following statements most closely reflects the philosophy of loose construction of the Constitution?

   (A) Judges should interpret the Constitution broadly to allow it to change with the times.
   (B) Judges should recognize that their role is to interpret the law rather than make the law.
   (C) Judges should stick to the literal meaning of the Constitution.
   (D) Judges should closely follow the intent of the framers of the Constitution.

3. The Supreme Court first claimed the power of judicial review in which of the following cases?

   (A) *Marbury v. Madison*
   (B) *McCulloch v. Maryland*
   (C) *Brown v. Board of Education*
   (D) *Plessy v. Ferguson*

4. An interpretation of the Constitution that favors limiting the authority of the national government while expanding the powers of the states is known as which of the following?

   (A) Strict construction
   (B) Loose construction
   (C) States' rights
   (D) Judicial review

5. The agenda of the modern Supreme Court (since 1937) has focused on which of the following sets of issue areas?

   (A) Civil liberties and civil rights
   (B) Foreign and defense policy
   (C) Regulatory policy
   (D) Social welfare policy

6. Which of the following federal courts is exclusively a trial court?

   (A) District court
   (B) Courts of appeal
   (C) Supreme Court
   (D) None of the above

7. How are U.S. district judges selected?

   (A) They are career civil servants, chosen through a merit hiring process.
   (B) They are appointed by the president subject to confirmation by the Senate.
   (C) They are elected by the voters in the states where they serve.
   (D) They are appointed by the president subject to confirmation by the House and Senate.

8. A liberal judge is more likely than a conservative judge to take which of the following policy actions?

   (A) To rule in favor of the government and against criminal defendants.
   (B) To rule in favor of workers and against corporate interests.
   (C) To rule in favor of state governments in federalism disputes with the federal government.
   (D) All of the above

9. What is the term of a federal district judge?

   (A) 2 years
   (B) 4 years
   (C) 6 years
   (D) Life, with "good behavior"

10. The "nuclear option" involved which of the following actions?

    (A) An attempt to increase the size of the Supreme Court
    (B) An effort to amend the Constitution to restrict the president's authority as commander-in-chief
    (C) An effort to eliminate the Senate filibuster for judicial nominees
    (D) An attempt to limit the jurisdiction of the Supreme Court to prevent it from hearing abortion cases

11. According to the U.S. Constitution, how many justices serve on the Supreme Court?

    (A) 7
    (B) 9
    (C) 11
    (D) The Constitution says nothing about the size of the Supreme Court.

12. The Supreme Court decides a case by a unanimous vote. Who writes the majority opinion?

    (A) The chief justice
    (B) The most senior justice
    (C) The chief justice either writes the opinion or assigns it to another justice
    (D) Opinion assignment is done randomly

13. Suppose that Congress passes controversial legislation that some people believe is unconstitutional. When, if ever, will the Supreme Court address the issue?

    (A) The Supreme Court will decide the issue when and if it accepts a case that involves a challenge to the constitutionality of the legislation.
    (B) The Supreme Court reviews legislation passed by Congress before it takes effect.
    (C) The Supreme Court will only review the legislation if Congress requests a review.
    (D) Never.

14. Why was *Brown v. Board of Education* an example of a test case?

    (A) The Supreme Court reversed an earlier decision (the *Plessy* case) when it decided *Brown*.
    (B) The case was prepared, presented, and financed by an interest group.
    (C) An interest group submitted a legal brief that discussed issues raised by the case.
    (D) *Brown* is considered a landmark decision in constitutional law.

15. How many justices must agree before the Supreme Court agrees to hear a case on appeal?

    (A) 3
    (B) 4
    (C) 5
    (D) 9

16. Daryl Renard Atkins was convicted of murder in the state of Virginia and sentenced to death. Under which of the following circumstances would the U.S. Supreme Court hear an appeal of his case?

    (A) All death penalty cases are automatically appealed to the U.S. Supreme Court.
    (B) State cases such as the Atkins case cannot be appealed to the federal court system.
    (C) His attorneys convince a majority of the justices of the Supreme Court that his case is interesting enough to review.
    (D) His attorneys raise national constitutional issues that at least four justices believe are worth considering.

17. A Supreme Court justice agrees with the outcome of a case but disagrees with the legal reasoning presented in the majority opinion. Which of the following actions would the justice take?

    (A) File a friend of the court brief.
    (B) Write a concurring opinion.
    (C) Write a majority opinion.
    (D) Write a dissenting opinion.

18. What is a friend of the court brief?

    (A) An opinion written by a member of a court who agrees with the court's ruling but disagrees with the reasoning behind it.
    (B) A judicial order directing the government either to release someone in custody or to justify why the person is being held.

    (C) A court case that is supported financially by a group.
    (D) A brief submitted by a group not directly involved in a case that is attempting to influence the outcome of the case.

19. What is a dissenting opinion?

    (A) It is a legal brief written by an interest group attempting to influence the outcome of a case.
    (B) It is an opinion written by a justice on the Supreme Court who agrees with the outcome of a case but disagrees with the reasoning contained in the majority opinion.
    (C) It is a document written by an interest group that disagrees with a ruling issued by the Supreme Court.
    (D) It is an opinion written by a justice of the Supreme Court that disagrees with the majority ruling on a case.

20. Assuming that the Supreme Court is fully staffed and that every justice participates in a decision, how many justices must agree to decide the outcome of a case?

    (A) 4
    (B) 5
    (C) 6
    (D) 9

21. What power does the Supreme Court have to enforce its rulings?

    (A) The Court can order law enforcement personnel to enforce its rulings.
    (B) The Court must rely on the other branches and units of government to enforce its rulings.
    (C) None. Court rulings are routinely ignored.
    (D) None of the above

22. Which of the following is a check on the power of the Supreme Court?

    (A) The president can appoint and the Senate can confirm new justices to fill vacancies on the Court.
    (B) The House and Senate can propose an amendment to the Constitution to overturn a judicial interpretation of the Constitution.
    (C) Congress and the president can rewrite a law to reverse a judicial interpretation of an act of Congress.
    (D) All of the above

Circle the correct answer.

1. A financial incentive given by government to an individual or a business interest to accomplish a public objective is known by which of the following terms?

   (A) Entitlement
   (B) Welfare program
   (C) Subsidy
   (D) Progressive taxation

2. "The nation is suffering a severe economic slump. Many companies have gone out of business and unemployment is at a record high." This statement describes which of the following?

   (A) Inflation
   (B) Recession
   (C) Depression
   (D) Supply-side economics

3. "Prices just keep going up. It sure seems like a dollar doesn't go as far these days as it used to." This statement describes which of the following?

   (A) Inflation
   (B) Recession
   (C) Depression
   (D) Supply-side economics

4. Which of the following is the most important tax source of revenue for the U.S. government?

   (A) Sales taxes
   (B) Payroll taxes
   (C) Corporate income taxes
   (D) Individual income taxes

5. An individual has a net income of $100,000, including $10,000 of income that is tax exempt. What is the individual's taxable income?

   (A) $100,000
   (B) $90,000
   (C) $10,000
   (D) It depends on the individual's tax bracket.

6. Your accountant informs you that you are in the 25 percent tax bracket. What does that statement mean?

   (A) You owe 25 percent of your gross income in taxes.
   (B) You owe 25 percent of your taxable income in taxes.
   (C) If you earn an additional dollar of income, 25 percent of it will go for taxes.
   (D) All of the above

7. You are in the 25 percent tax bracket. You have the opportunity to take an extra job that will allow you to earn an additional $1,000. How much of that money will go to income taxes?

   (A) $100
   (B) $250
   (C) $500
   (D) $1,000

8. Which of the following taxes is assessed on wage earnings but not on income generated by stock dividends and interest?

   (A) Individual income tax
   (B) Excise tax
   (C) Corporate income tax
   (D) Payroll tax

9. Federal payroll taxes fund which of the following government programs?

   (A) Social Security
   (B) Medicaid
   (C) Education
   (D) All of the above

10. Federal taxes on gasoline, tires, and airplane tickets are examples of which of the following?

    (A) Progressive taxes
    (B) Excise taxes
    (C) Payroll taxes
    (D) Tax preferences

11. The federal income tax is an example of which of the following?

    (A) Progressive tax
    (B) Regressive tax
    (C) Proportional tax
    (D) Excise tax

12. Which of the following taxes can be justified on the basis of the ability to pay theory of taxation?

    (A) Excise taxes on tobacco and alcohol
    (B) Payroll taxes to support Social Security and Medicare
    (C) Individual income tax
    (D) Excise taxes on tires and gasoline

13. An income tax that assesses the same percentage tax rate on all income levels above a personal exemption while allowing few if any deductions is a definition of which of the following?

    (A) Progressive tax
    (B) The ability to pay theory of taxation
    (C) Excise tax
    (D) Flat tax

14. Which of the following was a goal of the tax reforms associated with President George W. Bush?

    (A) Increase personal savings and investment
    (B) Increase taxes on upper income earners
    (C) Increase the estate tax
    (D) Make the federal income tax system more progressive

15. Assume that federal government revenues are $2.6 trillion and expenditures are $2.9 trillion. Which of the following statements is accurate?

    (A) The budget is balanced.
    (B) The government ran a surplus of $0.3 trillion.
    (C) The government ran a deficit of $0.3 trillion.
    (D) The national debt is $0.3 trillion

16. How does a deficit of $400 billion affect the national debt?

    (A) It has no impact on the national debt.
    (B) It increases the national debt by $400 billion.
    (C) It decreases the national debt by $400 billion.
    (D) The national debt is $400 billion.

17. Which of the following is *not* one of the top five major expenditure categories in the federal budget?

    (A) Foreign aid
    (B) Social Security
    (C) National defense
    (D) Healthcare

18. Which of the following is a factor negatively affecting the future of the Social Security program?

    (A) People are living longer.
    (B) The baby-boom generation is beginning to retire.
    (C) The generation following the baby-boom generation is smaller than its predecessor.
    (D) All of the above

19. Which of the following is an example of a means-tested program?

    (A) Social Security
    (B) Medicare
    (C) Medicaid
    (D) All of the above

20. Which of the following is *not* a result of welfare reform?

    (A) The number of welfare recipients has fallen.
    (B) The number of people living in poverty has decreased.
    (C) Most people leaving welfare have found work.
    (D) Most people leaving welfare still depend on the government for assistance.

21. Which of the following is an example of an entitlement program?

    (A) Social Security
    (B) Medicare
    (C) Medicaid
    (D) All of the above

22. Which of the following is *not* an example of mandatory spending?

    (A) Social Security expenditures
    (B) Interest on the debt
    (C) Spending for education
    (D) Payment for a weapons system contracted for in a prior year

23. Which of the following is primarily responsible for setting monetary policy?

    (A) Federal Reserve Board
    (B) Office of Management and Budget
    (C) Department of the Treasury
    (D) Congress and the president

24. The Federal Open Market Committee (FOMC) makes decisions that directly impact which of the following?

    (A) Tax rates
    (B) Fiscal policy
    (C) Interest rates
    (D) Social Security

25. An appropriation bill includes money to fund a mining museum for a small city in Alaska. This provision is an example of which of the following?

    (A) Entitlement
    (B) Means-tested program
    (C) Privatization
    (D) Earmark

Circle the correct answer.

1. The protection of the individual from the unrestricted power of government is the definition for which of the following?

    (A) Selective incorporation of the Bill of Rights
    (B) Fundamental rights
    (C) Civil rights
    (D) Civil liberties

2. Where is the Bill of Rights found?

    (A) It is the first ten amendments to the Constitution
    (B) It is found in Article I, Section 8, of the Constitution.
    (C) It is part of the Declaration of Independence
    (D) It is part of the Articles of Confederation

3. The Bill of Rights initially restricted the power of which of the following levels of government?

    (A) Neither the national government nor state governments
    (B) Both the national government and state governments
    (C) The national government but not state governments
    (D) State governments but not the national government

4. The selective incorporation of the Bill of Rights against the states is based on which of the following?

    (A) Due Process Clause of the Fourteenth Amendment
    (B) First Amendment
    (C) Equal Protection Clause of the Fourteenth Amendment
    (D) Thirteenth Amendment

5. Which of the following is the reason China has adopted a one-child policy?

    (A) To increase the size of the nation's population
    (B) To balance the population between men and women
    (C) To limit population growth in order to promote economic development
    (D) To force people to move to urban areas

6. Which of the following statements about constitutional rights is true?

    (A) All rights are equally important.
    (B) Rights are absolute, meaning that government cannot abridge rights guaranteed by the Constitution.
    (C) State constitutions can guarantee more rights than those found in the federal constitution.
    (D) All of the above

7. Which of the following statements is true about the fundamental rights protected by the Bill of Rights?

    (A) They are absolute and may never be abridged by the government.
    (B) They are guidelines, but government officials can abridge them when they determine it is in the public interest.

    (C) They can be abridged but only when the government can demonstrate a plausible justification.
    (D) They cannot be abridged unless the government can demonstrate a compelling or overriding public interest for so doing.

8. The Parker family is suing the local public school district. The Parkers, who are Mormons, complain that their children's school principal recites prayers over the school intercom and that the prayers are contrary to the family's religious beliefs. Which of the following statements is *not* true about this dispute?

    (A) The Parkers' lawsuit would be based on the First and Fourteenth Amendments of the U.S. Constitution.
    (B) The principal would likely successfully defend against the suit because he has the freedom of religion to express his religious views and that is protected by the Constitution.
    (C) The ACLU might be willing to assist the Parkers in their lawsuit.
    (D) The Parkers would probably sue in federal court rather than state court.

9. *Engel v. Vitale* dealt with which of the following issues?

    (A) Abortion
    (B) Freedom of religion
    (C) Freedom of speech
    (D) Establishment of religion

10. The local school district invites a local clergyman to speak at a high school assembly. At the end of his speech, the clergyman asks the students to join him in a recitation of the Lord's Prayer. Although most students and parents applaud the speech and the prayer, a few students and their parents object. Which of the following statements is true about this controversy?

    (A) No court would accept a lawsuit against this action because the clergyman has a constitutional right to express his religious beliefs.
    (B) No court would accept a lawsuit against this action because the majority of students and their parents do not object.
    (C) The parents of the unhappy students could sue the district based on the Establishment Clause of the First Amendment (and the Fourteenth Amendment).
    (D) This is an innocent event and nobody should complain.

11. A federal district judge rules that the display of a Ten Commandments monument on the grounds of the county courthouse violates the Establishment Clause. What if anything can be done to challenge his decision?

(A) Nothing. Federal court rulings are not subject to reversal because federal judges are appointed for life.
(B) The state legislature and the governor could pass a law to overturn the decision.
(C) Congress and the president could pass a law to overturn the decision.
(D) The county could appeal the decision to a higher court.

12. Which of the following types of expression would enjoy the highest level of constitutional protection?

(A) A book that accuses the president of the United States of trying to steal the election.
(B) A billboard advertising a diet supplement.
(C) A woman complains to the police that she has been receiving unwelcome sexually explicit telephone calls from a former supervisor.
(D) All of the above

13. Which of the following would be considered a constitutionally protected form of expression?

(A) A newspaper publishes an editorial critical of the president, declaring that the incumbent should be impeached and removed from office.
(B) A man flies the American flag upside down to protest American foreign policy.
(C) A woman passes out pamphlets on a corner attacking Judaism as a "gutter religion." Many people are offended.
(D) All of the above

14. Which of the following is an example of a hate crime?

(A) A group of young Latino and African American men break into the home of an Asian family. While robbing the family, they use racial/ethnic slurs, threatening the Asian family with violence if they don't move out of the neighborhood.
(B) A woman publishes a newsletter in which she attacks homosexuals as "godless pagans who spread disease."
(C) A white man who is fleeing from the scene of a crime shoots and wounds a police officer who is African American.
(D) All of the above

15. Which of the following statements is true regarding a right to privacy?

(A) The First Amendment guarantees people the right to personal privacy.
(B) The Supreme Court has interpreted various provisions of the Bill of Rights to create "zones of privacy."

(C) A right to privacy is the basis for *Brown v. Board of Education*.
(D) All of the above

16. Which of the following statements is true about *Roe v. Wade*?

(A) It is based on a constitutional right of privacy.
(B) It prohibited states from regulating abortion under all circumstances.
(C) The Supreme Court has subsequently overturned major parts of *Roe*.
(D) All of the above

17. The constitutional principle that government cannot deprive someone of life, liberty, or property without following fair and regular procedures is known as which of the following?

(A) Selective incorporation
(B) Parental choice
(C) Exclusionary rule
(D) Due process of law

18. *Mapp v. Ohio* is associated with which of the following?

(A) Prior restraint
(B) The *Miranda* warnings
(C) Double jeopardy
(D) Exclusionary rule

19. The right to a counsel is associated with which of the following cases?

(A) *Gideon v. Wainwright*
(B) *Engel v. Vitale*
(C) *Miranda v. Arizona*
(D) *Mapp v. Ohio*

20. *Employment Division v. Smith* dealt with which of the following issues?

(A) Establishment of religion
(B) Freedom of religion
(C) School prayer
(D) Abortion rights

21. What branch of government has had the greatest impact on civil liberties policy formulation and adoption?

(A) Judicial branch
(B) Executive branch
(C) Legislative branch
(D) State governments have been more important than the national government.

Circle the correct answer.

1. Which of the following constitutional provisions has the greatest impact on civil rights policymaking?

   (A) Equal Protection Clause of the Fourteenth Amendment
   (B) First Amendment
   (C) Second Amendment
   (D) Due Process Clause of the Fourteenth Amendment

2. Which of the following is a good description of the meaning of civil rights?

   (A) The right of an individual to be protected from the power of government when it comes to such matters as freedom of expression and freedom of religion.
   (B) The right of an individual not to be harmed or disadvantaged because of the individual's membership in a group based on race, ethnicity, gender, etc.
   (C) The right of an individual to be protected from the oppressive power of government.
   (D) All of the above

3. Which of the following branches of government plays the greatest role in civil rights policymaking?

   (A) Legislative branch
   (B) Executive branch
   (C) Judicial branch
   (D) The three branches are equally involved.

4. Under what, if any, circumstances can the government treat people of different races or ethnicities differently?

   (A) The government must demonstrate an overriding public interest in making the distinction and prove that it is achieving the compelling public interest in the least restrictive way possible.
   (B) The government must have a reasonable basis for making the distinction
   (C) The government must prove that the distinction is necessary to achieve an important governmental objective.
   (D) The government must treat all persons identically. The Constitution is color blind.

5. Which of the following distinctions among persons is *not* a suspect classification?

   (A) Ethnicity
   (B) Race
   (C) Citizenship status
   (D) Sexual orientation

6. The judicial decision rule holding that the Supreme Court will find a government policy unconstitutional unless the government can demonstrate a compelling interest justifying the action is known as which of the following?

   (A) Strict judicial scrutiny
   (B) Separate but equal
   (C) Civil liberties
   (D) Civil rights

7. The doctrine of separate but equal concerned what issue?

   (A) Separation of powers with checks and balances
   (B) Affirmative action
   (C) Voting rights for African Americans
   (D) Whether laws requiring separate facilities for whites and blacks satisfy the Equal Protection Clause

8. Which of the following statements about *Brown v. Board of Education* is/are true?

   (A) It was a test case promoted by the NAACP.
   (B) It overturned *Plessy v. Ferguson*.
   (C) It outlawed *de jure* segregation but not *de facto* segregation.
   (D) All of the above

9. Why is it that many public schools in the United States have student bodies that are all or almost all members of the same racial/ethnic group?

   (A) The Supreme Court overturned *Brown v. Board of Education* in *Parents Involved in Community Schools v. Seattle School District No. 1*.
   (B) The federal courts no longer enforce the *Brown* Decision.
   (C) Housing patterns in many cities isolate racial and ethnic groups.
   (D) Public opinion is heavily opposed to racial integration in public schools.

10. Suppose the government reinstates the military draft, but only drafts men and not women. Would it be possible for the government to adopt the policy constitutionally?

    (A) Yes, but it would have to demonstrate a rational basis for making the distinction.
    (B) Yes, but it would have to offer an "exceedingly persuasive justification" to make the distinction.
    (C) Yes, but it would have to demonstrate a compelling government interest in making the distinction.
    (D) No. Because of the Equal Protection Clause, any draft would have to include both men and women.

11. A state university decides to limit graduate student enrollment in its space physics program to American citizens, excluding permanent residents. Is such an action constitutional?

    (A) It is if the university can demonstrate a compelling governmental interest in making the distinction between citizens and noncitizen permanent residents.
    (B) It is if the university can state a rational basis for the distinction.
    (C) Yes. Permanent residents do not have the rights of citizens.
    (D) No. The Constitution prohibits distinctions based on citizenship status. Everyone must be treated equally.

12. Why did the U.S. Supreme Court overturn Colorado's Amendment Two in *Romer v. Evans?*

(A) The state did not have a compelling justification for its action.
(B) The state did not have an exceedingly persuasive justification for its action.
(C) The state failed to demonstrate a rational basis for its action.
(D) None of the above

13. What was the purpose of a grandfather clause?

(A) To exempt white people from voting restrictions placed on African Americans.
(B) To limit voting to older people.
(C) To prevent older people from voting.
(D) To establish different voting requirements based on age.

14. Which of the following was designed to discriminate against African American voters?

(A) Voting Rights Act (VRA)
(B) District elections
(C) Tests of understanding
(D) All of the above

15. Which of the following is *not* true about the Voting Rights Act (VRA)?

(A) It was designed to outlaw all sorts of voting discrimination.
(B) It has led to an increase in electoral districts designed to elect minority candidates.
(C) It has forced local officials in some parts of the country, especially the South, to get federal approval before changing election rules or procedures.
(D) Despite the Voting Rights Act, the Supreme Court has ruled that legislatures cannot create legislative districts based on the race of district residents unless it can demonstrate a compelling governmental interest.

16. What is a majority-minority district?

(A) A legislative district that is majority white but nonetheless elects a member of a racial or ethnic minority group to Congress.
(B) A legislative district whose population is more than 50 percent African American and Latino.
(C) A legislative district that is majority African American or Latino but nonetheless elects a white candidate to Congress.
(D) A legislative district with a population that has a majority of white voters.

17. What is the current status of deed restrictions that prevent property owners from selling their homes to members of racial and ethnic minority groups?

(A) They still apply because they are private agreements and anti-discrimination laws do not apply to private agreements.
(B) They are illegal because of the Voting Rights Act (VRA).
(C) The Supreme Court ruled them unenforceable in *Brown v. Board of Education.*
(D) The Supreme Court ruled them unenforceable in *Shelley v. Kraemer.*

18. Does the federal government have the authority to outlaw discrimination against racial and ethnic minorities in private businesses such as restaurants and hotels?

(A) Yes. The Supreme Court has ruled that Congress can legislate on the basis of its constitutional authority to regulate interstate commerce.
(B) Yes. The Supreme Court has ruled that Congress can legislate as part of its authority to enforce the Equal Protection Clause of the Fourteenth Amendment.
(C) Yes. The First Amendment gives the federal government the authority to prohibit discrimination.
(D) No. These are state issues, not federal issues.

19. What is the basis for sexual harassment law?

(A) Federal laws prohibiting gender discrimination in employment.
(B) First Amendment
(C) Equal Protection Clause of the Fourteenth Amendment
(D) Voting Rights Act

20. Which of the following cases dealt with affirmative action?

(A) *Shelley v. Kraemer*
(B) *Shaw v. Reno*
(C) *City of Richmond v. J. A. Croson Company*
(D) All of the above

21. Why did the U.S. Supreme Court uphold the admissions program at the University of Michigan law school?

(A) The Court ruled that the government has a compelling interest in promoting racial and ethnic diversity in higher education.
(B) The admissions program did not establish a quota system for admissions.
(C) The admissions program did not award a set number of points to applicants based on their race or ethnicity.
(D) All of the above

Circle the correct answer.

1. President George W. Bush identified all but which one of the following countries as part of an "axis of evil"?

   (A) Iran
   (B) Saudi Arabia
   (C) Iraq
   (D) North Korea

2. Why does the United States oppose Iran developing nuclear weapons?

   (A) Iran could provide a nuclear weapon to a terrorist group.
   (B) Iran could use nuclear weapons against American interests in the Middle East or against allies of the United States.
   (C) Iran could use its possession of nuclear weapons to bully its neighbors.
   (D) All of the above

3. Nations that threaten world peace by sponsoring international terrorism and promoting the spread of weapons of mass destruction are known as which of the following?

   (A) Rogue states
   (B) Nongovernmental organizations
   (C) United Nations
   (D) Postindustrial societies

4. Which of the following is an example of a nation-state?

   (A) United States
   (B) NATO
   (C) United Nations
   (D) All of the above

5. Which of the following is an international organization created to promote economic stability worldwide?

   (A) NATO
   (B) United Nations
   (C) WHO
   (D) IMF

6. Which of the following organizations would be involved in international efforts to control the H1N1 virus (swine flu)?

   (A) NATO
   (B) United Nations
   (C) WHO
   (D) IMF

7. Which of the following is a defense alliance?

   (A) NATO
   (B) United Nations
   (C) WHO
   (D) IMF

8. Which of the following organizations would be most likely to mediate a trade dispute?

   (A) NATO
   (B) World Trade Organization (WTO)
   (C) WHO
   (D) IMF

9. Greenpeace, Friends of the Earth, World Wide Fund for Nature, and the Nature Conservancy are all examples of which of the following?

   (A) Nation-states
   (B) Rogue states
   (C) Nongovernmental organizations
   (D) All of the above

10. Which of the following countries is *not* part of NAFTA?

    (A) Colombia
    (B) United States
    (C) Canada
    (D) Mexico

11. Which of the following statements about foreign aid is *not* true?

    (A) Foreign aid makes up about 10 percent of the federal budget.
    (B) Israel is a major beneficiary of American foreign aid.
    (C) Egypt is a major beneficiary of American foreign aid.
    (D) The United States has increased aid to countries whose assistance it needs in the war on terror.

12. The view that the United States should minimize its interactions with other nations is known as which of the following?

    (A) Diplomacy
    (B) Isolationism
    (C) Détente
    (D) Deterrence

13. Which of the following statements about the Cold War is/are true?

    (A) The Cold War ended with the disintegration of the Soviet Union.
    (B) The Cold War began in the late 1940s.
    (C) The Cold War was a struggle between the world's two great superpowers.
    (D) All of the above

14. The foreign policy calling for American support for all free peoples resisting communist aggression by internal or outside forces was associated with which of the following presidents?

    (A) Harry Truman
    (B) Richard Nixon
    (C) Ronald Reagan
    (D) George W. Bush

15. The American policy of keeping the Soviet Union from expanding its sphere of control was known as which of the following?

    (A) Balance of power
    (B) Containment
    (C) Deterrence
    (D) Preemption

16. Which of the following presidents asked Congress for a substantial increase in defense spending during peacetime in order to force the Soviet Union to choose between economic collapse and the end of the Cold War?

    (A) Richard Nixon
    (B) Ronald Reagan
    (C) George H. W. Bush
    (D) Bill Clinton

17. Which of the following is an argument offered by those people who believe that the United States should take an internationalist approach to foreign policy?

    (A) The United States should act in its own best interests rather than compromising with other nations.
    (B) As the world's most powerful nation, the United States does not have to accommodate the interests of other countries.
    (C) The United States needs the support of other nations if it hopes to accomplish its foreign policy goals.
    (D) All of the above

18. Which of the following statements is true about American defense spending?

    (A) In general, defense spending rises during wartime and falls during peacetime.
    (B) As a percentage of GDP, defense spending is greater today than at any time since World War II.
    (C) Defense spending has been falling in recent years despite the war on terror and wars in Afghanistan and Iraq.
    (D) All of the above

19. Tanks, personnel carriers, aircraft carriers, and so forth, are examples of which of the following?

    (A) Don't ask, don't tell
    (B) Conventional forces
    (C) Strategic forces
    (D) Mutual assured destruction (MAD)

20. "The Soviet leaders did not dare launch a nuclear attack against the United States because the American counterattack would have destroyed the Soviet Union and vice versa." This statement is an expression of which of the following?

    (A) Military preemption
    (B) Isolationism
    (C) Mutual assured destruction (MAD)
    (D) Don't ask, don't tell policy

21. The capacity of a nation to absorb an initial nuclear attack and retain sufficient nuclear firepower to inflict unacceptable damage on its adversary is known as which of the following?

    (A) Second-strike capability
    (B) Mutual assured destruction (MAD)
    (C) Deterrence
    (D) Military preemption

22. Why did Pakistan develop nuclear weapons?

    (A) To prevent the United States from attacking it
    (B) To sell weapons to other countries, including North Korea and Iran
    (C) To threaten surrounding countries in order to spread Islam throughout the region
    (D) To counter the development of nuclear weapons by neighboring India

23. "The United States needs to attack Iran to eliminate its nuclear capacity before it has the opportunity to attack us or provide weapons of mass destruction to terrorists." This statement is an expression of which of the following concepts?

    (A) Second-strike capability
    (B) Mutual assured destruction (MAD)
    (C) Deterrence
    (D) Military preemption

24. Which president is most closely associated with the concept of military preemption?

    (A) Richard Nixon
    (B) George W. Bush
    (C) Bill Clinton
    (D) Ronald Reagan

25. The don't ask, don't tell policy deals with which of the following issues?

    (A) The interrogation of terror suspects held in American custody
    (B) Gay men and lesbians serving in the U.S. armed forces
    (C) The ability of the armed forces to attract enough volunteers to staff the volunteer army
    (D) Intelligence leaks over American policy in the war on terror

Circle the correct answer.

1. How does Texas compare with other states in terms of educational attainment?

   (A) Texas has the lowest high school graduation rate in the nation.
   (B) The percentage of Texans with a college education is below the national average.
   (C) The percentage of Texans enrolled in higher education is below the national average.
   (D) All of the above

2. Which of the following groups of Texans is the best educated?

   (A) Latinos
   (B) African Americans
   (C) Whites
   (D) There is no difference among the groups.

3. Why does the National Center for Public Policy and Higher Education project that personal income per capita in Texas will decline by 2020?

   (A) Oil and gas will no longer be a major part of the state's economy.
   (B) A majority of the state's residents will be Latino.
   (C) The state's population as a whole will be less well educated in 2020 than the population is today.
   (D) Texas does not spend enough on education.

4. Which of the following statements about population growth in Texas is true?

   (A) The population of Texas is growing more rapidly than the population of the United States as a whole.
   (B) The population of Texas is growing more slowly than the population of the United States as a whole.
   (C) The population of Texas is growing at the same rate as the population of the United States as a whole.
   (D) Texas grew more rapidly than the nation as a whole during the 1970s and 1980s, but the state's population growth rate has now fallen below the national average.

5. Which of the following is *not* a reason for relative brisk population growth in Texas?

   (A) People live longer in Texas because of outstanding healthcare and nearly universal health insurance coverage.
   (B) The birthrate in Texas is one of the highest in the nation.
   (C) The population in Texas is relatively young.
   (D) Texas is the destination for a large number of immigrants from other countries.

6. Which of the following statements about illegal immigration is true?

   (A) Texas has more illegal immigrants than any other state.
   (B) A majority of illegal immigrants in Texas come from Mexico.
   (C) Illegal immigrants drag down the state's economy because they pay no taxes.
   (D) All of the above

7. According to a report by the Texas Comptroller of Public Accounts, what impact does illegal immigration have on the Texas economy and government?

   (A) Illegal immigrants contribute to economic growth.
   (B) Illegal immigrants pay more in state taxes than they receive in state services.
   (C) Illegal immigrants receive more services from local government than they pay in local taxes.
   (D) All of the above

8. Why was Texas awarded two additional seats in the U.S. House of Representatives after the 2000 Census?

   (A) The population of Texas surpassed 22 million.
   (B) The population of Texas included 1.4 million illegal immigrants.
   (C) The population of Texas grew more rapidly than the population of the nation as a whole during the 1990s.
   (D) The president of the United States was a Texan.

9. Which of the following statements about the population of Texas is *not* true?

   (A) A majority of state residents are Latino.
   (B) Latinos are the fastest growing racial/ethnic group in the state.
   (C) A majority of the Texas population are African American, Latino, or Asian.
   (D) A majority of Latinos in Texas are Mexican American.

10. African Americans are concentrated in all *but* which one of the following areas in Texas?

    (A) Houston
    (B) South Texas
    (C) East Texas
    (D) Dallas

11. Which of the following regions is the least densely populated?

    (A) West Texas
    (B) South Texas
    (C) North Texas
    (D) Gulf Coast area

12. Which of the following Texas cities is *not* among the ten largest cities in the United States?

    (A) Dallas
    (B) Austin
    (C) San Antonio
    (D) Houston

13. Which of the following regions of the state is growing the most rapidly?

    (A) Small towns
    (B) Rural areas
    (C) Suburban areas
    (D) Inner-city urban areas

14. Why is the petroleum industry a less significant component of the Texas economy today than it was 20 or 30 years ago?

    (A) Oil production in Texas has been declining for decades.
    (B) The international price of oil has been falling for years.
    (C) Most major oil companies have moved their headquarters from Texas to Louisiana and Oklahoma.
    (D) All of the above

15. Which of the following industries is *more* important now than it was in the first half of the twentieth century?

    (A) Cotton
    (B) Computers
    (C) Petroleum
    (D) None of the above

16. Which of the following is *not* an example of a high-technology industry?

    (A) Robotics
    (B) Telecommunications
    (C) Computers
    (D) Agriculture

17. Which of the following statements about the Texas economy is true?

    (A) The petroleum industry is the single largest component of the Texas economy.
    (B) The Texas economy is growing at a faster rate than the national economy.
    (C) Texas has the largest economy in the nation.
    (D) All of the above

18. Which of the following statements about the Texas economy is true?

    (A) Texas has the third largest state economy in the nation after California and New York.
    (B) Texas is a relatively poor state, at least in terms of individual and family income.
    (C) The poverty rate in Texas exceeds the national average.
    (D) All of the above

19. Which of the following groups of Texans has the highest household income?

    (A) African Americans
    (B) Whites
    (C) Latinos
    (D) Household income is roughly the same for all three groups.

20. Which of the following statements is true about income and wealth in Texas?

    (A) The income differential between the wealthiest and the poorest families is greater in Texas than it is in most other states.
    (B) The Texas economy is growing more slowly than the economies of most other states.
    (C) The poverty rate in Texas is lower than the national average.
    (D) All of the above

21. Which of the following terms is defined as the widely held, deeply rooted political values of a society?

    (A) Political science
    (B) Public policy
    (C) Politics
    (D) Political culture

22. Which of the following strains of political culture is *not* generally found in Texas?

    (A) Individualistic
    (B) Moralistic
    (C) Traditionalistic
    (D) Civic culture

23. Which of the following is a political culture that is conducive to the development of an efficient, effective government that meets the needs of its citizens in a timely and professional manner?

    (A) Individualistic
    (B) Moralistic
    (C) Traditionalistic
    (D) Civic culture

24. Where does Texas rank among the 50 states in terms of civic culture?

    (A) Texas has the highest level of civic culture in the nation.
    (B) Texas has the lowest level of civic culture in the nation.
    (C) Texas ranks below average in civic culture.
    (D) Texas ranks above average in civic culture.

25. Which of the following is true of a state with a high level of civic culture?

    (A) It has an innovative, effective government.
    (B) Citizen participation in the public policymaking process is low.
    (C) Citizens are intolerant of people with different ideas and lifestyles.
    (D) All of the above

Circle the correct answer.

1. Which of the following statements reflects the ruling of the Texas Supreme Court in *Edgewood v. Kirby*?

   (A) School districts should have the same amount of money.
   (B) School districts should have the same amount of money per student.
   (C) School districts with the same property tax rate should have the same amount of money per student.
   (D) School districts should have the same property tax rate.

2. The Robin Hood Plan included which of the following?

   (A) A provision requiring that all districts have the same amount of money
   (B) A provision requiring that wealthy districts transfer money either to the state or to poorer districts
   (C) A provision requiring that all school districts levy the same property tax rate
   (D) All of the above

3. Which of the following issues did the case *Neeley v. West Orange-Cove Consolidated ISD* address?

   (A) School vouchers
   (B) Racial integration of schools
   (C) Student test scores
   (D) Whether the state property tax cap amounted to an unconstitutional state property tax

4. Does the U.S. Congress have the authority to pass legislation that overrides a provision of a state constitution?

   (A) Yes. The U.S. Constitution and U.S. law take legal precedence over state laws and state constitutions.
   (B) No. The U.S. Constitution takes precedence over state laws but not over state constitutions.
   (C) It depends on whether the state constitution violates a specific provision of the U.S. Constitution.
   (D) No. State constitutions take precedence because states are sovereign entities.

5. Which of the following is a characteristic of both the U.S. Constitution and most state constitutions?

   (A) They provide for bicameral legislatures.
   (B) They provide for separation of powers.
   (C) They create a representative democracy.
   (D) All of the above

6. In which of the following ways do state constitutions typically differ from the U.S. Constitution?

   (A) State constitutions are shorter than the U.S. Constitution.
   (B) State constitutions have been amended less frequently than the U.S. Constitution.

   (C) Most state constitutions provide for the election of judges, whereas the U.S. Constitution provides for the appointment of federal judges.
   (D) All of the above

7. Which of the following statements about the Texas Constitution is *not* true?

   (A) It provides for a unicameral legislature.
   (B) It provides for a plural executive.
   (C) It provides for separation of powers.
   (D) It has a bill of rights.

8. Which of the following statements is true of the Texas Constitution but *not* true of the U.S. Constitution?

   (A) It has been amended many times.
   (B) It creates a plural executive.
   (C) It provides for the election of judges.
   (D) All of the above

9. The philosophy of Jacksonian democracy led to which of the following in Texas?

   (A) A school system funded with property taxes
   (B) Low election turnout
   (C) The long ballot
   (D) Branch banking

10. Which of the following factors influenced the drafting of the current Texas Constitution?

    (A) Reaction to the Reconstruction administration of E. J. Davis
    (B) The Grange
    (C) Jacksonian democracy
    (D) All of the above

11. Which of the following was a goal of the framers of the Texas Constitution of 1875?

    (A) To control the excesses of big business
    (B) To limit the power of government
    (C) To reduce the cost of government
    (D) All of the above

12. Which of the following provisions was included in the Texas Constitution written in 1875?

    (A) The constitution outlawed branch banking.
    (B) The constitution created a cabinet system of government.
    (C) The constitution provided for annual legislative sessions.
    (D) None of the above

13. Local-option elections deal with which of the following?

    (A) The selection of judges
    (B) The sale of alcoholic beverages
    (C) Branch banking
    (D) School finance

14. How does the Texas Constitution differ from the U.S. Constitution?

    (A) The Texas Constitution has a bill of rights, whereas the U.S. Constitution does not.
    (B) The Texas Constitution is longer and more detailed than the U.S. Constitution.
    (C) The Texas Constitution creates a unicameral legislature, whereas the U.S. Constitution creates a bicameral legislature.
    (D) All of the above

15. How does the Texas Bill of Rights compare with the U.S. Bill of Rights?

    (A) The provisions in the Texas Bill of Rights simply restate the provisions of the U.S. Bill of Rights.
    (B) The Texas Bill of Rights is shorter than the U.S. Bill of Rights.
    (C) The Texas Bill of Rights phrases the protection of rights positively, rather than prohibiting government from taking certain actions.
    (D) All of the above

16. Which of the following is the most important means for changing the Texas Constitution?

    (A) Change through amendment
    (B) Change through judicial interpretation
    (C) Change through practical experience
    (D) All three means are equally important.

17. A formal, written change or addition to the state's governing document is known as which of the following?

    (A) Constitutional revision
    (B) Judicial review
    (C) Constitutional amendment
    (D) None of the above

18. Which of the following is not a step in the process of amending the Texas Constitution?

    (A) The Texas House proposes an amendment by two-thirds' vote.
    (B) The Texas Senate proposes an amendment by two-thirds' vote.
    (C) The amendment goes to the governor for signature.
    (D) The voters ratify the amendment at the ballot box.

19. Which of the following statements about constitutional amendment elections in Texas is true?

    (A) Turnout for constitutional amendment elections is usually lower than turnout for elections between candidates.
    (B) The governor can use the veto to block an amendment from going on the ballot.
    (C) Voters must approve constitutional amendments by a two-thirds' vote.
    (D) All of the above

20. Which of the following changes has not come about because of the adoption of constitutional amendments in Texas?

    (A) A four-year term for the governor
    (B) Annual sessions for the legislature
    (C) Budget execution authority for the governor
    (D) Branch banking

21. Why does the state issue general obligation bonds?

    (A) To raise taxes
    (B) To amend the Texas Constitution
    (C) To borrow money
    (D) To ratify an amendment to the U.S. Constitution

22. Which of the following statements about constitutional amendment elections is true?

    (A) Turnout at amendment elections typically exceeds turnout at candidate elections.
    (B) In recent years, voters have rejected every amendment on the ballot.
    (C) Amendments cannot be ratified unless they receive a two-thirds' vote of the electorate.
    (D) None of the above

23. Which of the following universities does not benefit from the Permanent University Fund (PUF)?

    (A) Texas A&M University
    (B) University of Texas at Austin
    (C) University of Houston
    (D) All state universities benefit from the PUF.

24. What was the basis for the legalization of gay marriage in Massachusetts?

    (A) The Massachusetts legislature passed a law to provide for same-sex marriage.
    (B) The U.S. Supreme Court ruled that Massachusetts state laws against gay marriage were unconstitutional.
    (C) The voters of Massachusetts approved same-sex marriage in a referendum.
    (D) The Supreme Judicial Council in Massachusetts ruled that state laws against same-sex marriage violated the state constitution.

25. What is the legal status of the Texas homosexual conduct law?

    (A) It was overturned by a ruling of the U.S. Supreme Court.
    (B) It remains in effect because it was upheld by the Texas Supreme Court.
    (C) It was repealed by the adoption of a constitutional amendment by Texas voters in 2003.
    (D) It was overturned by the Texas Court of Criminal Appeals.

Circle the correct answer.

1. Why did Congress and the president enact the Real ID Act?

   (A) To reduce identity theft
   (B) To prevent terrorists and illegal aliens from fraudulently obtaining official state identification
   (C) To ensure that states raise the legal minimum drinking age to 21
   (D) None of the above

2. A political system that divides power between a central government, with authority over the whole nation, and a series of state governments is known as which of the following?

   (A) Representative democracy
   (B) Federal system
   (C) Democracy
   (D) Monarchy

3. Are states or the national government the dominant partner in the federal system?

   (A) States are the dominant partner because of the Tenth Amendment.
   (B) States and the national government are equal partners.
   (C) The national government is the dominant partner because of the National Supremacy Clause.
   (D) The Supreme Court determines which level of government takes precedence on a case-by-case basis.

4. Can states adopt laws that conflict with federal laws?

   (A) No. Federal laws take precedence over state law.
   (B) Yes. Both states and the national government are sovereign.
   (C) Yes, but only if the state law does not conflict with the U.S. Constitution.
   (D) Yes, but Congress can pass another law specifically repealing the state measure.

5. Which of the following programs provides health insurance coverage to children living in families with incomes just above the poverty level?

   (A) Medicaid
   (B) Social Security
   (C) Children's Health Insurance Program
   (D) Medicare

6. The gradual warming of the atmosphere that is reportedly caused by industrial pollutants and the burning of fossil fuels is known as which of the following?

   (A) Clean Air Act
   (B) Environmental Protection Agency (EPA)
   (C) Sierra Club
   (D) Global warming

7. Which of the following cases dealt with racial integration of public schools?

   (A) *Brown v. Board of Education of Topeka*
   (B) *Ruiz v. Estelle*
   (C) *Roe v. Wade*
   (D) *Edgewood v. Kirby*

8. Which of the following cases dealt with prison overcrowding?

   (A) *Brown v. Board of Education of Topeka*
   (B) *Ruiz v. Estelle*
   (C) *Roe v. Wade*
   (D) *Edgewood v. Kirby*

9. Which of the following cases dealt with abortion?

   (A) *Brown v. Board of Education of Topeka*
   (B) *Ruiz v. Estelle*
   (C) *Roe v. Wade*
   (D) *Edgewood v. Kirby*

10. Texas was forced to eliminate dual school systems because of which of the following?

    (A) *Brown v. Board of Education of Topeka*
    (B) *Ruiz v. Estelle*
    (C) *Roe v. Wade*
    (D) *Edgewood v. Kirby*

11. *Ruiz v. Estelle* dealt with which of the following issues?

    (A) School funding
    (B) School integration
    (C) Abortion
    (D) Prison overcrowding

12. An act of Congress adopting regulatory policies that overrule state policies in a particular regulatory area is known as which of the following?

    (A) Federal preemption of state authority
    (B) Federal mandate
    (C) Federal grant-in-aid
    (D) Federal matching funds requirement

13. A legal requirement placed on a state or local government by the national government requiring certain policy actions is known as which of the following?

    (A) Federal preemption of state authority
    (B) Federal mandate
    (C) Federal grant-in-aid
    (D) Federal matching funds requirement

14. What happens to Texas if its schools fail to comply with the provisions of No Child Left Behind?

    (A) State officials may go to jail.
    (B) The state will lose federal education funding.
    (C) The state will be embarrassed.
    (D) Nothing

15. The procedure through which Congress legislatively establishes a program, defines its general purpose, devises procedures for its operation, specifies an agency for implementation, and indicates an approximate level of funding is known as which of the following?

    (A) Appropriation process
    (B) Grants process
    (C) Authorization process
    (D) Appeals process

16. The procedure through which Congress legislatively provides money for a particular purpose is known as which of the following?

    (A) Appropriation process
    (B) Grants process
    (C) Authorization process
    (D) Appeals process

17. A federal grant-in-aid program that provides funds to state and local governments for a fairly narrow, specific purpose, such as removing asbestos from school buildings or acquiring land for outdoor recreation, is known as which of the following?

    (A) Formula grant program
    (B) Project grant program
    (C) Categorical grant program
    (D) Block grant program

18. A federal grant-in-aid program that provides money for a program in a broad, general policy area, such as elementary and secondary education or transportation, is known as which of the following?

    (A) Formula grant program
    (B) Project grant program
    (C) Categorical grant program
    (D) Block grant program

19. Which of the following is an example of an entitlement program?

    (A) Medicaid
    (B) School lunch program
    (C) Unemployment compensation
    (D) All of the above

20. A grant program that requires state and local governments to compete for available federal money is known as which of the following?

    (A) Formula grant program
    (B) Project grant program
    (C) Categorical grant program
    (D) Block grant program

21. A grant program that awards funding on the basis of a formula established by Congress is known as which of the following?

    (A) Formula grant program
    (B) Project grant program
    (C) Categorical grant program
    (D) Block grant program

22. The legislative provision that the national government will provide grant money for a particular activity only on condition that the state or local government involved supply a certain percentage of the total money required for the project or program is known as which of the following?

    (A) Formula grant
    (B) Matching funds requirement
    (C) Entitlement program
    (D) Federal preemption of state authority

23. Federal grant money flows to Texas to help fund which of the following?

    (A) Highway construction and maintenance
    (B) Mass transit
    (C) Public education
    (D) All of the above

24. How did the federal government force the state of Texas to increase its minimum legal drinking age to 21?

    (A) Congress passed legislation establishing a national drinking age.
    (B) Congress offered states a cash bonus if they would establish a minimum legal drinking age of 21.
    (C) Congress threatened to withhold federal highway funds from states that failed to establish a minimum legal drinking age of 21.
    (D) None of the above

25. Federal funds represent what percentage of the state budget?

    (A) 10 percent
    (B) 20 percent
    (C) 25 percent
    (D) 35 percent

Chapter 21: Political Participation in Texas

Circle the correct answer.

1. What percentage of the voting age population participated in the 2006 gubernatorial election?

   (A) 1 percent
   (B) 10 percent
   (C) 25 percent
   (D) 50 percent

2. Why did some white Texans organize chapters of the Ku Klux Klan after the Civil War?

   (A) To intimidate African Americans
   (B) To protect the voting rights of minority Texans
   (C) To fight against the Union forces occupying the state
   (D) To restore law and order

3. The poll tax had a negative impact on voter participation rates by which of the following groups?

   (A) African Americans
   (B) Latinos
   (C) Low-income whites
   (D) All of the above

4. Which of the following was *not* used to disfranchise African American Texans?

   (A) Retrospective voting
   (B) Poll tax
   (C) White primary
   (D) All three were used to disfranchise African Americans.

5. The white primary prevented African Americans from voting in which of the following elections?

   (A) Democratic primary
   (B) Republican primary
   (C) General election
   (D) All of the above

6. Which of the following elections was most important in late nineteenth-century Texas?

   (A) Democratic primary
   (B) Republican primary
   (C) General election
   (D) All of the above were equally important.

7. *Smith v. Allwright* dealt with which of the following issues?

   (A) Poll tax
   (B) Grandfather clauses
   (C) Abolition movement
   (D) White primary

8. George Parr is associated with which of the following?

   (A) Lyndon Johnson's election to the U.S. Senate in 1948
   (B) Duval County
   (C) Box 13 in Jim Wells County
   (D) All of the above

9. Lawrence A. Nixon is remembered for initiating legal challenges to which of the following?

   (A) Poll tax
   (B) Grandfather clauses
   (C) White primary
   (D) All of the above

10. Which of the following is *not* a requirement to vote in Texas?

    (A) You must be an American citizen.
    (B) You must live in the state for six months.
    (C) You must be at least 18 years of age.
    (D) All of the above are requirements to vote in Texas.

11. Are persons who have been convicted of serious crimes (felonies) eligible to vote in Texas?

    (A) No
    (B) Yes
    (C) Yes, but only after they have been released from prison.
    (D) Yes, but only after they have fully completed their sentences, including time served on parole and probation.

12. The election is next week and you want to vote, but you realize that you have not registered. What are your options?

    (A) You must register immediately because voter registration ends a week before the election.
    (B) You are out of luck because registration ended 30 days before the election.
    (C) You can register at the polls on the day of the election.
    (D) You can register now and vote early, but you cannot vote on the day of the election.

13. You hear on the news that early voting has begun for next month's election. Can you vote early if you just want to avoid the rush on the day of the election?

    (A) Yes. Anyone can vote early.
    (B) You can vote early if you are elderly or disabled, but otherwise you must vote on the day of the election.
    (C) You are required to vote early if you are over 65 years of age, but other people must vote on the day of the election.
    (D) You can vote early if you have a good reason, but otherwise you must vote on the day of the election.

14. You live in Houston, but you are attending college in Waco. What are your options for voting in the governor's election next fall?

    (A) You can change your voter registration to Waco and vote there.
    (B) You can vote early in Houston if you visit your parents during the early voting period next fall.
    (C) You can vote by mail.
    (D) All of the above

15. How does voter turnout in Texas compare with national turnout rates?

    (A) Turnout in Texas is about average compared with national turnout rates.
    (B) Turnout in Texas is below average compared with national rates.
    (C) Turnout in Texas is above average compared with national rates.
    (D) Turnout in Texas was once well above average but is now just below the national average.

16. Which of the following Texas elections would produce the highest turnout rate measured as a percentage of the voting age population?

    (A) A presidential election
    (B) A constitutional amendment election
    (C) A governor's election
    (D) A local election

17. Which of the following factors affects voter participation rates?

    (A) The average age of the population
    (B) The average level of education of the population
    (C) The average income level of the population
    (D) All of the above

18. Which of the following groups of Texans is underrepresented at the ballot box compared with its representation in the population of the state?

    (A) African Americans
    (B) Whites
    (C) Latinos
    (D) None of the above

19. Which of the following statements about the Texas electorate is not true?

    (A) Most Texas voters are white.
    (B) Most Texas voters are men.
    (C) Most Texans do not vote.
    (D) More Texans participate in presidential elections than in other types of elections.

20. The Texas electorate is representative of the population of the state of Texas in which of the following respects?

    (A) Racial/ethnic composition
    (B) Income
    (C) Education
    (D) None of the above

21. Which of the following groups of Texans is underrepresented at the ballot box compared with their representation in the population?

    (A) Whites
    (B) African Americans
    (C) Low-income Texans
    (D) All of the above

22. Which of the following groups is better represented among voters than among the population as a whole?

    (A) Asians
    (B) Latinos
    (C) Wealthy persons
    (D) All of the above

23. "I voted against the governor's reelection because I am unhappy with the direction the state is going." This statement reflects which of the following?

    (A) Democracy
    (B) Disfranchisement
    (C) Retrospective voting
    (D) None of the above

24. Which of the following statements about elections in Texas is true?

    (A) Newcomers must live in the state 90 days before they can register to vote.
    (B) Texans must register before they can vote.
    (C) Texas has term limits for all of its executive and legislative officials.
    (D) All of the above

25. Which of the following statements about elections in Texas is true?

    (A) Early voting is limited to people who will be out of town on the day of the election.
    (B) People who are out of town on the day of the election can use the Internet to cast their ballots.
    (C) In order to increase election turnout, the legislature recently changed state law to allow people to register to vote on the day of the election.
    (D) None of the above

Chapter 22: Interest Groups in Texas

Circle the correct answer.

1. Which of the following groups favored limiting noneconomic damages in medical malpractice cases?

   (A) Texas Medical Association
   (B) Texas Trial Lawyers Association
   (C) Consumer groups, such as Public Citizen
   (D) All of the above

2. The issue of tort reform deals with which of the following?

   (A) Protecting consumers against drunken drivers
   (B) School property tax rates
   (C) Immigration reform
   (D) Limiting damage awards in personal injury lawsuits

3. Which of the following is *not* an example of an interest group?

   (A) Texas Trial Lawyers Association
   (B) Texas Medical Association
   (C) State Board of Medical Examiners
   (D) League of United Latin American Citizens

4. The most powerful interest groups in Texas politics are which of the following?

   (A) Business and trade groups
   (B) Racial and ethnic minority groups
   (C) Religious groups
   (D) Organized labor

5. Which of the following interest groups would be most likely to favor the state having a "good business climate"?

   (A) Texas AFL-CIO
   (B) Christian Coalition
   (C) Texas Association of Business
   (D) LULAC

6. Which of the following would *not* be considered important to a good business climate?

   (A) Low tax rates on business
   (B) Tort reform
   (C) Regulations favorable to business growth
   (D) Strong labor unions

7. Right to work laws are designed to accomplish which of the following goals?

   (A) Limit the amount of money plaintiffs can recover from personal injury lawsuits
   (B) Ensure full employment in the state
   (C) Weaken labor unions
   (D) Guarantee workers the right to join a union

8. The Texas AFL-CIO would be most likely to favor which one of the following policy goals?

   (A) Increasing the state minimum wage
   (B) Prohibiting abortions in the state
   (C) Lowering property tax rates
   (D) Limiting punitive damages in medical malpractice lawsuits

9. Which of the following organizations would be most likely to advocate for the rights of Latinos?

   (A) NAACP
   (B) LULAC
   (C) MADD
   (D) AFL-CIO

10. Which of the following is an organization that supports the interests of African Americans?

    (A) NAACP
    (B) AFL-CIO
    (C) MADD
    (D) LULAC

11. Which of the following organizations would be most concerned about the problem of racial profiling?

    (A) Christian Coalition
    (B) American Federation of State, County, and Municipal Employees (AFSCME)
    (C) LULAC
    (D) Sierra Club

12. Which of the following organizations is typically allied with the Texas Republican Party?

    (A) LULAC
    (B) Christian Coalition
    (C) AFL-CIO
    (D) Sierra Club

13. Which of the following goals is *not* typically associated with conservative Christian organizations, such as the Christian Coalition, Eagle Forum, and American Family Association?

    (A) Repealing right to work laws
    (B) Prohibiting gay marriage
    (C) Limiting access to abortion
    (D) Restoring prayer to public schools

14. Which of the following groups is an environmental organization?

    (A) NARAL Pro-Choice Texas
    (B) NRA
    (C) Sierra Club
    (D) AARP

15. Which pair of interest groups would be most likely to agree on the issue of abortion?

    (A) Christian Coalition and Texas Association of Business
    (B) LULAC and AARP
    (C) Sierra Club and AFL-CIO
    (D) NOW and NARAL Pro-Choice Texas

16. Which of the following interest groups would be likely to endorse the Democratic candidate in the next Texas election?

    (A) AARP
    (B) Texas Medical Association
    (C) NARAL Pro-Choice Texas
    (D) Christian Coalition

17. An organization created to raise and distribute money in political campaigns is known as which of the following?

    (A) Political action committee (PAC)
    (B) Interest group
    (C) Political party
    (D) Issue network

18. What is the limit on the amount of campaign contributions a political action committee can give to candidates for statewide office or the legislature?

    (A) $5,000 per candidate per election
    (B) $10,000 per candidate and $100,000 overall
    (C) $200,000 overall
    (D) Texas allows unlimited contributions.

19. Which of the following PACs supports candidates opposed to tort reform?

    (A) Texans for Lawsuit Reform (TLR) PAC
    (B) Texas Medical Association PAC
    (C) Texas Trial Lawyers Association PAC
    (D) All of the above

20. What does "catching the late train" mean?

    (A) Contributing to the winning candidate after an election in which you backed the losing candidate
    (B) Changing political parties after an election defeat
    (C) Forming an interest group after losing a legislative battle
    (D) Changing the name of a PAC after an election defeat

21. What is lobbying?

    (A) Forming an organization to raise and distribute money during an election campaign
    (B) The communication of information by a representative of an interest group to a government official for the purpose of influencing a policy decision
    (C) Filing a lawsuit against a government agency that adopts a policy harmful to the position of an interest group
    (D) Endorsing candidates in an election

22. An open door through which an interest group hopes to influence the details of policy is known as which of the following?

    (A) Legislative access
    (B) Social lobbying
    (C) Lobbying
    (D) Catching the late train

23. Which of the following interest groups provided legal support to the poor school districts that sued the state over its education funding system in the case *Edgewood v. Kirby*?

    (A) Texas Federation of Teachers
    (B) Mexican American Legal Defense and Education Fund (MALDEF)
    (C) Texas Association of Business (TAB)
    (D) AARP

24. How do Thomas and Hrebenar classify the influence of interest groups in Texas?

    (A) They classify Texas as a state in which interest groups dominate the policymaking process.
    (B) They classify Texas as a state in which interest groups either must work with or are constrained by other elements of the state's political system, such as its political culture or a strong executive branch.
    (C) They believe that interest groups in Texas are subordinate to other elements of the state's political climate.
    (D) They believe that Texas alternates between interest groups dominating the policymaking process and sometimes having to work with other elements of the state's political system.

25. Which of the following statements most accurately describes the interest-group environment in Texas?

    (A) Groups that favor conservative public policies and groups that support liberal policies compete with one another on a nearly equal basis.
    (B) The most powerful interest groups in the state typically promote liberal policy preferences.
    (C) The most powerful interest groups in the state typically promote conservative policy preferences.
    (D) Interest groups are relatively weak in Texas because of the importance of political parties.

Chapter 23: Political Parties in Texas

Circle the correct answer.

1. A group of individuals who join together to seek public office in order to influence public policy is known as which of the following?

    (A) Political party
    (B) Political action committee
    (C) Interest group
    (D) Issue network

2. Which of the following statements best describes the nature of party politics in Texas from the Civil War era until the middle of the twentieth century?

    (A) Texas was a one-party Republican state.
    (B) Texas was a one-party Democratic state.
    (C) Texas was divided evenly between the two parties.
    (D) Third parties competed equally with Democrats and Republicans for control of state government.

3. An identifiable subgroup within a political party is known as which of the following?

    (A) Interest group
    (B) Third party
    (C) Political action committee
    (D) Party faction

4. Which of the following individuals was able to participate in a Republican precinct meeting after the March 2008 primary election?

    (A) Any citizen
    (B) Any citizen who voted in the primary election
    (C) Any citizen who voted in the Republican primary
    (D) Only elected party officials

5. Which of the following is *not* one of the purposes of a state political party convention?

    (A) To adopt a party platform
    (B) To elect a state party chairperson
    (C) To select party nominees for statewide office
    (D) To select delegates to the national party convention in presidential election years

6. Why were most native white Texans loyal members of the Democratic Party after the Civil War era?

    (A) They agreed with the Democratic Party on economic issues.
    (B) Most Texans were poor and the Democrats were the party of poor people.
    (C) They were hostile to the Republican Party because of its association with the Union during the Civil War era.
    (D) All of the above

7. The liberal wing of the Democratic Party favored which of the following positions?

    (A) Higher taxes on business and industry
    (B) More government spending on healthcare and education
    (C) Access to abortion
    (D) All of the above

8. Which of the following groups did *not* support the liberal faction of the Democratic Party?

    (A) Low-income voters
    (B) Businesspeople
    (C) African Americans
    (D) Latinos

9. Ralph Yarborough was a U.S. senator representing which of the following political groupings in Texas?

    (A) Conservative Democrats
    (B) Republicans
    (C) Independents
    (D) Liberal Democrats

10. Which of the following political groupings in Texas was helped most by the increased voting participation of minority Texans?

    (A) Liberal Democrats
    (B) Conservative Democrats
    (C) Republicans
    (D) Independents

11. John Tower was a U.S. senator representing which of the following political groupings in Texas?

    (A) Conservative Democrats
    (B) Republicans
    (C) Independents
    (D) Liberal Democrats

12. A Yellow Dog Democrat can best be described as which of the following?

    (A) Someone who always voted Democratic.
    (B) Someone who switched from the Democratic to the Republican Party.
    (C) Someone who called him- or herself a Democrat but often voted Republican.
    (D) Someone who switched from the Republican Party to the Democratic Party.

13. Which of the following factors helped the Republican Party emerge as a political force in Texas?

    (A) People were attracted to Franklin Roosevelt and the New Deal.
    (B) African Americans switched parties from the Democratic Party to the Republican Party.
    (C) Many conservative white Democrats became disenchanted with the national Democratic Party because they thought it was too liberal.
    (D) All of the above

14. Who was the first Republican governor of Texas in the twentieth century?

    (A) Bill Clements
    (B) John Connally
    (C) George W. Bush
    (D) Rick Perry

15. Which of the following statements is true about the current party balance in Texas?

    (A) A majority of the members of the Texas House are Republicans.
    (B) A majority of the members of the Texas Senate are Republicans.
    (C) All statewide elected officials are Republicans.
    (D) All of the above.

16. How does Texas compare with other states in terms of party balance as measured by the expressed party identification of state residents?

    (A) Texas is one of the most Republican states in the nation.
    (B) Texas is one of the most Democratic states in the nation.
    (C) The party balance in Texas is about average compared with other states.
    (D) Although Texas was once one of the most Republican states in the nation, the party balance between the two parties is now close.

17. Democratic candidates do best with which of the following groups of voters?

    (A) Upper-income voters
    (B) White voters
    (C) Latino voters
    (D) Suburban voters

18. Democratic candidates run the most strongly among which of the following groups of voters?

    (A) African Americans
    (B) Latinos
    (C) Whites
    (D) Asians

19. Which of the following regions is historically an area of Republican strength?

    (A) South Texas
    (B) East Texas
    (C) The border region with Mexico
    (D) West Texas

20. Which of the following areas would be most likely to support a Democratic candidate?

    (A) A rural county in West Texas
    (B) A suburban county outside a major city
    (C) A small town in Central Texas
    (D) An inner-city Houston neighborhood

21. Which of the following groups is *not* aligned with the Republican Party?

    (A) Religious organizations
    (B) Farm groups
    (C) Right-to-life advocates
    (D) Labor unions

22. On which of the following issues do the Texas Republican and Democratic Parties take opposing positions?

    (A) Minimum wage laws
    (B) Gay and lesbian rights
    (C) Abortion rights
    (D) All of the above

23. Which of the following is *not* a position taken by the Texas Republican Party?

    (A) Opposition to campaign finance reform
    (B) Opposition to gay marriage
    (C) Opposition to bilingual education
    (D) Opposition to the election of state judges

24. Which of the following factors may eventually lead to a resurgence of the Democratic Party in Texas?

    (A) An increase in minority voter turnout
    (B) The continued growth of suburban counties
    (C) An increased migration of white professionals from outside the region to Texas
    (D) All of the above

25. Which of the following is the best explanation for democratic party gains in Dallas county in 2006?

    (A) Demographic change
    (B) Popularity of George W. Bush
    (C) Republican candidates were hurt by scandal
    (D) Democrats became more conservative.

Circle the correct answer.

1. An election system that provides for the election of nearly every public official of any significance is known as which of the following?

   (A) Straight ticket voting
   (B) Long ballot
   (C) Split ticket voting
   (D) Retrospective voting

2. Which of the following elections is always held in November?

   (A) Primary election
   (B) Primary runoff election
   (C) General election
   (D) All of the above

3. Which of the following is an election contest between candidates of different political parties?

   (A) General election
   (B) Primary election
   (C) Primary runoff election
   (D) All of the above

4. In the fall general election, Republican A won 52 percent of the vote, Democrat B took 45 percent, and Independent C captured the remaining 3 percent. What is the outcome?

   (A) Republican A won by having the most votes.
   (B) Republican A and Democrat B face a runoff because they are the top two candidates.
   (C) Republican A won by having a majority of the vote. Otherwise, a runoff would have been held.
   (D) All three candidates are in a runoff.

5. In the fall general election, Republican A won 40 percent of the vote, Democrat B took 35 percent, and Independent C captured the remaining 25 percent. What is the outcome?

   (A) Republican A won by having the most votes.
   (B) Republican A and Democrat B face a runoff because they are the top two candidates.
   (C) Republican A won by having at least 40 percent of the vote. Otherwise, a runoff would have been held.
   (D) All three candidates are in a runoff.

6. In the March primary, Candidate A has 40 percent of the vote, Candidate B has 35 percent, and Candidate C has the remaining 25 percent. What is the outcome?

   (A) Candidate A won by having the most votes.
   (B) Candidates A and B face a runoff because they are the top two candidates.
   (C) Candidates A and B face a runoff because no one candidate had a majority and Candidate A and Candidate B are the top two finishers.
   (D) All three candidates are in a runoff.

7. You failed to vote in the March primary election. Are you allowed to vote in the primary runoff?

   (A) No
   (B) Yes, and you can vote in either primary runoff.
   (C) Yes, and you can vote in both primary runoffs.
   (D) Yes, but you can vote only in the runoff of the party in which you are registered.

8. Voter turnout is typically the greatest in Texas in which of the following elections?

   (A) Republican primary
   (B) Democratic primary
   (C) Primary runoff elections combined
   (D) General election

9. Which of the following characteristics is *not* typical of Republican primary voters?

   (A) Middle- and upper-income
   (B) Suburban
   (C) Latino
   (D) White

10. What is the purpose of a presidential preference primary?

    (A) To award state national convention delegates to presidential candidates
    (B) To determine which candidate wins the state's electoral vote
    (C) To select a president and vice president
    (D) To identify the people who will serve as electoral college electors for the state of Texas

11. Which of the following elections is typically held in odd-numbered years?

    (A) Primary election
    (B) Primary runoff
    (C) General election
    (D) Local election

12. Which of the following Texas elections is typically a nonpartisan election?

    (A) Election for mayor
    (B) Election for the Texas Supreme Court
    (C) Election for attorney general
    (D) Election for the state legislature

13. What is the purpose of a bond election?

    (A) To set the amount of money a criminal defendant must pay to get out of jail
    (B) To ratify constitutional amendments
    (C) To authorize local governments to borrow money
    (D) To remove an elected official from office

14. Which of the following officials is *not* elected in an at-large election?

   (A) State senator
   (B) Lieutenant governor
   (C) Attorney general
   (D) U.S. senator from Texas

15. What is the concept of one person, one vote?

   (A) Legislative districts should be drawn to have the same or nearly the same population.
   (B) Everyone should vote in order for democracy to function effectively.
   (C) People voting more than once are guilty of breaking the law.
   (D) Legislative districts must be redrawn every ten years.

16. What is the purpose of the Voting Rights Act (VRA)?

   (A) To ensure that legislative districts have nearly equal population
   (B) To prevent gerrymandering
   (C) To eliminate at-large elections
   (D) To protect the voting rights of racial and ethnic minority groups

17. The VRA has had which of the following effects in Texas?

   (A) To increase the number of minority legislators and members of Congress
   (B) To increase the number of Republicans in the legislature and in Congress
   (C) To require Texas to submit redistricting plans to the Justice Department for approval before they take effect
   (D) All of the above

18. Which of the following is responsible for redrawing state legislative districts every ten years?

   (A) U.S. Congress
   (B) State legislature
   (C) Governor
   (D) Federal courts

19. Why did Congressman Tom DeLay and the Republican leadership in the legislature want to redraw congressional districts in 2003?

   (A) To increase the number of Latino members of Congress from Texas
   (B) To increase the number of Republican members of Congress from Texas
   (C) To take account of major population shifts since the last census
   (D) To correct errors that took place in the redistricting that took place two years earlier

20. What is the most expensive cost for major statewide election campaigns?

   (A) Television
   (B) Polling
   (C) Travel
   (D) Consultants

21. How much money can a wealthy individual spend on his or her own campaign?

   (A) None
   (B) $5,000
   (C) $500,000
   (D) The amount is unlimited.

22. How much money can a wealthy contributor give to a candidate for governor?

   (A) $5,000
   (B) $500,000
   (C) $1,000,000
   (D) The amount is unlimited.

23. Why do incumbent members of Congress and the state legislature usually win reelection?

   (A) They are usually better known than their challengers.
   (B) They can usually raise more money than their challengers.
   (C) Most districts are stacked in favor of one political party, giving most incumbents a free ride in the general election.
   (D) All of the above

24. A political phenomenon in which a strong candidate for one office gives a boost to fellow party members on the same ballot seeking other offices is known as which of the following?

   (A) Retrospective voting
   (B) Electoral mandate
   (C) Coattail effect
   (D) Prospective voting

25. The expression of popular support for a particular policy demonstrated through the electoral process is known as which of the following?

   (A) Retrospective voting
   (B) Electoral mandate
   (C) Coattail effect
   (D) Prospective voting

Circle the correct answer.

1. How is the speaker of the House selected?

    (A) The speaker is selected by the voters in a statewide election.
    (B) The governor appoints the speaker.
    (C) The speaker is chosen by majority vote of the membership of the Texas House.
    (D) The speaker is chosen by a two-thirds' vote of the membership of the Texas House.

2. Which of the following statements about the Texas legislature is true?

    (A) The legislature holds regular sessions every other year.
    (B) Regular sessions of the legislature last for 90 days but can be extended by the governor.
    (C) The legislature meets in even-numbered years— 2008, 2010, and so on.
    (D) All of the above

3. Which of the following statements about the Texas legislature is true?

    (A) The Texas House has 31 members elected to serve two-year terms.
    (B) Members of the Texas Senate are elected to serve six-year terms.
    (C) The Texas Constitution limits the terms of members of the legislature to a maximum of eight years.
    (D) None of the above

4. In the 2008 election, how many members of the legislature had to stand for reelection?

    (A) All the members of the House and Senate
    (B) No members because they all stood for election in 2006 and will not run again until 2010
    (C) All members of the House but only half the Senate
    (D) Half of the members of the House and a third of the Senate

5. Which of the following statements about special sessions is true?

    (A) The governor, lieutenant governor, and speaker can call special sessions by majority vote.
    (B) A special session can consider any measure considered in the previous regular session of the legislature.
    (C) On average, the legislature meets in special session only once or twice every ten years.
    (D) A special session can last no longer than 30 days.

6. Which of the following groups is overrepresented among the membership of the legislature?

    (A) Women
    (B) Latinos
    (C) African Americans
    (D) Whites

7. How much do members of the legislature make?

    (A) $7,200 a year
    (B) $15,000 a year
    (C) $35,000 a year
    (D) $100,000 a year

8. How does the Texas legislature compare and contrast with legislatures in other states?

    (A) Most state legislatures meet in regular session every year, but the Texas legislature meets every other year.
    (B) Most state legislators are paid more than members of the Texas legislature.
    (C) Most state legislatures are bicameral and the Texas legislature is bicameral.
    (D) All of the above

9. What is the most important reason for turnover in the Texas legislature?

    (A) Term limits
    (B) Defeat for reelection
    (C) Voluntary retirement
    (D) Death

10. Which of the following is the most important figure in the Texas Senate?

    (A) Speaker
    (B) Lieutenant governor
    (C) Vice president
    (D) Majority leader

11. Which of the following is the most important figure in the Texas House?

    (A) Speaker
    (B) Lieutenant governor
    (C) Vice president
    (D) Majority leader

12. How is the lieutenant governor normally chosen?

    (A) The lieutenant governor is elected by the membership of the Senate.
    (B) The lieutenant governor is appointed by the governor.
    (C) The lieutenant governor is elected in a statewide election.
    (D) The lieutenant governor is elected running on a ticket with the governor.

13. An individual member of the Texas House is interested in becoming speaker in the next session of the legislature. What step does that individual take to accomplish his or her goal?

(A) Begin raising money and organizing a campaign for a statewide election.
(B) Lobby the governor for the appointment.
(C) Begin collecting pledge cards from other House members.
(D) None of the above

14. Which of the following agencies plays the greatest role in state budget policy?

(A) Legislative Redistricting Board (LRB)
(B) Legislative Budget Board (LBB)
(C) Land Commission
(D) State Board of Education (SBOE)

15. How are committee chairs chosen in the Texas House?

(A) They are elected by the membership.
(B) They are appointed by the governor.
(C) They are chosen on the basis of seniority.
(D) They are chosen by the speaker.

16. How are committee chairs chosen in the Texas Senate?

(A) They are elected by the membership.
(B) They are appointed by the governor.
(C) They are chosen on the basis of seniority.
(D) They are chosen by the lieutenant governor.

17. What is HB 201?

(A) A bill introduced in the legislature in 2001
(B) A bill introduced in the Texas Senate
(C) The 201st bill introduced in the Texas House
(D) The 201st bill introduced in the Texas Senate

18. A hearing on a bill is most likely to take place in which of the following?

(A) On the floor
(B) In standing committee
(C) In conference committee
(D) When it reaches the governor's desk

19. What is the purpose of a fiscal note?

(A) To indicate the cost of a measure to the state (if any)
(B) To indicate whether the measure is consistent with the Texas Constitution
(C) To measure the level of support for the measure in the legislature
(D) To indicate whether the governor supports or opposes the measure

20. What is the purpose of the House calendar?

(A) To determine when the legislature adjourns
(B) To set the priority order for consideration of legislation on the House floor
(C) To indicate the cost of a measure
(D) To assign House members to committee

21. What is the two-thirds' rule in the Senate?

(A) Legislation cannot reach the floor of the Senate unless two-thirds of the membership agrees to suspend the rules.
(B) Legislation cannot pass unless two-thirds' of the Senate votes for final passage.
(C) Constitutional amendments must be proposed by a two-thirds' vote.
(D) Two-thirds of the members of the Senate must be present in order to conduct official business.

22. Is the filibuster an effective weapon in the Texas Senate?

(A) Not usually, because it can be halted by majority vote.
(B) Yes, because it takes a two-thirds' vote to halt it.
(C) No, because Senate rules prevent the filibuster.
(D) None of the above

23. A bill passes the legislature and goes to the governor. Which of the following options does the governor *not* have for dealing with the bill?

(A) The governor can sign the bill into law.
(B) The governor can veto the bill.
(C) The governor can allow the bill to become law without signature.
(D) The governor can allow the bill to die by failing to sign it after the legislature has adjourned (a pocket veto).

24. Is the chair of the House Appropriations Committee a Democrat or a Republican?

(A) Democrat, because a majority of the members of the House are Democrats
(B) Republican, because a majority of the members of the House are Republicans
(C) Republican, because the Speaker of the House is a Republican
(D) Either a Democrat or a Republican, because the speaker chooses members of both parties to serve as committee chairs

25. Is the Texas House a partisan legislative body?

(A) No. Political parties are unimportant in the Texas legislature.
(B) Yes. The speaker is a member of the majority party and all committee chairs are members of the majority party.
(C) Not yet. Political parties play a more important role than they have in the past, but the Texas House does not yet meet the full definition of a partisan legislative body.
(D) No. Voting seldom, if ever, breaks down along party lines.

Chapter 26: The Executive Branch in Texas

Circle the correct answer.

1. How effective was Governor Perry's executive order to require Texas schoolgirls to be vaccinated against HPV?

    (A) The governor accomplished his goal because the vaccinations are now required for Texas school girls.

    (B) The governor failed because the Texas Supreme Court ruled that the executive order was unconstitutional.

    (C) The governor failed because the legislature passed a bill to overturn the order and Perry allowed it to become law because he knew the legislature would override his veto.

    (D) The governor failed because the Texas Health and Human Services Commission refused to carry out the order.

2. Which of the following statements about impeachment is true?

    (A) A governor who is impeached can be removed from office by a two-thirds' vote of the Texas Senate.

    (B) No Texas governor has been impeached.

    (C) The House and the Senate must both vote by a two-thirds' margin to remove a governor from office.

    (D) All of the above

3. What is the impact of the governor declaring a particular legislative measure an emergency?

    (A) Emergency measures receive priority attention on the floor of the House.

    (B) Legislators can introduce emergency measures after the deadline for introducing bills.

    (C) The action focuses legislative and public attention on a particular measure.

    (D) All of the above

4. The legislature passes a measure to authorize the construction of a medical school in El Paso. Which of the following options does the governor *not* have for dealing with this bill?

    (A) The governor can sign the bill into law.

    (B) The governor can veto the bill.

    (C) The governor can allow the bill to become law without signature.

    (D) The governor can sign the bill while issuing a line-item veto to remove parts of it that the governor does not like.

5. The legislature passes an appropriation measure to fund the medical school in El Paso. What are the governor's options for dealing with this bill?

    (A) The governor can sign the bill into law.

    (B) The governor can veto the entire bill.

    (C) The governor can sign the bill while issuing a line-item veto to remove parts of it that the governor does not like.

    (D) All of the above

6. Which of the following statements about special sessions is true?

    (A) The governor shares the power to call special sessions with the lieutenant governor and the speaker.

    (B) The governor sets the agenda for special sessions.

    (C) Special sessions may last no more than 60 days.

    (D) All of the above

7. Which of the following statements about the appointive power of the governor is true?

    (A) The governor appoints a cabinet, including an attorney general, a secretary of state, a comptroller, and a commissioner of agriculture.

    (B) The governor appoints the judges of the state's highest courts.

    (C) The governor's appointees must be confirmed by a two-thirds' vote of the Texas Senate.

    (D) None of the above

8. Which of the following is true of the judicial powers of the governor?

    (A) The governor appoints judges to fill vacancies in state district and appellate courts.

    (B) The governor has the sole authority to pardon individuals convicted of serious criminal offenses.

    (C) Although the members of the Texas Supreme Court are elected, the governor designates one judge as chief justice.

    (D) All of the above

9. Which of the following plays the most important role in drafting the Texas state budget?

    (A) Governor

    (B) Legislative Redistricting Board

    (C) Legislative Budget Board

    (D) Comptroller of Public Accounts

10. Which of the following officials participates directly in the budget execution process in Texas?

    (A) Comptroller

    (B) Governor

    (C) Attorney general

    (D) Chair of House Appropriations Committee

11. The governor has the authority to appoint which of the following executive branch officials?

    (A) Attorney general

    (B) Comptroller

    (C) Secretary of state

    (D) Commissioner of agriculture

12. Which of the following officials is elected?

    (A) Railroad commissioner

    (B) Secretary of state

    (C) Insurance commissioner

    (D) All of the above

13. Which of the following officials issues written opinions to interpret state laws and the state constitution?

(A) Agriculture commissioner
(B) Lieutenant governor
(C) Attorney general
(D) Comptroller

14. Which of the following officials estimates state revenues for the next biennium at the beginning of each legislative session?

(A) Agriculture commissioner
(B) Lieutenant governor
(C) Attorney general
(D) Comptroller

15. A businessperson operating a retail store would work closely with which of the following state officials on administering the state's sales tax?

(A) Secretary of state
(B) Comptroller
(C) Attorney general
(D) Land commissioner

16. If you suspect that the gasoline pump at the local service station is shortchanging purchasers, you should report your suspicion to which of the following state officials?

(A) Agriculture commissioner
(B) Attorney general
(C) Comptroller
(D) Land commissioner

17. Students doing research on state election results can find data at the website of which of the following state officials?

(A) Comptroller
(B) Attorney general
(C) Secretary of state
(D) Land commissioner

18. Which of the following agencies regulates oil and gas production in the state?

(A) Public Utility Commission
(B) Railroad Commission
(C) Texas Commission on Environmental Quality
(D) Land Commission

19. Which of the following agencies is led by a 15-member elected board?

(A) State Board of Education
(B) Railroad Commission
(C) Texas Higher Education Coordinating Board
(D) Public Utility Commission

20. The governor is unhappy with the policy decisions of the State Board of Education (SBOE). What can the governor do to influence its actions?

(A) The governor can remove its members and appoint replacements.
(B) The governor can remove the members that he or she appointed, but only with the approval of the Texas Senate.

(C) The governor can order the SBOE to change its policy position.
(D) The governor has little, if any, direct power to influence the SBOE.

21. The governor is unhappy with the policy decisions of the Texas Department of Parks and Wildlife. What can the governor do to influence its actions?

(A) The governor can appoint new board members as the terms of the old board members expire.
(B) The governor can remove its board members and appoint new ones.
(C) The governor can order it to change its policy position.
(D) The governor has little, if any, power to influence the agency.

22. You read in the newspaper that a local businessperson has been appointed to serve on the Board of Regents of Texas A&M University. What sort of job is that?

(A) University regents are responsible for running the daily affairs of the university.
(B) Serving as a member of a university board of regents is a full-time job.
(C) University regents earn $100,000 a year.
(D) The Board of Regents sets basic university policy.

23. The Public Utility Commission (PUC) is a rulemaking body. When the PUC adopts a rule, what is it doing?

(A) It is overriding a law passed by the legislature.
(B) It is adopting a legally binding regulation.
(C) It is recommending a new law to the legislature and the governor.
(D) It is adopting procedures for its own internal management.

24. The process that involves the government contracting with private business to implement government programs is known as which of the following?

(A) Rulemaking
(B) Privatization
(C) Budget execution authority
(D) Impeachment

25. An agency is scheduled for sunset review this year, but the legislature takes no action. What is the status of the agency?

(A) It will have to undergo sunset review in the next session of the legislature.
(B) It will have to shut down operations unless the governor signs an executive order to keep it in operation.
(C) It will have to shut down operations.
(D) Nothing happens to it.

Circle the correct answer.

1. Who are the litigants in a criminal case?

   (A) Civil defendant and prosecutor
   (B) Criminal defendant and crime victim
   (C) Prosecutor and criminal defendant
   (D) Judge and jury

2. Which of the following is a type of criminal dispute?

   (A) Misdemeanor case
   (B) Tort case
   (C) Contract case
   (D) All of the above

3. Which of the following is a misdemeanor, as opposed to a felony offense?

   (A) Aggravated assault
   (B) Murder
   (C) Robbery
   (D) Speeding through a school zone

4. Who has the burden of proof in a criminal case?

   (A) Prosecutor
   (B) Defendant
   (C) Crime victim
   (D) Judge

5. Who has the burden of proof in a civil case?

   (A) Defendant
   (B) Plaintiff
   (C) Judge
   (D) Jury

6. Assume that you are a member of a jury in a criminal case. After the evidence is presented, you think it is more likely than not that the defendant is guilty but it is a fairly close call in your judgment. How do you vote as a member of the jury?

   (A) You vote to convict the defendant because you think the defendant is guilty.
   (B) You vote to convict because the defendant has failed to prove innocence.
   (C) You vote not guilty because the prosecution has failed to prove guilt beyond a reasonable doubt.
   (D) You vote not guilty because the prosecution has failed to prove the case by a preponderance of the evidence.

7. Which of the following is *not* an example of a civil case?

   (A) A dispute over injuries suffered in an automobile accident
   (B) A trial of an individual accused of breaking into a home
   (C) A dispute over an estate
   (D) A child custody battle

8. Which of the following is an example of a tort case?

   (A) A personal injury
   (B) A divorce proceeding
   (C) A theft of property
   (D) A dispute over an estate

9. A procedure in which a defendant agrees to plead guilty in order to receive punishment less than the maximum for an offense is known as which of the following?

   (A) Adversary proceeding
   (B) Trial
   (C) Appeal
   (D) Plea bargain

10. Which of the following is characteristic of a trial but is *not* characteristic of an appellate proceeding?

    (A) A jury weighing guilt or innocence
    (B) A witness presenting testimony
    (C) A prosecuting attorney introducing evidence
    (D) All of the above

11. The taking of a case from a lower court to a higher court by the losing party in a lower-court decision is known as which of the following?

    (A) Adversary proceeding
    (B) Trial
    (C) Appeal
    (D) Plea bargain

12. A jury acquits a defendant of a criminal charge. New evidence subsequently emerges that indicates that the defendant is guilty after all. What, if anything, can the prosecutor do?

    (A) The prosecutor can do nothing because the Constitution protects against double jeopardy.
    (B) The prosecutor can appeal the acquittal to a higher court.
    (C) The prosecutor can ask a grand jury to reconsider the case.
    (D) The prosecutor can ask the judge to reconsider the original verdict.

13. Which of the following courts would be most likely to try a case involving a traffic ticket?

    (A) District court
    (B) County court
    (C) Municipal court
    (D) Texas Supreme Court

14. Which of the following courts would try a felony criminal case?

    (A) Municipal court
    (B) Justice of the peace court
    (C) District court
    (D) County court

15. Which of the following courts would try a misdemeanor case involving theft?

   (A) Municipal court
   (B) Justice of the peace court
   (C) District court
   (D) County court

16. Which of the following courts would try a multi-million-dollar civil suit?

   (A) District court
   (B) Court of appeals
   (C) Municipal court
   (D) Texas Supreme Court

17. Which of the following courts would neither try nor hear the appeal of an assault case?

   (A) District court
   (B) Court of appeals
   (C) Texas Supreme Court
   (D) Texas Court of Criminal Appeals

18. Which of the following courts would neither try nor hear the appeal of a medical malpractice lawsuit?

   (A) District court
   (B) Court of appeals
   (C) Texas Supreme Court
   (D) Texas Court of Criminal Appeals

19. Which of the following courts decides cases by majority vote of its nine members?

   (A) Court of appeal
   (B) District court
   (C) Texas Court of Criminal Appeals
   (D) Municipal court

20. Which of the following legal proceedings would take place in the Texas Supreme Court?

   (A) A divorce trial
   (B) The appeal of a burglary conviction
   (C) A capital murder trial
   (D) None of the above

21. Which of the following courts deals only with civil matters?

   (A) Texas Supreme Court
   (B) Texas Court of Criminal Appeals
   (C) Courts of appeals
   (D) District court

22. Which of the following courts has the authority to remove a judge of another court for misconduct?

   (A) District court
   (B) Texas Court of Criminal Appeals
   (C) Texas Supreme Court
   (D) All of the above

23. How are district court judges chosen in Texas?

   (A) Nonpartisan election
   (B) Missouri Plan
   (C) Partisan election
   (D) Gubernatorial appointment

24. Why are candidates for the Texas Supreme Court typically able to raise more money than candidates for the Texas Court of Criminal Appeals?

   (A) State law limits contributions for candidates for the Texas Court of Criminal Appeals and it does not limit contributions to Supreme Court candidates
   (B) The Texas Supreme Court hears appeals of cases from the Texas Court of Criminal Appeals, so it is more important
   (C) The litigants who appear before the Texas Supreme Court (insurance companies, bankers, businesspeople, etc.) have more money than the litigants who appear before the Texas Court of Criminal Appeals
   (D) All of the above

25. Which of the following steps is not part of merit selection, or the Missouri Plan, of judicial selection?

   (A) A commission draws up a short list of qualified candidates to fill a judicial vacancy.
   (B) The governor selects an appointee from the list.
   (C) The state Senate must confirm the appointment by a two-thirds' vote.
   (D) The Texas Supreme Court evaluates the judge's performance every four years and determines whether the judge stays in office.

Circle the correct answer.

1. Which of the following is true about the legal authority of Texas cities?

   (A) Cities must conform to state law.
   (B) Cities must conform to federal law.
   (C) Cities must conform to the Texas Constitution.
   (D) All of the above

2. Which of the following statements about a general-law city is true?

   (A) It may exercise only those powers specifically granted under state law.
   (B) It must have a city charter.
   (C) Voters must approve its incorporation.
   (D) All of the above

3. Which of the following statements about a home-rule city is true?

   (A) It can annex only with the approval of the residents of the area to be annexed.
   (B) It is bound by Dillon's Rule.
   (C) It must have at least 5,000 residents.
   (D) All of the above

4. A structure of municipal government in which the voters elect a mayor as the chief executive officer of the city and a council that serves as a legislative body is known as which of the following?

   (A) Mayor-council form of city government
   (B) Home-rule city
   (C) General-law city
   (D) City manager form of city government

5. Which of the following Texas cities uses the mayor-council form of city government?

   (A) Dallas
   (B) Houston
   (C) San Antonio
   (D) All of the above

6. Which of the following statements is *not* true about the mayor-council form of city government?

   (A) It is the traditional form of city government for large cities in the United States.
   (B) It is found in all the nation's major cities, including Houston, Dallas, and San Antonio.
   (C) In the strong mayor variation, the mayor prepares the budget.
   (D) The city council serves as a legislative body.

7. In which of the following forms of city government does the mayor have the most policymaking influence?

   (A) Mayor-council, strong mayor variation
   (B) Mayor-council, weak mayor variation
   (C) Council-manager
   (D) The mayor is equally powerful in all three forms of city government.

8. A structure of municipal government in which the city council/mayor appoints a professional administrator called a city manager to act as the chief executive officer of the municipality is known as which of the following?

   (A) Mayor-council form of city government
   (B) Home-rule city
   (C) General-law city
   (D) City manager form of city government

9. A local program that enhances the economic position of a community in its competition with other communities is known as which of the following?

   (A) Developmental urban policy
   (B) Redistributive urban policy
   (C) Allocational urban policy
   (D) None of the above

10. A city opens a series of neighborhood health clinics to provide basic healthcare to low-income families. This action is an example of which of the following?

    (A) Developmental urban policy
    (B) Redistributive urban policy
    (C) Allocational urban policy
    (D) None of the above

11. Police and fire protection are examples of which of the following?

    (A) Developmental urban policy
    (B) Redistributive urban policy
    (C) Allocational urban policy
    (D) None of the above

12. Texas cities provide all but which one of the following services?

    (A) Fire protection
    (B) Libraries
    (C) Garbage pickup
    (D) Public education

13. Which of the following is *not* a revenue source for Texas cities?

    (A) Sales tax
    (B) Property tax
    (C) Income tax
    (D) Franchise tax

14. What is the purpose of a homestead exemption?

    (A) To exempt homeowners from zoning laws
    (B) To give a property tax break to homeowners
    (C) To permit home-based businesses in a residential area
    (D) To grant homeowners the right to vote on annexation

15. A property owner can claim a homestead exemption on which of the following?

    (A) A primary residence
    (B) A rental house
    (C) A small-business establishment
    (D) All of the above

16. A program in which a local government promises to earmark increased property tax revenues generated by development in a designated area called a tax increment financing district to fund improvements in the area, such as roads, parks, sidewalks, and street lighting, is known as which of the following?

    (A) Homestead exemption
    (B) Redistributive urban policy
    (C) Extraterritoriality
    (D) Tax increment financing

17. What is the maximum amount of territory a Texas city of 100 square miles can annex in a single year (assuming that it annexed its full allotment in previous years)?

    (A) None
    (B) 100 square miles
    (C) 10 square miles
    (D) An unlimited amount

18. Which of the following is *not* a reason a city would annex a subdivision?

    (A) To expand its property tax base
    (B) To increase suburban shopping opportunities for inner-city residents
    (C) To prevent the incorporation of surrounding municipalities
    (D) To increase the amount of federal grant money it receives

19. Strategic Partnership Agreements are negotiated in regard to which of the following?

    (A) Annexation
    (B) Zoning
    (C) Tax abatement
    (D) Enterprise zones

20. You own property in the ETJ of a major city. What impact does that have on you?

    (A) If you build on the property, you must follow city construction ordinances and regulations.
    (B) You must pay property taxes to the city.
    (C) You can vote in city elections.
    (D) All of the above

21. The governmental designation of tracts of land for industrial, commercial, or residential use is known as which of the following?

    (A) Zoning
    (B) Deed restriction
    (C) Capital improvement
    (D) Housing code

22. Which of the following is a private agreement, as opposed to a governmental ordinance?

    (A) Zoning
    (B) Deed restriction
    (C) Capital improvement
    (D) Building code

23. The view that political power is held by a small group of people who dominate politics by controlling economic resources is known as which of the following?

    (A) Elite theory
    (B) Pluralism
    (C) Democracy
    (D) Political machine

24. The view that diverse groups of elites with differing interests compete with one another to control policy in various issue areas is known as which of the following?

    (A) Elite theory
    (B) Democracy
    (C) Pluralism
    (D) Political machine

25. The attempt of political candidates to deemphasize racially divisive themes in order to garner crossover support from voters of other races/ethnicities while receiving the overwhelming majority of support from voters of the candidate's own racial/ethnic group is known as which of the following?

    (A) Elite theory
    (B) Pluralism
    (C) Redistributive urban policies
    (D) Deracialization

Circle the correct answer.

1. Which of the following units of local government administer TAKS?

   (A) Counties
   (B) Cities
   (C) Independent school districts
   (D) All of the above

2. Which of the following units of local government have the authority to adopt home-rule status?

   (A) Counties
   (B) Cities
   (C) Independent school districts
   (D) All of the above

3. Which of the following is *not* a responsibility of county government?

   (A) Maintain records, such as births, deaths, marriages, and divorces
   (B) Law enforcement
   (C) Administer primary and general elections
   (D) Provide public education

4. Which of the following officials is a member of commissioners court?

   (A) County judge
   (B) County sheriff
   (C) County clerk
   (D) All of the above

5. Which of the following county officials is elected from a district smaller than the entire county?

   (A) County judge
   (B) County commissioner
   (C) County sheriff
   (D) County tax assessor-collector

6. The county judge has which of the following powers and responsibilities?

   (A) Veto power over the actions of the Commissioners Court
   (B) Authority to appoint the county sheriff
   (C) A vote on the Commissioners Court
   (D) All of the above

7. Which of the following units of local government have general ordinance-making power?

   (A) Counties
   (B) Cities
   (C) Municipal Utility Districts
   (D) All of the above

8. Which of the following officials administers the county jail?

   (A) County judge
   (B) County clerk
   (C) Sheriff
   (D) District clerk

9. Which of the following officials records legal documents, such as deeds, mortgages, and contracts?

   (A) County clerk
   (B) District clerk
   (C) County attorney
   (D) County tax assessor

10. Which of the following officials is the county election official?

    (A) County clerk
    (B) District clerk
    (C) County attorney
    (D) County tax assessor

11. Which of the following officials serves warrants and other legal papers on behalf of the justice of the peace?

    (A) Sheriff
    (B) County attorney
    (C) District attorney
    (D) Constable

12. Which of the following officials issues certificates-of-title for motor vehicles?

    (A) District clerk
    (B) Tax assessor-collector
    (C) County clerk
    (D) Justice of the peace

13. Which of the following officials is in charge of voter registration?

    (A) Tax assessor-collector
    (B) County clerk
    (C) District clerk
    (D) Sheriff

14. What is the main tax source for county government in Texas?

    (A) Sales tax
    (B) Income tax
    (C) Property tax
    (D) Inheritance tax

15. Which of the following county officials is elected?

    (A) Tax assessor-collector
    (B) County clerk
    (C) County treasurer
    (D) All of the above

16. Which of the following local officials is *not* elected?

    (A) Superintendent of schools
    (B) County tax assessor-collector
    (C) School board trustee
    (D) County sheriff

17. The board of trustees of an independent school district would make which of the following decisions?

    (A) Set the property tax rate
    (B) Hire a new superintendent
    (C) Approve a contract to build a new high school facility
    (D) All of the above

18. Which of the following statements accurately reflects the ruling of the Texas Supreme Court in *Edgewood v. Kirby*?

    (A) School districts with the same property tax rate should be able to raise the same amount of money per student.
    (B) School districts should all have the same tax rate.
    (C) School districts should all have the same amount of money.
    (D) School districts should all have the same amount of money per student.

19. The Robin Hood Plan requires which of the following?

    (A) Giving students in failing schools the opportunity to transfer to other schools, including private schools
    (B) Requiring property-wealthy districts to transfer funds either to the state or to other, poorer school districts
    (C) Forcing school districts to balance school enrollment by race and ethnicity
    (D) Basing school funding on TAKS scores

20. Which of the following is a publicly funded but privately managed school that operates under the terms of a formal contract with the state?

    (A) Independent school district
    (B) Special district
    (C) Municipal Utility District
    (D) Charter school

21. What is the theory behind the concept of school choice?

    (A) Schools will improve if they have to compete for students.
    (B) Poorly performing schools should be closed.

    (C) Schools with private management will outperform public schools.
    (D) Students will master English better in an English immersion class than a bilingual class.

22. Your child's school is rated exemplary. What does that mean?

    (A) It means that many parents chose the school as part of the parental choice program.
    (B) It means that the school has a healthy property tax base.
    (C) It means that the school receives more money from the state than other schools.
    (D) It means that the school's students do well on the TAKS test and have a low dropout rate.

23. A unit of local government created to perform specific-functions is known as which of the following?

    (A) Charter school
    (B) Special district
    (C) County
    (D) Independent school district

24. A family purchases a home in a subdivision located in an unincorporated area near a large urban center. The family will probably receive its water and sewer service from which of the following?

    (A) A Municipal Utility District (MUD)
    (B) The county
    (C) The nearby city
    (D) It will have to dig its own water well and septic tank.

25. Which of the following is the main tax revenue source for MUDs?

    (A) Sales taxes
    (B) Income taxes
    (C) Property taxes
    (D) Inheritance taxes

Circle the correct answer.

1. Which of the following taxes does the state of Texas *not* levy?

   (A) Personal income tax
   (B) General sales tax
   (C) Excise tax
   (D) Motor vehicle sales and rental tax

2. What is the most important source of tax revenue for the state?

   (A) Personal income tax
   (B) General sales tax
   (C) Excise tax
   (D) Property tax

3. Which federal program accounts for the largest single amount of federal money flowing to the state?

   (A) School lunch program
   (B) Children's Health Insurance Program (CHIP)
   (C) Medicaid
   (D) Temporary Assistance for Needy Families (TANF)

4. What is the general sales tax rate levied by the state of Texas?

   (A) 6.25 percent
   (B) 7.25 percent
   (C) 8.25 percent
   (D) 10 percent

5. Which of the following items is *not* subject to the general sales tax?

   (A) Breakfast eaten at a local diner
   (B) A box of cereal purchased at the corner grocery store
   (C) Blood pressure medicine purchased by prescription
   (D) All of the above

6. A tax levied on the manufacture, transportation, sale, or consumption of a particular item or set of related items is known as which of the following?

   (A) Sales tax
   (B) Severance tax
   (C) Franchise tax
   (D) Excise tax

7. Which of the following is an example of a sin tax?

   (A) Severance tax on oil and gas production
   (B) Motor vehicle sales and use tax
   (C) Cigarette tax
   (D) All of the above

8. Why has the relative importance of severance taxes on oil and gas production declined over the past 20 years?

   (A) Oil and gas production has been declining in the state.
   (B) People have purchased more fuel-efficient auto-mobiles.
   (C) The legislature has reduced the tax rate.
   (D) All of the above

9. Which of the following statements about the Texas Lottery is *not* true?

   (A) The lottery raises about 10 percent of total state revenue.
   (B) Lottery proceeds go into the Foundation School Program.
   (C) Lower-income people are more likely to purchase lottery tickets than middle- and upper-income people.
   (D) In addition to the Texas Lottery, state residents can participate in the Mega Millions lottery.

10. A levy whose burden weighs more heavily on persons earning higher incomes than it does on individuals making less money is known as which of the following?

    (A) Progressive tax
    (B) Regressive tax
    (C) Proportional tax
    (D) Sin tax

11. How does the tax incidence in Texas compare with that of other states?

    (A) Texas has a relatively progressive tax system.
    (B) Texas has one of the most regressive tax systems in the country.
    (C) The Texas tax system is somewhat regressive, but not more so than the tax systems in other states.
    (D) The Texas tax system is proportional because everyone pays the same sales tax rate on each purchase.

12. Which of the following taxes is based on the ability-to-pay theory of taxation?

    (A) Sales tax
    (B) Property tax
    (C) Personal income tax
    (D) Excise tax

13. The extent to which tax revenues increase as personal income rises is the definition of which of the following concepts?

    (A) Tax incidence
    (B) Performance-based
    (C) Tax elasticity
    (D) Progressive taxation

14. Conservatives oppose the adoption of a state income tax for which of the following reasons?

    (A) It would make the state tax system less regressive.
    (B) It would make the state tax system less elastic.
    (C) It would raise less money than other alternatives, such as broadening the sales tax.
    (D) It would slow economic growth.

15. When is the Texas sales tax holiday scheduled?

    (A) In December before Christmas
    (B) In early January
    (C) In May
    (D) In August before the start of school

16. Which of the following state spending categories has grown the most rapidly over the last two decades?

    (A) Public education
    (B) Health and human services
    (C) Criminal justice
    (D) Higher education

17. How does spending in Texas compare with other states?

    (A) Texas state spending is below the national average.
    (B) Texas state spending is around the national average.
    (C) Texas state spending is above the national average.
    (D) Texas state spending was once well below the national average but is now above the national average.

18. Spending in Texas is above the national average for which of the following services?

    (A) Welfare
    (B) Highways
    (C) Parks and recreation
    (D) Corrections

19. What is the most rapidly growing item in the state budget?

    (A) CHIP
    (B) Higher education
    (C) Medicaid
    (D) Public education

20. What is the goal of national welfare policy?

    (A) To move individuals and families from welfare to work
    (B) To ensure that welfare recipients have a minimal standard of living
    (C) To eliminate poverty in America
    (D) None of the above

21. A Personal Responsibility Agreement (PRA) is part of which of the following programs?

    (A) Medicaid
    (B) Temporary Assistance for Needy Families (TANF)
    (C) School lunch program
    (D) Annexation

22. Which of the following is the main source of funding for the Dedicated Highway Fund?

    (A) Motor fuels and lubricants tax
    (B) Lottery
    (C) Sales tax
    (D) Driver's license fees

23. Which of the following plays the most important role in preparing the state's budget?

    (A) Governor
    (B) Comptroller
    (C) Legislative Budget Board
    (D) Secretary of state

24. What impact does the line-item veto have on state spending?

    (A) None, the governor of Texas seldom issues a line-item veto.
    (B) Very little, the governor's vetoes typically account for less than 1 percent of total spending.
    (C) A fair amount, the governor's vetoes typically represent about 5 percent of state spending.
    (D) A considerable amount, the governor's vetoes typically represent about 10 percent of state spending.

25. A system of budget preparation and evaluation in which policymakers identify specific policy goals, set performance targets for agencies, and measure results is known as which of the following?

    (A) Incremental budgeting
    (B) Performance-based budgeting
    (C) Political culture
    (D) Sunset review

Chapter 31: Criminal Justice in Texas

Circle the correct answer.

1. "Ashley's Law" deals with which of the following issues?

   (A) Providing the possibility of life in prison without parole as an alternative to the death penalty
   (B) Making repeat child sex offenders eligible for the death penalty
   (C) Requiring sex offenders to register their addresses with law enforcement agencies
   (D) Making child murderers eligible for the death penalty

2. How does the crime rate in Texas compare with the national crime rate?

   (A) The crime rate in Texas is higher than the national crime rate.
   (B) The crime rate in Texas is lower than the national crime rate.
   (C) The crime rate in Texas is about the same as the national crime rate.
   (D) The crime rate in Texas was once higher than the national rate but is now below the national rate.

3. Which of the following criminal offenses is the most common?

   (A) Murder
   (B) Sexual assault
   (C) Larceny/theft
   (D) Robbery

4. How has the crime rate in the United States changed over the last 15 years?

   (A) The crime rate has been steadily climbing.
   (B) The crime rate rose in the 1990s but has recently been falling.
   (C) The crime rate fell during the 1990s but has recently been climbing.
   (D) The crime rate fell during the 1990s and has generally continued to fall but at a slower rate.

5. Which of the following is *not* a plausible reason for changes in the crime rate during the 1990s?

   (A) The population of young men increased.
   (B) The prison population increased.
   (C) The economy was strong.
   (D) Police departments developed and implemented new crime-fighting strategies.

6. An approach to law enforcement that seeks to reduce crime by increasing the interaction and cooperation between local law enforcement agencies and the people and neighborhoods they serve is known as which of the following?

   (A) Zero tolerance
   (B) Good time
   (C) Community-based policing
   (D) Adversary proceeding

7. Which of the following statements about the incidence of crime is true?

   (A) Homeowners are more likely to become victims than renters.
   (B) Whites are more likely to become victims than African Americans or Latinos.
   (C) Men are more likely to become victims than women.
   (D) All of the above

8. The reasonable belief that a crime has been committed and that a particular suspect is the likely perpetrator of that crime is known as which of the following?

   (A) Probable cause
   (B) Booking
   (C) Indictment
   (D) Probation

9. For which of the following crimes is the clearance rate the highest?

   (A) Sexual assault
   (B) Robbery
   (C) Burglary
   (D) Murder

10. An administrative procedure in which law enforcement personnel document a suspect's arrest is known as which of the following?

    (A) Probable cause
    (B) Booking
    (C) True bill
    (D) Indictment

11. What is the purpose of an arraignment?

    (A) To determine whether a crime has been committed
    (B) To determine whether an inmate should be released on parole
    (C) To determine whether a guilty defendant should be given probation
    (D) To formally charge a suspect with a crime and ask the suspect to enter a plea

12. What is the purpose of bail?

    (A) To raise money for the Texas Crime Victims' Compensation Fund
    (B) To punish an offender for committing a crime
    (C) To provide restitution to the victim of a crime
    (D) To ensure that a defendant shows up for later court proceedings

13. What does a grand jury do?

    (A) It hears evidence and decides whether to indict an accused person.
    (B) It decides the guilt or innocence of a person accused of a crime.
    (C) It determines punishment for someone found guilty of a crime.
    (D) All of the above

14. A legal procedure in which each side may present evidence and arguments to bolster its position, while rebutting evidence that might support the other side, is known as which of the following?

   (A) Adversary proceeding
   (B) Plea bargain
   (C) Indictment
   (D) Arraignment

15. Who has the burden of proof in a criminal case?

   (A) The defendant
   (B) The judge
   (C) The prosecutor
   (D) The jury

16. The suspension of a sentence, permitting the defendant to remain free under court supervision, is known as which of the following?

   (A) Parole
   (B) Plea bargain
   (C) Probation
   (D) Good time

17. Which of the following allows a defendant who pleads guilty to avoid having a conviction on his or her record?

   (A) Parole
   (B) Good time
   (C) Plea bargain
   (D) Deferred adjudication

18. What issue did *Furman v. Georgia* address?

   (A) Death penalty
   (B) Prison overcrowding
   (C) Juvenile justice
   (D) All of the above

19. Which of the following offenses would *not* qualify for the death penalty under Texas law?

   (A) Person A is robbing a convenience store with a gun pointed at the clerk. Even though Person A did not intend to use the gun, it accidentally goes off and the clerk is killed.
   (B) Person B hires Hitman X to kill her husband and Hitman X carries out the dirty deed.
   (C) Person C is baby-sitting his girlfriend's infant child. Person C grows exasperated when the baby cries; he shakes the infant and the baby dies.
   (D) Person D has held a grudge against a co-worker for years. One day Person D waits outside the co-worker's house and shoots him to death when he comes home.

20. Which of the following offenses would qualify for the death penalty under Texas law?

   (A) A drunken driver kills a family of four in an automobile accident.
   (B) A rejected boyfriend stabs his former girlfriend to death.
   (C) An angry wife runs over and kills her husband after she discovers that he is having an affair.
   (D) None of the above

21. How has the juvenile crime rate changed compared with the overall crime rate?

   (A) The juvenile crime rate has been falling faster than the overall crime rate has fallen.
   (B) The juvenile crime rate has been increasing faster than the overall crime rate has risen.
   (C) The juvenile crime rate has been falling, whereas the overall crime rate has been rising.
   (D) The juvenile crime rate has been rising, whereas the overall crime rate has been falling.

22. Which state has the largest prison system in terms of number of inmates?

   (A) Louisiana
   (B) California
   (C) Texas
   (D) New York

23. Which of the following offenders would be most likely to be housed in a state jail?

   (A) An inmate convicted of capital murder
   (B) A person accused of robbery and awaiting trial, unable to make bail
   (C) A juvenile convicted of a serious crime
   (D) An inmate convicted of fraud

24. A prison policy that credits inmates with time off for good behavior is known as which of the following?

   (A) Good time
   (B) Probation
   (C) Parole
   (D) Plea bargain

25. The tendency of offenders released from prison to commit additional crimes and be returned behind bars is known as which of the following?

   (A) Adversary proceeding
   (B) Recidivism
   (C) Clearance rate
   (D) Burden of proof

ANSWERS TO PRACTICE TEST QUESTIONS

Introduction: Government, Politics, and the Policymaking Process

1. A	11. D	21. D
2. C	12. C	22. C
3. C	13. C	23. D
4. C	14. A	24. A
5. A	15. B	25. A
6. D	16. B	
7. D	17. D	
8. A	18. B	
9. B	19. D	
10. B	20. B	

Chapter 1: A Changing America in a Changing World

1. B	11. C	21. A
2. B	12. A	22. D
3. C	13. C	23. C
4. A	14. C	24. C
5. A	15. A	25. C
6. A	16. B	
7. D	17. D	
8. B	18. D	
9. A	19. B	
10. A	20. D	

Chapter 2: The American Constitution

1. C	11. C	21. D
2. A	12. D	22. C
3. B	13. A	23. A
4. B	14. B	24. C
5. B	15. A	25. D
6. A	16. C	
7. D	17. C	
8. A	18. D	
9. D	19. B	
10. A	20. C	

Chapter 3: The Federal System

1. C	11. D	21. A
2. A	12. C	22. D
3. A	13. A	23. B
4. D	14. D	24. A
5. C	15. A	25. A
6. B	16. C	
7. C	17. D	
8. B	18. D	
9. B	19. B	
10. D	20. C	

Chapter 4: Public Opinion

1. A	11. C	21. D
2. A	12. D	22. C
3. C	13. A	
4. B	14. B	
5. D	15. B	
6. D	16. C	
7. C	17. C	
8. A	18. A	
9. B	19. D	
10. D	20. A	

Chapter 5: Political Participation

1. D	11. A	21. C
2. D	12. C	22. D
3. A	13. A	
4. D	14. D	
5. A	15. C	
6. B	16. A	
7. C	17. B	
8. D	18. C	
9. A	19. A	
10. C	20. A	

Chapter 6: The Media

1. D	11. B	21. A
2. A	12. B	22. B
3. B	13. C	23. D
4. C	14. C	24. A
5. A	15. D	25. A
6. D	16. B	
7. D	17. B	
8. C	18. C	
9. A	19. A	
10. D	20. B	

Chapter 7: Interest Groups

1. B	11. A	21. B
2. D	12. D	22. A
3. A	13. C	23. C
4. C	14. A	24. D
5. A	15. A	25. B
6. B	16. D	
7. D	17. A	
8. C	18. C	
9. A	19. D	
10. A	20. B	

Chapter 8: Political Parties

1. D	11. C	21. C
2. C	12. A	22. D
3. D	13. D	23. D
4. C	14. C	24. B
5. A	15. B	25. A
6. B	16. C	
7. D	17. D	
8. D	18. A	
9. C	19. B	
10. B	20. A	

Chapter 9: Elections

1. C	11. D	21. D
2. A	12. D	22. C
3. B	13. D	23. C
4. A	14. A	24. D
5. B	15. C	25. A
6. C	16. A	
7. B	17. B	
8. B	18. C	
9. C	19. C	
10. A	20. A	

Chapter 10: Congress

1. B	11. C	21. C
2. A	12. A	22. D
3. A	13. D	
4. B	14. A	
5. D	15. D	
6. D	16. B	
7. C	17. B	
8. A	18. C	
9. A	19. A	
10. D	20. C	

Chapter 11: The Presidency

1. B	11. B	21. C
2. D	12. A	22. B
3. D	13. D	23. D
4. B	14. A	24. C
5. D	15. B	25. D
6. B	16. C	
7. C	17. A	
8. A	18. D	
9. C	19. A	
10. D	20. D	

Chapter 12: The Federal Bureaucracy

1. A	11. C	21. D
2. C	12. B	22. C
3. D	13. A	23. B
4. A	14. C	24. A
5. B	15. D	25. A
6. D	16. A	
7. B	17. D	
8. C	18. C	
9. A	19. B	
10. B	20. D	

Chapter 13: The Federal Courts

1. B	11. D	21. B
2. A	12. C	22. D
3. A	13. A	
4. C	14. B	
5. A	15. B	
6. A	16. D	
7. B	17. B	
8. B	18. D	
9. D	19. D	
10. C	20. B	

Chapter 14: Economic Policymaking

1. C	11. A	21. D
2. C	12. C	22. C
3. A	13. D	23. A
4. D	14. A	24. C
5. B	15. C	25. D
6. C	16. B	
7. B	17. A	
8. D	18. D	
9. A	19. C	
10. B	20. B	

Chapter 15: Civil Liberties Policymaking

1. D	11. D	21. A
2. A	12. A	
3. C	13. D	
4. A	14. A	
5. C	15. B	
6. C	16. A	
7. D	17. D	
8. B	18. D	
9. D	19. A	
10. C	20. B	

Chapter 16: Civil Rights Policymaking

1. A	11. A	21. D
2. B	12. C	
3. C	13. A	
4. A	14. C	
5. D	15. A	
6. A	16. B	
7. D	17. D	
8. D	18. A	
9. C	19. A	
10. B	20. C	

Chapter 17: Foreign and Defense Policymaking

1. B	11. A	21. A
2. D	12. B	22. D
3. A	13. D	23. D
4. A	14. A	24. B
5. D	15. B	25. B
6. C	16. B	
7. A	17. C	
8. B	18. A	
9. C	19. B	
10. A	20. C	

Chapter 18: The People, Economy, and Political Culture of Texas

1. D	11. A	21. D
2. C	12. B	22. B
3. C	13. C	23. B
4. A	14. A	24. C
5. A	15. B	25. A
6. B	16. D	
7. D	17. B	
8. C	18. D	
9. A	19. B	
10. B	20. A	

Chapter 19: The Texas Constitution

1. C	11. D	21. C
2. B	12. A	22. D
3. D	13. B	23. C
4. A	14. B	24. D
5. D	15. C	25. A
6. C	16. A	
7. A	17. C	
8. D	18. C	
9. C	19. A	
10. D	20. B	

Chapter 20: The Federal Context of Texas Policymaking

1. B	11. D	21. A
2. B	12. A	22. B
3. C	13. B	23. D
4. A	14. B	24. C
5. C	15. C	25. D
6. D	16. A	
7. A	17. C	
8. B	18. D	
9. C	19. D	
10. A	20. B	

Chapter 21: Political Participation in Texas

1. C	11. D	21. C
2. A	12. B	22. C
3. D	13. A	23. C
4. A	14. D	24. B
5. A	15. B	25. D
6. A	16. A	
7. D	17. D	
8. D	18. C	
9. C	19. B	
10. B	20. D	

Chapter 22: Interest Groups in Texas

1. A	11. C	21. B
2. D	12. B	22. A
3. C	13. A	23. B
4. A	14. C	24. D
5. C	15. D	25. C
6. D	16. C	
7. C	17. A	
8. A	18. D	
9. B	19. C	
10. A	20. A	

Chapter 23: Political Parties in Texas

1. A	11. B	21. D
2. B	12. A	22. D
3. D	13. C	23. D
4. C	14. A	24. A
5. C	15. D	25. A
6. C	16. A	
7. D	17. C	
8. B	18. A	
9. D	19. D	
10. A	20. D	

Chapter 24: Texas Elections

1. B	11. D	21. D
2. C	12. A	22. D
3. A	13. C	23. D
4. A	14. A	24. C
5. A	15. A	25. B
6. C	16. D	
7. B	17. D	
8. D	18. B	
9. C	19. B	
10. A	20. A	

Chapter 25: The Texas Legislature

1. C	11. A	21. A
2. A	12. C	22. A
3. D	13. C	23. D
4. C	14. B	24. D
5. D	15. D	25. C
6. D	16. D	
7. A	17. C	
8. C	18. B	
9. C	19. A	
10. B	20. B	

Chapter 26: The Executive Branch in Texas

1. C	11. C	21. A
2. A	12. A	22. D
3. D	13. C	23. B
4. D	14. D	24. B
5. D	15. B	25. C
6. B	16. A	
7. C	17. C	
8. A	18. B	
9. C	19. A	
10. B	20. D	

Chapter 27: The Judicial Branch in Texas

1. C	11. C	21. A
2. A	12. A	22. C
3. D	13. C	23. C
4. A	14. C	24. C
5. B	15. D	25. D
6. C	16. A	
7. B	17. C	
8. A	18. D	
9. D	19. C	
10. D	20. D	

Chapter 28: City Government in Texas

1. D	11. C	21. A
2. D	12. D	22. B
3. C	13. C	23. A
4. A	14. B	24. C
5. B	15. A	25. D
6. B	16. D	
7. A	17. C	
8. D	18. B	
9. A	19. A	
10. B	20. A	

Chapter 29: Texas Counties, School Districts, and Special Districts

1. C	11. D	21. A
2. B	12. B	22. D
3. D	13. A	23. B
4. A	14. C	24. A
5. B	15. D	25. C
6. C	16. A	
7. B	17. D	
8. C	18. A	
9. A	19. B	
10. A	20. D	

Chapter 30: State Budget Policy in Texas

1. A	11. B	21. B
2. B	12. C	22. A
3. C	13. C	23. C
4. A	14. D	24. B
5. B	15. D	25. B
6. D	16. B	
7. C	17. A	
8. A	18. D	
9. A	19. C	
10. A	20. A	

Chapter 31: Criminal Justice in Texas

1. B	11. D	21. A
2. A	12. D	22. C
3. C	13. A	23. D
4. D	14. A	24. A
5. A	15. C	25. B
6. C	16. C	
7. C	17. D	
8. A	18. A	
9. D	19. D	
10. B	20. D	